D1642630

MRS BEETON'S GARDEN MANAGEMENT

Mrs Beeton's Garden Management

❖ ❖ ❖

ISABELLA BEETON

Wordsworth Reference

In loving memory of
MICHAEL TRAYLER
the founder of Wordsworth Editions

1

Readers who are interested in other titles from Wordsworth Editions are invited to visit our website at www.wordsworth-editions.com

For our latest list and a full mail-order service, contact Bibliophile Books, 5 Datapoint, South Crescent, London E16 4TL
TEL: +44 (0)20 7474 2474 FAX: +44 (0)20 7474 8589
ORDERS: orders@bibliophilebooks.com
WEBSITE: www.bibliophilebooks.com

This newly typeset edition first published in 2008 by Wordsworth Editions Limited
8B East Street, Ware, Hertfordshire SG12 9HJ

ISBN 978 1 84022 079 7

Typeset in Great Britain by Antony Gray
Printed and bound by Clays Ltd, St Ives plc

Contents

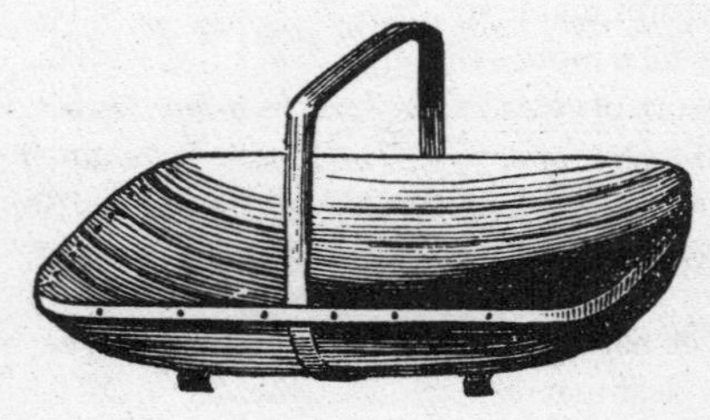

CHAPTER 1

The Origin of Gardening: its History and Progress from Remote Antiquity to the Present Time

> And the Lord God planted a garden eastward in Eden; and there He put the man whom He had formed. And out of the ground made the Lord God to grow every tree that is pleasant to the sight, and good for food. Genesis 2:8, 9.
>
> Neither is he that planteth any thing, neither he that watereth; but God that giveth the increase. 1 Corinthians 3:7.

1 The Garden is closely linked to, and intimately associated with, the history of the human race from the creation of Adam to the epoch of the final consummation of all things. The first man spent the early days of his life in a garden – the beauteous garden that God planted in Eden – ere he was driven out to till the ground whence he was taken, and to eat of it in sorrow all the days of his life. Our Blessed Redeemer, the second Adam, entered on the first phase of the bitter agony and suffering that crowned the purpose of His sojourn upon earth in a garden – the ancient garden of Gethsemane, on the Mount of Olives – where He was content to be betrayed into the hands of sinful men who sought to take His life. And in the closing chapter of the sacred volume our thoughts are directed to what may be spoken of as the second Eden – God's garden in 'that great city, the holy Jerusalem', in which appears once more the wondrous Tree of Life, which 'bare twelve manner of fruits, and yielded her fruit every month', whose leaves were for 'the healing of the nations'.

2 Viewed from this standpoint, and when it is remembered that the care and culture of a garden combined to form the very first vocation of man, chosen for him by his Maker – the very first kind of manual labour to which he was bidden to turn his hand – of a truth, Gardening, with all the work that is involved in it and can be included under the term, is invested with an interest that acts as a powerful magnet to draw us to its consideration, and entice us at participate actively in the pleasures that it affords. Of all callings and professions, save that alone which brings men more intimately acquainted with the complex structure of God's greatest work of creation, the human body, there is none, perhaps, that is better calculated to produce in man a reverent and humble spirit than a close association with, and a constant contemplation of, the diverse operations of Nature in the great plant-world – a study which can never fail to 'Lead from Nature up to Nature's God'.

3 Turn to whatever nation we may, whether in past ages, or in mediaeval or modern times, it is clear that the extent to which the art of gardening was carried by that nation is an excellent index of the height of civilisation to which it had attained. Among savages of the lowest type, no attention whatever is paid to gardening, and they possess no knowledge of it; but, on the contrary, amongst civilised nations, the greater the degree of civilisation among them, the greater is the fondness for gardening and the eagerness and skill with which the art is prosecuted. Architecture and gardening advance almost hand in hand, but the former has ever slight precedence. 'When ages grow to civility and elegancy,' wrote Lord Bacon, 'men come to build stately sooner than to garden finely, as if gardening were the greater perfection.' And truly the garden enhances the beauty of the building to which it is attached, or which it surrounds, as the jewel derives greater lustre from the setting in which it has been enshrined by the skill of the goldsmith.

4 Taking the manifest connection between civilisation and gardening as a keynote wherewith to guide and direct inquiry on the subject, it will be useful to take a rapid survey of the art of gardening, as practised by ancient nations, and to glance briefly at the peculiar styles by which it is marked among some of the leading peoples of modern times, selecting those whose features are so strongly marked as to place them conspicuously in the foreground.

5 It has been already shown that the very first kind of manual labour to which the attention of man was directed was that of gardening, and though there is no direct record of the fact, there can be no doubt that this and the sister art of agriculture was followed as closely as that of cattle farming, if I may use the expression, for we know that soon after Noah quitted the ark in which he and his family had been preserved during the Flood, he 'began to be a husbandman, and he planted a vineyard'. This is the earliest mention that we possess of fruit culture by man, and this, according to the received system of chronology, was done about 2347 BC.

6 Many years pass on and away before any direct allusion to gardening is made in the pages of Holy Writ, but at Taberah, in the course of their forty years' wandering in the wilderness, we find the children of Israel loathing the heaven-sent manna, and asking, 'Who shall give us flesh to eat? We remember the fish, which we did eat in Egypt freely; the cucumbers, and the melons, and the leeks, and the onions, and the garlic.' This proves that the Egyptians, whom we know to have been a highly civilised people, skilled in the arts of peace and war, paid considerable attention to gardening, and had brought the culture of herbs and vegetables to a high pitch of perfection, and this is abundantly confirmed by ancient Egyptian paintings and sculpture of historical and monumental character which have been exposed to view during the present century. The deliverance of the children of Israel took place 1491 BC, and we may reasonably infer that skilful gardeners were to be found in Egypt long before this time, and that the art was generally practised.

7 The land of Canaan was admirably adapted for the prosecution of agriculture and gardening. Its natural products were of the highest order: the slopes of the hills were clothed with forest and fruit-bearing trees; the banks of the rivers were fringed with flowering shrubs; and the fertile soil literally teemed with flowers and bulbs, among which the 'lilies of the field' were pre-eminently conspicuous. With the remembrance of the fruits and vegetables of Egypt ever uppermost in their minds, as it doubtless was by tradition, though not by actual experience, the Israelites, when settled in the Land of Promise, turned their attention with considerable zest to gardening and fruit-growing, for frequent mention of vineyards is made in Holy Scripture, and the act of sitting under one's own vine and fig tree is often used to denote a time of general tranquillity and immunity from internal commotion and foreign invasion.

8 Solomon himself, who died 975 BC, possessed an intimate knowledge of plants and trees, and wrote of them, 'from the cedar tree that is in Lebanon even unto the hyssop that springeth out of the wall' (1 Kings 4:33). He bears testimony to his fondness for gardening, which was undoubtedly shared by the people over which he ruled, for, when mentioning the various things that he had done in pursuit of pleasure, he says: 'I planted me vineyards: I made me gardens and orchards, and I planted trees in them of all kind of fruits: I made me pools of water, to water therewith the wood that bringeth forth trees: (Eccles. 2:4–6). Among the royal domains in different parts of the country were vineyards, which the monarch let out to fruit farmers of the time at certain fixed rents (Song of Solomon 8:11, 12), and in the remarkable poem from which this information is obtained there are many allusions to plants and flowers and fruit then in cultivation, and to garden work. The testimony adduced is sufficient to show that horticulture was well understood and commonly practised by the Jews.

9 Let us now turn to the history of other Eastern nations and nations dwelling on the seaboard of the Mediterranean, and see in what esteem gardening was held among them, and to what extent it was carried. The Greek poet Homer, who flourished between 960 and 930 BC, shortly after the time of Solomon, makes mention in the Odyssey of the gardens of Alcinous, King of Phaeacia, which were visited by Ulysses in the course of his wanderings on his return from the siege of Troy. Alcinous is reputed to have been fond of gardening and agriculture, and to have been well skilled in both. His gardens, and the gardens of the Hesperides, the three daughters of Hesperus, which are supposed to have been at or near Tangier, in Morocco, are mainly subjects of poetry and fable, but the very mention of them is sufficient to show that gardening was practised among the early Greeks, and that there must be a considerable substratum of fact underlying the fiction of which the accounts we have of them chiefly consist.

10 Far otherwise, however, is it with regard to the celebrated hanging gardens of Babylon, which, with the lofty and massive walls of that city, were regarded in ancient times as composing the fourth wonder of the world. These gardens, which are mentioned and described from tradition by Diodorus Siculus and other writers, although nothing is said of them by Herodotus, were made by Nebuchadnezzar, who reigned at Babylon from 605 to 562 BC, to gratify his queen Amytis, the daughter of Astyages, King of Media, for she found but little pleasure in the flat and monotonous country that surrounded Babylon after the well-wooded hills and mountains of Media, to which she had been accustomed from infancy to the time of her marriage. These marvellous gardens, of which the illustration given in Fig. 1 will convey an idea, covered a space four hundred feet square, and were composed of broad terraces, rising one above another on vast tiers of arches until the summit towered three hundred and fifty feet above the level of the plain below. The earth on each successive terrace was deep enough to allow large trees to grow and flourish in it, and the whole was watered with water drawn up from the river Euphrates by machinery specially devised for the purpose.

11 That the Persians were famous for their parks or pleasure grounds and gardens, and had been so, probably, from very early times, we learn from Xenophon, who lived between 445 and 355 BC, and wrote, among other works, the 'Cyropaedia', which is professed to be an account of the boyhood of Cyrus the Elder, otherwise called the Great, who wrested the sceptre of Babylon from the hands of Nabonadius or Belshazzar, about 557 BC. Be this as it may, Xenophon mentions many interesting facts with reference to gardening among the Persians, and he had ample opportunities for ascertaining them when he accompanied Cyrus the Younger, with a large body of Greek mercenaries, in his expedition against his brother, Artaxerxes, King of Persia, which was brought to an abrupt termination by the death of Cyrus in the battle of Cunaxa, 404 BC. Xenophon tells us that Cyrus the Elder considered a well-ordered *paradise* (παράδεισος, a beautiful pleasure garden) an indispensable adjunct to every royal palace in his dominions, and that he encouraged the formation of gardens and parks in every place in his kingdom which he happened to visit. The royal parks were in some instances large enough to form hunting grounds.

12 We know from later and more recent sources that the Persians from the earliest times were fond of gardens, and it appears from Pliny and other Roman writers that they were laid out much in the same way as those in our own times, the principal features in the larger ones being long straight walks and alleys, with borders on either side, having trees and shrubs at the back, or in the centre if the border happened to be between two walks, and having roses and sweet-scented flowers planted along the edges of the borders where they met the walks. This fashion seems to have spread westward and northward throughout Asia Minor, and to have passed into Greece, for the gardens in that country were laid out and stocked in the same manner, especially in and around Athens, where flowers were habitually sold in the public markets.

13 Public gardens were to be found in many of the principal towns in Greece, and these were the daily haunts of philosophers and men of leisure rather than of the people at large. Prior to the Christian era, Theophrastus, a Greek philosopher, who died 287 BC, and who was possessed of a famous garden, which he left to be preserved as a place of recreation and resort for men of letters, is the chief authority on gardening as carried on in Greece in his time. He wrote a 'History of Plants,' in which he gives many fanciful directions for gardening operations. It appears from what he says that the arts of pruning and grafting and the fertilisation of flowers by carrying the pollen from one to the other was known to the Greeks. Grafting, indeed, is said to have been known to Hesiod, who lived about 850 BC, but as to this there is no absolute certainty. That it was freely practised when Theophrastus lived, there is no doubt, and possibly the art was known and followed in all places in which gardening was in vogue, for St Paul alludes to it in Romans 11:17–24, and this he would not have done if it had

FIG. 1 *Hanging gardens of Babylon*

not been an operation that was well understood both by himself and by those to whom he was writing. The flowers chiefly cultivated by the Greeks, according to Theophrastus, appear to have been roses (of which both Greeks and Romans were extremely fond), violets, gilly flowers, hyacinths, larkspur, iris, white lily, myrtle, and ivy, with a few others. These furnished the wreaths and chaplets which were commonly worn at feasts and entertainments, mingled in some cases with parsley, a herb which it was supposed was possessed of power to repel and counteract the intoxicating effect of the wine that was drunk.

14 Among notable gardeners of ancient times it may not be out of place to mention Attalus III, King of Pergamus, who died 133 BC, and left his kingdom to the Roman people. He is said to have devoted much of his time, especially in the closing years of his life, to gardening, and even wrote a work upon the subject. Mithridates VI, King of Pontus, who lived from 120 to 63 BC, is also said to have been a skilful gardener. Both of these kings were curious in the culture of poisonous plants, possibly, to judge from some of their acts and deeds, for homicidal or suicidal purposes.

15 Not only are traces of extensive garden cultivation found among the Romans, but a garden literature also, which is supposed to have exercised some influence on our own. Even in early times, when Rome, yet in her infancy, was ruled by kings, gardens were not unknown, for when Sextus Tarquinius, son of Tarquinius Superbus, or Tarquin the Proud, seventh King of Rome, sent a messenger to his father, then in exile, to inquire what course he wished him to follow in the city, the monarch contented himself with striking off the heads of the tallest poppies that grew in the garden in which he received his son's envoy, bidding him return with speed to Sextus. This he did, but when Sextus asked him for his father's instructions, he said he had none to give: the King heard all he had to say, and moodily knocking off the heads of the tallest poppies within reach of his staff, as if meditating what answer he might best give, turned on him suddenly and told him to be gone. The son was by no means slow to catch the meaning of his father's act, nor averse to follow its prompting by putting to death the leading men in Rome, as opportunity offered, who were opposed to the King's return.

16 As we approach the Christian era, and pass that epoch, we come upon surer ground, and obtain more reliable information on gardening as it existed among the Romans. The Roman poets Virgil (70–19 BC) and Horace (65–8 BC), who lived and wrote in the time of the Emperor Augustus, afford us interesting glimpses of garden culture and garden lore at that period. In his *Georgics*, which are chiefly devoted to agricultural and bee-keeping, Virgil speaks of endive, celery, and plants of the gourd or cucumber tribe, with most of the flowers mentioned by Theophrastus, as being commonly grown in ordinary Roman gardens, but his catalogue of fruits, vegetables, and flowers is by no means an extensive one. In his *Odes*, *Epodes*, and *Satires*, Horace frequently adverts to the pleasures of country life, and he draws in his second Epode a graphic picture of a man who retires from business and seeks repose and relaxation in cultivating his garden and pruning his trees, but gives it up as suddenly as he took to it, returns to the city, and gets into harness again.

17 The Romans, being Epicureans in thought and habit, and belonging, as the great majority of them did, to the 'Eat-and-drink-for-tomorrow-we-die' school, carried everything to excess, whatever it might be, that they took in hand. They wasted money on flowers as a source of enjoyment to the same extent as on curious and costly dishes for the gratification of the palate. The passion for flowers pervaded all classes, and it was even found necessary to check extravagance in their use by the enactment of sumptuary laws. The Roman Emperors and most of the wealthy Romans had magnificent gardens, replete with groves, shady walks, trees, shrubs, parterres of bright and fragrant flowers, porticoes, summer houses, statues, and fountains. Lucullus, who died about 47 BC, had many villas in different parts of Italy, to each and all of which large gardens were attached, and introduced, as Loudon tells us, the cherry, the peach, and the apricot from the East. Sallust, who died 35 BC, was possessed of extensive gardens in Rome itself, on the Quirinal hill, which afterwards became the principal gardens of the Emperors with the city walls. Cicero, Rome's greatest orator, who took his name from a wen on his face that resembled a pea (*cicer*, chick pea or vetch), had his gardens, whose flowers formed one of his chief delights; and it is said that one of the principal charges brought against him by his opponent Verres, another orator of note, was that of having journeyed through Sicily, during his residence in that island as quaestor, in a litter that was strewn with roses and adorned with garlands of the 'queen of flowers'. Julius Caesar, the first of Rome's emperors in fact, if not in name, had his

> Private arbours and new planted orchards,
> On this side Tiber,

which doubtless roused the envy and malice of those who hated him to a yet higher pitch. Certain parts of Italy had a reputation above all others for certain fruits and flowers; and 'The Paestan roses, with their double Spring', in allusion to the fact that the roses of Paestum, in Lucania, blossomed twice a year, were as celebrated as the fruits from the gardens of Lucullus.

18 The chief sources from which reliable information can be obtained with regard to gardening as practised by the Romans are the writings of Columella, the author of a work on 'Rural Economy', in twelve books, one of which is entirely devoted to an exposition of the garden management of the time, and the works of Pliny the Elder and Pliny the Younger, uncle and nephew respectively. Columella, a Spaniard by birth, though a Roman citizen, flourished about 50 AD. Of the two Plinys, the uncle was born in 23 AD, and lost his life in 79 AD, during the terrible eruption of Vesuvius which destroyed the cities of Pompeii and Herculaneum. His chief work was his *Natural History*, in thirty-seven books, sixteen of which are devoted to a description of the principal trees, shrubs, fruits, flowers, and vegetables known and cultivated at the time, the medicinal properties of plants, and the arts of agriculture and gardening. The nephew was born in 61 or 62 AD, and, having lost his father when but a mere child, he was adopted and brought up by his uncle, and succeeded to his uncle's estates in various parts of Italy. He became a senator of Rome, and held various offices of State. Like his uncle, he was the author of many works, but of these only his *Epistles* and *Panegyric on Trajan* are extant, the former possessing the greater interest for those who are curious about the gardening of the ancients, because from his very elaborate descriptions of his various residences or villas, and the gardens, grounds, farms, buildings, and offices with which they were surrounded, we get the best idea of what Roman gardens really were in the best days of the Empire, and can trace the many points of resemblance that exist between them and the gardens of our own day. It will be useful to gather from Columella the description of tools with which the Roman gardener did his work; from Pliny the Elder, the fruits, vegetables, and flowers which were the chief objects of culture; and from Pliny the Younger, an account of one of his own gardens, which may be taken as a type of the arrangement that was commonly followed in laying out all gardens that belonged to men of wealth and eminence.

19 The tools or gardening implements of the Romans, according to Columella, were few and simple, being only seven in number. For working the ground, there was the *ligo*, or hoe, having a blade that was slightly turned inward; the *pala*, a tool with a broad, straight blade, resembling the modern spade; the *rastrum*, or rake; the *sarculum*, or weeding hoe, more like the hoe that is used now for hoeing turnips, and lighter than the *ligo*, which was better suited for digging, being more like our mattock; the *marra*, another kind of light hoe; and the *dolabra*, which answered to our pickaxe. For pruning purposes, there was the *securis*, or axe, which performed the same functions as our billhook; and the *falx*, or pruning knife, a strong tool with a curved blade, in some degree resembling the form of the half-moon.

20 With regard to *flowers*, those that were grown by the Greeks were chiefly cultivated by the Romans. The time had not yet come when every part of the world could be laid under contribution, as now, to yield additions to our floral treasures. Of *fruits*, they had apples and pears in many varieties, quinces, and medlars, peaches, apricots, almonds, plums, and olives, with cherries. They had also many kinds of grapes, from which excellent wines were made, mulberries, blackberries, strawberries, walnuts, chestnuts, hazelnuts, and filberts. Strawberries, however, were not an object of cultivation. Of *vegetables*, they possessed many varieties of the gourd tribe, including cucumbers and melons. They had many varieties of cabbages, with peas, beans, and runner-beans. They grew the turnip, carrot, parsnip, beet, skirret, and radish; and they had endive, lettuce, mustard, and other varieties of small salading. Asparagus was a special object of culture. Parsley, fennel, chervil, and other pot herbs were grown; and mushrooms were gathered and used for food, if not grown for that purpose, as in modern times.

21 Though they were well skilled in the art of warming their dwellings by artificial means, conveying the genial heat throughout the house when necessary by means of flues, and heating water for the bath, they never thought, it seems, of using similar means for forcing fruit and flowers. Hot beds, however, had been introduced in Pliny the Elder's time, for facilitating the growth of cucumbers and promoting the blooming of roses at all times of the year. These beds were formed of manure and covered over with *specularia*, which are supposed to have been frames in which talc was used in the same way as glass is used now, although Pliny and others represent them to be pieces of talc five feet in length. In this may be traced the germ of our present system of frame culture and forcing pits.

22 Before turning to the description of a Roman garden as given by Pliny the Younger, it will be interesting to note some of his reflections in his *Epistles* on gardening, and the extent to which it was carried by the Roman people nearly a century after the Christian era. 'At the present day,' he writes, sometime between 80 and 90 AD, 'under the general name of *horti*, we have pleasure grounds situated in the very heart of the city, as well as extensive fields and villas. The garden constitutes the poor man's field; from it the lower classes procure their food.' This shows that gardening was practised universally and by all grades of society from the highest to the lowest. But he then proceeds to complain that the cheap and simple luxuries of the garden were gradually being placed beyond the reach of the poor by the demands of the wealthy and luxurious for the monstrosities of high cultivation. 'Cabbages,' he says, 'are pampered to such an extent that the poor man's table is not large enough to hold them. Asparagus Nature intended to grow wild, so that all might gather it, but, lo! we find its cultivation carried to such a pitch, that at Ravenna heads are produced, three of which will weigh a pound. Alas, for the monstrous gluttony of the time.' This may be taken as evidence that market gardening was practised on an extensive scale at the time when Pliny the Younger wrote, and that horticulture had attained a high pitch of excellence.

23 After deprecating such high cultivation as a direct means of depriving the poor of their natural food, and stating that women were the chief cultivators of the kitchen garden among the Romans; that its appearance in the days of Cato the Censor was considered as the test of a good or careless housewife; and that the lower classes in Rome had their mimic gardens in the windows, as we have our window gardening; he continues: 'Let the garden, then, have its due meed of honour; let not its products, because they are common, be deprived of a due share of our consideration; for have not men of the highest rank been content to borrow their surnames from it? Have the Lactucini thought themselves disgraced by taking their name from the lettuce (*lactuca*), or the Fabii and Lentilii from the bean (*faba*) and the lentil (*lens*)? But we are ready to admit, with Virgil, that it is difficult by language to ennoble a subject, so humble in itself – "In tenui, at tenuis non gloria".'

24 In his *Epistles*, Pliny the Younger describes three villas of which he was the owner, namely, the Laurentian Villa, on the Tiber, near Paterno, now called San Lorenzo, about seventeen miles from Rome; the Tuscan Villa, near Frascati, in the Apennines, and also situated on the Tiber; and the Larian Villa, on the Larian Lake, now known as the Lake of Como. These descriptions have been noticed at length by Felibien, a French writer, in his *Plans and Descriptions of Pliny's Villas* (Paris, 1699); by Castell, in his *Villas of the Ancients* (London, 1728); and by Girardin, another French writer, in a work of which there is an English translation under the title of *An Essay on Landscape, with an Historical Introduction, etc.* (London, 1783). Felibien and Castell have given plans of these villas and the grounds that surrounded them, based on Pliny's account of them, and although in the construction of these plans they have necessarily drawn to a great extent on their imagination, it is considered, nevertheless, that they afford tolerably correct ideas of the country houses of the wealthy Romans, and the manner in which their environs were laid out.

25 Castell's plan of Pliny's Laurentian Villa has been reproduced in Fig. 2 from his *Villas of the Ancients*, and this has been selected because it is more simple in its character, and therefore more easy to understand when considering its various parts in detail. Those who are curious in the matter, and require further information on the subject, must be referred to the works mentioned above. The extent of the villa and the gardens and grounds about it is supposed to have been from three to four acres. The description that follows below has been written to suit the illustration. The writers that have been already mentioned are not in strict harmony with each other on every point as might be expected, nor are the descriptions given by each in perfect agreement with the diagrams with which it has been sought to illustrate them. This, however, should cause no surprise when it is remembered that both plans and descriptions are merely attempts by different minds to reflect as accurately as possible, from each writer's point of view, Pliny's accounts of his villas. For this reason it has been judged better to select a diagram which is sufficient in itself to show the points of similarity and dissimilarity between ancient Roman and modern English gardens; and to give a description that is absolutely suited to it, rather than to quote a description which is rather general than special, inasmuch as it does not cover all the details that should be touched on.

The illustration in Fig. 2 shows, as it has been said, the plan of the house and surrounding grounds which together formed Pliny's Laurentian Villa. Its aspect will be readily understood from the mark which shows the disposition and direction of the four cardinal points of the compass. The house itself and its offices are situated in the right-hand corner, and it will be as well to describe the gardens and grounds according to their relation to the house. Immediately in front of the building was the *atrium* (*a*), a large court, covered in on all sides, but open in the centre, which served as a cool shelter at all times of the day, and a place for the reception of guests and the transaction of business. From the atrium immediate access was gained to all parts of the grounds as well as to the house itself. To the left of the house was the *hortus*, or pleasure garden (*b*), consisting of flower garden and shrubbery, laid out so as to afford variety of scene, and to suit a multiplicity of requirements. Of this, the first feature that demands attention was the raised terrace, or *xystus* (*e*), from which a beautiful and unbroken view was obtained over the Bay of Ostia, and in front of which was a lawn of about the same width. At the back of the xystus, and in front of the lawn and to the left of both of them, was the flower garden (*b*), laid out in beds and broken with paths that gave access to every part. Without the flower garden, and surrounding it, was the *gestatio* (*c*), laid out in parallel paths, devoted to exercise on horseback and on foot. At the left-hand side this was disposed in the form of a semi-circle. Above it, and separated from it by a broad road, was the shrubbery proper, surrounded with trees and laid out in a quaint manner, with walks giving access to the principal positions within it, which were furnished with summer houses, each commanding a different view, and adorned with obelisks, pyramids, and statuary. Beyond the shrubbery lay the open country (*k*), well wooded and hilly, and to the right of it was a tract of land used as a vineyard, and containing spots and embellishments of a highly ornamental character. A stout fence divided Pliny's property from that of his neighbour, whose villa (*l*) is indicated in the illustration. To the right of the atrium was the vegetable ground or kitchen garden (*f*), surrounded by a fence of box and rosemary. This garden was small and not in proportion to the other parts of the grounds. At the back of the house, fronting the waters of the Bay of Ostia (*g*), and abutting on the shore (*h*), was the *gymnasium* (*i*), which was devoted to the athletic exercises in vogue among the Romans. To the right of the house, and in rear of the kitchen garden, were the stables and offices, consisting of the *equilia* (*m*), or stables proper, the *tecta vehiculis* (*n*), or coach houses, the *lignarium* (*o*), or shed for firewood, the *faenile* (*p*), or hayloft, for hay, corn, and fodder, the *piscinae* (*q*), or fishponds, used for storing and fattening fish, and at either end of the range of stables, *cellae cervorum* (*r*), or houses for deer, in which deer were kept as pets or to be fattened for table. Instead of these the Englishman would have his fowl house, etc., but when these minor points of difference are noted, it must be allowed that the Roman country house of eighteen hundred years ago bore a wonderful similarity to the modern English country residence in most of its arrangements.

To this may be added a few remarks gathered from the Introduction to Girardin's Essay and other sources, bearing on the general character of Roman gardens, whether on a large or small scale. In the towns, as shown by the paintings on the walls of Roman houses exhumed on the site once occupied by the cities of Pompeii and Herculaneum, the plots in front of the houses were laid out in a square formal style, much as ours are now, fenced in occasionally with trelliswork, over which and the doors of the houses climbing plants were trained. Flowers and fruits were also trained on rows of stakes, like our espaliers, and plants were placed in front of the windows and in different parts of the garden in vases and boxes. The prevailing characteristics of the larger gardens of country and suburban houses were platforms and terraces constructed chiefly with the view of commanding noteworthy points and objects in the surrounding prospect. Figs, vines, and mulberries were the fruits most commonly found in them, with apples and pears. The different gardens were surrounded by hedges of box and evergreens, which could be rendered close and compact by clipping, and the box trees were generally cut into fanciful

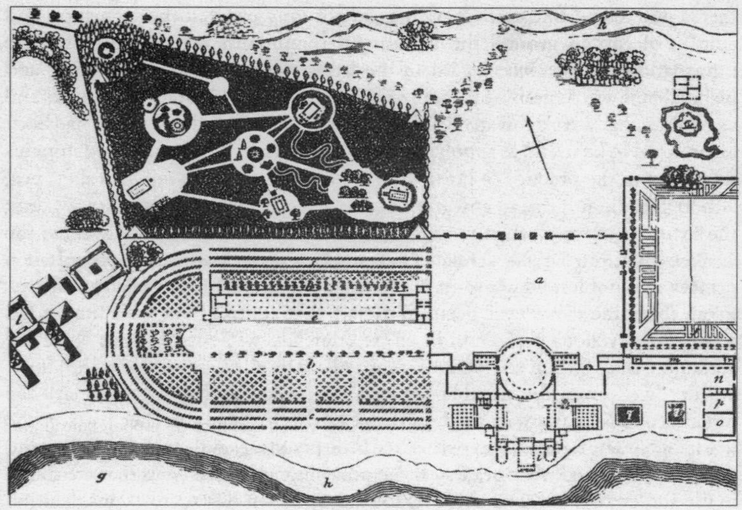

FIG. 2 *Plan of Pliny's Laurentian Villa*

shapes, such as figures of animals, letters forming names, etc., after the style that prevailed in English gardens of the Elizabethan period. When a higher fence, affording more shelter, was desired, bay trees and cypresses were planted to form it. Alcoves of marble, summer houses and seats of the same material, fountains and streams of water, partly for ornamental purposes and partly for irrigation, were to be found in all parts in which they could be placed, the position of the summer houses being regulated by the view that could be commanded from the sites on which they were placed.

26 The style of the ancient Roman garden has been dwelt on at some length here because it is on the gardens of Imperial Rome that the modern gardens of later European nations have been chiefly modelled. Hand in hand with the advance of civilisation in Rome, gardening gradually reached the high eminence it attained in the century that preceded and that which followed the Christian Era. It is now necessary to trace, as briefly as possible, its fortunes in the troublous times that attended the waning of the Roman Empire, and the influence Roman horticulture subsequently exerted on the efforts in this direction, both of nations that had not yet risen into importance, and of many that had not at this time been called into existence. To trace the decadence and subsequent revival of the art of gardening here at length is not possible. It must suffice to say that in the wars that marked the decline and fall of the Roman Empire, the art was gradually lost, as far as the people at large were concerned, and it was only by the monks, who carefully cultivated the gardens and grounds attached to their monasteries and religious houses, that the knowledge of horticulture was preserved and its practice sustained.

27 It was not until the time of Charlemagne, Emperor of the West, who was born in 742 and died in 814, that gardening experienced any decided revival, and this is due to the fact that Charlemagne not only ordered the formation and culture of garden ground throughout his dominions, but put forth for the information of his subjects a list of the fruits, vegetables, herbs, flowers, and plants that it was desirable for them to cultivate. These included the flowers and vegetables that were cultivated by the Romans and many others, which had been ascertained to be useful as supplying food or medicine. Thus a renewed impetus was given to the practice of horticulture, which never again fell into abeyance, although it did not rise to any great height, except in a few isolated cases, until the sixteenth century, when a revival of horticulture took place in Italy under the auspices of Alfonzo d'Este, Duke of Ferrara, Cosmo de Medici, and other Italian princes and nobles, which soon made itself felt in other European countries. From that time it has ever been on the advance, until in our own time it has attained marvellous perfection in all its branches, while its practice is viewed with increasing favour, and earnestly carried out by all classes of the community.

28 To dwell upon the peculiarities of gardens and gardening that mark the practice of horticulture in all the European nations, and in other parts of the world, would be tedious, and perhaps of little practical value. It will be sufficient, therefore, to glance very briefly on the prevailing characteristics that are found in the gardens of Italy, France, and Holland, and then pass on to a consideration of the rise and progress of gardening in our own country.

29 The modern style of gardening in Italy can only be regarded as a perfected continuation of that of the Romans, with whom it was an amplification of the house itself, for the Romans, when they spoke of a 'villa', meant not only the actual house, but the grounds and gardens by which it was surrounded, no matter what the purpose might be to which each part was devoted, and the Italians of the present day attach precisely the same meaning to the term. The Italian garden of today is, in fact,

> A pillared shade,
> With echoing walks beneath,

a series of broad paved and sunny terraces and shady colonnades connected in their style with the house. Marble fountains, statuary, and vases, and other vestiges of ancient art found in the ruins out of which they have been raised, are the chief characteristics of the magnificent gardens of modern Italy, and nothing can be nobler than this style when the accessories are all in keeping. In Fig. 3 will be found a picturesque example of the modern Italian garden.

> 'In spite of Walpole's sneer,' says Mr Bellenden Kerr, 'about walking up and down stairs in the open air, there are few things so beautiful in art as stately terraces, tier above tier, and bold flights of stone steps, now stretching forward in a broad, unbroken course; now winding round the angle of the terrace in short steep descents; each landing affording some new scene, some change of sun or shade – a genial basking-place or cool retreat – here the rich perfume of an ancestral orange tree, which may have been in the family three hundred years – there the bright blossoms of some sunny creeper – while at another time a balcony juts out to catch some distant view, or a recess is formed with seats for the loitering party to "rest and be thankful". Let all this be connected, by means of colonnades, with the architecture of the mansion, and you have a far more rational appendage to its incessantly artificial character than the petty wildernesses and picturesque *abandon*, which have not been without advocates, even on an insignificant scale.'

FIG. 3 *Modern Italian garden*

30 The French style of gardening may be said to be generally theatrical and affected, straining after effect with spectacle and display. Even at Versailles, whose gardens extend over two hundred acres, and represent an outlay of eight millions sterling, the geometric style of Le Notre differs in little from its predecessors or its fellows, except in its extent and magnificence. Here, as elsewhere, in the production of his school,

> 'Grove nods at grove, each alley has its brother,
> And half the garden just reflects the other.'

Its wonder was the labyrinth in which thirty-nine of Aesop's fables were represented by means of copper figures of birds and beasts, each group being connected with a separate fountain, and all spouting water. But we are speaking now of the characteristic features of French gardens, and not so much of gardening itself in France, for we have learnt much from modern French gardeners with regard to the training and management of fruit trees and vegetable culture, especially mushroom culture, which was very little practised in this country until French gardeners showed us what could be done in this direction by growing them for the Paris market in the catacombs of that city.

31 The Dutch style is marked by a great profusion of ornament on a small scale: 'Trees cut to statues, statues thick as trees'; canals and ditches made to accommodate the bridges thrown across them; caves, waterworks, banqueting houses, and the never-failing *lusthaus* or summer house, with a profusion of trelliswork and green paint, furnished, as Evelyn has it, 'with whatever may render the place agreeable, melancholy, and country-like', but abounding also in beautiful grassy banks and green slopes, unknown in French gardens.

32 In the United Kingdom and in the Colonies, gardening, as an art, much less as a science, is of comparatively modern date, but in no other country has it made such progress. The universal aspiration, 'Give me but a garden', pervades young and old of our race. Our travellers ransack the Old World and the New for new plants with which to beautify our gardens. The footsore and weary and rather eccentric Australian traveller in Leichhardt's *Overland Expedition* erected his tent, generally at a distance from the rest, under a shady tree or in a green bower of shrubs, where he made himself as comfortable as the place would allow by spreading branches and grass under his couch, and covering his tent with them to keep it shady and cool, *even planting lilies in blossom before his tent*, in order that he might enjoy their sight during his short stay. Under these circumstances, it is not surprising that our garden literature should be extremely copious.

33 For this taste, as well as the early rudiments of gardening, we are indebted to the Romans; for Strabo, writing in the first century, tells us that the people of Britain were ignorant of the art of cultivating gardens. The continual wars in which Britain was engaged from the fifth century, when the Romans vacated the island, probably rooted out all traces of an art so civilising as gardening, although there are indications that vineyards planted in the third century, under the Emperor Proteus, existed in the eighth century, when they are mentioned by the Venerable Bede; while William of Malmesbury, writing in the twelfth century, commends the vineyards of the county of Gloucester; and Pliny tells us that cherries, which Lucullus had introduced into Italy about a century before, were grown in Britain in the first century. Throughout the transition period which succeeded the Roman conquest, the warlike barons and discontented people were probably too much occupied in looking to their personal safety to think much of gardening. The opulent earls of Northumberland, whose household consisted, in 1512, of a hundred and sixty persons, had but one gardener, who, according to the *Household Book*, attended 'hourly in the garden for setting of erbes, and clipping of knottis, and sweeping the said garden clene'.

34 In Scotland – if we may trust to the authority of the royal poet James I – that poor country had already established some claims to the reputation which has since carried so many of her sons over the world as gardeners. In his poem called 'The King's Quhair', written early in the fifteenth century, when in captivity in the Tower of London, he speaks of

> A garden fair, and in the corneris set,
> An herbere green with wandes long and small.
> Railit about, and so with treeis set

Was all the place, and hawthorn hedges knet,
That lyfe was non, walkying there forbye
That might within scarce any wight espye,
So thicke the bewis and the leves grene.

35 Toward the end of the fifteenth and in the early part of the sixteenth century, the wise and politic Henry VII had nearly succeeded in rooting out the feuds of the Roses red and white, which are reputed to have commenced by the supporters of the rival claims of the houses of York and Lancaster plucking white and red roses as emblems of their respective factions; and a long reign of comparative repose had no doubt prepared the people for the revival of gardening, with the other arts of civilisation, which took place in the succeeding reign of Henry VIII. The royal gardens of Nonesuch, in the neighbourhood of Richmond, Surrey, so called by a play upon words, because none could then be found that equalled them, were laid out by this monarch with the greatest magnificence, and may be regarded as a fair type of old English gardens. The kitchen garden is said by Lysons to have been surrounded by a wall fourteen feet in height, and to have contained seventy-two fruit trees. On the west was a wilderness, or 'wild garden', extending over ten acres of ground, the kitchen garden being to the north of the palace. The King's private gardens were ornamented with fountains and statuary, and contained among the plants and trees that were to be found in it six lilacs grouped round one of the fountains, and a hundred and forty-four fruit trees. Before the palace was a bowling-green, surrounded by a balustrade of freestone.

Hentzner, in his *Travels*, which were translated by Horace Walpole, gives the following account of these gardens: 'Nonesuch is so encompassed with parks, delicious gardens, groves ornamented with trelliswork, cabinets of verdure, and walks so embowered by trees, that it seems to be a place pitched upon by Pleasure herself to dwell in along with Health. In the pleasure and artificial gardens are many columns and pyramids of marble; two fountains spout water one round the other like a pyramid, upon which are perched small birds that stream water out of their bills. In the grove of Diana is a very agreeable fountain, with Actaeon turned into a stag as he was sprinkled by the goddess and her nymphs. There is besides another pyramid of marble with concealed pipes, which spirt upon all who come within their reach.' Hence it appears that these gardens in their time might well claim pre-eminence, and justify the poet, who tells us,

This, which no equal hath in art or fame,
Britons deservedly do Nonesuch name.

36 Among other English gardens that were laid out in Henry's reign, those of Hampton Court, with its labyrinth or maze, covering a quarter of an acre, and containing half a mile of walks that turn and wind in every direction, were justly celebrated. During Elizabeth's reign, Holland and Hatfield Houses were both laid out. Of the former, part of the original plan still remains; of Hatfield, Hentzner says, 'The gardens are surrounded by a piece of water, with boats rowing through the alleys of well-cut trees and labyrinths made with great labour.' Mazes and labyrinths, by means of which visitors might find themselves lost, and wander hopelessly about until released by some one who had the clue, seems, indeed, to have been the taste of that day – a jocular sort of hospitality 'more honoured in the breach than the observance'. Some idea of the style and arrangements of old English gardens may be gathered from Fig. 4, which is a representation of the old palace at Hatfield.

FIG. 4 *The old palace at Hatfield*

37 In the reign of James I, the royal gardens at Theobalds, in Essex, were laid out, and are described by Mandelso, a French traveller who visited England in the reign of Charles I, as forming 'a large square, having all its walls covered with phillyrea, and a beautiful *jet d'eau* in the centre, the parterre having many pleasant walks, part of which are planted on the sides with espaliers, and others arched all over. At the end is a small mount, called the Mount of Venus, placed in the midst of a labyrinth, and which is, upon the whole, the most beautiful spot in the world.' At this time, the subject engaged the able and comprehensive mind of Bacon, with little immediate result; but the contempt he expresses for 'images cut out of juniper and other garden stuff' was not without its weight a few generations later, when a purer taste came to prevail.

38 Chatsworth and Wooton, and many other of the finest gardens in England, were laid out in the reign of Charles II; garden structures also began to be erected. Le Notre planted Greenwich and St James's Parks, under the immediate directions of Charles, Versailles being the model, although only at a humble distance. Clipped yew trees and other Dutch tendencies, scarcely redeemed by the magnificent gates and iron railings now introduced, became the rage in the reign of William and Mary – 'terraced walks, hedges of evergreens, shorn shrubs in boxes, orange and myrtle trees in tubs, being the chief excellences'. In 1696 an orangery with a glass roof was erected at Wollaton Hall, Nottinghamshire, said to have been the first structure of the kind in England, although greenhouses answering to the modern conservatory were brought into use in Italy in the sixteenth century. These gardens were laid out in the Italian style, with terraces, statues, fountains, and urns, and, next to Chatsworth, they seem to have been the finest in England. With the gardens of Powis Castle, and some other fine old terraced gardens, they were unfortunately sacrificed to the rage for improvement ushered in a century later by Kent and Brown and their followers.

39 The time was, indeed, fast approaching when an entirely new school of art in gardening and laying out grounds was to be initiated. Bacon's criticisms had paved the way; Milton's gorgeous descriptions helped to bring the stiff formality of the French and Dutch styles into disfavour; Addison and Pope, by their ridicule, completed their overthrow. Addison compared your makers of parterres and flower gardens to epigrammatists and sonneteers; contrivers of bowers and grottoes, treillages and cascades, to romance writers; while the gravel-pits at Kensington, then just laid out, were the writers of heroic verse. This ridicule had its due effect, and when combined with the imaginings of Milton, and the natural descriptions of scenery by Thomson and Shenstone, and the refined criticism of Pope, Gray, Warton, Whately, and Walpole, and the practical application of the poet's visions by Kent and Mason and their immediate predecessors, had a wonderful effect on English gardens and parks. The gardens of Paradise, as described by Milton, became the germ of many a palatial garden given up to the tender mercies of the artist. Many a garden emulated that of Eden, which

FIG. 5 *Chatsworth and its gardens*

'Crowns with her enclosure green,
As with a rural mound, the champaign head
Of a steep wilderness, whose hairy sides
With thicket overgrown, grotesque and wild,
Access denied.'

40 Nor is it to be wondered at that this gorgeous picture seized upon the imagination of the more enthusiastic landscape gardeners, roused to exertion by the mixed criticism and ridicule of the leading spirits of the age. The result was the establishment of a new school in art, which, in course of time, came to be recognised as the English style, and which, according to Gray, 'is the only taste we can call our own, the only proof we can give of original talent in matters of pleasure'.

41 Loudon and Wise were among the earliest innovators, and are highly praised in the *Spectator* for the manner in which they laid out Kensington Gardens. Bridgman followed, hewing down many a verdurous peacock and juniper lion. Kent, the inventor of the ha-ha, followed, and broke up the distinction of garden and park; and Brown – 'Capability' Brown, as he was called – succeeded him with round clumps and boundary belts, artificially winding rivers and lakes, with broad drives terminating in summer houses. Brown is admitted to have been a man of genius, and astonished the gardening world by the skilful manner in which he arrested the river and formed the beautiful lake at Blenheim; but he could not be everywhere, and he found many ignorant imitators.

Sir Walter Scott tells an amusing story of one of these conceited pretenders who was employed by Lord Abercorn in laying out the grounds at Duddingston. The house embraces noble views of Craigmillar Castle on the one side, backed by the Pentlands; on the other, by Arthur's Seat and the Salisbury Crags; and on a third the eye is carried past the precipitous rocks on which stands the Castle of Edinburgh, across the rich plains of Midlothian: the improver conceived it to be his duty to block out every glimpse of this noble landscape. Duddingston Loch is a beautiful piece of water, lying at the foot of Arthur's Seat: he shut out the lake also, and would have done as much for the surrounding hills, but they were too grand objects to be so treated. Lord Abercorn laughed at his absurdities, but was too indolent to interrupt his vagaries.

41 It is not surprising, perhaps, that the opponents of the old style rushed at a very early period to the opposite extreme; fine old gardens were recklessly pulled to pieces; in the words of Sir Walter Scott, 'Down went many a trophy of old magnificence – courtyard, ornamented enclosure, fosse, avenue, barbican, and every extensive monument of battled wall and flanking tower.' Sir Uvedale Price, who went a certain length with the prevailing mania, which he afterwards was still more active in arresting, expresses bitter regret for the destruction of an ancestral garden on the old system, which he condemned to destruction before he found out his error. He was afterwards led to write strongly in favour of the preservation of the remains of ancient magnificence still untouched, with modifications calculated to redeem them from the charge of barbarism.

42 'It was, indeed, high time that some one should interfere,' continues Sir Walter Scott. 'The garden, artificial in its structure, its shelter, its climate, and its soil, which every consideration of taste, beauty, and convenience recommended to be kept near to the mansion, and maintained as its appendage, has by a strange and sweeping sentence of exile been condemned to wear the coarsest and most humbling form.' Sir Uvedale Price soon recognised a threefold division of the domain. For the architectural terrace and flower-garden, in the direction of the house, he admits the formal style; for the shrubbery or pleasure-ground, a transition between flowers and trees, which he is willing to hand over to the improver; but for the park, which belongs to the picturesque – his own subject – he gives full scope to the most picturesque disposition, provided it is not frittered away in trifling details. This style of laying out, in which the lawn is imperceptibly lost in the distant park, has been called the 'English' style. 'Nothing,' says Scott, 'is more completely the child of art than a garden.' Who would clothe such a child in the gypsy garb, however picturesque it may be?

43 During the present century, this question, which at its commencement was one of chaos, has acquired form and consistency. The distinction which Sir Uvedale Price, Whately, and a host of writers sought to establish and simplify, has been ably continued by Sir Walter Scott, Sir Henry Stewart, Sir Thomas Dick Lauder – the able editor of the last edition of Price's work – Gilpin, and a host of writers, ably seconded by Repton, and another Gilpin – a professional landscape gardener – Sir Joseph Paxton, and other well-known practical gardeners; and it is now universally admitted that the garden surrounding the house, whether an architectural terrace or bedded lawn, must of necessity possess uniformity; that the shrubbery immediately adjoining must partake of the same character, somewhat modified; while the more distant portions and the park are willingly abandoned to the landscape gardener – a term, however, to which Sir Walter Scott takes exception.

44 Such is a very brief sketch of the rise and progress of gardening in Great Britain, and of 'palatial' gardening, which is necessarily the parent of all other styles worthy of name. The extent, however, to which the humbler class of gardens have been carried bears testimony how deeply rooted is the taste for flowers and gardening pursuits. While the higher order of gardening was settling down into the refined taste which has produced the ornamental gardens of Chatsworth, shown in Fig. 5, Trentham, Alton Towers, and Dalkeith Park, suburban gardening was also undergoing its own transition. The undoubted taste of Kent, Brown, and Repton was some protection to the places of which they had the immediate charge; but the humbler gardens, brought into form by their ignorant and careless imitators, had no such protection: with them a taste for the fantastic occupied the place which in a previous age had been devoted to the formal, and beds of bizarre forms and irregular outline were introduced, to the disfigurement of many a beautiful lawn. This style of arrangement, though still occasionally seen, has given place, like the same evil in more important places, to a purer and more simple style of arranging garden grounds. In villa gardening at the present time, the mixed garden holds a prominent place, and even the kitchen garden, pure and simple, is now no longer looked upon as a place devoid of interest; indeed, the beautifully-arranged kitchen gardens at Frogmore, where royalty does not refuse to visit, are proofs that utility is not necessarily unornamental. The cabbage and the onion were not excluded from 'the little garden of our ancestors, where they knew every flower because they were few, and every name because they were simple. Their rose-bushes and gilly flowers were dear to them, because themselves pruned, watered, and watched them – had marked from day to day their opening buds, and removed their fading blossoms.'

45 Gardens, as we have seen, were carefully cultivated by the Romans; the cottager's garden was the test of his worth as a member of the community; and we shall not be far wrong if we apply a similar test to our own rural population. The garden of the English cottager is, indeed, already remarked as one of our national distinctions; even in the midst of squalor and misery in London and some of our largest towns, we find frequently some poor artisan or charwoman growing auriculas, carnations, fuchsias, and geraniums in the greatest perfection, thus evincing the universal interest that is taken by all Englishmen and Englishwomen, high and low, rich and poor, gentle and simple, in this enthralling occupation. It has indeed been well remarked by a Quarterly reviewer, 'that when we see a plot set apart for a rose-bush, and a gilly flower, and a carnation, it is enough for us; if the jessamine and the honeysuckle embower the porch without, we may be sure there is the potato, the cabbage, and the onion for the pot within: if there be not plenty there, at least there is no want; if not happiness, there is the nearest approach to it in this world – content.

Yes! in the poor man's garden grow
Far more than herbs and flowers –
Kind thoughts contentment, peace of mind,
And joy for many hours!'

CHAPTER 2

The Formation of Natural Soils

46 Whoever travels in these days of railways and makes use of his eyes, must of necessity be struck, as he passes along between precipitous railway banks, with the variety of soils and subsoils which present themselves to view. White, red, and blue pass in rapid succession; soils, sandy and dry, pulverising readily under tillage, or stiff, wet, and unmanageable, may all be seen in a day's journey. In the absence of more exciting food for thought, the passing traveller, breaking through that indifference which takes all things for granted, may well ask himself whence arises this great diversity of soils, and what are their constituents?

47 The chemist will answer readily enough that they are compounded of a great many chemical substances, and he will repeat the names of about fourteen constituents, which are present in varying proportions in all fertile soils. The practical cultivator, however, will tell you that there are some five or six well-ascertained varieties of soil, characterised according to the preponderating proportions of silica, lime, clay, vegetable mould, marl, or loam, which they contain, according to his rough estimate.

a) *Sandy soils* contain 80 per cent, or thereabouts, of silica; that is, of the crumbling *débris* of granite or sandstone rock.
b) *Calcareous soils* contain upwards of 20 per cent of lime in their composition.
c) *Clay soils* contain 50 per cent of stiff unctuous clay.
d) *Peaty soils* or vegetable mould, the richest of all garden soils, contains from 5 to 12 per cent of *humus*; that is, decomposed vegetable and animal matter.
e) *Marly soils* is the *débris* of limestone rock, decomposed and reduced to a paste. It contains from 5 to 20 per cent of carbonate of lime.
f) *Loamy soils* is soil in which the proportion of clay varies from 20 to 25 per cent; sand, and various kinds of alluvium, making up the remainder.

In the *Elements of Agricultural Chemistry* by the late Professor J. W. F. Johnston, FRS, and Dr Charles H. Cameron, the following remarks are made on the leading characteristics of soils as above named:

> If an ounce of soil be intimately mixed with a pint of water, and it is perfectly softened and diffused through it, and if, after shaking, the heavy parts be allowed to settle for a few minutes, the sand will subside, while the clay – which is in finer particles and less heavy – will remain floating. If the water and fine floating clay be now poured into another vessel, and be allowed to stand until the water has become clear, the sandy part of the soil will be found on the bottom of the first vessel, and the clayey part on that of the second, and they may be dried and weighed separately.
>
> If 100 grains of dry soil, not peaty or unusually rich in vegetable matter, leave no more than 10 of clay when treated in this manner, it is called a *sandy soil*; if from 10 to

40, a *sandy loam*; if from 40 to 70, a *loamy soil*; if from 70 to 85, a *clay loam*; if from 85 to 90, a *strong clay soil*; and when no sand is separated at all by this process, it is a pure *agricultural clay*.

This pure clay contains silica and alumina in the proportion of about 60 of the former to 40 of the latter. Soils of pure clay rarely occur, it being well known to all practical men that the strong clays (tile clays), which contain from 5 to 15 per cent of sand, are brought into arable cultivation with the greatest possible difficulty. It will rarely, almost never, happen, therefore, that arable land will contain more than 30 to 35 per cent of alumina.

If a soil contain more than 5 per cent of carbonate of lime, it is called a *marl*; if more than 20 per cent, it is a *calcareous soil*. *Peaty soils*, of course, are those in which vegetable matter predominates very much.

48 Both chemist and cultivator, however, confine themselves to generalities. They tell us of the constituent elements of soils, and the proportions in which these elements exist in each variety; but we want to know something more of the origin of soils than we have yet ascertained, and for this we must turn to the geologist. From him we learn a strange and wonderful chapter in the history of creation. The framework of the globe we inhabit, he tells us, is a dense mass of primitive rock, the strata composing the earth's crust being divided into two great classes – the lower rocks, such as granite, basalt, etc., which are unstratified and crystalline, being due to the action of fire; and the higher series, which are stratified and very rarely crystalline, being attributable to the action of water. In the unstratified or fire-formed rocks no signs of animal life have ever yet been found, but in the stratified rocks of aqueous formation traces of animal life have been found in more or less abundance according to the priority of formation, and this at once forms a great and important mark of distinction between them.

49. By modern geologists the rocks that compose the earth's crust are divided into four great series, each named in reference to the fossils and remains of animal life that are found in them. Lowest of all are the primitive or crystalline rocks of igneous formation, which are called Azoic (Gr. ἀ, *without*, ζωή *life*), because no traces of the existence of animals coeval with them have ever been found in them. Next in order comes the Palaeozoic Series (Gr. παλαιός, *ancient*, ζωή, *life*), sometimes termed the Primary Series, and so called because in the rocks of which the series are composed are found the first or most ancient forms of life. After this comes the Mesozoic Series (Gr. μεσός, *middle*, ζωή, *life*), so called because the rocks of this period contain forms of life belonging to the middle period of the earth's existence. This series is also called the secondary Series. Lastly come the rocks of the Neozoic (Gr. νέος, *new*, ζωή, life), or Cainozoic (Gr. καινός, *recent*, ζωή, *life*) Series, also called the Tertiary Series, in which are found human remains, implements, and even dwellings formed by man, as well as the remains of existing and extinct quadrupeds of different kinds. By some geologists the latest formations are considered as forming another series, which is termed the Post Tertiary; but it will be enough here if we regard this as being the most recent formation of the Neozoic or Tertiary Series.

It will be useful to append here a table of the stratified rocks included in the above-named series, formed chiefly in accordance with Lyell's arrangement, showing the leading divisions and subdivisions in each, the formations that belong to them, and the fossil animals that have been found in them.

I – TERTIARY NEOZOIC OR CAINOZOIC SERIES			
i Post Tertiary or Post Pliocene	1 *Recent*	Marine strata, Danish peat	*Human remains, kitchen middens, bronze and stone implements, Swiss lake dwellings, etc*
	2 *Earlier*	Brixham cave, ancient valley gravels, glacial drift, ancient Nile mud, post glacial deposits in N. America, Australian breccias	*Flint knives, bones of existing and extinct quadrupeds, remains of Mastodon*
ii Pliocene	3 *Newer or Pleistocene*	Mammalian beds, Norwich crag	*Marine shells*
	4 *Older*	Red and Coralline crags (Suffolk; Antwerp).	*Marine shells*
iii Miocene	5 *Upper* 6 *Lower*	Bordeaux, Virginia sands and Touraine beds, Pikermé deposits near Athens, volcanic tufa and limestone of the Azores, brown coal of Germany, etc.	*Mastodon, Gigantic Elk, Salamander*
iv Eocene	7 *Upper* 8 *Middle* 9 *Lower*	Fresh-water and marine beds, Barton clays, Bracklesham sands, Paris gypsum, London, Plastic, and Thanet clays	*Palms, Birds, etc*
II – SECONDARY OR MESOZOIC SERIES			
v Cretaceous	10 *Upper*	British chalk, Maestricht beds, chalk with or without flints, chalk marl, upper green sand, gault, lower green sand	*Mesosaurus, Fish, Mollusks, etc*
	11 *Lower Neocomian, or Wealden*	Kentish rag, Weald clay, Hastings sand	*Iguanodon, Hylaeosaurus*
vi Oolite	12 *Upper*	Purbeck beds, Portland stone and sand, Kimmeridge clay, lithographic stone of Solenhofen	*Fish, Archaeopteryx*
	13 *Middle*	Calcareous grit, coral rag, Oxford clay, Kelloway rock	*Ammonites, Belemnites*
	14 *Lower*	Cornbrash, forest marble, Bradford clay, Great Oolite, Stonesfield slate, Fuller's earth, Inferior Oolite	*Ichthyosaurus, Plesiosaurus, Pterodactyl*
vii Lias	15 *Lias*	Lias clay and marl stone	*Ammonites, Equisetum, Amphibia, Labyrinthodon*
viii Trias	16 *Upper*	White lias, red clay, Cheshire salt, Virginian coal beds	*Fish, Dromatherium*
	17 *Middle or Muschelkalk*	This formation is not found in the United Kingdom	*Encrinus, Placodus gigas*
	18 *Lower*	New Red Sandstone of Lancashire and Cheshire	*Footprints of Birds and Reptiles, Labyrinthodon*
III – PRIMARY OR PALAEOZOIC SERIES			
ix Permian	19 *Permian*	Magnesian limestone, marl slates, red sandstone, shale, dolomite, kupfer-schiefer	*Firs, Fishes, Amphibia*
x Carboniferous	20 *Upper* 21 *Lower*	Coal measures, millstone grit, mountain limestone	*Ferns, Calamites*
xi Devonian	22 *Upper* 23 *Middle* 24 *Lower*	Tilestones, cornstones, marls, quartzose, conglomerates	*Shells, Fish, Trilobites*
xii Silurian	25 *Upper* 26 *Middle* 27 *Lower*	Ludlow shales, Aymestry limestone, Wenlock limestone and shale, Caradoc sandstone, Llandeilo flags, Niagara limestone	*Shells, Sponges, Corals, Trilobites*
xiii Cambrian	28 *Upper* 29 *Lower*	Bala limestone, Festiniog slates, Bangor slates and grits, Wicklow rock, Hasleets grits, Huronian system of Canada	*Zoophytes, Lingula. Ferns, Sigillaria, Stigmaria, Calamites, Cryptogamia*
xiv Laurentian	30 *Upper*	Gnesis in Hebrides, Labrador series N. of the St. Lawrence, Adirondack Mountains (New York)	
	31 *Lower*	Geniss, quartzites, inter-stratified limestones.	*Eoozon Canadense*, oldest known fossil, found in the limestone

50 The stratified rocks, which are due to the action of water, and which are comprised in the Secondary and Primary Series, are distinguished by their colour and structure, but above all by the fossil remains that have been discovered in them, by which the naturalist has been enabled to trace the history and progress of creation through a vast lapse of ages. It will be interesting to trace briefly the character and nature of the geological formations of each epoch, taking them in the order assigned to them in the preceding table, but proceeding inversely in order of their formation, from the earliest to the latest.

a The *Laurentian* (30, 31) and *Cambrian* (28, 29) formations, resting on the Azoic or Igneous system, and showing in themselves traces of the action of heat upon them, consist for the most part of hard, slaty rocks. Wherever these mica, slate, and gneiss rocks come to the surface, as does the Laurentian system in the north and west of Ireland, and in Argyleshire and Perthshire in Scotland, and the Cambrian in Cornwall, the counties on the west coast of Wales, the hilly parts of Cumberland and Tipperary, and the south-eastern parts of Ireland, the soil is poor and thin, and consists for the most part of heath and bog. Such soil is difficult to bring into cultivation, and requires good farming and lime as manure to quicken it.

b The *Silurian* formations (25, 26, 27), or clay-slate system, are a mass of sedimentary rocks, intersected here and there by beds of igneous origin, in the upper series of which are found the first vestiges of organised beings. They consist chiefly of sandstones and shales, with limestone interspersed, and are conspicuous in Wales and the south of Scotland. The soils formed by the decay of these rocks, consisting for the most part of '*muddy* clays', as Johnston terms them, are cold and barren. The best portions of them are produced from the limestone; but the clays require the addition of lime in the form of manure. Heath and bog in extensive tracts are the characteristics of land overlying the clay-slate system.

c The *Devonian* formations (22, 23, 24), or *Old Red Sandstone*, as they are sometimes called, can be traced by the naked eye, from the contrast they present to the grey slate of the Silurian and crystalline masses of the granite rocks. This difference in colour is the consequence of a change in the beds of ancient seas. During the formation of the Silurian deposits, the bed of the sea was occupied by blackish mud or clay, the *débris* of granite rock, decomposed by atmospheric influences and thrown down by the action of the waves. In the Devonian formations, so called from their prevalence in the county of Devon, this was succeeded by a sandy deposit, mixed with oxide of iron, to which the red colour is due. The soils from the red sandstones, red marls, and cornstones, as found in Devonshire, the counties in England and Wales watered by the Wye, parts of Scotland south of the Firth of Forth, Perthshire and the extreme northern counties, and in Waterford and Tipperary and the north of Ireland, in the belt of land between Dundalk Bay and Clew Bay, are for the most part of a deep rich red in colour and extremely fertile. The soil yielded by the harder sandstones is not nearly so good, being hungry and sandy.

d The *Carboniferous* system (20, 21), embracing the mountain limestone, rises in many places in close connection with the old red sandstone. The latter prevails to a large extent throughout Scotland and Wales, as it has been shown; but if we look to the southern slopes of the mountains, especially in the latter country, they are found to be of another shade, denoting the transition between the Devonian and the Carboniferous systems. The shales of the coal measures belonging to this period produce stiff, wet, and harsh clays, that are brought with difficulty into cultivation: the soil from the millstone grit is also poor, but that from the mountain limestone is well suited for pasture lands, and that from the limestone and shales in immediate contiguity makes good arable land suitable for oats, and, by judicious cultivation, for wheat. The carboniferous rocks develop themselves with great boldness in the vast basins of Glamorganshire, in Caernarvon, and in

Carmarthenshire, and again in Derbyshire, the picturesque character of this formation being most observable in the *dales* or gorges of the mountains. The limestone, which forms the base of the coal-measures, is exclusively of marine origin, as is made evident by the multitude of marine fossils found there; it also contains the first traces of the terrestrial flora, so abundant in the carboniferous formation, or coal-measures, deposited during an epoch of immense duration. It is supposed that, in the upper coalfields, where bed is heaped upon bed, the produce of ages upon ages, their formation was quiet and progressive; but that towards the end of the period it was marked by great convulsions; the masses of coal were broken, and thrown down in dislocated lines into separate basins, during which entrance is made on the next geological epoch.

e The *Permian* system (19) has left few traces in the British islands. It is, however, represented in Yorkshire, Derbyshire, and some other places, by accumulations of dolomite, of which we have examples in the stone used for the Houses of Parliament. The mountains of the system attain great height, but they are poor in fossils. Various-coloured marls, sandstone, and magnesian limestone characterise the formations of this epoch. The soil is poor and thin, and not good as pasture land, and it requires high farming to render it remunerative as arable land.

f The *New Red Sandstone* (18) is the most important formation of the Triassic period. In its features it is neither so striking as the old red sandstone, nor has it the bold and rigid aspect of the more primitive granite rocks. Its masses have formed the sandy bed of an ancient sea, of less depth than the seas of the preceding epochs. It is found chiefly in the northern and central counties of England. The soil produced from the red sandstone and red marls is arable land of the best quality.

g The *Lias* formation (15), consisting of blue clay, limestone, and marlstone, occupies a comparatively narrow belt, running through England almost from north to south, from the north-east of Yorkshire to the western extremity of Dorsetshire. The soil is a blue cold clay, which affords good pasture land, and is convertible into excellent wheat land when well drained.

h The *Oolite* formation (12, 13, 14) originates in the muddy deposits made in a calm sea. From Yorkshire on the north-east to Dorsetshire on the south-west, this formation extends across England, a system of rocks nearly thirty miles in breadth, which give a peculiar profile to the country. Its quarries furnish an excellent building material, as in the Bath and Portland stone. The clays on the sandstone and limestone of the *Lower Oolite* (14), appearing in the belt of land running north-east and south-west between the embouchures of the Humber and the Severn, furnish soils that are useful for both pasturage and tillage. In the *Middle Oolite* (13) the soils from the sandstones and limestones are excellent as arable land; but the clays, of a blue colour and very tenacious, found in most of the English counties from the Wash to the Severn, though furnishing good pasture lands, are extremely heavy, and are brought with difficulty and at much cost into cultivation. The soils of the *Upper Oolite* (12), found chiefly in Dorsetshire, are mostly serviceable as pasture land, but when mingled with the *débris* of the sandy limestones by which the clay is covered in some places, they are excellent for tillage.

i The *Cretaceous* or *Chalk* formation (10, 11) comprises green sands, chalk, marl, and flint, among its constituents. It is conspicuous in the eastern and southern counties of England; it is the base on which rests the great tertiary deposits of the London basin and the Wealden clay, and spreads over wide areas in France and Germany. If we traverse England in a slightly south-easterly direction, from Yorkshire to the extremity of Kent, a totally different outline characterises the plains and mountains, the colour of the rocks, and the character of the vegetation. Long ridges, having the appearance of coasts, may be traced in the interior of the country, with rounded headlands; at their foot stretch out undulating plains, richly wooded, clothed with herbage or with golden crops of richest cereals. Occasionally valleys are hollowed out without watercourses, the heights and downs on either side being often more or less denuded, their white and tempest-torn surface contrasting strangely with the red and broken rocks with which they are sometimes surrounded. In Oxfordshire, the Chiltern Hills may be instanced as presenting this aspect – chalky hills formerly covered with beeches. In Hampshire, at Selborne, is found a chalk formation of similar character; and in Kent, hundreds of similar spots maintain its character for beautiful scenery and richly productive soil. The *Wealden* formation (11), in the counties of Kent and Sussex, in the south-eastern corner of England, affords excellent land for tillage on the marls and limestone, but the clay lands are wet and cold, and require draining to bring them into remunerative cultivation. The chalks of the *Upper Chalk* (10) measures are useful for sheep pasturage and tillage, the chalk containing flints being more fitted for the former purpose, and the marly chalk without flints for the latter. But even the soil on the upper chalk is rendered highly productive of corn, beans, peas, and root crops by deep ploughing and fork husbandry, by which the soil itself and the upper portion of the substratum which immediately underlies it are mixed together, to the great improvement of the former. The clays of the green sands afford cold, wet lands, chiefly appropriated for pasturage; but the soil from the green sands and marls, especially when in combination, are fertile and well suited for hop growing. It is further enriched by the phosphate of lime furnished by the coprolites and other organic remains that are present in it in large quantities.

51 The formations of the Tertiary Period maybe regarded as the flesh which covers the bony skeleton of rocks that form the framework of the globe. This, indeed, belongs more properly to our subject; namely, the formation of soils. The lower strata, compressed by pressure into solid rock, and the upper portions, with the loose soil thrown on the surface, consisting of loosely-arranged beds of marine and freshwater origin, possess none of the grand characteristics which distinguish all the previous formations; but, in their place, we have the softened horizon, the rich plains, and smiling hills of a more civilising landscape. To the earlier geologists the Tertiary formation was a mere chaos of superficial deposits, which seemed to have no connection with any distinct epoch; but Sir Charles Lyell and recent geologists have deciphered this last chapter of an obscure history, dividing it, as previously explained, into (1) the Lower Tertiaries, or *Eocene*; (2) the Middle Tertiaries, or *Miocene*; (3) the Recent Tertiaries, or *Pliocene*; and (4) the Post Tertiaries, or *Post Pliocene*; each distinguished by the character of its fossiliferous deposits.

The most noteworthy features of the Tertiary formations are the clays of the Eocene period (7, 8, 9), known as the *London* and *Plastic Clays*. These are stiff, and dark in colour; but when mixed with sand, as the Plastic clays are, a good arable soil is the result. The stiffer clay soils require drainage and admixture with chalk or lime to render them fit for producing corn and root crops. The *Crag* of the Pliocene formations, found in the eastern borders of Norfolk and Suffolk, is formed of remains of shells mingled with sand and marl, and containing large quantities of coprolites, the principal ingredient of which is bone earth, otherwise known as calcium phosphate.

52 At the commencement of the Tertiary Period, there is every reason to believe that the British islands were merely a long straggling archipelago of rocky pinnacles, rising out of the great deep; and a geological map of the period may readily be constructed by laying under water every part of the country which does not rise 800 feet above the level of the sea. Taking the whole range of the country, it will be found that it is rugged and mountainous on the west, north-west, and south-west; extensive elevations, intermingling with valleys, dales, and intersected by rivers and plains much more extensive at the central, eastern, and south-eastern parts.

Commencing at Cape Wrath, an uninterrupted range of granite mountains, with groups of Silurian and sandstone formation, in some places rising perpendicularly out of the sea to a great height, occupy the west coast, culminating at Fort William, in Ben Nevis, where it is met by the mighty Grampians, the principal range of which, commencing a little to the east of Aberdeen, stretches across the country from east to west, culminating in Cairn-gorm and Ben Muic-dhu, the loftiest mountain in the island. The spurs of these two mountain ranges occupy pretty nearly the whole angle formed between Cape Wrath and the most easterly of the Grampians, while, on the south, it extends as far as Ben Lomond on the west and the Ochill Hills on the east. A broad valley, formed by the Forth and Clyde, and other watercourses, which even now nearly intersect the country, was still an ocean-bed; but, to the south, the Pentlands just raised their heads above the water, and formed, with the Lammermoor Hills, Black-hope Scaurs, Lothian Head, and the Liddles dale and Cheviot range, a small archipelago by themselves. South of the Tyne rose what has been called the Pennine chain, which includes Crossfell, Wharnside, and Holme Moss, terminating at the Weaver Hills in Staffordshire. This long range occupies the centre of the country for about 170 miles; while the Cumbrian group forms a quadrangular range nearly united with it for a considerable part of the distance, and may be considered the central range – the backbone, as it were, of the country.

FIG. 6 *Fort William*

A little to the south of the Weaver Hills, and considerably to the west, rising abruptly out of the sea, at Anglesea Bay, the British Alps, or Cambrian mountain-system, including the loftiest mountains of South Britain, commence. These extend their spurs over the whole west coast between the Bristol Channel and the island of Anglesea, and far into the interior of the country, gradually losing themselves in the Wrekin, in the plains of Salop and the tableland which extends between Nottingham, Birmingham, and Northampton. A few isolated groups of hills, as the Malvern Hills, the Cotswold Hills, the Cleave Hills, Inkpen Beacon, and some of the loftier of the South Downs, would just rise above the waters; but the whole of the east coast, to the foot of the hills named, now known as the eastern plains of England, of an elevation less than 800 feet, would, at the commencement of the Tertiary Period, be under water, and in course of formation, as well as the whole of the south and west coasts, except the high lands round Dartmoor and the Cornish hills.

Such is a brief sketch of the geological condition of the British islands at the beginning of the Tertiary Period; for the picturesque dales, and beautiful valleys, and rolling and undulating plains, which give beauty and variety to the country, were as yet at the bottom of the ocean, which swept the base of the mountain-ranges or lacustrine beds confined to the bosom of the mountains from which they had not as yet forced a passage. Undulating plains of verdure have succeeded to the ocean-wave. The rugged rocks of secondary formation, which now give character to the landscape, were still washed by it.

53 It will, perhaps, be asked how it is that the stratified rocks of the earth's crust, having been formed, as the term *stratified* implies, in a regular succession of layers at succeeding epochs, are found to present themselves at the surface of the earth, or at all events, a little below the surface, thrusting themselves upwards through strata that, according to the geologist, were formed at considerably later periods. This diversity of rocks at the very surface of the earth is due to forces – of volcanic character – generated in the interior of the earth, and producing dislocation and upheavals of the strata above them. The uniform course of the stratified rocks being thus broken, the strata on one side of the fracture have been thrown upward, while those on the other side have sunk. Thus the *ends*, so to speak, of masses of strata formed at widely different periods have been brought into juxtaposition, in some cases, far under the surface of the earth, producing a discontinuance of strata according to regular formation, or what are technically termed *faults*; while, in other cases, the upheaval of the expansive force acting below them has actually driven them to the surface. Nor is this change of position confined to the stratified rocks only, for the crystalline, or unstratified rocks, have been forced upwards to the surface by the same agency, right through the superincumbent layers of stratified rocks formed at later periods. Thus we find that *volcanic* agency is the first means to which the present disposition of rocks at the earth's surface is to be attributed.

54 The other agencies which have operated in the greatest degree in producing the present features of the country, and, indeed, in the formation of the various soils that cover its surface, are *chemical* and *mechanical*. The great *chemical* agent is the Oxygen contained in the atmosphere, for which many of the mineral elements possess a powerful affinity. Rocks have been broken up, and whole masses of them have crumbled into small fragments, which, by means of further accessions of oxygen, have finally crumbled into dust.

55 Again, *Carbonic Acid*, contained in great abundance in rainwater, has a powerful influence in dissolving the carbonate of lime present in limestone rocks: where a considerable proportion of clay is present, it crumbles into powder, furnishing what is known as marly soil. Even on felspars, granite, and other crystalline minerals, water exercises a highly-important action, decomposing them into alkaline silicates, yielding, in their turn, silica and carbonate of potash, and silicate of alumina – the chief constituents of clay; in other words, clay is produced; and highly-fertilising alkaline salts, which exist in these minerals, are changed into easily-soluble carbonates, which are thus rendered available for the immediate food of plants.

Plants and animals also take an active part in this disintegration of rocks. In the celebrated experiment of Von Helmont, he planted a willow tree, weighing five pounds, in two hundred pounds of earth, previously dried in an oven. After an interval of five years, he pulled up the willow and found that its weight had increased to a hundred and sixty-three pounds three ounces. During the five years, the earth had been duly watered with rainwater; but in order to protect it from any foreign admixture of soil, a piece of tin-plate was laid on its surface, pierced with small holes; the leaves which fell annually were not included in the weight. The earth was oven-dried and weighed, and was found to have lost only about two ounces of its original weight. Thus, according to Von Helmont, a hundred and sixty-three pounds of wood, and all the leaves of five years' growth, had

FIG. 7 *Dislocation of stratified rock*

been produced from water alone. Von Helmont's idea was that water generated earth, which is altogether fallacious; but the experiment is a valuable illustration of the power which vegetables have of decomposing carbonic acid and absorbing carbon. Subsequent experiments demonstrate the possibility of certain vegetables deriving the whole of the carbon necessary to their existence from water alone, as is shown in Scoffern's *Handy Book of the Chemistry of Soils*. Besides this, seeds of lichens and mosses floating in the air at last attach themselves to the rough and partially decomposed surface of the rocks, and, finding here sufficient food, germinate, and throw out roots, which penetrate into the crevices of the rocks like wedges, widening and separating them, and hastening their decomposition; for in their roots they retain the water, which finally acts upon them by its dissolving powers. Insects come to feed upon the mosses and lichens, and, finally, both die, leaving the rocky matter, originally purely mineral, a mixture of animal, vegetable, and mineral remains, or *humus*. A thin layer of fertile soil is thus formed, on which plants of a higher order spring up, all tending to produce the mighty results that have been hinted at.

56 *Wind, Water – above all, Gravitation* are the more *mechanical* agents in the disintegration of rocks. Water, aided by the tempest, having washed away all the softer supports of a mass of rock, this, in obedience to this irresistible law, soon falls, contributing its mass to fill up the valley below, the rocks being reduced in their fall to smaller pieces; and, finally, obedient to the chemical laws, they crumble to dust, more or less rapidly, according to their nature and the atmospheric influences.

Water, which thus acts as a chemical agent in destroying rocks, is also strong in its physical force. As falling rain, it washes down all loose particles into some riverbed, which again carries down the finer particles, held in suspension, till deposited in the delta, to form, at some future day, a field, a district, or a new country, as the case may be – rescued from the flood. Again, in the earlier geological epochs, when a vast portion of the earth was the bed of ocean, it may be imagined with what force the waves dashed against opposing granite rock. The chemical action was already at work, decomposing the crystalline fabric; while the waves, by their abrasive powers, were grinding and depositing the dark mass, which was to emerge, in due time, in the form of the slaty shale of the Silurian system. The action of the waves and the winds on the stratified rock is still more intelligible; accordingly, it is found that the London clay, embedded over the chalk to the depth of 700 feet, consists of layers of clay, of sand, and of gravel, sometimes marine and sometimes freshwater deposits, as the geologist easily learns by studying its fossil remains, which present every kind of vegetation, from the tropical coconut and acacia to the walnut tree; indicating that the country had passed from a tropical sun at one period to another extreme, when there is every indication that the temperature was that of the frozen zone. There were also shallow seas and lakes at the tropical period, when groves of palm trees existed, under whose shade tortoises basked; and rivers which swarmed with crocodiles, and forests in which the elephant and other tropical animals ranged; while the group of isolated islands became gradually united into small continents, and the rocks into islands, probably with small inland seas and lakes in their bosom.

57 As might be expected from the joint operations of the chemical and mechanical agencies above described, in promoting the formation of surface soil, the soil of any garden or field, when minutely inspected, will be found to contain – (1) Stones, sand, or gravel, in larger or smaller masses; (2) A lighter mass of friable soil, crumbling into dust between finger and thumb, and rendering it muddy when put in water; and (3) Organic matter, that is, vegetable and animal remains, or humus.

58 In order to effect a closer or chemical examination of the soil, it is necessary that a fair sample of the soil should be soaked in a glazed earthen basin, filled with rain or distilled water, agitating it occasionally, so as to break any hard lumps of earth. Where it is hard clay, rub the soil in a mortar with the pestle, adding water from time to time till dissolved. Allow the whole to remain undisturbed for a few minutes, when the sand, stony fragments, and organic matter will fall to the bottom, by reason of their specific gravity; the finer particles floating on the water. This muddy water is to be poured off into a glass vessel, and the deposit left washed repeatedly in clean water, till it comes off perfectly pure. The residuum is reserved for further examination.

59 The muddy water poured off first is suffered to remain at rest in the vessel till the fine mud has quite settled at the bottom, and the water is perfectly clear. The clear water itself must then be poured off into an earthen or porcelain vessel, and left to dry up by evaporation.

60 The sand and gravel, the mud, and the residue of the pure liquid, into which the soil has been separated, are mixed with organic matter. We can, therefore, only separate the soluble from insoluble matter, and the finer vegetable remains from the larger pieces of roots and stems. The soluble organic matter remains in solution, the finer portions with the mud, and the coarser with the gravel and sand. By heating a portion to red heat, in an iron spoon or platinum dish, the organic matter will first blacken the soil, and then disappear entirely. When the heat has been continued some time, and in an increased degree, the incombustible matter which is left behind is generally coloured red by the oxide of iron which is present in every soil. The organic part which burns is called the combustible part. Thus (1) stony fragments; (2) impalpable powder; and (3) soluble organic and inorganic matter, are obtained by the washing process.

61 The sand and gravel vary much in character, partaking of the rocks from which they emanate. The impalpable powder will be found a mixture of clay, with very fine fragments of stone and gravel, and organic matter. In it the chemist will distinguish alumina, silica, oxide of iron, oxide of manganese, lime, magnesia, potash, soda, with traces of phosphorus, sulphuric and carbonic acid; silica, or sand, predominating.

62 Organic matter is recognised by the black colour the powder assumes when heated over a spirit lamp. The watery solution evaporated to dryness leaves an inconsiderable residue, generally coloured brown by organic matter, which may be drawn off by heat. In the combustible residue, chemical tests will generally discover ammonia, humic, ulmic, cremic, and apocrenic acids, all known under the common name of humus. In the incombustible, potash, soda, lime, magnesia, phosphoric acid, sulphuric acid, silicic acid, chlorine, and occasionally oxide of iron and manganese, will be found, with nitre, iodine, and bromine; this latter, however, of very rare occurrence, and only in soils near the sea or near to salt springs.

63 All cultivated soils contain the above ingredients. When burnt, except in the case of chalk, they assume a red colour, which is due to the presence of ironstone. Out of this apparent sameness arise the greatest varieties of soils, from their proportionate admixture, and, especially, from the proportions of organic matter with which these chemical constituents are mixed.

64 Of this organic matter rich black garden soils long cultivated often contain from 20 to 25 per cent by weight, and in peaty soils it often amounts to from 50 to 70 per cent; in good garden land it may range from 5 to 12; and in good agricultural soils, from 4 to 8 per cent. This organic matter, so essential to soils, is chiefly of vegetable origin – the roots and stems of former crops, with a mixture of animal refuse. Decomposed under the influence of air, heat, and water, they produce, the brownish or blackish powdery substance known to the chemist and scientific gardener as humus. Humus exists in marly soils in which lime to the extent of 5 per cent is present, and loamy soils in which clay to the extent of from 25 to 50 per cent is present.

The practical analysis of the soil, washed and purified as described above, will be as follows: Any lime exisiting in the solution can readily be precipitated by the application of sulphuric acid, by which carbonic acid is liberated, and the soluble heavy body – sulphate of lime or gypsum – remains. Magnesia, which exists in all soils, and sometimes to an injurious extent, is precipitated when treated with hydrochloric acid; carbonic acid is thus evolved, and, by the addition of sulphuric acid, sulphate of magnesia, or Epsom salts, are precipitated, the amount being determined by washing, drying and weighing the resulting sulphate. Silica and clay will probably be the chief remaining ingredients in the solution; when dried, they are exposed to a red heat in a platinum or porcelain crucible, noting the loss sustained in drying. When ignited and cooled, a portion is weighed out accurately, triturated in a mortar of agate or Wedgwood stone, with about four times its weight of pure carbonate of soda, the whole mixture being transferred to a crucible of platinum, and exposed to a red heat for fifteen minutes. When cold, put the crucible and its contents into a porcelain evaporating basin; add water and hydrochloric acid, and leave the whole at rest for some time; the contents will gradually loosen and become dissolved. The solution will probably exhibit floating gelatinous particles; this is silica in combination with water, or hydrate of silica. When evaporated to dryness, but at a low temperature, a little hydrochloric acid is to be added, heat applied for a short time, and the whole filtered; the silica is retained on the filtering paper, the alumina has passed through in solution. After evaporation, wash the filter copiously with hot water, until a single drop of the water, caught on a slip of glass, no longer leaves a residuum when heat is applied. Hartshorn is now applied to the filtered solution; the precipitate is alumina in combination with water; and, if iron be present, it will be precipitated in the state of red oxide along with the alumina, which is to be evaporated and collected also on a filter, and the filtering paper carefully washed as before.

Having weighed each of the filtrates, the filters themselves and the crucibles are to be carefully dried, and finally severally ignited in a platinum crucible, and the amount of ashes yielded by the filter deducted in each case from the aggregate weight of the filter and precipitates; but if iron is present, it will be necessary first to separate the iron from the alumina by adding to the last filtrate a solution of caustic potash, which dissolves the alumina, leaving the oxide of iron untouched. This is to be accurately collected, washed by a process of decantation, and heated to a red heat, cooled and weighed; while the alumina, which we left dissolved in potash, is to be treated with the nitrate of ammonia, boiled, and collected by filtration, heated to redness, and finally weighed.

65 Soils, it is evident, are due to the disintegration of the solid rock, which has been going on for thousands of years; in the course of which time the surface of the country has thus been covered by a coating of disintegrated rock, varying in

FIG. 8 *Fingal's Cave, an example of Basalt rock*

depth and in character with the mineral nature of the neighbourhood. Sandstone has produced a light, porous, sandy soil; slaty shale has yielded a stiff, cold, impervious clay; from the crumbling limestone a calcareous soil has been formed; and the trap-rock of the primitive formation has yielded a rich, fertile, and generally reddish-grey loam. Basalt rock, which prevails over great part of Scotland and the north of Ireland, and here and there in England, gives a friable fertile soil, also of reddish grey; while the soils resting on the chalk formation generally partake of a dry, loose, friable character, congenial to many of the most useful forms of vegetation.

66 While useful to the gardener, an intimate knowledge of the characters of these soils is absolutely essential to the farmer. To a large extent, the gardener, operating on a limited scale, can prepare his soils, and ameliorate their nature, by the use of humus, or vegetable mould, the product of decomposed animal and vegetable manures. Of all the constituents of soils that have been named, humus performs the most important part in the direct food for the nutrition of plants; but whether it combines with organic matter and forms plant, or whether it only exercises a beneficial influence on vegetation by furnishing a continual source of carbonic acid by its decomposition, or by condensing ammoniac gas from the atmosphere, is by no means a settled question, the best chemists differing widely on the point; some of them denying altogether the efficacy of inorganic matter in soils. Recent experiments, however, show distinctly the great influences that inorganic matter exercises over the growth of plants; it is taken up by the roots, and may be traced in the ashes of plants; and it has been most satisfactorily proved that organic matter alone is incapable of supplying all the wants of the growing plant, certain inorganic substances being required by every plant, which, if not present in the soil, there is a barrier to its healthy growth. There can be no doubt that humus supplies plants with an essential part of their food; but it acts in various ways, which, as it has been said, are not very clearly ascertained.

66 All fertile soils thus contain, besides organic matter, a determinate quantity of eleven chemical substances; namely – (1) Potash; (2) Soda; (3) Lime; (4) Magnesia; (5) Alumina; (6) Iron; (7) Manganese; (8) Silica; (9) Sulphur; (10) Phosphorus; and (11) Chlorine.

Potash This substance is obtained from burning wood, small branches or leaves, the ash being washed in water, and evaporated in an iron pot and calcined. Add a small quantity of water, decant the liquid, and evaporate to dryness, and pearl-ash is obtained, which is an impure form of potash in combination with carbonic acid, or crude carbonate of potash. When this is boiled with newly-slaked quicklime, it is deprived of carbonic acid, which enters into combination with the lime, and the carbonate of potash is thus converted into pure or caustic potash, which can be separated into a silvery-white soft, metallic substance, potassium, and a gaseous element, oxygen. Many plants require a large amount of potash for their food, the only source from which it can be obtained being the soil. This accounts for the fact that wood ashes, which contain carbonate of potash, are so conducive to the healthy growth of clover, beans, peas, potatoes, and other plants whose ashes yield potash in return. The combination in which potash is found in soils is chiefly as silicates of potash. Some kinds of felspar, mica, and granite contain large proportions, as much as 15 to 20 per cent. It also enters into the composition of trap-rock, basalt, and whinstone, though in smaller proportions. As the rock crumbles, silicates of potash are set free, and rendered available for the plants. Clay, which is chiefly derived from felspar, invariably contains it; and it is partly for this reason that light land, in which potash is usually deficient, is benefitted by claying.

Soda This is obtained by burning seaweed; and plants growing on the seashore are rendered caustic by the same process. Its most common form, however, is sea-salt, or chloride of sodium. Seakale, asparagus, and similar plants are benefitted by its use.

Lime Chalk, marble, and limestone are carbonates of lime. Under heat, the carbonic acid is driven out, and pure or caustic lime remains. In its effects on animal and vegetable matters it resembles potash and soda, is slower in action, and is used most beneficially on peat land; its excess of organic matter is thus gradually destroyed, and converted into nutritious food for plants. Quicklime sprinkled with water absorbs it; heat is evolved, and it falls to powder, or is slaked. Slaked lime is a white powder, dry to appearance, but contains, in reality, water in an invisible form, chemically combined with lime. If exposed to the air, it attracts carbonic acid from the atmosphere, and becomes partially changed into carbonate of lime. Salts of lime are found in all ashes of plants; soils, therefore, capable of sustaining vegetable life, must contain lime in some form or other.

Magnesia This ingredient is never wanting in fertile soils. Magnesian limestone, which is a natural compound of the carbonates of lime and magnesia, contains 30 to 40 per cent; and in this form it exists in all dolomite and many other solid rocks. Soils containing much carbonate of magnesia absorb moisture with great avidity, and are generally cold soils. Silicate of magnesia enters largely into the composition of serpentine rocks. Soapstone and limestone frequently contain it. Compounds of sulphuric acid and muriatic acid with magnesia are also found in many mineral waters. Sulphate of magnesia, which is the name of the familiar Epsom salts, is formed from the decomposition of dolomitic rocks.

Alumina This is the compound of the metal aluminium with oxygen, or, in other words, oxide of aluminium. It occurs very abundantly in the mineral kingdom, both free and in combination with acids. In its crystallised state it forms the hard mineral known as corundum, and, in combination with oxide of chromium, the sapphire and the ruby; and emery is a dark-coloured granular variety of it. In an uncrystallised state it is a white, tasteless, powdery substance, obtained by adding a solution of carbonate of soda to alum. It constitutes a large proportion of shale and slate rocks, and is a principal ingredient, in combination with silica, in pipe, porcelain, and agricultural clays, to which it gives tenacity and stiffness. It is rarely found in the ashes of plants, and therefore not considered as directly contributing to their nourishment, although useful as a mechanical agent in absorbing ammonia from the atmosphere, and in detaining the volatile as well as the alkaline salts of manures, which would otherwise be dissolved by the first heavy shower, and carried into the subsoil beyond the reach of the roots of the plant.

Iron This metal, both in the black or protoxide, and the red or peroxide state, abounds in all soils, the red being most abundant, and easily observable from the red colour it communicates. Even soils in which the protoxide obtains, which are of a bluish-grey colour when brought to the surface, are changed to the red colour by the atmosphere, oxygen uniting with and acting on it. Oxide of iron is found in the ashes of all plants and in the blood of animals. The presence of iron is easily detected in soils by the ochry deposits in the beds of springs and ditches, where the oxide dissolved in carbonic acid produces the metallic-coloured deposit in question. Sulphate of iron also occurs in some soils, produced from iron pyrites: such soils are unproductive; for it is a compound of sulphuric acid with protoxide of iron, better known under the name of green vitriol. Lime added to such soils combines with the sulphuric acid, forming gypsum; and sweetens them and removes the injurious properties.

Manganese This metal, in combination with oxygen, associated with oxide of iron, occurs naturally in many soils. In the ashes of plants traces of it are also found; but iron usually predominates. The ash of the horse chestnut and oak bark is rich in manganese, with no trace of iron.

Silica or Silex This mineral occurs abundantly in nature, either in a free state or in the form of sand, sandstones, flint, chalcedony, rock-crystal, or quartz, and in combination with lime, magnesia, iron, potash, soda, and other minerals. Silica is insoluble in hot or cold water, and resists the action of some strong acids; but hydrofluoric acid dissolves it, when mixed with soda or potash, and exposed to the heat of a glass furnace. Silica is dissolved, or rather enters into combination with the alkali, and forms glass; or when the alkali is in excess, it dissolves into water. On the addition of muriatic acid, or sulphuric acid, to a solution of this silicate of potash, the silica separates into a gelatinous mass, in which form it is soluble in water, and thus becomes the food of plants.

Sulphur This compound, in the form of sulphuric acid, enters into the composition of all cultivated soils, chiefly in combination with limestone, magnesia, potash, and other bases. With hydrogen it forms sulphuretted hydrogen, a remarkably disagreeable-smelling gas, the product of the decomposition of organic matter contained in the soil and impregnating many medicinal waters, as at Harrogate.

Phosphorus This ingredient is a soft, waxlike, highly-inflammable substance, which combines with atmospheric oxygen, giving rise to phosphoric acid, which enters into the composition of all our cultivated plants, and is essentially necessary to a healthy condition of vegetable life. It exists in trap-rock, granite, basalt, and other igneous rocks, and in lime, ironstone, and most minerals.

Chlorine This is a highly-noxious, suffocating, yellowish, gaseous element, particularly disagreeable in smell. In soils it is found in combination with such bases as chloride of sodium, or common salt. It is more necessary as a plant-food to root crops than to cereals.

68 Soils, then – to sum up briefly that which has been stated in fuller terms above – may be said to consist of a mechanical mixture of four substances – (1) Silica, silicious sand, or gravel; (2) Clay; (3) Lime; and (4) Humus, with many of the chemical substances above mentioned, in varying proportions. Hazel loam, brown loam, clayey loam, fat soil, sandy soil, garden mould, which are continually spoken of by the gardener, have no specific proportions in themselves, but, nevertheless, on those proportions their fertility and capabilities depend.

69 Sandy soils are loose, friable, open, and dry, and for that reason easily cultivated. They rest chiefly on the old red sandstone, and granite and coal formations. When alumina and calcareous matter are absent, however, they are nearly barren: they absorb manures without benefit to the land. Where alumina and lime exist, they are more compact and adhesive, and grow good crops of beans, peas, spring wheat, and turnips. They are capable of improvement by admixture with clay, marl, chalk, and other adhesive soils, which communicate their constituent properties to them.

70 Calcareous soils resting on the upper chalk formation are usually deep, dry, loose, friable, and fertile in their nature; but others, resting on the shaly oolite, are stony, poor, thin soils. Leguminous plants, as peas, beans, vetches, saintfoin, and clover, do well on such soils, lime being essential to their growth. Where pure clay is present in such soils, they are called loams or calcareous clays; where silica is in excess, they are termed calcareous sandy soils.

71 Clay soils are characterised by stiffness, impenetrability, great power of absorbing and retaining moisture, and great specific gravity; they are, consequently, cold, stiff, heavy, and impervious, costly to cultivate, and often unproductive. Perfect drainage, burning the soil with wood faggots, branches of trees, grass sods, and vegetable refuse, and mixing chalk and sand, are the only remedies. Burning is the most efficient remedy; the burnt clay acting chemically as a manure, its constituents being rendered more soluble. Provided a moderate heat has been applied to the process, the potash is rendered soluble, and liberated from the clay in which it occurs in an insoluble combination. Thus treated, clay soils become the most fertile for all heavy crops.

It will be obvious to the reader that the process of analysis involves more minuteness of detail in carrying it out than it is possible to enter into here. Those who desire further information on the subject are referred to *The Handy Book of the Chemistry of Soils*, by Dr Scoffern, *The Elements of Agricultural Chemistry and Geology*, by the late Professor Johnston and Dr Cameron, and Professor Johnston's *Instructions for the Analysis of Soils*. These books are eminently practical, and enter into all necessary details in a manner which any intelligent reader may easily follow.

72 The chemical analysis of soils, as it has been inferred, and as it may be seen by any one who will refer to a tabulated statement of the results of an analysis, is manifestly an operation which requires professional knowledge and great care, skill, and nicety in its management. Few persons, perhaps, whether gardeners or amateurs, will take the trouble to attempt and carry out anything of this kind in the regular way, and for the information of such as these it is desirable to point out some simple means by which the natural properties of the different kinds of soils, and the presence of their chief and most important constituents, may be ascertained roughly, though not with any degree of precision or even approximately. Thus:

a) If there be Clay in any soil, the tenacity of the soil will indicate its presence.
b) If there be Calcareous matter, or lime or chalk, in any soil, its presence may be detected by pouring muriatic acid on it. If effervescence takes place freely, the soil thus tested is calcareous. Soils of this character, as well as clays, marls, and loams, are soft to the touch.

   Loudon says: To ascertain the quantity of calcareous earth present, dry soil thoroughly, and weigh a hundred grains of it, which gradually add to one drachm of muriatic acid, diluted with two drachms of water in a phial poised in a balance; the loss of weight will indicate the escape of carbonic acid, which will be 44 per cent of the quantity of calcareous earth in the soil.

c) If there be Sand in any soil, the soil will feel rough and harsh to the touch, and if a little of it be rubbed on a piece of glass, the glass will be scratched.
d) If the soil be Marly or Loamy, it will feel unctuous or greasy to the touch when rubbed between the finger and thumb.
e) If the soil contain Humus, or, in other words, decomposed organic matter, whether vegetable or animal, its presence may be ascertained by drying a portion of the soil thoroughly, and then, after weighing it, subjecting the soil so dried to a red heat. When withdrawn it must be weighed again, and the difference between its present weight and its weight before heating will show the proportion of organic matter in the soil.
f) If there be Iron in any soil – that is to say, oxide of iron – its presence will impart a reddish or yellowish colour, and sometimes even a greenish colour, to the soil.
g) If there be Salt in any soil, its presence will be shown by its saline taste, as well as by whitish effervescence or incrustation on the surface.

   Loudon gives the following methods for determining the specific gravity of any soil, and its capacity for retaining water:

1 *The specific gravity of a soil*, or the relation of its weight to that of water, may be ascertained by introducing into a phial which will contain a known quantity of water equal volumes of water and of soil, and this may be easily done by pouring in the water till it is half full, and then adding the soil till the fluid rises to the mouth; the difference between the weight of the soil and that of the water will give the result. Thus, if the bottle contains 400 grains of water, and gains 200 grains when filled half with water and half with soil, the specific gravity of the soil will be 2 – that is, it will be twice as heavy as water; and if it gained 165 grains, its specific gravity would be 1825, the water being 1000.

2 *The capacity of a soil for retaining water* may be thus ascertained. An equal portion of two soils, perfectly dry, may be introduced into two tall cylindrical glass vessels, in the middle of each of which a glass tube has been previously placed. The soils should be put into each in the same manner, not compressed very hard, but so as to receive a solidity approaching to that which they possessed when first obtained for trial. If, after this preparation, a quantity of water be poured into the glass tubes, it will subside, and the capillary attraction of the soils will conduct it up the cylinders towards the tops of the vessels. That which conducts it most rapidly, provided it does not rise from the weight of the incumbent column of water in the tube, may be pronounced to be the better soil.

73 In the absence of a geological or chemical knowledge of soils, many practical farmers and gardeners attach great importance to the vegetable products they throw up spontaneously, in the form of weeds, as an index to their nature and quality. Loudon has recorded, in his *Encyclopaedia of Gardening*, a vegetable index to soils, as it may be termed, based on this idea. He points out that the leading soils for the cultivator are the clayey, calcareous, sandy, ferruginous, peaty, saline, moist or aquatic, and dry; and he then proceeds to give for these different kinds of soil the following list of plants by which each is more especially distinguished in most parts of Europe. The scientific or botanic name of each plant follows the common name in every case in brackets.

a) **Argillaceous or Clayey Soil** Common coltsfoot (*Tussilago farfara*), the most certain and universal sign of a clayey soil, and the chief plant found on the alum grounds of Britain, France, and Italy; goose tansy (*Potentilla anserina*); silvery-leaved tansy (*Potentilla argentea*); creeping tansy (*Potentilla reptans*); yellow meadow rue (*Thaliclrum flavum*); sedge (*Carex*), many species; rush (*Juncus*), various species; tuberous bitter vetch (*Orobus tuberosus*); greater bird's-foot trefoil (*Lotus major*); small-horned trefoil (*Lotus corniculatus*); common soapwort (*Saponaria officinalis*).

b) **Calcareous Soil** Spiked speedwell (*Veronica spicata*); little bedstraw (*Galium pusillum*); common gromwell (*Lithospermum officinale*); purple-blue gromwell (*Lithospermum purpureocaeruleum*); clustered bell-flower (*Campanula glomerata*); hybrid bell-flower (*Specularia hybrida*); round-headed rampion (*Phyteuma orbiculare*); lychnitis mullein (*Verbascum lychnitis*); wayfaring tree (*Viburnum lantana*); common berberry (*Berberis vulgaris*); common dwarf sun-rose (*Helianthemum vulgare*); common pulsatilla anemone (*Anemone pulsatilla*); white vine, virgin's bower, or traveller's joy (*Clematis vitalba*); cultivated saintfoin (*Onobrychis sativa*).

c) **Sandy or Siliceous Soil** Three-leaved speedwell (*Veronica triphylla*); spring speedwell (*Veronica verna*); Italian viper's bugloss (*Echium Italicum*); smooth rupture wort (*Herniaria glabra*); hairy rupture wort (*Herniaria hirsuta*); English catchfly (*Silene Anglica*), and other species; red sandwort (*Arenaria rubra*); cornfield spurrey (*Spergula arvensis*); hybrid poppy (*Papaver hybridum*). scarlet poppy (*Papaver argemone*).

d) **Ferruginous Soil** Garden sorrel (*Rumex acetosa*); wood sorrel (*Oxalis acetosella*).

e) **Peaty Soil** Bilberry (*Vaccinium myrtillus*); bleaberry (*Vaccinium uliginosum*); cranberry (*Oxycoccus palustris*); heath (*Erica*); awl leaved spurrey (*Spergula subulata*); officinal septfoil (*Tormentilla officinalis*).

f) **Saline or Salt Soil** Glasswort (*Salicornia*); marine wrackgrass (*Zostera marina*); searuppia (*Ruppia maritima*); sea lungwort (*Pulmonaria maritima*); soldanella-leaved beanbind (*Calystegia soldanella*); whorled knotgrass (*Illecebrum verticillatum*); sea goosefoot (*Chenopodium maritimum*); shrubby goosefoot (*Chenopodium fruticosum*); kali saltwort (*Salsola kali*); whorlleaved honeywort (*Sison verticillatum*); marine sandwort (*Arenaria marina*); fringed orach (*Atriplex laciniata*).

g) **Aquatic or Moist Soil** Marsh marigold (*Caltha palustris*); common mare's-tail (*Hippuris vulgaris*); common butterwort (*Pinguicula vulgaris*); European water-horehound (*Lycopus Europceus*); dioecious valerian (*Valeriana dioica*); marsh violet (*Hottonia palustris*); Valerandi's brookweed (*Samolus valerandi*); marsh thysselinum (*Thysselinum palustre*); square-stalked willow herb (*Epilobium tetragonum*); willow-like lythrum (*Lythrum salicaria*); tongue-leaved crowfoot (*Ranunculus lingua*); spearwort (*Ranunculus flammeus*).

h) **Very Dry Soil** Red sandwort (*Arenaria rubra*); garden sorrel (*Rumex acetosa*); wild thyme (*Thymus serpyllum*); basil-leaved or common acynos, a thyme-like plant (*Acynos vulgaris*); field trefoil (*Trifolium arvense*).

It must be added that the indications of soils afforded by the presence of the above-named plants are not absolutely to be depended on even in Britain; and in other countries, says Loudon, they are sometimes found in soils directly opposite. Still, the cultivated saintfoin (*Onobrychis sativa*) is almost always an indication of calcareous soil; the common coltsfoot (*Tussilago farfara*), of blue clay; the red sandwort (*Arenaria rubra*), of poor sand; and garden or sheep's sorrel (*Rumex acetosa*), of the presence of iron or peat. The common reed (*Phragmites communis*) and the amphibious polygonum (*Polygonum amphibium*) grow on alluvial soils, which yield excellent crops if properly drained; but where the cornfield horsetail (*Equisetum arvense*) grows freely, it indicates a cold and retentive subsoil. The cornfield pimpernel (*Anagallis arvensis*), the cornfield madder (*Sherardia arvensis*), the cornfield gromwell (*Lithospermum arvense*), and the salad, lamb's lettuce (*Valerianella olitoria*), grow on cultivated lands where the soil is a strong black loam on a dry bottom; when such a soil is wet, the clown's heal-all (*Stachys palustris*) makes its appearance. A light sandy soil is known by the presence of the purple archangel (*Lamium purpureum*) and the shepherd's purse (*Capsella bursa-pastoris*). If the parsley piert (*Alchemilla aphanes*) is found, the soil is rather unproductive; if the cornfield spurrey (*Spergula arvensis*) grows very thick, the ground has likely been rendered too fine by the harrow; the common ragwort (*Senecio Jacobaea*) and the cornfield cirsium (*Cirsium arvense*) grow indiscriminately on strong light loams, but always indicate a fertile soil. The vernal draba (*Draba verna*) and the annual knawel (*Scleranthus annuus*) grow on soils that are dry, sandy, and poor in the extreme. The spiny rest-harrow (*Ononis spinosa*) is often found on dry pasture, and where the soil is incumbent on rotten rock. The aquatic, peaty, and saline soils are almost everywhere indicated by their appropriate plants – a proof that the climate and natural irrigation of plants have much more influence on their habits than mere soil.

74 If the presence of certain plants, indigenous to the soil in which they grow, is indicative to a certain extent – perhaps to a very great extent – of the character of the soil itself, and its nature and chief constituents, and it is fair to draw inferences therefrom as to the kind of culture for which the soil is suited, and the preparation and additions by way of manure that are necessary in order to render its cultivation remunerative, it is surely allowable to go a step further and to make other deductions from the appearance of certain plants in certain soils. It must be true that all plants, whether indigenous or exotic, thrive best in the soil whose constituents are by nature best fitted to promote their growth. All indigenous plants – call them weeds or wild flowers, or what you will – have their congeners in those that are the especial objects of garden cultivation. It is, then, surely worth while – nay, even desirable – that those who would excel as gardeners should note the effects of soil, climate, position, etc., on indigenous plants in places where they thrive best, and then test by experiment how far a like soil, aspect, and position is beneficial to the growth of plants of similar character that are under cultivation. Nature, at all events, can never be wrong; and any one who is seeking to read Nature can never do wrong by following Nature's teaching.

CHAPTER 3

The Mechanical Preparation of Soils

75 Speaking generally, there are two methods of preparing natural soils for the production of crops of all kinds, and these may be broadly distinguished as *mechanical* and *chemical*. The chemical means, so to speak, of improving soils, consists in adding to it such constituents as may render it better fitted to suit the requirements of the plants, be they what they may, that are to be grown in it, by supplying them with the plant food that they most require in order to bring them to perfection or as near to perfection as possible. This can be done only by adding manures to the soil in order to render it more productive. But before this is done it is necessary to have recourse to one or other of the mechanical means at our command for the preparation of natural soils; these mechanical means being *draining*, *burning*, and *digging*. Thus, the mechanical modes of preparing soils may be regarded as being the *primary* methods of effecting the object in view, and the chemical means as forming the *secondary* methods. Having shown, in the preceding chapter, what are the leading natural soils and their distinctive constituents, it is desirable to consider, in the present chapter, the three great mechanical means of bringing natural soils into cultivation, and the results which follow from their adoption.

76 The great improver, not of soils only, but even of the climate of whole districts when brought under its influence, is drainage. Within the present generation, localities which were formerly raw, cold, swampy, and unproductive, affording scanty and late harvests, if their products could be said to deserve the name, have become warm and dry, yielding highly-productive crops, at nearly the same time as the most forward districts, under the effects of drainage. The reason for the change is that under the influence of drainage the moisture is made to percolate through the earth to its lowest level, being drawn from a gradually extending circle until the surrounding soil is freed from superfluous moisture, and to give place to atmospheric air with its fertilising effects; while the atmosphere on the surface, which was formerly chilled by the effects of evaporation, is now rendered warm and genial; for water long retains its heat, and wherever water can flow, atmospheric air can follow.

77 While the general effects of drainage are so useful, however, it is difficult to give any specific directions on the subject that will be applicable to any and every case. Every kind of soil requires a different treatment, and some are capable of being seriously injured by injudicious draining. There are few gardens, however, in which it can be wholly dispensed with. As a general rule, a light loamy or sandy soil, with a gravelly subsoil, and a natural slope to some outfall, requires no drainage whatever – on the contrary, an admixture of clay is necessary to render it more retentive of moisture; but a tenacious clay soil and subsoil require thorough drainage to render them suitable for garden purposes. Before attempting it, however, even on a small scale, the locality, the soil and subsoil, the land-springs, and the average rainfall in the district, must receive careful consideration.

78 The great object of drainage is to prevent water from stagnating in the soil, by promoting its free percolation through it rather than by evaporation, which has a tendency to reduce the temperature. The water to be withdrawn arises from one of three sources, or from all three together; namely, from land-springs, or from rain, or from fountain heads at a higher level. One of these fountains, of a peculiar and somewhat mysterious character – namely, a reciprocating spring, is represented in Fig. 9. It is a sectional view of the flowing well of the Peak, in Derbyshire, and, although differing from most fountain heads, it will serve to illustrate the subject. All the phenomena, however, which are exhibited by this intermittent spring are not satisfactorily accounted for by the commonly-received explanation, which supposes an interior cavity, A, discharging its waters by a siphon-formed channel, B C D. When the water is sufficiently high, it overflows the level, C, running out until the water is too low to be forced over the vertex of the arch of the siphon. When forced into the channel, the waters descend through crevices in the rock, or they make for themselves a path to some porous strata, still descending, till they reach some impervious rock or clay basin, where they again accumulate and spread themselves until some new outlet is found at a lower level. Supposing this new basin to be impervious also, and the strata immediately over it to be a porous gravelly soil, or a clay soil with patches of gravel, the water will force its way upwards through those patches, partly by the pressure of the water at the higher level from which it is supplied, and partly by the force of capillary attraction. This is generally the source of land-springs, which sometimes baffle the most skilful efforts at thorough drainage.

FIG. 9 *Flowing well of the Peak, Derbyshire*

79 Other land-springs, collected in tenacious subsoils having no outlet, depend upon the fall of rain in the district. Water drawn from a higher level can only occur where the land is overlooked by neighbouring heights. In considering the amount of drainage requisite, it is to be borne in mind that the process of evaporation is a powerful agent in withdrawing water from the soil, surrounding it with a cold damp atmosphere, inimical to vegetation; while percolation through the soil assists in preserving its warmth. The average fall of rain and evaporation in the ordinary soils round London may be stated as follows:

	Inches of Rain	Evaporation, in inches
From January to May	8.75	4.45
From May to August	7.0	6.80
From August to October	5.50	3.75
In November	3.75	0.60
In December	1.75	0.17

80 The first subject of inquiry before commencing drainage is the nature of the soil to be operated upon. Where its base is an aluminous clay, the soil will be found to be exceedingly tenacious of moisture; but a silicious deposit, on the contrary, admits of very free percolation: from limestone rocks a chalky, friable, and moderately tenacious soil is obtained. On the proportion of each of these substances contained in the soil and subsoil, therefore, will depend the extent of drainage requisite.

81 As an example of what is meant, let us first suppose that the land to be drained, shown at A in Fig. 10, lies in a basin-shaped hollow, having a retentive clay, B, below it as its subsoil, and surrounding it on all sides, as shown in the illustration, which is known to be superimposed on a stratum of sand or gravel, C, which, in its turn, rests on retentive clay of the same kind as that which is above it, and which is also lettered B in the diagram. It is obvious that in order to render the drains, D, D, D, effective, it will be necessary to pierce the stiff clay, B, in order to carry the surplus water into the looser soil, C. This is done by draining A by means of the drains, D, D, D, in the usual way; but at their outfall, or lowest part, the clay, B, is pierced by an auger, as shown by the spaces left without shading, and a passage made for the water into the gravelly stratum, C.

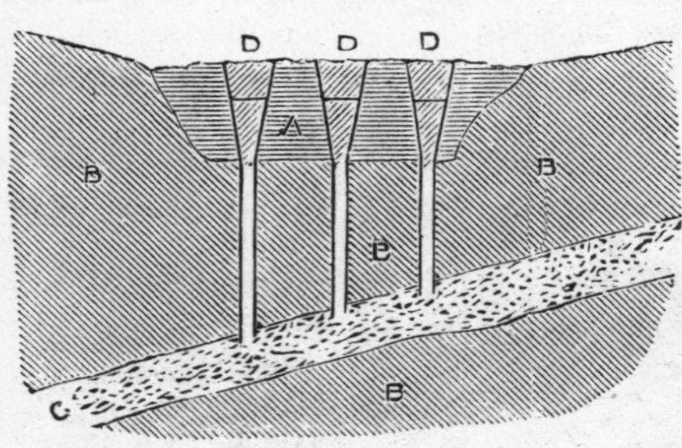

FIG. 10 *Drainage of basin on clay*

82 Another case, of not very uncommon occurrence, arises when a loose sandy or friable soil, A, rests on a substratum of clay, B, as shown in Fig. 11. Here all the moisture not taken up by evaporation is either diffused through the gravel or absorbed into the tenacious subsoil, from which it has no escape through the soil, B. Sinking drains to the bottom of the soil, as shown at D, D, D, will not here serve the purpose, unless they are sunk sufficiently deep into the subsoil, B, to remove the moisture absorbed at the surface of the substratum, where the soil and subsoil come into contact, although a false economy, and the advice of ignorant workmen, might recommend such a course.

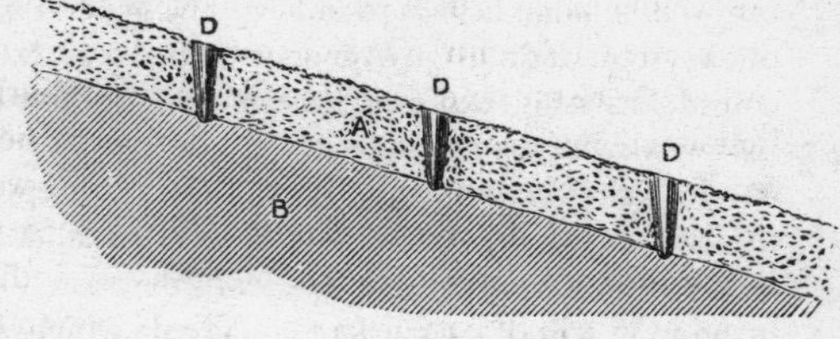

FIG. 11 *Drainage of light soil on clay*

83 In a third case, nearly resembling the above, where a porous soil, A, rests on stiff tenacious subsoil, B, as shown in Fig. 12, but crops out, or terminates, in a gravelly porous soil, having no power to retain water, it is evident the water would follow the surface of the retentive soil, in the direction of the arrow. To obviate this, a main drain is required at D, which will intercept and carry off the water from the porous soil, A.

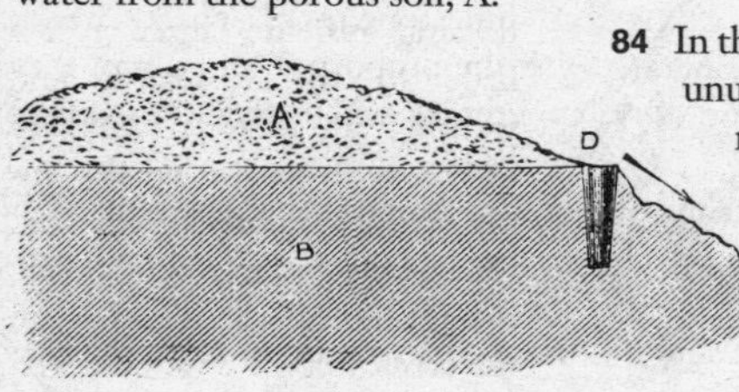

FIG. 12 *Drainage of porous soil on stiff subsoil*

84 In the neighbourhood of rivers it is not unusual to find a retentive soil, B, resting on a porous subsoil, A, as shown in Fig. 13, rendered wet and spongy by the presence of land-springs, S, S, S, which force themselves up through the retentive soil by capillary attraction. In this case, a drain, D, should be cut through the retentive soil below the lowest spring, whose position must be ascertained by closely watching the moisture in the dry season.

85 It is wholly unnecessary, and, indeed, it is neither desirable nor possible, to enter here into a description of the various geological formations and the respective relations of soils and subsoils which must perforce exert an influence upon the system of drainage to be adopted, that it is impossible to ignore. From what has been already advanced, it will be obvious to all, that in effecting the drainage of a large tract of land on scientific principles it will be needful to have recourse to the advice and guidance of those who have made this subject their study and thoroughly understand what they are about. All that

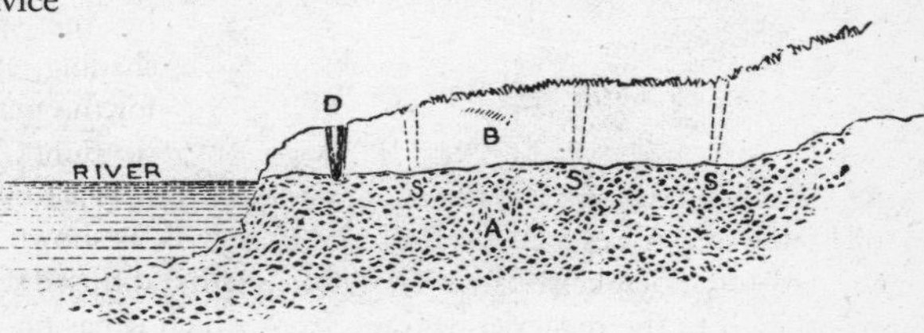

FIG. 13 *Drainage of retentive soil on porous subsoil*

can well be done here is to indicate the general method of procedure in laying out a system of drainage over an extended area, by taking a hypothetical case for consideration and explaining the general arrangement of drains, large and small, that would be best suited to it.

86 In laying down a system of drainage, attention must first be directed to the surface of the ground. Is it level or undulating? Is it commanded by neighbouring heights? The next consideration is the question of outfall. Let us imagine an area of say ten acres and a half, which is to become the site of a house and range of gardens, and let us suppose that the accompanying diagram, Fig. 14, exhibits a rough plan of its general features. Its southern boundary is a river, R, flowing from west to east, or nearly so. On the eastern side rises a gentle hill, sloping off towards the river – light sandy soil with clay subsoil. Beyond it a brook, BB´, drains its eastern slopes, flowing into the larger river a little to the eastward, and forming the eastern boundary of the area: to the north, this hill inclines slightly to the west. On the west rises a similar hill, the profile of which is seen in the cross section, Fig. 15, taken along the dotted line, AA´. This height rises rather abruptly from the river, slopes off towards the north, but rises again, the heights running nearly parallel to the eastern range, leaving a gentle undulating valley between them, sloping off towards the river. The western boundary of the area is indicated by the dotted line, BB´, running along the crest of the ridge of hills to the west. This site, it will be observed, is one that is possessed of great capabilities in a picturesque point of view, when it is laid out as gardens and filled up with trees.

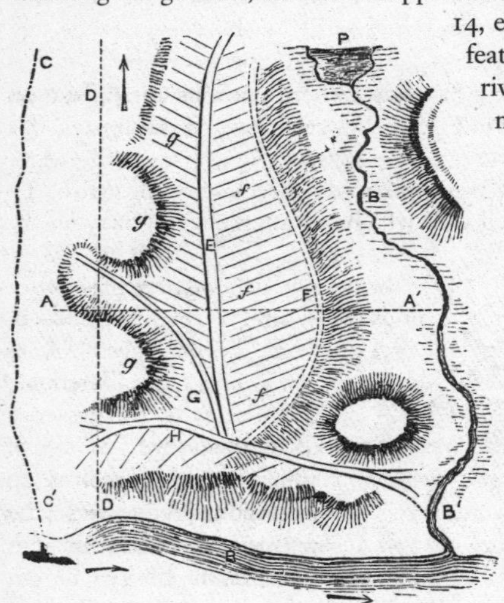

FIG. 14 *Plan of ground to be drained*

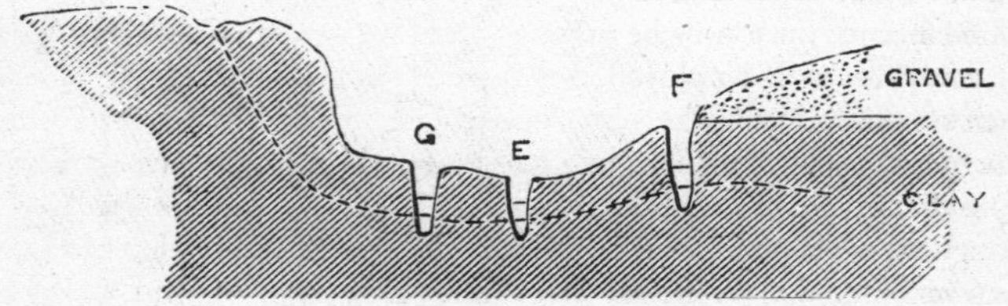

FIG. 15 *Cross section along AA' in fig. 14*

87 Having surveyed and mapped out this area, which may be done either by means of the theodolite, or by a spirit-level and actual measurement, it will be found to contain a small valley ranging from north to south, surrounded on three sides by gently-rising ground. The bed of the valley is a stiff clay, and somewhat marshy, from the overflowing of the brook which occupies its eastern extremity. The heights to the east range away for about 1000 feet to the north, the summit being a bed of gravel, which crops out, and joins the clay at the line indicated in the large central drain running from north to south. Beyond the rising ground to the north a small pond or lake, P, collects the waters from the surrounding gravel beds, and has retained them until they have forced their way into the valley. Two gentle elevations, with a depression between them, occupy the west, an ancient pasture ground, that best of all material for forming a garden. To the south the land falls off gently to the bed of the river, which flows from west to east, some half a mile distant. The profile of the western hill taken in section along the dotted line, DD′, is exhibited in Fig. 16.

FIG. 16 *Profile of western hill along DD' in fig. 14*

88 On reference to the map of the area that has been made, we find that it extends about 1000 feet, ranging towards the north and north-west, the mouth of the valley, where it opens out towards the river, being about 400 feet wide, the country falling in undulating scenery beyond. In order to secure the thorough drainage of this site, a deep main drain, E, must run from the foot of the northern heights to another main drain, H, intersecting it at the lower part of the valley, and carrying the accumulated waters into the brook lying to the east. These two drains are, of course, the key to the whole system, and should either be barrel-drains, or pipe-drains of the largest size, fitted in with glazed pipes properly jointed, with socket-joints and elbow-joints to receive the lateral drains. The size and kind of drains, however, should be matter of very exact calculation, based on the average fall of rain in the neighbourhood, and the arrangements for securing the house sewage within the grounds. Nothing but the overflow should be suffered to escape through these drains; but they must be of sufficient size to provide for any possible fall of water.

89 As reference must now be made to different modes of constructing drains and the various tools employed in the operation, it will be as well to leave the further consideration of the system of drainage to be carried out on the plan before us for a while, and turn our attention meantime to the various methods of making drains, the materials employed, and the tools that are used. When all this has been explained, it will be easier to understand the mode of carrying out and completing the system of drainage of the piece of land that we have supposed to be under treatment, and to apply the principles of laying out and constructing drains to actual practice.

90 The materials employed in covering drains are very varied – brushwood, rubble, stones, bricks, and pipes being all in use; and in clay countries it has not been unusual to form pipes with the clay itself, by inserting an arched framework of wood, and withdrawing it when consolidated. The best and cheapest drains, however, are drainpipes, which are new obtainable everywhere on moderate terms.

91 The implements used in drainage are a spade, or, in deep draining, and in a clay soil, a series of two or three spades, varying in size, and each sloping to the point, and slightly rounded, so as to make a circular cut; a spoon-like implement for lifting the loose soil clear out of the bottom of the trench; and a level, commonly called, from its shape, an A level. This may easily be formed by fixing three perfectly straight-edged boards in an upright position and in a triangular form, held together by a vertical board in the centre, with an opening at its base for a line and plummet. The spades and scoop are shown further on in Fig. 19. The A level and its construction is exhibited in Fig. 17.

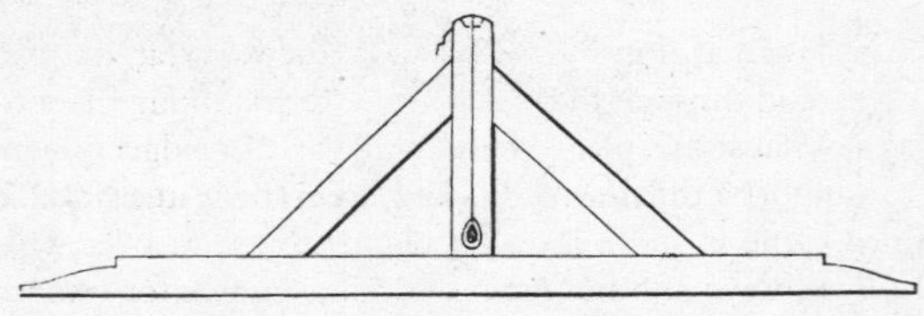

FIG. 17 *A level used in draining operations*

92 When the general system of the drainage and the direction which the drains are to take have been determined, the next points which present themselves for settlement are the depth and size of the drains, as well as their distance from each other – considerations which will depend on the nature of the soil and subsoil. Whether deep or comparatively shallow drainage was better, was long a question of great doubt, the advocates of deep drainage in heavy soils contending that water will find its level, which is in the bottom of the drain, through holes and crannies innumerable, and that the deeper the drain the wider is the area affected; on the other hand, however, it was contended that, while this doctrine is founded in truth, it has its limits, and that beyond a certain depth the influence of the drain is lost. A sort of compromise has been the result, and very deep drainage has been nearly abandoned.

On this subject the views expressed by Mr Chitty, in the following remarks, probably express the opinion of the majority of practical men. 'Observe,' he says, 'that the depth should vary with the nature of the soil. If the subsoil is a stiff retentive clay, care should be taken to go no deeper than is necessary to be out of the way of the spade in digging and trenching, or to give the necessary fall; for every ground workman knows that water does not readily filter through clay, and draining land is for the purpose of drawing the water quickly off the surface, to prevent stagnation, and to admit of going on it immediately after rain; therefore, to lay drains so deep into the clay that water would be weeks in filtering to them would be the height of folly. If the ground be more porous, let the drains be three, but not more than four, feet deep. Having got the trenches ready, lay in the pipes, and cover them for a few inches with rough porous rubbish, or broken crockery, or any such material, and the drains will be effective and permanent. The mode I prefer is to lay soles or flat tiles, and on these to set half-pipes or bridge-pipes, which are of a tunnel shape, and on these to lay the rough stuff, and fill in with earth, which should not be rammed or trodden very tight, but allowed to settle. If the trenches are merely filled with rough stuff to the thickness of a foot or so, it will be effective, but not so permanent; even brushwood will do, and sometimes last for many years in clay soils.'

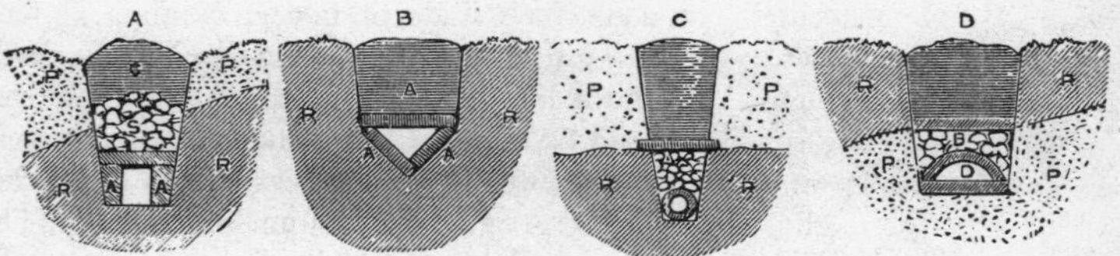

FIG. 18 *Four different modes of constructing drains*

93 The drain shown at *A* in Fig. 18 is cut through a stratum of porous soil, P, for about 2 feet, and through the clay subsoil, R, for about 2 feet 6 inches. A, A, are two pieces of flat stone, placed perpendicularly on edge, one on each side of the drain, to support a third, which is laid upon them in a horizontal position: over this third stone is laid a layer of round stones, S, over which the soil is replaced. In *B* is shown another form of drain, suitable for retentive soils. The construction is the same: two stones or tiles, A, A, placed at right angles, rest against the sides, and a third, similarly lettered, is placed horizontally over them; the soil is replaced, the looser and coarser parts being at the bottom. In *C* is represented the most perfect of all drainage: a circular drainpipe is laid at the bottom of the trench, carried down through the porous soil, P, below the surface of the retentive subsoil, R, over it are laid, first, the roughest rubble that is available. A slate or tile is laid across over the rough stones in order to prevent roots penetrating to the pipes, as well as the earth from falling in through the stones. In *D* we have an arrangement which is convenient, especially for porous subsoils. A serviceable flat tile or sole, D, is laid flat in the bottom of the open trench, resting on a solid and perfectly level bed, gently falling from the higher ground to the outflow; over the tile is laid a semicircular tile, forming an arch extending uninterruptedly along the length of the drain; over this is thrown a layer of rough stones and rubble, B, 6 or 8 inches thick; over this another flat tile, to keep out sand, roots of trees, and other destructive agencies; and over the whole the surface soil is again filled in.

94 We can now return to the plan of the ground that has been supposed to require drainage, and consider the method

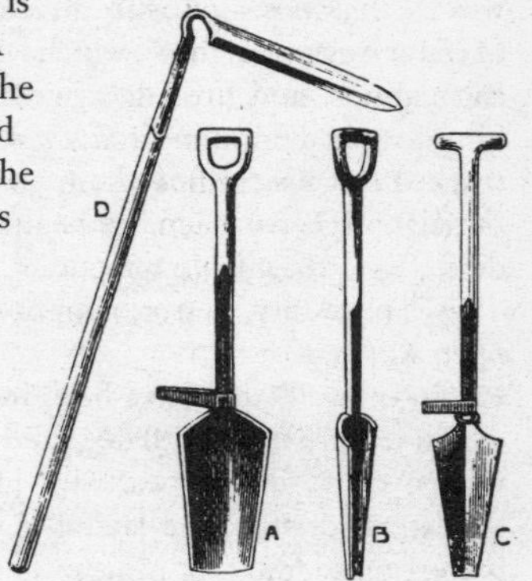

FIG. 19 *Tools used in cutting drains*

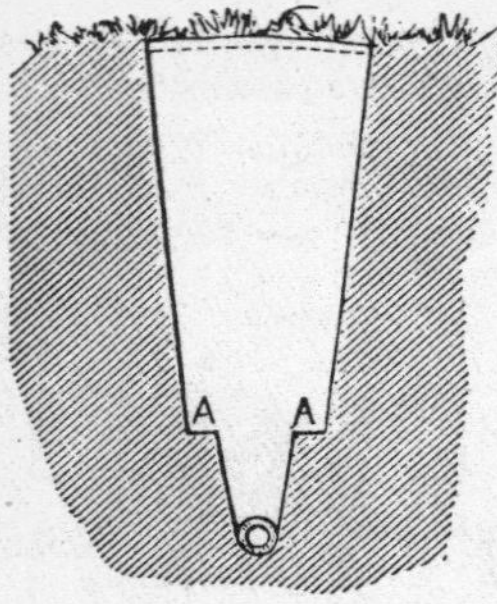

FIG. 20 *Section of drain*

pursued in cutting trenches for drainage and making the drains in direct reference to it. In excavating the drains, the first operation is to cut the intersecting drain, H, beginning at the outfall near the brook. The depth will depend upon the level of the brook when full; but, supposing there is a good fall, it should not be less than 4½ feet. The width at the surface should be laid out neatly with the line and reel, and the first spit removed should be of a width in which a man can work conveniently. From the surface the excavation should taper gradually towards the bottom. The earth, as it is removed, should be thrown to the lower side of the drain – partly because it is easier for the workmen, and partly to prevent a slip of the soil caused by the incumbent weight if heavy rains occur while the work is in progress. Having dug out the soil to within 8 or 9 inches of the bottom, for which the draining-spade, A, in Fig. 19, is generally used, the bottom being of a breadth convenient for the workman, the remaining space is required to be much narrower, as shown in Fig. 20, and is excavated by means of the bottom-tools, B and C (Fig. 19), the workman standing on the shoulders, A, A (Fig. 20,), the bottom being made smooth and level by means of the scoop, D (Fig. 19), of which several sizes are in use. This drain having been opened along its whole length, the main drain, E, is next excavated in the same manner, care being taken that, while the bottom is left smooth, it should have a proper fall throughout its whole length, and that if there is no natural fall in the land, one should be produced by making the head of the drain shallower than the outfall. If the soil is clay, and likely to bear the exposure without falling in, it will greatly facilitate the work to open the other main drains, F and G, both of which are to be executed in the same manner. The advantages of this are twofold: the person charged with the work will see that these drains are all at the proper level; he will see, also, the quantity of water flowing in them, which will, in many instances, enable him to check his calculations, and provide against unexpected land-springs. Having satisfied himself that his main drains are in proper order, and laid down the pipes, marked out his feeding drains, and inserted pipes with elbow-joints at their outfall to receive them, he begins by opening those at the head of the main drain, E, farthest from the outfall, filling in each as fast as the pipes can be laid. This is necessary, as frosts might occur, and cause considerable damage to the open works.

95 In the soils that have been indicated, the central main drain, E (Fig. 14), would require to be both deep and strongly constructed, probably four feet, laid with 9 or 12-inch pipes, with junction-sockets and elbow-joints to receive the lateral drains. The lateral main drains, F, G, should be three feet deep, increasing to four feet near to the junction, entering the main drain, H, with a fall of six inches in the last six feet, the pipes being from four to six inches in diameter, but the diameter in any and every case being determined by close calculation of the water to be carried off. The depth of the main drain, H, has been already stated as being 4½ feet.

96 The feeders, *f, f, f,* to the main drain, E, should be 3-inch pipes, their depth beginning at three feet, and increasing to three and a half, as in the former case; while for the feeders, *g, g,* of the lateral main drains, 2-inch pipes will probably suffice. Each of the feeders should be from 15 to 20 feet apart for garden purposes. These should enter the main drain obliquely, as shown in the engraving, and on no account at right angles.

97 Where house sewage and the overflow of cisterns have to be provided for, a barrel-drain will probably be requisite; and its size will be a matter of calculation before construction. As in the case of the lateral main drains, so the fall in the feeders at their junction with the drains into which they empty themselves should not be less than three or four inches. They may be, as it has been said, from 15 to 20 feet apart, according to the nature of the soil, and their minimum depth 30 inches: this will allow for the deepest trenching without disturbing the drain.

98 The best pipes for the feeders are 2-inch pipes, which are generally made from 12 to 15 inches in length, and cost from 10s. to 15s. per 1000. They are sometimes laid with collars – that is, short pieces of piping sufficiently large to receive the ends of two pipes – thus keeping them firmly in their place. These collars are sometimes perforated on the upper surface to admit the water. Sometimes the pipes are bound together by bands of tempered clay at the junction, which answers very well; but in this case the upper sides of the pipes are perforated with holes for the reception of the water, so that the solid junction of the pipes is not objectionable on that account. It is not usual, however, to do more than lay the pipes in a straight line when the workman is left to himself; and few will do that unless very closely watched. In the junction with the main drains the union should be carefully made, either by clay or cement, where permanent drainage is expected.

The *rationale* of drainage is very happily set forth and explained by Mr D. T. Fish, who has written much on every subject connected with gardening:

> Drainage as popularly understood, means the art of laying land dry. This, however, is a very imperfect definition, either of its theoretical principles or practical results. Paradoxical as it may appear, drainage is almost as useful in keeping land moist as in laying it dry. Its proper function is to maintain the soil in the best possible hygrometrical condition for the development of vegetable life. Drainage has also a powerful influence in altering the texture of soils. It enriches their plant-feeding capabilities; elevates their temperature, and improves the general climate of a whole district, by increasing its temperature, and removing unhealthy exhalations and foetid miasmas, the fruitful hotbeds of fevers and agues, which desolate all damp districts. It lays land dry, by removing superfluous water; it keeps it moist, by increasing its power of resisting the force of evaporation; it alters the texture, by the conduction of water, and by filling the interstices previously occupied by that fluid with atmospheric air; it enriches the soil, by separating carbonic acid gas and ammonia from the atmosphere, and by facilitating the decomposition, absorption, and amalgamation of liquid and solid manures. It heightens the temperature of the earth, by husbanding its heat, and surrounding it with an envelope of comparatively dry air, and by substituting the air for water withdrawn through the interstices of the soil; for while the tendency of excessive moisture in the soil is to bind the whole mass into an almost solid substance, so the tendency of air is

to separate its particles into separate atoms, and render it porous; and the more porous a soil is, the greater is its power of resisting evaporation. For this reason, porous soils are more moist in hot weather than those of a more tenacious character.

Drainage enriches soils in another way. All rainwater is more or less charged with carbonic acid gas and ammonia. Now, the larger the quantity of rainwater that passes through the soil, the greater will be the amount of these gases brought in contact with the roots of plants. Nor is this all: solid manures of the richest quality are comparatively useless on wet heavy soils; for while a certain amount of moisture is essential to the decomposition of manures, an excess arrests the process, and all the most soluble portions are washed out long before it is sufficiently decomposed to enter into the composition of plants. Judicious drainage, therefore, places the soil in a proper hygrometrical condition for performing its important function.

99 The general principles that influence and govern the laying out of a system of drainage and the construction of the drains of which the system is composed, are the same for all areas of land, whether large or small, and must be applied in like manner in all cases, although the extent and degree of application may differ considerably. In treating the large superficial area that was taken and described under certain conditions of surface and aspects in order to set forth and explain these principles so as to render them intelligible to all, we have learnt, firstly, that the entire system must form a gradual slope, descending by a gentle, and in some cases almost imperceptible, fall, from the further extremities of the lateral feeders to the outlet of the entire system. This is absolutely necessary, whether the system be large or small – that is to say, whether it consists of many distinct parts, as in the example taken, or of a simple drain consisting of a single line of pipes. Then we learn that, if the system be a complex one, the chief main drain, at one end of which is the outlet, must have a fall of its own, from beginning to outlet, and that in every part it must be lower than the tributary main drains at the points at which they enter it and discharge into it the waters that they have received from the feeders. In the same way, the feeders must fall gradually, from their commencement to their outfall, into the tributary main drains, and these must be lower than the outfalls of the feeders at the points at which the feeders discharge themselves into them. Drains, then, to be efficient, must be constructed with a sufficient fall, and the greater the fall, having due regard to the depth of the outlet, the more quickly will the collected water be carried off.

100 It has been said that from 15 to 20 feet is a sufficient distance between the feeders for garden purposes; but it must be remembered that the foregoing remarks have been made in reference to the drainage of an extended area to be laid out in a series of gardens, rather than to a single small garden. With regard to smaller gardens, let us look at the drainage of, say, an acre of ground. Now, an acre is a piece of land that contains 160 square poles, perches, or rods – the pole or land rod being 16½ feet in length, or 4840 square yards, or 43,560 square feet. Supposing, then, that our acre is 16 rods or 264 feet in length and 10 rods or 165 feet in breadth, if the configuration of the land be such that it consists of a gentle slope on each side, falling gradually to a depression in the centre, it is clear that, outlet permitting, a main drain must be laid down in the central depression throughout the length of the garden, and that from 13 to 18 feeders, placed obliquely to the main drain, must be cut and led into it on each side. If, on the contrary, the land be high in the centre and slopes from a central ridge on either side, two main drains must be cut, one on each side of the ground, and feeders carried from the central ridge down each slope into the main drains. And the main drains must each have its outlet, or be led into another deeper drain at one end of the garden, which will act for the system in the same manner as the chief main drain acted for the larger area.

101 With regard to gardens that are even more limited in area than an acre, and small plots of ground attached to houses in the suburbs of large towns, if drainage is required, as indeed it very often is, the drains should follow, as far as possible, the course of the walks, and the water should be carried into the drain of the house, to be conducted thereby into the sewer in the roadway. But if there be no means of escape of this kind for the water, the only thing to be done is to lead the drains into a small cesspit of sufficient size to receive the surplus water even in the heaviest rainfall, and to hold it while it escapes through natural fissures or porous soil below, or into a tank constructed at a sufficient depth below the surface to give a proper fall to the drains that run into it. When caught in a tank, the water thus collected may be utilised for garden purposes if a small pump be inserted in the tank by which the water may be raised when required. This is one means, and perhaps the best means, for providing for the drainage of a *level* piece of ground that is surrounded by other gardens and buildings, and for which no outlet can possibly be found. Cases of this kind will frequently be found in towns which possess no system of urban drainage, and in which the old cesspit system for the disposal of sewage is still maintained, or the dry-earth system for the reception and utilisation of excreta has been introduced.

102 Next to drainage, fire, the second of the *mechanical* means employed in bringing land into cultivation, is the great ameliorator of soils; and in laying out garden grounds, where clay forms the soil or subsoil, calcination will be found a most effective fertiliser. The land being thoroughly drained, and the paths marked out according to the working plan, it will be necessary to fill up all inequalities of the surface; for a garden or lawn should present no inequality beyond a gentle slope. This inequality is to be removed by levelling the high parts and filling up all hollows with the earth removed from them, and by grubbing up all trees and shrubs which are not intended to stand: as a general rule, none such should be left. When the surface soil is of a loamy, friable description, the first spit, for eight or nine inches, should be carefully preserved in a heap with its herbage: it is the most valuable compost the gardener possesses. Even when it is a stiff clay, a mixture of sandy soil and lime will impart all the best fertilising characters to it. When the soil is a stiff, unmanageable clay, calcination will render it a valuable garden soil, and when there are trees and shrubs to be grubbed up, these should be burned with the clay, for the wood ashes thus obtained will impart highly fertilising constituents to the soil.

103 Stiff clay soils are chiefly susceptible of improvement by burning, because the silicates of alumina that they contain become soluble when acted on by heat, and therefore are rendered capable of being acted on by air and water, from which they absorb oxygen, carbonic acid, and other chemical constituents that support vegetable life. Calcareous soils are also sometimes improved by calcination, and even marls, especially red marls from the red sandstone. In calcareous soils acted on by fire, the process of burning expels the carbonic acid that is contained in them, leaving pure lime behind. This lime reabsorbs carbon from the air in the form of carbonic acid gas, and under its influence becomes a fine powder, which readily mixes with and fertilises the soil. Loudon says:

> The advantages of burning are, that it renders the soil less compact, less tenacious, and less retentive of moisture, and, when properly applied, may convert a matter that was stiff, damp, and, in consequence, cold, into one powdery, dry, and warm, and permeable by air and water. Burning also improves all soils containing clay, by increasing their power of absorbing and condensing from the air, ammonia, carbonic acid, and other gases necessary to the growth of plants. The soils improved by burning are all such as contain too much dead vegetable fibre, and which consequently lose from one-third to one-half their weight by incineration; and all such as contain their earthy constituents in an impalpable state of division – that is, the stiff clays and marls – are improved by burning; but in coarse sands, or rich soils containing a just mixture of the earths, and in all cases in which the texture is sufficiently loose, or the organisable matter sufficiently soluble, the process of torrefaction cannot be useful.

104 The calcining process is commenced by building up a temporary dwarf wall of bricks or stone, with some iron bars laid across the wall thus formed for the free admission of air below the burning mass when it is fairly alight. On this a fire is lighted, with such material as there may be at hand: over that a layer of clay is placed, to which the fire soon extends. More clay is added, and the heap is extended in all directions, care being taken that ventilation is kept up under it, and that clay is added by degrees, mixed with fuel. In this manner the whole surface of the ground may be pared, calcined, and afterwards made smooth and levelled by rolling, and the turf replaced on places where it is to be preserved.

105 Highly-burnt clay is further useful as a covering for roads and paths where gravel is inaccessible; its chief objection, as a surface material for paths, being its colour, for the oxide of iron present in all clay soils, uniting with oxygen, gives it a dark red brick-colour. This property is usefully applied in the modern style of laying out flower-beds with variegated paths; marble and granite chips being used for white and grey paths, gravel for yellow, and burnt clay for red, with a very happy effect.

The mode of burning clay varies in different counties. Some clays burn hard when dry, others when wet. In some places, where it is only required as manure, the waste corners of fields and scourings of the ditches are burnt in heaps and scattered over the ground. When all the land is burned, as many as forty heaps are scattered over an acre, and when reduced to about half their bulk, the fires are extinguished. Sometimes, however, the burning takes place in large heaps, varying from two to three hundred loads, fresh materials being added as the fire makes its appearance outside. The object not being to burn the clay into a hard red brick, however, it is just heated sufficiently to disintegrate the clay, so that it crumbles into dust between the finger and thumb. Where the burning is taken by the piece, and in large heaps, the cost of digging and burning is from 5d. to 7d. the yard of ashes. When the burning is in heaps forty to the acre, it costs about 8s. This cost, however, increases with the purity of the clay; but the benefit derived from the process increases also, especially if it is not confined to simply paring and burning the surface, but removing the stiff subsoil itself, and exposing it to calcination. The secret of burning strong clay is to throw it wet upon the burning heap, raking it down flat as the lumps begin to crack, thus increasing the surface exposed to the action of the heat and atmosphere; taking care, in windy weather, to apply the fresh material on the leeward side, or that side will be burnt before the other is touched. Burnt in this way, the lumps will crumble under the rake in a short time; if applied dry, on the contrary, the hard lumps will become harder.

106 That the process of burning is highly beneficial in some cases there can be no doubt. The garden at Hardwicke Court, Gloucester, consisted of a stiff sterile clay, but by digging out the soil three feet deep and burning it, it was rendered as remarkable for its fertility as it had been before for the reverse. Authorities, however, are not agreed as to the causes of this increased fertility. In the natural state of clay, it may be digested for hours with concentrated sulphuric acid without dissolving; but, when slightly burnt, it dissolves in acids with great ease, while the silica is separated into its gelatinous and soluble form. The soil is rendered accessible to air, oxygen, and carbonic acid, according to Liebig; and these are the principal conditions favourable to the development of roots. Common potter's clay contains within it all the constituents necessary to the luxuriant growth of plants; but they must be presented in a state fit to be taken up by the roots of plants: gentle calcination communicates these properties.

107 Burning the soil thus operates by chemical as well as by mechanical agency; the compact clay has been hitherto impervious to atmospheric influence; the half-decomposed remains of former crops have remained in the soil an inert mass of organic matter. By burning, the saline constituents of former crops are unlocked and rendered soluble in water, and become available as food to the plants. Moreover, the application of heat has rendered the surface porous and friable – its mechanical condition has undergone an entire change; and Liebig considers that its power of attracting ammonia from the atmosphere is increased far beyond that of any natural soil; while Dr Voelcker regards potash, which is liberated on burning the clay, as the chief source of its efficacy.

108 Burning is attended with especial advantage to peat soils, in which the accumulation of organic matter is prejudicial to all vegetation. In burning, the sour humus which is formed by marshy soils is destroyed, and the insoluble particles occurring in it rendered soluble and available as fertilisers.

109 Next in importance to drainage and burning is the introduction into the soil of atmospheric air, which is a combination of oxygen and hydrogen – one of the objects of drainage being to admit oxygen, with the other constituents of atmospheric air, into the soil. We are now brought on to a consideration of digging as the third and best known, because most frequently practised, of the three great mechanical means by which natural soils are prepared and brought into cultivation. The admission of atmospheric air, which is promoted in the first place by draining, is facilitated by the deep trenching which usually follows the thorough drainage of a garden ground. The immediate object of trenching is to deepen the soil, and prepare the subsoil to nourish the fibres of deep-rooting plants. The operation is commenced by throwing out the top spit to a convenient breadth for the workman, and wheeling it to the farther end of the bed or quarter; the second spit is treated in the same manner if the trenching is to be three spades deep. This done, the bottom of the trench is dug up as roughly as possible, so that it is left level. The top spit of a second portion of the ground is now removed and placed alongside the first, and the second spit of this portion is dug up and placed roughly over the first trench. The first spit of a third portion is now removed and placed in as large masses as possible over the first trench: the bottom of the second trench is now dug up in the same manner as the first, and so on till the whole is finished.

110 To render the operation of trenching three spades deep fully intelligible, it may be as well as to make the description that has just been given yet more clear by reference to a diagram. Thus, in Fig. 21, a plan of the ground to be trenched is shown divided into trenches, A, B, C, etc., of convenient width, say 12 inches; and in Fig. 22 a longitudinal section of the ground, showing it divided into layers 8 inches in depth, and into trenches 12 inches wide, so that the trenching is carried to the depth of 2 feet. The operation of trenching is commenced by taking out the top spit from the trench A and wheeling the soil to the other end of the piece of land to be trenched, placing it at H in a long row, the length of the row being equal to the width of the land to be trenched, and at a sufficient distance from the space to be occupied by the last trench to allow the second spit from A to be placed at K, alongside of the mould at H, and nearer the last trench, G, than the mould at H. The top spit from the second trench, B, is then to be wheeled to L. The disposition of the first and second spits from A and the top spit from B is thus made to bring the mould into a convenient position for filling in the trenches F and G at the completion of the trenching; for as the second spit in G is thrown into F to form the second spit of that trench, the top spits from A and B being thrown into F and G to form the top spits of those trenches. It will manifestly be easier to throw the mould of the second spit from A into G from K than if it had been placed to the rear of the top spits from A and B, and when this mould has been put in its place, the mould of the top spits from A and B may be thrown over the second spits in F and G just as the mould comes to hand. In the sectional view in Fig. 22, the transfer of the spits of earth from trench to trench is shown by the arrows. No further mention

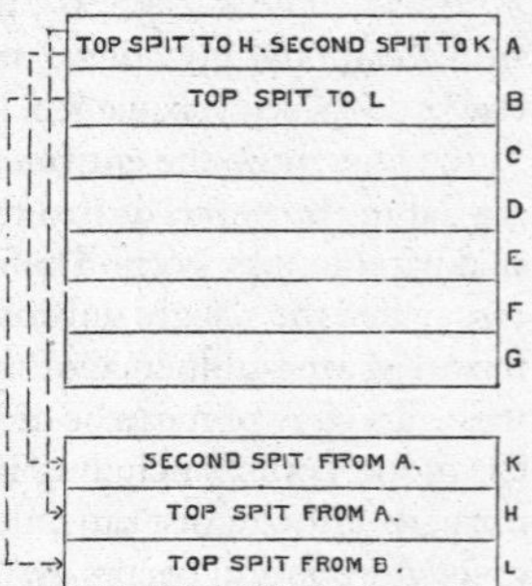

FIG. 21 *Plan of ground marked for trenching*

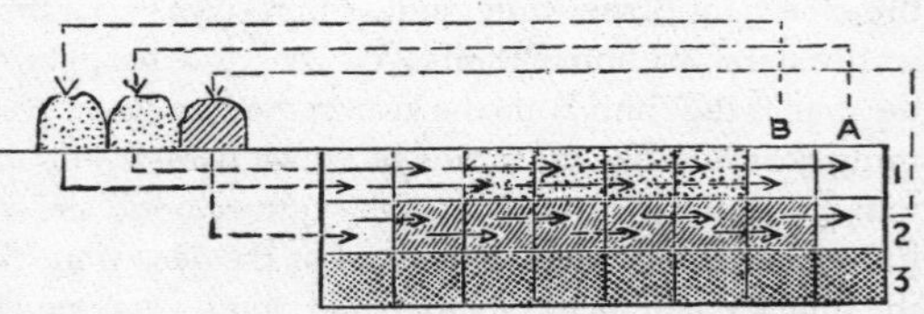

FIG. 22 *Sectional diagram showing transfer of earth from trench to trench in trenching*

need be made of the temporary removal of the first and second spits in A and the top spit in B to the rear of the ground to be trenched. In the diagram, the third spits are distinguished by crossed irregular lines. This spit in each trench is broken up into rough lumps when the spits above it have been removed. The second spits are shown by diagonal lines, and the transfer of the spits from B to A, from C to B, etc., is shown by the short arrows. The top spits are shown by dotted spaces, and the transfer of the spits from C to A, from D to B, etc., is shown by longer arrows. When the second spit in H has been removed to a similar position in G, and the top spits in G and H to similar positions in E and F respectively, the vacant spits which are left white in the diagram are filled in with the mould previously removed from the trenches A and B in the manner and order already explained.

111 Thus, while the entire soil in the ground that has been trenched has been stirred to the depth of two feet, it still retains the position, in point of depth, that it held in the ground before it was trenched; the surface being left exposed for a time in rough unbroken lumps, till it crumbles naturally under the disintegrating influence of the atmosphere. Oxygen enters into combination with all soils; and it can be demonstrated that about one-half of the materials of the globe's crust, including its animal and vegetable products, is composed of oxygen. The chemist can only obtain it as a gas; but when combined, it assumes divers forms, and occurs as liquids and solids, as well as a gas. About a half by weight of flint, rock-crystal, and other forms of silica, is oxygen; about a third of alumina, or pure clay, by measure, and a fifth of the atmosphere by weight, are oxygen; and no plant or animal can exist without oxygen entering largely into its constitution.

112 In the description of trenching given above, the width of the trenches has been stated at 1 foot. In practice it will be found convenient to make the width 18 inches or 2 feet, and in some cases, according to the nature of the soil and subsoil, it will be necessary to extend the width considerably, putting it at from 3 to 5 or even 6 feet, especially when the ground is uneven, and depressions and hollows have to be filled up. When the space to be trenched is very long, in order to save the time and trouble involved in wheeling the soil taken out of the trenches A and B to the rear of the ground, it is better to divide the ground longitudinally into two equal parts, as shown in Fig. 23. The topmost spit from the trench A can then be placed at D, the topmost spit from B at E, and the second spit from A at F, as shown by the dotted

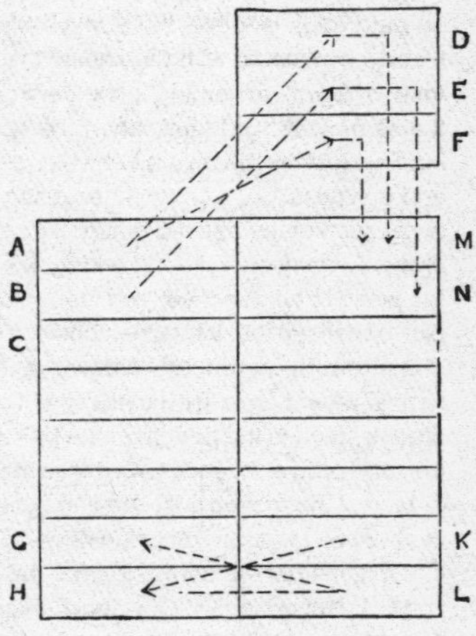

FIG. 23 *Diagram showing mode of trenching without wheeling soil to rear of ground to be trenched*

lines and arrow heads. On arriving at the other end of the first portion of the ground, the topmost spit from L will go to G, the second spit from L to H, and the topmost spit from K to H. The second portion will then be trenched backwards; and, to complete the operation, the second spit of soil from A deposited temporarily at F will form the second layer in M, and the topmost spits from A and B, at D and E, will be transferred to M and N, and form the topmost spits of these trenches.

113 It must not be supposed from what has been said about trenching that it is absolutely necessary at all times to trench ground to the depth of 2 feet, or, in other words, three spits deep. In ordinary cases it is sufficient to carry the trenching to two spits in depth, or 16 inches; but in this the *modus operandi* is precisely the same, although the removal of the soil in the topmost spit of the first trench, either to the rear of the ground, or as in Fig. 23, to the topmost end of the second portion to be trenched, is all that is required. Nor is it an invariable rule that the original position of the three spits or strata is to be retained, for sometimes it is found necessary to reverse it, and to deposit the surface soil at the bottom of the trench, while that which is below it is brought to the top.

'Trenching,' says Loudon, 'is a mode of pulverising and mixing the soil, or of pulverising and changing its surface, to a greater depth than can be done by the spade alone' – that is to say, by thrusting the spade as far as possible into the ground and turning over the earth that can be lifted at one time by it, for, after all, trenching to any depth is performed by aid of the spade. 'For trenching with a view to pulverising and changing the surface, a trench is formed like the furrow in digging, but two or more times wider and deeper.' The term 'digging', it should be said, is applied by Loudon to the act of simply turning over the surface of ground with the spade. 'The plot or piece to be trenched,' he then continues 'is next marked off into parallel strips of this width, and beginning at one of these, the operator digs or picks the surface stratum, and throws it in the bottom of the trench. Having completed with the shovel the removal of the surface stratum, a second, and a third, or fourth, according to the depth of the soil and other circumstances, is removed in the same way, and thus, when the operation is completed, the position of the different strata is exactly the reverse of what they were before. In trenching, with a view to mixture and pulverisation, all that is necessary is to open, at one corner of the plot, a trench or excavation of the desired depth, 3 or 4 feet long, and 6 or 8 feet broad. Then proceed to fill this excavation from one end by working out a similar one. In this way proceed across the piece to be trenched, and then return, and so on in parallel courses to the end of the plot, observing that the face or position of the moved soil in the trench must always be that of a slope, in order that whatever is thrown there may be mixed, and not deposited in regular layers as in the other case. To effect this most completely, the operator should always stand in the bottom of the trench, and first picking down and mixing the materials from the solid side, should next take them up with the shovel, and throw them on the slope or face of the moved soil, keeping a distinct space of 2 or 3 feet between them. For want of attention to this in trenching new soils for gardens and plantations, it may be truly said that half the benefit derivable from the operation is lost.'

Mr J. Robertson, of Cowdenknowes, writing in *Gardening Illustrated*, thus insists on the importance of trenching and double digging. November, he points out, 'is the time to get as much of the garden dug over as possible,' and then, turning to the main part of his subject, he continues: 'It is a good plan to trench part of the garden every year, exposing as much surface to the frost as possible. The piece of ground intended for carrots, parsnips, beet, salsify, scorzonera, chicory, and all such things with long roots, should be trenched; by so doing, the roots are not so apt to fork. Peas and potatoes also do well on newly-trenched ground. When commencing to trench a piece of ground, I take an opening out three feet wide and three spades deep, and wheel the soil to the other end for filling in the last trench. I make each trench the same width. After two spits deep is turned over into the trench, I then put the manure on the top of that, the last spit going on top of the manure in form of a ridge. It is best to lay the soil up in ridges, and as rough as possible, exposing as much surface to the influence of frost as can be done. If the garden has a gravelly or sandy bottom it will be sure to be dry in summer. When trenching such ground, put into the bottom of the trench all old cabbages that are past any use, cauliflower leaves, and all such vegetable refuse; by doing so, it helps to retain the moisture in dry seasons, and it will be found to help substantially the growing crops in summer. When manure is plentiful it should not be spared when trenching, putting a layer between every spit. In gardens, where there is time, instead of digging one spade deep, and laying up rough for winter, it is a good system to double dig, laying up in ridges. Take out an opening two spades broad and two deep, and spread the manure on the surface, digging it into the bottom with the first spit, the last spit going on the top in the form of a ridge. By ridging there is a vast amount more surface exposed to the action of the frost than there would be by level digging; and in spring, when it is levelled down to get in the crops, it will be found that the frost has torn it asunder and pulverised it so nicely that it goes down like meal, and is in splendid condition for receiving seeds. By adopting a course of trenching and double digging, in a few years the effect will be apparent. A nice depth of rich, easy-worked soil will be secured, which most vegetables will take to and root in readily, and when vegetables do so, whatever the sort may be, we have prospects of a good crop. Where the soil is of a clayey nature, it is a good plan to work in, while trenching and double digging, plenty of leaf-mould, old lime rubbish, sand, ashes, or anything of a light nature that will help to keep the soil open and sweet.'

114 Trenching, therefore, may be managed in two different ways – one in which the relative position of the spits or strata is preserved, nothing more in change of position of each spit being effected than in turning it upside down, breaking into pieces, as far as may be possible, with the view of admitting air between the pieces, in order to produce further pulverisation; and the other in which the strata are broken up and thoroughly commingled without any attempt being made to preserve their original position. The first method is the best for garden ground already under cultivation, or in process of renewal; and the second for ground that is broken up for the first time: but even in this case the nature of the soil and subsoil will indicate the kind of trenching that may most profitably be applied to it.

115 In trenching new ground that it is sought to bring into cultivation by deep digging, it should in many cases be accompanied by the incorporation of lime with the soil, which sweetens, quickens, and enriches it. The action of lime, however, is chemical and not mechanical, and must therefore be noticed more particularly when the application, nature, and properties of manures are brought under consideration in the next chapter. Lime itself, as a manure and as an important fertiliser of the soil, is mentioned here because the operation of trenching affords the most favourable opportunity that can be obtained for its introduction into, and admixture with, soil that will be benefitted by its quickening influence.

'Lime, employed as a manure,' says Scoffern, 'performs three well-marked functions at least, perhaps more: in all it is a powerful ameliorator of soils, and under two series of conditions it should be used in different forms. New-burned caustic lime is a powerfully corrosive body; when brought into contact with animal and vegetable tissues, it rapidly disorganises them. Even if the tissues be living, still the quicklime will effect their disorganisation. Hence arise the following deductions. When we have to deal with a rank new soil, teeming with noxious seeds, and with seeds ready to spring into life on the first opportunity, or when the object is to convert hard animal tissues, such as horn or kelp, or even softer ones, as clippings of woollen cloth, into a useful manure, unslaked lime is employed. On the other hand, when the object in adding lime to the soil is to supply the calcareous element as a mechanical means of ameliorating the texture of the soil, and a physiological means of supplying food to certain crops, and where there are no weeds nor noxious germs to destroy, nor organic tissues to decompose, then the employment of lime should be in the mild or slaked state.' In both its forms, therefore, lime is a powerful agent in the improvement of soils, especially those in which clay and peat exist to any extent.

CHAPTER 4

Manures, Natural and Artificial; Preparation of Composts, Liquid Manures, etc.

116 In the preceding chapters the origin of various soils has been traced, and it has been shown, from natural causes and influences, how it is that one kind of soil is to be found in one place and another in another, and how different soils are often found in juxtaposition, although proceeding from the disintegration of strata that have been deposited at widely distant periods of the world's life. The three great mechanical methods by which soils are primarily prepared for cultivation have also been noticed, and this done, before entering directly upon garden work, it is desirable to consider briefly the nature of the natural manures and appliances that are combined with the soil in order to render it fertile or to increase its fertility, to mention some of the leading artificial manures and the purposes they are intended to serve, and to dwell awhile on the preparation of composts for garden use. Before beginning garden work in practice, it is but reasonable that we should know something of the manures that either form the food of plants to a certain extent, or, by acting on the ground in which they are grown, sometimes chemically, and sometimes even mechanically, tend to render it better fitted to promote their growth from germination to maturity.

117 Plants derive the chief part of their food from the soil, and as the growth of different species of plants is promoted by certain substances taken up in different proportions from it, which require to be replaced in order to reproduce the same crop, it is obvious that this renovation of the soil is a very important part of gardening, as it is of cultivation on a greater scale. Much discrimination and judgment is therefore required in the preparation of composts and arrangement of the manure heap. A rough analysis of natural soils usually presents a percentage of silica, oxide of iron, alumina, potash, and other substances, which enter into their composition with certain organic matters, to which they owe much of their fertility. The organic matter is of a very complex character, and owes its origin in a great degree to vegetable remains, as the roots and stems of former crops; but also, in part, to decayed animal remains, both of which are found to decompose under the influence of water, air, and heat, producing a blackish-brown powdery substance on analysis, known as *humus* – a substance which includes a great many vegetable acids in its composition.

'The opinion of chemists is much divided,' Dr Scoffern remarks, in his *Chemistry of Soils*, 'as to whether the humic acid bodies, when dissolved, are actually absorbed by plants, as nourishment in that condition, or whether complete decomposition into gaseous elements must be the preparatory step to their appropriation. In either case the alkalies must be efficacious, for the solvent action which they exercise advances by one degree at least their final decomposition. That some important function of these bodies is intimately associated with their extreme avidity for alkalies, especially for ammonia, can scarcely be doubted. So great is their tendency to unite with it that it is exceedingly – difficult to procure acids of this series free from it. Not only do they absorb all of this alkali they come in contact with, but it is suspected that they actually, like many other porous bodies, promote the combination of oxygen and hydrogen, and form ammonia – a beautiful provision of Nature, by which the products of natural decomposition to which vegetables are disposed are endowed with the property of generating that which is necessary to their own solution, and consequently to their assimilation as food; not merely of collecting, but of generating ammonia for their own use.'

118 In order, however, to accomplish the production of decomposed organic matter suitable for the food of plants, certain elements must be supplied; and all who have examined this question admit that the value of manures is in proportion to the nitrogen or phosphates which they contain, more especially the former; for nitrogen is almost synonymous with ammonia, that being the chief source of nitrogen for plants. It should be the first business of the farmer and gardener, therefore, to take care of the ammonia and phosphates at his command, and to take steps to prevent the loss of all soluble matters from his compost heap.

119 *Farmyard Manure* The first and most important source of these elements is farmyard manure, which, in its fresh state, consists of the refuse of straw, of green vegetable matter, and the excreta of domestic animals. Horse dung varies in its composition according to the food of the animal, being most valuable when fed upon grain, being then firm in consistence and rich in phosphates. Sheep's litter is a very active manure, and rich in sulphur and nitrogen; for if a slip of white paper, previously dipped in a solution of lead, be exposed to the fumes of fresh sheep's dung, the paper will be blackened: and the blackening is a sure test of the presence of sulphur. Cow litter is cooler and less rich in nitrogenous matter than is horse dung or sheep's dung; but it is rich in salts of potash and soda, and thus better adapted for delicate and deep-rooted plants. Swine's dung is highly nitrogenous, but more watery, and full of vegetable matter, often containing seeds not dead, but ready to germinate.

120 The most important of all manures is the urine from the stables and drainings of the dung heap, which is wasted daily to an enormous extent. The urine of all carnivorous animals is rich in urea and uric acid. In the urine of herbivorous animals, except the pig, hippuric acid takes the place of uric acid; but in all cases urine is rich in nitrogen, and, when allowed to putrefy, ammonia is evolved from it. Urine is thus one of the most important constituents of farmyard manure.

In the *Elements of Agricultural Chemistry and Geology*, by Johnston and Cameron, the following remarks are made on the value of the excreta obtained from the cow, the horse, the sheep, and the pig: '*Cow dung* is the most abundant and least valuable in composition of the animal manures; it decomposes slowly, giving out but little heat, hence it is said to be a *cold* manure. This is quite correct, for manures, such as horse dung, which decompose rapidly in the soil, warm the latter. Decomposition in such cases is really a slow combustion. *Horse dung* is more valuable than cow dung. It contains less water, is not so coherent, and does not form, during its decomposition, an unctuous mass such as cow dung does. Horse dung decomposes rapidly, and is therefore a *hot* manure. It is a useful addition to cow dung, as it renders the latter more friable, whereby it can be more equably distributed throughout the soil. *Sheep's dung* decomposes more rapidly than cow dung, and not so quickly as horse dung. It is richer in solid matters than the former. *Pig's dung*: The pig being almost an omnivorous animal, its excrements vary in composition according to the nature of its food. Its dung is soft and compact, and it decomposes slowly. It is one of the richest kinds of animal manure, but it is alleged that when used alone as manure it gives a disagreeable flavour to roots. *Bird's dung*: The bird voids but one excrement, which partakes more of the nature of urine than of faeces. It is a good manure, but it is not usually obtained in these countries in large quantities. The manure from the poultry yard, such as it is, should be carefully gathered up and added to the compost heap. The same observation applies to the dung of pigeons, which in some farmsteads is occasionally produced in great quantities.'

From what has been stated above, it is clear why cow dung is best suited as a manure for roses, why horse dung is most suitable for mushroom culture, and why sheep's dung, when infused in water, forms an excellent liquid manure for plants. The following table of the composition of animal faeces is compiled from various statements put forth by Stockhardt, Cameron, and Anderson, and given in the *Elements of Agricultural Chemistry and Geology*.

COMPOSITION OF ANIMAL FAECES

1000 Parts of each contain:

		Cow		Horse		Sheep		Pig	
	Constituents	Dung	Urine	Dung	Urine	Dung	Urine	Dung	Urine
Cameron	**Water**	860.0	915.0	750.0	900.0	640.0	950.0	760.0	976.0
	Nitrogen	3.6	9.0	6.0	11.0	6.0	8.0	7.0	3.0
	Phosphoric Acid	3.0		4.0		5.0		5.0	1.2
	Potash and Soda	2.2	16.0	3.5	14.0	3.0	8.0	6.5	2.0
	Other Solid Matters	131.2	60.0	236.5	75.0	346.0	34.0	221.5	17.8
		1000.0	1000.0	1000.0	1000.0	1000.0	1000.0	1000.0	1000.0
Stockhardt	**Water**	840.0	920.0	760.0	890.0	580.0	870.0	800.0	750.0
	Nitrogen	3.0	8.0	5.0	12.0	7.5	14.0	6.0	30.0
	Phosphoric Acid						.5		1.25
	Potash and Soda	1.0	14.0	3.0	20.0	3.0	20.0	5.0	20.0
	Other Solid Matters	156.0	58.0	232.0	78.0	409.5	95.5	189.0	198.75
		1000.0	1000.0	1000.0	1000.0	1000.0	1000.0	1000.0	1000.0

1000 Parts of each contain:

	Constituents	Hen	Pigeon
Anderson	**Water**	608.8	583.2
	Organic Matter	184.8	265.0
	Ammonia from Organic Matter	7.4	17.5
	Phosphates	44.7	26.9
	Calcic Carbonate	78.5	17.5
	Alkaline Salts	10.2	18.9
	Phosphoric Acid = Tricalcic Phosphate	.7	1.0
	Sand	66.9	70.0
		1000.0	1000.0

121 The composition of manure is a very heterogeneous mixture. It may be broadly viewed as a mixture of humic acid bodies fixed in alkaline salts, and nitrogenous bodies capable of yielding ammonia; and it becomes an important question how its strength is best economised. Some advocate the practice of allowing the compost heap to be entirely decomposed into an earthy mass, but this permits the whole of the ammonia to escape; others, again, have gone so far as not to permit of any fermentation at all, stopping all action by continual turning. It is a bad practice to allow so valuable an agent as ammonia to go to waste; but this is the inevitable result of permitting manure to undergo its last degree of fermentation. Again, it is doubtful whether the beneficial qualities of the manure can be brought into play if it has not been submitted to incipient decomposition. Nevertheless, means exist by which the ammonia may be fixed and retained in all its strength, while it is reduced to a state suited for assimilation as food for plants. It may be absorbed by gypsum or sulphate of lime, which, being cheap, is often mixed with the compost heap for the purpose; the ammoniacal salts thus formed being afterwards decomposed by the vegetable organism, or by its agency combined with atmospheric influences.

122 It appears, then, from what has been said, that the chief value of farmyard manure – independent of the fact that by its incorporation with the soil it renders the latter lighter, more porous, and more friable – consists in the ammoniacal salts that it contains, which form an important, perhaps the most important, constituent of plant food; because it is from ammonia that plants seem to derive the chief proportion of the nitrogen that they take in from the soil through their roots. Being given off by animal and vegetable substances in course of decomposition, it rises into the atmosphere, and there remains until it is brought down to the ground once more by the rain, which carries it into the soil. It is present in considerable quantities in farmyard manure, and chemical analysis has shown that the liquids of the farmyard contain a much greater proportion of it than the solids.

123 From this the chief deduction is that it is desirable to preserve as much of the liquid manure of the farmyard as possible, and in such a manner as will best promote the retention of the ammonia. To this end it is desirable that farmyard manure should be stored under cover – that is to say, under a structure composed of a roof supported on posts, and open on all sides. This prevents the manure that is stored in the shed from having its best constituents washed out of it and carried away by direct down pouring of rain, as it inevitably must be if not kept under cover, and at the same time the open sides of the structure prevent it from giving out a strong, pungent, and objectionable smell, as it must do if it is kept in a close and confined place. And as it is clear that it is the liquid portion of the manure that is most valuable, the floor of the shed should be concreted, and made to slope gently from all sides to the centre, in which a grating should be placed through which the liquid part may find its way to a concreted reservoir below, from which it could be raised by a pump, and mixed with water to a sufficient degree to admit of its application with safety to grass lands and growing crops.

124 It will be argued that it is out of the power of the ordinary gardener, whether professional or amateur, either to obtain or preserve liquid manure for use in the manner above stated. This is not the case. In every garden that has any pretension to be called a garden, even in suburban localities, there will be a corner which can be divided off and masked in a variety of ways for the storage of compost and the formation of a compost heap. If a horse be kept, there will in all probability be due provision for the storage of manure from the stable without such a corner; but if not, let the most remote and unprofitable nook in the garden be appropriated for a compost yard, and here, under a roof, let the vegetable refuse of the house, the droppings of the fowls and pigeons, if poultry be kept, and everything of this kind that is available, be consigned. Over this let the slops of the house, the soapy water made on washing days, be poured occasionally, if not every day, to percolate through the decomposing heap into a tank constructed below, from which it may be pumped up at pleasure to be used, when diluted, as liquid manure for the garden.

125 On the heap, animal refuse may be thrown as well as vegetable. It will be better, however, to keep from it all such things as cabbage-stalks, the stems of plants, and anything whose hard, woody fibre would prevent it from rotting quickly, and destroy these, when dry enough, by burning. The ashes that are obtained by this means should not be put on the compost heap, but rather stored in a place set apart for them for transference to any border, or for incorporation with soil that is specially reserved for potting plants. No apology is necessary for these apparently trivial details, for it is requisite to afford limits for the collection and storage of manure on a small scale as on a large one.

126 We have now fully considered the advantages to be derived from farmyard manure pure and simple, or manure consisting of excreta and urine mingled with decomposing animal and vegetable matter. This is the first and cheapest natural manure arising from natural causes, and which must be applied direct to the ground as a fertilising agent. Farmyard manure, although in itself a compost, inasmuch as it consists of several ingredients placed together, must not be confounded with the *compost heap*, which, properly speaking, consists of ingredients brought together for the sake of the fertilising properties which they contain, but which rather forms a soil that is beneficial and useful for the growth of plants therein rather than a manure. Potting earth, for example, is a *compost*, but it cannot be viewed as a manure in the same light that the gatherings of the farmyard are looked upon as such. It is only when spent and thoroughly rotted that farmyard dung becomes a suitable ingredient for the compost heap as it is here regarded; as, for instance, when it has done its work in the hotbed employed in raising cucumbers and melons. We will now proceed to consider other ingredients that are suitable for the compost heap, but which are nevertheless natural manures, or have a good claim to be so considered.

127 *Leaf-mould* This is a substance complex in its nature, and its functions, except so far as its heating properties are concerned, are imperfectly known. The substance of all plants and leaves yields by slow decomposition results of the highest importance to the cultivation of the soil; and when exposed to a sufficient amount of heat, and under the full play of atmospheric air or oxygen, they burn, yielding water and carbonic acid, leaving only a trifling amount of organic matter behind. Natural decay is just such a slow combustion of moist organic matter as is required; it is decomposed when freely exposed to the oxygen of the air by slow burning, and the result is that when the gaseous fumes evolved by decomposition are given off, a blackish-looking mass remains, consisting of bodies of the humic acid series. When reduced to this state, they are, to all physical appearance, like dark-brown soil, or earth; and it is to their presence that garden soils owe their peculiar colour. On ultimate analysis, these brownish bodies are found to consist of *humic*, *ulmic*, and *geic* acids, neither of them soluble in water, but all soluble in alkalies, with which they have a strong affinity. Hence their tendency to unite in the ammonia, and their value as manures in connection with alkali.

'Not only do they absorb such of this alkali as they come in contact with,' says Dr Scoffern, 'but it is suspected that they actually, like many other porous bodies, promote the combination of oxygen and hydrogen, and *form* ammonia by catalytic agency – a term used by Berzelius to express the result of the contact of a third body upon two others, without being itself changed in its character – a beautiful provision of Nature, by which the products of natural decomposition are endowed with the properties necessary to render them fit for assimilation as food for vegetables.' From this it is clear how important it is that not a leaf should be suffered to run to waste, but should be swept up as they fall, and conveyed to a heap, taking care to keep them by themselves, and apart from other manures, until they are in a state fit for mixing into composts.

The manner in which these influences operate is an interesting subject to the gardener. The fertilising properties of manure are in proportion to the nitrogen contained in it, this gas being absorbed by plants in combination with hydrogen in the form of ammonia, which is composed of 14 parts of nitrogen and 3 parts of hydrogen *by weight*. When this is borne in mind, and the fact that the atmosphere is another source from which plants derive this substance, the great utility of trenching becomes evident, especially to those plants which easily give off their nitrogen to mix in the atmosphere rather than in the soil. Leguminous plants are valuable in this respect, for it enables the cultivator to enrich the ground which has been exhausted by excessive cropping. That the atmosphere holds ammonia sufficient for the development of plants is due to the decomposition of organised bodies, which all contain a greater or less quantity of nitrogen; but it is particularly in the bodies of animals that this agent exists. It enters into the composition of all their organs, and when, after death, animals are left to the chemical action of Nature, all the elements of which they were constituted are separated, and immediately form new, and for the greater part, gaseous compounds, and amongst them ammonia, which is dissolved in the atmosphere by the water with which the air is always charged.

Another source of this agent has been traced to the electric discharges in a thunderstorm. Carbonate of ammonia, according to Boussingault and Liebig, pre-exists in all organised beings. 'The phenomenon of the constancy of thunderstorms,' M. Boussingault says, 'would seem to justify this opinion. It is said, indeed, that every time a series of electric flashes pass in the humid atmosphere, there is a production and combination of nitric acid and ammonia; the nitrate of ammonia, besides, always accompanies the rain which falls in a thunderstorm; but this acid being fixed in its nature, cannot be maintained in a state of vapour. When we consider the reaction which takes place between the different compounds in question, it may easily be conceived that the nitrate of ammonia, which is drawn to the earth by the rain, and which comes in contact with the rocks or calcareous soil, is afterwards volatilised to the state of carbonate at the next drying of the soil. There can be no doubt at the present day, that the carbonate of ammonia is the most active agent of vegetation, and without which all the others would be useless; but this carbonate is gaseous, and for this reason cannot be employed directly by the cultivator, who, were he to try to create an atmosphere of the carbonate of ammonia under his ground, would spend a great deal of money without obtaining any benefit whatever, since the slightest movement of the air would instantly produce evaporation of this volatile manure.'

128 Ammonia, indeed, whether in the atmosphere or the soil, is the great source of fertility; but natural soils are themselves of much importance in plant cultivation. Rich black mould often contains 20 per cent of its own weight of organic matter, derived from the decomposition of animal and vegetable matter. In peat-earth, the proportions vary from 50 to 70 per cent; in good garden land, the average amount is 10 to 12 per cent, and sometimes even twice as much in soils that have for a long period been well cultivated; and in average arable soils of the fields, it may be from 4 to 8 per cent.

129 *Sand and Clay* Sand in its various phases, from silver to yellow, is an important part of the compost heap, more for its mechanical than its fertilising properties, although it forms a constituent of many plants; and clay, besides its stiff, tenacious character, which enables it to sustain the more vigorous vegetable growths, is found to be highly attractive of ammonia; so highly attractive, according to Mr Way – who published the result of his experiments on the power of soils to absorb and retain manure in the Journal of the Royal Agricultural Society in 1850, 1852, and 1855 – that an ammoniacal sulphate, or nitrate, or muriate, being filtered through a collection of clay soils, real chemical decomposition resulted, the ammonia being retained, and the associated acid passing into some new state of combination. Pursuing his experiments, Mr Way finally determined the question by tracing silicates of lime, of soda, and potash among the constituents of clay, which were the absorbing agents in question.

130 It is thus a matter of great practical importance that the soils for gardening purposes should not only be judiciously, but carefully collected and stored for future use. All the care bestowed on a plant in potting and watering is so much labour thrown away if the soil is unsuitable; but if a suitable soil be employed, it is wonderful with what tenacity a plant will cling to existence, even under the most unfavourable circumstances. The sweeter a soil is – that is to say, the more it has been exposed to atmospheric influences – the more suitable it becomes for all horticultural purposes.

Even maiden soil from an upland pasture, where it has been well drained, is materially improved by exposure to atmospheric changes for a few months; while soil from a wet locality should never be used, under any circumstances, until it has been exposed to the varied changes of an English winter; and if it be also exposed for a month or two in summer it will be much improved. The improvement arises principally from the expulsion of deleterious matter, the decomposition of vegetable substances, and the thorough disintegration of the whole mass. When a soil is very strong and adhesive, it is necessary to expose it in thin layers to the action of frost, removing the frozen part as often as it becomes frozen to a sufficient thickness, and placing it where it can be thoroughly dried. Soil thus prepared will generally be found clear of insects – a matter of considerable importance in the cultivation of choice plants.

131 *Peat* This important material should be in layers not more than two or three inches thick, firm in texture and fibrous, the upper surface covered with dwarf heath, and the under surface resting on sand. It will generally be found in upland situations. This, when brought home, should be carefully looked over, and the upper surface divested of all rough herbage, and the lower of every particle of sand; and then placed in ridges, so that the air can act on all parts of it: it should be turned occasionally until the rains of autumn render it necessary to stack it.

If not wanted for use before the following summer, build some turf-pits with it, which may be turned to good account for protecting lettuce or cauliflower plants, leaving the peat exposed to the action of the weather on all sides, which will much improve its texture and mellow its properties. If not used for that purpose, however, stack it in narrow ridges four feet in height, the base three feet wide, and tapering to a single turf at the top, placing the turves at short distances apart, so as to admit of the air percolating freely among them, and run an air-drain longitudinally through the centre of the stack, or introduce old pea-sticks between each alternate layer of peat, so that the surface-water may be carried away as it falls.

132 When peat is required for immediate use, and there is not sufficient time to mature it by exposure to the action of the air, the outer surface should be charred. The turves should be cut into pieces three inches wide, to allow every part to become equally heated. Loam prepared for immediate use should be charred in the same way; indeed, leaf-mould and composts of all kinds will be materially benefitted by charring, especially when intended for raising small seed, so as to destroy the insects and vegetative power of any seeds they may contain.

Charred cow dung is an excellent manure for almost all purposes, and by charring it, it is immediately fit for use. Take some old wood and build a cone two or three feet high; then procure some green cow dung, and cover the cone nine inches thick; let it drain for a day or two; cover it with weeds or rubbish, and set fire to the wood, regulating the draught so as to prevent the fire burning too fiercely; and by the time the wood is consumed, you will have a fine crust of charred cow dung. To mix, when broken up, with composts, or to place a few pieces at the bottom of the pots in which calceolarias, pelargoniums, cincrarias, or pines or vines are grown, this will be found a most excellent manure.

133 *Grey or Silver Sand* This substance is an indispensable ingredient in all composts for plant culture. In its purest state, silica or sand is the *débris* of quartz, or rock-crystal, which is composed almost entirely of silica, hard sand being the result of the disintegration and decomposition of rocks by the chemical agency of the atmosphere, assisted by the mechanical powers of the winds, of rain, and abrading waters. It varies much in its composition; oolitic rocks, granite, limestone, and red and green sandstone, all furnishing their quota. As an impalpable powder, it occurs in all soils. In its chemical character silica is an important constituent of organic life, being found, on analysis, in most plants. Mixed with soda, and heated to redness in an iron ladle, silica dissolves to a fused mass; if thrown into water, it will completely dissolve; and if nitric acid be added, it becomes gelatinous – indications of the means by which silica is treated in the great alembic of Nature, and adapted for absorption into the tissue of plants.

In preparing sand for the more obvious mechanical purpose which it serves in plant culture, it is divested of the other constituents of the soil, by washing and sifting through a fine sieve. In this way, all soils will yield a portion of this element, and dry; but the best mode of procuring it is to proceed to some stream running through any of the sandstone countries. In such a stream there are few places where the winding eddies have not formed a sandbank, and one of these will generally furnish an ample supply. In towns and in country places where access cannot conveniently be obtained to running streams or to the seashore, in some parts of which fine sand is found, which is most useful for gardening and agricultural purposes, the sweepings of the streets and roads, especially the grit blown on to the side-walks of streets in windy and dry weather, will furnish sand of an excellent quality for plant culture. And the sand that is washed by heavy rainfalls down roads or the channels of streets, between the curb of the side-walks and the roadway, and deposited in some hollow under the hedge in the former, or at the mouth of a gully-hole in the latter, is equally desirable. Grit of this kind is known as road sand. It forms a useful ingredient in compost for the culture of the auricula.

When thoroughly washed, and all particles of clay extracted, let the sand be thrown into a heap, sheltered from the rain, and turned until it is thoroughly aerated; it should then be stored in a dry place till wanted for use. Silica is a constituent of all the grasses, and is absolutely necessary in the cultivation of all those of the family cultivated in our hothouses and gardens: it is also a necessary ameliorator in all clay soils. Its value is therefore beyond calculation to the gardener.

134 After soils are collected for use, they should not be washed by excessive rains, and for that reason they should be in narrow upright ridges, so as to throw the rain off; and after they have been turned a time or two, it may be necessary to protect them by a slight covering of weatherboarding.

135 Reference has been already made to lime as a fertiliser that it is desirable to commingle with soil that is being brought into cultivation, especially when it is trenched for the first time, but its importance as a manure is so great that it is necessary to refer to it again. It is found chiefly in the form of limestone and chalk; it enters into the composition of all marls in the form of calcic carbonate in various proportions, ranging from 5 to even 90 per cent; and it is a large constituent of all shells and shell sand and of corals.

136 Limestone and chalk, from which the chief part of the lime used in agricultural and gardening purposes is derived, consist of calcic carbonate and carbon dioxide in the proportion of 14 parts of the former to 11 parts of the latter. When subjected to the action of fire in a kiln, the carbon dioxide is liberated and driven off in the form of carbonic acid gas, a shimmering vapour that may be seen rising from the mouth of any kiln that is alight, and leaves the lime behind it in a pure or nearly pure state. In this condition it is known as *caustic* or *quick lime*. When water is poured on it, it heats almost immediately, pours forth steam, and ultimately falls to pieces, assuming the form of a white powder, which is known as *slaked lime*, the operation of reducing the lime to powder by the agency of water being termed *slaking*. By chemists slaked lime is called *hydrate of calcium*. The powder thus obtained is composed very nearly of 3 parts of lime to 1 part of water. If quicklime is exposed to the action of the air, it first takes in water from the atmosphere, and then falls to powder in the same way as it does when water is poured directly upon it, though not so quickly. Lastly, the slaked lime, whether converted into powder rapidly by water or slowly by the air, gives off the water that it has retained, absorbs carbonic acid from the air, and ultimately becomes calcic carbonate, reverting as it were to the state in which it existed before it was burnt in the kiln; the advantage arising from burning being chiefly that it is brought into a state and condition suitable for admixture with the soil.

The advantages of burning lime are thus set forth in the *Elements of Agricultural Chemistry and Geology*, by Johnston and Cameron:

'If the lime return to the same chemical state of carbonate in which it existed in the state of chalk or limestone, what is the benefit of burning it? The benefits are partly mechanical and partly chemical.

a We have seen that on slaking the burnt lime falls to an exceedingly fine bulky powder. When it afterwards becomes converted into carbonate, it still retains this exceedingly minute state of division; and thus, whether as caustic hydrate or as a mild carbonate, can be spread over a large surface, and be intimately mixed with the soil. No available mechanical means could be economically employed to reduce our limestones, or even our softer chalks, to a powder of equal fineness.

b By burning, the lime is brought into a caustic state, which it retains, as we have seen, for a longer or shorter period, till it again absorbs carbonic acid from the air or from the soil. In this caustic state, its action upon the soil and upon organic matter is more energetic than in the state of mild lime; and thus it is fitted to produce effects which mere powdered limestone or chalk could not bring about at all, or to produce them more effectually and in a shorter period of time.

c Limestones often contain sulphur in combination with iron (iron pyrites). The coal or peat with which it is burnt also contains sulphur. During the burning, a portion of this sulphur (oxidised) unites with the lime to form gypsum, by this means adding to the proportion of this substance which naturally exists in the limestone.

d Earthy and silicious matters are sometimes present in considerable quantities in our limestone rocks. When burnt in the kiln, the silica of this earthy matter unites with lime to form *calcic silicate*. This silicate being diffused through the burnt and slaked lime, and afterwards spread in a minute state of division over the soil, is in a condition in which it may yield silica to the growing plant, supposing silica to be essential.

'Thus the benefits of burning are, as we have seen, partly mechanical and partly chemical. They are mechanical, inasmuch as by slaking the burnt lime can be reduced to a much finer and more bulky powder than the limestone could be by any mechanical means; and they are chemical, inasmuch as by burning the lime is brought into a more active and caustic state, and is, at the same time, mixed with variable proportions of sulphate and silicate of lime, which may render it more useful to the growing crops.'

137 It is not possible to lay down any precise rule for the application of lime as a manure, and the quantity to be used must depend chiefly on the soil itself and its special character. When ground is first taken into cultivation it may be applied in considerable quantities, but on land that has been already utilised for the production of crops it must not be used so freely. On clay lands a plentiful admixture is beneficial, and on soils on which much vegetable matter is dug in it is equally serviceable. On light lands it must be used but moderately, and even then it is better to mix it with soil, turf in course of disintegration, etc., so as to form a compost. The effect of lime is not immediately apparent, but shows itself the second or even third year after application. This, of course, does not apply to its use for the destruction of worms, slugs, grubs, etc., which promptly feel and acknowledge the application of caustic lime and lime just slaked. Stiff and heavy lands are lightened and mellowed by its presence, and the crops that are yielded by land judiciously limed are heavier, better, and earlier than those which it produced before liming.

138 It is unnecessary to say much here upon sewage, which is better suited for manuring farm lands than for dressing garden ground. House slops are valuable on account of the urine and alkaline salts that they contain, and are therefore useful for gardens. Night soil is undesirable for small gardens, although it is useful in market gardening on a large scale. The conservation and application of human excreta to garden ground is best effected by means of the earth closet, of which that which is constructed on Moule's patent appears to be the best. The manure obtained from this source is possessed of considerable fertilising properties, which are augmented by mixing a little pulverised charcoal with the earth. Indeed, it has been said that manure from earth closets would be all the more valuable if the earth were dispensed with altogether and charcoal used in its stead.

139 Guano, which is nothing more than the droppings of sea-birds, dried and pulverised by the heat of the sun, is an important manure, which is collected in small islands on the coast of Peru and some other parts of the world, and imported in large quantities into the United Kingdom. Its weight per bushel is about 70lb.; if heavier than this, the additional weight per bushel would tend to show that it has been subjected to adulteration. By analysis it has been found that very nearly one-half consists of organic matter, of which about a fifth part is ammonia; about a fourth part of the entire mass is calcic phosphate, and of the remaining fourth, about two-fifths are alkaline salts, a considerable part of which is phosphoric acid. There is no doubt that guano affords a valuable manure, useful for all purposes in the garden. It is very similar in its constituents, and the relative quantities of each that it contains, to farmyard manure, but being more highly concentrated and therefore less in bulk, and differing from the latter in being dry instead of wet, it is more handy for use in small gardens, and therefore demands the attention of all whose gardening is restricted to space and operations that are alike limited in character.

140 We must now glance briefly at some of the more notable manures derived from animal and vegetable sources, with other saline and earthy manures that have not yet received notice, and bring this chapter to a close with a few remarks on some of the best known artificial manures that are now in use, and the preparation and administration of manures in a soluble condition, commonly known as liquid manures.

141 *Animal manures* that is to say, manures derived from certain parts and portions of larger animals, such as the flesh, blood, hides, horns, hoofs, wool, and bones of horses, oxen, sheep, etc., and from small kinds of fish, such as herrings, pilchards, sprats, etc., when caught in great quantities – are better suited for the farm than for the garden. All animal manures should suffer decomposition before they are applied to the soil, and be mixed with other ingredients, such as clay, stiff soil, and quicklime, in order to form a compost. They are then valuable on account of the ammonia, bone phosphate, and potash that they contain. The hides, hoofs, horns, etc., or rather refuse leather and horn from the workshops of the shoemaker, the saddler, and the comb-maker, require digestion by means of sulphuric acid in order to render them soluble and fit for assimilation as plant food. The blood is most speedily available as a manure. It may be formed into a compost with an equal quantity of wood ashes and pulverised or crushed charcoal, but the compost thus made is not fit for incorporation with the soil under a year. Fish are sometimes thrown on the ground and ploughed in, and sometimes mixed with clay or peat earth to form a compost. In neither way, however, are they suitable for garden ground.

It has been supposed that it is beneficial to trees, especially fruit trees, to bury a dead animal close to their roots. A vine, it is well known, is what is commonly called a gross feeder – that is to say, it requires an abundance of plant food of a character suited to it. The idea, however, has got abroad, and taken pretty deep root among gardeners of a certain class and capacity, that a vine is a gross feeder or omnivorous plant, in much the same way that a pig or a duck, which will swallow almost any kind of garbage, is said to be a gross feeder, and therefore it has been recommended to bury dead dogs, cats, blood, etc., at the foot of a vine, or under a young tree when planting it. It will take a considerable time before the carcases and blood are sufficiently decomposed to be useful as plant food, and until they have arrived at this state they are useless. No manure is serviceable to plants until it is fit for absorption and assimilation by them in the form of plant food.

142 The portions of the animal that are most useful as manure and can be most speedily converted into a manure suitable for plant food are the bones, which consist of about one-third organic matter and two-thirds inorganic matter, the chief constituents of the latter being – Carbonic dioxide, 6 parts; phosphoric acid, 40 parts; and lime, 54 parts. It is, however, next to useless to put bones as they are into the soil, because many years will elapse before they are sufficiently decomposed to serve as plant food. If they could be reduced to powder without difficulty, the bone powder would speedily furnish an excellent manure, but it is no easy matter to crush bones, and very powerful machinery is necessary to do it with proper effect. Bones may be more easily brought to a condition suitable for manure by fermenting them, which is done by mixing two parts of bones with one part of clay, the parts being taken according to weight, and then soaking the compound in urine, covering the mass with a three-inch layer of clay to prevent the escape of the ammonia.

In the *Elements of Agricultural Chemistry and Geology*, the following method of preparing bones for bone manure is given: 'Provide a wooden trough, 12 feet long, 4 feet wide, and 1½ feet deep. Protect its interior from the action of the acid by a coat of pitch. Spread over the bottom of this vessel the bones, etc., to be vitriolised, and add about one-third of their weight of water; next pour uniformly over them half their weight of brown acid, or one-third of their weight of white acid; mix quickly with a wooden spade, and let the mixture stand for an hour or so. The manure may then be removed to a covered shed and kept until required, which should not be for a month or two at least. As the cost of the carriage of oil of vitriol from one place to another is sometimes considerable, it may, under certain circumstances, be found more economical to use the white acid, though it is the dearest. One pound of white sulphuric acid is equal to 1¼ lb. of brown acid and 1¾ lb. of chamber acid.'

143 Bones prepared by mixing them with sulphuric acid, in order to procure their disintegration, form a manure which is well and widely known as *superphosphate of lime*. There is no necessity here to enter into a description of the chemical changes which are brought about by the action of the acid on the bones. It is enough to say that by the process the bone phosphate, previously insoluble, has been converted into a phosphate which is soluble and therefore useful as a manure. The 'superphosphate' now in use is chiefly made of mineral phosphates, such as the coprolites of the Eastern Counties, supposed to be fossilised bones, or excreta of ancient and extinct animals, and products from various parts of the world rich in calcic phosphates, treated with sulphuric acid. Bone-ash and bone-black from sugar refineries are also used. A useful manure may be obtained by subjecting bones to the action of fire until calcination takes place, but the smell given forth by the burning bones is horrible, as any one may find out for himself if he put a bone on the kitchen fire and await the result. Superphosphate is beneficial to root crops and leguminous crops.

The admixture of a small portion of bone dust, or superphosphate, in the soil in which various plants have been grown, has proved very beneficial, and caused them to produce stronger and more healthy growth. This effect is noticed in plants of a slender, delicate habit, as *Tropaolum tricolorum*, and a great variety of others. By thus enriching the soil, it was found that plants throve in smaller pots than usual, and did not apparently suffer in the same degree for want of shifting to larger pots. Bone dust, as a fertilising agent, in due proportions, appears to be applicable to a greater variety of plants than almost any other yet noticed, having one property attached to it that is not generally common to others, namely, acting as a mechanical agent in adding a greater porosity to the soil by its slower decomposition. Bone dust, mixed with dry sifted loam or soil, and sown thickly broadcast (with after rollings), forms an excellent ingredient in restoring and quickening the verdure of decaying grass plots in gardens and pleasure grounds, etc.

144 Vegetable manures, unlike animal manures, can be applied immediately to the soil without having undergone decomposition, and this is why weeds that have not gone to seed, growing crops of various kinds, grass, clippings of various kinds of plants, potato haulms, cabbage leaves and stumps, are beneficial as manures when buried in the ground direct, without being advanced in the stage of decomposition by undergoing a chemical change in the stomachs of animals on its way to the manure heap in the farmyard. Green refuse of any kind will enrich the soil when ploughed or dug into it, but when there is much woody fibre with it, which would take some time to decompose, such portions should be burnt.

Speaking of growing crops as green manures, Johnston and Cameron say, in the *Elements of Agricultural Chemistry and Geology*: 'When grass is mown in the field and laid in heaps, it speedily heats, ferments, and rots. The same is true of all other vegetable substances – they all rot more readily in the green state. The reason of this is that the sap or juice of the green plant begins very soon to ferment in the interior of the stem and leaves, and speedily communicates the same condition to the moist fibre of the plant itself. The same rapid decay of green vegetable matter takes place when it is buried in the soil. Hence the cleanings and scourings of the ditches and hedge-sides form a compost of mixed earth and fresh vegetable matter, which soon becomes capable of enriching the ground. When a green crop is ploughed into a field, the whole of its surface is converted into such a compost – the vegetable matter in a short time decays into a light black mould, and enriches, in a remarkable degree, the soil. Indeed, a green crop ploughed in is believed, by some practical men, to enrich the soil as much as the droppings of cattle from a quantity of green food three times as great.'

145 The advantages of decayed leaves, when mixed with the soil, have already been mentioned, and every gardener, though he turn in the leaves of cabbages, potatoes, etc., will preserve the leaves of trees to ferment and furnish leaf-mould. Malt dust affords an excellent manure for potatoes, and by some it is used for turnips. Peat and bark from tanyards are good as manures, either worked up with other ingredients, such as lime, bone dust, ammoniacal liquor from gas works, and a little salt, or reduced to ashes by burning. Sawdust may be utilised in the same way, and it may be used to disintegrate and lighten stiff soil, but as a manure by itself it is not worth much. Seaweed in a green state, or when rotted and formed into a compost, affords an excellent manure for potatoes and asparagus, which is always better for being dressed with salt or with manure that contains saline matter; but the smell of rotting seaweed is as disagreeable as that of burnt bones, and no decomposing heap of this material should be allowed to be near any house.

146 Charred vegetable matter of all kinds, as it has been already said, constitutes a most valuable manure. The ashes obtained from peat that has been brought into such a state by the action of fire so that it may be easily crumbled into a rough, coarse powder, affords a good dressing even when used alone, but it is still more serviceable when formed into a compost with other ingredients as described above. Charcoal, which is wood so highly charred that it may be broken into small pieces, or even reduced to powder, is highly beneficial as a surface dressing, especially for flowers, whose colours it deepens, while it imparts a richer and darker green to the foliage. Charcoal is an antiseptic – that is to say, it arrests the progress of decay, and absorbs and neutralises offensive emanations from the soil and baneful gases in the air. It also prevents the rising of harmful vapours from decaying animal and vegetable matter. For these reasons it forms a valuable addition to the compost heap. Soot is also a powerful and beneficial manure, both for root-crops and when used as a top dressing for grass and flowers, to which, especially when in pots, it is best applied in the form of liquid manure. Soot is considerably impregnated with ammonia, and gypsum and nitric acid are also present in the inorganic matter of which it is largely composed.

147 There is no better way of getting rid of branches cut from trees, the stalks of plants, and green vegetable matter and weeds in a half dry state, than by burning. In order to make charcoal and wood ashes to be preserved for potting and other purposes instead of being worked at once into the soil, lumps of wood (for charcoal) and refuse branches, sticks, etc. (for wood ashes), should be packed close in the form of a mound or cone, and thus set on fire, kept closely covered with good tough grass clods about three inches thick. The heap should be watched by day during combustion, and even by night, if possible, an additional clod being added here and there, when and where necessary, to prevent the escape of flame. When the charcoal is made, the heap should be opened and cooled with water.

148 Mention may be made of a few more substances that are useful as manures, such as gas liquor, and lime from gasworks, nitrate of soda, gypsum, and common salt, which are derived from mineral sources, and therefore cannot be classified with manures derived from animal and vegetable sources. Gas liquor, which results from the means taken to purify coal gas before it is utilised for lighting, and which is impregnated with ammonia, sulphuretted hydrogen, and various acids liberated from the coal when subjected to the action of fire in retorts, is valuable on account of the ammonia it contains. It should be mixed with water, in the proportion of 1 part of gas liquor to 4 or 5 or even 6 parts of water, for application to lawns and grass plots. For garden ground it is more beneficial when mixed with charred peat or charcoal, or poured on the compost heap. Lime from gasworks, which contains a large percentage of gypsum, requires exposure to the air for some time before it is used, as, when first brought from the works, its chemical composition is of a character that would render it injurious to vegetable growths.

149 Nitrate of soda contains about 15 per cent of nitrogen, and on this account its use as a manure is advantageous to plant life. It is highly beneficial to root crops and grass, and it may be used with good effect for leguminous plants, onions, etc. Gypsum, an abundant source of lime and sulphuric acid, is also beneficial as a manure for peas, beans, grass, etc. It forms the chief constituent of all mineral or natural superphosphates. Salt is destructive to insect life, and is absolutely necessary as a manure for asparagus, and is beneficial to seakale and root crops generally. Its use tends to destroy weeds and moss on grass, and to increase the fineness of the grass itself. In the compost heap it is useful as an agent which acts chemically on calcic phosphates and nitrogen contained in an insoluble form in various manures, rendering them soluble, and therefore reducing them to a condition in which they are capable of assimilation as plant food.

The effect of common washing soda on young onions is surprising. If some of this be reduced to powder, and sprinkled over a bed of onions, just before rain, if possible, the effect will be shown in a very few days by the deepened colour of the leaf and the strong growth of the root, the leaf assuming a rich bluish-green tint. It is better to apply the soda as a dressing on the surface of the soil just before rain, because it must be washed into the soil in order to prove beneficial to the plants. If given in the form of liquid manure it is not so good. Onions, indeed, should never be watered, for if watering by artificial means is commenced and subsequently withheld, the leaves have a tendency to turn yellow at the tip.

150 Of late years many artificial manures have been introduced which are specially useful to window gardeners and to gardeners in a small way, because they are supplied in small quantities and are cleanly to use, a great desideratum to ladies and others who could not or would not deal with the grosser and more offensive kinds of manure. Of these it will be sufficient to name Amies' Horticultural Manure, manufactured by Amies' Chemical Manure Company, Limited, 75 Mark Lane, London; Clay's Fertiliser, manufactured by Messrs Clay and Levesley, Temple Mill Lane, Stratford, London; Beeson's Rose, Vine and Plant Manure, manufactured by Mr W. H. Beeson, Carbrook Bone Mills, Sheffield; and Booty's New Insect Manure, manufactured by Messrs Arthur Booty & Co., Rose Villa Nursery, High Harrogate. These manures may be regarded as forming a representative group of stimulants to plant growth and renewers of exhausted soils especially suitable for use in gardens and greenhouses. They are supplied by the manufacturers, but can be obtained of all nurserymen, seedsmen, and florists, and those who deal in horticultural requisites, in large or small quantities as follows:

Amies' Horticultural Manure – In bags, 2lb., 1s.; 7lb., 2s. 3d.; 14lb., 4s.; 28lb., 7s.; 56lb., 11s. 6d.; 112lb., 19s.

Clay's Fertiliser – In packets at 6s. and 1s.; in bags, 7lb., 2s. 6d.; 14lb., 4s. 6d.; 28lb., 7s. 6d.; 56lb., 12s. 6d.; 112lb., 20s.

Beeson's Rose, Vine, and Plant Manure – In packages at 1s.; in bags, 112lb., at 12s.
Booty's New Insect Manure – In sample tins, 1lb., 1s.; 7lb., 4s.; 14lb., 6s.; in bags, 28lb., 7s. 6d.; 56lb., 12s. 6d.; 112lb., 20s.: tins and bags free.

There can be no reasonable doubt that the chemical manures named above may be taken as general types of manures of this character, and it will be useful, as far as may be possible, to describe the constituents of each and the manner in which it should be applied. Each composition, as a matter of course, differs from the others in the nature, perhaps, and certainly in the proportions, of its various constituents, but all are compounded with the view to promote vegetable growth. Care should be taken not to use more than is recommended in the directions issued by the manufacturers, as if used in excess any and all of them are calculated to afford too great a stimulus to plant growth, and thus to injure the plants to which they are applied rather than to benefit them.

Amies' Horticultural Manure Taken roughly and at a general average, 100 parts of this manure may be stated to be composed of the following constituents: Moisture, 4; Organic Matter, Carbon and Salts of Ammonia (containing Nitrogen), 24; Phosphoric Acid, 20; Lime, 27; Oxide of Iron, 6; Sulphuric Acid, 8; Alkaline Salts and Magnesia (containing Potash), 5; Carbonic Acid, 2; Insoluble Siliceous Matter, 4. Dr Voelcker, speaking of this manure, says: 'In addition to a high percentage of phosphate of lime (bone phosphate), it contains, in well-balanced proportions, salts of ammonia, yielding about 4 per cent of ammonia, potash salts, and other useful fertilising ingredients, and thus differs materially in its constitution from purely ammoniacal manures, which, containing exclusively or in excessive proportions, ammonia, are apt to cause over-luxuriance of the leafy parts of plants at the expense of their vigorous growth and proper maturity of horticultural produce.'

Clear and ample directions for the use of the manure are issued by the Company, and those who wish to make trial of it must be guarded by these. Different fruits and plants require it in different quantities, but for general garden culture from 3oz. to 6oz. is considered sufficient for every square yard of ground, and the reader must remember that by this is meant the square yard that contains 9 square feet, and not the square rod, pole, or land yard, which contains 272¼ square feet. In all cases the manure should be thoroughly incorporated with the soil. The best results are obtained by applying, where practicable, half the quantity that it is intended to use before sowing or planting out, and the remainder at the time of sowing or planting. When intended as a stimulant it should be applied early and liberally as a top dressing, and well forked in. Equal distribution over and with the soil is better effected by mixing the manure with fine dry mould or ashes. A good liquid manure, to be used preferably when the flower-buds appear, is made by mixing 8oz. with 12 gallons of water. When prepared at this strength, it may be used frequently. A stronger solution, that may be used for soft-wooded plants, is prepared by mixing from 1oz. to 3oz. with 1 gallon of water. In using the manure thus it is better to apply a weak solution at first and then gradually to increase its strength. It is equally suitable for flowers, fruits, and vegetables, and acts as an insecticide. Special manures are prepared by the Company for dressing potatoes, vine borders, etc.

Clay's Fertiliser This manure is a plant food suitable for window, conservatory, and garden culture in a highly concentrated form. It contains all the elements which enter into the composition of plants in such proportions as are necessary for luxuriant vegetation. Its important and active constituents are in a perfectly soluble condition, and are so fixed that they cannot escape by atmospheric influences. It is serviceable either by incorporation with the soil, or as a top dressing, but not for the preparation of liquid manure. In the preparation of a compost for potting, mix 1 part of the manure with 80 or 100 parts of mould; for top dressing a plant in a pot, use a small teaspoonful for a 5-inch pot, and for plants in larger or smaller pots in proportion. For ordinary gardening operations use from 1½oz. to 2oz. to the square yard, and from ½lb. to 1lb. for vine-borders, forked in and afterwards well watered.

Of this manure, as of others of the same kind, it is desirable to use sparingly, and to use it a second time if it appear that more is required than was given at first.

Beeson's Rose, Vine, and Plant Manure This manure is a compound of fresh raw bones and fresh blood, with the addition only of such ingredients as are necessary to preserve the constituents that render it valuable as a manure from evaporation through exposure or climatic changes. This being the case, it is clear that it contains all the elements that constitute the fertilising properties of blood and bones, which, as it has been already shown, cannot easily be rendered fit by operations on a small scale for assimilation by plants as plant food. Although it is a most valuable manure for all general horticultural purposes, it is specially useful for dressing roses and vines, causing the latter, when manured by repeated top dressings during the growing season, to yield large and handsome bunches of grapes, the berries of which show marked improvement in size and colour, and enabling the former to make strong and healthy growth in spite of the cold winds that so often prevail from the beginning of March to the end of May, and destroy the early shoots: it also prevents injury to roses from blight and mildew and the ravages of the aphis or green fly. The manure, which shows its influence for some time after it has been put on the soil, may be well incorporated with the soil by digging, or used as a top dressing, mingled with it by hoeing or 'pointing' the ground with a fork. For general use, about 1lb. to each square yard of ground is necessary; for roses in pots, 3oz. as a top dressing, loosening the soil at the surface, and then watering with a fine rose; for chrysanthemums, ½lb. to 1 peck of potting compost, and a good top dressing when the buds are swelling; for roses in beds and borders, apply, just before a shower, a small handful round each plant, about four times during the season of growth, raking the manure well in. It is highly beneficial for fruit trees. For cabbages, etc., of every description, the manure should be well dug in just before planting, but for peas and all kinds of seeds the drills should be made a little deeper than usual, a little of the manure sprinkled along the bottom of the drill and covered over with a small quantity of soil, on top of which the seed must be sown in the usual way. It is useful to note that the manufacturer supplies pure crushed, unboiled bones, in pieces 1in., ½ in., or ¼ in. square, as desired, and bone meal for vine borders, potting, etc. For vines, crushed bones are a desideratum, if not an absolute necessity.

Booty's New Insect Manure The *raison d'être* of this manure, gathered from the statement of the manufacturer, is somewhat curious. A friend of the maker, travelling in China and Japan, was struck with the luxuriant growth of the plants and the brilliant colouring of the flowers that he saw in many parts. He found, on observation of the mode of culture adopted, that this was mostly due to the use, as a manure, of dead silkworms and their deposits, obtained during the time that the insects are feeding, from the period of emergence from the egg to the formation of the cocoon. Arrangements were at once made for the collection and importation of large quantities, from which the manure is prepared for sending out in proper condition for plant growers to use. Mr James Baynes, jun, FCS, of the Chemical and Assay Laboratory, Hull, gives the following as his opinion of the manure. He says: 'I have analysed the New Insect Manure, manufactured by Messrs A. Booty and Co., and can, with confidence, testify to its peculiar adaptibility as a manure for fruit, plants, and flowers. It is rich in phosphates, ammonia, and alkaline salts, and these are judiciously blended, and are in such a condition as to impart a gentle but continuous supply of phosphoric acid and ammonia to the soil. In addition to its high fertilising properties, the ingredients used in its manufacture are thoroughly incorporated, and, what is very essential, the mechanical texture is perfect, which makes it not only easy of application, but also most efficacious in its results.'

151 *With's Improved Carbon Universal* This is another excellent chemical manure for use in the flower garden, greenhouse, and vegetable garden, to which attention must be especially directed. It is the invention of Mr G. H. With, FRAS, FCS, Chemist to the Hereford Society for Aiding the Industrious, and is manufactured and sold by the Society at their Experimental Garden, Bath Street, Hereford. It is supplied in sacks of 28lb. at 2s., 56lb. at 3s. 6d. and 112lb. at 7s. It is, therefore, a cheap manure. Directions are issued for its use, and those who wish to mix it for themselves the Society will supply with the compound of charcoal and chemicals that is required for its preparation. Among other fertilising compositions that are due to the research of Mr With, who for some years has devoted his entire time and attention to the study of agricultural chemistry and matters connected with plant life and growth, are his Liquid Plant Food Compound, for use in the greenhouse and garden, and his Food for Fruit Trees. The former is supplied in 2lb, 5lb., and 10lb. bags, sufficient to make 32, 80, and 160 gallons respectively, at 1s., 2s., and 3s. 6d.; and the latter in sacks of 14lb. at 2s. 6d., 28lb. at 4s., 56lb. at 7s. 6d., and 112lb. at 14s.

It is unnecessary to dwell at length on the mode of application of With's Improved Carbon Universal Manure, because this can be learnt from the pamphlets issued by the Hereford Society. It is enough to say that it is a chemical compound of remarkable efficacy for horticultural purposes, and bears the name of Universal Manure because it is universally applicable to the cultivation of vegetables, fruit trees, and flowers, whether out of doors or under glass. 'No other manure whatever, it is alleged, 'is needed where the Carbon Universal Manure is used. It is, at least, as cheap as stable manure, while it is superior in its fertilising power, and much more speedy and certain in its action.' I am enabled, by the courtesy of Mr With and the kindness of the Committee of the Hereford Society, to give here the inventor's theory of the Universal Manure. He says: '*A perfect manure* should contain, in sufficient quantity, in suitable proportions, and in the best form, all the substances which are essential to healthy, vigorous, and *rapid* plant growth. Those substances should be present in such a form that, when used in proper quantity and in a proper manner, they shall not injure the delicate absorbing skin and almost microscopic hairs by means of which the plant takes its food from the soil. It is evident that any injury to these parts of the plant must check its growth by lessening its power to take in food. Part of the plant food should exist in the manure in the special form of a *tonic*, or strengthener of the system of the plant – that is, it should be to the plant what iron is to the human being. With the tonic there should also be a due proportion of *stimulant*. Some of the stimulant should be in a condition immediately available by the plants, and the rest so locked up as to be furnished by degrees to carry on the growth. In addition to the tonic and the stimulant there must, of course, be *a sufficient supply of substantial food*. In the Universal Manure these somewhat difficult conditions are perfectly satisfied. A series of careful trials by a large number of skilled men – to say nothing of my own experiments during a period of five years – has shown that it contains abundantly, in due proportion and in an appropriate form, all the substances best fitted for the rapid production of vigorous plant life. It has also been proved that it may be applied, in suitable quantity, very close to the roots of the plant – even to those of the most sensitive hothouse plants – without checking the growth. Some of the food is ready for the immediate nourishment of the plant; the remainder will become so, under the influence of the chemical agencies at work in the soil, as the plant advances in growth. There are also the tonic and the stimulant, also partly available immediately, partly by slow degrees. The remarkable vigour, healthfulness, and quickness of growth of plants fed by this manure are the best possible testimony to the suitableness of the condition in which the manurial substances exist in it.'

In a communication with reference to the qualities of the Improved Universal Carbon Manure, and the advantages to be derived from its use, Mr With thus enumerates some of the benefits attending the application of scientifically-compounded and honestly-made artificial manures. '(1) They contain exactly the food required by the plant. (2) They do not introduce into the soil the seeds of weeds or the eggs of insects. (3) They do not breed fungoid growths. (4) They can be applied as a top dressing just when and where they are needed. (5) They are cleanly, inoffensive, absolutely certain in their action, and their use saves labour to a very great extent. (6) Their use allows a constant succession of intercropping in the vegetable garden. (7) They do not exhaust the land. (8) The ground being once dug, the weakest person can apply an artificial manure, and thus find in the cultivation of the vegetable and flower garden an easy and pleasant occupation. The objections to the use of stable manure in gardening operations are too well known to need recapitulation.'

152 *Jensen's Norwegian Fish Potash Manure* Another powerful and highly concentrated manure, said to be a perfect and invaluable fertiliser for garden and greenhouse use, is the Norwegian Fish Potash Manure, manufactured at the Loffoten Islands, Norway, and sold by the manufacturers, Messrs J. Jensen and Co., at their London offices, 10 St Helen's Place, London. The value of fish as an animal manure is fully recognised by farmers, but the odour emanating from the 'harvests of the deep' when undergoing decomposition is so offensive as to render the use of fish manure in a natural form highly objectionable. It is well known that in the cod and herring fisheries carried on in Norwegian waters there is considerable waste, and it occurred to Messrs Jensen and Co. that the refuse, which was formerly considered of no value whatever, might be treated and combined with mineral ingredients so as to form a valuable manure – as valuable, indeed, and possessed of fertilising qualities as great as those of Peruvian guano. The result of their researches is to be seen in their Fish Potash Manure or Fish Guano, which is fish, flesh, and bone, dried and reduced to powder, and then combined with pure double salts of potash and magnesia. Thus the three ingredients essential for complete fertilisation – namely, ammonia, phosphates, and potash – are obtained in a perfect form. When applied to plants, by reason of its being a highly concentrated manure, a very little of it produces a speedy and marked effect, and being free from any acid injurious to plant life, it can, with discretion, be applied to the most delicate plants, as well as to those of the strongest habit, inducing good root growth, fine foliage, and a satisfactory development of flowers and fruit. The average manurial constituents in 100 parts are as follows:

	Ammonia	*Phosphates*	*Potash*	*Magnesia*	*Organic Matter, etc.*	*Total*
Cod Fish and Potash	7	20	16	11	46	= 100
Herring and Potash	7	8	16	11	58	= 100

or, in other words, a ton of cod fish and potash is composed approximately of 10 cwt of dried fish flesh (organic matter), 4 cwt. of dried fish bone (phosphates), 3 cwt. of sulphate of potash, 2 cwt. of sulphate of magnesia, and 1 cwt. of moisture and ingredients possessing no value as manure. The prices of the Fish Potash Manure are: 28 lb., 6s. 6d.; 56 lb., 10s. 6d.; 1 1/4 cwt., 20s.; 2 cwt., 30s.; 5 cwt., 60s. – bags free; or in larger quantities, £9 per ton for the herring manure, and

£10 for the cod manure – bags included, on rail in the docks. The higher charge for the cod manure is owing to its containing a greater percentage of phosphates. The manure is in the form of a brown and white granulated powder, and although its odour bears unmistakable testimony to the source from which it is derived, it is far from being unpleasant; indeed, the most fastidious person could not object to its use out of doors or indoors.

153 With regard to the use of the Norwegian Fish Potash Manure, the manufacturers guarantee that it will fertilise the most exhausted soils, give renewed vitality to pot-bound plants, and impart exceptional health and vigour to all plant life. For *grass*, about 2 oz. per square yard should be strewn over it in showery weather. The impetus given by it to fine lawn grasses produces close growth, and tends to keep down weeds and destroy moss. For *potting and planting*, it should be incorporated with the soil; the ingredients work in with it, and are absorbed in it speedily, so that the young roots are furnished with the plant food that they can readily take in, and assimilate as soon as they are formed. When this manure is used, plants may be placed in smaller pots than those which are generally used for them. *Bulbs*, as hyacinths, etc., need only a moderate dusting on the surface. For *shrubs, hard-wooded plants, and greenhouse plants*, and for roses, camellias, azaleas, fuchsias, rhododendrons, pelargoniums, primulas, cinerarias, gloxinias, chrysanthemums, etc., from 3 to 5 parts in 100 should be mixed with the soil for plants in pots, or from ½ oz. to 8 oz. per square yard, forked into the soil, for plants in borders. *Plants in large pots*, especially those that are pot-bound, may have ½ oz., mixed with a little fresh surface soil, applied to them as a top dressing. *Ferns, fruit trees, and vegetables of all kinds, bush fruit, strawberries, and raspberries*, soon show the effect produced on them by this manure by the dark rich colour of their foliage and the size and flavour of well-developed fruit. When used in the kitchen garden and fruit borders, it must be spread on the surface and forked in. A shower after application, or a gentle watering both of plants in borders when the weather is hot and dry and of plants in pots within doors, will soon carry the fertilising constituents of the manure to the roots.

The testimony given with regard to the Fish Potash Manure by those who have used it shows that it is most valuable dressing, suitable for any crop and lasting in its effect, requiring moisture to produce its best effect on the soil. It should be spread over the soil and dug in, rather than sown with seed, etc., in drills. Mr Roe, of The Pinetum, Bache Hall, Chester, writing to Messrs Jensen and Co., in 1884, said that its effect on pelargoniums was marvellous, the trusses of bloom produced by them being six inches across and bright in colour, while the foliage was good. All greenhouse plants did well with it, and roses to which it was applied grew grandly. Cauliflowers were obtained twelve inches across the head, and ash-leaf potatoes yielded about twenty tubers to each root. The vines were much improved by its use, and fruit trees, such as pears, apples, and peaches, that were dressed with it, and raspberries and strawberries, produced fruit greater in point of size and better in flavour than in former years. Hollies treated with it made new wood twelve inches in length in a few weeks, with foliage of a rich dark colour. Its effect on grass land was remarkable. A breadth of grass that had not been dressed for twenty years was strewn with it in showery weather, and in three weeks' time there was a thick bottom grass ten inches high. After the month of June it was cut three times, and of the yield obtained at each cutting the last was the best.

154 *Bracher's Moss Litter* Until the last few years nothing but straw was used as bedding for cattle, and farmyard manure consisted entirely of this material, incorporated with the droppings and saturated with the urine of animals whose stalls had been strewn with it. Of course, where fern and bracken could be obtained, the leaves and stalks could be utilised as bedding, but, owing to the size, hardness, and toughness of the stalks and midribs of the leaves, these parts were long in decaying, and caused the manure to be coarse and stringy, if such a term be admissible. Now, however, a more suitable substitute for straw has been found in Moss Litter, a product of peat, introduced by Messrs P. H. Bracher and Co., 77 High Street, Wincanton, who are the inventors and patentees of a machine known as Bracher's Peat Breaker, by which dried peat from moorlands and peat bogs is disintegrated and rendered fit for litter. The peat is first cut and stacked, in order to dry, and is then broken up by the machine. Being akin to charcoal in its nature, peat acts as a purifier and deodoriser, and therefore possesses a considerable advantage over straw in neutralising any smell that would otherwise be thrown off from the manure. In addition to its capacity for retaining smells, it is highly absorbant, being able to take in six times its own weight of moisture, and, being very short, it passes into the state of manure fit for incorporation with the soil far more quickly than long straw, and is therefore more easily handled. Its use, therefore, in stable and farmyards is to be advocated, and it may also be employed with advantage in the earth-closet system in schools, hospitals, factories, workhouses, railway stations, and dwelling-houses, rendering drains no longer absolutely necessary, as by its use all sewage matter can be readily converted into manure. The machines for breaking the peat are made in five sizes, from No. 1 to No. 5, the width of hopper being in each size respectively 6, 9, 12, 18, and 24 inches, and the prices £5, £8, £10, £15, and £20.

155 It will be clear, even to the most superficial observer, that all manures, or the fertilising constituents of manures, must be dissolved in water before they can be taken into and assimilated as food by the growing plant, and that accordingly liquid manure is the form in which these constituents can be carried most speedily to the roots of plants and in the form most suitable for their reception. A few recipes for the composition of liquid manures are therefore appended here, which may prove useful.

1. *Superphosphate of Lime.* – When diluted in the proportion of a quarter of a pound to a gallon of water for each plant, and thus applied to a given number, after the lapse of a few weeks it is found to impart additional vigour and a very rich dark-green hue, so much so as to distinguish the plants thus watered out of hundreds of similar-sized growth. As a fertiliser, the superphosphate is highly commended, since it seems almost universally applicable, and, unlike some other artificial manures, it may be applied in varying proportions without the least risk of injury. When a small portion of it is mixed with seeds when sown, in sufficient quantity to give them the appearance of being limed over, the seeds germinate quicker and stronger, more especially in the case of old seeds; and it is also found that the plants are less liable to 'damp off', or otherwise to be injured by insects.
2. *Sheep's Dung.* – Dilute thirty gallons of pure water with one peck of sheep's dung. After remaining half a day, strain it through a coarse bag or cloth, and apply the liquid

as required. Cow manure mixed with water in the same manner is nearly as beneficial.

3 *Guano Water.* – One pound of guano to twenty gallons of water will be sufficiently strong for a single watering to fruit trees in pots, each week, and more efficient than repeated waterings with weaker solutions.

4 *Guano and Soot.* – One pound of guano to thirty gallons of water, and about a spadeful of soot, tied up in a bag or coarse cloth to prevent it from swimming on the surface, will make liquid manure fit for any gross-feeding plant, as pelargoniums, calceolarias, achimenes, and clerodendron, etc., etc. Drain it off as clear as possible to prevent the materials forming a turbid state. For growth, use the liquid twice each week, but for developing the greatest size of flowers (after the colour appears), once each week should seldom be exceeded. For growing vegetable crops, it may be given twice each week, and for developing flowers, as soon as the calyx or flower-cup begins to burst, it should be applied but once a week. A cloudy atmosphere is the best condition for giving water, and early in the evening the best period in summer months. The liquid which soaks from common farm and poultry yards, with some soot added, is the cheapest; but where such is not procurable, the plan recommended above is the best.

5 *Soot.* – This substance, when used as a liquid, not only acts as a fertiliser, but expels worms, maggots, etc., from plants in pots, and drives them from the soil in the open ground. When applied in the form of liquid manure, the soot should be tied up in a coarse cloth, and allowed to soak in water placed in a small tub. When used, the water should be drawn off and applied in a clear state. To obtain it in this condition it is necessary that the soot should be tied up in a coarse cloth or canvas bag, and not simply mixed with the water. About one gallon of soot is sufficient to impregnate ten or fifteen gallons of water.

6 *Nitrate of Soda.* – This substance, dissolved in water in the proportion of a quarter of an ounce of the former to one gallon of the latter, is said to be a useful stimulant for bulbs.

156 This chapter may be fitly brought to a conclusion by reference to a material of vegetable origin which, if not precisely a manure, is one that is most useful for a variety of horticultural purposes, and especially in potting. This material is coconut fibre. When used in striking cuttings, it induces the formation of roots in plants perhaps quicker than anything else. Indeed, cuttings of all common bedding plants – verbenas, petunias, calceolarias – will strike and make good plants very freely in it. Spent hops may be used instead of coconut fibre, but they are not so good. In making compost with peat, leaf mould, or potting earth, in the proportion of 1 part of coconut fibre to 3 parts of the other material or materials used, it tends to lighten the mixture and render it better suited for the growth and running of the roots of the cuttings. When fairly growing, however, plants, whether struck in coconut fibre alone or in soil in whose composition it enters largely, should be removed and repotted, as the fibre is highly retentive of moisture, and this in itself has a tendency to cause the rootlets to decay. It is equally useful for mulching and for lightening stiff, heavy soil, which is apt to cling together in lumpy masses, especially when the ground is very moist, hardening to such a degree that it can be with difficulty broken up when a long period of dry weather ensues. As a material in which to plunge pots containing plants at any time of the year, it is most useful, for, owing to the quality it possesses of retaining moisture, it keeps the exterior of the pots in a moist condition in the hottest months of the year, preventing the roots of the plants that are in them from becoming injured by exposure to too great heat and dryness, and in the winter it tends to preserve an equable temperature round them, and to prevent the access of frost, if not too wet. Among its other good properties, it may be said that it does not harbour insects.

For potting purposes, and for the preparation of composts of various kinds, coconut fibre, peat of various kinds, loam, leaf mould, peat mould, and coarse silver sand are requisites that should be kept at hand by every gardener. They may be purchased of any local nurseryman, seedsman, or florist; but if there be any difficulty in procuring them they may be obtained without trouble or delay of such firms as Messrs Chubb, Round, and Co., West Ferry Road, Millwall, London; Messrs J. H. Vavasseur and Co., Coconut Fibre Mills, Cowley, near Uxbridge, Middlesex; Mr H. G. Smyth, 21 Goldsmith Street, Drury Lane, London; and Messrs W. Herbert and Co., 2 Hop Exchange Warehouses, Southwark Street, London. Prices rule about as follows:

1 *Coconut Fibre Refuse* – Sacks, 1s. 6s. each; 10 sacks, 13s.; 15 sacks, 18s.; 20 sacks, 23s.; 30 sacks, 36s.; truckload, free on rail, 40s. A superior quality is supplied by some dealers at 2s. 6d. per sack, which appears to be the granulated portion of the refuse divested of the long hair-like fibres that are generally found in it.

2 *Fibrous Brown Peat*, best quality – Sacks, 4s. 6d.; 5 sacks, 20s.

3 *Fibrous Black Peat*, best quality – Sacks, 3s. 6d.; 5 sacks, 15s.

4 *Selected Peat*, for orchids – Sacks, 5s.

5 *Silver Sand*, coarse, from 1s. 3d. to 1s. 9d. per bushel.

6 *Best Fibrous Yellow Loam, Leaf Mould, Peat Mould, and Prepared Compost for Potting*; all at 1s. per bushel, including sacks by some firms, while by others an extra charge of 4s. per sack is made. Any firm will send price lists of garden requisites, such as are mentioned above, on application. The carriage, except for very large quantities, is paid by the purchaser.

FIG. 24 *Gymnostachyum verschaffelti*

CHAPTER 5

The Choice and Selection of a Garden Site

157 In the preceding chapters, the History and Progress of Gardening have been briefly traced, and the relations of Geology and Chemistry to the art of Horticulture have been considered in the account that has been given of the formation of natural soils, the steps that must be taken for bringing them under cultivation by mechanical means, and their enrichment and fertilisation by manures of different kinds, whose use tends to the production of crops heavier and better in every way than those which the ground would yield if left in a natural state. Having thus cleared the way, before entering on the actual work that is necessary in a garden, whether large or small, we may now dwell for a time on the circumstances and qualities that should influence us in the selection of a piece of ground that is to be converted into a garden, and the preliminary work that must be done before it can be called a garden in very truth – the work, indeed, that is involved in laying out a garden. The time spent in the consideration of these matters will in no way be wasted: it is necessary in gardening, as in everything else, to begin at the beginning, and to proceed steadily onwards and upwards until the elements are mastered, and we are in a position to enter on the higher work of Horticulture, in full consciousness that everything has been done that is necessary to promote and deserve success, if not absolutely to secure it.

158 There are few localities in this country, from the extreme north to the Land's End, where a suitable site for a garden may not be found. Wherever a crop of wheat will grow and ripen, a good garden may be formed. While the difficulty of giving special directions as to site is much enhanced by the innumerable variations of scenery, climate, and other circumstances, there are still a few characteristics in which every desirable site must agree. These appear to be *security*, *healthfulness*, *beauty*, *congruity*, *utility*, and *variety*. These prominent characteristics of a desirable site being self-evident, the site which exhibits them cannot be otherwise than satisfactory, and its possession and cultivation must, or ought to, afford the highest possible amount of happiness.

159 *Security* is still the first consideration; for, even in our peaceful days, the first thing generally done after fixing on a site is to enclose it. In the olden time, the idea of safety was the chief thing considered, and the site for a house and garden was chosen much upon the same principle as the site of a fortress is now fixed on. In those days, every man's – at least, every great man's – house was his castle in a very different sense to what it is now. Homes were not then so much sacred retreats from vulgar intrusion as citadels of defence or the strongholds of petty tyrants. Hence, houses were erected on the summits of bleak rocks, or in deep and secluded valleys, where artificial barriers of rocks almost perpendicular, strong walls, and a broad and deep moat, rendered them almost impregnable. These moats, when they came to be filled up in more peaceful times, supplied to some of these strongholds gardens of a most picturesque character; for many of these feudal fortresses were built in situations of great natural beauty. Now, although the idea of safety from danger and security from intrusion still lends a charm to every happy home, it need no longer be the primary object of selection; for, thanks to advancing intelligence, efficient laws, and improved morals, every one can now dwell in peace under his own vine and fig tree, none daring to make him afraid. It is more pleasant, however, not to be overlooked while sitting there; and therefore a site for a house, as well as a garden, should be thoroughly enclosed – not too close to a public path, and as much within its own grounds as possible.

160 *Healthfulness or Salubrity* The second, and, indeed, the most important point, is the healthiness of the situation. Without health, nothing can be enjoyed; with it, the humblest home and smallest garden may become a constant and lasting source of happiness. Men rarely build a house or form a garden more than once in a lifetime; and an unfavourable choice will not only cause disappointment, but engender petty misery throughout an entire lifetime; and too much caution cannot be exercised on this point. Data should be collected from the bills of mortality, by visits to the graveyards, by converse with the people, by observing the number and condition of the aged inhabitants, by the presence or absence of epidemic diseases, by the nature of the soil and subsoil, by the state of the crops, and by the physical stamina and moral condition of the inhabitants. No advantageous offer of a cheap plot of land; no contiguity to a town or railway; no desire even to be near your business, beyond what necessity requires, or to be near old friends; no theoretical fancies about the ameliorating influence upon climate of thorough drainage, or the effect of scientific cultivation, should induce anyone to build in an unhealthy locality.

161 Four sufficiently striking characteristics will generally distinguish a healthy site. It will be dry, warm, liberally supplied with pure water, and elevated more or less above the surrounding country. Let us consider each of these characteristics in their order, treating them, on account of their manifest importance, as principal divisions of the main subject now under notice, although, in point of fact, they are but sections of one of these divisions.

162 *A Dry Soil and Subsoil* together constitute the first condition of a healthy situation. The soil, indeed, can be made dry by drainage; the latter can scarcely be altered by the power of man, unless at a ruinous expenditure of labour and money. Hence the importance of choosing a chalky, rocky, or gravelly subsoil, as the best site for building or gardening purposes, and of rejecting a green sand or heavy clay as the worst that can be for the object in view. Where the fall is ample, the worst of clays may to some extent be dried by efficient drainage; but the percolation of water through them is exceedingly slow, and is sometimes almost counteracted by the rapid conduction of water to the surface by the process of capillary attraction. It is this power that conducts the moisture up walls and through walks made on such soils. The same cause also imparts that peculiarly unhealthy musty odour that is eminently characteristic of houses and gardens in damp situations. Papers on the walls are moulded, carpets rotted, furniture ruined; the roots of fruit trees and other plants and shrubs literally starved by having their tender spongioles thrust into and kept in a perpetual cold bath by the excessively active capillary power possessed by heavy soils, which originate sterility, stunted growth, disease, and death among them; producing, also, the greatest of all miseries in a garden – a wet adhesive soil and hard-baked surface. All, therefore, who value health, or wish to possess a garden as a means of contributing to their happiness, must choose a dry site, if they would enjoy it.

163 *Warmth* The second condition of a healthy situation is warmth, using the word comparatively, and with a special application to our own climate. It is well known that localities within a few miles of each other vary considerably in temperature. Other conditions being favourable, then, the warmer any given spot is the better is it adapted for a garden site. A dry situation is much warmer than a wet one, because moist air is a rapid, and dry air a slow, conductor of heat; and not a drop of water can be raised or evaporated from the surface of any body until it has been rendered buoyant by the absorption of heat from that body or the surrounding air; consequently, the greater the evaporation of water from the earth's surface, the colder, of necessity, that surface must become. The air is not sensibly heated by the direct communication of warmth by the sun's rays, but by its contact with the warm surface of the earth; whatever cools that surface must, in the same proportion, lower the temperature of the air. Water, in fact, is the passenger to be conveyed; heat is the carriage that conveys it. Each passenger requires a separate carriage; consequently, the more drops requiring removal, the greater the absorption of heat, and, of necessity, the colder the earth and air in contact with it become. Every drop of water that passes through a porous soil, while it raises the temperature of the soil by communicating its own heat, also prevents the surface from being cooled by its removal; the air is thus maintained in a dry state. The free percolation of water through the soil assists in warming the earth, and has thus a threefold influence in increasing its temperature. It not only, as we have just shown, adds to and prevents the destruction of the heat, but it envelops the earth in a stratum of dry air, which is one of the most efficient obstacles to the conduction or withdrawal of heat.

164 *Shelter*, again, is also a most efficient means of husbanding and preserving heat, and should always be given from the north and north-east winds, by judicious planting. The site should be freely exposed to the south-east, south, south-west, and west, unless it is near the west coast, when some shelter may be necessary from the fierce winds of the Atlantic Ocean. But shelter on the north and north-east is indispensable in our climate, unless we choose to see our crops shrivelled up by the piercing winds that have just been robbed of all their heat by contact with the gigantic icebergs of the polar seas.

165 *Pure Water*, liberally supplied, is essentially necessary to a healthy site. If a brook, spring, or river, originates in or passes through it, so much the better; but as this charm cannot always be secured, see that the water is bountifully supplied, easily got at, and of the purest quality. It should be tested by chemical analysis, and every means taken to prove that it is not tainted with vegetable or mineral poisons. Neither vegetables nor animals can long continue to enjoy health, unless this primary necessity of their very existence is provided to them in a pure state.

Rainwater is the purest that can be obtained without having recourse to distillation: it contains carbonic acid and oxygen, absorbed from the atmosphere. Spring-water, filtered through granite and silicious rocks, is tolerably pure; but springs which pass through limestone or chalk are impregnated with considerable portions of these substances. Lake or river water partakes of the soil which forms its bed or basin; and marsh waters abound in decomposed animal and vegetable matter. Pure water is tasteless and inodorous; the presence of carbonic acid renders it bright, sparkling, and more or less acidulated, as in the Carlsbad and Seltzer waters. When iron is held in solution by the carbonic acid, the water becomes chalybeate, as in the Cheltenham and Tunbridge waters. The presence of sulphuretted hydrogen distinguishes the Harrogate, Moffat, and many other medicinal springs. Hot springs are produced by silica held in solution by free soda, and formed in the vicinity of volcanic or other igneous rocks.

The saline taste in water arises from impregnation with earthy salts of lime, of magnesia, of common salt, and sometimes the bicarbonate of soda and potash. Iron gives an inky taste to the water, and a yellowish tint to linen washed in it. These salts are the cause of hardness, which filtration has no effect in removing; but water that contains them is softened by exposure to the air, and sometimes by boiling.

Availing himself of the chemical properties of chalk and lime, Dr Clarke, of Aberdeen, invented a process for purifying waters impregnated with lime or chalk, a combination very common in the water round London, and in many parts of England, especially in Kent and Devonshire. When burnt in a kiln, a pound of chalk loses seven ounces of its weight by the withdrawal of carbonic acid, and becomes quicklime soluble in water; but it requires forty gallons to reduce it to lime-water. Another mode of rendering chalk soluble in water is the very reverse of this: in place of withdrawing the seven ounces of carbonic acid from the chalk by calcination, seven ounces of carbonic acid are added to it, and it is then soluble in water, without perceptibly changing its appearance; in fact, the Thames water, after filtration, as it is now delivered to the inhabitants of London, contains a pound of chalk held in solution by this proportion of carbonic acid for every 560 gallons. Now, it is found that, on mixing forty gallons of lime-water, or water in which nine ounces of quicklime is dissolved, with 560 gallons in which a pound of chalk is held in solution by seven ounces of carbonic acid, a haziness first occurs in the water, then it deepens into a white liquid, and soon assumes the appearance of a well-mixed whitewash. When the agitation subsides, it is found that the nine ounces of quicklime have again absorbed the seven ounces of carbonic acid, and that both the quicklime and the pound of chalk have been precipitated, leaving the water over it perfectly pure. Availing himself of these apparently opposing properties of chalk, Dr Clarke proposed, when water is impregnated with lime or chalk, to have two cisterns, one in which lime-water is prepared, and another fourteen times larger, in which chalk is held in solution by the addition of the above proportion of carbonic acid; with a third cistern, in which the pure water can be drawn off.

Lime and chalk being the chief agents in rendering water hard and unsuitable for domestic purposes, this mode of purification presents itself at once efficient and practicable. Where the more subtle salts are present in sufficient force to impart an offensive flavour, good water must be sought elsewhere.

166 *Elevation* To be perfectly healthy, a site for a house and garden should also be elevated above the general level of the surrounding country. For many reasons, the south aspect and the side of a hill is the best of all positions. It will either be naturally dry, or capable of being easily rendered so by efficient drainage. It will be warm, by absorbing the greater part of the sun's rays and being sheltered by the rising hill behind it. It may generally be economically watered by diverting the course of some trickling stream for the purpose; or, if a well is dug at the highest part of the ground, the water may be easily and cheaply conveyed wherever it is wanted. Such positions also enjoy immunity from those heavy fogs and blinding mists that are so characteristic of many of our most beautiful valleys. Where these mists abound, some of the most picturesque houses and most beautiful gardens are enveloped in a thick covering of watery vapour during the most enjoyable hours of the morning and evening. Nothing is more antagonistic to health or opposed to true enjoyment than a garden so enwrapped in early morn and dewy eve. The dreamy hour of twilight cannot be enjoyed in the garden, except at the risk of sore throats, catarrh, and lung disease. The more charming the scene, the greater the deprivation – the greater the danger to health. To be driven out of the garden by a sudden invasion of fog; to be compelled to shut the drawing-room windows amid the departing glories of the setting sun, is by no means pleasant. An elevated position is also free from the noxious effluvia so prevalent in low marshy localities, which will take their course up the bottom of a valley for miles, saturating the air with its noxious perfume; for the elevation of this moist polluted air may be almost as clearly defined as the tidal wave upon the seashore. Every consideration of health demands that the site for a garden or house should be chosen at a considerable altitude above the surrounding country. Such a site escapes – from the dryness of its air – the early spring and autumn frosts, which curtail the summer at both ends, and are often so fatal to the beauty as well as the productiveness of the garden.

167 *Beauty* Of this characteristic of a locality suitable for a garden, there is little need to say much. A site, to be desirable, should be beautiful, as well as healthful and secure. Some gardens are so situated as only to make more apparent the surrounding barrenness, desolation, and deformity; others throw their own beauty over scenes of equal brightness, harmonising with and heightening the beauty of the surrounding scenery.

But here tastes and dispositions interpose in endless variety. One man prefers to be near the busy town: another considers most pleasant that lonely but grand position pictured by Pollok in his *Course of Time*:

> A solitude of vast extent, untouched
> By hand of Art; where Nature sowed herself
> And reaped her crops; whose garments were the clouds
> Whose minstrels, brooks; whose lamps the moon and stars;
> Whose organ-choir the voice of many waters;
> Whose banquets, morning dews; whose heroes, storms;
> Whose warriors, mighty winds; whose lovers, flowers;
> Whose orators the thunderbolts of God;
> Whose palaces the everlasting hills;
> Whose ceiling, heaven's unfathomable blue;
> And from whose rocky turrets, battled high,
> Prospect immense, spread out on all sides round;
> Lost now between the welkin and the main,
> Now walled with hills that slept above the storm.

Philosophers, poets, ancient and modern, as well as landscape gardeners, all agree in this, that the site should be elevated above the surrounding country. Hence we have the inspired writer exclaiming, 'Beautiful is Mount Zion'. And Milton speaks of the

> Rural mound and verdurous wall of Paradise,
> Which to our general sire gave prospect large.

This 'prospect large' constitutes, unless in very moist localities, one of the chief beauties of every garden; it not only confers dignity and importance upon, but virtually extends the boundary of, the domain:

> O'er hill and dale, o'er wood or lawn,
> And verdant fields, and darkening heath between,
> And villages embosom'd soft in trees,
> And spiry towns by surging columns marked.

168 *Congruity* The charm of variety, which will be touched on presently, is quite consistent with another characteristic of a good site – congruity. There is no necessity for throwing a number of beautiful things higgledy-piggledy together; and it is seldom necessary to form a garden in such a situation where the surrounding scenery can neither be made to add to its charms nor harmonise with its beauty. Milton is a master of the art of congruity: crowded as his picture is, there is no confusion: everything seems placed in the best position for displaying its own beauty without detracting from the beauty of others. To speak of the internal arrangements of the garden, which must form the subject of future elucidation, it will suffice here to remark that Milton's views were far in advance of those of many great gardeners even now, who compel us to admire flowers in juxtaposition with cabbages, onions, and potatoes, and set all the laws of congruity at defiance.

It must not be thought that this is intended in disparagement of the 'mixed' garden, so called, in which fruit, flowers, and vegetables are grown in close proximity, without detriment to either. It applies rather to the arrangement of gardens on a large scale, in which a suitable locality should be assigned to each department of horticulture, and each kept strictly in its own place. In the mixed garden, which is so of necessity because it is a small garden *per se*, and not one of a range of gardens, each devoted to its own purpose, congruity is observed as far as it is practical to do so, for although no fence divides them one from another, the portions occupied by fruit, flowers, and vegetables are each and all of them clearly marked, the vegetables being kept together in the central parts of the larger plots into which the garden is divided, the flowers in borders flanking the alleys, and the fruit trees on espaliers between the flowers and the vegetables, or suitably placed here and there with due regard to the general effect.

169 *Utility* The usefulness of a garden will very much depend upon the quality of its soil and the facilities it affords for easy access. At one time, a good soil was the main, if not the only, consideration in choosing a garden; and it is still considered of great, though not of primary importance; for it is obviously more immediately under control than any of the other essential characteristics. Shallow soils can be deepened by trenching; wet soils dried by draining; poor soils enriched by manuring; stiff soils rendered workable by skilful admixture or by burning; light sandy soils brought to the proper texture by the application of marl; barren soils, if such there be, rendered fruitful by manuring; and incorrigibly bad soils bodily removed, and good soil substituted in their stead. Of course, any and all of these operations involve a considerable outlay of money; but they are less expensive and more practicable than improving the sanitary condition of a whole neighbourhood, conveying pure water for miles, and converting a flat, uninteresting country into a beautiful landscape. While elevation continues to be a most desirable object in the site of a garden, the garden, nevertheless, must not be on a hill so steep as to render it difficult or dangerous to reach it at any hour of the day or night; for if it be so situated, both the pleasure to be derived from such a garden, and its utility as well, will be much impaired. It should be within an easy distance of a good public road, as road-making involves a large outlay, and road-keeping is a heavy item of expense. The length of a private or carriage road to house or garden should be regulated, to a great extent, by the size of the house and extent of the grounds; a long winding road may be a very pretty object in itself, but it is disappointing if it leads to nothing. For ducal parks, or large estates, where expense is no object, so long as a road appears to be going in the direction of the house, the longer it is, the stronger is the impression of extent produced, provided it terminate at a splendid mansion. But not only the length, but even the width of the carriage road should correspond with the extent of the demesne; it is in bad taste to have a bold road skirting the boundaries of a small estate, and leading to nothing more than a villa residence. On economical grounds, to save the expense of making and keeping the roads, and as a matter of convenience for the carting of manure, and all other utilitarian purposes, it is desirable that a site be easily and quickly accessible from a public road.

170 *Variety* is also characteristic of a good site. Milton crowds almost every kind of natural beauty into his glowing pictures; and in this he reveals his complete knowledge of human nature. No beauty can continue to satisfy that is destitute of the fascinating charm of variety. Nature itself presents one magnificent series of incessant and never-ending change; the surface of the earth is variegated with sea and land, hill and dale, forests and burning sands; lofty mountains, sublime in their rugged grandeur, and flat prairies, like placid oceans of land. He who has an absolute power of choice, therefore, will do well to secure, not only a beautiful situation, in some such position as has been indicated, but one where the scenery is varied, and the landscape crowded with interesting objects.

It is desirable, in short, for variety's sake, in fixing on a garden site, to endeavour to get a spot from which may be obtained a distant glimpse of tapering spires, of rugged rocks, of the rushing train, and the everlasting mountains; of modern towns and crumbling ruins; of ducal parks and factory chimneys; of grazing flocks and bounding deer; and of the full expanse of the cloud-flecked heavens, whether at morn or eve, in the busy stir of day or in the hush of night. If the hand of taste cannot create, it can at least develop and assist at the exhibition of these charms – in the words of Mason, it can make

'Yon stately spire
Pierce the opposing oaks' luxurious shade;
Bid yonder crowding hawthorns low retire,
Nor veil the glories of the golden mead.
Hail! sylvan wonders, hail! and hail the hand
Whose native taste thy native charms display'd!
Teaching one little acre to command
Each envied happiness of scene and shade.'

And if all this variety of scene cannot be secured, at least let us choose as many of them as circumstances permit. Nature's own variety of the seasons, at least, may be secured – Spring with its freshness, Summer with its beauty, Autumn with its rich warmth of glory, and pale Winter

> Casting his silvery mantle o'er the woods,
> And binding in crystal chains the slumb'ring floods.

And the innumerable phases of variety which pervade the elements of earth and air, the sea, and flowing waters, may be obtained; or, as Pollok has it, of

> Day
> And night, and rising suns and setting suns,
> And clouds that seem like chariots of the saints
> By fiery coursers drawn; as brightly hued
> As if the glorious bushy, golden locks
> Of thousand cherubim had been shorn off,
> And on the temples hung of Morn and Even.

FIG. 25 *Rustic approach to terrace in garden*

CHAPTER 6

On Various Styles of Gardening and the Arrangement of Gardens

171 The site being fixed upon, before commencing the actual work of laying out the garden, making the roads that shall afford access to it, raising the fences that shall enclose it, and building the various structures that shall serve for embellishments on the one hand, and add to its utility on the other, it is desirable – nay, more, absolutely necessary – to consider the disposition of the spot, and the natural formation of the ground, in order that the work to be done may be so ordered as to tend to the improvement of its existing features and conformation, and the skilful adaptation of them to meet the views and requirements of the owner rather than to effect any radical alteration, which, to say the least of it, is both difficult and costly. It is also necessary to determine on the general style to be adopted, which shall impart character and individuality to the garden, and give distinctive emphasis to every part of it when viewed together as a whole. To do this effectually, it is needful to know something of the styles that already prevail in existing gardens, and the plans on which they have been laid out and arranged, and to this end the present chapter is devoted to a consideration of various methods of arranging and laying out gardens of all kinds, large and small, taking them as types which shall afford useful aid in the construction of gardens yet to be made, or possibly remodelled, not indeed to be copied with slavish adherence to every feature, but to be modified and altered and adapted in such manner as may best suit the conformation of the locality under treatment.

172 Gardening in itself is an Art of the highest order, but its chief object as an Art should be not to revolutionise Nature, if the expression may be permitted, but to render Nature still more charming:

> For Nature ne'er deserts the wise and pure;
> No plot so narrow be, but Nature there,
> No waste so vacant, but may well employ
> Each faculty of sense, and keep the heart
> Awake to love and beauty.

Not, however, that Art should ever strive to imitate so as to be mistaken for Nature: this, if possible, is not desirable – it would rob Art of half its merit, without attaining either beauty or grandeur; for, after all, the gardener operates on a very limited scale, even when the widest scope is given to his genius. A garden is a work of art, and Art ought to be avowedly present in every part of it. The meandering path, winding through tangled thickets, beneath the spreading cedar, of which the 'lichen staineth the stem', is as much a work of art as the highly-embellished geometrical garden, the architectural terraces and vases which overlook it, or the fountain which occupies its centre. Nature, in dishabille, is beautiful in a wood, at home on the bleak moor and rugged mountain – often admissible in a park, but, strictly speaking, Nature would be incongruous and misplaced in a garden; and where such features have been introduced, on the pretence of making 'natural gardens', the results produced are a libel on good taste. A dwelling-house might, with as much propriety, be built in imitation of a natural cave, as an artificial garden so arranged as to be mistaken for a bit of natural scenery. On the other hand, by proceeding with the idea that Art is to be apparent, the capabilities of the site and resources of the garden will be fully developed, if the designs are tasteful and skilfully carried into execution.

173 Although it may appear somewhat early to speak of glazed buildings in connection with the garden, it is prudent to allude to them at the very first, for in the present day a 'bit of glass' is an almost indispensable adjunct even to the smallest and most unpretentious gardens, while in gardens on a considerable scale the arrangement of the glass structures is a matter of greater importance than it appears to be at first sight, and requires much more attention than it has sometimes received. Glass, sufficient to form a magnificent block of houses, is frequently scattered over the grounds, creating an appearance of confusion, and interfering most unnecessarily with the economy both of space and labour. To say nothing of the additional expense of working detached houses, they are often so placed as to become an intolerable nuisance, instead of a source of comfort and enjoyment to their possessor.

174 All glass structures should be distinguished by utility, ornament, and convenience. The first is often sacrificed to antiquated routine, and houses, built for the culture of tropical plants and fruits, are constructed so as to exclude more than half of the little light we can afford them. But the genius of Routine waves her wand, and *lean-to* houses, with opaque backs – these antiquated receptacles for plants – still arise at her bidding; ornamental glass houses that admit the light on every side being, to all appearance, studiously shunned in many gardens, as if, the uglier houses could be made, the better they must needs be adapted for their intended purposes. Nevertheless, a large measure of structural and decorative beauty is compatible with the highest cultural advantages, and consistent with the severest economy; and this should be steadily and persistently kept in view in the construction of all glazed buildings, be they what they may, for horticultural purposes.

Glass houses are a never-failing resource on wet days, when other amusements fail and outdoor exercise becomes impossible, and it is then that they should contribute their largest quota of enjoyment. They should therefore be always accessible from the drawing-room, without the necessity of going out of doors. Probably, the best possible arrangement is to attach the conservatory to the mansion; and, where there are other houses, to connect all with the conservatory, by the intervention of a glass passage or verandah. Of course, where there is only one house, whatever its form and designation, this applies with even more force. All glass houses ought to be span, curvilinear, or ridge-and-furrow roofed, and should be placed, if possible, at right angles with the verandah, their end doors communicating with it. They should run north and south, and present east and west aspects to the sun's rays, which is decidedly the best for general purposes.

Rooms for the gardeners employed, fruit rooms, mushroom pits, retarding and propagating houses, potting and tool sheds, etc., should also be placed near to them. Perhaps a span-roofed building, divided in the centre, and running up at one point to the glass, with a building at one end for the reception of a boiler to heat the whole range, would be the very best, and certainly the most economical arrangement. The gardener's cottage might also be placed either here or at the extremity of the centre walk in the kitchen garden, where a terminal Tudor façade would be ornamental as well as convenient. The glass arcade or verandah should terminate in a handsome fountain or vase, and have an outlet into the kitchen garden. It might also branch off to the stables, and thus bring the whole of the home attractions within easy and comfortable access of the dwelling-house in all weathers. The frame ground should be placed close to the stables, and be large enough to answer the purposes of a soil yard as well as a reserve garden.

175 Having settled the position of all the necessary buildings, the next point is the sewage removal and water supply. All the sewage from house and stables should be conveyed into one large tank in the frame-ground. In no other country is there such waste of the richest manure as in these islands, where it may be safely asserted that many millions sterling annually are permitted to escape into our brooks, poisoning man and beast; for, when thus disposed of, the liquid manure thrown away is truly 'matter in the wrong place', as Lord Palmerston has well said. Applied in a proper state of dilution, nothing can be more valuable to growing crops of every description. The tank would, of course, be covered or domed over, furnished with a pump for raising the liquid, and an outlet for an overflow: the outlet, however, with proper management, would seldom be brought into use.

176 In many situations, especially on the side of a hill, abundance of water is to be found at a higher elevation than the house; and in these cases the supply of water to house and garden is simply and easily effected. All that is needful is to form a reservoir, and lay down pipes; generally, however, spring-water has to be raised from a considerable depth. The great point is to form the tank high enough to enable the water to come down by its own specific gravity to wherever it is wanted afterwards. On the same principle, tanks for rainwater should be built as much as possible above the level of the surface, to obviate the necessity of raising it for use; and as the operation of laying down pipes involves the removal of large quantities of earth, this should always precede any direct operations on the garden. The position of fountains, ornamental water, and waterfalls, should also be determined, in order that their future supply may be provided for, by laying the necessary pipes at once. The direction of the sewers, drains, and water-pipes should also be carefully delineated on the plan, as well as indicated on the grounds by specific marks.

177 All modern writers and practitioners now agree that the pleasure garden should be contiguous to the house. The fact of its contiguity to the mansion will have much influence upon the character of the garden. Certain styles of architecture require corresponding styles of gardening as their proper accompaniments. An imposing and highly-finished façade seems to demand formal terraces and geometric gardens as a proper and congruous base. Hence we have Gothic, Italian, French, and Dutch styles of gardening, which are all branches of the formal or geometric style, and may be described as presenting regular forms, or groups of figures, arranged in mathematical lines, either regularly straight or curved, and at regulated distances. This is much the most useful and effective style of flower garden. The groups may be sunk beneath the surface, when they are called Dutch gardens, or the figures can be edged with stone or tiles, and thus be constituted architectural gardens; the character and design of the edging corresponding with the architecture of the house, often supported by retaining walls, with massive piers for vases, and embellished with fountains. As a transition from the house to the garden, nothing can be more pleasing than a pleasure-garden in the 'Geometric' style, laid out in turf or gravel, connected with the house by an upper and lower terrace, and descending by broad stone steps, notwithstanding Horace Walpole's satirical remark about 'walking up and down stairs out of doors'.

178 The 'Gardenesque' style may be described as a skilful disposition of trees and shrubs, in regular or irregular figures, or singly and at equal or unequal distances, preserving, amid apparent irregularity, a certain degree of uniformity. The chief feature of this style is, that no two plants shall be planted so close together as to touch each other, and that no indiscriminate mixture of flowers of different species shall be permitted in the same clump. This style is generally employed in arboretums and pinetums, and is the only one capable of exhibiting individual plants, shrubs, and trees in perfection. It forms a tasteful gradation between the 'Geometric' style and the 'Picturesque' style.

179 The 'Picturesque' style is defined by Mr Loudon as an imitation of Nature in a wild state, according to Art. He also gives an example of how this can be done: 'A gravel pit would be improved, according to Art, if foreign trees, shrubs, and plants, even to the grasses, were introduced instead of indigenous ones; or a Swiss cottage instead of a hovel. Rock scenery, aquatic scenery, dale or dingle scenery, forest scenery, copse scenery, and open glade scenery, may all be imitated on the same principle; viz., that of substituting foreign for indigenous vegetation, and laying out regular walks. This is sufficient to constitute a picturesque imitation of natural scenery.'

180 Thus the 'Picturesque' style may be said to consist of irregular groups of figures, masses or clumps, disposed at irregular intervals; for, in this style, the grouping is everything – individual effect nothing. It is the connecting link, as it were, between the garden and the natural scenery outside. Notwithstanding all that has been written about the importance of purity of style, it seems to be desirable that every large garden should combine all the three styles. This it has been attempted to set forth in the design exhibited in Fig. 26. Furnishing the house with a broad and elevated base of gravel to stand upon, a geometrical flower garden succeeds it, supported by an ornamental wall, which may be said to terminate in the architectural alcove at each end of the west walk. The lawn itself is laid out in the Gardenesque style, and all beyond the serpentine walk, on the east side, belongs to the Picturesque style. The transition from the highest artistic finish to nature undressed is gradual and easy, and, as it appears to me, satisfactory to the mind.

181 In the accompanying typical range of garden and pleasure grounds, in which it has been sought to embody these principles, the prayer of Cowley:

Ah! yet ere I descend into the grave,
May I a small house and large garden have –

has not been disregarded. The house is modest in its pretensions – the garden ground from north to south and from east to west covering an area of about a thousand feet by four hundred; or, including house and offices, a little more than nine acres. The entrance lies towards the north, being approached by a sweeping drive from the north-west, through shrubberies on ground rising towards the north-east; so that it is well sheltered in that direction. The principal apartments look to the south and west, the circular windows looking out on geometrical flower beds, margined with turf, and surrounded by a broad gravel path; while corresponding beds occupy the whole width of the lawn to the south, forming together a raised terrace round the house, from which flights of steps lead down to the lawn; a dwarf wall with balustrades and climbing roses supporting it. At the foot of this wall, a ribbon border, or mixed herbaceous border, may be laid out with very good effect. From the north-west corner of the house, a broad belt of sloping lawn sweeps round the shrubbery, separated from the park by an iron wire fence. An elegant ribbon border facing the drawing-room occupies the front of this lawn, backed, at a little distance off, by a bank of choice rhododendrons, sheltered by a thick hedge of low-cut hollies. Beyond these the ha-ha fence admits an extensive prospect of the adjacent country.

182 Towards the south, the ha-ha fence stretches for about eight hundred yards in a south-easterly direction, giving a circular termination to the grounds, extending all round the enclosure. The details of the plan will, however, be better understood by the following references to it:

A Farmyard, poultry yard, etc.
B Turf bins and manure yard, with tank for house sewage, led through drain indicated by dotted line from house.
C Frame ground and reserve garden.
D Stables, coach house, and yard.
E Shady yard for plants in summer.
F Kitchen entrance to house.
G Forcing houses, vinery, etc.
H Fruit and kitchen garden in compartments.
I Small orchard.
J Tank and fountain.
K Gardener's cottage and offices.
L Chain border.
M Ribbon border and shrubs.
N Ribbon beds and scroll beds.
O Pinetum.
P Rosary or rose garden.
Q Heaths and ferns, with rockery in the rear as background.
R Dahlias, hollyhocks, etc., in beds.
S Syringas and other ornamental shrubs, with ruin and river behind.
T American plants.
U Verbena garden, interspersed with dwarf trees and shrubs.
V Clumps of Ghent azaleas.
W Elms, sycamores, and forest trees, with a belt of shrubs in front.
X Geometrical flower garden.
Y Ribbon border opposite drawing-room on west side of house.
Z Clump of choice rhododendrons.
a Wide carriage approach and sweep in front of house.
b Road to stables, farmyard, gardens, etc.
c Gravel walk, 10 feet wide, extending across grounds.
d Gate of iron, with ornamental arch, giving access to kitchen garden.
e Conservatory attached to house
f Verandah leading from conservatory to fruit room.

g Stokehole for forcing houses.
hh Gravel walk, with arches of roses overhead, or orangery.
ii Broad gravel walks.
jj Dotted line from reservoir in front of house indicating course of brook, which runs under forcing house and part of the grounds.
kk Wall and balustrades, with ribbon border in front.
ll Turf, with standard Portugal laurels, 20 feet apart.
m Terrace walk, with stone steps at the north end, and alcove at the south end.
nn Portugal laurels, etc., on east of terrace walk.
o Reserve garden.
pp Pathway leading from kitchen to manure yard and frame ground.

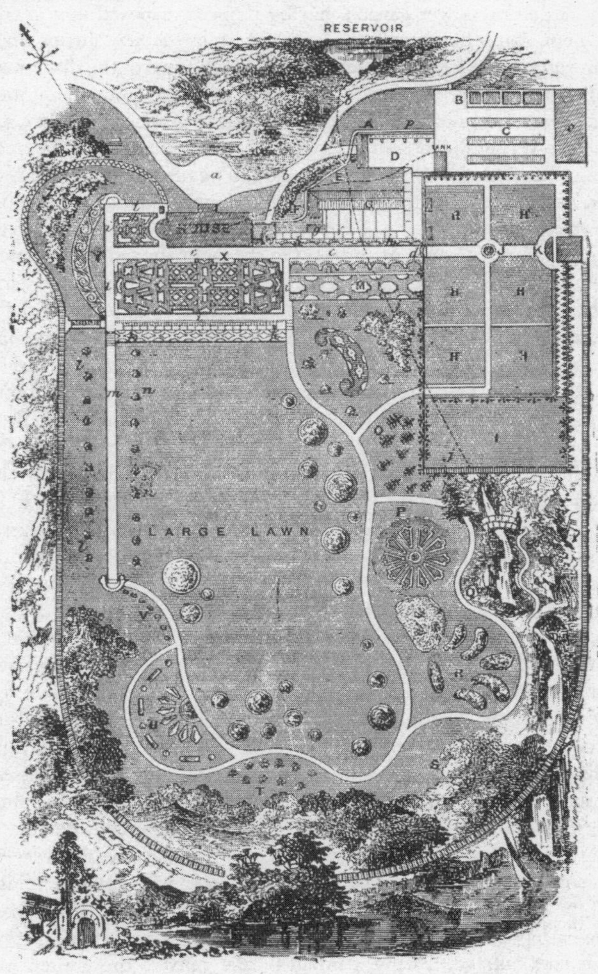

FIG. 26 *Example of garden and grounds in picturesque style*

183 Descending the steps adjoining the geometric flower garden, a broad gravel path, ten feet wide, stretches, in a direction parallel with the ha-ha, for about two hundred and thirty feet, bordered on either hand with Portuguese laurels and other choice standard trees of a size, planted on the turf. This terrace walk terminates in a circular alcove. Behind the alcove may be planted, or rather transplanted, so as to be regulated in size, some of the larger trees, such as elms, sycamores, and other forest trees. A broad sweeping path leads off here in an easterly direction, bordered on the left by a series of circular beds, and on the right by clumps of Ghent azaleas. A little onwards is a semicircular verbena garden or flower garden, having its beds disposed in a geometrical arrangement, backed towards the south-west by choice shrubs and trees, through which vistas have been left, affording glimpses of the distant country; in the distance, a river flowing from west to east, the landscape dotted with farms, cottages, and occasional spires. Groups of American plants, syringas, and other flowering shrubs and trees, backed and blending with the trees up to the ha-ha fence, occupy the south boundary. The main path, which is ten feet broad in its whole length, pursues its winding course back to the steps at the eastern extremity of the terrace, dotted on the left by circular beds varying in size, and occasional clumps of shrubs. On the right the path is flanked by the dahlia and hollyhock garden and rosary, succeeded by the pinetum, where the more choice araucarias, deodars, and other pines are sheltered by the garden wall. Beyond the pinetum the lawn is decorated by an elegant ribbon border in a scroll, and dotted with choice deciduous shrubs, up to the dwarf wall of the terrace. An arch of roses, growing from each side, covers this part of the broad gravel path, which extends the whole breadth of the grounds, from the centre of the rhododendron beds on the west to the kitchen garden on the east. Behind the roses a glass arcade or verandah leads from the conservatory attached to the east end of the house to the kitchen garden, passing in front of the range of forcing houses. The roses may be dispensed with if preferred, and on the north side of the path an orangery may be constructed fronting the south, and forming the back of the arcade or verandah, which may be so built as to be shut in by glass sashes in the winter.

184 Farther to the south-east, while the main path pursues a winding course back to the terrace, a secondary path winds through the shrubberies, having the dahlia and hollyhock garden on the left, and choice syringas and other flowering shrubs on the right. A little further on, on the left, is a formally-laid-out rose garden cut in the turf, sheltered on the north and east by groups of American and other pines on either side of the path. Here the brook, which rises in the high ground to the north of the house, and which has been carried under the ground for some distance, issues from the orchard in a considerable stream, tumbling over artificial rocks placed here – a very pretty and very musical cascade; surrounded by rugged banks of rock-work, a fernery extending to the edges of the brook, and in front of the path a collection of hardy heaths.

185 The ha-ha fence, which surrounds the whole area, proceeds as far north as the gardener's cottage, leaving a broad border outside the garden walls, on which some of the most choice fruit trees are planted: the aspect being a south-east one, it receives all the benefits of the morning sun, and it is sheltered from the east winds by a belt of young trees outside, and a holly hedge planted on the top of the ha-ha inside. The orchard on the south side is protected by an efficient iron railing in place of a wall. On the west, the wall is a continuous one up to the broad gravel walk, and a fair sprinkling of choice fruit should be found on it in the proper season. The reserve garden occupies the slope north of the gardener's cottage, the manure yard and farm ground adjoining them; a sewer from the house, leading through the yard behind the forcing houses and past the stables, conveys all the sewage both of house and stables to the manure tank.

There can be no question that this principle of gradation is the true theory of laying out grounds, although the mode of its application may be infinitely varied. The Geometrical style, for instance, may be carried on through a series of terraces, sloping banks, flights of steps of turf or stone, retaining walls, etc., until it occupies the whole of the enclosed lawn. Beds in scrollwork patterns, edged with box, and with the intervening paths made up of gravel, broken red or white brick, Derbyshire spar, blue slate, or limestone chippings, the interstices being filled with silver, yellow, or red sand, may also be introduced with pleasing effect. The Geometrical garden may be formed on a level surface, and all fountains, steps, banks, and walls dispensed with; it may be raised above the surface, supported by stone edgings, or be sunk beneath it, which is an excellent arrangement where the height of the flowers would mar the effect of the more distant flower beds. In fact, the Geometrical style is capable of endless variation and the most facile adaptation; and, in addition to those here given, others might follow it in succession upon different levels, until the whole front lawn was thus furnished, the central part of the lawn being preserved and carefully kept for croquet, lawn tennis, and any of the outdoor games of this sort in which both ladies and gentlemen can take part. The shape of these groups of beds is of less importance than might be supposed, and could be altered every few years, to give fresh interest and variety to them.

In all cases, however, where it occupies the whole of the enclosed space, the park, for a certain distance beyond, should be laid out in the Gardenesque style. The boundary walk should also be kept at the distance of from twenty to fifty feet from the fence which separates the lawn from the park. The practice of leading the walk within a few feet of the boundary, or fence, cannot be too severely reprehended. It not only makes the boundary line offensively apparent, but compels the eye to travel along the bottom of an unsightly ditch. Some landscape gardeners recommend planting the inside edge of the ha-ha with choice shrubs or flowers; but this expedient only makes bad worse, by bringing the eye to admire beauty in juxtaposition with its opposite. The plants so placed will also be in dangerous proximity to points whence injury may accrue to them from the browsing propensities of cattle. No pleasure can possibly be derived from seeing easily-injured objects placed in seeming danger, especially where the impression may be so easily avoided, and substantial advantages gained, by keeping the walks at a sufficient distance from the boundary line. Ideas of grandeur and extent may be imparted, and the boundary line broken and almost hid by planting standard laurels or bays, and laying down clumps of choice shrubs on the intervening space, thus forming a foreground for other clumps planted on the Gardenesque principle. The effect, as seen from the house and other parts of the grounds, should be to destroy entirely the sharp line of demarcation between lawn and park; to extend indefinitely the appearance of the former, and virtually include the latter, as far as the organ of vision is concerned. The more distant part of the park should then be planted and grouped on the Picturesque principle, assuming in the extreme distance the rougher, bolder, and consequently more picturesque outlines of natural scenery.

Upon the same principle, a place may be laid out entirely in the Gardenesque style, the Geometrical being entirely dispensed with. In this case, the Picturesque groups in the park should harmonise with the Gardenesque groups on the lawn, and apparent extent and congruous variety be obtained. The Picturesque style is only admissible beside Swiss cottages or rural residences, and can never be made to harmonise with the broad square outlines of any more imposing style of architecture. The worst possible arrangement is to surround the house with picturesque objects, with the highly-embellished Geometrical garden farther off; and yet we sometimes see a tangled thicket of furze-broom, thorns, and brambles, up to the very door, with a ravelled skein of wild roses, sweetbrier, and honeysuckle peeping in at the windows; while the highly-dressed garden is placed entirely out of view. This arrangement, however romantic, is altogether opposed to correct taste, and incompatible with the comfortable enjoyment of either house or garden.

The practice of planting the park and lawn so as to constitute an indivisible and perfect whole may be objected to, because it practises a deception on the eye of the beholder. Burke, on the other hand, remarks 'that no work of art can be great but as it deceives.' Without contending very strenuously for the entire truth of this sentiment, it must be admitted that it is not only allowable, but one of the chief merits of Art, to conceal the modes by which its effects are produced. If it is apparent that a splash of white paint is used to represent water or moonlight in a landscape, the merit of the picture must be of the most mediocre description. When we look at a good painting, we think nothing of brushes, easels, and colours, but only of the marvellous beauty and truthfulness to nature of the representation. The canvas speaks, but it speaks to us only of light and shade, of depth, softness, and intensity of tone, and apparent extent, which are all admired; but the mode of their production is concealed. Bald, bare outlines and sharply-defined boundaries are hidden on canvas by a dash of paint, and in the natural landscape by a group of shrubs and trees; and the latter deception, if such it can be called, is as consistent with the highest principles of artistic taste as the former. While, therefore, an occasional boundary line, where the prospect is commanding, may be visible, as a rule, it should be at least partially concealed.

186 As a remarkable example of gardens laid out in a style that is at once imposing and effective, but at the same time satisfactory to the eye and pleasing as a *coup d'oeil*, reference may be made to the gardens of the Royal Horticultural Society at South Kensington, which are laid out in the formal or Geometrical style; but as these beautiful gardens are, in point of fact, public gardens intended for architectural and horticultural display, and to accommodate exhibitions of the Society and gatherings of large numbers of people, and not in any way a demesne calculated to promote the pleasure and enjoyment of the members of a private family and their friends, it is useless to give more than a brief general description of them, because everything in connection with them is carried out on far too large a scale to be susceptible of imitation elsewhere, and it is merely necessary to refer to them here as being the gardens that are immediately under the management of a body of scientific men, whose authority is pre-eminent in the United Kingdom in all matters pertaining to every branch of horticulture, and to which the attention of gardeners and all who love a garden may be naturally directed, as supplying the best and most noteworthy example of that which a garden on so colossal a scale might with reason be expected to be.

The gardens of the Royal Horticultural Society occupied a considerable portion of the garden grounds attached to Gore House, but owing to the erection of the International Exhibition buildings, their extent is now greatly curtailed. The area originally covered about 23 acres, and was about 1200 feet in length and 800 feet in breadth, sloping gently from the northern to the southern limit, with a fall of about 20 feet through its entire length. The soil and subsoil are of the most favourable description, the former being a rich black earth of considerable depth, similar to that of the market gardens of the neighbourhood, and the subsoil the gravel of the district mixed with a little clay.

It was determined to lay out the ground in a succession of terraces, and the formation of these was greatly facilitated by its natural inclination; and this may serve as a useful hint in the formation of gardens under similar conditions of slope and configuration of surface, though on a smaller scale. The natural inclination of the ground greatly facilitated the formation of the terraces. The ante-garden at the south extremity, an oblong square of 800 feet by 400, occupied the lower level; the earth taken from its more elevated part served to form a raised bank of a foot and a half along its whole breadth. This second level extended for about 300 feet at this level, when another rise of two feet occurred – broad raised verges 12 feet wide all round, and sloping ramps leading by a grass promenade to the gravel walks round the canal, at the same level as the ante-garden, with their embroidered flower beds and evergreen clumps and scrolls. Another space of about 360 feet, and a third rise of five feet occurred, which was attained by two flights of steps on either side of the basin. The gardens on this third level brought before the spectator much of the architectural display of the place, and led to the fourth level by three flights of steps in the path and grassy slopes in the grounds. The conservatory terrace is attained by an additional flight of steps and grass ramps. As the necessary excavations were made, the various earthworks were raised by the material removed in excavating, the surface soil, a fine, friable loam, being reserved for the surface of the sloping banks and level ground. This should be noted and acted on by all who are engaged in making a garden whenever the surface soil is of a nature to warrant its retention.

The system of surface drainage and the arrangements for watering were of the most complete description. A deep drain, laid with 18-inch glazed pipes, cemented at the joints, ran under the central cross walk of the ante-garden, received all the surface drainage, and communicated with the sewer in the adjoining street. Two other main drains, laid with 12-inch glazed pipes, traversed the gardens from north to south on each side of the central walk, about 80 feet apart. Two other drains, parallel with these, laid with 9-inch pipes, ran down the side of each corridor, outside the gravel, entering the main drain in the ante-garden. Into these main drains, lateral drains, with pipes of 4 or 6 inches diameter, according to the extent of surface they have to drain, collected and led the surface waters over the whole area; these smaller pipes being jointed with clay or cement, and having elbow-joints for the reception of other pipes, which ramify in a different direction. Efficient arrangements were made for watering the gardens, as well as for draining them; but these do not require description.

The walks which traverse the gardens were equally perfect as models of workmanship and design, forming noble promenades round the whole area, with a broad central path and cross walks at convenient distances: they were made of the subsoil gravel excavated for the canals and sunken grass promenades. The central and principal cross walks were throughout 40 feet wide, with the slightest possible curve in the centre, which was on a level with the side verge of turf. They were excavated to the depth of 18 inches in the principal walks, and 9 inches of brick-and-lime rubbish laid down and heavily rolled in. After setting a short time, 6 inches of coarse gravel was laid down, and a further layer of finer gravel added as a finish, and the whole well rolled. The cross and corridor walks, about 20 feet wide, contained 9 inches of brick-and-lime rubbish and 6 inches of gravel, applied in the same manner. Neat iron gratings, at regular distances, received and conveyed the rainwater into the nearest drainpipes. When the various earthworks, ramps, and glacis were completed, and the soil had settled, the ancient turf, which had been carefully preserved, was again laid down.

187 In all made gardens of considerable size and extent, the terrace is an artificial formation which forms a conspicuous feature in the *tout ensemble* when the ground has been laid out, and its construction demands notice and its various parts some brief explanation. It is almost unnecessary to say that it is a platform or level surface of earth, supported on one or both sides, as the case may be, by a wall or by a sloping bank of earth, covered with turf. In some situations, where the terrace is of no great length, it is possible to convert the slope into a rockery; but in the majority of cases in which a terrace is constructed, the rockery would be out of place, and not in strict keeping with the surroundings of the platform and the main object for which it is constructed, namely, to obtain a better view of some distant prospect, or to command the entire garden, or the greater part of it, spreading out before it and exhibiting more completely to the view every noticeable feature that it contains. The term 'terrace' is derived directly from the Italian *terrazze* or the French *terrasse*, which in their turn are obtained from the Latin *terra*, earth, the material of which the terrace is made. It is used by and possibly borrowed from military engineers, by whom a level surface within a fort is called the terrace, and Hackluyt speaks of 'the terrace of the fort'.' Access is usually gained to the higher level of a terrace in a garden by steps, and the terrace thus constructed and upheld by a wall in front, surmounted by a balustrade, formed a prominent feature in Elizabethan gardens, and a suitable base to the architecture of that period. In the present day the terrace consists of a raised walk in various parts of the gardens rather than a platform immediately in front of the principal façade of the house or some other of the frontages that it possesses, and is bounded and contained by a slope covered with turf, as it has been said. Care must be taken to give sufficient inclination to the slope, to prevent any chance of its falling away either by action of the weather, or by the weight of the body when it is found necessary to walk or stand on the slope for the purpose of cutting the grass or any other needful operation.

The following facts, taken from Laxton's *Builder's Price Book*, may be useful to those who are engaged in the formation of terraces when laying out a garden. 'In loose ground a man can throw up about 10 cubic yards per day, but in hard or gravelly soils 5 yards will be a fair day's work. Three men will remove 30 yards of earth a distance of 20 yards in a day. With regard to the weight of materials 19 cubic feet of sand, 18 ditto of clay, 24 ditto earth, 15½ ditto chalk, 20 ditto gravel, will each weigh one ton. A cubic yard of earth before digging will occupy about 1½ cubic yard when dug. Sand and gravel does not increase more than one-third as much as earth in bulk when dug, but will decrease in height one-fourth more than earth. A wheelbarrow (that is to say, the broad, shallow barrow used by navvies) holds ⅒ yard cube. A cubic yard, or 27 cubic feet of earth, is a single load, and contains 20 bushels; 1 cubic yard of gravel contains 18 bushels in the pit; when dug it will increase nearly one-third in bulk, but will subside nearly one-fourth in height, and decrease one-fifth in bulk when formed into embankments. When earth is well drained, it will stand in embankment about 1½ to 1.' That is to say, if the height of the embankment be 1 foot, or 1 yard, or 12 yards, as the case may be, as shown by BC, in Fig. 27, the length of the slope, AC, may be 1½ feet, 1½ yards, or 18 yards respectively. Or, what is the same thing, the slope, AC, should form an angle of 40° or 41° with the horizontal base line, AB. This will prove a useful rule in throwing up terraces, embankments, mounds, etc., in the grounds or gardens. If revetted, to use an engineer's term, or covered with turf, the inclination may be at a greater angle, and therefore steeper, because the roots of the grass bind the surface earth together, and keep it from being washed down by heavy rains. This will be evident from the inspection of the side of a hedge or bank covered with turf, which may be inclined to the horizontal base line at angles ranging from 10° to 20°, but such steep inclines are not suited for the embankments of terraces, in which the slope should be easy and gentle.

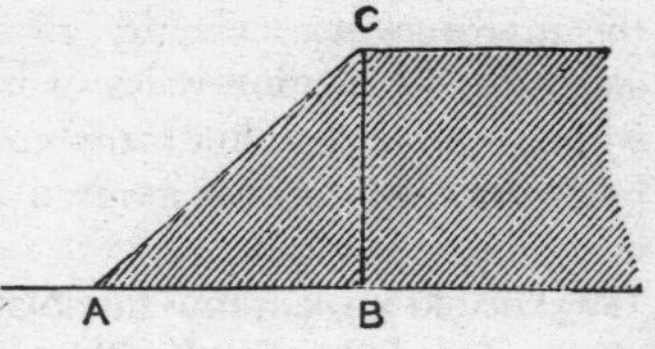

FIG. 27 *Slope of terrace or embankment in section*

In speaking of the formation of the terraces and raised earth works in the gardens of the Royal Horticultural Society, the terms 'glacis' and 'ramp' have been used, and it may be remarked that, while the latter is applicable to garden work, the former is not so suitable. A glacis, in military parlance, is the exterior surface of a bank of earth gently sloping to the level country, about eight feet high at the crest, and about one hundred and fifty feet wide, serving to shelter the defenders of the covered way from one part of the works to another outside the main wall, and to protect in a measure the masonry revetment of the inner works from cannonade. The glacis bears the same relation to the embankment as the slope, AC, bears to the entire terrace in Fig. 27, but the slope, AC, can only be called a glacis on account of its similarity to the glacis proper in position and construction. It is a French word imported and adopted into the English language, and derived from the Low or Mediaeval Latin *glatia*, smoothness. The ramp, from the French *ramper*, to creep, or in old French, to climb, is a road or pathway cut obliquely into, or added to, the interior slope of a rampart or parapet, and it has a slanting face, as AC in the above diagram. The ramp serves as a step, giving means of access from a lower level to a higher, and as the higher level is not very far removed above the lower level, the term ramp is more appropriately applied to the external incline of a terrace or raised earthwork in gardening than that of glacis, which, as it has been shown, belongs to a far more important and imposing construction. The ramp, as used in gardening, and the purposes to which it is put, is shown in section in Fig. 28, in which are four ramps or slopes, AB, CD, EF, GH, forming embankments to small raised terraces, BC and FG. It may be used, and beneficially, in forming the enclosure of a level piece of turf for croquet, lawn tennis, or similar games, as shown by DE, and the terraces, BC and FG, may be utilised in a most desirable manner, if wide enough, as long narrow beds for flowers. Such a position is suitable for roses, and for pinks and carnations, which like good drainage and do not object to raised ground, such as is shown in the diagram. The ramp may be modelled in curved as well as straight lines.

FIG. 28 *The ramp shown in section*

188 There are many gardens, chiefly derived from the Italian school, in which terraces form an important feature, and where much of the beauty immediately surrounding the house is derived from architectural display. In some parts of the Continent where the orange is cultivated, those noble plants, in their massive square tubs, form a grand and appropriate decoration to terrace walks. The glacis at Glamis Castle and the terraces of Powis Castle, and many other equally beautiful specimens of terraced garden style of gardening, fell before the improvers of last century, giving place to the more tame, undulating, turfy sward and serpentine walks of more modern times – the gem, as it were, without the setting. But many noble specimens were spared, and others have been since added, the terraced gardens at Windsor Castle presenting no insignificant example.

189 The old gardens thus immolated to the rage of fashion were generally laid out so as to correspond with the main lines of the building, and no doubt architectural unity requires that this should always be the case, but it is not always necessary to terrace effects that architectural decorations should be introduced; simple embankments of a noble character, blending most happily with the surrounding landscape, may be produced by very simple means. A notable example of the geometric garden may be seen at Rome in the Papal gardens of the Belvedere behind the Vatican, which is elegant in its simplicity. The geometric figures are produced by deep box edgings; and the symmetrical effects given to the variety of elevation by the embankment 'are evidences,' says Mr Humphreys, 'of true feeling for the gardenesque in the designer.' The effects to be produced by deep box edgings, and the general effect of sloping banks and terraces without too much elaboration, were also to be observed in the Horticultural Society's Gardens at Kensington.

190 Many writers have given descriptions of gardens which, although they may be due in a great measure to the imagination, must, nevertheless, be based on existing gardens that have been seen and enjoyed to the utmost by those who have pictured the beautiful retreats which they have assigned to one or other of the beings who have been born in thought. And those who can thus describe gardens must truly love gardens and appreciate them. The mind of many a reader will here revert, in all probability, even before his eye lights on the coming words, to the charming garden of Lady Corisande, described by the Earl of Beaconsfield in his novel *Lothair* – a garden which was doubtless suggested by many of the features that were familiar to him in the gardens that encompassed Hughenden. From such descriptions as these there is many a useful hint to be gleaned, and many an apt suggestion given, but it is not possible to find room here for more than the following extract, which is abridged from *The Carthusian*, and which cannot be excelled as a vivid word painting of a garden which, as a garden, must indeed have been perfection. The writer says:

> My garden is south of the house, the ground gradually sloping for a short distance till it falls abruptly into the tangled shrubberies. A broad terrace runs along the southern length of the building, extending round the west side also, for I would catch the last red light of the setting sun. Musk and Noisette roses and jasmine must run up the mullions of the oriel window, and honeysuckle and clematis, the white, purple, and blue, climb round the top. The upper terrace is strictly architectural; no plants are to be found there. I can endure no plants in pots – they are like birds in a cage. The gourd alone throws out its tendrils, and displays its green and golden fruit from the vases that surmount the broad flight of stone steps that lead to the lower terrace; while a vase of larger dimensions and bolder sculpture at the western corner is backed by the heads of a mass of crimson, rose, and straw-coloured hollyhocks, that spring up from the bank below. The lower terrace is of the most velvety turf, laid out in an elaborate pattern in the Italian style. Here are collected the choicest flowers of the garden in masses – the purple gentianella, the dazzling scarlet of

> the verbena, the fulgent lobelia, the bright yellow and rich brown of the calceolaria, here luxuriate in their trimly-cut parterres, and 'Broider the ground with rich inlay'.

191 Contrasts are charming even in descriptions, and lest the reader should think from this word painting that costly works and appendages are absolutely necessary to garden decorations and the laying out of gardens, let us turn for a moment from the stately but beautiful outline filled in with glowing colouring on which we have just been gazing, to another picture, whose charm lies in its simplicity, but in which the adoption of the terrace in the construction of a garden is urged with equal weight and reason by a practical writer of unexceptionable taste – Mr Noel Humphreys. This is his opinion on the matter, and it is one which may be easily followed by anyone who is disposed to do so, the circumstances of the site and its surroundings always permitting. Mr Humphreys says:

> 'I think that even a simple turfed embankment, surmounted by a low-cut hedge, formed of some hardy evergreen shrub, cropped very square, and flat at the top, might, either with or without the addition of a single flight of steps and with a few appropriate pedestals and vases, be sufficient to produce much of the desired effect. In accordance with the more irregular and picturesque forms of cottage architecture, the terrace might be guarded by balustrades of simple rustic work or branches. Even a rustic cottage requires to be accompanied by a moderately broad esplanade or terrace on its principal side, which, however, does not absolutely require expensive architectural embellishment; a neatly turfed embankment, raised a few feet above the surrounding garden, suggests the idea, even in that simple form, that a sufficiently high situation has been selected, and gives a pleasing air of propriety to the site of the dwelling. First, it suggests that a sufficiently high situation has been selected; secondly, that an amply sufficient space has been prepared for the erection of the building, and by its means is carried beyond the mere form of the house itself, in a manner that causes its vertical and horizontal lines to blend by degrees with the outline of the surrounding vegetation and the undulations of the ground.' With a trifling increase of expense, also, a rustic and somewhat more architectural approach might be given to this terrace, as shown in Fig. 25.

192 Having thus placed side by side, in immediate contrast, the more elaborate treatment of a terraced garden in keeping with a house of some pretension, and the simpler management, though similar in the principal feature that gives character to both, of a garden more in accordance with a dwelling that is at the same time smaller and less marked by architectural beauty, let us return to the garden scheme, if not the description of a garden in actual existence, set forth by the writer in *The Carthusian*.

> Pausing for a moment to call our attention once more to the 'mass of gorgeous colouring' that distinguishes the portion of the garden that we have already visited in fancy, and the two pretty fountains that play in their basins of native rock on either hand, he bids us 'descend the flight of steps, simpler than those of the upper terrace, and turn to the left hand, where a broad gravel walk leads to the kitchen garden through an avenue, splendid in autumn with hollyhocks, dahlias, China asters, nasturtiums, and African marigolds.
>
> 'We will stop short, however, of the walled garden to turn off among the clipped edges of box and yew and hornbeam, which surround the bowling-green, and lead to a curiously-formed labyrinth, in the centre of which, perched on a triangular mound, is a fanciful old summer house, with a gilded roof, that commands the view of the whole surrounding country. Quaint devices of all kinds are found here, for the garden is an ancient one, to which modern improvements have been added. Here is a sundial of

flowers arranged according to the time of day at which they open and close. Here are peacocks and lions in livery of Lincoln green. Here are berceaux and arbours, and covered alleys and enclosures, containing the primest of the carnations and cloves in set order, and miniature canals, that carry down a stream of pure water to the fishing-ponds below. Farther onwards, and up the south bank, winding towards the house, are espaliers and standards of the choicest fruit trees. Here are strawberry beds, raised so as to be easy for gathering; while the round gooseberry and currant bushes, and the arched raspberries, continue the formal style up to the walls of the enclosed garden, whose outer sides are clothed alternately with fruits and flowers, so that the "stranger within the house" may be satisfied without being tantalised by the rich reserves within the gate of iron tracery, of which the gardener keeps the key.

'Returning to the steps of the lower terrace, what a fine slope of green pasture loses itself in the thorn, hazel, and holly thicket below, while the silver thread of the running brook here and there sparkles in the light. And how happily the miniature prospect, framed by the gnarled branches of those gigantic oaks, discloses the white spire of the village church in the middle distance; while in the background the smoke drifting athwart the base of the purple hill gives evidence that the evening fires are just lit in the far-off town. At the right-hand corner of the lower terrace the ground falls more abruptly away, and the descent into the lawn, which is overlooked from the high western terrace, is by two or three steps at a time, cut out in the native rock of red sandstone, which also forms the base of the terrace itself. Rock plants of every description grow freely in the crevices of the rustic battlement which flanks the path on either side; the irregularity of the structure increases as you descend, till, on arriving on the lawn below, large rude masses lie scattered on the turf and along the foundation of the western terrace.

'A profusion of the most exquisite climbing roses, of endless variety, here clamber up till they bloom over the very balustrades of the higher terrace, or creep over the rough stones at the foot of the descent. Here, stretching to the south, is the nosegay of the garden. Mignonette, "the Frenchman's darling", and the musk-mimulus, spring out of every fissure of the sandstone; while beds of violets "strew the green lap of the new-come spring", and lilies of the valley scent the air below. Beds of heliotrope flourish around the isolated blocks of sandstone; the fuchsia, alone inodorous, claims a place from its elegance; and honeysuckle and clématis, of all kinds, trail along the ground, or twine up the stands of rustic baskets filled with the more choice odoriferous plants of the greenhouse. The scented heath, the tuberose, and the rarer jasmines, have each their place here; while the sweetbrier and the wallflower, and the clove and stock gillyflower, are not too common to be neglected. To bask upon the dry sunny rock, on a bright spring morning, in the midst of this "wilderness of sweets", or on a dewy summer's eve to lean over the balustrade above, while every breath from beneath wafts up the perfumed air, "stealing and giving odour", is one of the greatest luxuries in life.

'A little farther on the lawn are the trunks and stumps of old pollards hollowed out, and from the cavities, filled with rich mould, climbers, creepers, trailers, and twiners, of every hue and habit, form a singular and picturesque group. The lophospermum, the eccremocarpus, the maurandia, the loasa, the rhodochiton, verbenas, and petunias, in all their varieties, festoon themselves over the rugged bark, and form the gayest and gracefullest bouquet imaginable; while the simple and pretty snapdragon* weeps over the side, till its tiny pink threads are tangled among the feathery ferns that fringe the base of the stump.

* The writer does not mean the *Antirrhinum*, to which this name is given from the fancied resemblance of its flowers to the nose or snout of an animal, and which is called in familiar parlance the *snapdragon*, from the peculiar way in which the flower opens when pressed from behind and at the sides, and closes again when the pressure is relaxed, but refers to *Silene antirrhina*, a variety of the 'Catchfly' family, suitable for knolls and rockwork.]

'The lawn now stretches some distance westward, its green and velvet surface uninterrupted by a single shrub, till towards the verge of the shrubberies, into which it falls away in irregular clumps of evergreens and low shrubs, which break the boundary line of greensward. Here are no borders for flowers, but clusters of the larger and bolder kinds, as hollyhocks and peonies, rise from the turf itself. Here, too, in spring, golden and purple crocuses, daffodils, aconites, snowdrops, bluebells, cyclamen, wood-anemones, hepaticas – the pink and the blue – chequer the lawn in bold broad strips, the wilder sorts being more distant from the house, and losing themselves under the dark underwood of the adjoining coppice. The ground here becomes more varied and broken, clumps of double-flowering gorse, 'The vernal furze, with golden baskets hung'; the evergreen barberry, the ilex, in all its varieties, hardy ferns, bordering the green drive which leads to the wilder parts of the plantations.'

193 Such a garden as that which has just been described could not have embraced less than three acres, and it may have extended over even a greater area. We will now consider another typical garden which Mr Loudon, whose authority is great on such questions, describes and figures in his *Cottage, Farm, and Villa Architecture*, and which, in his opinion, when the size of the residence itself and the accommodation that both house and grounds afforded were taken into account, was as near perfection as possible, being more convenient and laid out to better purpose than any place of similar extent that he had ever seen. It should be said that the house had been built and the garden laid out by an architect for his own occupation. The land enclosed was two acres and a half, extending longitudinally from north to south, so that it would be, judging from the plan, 200 yards from north to south and 110 yards from east to west.

194 The following is the description given by Mr Loudon of the general plan of the house and grounds, which is represented in Fig. 29. He says: 'In this plan, A, on the south-east, is the main entrance; B, the entrance portico of the house; C, the kitchen and stable yard; D, the stable and coach house; E, a door in the wall bounding the entrance court, by which the grounds are entered without passing through the house; F, a circular bed for geraniums and other showy greenhouse plants; G, a billiard-room: H, a rosary in the horseshoe form, having a dial in the centre; I, a marble basin with a bronze fountain as the centre, the space of turf lawn between it and the gravel walk having beds of choice herbaceous plants; K is the tool and potting houses and working sheds; L, a grotto, having the appearance externally of a rock covered with ivy and creepers; M, a clump of American plants with ornamental vases, statues, and pedestals; N, a collection of choice herbaceous plants; O, wooded knoll, having an open grove of pine trees on the summit; P, shady grass walks; Q, a wire fence on the top of a concealed wall, or ha-ha; R, wall and fruit border facing the south; S, gardener's cottage; T, a plot for aromatic herbs; U, melon ground, sunk three feet beneath the general surface, and surrounded by a box hedge; V, the kitchen garden; W, a piece of rockwork projecting into the lake, and covered with creepers and rock plants on the west side; X, a fruit wall and border, with western aspect; Y, an octagon arbour or summer house, in the centre of which the proprietor has placed a magnificent vase from the antique, but in which position a statuette or jardinière would look equally well and be quite as appropriate; Z, a descent of three steps from the drawing-room to the garden.

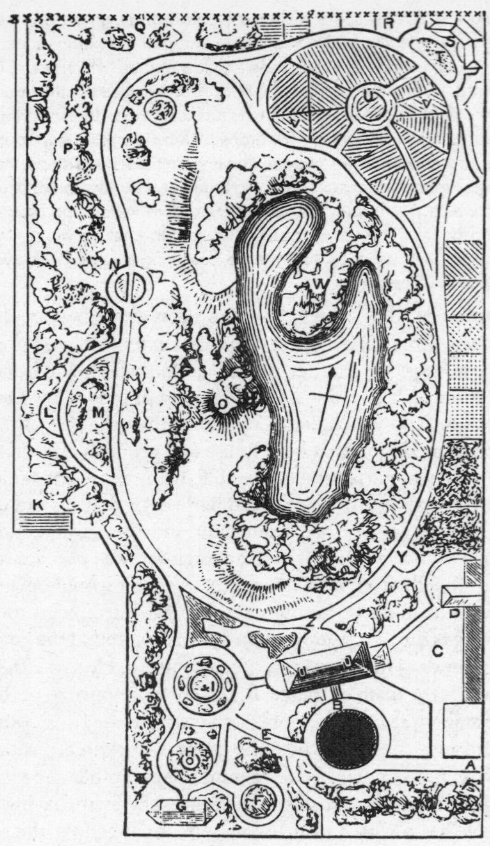

FIG. 29 *Plan for garden and grounds of two and a half acres*

195 The objects attained by this arrangement of the ground are, the utmost amount of space for exercise within the wall, with as much of variety and privacy as is consistent with views of the surrounding scenery, and the usual supply of fruit and vegetables. The more choice peaches and nectarines are placed on the wall R, which has a due south aspect; the wall X, with a western aspect, being covered with choice figs, apricots, and the more choice cherries, plums, and pears; apples, pears, plums, and cherries being also distributed through the grounds, as standard trees, along with some walnuts, eating or Spanish chestnuts, mulberries, quinces, medlars, and service trees. Mr Loudon's objection to this design, which, however, he considered almost perfect, was, that the lines were too formal and unbroken, and he proposed to remedy it by substituting for the defined margin of the American clump, M, the same plants, the lines being gradually lost on the turf, and by the introduction of more formal-shaped beds. The kitchen garden at V he considered a necessary evil, having no beauty as such, but placed so as to interfere as little as possible with the area of space sought to be created.

196 Hitherto our attention has been directed to gardens of considerable extent; let us now see how we may best deal with a single acre of land, which is to include house and offices as well as garden.

197 Even in the area of an acre much the larger portion is usually devoted to lawn, flower garden, and shrubberies, say two-thirds, which leaves one-third for the kitchen garden, exclusive, we will suppose, of melon ground, or, to speak more generally, a space devoted to the accommodation of frames and forcing pits. The latter ought to be about twenty yards square, walled or fenced round to the height of six feet, with a gateway leading into it large enough to admit a horse and cart. The drainage of the forcing ground should be perfect, the water from the pits and houses falling into a tank placed sufficiently deep in the ground to receive all the drainage from the dung beds and compost heaps. If this tank is within the kitchen garden, it will be an advantage, as the liquid manure that is obtained from it is invaluable in the cultivation of flowers and vegetables. In the space devoted to frames should be placed the potting sheds, and sheds for the preparation of composts, which should always be prepared under cover; and as the yard is by no means ornamental, it should be located as far as possible from the house.

198 In the plan exhibited in Fig. 30, A is the house; B, the conservatory; C, clump of American plants, consisting some of rhododendrons, ledums, and heaths; D, roses; E, flower beds, with coniferae in the centre; F, flower beds; G, jardinette, with fountain; H, borders planted with Alpine plants; I, vines or ornamental climbers; J, pears, cherries, etc., trained against the wall; K, verandah with climbers; L, carriage drive; M, arches over path for climbing roses and other ornamental climbers; N, fernery; O, turf lawns; P, shrubberies; Q, summer house; R, flower beds, with deodars in the centre, surrounded by turf; S, shady walk; T, flower border, fronting conservatory; U, flower border fronting shrubberies; V, melon ground and compost yard; w, back entrance, wide enough for carts to enter; X, range of three forcing pits; Y, vinery and forcing house; Z, tool house; A′, frames; B′, manure beds; C′, garden entrance; D′, tank for liquid manure.

199 The kitchen garden being thoroughly drained, trenched, and manured, and the walls in order, the following will be its first order of cropping: *a*, Jerusalem artichokes and horse radish; *b*, gooseberries; *c*, raspberries; *d*, red, white, and black currants in rows; *e*, strawberries, seakale, rhubarb, and globe artichokes; *f*, a row of pyramid plum trees, asparagus, seakale, and celery; *g*, pot herbs, potatoes, and peas; *h*, a row of pyramid apple trees, parsnips, carrots, and turnips; *i*, pyramid pear trees, cabbages, broad beans, scarlet runners, cauliflower, and early broccoli. On the south wall, peaches, nectarines, apricots, plums, and cherries. A walk, six feet wide, separates the main part of the kitchen garden from the broad south border, on which lettuces, radishes, early potatoes, early peas and beans, kidney beans, early strawberries, spinach, and early horn carrots, are to be cultivated.

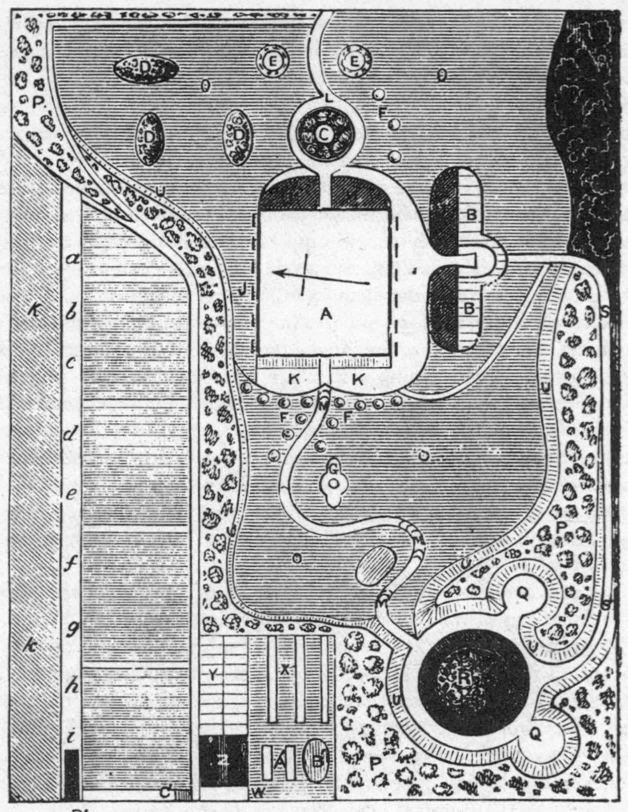

FIG. 30 *Plan for garden and grounds of one acre*

It will be understood that the above scheme for the disposal of the space allotted to the kitchen garden is general rather than special and positive, and serves as an indication of what may be done rather than what *must* be done; in all cases, the allotment of the area at command to particular fruits and vegetables must be influenced by the requirements of the family, and the preferences and predilections of those persons of whom it is composed. It will be noted that the suggestions are made for the first order of cropping only, and with the view to secure as much fruit as possible of all kinds. The main part of the kitchen garden, divided as it is into several small plots, might have the edges of each plot devoted to espalier apples and pears, or trees of these kinds trained on the cordon system, with pyramid trees at the angles, the central portions being devoted to vegetables. Nothing can be said here about succession of crops, which will be treated elsewhere, for it must not be supposed that the above system is intended to be permanent; it is given only as the first order at the formation of the garden.

200 In all theoretical gardening it is forbidden to crop the border on which wall fruit is planted; but this is rare in practice. The crops indicated above generally occupy such borders; but probably a line might be drawn beyond which such crops should not approach the wall. Supposing such a border to be sixteen feet, twelve feet might be devoted to such crops in the kitchen garden as require a warm, sunny border.

201 Where it can be so arranged, the garden should be a rectangular oblong. A very convenient form will be found in an oblong that is a length of 100 yards from east to west and a width of 30 yards from north to south, and about the proportions laid down in the plan given in Fig. 31. This allows the vegetables to range from north to south, which is always to be preferred, otherwise they get drawn to one side by the side light of the sun. The arrangement of the entire garden is as follows: A, the site of the house; B, the conservatory; C, a clump of trees and shrubs fronting the main entrance; D, coach house and stables; E, tool house; F, manure and frame yard; G, flower borders and shrubberies; H, ferns and American plants; I, rose clumps; J, circular beds for hollyhocks, dahlias, and other free-blooming plants in summer, and thinly planted with evergreens to take off the nakedness in winter; K, arbour; L, flower beds; M, lawn; N, paths; O, beds for placing out flowers in pots; P, kitchen gardens; Q, peach wall; R, west wall for plums, cherries, and pears.

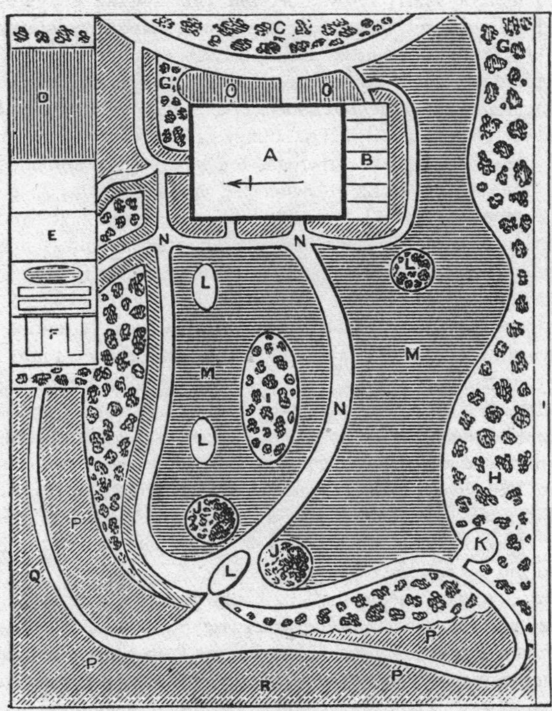

FIG. 31 *Plan for garden and grounds of about half an acre*

202 It is sometimes advantageous to have buildings and even groups of large trees contiguous to gardens: where these are situated to the north of the garden, they not only break and turn aside the cold winds, but concentrate the heat of the sun, a great advantage when early crops are required. They also preserve the crops during winter. Buildings have this advantage over trees, that they afford the shelter without robbing the soil of the food necessary for its legitimate crop. In the accompanying plan it will be observed that the whole frontage north of the house is laid out as lawn, and to the south, that the breadth of the house and offices is disposed in the same way; a single winding path running through it. South of the house lie the conservatory and offices, sheltered by a belt of shrubbery which runs round the whole lawn. The kitchen gardens occupy the north-west side of the ground, and adjoining it at the western extremity may be vineries, forcing houses, and orchard houses. The eastern boundary is a dwarf wall with green iron railings.

203 The gardens attached to villa residences in the suburbs of towns and cottages in the country vary in size, shape, position, and aspect: some are square, some – perhaps the greater number – oblong, and others irregular in form, ranging in size from a couple of rods, or about 60 square yards, to a quarter of an acre, or about 1200 square yards. The mode of laying out any garden must be influenced and ultimately determined by the size, shape, position, and aspect of the piece of ground to be treated. Let us endeavour to lay, down some general rules for our guidance in the disposition of small gardens, and then we shall be in a better position to apply them to a special piece of ground that may be taken as the prevailing type of a small villa or cottage garden.

204 First, then, in laying out a small garden, economy recommends simplicity of design, for intricate plans only increase the labour, and do not yield an adequate compensation. Still, there is a limit even to simplicity of design, and this should be carried only so far that it may not interfere with as much diversity as possible, for there is nothing that increases the pleasure to be derived from a small garden, or apparently adds to its extent, than as many objects as possible prominently brought out here and there to attract and rivet attention by turns as each comes under notice in a walk round the garden, whenever it may be taken. Supposing the frontage to be laid out as a flower garden, let the walks present curves rather than sharp angles, let the beds be circular or oval rather than pointed, and let the space for flowers be as open as possible. Nothing is more beautiful than a small green plot of grass on which one or two of the smaller ornamental trees may be planted, such as the silver birch or copper beech, or some sort of conifer, as a pine or cypress, an araucaria, now easily procurable, or a deodar. These do not create such a litter with their leaves as freer-growing plants, and will not so soon overcrowd the place.

205 Let the edgings of the flower beds, where edging is necessary, be of box, if obtainable – nothing is so handsome; otherwise thrift, white alyssum, or some of the ornamental grasses; or ornamental tiles are both cheap and elegant, and a grass verge from 6 to 9 inches wide, if kept in order, is always pleasant and attractive to look on. The path should be of gravel, if possible, or of coarse sand – even road sand is capital for kitchen garden walks, so also is burnt clay. In the present day, walks are sometimes made of a concrete of tar and pebbles, rolled and faced with sand, or of asphalt, but these kinds of walks are not desirable, except in such positions where it is desirable to find the path firm and dry even immediately after heavy rain.

206 Let the main parts of the ground be devoted to kitchen crops. If drainage is necessary, ascertain whither the water can be carried. Open a trench along the whole breadth of the plot, either into the intended outlet or into a well sunk in the ground, and into this trench lead the several drains from the higher part of the ground from one end of the garden to the outlet, gradually sloping towards the lower trench. If this be left open and kept clear, it will carry off all superfluous water; but if some brushwood is laid along the bottom, it may be covered and cropped over. Brickbats or stones will do, but pipes or tiles are to be preferred. Having done this, see to the construction of the walks: if pleasure be the object, do not grudge the space to be given up to them; but if profit be sought after by keeping as much of the ground as possible for cultivation, let one main walk pass through the centre, of about five feet wide, or more if it is to be made a drying ground. At the end of this main walk an arbour may be formed of the common white clematis or 'traveller's joy' (*Clematis vitalba*), of the white jasmine (*Jasminum officinale*), or yellow winter-flowering jasmine (*Jasminum nudiflorum*): these are suitable for the purpose, being of dense growth and habit, and very cheap. On each side of the arbour flowers or herbs may be grown. On the sunny sides of the house let a vine, apricot, peach, or nectarine be planted, seeing that a proper station is prepared for them, If there is a wall having a southern aspect, let it be devoted to some of these also; if not required for home use, they are saleable.

207 In the portion of ground devoted to kitchen crops, follow out a system of rotation cropping, and use a little caution in the application of manures; which, if unprepared by time and the action of the weather, or consisting of rank-smelling dung, breed no end of insects, which do injury to the crops. In preparing manures – which, however, are essential for maintaining the fertility of the soil – let it be remembered that all animal and vegetable refuse will be useful, when properly mixed. The droppings of cattle, sheep, pigs, and all house-sewage, should be collected and saved, and mixed with rather more than the same quantity of garden soil; the application of a little quicklime will remove any offensive smell. Let the offal, dung, etc., be laid in layers, about nine inches thick, mixed with similar layers of garden soil and quicklime, remaining so till a good heap has accumulated, when it should be turned over and mixed thoroughly before dressing the ground with it. Applied in this way, it is not so likely to breed insects, and is more efficacious. The system of grouping and rotation of crops cannot be discussed here for reasons already given, but must be reserved for a subsequent chapter.

208 We can now apply what has been said to a small garden attached to a cottage or villa residence, and we will take as our typical garden a rectangular piece of ground, measuring about 40 yards one way and 20 the other, this being the form that generally prevails in estates parcelled out in lots as building ground. We will suppose that, as in the plan shown in Fig. 32, the length of the

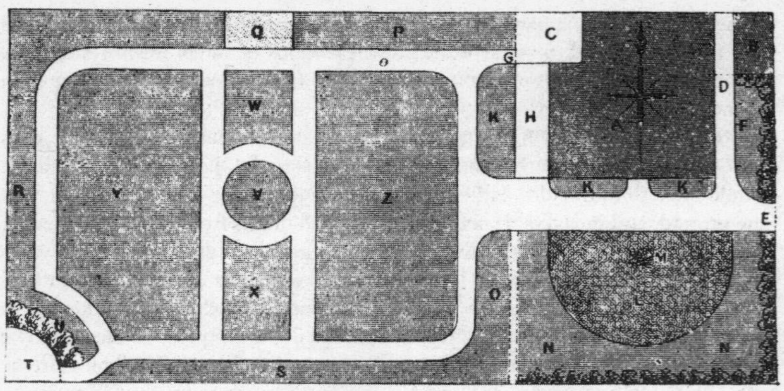

FIG. 32 *Plan for small villa garden and grounds of about* 800 *square yards*

garden lies east and west, and the breadth of it north and south. By such a disposition, we are enabled to obtain a good stretch of south wall. In this, as in former plans, A indicates the house, placed at the eastern end of the ground, or, in other words, very nearly in the north-east corner. In this position the house itself acts as a protection to a great part of the garden against north-easterly winds, B is a small court, well out of the way, reached from the back of the house, and appropriated to the dustbin and offices that it is desirable to keep out of sight. A door at D – a trellised door is sufficient – gives access to a path which enters the main path near E, the entrance from the roadway. The court D is masked by creepers and shrubs, disposed along a border, F, whose frontage is devoted to flowers that will grow in the shade. A piece of trellis divides the court C from the garden, which is entered from C by the gate G. A conservatory on the west side of the house is shown at H, and beds before the conservatory and house at K, K, K. Before the house is a broad gravel path, leading in a straight line from the entrance, E, to the main part of the garden. These and all the other paths are so distinct that no letters are required to distinguish them. Immediately in front of the house is a grass plot, L, nearly semicircular, with an ornamental tree at M. Surrounding this is a broad border, N, planted at the back with shrubs, in front of which are flowers. A dwarf wall may separate the shrubbery from the kitchen garden on the west side, and on this vases for flowers may be placed at intervals.

209 Thus, a third of the ground is devoted to the house and a small ornamental flower garden, and the remainder is available as a kitchen garden. The border K may be a vine border, if it is intended to grow grapes in the conservatory, H; the corresponding border, O, may be sloped as a bank, and appropriated to strawberries. Under the south wall, or wall which faces the south, on which peaches, apricots, nectarines, etc., may be grown, is a broad border, P, useful for early vegetables and the more tender crops. In the centre of this border, breaking its continuity, is a space, Q, which may be utilised as a frame for melons or cucumbers, or as a summer house, according to taste. R is a border before the east wall, on which plums may be grown: this border may be broad, as P, or narrow, as the border, S, in front of the north wall, on which plums and morello cherries may be grown, the border being utilised as a reserve garden in miniature. The corner, T, is set apart for manure and the reception of such rubbish as will accumulate in a garden, but cannot be immediately disposed of on the spot. Before it is a rockery and narrow border, U. In the centre is a circular bed, V, which may be devoted to a variety of purposes, as, for example, a rosary on a small scale, or a bed with a sundial, or even a fountain in the centre, or it may be converted into a circular basin for aquatic plants, with a fountain in the middle of it or piece of statuary, W, X, Y, and Z are pieces of ground which may be assigned for such purposes as the owner of the garden may prefer; for instance, W and X may be planted with currants, gooseberries, raspberries, etc., and vegetables raised in Y and Z. Pyramid apple and pear trees may be placed at the corners of these pieces, and espalier or cordon trees be trained between them. The object in forming this garden plan has been to get as much variety as possible into a limited space.

210 It is undesirable to quit this portion of the subject without a word or two on the disposition of allotment gardens and of ground appropriated to this purpose. It is unnecessary to linger in order to point out the many and great benefits which result from the allotment of a small portion of land for a garden to every cottage. These are so obvious that we may take them for granted here, and proceed at once to show how such allotments may be disposed to the best advantage. Many cottages, especially in small agricultural parishes, have land enough attached to them for the purpose of forming a garden which shall supply the wants of the family. The case, however, is different with cottages situated in populous villages and on the outskirts of large towns. Here, for the most part, a rod or two of land in front, and the same quantity for a yard at the back, the cottages being generally built in rows, is all that can be attached to each: now, under such circumstances, the want of a garden is well supplied by the allotment system. The field selected for garden allotments should, of course, be situated as near as possible to the cottages for which they are required, and it should have the convenience of a supply of soft water either from a pond or running stream.

The rent at which allotments are let must be determined by the value of land in the neighbourhood. It should include all rates, taxes, and other outgoings of a like nature, and may be fixed somewhat higher than the rent of ordinary farm land, but not so high as market garden ground. The extent of each allotment should be not less than a quarter of an acre, nor more than half an acre. Little benefit can be derived from less than the former quantity, and if half an acre be exceeded there is great danger that the cottager will become unsettled as a day labourer or mechanic, while his occupation will not be large enough to make him either a farmer or market gardener. Spade husbandry must be insisted upon, and each allotment, to all intents and purposes, be treated as a cottage garden. In an allotment of half an acre it is quite allowable that one-fourth may be cultivated in wheat or some other cereal and one-fourth in potatoes each year, or half in wheat and half in potatoes in alternate years; but certainly, in all cases, one quarter of an acre should be stocked with what are properly called garden vegetables. The same portion of land should not be cropped with wheat and potatoes in continual succession, but after two years a change should be made with the other portion which has been cropped with garden produce. Indeed, the soil must naturally be very good, and also be well done by, to admit of such a close succession of wheat and potatoes. Barley or rye may, with advantage, be made now and then a substitute for wheat, and mangold wurzel will at times profitably take the place of potatoes; some provision, of course, having been made for a sufficient quantity of these for the use of the family. In agricultural parishes, the growing of seeds – turnip, mangold wurzel, carrots, and parsnip seeds – either on a portion of the allotment ground, or, what is better, on the land attached to a cottage, is found profitable, especially where there are children who can assist in keeping off the birds while the seed is ripening. Seed-sowing will make a good change with wheat and potatoes; but it should not be encouraged, except in cases where the allotment exceeds the quarter of an acre.

211 The laying out and division of a field into its proper allotments is a matter of taste, and must be regulated by the shape of the enclosure. A square field of ten or more acres may be divided by two walks cutting each other in the centre at right angles; and another walk may be made along each side, and at such a distance from the hedge or enclosure as the size of the field may suggest. These walks, if thought desirable, can be made broad enough for a small cart to pass along. Beyond these, all that is required would be alleys or small walks between the different allotments: these last may be measured into the allotments, half to each occupier; but the larger and more important walks should not be measured in. If the field be enclosed with a bank and hedge, these should be kept in order at the joint expense or labour of the different occupiers of the land; and so also should the garden pump, if, from the absence of any supply of soft water, it should be necessary to sink a well. Dwarf apples and pears, etc., and all bush fruit, should be considered admissible; but no high trees should be allowed, as they may do harm to a neighbouring allotment, nor should any occupier be allowed to erect a greenhouse or shed, except under especial permission. Ordinary garden frames can, of course, be used, wherever they are desired. The land taken for allotment gardens, previous to being let to the different tenants, should be drained, and proper water courses provided.

Many persons recommend the building of a large shed for garden tools, etc., for the joint occupation of the tenants; but, as far as our experience goes, this is better avoided. Much ill feeling is often engendered among the tenants by the taking of each other's implements, and where property is left upon the ground in this unprotected state, an opening is given to petty thieving. It can be no great difficulty for a man, whenever he has an hour or two to spend in his garden, to take with him on his barrow, his spade, rake, and hoe, or whatever he may require, and if the allotment be too far off for him to carry these things to and fro, in our opinion, he is better without it. Very strict attention should be given to the payment of rent. The land should be let from Michaelmas to Michaelmas, and the rent paid half-yearly – the first half year's rent to be paid on account at Midsummer, and the remaining half at the year's end. No cottager, except of good moral character, should be accepted as a tenant. Proper cultivation, neatness, and order should be strictly enforced, and, where these are not attended to, the tenant should have notice to quit; a three months' notice, expiring at Michaelmas, is the fairest arrangement for all parties. Allotment gardens are best managed under direction of a small committee. A piece of glebe land, if such lie convenient, is perhaps the best that can be occupied for the purpose, and the clergyman of the parish should be chairman of the committee.

212 It has been thought better to make these general observations, which are the result of many years' experience, than to give copies of rules which are actually of no use; for all rules, though they embody the principles which we have laid down, must be adapted to their own particular cases. With regard to the cropping of allotment ground, the remarks on this subject which will be found elsewhere in this volume, and on rotation of crops generally as practised in villa and cottage gardening, will supply ample information.

FIG. 33 *Aralia papyrifera*

CHAPTER 7

Levelling and Laying Out

213 Having selected, enclosed, drained, and mapped out the site for house and garden, determined upon the lines of roads and principal walks, and decided upon the leading features of the place, the next step is to operate upon the ground itself; and in this, if in anything, it is desirable, and even necessary, to understand clearly each step that must now be taken in due succession, and, in short, everything that ought to be done, and how and why it should be done, in order to avoid alterations during the progress of ground work, which are vexatious to the workman and ruinously expensive to the owner of the ground. Perhaps there is no better mode of preventing such evils than by the formation of a model of the centre garden, on a small scale, in a box of sand, or on a large scale on a piece of ground. Not only can the mere outlines of walks, forms of beds, positions of vases, fountains, etc., be indicated by this means, but every irregularity of surface, depth and inclination of terraces, and even the effects of planting, can be thus vividly illustrated.

214 Having discovered by this, or any other method, what your garden is to be, the next point demanding attention will be the form of the surface and character of the soil. It is seldom that either will be found exactly adapted to our tastes or necessities; the former will generally require improving in form, and the latter in quality. Smoothness or evenness of surface is not only one of the elements of beauty, but constitutes the chief charm of every garden: not that the surface need be level; but the fall should be regular, the elevations nicely rounded off, and all small irregularities removed. The best form is to have the ground level for twenty or fifty yards round the house, and then a gentle incline beyond it. Occasionally, however, grounds will look very charming if they have a gradual rise at a distance of 100 to 200 yards from a dwelling-house. A very beautiful garden, which was in every respects satisfactory to the eye, was the result of the arrangement exhibited in section in Fig. 34, in which A represents the house, B a gravel walk, with grass plot, C, descending by a sloping bank, D, to a lawn, E, on a gentle incline, at whose base was a flower garden, F, extending to the edge of a bank, G, which sloped down to the water, H, which may be either an artificial canal or a natural river, the opposite bank, K, being laid out as a shrubbery. If the opposite bank had been nicely sloped down to the water, and planted with rhododendrons, the effect would have been even still more perfect. Such a garden as this would lose much of its attraction if the shrubbery were left rough and apparently uncared for, and an irregular run of ragged edges of earth exhibited along the water's edge throughout its entire length. The banks of all ornamental water in dressed pleasure grounds, whether composed of turf or stone, should descend several inches below the water line.

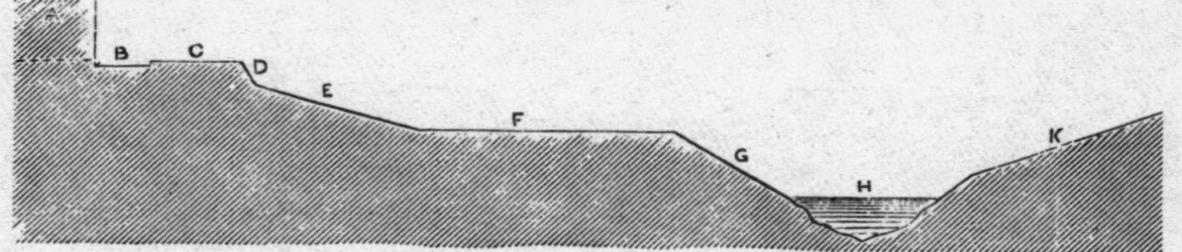

FIG. 34 *Section of ground with gradual rise from flower garden to house*

215 Another example of good taste in laying out gardens and ornamental grounds is shown in Fig. 35, which was taken originally from a gentleman's country seat in the county of Norfolk. The house stood on the side of a hill, sloping down to a most extensive, rich, agricultural, wooded valley beyond. It was surrounded with wide terraces, supported with massive walls finished with rich balustrades, the different levels being reached by magnificent flights of steps. Fig. 35 exhibits a rough section of the shape of the ground about the centre. A is the position of the house; B, the grand terrace, of different widths and levels, edged with scrollwork of box and white sand, filled up with deep bedding plants; C is the massive stone wall; D, a border for geraniums, with patches of hollyhocks, etc.; and E, a sloping lawn, furnished in some parts with fine large trees, in others with regular-shaped beds for bedding-out plants. At F is indicated a broad gravel walk, which skirts along part of the wood that occupies, in one part, the second slope, G; this slope being diversified at some points with clumps of trees, etc., and in others made available for ferneries, and enriched in colour by a ribbon border of dahlias, perhaps 200 yards long. A broad promenade of turf, H, probably 1500 yards long and 30 feet wide, bounded one side of the nearly level space, K, which was occupied with a succession of gardens in almost every variety of style, from tastefully embroidered patterns of box, sand, and flowers, through a succession of beautifully-grouped flower gardens, and bits, here and there, of the most perfect imitations of natural scenery. On the other side of these gardens was a walk, winding through beds of flowers, groups of shrubs, etc., laid out in the picturesque style; the whole being bounded beyond the walk by a belt of wood, and at each end by an extensive park.

216 Doubtless such positions as those which have just been described are the most commanding, and afford great scope for the display of cultivated taste and inventive genius. Sometimes, however, the grounds are level, and it is desirable that a distant view should not be obscured by a garden on the surface: in such cases, the ground is shaped as in Fig. 36; A being the house, B the gravel walk, C

FIG. 35 *Section of ground with successive slopes from terrace*

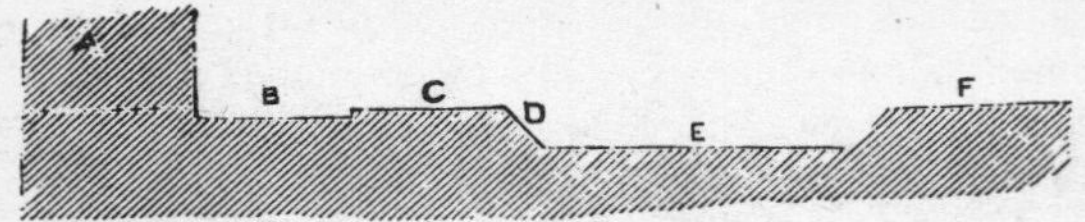

FIG. 36 *Section showing garden sunk below ground level*

The turf lawn, D a sloping bank, and E the garden, with rising bank, F, beyond. Occasionally, again, the ground rises from the house, and a garden has to be looked up to, as in Fig. 37; in all such cases, A being the house, and B a broad gravel drive in front of it, the ground should be levelled as far as C, and then either rise gradually, as shown at D, or suddenly, as at D in Fig. 38. When a garden is formed on the rising slope, the former method is generally best, as the beds meet the eye better. In the case of a site in which the ground rose rapidly towards the east, and was level on the south front, which commanded a magnificent view, it was determined to keep the front perfectly clear, and the garden was formed on the rising ground east of the house, as shown in Fig. 39, in which A represents the house, B a level esplanade in front of the house which looks towards the south, and C the garden.

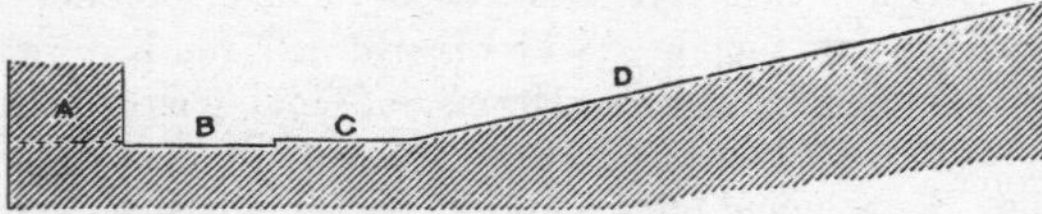

FIG. 37 *Section of ground rising from front of house*

217 Brick or stone walls will sometimes be better and more effective than earth banks for maintaining the different levels; they should incline towards the bank from 1 to 1½ inch, according to their height. Generally, it will be best to finish them with balustrading and vases: occasionally, however, the wall will look best if rendered altogether invisible from the inside, with a plain wall or walls on the outside – a kind of ha-ha. In all cases where walls are used, the different levels must be connected by flights of stone steps. The breadth of these from front to back, technically called the tread, may range from 15 inches to 2 feet, and the rise need not be less than 4 inches, but should not be more than 8 inches in depth. Turf steps should never occur on a gravel walk, nor stone on a turf bank.

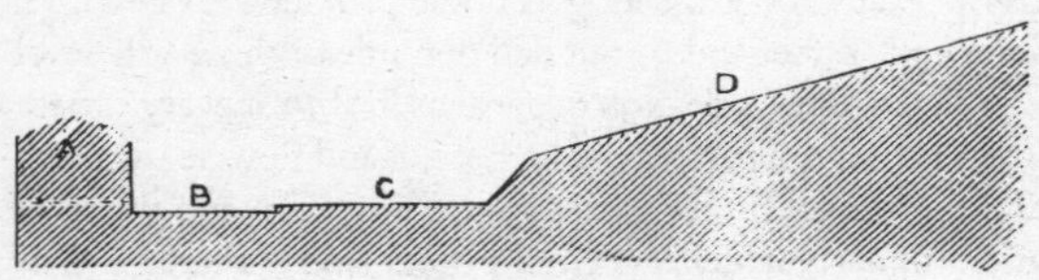

FIG. 38 *Alternative from for ground rising from front of house*

FIG. 39 *House with garden on rising ground at side*

218 But it is not possible, if it were

desirable, to lay out all gardens either upon level ground or on such as has a regular slope. Sometimes the intervention of rocks, the enormous quantity of material to be moved, and even the style adopted, may render this absolutely impossible or not desirable. As a rule, all geometrical gardens look best, and appear largest, on level surfaces; such a surface is also most effective for displaying the Gardenesque style. In the Picturesque style irregularities of surface may not only be useful but highly desirable. The sketches A, B, C, D, E, in Fig. 40, which represent bits of undulating or rising and falling country, partly in section and partly in superficies, will illustrate what is meant. It is obvious that if trees, shrubs, etc., are planted on these knolls, they will appear much larger and more effective than if placed on a level surface.

219 Having now considered a few of the many varieties of natural surface forms that may occur in ground selected for a garden site, and the modifications that it may be desirable to effect in them, let us now turn our attention to the means by which these modifications may be produced. No operation can well be more simple than that of levelling ground. All that is absolutely necessary are a few straight stakes of varied length, a mallet, an ordinary spirit level, and a straight-edge, as it is technically called, or a straight-edged piece of wood 10 or 12 feet long, 4 inches deep, and 1½ inch thick. It is necessary in this straight-edge that its upper and lower edges should be perfectly level and parallel throughout; as then, in order to ascertain that points on

FIG. 40 *Irregularities of surface in picturesque style*

two rods, at a distance from each other less than the length of the level, are themselves in the same level horizontal straight line or otherwise, the lower edge of the straight-edge may be applied to the points and the spirit level laid on the upper edge in a position equidistant from each of them. The bubble of air in the spirit level will then indicate whether the points are level, or if not so, which is too high or too low, as the case may be, to be level with the other. In some cases, the straight-edge and spirit level are combined, as shown in Fig 41. In this the upper edge of the straight-edge is not level with the lower edge throughout, but it is made of about twice the depth in the centre to admit of the insertion of the level in the centre midway between the ends, in such a manner that the upper surface of the glass tube of the spirit level is in the same straight line with the upper edge of the straight-edge on each side. Practically, the effect thus produced is precisely the same as if the straight-edge had been of one and the same width throughout and the spirit-level were laid upon it when the lower edge was applied to two points to test their relative position.

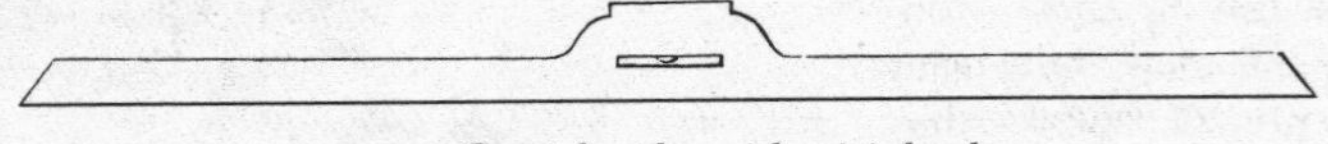

FIG. 41 *Straight-edge with spirit level*

220 Let us now see how these simple appliances may be made use of in levelling land. Suppose, then, that in Fig. 42 the solid line between A and B represents the natural surface of the land in section, and the dotted line the level to which it is desired to reduce it. Drive a stake into the surface of the soil at *a*, insert another at *b*, and ascertain that their tops are on a level, by applying the straight edge and level to them. Next drive in a third stake at *c*, and so proceed, inserting stakes at *d*, *e*, *f*, *g*, and *h*, and testing the level of their tops with the straight edge, until you have a level line of stakes throughout, from *a* to *h*. It is necessary that the stakes should be in a straight line, and this is best effected by driving in two stakes at, say, A and B, and then keeping the intermediate stakes in a regular row by glancing from A to B as each successive stake is driven in. Then, having determined the distance from the level line running along the tops of the stakes *a*, *b*, etc., to the level to be adopted, as shown by the dotted line AB, measure the same distance down from the top of each stake which is more than this distance above the natural surface of the soil, as *b*, *c*, *e*, *g*, and *h*, and a straight line passing through the points thus obtained must obviously furnish the required level, AB. It is manifest that all the stakes will not be driven to the same depth in the ground, as shown in the illustration, and this is the reason why stakes of various lengths are necessary, for while long stakes are wanted at *b*, *c*, *e*, *g* and *h*, and also at A and B, shorter ones can be used at *a*, *d*, and *f*. Nor is it absolutely necessary that all their tops should be absolutely on the same level, for it is enough to take any point in *a*, either *at* or *above* the surface of the soil, and to mark points on the other stakes at the same level, by aid of the straight-edge, from which the measurement can be made in a downward direction to determine the required level AB. This is shown by the short marks crossing the stakes, on a level with the natural soil at the spot into which the stake *a* is driven.

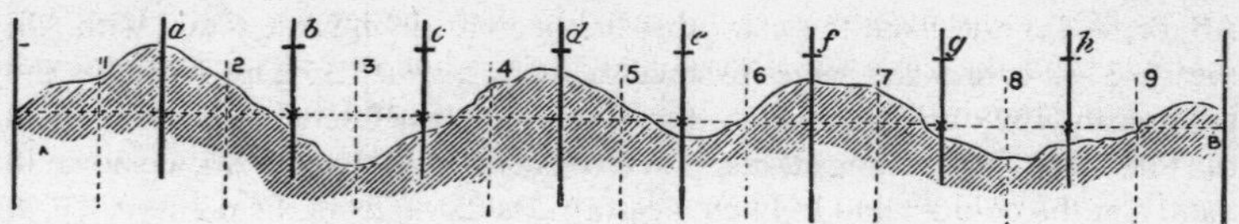

FIG. 42 *Method of levelling ground*

221 In the section that is exhibited in Fig. 42, there will be rather more earth to be moved than will be required to fill up the depressions on the surface. Sometimes this is an advantage, as the earth may be wanted elsewhere; but if it is otherwise, an excess of soil must be guarded against by a careful survey and correct measurement of the surface. Where this is the case, one of the simplest methods for arriving at a correct estimate is to dig out narrow trenches across the ground to be levelled, at distances of 20 or 30 feet apart, reducing these trenches to the requisite level. By carefully measuring the elevations and depressions in the ground left which the correct basis thus provided furnishes, the necessary data for the exact level which can be maintained by the soil on the spot can be correctly estimated. The trenches themselves can then be elevated or depressed at pleasure, supposing the level at which they were originally formed not to be the actual level that is required. When this plan is adopted, the dotted line AB would represent the trench formed, and the dotted vertical lines, numbered from 1 to 9, the levelling stakes. Of course, it will be understood that the trench can only be taken out in those portions of the ground which rise above the height of the line selected as the level. If it be desired to complete the level throughout the entire length of AB, the depressions between the elevations must be filled up to the necessary height.

222 Grounds with a regular slope in any one direction are managed in a similar manner. Supposing that it has been determined that the soil shown in section in Fig. 43 is to have a fall of 20 inches in 200 feet, proceed thus: Level the distance from A to B, having driven in the stakes *a* and *b* into the ground at AB. Look along the line AB, and at the distance of 200 feet from A drive in the stake *g*, and bring the top of this stake on a level with AB, or, what is precisely the same thing, if the top of the stake be above the level of AB, as shown in the illustration, make a mark on *g* that is in the same straight line with AB, as shown by the dotted line A*g*. Then on the stake *a* measure *upwards* from A the distance of 20 inches; and from the top of the stake *g*, if the top of the stake be on a level with

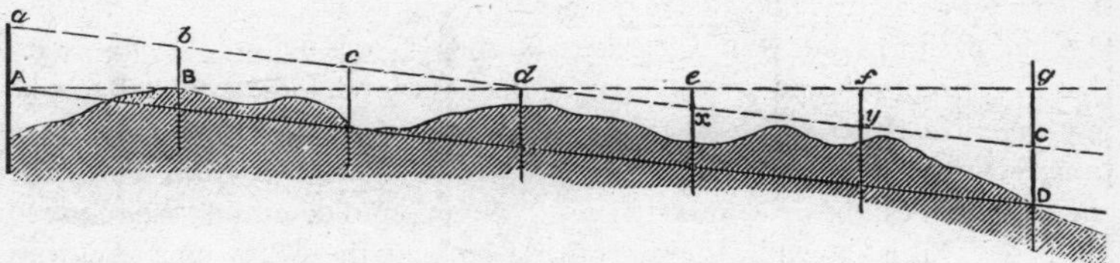

FIG. 43 *Levelling on regular slope*

AB, or, if it is not, from the mark that has been made in it on a level with AB, measure *downwards* the same distance, namely, 20 inches. This will give the point c, and the straight line from *a* to C will show the line which should touch the tops of the intervening stakes, as at *b*, *c*, and *d*, or intersect them, as shown in *e* and *f*, at the points *x* and *y*. Then measure *downwards* from the points *b*, *c*, *d*, *x*, *y*, and C, a distance equal to that from A to *a*, which in the case under consideration is 20 inches; and the straight line AD, which intersects each part at a distance of 20 inches from the top in the stakes *b*, *c*, *d*, and 20 inches from the marks *x*, *y*, and C in the stakes *e*, *f*, *g*, shows the line of the even slope from A to D that is required.

223 The theory of levelling on a regular slope is explained clearly, it is to be hoped, in the preceding section, but it is now necessary to show the mode of procedure that is adopted in actual practice in determining a regular fall by the aid of a spirit level. Let us suppose, as before, that an incline having a regular fall of 20 inches in 200 feet is required. Now, it does not take much calculation to show that, at this degree of inclination, the amount of fall in every 10 feet will be 1 inch. Taking AB in Fig. 44 to represent in section the natural disposition of the ground for 30 feet or rather more, drive in at A the stake *a*, leaving the top at such a height above the surface of the soil that the tops of all the stakes driven in at intervening points between A and the utmost extent of the ground to be regularly sloped may also be well above the surface. Then, at the distance of 10 feet from the stake *a*, drive in another stake, *b*, and as the fall in 10 feet is 1 inch, place a piece of wood 1 inch thick on the top of *b*, and drive the stake into the ground until, by the repeated application of the straight-edge and level, it appears that the top of the stake *a* and the upper surface of the piece of wood *x* are on the same level, as shown by the dotted line *ax*. Then remove the wood, and having driven in the stake *c* at the distance of 10 feet from *b*, put the wood on the top of *c*, as shown by *y*, and proceed as before, until the spirit level shows that the top of the stake *b* and the upper surface of the block *y* are on the same level, as shown by the dotted line *by*. The same process is carried out between the stakes *c* and *d*, and so on in like manner until the eleventh and last stake from *a* is reached. The tops of the stakes, *a*, *b*, *c*, *d*, etc., will now be in a straight line, as shown by the dotted line, *ad*, which indicates the slope required as far as inclination goes. In order to get the actual slope or inclined surface of the altered ground, it is only necessary to measure downwards an equal distance from the top of each stake, in order to get the true surface, AC, which corresponds exactly

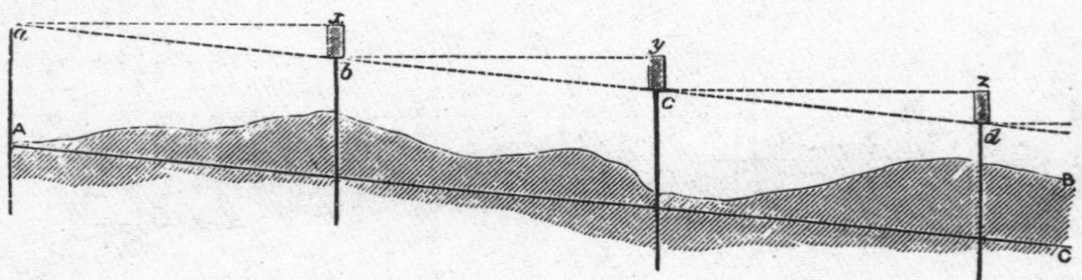

FIG. 44 *Determining regular slope with spirit level*

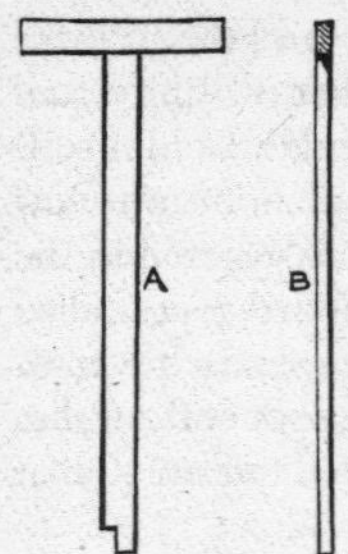

FIG. 45 *Borning piece*
A. Front elevation
B. End elevation

in inclination to the dotted line, *ad*, or, in other terms, is parallel to it. Thus, the amount of fall in any length being given, and the distance between the stakes ascertained, which, however, must be regular and equal from stake to stake, the thickness of the block required, as used at *x*, *y*, and *z*, will be at once determined.

224 But ground for which an even fall is required is perhaps most expeditiously levelled by the aid of three sighting pins, or 'borning pieces', as they are technically called, the term being derived from the French *borner*, to bound. The borning piece is made, as shown in Fig. 45, of two pieces of wood attached to each other at right angles, the vertical portion being from 3 to 5 feet long, 1 inch thick, and from 2 to 3 inches wide, and the shorter, or horizontal piece, being from 1 to 2 feet in length, but otherwise of the same dimensions as the upright piece. These pieces may be halved together or connected by mortise and tenon, so that when the instrument is complete it has the form of a **T**. A notch is cut in the bottom of the upright, as shown in the illustration, for the purpose of resting the borning piece on the top of a stake driven into the ground when it is necessary to do so. The pieces may be painted white, and the three should be of precisely the same height, and be notched, each and all of them, to exactly the same depth at the bottom. In order to use the borning pieces, having ascertained the level, as in Fig. 46, between two distant points, A and B, and having driven in a stake, *a*, at A, and another, *b*, at B, so that their tops are on a level, one of the borning pieces, C, is rested on the top of the stake *a*, and another, D, on the top of the stake *b*. Now, as the tops of the stakes *a*, *b*, are on a level, and as the length of the borning pieces, C, D, and E, are precisely the same, from the surface of the horizontal piece in each to the notch at the foot, it follows that the tops of the pieces C and D in the illustration are in the same straight line and on a level. An assistant must now be sent along the line of ground between A and B, to insert the stakes *c*, *d*, *e*, *f*, and *g*, as many as may be required, at equal distances, carrying the third borning piece with him. Each stake, when driven in, is tested, as shown at the stake *e*, by placing the borning piece on top of it, as shown at E. If the top of the horizontal piece appears in one and the same plane with the tops of the pieces at each end, the top of the stake thus tested is on a level with the tops of the stakes at A and B; but if

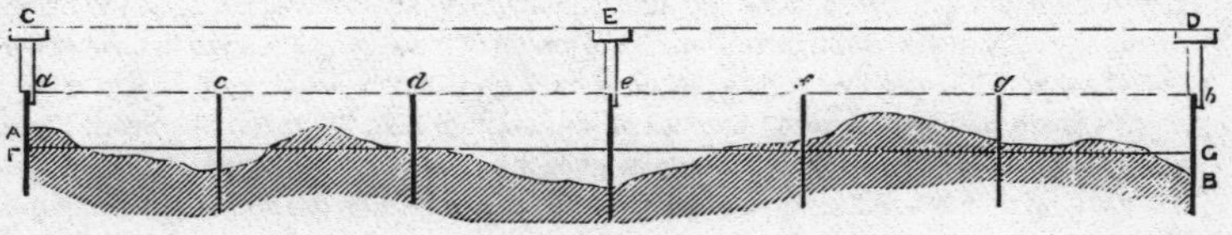

FIG. 46 *Levelling by means of borning pieces*

it shows above the plane, the stake must be driven in further, until the accurate level is obtained, and if it is found to be below it, the stake that is being tested must be raised. If the distance is too great to see the entire length from A to B with convenience, the observer, instead of continuing at one end, can follow within a few stakes of his assistant, or a borning piece may be inserted in the centre as well as at each end of the length to be levelled, and a fourth piece called into requisition to test the accuracy of level of the tops of the stakes driven in between the centre stake and the stake at each end. When the tops of the stakes have been brought on a level, as shown in Fig. 46, by the dotted line *ab*, all that is necessary to determine the required level of the soil, as along FG, is to measure *downwards* the same distance throughout from the top of each stake. After all that has been said, the application of the borning pieces to determine any regular inclined slope is obvious. In determining a dead level, the borning pieces may be placed on the stakes so as to look along the length of the horizontal piece from end to end, as shown in Fig. 46, or turned, as in the end elevation at B in Fig. 45, so that the eye may look from one to the other across the breadth of the horizontal pieces; but in determining inclinations, it is better to place the borning pieces on the stakes in the latter way.

Borning pieces are used for other purposes than the mere levelling and laying out large areas of ground. The borning piece is defined in *Chambers's Encyclopaedia* as 'a common and very simple implement used by gardeners in laying out grounds, to make the surface either level or of a perfectly regular shape. It consists of two slips of boards, one about 18 inches long and the other about 4 feet, the shorter fastened by the middle to one end of the longer, and at right angles to it. One borning piece being placed at one end of a line drawn in the piece of ground which is being laid out, with the edge of the shorter slip of board along the line and the longer slip erect, others of the same size are similarly placed at the other end and in other parts of the line; and the requisite uniformity of surface is obtained by filling up with earth or removing it, until, looking along their summits, it appears they are all in the same plane. The name is perhaps derived from the frequent application of the implement to borders or edgings.' The feet of the borning pieces used for levelling borders or edgings need not be notched. Loudon says that 'where box edgings are to be planted with accuracy and beauty, the use of these implements cannot be dispensed with.'

There are, of course, other methods of determining the levels of lines in gardens, and laying out ground, than those which have been described above; and the following mode of doing so, in determining the level of a line such as that which is intended for the edging of a walk, is simple and merits attention. It is taken from Thompson's *Gardener's Assistant*. The writer says: 'Prepare a lozenge-shaped piece of wood (as shown in Fig. 47) about 6 inches broad; paint it white, with the exception of an inch all round the margin, which should be black; also a strong black line across from angle to angle. A square hole cut on the upper side of the cross line admits of anything against which it is placed being marked exactly at the height of that line. If the length of the edging intended to be levelled do not exceed 600 feet, let a rod be placed at each end, and the instrument (that is to say, a spirit level) half way between these. Let an assistant hold the lozenge-shaped mark against the rod at one extremity of the line, while the person at the instrument directs him to slide it up or down till the line across its centre coincides with the line of sight from the instrument when the bubble is in the middle of the spirit-tube. Mark the rod at the height of the cross line, and in the same way the rod at the other end of the walk. The two points so marked on the rods at each extremity are in the same horizontal line.

FIG. 47 *Lozenge-shaped board for levelling*

'The instrument may now be removed, and a rod put in its place. By placing the cross line of the lozenge slide on one of the points to which the level was directed, and then viewing from the point at the other extremity, the rod placed in the middle can be marked at a point which will be in a horizontal line with the other two. There will then be three ascertained points on the same level; and by viewing between any two, as many more may be marked along the line as may be found necessary. Thus, on the rods placed between the two extremities, a series of points may be marked, all of which shall be in the same horizontal line. By measuring down a uniform distance from each of these points, the horizontal line which they marked may be transferred to the ground or to the height to which the edging is to be worked. If this height be determined at any place, then it is only necessary to measure down to it from the level point originally marked on the rod, and to the same distance below each of the level points the whole edging should be formed.

'But instead of being level, the walk maybe required to have a uniform slope, so that one end of it shall be, say, two feet lower than the other. In this and similar cases find the horizontal level points at each end as before; then mark a foot higher than the level point at the one end, and a foot lower at the other, and thus there will be a difference of two feet between these new points, and a straight line from one to the other will have the required slope.'

225 In bringing a certain area of ground to an even surface, whether on a dead horizontal level or on a regular incline, it is desirable to fix the level in such a manner as to prevent the necessity of casting away any quantity of soil to another spot, or of finding oneself compelled to bring soil to the place in order to make up for any deficiency. For example, a row of level points having been determined, as at *a*, *c*, *d*, *e*, *f*, *g*, and *b*, in Fig. 46, it is desirable to know as nearly as possible by calculation how far the level line FG ought to be below the level line *ab*, so that the elevations of the ground, when taken off, may exactly fill the depressions, or as nearly so as possible. The method that is generally adopted to effect this is to measure the depth from the top of each rod to the surface of the ground, to add the amounts thus obtained together, and to divide the total by the number of the rods. This gives the mean depth which should be measured downwards from the top of each rod, along each rod, to determine the line FG.

This method, however, is somewhat of a rough and ready mode of arriving at the result desired; and Thompson, in his *Gardener's Assistant*, proposes the adoption of the following mode as being more correct. Supposing that ten rods have been placed along the line, he says: 'To half the sum of the first and last perpendiculars, add all the others, and divide the sum by their number less 1; the quotient will be the mean depth of the space between the ground and horizontal line, and a line traced at that depth below the horizontal line will be the ground level to which, if the high parts are taken down, the soil from them will exactly fill the hollows. Suppose the distances from the ground to the level points marked on the ten rods' to be as per table below, and the mode of reckoning that has been described to be carried out, the average depth will be 3 feet 8½ inches.

'The sum of all their depths divided by their number,' continues Mr Thompson, 'would give an average of 3 feet 7½ inches, which is not far from the truth, because a considerable number of depths were taken. But supposing the number of perpendiculars had been only five, and that their lengths were respectively 4ft. 6in., 3ft. 6in., 4ft., 2ft. 6in., 5ft. 6in., then their whole sum, 20 feet, divided by 5, their number, gives 4 feet; whereas the correct mean depth of the space is only 3ft. 9in., the error being 3in.; but this would amount to an excess of 50 loads of earth in a border 300 feet in length by 20 feet in breadth.'

Rod 1	4ft 6in.

Rod 2	3ft 6in.
Rod 3	3ft 0in.
Rod 4	2ft 6in.
Rod 5	3ft 0in.
Rod 6	4ft 6in.
Rod 7	5ft 0in.
Rod 8	4ft 3in.
Rod 9	4ft 0in.

Rod 10	2ft 6in.

Sum of the first and last divided by 2	3ft 6in.
Sum of the other depths	29ft 9in.

Number of depths less 1 = 9	33ft 3in.

	3ft 8½in.

Mr Thompson, however, is in error when he says, 'The sum of all their depths divided by their number would give an average of 3ft. 7½ in.,' for the sum of the depths of the ten rods amounts to 36ft. 9in., and this divided by 10 gives an average of 3ft. 8⅒ in., which corresponds very closely with the average, 3ft. 8½ in., obtained by Mr Thompson's process. If a number of depths be taken, it will really matter but little which mode of calculating we use; but the greater the number of depths taken along the line, the closer will the result obtained be to absolute accuracy. Of course, in order to obtain a greater number of depths along any line, all that need be done is to insert intermediate rods or stakes between those that have been already driven in.

226 For levelling extensive tracts of country for railways, canals, etc., a theodolite, which is a spirit level raised on three legs and furnished with a telescope, is the instrument employed; but there is no necessity to do more than touch very briefly on the method that is adopted for levelling on a scale far larger than that which is involved in laying out garden ground. A quadrant is also frequently used for the same purpose, and for determining the level of drains, etc. The diagram exhibited in Fig. 48, and remarks, are taken from Loudon's *Self-Instruction for Young Gardeners*, the last contribution of that great and good man to a science that he loved better than his life.

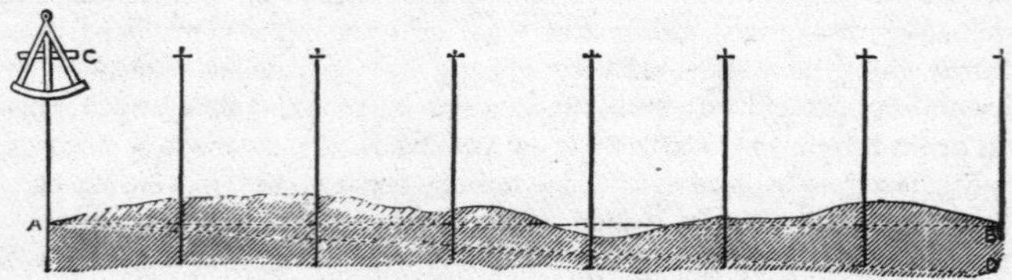

FIG. 48 *Levelling ground with quadrant*

227 'Suppose it were required to run a level through the ground indicated, AB, from the point A. Provide a few staves proportioned in length to the work in hand, and let them have cross pieces to slide up and down; then, having firmly fixed the staff, to which the quadrant is attached, in the ground, at the point A, set the instrument in such a position that the plumb line shall hang exactly parallel to the perpendicular limb of the quadrant; the upper limb will then be horizontal. This done, direct the eye through the sights, and, at the same time, let an assistant adjust the slides on each staff so as exactly to range with the line of vision. Then suppose the height AC to be 5 feet downwards from the upper side of the slide upon each staff, so shall the dotted line AB represent the level line required. Suppose the operation had been to determine a cut for a drain, to have a fall of 3 inches in every 20 feet, the distance between each staff in the above figure may be supposed to be 20 feet, then 5 feet 3 inches would have to be measured down the first staff, 5 feet 6 inches down the second, 5 feet 9 inches down the third, etc., etc. The dotted line AD would then represent the line parallel to the bottom of the intended drain.'

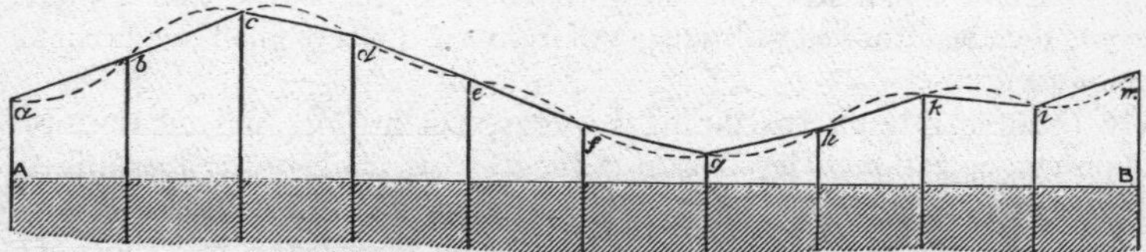

FIG. 49 *Outline of artificial elevation with stakes and cord*

228 Where elevations or mounds are to be thrown up, stakes should be inserted of the desired height, and a line stretched across their tops to show the conformation of the surface, as in Fig. 49. These stakes, in all garden operations, should range from 10 to 20 feet apart, 15 being a good average; they are not only necessary for ascertaining the levels, but enable the men to perform their work with the utmost ease and certainty as to the result. In the illustration of this method of producing the outline in section of an artificial mound or elevation by means of stakes and a cord, the stakes *a* to *m* are driven into the original surface, AB, which for convenience is supposed to be level, and the cord is then stretched from top to top, as shown by the solid line *abcdefghklm*. The cord should be drawn as tight as possible, and notches for its reception should be cut in the tops of the stakes. The outline afforded by the cord is approximate only, and consists of a series of straight lines from top to top of adjacent stakes. The outline that the soil will take when placed in position is indicated by the dotted line from *a* to *m*. The mode of procedure would be precisely the same if the surface AB were inclined or undulating.

229 One of the chief things to be attended to in levelling is to retain all the best soil for the surface: this increases the labour and expense, but is of the first importance in all garden operations. However, if judgment is exercised in the performance of the work, the surface soil can generally be passed over on to the

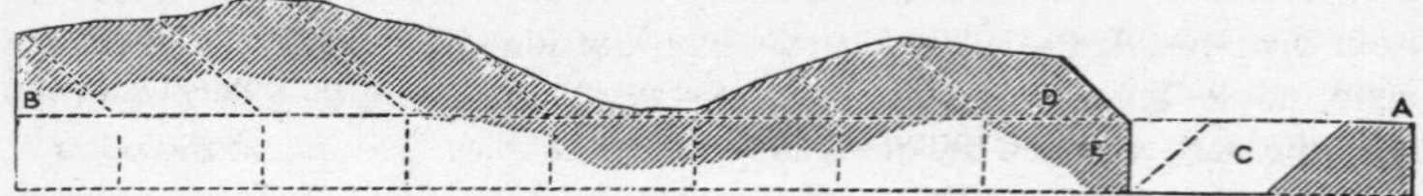

FIG. 50 *Mode of removing subsoil and retaining surface soil in levelling*

new level without the intervention of carts or barrows. This will be obvious from the section shown in Fig. 50, in which AB is the desired level, C an open trench from which the worthless subsoil below the line AB has been removed, and D the section of the next ground to be levelled. Of course, the surface soil would be thrown from D into the trench C, up to the level of the line AB, the fresh soil thus transferred assuming the form indicated by the dotted lines, being thrown against the soil already placed in position at A. The subsoil under D would then be carted or wheeled where it was wanted, forming a new trench at E, and the same process be repeated throughout the entire section, as shown by the dotted lines indicating the successive trenches from A to B. The new level would then be furnished with a depth of from 2 to 3 feet of good soil, fit for all cultural purposes.

230 Drains may be inserted during the progress of the work, and thus the three important operations of levelling, trenching, and draining, proceed at once. All garden ground should be trenched; for most purposes, from 3 to 4 feet is a good depth: even grass will *burn* less in hot weather, and look better at all times, if it has a depth of from 18 inches to 2 feet of good soil to grow in. The different effects of dry seasons upon lawns in the same localities arise chiefly from the varying depths of their soil: this has even more influence than their quality, for almost any poor soil will grow lawn grasses; and if too rich, the grass will become coarse, and militate against that elastic carpet appearance which constitutes the inimitable charm of British lawns. Where this is the case, part of the rich soil should be removed, and some of the poor soil mixed up with the surface intended for grass. Sometimes the soil of other parts is so poor as to be much benefitted by a liberal application of well-rotted stable or other manure. Generally, however, if it is well mixed, and not simply inverted, in the process of trenching, moved to a sufficient depth, and properly drained, the soil on the spot will grow most of the garden plants well. Roses, etc., will require a richer soil, and azaleas, thalmias, etc., peat earth to grow in. Rhododendrons generally grow almost as well, and flower better, in stiff sandy loam than in any other soil whatever. Where peat cannot be procured, rotten leaves converted into mould are the best substitute. If possible, all special soils should be introduced during the performance of the heavy ground work incident to levelling, trenching, etc. This will prevent newly-made lawns from being injured by wheeling on it before they are properly consolidated. Walks should also be made, walls built, and steps erected at this stage of the proceedings; but the surface gravel ought not to be put on until the turf is laid and all the rough work finished.

231 And now, having got the ground into shape, and all the heavy work completed, if operators and proprietors could only be induced to rest from their labours for nine or ten months, they would speedily gain double that time in enhanced rapidity of growth of trees and plants of every description, and obtain more satisfactory results. The fact is, the ground ought to be furnished with a *green crop* of some description, to ameliorate its texture and clear it from weeds. Any part, too, that had been made up from a greater depth than others would have time to subside between the time of levelling and laying out the ground, which should be commenced and carried out preferably in October and November, and the following October. However firmly the earth may be rammed, subsidence or settlement is, to some extent, unavoidable; and the intervention of a green crop would allow the whole surface to be overlooked, and little inequalities remedied before permanent turfing or planting. Nothing can well be worse practice than planting upon crude newly-exposed, fresh-drained land. Such land is often more or less puddled during the operation; and it will be several years before the action of drains and the percolation of rainwater will remedy this evil. As but few, however, will have patience thus 'to labour and to wait', and as what may be termed 'garden geometry' is a necessary sequel to and an essential part of, levelling and laying out garden ground, it is convenient to proceed at once with practical directions for laying down flower beds, etc., though, practically, it is far better that every one who has drained, trenched, and levelled his ground should prepare for a crop of turnips, carrots, and potatoes, and carry out these instructions next year.

232 In laying out a garden, whatever may be the purpose to which it is to be devoted, a working plan is absolutely necessary. All working plans, as they are termed, should be drawn to a correct scale, the larger the better – a quarter of an inch to a foot is a convenient size. Having provided ourselves with a strong garden line; several smooth round stakes, from 5 to 6 feet long; a quantity of small stakes to define the beds; a pair of wooden compasses, 5 feet in length, the legs being connected together with a perforated quadrant-shaped piece of iron, for fixing them at any distance required; a straight-edged piece of wood, say 10 feet long; and a square, with one limb about the same length – we proceed to business.

Mr McIntosh, in his *Book of the Garden*, gives a diagram and description of a very useful instrument, which it would be desirable to procure where there is much work to be done, although a line in a proper loop round a stake will perform the same work, but not quite so expeditiously. The instrument described by Mr McIntosh is 'an upright pole 2 feet in length, shod with iron, upon which revolves a metallic tube, with a projecting shoulder, to which is attached by a screw a wooden rod, 8, 10, or more feet in length, marked in feet and inches. Upon this rod there is a movable iron slide, with an iron sharp-pointed stud. The 2-feet pole being placed in the centre, or point from which the figure is to be described, the slide is moved along the rod to the proper distance, and fixed there by means of a screw. An iron handle, turned up at the end of the rod, about 18 inches in length, is taken hold of; and, as it is moved round, the iron stud in the horizontal rod describes the figure intended. This instrument is shown in Fig. 51.

233 The first operation in laying down a garden will generally consist in determining the centre of the ground to be occupied, and then drawing a baseline, intersected by a perpendicular, the whole length and width of the space to be occupied. These lines will furnish the starting-points of most of our

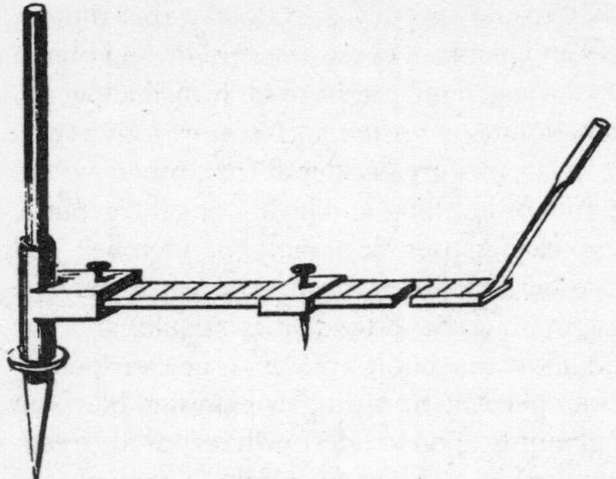

FIG. 51 *McIntosh's substitute for compasses in striking circles and arcs of circles*

measurements, and it is of the first importance that they should intersect each other exactly at right angles. Everybody knows how to make a circle, and all figures whose sides are part of a circle are formed by its division into different parts. For instance, a pentagon is a circle whose circumference is divided into five, a hexagon six, a heptagon seven, an octagon eight, and so on. If the operator is not furnished with a pair of large compasses, all regularly-curved lines can be described by a cord running loosely round a strong stake in the centre of the curve, and the divisions of the circumference can be easily made to furnish the polygon required by means of straight lines drawn from point to point. All regular figures, from an equilateral triangle to an octagon, are represented in Figs. 52, 53, 54, 55, 56, 57. These are so clear and suggestive of the method employed in describing them that little more need be said about them.

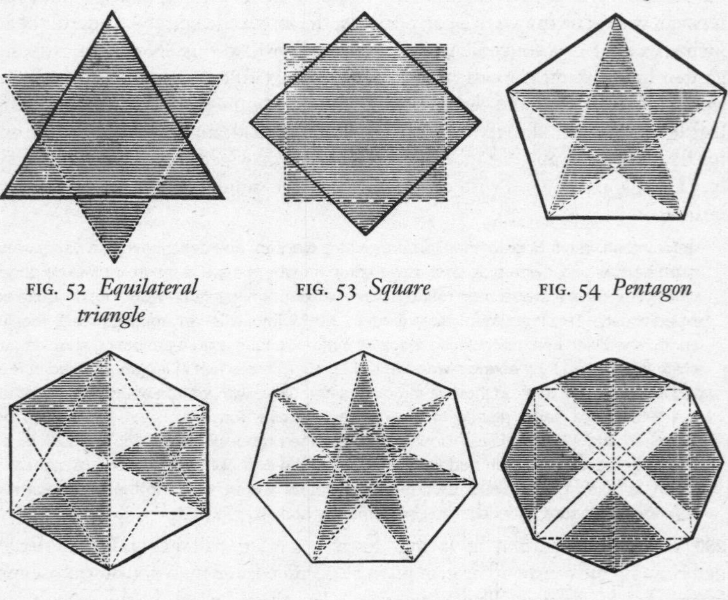

FIG. 52 *Equilateral triangle*

FIG. 53 *Square*

FIG. 54 *Pentagon*

FIG. 55 *Hexagon*

FIG. 56 *Heptagon*

FIG. 57 *Octagon*

It is obvious that in a work like this, though it is necessary to touch on geometry, it is impracticable to give directions in detail for the construction of each figure, and for this reason any reader who desires further information of this kind must be referred to a work on Practical Geometry, of which there are many in existence. The mode of describing a circle has been described, and it has been said that any regular polygon can be formed by dividing the circumference of the circle into as many parts as the figure has sides, and drawing straight lines between each pair of adjacent points. Now, the hexagon is the easiest figure to construct, because the circle in which it is inscribed may be divided into six equal parts without any alteration of the width between the extreme points of the legs of the compasses, because any and all the sides of a hexagon are exactly equal to the radius of the circle on which it is inscribed. Thus, if the radius of the circle be 3 feet, each side of the hexagon inscribed in it will be 3 feet, and so on. The equilateral triangle is equally easy to describe, when it is said that the circumference of the circle may be divided into six equal parts as for a hexagon, and the triangle completed by drawing straight lines between the *intermediate* points. The four points of a square may be easily determined by drawing or marking out on the ground two straight lines of sufficient length, and from the point of their intersection as a centre describing a circle cutting the straight lines already drawn at right angles to each other. The points in which the circumference of the circle cuts the straight lines at right angles to each other are those which must be joined by drawing straight lines between each pair of adjacent points in order to form the square. The pentagon and heptagon can be readily determined by geometrical process, but as they are too long to enter on here, the points of division in the circumference of the circle must be determined by trial. The octagon can be easily made by describing a square within a circle first of all, and then dividing into two equal parts each portion or arc of the circumference subtended by a side of the square. When straight lines are drawn from point to point in succession of the eight points thus found, the octagon will be formed. All that has been said above will be apparent on examination of Figs. 52 to 57 inclusive, but if the reader will look closely at each of these figures, and note the effect of the dotted lines drawn across them from point to point, he will see how many additional regular figures may be gained from them. These figures are indicated by the shaded parts, the original figure in each case being bounded and contained by solid black lines. Thus, the overlapping of two equal and similar equilateral triangles, as in Fig. 52, forms a six-pointed star, and a similar disposition of two squares, as in Fig. 53, gives an eight-pointed star. By drawing straight lines from each point of the pentagon, as shown in Fig. 54, to the extremities of the side that is opposite to it, a five-pointed star, known in heraldry as a mullet, is obtained. A similar procedure with regard to the hexagon gives a six-pointed star of the same form as that shown in Fig. 52, or three equilateral triangles meeting in a point, as shown by the shaded parts in Fig. 55. Finally, by treating the heptagon in the same way as the pentagon was treated, a seven-pointed star is formed, as in Fig. 56; and Fig. 57 suggests the formation of four rhomboidal beds, which should be divided by an intervening space of turf or gravel path.

234 Ellipses, or ovals, are figures which frequently occur in gardens, and as these present more difficulty in their formation than the circle or any polygonal bed based on the circle, it is better to describe here various ways of forming them to which the operator may have recourse. The chief point to bear in mind concerning them is that the length must always correspond with the width. In cases where both the length and the breadth are given, the easiest way to proceed is as follows: Mark out a line, AB, Fig 58, equal to the given length, and another, CD, equal to the given breadth, and intersecting AB at right angles at E, itself being also intersected by AB in the same point, E. Now take a distance

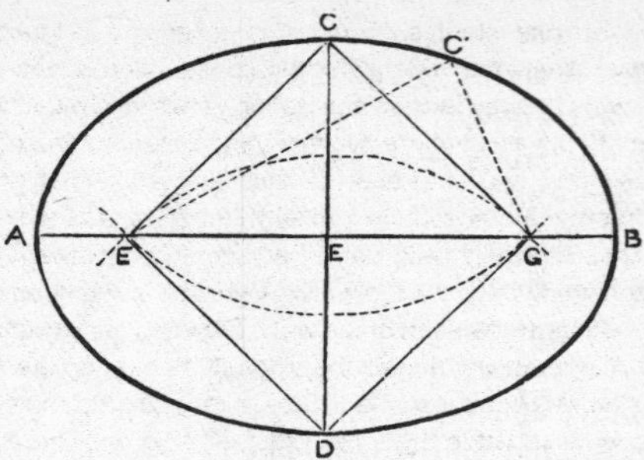

FIG. 58 *Ellipse whose length and breadth are known*

or radius equal to half the length of the ellipse – in this case equal to AE or BE – and with this radius, from the points C and D as centres, describe the dotted arcs shown in the figure which cut each other and the length of the ellipse, AB, in F and G. Drive two stout stakes into the ground at F and G, and having taken a piece of cord with a loop at each end, equal to AB, including the loops, slip one loop over F and the other over G, and then tightening the cord to the utmost with a stick or iron stake extend the cord till it touches the point A, and, keeping it tight, trace the curved line, ACBDA, which is the ellipse required. Thus it will be seen that the distance from any point in the circumference of the ellipse to F and G, taken conjointly, is the same in all cases, for FA + AG = FC + CG = FC′ + CG = FB + BG = GD + DF, and so on for any other point in the circumference of the ellipse that may be selected.

235 Ovals can also be formed by the aid of two, three, or four circles, as shown below. In Fig. 59, three circles are formed on AB, the centre line of the oval, whose length is given. The outer edges of the two end circles form the ends of the ellipse. Then draw CD at right angles to AB at the point of contact of the end circles, and also draw the straight lines, *de*, *ec*, *af*, and *ag*. Then from *a* as centre, with the radius *ag* or *af*, describe the arc *gf*, and from *e* as centre, with the radius *ed* or *ec*, describe the arc *dc*. The four arcs, *dg*, *gf*, *fc*, and *cd*, together make up the circumference of the required ellipse.

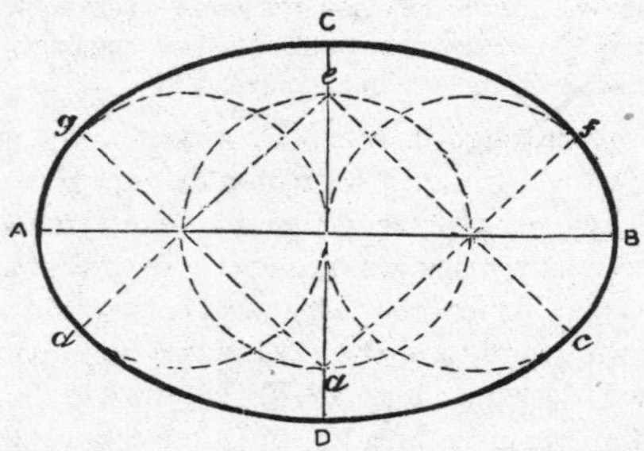

FIG. 59 *Oval formed of arcs of circles*

236 To make the ellipse shown in Fig. 60, describe two circles, A and B, whose circumference will touch each other. Take the diameter of one of these circles as a radius, and placing one foot of the compasses first in the centre of one of these circles and then of the other, draw arcs, as shown in the diagram, intersecting each other at the points *a* and *b*. Then from *a* and *b* as centres draw two more circles of the same diameter as those first described, to form the ends of the oval. Then draw straight lines through A and *b*, *b* and B, B and *a*, and *a* and A, as shown in the diagram. Lastly, from A as centre, with a radius AC or AD, describe the arc CD, and from B as centre, with a radius BE or BF, describe the arc EF. The four arcs, CD, DE, EF, and FC, together form the circumference of the ellipse, and the figure is complete. These circles may all be formed by means of a stake, to which a string is attached.

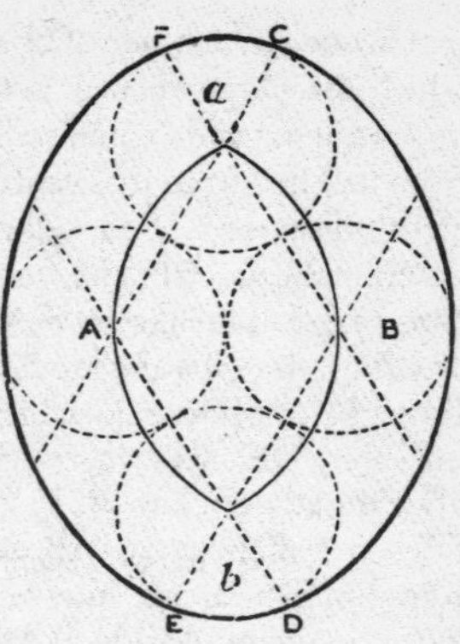

FIG. 60 *Another oval of arcs*

237 The method shown in Fig. 61 is still more simple. Divide the length, AB, into three equal parts, AC, CD, and DB, and let the two points C and D thus found be the centres of two circles, whose outside edges will form the ends of the oval. From the points E and F, in which the circles intersect each other, draw through C and D the straight lines, EG, EH, FK, FL. Then from E as centre, with EG or EH as radius, describe the arc GH, and from F as centre, with FK or FL as radius, describe the arc KL. The four arcs, GH, HL, LK, and KG, as in the cases already explained, make up the circumference of the oval.

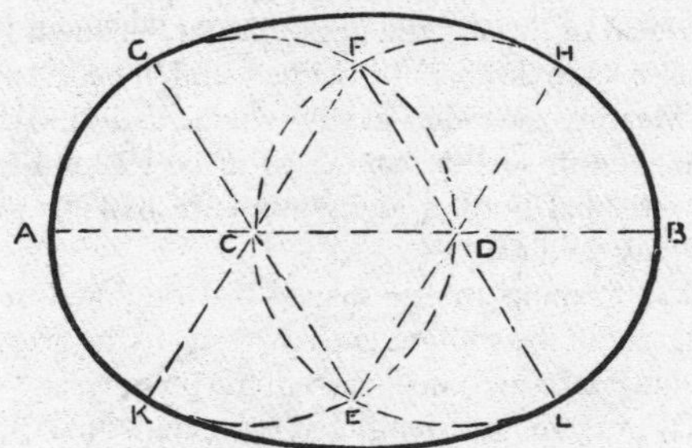

FIG. 61 *Third oval of arcs*

238 It has been supposed that everyone knows how to erect one line perpendicular to another. In case, however, this assumption is wrong, it will be as well to explain the very simple process by which this operation is effected. In Fig. 62, let AB be a straight line to which it is required to erect a perpendicular at C. Take any point, D, in CA, and make CE equal to CD, thus getting two points in AB, one on each side of C, at which the perpendicular is to be erected, and equidistant from it. Then from E as centre at the distance ED as radius, describe the arc DF, and from D as centre at the distance DE as radius, describe the arc EF. From F, the points in which the arcs DF, EF, intersect, draw the straight line FC to C; FC is perpendicular to AB. By continuing the arcs to intersect in G, on the other side of AB, and joining F and G, a straight line, FG, is obtained, which passes through AB at right angles to it.

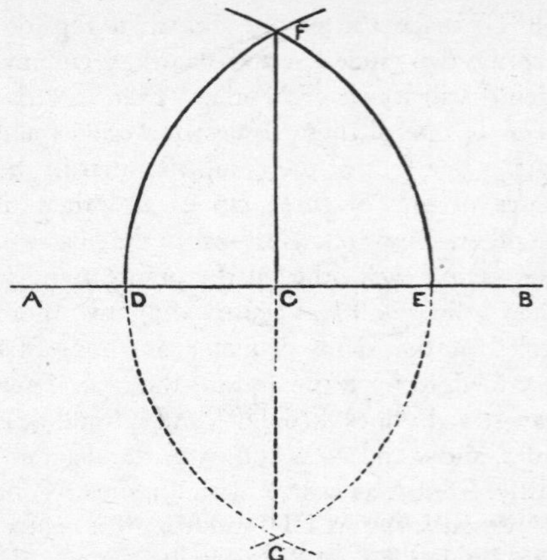

FIG. 62 *Mode of erecting perpendicular to a given straight line*

239 There are no better methods of forming curved spiral lines than the following systems: (1) *To form a volute with numerous spaces:* Make a circle around the centre of your intended volute, as much in circumference as you intend the breadth of your circuitous border to be. Stick the circumferential line full of pegs, and tie one end of a garden line to one of them; then, taking the other in your hand, go out to the point where you intend the volute to begin, and, as you circumambulate, holding the line strained tight, you will delineate on the ground the figure required. (2) *To form a spiral line where the border is narrower, towards the centre, like the shell of a snail*: Make a circle as before, and, instead of driving the pegs upright, let them form a cone; or, instead of pegs, use a large flowerpot whelmed, and, if necessary, a smaller one whelmed over it. Measure the radius of your volute, and wind that complement of line round the cone in such a manner as to correspond with the varying breadth of your intended border, and commence making the figure at the interior by unwinding the line.

240 The method of forming an egg-shaped bed exhibited in Fig. 63 will be found useful. First set out the straight line AB, equal to the greatest width of the bed required. Divide it into two equal parts in the point C, and through C draw the straight line DE, of indefinite length, at right angles to AB. Then from the point C, where AB and DE intersect each other, with the radius CA or CB, describe the circle AFBG Next, taking A and B as centres, with AB and BA as radii, describe the arcs BH, AK, and from the same points A and B draw through G – one of the points in which the circle AFBG cuts the straight line DE – the straight lines AL, BM, respectively cutting the arc BH in the point O and the arc AK in the point N. Lastly, from G as centre, with the radius GN or GO, describe the arc or quarter circle NO, which completes the figure. The outline of the bed thus obtained is shown by the solid line.

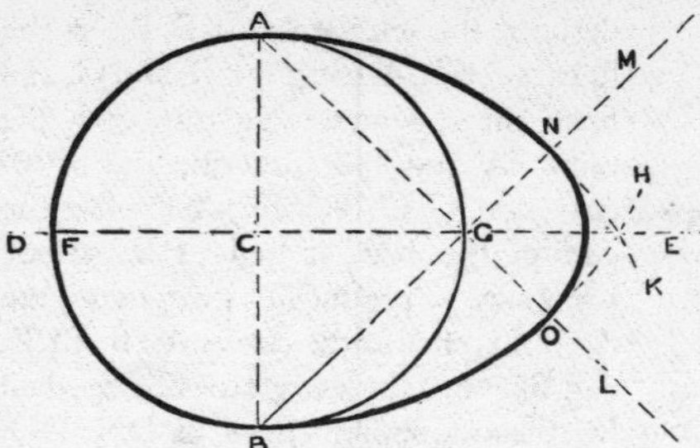

FIG. 63 *Egg-shaped bed*

241 The forms shown in Figs. 64, 65, 66, 67, and 68, are frequently found in beds cut in turf, or formed with box edging; and it may be useful to show as briefly as possible the modes by which they may be conveniently laid out. In Fig. 64, the first step to be taken is to lay out two straight lines, AB, CD, intersecting each other at right angles in E. Then from E as centre, with any length of radius that may be determined on, describe the circle FGHK. In this circle inscribe a square, FGHK, and from the points, L, M, N, O, in which the sides of the square intersect the straight lines AB, CD, describe the arcs FPG, GQH, HRK, KSF. A bed of the form shown by the solid arcs of circles will then be formed, consisting of four semicircles described on the four sides of a square. The simplest method of construction is to lay out a square first of all, as FGHK, next to bisect the four sides of the square in the points L, M, N, O, and from these points as centres to describe the semicircles FPG, GQH, HRK, and KSF, that form the bed; but the more elaborate mode of procedure has been given because it is suggestive of the formation of other beds – as a crescent, formed by the solid arc FPG and the dotted arc FG, which is a fourth part of the circumference of the circle FGHK. Other forms are those which are bounded by the solid arc FPG, and the dotted arcs FE, GE, or by the dotted arcs FG, GE, EF.

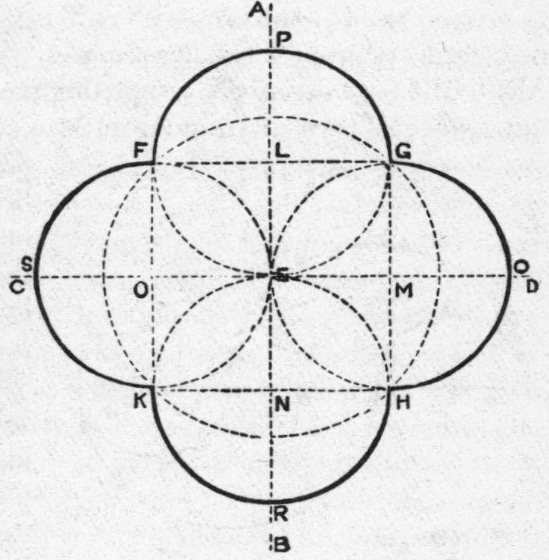

FIG. 64 *Bed formed by semicircles described on sides of square*

242 In Fig. 65, a semicircular ribbon bed is shown. To lay out a bed of this form, a straight line, AB, equal in length to the distance between the outer edges of the border, is drawn, and this is divided into any number of equal parts, according to the width of the bed that it is intended to make: if narrow, a greater number of parts will be required; if wide, less. In this case it is supposed to be divided into four equal parts, in the points C, D, and E. From the centre, D, at the distance, DA, describe the semicircle AHB, and from the same centre at the distance DC

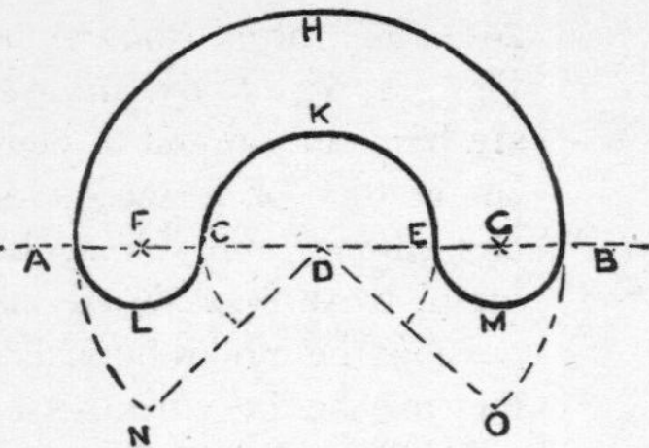

FIG. 65 *Semicircular ribbon of horseshoe bed*

describe the semicircle CKE. Bisect the lines AC, EB, in the points F and G, and from these points as centres, with the radii FA and GB, describe the semicircles ALC, BME, which complete the end of the bed. A bed of horseshoe form may be produced by extending the circumference of the circles AHB, CKE, and forming the extremities of the bed by drawing straight lines, as DN, DO, intersecting the circumferences of the circles. From Fig. 65, it may be easily seen how to form a bed of an **S**, or serpentine form, by repeating the process already described on the line AB produced towards A or B, or continuing it on the lines DN or DO produced towards N or O.

243 A bed in a serpentine form is shown in Fig. 66 which is very easily laid out. Firstly, a straight line, equal to the length of the bed from end to end, as AB, is marked out, and this is divided into three equal parts in the points C and D. The divisions AC, DB, are again subdivided into two equal parts in the points E and F. From E and F, as centres, with radii EA, EB, the semicircles AGC, BHD are described, and from C and D as centres, with radii CA and DB, the semicircles AKD, BLC, are described, completing the outline of the bed. By dividing AB into two equal parts in M, and from M as centre, with the distance MA on MB, describing the dotted circle ANBO, a bed of a curved pear-shaped form is obtained, as AGCLBO. The fault of the serpentine bed shown by the solid lines in Fig. 66 is that it is too sharp at the extremities. Another serpentine form that has not get this fault is shown in Fig 67. In this the straight line AB is divided, as in the above, into three equal parts, and each of these parts is again subdivided in E, G, and F. Perpendiculars on opposite sides of AB are erected to AB at E and F, as EH and FK. In EH, take EL, equal to EA or EC, and in FK take FM, equal to FB or FD. Join LM, and from L through C draw LN, and from M through D draw MO. Then from L as centre, with radius LC, describe the arc ACP, and from M as centre, with radius MD, describe the arc BDQ, and next from the same centres, with radii LQ, MP, describe the arcs QR, PS. Join AR, BS, and bisect them in T and U; erect perpendiculars TV, UX, to AR, BS, at the points T and U, and from V and X (where these perpendiculars cut LR, MS) as centres, with radii VR, XS, describe the arcs AR, BS, which complete the figure.

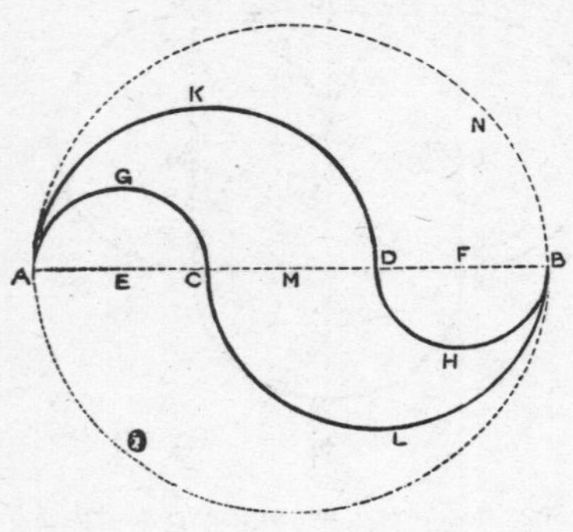

FIG. 66 *Serpentine bed*

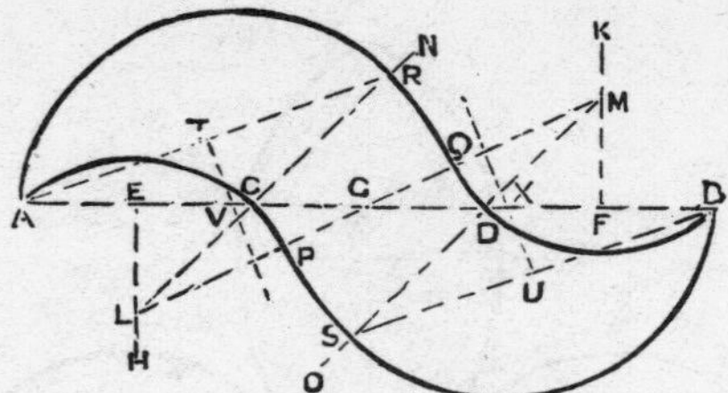

FIG. 67 *Another serpentine bed*

244 A cordate or heart-shaped bed is formed as in Fig. 68 by dividing a line AB into four equal parts in the points D, C, E. Then from D and E as centres, with radii DA and DB, the semicircles AFC, CGB, are described, and from the same points as centres, with radii DB, EA, the arcs BLH, AKH, are described, which intersect each other in H, and complete the figure. By dividing AB into six equal parts in the points M, N, C, O, P, and by describing the semicircle AQB from C as centre, with radius CA or CB, and the semicircles ATN, NRO, and OVB, from M, C, and P as centres, a fan-shaped figure enclosed by dotted lines is obtained, and by completing the circle AQBS, a bed similar to that shown in Fig. 65, but in different proportions, is exhibited. Lastly, by the larger and smaller semicircles disposed about the straight line AB, a birdlike figure, with symmetrical wings, is shown; and another bed, bounded by the semicircles AFC, CGB, above the line AB, and the semicircle ASB below it. All these forms may prove useful in various positions, and will suggest modes of setting out geometrical gardens in curved lines.

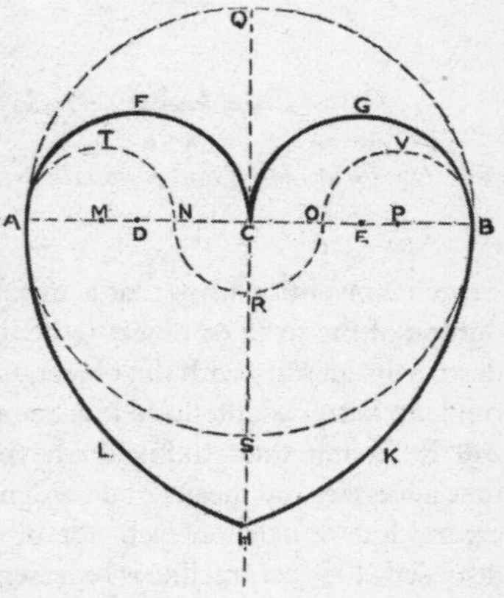

FIG. 68 *Heart-shaped and other beds*

245 At times it happens that a bed is desired whose form is not in strict accordance with any of those figures whose construction is treated and explained in works on geometry. For example, a fleur-de-lys might be required; and for the sake of showing those who may wish to mark out their own beds how figures may be formed on geometrical principles, however difficult their outlines may appear to be, it will be helpful, perhaps, to show how a fleur-de-lys may be drawn geometrically, being mainly formed by arcs struck from certain centres. It is in the determination of these centres that the difficulty chiefly lies in laying out this or any other bed whose outline is chiefly composed of arcs of circles. The design is

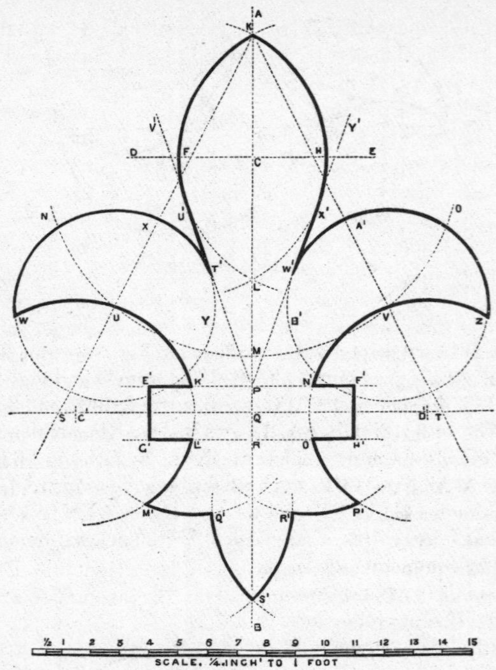

FIG. 69 *Fleur-de-lys conventionally treated and geometrically laid out for flower bed*

treated conventionally – that is to say, such changes are effected in the general outline of the form or object to be delineated as, while they do not in any way destroy its identity with the object, natural or otherwise, from which it is taken, render it better adapted and more suitable for the purpose it is intended to serve.

246 Referring, then, to Fig. 69, having determined the position of the bed, it is first necessary, by means of a garden line and a couple of stakes, to lay down a central line or axis, on each side of which the bed itself will be symmetrically disposed. This central line is represented in the figure by the straight line AB. In this straight line, at a suitable distance from the end A, select a point C, and through C draw the straight line DE at right angles to AB, and measure off along the line DE, CF and CH, each equal to 2½ feet. The figure is constructed on a large scale, and is shown on a scale of ¼ inch to a foot; the size of the bed, however, may be regulated at pleasure by changing the scale – for example, if the scale of the bed be taken at ½ inch to a foot, then CF and CH will be each equal to 1¼ foot, and the actual size of the bed when cut will be just one half of what it would be if carried out on a scale of ¼ inch to a foot. By what has been done we have now obtained two points, F and H, at a distance of 2½ feet from the point C, and therefore at a distance of 5 feet from each other. From the point F, with the radius FH, describe the arc KHL, and from the point H, with the radius HF, describe the arc KFL. These arcs give the outline of the upper end of the central lobe of the fleur-de-lys. To trace these arcs, drive in stakes at F and H, and have a piece of garden line with a ring at one end that may be slipped over each stake in turn, and a pointed iron at the other, round which the free end of the line may be wound until the required length of radius is obtained.

247 From C now measure off along AB and towards B, CM = 7 feet if the scale be taken at ¼ inch to a foot, or = 3½ feet if taken at ½ inch to a foot, and from C as centre, with the radius CM, describe the arc NMO. From the point M set off along AB, and towards B, MP, PQ and QR, each equal to 1 foot (I shall from this point leave off calling attention to any difference in reading the scale, as my readers can work this out for themselves), and through Q draw the straight line ST at right angles to AB. Along this line, in opposite directions from Q set off QS and QT, each equal to 6½ feet, and from K draw the straight lines KS and KT, through the points S and T. These lines cut the arc NMO in the points U and V, at which, as also at the points P and R, stakes should be driven in. From the point U, with the radius UX, equal to 3½ feet, describe the circle WXY; and from the point V, with the radius VA′, describe the circle ZA′B′. In these circles we obtain the upper arcs of the side lobes of the figure, whose extent will be determined presently.

248 Through the points P and R, now set off the straight lines E′F′ and G′H′, each at right angles to AB, and therefore parallel to the central line ST, and along ST, in opposite directions from Q, set off QC′ and QD′, each equal to 6 feet. Then, from C′ as centre, with radius C′U, describe the arc WK′L′M′, cutting E′F′ and G′H′ in K′ and L′, and from D′ as centre, with radius D′V, describe the arc ZN′O′P′, cutting E′F′ and G′H′ in N′ and O′. In the arcs WK′ and ZN′ we obtain the lower arcs of the side lobes the figure, and the arcs L′M′ and O′P′ of the extremity of the figure below the transverse bar. Now set off PE′ and PF′ in opposite directions from P along the straight line E′F′, each equal to 3½ feet, and RG′ and RH′, each equal to 3½ feet, along the straight G′H′ from R, and also in opposite directions from this point. Join E′G′, F′H′, and the transverse bar of the fleur-de-lys is completed. Then from K′, with a radius equal to 4½ feet, describe the arc M′Q′, and from N′, with the same radius, describe the arc P′R′. Lastly, from P′ as a centre, with a radius equal to 5 feet, describe the arc Q′S′, and from M′ as centre, with the same radius, describe the arc R′S′.

249 The lower part of the figure is now completed, and all that is left to be done is to connect the upper part of the central lobe with the upper arcs of the side lobes. This is done by laying down from P the straight line PV′, touching the circumference of the circle WXY in T′ and the arc KFL in U′, and the straight line PY′, touching the circumference of the circle ZA′B′ in W′ and the arc KHL in X′. By the addition of the straight lines T′U′, W′X′, the outline of the fleur-de-lys is now completed in every part, and is exhibited in the diagram by a thick and solid line, the portions of arcs and straight lines that are not included in the outline of the figure being in dotted lines. If space permitted, a handsome cross might be formed of four beds similar to this, disposed so as to bring the lowest point S′ in each to the distance of about three or four feet from each other.

250 It is possible that many gardeners, professionals as well as amateurs, may find a little difficulty in setting out straight lines at right angles to each other, or, in other words, in setting out one or more straight lines at right angles to another straight line, as the straight lines DE, E′F′, ST, and G′H′ at right angles to the straight line AB in Fig. 69. A contrivance for doing this without any trouble whatever is shown in Fig. 70, and this may be easily made by anyone who can accomplish a little simple joinery. The first thing to be done is to cut out and plane up two slips of wood, 3 or 4 feet in length, about 3 inches broad, and ¾ inch thick, as represented by BC, DE, in the figure. These pieces, when accurately halved together and secured by screws, will present the form of a cross, whose arms are at right angles to one another. Notch the ends of the arms of the cross with rectangular notches, their points or apexes being exactly in the straight line running through each slip from end to end, equidistant from its edges. Paint the cross itself black, and the straight lines forming the central line of each slip white, and at their point of intersection at A bore a hole from ½ inch to ¾ inch in diameter. Now when a straight line has been set out by means of stakes and a garden line, as AB in Fig. 69, it is manifest that when the cross is passed *under* this line – that is to say, the garden line – the line itself will lie along the white line DE, if DE be the slip that is placed beneath it, and that when the hole at A is brought directly over the point C in Fig. 69, and another line is laid along and over the white line BC, the line thus laid down will be at right angles to the first line, AB. And provided that the four arms of the cross are of equal length, as they should, be, a square, BDCE, may be immediately and quickly traced by putting in stakes in the ground, one in each notch at the ends of the arms, and laying down lines from stake to stake. Or if marks be set between A and B, and A and C, at equal distances from A, as at L and M, a diamond may be formed by laying down the lines DL, DM, EM, EL; and, by turning the cross so that the white line DE is brought into the position FH, and BC into that of KG, by laying

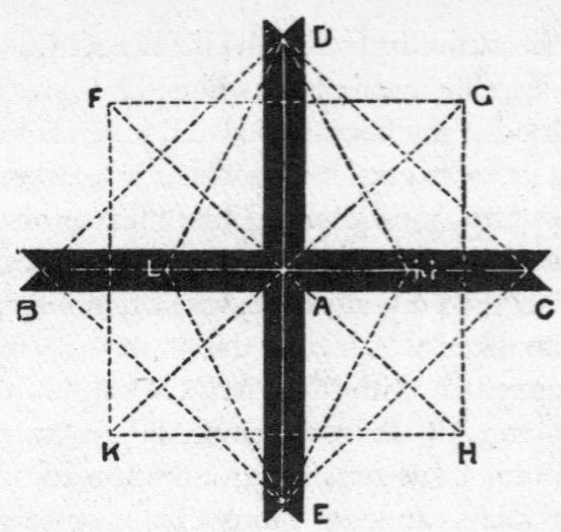

FIG. 70 *Contrivance for setting out lines at right angles*

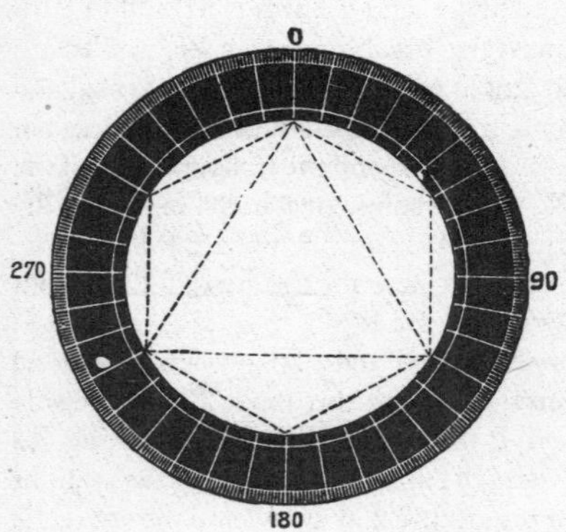

FIG. 71 *Protractor for gardeners*

down the lines FK, KH, HG, GF, forming another square, an eight-pointed star, having the points B, F, D, G, C, H, E, K, will be produced.

251 In laying out beds and determining the inclination of straight lines at certain angles to each other, a protractor on a large scale, as shown in Fig. 71, will be found useful. This will assume the form of a broad ring, whose inner and outer edges are concentric circles. It may be easily made by cutting out arcs of wood of the necessary radius, in board ⅜ inch thick, and arranging them in a double circle, so that the joints in the circle above come about the centres of the pieces forming the circle below, and vice versa, and then screwing the whole firmly together to form a solid ring of ¾ inch in thickness. For the inner edge of the ring, 2 feet will be found a sufficient radius, and from 2 feet 4 inches to 2 feet 6 inches for the radius of the outer edge. The surface of the ring should be painted black, and two circles traced on it, one at the distance of 1 inch within the outer edge, and the other at the same distance within the inner edge. The inner zone thus formed, and the central zone also, may be divided into spaces of 10 degrees, but the outer zone should be perfectly graduated in spaces of 1 degree, as shown in the figure. It will be useful to indicate the common centre of the concentric circles forming the ring, and traced upon it by wires traversing the central space from the points marked 0 and 180, and 90 and 270. These wires are not shown in the illustration.

The circumference of a circle, it is almost needless to say, is divided into 360 degrees, a semicircle into 180 degrees, and a quadrant into 90 degrees. The number of degrees in an angle at the centre of any regular polygon, subtended by the side of the polygon, is obtained by dividing 360 by the number of sides in the polygon; thus, the angle subtended by the side of an equilateral triangle is obtained by dividing 360 by 3, which gives 120. If, then, stakes be placed at intervals of 120 degrees round the inner or outer edge of the protractor, and straight lines traced from stake to stake, an equilateral triangle will be formed, as shown by the dotted lines traced in the interior of the figure. Similarly, as an angle of 60 degrees is subtended by the side of a regular hexagon, or six-sided figure, this figure may be obtained by setting stakes round the protractor at intervals of 60 degrees, and drawing lines from stake to stake, as also shown in the interior of Fig. 71. Larger figures may be obtained by laying out lines from the centre across the proper marks of division to any extent, and taking points in the lines thus obtained, equidistant from the centre, from which to lay down lines to form the boundary of the regular figure required.

Polygon	Number of sides	Angle at centre of Polygon	Polygon	Number of sides	Angle at centre of Polygon
Equilateral Triangle	3	120° 0′	Decagon	10	36° 0′
Square	4	90° 0′	Undecagon	11	32° 44′
Pentagon	5	72° 0′	Dodecagon	12	30° 0′
Hexagon	6	60° 0′	Polygon of 13 sides	13	27° 42′
Heptagon	7	51° 26′	Polygon of 14 sides	14	25° 43′
Octagon	8	45° 0′	Quindecagon	15	24° 0′
Nonagon	9	40° 0′			

In the preceding section it has been shown that the number of degrees in an angle subtended by the side of any regular polygon is obtained by dividing 360 by the number of sides in the polygon. It may be convenient for many to have a table showing the angles at the centres of regular polygons subtended by each side of the polygon, to which recourse may be had when using the protractor illustrated in Fig. 71. The angles are given for all regular polygons, from the equilateral triangle to the quindecagon, in degrees and minutes, as closely as can be done without resorting to seconds and fractions of seconds.

		SCALE		
MEASUREMENTS		½ inch to 1 foot	½ inch to 1 foot	½ inch to 1 foot
Semi radius, CF = CH	=	2½ feet	1⅞ feet	1¼ feet
Radius FH = HF	=	5 feet	3¾ feet	2½ feet
Radius CM	=	7 feet	5¼ feet	3½ feet
MP = PQ = QR	=	1 foot	9 inches	6 inches
QS = QT	=	6½ feet	4⅞ feet	3¼ feet
Radius UX = VA′	=	3½ feet	2⅝ feet	1¾ feet
QC′ = QD′	=	6 feet	4½ feet	3 feet
PE = PF' = RG′ = RH′	=	3½ feet	2⅜ feet	1¾ feet
Radius C′U = D′V	=	4 feet	3 feet	2 feet
Radius of arcs M′Q′, P′R′, from centres K′, N′	=	4½ feet	3⅜ feet	2¼ feet
Radius of arcs Q′S′, R′S′, from centres P′, M′	=	5 feet	3¾ feet	2½ feet
E′G′ = F′H′	=	2 feet	1½ feet	1 foot

These tables, without doubt, will be suggestive and helpful to many, both professionals and amateurs, in designing and tracing the outlines of flower beds on geometrical principles.

252 A design for a geometrical garden is shown in Fig. 72, which maybe cut in turf or formed with box edging, with gravel walks between the beds. The entire centre of the design is shown in the illustration, and a full quarter in the upper right-hand corner. From this a working drawing, showing the garden complete, may easily be made. In forming this design, the first step will be to drive in a stake at A, which is the centre of the eight concentric circles that form the main path in successive rings, from the middle to the exterior limit of the garden. This done, set out the straight lines BC, DE, intersecting each other in A at right angles, and the diagonals FG, HK, which also intersect each other in A at right angles, and make angles of 45° with the lines AB, CD, at the common point of intersection, A. If a point be taken on any of the straight lines passing through A, midway between Nos. 2 and 3 of the concentric circles, and another concentric circle be struck through this point, as M, for example, the centres, L and N, of the circles in the first zone of borders next the borders forming the centre, and the centres, K, M, H, G, of the inner curves of the elliptic borders arranged round the central border, and of the curves of the central border itself, will be found at the points in which the dotted concentric circle intersects the straight lines proceeding from the central point, A. The centres, O, P, Q, of the small circles of the outer zone of borders are in the points in which the straight lines drawn through A are intersected by another concentric circle described from A as its centre midway between the circles numbered 6 and 7. With regard to the curves that form the beds in the second zone of borders, R is the centre of the curves lettered T and U, and s the centre of the curves lettered V and W. Lastly, X and Y are the centres of the curves that form the spearheaded corner bed at F and the paths on the inner sides of it. From the data given, the figure can be easily completed. With the corner beds, the design may be used for a square geometrical garden; without them, it represents a circular garden.

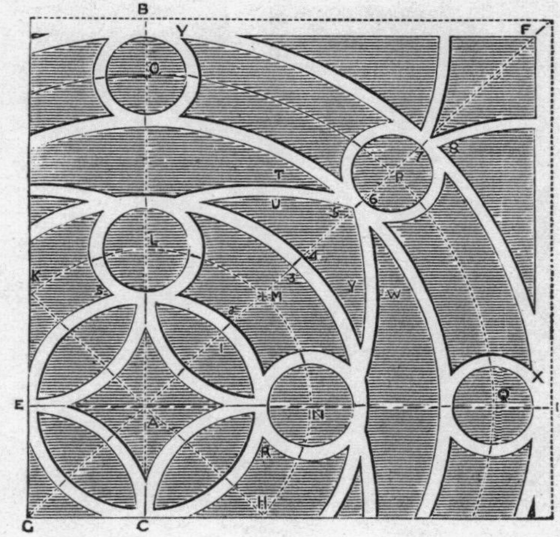

FIG. 72 *Design for geometrical garden*

253 Fig. 73 represents the centre and a quarter of a garden in the Dutch or French style. It is most readily formed by drawing the centre and the four semicircles at the sides, then drawing the diagonal lines, and, finally, the straight ones. This garden, if sunk about 18 inches or 2 feet beneath the surrounding surface, would have a beautiful effect when looked down upon.

FIG. 73 *Design for geometrical garden in dutch of French style*

254 Fig. 74 represents a quarter of a geometrical garden in a more stiff and formal style, the other three parts being exactly the counterpart of that which is given. Beginning at the centre, it would be easily transferred to paper by dividing the dotted

FIG. 74 *Formal geometrical garden*

circle into an octagon, having the horizontal sides at top and bottom, and the perpendicular sides to right and left, longer than the four diagonal ones; the other lines being mostly straight, no instructions for their construction are necessary.

255 Irregular figures and elaborate patterns in box are not so easily managed as beds cut in turf, although many of them are susceptible of being formed upon certain and easily-ascertained principles. In cases, however, where it is otherwise, and the tracery is capricious and difficult to reduce to rule, there is no better mode of transference to the ground than by running lines across it in all directions, so that the ground is divided into a series of squares of equal size, corresponding to the same squares on the paper reduced to a scale. Holding the paper in one hand and a pointed stick in the other, almost any design may be copied in this manner. Of course, the plan on the paper will be divided into squares in the same manner as the ground. It would also facilitate the transference of all plans, if the chief points of formation were boldly indicated.

256 Generally, gardeners make rough plans for their own use; and certainly every design must be fully mastered on paper before there can be the slightest hope of success in placing it on the ground. It will be observed in the plans that are given in Figs. 72, 73, and 74, that the spaces between the beds are of uniform width throughout. No plan ever looks satisfactory on the ground if this desideratum is not carefully observed. Sharp, irregular, angular pieces of turf or gravel, leading nowhere, may look very well on paper, but are most disappointing on the ground. Unless there are embroidery patterns of box or different-coloured surfaces, lay it down as a rule never to be infringed that the spaces between the beds, whether occupied with turf or gravel, shall be of one uniform width throughout. The distance between them and the main walks should also be the same at all points; and, as a rule, this distance should be greater than the width between the beds. The distance of one figure from another must be determined by the size of the figures. On grass, however, it should never be less than 3 feet, and need never exceed 12 feet. Small gardens on gravel may have the figures closer together; but if the paths between them are much under 3 feet, the beds will have a miserable puny appearance. For large gardens, 5 feet will be a good average width for the paths; for large gardens on grass, 6 is also an excellent average; and 5, 4, down to 3, for those of smaller dimensions.

257 Sometimes gardens are laid down on a mixed plan of grass and gravel. When each bed is edged with brick, stone, tile, or cement, these edgings are occasionally surrounded with from 2 to 4 feet of gravel, succeeded by the same or a greater width of turf. Flagstones are also used for this purpose instead of gravel, as well as to subdivide groups of figures close to the dwelling-house. Beds on grass, however, unless much elevated above the surface, are most effective without any edgings whatever; although, in certain situations, raised beds, with massive edgings of stone or rustic work, look well. Single beds of this description often have their tops converted into the form of baskets, tents, etc., to be covered with climbing plants or roses, with excellent effect. For beds on gravel, an edging of some kind becomes imperative. Of all living edgings, box is the best; thrift, echeverias, sedums, and saxifrages of various kinds, follow each other in value and adaptability for this purpose, in the order in which they are here named. Ornamental stone, tile, brick, or cast iron edgings, are probably better than any living edging whatever. They can neither harbour insects, exhaust the soil, nor look patchy through dying off; and, although perhaps more expensive in the first instance, the first expense is the only one. They can be purchased on the most reasonable terms, and of the most chaste patterns and varied and elegant designs. Whatever edgings are used, they must vary in height and thickness with the size of the beds they define. Nothing can be in worse taste than a heavy, massive edging surrounding a small, delicate pattern, or vice versa.

258 On sterile, uncongenial soils, it has been recommended by Mr Loudon and others to enclose all the flower beds with a brick wall to the depth of 2 or 3 feet, so that the soil may be entirely removed at pleasure. Where this is attempted, the walls would form an excellent base for the edging to rest on; and where such an operation is unnecessary, a layer of concrete 6 inches deep will afford the requisite solidity and stability. Groups of beds, or single figures for roses, may often be edged with tiles of good design and embellished overhead with Gothic or other arches of wire-work, to be covered with the climbing varieties. Such erections, while objects of great beauty in themselves, also diversify the sky outline of our gardens, and relieve that monotonous beauty which seems almost to be incident to our present methods of furnishing them.

259 As the art of laying out grounds has now been set forth in such a manner as to enable every lover of a garden to form his own, and thus heighten his enjoyment by adding to his other pleasures the high and satisfying pleasure of constructing, and even carrying out, if needs be, his own designs without the assistance of others, a few hints may now be given concerning other special departments.

260 *Reserve Gardens* Utility, or fitness for the object in view, must be the principle embodied in laying out this department. This, however, is quite compatible with neatness and order; in fact, these are well nigh indispensable to utility. To manage any piece of ground on the haphazard rule-of-thumb want of principle is the surest mode of making it of the least possible use.

261 No better system of laying out a reserve garden can be adopted than making a few good walks through the ground, and forming the remainder into beds, say four feet wide, and of any convenient lengths. Part of the ground can be left without division into beds, for raising hollyhocks and other large-growing plants, or for growing dahlias, etc., for exhibition or other special purposes. The beds will be used for raising annuals or biennials, for propagating choice varieties of pinks, carnations, polyanthuses, etc., and for providing a reserve stock for verbena borders and flower beds, and performing any operation that might render other departments unsightly. Roses might be budded, choice shrubs layered, seedling rhododendrons, etc, raised and nursed, new varieties of all bedding plants preserved, and any desirable or necessary experiments to find out the capabilities of any given plant made, in this department. Rich beds could also be provided for growing and layering chrysanthemums, salvias, etc., for potting in the autumn. The beds need not be divided by any formal walks of gravel; alleys cut off with the spade, from one foot to eighteen inches wide, will suffice. The relative position of beds and paths could then be changed every second year, and the whole ground enjoy the benefit of the highest culture.

262 In wet weather, a few boards may be thrown down on the earth paths by the men, when they come for the plants for transplanting, in order to keep the walks clean. A dry soil – of great importance everywhere else – is essentially necessary here; as the three great agents in the germination of seeds are heat, moisture, and air. An excess of moisture, however, by reducing the temperature and excluding the air, decomposes the seed before the vital principle can develop itself. Hence the frequent complaint of bad seed on wet soils. This will be rendered still more obvious by the accompanying diagrams, which prove the beneficial influence exercised by drainage upon the soil, and which were

FIG. 75 *Soil in perfectly dry state*

FIG. 76 *Soil in perfectly wet state*

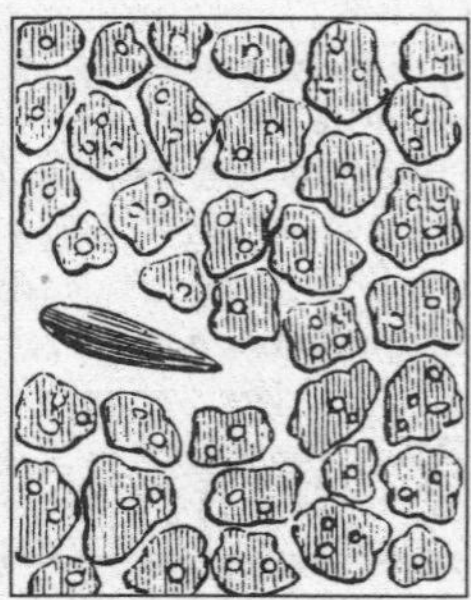

FIG. 77 *Soil in proper condition for germination*

exhibited before the Highland Agricultural Society by Dr Madden, of Penicuik, at a time when the beneficial effects of draining were not so well understood as they are now. They are highly magnified sections of soil in three different conditions. Under the microscope, soil is seen to be made up of numerous distinct porous particles. Fig. 75 represents it in a perfectly dry state; both the soil and the channels between being quite dry. Fig. 76, on the other hand, represents a soil perfectly wet; the particles themselves are full of water, and so are the channels between them. In Fig. 77 the particles are moist, while the passages between them are filled with air. These diagrams show that soil in the condition exhibited in Figs. 75 and 76 was totally unfit for the germination of seed. In Fig. 75 there is no water; in Fig. 76 there is no air; in Fig. 77 both are present, in the proportions favourable to the growth of seeds, and those are requisite to insure the vigorous growth of the plant throughout all its stages; therefore, Fig. 77 is the condition of soil desiderated for all cultural purposes, and exhibits that congenial admixture of earth, water, and air, that plants delight in, and which efficient drainage only can provide for them.

263 No better form can be devised for a kitchen garden than a square, subdivided by two centre walks, as in Fig. 78, or a long parallelogram, as Fig. 79. Something like Fig. 80 has also been recommended by Mr Loudon and others, and the rounded part would make a beautiful fruit garden. This figure might also be rounded at both ends. The centre walk should pass through close at each end. *a* represents the wall; *b*, fruit tree border, 10 feet wide; *c*, walk, 6 feet wide; and *d*, border for dwarf trees or bushes, or the culture of strawberries, etc., 6 feet wide.

Whatever shape is adopted, borders should always be introduced on each side of the main walks. Nothing tends more to relieve the heavy appearance of large masses of vegetables, and to confer an air of elegance to a kitchen garden, than such borders. They should be separated from the main vegetable compartments by small walks, from eighteen inches to two feet wide. These walks can be edged with pebbles, and have a sprinkling of gravel, or simply cut off as alleys, and be left solid earth, at pleasure. If they are formed of some hard substance, all the wheeling can be performed on them instead of on the main walk.

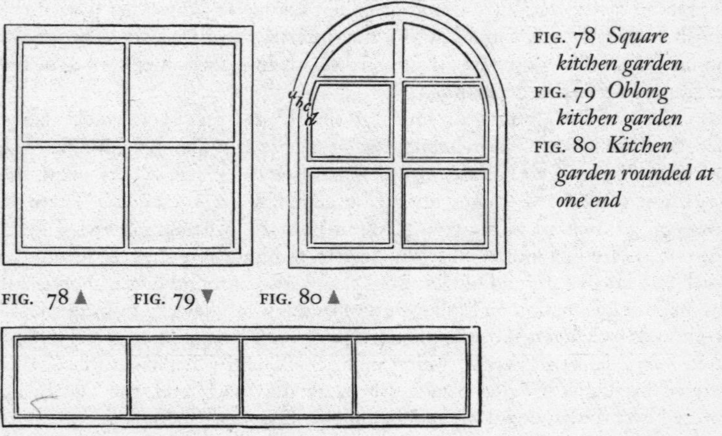

FIG. 78 *Square kitchen garden*
FIG. 79 *Oblong kitchen garden*
FIG. 80 *Kitchen garden rounded at one end*

FIG. 78 ▲ FIG. 79 ▼ FIG. 80 ▲

264 Perhaps the nearer to a level a kitchen garden can be formed, the better. A slight inclination to the south-east, south, or west, might be an advantage; on no account should it incline to the north. Where a kitchen garden is nearly level, it may often be desirable to give fruit tree borders a considerable inclination, to get the benefit of the sun's rays and insure thorough drainage. Borders against the wall may be sloped in directions opposite to those which line the inner side of the walk. These borders have also a good effect laid on in round ridges.

In level kitchen gardens it is often desirable to throw up sloping banks or zigzag ridges for early and late crops. The south front of such banks, especially if a thatched hurdle or some other check to the wind is placed on the top, is equal to a south border; and the north side is equally useful for late strawberries, salading in hot weather, etc. Such banks are also most useful for training peas, etc., on table-trestles, within one foot or eighteen inches of the surface. Some of the borders at the side of the walk might also be occupied by iron wire for training trees or espaliers, table-trestles, etc. One should be devoted to raspberries, planted three feet from the walks, and trained to a handrail at the side of the walk, from three to four feet high. The advantages of this system, on the ground of beauty, doing justice to the young wood, and the facility and pleasure of gathering, must be at once apparent.

265 The size of the kitchen garden must depend upon the demands upon it, and the mode of culture adopted. It is bad policy to have it too large. It should be kept in the highest state of cultivation, and its productive powers stimulated to the utmost by liberal dressings of manure. The soil should be trenched at least four feet deep, and drained a foot deeper. All the coarse vegetables, such as Jerusalem and globe artichokes, horseradish, rhubarb, etc., should be grown outside the walls, if possible, in a slip by themselves. Herbs should have a border devoted to them, and be grown in beds three feet wide. Thus cultivated, the back garden becomes a source of interest and an object of beauty, and they are easily accessible. All that has been here advised is as applicable to a plot a few yards square as to a nobleman's garden of ten or twenty acres. There is no reason why the kitchen garden should not bear the impress of order, design, and high keeping, as much as any other part of the grounds, or why this should in any way interfere with securing the largest amount of produce of the best quality from a given space, which should be the leading object in this department.

266 *Orchard* The grafting of most of our fruit trees upon stocks being calculated to produce short stunted growth, has considerably modified the practice of hardy fruit culture. Unless the demand for fruit is very great, the formation of orchards ought not to be generally recommended. There is, however, an orchard in the plan given in Fig. 26, in paragraph 182, and its position is carefully indicated. It will be seen to be entirely sheltered from the north and north-east, and hidden from the pleasure ground by shrubberies. It has a gentle inclination and full exposure to the south, and, both in form and position, is well adapted for its intended purpose. The soil is supposed to be a good loam, 4 feet in depth, resting upon chalk, and it has been thoroughly drained by drains inserted 6 inches beneath the chalk level, the tiles being covered over to that depth with broken stones. The permanent trees, which, as it is intended to lay the orchard down to grass, must be standards and half-standards, with from 4 to 6 feet of clear stem, should be planted in rows, from 30 to 40 feet apart, and in what is termed the *quincunx* style, thus:

The north or coldest side of the orchard should be planted with walnuts, cherries, medlars, chestnuts, etc., to provide shelter for the others. They might be succeeded by the hardiest plums and apples, to be followed by the tender pears on the south or warmest side. If a gradation of height were also followed, the shelter provided would be more efficient, and the general effect more pleasing. Filberts, mulberries, and service trees, may also be introduced. But these temporary trees should be inserted as nurses between the permanent trees. Firm-growing varieties that come early into bearing should be chosen for this purpose, and they will not only encourage the growth of the permanent trees, but pay their own cost a dozen times over before they will require removal. They must, however, be carefully watched, lest they weaken the energy or destroy the symmetry of the permanent trees. The rows in this case will run east and west, which is, perhaps, as good an arrangement as any.

267 Though, from the introduction of dwarf trees, upon which, in a good kitchen garden, as much fruit may be grown as will be required for the consumption of a family, an orchard is not now so necessary as it was some years ago, still it is not desirable to see this useful appendage of the country house wholly neglected. A piece of pasture where the soil is good may be very profitably employed as an orchard. It will yield both a crop of fruit and a crop of grass, and if the former be not required for consumption, there is at all times a ready sale for it. Apples, pears, and cherries are the fruits properly cultivated in orchards; but plums, walnuts, and filberts are not unfrequently considered as orchard fruit, and in cases where there is only one orchard, all these fruits may, with advantage, be included in it.

Upon the nature of the site and soil best suited for an orchard, Abercrombie observes: 'Land sloping to the east or south is better than a level; a sheltered hollow, not liable to floods, is better than an upland with the same aspect, and yet a gentle rising, backed by sufficient shelter, or the base of a hill, is eligible. A good loam, in which the constituents of a good soil predominate over those of a hot one, suits most fruit trees; the subsoil should be dry, and the depth of mould thirty inches or three feet. Before planting, drain, if necessary; trench to the depth of two feet, manure according to the defects of the soil, and give a winter and summer fallow; or cultivate the site for a year or two as a kitchen garden, so that it may be deeply dug and receive a good annual dressing.'

In forming an orchard, Dr Lindley recommends, and we quite agree with him, the early transplanting of the different trees. 'They cannot,' he says, 'be removed from the nursery too soon after the wood has become ripe and the leaves have fallen off, for between this time and the winter many of them will make fresh roots, and be prepared to push forth their young shoots with more vigour in the spring than those whose transplanting has been deferred to a late period of the season.' All young trees should be carefully staked and protected from the wind, and, if a dry spring should succeed the autumn of their planting, they will require to be watered, or, what is better, to have manure laid round their roots and be watered through it. Pruning and training are necessary; but, as a general rule, the knife should be avoided, if it is possible to bring the tree into a good shape without it. Pear trees will thrive in a lighter soil than apples, and they are generally more hardy, and bear the wind better. In a good soil, the distance at which trees should stand from each other is from twenty-five to thirty feet; if all free-growing varieties are planted, it may perhaps be desirable to give from thirty to forty feet between them, and in all cases the quincunx mode, as we have already stated, is the best.

In selecting apples and pears for planting, and, indeed, all fruits that admit of sorts, it is of the greatest importance to take into consideration not only soil but climate. Very little good is gained by selecting the best varieties if they, or any of them, are not suited to the locality. Disappointment too often follows want of judgment in this respect. Whoever intends to plant an orchard, especially of apples and pears, should ascertain, in the first instance, what sorts flourish best in his part of the country. He should then select the best of these and introduce such other sorts as, from their resemblance to them, may seem likely to answer. A list of good sorts of apples and pears suitable for cooking and for dessert will be found in another part of this volume.

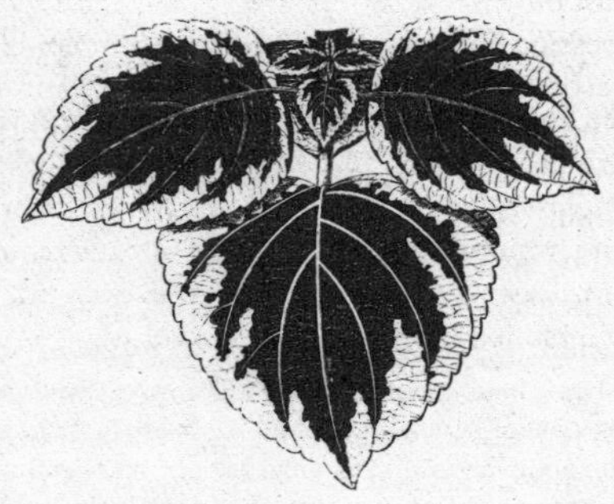

FIG. 81 *Coleus veitchii*

CHAPTER 8

Fences, Walls, and Shelters

268 The idea of enclosing land is one of the most conclusive proofs of a high state of civilisation; indeed, a history of fencing, from the rude landmarks of ancient times up to the almost perfect fences of the present day, would, to a great extent, be a history of social progress and moral advancement. Even now, the character of districts and countries is fairly indicated by the nature and condition of their fences. The social status, tastes, and pecuniary resources of individuals may often be determined in the same manner. In this, if in anything, those who judge by the outward appearance only may generally judge correctly. Fences are so obtrusively conspicuous that they at once arrest our attention and challenge an opinion. They convey to us our first impressions of a domain, and we may thus almost determine at sight the estate of a spendthrift or a property in Chancery. Fences not only define boundaries and ensure security, but they also convey ideas of possession and seclusion, and impart a reputable or disreputable character to a property, according to the taste, or the want of it, by which they are distinguished. The character of the fence itself, and its efficient preservation afterwards, therefore, become objects of the highest importance.

269 In a thickly-populated country like England, it is scarcely left optional whether estates shall be enclosed or not; but the character of the fence used is a matter of taste. Neither is there any lack of materials; for earth, water, hedges, formed of a great variety of plants – wooden fences of every type, from the rude post, surmounted by a single rail, to the highly-finished and beautifully-designed rustic park fence – iron of every thickness and every pattern – brick, stone, and concrete wall – all are used. And, perhaps, each of these materials is in itself the best for special localities. A ditch, two yards wide and four feet deep, with one or two feet of water in the bottom, is a capital fence, or substitute for one, on swampy, fenny lands. A steep earth bank, with a small ditch at bottom, containing water, may also serve all the purposes of a fence on heavy clay lands. On poor uplands, a wall of turf may answer very well, and stand for twenty years. But, however useful such expedients may be on the soils or localities indicated, they would be of no use whatever on more cultivated properties. Fences are required for four leading purposes – namely, for subdivision of an estate or farm into fields; for defining the boundary of a park, and adding dignity to its appearance; for protecting clumps of trees and plantations; and for maintaining a separation between park and gardens and adjacent fields, or, as some writers have it, between the grass that is mown and the grass that is fed.

270 The fence that forms the boundary of a park, of whatever material it should be formed, should always be of sufficient height and strength to prevent the ingress or egress of cattle at their own pleasure; it should also be more or less ornamental. A strong fence of wood, brick, stone, or iron, from 3½ to 4½ feet high, or even 6 or 7 feet in height where deer are kept, is well adapted for the enclosure of a park. Hedges, however excellent, can never confine deer, and are seldom efficient for cattle. An excellent park fence of wood, about five feet above the surface of the ground, may be formed as follows: Larch trees, averaging from 6 to 9 inches in diameter, should be barked and cut into lengths measuring from 8 to 9 feet for posts. Holes should then be dug in the ground from 3 to 4 feet in depth, and the posts placed in them and rammed firmly with earth, stones, brickbats, etc., care being taken to keep the posts upright by means of a plumb-level, and ranged in a regular line, straight or curved, as the case may be.

FIG. 82 *Arris rail*

The posts may then be connected by three strong rails of Scotch fir, notched into the posts about 3 inches deep from their front surface. The rails may be from 2 to 3 inches thick, and about 4 or 5 inches wide. Arris rails, or rails of a triangular shape made by sawing asunder a square rail diagonally throughout its length, as shown in section in Fig. 82, may be used if preferred to flat rails. Vertical rails of barked larch, formed by sawing young trees down the centre, should then be nailed on, leaving a clear space of about 2½ inches between them. The splints will average about 4 inches in width, and should be pointed at the top, as shown in Fig. 83. No fence of wood can well look neater or stronger than this; and if the posts are partially charred for a foot above and below their junction with the soil – that being the point where wooden posts always decay first, and, consequently, where the antiseptic property of charring would be most valuable – and the whole coated with anti-corrosive paint, or, better still, where the colour is not objectionable, a varnish of Stockholm tar, fences thus formed will last for many years. The construction of this kind of fence is shown in Fig. 83, in which A exhibits the elevation and B the plan when viewed from above, as well as a section, the dotted line across the post showing the extent of notching required to let in the horizontal rail. In Fig. 83, in the top and bottom horizontal rail, the method of cutting the ends of these horizontal rails, so as to effect their junction against the principal posts, is clearly illustrated. It is better to notch the rails into the posts only to such a depth that their outer surface is flush with the front surface of the posts, and by way of imparting a better finish, an upright similar to those shown to the right of the illustration may be nailed to the face of the post. This upright is

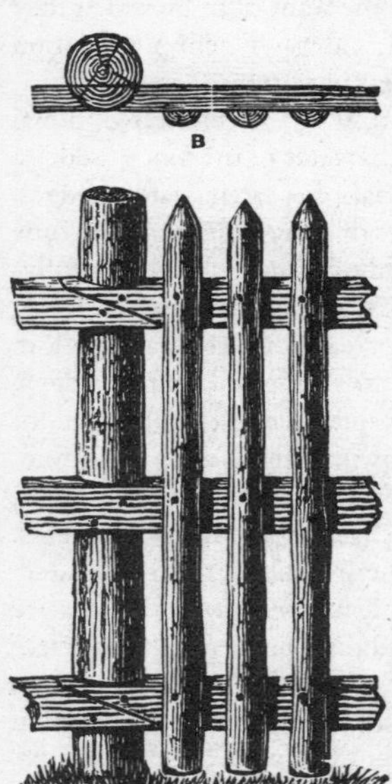

FIG. 83 *Larch and scotch fir park paling*

not shown in the illustration because its introduction would render the mode of joining the rails less plain and perhaps less intelligible. The paling may be strengthened to resist any attempt to destroy it by nailing horizontal strips of hoop iron both inside the rails and on the outer side, curving them round the uprights, and nailing them to the rails as well as the uprights.

271 A similar kind of park fence, as sightly in appearance and still more durable, may be made of posts formed of oak instead of larch, the horizontal and vertical rails being also sawn out of oak or out of good sound deal. This fence may be coated with Stockholm tar, or the wood may be painted or varnished only, according to taste, though varnishing will be found somewhat expensive. Coal tar should never be used for park fences: it is useful for common wooden fences that are not conspicuously brought into sight, or on the score of economy; but Stockholm tar is lighter in colour and more transparent than coal tar, and is therefore better suited for the better class of wooden fences, when tar is used as a protective coating against wet and the action of the weather.

272 Another handsome kind of wooden fence is that which is ordinarily known as 'park paling', and which is illustrated in Fig. 84. In this fence, as in the larch used for fence shown in Fig. 83, the method adopted in its construction is the same, though the details are different, for the posts are of the same length, and set in the ground at the same distance apart and to the same depth; they are, however, square in shape, being sawn out of pieces of oak, in order to bring them into this form, but they are squared only so far as they appear above the surface of the ground: below the surface they are left in their original state, for the sake of imparting additional strength and solidity to the fence, and better holding power when set in the ground. From post to post, at the base, and touching or even entering the ground, boards from 8 to 12 inches in width, called gravel boards, are placed, the ends being let into notches cut in the posts to receive them, or butted against clumps of wood nailed to the sides of the posts; a combination of these two modes will form the strongest fencing at this part. Above the gravel board, three rows of arris rails are mortised into the posts, the ends of the triangular rails being cut in a rectangular form, and when inserted they are held in place by pegs or tree-nails of oak driven into holes bored into the posts and through the rails by a bit-and-brace. When this is done, staves of rent oak, about 4 or 5 inches in width, are nailed against the rails as shown in Fig. 84 in the elevation of the fence at A and the section at B, each overlapping the stave

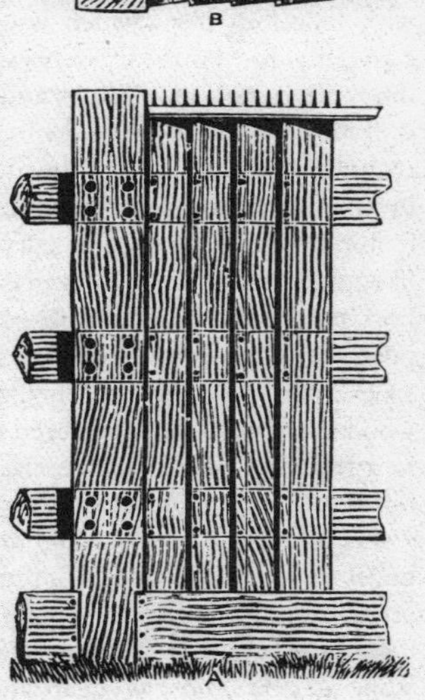

FIG. 84 *Park paling of oak*

that has been fixed immediately before it, after the manner of weather boarding. This is shown so clearly in the illustrations, the dotted lines showing the extent of overlapping of the staves and the direction of the arris rails, that no further explanation is needed. The fence is finished at the top by a capping of deal, through which, before it is nailed in position, strong nails have been passed, front uppermost, so as to form a series of short spikes along the top. When finished, such a fence as this should be varnished.

273 In these fences examples have been given of a good open fence and a good close fence – of a fence that is comparatively cheap and involving but little labour in its construction, and of another that will be more costly both on account of the material that is used in it and of the labour that must be expended on it. Such a fence as that which is shown in Fig. 84 may, perhaps, be improved by the substitution of brick work for the gravel board at the bottom, and when made on this principle such a fence would be inferior only to a brick or stone wall for garden purposes. For gardens of the ordinary kind, open fencing of sufficient strength may be made by posts connected by two series of rails, one about 9 inches from the top, and the other about 12 inches from the surface of the ground, with palisades from 2 to 3 inches in width nailed to the rails at the same distance apart. These palisades should be from ¾ inch to 1 inch in thickness. Such a paling is obviously suited for cottage gardens only, but in a work like this no class of garden should be neglected; and it is more convenient when treating of any particular kind of fencing to show how it may be modified in detail so as to meet all requirements.

274 It is, however, only by reason of the greater shelter provided by wooden fences, and their less cost in the first instance, that they can in any way compete with fences of iron, which is doubtless the best of all materials for fences, especially for boundary fences. In point of ultimate economy, efficiency, durability, and beauty, iron stands unrivalled. Before erecting a boundary fence, everyone who is about to do so should consult the circulars of our great wire manufacturers. They offer the most tempting variety of designs, at astonishingly low prices; and by means of strained wire, iron hurdles, and the flexibility of the material used, the sharpest curves can be followed to a nicety, and the most irregular outline correctly traced. An iron fence for deer, six feet high, with horizontal rods, iron posts seven feet apart, and a handsome massive straining pillar for every hundred yards of fence, will be delivered at any railway station at 2s. 2d. per lineal yard. A fence of the same height, the proprietor finding the wooden posts, will be delivered at 10½d. per lineal yard. A heavy cattle fence, four feet high, of a similar description, complete, can be delivered for 1s. 4d. per lineal yard, or, the proprietor supplying wooden posts, for 7½d. per lineal yard; a sheep fence, three feet high, complete, with five horizontal rods, 10d. per lineal yard; wooden posts supplied by proprietor, 3d. do. do.; and so on in proportion. Nothing can well be cheaper, and certainly nothing more efficient, than these fences. In districts where stone is plentiful and labour cheap, a wall of stone may be almost as cheap, and, although less elegant in appearance, is quite as efficient for protection, and more useful for shelter. Some will prefer brick; and walls of either brick or stone, four feet high, will be sufficient for bullocks

FIG. 85 *Stone wall surmounted by coping and dwarf iron railing*

and horses. For deer, the walls must be either two feet higher, or surmounted by one or two horizontal iron rails, supported by stone piers or iron posts, to give additional height, fixed in a coping, as shown in Fig. 85.

275 In situations where the extremities of parks are mostly bounded by plantations of wood, or where they are grazed by sheep only, a most useful and ornamental hedge-and wall fence may be thus formed: Build a wall from 2½ feet to 3 feet in height, and plant a hedge of holly, hawthorn, hornbeam, beech, or other shrub suitable for the purpose, on a bank of earth thrown up against its inner edge, as shown in elevation in Fig. 86, and in section in Fig. 87. The outer face of the wall should not be perpendicular to the surface of the ground, but be built so as to show a slight inclination inwards. Behind the wall a bank of earth should be thrown up, either level with the top of the wall or a little below it as shown, and on the top of this the quick hedge may be planted. The face of the bank should be sloped and revetted with turf, or sown with grass seeds.

FIG. 86 *Hedge-and-wall fence. Elevation.* FIG. 87 *Hedge-and-wall fence. Section.*

276 Such a fence as this not only presents an impassable barrier from the outside, but is one of the most beautiful combinations of a living and dead fence that can be imagined. Hedges of quickthorn alone will form excellent boundary fences for sheep, and on the best soils, with extremely good management, for cattle also. They are generally planted thus: A ditch is cut, and with the material

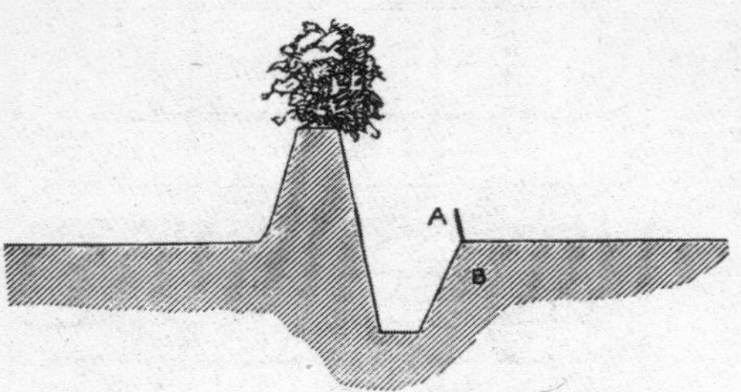

FIG. 88 *Bank and ditch, with hedge or bank*

taken from it a bank is formed along one edge of the ditch, as shown in Fig. 88. Sometimes a ditch is made on both sides, to give additional security, and the angle of the banks varies in different localities, and according to the soil. The plants are inserted, sometimes on the very top of the bank, at other times a foot or more down; but the principle is always the same. It will at once be seen that the chief use of both ditch and bank is to increase the obstructive power of the hedge placed on its summit. A temporary fence of wood or iron will, however, generally be necessary to protect the hedge plants in their young state. A single or double rail, A, standing out from the bank, B, as above, will answer the purpose perfectly well.

277 For temporary fencing round groups of trees, nothing, except where wood is very cheap and plentiful, can equal iron hurdles. Iron or hedges are also the best fences for permanent woods. No group in a park should be permanently fenced. Whatever the trees are of which it is formed, as they grow larger they should either be pruned to a sufficient height to protect them from the browsing of cattle, or intermixed with thorns and hollies, which will form an impenetrable undergrowth of such a formidable character as to protect the other trees under which they are growing. These spiny plants will also add to the picturesque effect of the groups. Trees planted on the Gardenesque principle may be protected, when young, with iron guards, but as they advance in growth, their lower branches must be pruned off. This may prevent their ever becoming perfect specimens; but such practice is better than surrounding them with permanent fencing. Trees thus treated will form pleasing contrasts to those which are allowed to sweep the turf of the pleasure ground with their lower branches. Care must be exercised to vary the height of pruning different trees, so as to destroy the insipid sameness and tiresome uniformity of the browsing line in parks.

278 The fence separating the garden from the park now claims our notice. It must be strong enough to exclude all sorts of cattle, and fine enough to keep out the smallest rabbit. It must either be partially or entirely invisible, or highly ornamental, or both – that is, it need not be of one uniform character throughout. Where a splendid prospect challenges our admiration, it should be invisible – that is to say, formed of horizontal wires run through light iron standards – such a fencing, although strong, being so slight as nearly to escape observation; but where a factory chimney, in a bleak locality, requires concealing, an ornamental wall will best serve the purpose in view. Part of the fence given in Fig. 26 is a strong iron rabbit-proof one, six feet high, which imparts better ideas of security and strength, near the carriage entrance, than

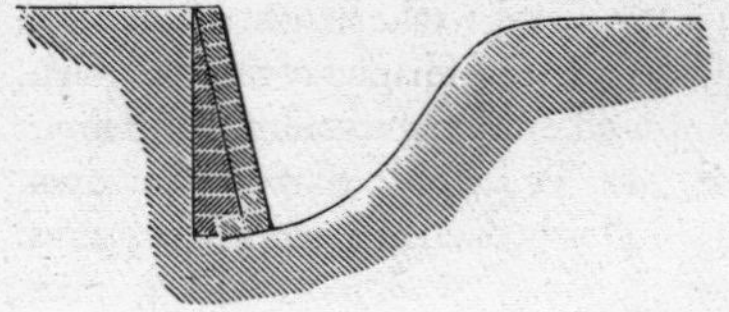

FIG. 89 *Ha-ha with wall*

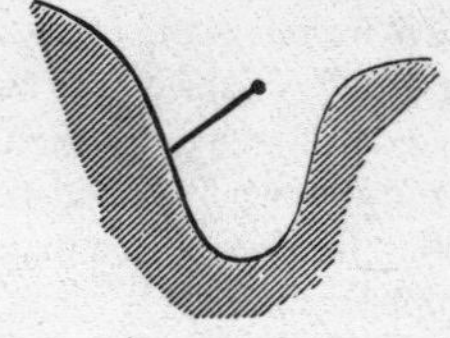

FIG. 90 *Ha-ha with iron fence projecting outwards*

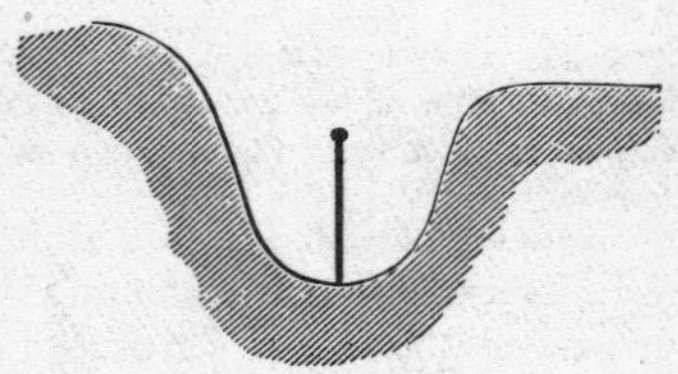

FIG. 91 *Ha-ha with upright fence set in bottom of ditch*

FIG. 92 *Ha-ha surmounted by dwarf wall*

anything else, save brick or stone, could have given. The same or a similar kind of fence might run along most of the east side, reserving the west and south for the ha-ha. The object of the ha-ha is to make a fence entirely invisible, or to make what is a very dwarf fence from the inside a tall one from the park. Invisible ha-ha's are thus formed, as in Fig. 89, with the aid of a brick wall from four to six feet high, which should slope inwards slightly; or the wall may be dispensed with, and a small iron fence, projecting outwards, substituted for it, as in Fig. 90. Sometimes an upright fence is placed in the bottom of the ditch, as in Fig. 91; but this is the worst of all forms of the ha-ha – if, indeed, it deserves the name at all. Another form of ha-ha is to have the inner part of the ditch faced or revetted with brick r stone, as shown in Fig. 92, surmounted by a dwarf iron fence, as shown in Fig. 85, or with a dwarf wall of

FIG. 93 *Ornamental fence with ha-ha*

the same materials as the revetment of the ditch, rising to the height of one, two, or three feet. To walls of this kind a highly ornamental character may be given, as exhibited in Fig. 93, in which the wall imposed on the revetment of the inner face of the ditch has a solid base, but the greater part is composed of open balustrades, finished with a massive coping, and is broken at intervals by pillars, which support vases.

The following diagrams and remarks, from Repton's *Landscape Gardening*, will show the importance of having these walls of the right height and at the proper distance. Mr Repton says, where the ground falls from the house in an inclined plane, the distance of the fence can only be ascertained by actual experiment on the spot; and of course, the steeper the descent the nearer or lower must be the terrace wall.

The eye sees the ground over the fence at A (Fig. 94), but if carried to B, all view of the ground will be lost to a person standing on the floor-line C. If the ground be flat, as at C, in Fig. 95, or rises from the house to D, the fence may be placed much farther from the house without obstructing the view of the park from A.

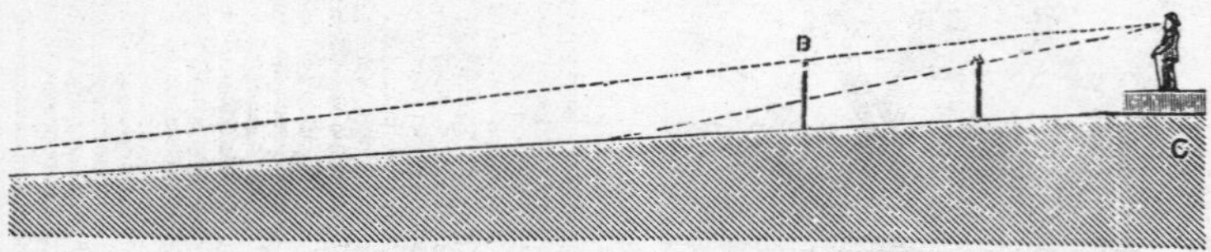

FIG. 94 *Position of fence on ground inclined from the house*

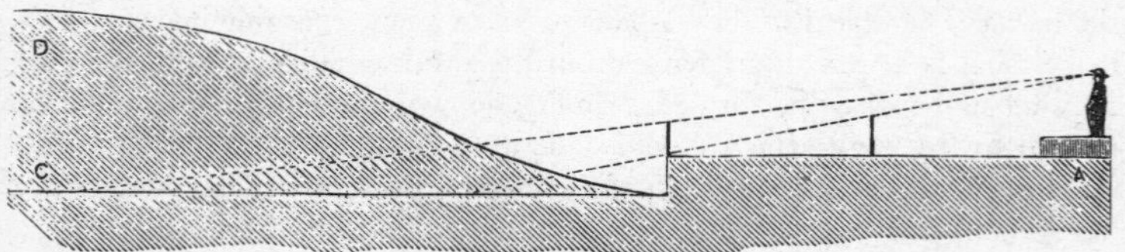

FIG. 95 *Position of fence on flat ground of ground rising from the house*

279 An invisible wire or ornamental iron fence may also be placed on the top of the ha-ha; but generally it is best finished with an ornamental wall, as shown in Fig. 93, or left level with the inside or garden surface. At one time, rustic fences were much used for separating the park from the pleasure ground. While they are among the most beautiful, they are certainly the most expensive of all fences. They might still be used to separate one part of the grounds from another – the rabbit-proof garden from the outside pleasure ground – where labour and expense are no object. The designs given in Figs. 96 and 97 are simple but pretty, and they can be made of hazel, larch, spruce, or indeed any young trees. The bark should always be left on, and the more numerous and rougher the knots, the more rustic the fence will be. Fig. 96 represents a fence in rustic trellis work. The bars of which it is formed should be slightly notched one into another at the points in which they cross, so that they may have a better bearing one against another and a firmer holding than round sticks could possibly have if nailed together without notching. For the rustic mosaic work shown in Fig. 97, sticks of hazel, maple, willow, cherry, etc., must be sawn in sunder lengthways, and then cut into pieces as required to form the mosaic. These pieces must be nailed against a backing of stout boards. It is more suitable for summer houses, window boxes, etc., than for fencing. Wire fences look better than these, and their patterns and prices are endlessly varied, to suit the means and tastes of all. The patterns shown in Figs. 98 and 99 look as well as any.

FIG. 96 *Dwarf fence of rough stakes disposed in rustic trellis work*

FIG. 97 *Dwarf fence in rustic mosaic work*

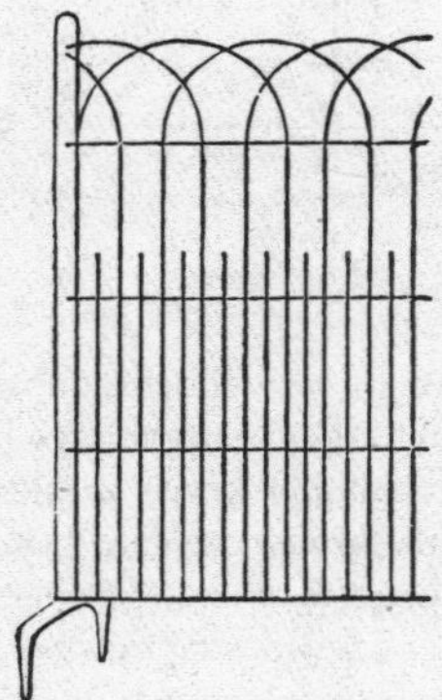

FIG. 98 *Wire fence*

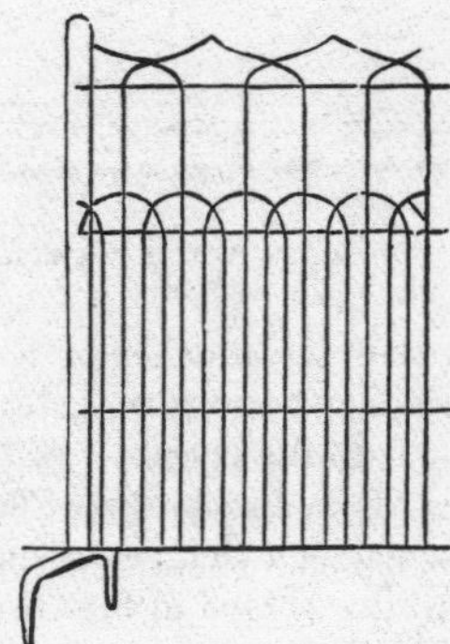

FIG. 99 *Wire fence*

280 Walls are occasionally introduced into flower gardens, either for the shelter they afford in bleak localities, their architectural effect near dwelling houses, or the culture of the more tender plants in the open air. In all such cases they should be formed of the best materials, and either panelled or rendered otherwise ornamental. They should seldom be more than ten or less than six feet high, although those who have seen the enormous magnolia walls at White

Knights Park, near Reading, will feel inclined to double the maximum given. As a rule, however, the elevations named will look best and be most suitable for cultural purposes. It would be worth going a hundred miles to see a wall six feet high and fifty yards long, furnished with a collection of tea roses in full bloom. If the wall were furnished with a coping projecting four inches, so constructed as to prevent the drip of water, and the roses were slightly covered in winter with spruce branches, and sheltered with canvas covering from early spring frosts, such a sight might be realised, and a wall affording alike shelter and fence on one side become an object of surpassing loveliness on the other.

281 For single gates across a carriage road, across a pathway, or anywhere else, Fig. 100, being of an ornamental character, will be found appropriate. The number of bars and patterns of such gates can be made to suit every purpose and gratify every taste. On carriage roads, gates should never be less than four, and seldom need be more than six feet in height; five feet being an excellent average. The construction of these gates cannot be described at length here, but the principles involved are explained by the sketches themselves, from which any carpenter of average intelligence, or any amateur who can use a saw, plane, hammer, and chisel, might easily make them.

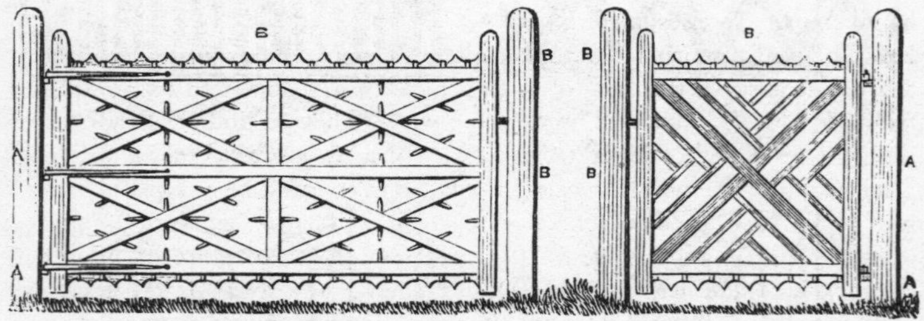

FIG. 100 *Designs for gates across roads and pathways*

282 These observations upon fencing may be brought to a conclusion with a few more observations on gates. As a general rule, they must always be in harmony with the character of the fence. Occasionally, however, in pleasure grounds, where a rabbit-proof fence is hidden with shrubs, the gate spanning the walk may be much better and more elegant than the fence, of a character similar to that shown in Fig. 101. Beautiful gates of this description are now supplied by the Coalbrooke Dale Company in Shropshire, from whom, as well as from other manufacturers, gates may be had in iron in more or less elaborate styles, according to price. Lodge or entrance gates are most effective in pairs, as in Fig. 102. They should neither be too massive nor too light – of sufficient width to prevent anxiety about wheels or posts; of elegant pattern, strong construction, and a colour that can be easily discerned at night. Nothing can equal, in ultimate economy, nor exceed in usefulness and beauty, a well-raised, carefully-hung pair of wrought-iron gates, ten or twelve feet wide, and painted a light stone colour, or in imitation of bronze.

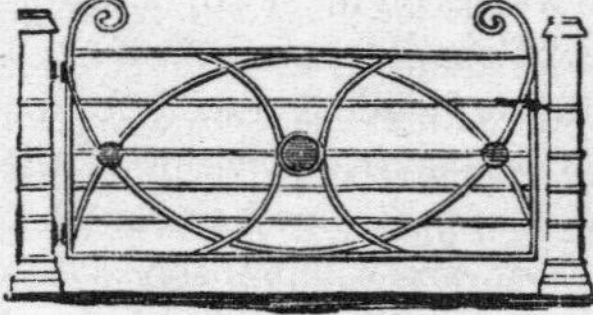

FIG. 101 *Ornamental iron gate*

FIG. 102 *Iron gates for entrance*

283 The Garden Wall is as the setting to the gem; without its enclosing fence, the garden would be undistinguishable from the neighbouring fields, and its contents exposed to the depredations of man and beast, as well as to the 'pitiless pelting' of every storm. But besides the protection it affords in this sense, the properly-constructed garden wall has other important conservative duties. Dr Wells, in his interesting experiments on the origin of dew, found that a thermometer protected by a handkerchief sustained horizontally over it marked a temperature from four to six degrees higher than the corresponding instrument placed in the open ground. The wall and its coping exercise a conservative power in preventing the radiation of heat in the one case which the handkerchief exercises in the other.

284 The wall performs another equally important office: during the heat of the day it absorbs the sun's rays in a ratio proportioned to its aspect and inclination to the sun; and, in common with all heated bodies, it radiates its heat in a ratio proportioned to the square of its distance; so that if an object placed a foot from the wall receives 1° of heat from it, at one inch it will receive heat equal to 144°. The reflection, also, of all unabsorbed rays impinging on the surface of the wall, greatly increases the temperature of the air in immediate contact with it. Besides this power of absorbing heat, moisture is also absorbed, both from rain and from the atmosphere, and, with the heat, is given out by radiation, tempering the atmosphere during the night. A wall is thus, in every sense, a source of protection; and it is of considerable importance that its height and form, as well as its workmanship and materials, should be well considered.

The countries of Southern Europe, and especially Italy, can dispense with some of the conservative properties of the wall, and render architecturally ornamental that which we must make strictly utilitarian. The walls of Italian gardens are, therefore, frequently decorated with alcoves and balustrades, with a full complement of statuary and vases.

285 It has been already mentioned that the ha-ha fence, invented by William Kent – a painter, sculptor, and architect, who attained great celebrity for his skill as a landscape gardener, and who was born in 1684 and died in 1748 – has been considered the best form of external fence, because it affords protection from without, and does not obstruct the view, but carries the eye uninterruptedly into the neighbouring domain, while a light wire fence offers the best possible protection from game, rabbits, and other wild animals. A holly or privet hedge may with advantage surmount the ha-ha on the east and west, especially if it is intended to have borders outside the garden wall, either for wall trees or vegetables. Where circumstances permit, a belt of trees on the north or north-east side of the ha-ha will also afford a desirable shelter.

286 Within this external fence the kitchen and fruit gardens usually form a separate enclosure, more or less extensive, according to the means of the proprietor; and the wall surrounding this enclosure we have now to consider. Garden walls have long been a subject for discussion, and will probably always remain so: like everything else connected with gardening, they depend on local circumstances of climate, elevation, extent, and undulation. The walls which would be suitable for a moderate-sized kitchen garden, in a flat or thickly-wooded country, would be very unsuitable for a loftier site, on the side of a hill, or in an open, undulating country; while the enclosure of a plot of small extent by walls 14 or 16 feet high would be in-admissable both on artistic and physiological principles: on the first, such walls would seem as the walls of a prison; on the second, they would literally be so, for they would tend to hinder the free admission and circulation of air, which is essential to the growth of plants.

287 On these grounds, the best practitioners consider that, for small gardens, 8 feet walls are most suitable, provided the trees on them are planted so far apart as to admit of their horizontal extension. For gardens of larger size, 10 feet walls, and for an extensive garden, walls of 12 and even 14 feet in height, will not be too great. Nicol thinks 10 or 12 feet a height convenient for pruning, watering, and gathering the fruit, and one which gives ample space for the expansion of the branches of most trees; but he adds, this should be influenced by the extent, or apparent extent, of the ground, the latter depending upon its cast. If it be a lengthened parallelogram, for instance, the ground will seem larger than it really is; if an exact square, it will seem smaller. So, if it is flat, it will seem smaller than if it is either undulating or sloping; while, on an elevation, loftier walls will admit a larger amount of atmospheric air than if the garden happens to be placed in a hollow, or even in a flat country. Where an acre of ground, in the form of a parallelogram, is enclosed on a gentle elevation, he recommends a north wall 14 feet high, and that the east, west, and south walls should be only 10 feet in height; if the slope of the ground is considerable, the difference may be less. In gardens of greater extent – enclosures of four acres, for instance – the walls may be higher, but in no instance more than 18 feet high for the north wall, 15 feet for the east and west walls, and 12 feet for the south wall.

288 In a parallelogram 400 feet in length by 300 feet in breadth, which is a superficial area of about two acres and three quarters, and a well-proportioned piece of ground, if the lie of the land is an easy slope, McIntosh recommends a wall 16 feet high for the north wall, 14 feet for the east and west walls, and 12 feet for the south wall; but on level ground, while the north wall is still 16 feet, he would make the east and west walls 13 feet, and the south wall 10 feet. Rogers considers low walls much more convenient in management, and more easily protected; and, seeing that the fruit trees are most productive under horizontal training, he recommends two walls of 6 feet high, with the trees planted at good distances from each other, and asserts that such walls will produce more fruit in any given number of years than one 12 feet wall. 'Low walls give free

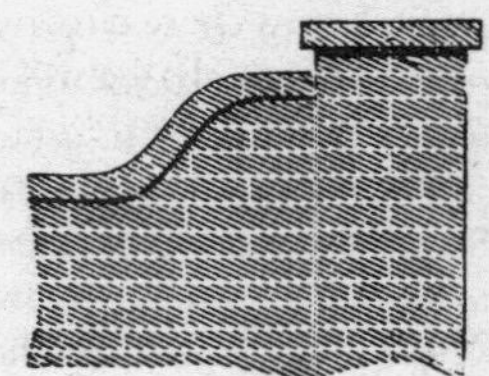

FIG. 103 *Rise in wall from lower to higher level*

ventilation,' he adds, 'which is necessary at all times: even high winds do less damage than foul stagnant air, pent up within four high walls.' Walker thinks walls should not be under 8 feet from the ground level to the coping, but 10 feet he considers the most useful height for general purposes; but where the garden area is flat, the appearance would be improved by raising the north wall a foot or two higher, carrying the rise round the north-east and north-west angles, and proceeding from the lower to the higher level with an appropriate rise or ramp, as indicated in Fig. 103.

289 The materials of which walls are formed must always depend upon local circumstances; brick, stone, clay, chalk, and oak fencing, being all in common use for the purpose. Of all these materials, brick seems to be the favourite, being most convenient, absorbing most heat, and being most enduring. Forsyth says, 'Where brick cannot be had, it is better to dispense with walls altogether, and adopt wood.' Brick walls are, therefore, considered the best for all practical purposes; they are most convenient for training, and they absorb and retain most heat. Whinstone, a species of basalt rock common in the northern counties, is looked upon as coming next to brick in regard to these qualities, while its close grain rejects moisture.

290 It has also been a question whether inclined or vertical walls are most favourable to the produce of wall fruit. Zigzag walls, and walls with deep recesses, have also been experimented on; and, latterly, glass walls, which, after all, only amount to an arcade enclosed with glass and lined with vines, fruit trees, and exotics – an arrangement that is beautiful to look on, without doubt, but one which will certainly cost more than it is worth, and can only be regarded as an expensive luxury that will never afford remuneration for the outlay expended on it.

In reference to the really practical question of walls, the Caledonian Horticultural Society instituted, some years ago, a very interesting series of experiments on the comparative merits of a wall coloured black, an inclined wall at an angle of 50°, and a vertical wall of the same freestone. The results were very varied. At 6 p.m. in April, the average temperature of the sloping, the black, and the freestone wall was the same – the brick wall was one degree lower. During May the temperature of the brick wall was considerably higher. At one o'clock in the day the average temperature of the sloping wall was seven degrees higher than the brick wall – the whinstone wall was three degrees, and the freestone five degrees, lower than the sloping wall; and at six o'clock the sloping wall was two degrees higher than the freestone and brick wall, and five degrees above the whinstone. But in frosty weather the sloping wall was three degrees colder, in the night, than any of the others. It may therefore be assumed that, for all practical purposes, the brick and whinstone walls are nearly equal, and only a shade in advance of the freestone wall.

291 The position of the walls being determined, as well as the material, trenches for the reception of the foundations should be excavated. Their depth must depend upon the subsoil, and the workmen should dig until they reach a solid homogeneous bed. The trench completed, it should be filled up with concrete, consisting of six or seven parts of coarse gravel, stones, or brick rubbish, to one part of freshly-slaked lime and one part of cement. This material should be mixed thoroughly in a heap, and thrown into the trench from a platform of scaffold boards raised two or three feet above the level of the ground. The effect of throwing the concrete from a position a few feet above that in which it is intended to remain is to consolidate the wall, the force and weight of the descending material tending to drive the particles closer together. The trench may be filled with the concrete that is to serve as a foundation for the walls up to the surface of the ground, or it may be carried a few inches above it. This would tend to keep the wall dry at the base, for if the brickwork is below the surface of the soil, as bricks are more or less porous they will absorb moisture from it.

292 But garden walls may be built altogether of concrete, which is a manifest advantage in districts in which gravel is plentiful, but where bricks and stones are not so easily obtained. When the surface of the ground is reached the remainder of the wall above ground is formed in successive stages by concrete thrown into a space the width of the wall, and formed into the shape of a trough of the wall's thickness, by means of boards placed on either side of the wall, and sustained in a framework specially contrived for the purpose. The corners or 'returns' of the walls are managed in a similar manner. Thus walls of any length may be raised to any height at comparatively little cost. It must be remembered, however, that concrete, when properly made, is so hard that it is not possible to drive nails into it as into brickwork. It is therefore desirable, and indeed necessary, to provide means for training fruit trees and the support of climbing plants, etc., during the building of the wall. This is best done by inserting, at distances from 8 to 12 feet, vertical pieces of wood in the face of the wall along its entire length. These should be made of a dovetailed form in section, as shown in Fig. 104, which represents a horizontal section of a concrete wall thus treated. The wall, as it has been said, is formed, or moulded, by throwing concrete between boards placed along its inner and outer face – that is to say, along PQ, the inner surface, and RS, the outer surface. The uprights, as shown at A, which should be prepared some little time before they are wanted for use, and well dressed with tar, or painted, if it be preferred, are then placed at intervals along the boards that form the inner face, to which they may be temporarily attached by screws *driven into them from the outer surface of the boards*, in order to keep them flush with the surface of the wall. As they are keyed into the wall, by being wider behind than they are in front, it is not possible for them to be pulled out as pieces rectangular in section might be, owing to the shrinkage of the concrete. These vertical slips of wood, which may be from 2 to 3 inches in thickness, and from 3 to 4 inches in width, will then afford means for inserting screw-eyes to carry wires along the surface of the

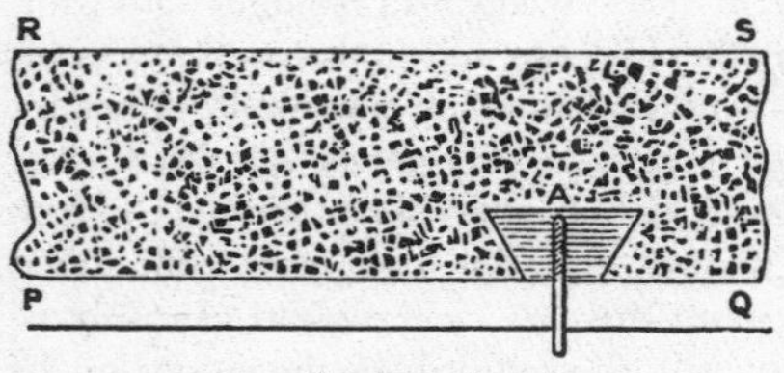

FIG. 104 *Supports for wires along face of concrete wall*

wall, as shown in the illustration, and for the support of the apparatus that is required to strain the wires and keep them at a proper tension. Therefore, if it be intended to enclose a garden with concrete walls, it is necessary, before beginning to build it, to provide means for training trees, etc., as described, as it can only be done with considerable difficulty after the wall is built, and then only in a manner which affords far less satisfactory results.

293 Of late years, other means and materials have been introduced by which garden walls may be very easily and speedily constructed. These are the Patent Concrete Slabs, manufactured and sold by Mr W. H. Lascelles, builder, 121 Bunhill Row, London, and the Croft Adamant Slabs, made and supplied by the Croft Granite, Brick, and Concrete Company, Croft, near Leicester. The slabs made by Mr Lascelles are uniform in size, being 3 feet in length by 2 feet in width, but they are different in external appearance and thickness. Thus, the Fish Scale Tile Slabs, with an ornamental exterior, and used for building cottages, etc., are coloured red, and furnished with a rebate along the lower edge which fits over the thin upper edge of the slab immediately below it. These slabs cost £12 10s. per 100, or 2s. 6d. each, being equal to 5d. per foot super. There are two kinds of plain slabs, suitable for garden walls, grey in colour. Of these, the thicker slab, 1½ inch in thickness, is sold at £10 per 100, or 2s. each, being equal to 4d. per foot super, and the thinner slab, generally called the 'lining slab', because it is chiefly used as a lining for houses and cottages, is sold at £8 15s. per 100, or 1s. 9d. each, being equal to 3½d. per foot super. In building walls with these slabs, a concrete foundation must first be made, and on this a framework of wood or iron must be raised, or vertical studs planted in a wooden sill buried in the concrete foundation, at intervals of 2 feet 9 inches, supposing them to be 3 inches in width. To these uprights the slabs are attached by screws, and the wall is surmounted by a coping of concrete studs, 8 feet long, 4 inches wide, and 4 inches thick, supplied at £11 15s. per 100, or 2s. 4d. each, a price equivalent to 3½d. per foot run. From the data given it is easy to calculate the cost of a wall made of these slabs. The wooden uprights will carry wires for training trees, etc.

294 The Croft Adamant Slabs are used for building silos, cottages, etc., and for roofing purposes are made no thicker than ⅜ inch; but for walls, etc., slabs 1½ inch thick are used. In superficial extent these slabs are 4 feet long and 2 feet 6 inches broad, and are sold at £16 13s. per hundred, which shows the price of each slab to be 3s. 4d., or 4d. per foot super. They possess this advantage in a structural point of view over Lascelles's Patent Concrete Slabs, that in building with them no screwing is necessary, and therefore walls and buildings constructed with them can be more easily taken down and removed from place to place, and with less chance of damage to the material, if the parts are not cemented together. Grooved plinths or sills, uprights, and copings of the same material are provided, the plinths having sockets in them in which the tenons of the uprights are planted, similar tenons in the upper ends of the uprights entering the sockets in the coping. A grooved framework is thus formed, resembling, so to speak, the frame of a school slate, into which the slabs are inserted in the same manner. Iron uprights, formed thus **I**, are also used for the reception of the slabs, and these are lighter in appearance than the Croft

Adamant uprights. If intended to remain permanently in the place where they are erected, it is of course better to cement slabs and uprights together by cement, but if not, a perfectly airtight structure can be obtained by laying a piece of tarred cord along the joints of the slabs, and caulking the uprights. The slabs themselves are tongued and grooved, which assists materially in obtaining a perfect fit and airtight joint in silos and cottages. For walls this is not absolutely necessary.

295 But we must now return to the consideration of the garden wall when built of brick. The thickness of the wall must depend on its height, and the foundation should be thicker by 3 or 4 inches than the wall itself – this thickness rising 5 or 6 inches above the surface level. For a wall 6 or 7 feet high, a single brick, or 9 inch wall, will suffice; for higher walls, it will require a brick in length and another in breadth, or 14 inches; beyond 12 feet and up to 18, two bricks in length, or 18 inches. Walls of these proportions are capable of supporting a lean-to greenhouse of corresponding height, if they are properly bonded and hot lime or good cement is used. It should be the chief aim of the gardener, if he is charged with the superintendence of the work, to see that the workmen use good bricks, and that they are bedded in a moderate quantity of mortar made of fresh-slaked lime and good sand.

The following hints on bricklaying and building brick walls, gathered from *Every Man His Own Mechanic*, may be useful to amateurs who undertake the superintendence of the work that is being executed for them, or gardeners who may be charged with looking after the erection of brick walls. The author of this work says:

Chalk lime (as supplied in Kent) by the yard or hundred is 13s., but per bushel *1*s. Stone lime (as supplied in Devonshire) is 16s. per hundred and 1s. 2d. per bushel. In the immediate neighbourhood of kiln in any locality lime can, of course, be procured at a lower rate than those named. Blue lias lime is charged 24s. per yard. Sand or road grit varies very much, according to the locality and the ease with which it can be procured. Road grit may be valued at 4s. per yard or 4d. per bushel, and sand at an average of 5s. or 6s. per yard or 6d. per bushel. Mortar, when supplied by a builder, is charged at 7d. per hod, and a hod contains half a bushel, which brings the cost to about 1s. or 1s. 2d. per bushel. The amateur should never use sand from the seashore in making mortar; it is excellent for all farm and garden purposes, but the presence of salt from the sea water renders mortar made of it liable to attract moisture in damp weather. If good, clean road sand cannot be got, the best thing to use is sand from the nearest gravel pit. One or the other can always be obtained. Finely-sifted cinder ashes may be mixed with lime, but this will, of course, impart a dark colour to the mortar. The following are the prices per hundred at which bricks are quoted: Place bricks, 4s. 6d.; grey stocks, 5s.; red stocks, 6s.; malms, 9s.; cutters, 11s. 6d.; and red rubbers, 8s.

To proceed, however, with bricklaying, or building with bricks, the amateur must remember that it is a fundamental rule that *in no two courses of bricks immediately contiguous shall the joints between two bricks in each course be continuous, or form a straight or unbroken line.* This must be rigidly observed; the disposition of the bricks caused by the observance of this rule is called 'breaking bond'. A layer of bricks lengthwise throughout a wall is called a 'course', and when bricks are so laid that their length is in the direction of the course, and their sides appear in the face of the wall, they are called 'stretchers', and a course thus formed a 'stretching course', but when they are laid across the line of the course so that their ends or heads appear in the face of the wall, they are called 'headers', and a course thus laid is called a 'heading course'.

FIG. 105 *English bond*

FIG. 106 *Flemish bond*

There are three kinds of bonds used by English bricklayers, called respectively 'garden bond', 'English bond', and 'Flemish bond', and of these the last named is most commonly used. Garden wall bond is used only for 9 inch walls, and consists of courses of three stretchers and one header in regular succession throughout the course. English bond consists of alternate courses of stretchers and headers, as shown in Fig. 105. It is reputed to be the strongest bond used in bricklaying, but it is not so ornamental, and therefore pleasing to the eye, as the Flemish bond, shown in Fig. 106, which consists of courses composed of headers and stretchers in alternation, every successive course being so arranged that the header in the course above rests immediately on the middle of the stretcher in the course below, while the stretcher in the upper course extends over the header in the course below it, and has its ends resting on the ends of the stretchers on either side of the header in question. The difference in the appearance of English and Flemish bond is clearly shown in the illustrations.

296 An economical wall is sometimes constructed of bricks laid as stretchers on each side, the space between being filled up with concrete similar to that prepared for the foundation. This adheres to the brickwork. Headers, or bricks across, are used occasionally as bonders, to hold the two sides together. A wall of 13½ inches, or even 18 inches, if built in this manner, would require, roughly speaking, the former only two-thirds of the quantity of bricks employed in building a solid wall of brick, and the latter not more than one half, while the cost of the concrete is comparatively trifling. In countries where brick is not easily come by, a very good wall may be constructed with a brick in front and stone behind, where one front only is required for use. In Fig. 107, a section of a wall 18 inches, or two bricks, thick, is shown faced on each side with brick, and filled with concrete, and in Fig. 108, an end of the same wall.

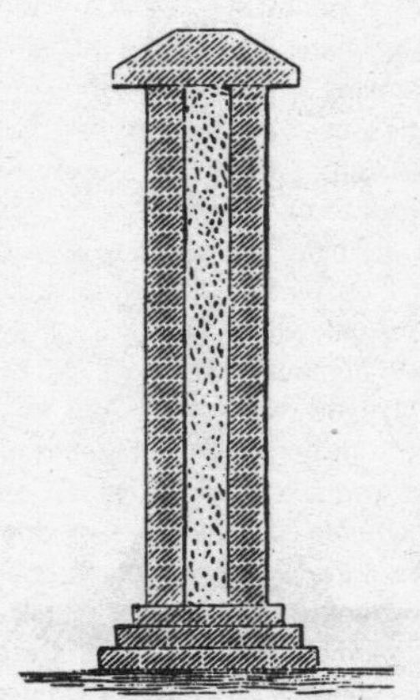

FIG. 107 *Wall filled with concrete*

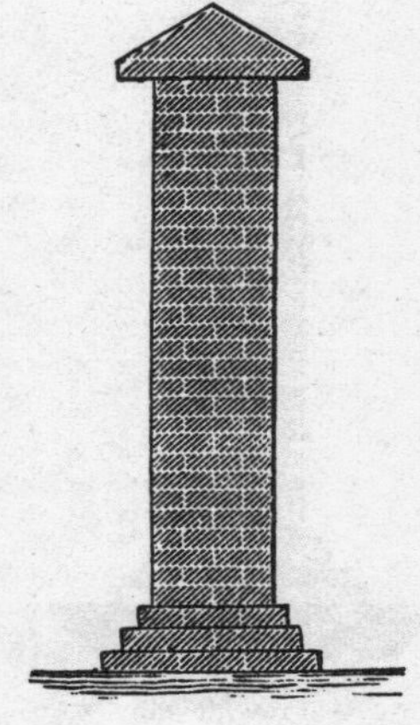

FIG. 108 *End of 18-inch wall*

297 The introduction of hollow bricks is supposed to be conducive to dryness and free ventilation, while it greatly reduces the pressure on the foundation; but it does not appear that we have any great experience as to its result on garden walls.

298 Stone walls for gardens should be built in courses of four or eight inches thick; the stones hammer-dressed on the external surface, the mortar bed not too thick, and the joints pointed and drawn clean. In stone walls – perhaps in brick walls also – copper or iron nails with eyes should be let into the interstices of the wall, to tie down the branches of the fruit trees, taking care that they are let in with the eye close to the wall; for the radiation of heat from the wall is in proportion to its distance, and the heat which is one degree a foot off the wall, is, as we have seen, a hundred and forty-four when in contact with it. The advantage of the eyed nails consists in preserving the wall. Thread dipped in pyroligneous acid, or flexible wire, may be used for the purpose.

FIG. 109 *Eyed nail*

The chief difficulty in the use of eyes in a stone or brick wall arises when they happen to have been driven in at equal intervals horizontally and vertically after the wall is built and before the trees are *in situ* or ready for training. It is better to insert the eyes when engaged in training trees, as then the eyes may be put in exactly where they are wanted. It is better to strain wires along walls, pulling them as close to the surface as possible, for the reasons given, than to tie down the branches to eyes.

299 Hollow walls are sometimes found in gardens of lofty pretensions, where very high cultivation is adopted; but there is reason to believe that in many quarters where they exist they are rarely used. The following very good reasons have been given for their use by Mr Bailey, formerly gardener at Nuneham Park; and certainly, where expense is no object, every gentleman would like to see his walls covered with fruit in its season. 'Apricots,' says Mr Bailey, 'when placed on a south wall, are soon excited by open sunny days in spring: the sap vessels become filled with watery sap. In this state, if a severe frost occurs, the sap vessels are burst by the freezing fluid, and the whole

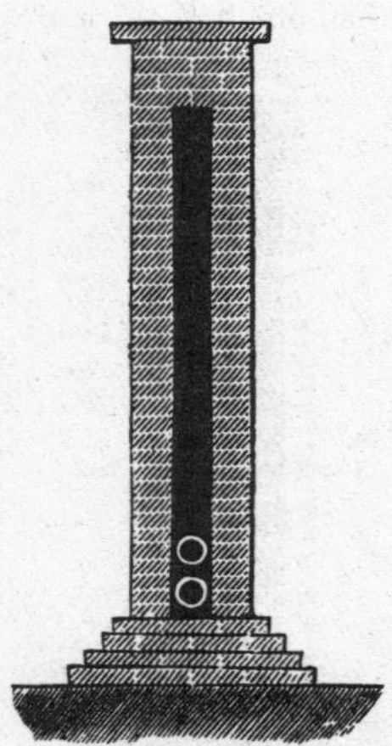

FIG. 110 *Hollow brick wall, enclosing water pipes to heat both sides*

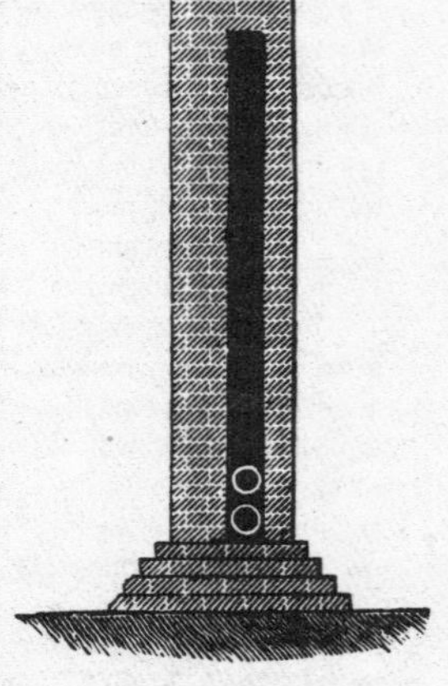

FIG. 111 *Hollow brick wall, heated on one side only*

economy of the plant deranged. Some parts of the tree suffer more than others. The branches most affected, having consumed the sap inherent in them, can draw no further supply, and on the first day when the solar influence is sufficient to cause perspiration, they languish and die. The cause of the injury is not always apparent at the time; but in a ratio proportionate to its extent, it will show itself in a year or two.' Mr Bailey thus accounts for the paralysis which so frequently overtakes this highly-esteemed fruit – first a branch, then a whole side dying away, in the fine sunny days of spring, to the surprise of the gardener; the Moorpark variety being especially subject to such sudden mortality.

300 The walls that were erected at Dalkeith Palace by Mr Charles McIntosh, while in charge of the magnificent gardens there, are 12 feet high and 18 inches thick. The following description of them, and Figs, 110 and 111, are taken from McIntosh's *Book of the Garden*: 'Upon a solid rubble-stone foundation rising to within 6 inches of the surface, nine courses of brick are laid on bed, and form the side of the wall; the tenth course on each side has headers laid across and meeting in the middle at every 3 feet, which binds the wall; these headers being 10 inches long, have 2 inches cut off the end of each, and have a whole brick laid over them; the open space below is occupied by the hot-water pipes, as in Fig. 110. The same is carried on upwards, only changing the place of the headers, so that they shall not be immediately above each other; the last three courses at the top are built solid, to prevent the escape of heat through the coping.' This wall gives equal heat on both sides, and in place of headers pieces of hoop iron may be employed as binders, the iron being bent at the ends, and turned down about 3 inches on the outer side. When one side only is to be heated, a brick and a half, or 14 inches, will occupy one side, and brick on bed the other, as in Fig. 111.

Dearn's system of building hollow walls is a useful one, respecting which the following remarks are made in *Every Man His Own Mechanic*:

> Suppose, for example, that it is desired to construct one or more longitudinal flues in a brick wall. In such a case it is manifest that Flemish bond will not do, because the headers in each course would prove an obstruction. English bond must, therefore, be resorted to, which, as the reader will remember, consists of alternate courses of stretchers and headers. The wall must be built up in the ordinary manner, a layer of stretchers and a layer of headers alternately, until the height is reached at which it is proposed to construct the flue. The last course laid, which, it must be observed, forms the bottom of the flue, must be a course of headers. This course is shown at A in Fig. 112, which represents the vertical and transverse section of such a wall as that which is being described, and which was introduced by a builder named Dearn, whence it was commonly called 'Dearn's Wall'. On either side of the course of headers A, a line of stretchers, B, B, laid on their sides, is placed, and as a brick is 9 inches long and 2½ inches thick, a longitudinal opening, D, 4 inches wide and 4½ inches high, is left in the centre of the wall. This opening is covered in by another course of headers, C, on which the wall is continued with a course of stretchers, and so on. When a wall is built hollow, as above described, other

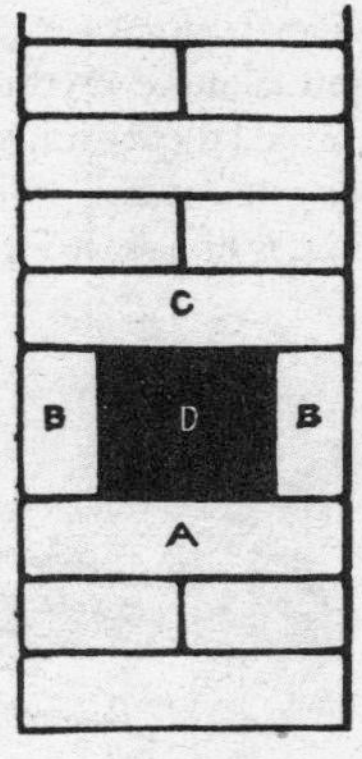

FIG. 112 *Dearn's wall*

ends are effected besides the mere making of a flue, for by the ventilation afforded damp is prevented, and there is a great saving of materials. It was indeed rather for these purposes than for making flues that the hollow construction of walls was proposed by Mr Dearn, and is still followed in many cases. If bricks were scarce and expensive in the locality, a saving of about one-third might be effected by building the wall from the level of the ground with alternate courses of headers and stretchers laid on their sides, as shown in Fig. 112. The wall would not be so strong, it is true, as a solid 9-inch wall, but if solidity were a *sine qua non*, it might be gained by filling the hollow at D with gravel concrete.

301 Mr Walker recommends a mode of heating by hot air as shown in Fig. 113, the apparatus being a furnace, placed below the ground level of the wall, and as much as practicable at the lowest point. The furnace, *a*, with hearth, *m*, below, is bricked in, so that the coal may coke, both for economy of fuel and labour. The air in contact with the plates *b*, *c*, being expanded by heat, will flow into the hot air chamber, *f*, through the flues *e*, *e*, coming in contact with the colder air there. Here it acquires a rotatory motion, retaining a tendency to ascend in the ratio of its rarefaction, flowing along the flue *g* in the direction of the arrows, into the flues *h*, *h*, through the narrow opening left. The sliding of the door *i* will accelerate its circulation. This system obviates the necessity of cleaning the flues, which is found difficult in practice; while hot water, which is advocated in some places, is found too expensive for ordinary use.

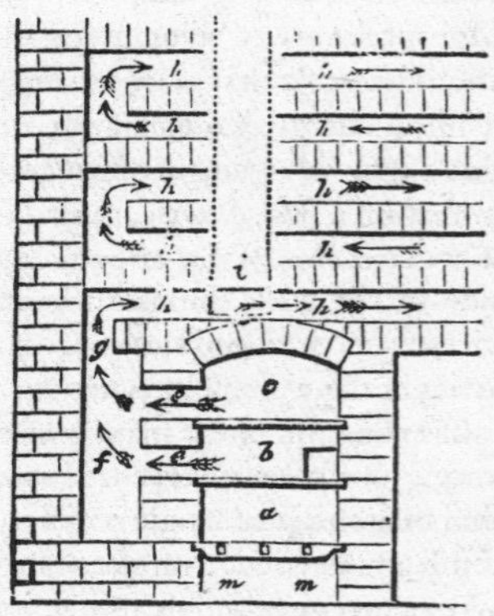

FIG. 113 *Walker's method of heating walls by hot air*

302 Coping to garden walls has been a 'much-vexed' question, and probably many practical men retain their own system, without paying much attention to theories; for, in gardening, a common-sense application of the means at hand, and taking everything at the right time, is of more importance than the best-formed theory imperfectly carried out. It seems very well settled, however, that a stone coping, projecting an inch or two over the wall on each side, as in Fig. 114, is necessary for the protection of the wall from the effects of rain, and that,

FIG. 114 *Flat stone coping on wall*

FIG. 115 *Coping of tiles*

to that extent, the coping is useful in retarding the radiation of heat. Such a coping is formed of flat stones, cemented at the edges to prevent any access of moisture to the top of the wall. Another coping may be formed of roofing tiles, or even of slates, as shown in Figs. 115 and 116, when stones cannot be readily procured. Copings are generally recommended as improving the appearance of the wall, and as being necessary for protecting it from the weather. A coping of slate flags, two inches thick, bevelled off to three-fourths of an inch at the edges on each side, is one of the simplest and most efficient, and is easily obtained in any part of the country where slates are quarried. The projections of the coping greatly enhance the conservative power of the walls. The practice of fitting wire or wood trellis on the face of the wall is condemned by many practical men as interfering with this conservative power, for a space intervenes betwixt the trees and the wall, where the heated air escapes at the small angle of divergence, in consequence of the greater lightness of the air, caused by rarefaction, while the constant flowing of the denser and colder current to supply its place produces a current which destroys the forcing power of the wall.

FIG. 116 *Coping of bevelled slates*

Coping should be always 'throated' when made of stone or slate; with tiles it is neither possible nor necessary to do this. By 'throating' is meant a narrow groove or channel cut in the coping as close to the edge as possible on the lower side, to prevent the water from making its way back against the face of the wall. When the inner face, or one face only, of the wall is used for training trees, the coping may be so put on as to slant in the direction of the face against which no trees are nailed. By this means the water is thrown entirely to the side of the wall that is not stocked with trees. When a stone coping is put on in this way, the higher edge of the coping should be throated; there is no necessity for treating the edge on the lower side in this manner. York paving, six inches thick, Caithness flag, Ackworth paving stone, and various heads of slate of the Pembrokeshire and other Welsh counties, make excellent coping stone. Roman cement has been tried; asphalt has also been tried successfully. Glass, six inches thick, and bevelled, has been thought the best material for coping, being perfectly indestructible by the weather; and cast iron has been found to answer. As to shape, the flat coping, with a groove to carry off the water, is considered to be excellent. A very good coping is sometimes formed of brick and cement, in the style of Fig. 115. Another form of coping strongly recommended are stones, sloping on each side, laid on flat ones placed horizontally along the top of the wall.

303 Admitting that a coping projecting to the extent of two inches is necessary for the protection of the wall, and beneficial to the tree, the best horticulturists come to the conclusion that temporary copings, extending eighteen inches beyond the wall, as shown in Figs. 117 and 118, with protecting curtains depending from them, are very useful during the spring months; and Mr Errington considers that by using them in autumn a fortnight is added to the summer, and time given for the ripening of the young wood. He recommends a

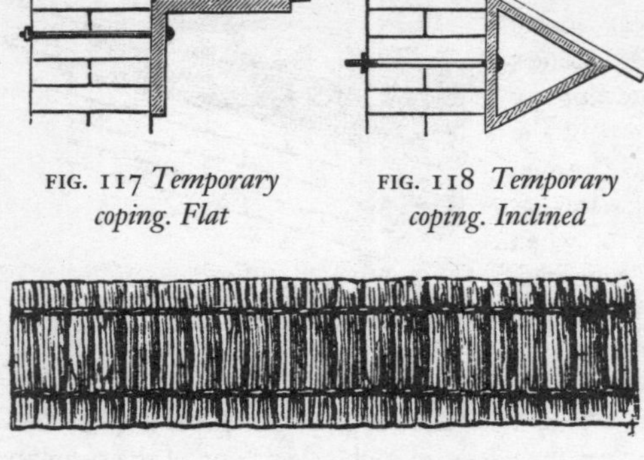

FIG. 117 *Temporary coping. Flat*

FIG. 118 *Temporary coping. Inclined*

FIG. 119 *Straw protectors for fruit trees*

temporary coping, seven or eight inches, in the summer and autumn, and twice that in April and May. Mr McIntosh considers wet walls in summer as robbers of heat, and that a wall with a good projecting coping, capable of being moved in the heat of the day, is invaluable after sunset. The portable coping at Dalkeith is a boarding nine inches wide, supported on iron brackets secured by bolts and nuts passing through the wall. The boards are attached to the brackets by screws. In the coping shown in Fig. 118, the iron brackets are constructed in the form of a triangle instead of in the ordinary way, as in Fig. 117; but they are secured to the wall in the same manner. This construction admits of the temporary coping being placed in a slanting position.

304 Copings projecting too far are said to deprive the leaves of the vigour they derive from summer rains and heavy dews, although they are useful in spring, when the trees are in blossom, and up to the time when the fruit is set. At this season, even in the drier climate of France, it is found necessary to protect the tender blossoms from the late frosts, hail, snow, and cold rains of spring, which are very fatal to stone fruit; the walls in France being generally trellised, in order to protect the trees from the intensity of the heat produced by radiation, as distinguished from our own moist climate, where the practice is reversed. To carry the protecting material, an angular framework of wood is attached to the trellis, projecting some twenty inches or so from the wall, at an inclination of 50°. When the tree begins to vegetate, toward the second week of February, hurdles of straw attached to rods of wood, 7 feet 4 inches in length by 2 feet broad, as in Fig. 119, are placed on triangular frames, as shown in Fig. 120, so as to shelter the tree at the time when it is in blossom, till it has begun to stone. In these frames the piece B is passed behind the trellis, the piece A takes and supports the protector, C acts as a strut against the wall to sustain the straw hurdle and its support A, and D is a connecting upright to stiffen the frame. When the trellis is absent, projecting rods of wood are attached under the coping, as in Fig. 121, upon which the hurdles are laid in lengths, at a similar angle. This shelter, M. Du Breuil declares, is indispensable

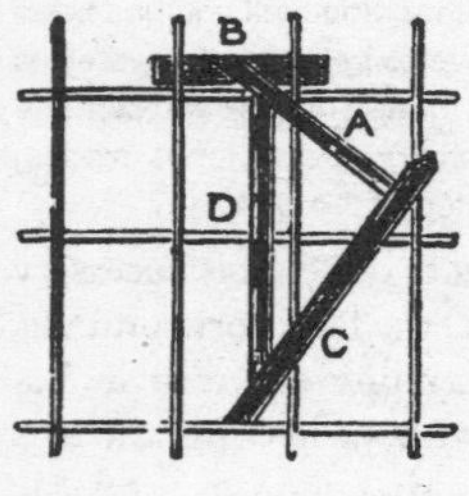

FIG. 120 *Bracket for straw hurdle*

for stone fruit. Apples and pears are also benefitted by the shelter, especially when exposed to a north or west aspect, or in damp localities. This protection, however, according to the same authority, which suffices while the temperature stands at 1° or 1½° below zero, becomes useless when it descends to 3°, or even 2°, which too frequently sweeps away the hopes of the fruit gardener. The walls should then be protected by means of a rough canvas, such as is used by paperhangers to cover walls before papering, which is attached to the projecting hurdles, A, in Fig. 122, under the coping at B, and at the bottom, C, to posts, D, driven into the ground at a sufficient distance in front of the wall. The canvas covering permits the light and air and warmth to pass; the vegetation is uninterrupted, but the protection is sufficient to exclude the strongest spring frosts.

FIG. 121 *Rods of wood to support straw protectors*

Mr Gorrie, a well-known and experienced horticulturist, found that the projecting coping added greatly to the warmth of the walls, the difference being from 4° to 11°; and it will be readily conceded that this advantage is a very important one. At the same time the cost of permanent coping adds greatly to the cost of the wall. Mr Gorrie proposed to train the Ayrshire rose on a projecting trellis under the coping, so as to give shelter to the fruit trees while in blossom, the rapid spring growth of this rose being favourable for the purpose, while its deciduous habit admits of the full play of the wind in winter.

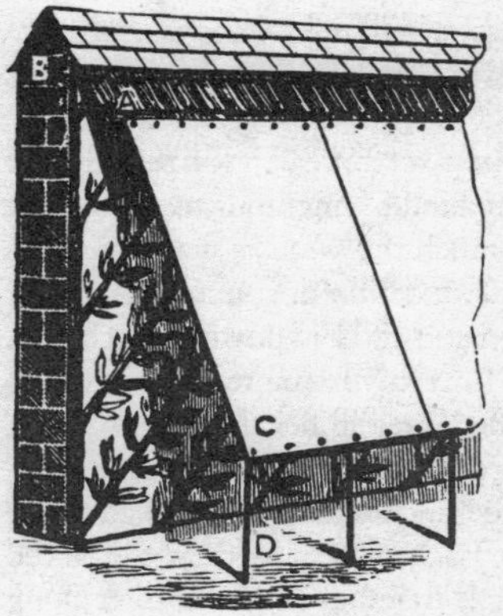

FIG. 122 *French shelter of canvas for fruit trees*

305 Among the causes of barrenness to which the Rev. John Lawrence, one of our oldest and best writers on fruit trees, directs attention are – cold seasons, but especially *frosts* and *blasts* in the spring. Having recourse to mats, although sometimes successful, has many objections, which put him to considering something more efficient, and it occurred to him that horizontal shelters presented the one needful remedy. He experimented with thin bits of board or tile, fastened to the wall, and found them to succeed to a marvel, securing fruit wherever they were placed. For this purpose he proposes to lay rows of tiles in the wall at distances regulated by the space between the lateral branches of the tree, and jutting forward from the plane of the wall about an inch and a half, not in continuous rows, but with gaps to receive the branches of the tree. By the help of these shelters, says Mr Lawrence, 'even in the most difficult year, a good quantity of fruit may *almost* be depended upon from such blossoms as are sheltered by the tiles. The fruit thus sheltered from cold and blasts I have experienced to be much larger, better, and finer-tasted, than those of the same tree where exposed. They are also forwarder and earlier ripe than the others.'

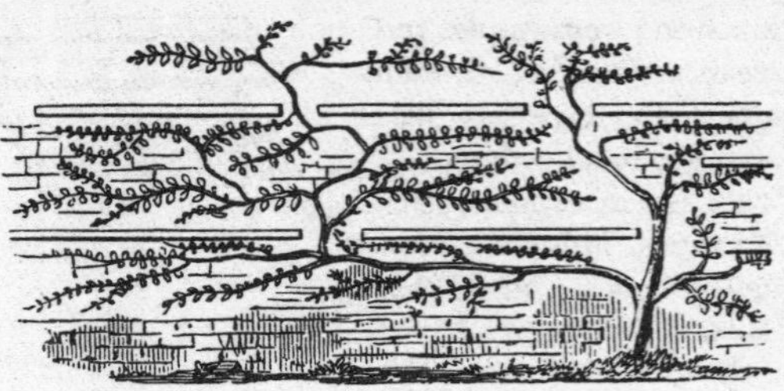

FIG. 123 *Lawrence's method of protecting fruit trees*

306 Besides brick and stone, chalk and earth have been sometimes employed in erecting garden walls with success. In the case of chalk, the lumps should be used in much the same way as irregular blocks of rag-stone, and bedded in mortar: it is, however, a brittle material, and one that is undesirable in many ways and for many reasons, and should only be used in cases of absolute necessity. It is said that an entire house with garden walls has been erected on this principle in chalk, but we are not told whether or not it was a success. It is, however, an interesting question, as the cost of such a house, where the subsoil is chalk, is confined to the labour – and labour of the most ordinary kind – the soil dug out yielding all the material.

307 In the case of building with earth – the best sort of earth for this kind of building is what is termed 'brick earth', or any kind of unctuous marly soil, or gravelly earth full of pebbles – the process is much the same as that which has been described for building concrete walls. A foundation of concrete, brick, or stone, having been laid, a wooden frame is prepared and laid down on each side, of the exact thickness of the intended walls. Into this frame the earth, which should first be broken to pieces, freed from the larger stones that may be in it, and moistened with water sprinkled over it through the fine rose of a watering-pot, is mixed with straw cut in pieces from 3 to 6 inches long, and placed in the frame in successive layers about 6 inches thick. Each layer of earth as it is placed in the frame is consolidated by ramming it closely together with a rammer along the whole length of the wall. In this way the work proceeds layer by layer until the intended height is attained, when a coping of stone or other material is bedded on it with cement or mortar, in order to complete and protect the wall.

308 It will be readily enough understood that this sort of wall would be only resorted to in the present day where bricks and stone are nearly inaccessible, but in the olden time, and indeed in the commencement of the present century, such walls were common enough in Devonshire as garden walls and the walls of labourers' cottages and outbuildings. They were warmer than walls of brick and stone, and by no means unsightly. They were known in the western counties as 'cob' walls. When taken down and broken into small pieces they were found to furnish an excellent manure for grass lands. Wooden slips, as shown in Fig. 104, should be inserted vertically in the face of such walls as these, in order to take wall-eyes, or to which to attach horizontal bars or wires, to which the branches of the trees might be tied down when training them. In fact, an earth wall is as much too weak for the reception and retention of wall rails as concrete is too hard, and means for training the trees must be adopted without fail, and attached to the walls while their erection is in progress.

While treating of walls and laying out gardens, let us give the reader an excellent piece of advice from quaint old John Lawrence: 'To those who are to form a garden anew, I say that thirty or forty yards square is abundantly enough for that you intend for your best garden, where you would have your choicest fruit to grow. More would only make you uneasy, to keep and manage it as you ought.' Returning again to this argument, he gives in detail the produce under his own management of forty yards square. On his north wall, or south aspect, he has seven peaches trained with his horizontal shelters. Of these he reckons each tree under proper management will produce a hundred of large fair fruit; 'but, lest that number may be thought too large, let us take half, and say fifty; the seven peaches on the best wall will thus produce, at a very moderate computation, three hundred and fifty.' On the same wall he allows three of the 'large Turkish apricot, which hath a noble flavour', and on another wall five. 'If they be managed as they ought, and at full growth, I cannot say that I remember a year when they have afforded me less than a bushel of fruit.' On his best wall he allows room for four or five of the best French pears, which are so little inferior to stone fruit, and yet come to their maturity when the other is gone. With good management each tree will yield half a bushel. 'On the east, west, and south wall I allow room for some of the best plums.' Upon the whole, here is a square wall, forty yards square, which will afford room for forty trees suited to its several aspects, which, with the dwarf pears, plums, and cherries, which occupy the centre of the square, which, he reckons, yield, on estimate, fourteen bushels of finest pears, and an 'abundant provision for the table, throughout the season, of cherries and plums'; while vines, figs, and winter pears are not forgotten, each sort suitably placed to the sun, which, with good management, may reasonably afford every year a sufficient variety as well as quantity of the best fruits.' Such is the opinion of the Rev. John Lawrence, based on the result of his own skilful management.

309 The introduction of orchard houses has, to a certain extent, revolutionised the whole practice of the culture of tender fruit in the open air. Except in the most highly-favoured localities, it is not desirable to furnish walls with peaches and nectarines, unless provision be made for covering them with glass in early spring and in late wet autumns. The safety of the blossom and embryo fruit, and maturation of the wood, would thus be insured. It is wiser, however, to devote the best walls to the culture of pears and plums, and to erect orchard houses for all other stone fruit, and the tenderer varieties and choicer sorts of plums. Orchard houses, most assuredly, are cheaper, more efficient, and certain than glass walls, but many horticulturists of repute are still in favour of planting the trees out rather than growing them in pots. Success is probable and possible enough by pot culture; with ordinary care it is certain, if the trees are planted out in good loam.

310 But it has been so long the custom to grow peaches and nectarines on walls, that many will still insist upon doing so; and therefore the best descriptions of walls, most approved methods of protection, etc., continue to be subjects of the first importance. To sum up all that has been said on the subject, with some slight additions: No material for kitchen garden walls can equal good red brick of medium hardness of texture. The joints should be as narrow as possible, and should be formed of the best lime and sharp sand: they can either be left white, or the lime can be coloured a few shades lighter than the bricks. The bricks are better without any colouring whatever. This is not only the best-looking wall, but the plants are easier trained to it, and are probably subject to fewer alterations of temperature upon its surface than they would be upon a wall of any other substance or colour. Walls should never be less than 8 or more than 14 feet high, and may vary from 9 to 22 inches in thickness. From 10 to 12 feet is a good average height, and 14 inches in thickness will impart strength enough for that height. Sometimes walls from 4 to 6 feet in height are built only 4½ inches thick; but when they are built in this thickness, a *quasi* buttress, 9 inches thick is placed at intervals of 10 or 12 feet, to impart strength and to give stability to the wall. The superstructure is carried up on the foundation in the thickness of 9 inches to the level of the ground or a few inches above it, and a coping of one or two courses laid in the ordinary way, and a third course of headers placed on the side is used to finish the wall, giving it the appearance of being built in panels. When built without piers or buttresses, the wall is frequently erected in a curved form, as shown in Fig. 124, as a 4½ inch curved wall of this form will resist as much pressure as a straight wall 9 inches thick without piers. As a rule, however, all kitchen garden walls should be straight; and they are not safe without piers, unless they are a brick and a half, or 13½ inches, thick.

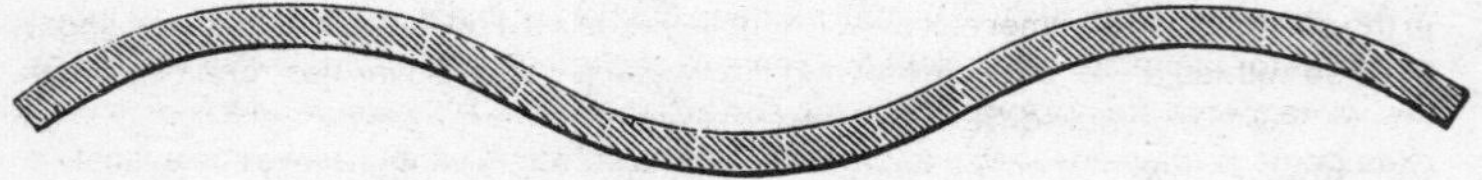

FIG. 124 *Curved from 4½ inch wall*

311 All walls for fruit trees should also be furnished with a coping of stone, slate, or some other hard, durable material, of sufficient width to project four inches on each side of the wall. The top of the coping should be slightly convex or sloping towards each face of the wall, and the under surface as much concave, to facilitate the removal of water. A groove, or 'throating', should also be formed ½ inch deep, and ¾ inch from the outside edge of the lower side, to intercept and throw off all drip. The coping should also be made in as long lengths as possible, to reduce the number of joinings. If stone is used, the joints should be formed of the best Portland cement; if slate, a mixture of white and red lead must be used. It would also be advisable to have the copings overlap, as in Fig. 125, as they are comparatively useless unless waterproof. As in fine weather frost falls in nearly perpendicular or vertical lines, a coping projecting over a wall will often protect the trees on its surface; and it will do this the more effectually if it has previously preserved them in a dry state.

FIG. 125 *Coping rebated to overlap*

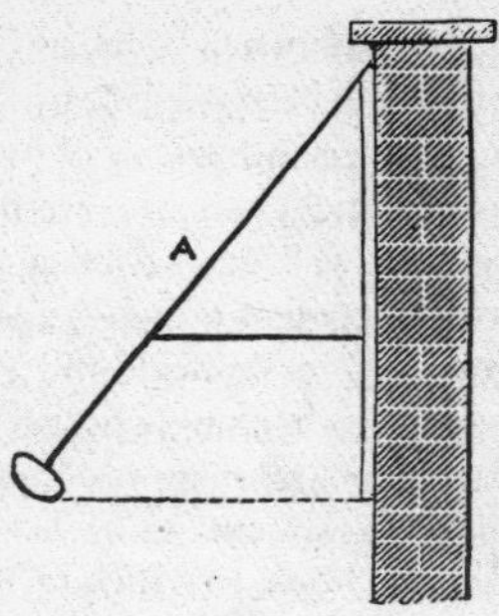

FIG. 126 *Bracket for broad slate coping*

Permanent and temporary copings of much greater widths are frequently used, as it has been already stated. The section in Fig. 126 represents a bracket for supporting a wide slate coping that is sometimes brought into temporary use. The top surface, A, of the bracket consists of a bar of iron two inches wide, on which the slate slabs meet. Any length of slate may be used, but the longer and stronger the slabs, the fewer the brackets required, and vice versa. An iron gutter runs along the rings in front, to convey the water into a drain at the end. A great drawback to such copings is, that the trees are deprived of the natural rains and dews. This, however, may be remedied, to some extent, by syringing. Such brackets would be invaluable for applying temporary copings of wood for a few weeks in spring and autumn. Notwithstanding all that has been written against the practice, there can be no doubt that it is desirable to afford protection to the surface of wall trees when in blossom. No copings, wide or narrow, permanent or temporary, will shelter them from cutting frosts driven in upon them at that time by a sharp wind. Of course, every gardener is fully aware of the great importance of thinning both wood and fruit, getting the former thoroughly matured, and preserving the tree in the most robust health; but it is difficult to see how this precludes us from protecting the blossoms in the spring. Good summer culture will doubtless secure a good show of fruit, and endow the tree with sufficient strength to bring it to maturity; but it never has, and never can, enable the tender blossoms of peaches and apricots to withstand a frost of 2° without protection. The great merit of the covering suggested above consists in the facility with which it can be removed and applied at pleasure; for it is better not to protect at all than to apply a permanent covering of any description. The artificial tenderness and extra liability to the attraction of insects, in consequence, would be more disastrous than the frost itself. No valid objection can, however, be urged against temporary protection, applied only in cases of absolute necessity, and at no other time. So particular are some gardeners upon this point that they have sallied out to place copings or coverings of some sort over the trees even at midnight when the weather has been uncertain.

312 Blinds or screens of canvas, netting, or tiffany, form excellent temporary protection for trees, and the following is a description of the method by which they may be prepared and attached to the walls for use: About 1 inch below the coping a splint of wood, 2½ inches wide and 1½ inch thick, is firmly secured to the wall. This splint is furnished with hooks about 1 inch long, and 1 foot apart. Pairs of pulleys, 1½ inch in diameter and ¼ inch deep, attached to iron plates, are fixed on this splint, at intervals of 8 feet apart, all along the wall. They are let

FIG. 127 *Pulleys in splint*

into the splint at a bevel, by cutting off part of the top and front surface; and each is firmly kept in its place by four screws, as in Fig. 127. Small eyes are also placed below every other pair of pulleys thereon, at distances of 16 feet apart. Pairs of posts, 4 inches square, are firmly inserted in the ground, about 4 feet 6 inches from the wall, and 16 feet apart, leaving about 3 inches above the surface. These posts are 2 feet 6 inches apart, and connected together with a strong piece of wood, 1½ inches wide and 3 inches deep, nailed on the inner or wall side of the posts. Another single post is placed in the centre of the space between the pairs, leaving a clear space of 8 feet between. The tops of the posts are cut out in the middle, as shown in Fig. 128, and the single one is furnished with a double hook, to which to attach a cord. Splints of wood, ½ inch square and 10 feet 6 inches long, are then attached to the hooks already referred to, by an iron eye attached to the upper end, the bottom end resting in the opening of the centre of the post. Canvas screens, 2 feet wide, attached to two similar splints of wood, are then hooked on to the top of the wall, resting on the pair of posts already adverted to. Wooden rollers, 16 feet long and 3¼ inches in diameter, furnished with a cast-iron wheel at both ends, 4½ inches in diameter, 1½ deep, and 1½ wide across the mouth, for the reception of cord, are then attached to the bottom of broad pieces of canvas to be used as blinds, between the pairs of posts. The top of the canvas has pieces of zinc an inch square, with a hole in the centre, firmly sewn to it, a foot apart. These are for attaching to the hooks on the splint at the top of the wall, and the cord is then passed over the hooks, *b*, *b*, carried round the pulleys at *e*, *e*, then over those at *d*, *d*, and fastened to the ends of the roller at *c*, *c*, so that by pulling the cord passed over the hooks, *b*, *b*, the roller and canvas attached to it is drawn up to the splint. It will be seen that each roller is thus furnished with four pulleys and two cords, and it can be moved up and down with the greatest dispatch. The canvas screens fixed on the pairs of posts, while they support the ends of the rollers, also allow plenty of space for the rollers to work in, without coming in contact with each other, and without leaving a vacancy between. Angular screens are also provided for filling the spaces at the ends, so that it forms a complete canvas house when the blinds are down, and it can be removed or applied in one half the time taken to describe it.

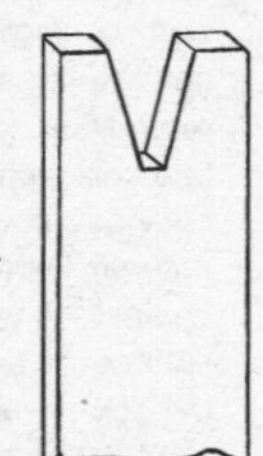

FIG. 128 *Top of posts in pairs*

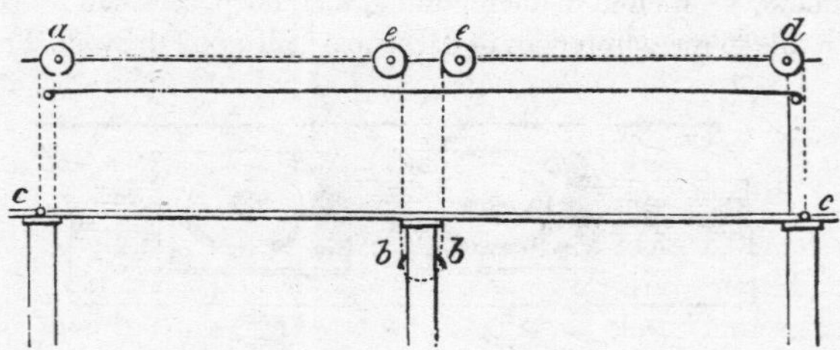

FIG. 129 *Diagram illustrative of application of canvas screens for fruit trees*

Such blinds as those described above, if carefully used, will last a dozen of years, and often save a crop in a single night; and they are equally as useful in autumn in maturing the wood as in spring for protecting the blossoms. In cold districts they would be most useful for pears, plums, etc. Flued walls, carefully managed, may often ensure a crop, also; but great care is necessary to prevent an excess of heat: combined with canvas covering, less heat would be necessary. Provision should be made for easily and expeditiously cleaning them, as a flued wall on fire is certain death to the trees. Hot water would, of course, be infinitely better, attended with no danger and certain benefit. Its first expense, however, is great, although its working would be cheap; for, no aperture being required, a very gentle heat would suffice. Both for flues and hot water, of course, the walls would be partly hollow, and, apart from heating altogether, some recommend hollow walls. There can be no possible objection to their use: they would possibly be drier at all times, and certainly the air contained in their interstices, being dry, would retain its heat for a considerable time, and raise the temperature of the wall when the heat might be most wanted. The grand secret of successful fruit culture on the open walls, however, is to have the wood well ripened in the autumn, retarding it from blooming early in the spring, by removing it from the wall. Finally, trees should always be attached to the walls by nailing, when it is possible to do so, and not tied to wall eyes, etc., however close they may be fixed to it. Nailing is not only more expeditious, but better for the trees than tying.

313 Hedges have already been slightly alluded to in the foregoing pages, but they merit further consideration; for, properly managed, they undoubtedly constitute the cheapest and most lasting, as well as the most ornamental, of all the artificial divisions of land. Few persons will object to the opinion, that the country where fields are divided by the common white thorn presents a far more agreeable appearance at all seasons of the year, and especially during spring, when the thorns are in blossom, than those parts where dwarf stone walls are made to answer the same purpose. The white thorn, however, though most commonly employed, is not the only plant that can be made use of for separating one piece of ground from another. Though for fields it is, perhaps, as useful as any, still, for park and garden purposes, there are many other plants which may be advantageously employed.

314 The different kinds of thorn certainly embrace all the constituents of a good hedge: they are of easy culture, quick growth, and capable of being trained in any direction; they branch out and thicken under pruning, and are not over particular as to soil; but there are many other plants far more ornamental which will fulfil all these conditions equally well. For some time the chief objection to the general introduction of most of these – the price – an objection that is rapidly being got rid of, for hollies and evergreens suitable for hedges have recently been getting cheaper and cheaper every year. And there is no reason why they should not be cheap, for hollies and several other evergreens can be raised at almost as small an expense as thorns. Upon every large estate the woodman should have his seed bed of hollies, evergreen oaks, and other things that can be used for hedge purposes.

315 Few things have a better appearance than a well-kept holly hedge. The best variety for the purpose is *Ilex aquifolium*, the Common Holly. In forming a holly hedge, the ground should be prepared by trenching, and, if the soil be poor and sandy, it will be well to let it have a dressing of manure. The best plants are those of three years' growth, which have had one shift from the seed bed. They should be taken up carefully, with as much soil on the roots as possible, and planted soon after Midsummer – if possible, during the rains of July. A board trench should be dug, capable of receiving the plants, which should be placed in it singly with their roots well spread out. If the weather be dry at the time, the best plan is to water the bottom of the trench and to give no water afterwards, unless a severe drought should set in. The next season, if they be well rooted, the young plants may be moderately pruned with the knife, after which they will branch out and form themselves into a good hedge.

316 Next to holly for forming a compact and durable hedge is the Yew. It bears close clipping, takes up but little space, and is a good shelter throughout the year. The yew, however, must only be used for garden purposes, or, at any rate, in places where cattle can be kept from it, for horses and all cattle are very fond of the yew, and will eat greedily the young spring leaves, though they are very injurious, and often fatal to them. The same objection attaches to two other plants which make very useful and ornamental hedges – the box and the privet. Both these should be kept out of the way of cattle. In gardens and pleasure grounds they may be used with very good effect, for they bear clipping almost better than anything else, and are very neat and compact. The privet mixes well with the thorn, where greater strength is required than can be had by using privet alone.

Those persons who have travelled in Holland and Belgium have no doubt noticed the neat manner in which small enclosures of land are separated from each other by their thrifty and industrious owners. The hedges are trained along stakes and rods placed for the purpose, and to these the plants of which they are composed are tied with pieces of osier. In this way every slender branch is laid in, and as they are made to cross each other frequently, a regular network is formed. These hedges, when in leaf, are very close and tight, they take up very little room, and form scarcely any harbour for small birds. Many of our ornamental shrubs might be thus trained to form hedges – the *Cydonia Japonica*, for instance, which is close, quick-growing, and bears a most beautiful flower. This plant is as hardy as any native British plant, and very easily propagated.

The Cotoneaster, again, may be employed for the same purpose and in the same way. Cuttings of the Cotoneaster taken in August, and put into the shade, will be rooted well enough for planting out next spring. When planted they should be about one foot or a foot and a half apart, and have a trellis of stakes or hazel rods to support them. This hedge will require, at first, a good deal of attention in training and entwining the branches; but when three or four feet high, it may be clipped and thus kept in shape.

The different Veronicas also make firm hedges, and are very handsome when in flower. Strong bushes may be planted three feet apart, and trained to stretched wires, which, in this case, are better than stakes. In Guernsey, the Hydrangea is sometimes used to form a hedge to a grass field, and nothing can be more beautiful. Both this and the veronica, however, are not sufficiently hardy to admit of their being used except in the extreme south. Such, however, is not the case with the Aucuba, which is so hardy that it might be used in most parts of England. It is easily cultivated, and might be trained to stretched wire.

An American writer recommends the Common Barberry, *Berberis vulgaris*, as a hedge plant. 'A hedge plant,' he says, 'to become popular, must be perfectly hardy and easy to propagate. It should also be vigorous enough to grow well in ordinary soil without manure. It should be thorny to keep cattle off, and low enough to require little or no pruning. The Common Barberry combines these qualities better than any plant that I am acquainted with. It is remarkably hardy, thriving well in a great variety of soils, and is said to live for centuries. It has a shrubby habit, growing from six to ten feet in height, yellowish, thorny wood, leaves in rosettes, yellow flowers on drooping racemes, and scarlet oblong berries, very acid, but making delicious preserves. We have a barberry hedge,' he continues, 'in our grounds at Wallingford, Connecticut, twenty-four rods long, and nine years old, from the seed. Two rows of plants were set, the rows one foot apart and the plants one foot apart in the rows, and set alternately to break joints. This hedge has been clipped a little two or three times to keep it even, and is now six or seven feet high, with a firm, compact base, perfectly impervious to the smaller animals, and stout enough to turn ordinary farm stock. An important item, as regards this plant, is its habit of sending up suckers from the bottom, by which, in a few years, it comes to have a base six to twelve inches in diameter.'

317 There is no doubt that very many conifers would make excellent hedges, all that is required being that they should be supplied at a suitable price. Most, even of the choicest varieties, may be raised very freely from cuttings as well as from seed. We know that the common Scotch fir is used, with very good effect, both as a fence and shelter along many of our lines of railroad. When headed down this fir throws out strong laterals, which, interlacing each other, make a very substantial and lasting hedge. The young plants should be set closely, and as they grow up, any weak places can easily be stopped by rails crossing the stems. Like all other hedges, these require occasional training and attention.

318 In forming any hedge, it is, of course, necessary to take into consideration the aspect, the quality of the soil, and all other particulars that conduce to the healthy state of vegetable life. The skill of the gardener is hardly anywhere more discernible than in the exercise of that statesmanlike quality which consists of putting the right thing in the right place. All plants will not suit all climates, all situations, and all soils. It is wise, therefore, to consider that though there are many ornamental plants and shrubs that will make good hedges, it is not all of these that may choose to flourish where we wish our hedge to grow. As a general rule, the knife may be used unsparingly in all things suitable for hedges, and the hedge itself will be greatly improved by its use. All hedges, but especially those that bear the shears or clippers, should be cut upwards to a narrow ridge, for, by this means, the lower part, not being overshadowed by the upper, will be kept thick, and the hedge will last sound much longer. After they have been planted several years, hedges of most materials will require to be cut down, the soil renovated, and, perhaps, new plants introduced. This necessity, however, is very generally the result of neglect in early years, for, where proper care has been bestowed, and annual pruning given, hedges will last as long as brick walls.

CHAPTER 9

Roads, Walks, Bridges, and Garden Buildings

319 In the formation of all roads and walks that give access to the house itself, and to the gardens and grounds, and the various parts of which they are composed, it will be useful to bear in mind that the main principle of perfect transit is found in the ability to reach distant places by the nearest route, with the greatest ease, and in the shortest time. It is true that this applies chiefly to the means of communication between one town and another, whether by road or rail, but the principle, nevertheless, should be carried out even in private roads and pathways, and should be remembered when laying them out, unless any valid reason exists for adopting a different plan. A carriage road, for instance, should always appear to be the best and most direct route to the house. If this principle is not violated, it matters little whether the road be long or short, straight or curved, level or undulating, carried through parks stocked with deer or noble woods abounding with game; but let it once become obvious that the road is unduly lengthened for the sake of effect, and the charm vanishes at once – the same scenery that delighted and pleased becomes tame and tiresome. There is no good reason, however, why the carriage road may not be carried through some of the most picturesque scenery, and rendered as interesting and commanding as is consistent with convenience. A distant glimpse of the house may sometimes be permitted with excellent effect, as being satisfactory to the eye for its beauty, and as indicating a termination to the journey.

320 Nothing contributes more to the importance of a carriage road and the effect that it produces at starting than the manner and line of its divergence from the public road. The farther in reason that the angle of divergence can be removed from a right angle, the more graceful will the entrance be. In some cases it may be impossible to place the carriage road at any other angle to the public road than that of a right angle, but even here much may be done to modify the otherwise obvious disadvantage. Thus, in Fig. 130, the carriage road, B, enters the public road, A, at right angles. Now, any enclosure following the rectangular lines that define the public road and the carriage road would be stiff and formal, but by erecting an ornamental fence where the dotted lines occur, placing the entrance gate at C, and laying down the parts D, D, between the roads and the railing, in grass, the offensive impression of stiffness is at once removed. But even here the sharp turn into and out of the public road at right angles is still preserved, and nothing but the stiffness of appearance is removed. It is better, then, under such circumstances, to make, as in Fig. 131, a double approach, as shown by B, B, to the entrance gate, C, from the public road, A. The triangular space, D, may be laid down in grass, and protected by stone pillars or wooden posts connected by iron rails, or by a massive iron chain, or, if

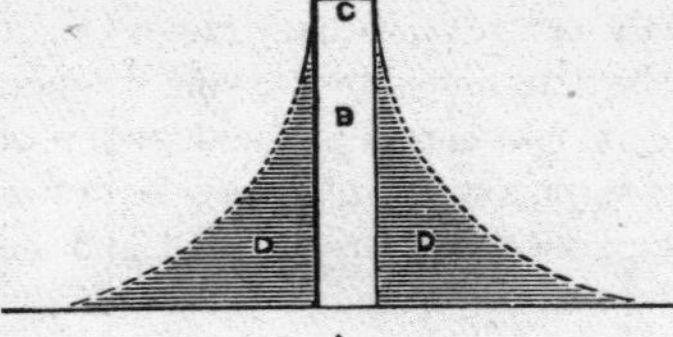

FIG. 130 *Private road at right angles to public road*

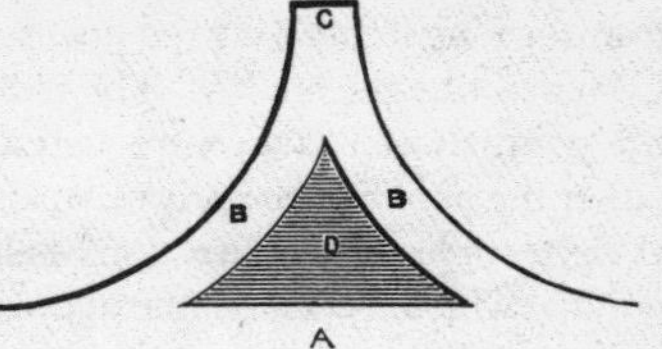

FIG. 131 *Double approach in order to avoid right angles*

large enough, planted with ornamental shrubs and trees. Of course, neither in Figs. 130 or 131 need the precise circular form of sweep be preserved; on the contrary, the longer the curves B, B, in Fig. 131, and the longer the frontage the space D presents to the public road, the better will be the general appearance of the entrance. Whatever may be the curvature of the sweep, it is desirable that a liberal space should be left outside the entrance gate; the form of the space D is of less consequence than its size. When small, it will be better to lay it down in grass, but when large, it will form a pretty and effective shrubbery.

321 We may now take representative cases in which the divergence from the main road is effected at angles other than that of a right angle, as in Figs. 132 and 133, in which the latter exhibits a separation at a very acute angle, and the former a turning off at a considerably wider angle – in fact, at an angle of about 50 degrees. Now, in each of these cases, the mode of treatment is the same, and in each the same lettering has been adopted, A, as before, representing the public road, and B the private road, their relative positions in each diagram being shown by the solid lines. It is desirable to see what may be done in order to divest the approach from the public road of its stiffness and angularity, and at the same time to determine at what position in the private road the entrance gate may best be placed. This may be done on mathematical principles, if desired, and not in dependence on chance curves determined by the eye, which may present a good appearance from certain aspects, but look unsightly from others. The first thing to be done in each diagram is to bisect the angles at C and D, and to set out the dotted lines of bisection, CE and DF. Then, having determined suitable positions in CE, DF, for the centres E and G, from the centre E, with the radius EH or EK, describe the arc HK, cutting off the angle at C and

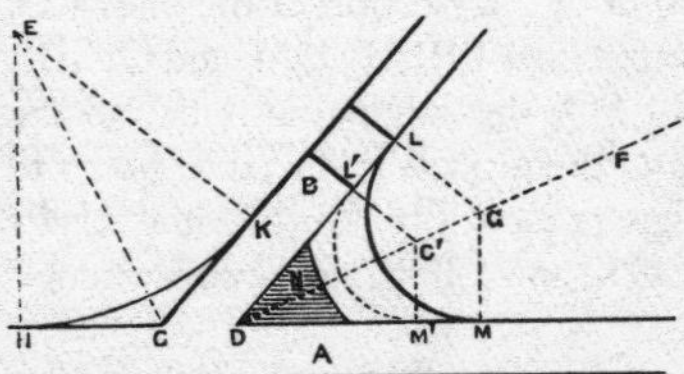

FIG. 132 *Private road at angle of 50° to public road*

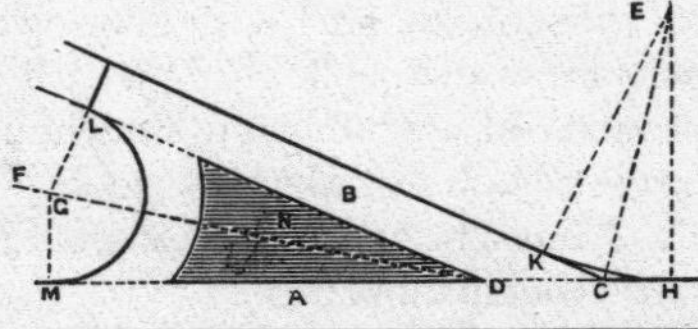

FIG. 133 *Private road at an angle of 25° to public road*

transforming it into a curved line, and from the centre G, with the radius GL or GM, describe the arc LM. The radius may be determined by drawing through the point chosen as a centre a straight line at right angles to the direction of either the public or the private road; or, vice versa, a straight line may be drawn at right angles to the direction of either the public or the private road, and the point at which it cuts the line of bisection of the angle formed by the inclination of the direction of the roads will be the centre from which to strike the sweep. The entrance gate may be placed across the private road at L. In Fig. 133, the space N may be railed in and laid down in grass, or planted with shrubs, but in Fig. 132, this space is too small for treatment in this manner, and it will be better to throw the whole space between the curves into the roadway, or bring the entrance gate nearer to K, placing it at L´. and form the sweep to the right hand by the arc L´M´, struck from the centre G´. Very little, however, is gained by doing this, and the general effect of the entrance is considerably impaired by the diminution of the sweep on the right hand.

322 It is not always the case that public roads run in a straight line at the part at which they are entered by the private road; they may, on the contrary, be serpentine in form, and present an appearance somewhat similar to that shown in Fig. 134. But here again a convenient approach from the public road, A, to the private road, B, may be laid out in the same manner as in the case of roads entering straight public roads at various angles. Let C be fixed on as the position of the entrance gate. Then from D to E, the innermost point in that part of the direction of the public road, draw the Straight line DE. Bisect it in F, and draw FG at right angles to it. From D draw DH at right angles to the course of the private road, and from the point of intersection of FG, DH, which is not shown in the diagram for want of room, but which can be easily determined by producing the lines until they meet, describe the arc DE, converting the angle at A into a sweep that is in harmony with the curvature of the road. A point, K, being similarly selected to the right, join LK, and bisect it in M, draw MN at right angles to LK and LO at right angles to the direction of the private road. Then from O, which is the point of intersection of the lines LO, MN, describe the arc LK. By drawing the dotted lines ER, EP, QM, and QK, the portions of the public road on each side of PQ, the original entrance to the private road, are brought to straight lines, and the process involved is shown to be the same as that which was adopted in Figs. 132 and 133, for the same results are obtained by bisecting the angles EPD, LQK, and following the construction carried out in those figures.

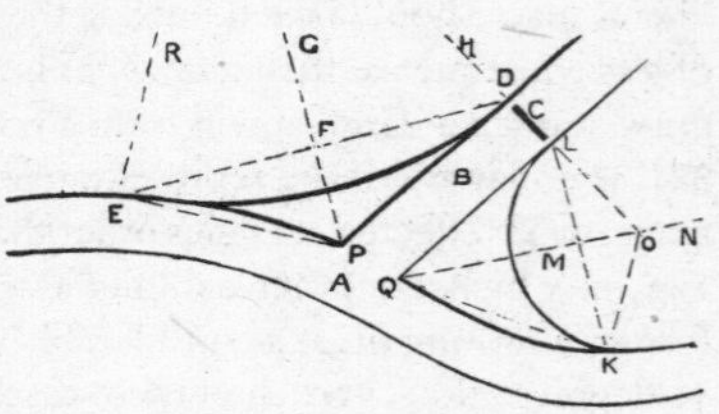

FIG. 134 *Sweep from winding public road into private road*

323 In some cases, and especially in the entrances to residences in the outskirts of towns where the grounds are immediately contiguous to the public road, the entrance gate is set back from the road, and a space is left in front of it for the

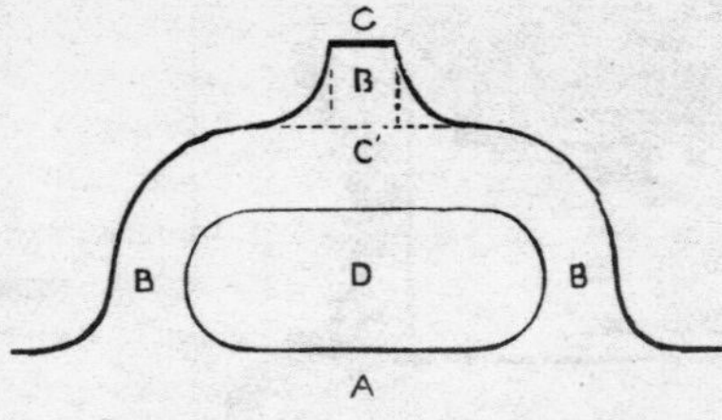

FIG. 135 *Space in front of entrance gate between gate and public road*

more convenient ingress and egress of carriages, as shown in Fig. 135, in which A is the public road, and B the private road outside the entrance gate, C. Various forms have been recommended, but the best, perhaps, is that shown in Fig. 135, in which anything in the form of an angle is avoided. If the recess is deep enough, a grass plot, D, protected by posts and chains, may be introduced with good effect; but if it be narrow, and the gate is placed at C′, the grass plot should be omitted, so as to permit carriages to obtain easier access from the public road to the entrance gate than they could have if a grass plot was introduced. Fig. 135 exhibits a useful form for a sweep in front of the portico of a house, but the grass plot D may be made to assume other forms, as a circle, a semi-circle, or an oval, according to taste or circumstances of position. In determining the form of access from a public road to the entrance to the grounds of a house, or to a private road leading to a house through its grounds, the great points are to secure abundance of space for convenient ingress and egress, and convey, at the same time, the idea of liberality in the disposition of private property.

324 Similar principles should govern the shape and extent of the gravel sweep in front of the chief entrance to any house of importance. In the plan given in paragraph 182 this is shown as a circle; but an ellipse, square, parallelogram, a pear-shaped form (as in Fig. 136), or any other shape, such as an irregular octagon or hexagon, may be chosen at pleasure, provided only that the space is large enough. Where a house is close to a public road, the centre of the gravel is often planted with shrubs, as indicated by the dotted circle in Fig. 136. The size must likewise be in proportion to the magnitude of the house and the nature of the traffic expected: a ducal residence might demand 3000 square yards; for the house of a quiet country squire 500 would suffice – it should never be less than 300; from 400 to 500 yards is a good medium. A circular or oval form has the advantage of being easier kept, and of enabling carriages to turn within a smaller compass, than any other shape.

FIG. 136 *Pear-shaped from of gravel sweep before house*

325 In the plan shown in Fig. 137, the carriage road, B, approaches the house, A, through a winding shrubbery, which conceals the servants' entrance, R, and the stable-yard, C, on the left. The space in front is an oblong, 180 feet by 90 feet, supported by a retaining wall, DD, ten feet from the surface of the lawn without, and three feet above the level of the space in front of the house, which, it need scarcely be said, is seven feet above the lawn. The portion of the retaining wall that appears above the level of the space is formed of open

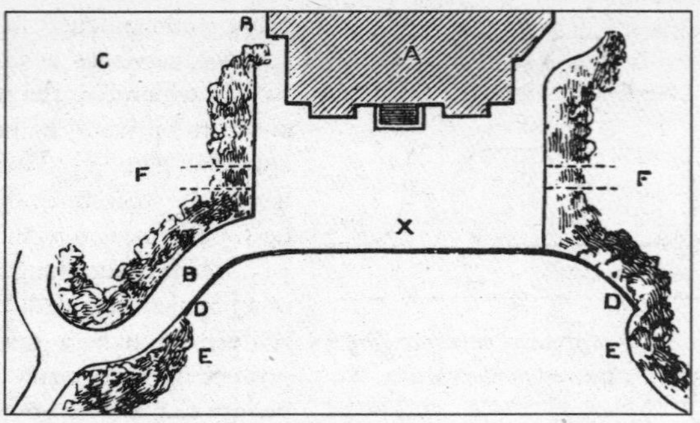

FIG. 137 *Plan of carriage approach to house*

stonework, surmounted with massive coping. The wall terminates on each side at D, and is continued from these points by the shrubbery and a wire fence, E, E. The wall runs up to the house on both sides, and is ornamented with handsome vases. The most convenient entrance to the carriage front is at one end, as shown in the diagram, or in the centre of the space, as indicated by the dotted lines at F, F. When the stables are placed to the right of the house, the carriage should pass right through and across the space, as shown on the plan; occasionally, however, it may be best to enter in the centre of the space opposite the front door, as at X; indeed, no absolute rule can be laid down upon the subject. Whenever grass is introduced in the centre of the space, it will be best to enter in the centre, and drive round the turf up to the door. When the road is carried right through to another gate, and carriages have not to return by the same route as they entered, a smaller space will suffice.

The line or direction of the road itself must be determined by the characteristics of the locality and the taste of the proprietor. Notwithstanding all that has been said about a curved line being the line of beauty, the grand old straight carriage roads, with their accompanying avenues, that sometimes form the approach to ancient houses, cannot fail to obtain the admiration of all who see them. Nothing imparts such ideas of magnificence and grandeur to a domain as trees planted in this manner. Deciduous trees are very effective; but an avenue a mile long of cedars of Lebanon would confer regal dignity upon any property. The *Cedrus deodora, Araucaria imbricata*, and similar trees, are better adapted for lines than for overhanging arches; but they would look rich and beautiful, nevertheless. The *Wellingtona gigantea*, being so hardy, and such a rapid grower, would also do well. Those who have seen the magnificent specimens of the common spruce in the grounds of Sandhurst College may try to imagine the marvellous effect of two lines of such trees bounding a carriage road of this length. Without in any way advocating the general and indiscriminate introduction of straight carriage roads and avenues, yet, in suitable circumstances, their formation may certainly be encouraged and advised. Whatever may truthfully be said against the use of straight lines, there can be but few, if any, who do not admire them in vistas, or straight forward views, in the landscape. In looking from one object to another, the line of vision, which is to us the only line of beauty, is always, to our perceptions, a straight one: the advocates of straight roads are, therefore, not quite so unphilosophical or unnatural as has been supposed; and it is a thousand pities that so many of their grand works have been destroyed by the mischievous zeal of the extreme picturesque school. However, in many cases it will be impossible – and undesirable if possible – to make roads straight; and then they must be boldly and tastefully curved. The extent and form of the bend must, to a great extent, be controlled by the width of the road. Repton, or some other landscape gardener of repute, has laid it down as a principle that no two sweeps shall ever be visible from the same spot; for a curve that might by itself look beautiful and bold, even in a narrow walk, might look puny and poor on a wider road when thus repeated.

Another principle, of great importance, is, that the curves must not appear to be capricious; the shape of the grounds must be so arranged as to be furnished with trees and shrubs. The direction must appear to be the best for reaching the house; commanding views of beautiful scenery must be introduced, giving apparent or real design to every bend on a road. Neither must the same curve be too often repeated; this would show poverty of invention, and become tiresome and monotonous. Keeping these principles in view, and adapting the curves to the nature of the surface traversed by the road, almost any possible line of inclination, from a square to an arch, may be used with propriety. Neither is a curved road necessarily so much longer than a straight one. Edgeworth, in his *Essay on the Construction of Roads*, says: 'A road ten miles long and perfectly straight can scarcely be found anywhere; but if such a road could be found, and it were curved so as to prevent the eye seeing farther than a quarter of a mile of it in any one place, the whole road would not be lengthened thereby more than 150 yards.'

326 If it were possible, it is not often desirable to make roads level, nor of one uniform gradient throughout. Undulations are charming to the eye, and give intermittent seasons of work and rest to the horses. No angle of ascent, however, on a carriage road should exceed 1 in 25, and 1 in 30 or 40 is better; for an ascent of 1 in 25, which is a rise of very nearly 200 feet in a mile, is rather too steep, in fact, to drive rapidly up and down with perfect safety, and consequently a gradient of 1 in 30 or 40, which implies a rise of 176 feet in a mile in the former and 132 feet in the latter, is as much as can be recommended.

327 The surface of roads should be slightly convex, as in Fig. 138. When formed across a steep hill, they may often slope inwards with a fall of two, three, or four inches towards the hill, as at A in Fig. 139, instead of being formed with a similar degree of slope outwards, as shown by the line B. For the proper drainage of the road, a cutting may be formed at C, and drain pipes laid as at D, or the cutting may form an open ditch. If necessary, provision may be made for carrying off the water at intervals by drains laid across the road along the line B, discharging themselves outwards on the hill side. The form of road indicated in Fig. 139 is an excellent shape in such positions, as it throws the whole inclination of the carriage towards the safe side. Carriage roads may vary in width from 12 to 24 feet – they are sometimes only 8 or 9; but this gives a mean appearance to a place: they should never be less than 12, and need seldom be more than 18 feet

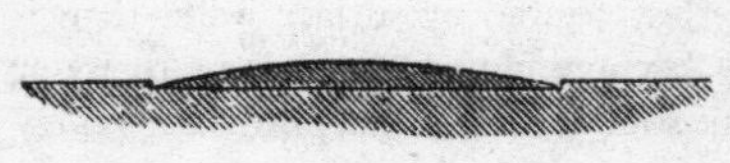

FIG. 138 *Convex from of surface of road*

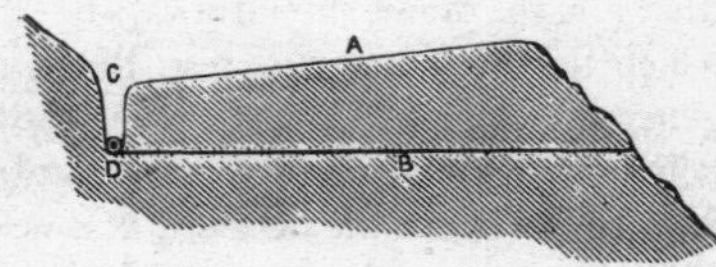

FIG. 139 *Road cut on side of hill*

wide. For a 12-feet road, 3 inches of convexity will be enough; an 18-feet road would be the better for 4 inches.

328 Except where it proceeds direct from a public road, the back road to a house should always diverge from the carriage way at right angles with it. It should also be, say, two feet, narrower than the carriage road, and should leave it at some considerable distance, so as to be out of view of the house; it may then proceed by the nearest route to the stables, kitchen garden, and kitchen court, terminating on the gravel at the kitchen door: it will thus answer the double purpose of a back road and a stable road. Where the above hints are not attended to, the back road is sometimes mistaken for the chief carriage road. For example, in Fig. 140 is shown the disposition of the roads in a place laid out by a famous landscape gardener. The carriage road, B, which is entered from the public road, A, proceeds in a straight line to the farm in the direction of the arrow, and branches off in C at a right angle to the dwelling house at D. By this arrangement the road B is sometimes followed by those who are unacquainted with the place as being the road that leads to the house, for naturally enough the road C is regarded as a side road, which has in itself a comparatively unimportant termination.

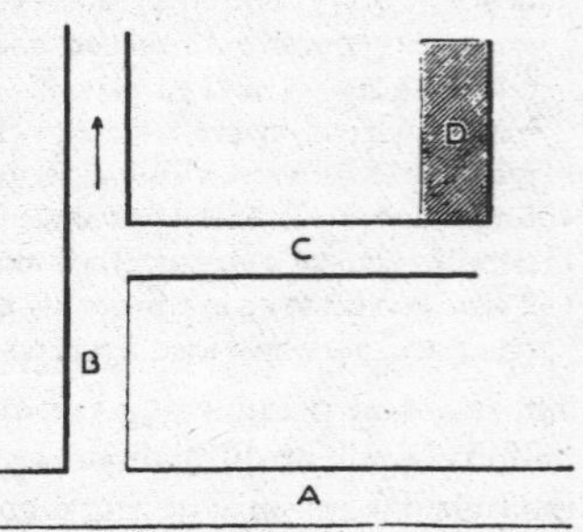

FIG. 140 *Bad disposition of roads*

329 Having designed the line of roads and paths, and the entrance, form, and termination of each road, the next operation *is to make them*. The first process is to remove the top spit of soil to a depth of 6, 9, or 12 inches – although some road makers say 15, and even 18 – according to the nature of the subsoil and the quantity of hard material that may be available to form the road; perhaps about 9 inches or 1 foot may be named as being a useful average depth. The loose pieces of soil should also be thrown out, leaving the surface smooth and hard for the reception of the stones. Some are inclined to think that the bottom of the road should be of the same shape as the top, others recommend that it should be level, and some contend that it should be convex in the middle, so that by placing the roughest materials here the crown of the road may be kept dry.

330 When roads are made on wet soils, drainage of some kind will be necessary, and drains may be inserted on each side, or in the centre, or on one side only, according to the form of the ground, the disposition of the strata, and the direction of land-springs. The great point is to keep the bed of the road dry; and therefore the drains should always be sunk a foot or more below the solid earth on which the road materials rest. Roads are less injured by surface water than is generally supposed; if well formed, they become almost impervious to water falling upon them; but no road can continue sound which rests upon a soft spongy foundation: hence the necessity of intercepting and carrying off ascending water.

331 A carriage road always looks best when it is placed at the same level, or nearly so, as the ground it passes over; but when it has to be carried over marshy ground, to make a sound road, it has to be raised above the surrounding level, as shown in Fig. 141. The space occupied by the dark lines may often be advantageously filled with faggots of wood: these not only afford an excellent base for the hard materials of which the road is formed, and efficient drainage, but impart a marvellous degree of elasticity to the road itself. Neither is the effect so evanescent as might be supposed; a road thus formed will be less noisy and more elastic than an ordinary road, and last at least half a century.

FIG. 141 *Carriage road on marshy ground*

332 But whatever the nature of the bottom of a road, from 9 to 12 inches of hard material, consisting of three layers of different-sized stones or gravel, will be necessary in its formation. Within certain limits, the smaller the stones are broken, the smoother and more durable the road will be. The bottom layer may consist of some 3 inches in diameter, weighing 7 or 8 oz.; the second layer, 2 inches, weighing 5 to 6 oz.; and the top layer of clean binding gravel. The layers may be all of the same depth, or the bottom be 5, the second 3, and the top, of gravel, should never be less than 4 inches in thickness. Such a road, well raked and rolled until it binds, and properly kept afterwards, will last for an indefinite period. Good roads may also be made with concrete for their foundation or their chief material, covering it with 3 or 4 inches of good gravel on the top. In districts where chalk or lime is plentiful, and the soil and subsoil tolerably dry, perhaps a concrete road, from 5 to 6 inches thick, with its surfacing of gravel, would be the cheapest and best of all roads.

333 When the soil along the course selected for a roadway is clayey, it may be converted into 'ballast', as it is called, which affords a useful material for making roads and mixing concrete. A fire is made of small coal or culm, cinders, ashes, etc., which is covered in with lumps of clay. More fuel is scattered over the clay, and then clay on the fuel, alternate layers of each being deposited one over the other until a large heap is made. The mass takes some time to burn through, but when the fire has burnt out the clay has assumed the appearance of brick rubbish, and has hardened into a tolerably good material for road making. Reckoning coal at from 15s. to 18s. per ton, this material will cost from 2s. to 2s. 6d. per cubic yard. It will be found very useful, when no better hardening material can be obtained.

334 Various descriptions of wood and iron pavements, and every variety of stone, have been recommended for roads, but none of these are suitable for carriage roads, which, in all cases, require that high finish which a gravelled surface alone can impart. At the same time, the character of the material used must of necessity vary with the character of the district; in many parts of the country nothing can be had but flints, and the harder and tougher flints are good materials for the bottom and body of a road. The best road materials, however, consist of the different varieties of greenstone, basalt, porphyry, limestone, and granite, broken into small square pieces. Some recommend a large admixture of chalk, but this is not generally approved of, and certain it is that good road-metal binds equally well without it.

335 Generally speaking, it will be desirable to furnish gratings on the sides of roads for the removal of the surface water; in no case, however, should these gratings communicate directly with the drains, as the sand soon chokes the latter up. The gratings should be placed over a well, C, as in Fig. 142, formed of brick, 1 foot or 18 inches square, and of sufficient depth to leave a space, B, of 1 foot or 18 inches below the level of the drain, A, for the deposition of sediment. The space B should be cleared out occasionally, and the drains will work for centuries.

FIG. 142
Construction of drainage for roads

336 Since the introduction of Fleming's salting machine, and the practice of applying dry salt in fine weather for the destruction of weeds, the keeping of roads clean has become both cheaper and more effective. Wherever the nature of the edging renders it practicable, it will be found that pickling the weeds off the surface of stones and gravel is better than any of the usual methods of turning, scarifying, hoeing, and raking the surface. This operation, performed in spring and autumn, with attention to raking in the ruts where any are made, and frequent rollings after heavy rains, will keep roads in the highest state of efficiency and cleanliness, and impart that bright sparkling appearance which is an additional recommendation of the salting process. Roads formed and kept as here recommended will seldom, unless the traffic is unusually heavy, require any further repair than an occasional slight top dressing of gravel.

337 The grass edges on the sides of carriage roads should never exceed an inch, or at most 1½ inch, in height, and should be neatly cut with an edging knife once or twice a year, and clipped once a month during the growing season. Nothing imparts such a charm to a road as a sharply-defined well-kept edge, of one uniform height throughout. The best coloured gravel for roads is the reddish yellow, so common in the neighbourhood of London; light shades of gravel impart an impression of coldness to roads, and seldom wear so well.

338 Nearly all that has been said about roads is applicable to walks: for roads may be defined as larger walks, made in a more substantial manner, to bear heavier traffic; and walks as narrow roads, designed for pedestrian or light carriage traffic only, bearing the impress of greater refinement and a higher style of finish. With these distinctions, arising from their different uses, the same principles apply to the formation of both. The quantity of material used need not be so great in depth, and its texture should be finer for walks; but the mode of its application, and the functions it performs, are in both cases alike. A good walk may be formed of concrete, consisting of six parts of coarse gravel and one of lime, 4 inches deep, with an inch of fine-sifted gravel sprinkled over and well rolled into the top; and 6 or 7 inches deep, including gravel, will be a good average for walks formed of stones, etc., in the ordinary way.

339 But as garden walks are necessary parts of every garden, whether large or small, it is necessary here to give, as exhaustively as possible, a description of the different methods that are employed in their formation. The chief thing to be done in every case is to provide a solid but yet porous substratum, which will afford sufficient support to the materials of which the upper part of the walk, or rather its surface, is made, and yet allow of the rapid passing away of the water that may fall on the walk in the form of rain. Of course, we are now supposing that the walk is made in the ordinary way, and coated with gravel, which is used for walks and paths in the same manner that 'metalling', as broken stones are technically called, is used for broader roadways, especially those of a public character.

340 The course of the path or walk must first be marked out with stakes, and the surface soil removed, as in roadmaking, to the depth of from 12 to 18 inches, if there be no lack of material to fill up the trench thus made. From one-third to one-half the depth must then be filled up with rough stones, brickbats, clinkers from the brick fields, slag and scoriae from the iron works, and any coarse, hard rubbish that can be gathered together. The greater part of the remainder of the trench must then be filled up with coarse gravel, shingle, etc., which may be mixed with a little earth, to give consistency to the whole, and finally coated with good gravel to the depth of 2 or 3 inches. This superficial layer must be constantly rolled with a heavy garden roller until the path is hard and solid.

341 The section of a garden walk made in this manner is shown in Fig. 143, in which A represents the stratum of brickbats, etc., B the layer of gravel or shingle, intermediate in size between the brickbats below and the gravel, C, above. The top of the gravel, and, indeed, of every walk, should be gently rounded, as at DD, in order to allow any rain that may fall to trickle off on either side, whence it soaks away into the earth at E, E. Supposing, as is sometimes the case, that the ground is of a loose porous character, or wet and marshy, and, therefore, not calculated to afford a solid basis to the pathway, it is a good plan to make the trench deeper, and to lay faggots or brushwood in the bottom as recommended for roadmaking, before throwing in the rough rubbish. The faggoting not only furnishes a firm and desirable foundation for the pathway, but it also helps to drain the ground on either side of the walk, carrying the water off to the lowest part, if the walk slopes from higher ground to lower.

FIG. 143 *Section of garden walk*

342 In some cases it may be desirable to have a solid facing to a garden walk, so that it may be impervious to rain, and in this case it is of importance that the surface of the walk should be rounded – higher in the centre and sloping down on either side. The water will escape into the earth or turf by which the walk is bordered, or, if desired, a gutter can be made to carry the water to a tank formed for its reception in some part of the garden. The gutter may be moulded in the material of which the path is made, or it may be constructed below the surface, like a drain, and hidden from view. In this case, gratings should be inserted along the edge of the path at intervals, to allow of the escape of the water into the gutter.

343 In making a path with a solid surface, resort may be had to one or other of three different kinds, namely, asphalte paving, tar paving, and concrete paving. Asphalte pavement consists of a surface of asphalte or bitumen, brought to a semi-fluid condition by means of heat, and spread over a concrete bed. Such a pavement as this requires special plant and special skill in its construction, and should not be entrusted to men who are unaccustomed to the work. Indeed, if expense be no object, the work should be carried out by one or other of the public companies who make it their business to lay down roadways of this material in the streets of London and our larger towns.

344 Tar pavement may be easily laid by ordinary labourers, although it is better to leave even this to practised hands. The surface of the walk must be skimmed off to the depth of 3 or 4 inches, and the new surface thus exposed should be consolidated by beating. Some thick coal tar must now be poured over a heap of shingle or coarse gravel, and the whole worked together with a spade or crooked fork until the gravel is thoroughly impregnated with the tar. This composition must be spread over the beaten surface and rolled down with a heavy roller. Another mixture must now be made of tar and finer gravel, or sifted ashes from the dust bin, and a thin layer spread over the layer of rougher stuff first put on. Fine sand or gravel must then be sprinkled freely over the top of this, and the whole once more rolled with the roller. This material forms an excellent walk, but if laid down in a situation that is fully exposed to the sun's rays, it is apt to 'give' in summer time.

345 Concrete pavement, which has already been mentioned, is put down in the following manner: The earth is first removed from the surface of the path to the depth of 8 or 9 inches, and the shallow trench thus made is filled up to about two-thirds or three-fourths of its whole depth with stones, broken brickbats, and coarse gravel, well rammed together, so as to present a level surface. Portland cement must now be mixed in a tub with water, until it is of the consistence of thick cream or custard, and poured over the gravel. This must be spread about with a bass broom to level the surface, and send it into the interstices of the first rough coat of stones and gravel. On this a coating of Portland cement and gravel, mixed with water, must be spread, bringing the surface very nearly up to the height of the path; and when this has hardened, a finishing coat must be put on, composed of clean sharp sand and Portland cement in equal parts, and brought, when mixed with water, to the consistence of mortar. The surface must be rounded and brought to smoothness by the aid of a float – a piece of wood with a handle at the back, something like the flat iron used by laundresses, but larger, with which plasterers finish the surface of walls and ceilings. No one should be allowed to tread on the surface of a walk thus made until it is perfectly dry and hard.

346 The cost of garden walks may be estimated as follows, at per square yard: The ordinary gravel walk, when properly made, at 1s. 8d.; tar pavement, consisting of gravel mixed with tar and sprinkled with sand, at 2s. 9d.; and concrete pavement, consisting of concrete faced with cement, at 3s. 6d. Asphalte pavement, at a rough computation, ranges from 5s. to 15s. per square yard, the cost being regulated by the thickness of the coating of asphalte and the concrete substratum below, and the greater the area covered, in some cases, the lower is the cost. It costs more to lay asphalte pavement in the country than it does in London, on account of the carriage of materials. The above prices, it must be understood, are approximate only.

347 Occasionally it is necessary, in cases where a piece of garden ground is acquired at some little distance from the house, either for temporary purposes, or as a means of extending the garden accommodation at the house itself, which in the outskirts of many towns is but limited, to form the garden paths of turf, which is cleanly in itself, and sufficient for all practical purposes when the garden is not a daily resort. If the land is grass land, then nothing more need be done than to mark out the beds and plots to be devoted to the growing of fruit and vegetables, and to turn and trench these parts, leaving the turf between them to form the paths. It can easily be kept short with a mowing machine, and by constant cutting will become a close and verdant carpet. If the garden be on arable land, as the cost of turf is no more than 3d. per square yard, it will be as well, if the season of the year be favourable, to mark out the paths and proceed at once to lay them down with turf. Many pieces of land to be let or sold for building purposes are previously utilised as gardens, and by having paths of turf there is less loss if the land has to be given up on short notice.

FIG. 144 *Walk below general level*

FIG. 145 *Walk above general level*

FIG. 146 *Walk level with surface of ground*

348 Perfect dryness is even of more importance upon walks than roads, as they should be clean and comparatively impenetrable in all weathers and at all seasons. Although some recommend walks to be sunk below the general level, as in Fig. 144, and others above it, as in Fig. 145, yet walks, generally look best on a level with the surface, as in Fig. 146. When thus constructed, they must be sunk about an inch at the edge, to leave this height of verge, which ought never to be exceeded in pleasure ground walks. Walks themselves should also be nearly level, an inch affording sufficient convexity for a 10 feet walk. The wider the walk the smaller is the permissible rise in the centre, as nothing detracts more from the appearance of a gravel walk, of say 15 or 20 feet, than variations in the level of its surface. A 6 feet walk, with 2½ or 3 inches rise in the centre, would not be so offensive to the eye as the same amount of convexity in a walk 15 feet wide; all broad terraces and promenades should therefore be perfectly level, and if the removal of water renders a fall necessary, it should be so slight as to be imperceptible to the eye. For similar reasons, gratings are hardly ever admissible on such walks; rough stones, or rubble connected with underground drains, cropping out to within a few inches of the surface, being used instead for the removal of surface water. The longer and wider a walk of this description is, the more offensive to good taste is the incongruous appearance of an obtrusive grating and other petty irregularities of level. These views apply with double force to straight walks, and there are few gardens of any pretensions where either are now to be found.

349 With regard to walks in a curved or serpentine form, however beautiful they may be in the pleasure grounds that surround the dwelling – and they are exceedingly beautiful – they can never be made to harmonise with the straight lines of architecture, and therefore should not be introduced near the mansion. Generally, there will be found plenty of scope for the introduction of both straight and curved walks; but where there is not, the former should have precedence, and the curved lines be introduced in and beyond the pleasure grounds, in which should be found objects of attraction, such a arbours, seats, summer houses, fountains, statues, grottoes, etc., contrived and constructed so as to be in character and keeping with the scenery that surrounds them, and the paths by which access is obtained to them.

Notwithstanding the dictum of Shenstone, who was a greater landscape gardener than poet, perhaps, and who tells us 'that when a building or other object has been once viewed from its proper point, the foot should never travel to it by the same path which the eye has travelled over before,' a handsome seat or temple, a beautiful fountain, or a statue, affords a pleasing termination to a walk of 100 to 500 yards long. Certainly the rest the seat affords, and the pleasure imparted by the other objects, will not be the less refreshing or satisfactory because we are made aware of their proximity by walking right up to them. The size and importance of the terminal objects must, however, always correspond in magnitude and importance with the length and width of the walk, and architectural objects only are suitable termini for straight paths. Curved walks may have rustic buildings, moss, root, or heath houses, of every variety of pattern and design, simple seats, secluded grottoes with suitable inscriptions, ornamental bridges of antique shape, and rustic fountains, either as embellishments or as termini to them; for there is great truth in Shenstone's remark, that a rural scene is never perfect without the addition of some kind of building. The following very effective mode of treating a view of country scenery is one which may be carried out with success in many places. A pretty path, embowered with shrubs and ornamental trees, which completely concealed the beautiful view at the termination of the walk, gave access to a simple rustic structure, with a small aperture in the back, fitted with a frame for a mirror. There was no glass in it; but on approaching the opening the surprised beholder suddenly came in view of one of the most lovely landscapes in this country; and the effect was charming.

350 Generally, a walk should never terminate at any object to which it forms an approach: it is unsatisfactory to be compelled to return by the same route as we advance. Other walks should diverge from it, to give the option of choice. The proper line of divergence is of consequence; Repton says, where two walks separate from each other, it is always desirable to have them diverge in different directions, as in Fig. 147, so as to give the idea to those who traverse them that the walks are really trending in widely different directions, rather than give the idea of contiguity, as in Fig. 148, which conveys the notion that the walks are parallel, or merely separated for a short distance by a narrow belt of shrubs, presently to merge again into one another. When two walks join each other, it is generally better that they should meet at right angles, or nearly so, rather than

FIG. 147 *Divergence suggesting actual difference of direction*

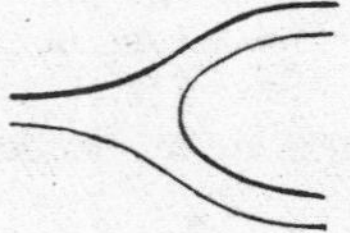

FIG. 148 *Divergence suggesting contiguity*

FIG. 149 *Walks meeting at too sharp an angle*

to leave too sharp a point, as in the acute angle at A in Fig. 149. The great thing is to avoid a stiff uniformity, and give meaning to the curves on a walk by judiciously planting firs, limes, etc., as shown at A, B, C, in Fig. 150, so as to escape the force of such severe lines as these:

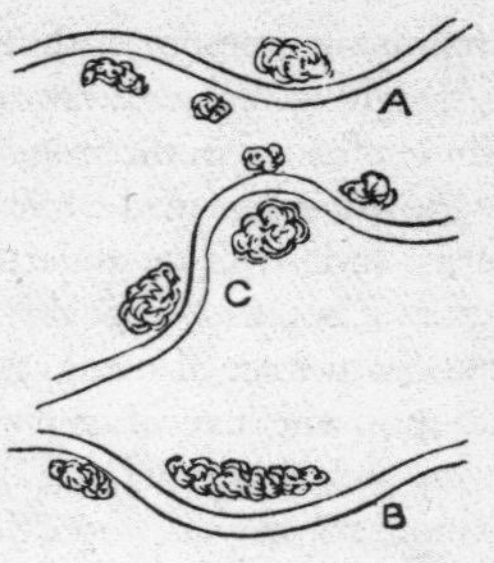

FIG. 150 *Trees by side of winding walks*

Prim gravel walks, through which we winding go,
In endless serpentines, that nothing show;
Till, tired, I ask, 'Why this eternal round?'
And the pert gardener says, ' 'Tis pleasure ground.'

Walks should always avoid skirting the boundary of pleasure grounds, although they may occasionally approach it, and, as a general rule, one should never be *vis-à-vis*, for any great distance, to another; and then they should be of different widths, according to their relative importance; but each walk should maintain the same width throughout, unless it passes through rockwork, when it should be distinguished by irregularity of width, abrupt bends, and capricious undulations; the trim walk should then be lost in rugged attempts at the mountain path, although the idea of safety must still be preserved. Grass walks are not so common as they were. On well-drained lawns the whole surface becomes a walk at pleasure, and grass walks ought never to be depended upon as necessary routes to or from any given place. When of great length, and 12 or 18 feet wide, however, they have a noble effect. The late Mr Loudon recommends, where there is much traffic on grass walks, that their bottom should be formed with stone, as if for gravel; but it will be more satisfactory to make good gravel walks for the general traffic, and reserve the grass walks for delightful promenades in fine weather.

351 In reference to statues, rustic houses, bridges, etc., which are often more attractive at a distance than enjoyable when reached, Shenstone's principle of the eye and foot reaching them by a different route may be often applicable. Occasional ruins and bridges may be introduced to please the eye, that are never intended to be reached by the foot at all; it is bad taste, how ever, to erect a bridge where there is no water or other apparent reason for its existence, apart from its mere effect upon the landscape; but wherever the nature of the ground requires a bridge, a distant view of it ought to be obtained, as few objects can be made more effective in a landscape. Viewed at a distance, the mind contemplates its features of beauty only; as we approach it, considerations regarding its strength and security predominate. Hence, every bridge in a pleasure ground, whether formed of iron, as in Fig. 151, stone, or wood, of the most elaborate

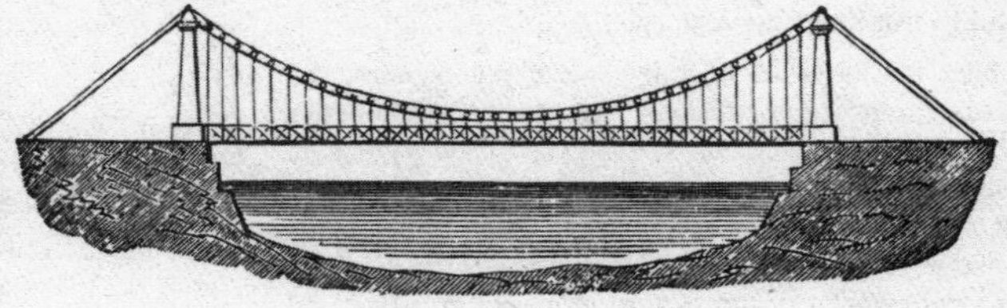

FIG. 151 *Iron bridge for a park*

architectural design or the rudest rustic form, should not only be, but appear at first sight to be, perfectly safe; if there is the slightest doubt on this ground, the whole pleasure of the scene will be lost. Of whatever form or substance the sides of the bridge are made, they should be so high as to prevent any danger of falling over, and so close together that neither child nor dog can fall through. Approaches to a bridge through a raised archway are admissible in certain cases.

352 Statues are also admissible in garden scenery, and should be large, as they are most effective when viewed at a distance; consequently, the outline of their form should be bold, the drapery rough, and the figure so commanding as to assume its proper proportions at a distance of from 50 to 100 yards from the spectator. The best materials are stone, bronze, iron, and lead, the two last named materials being painted to resemble stone. They are sometimes very effective in alcoves, summer houses, etc., and sometimes impart the charm of sudden surprise as suitable terminals to winding paths.

FIG. 152 *Perspective view of summer house*

353 Seats should be provided in every garden, and the state of our atmosphere renders it almost imperative that they should be protected from the weather. Hence the origin of rustic and architectural summer houses, Doric and other temples, etc., which are not only ornamental but highly convenient. A perspective view and plan of a rustic summer house is given in Figs. 152 and 153, but to enter here on a description of the manner and method in which such structures may be erected would tend to extend this chapter to too great a length, and therefore no more can be done here than to indicate the purpose and nature of such garden buildings, and to show how desirable it is that they should be found in gardens of all kinds, from the cottager's 'bit o' ground' to the extensive domains of the wealthy country gentleman, in which they may be found in number and variety.

Under the influence of that peculiar half-painful, half-pleasant lassitude which a succession of beautiful scenery so often induces, nothing can be more pleasant than the welcome shade of rustic root house, cool grotto, or sheltering temple, sacred to Flora, Poetry, Friendship, or Love. Rogers, the poet, used often to sit in an alcove in the garden at Holland House, Kensington, which still bears this inscription:

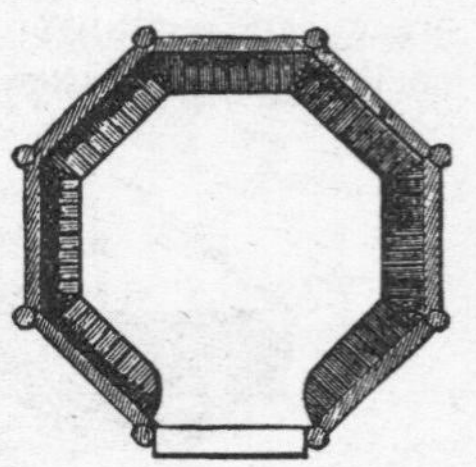

FIG. 153 *Plan of summer house shown in Fig. 152*

'Here Rogers sat, and here for ever dwell
With me those pleasures that he sung so well.'

And, doubtless, Byron, Campbell, and Moore, have often done the same when they visited this princely domain. Scott and Shenstone were not only enthusiastic admirers, but successful creators of beautiful landscapes; and the latter studded his whole estate with summer houses, temples, alcoves, caves, statues, obelisks, and seats. According to Dodsley's description of the Leasowes, there were about three dozen of seats placed in the best possible positions, besides the rustic and architectural buildings already noticed; and the majority of them were furnished with appropriate inscriptions. Doubtless this is a legitimate means of deepening the impression arising from the contemplation of beautiful scenery, of inculcating moral lessons or of setting forth the charms of retirement and rural life. Shenstone, and some others, may have multiplied inscriptions and seats to excess, but that is no reason for their total abolition. There is a great want of *sitting* accommodation in most of our best gardens, and yet nothing can be easier to provide. Many of the seats of the Leasowes consisted of a single slab fixed at the root of one, or upon the stumps of two trees. Unless in very wild scenery, such seats are scarcely admissible; but stone, wood, and cast iron are available everywhere; and, in many positions, rustic wooden chairs are the most appropriate and useful.

Summer houses and seats, as we have already observed, are very desirable, and add much to the comfort, as well as the ornament, of pleasure grounds and gardens. Almost any clever carpenter can put up a rustic arbour – at any rate, with the assistance of a few hints. Arbours, however, as well as seats, can be bought ready made. Very neat buildings may be formed with young oak stands, ornamented with pieces of oak billet and thatched with reed; also of Scotch fir poles split or sawn in two lengthways, showing the bark on the outside. Such summer houses as these may be boarded inside and lined with matting, or made more ornamental by a panelling of spilt hazel worked into different patterns. The flooring can be of brick or stone. More substantial houses can be built wholly of flint or stone, and fitted up accordingly.

Of garden seats the variety is infinite. In the wilder portions of the plantations and shrubberies the more simple and rustic these seats are, the better. The stump of a tree or the stem placed lengthways may be fitted up for the purpose. Seats shaped like large mushrooms placed here and there under trees are not only very comfortable, but they have the great advantage, from their peculiar shape, of always being dry. Of late years cast iron garden furniture has been introduced, and very good imitations of oak chairs and tables are made in this material; but preference should be given to wood. The price however, of this cast iron furniture is so moderate that many persons may be inclined to adopt it, especially as it is so durable that, unless broken by a sudden blow or fall, it will last for ever. For gardens and pleasure grounds near the house, what is called the Leicester garden seat is well adapted. It is a combination of wood and wrought iron, and forms by no means an uncomfortable seat. It is light, and being fitted with bolts and nuts, it can readily be taken to pieces and put away during the winter. The garden seats and chairs made by Barnard and Bishop, of the *Norwich Iron Works*, are excellent, not only as regards make, but also for design. These chairs have frameworks of wrought iron, and seats of a chain or network of galvanised wire. They are very elastic, and almost as comfortable and soft as a stuffed cushion. They are made of various shapes and sizes, and the single chairs can be folded up, and are so light that a child can carry them.

354 With reference to garden structures other than summer houses, almost every garden requires some buildings the construction of which may serve to call into exercise the good taste of its proprietor. When the grounds are of sufficient extent, the gardener's cottage should be contained within them, and the proper situation of this will be as near as possible to the hot houses and melon grounds. This cottage should be in keeping with the mansion and its lodges. It should be so arranged as to contain within it the fruit-room and a storeroom for seeds. In this storeroom all seeds may be dried, cleaned, and put away. There should be a table in the centre and dressers round the room; drawers and nests should be provided for the different seeds and bulbs. One or two cross beams in the roof will be very handy, for when provided with hooks all pod seeds can be hung up and dried; onions also, in ropes or bunches, can be suspended from them. Sieves, bags, a quire of coarse brown paper, and a ball of string, with a packing needle, are essential requisites in such a storeroom; a small hand threshing machine and a small fanning machine also will be found very convenient.

355 The tool house may be attached to the gardener's cottage or placed at the back of the hothouses, if such a situation be found more convenient. In every well-planned tool house there should be contrivances of different sorts for hanging up the tools – rakes, hoes, spades, etc. – which should all be well cleaned before they are put away. If many men are employed in the garden, each one should have a proper place for his own tools. Watering pots, syringes, garden engines, should have their moveable parts separated and be reversed, in order that they may drain and dry. The mowing machine should be kept thoroughly clean and oiled, and so should all clippers and pruning instruments. A bench with a vice attached to it will be found very useful in a tool house; also a grindstone and hones for the sharpening of different tools.

356 A large house in the country can hardly be said to be properly provided unless it has, somewhere in the grounds, an ice house. Ice is a very inexpensive luxury to those who live in the country, and who have the means of keeping it. The construction of an ice house is very simple, and the management of one extremely easy. On any dry spot of ground, under shade of trees, on the slope of a hill, or where drainage can be obtained, let a well be sunk of any convenient size. It is a mistake to suppose that it need be very deep, for ice keeps best in a broad, solid mass, as we may prove by examination of any ice house, where we shall find that melting always begins next to the side walls. At the bottom of this well faggots should be laid to form a drainage, and upon these a bed of dry straw or reeds to receive the ice. From the bottom of the well, under the faggots, there should be a brick drain, trapped on the outside with a syphon, so that all water may be carried off and no air admitted. The walls of the well are best built hollow, and the top arched. The ice house should be provided with two doors – an inner one on the top of the well, and an outer one some few feet from it. The interval between these doors should be filled up with straw, and the entire outer covering of the whole building should be a mound of earth. This mound may be planted with John's wort, periwinkles, and other creepers, and in this way it will be rendered a pleasing object. It hardly comes within the design of this work to explain how ice may be best kept: it may, however, be observed that the thinner the ice is, the better; for, to keep well, it must be broken into small pieces and thoroughly rammed down so as to form a solid mass.

CHAPTER 10

Fountains, Fishponds, Ornamental Waters and Rockwork

357 'Fountains and Sculpture,' says Sir Uvedale Price, 'are among the most refined of all garden ornaments.' When judiciously combined, the effect is most brilliant. It has been objected that fountains are not natural objects; but we have already seen that the garden is altogether a thing of art –

> That which increases every charm revealed
> Is that the art which wrought it lies concealed.

And the fountain differs in no respect from other accessories to the embellishment of a garden. But it is only in the long days of summer that fountains add a charm to the scene in our variable climate. It is not, therefore, very surprising that the efforts to establish fountains have not been fortunate either in our gardens or public places. Besides, they are very costly luxuries. A day of the waterworks at Versailles, when in full operation, involves a cost of some hundreds of pounds; and the water to supply the fountains at the Crystal Palace is pumped up by steam-power to the summit of the two lofty towers, whence it descends, producing for a short time a very magnificent display. But it will be easily understood that this is effected at a very considerable cost, and cannot be continued for any lengthened period. In no case, therefore, except in the midst of mountain scenery, where water is retained by some peculiarity of the soil or by artificial embankments, can fountains and *jets d'eau* be brought into frequent use, and in the midst of these wild scenes the natural cascade supersedes all thoughts of the artificial one.

358 The *jet d'eau* at Chatsworth is, perhaps, the most perfectly satisfactory instance we have where advantage has been taken of Nature, so as to bring it efficiently to the aid of Art! Here, we may say, in the words of Shakespeare,

> Is an art
> Which does mend Nature – change it, rather;
> But the art is Nature's self.

In the gardens and pleasure grounds of the ducal house of Devonshire, which, in the words of its poet,

> Stands in the middle of a falling ground
> At a black mountain's foot, whose craggy brow
> Secures from eastern tempests all below,

advantage has been taken of the heights in question to collect the waters in a lake at a great elevation, and connect them with the *jet d'eau* which forms the Emperor Fountain in the centre of the grounds. This magnificent and massive column of water rises, by its own natural force, 297 feet – the largest artificial *jet d'eau* in the world. The nearest approach to this is the Wilhelm Fountain, at Hesse-Cassel, which rises 190 feet. At St Cloud the jet rises 160; that at Peterhoff, at St Petersburg, 120; and the Old Fountain at Chatsworth, which supplies the copper-tree and other deceptive waterworks at that palace, rises 90 feet – the height, also, of the principal *jet d'eau* at Versailles. The lake which supplies the fountains at Chatsworth covers eight acres of ground, having been enlarged by artificial means when the Emperor Fountain was laid down; but so great is the demand upon it while the fountain is in operation that a foot of water, it is said, disappears every three hours.

359 It will be readily understood that fountains, even on the smallest scale that has been indicated above, can only be constructed in gardens and pleasure grounds of great size or of considerable importance, whether they be private gardens restricted to the use of the owner and his friends and those whom he may choose to admit, or public places of resort which are visited daily by immense numbers, and on whose maintenance large sums of money can be expended freely and without stint. The great objection to fountains as garden decorations is to be found in the fact that they cannot be always in operation, and that they must be set in action like a musical box, and, like a musical box, will only remain in action until the motive power is exhausted. In small gardens they can only be carried out on a small scale, and it is doubtful if the temporary effect that is produced now and then for a brief period is worth the cost of production. Fountains in miniature in ferneries and conservatories are admissible, and even desirable, as pretty adjuncts in the right place, whose maintenance at certain seasons can be managed by artificial means which in themselves are not overburdensome by reason of their cost; but in small gardens the introduction of a fountain savours somewhat of pretension. A tank or basin for the display of water lilies and aquatic plants is a different thing altogether, but it should be kept scrupulously clean and free from the stains caused by vegetation that asserts itself on stone surfaces, etc., which are always, or nearly always, damp, and be constructed without the dumb waiter-like centre piece, surmounted by the inevitable figure of a boy holding an erect squirt, which is seldom brought into requisition. It is better in all cases to ignore the intermittent fountain altogether, but if anyone be so fortunate as to have a brook or streamlet running through or bordering the grounds, and the general formation of its course so permit, a suitable opportunity offers of so manipulating and managing the natural course of the brook, that cascades, pools, and rapids – those picturesque charms of lake and river scenery – may be imitated on however small and humble a scale, and be made to perform all the services with regard to the culture of aquatic plants, and the keeping of gold and silver fish, etc., for which the garden tank or basin is usually brought into requisition.

360 It is altogether contrary to human experience, however, to expect that all who consult this work will be content with the opinion that has been thus strongly expressed. There are many who will have a fountain by hook or by crook, as the old saying goes, and it is therefore necessary to explain the principles on which fountains may be constructed.

361 Water, unless interrupted in its course, will, in ordinary circumstances, find its natural level; that is to say, if a body of water, A, in Fig. 155, underlying an impervious stratum of clay, as B, is pierced at C, and a tube inserted, the water will rise in a jet to the highest level of the water A, as shown by the horizontal dotted line. Or if a glass tube, A, in Fig. 156, having a funnel-shaped mouth, be carried through the cork, B, of the jar C, and a small tube, D, also inserted in the same cork, so as to be in free communication with the fluid poured into the funnel, it will be found that when the jar C is filled by pouring water through the tube A, the water will force its way upward through D in a small jet, and continue to do so as long as liquid is poured into the funnel, the jet being proportioned in height to the height and diameter of the tube.

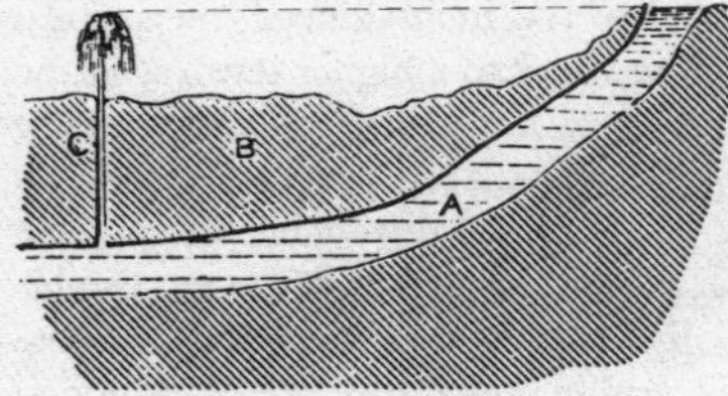

FIG. 155 *Diagram showing how water finds its own level*

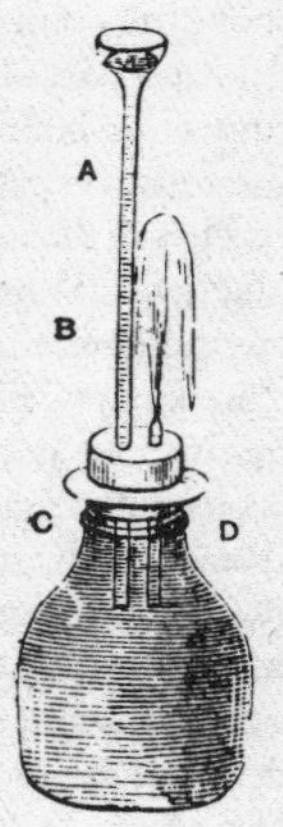

FIG. 156 *Principle of the fountain explained*

362 Jets exceeding the fifteenth of an inch in size never attain the natural surface level; friction at the orifice, the diffusion of the power by the spreading of spray, and the resisting power of the atmosphere, all tending to prevent its doing so. Great jets rise higher in proportion than small, except when the horizontal tube leading to the orifice of the jet is very narrow, when small jets rise highest.

The form of the orifice also influences the height of the jet, as was ascertained in a series of interesting experiments made by the French physicist, M. Brisson, to test the power of water. He prepared an upright vessel, A, in Fig. 157, with a narrow horizontal tube, P, on one side, and a larger horizontal tube, Q, on the opposite side. The first was perforated with three simple orifices – M two lines, L four lines, and K eight lines, in diameter. Turning on these jets, the first rose 9 feet 11 inches vertically, the second 9 feet 7 inches, and the last, 7 feet 10 inches. In the larger horizontal tube, Q, he made five small orifices – D, with a cylindrical orifice 70 lines, which rose 9 feet 1 inch vertically, and 9 feet 3 inches on an incline; E, from a conical orifice 94 lines by 70, rose 9 feet 6 inches vertically, and 9 feet 8 inches on an incline; F, G, and H rose-respectively, with simple orifices of eight, four, and two lines, 10 feet 6 inches, 10 feet 5 inches, and 10 feet, vertically. It thus appears that the smaller cylindrical tube was the least effective; that the conical orifice threw the fluid much higher, and the simple orifice, with the largest opening, the highest of all.

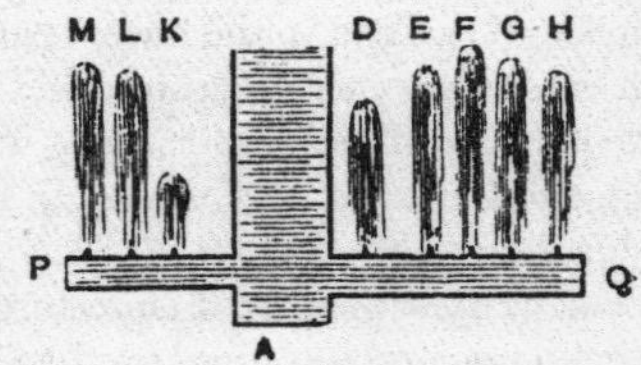

FIG. 157 *Brisson's fountain*

363 Practically, a jet will rise to within a few inches of the bottom of its fountain- head. For the artificial cascade, the water-service need not be higher than the point at which it flows over the ledge or lips of the tazza; the ledge should be perfectly level, in order to keep up a regular flow of water: a notch or other irregularity would destroy the cascade and produce a stream. On the other hand, if it is to be forced upwards, the bottom of the fountainhead must be some inches above the point to which the jet is to rise, and the supply pipe should lead from the lowest part of the basin, descending in a continuous and uniform line, without break or bend, to increase the friction. Any such departure from the direct line must be calculated in the result; the usual calculation being that a head six inches in diameter will force a column of water up a jet one-eighth of an inch in diameter. Where iron pipes are used, the deposit of calcareous matter soon stops them up; they are useless, therefore, when less than three-inch pipes, unless coated, outside and in, with some composition for preventing oxidation.
364 When the jet is to be forced higher than the fountainhead, mechanical force becomes necessary, either to pump the water to a higher level, as at the Crystal Palace, or by means of the hydraulic ram, a machine contrived to raise water by its own momentum – a sort of reciprocating process in which a comparatively small quantity of water is forced up at a time; but the process being continuous and self-acting, great aggregate results are obtained. By this process the *jet d'eau* in the gardens of the Nymphenberg at Munich rises to the height of 90 feet. These few remarks will readily account for the failure of all attempts to introduce effective fountains into our public places. According to our system of finance, public money cannot be applied in any considerable amount to such purposes; and without a large expenditure no grand result can be attained.
365 Thus it is only where the pleasure garden is surrounded by high grounds that effective fountains can be constructed. It was by taking advantage of the rocky slopes of the Apennines, in the neighbourhood of Tivoli and Frascati, that the Italian villa gardens became such noble models for terraces and fountains. The Villa d'Este, below Tivoli, although its terraces are crumbling to ruin, and its fountains dry, is yet a wonderful creation of Art, which could only have existence on the declivities of a hill side. But, though the fountain can only act where the water lies at a great elevation, or can be forced up by artificial power, there are other forms in which water becomes ornamental in a garden as well as useful.
366 Where water can be obtained from a higher level than the garden, after having performed a *tour de force* as a jet in the vicinity of the house, it may be made to descend to the lower level of the grounds, step by step, until it finally feeds shallow canals, constructed for growing such ornamental aquatic plants as require the stimulus of running water. Mr Noel Humphreys has proposed an ingenious design for forming an ornamental canal of this kind, of which the illustration shown in Fig. 158 is a copy. The basin is supposed to have stone or cement dressing of an architectural character. On each side is a small and still shallower canal, prepared for the reception of the rarer aquatic plants for which

FIG. 158 *Noel Humphrey's ornamental geometric flower tank*

more careful treatment is required. In these canals receptacles are prepared for the soil, sufficiently massive to retain their places, or having spaces left in the bottom for the reception of a basin (Fig. 159), in which the soil is placed and the root planted; it is then sunk into its place at the bottom of the canal, and the cover, A, fitted into it, and, in due course, the plant throws up its stem through the apertures in the lid. The soil is thus kept in its place, and the water remains pure, even amid considerable agitation. The basin and canals might be formed of Portland cement, moulded into architectural form, or the coping might be of the ordinary dressed freestone of the quarries. The water enters at the upper end, being obtained either from the overflow of some fountain at a higher level, or from an artesian or other well. It flows in a thin sheet over a dam forming a gentle cascade, flowing away in a similar manner at the lower end, being so contrived that only as much is drawn off at one end as is permitted to enter at the other. Gravel walks surround the basin, with weeping willows and other drooping trees, for shade and shelter.

FIG. 159 *Basin for aquatic plants*

367 The first requirement for the formation of a basin of this kind is water. A small brook or spring, in the absence of water at a high level, or an artesian well, as we have said, is necessary, the water from either source being brought under ground to the head of the basin. A level spot being selected in the lower part of the grounds, and care taken to secure an outfall for the water, the larger basin is excavated to the depth intended. The design is supposed to be 24 feet wide by 48 long, the excavation for the basin 2 feet 4 inches, and for the side compartment 1 foot 4 inches. When bottom and sides have been rendered perfectly smooth with the spade, and made quite dry, a bed of concrete is laid down, 8 or 10 inches thick; over this, layers of tiles in Portland cement are laid. In some structures of this kind four such layers of tiles have been placed round the bottom and sides. When perfectly dry, a coating of cement will complete the basins.

368 The walls separating the basin from the side canals are single-brick, laid across, set in cement, and covered with cement when dry; the parts designed for the entrance and exit of the water being formed in the same manner. The moulding is now formed by running the moulding tool along the whole, while the cement is soft, in a manner well known to every workman.

369 This, of course, is a case where brick or tiles and cement are used; where stone is the material employed, the stonemason will be employed to dress the stone after the design of the architect.

370 A canal of geometric figure, such as has been indicated, should be surrounded by a broad gravel walk, approached by other walks of some length, marked by vases on pedestals or other semi-architectural design, with geometric flower beds and some shrubs, so placed as to conceal it from the rest of the pleasure grounds. The plants for the central or deeper canal may be our native water crowfoot, the marsh marigold, white and yellow water lilies, frog-bit, floating plantain, and other hardy exotics; in the shallow side slips, the yellow iris, the flowering rush and arrowhead, and the greater and lesser water-plantain, and the elegant Cape arum.

371 But this does not necessarily exclude more formal geometrical flower gardens. On the contrary, in the immediate vicinity of such a piece of water, side walks, lined with yew, privet, or holly, might be made to lead to a circular grove of newly-planted poplars and cypresses, surrounded by closely-cut square hedges of yew; the centre occupied by a geometrical flower garden, where certain shade-loving plants which suffer from the sun might be cultivated. If the ground happened to be on different levels, much interest might be added by training the water in gentle cascades round such a garden, before it reaches the basin. Stages for vases and ornamental flowerpots might be placed, and in the rear it might lead with propriety to more tangled meanderings, where Art need not strive very hard to conceal itself.

As a means of removing the impression of flatness which the geometrical flower garden is calculated to convey where bounded by walls, Mr Humphreys has suggested the introduction of formal groups of tall trees, such as poplars or cypresses, where the climate is not too severe for them. 'I will imagine a space,' he says, 'only suitable to one group, which in this case would, of course, be central. The hedges might be privet, some of the new berberries, or other quick-growing evergreens; some hardy tree of spiral growth suited to our climate should take the place of the "sky-cleaving cypress" of the Italian gardens. By this means the monotony of the geometrical flower garden would be broken up and turned by a few lofty and finely-grouped objects. Other advantages would also be gained; for instance, within the newly-enclosed circuit of tall trees there would be a space

FIG. 160 *Italian theatre of cypresses*

> where certain plants which suffer from too much sun might be successfully cultivated; and even on the north side of these trees, certain shade-loving flowers would find an appropriate situation. A certain degree of intricacy would also be attained, which is always agreeable. Something choice would be imagined beyond the well-hedged circle; and, in reality, beyond it, on either side, would be certain partially-covered portions of the flower garden. As a good centre to a geometric plan an imitation of the Italian theatre of cypresses, copied from the gardens of a celebrated Italian villa, could not be otherwise than effective and agreeable; it would also be a novelty in modern gardens, where dislike to cropping has run into the other extreme, and bowers, avenues, peacocks, and other formal figures clipped in yew, have been swept away with relentless rigour.'

372 As regards fishponds, the monks of old well understood the management of them, and traces of them may be found near the ruins of many an old abbey. It is a well-known fact, that in certain waters and soils the fish breed, but do not increase in size, while in others the reverse is the case; the cause of this, however, remains a mystery. Fishponds may become a costly luxury; but where water exists already, it might as well be utilised, and a basin such as that which has been described above might be readily adapted to the purpose. Fish cannot exist in foul or impure water; therefore, no dead leaves or rotten branches should cumber the pond. Shrubs and flowers growing at the sides and on the surface should be kept trim and neat, and decayed, flowers and leaves raked carefully off. Shelter of some kind should, however, be furnished, to keep off the glare of the noonday sun, if the fish are to increase and multiply; and food must be supplied also. The Chinese excel all other people in the care they take of their fishponds, and the favourite food is said to be a hard-boiled egg crumbled into small pieces and put in the water. Overshadowing trees on such a basin as we have described would be inadmissible: the foliage of water plants or artificial rockwork must here serve the purpose. But in a more natural pond or river, trees rooted in the bank, and overhanging the water, give a grateful shade and shelter to the fish.

373 Rockwork is a natural adjunct to water, and requires its aid to render it perfectly successful where ferns are to form one of its accessories. Rockwork, where it is artificial, is usually raised as a screen between two styles of gardening, or as a surprise to the visitors. Where it is wholly artificial, large mounds of earth, sometimes mingled with roots of trees, are formed, over which angular masses of rock are placed – in apparent confusion, but with real symmetry; some of them advancing beyond the line, others receding, so as to conceal their more artificial foundation. A running stream, even where it only trickles over the rocks, is necessary to complete the deception, and produce healthy-looking ferns; but there are other rock plants, for which a warm dry soil is requisite. Here, walks curving round the base of the rocks, and winding up the mimic cliffs, with rustic balustrade and trelliswork, on which climbing roses, clematis of various sorts, glycines, such as the well-known Chinese twining plant, *Glycine Sinensis*, and other climbing plants, or the humbler Alpine creepers, are festooned. The graceful yellow broom, the double-flowering furze, and the hardy cistuses, may be planted among these rocks. The detached pieces of rock should, if possible, be blocks of the real stone found in the neighbourhood.

Attempts have sometimes been made to imitate or make models of real Alpine scenery, but with indifferent success, as may be supposed. In this manner a model of the mountains of Savoy was chosen for imitation in the rockery at Hoole House by a former owner of this property. With great trouble the outline of the mountains was successfully preserved, the Mer de Glace being imitated in grey limestone, quartz, and felspar. After six years' labour had been bestowed on this rocky boundary to the flower garden, it was described as an exquisite piece of workmanship, completely covered with rare and beautiful Alpine plants, except where snow, glaciers, and the pinnacles of rock were present; the first two of these being represented by glittering spar and white marble. Each plant was placed in a bed of soil of suitable character, and protected by broken fragments of stone, clean-washed gravel, moss, and other suitable materials; stones being selected for certain subjects, according as they reflected or absorbed the heat. Among the plants which abounded in this rocky bed were saxifrages, sedums, rock pinks, anemones, myosotis, heaths, violas, the Alpine lychnis, campanulas, oxalis, hepaticas, anagallas, cyclamens, calceolarias, dwarf veronicas – in short, every gem of the garden that will grow in such soils found a place in this choice rockery.

374 Rockwork in combination with water may, under proper treatment, be rendered highly attractive. Even where fountains are not attainable, tanks are not only useful, but may be made exceedingly ornamental, either in flower or kitchen garden, after the manner shown in Fig. 158. The position in the latter should be in the centre of a broad grass walk lined with pear trees and standard roses as described above. It should be made with an asphalt composition, and surrounded by rockwork covered with sedums and the different kinds of saxifrage. In the flower garden its position must be determined by circumstances. It forms a useful and beautiful centre to a hardy fernery; and, if near enough to the house, may frequently, at a very small expense, be provided with a fountain by means of a small gutta-percha tube in connection with the cistern, which is supplied by the force pump of the house. This tube should be so managed as to be removable in winter, for fear of frost.

375 Nothing should be attempted in rockwork as an imitation or copy of natural scenery, unless it can be carried out on a very large scale, and thus be rendered grand and imposing. Rockwork of this description, moreover, is suitable only for pleasure grounds of considerable extent, and is by no means appropriate for gardens, in which it should be of the simplest character, and show as few traces as possible of its artificial origin. Rockwork may be made useful for various purposes apart from the primary object of growing a class of plants that will neither do as well, nor be seen to advantage, in the open border. Thus, it may be utilised as a screen to conceal some unsightly object, either wholly or partially, instead of a hedge or wall, or it may be piled up against the wall in order to conceal, as far as possible, its flat and uninteresting character, especially if it be of brick. And again, it may be used to break any continuous line of too great a length, or any stretch of level ground that from its length and uniformity is apt to become monotonous, if not tiring to the eye.

376 There will be many who will wish to know the mode of construction employed in building rockwork for the purposes above noted. For the rockery in some secluded corner of an extensive garden, where much space can be devoted to the purpose, a few large masses of stones and boulders, scattered here and there, and arranged with a view to artistic effect, although there should be nothing in the arrangement to indicate that art has been at work, will look far better than a rockery which exhibits indubitable traces of its origin, as all heaps of stones piled one upon another must do, however skilfully they may be thrown together. In constructing a rockery of this kind, whether to fill a bare and ugly corner, or to conceal a space which serves as a receptacle for rubbish, or the compost heap, a bank or mound must first be thrown up on the area of ground that is to be thus occupied.

377 It is desirable that this mound should not be formed entirely of earth, but of soil mixed with stones and brick-and-lime rubbish, which will afford the necessary drainage for the roots of the plants, and prevent the consolidation of the soil into a hard mass, which is the invariable result when earth, and earth only, is used in making it. A rugged and irregular exterior may now be given to the mound or foundation of earth by covering it with flints, burnt masses of bricks that have become partially fused and run together when burning in the kiln or clamp, cinders and scoriae from the refuse taken from furnaces for smelting iron, and rough bits of coke covered and coloured with cement made in the form of batter and poured over them. The materials, be they what they may, should be so put together that interstices or pockets may be left between them for the introduction of the plants, the pockets themselves being filled with soil suitable for the plants that are to grow in them. And the pieces should be so disposed, that the highest parts surrounding any interstice should be in the direction of the north or east, and so render protection to the plants from cold winds coming from those quarters.

378 In close connection with the subject of rockwork is the utilisation of dead walls in gardens attached to small houses, so that they may serve as ferneries, or for the culture of such plants as will grow in dark and shady corners. It frequently happens that in the small space of ground attached to small houses in crowded towns one or more of the walls either hides, or is in the shadow of some other wall that hides, the sunlight, which is absolutely necessary for the culture of flowers. After many futile attempts the occupant of the house and garden at last comes to the conclusion that *nothing will grow on that side*. Now, in nine cases out of ten, that is just the spot in which a most successful attempt at fern cultivation may be made. It will be somewhat of a dirty job, and will entail a little hard work, but the result obtained will amply repay the expenditure of money, time, and labour.

379 The materials required are 2 or 3lb. of 2-inch nails, a sack or two of coke from the gas works, and some Roman cement and washed sand. Having broken up the coke into pieces of a suitable size, plunge them in a thin batter of cement. Next knock a number of nails into the crevices of the brickwork or material of the wall at irregular intervals, to afford lodgment for the material that is to be applied to the wall, and for another purpose that will be mentioned presently. You are beginning, of course, at the bottom of the wall, or at the summit of a bank thrown up against its lower part. Now take some flowerpots of various sizes and cover them with paper, and then attach them to the wall in a slanting position by passing pieces of string round them in order to tie them to the nails. Build up the spaces that surround the pots with the pieces of coke that have been dipped in the cement batter; these pieces should be about the size of a walnut. When each pot has been surrounded fill the interstices with cement, putting larger pieces of coke between the pots in

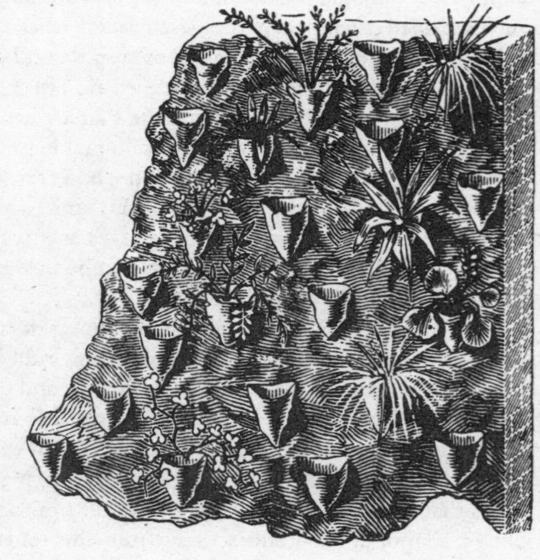

FIG. 161 *Wall over with pocket in cement for ferneries*

order to give breadth and character to the rockwork. The cement now used should consist of three parts of good Roman cement to one part of sharp clean sand.

380 The flowerpots covered with paper act, as the reader will have surmised, as moulds for the interstices or pockets in which the ferns are to be placed, and when the cement is set, withdraw the flowerpots, which will be found perfectly easy, as the cement will not stick to the paper. It is better not to attempt to cover too much wall space at once, and to give the cement full time to set before the flowerpots are withdrawn. The more irregularly and roughly this work is done the better it will look. Fig. 161 will afford a general idea of its appearance when complete. As soon as the work is perfectly hard and dry, and tinted over with touches of green and brown paint, the pockets may be filled with soil and planted with ferns and creepers, those which require the most moisture being placed nearest the bottom. Let the rockwork be extended outwards at the bottom as far as may be convenient, and when watering the plants use a syringe. Always keep the rockwork as damp as possible, as this favours the development of mosses, lichens, etc.

381 A new patent material for rockwork has been recently introduced by Mr W. H. Lascelles builder, of Bunhill Row, Finsbury, London. The blocks are flat on the under side for laying on the soil or on the top of the wall as an ornamental kind of coping suitable for the prosecution of 'wall gardening' or the growth of wallflowers, antirrhinums, toad-flax, and similar plants, on wall tops, and rough and jagged all around and at the top. They are made in a variety of suitable colours, and though irregular in shape, average, as nearly as may be, 9 inches square. They are sold at 9d. each, or 75s. per hundred. It is obvious from their size that a few of them will cover a considerable area. The material of which they are made is highly porous, and of a nature that will encourage the growth of lichens and other vegetation.

Tagetes signata pumila

CHAPTER 11

Old Gardens and Their Renewal

382 In the preceding chapters attention has been paid wholly and solely to the formation of a new garden out of maiden ground – that is to say, out of ground which has never before been appropriated to garden purposes of any kind. On this account, considerable stress has been laid on every branch of garden lore and operations on ground that is intended for a garden that must of necessity be pondered over and performed, in order to make any ordinary piece of land bud and blossom as it were into a trim and well-kept garden, or one that is capable of being well kept when all the preliminary work has been gone through. This, as a matter of necessity, has involved the consideration of the formation and constituents of natural soils; their improvement by drainage, trenching, and other artificial means; their enrichment by manures and compost, the operations that belong to the preparation of ground in order to render it well fitted for the production of fruit, flowers, and vegetables; its protection by suitable walls and fences; and the construction of various adjuncts, such as fountains, fishponds, rockwork, etc., which are highly ornamental in themselves, but which, as it has been seen, may be easily made to serve some useful purpose beyond that of mere decoration. It should be the aim of every gardener, whether professional or amateur, to contrive that everything that is constructed or put up in the garden with a view to ornamentation in the first place, should, in the second place, serve some useful purpose; for it is only by doing this that we can hope to reap from our gardens that advantage and satisfaction to which those who labour therein, whether in designing or in actual doing, are in every way entitled.

383 But, after all, it is not every one that can enjoy the pleasure of laying out his own garden and moulding it to his pleasure as he will, for the majority in this country, whether owners or occupiers, have to take to gardens secondhand which have been made, and perhaps marred, by others, and which in nine cases out of ten in all probability must be adapted and manipulated in order to render them what they might be and what they ought to be. Old gardens, it will be found, will often require renewal, but it will depend very much upon circumstances what the renewal may be that is absolutely required. In one class of gardens – the gardens that have been made and cultivated by generations long since passed away – the renewal that is required is a course of treatment that will restore the soil itself, the garden, the walls, the trees, the shrubberies, to their pristine excellence; in another class – the gardens of later times, especially those attached to houses recently built in the suburbs of our towns and cities – the work of renewal will be that of re-formation, a mode of treatment which, while the original design is in a great measure preserved, tends to soften its harshness and crudeness, and to render the garden at least passable and pleasing if it cannot be rendered exactly that which is desired and desirable.

384 There is something to reverence in the very idea of an 'old garden'. To the imaginative it suggests recollections of old baronial fortalices of the York and Lancaster wars, whose walls and battlements were levelled under the firmer policy and more peaceful times of the Tudors; grey weather-beaten stone walls, deep oriel windows, heavy clustering chimneys, half hidden, half revealed, by masses of dark glossy ivy; broad gravel terraces, with retaining walls and balustrades, decorated with Italian vases, resting on the foundations of the old battlements, with rich green lawn, and shrubbery, and park – cornfields, meadows, villages, and spires, extending far beyond, until lost in the distance. This lordly picture may be replaced by the more humble priory houses or abbey wrested from the Church, whose gardens were laid out by the 'monks of old', who well knew how to select a pleasant and fertile site, and how to use it; or, it may be, by some snug Elizabethan cottage, so called, just far enough removed from the village, and at its best end, to give its inhabitants room to breathe – a place of 'lettered ease'; with mullioned windows, as in Fig. 163, covered with creepers and perpetual roses; with dormered roof and many-angled gables, standing in a lawn, smooth, green, and short as the velvet pile which decorates its drawing-room, with broad flower border, and interspersed with flower beds, filled with old-fashioned bulbs and herbaceous plants and ribbon grass, with just an amount of massed and bedded-out plants as show that the inhabitants, while preserving the antique character of the garden, are also alive to modern improvements.

FIG. 163 *Tudor mansion and its garden*

385 There is another recollection of an 'old garden' which haunts many wayworn travellers on the path of life – the garden of early youth and childhood, where they were permitted to taste the first peach of the season, or to partake of the earliest and sweetest of gooseberries or strawberries, or feast on the earliest of mellow pears. Memory carries one back to such days, and to a grim Cerberus of a gardener, who kept the keys of such a garden, enclosed in walls too lofty to be scaled. But then the sweetness of those pears and gooseberries and strawberries when by good luck or favour they were obtained! No fruits of these days have a flavour like them. And what a glow of colour did that broad flower border present in the glorious summer sun; for even the sun has lost the brilliancy it had while the century was yet in its 'teens'.

386 But every medal has its reverse, and where one old garden brings golden recollections with it, nine others tell of indolence and neglect. Listen to the Rev. John Lawrence, the author of *The Pleasure and Profits of Gardening*, to which allusion has already been made, who had always had an 'earnest desire to have a garden', and at last, 'by the providence of God and the bounty of a generous patron', got a rural living and a garden. 'Adjoining my house, when I came here,' he says, 'I found what they called a garden, of about thirty-two yards square, mounted with low mud walls, quite overrun with couch or twitch grass, nettles, and a few stunted gooseberry bushes, a worn-out soil, and a wet white clay within half a foot of the surface. The earnest desire I always had to have a garden made me look on with grief; but yet I instantly resolved to do something, that no time might be lost.

387 'I was dissuaded by most of my neighbours, as thinking it a very vain attempt, and that I should lose my labour and charge as others had done. Not discouraged, however, I resolved to pull down the mud wall that faced the south-east, and to build me a brick one in its stead, nine feet high; which I did, by the help of my neighbours, the same summer. What methods I used to give myself any hopes of fruit in such a garden were made almost *invita Minerva*, and will appear elsewhere. I can only say here, to encourage my friends, that in three years' time I began to taste the fruits of my labour, and ever since I have had plenty, even greater than I could reasonably expect.'

388 Most of our gardening friends will be familiar with another phase of 'old gardens', in which the soil has been manured year after year, and cropped without any system of rotation, until it has become a mass of black pasty-looking earth, rich, but altogether unsuitable for growing the ordinary garden crops and fruit trees. The truth is, the soil is choked up with undecomposed dung, which is unfitted for the food of plants; and it has been cropped year after year with the same vegetables until it is completely divested of the particular constituent of soils which is necessary for the further production of that particular crop. The consequence is, the vegetables cease to thrive; the fruit trees run to wood; peaches, nectarines, and apricots canker and die, branch by branch; plums refuse to bear; apples are infested with American blight; pears make woody branches; gooseberries and strawberries produce large leaves and small fruit, or none. These evils prevail everywhere, except in the best cultivated gardens, or where the proprietor thinks for himself: especially do they prevail in farm gardens, the place where one would expect a priori to find a better state of things; in the suburbs of large towns, where the gardens are excluded from light by overlooking buildings, where the pure oxygen of the air is overloaded with carbon, the evils of indigestible manure exist in great force.

389 The remedy for these evils depends on a vast variety of circumstances. Is the soil clay or loam? or does sand, gravel, or chalk prevail? – above all, is the drainage perfect? Few old gardens, unless they have been renovated during the last thirty years, can boast of thorough drainage, and without it all attempts at amelioration are vain. Let the proprietor, in this case – unless, indeed, the soil and subsoil are both sufficiently porous for water to percolate through readily – sacrifice his year's crop, drain it thoroughly at once, and either give the ground a good coat of lime, and trench and ridge it up for the season, or trench and take a crop of turnips or carrots from it, and re-arrange it for cropping in the autumn and spring.

390 When the drainage is in proper order, and the soil and subsoil such a wet tenacious clay as that described by Mr Lawrence, two modes of dealing with it present themselves. The most efficient would be to dig the soil three feet deep, and pile it up in heaps for burning as described in Section 105, taking care that the soil is only burnt sufficiently to crumble between the finger and thumb on being rubbed.

391 When the soil is a porous one, the only remedy is to mix it with a more tenacious soil while digging, thoroughly incorporating the two soils together, and enriching them with a liberal supply of thoroughly decomposed dung or leaf-mould, in proportions suited to the intended crops.

392 Returning for a moment to Mr Lawrence and his thirty-two square yards of wet clay full of noxious weeds. 'The first care,' he tells us, 'is to destroy these, so that what is sown or planted may not perish by *their* spreading luxuriant growth. For this purpose I have found no way so certain and effectual as laying the whole ground fallow all the summer, by digging it over two or three several times, always observing to do it during the greatest heats and droughts. This not only kills all the weeds, but it mellows and enriches the ground exceedingly, as all good farmers know very well. Most are naturally desirous to improve their ground; but if they sow with expectation of fruit while it is full of weeds, 'tis but labour lost, and they will repent it.' 'I do not speak thus, with respect to planting fruit trees,' he says further on, 'for I would lose no time in planting them, for, as it takes years to produce a crop from them, the season should not be lost.'

393 Where the evil arises from a system of over-manuring, the remedy is to clear a good portion of the richest earth away. 'Generally speaking,' says a correspondent of the *Gardener's Chronicle*, 'there are few places where an exchange of fresh earth may not be made; for this garden soil forms one of the most valuable dressings for pasture or meadow land which can be met with. It is not always possible to get turf, or even soil, from pasture land, which is the very best for garden purposes; but failing this, that from arable land, if moderately fresh and loamy, will form no bad substitute. When the rich top soil has been removed, spread a good dressing of quicklime over the lower surface and fork it in – if the lime is an inch in thickness it will not be too much. Afterwards road-scrapings or old mortar may be added when the soil is heavy, and marl or a dressing of the scourings of ditches when it is light. When this is well mixed with the lower spit, bring in the fresh earth and thoroughly incorporate the whole together.

394 'Rather than do this imperfectly, it will be better that only a small portion should be done at once, commencing with those portions on which peas, cauliflowers, cabbages, onions, and carrots are to be grown, leaving the parts appropriated to asparagus, seakale, and rhubarb for after consideration. Above all, the fruit tree borders, if they cannot be entirely renovated, should only have one half of the old soil removed and replaced by fresh loam, having previously made a good rubble bottom one foot deep, over which two feet of the above compost should be placed for the trees. Many kinds of fruit trees may safely be lifted, if done carefully, and the roots laid in any spare piece of ground while the borders are being renewed – more particularly pears, plums, and apricots, which will grow on richer soils than the peach and cherry.' Thorough drainage is indispensable in all these improvements both in the garden and fruit borders. In the latter, intersecting surface drains are recommended for aerating the soil as well as for removing moisture.

395 'Where it is found impracticable to remove any portion of the over-rich earth, the next best thing is to employ those materials which are found by practice to counteract soils containing superabundance of organic manures. Lime is the best and the most readily procurable. A mixture of 64 bushels and 2 cwt. of salt is a valuable compost for old gardens, and is sufficient for one acre. Superphosphate of lime mixed with a small quantity of nitrate of soda is the next best; but it is more expensive. Both these applications should be forked in directly they are spread over the ground. A dressing of hot lime given every third year, adding phosphate of guano occasionally, would be a great improvement on stable dung, no opportunity being lost of applying road-scrapings and marl, or calcareous soil, where much manuring is necessary. Liquid manure is a better material than stable manure for these gardens, as it is more easily taken up by plants, and, with chalk or lime occasionally added, will tend to form a better and more productive soil, and one capable of keeping in good heart for years, without the danger of getting over-rich.'

396 Thus much for the treatment of the soil in old gardens, according to its composition and condition. There is no necessity to dwell any longer on this point, for all has been said on it that is absolutely necessary. We may pass at once from old garden ground to old garden walls, which are troublesome things to a gardener, when years of nailing have loosened the mortar joints, and left even the bricks full of holes; but they are even more troublesome as harbours of refuge for insects and all sorts of garden pests.

397 When garden walls get into this state, the first convenient opportunity should be taken for thorough cleansing and repair. In autumn, after the fruit is gathered, or in early spring, the weather being dry but not frosty, let every tree be un-nailed, the branches tied carefully together with hay bands to prevent injury from the wind, and the stem of each tree drawn gently away from the wall as far as can conveniently be managed without injury to the roots, and kept there by means of a rope placed round it about two-thirds of its height, which rope can be made fast by a stake driven round the border, at a little distance from the stem. The wall, being cleared, should be scraped to remove all moss and every kind of parasite that may be growing upon it. After this, if the weather be quite dry at the time, it will be found a very good plan to give the wall a thorough dressing with very thin size, put on boiling hot with a large plastering brush: this will effectually destroy all larvae and eggs of insects that may remain after scraping. The wall can now be pointed in the usual way, using either cement or mortar made of newly-slaked lime and river sand, great care being taken that all the old loose mortar in the joints is removed; otherwise the new jointing will not bear the nailing to which it is to be subjected.

398 From the walls themselves transition is natural to the trees that are attached to them. How frequently do we find the inheritor of an old garden praising loudly bygone times in reference to some noble pear tree against a wall, or covering perhaps one whole side of his house, calling to mind the bushels of fruit borne by it when he was a boy, and lamenting its present diminished produce. What is to be done with it? is the inquiry. The tree is, to all appearance, full of vigour, and it would be a shame to cut it down; besides, it must take years for another to fill up the space it occupies. Perhaps, also, there is some little fruit on it each year, though nothing to what a tree of the size ought to produce, for the centre never has a single pear or blossom bud upon it. Look to Nature! is the only answer to be made to one so inquiring; and you will find that all the fruit and all the blossom of the fine old pear tree is upon the young wood at the extremities of its branches. The case is clear, then: young wood must be encouraged, and old wood got rid of.

399 In order to do this, let anyone try the following plan, and he will not be disappointed. Cut out, at pruning time, all the lateral branches within one eye of the stem: but, in order to balance the tree, and give employment to the roots, let this be done by degrees; let every alternate lateral, on either side, be cut out each year; and in a year or two, when fresh wood is filling up the bare spaces, the whole tree will be covered with bearing wood. Old and exhausted Chaumontel pears will well repay anyone who will bestow this treatment upon them. It may also, with benefit, be applied to all espaliers, whether apples or pears, which are found to fall off in bearing, especially when they are found to bear, as is so often the complaint with old trees, only at the extremities of their shoots. When the vigour of the old tree is expended in producing wood and leaves, with an inadequate supply of fruit, it probably arises from over-vigorous root action. The remedy of root pruning, described in another part of this volume, may be applied with advantage.

400 To renovate old and exhausted apple trees, open a deep and wide trench all round them, remove the soil and fill in with fresh rich loam, with a good top dressing of well-rotted manure, that can be washed into it with every shower. It will do no harm to cut through a few of the roots, especially at some distance from the stem. After this, in early spring, scrub the bark of the stem and larger branches with a strong brine, rubbing in the solution with a hard brush.

This operation was very commonly carried out in early spring in Devonshire orchards thirty or forty years ago, and is doubtless resorted to at the present time with as much benefit to the trees as heretofore. The brush to be used should not be an ordinary scrubbing brush, because the tufts of hair or bristles in brushes used for scrubbing floors are two short and too closely set together to penetrate effectually into the cracks and crevices of the old bark. The best brush for the purpose is one that is used in stables, with a slightly rounded back, ends that may be described as pointed rather than round, and bristles or fibre about 1½ inch long, and not too closely set together. With this it is possible to get well between the cracks, and make it thoroughly uncomfortable for any insects that may be lurking in them. If portions of the outer bark are carried away by the scrubbing, no harm will be done, as it will be merely dead bark, that rather militates against the health of the tree than encourages it. In fact, it bears much the same relation to the tree that the scarf-pin or epidermis does to the true skin of the human body, whose removal, when it has perished and has been replaced by a new cuticle below, by means of a rough towel, after a bath, is eminently desirable.

401 With regard to the renovation of border edgings, that which is formed of box is the only kind which absolutely requires notice here. Nothing gives a more neat and agreeable appearance to a garden than well-kept box-edgings; the only drawback to them is that they afford a better harbour for slugs and snails than any other edging, and this, in a measure, militates against them. The sort of box in use for this purpose is a dwarf variety of the common box tree, or *Buxus sempervirens*. This, with a little attention, may be kept in order for several years; but, if neglected, as is too frequently the case, it very soon gets out of order. In old gardens, the box edgings often look coarse and bushy, and full of gaps; for this there is no remedy but to take all up, and replant.

402 The plan to be followed is this: Fork up the old box, and pull it into small pieces, with not more than one or two stems each, selecting the youngest and freshest pieces for immediate planting. These should be cut with a sharp spade or garden shears, so as to be even at the top and also at the roots, leaving each piece about three or four inches in length. The old wood may be served the same way; but, before these are used to form box edgings, it will be better to plant them out in the reserve garden for a season, in a rich light soil, to give them a start, without which they cannot be considered fit for edgings, as they will certainly not recover from their rusty and shabby appearance for a year or two. As box edging, under the best treatment and greatest care, can hardly be made to last and look well longer than eight or ten years, it is very desirable to have a reserve of young fresh plants always on hand.

403 The method adopted in planting box edging is simple enough, but it should be carried out in strict accordance with the directions about to be given in order to ensure regularity of setting and evenness of growth. The mode of procedure is illustrated in Fig. 164, and it is scarcely necessary to say that it is precisely the same both in planting a box edging for the first time and in renovating, or rather replanting, an old edging. The old plants having been

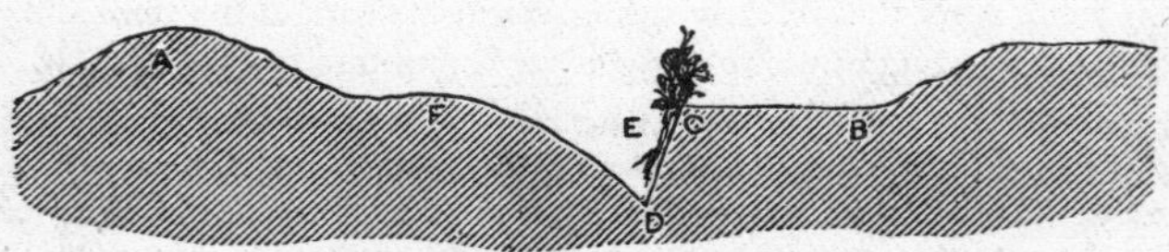

FIG. 164 *Method of planting box edging*

pulled to pieces, and prepared for planting, if the path be already gravelled, the gravel must be drawn back from the edge of the border towards the middle of the path, as at A in the annexed illustration in section in Fig. 164. The edge, B, of the border must then be dug over with a fork, and the soil along the edge be brought to a level and even surface, and rendered firm and solid by beating it with the spade. A garden line is then stretched along the edge of the border, from end to end, as at C, so as to clearly define the edge and show the exact line that is to be occupied by the box. A shallow trench, E, about 3 inches deep, is then made with the spade, and the earth is drawn out on the path, as shown at F. The edge of the bed then assumes the form shown at BCD, and the side of the edge, CD, is rendered as firm and solid as the surface, BC, by beating and flattening it with the spade. It will be noticed that the side of the edge, CD, is in a direction slanting outwards. This is done in order that the roots of the box may strike outwards into the gravel, and thus be kept from too luxuriant growth. The pieces of box are then placed along the slope, CD, as shown in the illustration; the soil at F is returned to the trench, E, and trodden in firmly against the box, and, lastly, the gravel at A is restored to its original position. It must be understood that the soil at F is not earth only, but earth mixed with a large proportion of gravel. When the work is done, the freshly-planted box should be from 1 inch to 1½ inch above the surface of the gravel on one side and the surface of the border on the other. After the gravel has been put in its place, the plants should be well watered.

404 Box edging may be planted either in the spring or in the autumn, but the autumn, say October, is considered to be the better time. If planted in the late spring or in early summer, it will require frequent watering during the summer months. The best time for clipping box is in June, because, if well watered after the clipping is done, the plants will send forth short shoots, which will do away with the formal appearance caused by the clipping. For dimensions, an edging of box should not be more than 3, or at the utmost 4, inches in height, and about 3 inches broad at the bottom, and just half that width at the top. An edging of box, when clipped every year, will continue to retain a good appearance for about seven years, when it is desirable to replant it. When left unclipped and uncared for, the plants will attain a height of 9 inches, and while the top is broad and green, the bottom will be utterly bare and naked. This is often seen in old gardens, and persons, instead of replanting the box, are content to leave it as it is, or to clip the sides and top in a formal manner, so that the edging looks like a broad mass of greenery, supported on a closely serried line of brown sticks and twigs utterly devoid of leafage.

405 During spring and the early summer months, all garden turf and lawns will require very great attention. If they are to look well for the rest of the year – and we must remember that the general appearance of the whole garden depends much upon the state of the turf – it is now that the broom and the roller must be kept in constant use. If the grass, from the nature of the soil, is inclined to grow rank and coarse, it will be much improved by a good dressing of sand all over it; if, on the other hand, it has a tendency to scald and burn up, it will receive great benefit from a sprinkling of good guano or soot just before a shower of rain.

406 Just before regular mowing commences, it will be well to go over all grass, carefully removing rank and unsightly weeds, daisies, dandelions, the little buttercup, etc., etc. Wherever the turf is mossy, it is a very good plan to rake it well with a sharp five-toothed rake; but it must be borne in mind that under-draining is the only effectual cure for moss. Daisies should never be allowed to flower: a good daisy rake, with a little trouble, will remove all flowers as they come out; but the only plan to clear a lawn effectually of these disagreeable weeds is to take them out with the *daisy fork* wherever they are found. This handy little tool is made in different forms, or rather with handles of different lengths, but the principle is the same in all. A short form of the fork is shown in Fig. 165. This consists of an iron shaft about ½ inch square, set in a wooden handle. The extremity of the iron is formed into a cleft fork, as shown at A. This fork is thrust into the ground, so as to take the daisy plant between the prongs or tines. The iron ring which is attached to the iron is then pressed against the ground, and acts as a fulcrum, on which the cleft end is raised when the handle is pressed downwards. The raising of the cleft end lifts the daisy out of the ground. It is sometimes used to remove docks and dandelions, but it is not so effectual for these weeds, which have long tap roots which are firmly secured to the ground, and generally break when an attempt is made to lift the plant. Daisies, and indeed all weeds, are more easily removed in wet weather, or after a shower, than when the ground is dry. The tool may be used by any lady or child; and in process of time the most hopeless pieces of grass may be cleared by it. Turf, quite white with daisies in the spring, may be cleared entirely in the course of a season. The neat appearance of the lawn will well repay the time and trouble spent in the continual use of the daisy fork.

FIG. 165 *Short form of daisy fork*

407 A daisy rake is very easily made. Its form and construction is shown in Fig. 166. First of all a thin plate of iron is obtained, and cut into broad teeth along one edge: the iron should be just so thick as not to bend easily to pressure or any resistance. Two slips of ash are then cut out, each being of the length of the iron, and about ⅝ inch in thickness and 2 inches wide. These are bevelled towards the inner edge – the upper one but slightly, and the other to the thickness of ¼ inch. The iron is placed between them, and the two pieces of wood and the iron are all firmly fastened together by stout screws or rivets. A handle is then put into the rake, is shown in the illustration. Holes should bedrilled through the iron plate to admit of the passage of the rivets and handle. The teeth of the rake should be slightly bent upwards.

FIG. 166 *The daisy rake*

408 We may now take into consideration the renewal of the shrubbery. In old gardens, it is no unfamiliar thing to find the lawn and borders skirted by long, unbroken belts of shrubs, intermingled in pell-mell fashion, the lower part of most of the deciduous shrubs lean and naked, having been long since denuded of their smaller twigs. Confusion rather than order seems to have been encouraged. Stems bare and naked at the roots show only straggling wiry branches towards the summit. When the shrubbery has acquired all or any of these characteristics, renovation, in whole or part, has become indispensable.

409 Shrubberies skirting winding paths, either as a screen to unsightly objects or as shade and shelter from sun and wind, are perhaps the most agreeable portions of a garden; but in order to be so the shrubs must be cultivated with as much care as is the most choice individual plant of the parterre. They should be selected for their close and evergreen habit of growth, and the habit increased by high dressing, judicious pruning, and pegging down. This compact habit of growth, however, can only be maintained in its beauty for a number of years by planting the shrubs so far apart that they may not touch, every one having free liberty to show and preserve its individual habit, no two shrubs being suffered to touch each other; the ground between must be kept clear by frequent raking and hoeing. There are some happy exceptions to this rule of planting. The rhododendron does well planted in masses, and where the shoots are pegged down, they soon present a broad mass of green on the margin of the clump or shrubbery, when the turf can be carried up to its lowest branches. Behind these dense shrubby evergreens, the taller thorns, Turkey oak, the *Pyrus sorbus* (or service tree) in its three varieties, the broad-leaved Pyrus, the deeply-cut-leaved Pyrus, and other trees of moderate height of the fancy arboretum varieties, might be planted at intervals for shade and breadth of effect.

The pear, the apple, and the service tree, in all their varieties, belong to the *Pyrus* family, the scientific name of the pear being *Pyrus communis*, that of the apple, *Pyrus malus*, and that of the service, *Pyrus sorbus*. The quince, *Cydonia vulgaris*, and the medlar, *Mespilus Germanica*, are closely allied to the pyruses, all belonging to the same natural order, *Pomaceae*, or Appleworts.

410 Shrubberies on the verge of the lawn would naturally be planted with the best small flowering shrubs on the margin, either in masses or single: if in masses, the shrubs should be pegged down, so as to present a continuous mass of vegetation along the whole margin, relieved as before with a background of ornamental trees; leafy masses of rhododendrons, brought down to the margin of the turf by pegging, form an admirable connecting link between the grassy sward and the individual shrub and dwarf trees behind them. Where the shrubbery is planted for individual effect, those of an enduring growth and elegant habit should be chiefly used. Where there is space for such display, the lawn adjoining the shrubberies may be advantageously dotted with single evergreens and some of the more eloquent-flowering deciduous shrubs; an occasional hemlock-spruce (*Pinus Canadensis*), with its weeping plumes; a holly whose lower boughs, still fresh, sweep the turf on which it is planted; or the graceful *Cedrus deodara*, or *Araucaria imbricata* (or Chili pine), better known in this country as the Monkey Puzzle, in order to break the outline and relieve the meagreness arising from the single mode of planting the deciduous shrubs. Another mode of relieving the nakedness of newly-planted shrubberies is the introduction of hardy flowering plants: this may be adopted with excellent effect until the lower branches have made sufficient growth to admit of the surface being turfed up to meet them.

411 In planting or renovating the lawn and shrubberies, due attention should be paid to the different seasonal effects of the trees and shrubs that are introduced. There are a few which herald in the spring; such as *Chimonanthus fragans* and the cornel tree (*Cornus mascula*), the Mezereon (*Daphne Mezereum,*), the red-flowering currant (*Ribes sanguineum*), the *Kerria Japonica*, formerly better known as *Corchorus Japonicus*. In conjunction with these, the strongly-characterised Japan cedar (*Cryptomeria Japonica*), the Canadian spruce (*Abies Canadensis*), some trees of the sumach family, deciduous cypresses, purple beech, and weeping laburnums, might be planted with effect. There are so many noble trees which present rich gradations of tint in autumn, that it is almost needless to name them. The old Virginian creeper (*Ampelopsis hederacea*), and the new variety of this climber, *Ampelopsis Veitchii*, are more beautiful in their autumn costume than in their vernal hues. The scarlet and other American oaks, the wild cherry (*Cerasus vulgaris*), the *Koelreuteria paniculata*, and many others, have a splendid effect either by themselves or on the skirts of the shrubbery; and all the new conifers recently introduced are treasures by themselves, and well adapted to fill up the background of the shrubbery. Pillared roses may also be introduced with excellent effect.

412 But high-keeping is the great element of success in the shrubbery as in the flower and kitchen garden. Keep the soil in good heart by dressing with properly prepared composts. Remove all traces of disorder in the soil by constant use of the rake; let no trace of weeds appear; study the natural habit of every shrub, and keep it under control by the timely removal of exuberant growth; remove all decaying blossoms not required for seed; peg down early and continuously, in order to encourage the development of trusses of flowers, giving to each and all a combined air of freedom and trimness, and the result will be order, elegance, and beauty. Appended is a list of choice deciduous flowering trees and shrubs (the figures, when appended, indicating the height in feet).

413 *Choice Deciduous Flowering Trees and Shrubs and Climbers*

Althaea frutex, or Shrubby Althaea (sometimes called *Hibiscus Sinensis*) – bears various-coloured flowers, like single hollyhock; blooms early.

Almond (*Amygdalus*) – dwarf (2) and tall (15); bears pink flowers; very early.

Azaleas (4) – These may be had of many colours – scarlet, red, orange, yellow, pink, bronze-colour, and shaded; blooms early.

Berberry (3–6) – flowers in bunches, yellow, and succeeded by scarlet berries.

Buddlea globosa (15) – orange-coloured flowers.

Calycanthus floridus (6) – allspice-scented wood, with brown flowers.

Cherry – double flowering (15).

Chimonanthus fragrans (6) – dull-coloured; flowers in the winter, highly scented, and before the leaves appear.

Clematis (various). – The common clematis, called Virgin's Bower, Traveller's Joy, or Old Man's Beard, is very hardy and fragrant (20).

Clematis Sieboldii (10) – purple.

Clematis coerulia grandiflora (10) – rich purple.

Crataegus (Thorn) (15) – red, double and single; pink do.; white do.; and many varieties of fruit and foliage.
Cydonia (*Pyrus*) **Japonica** (4) – scarlet flowers; blooming several months in the year.
Cytisus (*Laburnum*) – yellow, purple and other varieties (15); flowering early in the spring.
Daphne Mezereum (4) – pink.
Deutzia scabra (6) – flowers white.
Guelder Rose (*Viburnum opulus*) (10) – bears white balls of bloom.
Jasminum nudiflorum (15) – yellow.
Jasminum officinale (15) – white.
Lilac (10) – purple, pale, white, Persian, and other varieties.
Lonicera (Honeysuckle) (3–15) – an immense number of species and varieties, and nearly all good
Magnolia grandiflora (20) – white.
Magnolia Exoniensis (20) – white.
Magnolia purpurea; and many other excellent species and varieties.
Peach – double flowering; red (15).
Philadelphus (Syringa or Mock Orange) (8) – highly-scented white flower; leaves small, with a flavour like the cucumber.
Ribes sanguineum – crimson flowers (6).
Ribes album – white do. (4).
Ribes aureum – yellow do. (8).
Ribes speciosum – crimson (4), a double variety; and many others.
Robinia hispida (Rose acacia) (10) – pink flowers; several varieties.
Roses – A list of the best varieties and species will be given elsewhere.
Spiraea (2–4) – many varieties, and all pretty.
Virginian Creeper – will grow to the top of a house, and the foliage turns crimson in autumn.

414 Few things afford stronger indications of the necessity of renovation and reform in a garden than the state of the evergreens and hedges. These are so easily and so insensibly suffered to grow wild, and are so seriously injured by want of care and the proper use of the knife, that neglect cannot go on very long without its ill consequences becoming manifest. Portugal laurels (*Cerasus Lusitanica*) and many other evergreens may be cut in; but with the common laurel it is a saving of time to cut it down at once; so also with the arbutus or strawberry tree, and sweet bay (*Laurus nobilis*). Thorn, privet, and holly edges, which from years of neglect are found to be occupying too much space, must be cut in. Thorn and privet hedges may often be cut down with advantage to within a few inches of the ground, and holly hedges cut close on all sides to the single stems. In a few years new and fresh wood will fill up all vacant spaces, provided the soil is enriched and kept free from weeds. Nothing is more beautiful than the quickset or hawthorn hedge when kept up properly; and among other things the railways did for us, they taught us practically that the hawthorn required to be controlled and cultivated like other plants, in order to perform its office in civilised life as distinguished from its wild state.

415 All these hedge plants do well in a stiffish loamy soil, and if such is not the natural soil in which they are to be planted, they will repay the trifling expense incurred in making it. In making a new hedge, whether of hawthorn, privet, or holly, the plants are taken from the nursery when well rooted and about a foot high. The bed is prepared for them by raising a bank more or less high according to circumstances, digging the centre about a foot broad, and in the middle of this plant the young shrubs. The banks may be turfed, or grass seeds sown on them, but the summit of the ridge on which the hedge is planted requires to be stirred occasionally, and kept perfectly clear from weeds. The young hedge, if properly planted, requires little further care except watering if dry weather follow the planting, stirring the earth from time to time, and careful weeding: here, as in other branches of cultivation, the soil cannot feed two masters.

416 There are several species of the beautiful *Cratoegus*, or thorn, suitable for hedges, and a mixed hedge of the white and pink hawthorn and scarlet thorn, or the Glastonbury thorn, a variety of the common hawthorn, or *Cratoegus oxycantha*, would be a beautiful object in any garden and an excellent fence between fruit and kitchen or flower garden. Meanwhile, if a screen be needed in the garden, it may easily be managed, and with a very good effect, by means of hollyhocks and chrysanthemums. Hedges of either of these flowers will serve to shut out from view anything that may be required, and at the time produce a beautiful effect. Hollyhocks can be staked separately in the line where they are wanted; but with chrysanthemums the best plan is to stretch a rough wire fence to which they may be trained. This may be made of a few rough stakes supporting three or four rows of wire, over which on both sides the plants may be trained after the fashion of espaliers, so as to cover all the framework. There are many other plants also which will suggest themselves to every gardener as capable of forming a pleasing and effective temporary hedge.

417 The last subject requiring notice in connection with the renewal of old gardens is the flower border. In these the flower border was an important object, nor is it superseded even now by the more modern bedding out, massing, and clumping system. It is the natural abode of the pink, carnation, stock, gillyflower, the wallflower, hyacinths, roses and heliotropes, with many other gems whose fragrance loads the atmosphere, while their beauty charms the eye; and of the gaudy tulip and paeonies, white, crimson, rose-colour and pink, whose brilliant colours are highly attractive to the beholder, although they yield no perfume. Such mixed borders, when kept highly dressed and judiciously planted, well selected and arranged, possesses great interest. But it is the tendency of many of the herbaceous plants to become crowded, and to exhaust themselves. Phloxes, asters, monardas, delphiniums, and other free-growing plants, soon choke their delicate companions, leaving little room for the more graceful gentians, aquilegias, camassias (hardy bulbs allied to the *Scilla*, or squill), lychnises, and gnaphaliums (a variety of plants allied to the helichrysums). Unless these are parted, dressed in the spring, and re-arranged every season, all arrangement and proportion is destroyed. The plants of courser habit expel the more delicate flowers, and with their expulsion vanishes all idea of order and proportion, on which so much of the beauty of the garden depends.

418 Supposing this state of things has gone on until entire renovation has become necessary; that the border is exhausted by continually growing the same thing for years, and a radical remedy is required – there is only one which is effectual. Remove the plants to a place of safety, and either dig out the old soil to the depth of two feet, and fill up again with a rich light compost of sandy loam and leaf mould, or, if the base of the soil is pretty good, mix it with equal portions of the same compost, with a copious manuring with well-rotted dung, and trench it two feet deep, taking care that the drainage is in proper order. Where fruit trees occupy the walls on such a border, it will be well to leave a space of two feet from the wall, slightly raised above the general surface of the border, unplanted, for the benefit of the trees.

419 On a border thus prepared the plants may be replaced, taking care that young plants of phloxes, asters, pentstemons, and similar exhausting plants, are selected, leaving the old stools in the reserve beds to propagate from; for it is found that young herbaceous plants, propagated from old plants the previous summer, yield the best flowering plants for the beds or borders. In replanting, strict attention should be paid to their height, the dwarfish kinds being in the first row, the next in size in the second, and so on, placing the tallest sorts behind. The same attention should be paid to their colour and time of flowering, so that the green of the late-blooming kinds should blend harmoniously with the colours of early bloomers, and these with each other, and vice versa.

420 Where a very choice selection of border flowers is aimed at, it is desirable to plant close to the wall, at distances varying from two to three feet, dwarf-growing varieties of tea-scented, Noisette, and other continuous blooming roses, of which a selection may be made from the list of all kinds of this beautiful flower that will be found in another part of this volume.

421 Between the roses and the wall, plant *Thunbergia grandiflora*, *T. aurantiaca*, and *T. alba*; *Alstroemeria pulchella*, *A. aurea*, *A. Hookerii, and A. psittacina*; *Gladiolus Gandavensis*, *G. Brenchleyensis*, *G. cardinalis*, *G. psittacinus*, and any of the beautiful gladioli that have been introduced of late years; *Amaryllis Belladonna*; *Camassia esculenta*, etc. In the front, between the roses and the edging, plant ixias, tritonias, watsonias and sparaxes, which, in such situations, if planted five or six inches deep, will flower well. These may be intermixed with the beautiful *Anomatheca cruenta* and *A. juncea*; *Calochortus venustus* and *C. splendens*; *Vieusseuxia pavonina*; *Sternbergia lutea*; *Oxalis floribunda*, *O. Bowiei*, and *O. Deppei*. Patches of *Tigridia pavonia* and *T. conchiflora*, planted judiciously here and here, with *Anemone Japonica* and *A. Japonica hybrida*, planted in peat, will also be suitable occupants of such a border, in which some of the best dwarf bedding-out plants may be planted out in summer to fill up vacancies. Many of these are surpassingly beautiful, and a portion would be in flower from early spring till the frosts set in, when the whole border should be covered with a layer of decayed leaves, at least four inches thick.

422 It not unfrequently happens, and that in gardens once famed for the luxuriance of their plants on bog or peat borders, that a period of decay arrives. Rhododendrons become sticky, moss accumulates about their roots, and their leaves flag and look sickly at the slightest drought. Kalmias, also, have continually dead branches to be removed, and azaleas do not make the new wood they ought. These are undoubted evidences that renovation is required, and should be forthwith attended to. A top dressing of the soil, with a mixture of well-rotted manure from the cowyard, and fresh peat or bog, may do some good; but if evidences of decay are very striking, it will be far better to take up all the plants and dig in a good change of soil. Bog-earth which has been kept for a season, and turned two or three times, is, of course, the best; but, in the absence of this, leaf mould and cow dung may be used.

423 Those rhododendrons which have run too far from home, and bear leaves only at the extremities of long sticky branches, must be cut down. The season of the year best suited for pruning rhododendrons is immediately after the flowering season, that they may have all their growing period of the year before them to make fresh shoots. Rhododendrons of any size may be taken up and removed, and not unfrequently with great benefit, as far, at any rate, as flowering is concerned, if care be taken that the mould about the stem and roots be not disturbed. In cases, however, where bog plants come up very easily, having no hold in the ground, and with a hard ball of earth about the roots, which appears disinclined to blend with the surrounding soil, it is frequently of great advantage to loosen this ball and open the roots a little before the plants are placed in their fresh bed.

424 In speaking of the renewal of old gardens, it was inferred that the work of renovation belonged rather to the trees, shrubs, and plants with which they are stocked than to the laying out of the garden and grounds, and that the latter required attention in modern gardens only. It may be the case, however, with many an old garden that a little alteration of the paths, lawn, shrubbery, and flower borders may prove highly desirable, but in these the alterations that are required must be governed by existing circumstances, as well as in small gardens. They will, in nine cases out of ten, suggest themselves, and therefore it is undesirable, even if it were possible, to attempt even to offer advice respecting them, much less to lay down rules for the guidance of those who may find themselves engaged in such a task. Alterations in the mode of laying out gardens, it may be said, are less required in gardens of considerable size attached to old houses, because their extent tends to render their defects less conspicuous. With small gardens appended to houses of later date, however, the confined space that is assigned to them only serves to render the faults of their arrangement and laying out all the more glaring, and more especially because it is in the stereotyped form so common to the gardens of so-called villa residences in which straight lines are the rule, and anything approaching to a curved line a rare exception.

425 In order to make the meaning of that which has just been said perfectly clear, let us take the case of a small semidetached house, having a frontage to the roadway of 40 feet, and a depth from roadway to rear of 75 feet, and show, firstly, how the garden both in front and rear was laid out, and then what additions were made, and what improvements and modifications were introduced, so that a very bare and ordinary form of garden was transformed, without very much trouble and expense, into one that was extremely pretty and attractive, despite the smallness of the field of operation and the necessarily restricted size of its various features. The example given will serve as a suggestion for the modification of gardens laid out on the strictly rectilinear principle: it may be followed in its leading features, although the outline of the block that shows the form of the house that stands in the garden may, in the great majority of cases, prevent its adoption in all its entirety.

426 The plan of the house and garden is shown in Fig. 167, on a scale of 1 inch to 12 feet, which has been adopted so that the extreme length of the diagram, if drawn on a larger scale, might not necessitate the omission of the ground occupied by the house. The shaded block indicates the house itself, whose

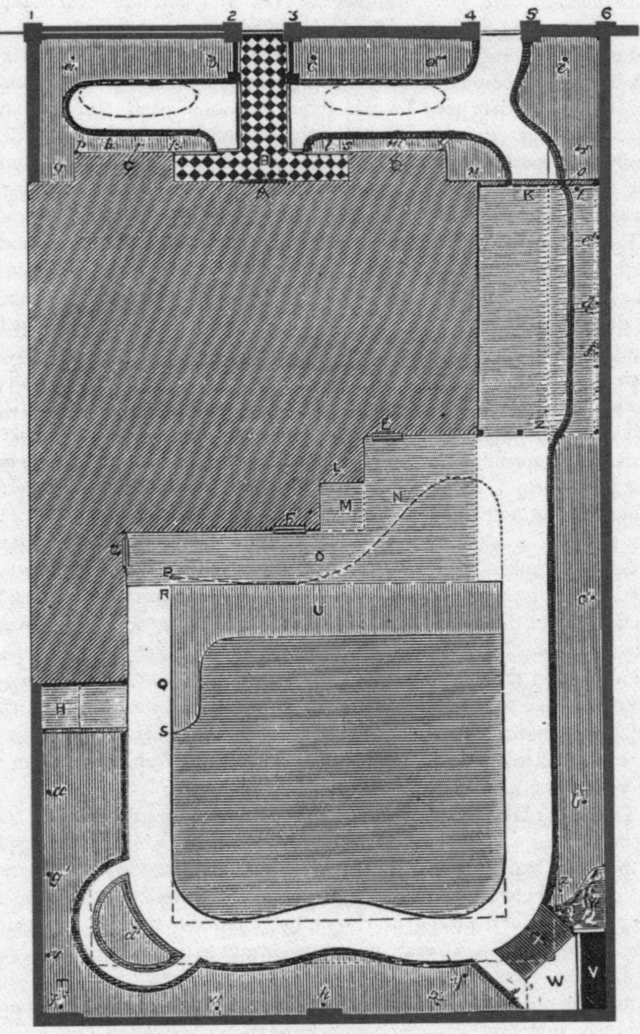

FIG. 167 *Diagram showing renovation of garden badly laid out*

structure, as a matter of course, was permitted to remain unaltered, except in one particular, which will be mentioned presently. The house, as will be seen, is double-fronted, having the entrance in the centre of the front. Two square bays project from the front, and the space between them is occupied by a shallow verandah, which affords shelter to anyone seeking admission to the house, and which is partly enclosed on each side by Japanese trellis work, connected by an arch in the same style. Thus, A shows the front door, and B the covered space in front of it, between the square bays C, D, which contain the windows that light the dining room and drawing room. At E in the drawing room is a French window, giving access to the garden; F is the back door, and G the back-kitchen door. This is all that need be said about the house itself, and we may now proceed to the garden, merely pausing for a moment to say that the wall at the bottom of the garden, on the left side, and in the front, with the piers numbered 1 to 5, belong to the house, but that pier No. 6, the wall, and the building in the centre of it, or nearly so, to the right, belong to the house next on the right.

427 With regard to the laying out of the garden, which was done doubtless in accordance with the ideas, limited, of the builder who built the house, it was of the baldest, barest, most severe description. It is indicated in the diagram by faint dotted lines, and consisted of a border 3 feet 6 inches wide, including edging from the front wall between piers 5 and 6 straight away to the back wall, and continued in the same monotony of treatment in front of the wall at the bottom and on the left until it met that disgrace to modern civilisation and urban sanitary authorities, the inevitable dustbin, which thrust its boxlike form into unpleasant prominence at H. The walk on the right side and at the bottom of the garden was 3 feet 6 inches in width; but on the left it was increased to 6 feet in width, presumably because the builder had not the slightest idea how it might be made to harmonise in width with the rest of the pathways. The space between the front of the house and the front wall, from the wall between the house and pier 1, on the left, to the beginning of the bed on the right, was a bare stretch of gravel, diversified by two little oval beds, edged with box, which were planted like oases in the gravel desert, one in front of each window. These are also indicated by faint dotted lines. Turning to the rear of the house once more, the central space between the pathways was occupied by a grass plat, with the tasteful sweep indicated at the top where it approached the house. Surely there is no one who will not say that under all the circumstances renewal and renovation in every way was a thing that was much needed.

428 The walls of the house, the walls that enclosed the garden on each side and in front and rear were of brick, but the builder had not put good and new bricks into the walls, and consequently they were all the worse for wear. There were entrance gates between piers 2 and 3 and between piers 4 and 5. Between piers 1 and 2 and piers 3 and 4 was a dwarf wall, surmounted by a cast-iron ornamental railing, or rather a cast-iron railing that was meant to be ornamental. It has been said that the space in front of the house was entirely gravelled, with the exception of the oval beds and border to the right, consequently there was neither tree, nor shrub, nor climber to clothe the walls and hide their forbidding aspect. The house in question had been built about five-and-twenty years, and it is a fact that neither owner nor tenant had gone to the slightest trouble or expense in stocking the garden. But of this more presently. The first thing that was done was to secure the privacy of the garden in the rear as far as possible by putting up a strong fence at K. This consisted of a trellised door in the centre with trellised compartments on each side of it, the upper portion consisting of trellised panels, and the lower part of closed panels of match boarding placed diagonally. Each of the four posts on which the fence was framed was surmounted by a finial in the form of a small pinnacle, and between the finials were pieces of ornamental cresting.

429 The front garden was then remodelled, and how this was done is shown by the illustration. Firstly, the approach from the front gate, between piers 2 and 3, to the front door, was paved with tiles. Two dwarf walls, or rather rows of bricks, were carried along the approach on either side of it for a short distance, and terminated by low piers surmounted by square red tiles. The piers were about 14 or 15 inches high, including the tiles. The primary object was to prevent anyone from stepping on the beds that were about to be made when coming through the front gate, and the dwarf piers further served as pedestals for flowers in pots. Beds were then formed as shown; a narrow border about 15 inches wide, including a grass verge of 6 inches, being made close to the house under the windows, and a wider border of 3 feet 6 inches, including grass verge of 6 inches, being made within the front fence. The end of the border between piers 5 and 6 was remodelled as shown, and the path, which was now wholly central, was gravelled after the earth had been removed to some depth and filled with brickbats and rough stones. This being done, a laburnum was planted at *a*, a white thorn at *b*, a scarlet thorn at *c*, a double-flowering cherry at *d*, an almond at *e*, and a mountain ash at *f*. At the base of the garden walls and fencing surrounding the front garden, Irish ivy (*Hedera Canariensis*) and some large varieties of variegated ivy were planted, and in a short time the walls, piers, and iron railings were completely covered by a sheet of ivy, which hid their ugliness and gave character and individuality to the entire front of the house. Further, Virginian creepers were planted at *g* and *o*, a white jasmine at *n*, yellow jasmine (*Jasminum nudiflorum*) at *p* and *q*, *Cydonia Japonica* at *h* and *m*, *Kerria Japonica* at *r* and *s*, and clematises against the verandah at *k* and *l*. This completed the work of renovation in the front of the house.

430 The alterations in the garden at the rear of the house were as follows: First, a closet at L, which was entered from the garden, and which served as a tool house and a receptacle for many odds and ends, was taken into the house by a change of entrance and converted into a china and store closet, and its place was supplied by another similar closet built at M, and a conservatory, entered from the drawing room by the French window at E, was constructed as shown at N. By this means the back of the house, instead of being twice recessed, was brought into one line, and an opportunity was afforded for putting up a glazed verandah running all the way from the back kitchen door to the outer corner of the conservatory, which, as the back of the house fronted due south, served admirably as a vinery on a small scale. A trellis had originally been placed from P to Q. This was altered to run from R to S, in which position it screened both the back-kitchen window and dustbin, H, which was still further concealed by having an auricula house built over it, panelled below with wood, in the centre with open trellis work in Japanese style, and glazed at the top and just above the open panels; the end being left open for access to the house and dustbin. The narrow bed beyond H was brought out to the same width as the back-kitchen, the lower corners of the grass plat were rounded off, and the bottom treated as shown, and in order to give access to the corner at T, for several reasons, a small crescent bed was taken out as drawn. A broad border was made at U, in front of the verandah and trellis, to take the vines and be planted with flowers. In the lower right-hand corner a bin was made at V for the reception of grass cut from the lawn and hedges, soot, etc. – in fact, to serve as a compost pit. Before it was a small court, W, entered by a trellised door indicated by the dotted line. The court and compost pit were masked by a small summer house at X, and a rockery at Y. The space by the side of the house from K to Z it was resolved to cover in with a glazed roof, leaving the ends open so as not to interfere with the use of the border by the side.

431 As for the trees that were in the garden before the work of renovation was commenced, there was a large laburnum in the corner at V, with two limes close to it, one of which had been polled, and was therefore anything but ornamental. These were, of course, uprooted and converted into firewood. Instead of these, some fruit trees were put in as follows: Prince of Wales plums at *t*, *u*, *v*, a Victoria plum at *w*, a. Morello cherry at *x*, an apple (Lady Henniker) at *y*, another (Blenheim Orange) at *z*, an amber heart standard cherry in the crescent bed at *a*′, a Cox's Emperor plum at *b*′ a William's Bon Chrétien pear at *c*′, a Louise Bonne de Jersey pear at *d*′, and black-heart cherries at *e*′ and *f*′. These cherries fill the lower panels of the dwarf wall against which they are planted, while the pears will be trained above them on the fence of wood that will be raised above the wall to enclose the garden more effectually. A white jasmine is planted at *g*′*f*, Irish ivy at *k*′ and *l*′, and a *Cotoneaster Simonsi* at *h*′.

432 With the vines and climbers in the border at U, it is clear that an effort has been made to make the best of the space and materials at command. If any one will take the trouble to make a sketch of the house and garden as it originally presented itself, according to the run of the faint dotted lines, and compare it with Fig. 167, this will be very plainly shown. Space and time fail to speak of other adjuncts which have been introduced for the ornamentation of the garden in the form of covered trellis to mask buttresses in the walls, the buttresses themselves being capped with boxes for wall gardening, and which could not be understood without elaborate illustration. In that which has been said it has been sought to show how easily, and with what little departure from the original plan, a stiff and formal garden may be rendered pretty and attractive as well as useful. It will be found, moreover, that any garden which is treated in this manner will give the beholder the idea of being larger than it really is. This is owing to the simple fact that it takes the eye a longer time to pass over it and recognise every separate item and article, and that the eye cannot glance so rapidly along a curved line as it can along a straight line. Hence the desirability, especially in small gardens, of avoiding as far as may be possible the disposition of everything in the garden in straight lines.

CHAPTER 12

Furnishing the Garden – Rotation of Crops

433 From the digression in the last chapter respecting the renovation and renewal of old gardens and gardens that have been badly laid out, we must now return to a consideration of the land that we have supposed to have been duly prepared, and for the first time brought into a suitable condition for the practice of horticulture in all its branches. From this point it may be said that the treatment of the newly-made garden and of the garden that has been renewed will be in every important particular the same, or very nearly so, and that the instructions that are applicable to the new garden will be found to be equally suitable for the renewed garden.

434 The new ground having been duly levelled and drained, and the foundations laid for the walks, so that only a last coating of fine gravel is required to give the finishing touch to them, the portion intended for cropping and for flower beds, as already intimated, should either lie fallow for a season, or be sown with some preparatory crop, such as turnips or carrots. From this treatment, however, we must certainly except the *Reserve Garden*, on which the appearance of the flower beds in the following summer must depend; the *Orchard* and the *Fruit Garden*, in which the young trees will take many years to arrive at a mature state; and perhaps the *Kitchen Garden* also, which may be cropped with such vegetable products as are found to be preparers of the soil.

435 Firstly, with regard to the Reserve Garden, this, as its name imports, is not meant to be a special object of beauty in itself, but to provide the means of upholding a continuous display of beauty elsewhere. Many plants that are totally unfit, from the short duration of their bloom, to enter the flower garden as permanent occupants, may, with perfect safety, be transplanted there for the display of their floral beauty, and be returned, as they fade, to the reserve garden. Of this class is the whole race of polyanthuses, hepaticas, hardy auriculas, primroses, and violets. The winter aconite, the Christmas rose (*Helleborus niger*), the spring arabis (*Arabis verna*), the rock alyssum or madwort (*Alyssum saxatile*), all the saxifrages, sedums, campanulas, early-flowering phloxes, adonis, orobus, and other similar plants, should also be found here. All these, and any other plants of similar habit, may be moved into the flower garden after the bedding plants are cleared off in October or November, and taken back to the reserve garden in April or May, to make room for the more permanent flowering plants.

436 Most of the temporary tenants of the reserve garden are propagated by division of the root; and at the time they are taken back to their summer quarters in the reserve garden will be the best period thus to increase the stock. When they are severally subdivided, it may be necessary to shade them for a time, as the profusion and perfection of next year's blossoms are dependent upon the healthy growth of their summer leaves. In no case, however, should shading be resorted to if the plants will bear full exposure to light and air without it, as direct sunlight is the great agent in elaborating the sap and inducing the production of flowers. The roots of some of the species, of which the Russian violet may be accepted as a representative, should be divided and young plants formed annually. Others, of which the *Alyssum saxatile* is a type, flower better and are much more effective as large plants or patches.

437 The reserve garden is also the proper place for sowing hardy annuals in the autumn, for embellishing the flower garden in the spring. They should be sown thinly broadcast in beds, in September or October, and the oftener they are pricked out or transplanted the better. The checks incident to such operations ensure profusion of bloom and hardiness of constitution.

438 In rapid-growing plants the sap is not only more abundant, but also more watery, or thinner, than in those of slower growth. The affinity of frost for water especially exposes plants in this state to the full force of its blighting power. The thicker or more highly elaborated the sap, not only the more profuse the bloom, but the greater the power of the plant to resist cold. Hence arises the safety of broccoli that has been heeled over, and of stocks that have been transplanted, when either, if left to grow freely, are killed by the frost; and hence, too, the benefit of transplanting annuals that are intended to withstand the severity of the weather.

439 The following annuals are among the best for this purpose: *Calliopsis* (or *Coreopsis*) *Drummondii*, *Calliopsis tinctoria*, *Clarkia pulchella*, *Clarkia pulchella alba*, *Collinsia bicolor*, *Collinsia grandiflora*, delphiniums or larkspurs of different sorts and colours, *Bartonia aurea*, *Erysimum Perovskianum*, *Eschscholtzia Californica*, *Gilia capitata*, *Gilia tricolor*, all the annual varieties of candytufts (*Iberis*). *Leptosiphon andrasaceus*, *Leptosiphon densiflorus*, white and pink Virginian stocks, *Limnanthes Douglasii*, all the varities of nemophila, dwarf schizanthus (*Schizanthus pinnatus humilis*), *Schizanthus porrigens*, *Schizanthus Priestii*, and the rock lychnis (*Viscaria oculata*), will also stand through ordinary winters, and be useful in furnishing the flower garden in spring or early summer.*

440 Many of the spring-sown hardy annuals would also be raised in the reserve garden, although in most gardens where they are extensively grown, the majority of them are sown either in patches or lines where they are intended to flower.

441 The reserve garden is also the proper nursing place for the whole race of half-hardy annuals. Stocks, asters, marigolds, clintonias, calandrinias, lobelias, mesembryanthemums, portulacas, oenotheras, the phloxes (including the

* In order to save space and to prevent undue repetition, it is usual in all works on gardening, when the name of a variety of any family of plants has been given at full length, and is followed by another of the same family, to give the initial letter only of the family name or generic name. Thus, *Calliopsis tinctoria* would be written *C. tinctoria*, and *Clarkia pulchella alba*, *C. p. alba*, because in each case the names of the flowers thus distinguished are preceded by the name of another member of the family, whose name has been given at full length. This plan will be followed in future pages.

varieties of *Phlox Drummondii*), salpiglossis, maurandyas, tropaeolums, etc., raised on a slight hotbed, must be gradually hardened off, and planted in rich soil in a warm corner, to be moved in due time to their blooming quarters. Hardy biennials, such as wallflowers, Brompton stocks, sweet williams, foxgloves, etc., etc., should also be sown here in May or June, and receive their proper culture throughout the summer. Any perennials, such as hollyhocks, that are raised from seed, should likewise be sown in the reserve garden, and treated the same as biennials. Cuttings of any plants that will root in the open air should also be inserted here; and a corner should be devoted to shrubs that are intended to be increased by layering. Provision should also be made in this department for affording temporary shelter, and the means of gradually hardening off the whole stock of bedding plants. Even in small gardens, the north border or a portion of it should be utilised as a reserve garden.

442 In places of any extent, the reserve garden should be furnished with ranges of cold and partially-heated pits and frames; and beds of rich soil, with raised edgings of brick, stone, or wood, spanned over with hoops, to support mats, canvas, reed coverings, etc., in cold weather.

443 In most gardens there is a sad lack of means for gradually transferring plants to the open air, and several months of beauty in the flower garden are often lost in consequence. These raised protected-at-pleasure beds will also be the best possible positions for growing the choicest sorts of tulips, hyacinths, anemones, and other favourite flowers of early summer. I consider it better to plant hardy bulbs, such as crocuses, snowdrops, and the commoner tulips, say from one foot to eighteen inches deep, and leave them permanently in the flower beds or borders, than to remove them out of the way of the bedding plants annually. Those, however, who object to this treatment will of course provide space for them in the reserve garden, and remove them thither when they plant out regular bedding plants in May.

444 All surplus stock, to fill blanks or repair accidents, should be neatly plunged in pots, ready to be moved when wanted. Others, that root more freely, and bear moving better, may be planted in rich soil for similar purposes; if not required to fill up gaps in the flower beds, they will furnish strong early cuttings and cut flowers throughout the season. When the reserve garden is of sufficient dimensions, the whole of the cuttings and cut flowers should be derived from it, thus leaving the flower garden in full perfection throughout the season. For want of such a reserve to fall back upon, some gardens have no sooner arrived at perfection than they are fearfully mangled, and their beauty marred, by the imperious demands of the propagator and decorator. Choice collections of pinks and carnations, dahlias, roses, and chrysanthemums, for show flowers, should also be grown in the reserve garden. The arrangements and special culture that some of these flowers require to produce them in the highest perfection, are hardly consistent with the high finish and refined enjoyment which should be the leading characteristic of every well-kept garden.

445 When the flower garden is furnished with shrubs for winter, space must be found for them in the reserve garden in summer. Small plants of hollies, laurels, box, acacias, berberries, sedums, kalmias, rhododendrons, and other flowering shrubs, are very effective and useful for this purpose. They may be either grown in pots or carefully moved without pots. After a few years' transplanting in good sound loam, they will be furnished with such compact balls of roots as to be moved with impunity at almost any period of summer or winter. Living plants are much better than branches of shrubs for relieving the bald outlines of flower beds in winter. By studying the various shades of green, intermixing variegated varieties, and edging the shrubs with bulbs or other plants, to increase the effect, the garden may be made almost as interesting in winter and spring as at any other period.

446 The soil in the reserve garden should be varied, to suit its special uses. That most generally serviceable will be a rather heavy loam, which, by the addition of sand, leaf mould, etc., will produce almost every conceivable variety best adapted to the varied purposes of this department. Some beds of peat should also be provided, and composts of various kinds laid up within easy distance. The size of the reserve garden will entirely depend upon the demands upon it. A few square yards, according to the size of the garden itself, may suffice for an amateur; a quarter or half an acre may be needful for some of our largest places. No garden, large or small, can be complete without one: for what the propagating, store, and growing houses are to the conservatory and drawing room, the reserve garden is, or should be, to the flower garden. It should not only be a great manufactory of raw material, but an inexhaustible warehouse, filled to overflowing with finished goods ready to be delivered whenever and wherever a supply is demanded.

447 From the Reserve Garden we may pass on at once to the consideration of the Kitchen Garden. Kitchen gardening is certainly the most profitable purpose to which a piece of ground can be applied; a shilling's worth of cabbage seed will produce plants enough to crop several rods of ground, and will furnish greens in winter and cabbages in summer for a large family; but few who possess a piece of ground are contented with the mere cultivation of cabbages. The crops required for the kitchen are both numerous and varied; delicacies must be produced in season and out of season, and this requires both judgment in arranging and skill in growing them.

448 In laying down a plan of operations for kitchen gardening, it is necessary to have an eye to the means of those for whose service it is intended. A kitchen garden suitable for a gentleman's country seat would be of little or no use to the cottager, and vice versa; but although the minor details would be different, the broad principles are the same – the soil and situation are to be adapted to the vegetables required, and the ground turned to the best possible account in both cases.

449 Although much has been said about soils and sites for gardens in preceding chapters, it will be useful to glance briefly here at a few important points in connection with these subjects and the desirability of suitable protection for gardens in certain quarters, as they have much to do with both the furnishing of the garden and the rotation or succession of crops. The best soil for kitchen garden purposes is a mellow holding loam – that is, loam which crumbles to pieces in working it, and yet is retentive of moisture. But it does not follow that other soils are not suitable for growing good crops, for under proper management and a proper system of cultivation, good vegetables may be grown on a light black loam with a gravelly subsoil, and also on heavy clay. Both may be worked advantageously by adopting the necessary tillage. A light gravelly soil, for instance, quickly loses moisture, the principal support of all vegetation, for the surplus water quickly percolates through the soil or escapes by evaporation. But excessive evaporation may be prevented, and the plants invigorated at the same time, by a system of manuring the ground by mulching – that is, by spreading a layer of long stable dung over the light soils, and a good crop of vegetables will be ensured.

450 Where the soil is heavy and retentive, as all clay lands are, it is necessary to dig or trench the ground a few weeks before cropping it; if it is laid in ridges in November or December, for instance, or dug level and left in coarse lumps, round and between which the air constantly permeates, after a frost it will all crumble to a coarse powder under the March winds; while in summer, when it is sometimes necessary to dig and crop it, the ground is dug or trenched, and left in a rough state; the first drying day will render every lump as hard as granite, but a shower of rain makes them fall to pieces. If cropped while in this state, before the surface gets quite dry, the soil will work easily enough. This is of some importance; for in sowing small seeds it is necessary that the ground should be smooth and well pulverised, otherwise the seed will remain uncovered. Again, light soils quickly lose moisture, which is absorbed by the air; but quickly revive again, and the air is rendered mild and genial by the moisture that has been taken from the ground; it is therefore evident, that certain crops which come in early, and are of short duration, are most suitable for such soils.

451 In the early spring months, a few sunny days, which make no impression on clay land, render the light ground quite warm, and plants and seeds start into growth at once. On a warm sunny border of light soil early salads and vegetables may be produced a month or six weeks earlier than on heavy retentive soils; on the other hand, heavy ground receives both heat and moisture slowly, and is very retentive of the moisture, retaining it after many weeks of dry weather: the heaviest and grossest feeding crops are therefore most suitable for it during the summer, and will continue growing on it further into the winter if the water is not allowed to stagnate. Heavy summer and autumn and late winter crops will therefore repay the cultivator on such soils; but it is always advisable, where the soil is in either extreme, to dress it so that the light soil shall become more tenacious and the heavy more porous: this is done by mixing light soil with equal parts of fat unctuous loam, and the manure and mulching recommended above. The loam should feel doughy in the hand, and is best obtained from meadow land, taking the whole top spit, herbage and all, which is itself an excellent fertiliser. Where the common buttercup flourishes, there will mostly be found loam suitable for the purpose. Where the soil is a heavy clay, and there is no light soil available, burn a portion of the clay and mix it with the rest: this may be done either by mixing the burnt soil with the dung and applying it as manure, or by mixing them up in trenching; but an admixture of light sandy soil mixed with the manure is more economical and equally effective.

452 The same remarks apply to stony or sandy soils. A stony soil may be retentive and none the worse for being stony, except in working; good crops may be grown even on light stony soils. If the soil is sandy, let mulching form one of the chief items in its tillage, and it will repay the cultivator.

453 In selecting a piece of ground for garden cultivation, its situation as to hills, large trees, buildings, and to water, is important. Generally speaking, land situated on the banks, or very near large pieces of water, is cold and bleak; the process of evaporation, continually going on, renders the air cold and raw in such localities; and cold air, cutting winds, and cold soil, are most unfavourable to gardening. A thick brick or stone wall and row of trees on the water side would reduce the one, and if the ground slope down to the water with a sufficient fall, good drainage will remove the coldness of the soil. If the land lies too low to be drained, the water lies stagnate, and the roots of the crops, consequently, are always in an unhealthy cold bath, a situation in which few things will flourish.

454 In no case should trees be so close to the kitchen garden that their roots obtrude into the borders; no culinary plant can get its proper supply while the fibres of a vigorous tree are appropriating the lion's share of the sustenance afforded by the soil. Another objection to trees as a shelter is, that when most required they are least efficient. Denuded of their leaves in these seasons, they afford little shelter in the winter and early spring months. Where trees or buildings lie between the garden and the sun, crops which do well in the shade should be grown there. There are not many vegetables which prosper in such situations; certainly it would be useless to try peas, beans, potatoes, or cabbages, under such circumstances; but rhubarb, seakale, Scotch kale, and salads may do. On the other hand, it may be observed as a rule that where a cabbage will grow vigorously and make a good heart, there any kind of kitchen crop will flourish. Hilly ground may be favourably situated or otherwise, according to the aspect. A northern aspect will probably be bleak, a south one warm and sheltered; but success or failure depends on a combination of, rather than on, particular circumstances; and a useful lesson in cultivation may be drawn from the weeds which flourish on the natural soil in the neighbourhood. If buttercups, docks, thistles, couch grass, and suchlike weeds grow luxuriantly, peas, cabbages, celery, etc., may be made to flourish; the presence of such weeds is an excellent criterion of the fertility of the soil.

455 The kitchen garden suitable for a suburban villa will altogether depend on the extent of ground attached to those residences. Let us, however, take one of medium size, enclosing an acre of ground, arranged as a pleasure and kitchen garden, as far from the house as possible, beyond bad smells; although these may be prevented by means of lime, charcoal, or some other deodoriser. The melon ground, like the kitchen garden, Will be greatly benefitted if some trees of dense habit, such as a belt of larch or other pines, happen to be planted about fifty yards to the north or east of it, to break the force of cutting north winds.

456 As the question of brick walls has already been fully discussed, it is only necessary to remark here that there can be no question about the advantages they offer, especially with a southern aspect. Walls constructed with curvatures or piers to protect the wall trees from cold winds are practically no better than walls that are straight or unbroken by projections, for everybody knows that wall trees bear yearly, for many years, an excellent crop of fruit, which ripens well without any such assistance on a wall facing the south, without any protection. But the trees should be planted on a good holding loam; they should be young healthy trees when planted, and they should be kept in a healthy state by judicious management, in which disbudding is used more than the knife. In such soil and under such management it is not probable that fruit trees will fail in producing good crops, weather permitting.

457 Respecting the paths, etc., the main object is to have them strong and durable, for a kitchen garden should be so in reality; and whatever is done to make it ornamental beyond keeping it very clean and sweet must and does detract from its true purpose. In a kitchen garden there is a great deal of wheeling in of manure and wheeling out of rubbish to be performed. Therefore, in forming paths, let strength and solidity be the chief considerations; see that the paths are high enough to allow for sinking, which is the result of constant wheeling upon them; and, as regards drainage, if paths are made very solid, they will not absorb water, and, if they are made sufficiently high and rounded, water will readily run off and find its way to the drains. If the walks are rendered impervious to wet, a good foot of ballast or coarse gravel will be sufficient; and if on this is placed a thin layer of fine gravel or coarse sand, it will take off the roughness. Where gravel can be procured, nothing can be better; but, if not easily procurable, well-burnt clay is equally efficacious.

458 In large kitchen gardens it is desirable to have two or three main walks, both for the greater convenience of cropping and working, and for more effectually carrying out a system of rotation cropping. Then, again, with regard to extent, an acre of ground may be both a large or a small kitchen garden, according to what it is desired to grow in it. In places where the orchard is a separate department, and the kitchen garden is devoted exclusively to vegetable culture, an acre of ground will yield vegetables for a large family; but, if it is thickly planted with fruit trees in the form of standard dwarfs and espaliers, an acre will be insufficient. And, be it observed, the vegetables will not be so good; for good healthy vegetables require to be open to the sun and to the free circulation of air. Where there is room, let the orchard be apart from the kitchen garden, and the result will be a thousand times more satisfactory.

459 In conjunction with a large kitchen garden, there will necessarily be forcing pits or houses; and it will be the province of the garden to grow subjects for them to a certain extent. The structure of glazed houses and shelters of all kinds, orchard houses, etc., will be treated in another part of this volume.

460 When the same crops are grown successively on the same piece of ground year after year, without addition to the soil, it has been found that the soil is impoverished for that particular crop, but that properties are still left in it which are nutritive to others; thus, a crop of peas and a crop of wheat being sown on the same ground, and under precisely the same circumstances, it has been found that the wheat will absorb all the silica from the soil, while the pea leaves this component part of the soil untouched. Some plants, according to Dr Daubeny, absorb strontium; the spiral-rooted polygonum, while it takes up common salt, refuses acetate of lime; and so with many other plants. Cropping the land, therefore, year after year with the same plants has long been abandoned.

Touching on the exhaustion of certain constituents in the soil in connection with the rotation of crops, Loudon says: 'When the particular earths that a plant requires have been exhausted in any soil by a crop of that particular plant having been grown in it, it is evident that another crop of the same plant cannot be grown in the same soil until it has recovered a sufficient quantity of that substance which had become exhausted; but it is equally evident that another crop, requiring a different substance, may be grown in the same soil the following year. Thus, plants that require potash, such as the beet, the mangold wurzel, and the turnip, may succeed plants that require lime, such as beans, peas, etc., and thus the same result is obtained as was proposed by the former hypothesis' (namely, that of De Candolle and others, who supposed that growing plants threw off into the soil in course of growth excrementitious matter that was injurious to plants of its own kind but not to others, and therefore that the same kind of crop could not be grown to advantage two years running in the same soil), with this difference, that the real cause why a rotation of crops is advisable being now known, the necessity for it may be avoided by supplying the soil, after each crop, with the mineral substances that had become exhausted, and thus the same crop may be grown on the same soil for twenty years in succession.

'If no artificial means are used, Nature gradually restores the mineral substances which have been exhausted, and which the soil obtains from the atmosphere, the rain, and other sources. The restoration, when left entirely to Nature, is slow, and thus it was the custom to let five or even six years elapse before the same crop was grown twice on the same land, unless the process of restoration was aided by fallowing or by irrigation.'

In Johnston and Cameron's *Elements of Agricultural Chemistry and Geology*, the following remarks are made on the subject now under consideration: 'The experiments of Lawes and Gilbert show that soils become exhausted of certain of their constituents sooner than of others. The substance which disappears soonest in the case of certain kinds of cropping is nitrogen (ammonia); but there are other crops which deal gently with nitrogen and draw largely on some of the mineral ingredients of the soil. During the growth of leguminous crops, nitrogen accumulates in the surface soil.

'If two crops of unlike kinds be sown together, their roots suck in the inorganic substances in different proportions – the one more potash and phosphoric acid, perhaps; the other more lime, magnesia, or silica. They thus interfere less with each other than plants of the same kind do which require the same kinds of food in nearly the same proportions. Or the two kinds of crop grow with different degrees of rapidity or at different periods of the year; while the roots of the one are busy drawing in supplies of inorganic nourishment, chiefly from great depths, those of the other are only able to take up food from the surface soil.

'If each crop demands special substances, or these substances in quantities peculiar to itself, or in some peculiar state of combination, the chances that the soil will be able to supply them are greater the more distant the intervals at which the same crop is grown upon it. Other crops do not demand the same substances in the same proportions; and thus they may gradually accumulate on the soil till it becomes especially favourable to the particular one we wish to grow.

'Suppose the soil to contain a certain average supply of all those inorganic substances which plants require, and that the same corn crop is grown upon it for a long series of years – this crop will carry off some of these substances in larger proportions than others, so that year by year the quantity of those which are chiefly carried off will become relatively less. Thus at length the soil, for want of these special substances, will become unable to bear a good crop of this kind at all, though it may still contain a large store of the other inorganic substances which other plants do not specially exhaust. Suppose bean or turnip crops raised in like manner for a succession of years; they would exhaust the soil of a certain set of substances till it became unable to grow them profitably, though still rich perhaps in those things which cereals especially demand.

'But grow these crops alternately, and then the one crop will draw especially upon one class of substances, the other crop upon another; and thus a much larger produce of each will be reaped from the same soil, and for a much longer period of time. On this principle the benefit of a rotation of crops in an important degree depends.'

In the preceding remarks, gathered from the writings of competent authorities on the subject, the reasons which show that the rotation of crops, both in farming and gardening, is not only desirable but highly necessary, are duly set forth and explained. The importance of the subject, coupled with the indisputable fact that it is one which should be thoroughly understood by all gardeners, renders any apology for the length of the extracts unnecessary. And here the importance of chemistry in its relations to agriculture and horticulture clearly appears, for when the constituents of plants have been determined by chemical analysis, and the composition of the soil or soils with which the gardener has to deal, it requires but little reasoning to show (1) what plants are best suited to the soil as it stands; (2) what manures are most necessary for the amelioration of the soil and to render it better fitted for other kinds of plants; and (3) what succession or rotation of crops should be adopted in order to husband and utilise to the fullest extent the fertilising elements that the soil contains.

461 In the garden, where it is more difficult, from the limited space and numerous crops, to obtain a perfect system of rotation than it is in the farm, it is sought to renew the constituents withdrawn from the soil (1) by manuring, (2) by ridging up vacant ground so as to expose the largest possible surface to the action of the atmosphere and the salts contained in the winter's snow, and (3) by the admixture of virgin soil; but wherever it is possible, rotation of crops should be adopted. In ordering the rotation, there are certain rules to be observed which have been deduced from the experience of practical gardeners. These may be epitomised as follows:

1 Plants which belong to the same natural order, and which, therefore, have a close affinity to each other and resemble each other in structure and habit, should not succeed each other. Thus, cruciferous plants, such as cabbages, turnips, etc., should be followed by leguminous plants, such as peas, beans, etc; and deep-rooting plants, such as beet, carrots, parsnips, etc., that draw their nutriment from a considerable depth below the surface, should be followed by spinach, lettuce, etc., which do not strike deeply into the earth, but send out their rootlets into the surface soil; and in the examples given the converse also holds good.

2 Plants, for the sake of their roots or bulbs, should not follow or be followed by others grown for the same purpose, nor, by parity of reasoning, should plants grown for their fruit or seeds, or plants grown for their leaves, follow or be followed by plants that are grown for similar purposes. And it should be noted that plants grown for the sake of their seeds are more exhausting or take more from the soil than those which are grown for the sake of their leaves.

3 Perennial plants, which occupy the ground for many years, should never succeed each other, but be followed by plants which remain on the ground for a short time only. Thus, asparagus, seakale, globe artichokes, or

strawberries should never follow each other, but be succeeded by such crops as onions, leeks, lettuces, which are annual crops that remain for a short time, comparatively speaking, on the soil.

4 No crop of an exhausting nature should follow another crop of the same character in this respect, but any exhausting crop should be preceded and followed by a crop that does not take so much out of the ground. Thus, cabbages should be preceded or followed by lettuces, etc.

462 In his *Book of the Garden*, McIntosh quotes with approval an article on rotation cropping that appeared in *The Gardeners' Chronicle*, and it is certainly one that is most practical, useful, and illustrative of all that has been just advanced, but it has this fault, namely, that as the months in which the various operations of sowing, planting, and clearing take place follow indiscriminately throughout the paper, without any regard to the succession of the years in which the months mentioned occur, the reader naturally gets confused, and in his confusion soon loses all touch of the sequence of the years, which deprives the whole description of its utility. Instead, therefore, of quoting the article in question, or even giving the pith of it briefly, I have thrown it into the form of a table, in which the successional order of the years is plainly exhibited.

463 *Table Exhibiting a Rotation of Crops Over a Period of Seven Years.*
See facing page.

A few words of explanation may be necessary in relation to the above table, and these will be best given *seriatim* in connection with the reference letters that appear in it. (*a*) Here it is meant that the *early* peas will be cleared by the end of June, to be immediately succeeded by early broccoli, and that the peas will be under gradual clearance until September, to be followed by other plants included in the list of those in the second order of rotation, (*b*) The ground should have a slight dressing for these crops. The early broccoli will be cleared, perhaps, by the end of November, and should be ridged up all the winter, and remain so until April, when a crop of carrots will be sown as early as it is possible to do so. The other crops will be gradually cleared and the ground free by April, (*c*) As soon as the plants in the third order are cleared, which will be accomplished by November, the ground must be ridged up for winter, and heavily manured for the coming crops in the fourth order, of which the garlic and shallots should be planted in November, and the turnips sown in April. Potato-onions, or 'underground' onions, as some call them, may be put in at the same time as the shallots. These crops are set in Devonshire on the shortest day – St Thomas's Day, December 21 – and taken up on the longest day – St John Baptist's Day, June 24. They occupy but little room, so that by far the greater part of the ground can be ridged up. (*d*) By secondary crops are meant all short-lived crops, such as lettuces, radishes, and small salading, sweet herbs sown annually, and very early peas, beans, cauliflower, turnips, and potatoes, which are sown and planted in November, and require a warm south border. In this, the fifth series, the autumn spinach and endive will succeed the cauliflower that is cleared by July, and the shallots also; the winter spinach will follow the onions that will be cleared later, and the spring onions, winter lettuce, and

No.	Crops.	Operation	Sequence of years.						
			1st	2nd	3rd	4th	5th	6th	7th
1	Peas and Beans (*a*)	Sowing Clearing	Feb.–June	 June–Sep.					
2	Early Broccoli, Late Broccoli,Savoys, Borecole, Brussels Sprouts, Collards or Coleworts, Spring Cabbage (*b*)	Planting Clearing		June–Sep. Nov.–April					
3	Carrots, Parsnips, Beet, Scorzonera, Salsafy, etc. (*c*)	Sowing Clearing		April Nov.					
4	Cauliflower, Onions, Garlic,Shallots, Turnips	Sow and Plant Clearing			{Nov.–April July–Sep.				
5	Autumn Spinach, Endive, Winter Spinach, Spring Onions, Winter Lettuce, and other Secondary Crops (*d*)	Sowing Clearing			July–Sep.	 May			
6	Winter Greens, Red Cabbage, Savoys, Cauliflower, Leeks (*e*)	Planting Clearing				May	 April		
7	Potatoes (*f*)	Planting Clearing					April	 Sep.	
8	Spring Cabbage, Turnips, Late Broccoli (*g*)	Sow and Plant Clearing						{July May	
9	Celery, Cardoons, and Secondary Crops (*h*)	Sow and Plant Clearing						{May	 Mar.
10	French Beans, Scarlet Runners, Cauliflower, Cucumbers, Tomatoes	Sow and Plant Clearing							{April Nov.

secondary crops, the turnips, which will be off the ground in September, (*e*) For the plants included in the sixth series, the ground should be manured moderately. (*f*) The potatoes will be cleared gradually as the successive sorts come into use, the earlier sorts being off the ground in July and August for the turnips and other crops of the eighth series. (*g*) The turnips, etc., will make way in May for the celery and cardoons, which must be set in deep trenches. If all the ground is not required, the cabbages may be allowed to remain to furnish sprouts, which they will do all the summer. (*b*) The ground must be heavily manured for celery, etc., and the secondary crops, such as lettuce, etc., may be planted in the spaces that intervene between the trenches. As the ground occupied by the ninth series of plants is cleared, the ground should be trenched, and remain so until it is required for the plants of the tenth and last series. In the eighth year, the rotation may be commenced anew with peas and beans as shown in the table.

464 It will appear from the table given above, that two kinds of crops are sometimes grown on the same piece of ground at the same time, namely, the main crop and another crop, which, partly on account of the shortness of its duration and partly because it is subsidiary in a measure to the main crop, is called the secondary crop. When carried no further than this no harm can result from it, but when crops of importance are interlined, as it were – that is to say, when rows of cabbages are planted between the lines of potatoes – the ground is subjected to greater exhaustion, and in no case can the different crops thus grown turn out as well as they might have done had they been grown separately.

On this subject Thompson says, in *The Gardener's Assistant*: 'Two modes of cropping are adopted in gardens. The first may be termed separate cropping, the second simultaneous cropping. In the former the ground is only occupied by one crop at a time, in the latter by several. For instance, summer spinach may be sown between the rows of peas and beans, radishes along with carrots, or lettuces together with onions, or planted between the rows of celery. With regard to the comparative merits of these two modes of cropping there is much difference of opinion. The finest productions are undoubtedly obtained by the separate system; whilst a greater weight of produce of all sorts, but generally of inferior quality, is obtained by the simultaneous mode. To carry out the latter properly the soil must be rich and frequently manured; whilst by the other mode, good vegetables may be grown without so much artificial enrichment. Upon the whole, we consider that the separate mode of cultivation is the best adapted for large gardens; that simultaneous cropping may be advantageously adopted in those of small extent; and that in gardens of medium size, from which a great variety of productions are required in considerable quantity, both systems may, to a certain extent, be combined. Thus, succession crops of spinach, lettuce, likewise coleworts and borecole, may occupy the ground between other crops.'

465 Reverting once more to the Seven Years' Table of Rotation of Crops that has been given, it may be said that many modifications of the arrangements proposed will be found necessary in actual practice, but that something closely approaching it may be studied with advantage. Some crops, such as Jerusalem artichokes, a valuable, wholesome, and delicious vegetable, are altogether omitted in it; and, again, there are, besides the crops mentioned, permanent crops, such as asparagus, seakale, and globe artichokes, for which no such rotation can take place. Among all the systems of rotation and grouping that have been proposed, perhaps there is none so complete and so thoroughly practical in all its details as the following, which was devised, as well as the peculiar classification of crops set forth in it, by Mr Errington, formerly gardener at Oulton Park, Cheshire. In his system of grouping, Mr Errington places first:

466 The *Deepeners*; comprising asparagus, seakale, rhubarb, horseradish, and globe artichokes. These will require a deep soil; so that, before planting them, it is necessary to work the ground at least 3 feet deep, and, if the soil is good to that depth, 4 feet is better; they bear well the third year, and should not occupy the ground more than ten or a dozen years, as young plants are more productive than old, besides their use as deepeners of the soil for other crops.

467 The *Preparers*, which are all root crops, as potatoes, carrots, parsnips, turnips, salsafy, and scorzoneras, but Jerusalem artichokes, peas, beans, including scarlet runners, celery, onions, and suchlike crops, being all, with the exception of salsafy and scorzoneras, of less than a year's growth, and, with the exception of most of the root crops, requiring plenty of manure.

468 When these crops come off, the ground should be well manured; it will then be in first-rate condition for the next group, namely, Surface Crops. These consist of saladings, such as lettuce, endive, radishes, corn salad, rampion, American cress, parsley, spinach, French beans, early horn carrot, and such light crops, being mostly of not more than six months' growth. These always do best on a very rich surface soil, containing plenty of manure, but requiring no deep digging. When these crops come off, the ground should have a dressing of manure mixed with fresh loamy soil; and, if the ground is heavy, a portion of burnt clay will improve it. This should be dug in one spit deep, or the ground may be bastard-trenched – that is, keeping the top spit on the top, and digging the subsoil two spades deep. It has been found that bringing up too much of the under soil engenders clubbing. Having so prepared the ground, it is in a condition to receive that group which is the most scourging and exhaustive crop of any, that is:

469 The Cabbage, or *Brassicae* tribe, or *Deteriorators*, as Mr Errington calls them, which are mostly biennials, and occupy the ground about a twelve-month – some more, others a little less. This latter group forms a much larger proportion of kitchen crops than any of the surface group; consequently, the ground occupied by the latter will not generally be sufficient for it; if there is ground to spare, it is advisable to let it lie fallow till the winter crops are ready to plant out, stirring the surface frequently so as to expose as much of the soil as possible to the air.

470 In the plan in Fig. 168, which is that of the kitchen garden shown in Fig. 30, and repeated here for the sake of clearness on a larger scale, the quarters A to K of the kitchen garden are supposed to be cropped for the first time, and somewhat in accordance with this scheme, D and E being the deepeners, with a row of plum trees occupying the dotted line between them, and a bed of strawberries at each extremity of the quarter, in the following order: 1, Strawberries; 2, seakale; 3, rhubarb; 4, globe artichokes; 5, plum trees; 6, asparagus; 7, horseradish; 8, strawberries. F and G are occupied by the preparers and surface crops, with a row of espalier or pyramid apple trees on the dotted line, in the following order: 1, Scorzoneras, salsafy, etc.; 2, potatoes; 3, peas; 4, apple trees; 5, parsnips; 6, carrots; 7, turnips. The quarter composed of H and K is devoted chiefly to the deteriorators, or cabbage tribe, in the following order: 1, Cabbages; 2, celery; 3, broad beans; 4, runner beans; 5, pear trees, as espaliers, on the dotted line; 6, runner beans; 7, broad beans; 8, cauliflowers; 9, early broccoli. The angular corner, A, is devoted to Jerusalem artichokes, and the quarter composed of B and C to – 1, Gooseberries; 2, black currants; 3, a row of cherry trees, on the dotted line; 4, red currants; 5, white currants; an alley, two feet wide, separating each quarter.

471 The broad border under the south wall, or wall that fronts nearly south, is cropped with spring lettuces, radishes, early potatoes, early peas, early beans, kidney beans, early strawberries, early-horn carrots, and other crops requiring a warm border, but the positions of these are not shown, nor is it necessary to define them. The border itself should not be less than 8 feet, and, if the wall is covered with peaches, it should be 12 or 16 feet. When the front border is occupied with vegetables, it is desirable, in the interest of the wall fruit, that a portion about 2 feet, sloping gently from the wall, should be reserved, elevated an inch or two above the border; thus forming a slight terrace, to be left uncropped, and kept free from weeds. On the north wall, if there be a north wall, which is not the case in the diagram under consideration, plums, cherries, and pears should be planted. In gardening parlance, a north wall, it must be remembered, is a wall that fronts the north or has a north aspect. The walls of a garden are always designated in reference to their *aspects.* Every wall has two faces, so the north wall for one garden is the south wall of the garden on the other side of it.

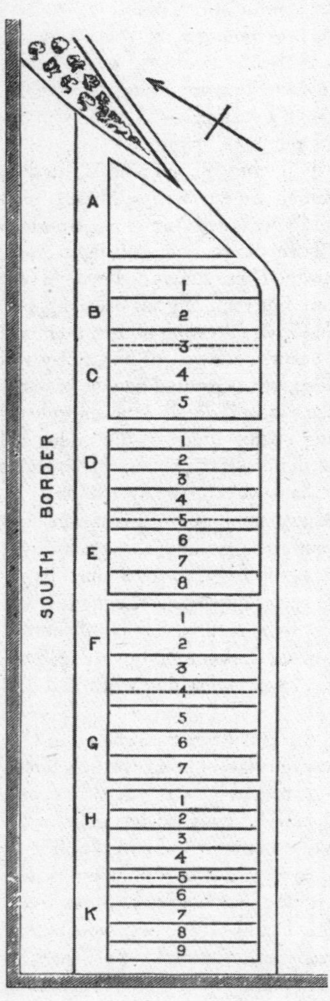

FIG. 168 *Diagram illustrative of cropping of Mr Errington's*

472 In dealing with asparagus, seakale, and other crops usually termed permanent crops, Mr Errington selects from the beds what he wants each season for forcing, planting as much every year as he removes; those removed are replaced by celery, and the celery by the *preparers*, and these in their turn by the *Brassiccae*, or *deteriorators.* The portion devoted to permanent crops, as well as the quarters devoted to bush fruit, are thus brought into his system of rotation cropping.

Principal crops	Crops it may follow	Crops it may not follow	Crops it may be followed by	Crops it may be followed by	May plant between rows
Beans	Borecole, broccoli, cabbages, parsnips, carrots, potatoes	Leguminous plants of its own natural order, *i.e.*, peas, etc.	Celery, leeks, let tuces, turnip, and any of the Cabbage tribe.	Leguminous plants of its own natural order, *i.e.*, peas, etc.	Borecole, Brussels sprouts
Beet	Cabbage tribe, and any crops but those specified in next column	Spinach, turnips, parsnips, carrots, salsafy, and scorzonera	Peas, beans, cabbages, cauliflower, lettuces, and any spring-sown crop except those in next column.	Spinach, turnips, parsnips, and carrots.	Nothing
Borecole and Brussels Sprouts	Peas, beans, lettuces, potatoes	Cruciferous plants of own order, *i.e.*, any of Cabbage tribe, turnips, etc.	Peas, beans, beet, carrots, parsnips, onions, potatoes, kidney beans.	Cruciferous plants of own order, *i.e.*, any of Cabbage tribe, turnips, etc.	Beans
Broccoli	Peas, beans, kidney beans	Cruciferous plants of own natural order	Any crop to be sown or planted when cleared off.	Cruciferous plants of own natural order.	Nothing
Cabbages	Peas, beans, kidney beans, potatoes, lettuces, onions, leeks, celery, etc.	Cruciferous plants of own natural order	Peas, beans, kidney beans, potatoes, lettuces, carrots, parsnips, beet, salsafy, celery, etc.	Cruciferous plants of own natural order.	Coleworts
Carrots and Parsnips	Any crops except those in next column	Any crops except root crops and umbelliferous plants, as celery, parsley, etc.	Any crops except those in next column.	Any crops except root crops and umbelliferous plants, as celery, parsley, etc.	Nothing
Cauliflower	Peas, beans, potatoes, celery, kidney beans, onions, carrots, lettuces, beet	Cruciferous plants of own natural order	Peas, beans, potatoes, celery, kidney beans, onions, carrots, lettuces, beet.	Cruciferous plants of own natural order	Spinach, lettuces, endive
Celery	Any crop except those in next column	Parsnips, carrots, parsley	Peas, beans, kidney beans, potatoes, turnips, and any of the Cabbage tribe.	Parsnips, carrots, parsley.	Lettuces, endive
Endive and Lettuce	Potatoes, peas, beans, and any of the Cabbage tribe	Chicory, salsafy, scorzonera, artichokes, cardoons, and any plants of the natural order *Compositae*	Any crop suitable for borders	Chicory, salsafy, scorzonera, artichokes, cardoons, and any plants of the natural order *Compositae*.	Nothing
Kidney Beans and Peas	Potatoes, carrots, parsnips, turnips, broccoli, and any of the Cabbage tribe	Beans and leguminous plants of own natural order	Broccoli, cabbages of any kind, spinach, turnips, late celery	Beans and leguminous plants of own natural order.	Summer spinach, radishes; borecole and Brussels sprouts between dwarf sorts
Leeks, Onions, Shallots, etc.	Cabbage tribe, celery, potatoes, peas, beans, kidney beans, lettuces, endive, spinach	Garlic, rocambole, chives, and any crop of alliaceous nature	Cabbages and coleworts	Garlic, rocambole, chives, and any crop of alliaceous nature.	Nothing
Potatoes	Any crop except those specified in the next column	Carrots, parsnips, beet, salsafy, scorzonera	Any crop requiring a loose, clean, well-worked soil, and all cruciferous plants	Root crops generally, as carrots, parsnips, beet, etc.	Brussels sprouts, borecole, broccoli, and late celery if there be space enough for trench
Seakale	Potatoes, peas, beans, carrots, parsnips, beet, celery, etc.	Cruciferous plants of own natural order	Potatoes, peas, beans, carrots, parsnips, beet, celery, etc.	Cruciferous plants of own natural order	Nothing
Spinach	Peas, beans, kidney beans, cabbage, cauliflower, lettuces, etc.	Beet	Peas, beans, kidney beans, cabbage, cauliflower, lettuces, etc.	Beet	Nothing
Turnips	Potatoes, spinach, peas, beans, lettuces, etc.	Cruciferous plants of own natural order	Potatoes, spinach, peas, beans, lettuces, etc.	Cruciferous plants of own natural order.	Nothing

473 Having regard to the sequence of crops when planted in rotation, the following tabular statement, compiled from *The Gardener's Assistant*, showing what certain principal crops may follow, by what they may be succeeded, and what and when to plant and when not to plant between the rows, will be found useful. It is a general table, but, with modifications to suit soil, site, aspect, and other circumstances, it will be found to be such as may be conveniently followed in any garden.

With reference to the preceding table, it may be said that the directions as to sequence of crops, etc., may not, as a fixed rule, admit of being followed exactly, especially in small gardens, where but little space is available for a set rotation of crops, and where one crop may, perhaps, have to follow another of the same nature, and in the case of backward seasons, when crops may be cleared too late to admit of the proper succession. As a rule, however, whenever the ground must be occupied by two crops of the same kind in succession, as for example, when onions have to follow onions, it should be dug over two spades deep, and well manured.

Certain natural orders of plants have been mentioned in the table, which require a few words of explanation, namely, *Cruciferous* plants, *Leguminous* plants, *Umbelliferous* plants, and *Composite* plants. The distinguishing feature of the *Cruciferae*, or *cross-carrying* plants, is that the flowers have a calyx of four sepals, which fall off after flowering, and a corolla of four petals, which are arranged in the form of a cross and in alternation with the sepals. No plant belonging to this order is poisonous, and those that are eaten as food are antiscorbutic. The cabbage, cauliflower, broccoli, colewort, and all plants of the cabbage tribe, turnip, rape, radish, cress, seakale, mustard, horseradish, scurvy grass, all belong to this order, which includes the wallflower, stock, oenothera, and other well-known garden flowers. The *Leguminosae* are plants that bear seeds that are eaten for food, and include peas and beans of all kinds grown in the field and garden, the vetch, clover, trefoil and lucerne, used as fodder for cattle, and many flowering trees and shrubs, as the laburnum, furze, broom, cytisus, etc. The *Umbelliferae* are plants whose flowers spring from one common stalk, and are carried on a number of stalks of less size, diverging from the common stalk, having an umbrella-like appearance. The carrot, parsnip, parsley, celery, fennel, carraway, etc., belong to this order. Lastly, the *Compositae* are plants whose flowers consist of a great number of little florets, which nevertheless are perfect flowers, all gathered together on a common receptacle, surrounded by bracts, forming a leafy or scaly envelope to it. To this order belong the globe artichoke, Jerusalem artichoke, scorzonera, salsafy, endive, lettuce, chicory, and among other plants that are included in it are the sunflower, daisy, aster, thistle, dandelion, camomile, etc. The distinctive character of the blossoms of plants of these natural orders are shown in Figs. 169,170, 171, and 172

FIG. 169
Cruciferae
(Radish)

FIG. 170
Leguminosae
(Pea)

FIG. 171
Umbelliferae
(Parsley)

FIG. 172
Compositae
(Globe artichoke)

474 The subject of cropping in rotation may be suitably brought to a close by the following description of an eight years' rotation of crops for a kitchen garden, from the pen of a gentleman who has made trial of it for some years, with admirable results, both in the harsh uplands of Warwickshire and in a Sussex valley in which the surface soil is thin rich humus, resting on chalky marl and flint, with chalk rock below, and who communicated his plan to *Gardening Illustrated*, whence this is taken. He apparently divides his garden ground into thirteen plots, which are occupied as follows:

Plot 1 Potatoes, early autumn sorts, followed by cabbage, winter spinach, lettuce, and parts left for onions. – *As soon as the potatoes are taken up, the ground is trenched and manured, and then planted with cabbages.*

Plot 2 Cabbage, winter spinach, lettuce, and onions, followed by celery, leeks, and cardoons. – *Onions sown in with wood ashes; ground enriched with good rotten manure in the bottom of celery trenches, and liquid manure applied during growth.*

Plot 3 Parsnips, carrots, scorzonera, salsafy, and beet. – *Sown in with wood ashes mixed with fine mould: as soon as the roots are cleared the ground is thrown up in high ridges, and bottom between ridges forked and left to chasten during winter. So with any plot throughout which becomes vacant during winter.*

Plot 4 Tall later peas with winter greens, *e.g.*, Brussels sprouts, savoys, kale, etc., two rows planted in between each row of peas later on. – *A little rotten manure in the bottom of the trenches for peas. The peas shade the Brassicae, and thus cause them to make vigorous growth.*

Plot 5 Potatoes, later sorts. Broccoli and sprouting broccoli planted out, a row between each row of potatoes, except in a part to be kept after potatoes for small late turnips. – *See under Plot 4 on advantages of shading.*

Plot 6 Cauliflower, couve-tronchuda, and dwarf French beans. – *The ground is dug up all over; the dwarf French beans are planted where rows of broccoli were. Then manure is dug in between later on, and cauliflowers planted where rows of potatoes were.*

Plot 7 Potatoes, middle crop. – *After potatoes are lifted the ground is ridged up for winter as directed for Plot 3, which see.*

Plot 8 Broad beans, followed by middle crop of turnips. Runner beans on outsides of remaining ground, with two or more rows of dwarf peas in between, and rows of early turnips between both. – *These turnips are left for spring tops and the early blooms left for bees, till potatoes are required to be planted; or bloom may be left still longer, and be arranged that the potatoes shall come between the rows.*

With regard to the eight plots whose cropping and culture has been described, the crop which is on Plot 1 will come on Plot 8 in the next year, Plot 2 on Plot 1, Plot 3 on Plot 2, etc., etc., and so on from year to year in succession.

Plot 9 Strawberries are grown in this plot, and are changed one-third every year to the next plot of ground, and so back again. This does not, therefore, interfere with the rotation, but only causes portions of two contiguous plots to be taken and counted to make up one. – *Mulched with rotten manure in autumn after the leaves are cut off, and then spread with fresh seaweed in spring.*

Plot 10 Earliest peas, earliest potatoes, and earliest winter lettuce and spinach are grown on a separate sunny border, near a wall with southern aspect, changing places with each other yearly, one-third of the ground being given to each crop. – *Earliest peas dressed with rotten manure; potatoes put in with fresh seaweed or plenty of rotten manure; lettuces with rotten manure.*

Plot 11 Globe artichokes and asparagus have each separate beds. – *Mulch round crowns of globe artichokes with manure after stems are cut down, and with seaweed, not put over crowns, in spring. After stems of asparagus are cut down, fork up beds roughly, and then manure heavily with fresh manure. In February throw mould from alleys on beds, and spread layer of fresh seaweed on top.*

Plot 12 Rhubarb and seakale, but it is proposed to gradually change these one with the other. – *Mulch rhubarb with long manure and beech leaves, kept off ground with sticks. Earliest seakale forced with beech leaves mixed with stable manure; main crop with fresh seaweed, two feet deep, till shoots begin to appear through; this is not kept off the crowns with sticks.*

Plot 13 Jerusalem artichokes and horseradish have a nook where they cannot trespass on other crops. – *Jerusalem artichokes are dug up every year, and the ground carefully cleaned, manured, and replanted. Half bed of horseradish dug one year, the other half the next; crowns replanted 2 feet deep, with manure at bottom.*

475 There are certain permanent crops, both of vegetables and fruit trees, which will occupy the gardener in the autumn months. To begin with the borders. In preparing them, dig out the soil to the depth of 4 feet, and in this trench place first about a foot in thickness of brick rubbish, or any coarse stuff, which, when rammed down hard, will prevent the wall trees forming tap roots.

476 If the soil is naturally good loam, no more is required than to mix a quantity of well-rotted dung with it before throwing it back into the trench, making the border slope gradually towards the path. If the soil requires improving, get a quantity of friable loam, mix rotten dung with it in the proportion of one part dung to three parts loam, and mix this again with the soil of the border where the trees are to stand. Plant healthy young trees of peach, nectarine, and apricot, and, if desirable, grape vines and figs: these ought to be placed 12 or 15 feet apart. The following is a very convenient plan of growing grapes on a wall between the peaches. The peaches were placed 15 feet apart, and a vine planted in each space halfway between; the vine was carried in a single stem to the top of the wall, where it divided into two stems, which were trained right and left under the coping; and as they were pruned on the spur system, they took up little room, and did not interfere with the other trees. On the east and west walls plant trained trees of plums, cherries, pears, and mulberries, after the same rule, but without the same precaution as to soil, as these are not so particular. On the north wall plant plums and morello cherries, but select such plums as are suitable for this position.

477 In draining the kitchen garden, one of the drains ought to run the whole length of the south border; for where peaches, nectarines, and especially apricots, are to be cultivated, the ground should be thoroughly drained. It is not desirable, as a rule, to proceed beyond this, in cultivating wall fruit in the kitchen garden. Curvatures in the wall, projecting piers, leaning walls and fences, covering the whole soil of the border occasionally, and suchlike nostrums, are as well left alone, and the money spent on matters of real utility, such as orchard houses.

478 In disposing of the main body of the garden, if the form be such as will admit of doing so, divide it into four equal compartments, by means of cross walks three or four feet wide, as it has been already recommended in a previous chapter. If it is desired to have fruit trees, plant a row through the centre of each quarter from north to south, and no more, for it should be remembered that the more trees there are the less and poorer will be the crops, both of fruit and vegetables. As regards gooseberries, black, red, and white currants, and raspberries, it is far better to plant one of the quarters with these, instead of resorting to the very common practice of bordering the quarters with them. This is done on a false notion of economy, while, in fact, it is a great waste; it is also done with the view of being ornamental – it is, in reality, the contrary; and it involves the loss of these bushes as renewers and preparers of the soil for ordinary kitchen crops in connection with a system of rotation of crops, which will keep the ground in good heart without any intermission in the produce. It will not be difficult to point out the converse of this in some old suburban kitchen gardens, which do not return the worth of the seed sown in them; where the soil is swarming with grubs, maggots, and mildew; where cabbages club and rot, tap roots canker, and potatoes produce no tubers; – and why? – because the soil has been for many years over-tasked, cropped highly, and injudiciously manured; whereas a proper system of rotation-cropping would have kept the ground in good heart.

479 In most large kitchen gardens seeds of all the different vegetables in use are saved from year to year. This practice is recommended not only by economy, but by every consideration of good management; for, in this way, sorts that have been found to suit the soil and situation are effectually preserved. To save seeds, however, is a work of some trouble. It causes a great waste of ground, exhaustion of the soil, and also involves much labour. Moreover, in a thickly-wooded country, the birds are generally so troublesome, that, if they do not prevent the saving of seeds, they add much to the expense of it. Wherever, therefore, ground is limited, birds troublesome, and there are no spare hands, it is better, perhaps, to give up the practice, or, at least, to limit the saving of seeds to a few favourite sorts.

480 Good seeds can now be purchased at a very reasonable rate, and novelties in every kind of vegetable are continually being introduced. Most seedsmen publish lists of seeds, with prices, suitable in quantity to gardens of all sizes, and as the demand for seeds is an annual one, no man of character will venture to hazard his reputation and his interest by sending out bad seed. It is very easy to test the growing qualities of seeds, and this should be done before they are packed up and offered for sale. This is done, it is said, with all seed supplied by Messrs Richard Smith and Co., of *Worcester*. Their collections of kitchen garden seeds are so varied in sorts, and so moderate in price, that the generality of gardeners may well be spared the trouble of saving seeds, and use their land for some useful crops. The following is an enumeration of the seeds necessary for a year's supply, with quantities and prices to suit gardens of five different sizes.

481 *Collections of seeds for one year's supply.*

Name	£3 3s. 0d. Collection	£2 2s. 0d. Collection	£1 11s. 6d. Collection	£1 1s. 0d. Collection	10s. 6d. Collection
Peas, best varieties for succession	18 quarts	11 quarts	8 quarts	6 quarts	4 pints
Beans, broad, the best sorts	6 quarts	4 quarts	3 quarts	2 quarts	2 pints
Beans, French, dwarf varieties	2 pints	1½ pints	1 pint	1 pint	1½ pints
Beans, French, Runners	2 pints	1 quart	1½ pints	1 pint	1 pint
Beet, Dell's and other sorts	2 packets	2 packets	1 packet	1 packet	1 packet
Borecole or Kale, best sorts	4 packets	3 packets	3 packets	2 packets	1 packet
Broccoli, best early and late sorts	8 packets	6 packets	5 packets	4 packets	2 packets
Brussels Sprouts, finest	1 packet	1 packet	1 packet	1 packet	1 packet
Cabbage, best sorts for succession	7 packets	6 packets	5 packets	4 packets	2 packets
Cabbage, Savoy, best sorts	3 packets	2 packets	2 packets	1 packet	1 packet
Capsicum	1 packet	1 packet	1 packet		
Carrot,for forcing and general crop	14 ounces	8 ounces	4 ounces	3 ounces	1½ ounces
Cauliflower, best for succession.	2 packets	2 packets	1 packet	1 packet	
Celery, of sorts	2 packets	2 packets	2 packets	2 packets	1 packet
Couve Tronchuda	1 packet	1 packet	1 packet	1 packet	
Corn Salad	1 packet	1 packet	1 packet		
Cress, plain, curled, etc.	½ pint and 6 ounces	8 ounces	6 ounces	4 ounces	2 ounces
Cucumbers, of sorts	4 packets	3 packets	2 packets	1 packet	
Endive, best sorts	3 packets	2 packets	1 packet	1 packet	1 packet
Herbs, of sorts	6 packets	4 packets	3 packets	2 packets	2 packets
Leek, best sorts	1 ounce	1 packet	1 packet	1 packet	
Lettuce, best Cos and Cabbage	6 packets	4 packets	3 packets	3 packets	2 packets
Melon, finest sorts	3 packets	2 packets	1 packet		
Mustard, white	1 quart	2 pints	½ pint	4 ounces	2 ounces
Onion, White Spanish and others	12 ounces	8 ounces	6 ounce	3 ounces	1½ ounces
Orach	1 packet	1 packet	1 packet		
Parsley, garnishing, etc	2 ounces	1 ounce	1 packet	1 packet	1 packet
Parsnip, Hollow Crowned	4 ounces	3 ounces	2 ounces	1 ounce	1 packet
Radish, bestsorts for succession	1 pint and 11 ounces	9 ounces	6 ounces	4 ounces	2 ounces
Rampion	1 packet	1 packet	1 packet		
Salsafy	1 packet	1 packet	1 packet		
Scorzonera	1 packet	1 packet	1 packet		
Spinach, summer and winter sorts	2 pints	1½ pints	1 pint	4 ounces	2 ounces
Tomato	1 packet	1 packet	1 packet		
Turnip, Snowball and others	12 ounces	5 ounces	8 ounces	3 ounces	2 packets
Vegetable Marrow	2 packets	1 packet	1 packet	1 packet	1 packet

CHAPTER 13

Garden Tools, Implements, and Appliances Required for Working the Soil, Measurement, Sowing, Planting, Transplanting, Potting, and Watering

482 The tools, implements, and appliances that are required and used in gardening are both numerous and various, and all that are now in existence are perhaps equally handy and desirable, each for the particular purpose it is intended to serve. Yet, notwithstanding this, it is surprising how few tools are absolutely necessary to a handy man who knows and likes his work. It is the bad workman, generally speaking, who is mostly on the look out for new appliances and anxious to acquire them, vainly hoping that their possession and use may tend at least to disguise, if not to remedy altogether, his want of skill, forgetful of the fact that he himself is the controlling power of the machine he uses, whatever it may be, and that the effect produced is due as much, if not more, to the manual skill and dexterity of the operator, as to the excellence of the appliance that he sets in motion. The good workman, on the contrary, will manage to do all that is required of him in a satisfactory manner with the sorriest of tools, and his work when done will present a far better appearance than that which is turned out by the less skilful hand with the best tool that money can procure. In advancing this there is no intention to attempt to persuade the gardener, whether professional or amateur, against providing himself with the best tools and appliances in the market, or even two or three of the same kind, if he likes to do so and can afford it. On the contrary, it is only sought to insist on the fact that to the man who understands what he is about, a few tools, and those of the simplest character, are all that are really necessary to him in order to attain the end that he has in view.

483 The easiest way to get at the tools that are required and supplied for garden work of all kinds, and, at the same time, to produce a general classification of them according to the purposes for which they are used, is to consider in the first place what may be the various operations that a gardener is called upon to perform in his daily work, and then to arrange in groups, under each operation, the tools that are requisite, more or less, for carrying it out. Of these, the first operation that will suggest itself to anyone who takes the trouble to consider the subject in all its bearings will be the working of the soil, which involves its preparation for crops, and keeping it free from weeds, etc., while the crops are growing. Then it will be remembered that the ground has to be marked out and measured, and formed into beds and plots for the reception of crops, and that from this it is but a short step to sowing, planting, and transplanting, and the closely allied work of potting, etc. Growing plants require care in many ways, and this causes us to think of watering, and the various means and modes of support that must frequently be supplied. Then, again, trees require pruning, training, grafting, and budding, and these, as well as seed crops and growing plants, stand in need of distinction one from another by appliances contrived to meet the purpose of designation, and they will also require in some cases protection by shelters of various kinds. Shrubs must be clipped at times, and hedges must be trimly cut, grass lawns and edgings demand attention, and walks and paths must not be left neglected and untouched. Means must be provided for the transfer of manure, soil, and even plants from place to place, and the attacks of insects and vermin must be guarded against and warded off. But even when the tools and appliances that are desirable and even necessary for carrying out and providing for these various operations and requirements have been mentioned and described, there will yet be some that cannot conveniently be placed under any kind of work that has been mentioned, and these must consequently be relegated to an especial section of their own.

484 This done, we are now better able to name and classify, without much trouble, the different tools that are required for the various operations that have been enumerated, and to arrange them in a fair show of order, under each heading, as follows:

1 *For Working the Soil* – Pick, mattock, spade, shovel, fork, hoe, rake, tool cleaner.

2 *For Measurement and Direction* – Garden reel and line, measuring rod.

3 *For Sowing, Planting, and Transplanting* – Dibber or dibble, drill, trowel, transplanter.

4 *For Potting* – Stage, screen, sieve, pots, water saucers, tubs, boxes, window boxes.

5 *For Watering* – Water pot, syringe, hydropult, hose and hose carriage.

6 *For Support and Training* – Flower stakes and sticks, poles, pea sticks, espalier stakes, trellises, wires on walls and fences with straining apparatus, holdfasts, etc.

7 *For Pruning, Grafting, Budding, etc.* – Knife, chisel, billhook, axe, saw, averruncator, hammer, pincers, list, nails, ladders, fruit gatherers, etc.

8 *For Distinction and Designation* – Sticks for names and numbers, labels, tallies.

9 *For Protection against Weather, etc.* – Copings, canvas, netting, small glass structures and shelters, hurdles, etc.

10 *For Shearing, Clipping, etc.* – Scythe, mowing machine, raser, roller, shears, weeders, broom or besom.

11 *For Carriage and Transfer* – Handbarrow, wheelbarrow, mould scuttle, pot carrier, basket, planks.

12 *For Protection against Animals, Vermin, etc.* – Traps of various kinds, bird scarers, cat teasers.

13 *For Miscellaneous Purposes* – Fumigator, thermometers, sulphurators, etc. During the Peninsular War, when any minor matter was brought under the notice of the Duke of Wellington for which he had omitted to provide, he was accustomed to meet the matter and dispose of it at once

by saying, 'One cannot think of everything.' No one who has attempted to draw up a list similar to the above will be inclined to dispute the Duke's assertion. It is fairly exhaustive, but if it be not absolutely so, it may be said with truth that it is sufficient, and amply sufficient, for all practical purposes and ordinary requirements.

485 *Tools Requisite for Working the Soil* Of these it may be generally observed that they require the use of both hands and arms, and some of them the whole muscular force of the frame. They generally combine the principle of the lever and the wedge, the blade of all of them being employed to separate particles of matter by the application of lever power which lies in the shaft or handle. When the handle is intended to be grasped and held firmly at one spot, as in the spade, it is fitted with a transverse bar, for that purpose; but when it is necessary that the hand should slide along it, the handle should be quite smooth and round. Such is the form of the handles of the rake, the pick, and all similar tools. Ash is the best material for all handles in which strength is required, but willow is lighter than ash and strong enough for tools such as the rake, the hoe, and others for which it is desirable that the handle should be of some length. Suitable handles for rakes, hoes, etc., may also be made of pitch pine, deal, etc., nicely and neatly rounded with the plane. All tools should be kept in a shed or tool house, in which they will be protected from the weather when not in use.

In a small garden, but few tools will be required, and these may be put away in a tolerably small space. Accommodation may be found for them under the stage in any tiny greenhouse or glass structure, if the garden can boast of one, or the dustbin may be covered over with a roof, and the space above it, or at its side, thus utilised for the purpose. In larger gardens, a shed is often available, or even a closet, attached to the house, and constructed for the purpose, with a door opening on the garden only, and having no means of access from the house itself. Where there is a greenhouse of some size, to which a potting shed is attached, the shed itself may be of sufficient size to receive all the tools and appliances that are required for the work of the garden. Failing anything of this kind, it is not difficult, even in the gardens attached to suburban villas, to find a suitable corner in which a shed may be erected at trifling expense. If there be a summer house, this may be brought forward a little, if necessary, so as to gain a little space behind it, and a shelter for the garden tools may be improvised here. If it be found necessary to erect a tool house, either attached to another building or forming a completely detached structure, a building from 4 to 6 feet square will be found sufficiently large to contain everything that is wanted, including roller, mowing machine, and garden hose, and even a set of steps or a folding ladder, and the structure itself may consist of a framework of quartering 2 inches square, having a door in any convenient position, with a light over it, and covered at the sides and roofed in with feather-edged boards, or 'weather boarding', as this kind of boarding is usually called, or even with sheets of corrugated iron. Those to whom cost is no object may obtain an excellent wood shed made of weather boarding, on a strong frame, painted with three coats of oil colour, 8 feet wide, 6 feet deep, and 9 feet 6 inches high, with span roof, for £8 15s., of Messrs Deane and Co., 46 King William Street, London Bridge, London. Other sizes may be had at proportionate prices.

486 *The Pick* This tool is a bent, or compound lever, when regarded as a mechanical power, as may be seen when it is employed in lifting a paving stone, for example. The paving stone then is the weight to be raised, and is at one end of the short arm of the lever, which is formed of that part of the head which lies between the extreme point and the socket in which the handle is set. The handle itself forms the other arm of the lever, the ground on which the head rests is the fulcrum, and the power is the pressure applied at the upper end of the handle by the man who is using it. The blade, or head, should be made of the best wrought iron, tipped or pointed with steel. Both ends are alike in this tool, and both are pointed, as shown at A in Fig. 173. The handle should be made of sound, well-seasoned ash. The head is slipped over the upper end of the handle, and forced into its place at the other end, by letting this end fall in a succession of blows on a block of wood, or stone, or even hard and solid ground. It is released by going through the same process with the upper end of the handle. The handle should be from 2 feet 8 inches to 3 feet in length, according to the height of the person who will mostly use it. A form of pick better adapted for garden use is shown at B, one end being pointed as in the ordinary pick, and the other broad and in the form of a wedge-shaped blade. This end is used for cutting through roots as well as for digging. The chief use of the pick in gardens is to loosen hard soil, pick up old paths, and to do any work of this nature for which a strong and heavy tool is required.

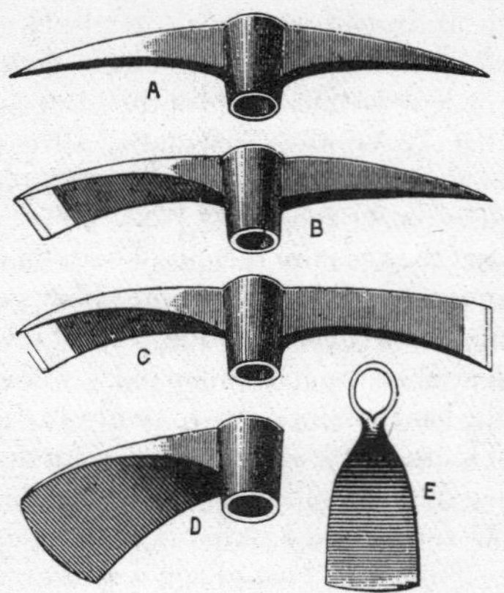

FIG. 173 *The pick and tools allied to it. A. Pick proper. B. Pick for garden use C. Pickaxe. D. Mattock. E. View of Mattock from top, showing shape of iron*

487 *The Pickaxe and Mattock* These are tools which are closely allied to the pick, being modifications of it in form. The pickaxe is shown in Fig. 173 at C. It will be noticed that one arm is in the form of an axe, and the other in the form of an adze, as in the left-hand side of the garden pick shown at B. Sometimes this form of pick has one of its arms in the form of an axe, instead of taking the adze form; but whatever its shape may be, whether adze-like or axe-like, it is used for the same purpose, namely, for loosening hard soil and for cutting roots. The pickaxe, as at C, with one arm like an axe and the other like an adze, is used more especially for taking up the roots of trees that have been felled, or for uprooting trees. Another form of pickaxe, known as a mattock, is shown at D. It has a broad adze-like blade on one side of the socket only. Its shape, when viewed from the top, is shown at E. It is used for loosening surfaces and masses of earth that are not so hard as to necessitate the use of the pick. It is also used for taking up trees, shrubs, etc., from which it is sometimes called a grubbing-axe, and for earthing up potatoes, from which it is frequently called a hoe-axe, as it combines the functions of the two tools, namely, that of the axe in loosening the soil between the rows, and that of the hoe in drawing the earth up to and around the haulm of the potato in the form of a small bank or mound. The mattock is sometimes called a grubbing-axe, or grubbing-hoe. It is sold by weight, and varies from 3 lb., the smaller size, to 5½ lb., the largest size, there being a difference of ½ lb. in all the intermediate sizes. Hoes, on the contrary, as will be seen, are estimated by the length of the edge of the blade in inches, and rakes by the number of teeth that they contain. Picks and pickaxes are supplied in three sizes, known as small, medium, and large; the prices respectively being about 3s., 3s. 6d., and 4s. These prices include handles.

488 *The Spade* This indispensable tool is a broad blade of plate iron, rectangular in form, attached to a handle of tough ash, the upper end of which is in the form of a **D**, or fitted with a transverse bar, like the head of a crutch. The **D** form is most convenient for digging. The lower part, or edge of the blade, should be of steel, and the upper part of the best scrap iron, well welded together. The blade is hollow at the top, for the reception of the lower end of the handle, and from it run in an upward direction two straps, one in front and the other behind, which are fitted to the handle, and secured to it by rivets. The space between the front and back part of the blade is covered with a narrow iron plate, called the tread, which affords support to the foot of the operator when it is pressed on the blade in order to force it into the soil. The transverse bar of the **D**-shaped handle is apt to split, as the grain runs transversely to its length. It should therefore be strengthened by boring a hole of small diameter through it, into which is inserted a piece of iron wire, riveted over a small plate at each end. All the best spades are made in this way. There are many different varieties of spade for trenching and digging, distinguished by some slight peculiarity of construction; but all of them are sufficiently similar to the type shown in the London treaded spade, in Fig. 174, to require no separate description. The gardener's spade is made with a broad straight edge, because this form is better calculated to hold and lift masses of earth, and to penetrate equally all over the bottom of the trench, than a pointed tool. Spades suitable for the gardener's use are made in four sizes, numbered 1, 2, 3, and 4, proceeding from the smallest to the largest. Of these, Nos. 2 and 3 are useful sizes for amateurs. Common spades, according to these sizes, are supplied at 2s. 2d. for No. 1, with an increase of 2d. for each size; cast steel spades at 3s. 3d. for No. 1, with an increase of 3d. for each size; cast steel spades, with centre strap, in sizes 1, 2, and 3, at 3s. 6d., 3s. 9d., and 4s., respectively.

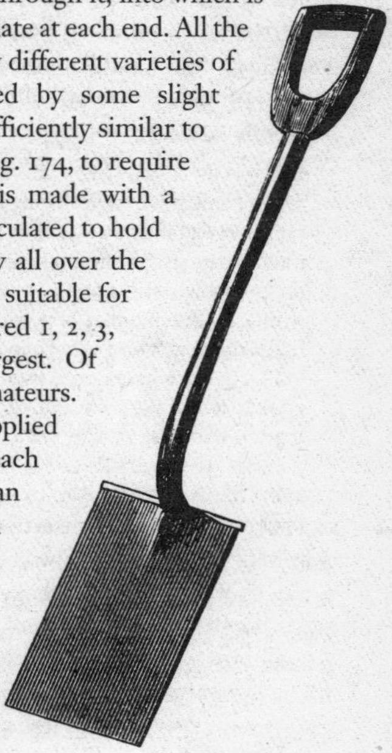

Although it is only *garden tools* that are now under consideration, it may be as well to point out that spades of other forms are used for other purposes than those of trenching and digging with better effect; thus, for working in clay and stiff adhesive soil a spade with a hollow or slightly curved blade is preferable and for cutting trenches in draining a spade with a very narrow blade is used. Spades adapted for this purpose are illustrated in Fig. 19, in paragraph 94.

FIG. 174 *London treaded spade*

489 *The Shovel* This implement differs from the spade in many important particulars. As a rule, the blade is broader, has no tread, and the handle, which is long and slightly bent, is inserted into a socket proceeding from the top of the blade instead of being attached to the blade by means of straps. The shovel is not used for digging, but for clearing trenches, etc., or for lifting soil, gravel, manure, etc., that requires removal into a barrow or cart, though manure from the heap can be handled more readily by means of a fork. As the blade is pointed, as shown at A and B, or, at least, narrow at the edge, although straight, as shown at C in Fig. 175, which illustrates various forms of shovels, it can be thrust into masses of loose soil more easily than the stiffer blade of the spade, because it encounters less resistance, and is thus more capable of penetration. Being broader than that of the spade the shovel blade will receive and lift a greater quantity of mould, etc., and as the handle is longer the person who is using it has not to stoop so much in thrusting the shovel into the mould, etc., and can maintain his position while throwing the material to be removed into the cart. The length of the handle, in fact, gives better leverage in lifting, which is an essential in work of this kind. The handle should be made of ash, and should be perfectly smooth.

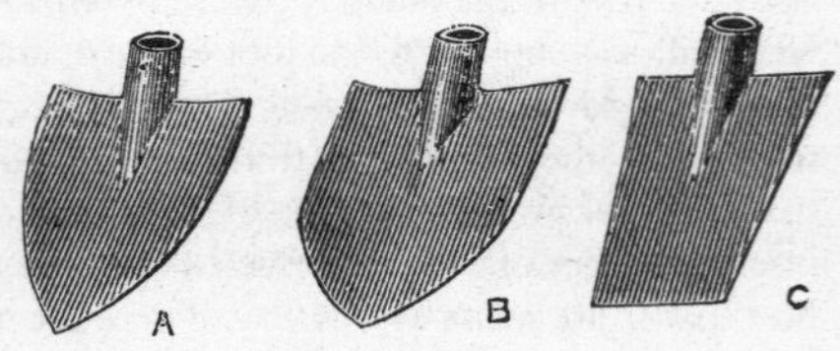

FIG. 175 *Various forms of shovels*

Shovels that are used by navvies, miners, coal-heavers, etc., are different in construction to the garden shovel, and may always be distinguished from it by their handles, which are short, like that of the garden spade, and terminate, with one or two exceptions, in a crutched head. The blades of shovels used for railway work and pit work are mostly of the shape shown at A and Bin Fig. 175, but they are secured to the handles by straps and rivets, or the handles are let into long cylindrical sockets, and riveted. Shovels for handling ballast and coal have handles of the same length attached in the same way, but the blades are very large, square in form, and have the edges turned up at the back and on both sides, like a fire shovel. They are described here that the purchaser of a shovel for garden use may not be induced to buy an article which, being intended for a different purpose, will be of little use to him. The blade of a garden shovel should be of one or other of the forms shown in Fig. 175, and should be furnished with a socket for the reception of the handle, which, as it has been said, should be long and slightly bent.

490 *The Turf Spade or Turfing Iron* Closely allied to the shovel in form, though it is used for a very different purpose, is the turf spade or turfing iron, illustrated in Fig. 176. This implement, which is required only by professional gardeners, unless the garden or series of gardens may be large enough to bring it occasionally into requisition, either for cutting fresh turf or for removing the sward from the surface already covered in order to remedy inequalities, is a heart-shaped steel blade, riveted to a bent shank terminating in a socket for the reception of the handle. It is thus formed that the blade may be thrust under the turf in a direction parallel to the surface, without inconvenience. Turf is generally marked out into rows 1 foot in breadth, and the edges of the rows are cut from end to end with a spade or any sharp instrument. The rows are divided in the same way into lengths of 3 feet. The turf spade is then passed under each length, and they are then rolled up for removal. When the removal of any inequality of surface is the object in view, the turf need only be rolled or lifted back, so as to lay bare the spot to or from which some soil is to be added or taken away, as the case may be. It is also useful for cutting turf from pasture ground to be laid by in heaps to rot, and thus form mould, although for this purpose turf may be cut well enough with a spade or shovel. The numbers, indicating sizes, and the prices of cast steel turfing irons are as follows: No. 0, 6s. 6d.; No. 1, 7s. 6d.; No. 2, 8s. 6d.; No. 3, 9s. 6d. If handles are required, they are supplied at 1s. extra.

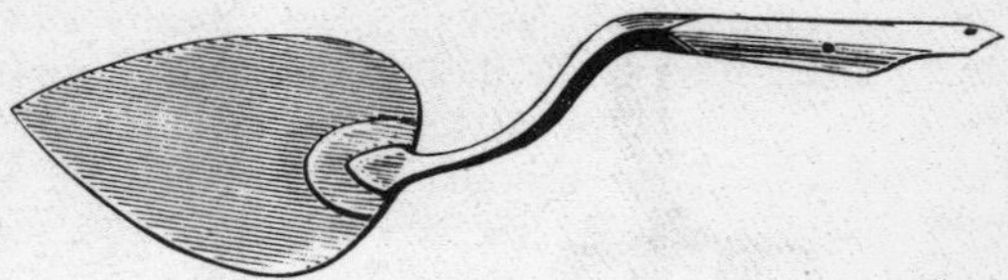

FIG. 176 *Turf spade or turfing iron*

491 *The Fork* This tool is as indispensable as the spade, and even more so, for it is possible to do all the necessary work in a small garden containing nothing more than a few borders for flowers with an ordinary border fork. It is handled in much the same manner as the spade, the only difference being that the handle is inserted into a socket proceeding upwards from the centre of the head of the fork, and does not enter the top of the blade as in the spade. For gardening purposes, forks are made with three, four, and five prongs; but for digging and trenching, a fork with four prongs is the most suitable. The lower part of each prong should be of steel, and the upper part and the tread and socket of the best scrap iron, and the prongs of all forks used for digging and trenching should be slightly curved. Fig. 177 shows the ordinary digging fork, and this may be taken as the general type of tools of this class, the prongs being about 9 or 10 inches in length. This fork will serve for all ordinary purposes, but for trenching and breaking up ground at some little depth below the surface, a fork with stronger and broader prongs should be used, such as the Demerara trenching fork, which is illustrated in Fig. 178. In order to impart as much strength as possible to this implement, the front strap is carried almost up the top of the handle, to which it is secured by several rivets. The ends of the prongs are square and broad. In Fig. 179 the border or lady's fork is shown, a tool with slight prongs, square above and pointed at the extremity, similar in structure to the ordinary digging fork, but much smaller, the prongs being about 6 or 7 inches in length. The smaller fork is most useful for border work in stirring the surface soil to the depth of two or three inches, an operation which is known as 'pointing'. When borders receive a top dressing of well-rotted manure in the late

FIG. 177 *Ordinary digging fork*

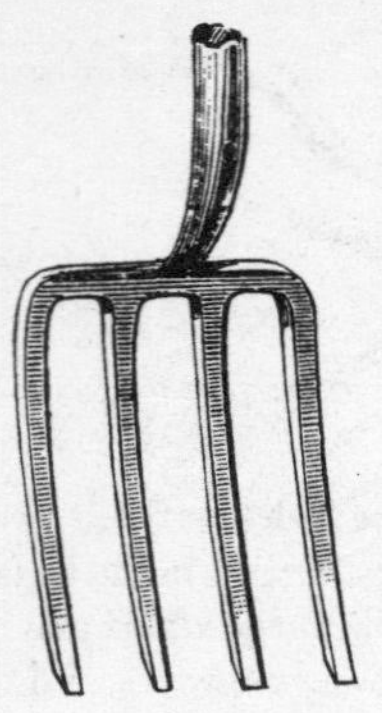

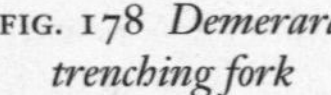

FIG. 178 *Demerara trenching fork*

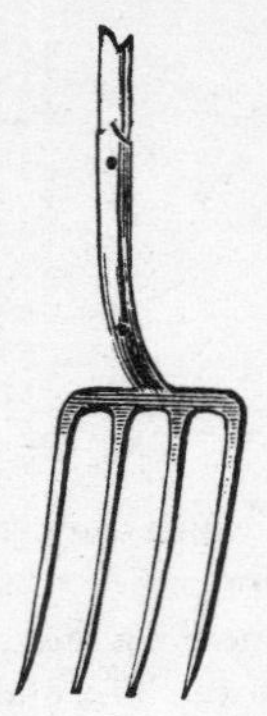

FIG. 179 *Border fork*

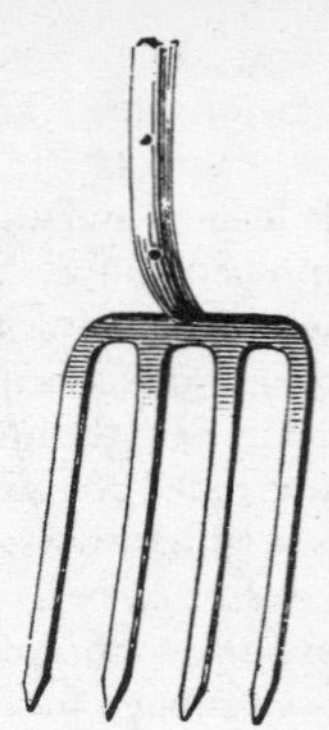

FIG. 180 *Flat prong potato fork*

autumn or early winter, it should be mingled with the surface soil by pointing with this fork. Being light and small, and having the prongs tolerably close together, it is possible to finish the surface of a border as neatly with this fork as with a rake, any large stones, pebbles, etc., that are brought to the surface being picked off with the hand. The potato fork, which is used for digging potatoes, is somewhat similar in form to the trenching fork, but the prongs are pointed and not so much curved. By its aid large masses of earth can be lifted and shaken or knocked to pieces, so as to expose the potato tubers without injury. Digging forks are sold at the average prices of 3s. for three-pronged forks; 2s. 9d. and 3s. 6d. for four-pronged forks, according to size, the former being a nice light tool for pointing borders; and 4s. 6d. for five pronged forks. Potato forks, with three prongs, are sold at 3s. 6d.; with four prongs, at 4s. Trenching forks, with four prongs, are supplied at 5s. 3d. each. The Demerara trenching forks, manufactured by the Hardy Patent Pick Company, Limited, Heeley, Sheffield, whose London office is in Walbrook, London, are supplied at about the following rates: with three prongs (13½ inches by 7½ inches), 4s. 6d. each, and with four prongs (13½ inches by 8 inches), at 5s. 6d each.

492 *The Manure Fork* The forks used for lifting manure and turning over manure heaps are lighter in structure than digging forks, the prongs being slighter and having more space between them. A useful form is shown in Fig. 181, which represents the Anglo-American Manure Fork, manufactured by the Hardy Patent Pick Company, Limited, Heeley, Sheffield, and Walbrook, London, who turn out excellent tools of all kinds for gardening purposes. Manure forks are supplied with long or short handles as may be preferred. The long-handled fork is preferable for lifting manure into a cart, but the short handled fork will do very well for turning over a heap, lifting it into a barrow, or spreading it over the ground. It must be understood that manure forks are only necessary in dealing with farmyard manure: they are not wanted for the compost heap, unless considerable quantities of grass and vegetable refuse be thrown on

FIG. 181 *Manure fork*

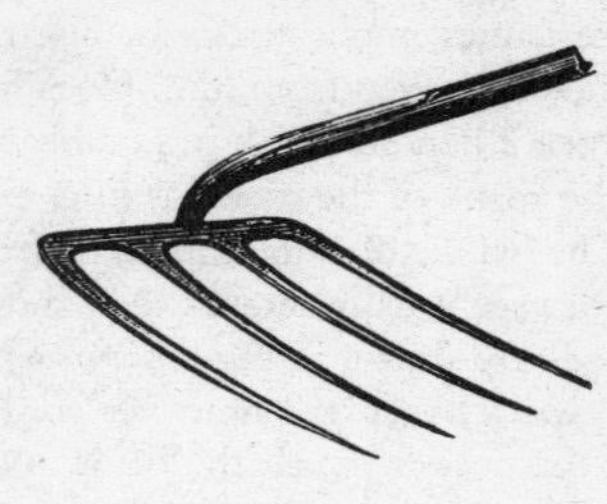

FIG. 182 *Manure drag*

it. The Manure Drag shown in Fig. 182 is to all intents and purposes a fork, so bent that it is no longer available for the purposes for which a manure fork is required, but must be used as a rake. It is always fitted with a long handle. The cost of good ordinary manure forks, with long handles, black, range from 3s. 6d. to 4s. 6d., according to size; bright forks and forks of better quality are higher, say 1s. more. Drag forks cost about 4s. 6d. each.

493 *Hand Fork or Garden Fork* This handy and useful form of fork is supplied with a long handle, as shown in Fig. 184, or with a short handle, as shown in Fig. 183. Either kind may be used with one hand. The prongs are broad and pointed. These forks will be found useful and serviceable in transplanting border plants, and in working the surface of the soil in borders in which growing plants stand closely together – too closely, in fact, for the safe use of the pointing fork. They are also useful for taking up asparagus and other roots that are not too large for removal by such means, and for putting aside bark, cocoanut fibre, etc., for pots that require plunging in these materials. Garden forks, or weeding forks, as they are sometimes called, with short handles, are sold in three sizes, and range in price from 1s. to 2s. 6d. each, according to quality; and the prices of those with long handles are much the same, the extra length of handle making but little difference.

FIG. 183—*Garden fork with short handle* FIG. 184 *Garden fork with long handle*

494 *The Hoe* As the pick is used for loosening hard soil, and the spade and fork for preparing and working mould that is sufficiently loose in itself to be readily penetrated by this implement, so the hoe may be said to have its special use for cleansing purposes, though it is also serviceable in loosening and stirring the surface of the soil amid growing crops, as well as for destroying weeds. Hoes are of many forms, but they may be broadly classified as draw hoes and thrust hoes. As these names imply, the draw hoe is pulled towards the operator, and the thrust hoe is pushed from him. Hoes for the most part are made with sockets, into which a handle of ash preferably, but sometimes of pine, is inserted, and when the shank of the socket is long enough it is secured to the handle with a rivet. The handle of a hoe should be from 4 to 5 feet in length. The handles of draw hoes are usually shorter than those of thrust hoes. The chief varieties of draw hoes are shown in Fig. 185, in which A represents the short-neck hoe, B the long-neck hoe, C the swan-neck or Bury hoe, from the bent formation of the part of the neck between the blade and the socket, and D the triangular hoe. This last form of hoe is convenient for cutting up weeds, as its corners are sharper than those of the hoes with square blades, and the corners of the blade are always used for cutting out and pulling away weeds from the soil. Sometimes hoes were made with a slight wedge-shaped shank, like the tang of a chisel, etc., which was driven into the end of the wooden handle, splitting being prevented by encircling the end of the handle with an iron band ring, about ½ inch or ¾ inch wide. The varieties of the thrust hoe are shown in Fig. 186, for the weeding tool called a spud may be regarded as a variety of thrust hoe. The Dutch hoe, or scuffle, as it is sometimes called, is shown at A. It consists of a sharp and comparatively narrow blade, attached to the socket by two arms, which spring from the lower end of the latter, and are fastened at their extremities to the blade, one on one side and one on the other. The blade of the hoe being thus attached forms an angle with the handle, and by this means is almost parallel to the surface of the soil when in use. The edge is thrust into the earth with a pushing motion and cuts up the weeds, which, with the surface soil, pass through the aperture between the arms. By this arrangement the tool meets with far less resistance, and the labour is rendered far lighter than it would be if the opening was closed, or even if the socket for the handle proceeded immediately from the centre of the blade. The spud, shown at B, consists of a

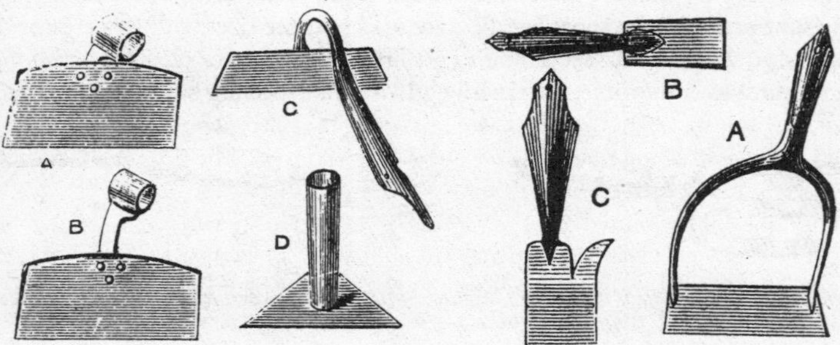

FIG. 185 *Varieties of draw hoes. A. Short-neck; B. Long-neck; C. Swan-neck or bury; D. Triangular.*

FIG. 186 *Varieties of the thrust hoe. A. Scuffle of dutch hoe. B. Spud C. Combined spud and weed hook*

stiff narrow blade, with a socket to admit of its attachment to a handle. It is used for cutting up docks, dandelions, thistles, and other weeds. There is another form shown at C, with a horn proceeding from the upper left-hand corner of the blade. This projection is utilised as a hook for pulling up weeds, or hooking down any tangled growth, etc. All kinds of hoes, except the swan-neck, the triangular hoe, and the spud, are made in sizes ranging from 3 inches to 10 inches, measuring along the edge of the blade, increasing by 1 inch from the smallest to the largest. The smallest size of swan-neck hoe is 4 inches: the largest size of triangular hoe 8 inches, the former going up to 10 inches, and the latter commencing at 3 inches. Spuds are made in three sizes, namely, 2 inch, 2½ inch, and 3 inch. Short-neck, long-neck, and swan-neck hoes are also made with blades having a curved or crescent-shaped edge, in which case they are called half-moon hoes. The prices of hoes of different kinds are as follows, according to the width of the tool from point to point of the cutting edge in inches, and in solid cast steel:

	3 in.	**4 in.**	**5 in.**	**6 in.**	**7 in.**	**8 in.**	**9 in.**	**10 in.**
Short-necked	6d.	8d.	10d.	1s. 0d.	1s. 2d.	1s. 4d.	1s. 6d.	1s. 8d.
Long-necked	7d.	9d.	11d.	1s. 1d.	1s. 3d.	1s. 5d.	1s. 7d.	1s. 9d.
Triangular	8d.	10d.	11d.	1s. 1d.	1s. 2d.	1s. 4d.	—	—
Bury	—	10d.	1s. 0d.	1s. 2d.	1s. 4d.	1s. 6d.	1s. 9d.	2s. 0d.
Dutch	9d.	1s. 0d.	1s. 3d.	1s. 6d.	1s. 9d.	2s. 0d.	2s. 3d.	2s. 6d.

These prices do not include handles, which are supplied at from 8d. to 1s., according to size of hoe. Half-moon hoes, whether short-necked, long-necked, or Bury, are sold at the above prices according to sizes as given. Round-prong hoes, with 4-feet ash handles, are sold at 2s. with three prongs, 2s. 6d. with four prongs, and 3s. 6d. with five prongs. Spuds and weed hooks are supplied at 7d. each, 3 inches wide; 8d., 2½ inches; and 10d., 3 inches; but if handles are required 7d. must be added to each of these prices.

495 *The Rake* This is a tool that is not so much required in the flower garden as in the vegetable garden, where its use is necessary in order to bring the surface of the soil to some uniformity of fineness, and to draw the earth over seed that has been newly sown, either in drills or in patches. It is also necessary for drawing weeds, stones, etc., together into a heap prior to removal. The rake itself consists of a straight flat bar of iron from ½ inch to ¾ inch wide, in which teeth, resembling round pointed nails, are set at right angles to the under surface of the bar. The teeth are usually slightly curved, but sometimes they are straight, and sometimes, instead of being like a cylindrical curved peg, they are flat, and as wide as the bar of the rake, but set in the bar with the width of the tooth transversely to the bar, so that the edges of the teeth meet the soil, etc., when the rake is in use. The teeth of rakes are generally 1 inch apart, and the rakes are made in sizes containing from 4 to 12 teeth in light rakes, and from 4 to 16 teeth in strong and extra strong rakes. A socket is attached to the bar at right angles to it, and in this a round straight ash or deal handle, of about 5 feet in length, is

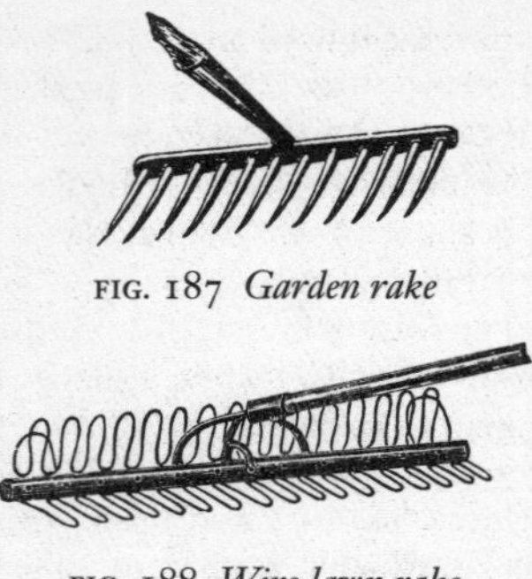

FIG. 187 *Garden rake*

FIG. 188 *Wire lawn rake*

FIG. 189 *Patent steel. Hay rake*

inserted. There are other varieties of rakes used in gardening, such as the ordinary haymaker's wooden rake, and the Wire Lawn Rake, represented in Fig. 188, which are used for the removal of grass, etc., from lawns. A new and light steel rake for lawns, illustrated in Fig. 189, has been introduced of late years. Being constructed entirely of steel, it is both strong and light, and though costing 1s. 9d., or nearly three times as much as an ordinary hay rake of wood, its durability, strength, and lightness render it a far more desirable implement to possess than the wooden rake. The daisy rake has been illustrated and described in p. 188. The prices of garden rakes are regulated by the number of teeth in them, and may be stated as follows:

	4	5	6	7	8	9	10	12	13	14
Light	4d.	5d.	6d.	7d.	8d.	9d.	10d.	1s. 0d.	—	—
Strong	6d.	7½d.	9d.	10½d.	1s. 0d.	1s.1½d.	1s. 3d.	1s. 6d.	1s. 9d.	2s. 0d.
Extra Strong	8d.	10d.	1s.	1s. 2d.	1s. 4d.	1s. 6d.	1s. 8d.	2s. 0d.	2s. 4d.	2s. 8d.
Solid Teeth for Roads				3s. 6d.	4s. 0d.	4s. 6d.	5s. 0d.	—	—	—

Handles for garden rakes are charged at from 8d. to 1s. extra, according to size; for handles for road rakes, 1s. 6d. is charged. Daisy rakes are regulated by width, and are made in sizes from 10 inches to 24 inches, and sold at prices ranging from 3s. 6d. to 6s., according to width, from 1s. to 1s. 6d. extra being charged for handles if required. The patent hay rake of Bessemer steel, with a 6-foot handle, is sold at 1s. 9d.; the wire lawn rake at about 2s. 3d.

Loudon says: 'Rakes vary in size and in the length and strength of their teeth: they are used for covering seeds or taking off weeds or cut grass, for smoothing surfaces, and for removing or replacing thin strata of pulverised surfaces, as in "cuffing", which is a mode of covering tree seeds sown in beds, by spreading the earth previously drawn off to the sides, over the seeds, by a smart blow or cuff with the back of a rake.' Indeed, the back of the rake is frequently used in pulverising and knocking to pieces clods of earth before raking the surface of a bed for the reception of seeds, and one end of the bar is often utilised for tracing drills for the reception of seed. Thus the rake may be made to serve more purposes than one.

496 *Tool Cleaner* All tools should be kept scrupulously clean, and should therefore be freed from all adhering particles of soil, etc., before they are put away in the tool house. For scraping off dirt from spades, picks, forks, hoes, etc., a piece of wood about ½ inch thick, cut in the shape shown in Fig. 190, with the bottom part a little thinner at the edge than at the shoulder, will be found useful, and a finishing touch may be imparted by a brush consisting of a number of wire ends bound round a short stick, or one of the cocoanut fibre brushes or rubbers that are now seen among the varied stock kept by seedsmen. The cleansing of the tool allows it to dry more quickly than it otherwise would, and prevents rust from the action of the oxygen of the air. When tools are likely to be put away for some time, the application of a little blacklead with a blacklead brush acts as a preservative. The spatula-shaped tool shown in Fig. 190 is frequently brought into use for clearing the spade or fork from earth which will inevitably cling to it when it is used in working heavy adhesive soil.

FIG. 190 *Tool cleaner*

497 *Miniature Tools* For ladies' and children's use, sets of tools, consisting of a spade, rake, and hoe, or of a spade, rake, hoe, and fork, are sold at prices ranging, in accordance with size, from 3s. 6d. to 10s. They are light and pretty in appearance, the handles being turned and attached to the tools in every case by sockets proceeding from the blades, and may serve for an hour's amusement in the flower garden now and then, but are in no way calculated for serious and actual work carried on in earnest. The same may be said of the boxes of Floral Tools, so called, consisting of a small rake, hoe, fork, and trowel, and sold in a box complete for 2s. 6d.

498 *Tools Requisite for Measurement and Direction* Many of the appliances required in preliminary operations in garden work, such as levelling, laying out roads, paths, etc., and constructing borders of different shapes, including the level, staff, straight-edge, borning pieces, etc., have been described in Chapter 7, and there is no necessity for more than a passing reference to them here. There are, however, two instruments that will require description, because they are so frequently required in garden work. These are the garden reel and line, and the measuring rod.

499 *The Garden Reel and Line* Practically, a couple of stakes and a piece of strong cord are all that are absolutely necessary for marking out a straight line between any two points, but far less time is taken up in winding a line round the frame which forms part of the garden reel than in turning and turning it round a stake a little thicker than one's thumb. The shape shown in Fig. 191 exhibits a very common form of garden reel and line, but whatever the form may be, the principle is alike in all. The reel consists of a central stake or pin of iron, sharpened to a point at the lower end, and so constructed above that an iron frame, consisting of top, bottom, and two sides, revolves upon it easily. The pin passes through holes made for its reception in the top and bottom piece of the frame. One end of the line is secured to the pin or tied to one side of the frame, and then wound round the sides of the frame. As the frame may be made to revolve on the pin with great rapidity, it is manifest that the line, even if entirely unwound,

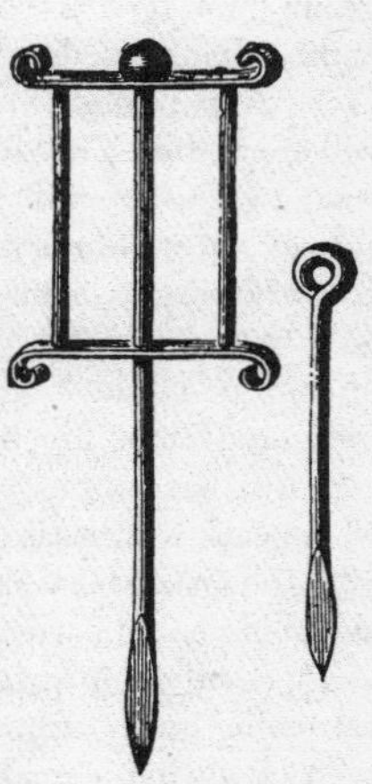

FIG. 191 *Garden line and reel*

can be wound up again very quickly. The other end of the line is tied to an eye projecting from another stake or pin, as shown in the illustration. When it is necessary to stretch the line, either for the purpose of defining the edge of a path or border, or for tracing a drill for seed sowing, this stake is pressed into the ground, usually by the hand of the gardener, or, if necessary, by the pressure of his heel. The line is then unwound from the frame as far as is necessary, and the pin passing through the frame is pressed into the ground at the point required; the line is then turned round the pin just below the frame, and is tightened by screwing the stake round and round. When the necessary tension has been obtained, pressure is exerted on the frame and its stake to force them into the mould, so that the line may not slip or slacken. A strong and well-made garden reel of wrought iron is supplied by Messrs J. J. Thomas and Co., 87 Queen Victoria Street, London, for 2s. 6d., and flax garden lines, 40 yards in length, at 1s. 6d., and 60 yards at 2s. Garden lines of the best hemp are supplied by Mr Benjamin Edgington, 2 Duke Street, London, in lengths of 60 yards at 1s. 6d., 2s. 3d., and 3s. each, according to size and stoutness of line. It may be desirable to add here that soft tarred hemp twine of the best quality, for tying plants to espaliers, trellises, etc., may be purchased of Mr Edgington for 9d. per skein, and the best tarred hemp-laid twine at 1s. per lb.

500 *The Measuring Rod* This is a piece of deal or pitch pine, 6, 8, or 10 feet long, from ½ inch to 2 inches wide, and from ½ inch to ⅝ inch thick, or from 1 to 1½ inch square, as may be preferred. It should be nicely planed up, painted black or white, according to taste, and then divided by white marks on black, or black marks on white, into feet, which should be numbered consecutively, the feet being subdivided into spaces of 3 inches or quarter-feet, and the first foot into inches. A rod of 6 feet in length is sufficient for a small garden, but for a large garden one of 10 feet will be found more handy. A white rod is easier seen on the ground, but it soils more readily than a black one. It is used for measuring the width of paths, beds, drills, etc., so as to ensure parallelism between them, and, in the case of drills, to place them apart at equal distances. The jobbing gardener will effect this by cutting notches on his rake, or on a stick, but this is a slovenly way of going to work, and spoils the handle of the tool that is thus notched. It should never be resorted to in a well-ordered garden, in which a properly constructed measuring rod should be always at hand when wanted.

501 *Tools Necessary for Sowing, Planting, and Transplanting* It is clear that the operations of sowing, planting, and transplanting, form together one of the most important functions of the gardener. Each is simple enough in itself, perhaps, but, notwithstanding its simplicity, there are circumstances under which each will require some special appliances to aid in its performance.

502 *The Drill and Drill Rake* The drilling and sowing machine, although it may be useful in market gardening on a large scale, when large areas of land have to be sown, is rather an agricultural appliance than a horticultural implement, and in gardening on an ordinary scale is wholly unnecessary. It is desirable, however, even in sowing a small bed of seed, that the rows in which the seed is sown should be even and regular. It has been shown above how drills may be traced by aid of the garden reel and line and the measuring rod; but this is a tedious

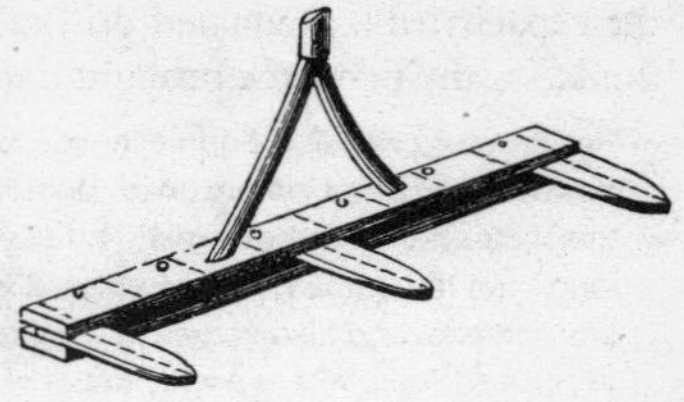

FIG. 192 *Drill rake*

process, as it involves, first of all, the marking of the distances between the drills with small sticks at each end of the bed, and then the transference of the line from mark to mark, and the tracing of the drill with the point of a stick or the end of the bar of the rake, or even with the hoe. The quicker way is to set the line along one side of the bed as a guide for the first row, and then to trace the drills, three or four at a time, with a drill rake. When this instrument is used there is no need to move the line, for the last of the first series of rows formed by the rake will serve as a guide for the first of the second series, the first tooth of the rake being drawn along it. The drill rake, it should be said, is only requisite for small seeds, such as onions, carrots, parsnips, etc.: for larger seeds, such as peas and beans, it is better to take out single rows with the line and hoe, on account of the distance between them, which prevents the use of a drill rake. The mode of making a drill rake is shown in Fig. 192. A handle similar to that of a wooden hay rake, or a straight handle like that of an iron garden rake, if it be preferred, is let into a flat piece of wood, from 20 to 26 inches in length, 2 inches wide, and ½ inch thick. Another piece of the same size is also required, and a third strip, about ¾ inch wide, but of the same length and thickness as the other two. This piece is placed between the wider pieces, so that the back of each is in one and the same plane, and they are then firmly screwed together. The bar of the rake thus assumes the form of a piece of wood 2 inches wide and 1½ inch thick, with a deep groove 1¼ inch in depth and ½ inch wide in its inner side. In this groove, teeth about 6 inches long, ½ inch thick, and 2 inches wide at the base, brought to a blunt point in front, are inserted, as shown in the illustration, and if they are made to fit with tolerable tightness, and the bar and teeth are preserved from damp, no fixing will be necessary – that is to say, no fixing with nails or screws. The convenience in having movable teeth lies in this, that one bar may be made to serve for drills of any desired distance apart. To effect this, a line should be drawn up the centre of each tooth, as shown by the dotted lines in the illustration, and the top of the rake bar should be graduated at regular intervals, proceeding each way from the centre. Now, supposing that the bar in the illustration is 26 inches long, and a tooth 2 inches wide is inserted at each end, it is manifest that the distance between the points of the teeth will be 24 inches, and this is the reason why a length of 20 or 26 inches was named for the bar, so as to allow 1 inch for half the breadth of the teeth when placed at each end, so that there might be a positive distance of 18 or 24 inches between the points. If, then, the upper surface of the bar be graduated in inches, between the central mark and the marks at the ends, which are distant 12 inches from the centre, it is clear that, by the insertion of teeth in the groove at the required distance apart, we may contrive to make drills at any distance apart from 2 to 24 inches. For example, we can get 13 drills at 2 inches apart, 9 at 3 inches, 7 at 4 inches, 5 at 5 and 6 inches, 4 at 7 and 8 inches, 3 at 9, 10, 11, and 12 inches, and 2 at any distance from 13 to 24 inches. Such is the capacity of a graduated drill rake with a bar of 26 inches, which is now, I think, for the first time brought under the notice of gardeners.

Far greater precision and utility can be claimed for this drill rake than for the drill rake described by other writers on gardening. Let us take, for example, Loudon's description of this instrument. 'The drill rake,' he says, 'has large coulter-formed teeth, about 6 inches long, and the same distance apart; it is used for drawing drills across beds for receiving small seeds, and also serves to stir the soil between the rows after the seeds come up. In very loose soils, where a wide drill is required, a sheath of wood may be fixed to the upper part of each prong, in order to spread the earth, but this is seldom necessary. When the drills are not to be quite so wide as 6 inches, the operator has only to work the implement diagonally.' But in this way it is impossible to determine with exactness the distance between the rows.

503 *Hopper for Seed Sowing* It is surprising to note the exactness with which gardeners will distribute the contents of a packet of seed over a certain area – how they will make an ounce of onion seed suffice for a bed marked out in drills, or a quart of peas for a certain length of row, exhausting the seed precisely as the end of the row or of the last drill is reached. This facility can only be gained by practice, and for those who cannot have much practice in this kind of work, it is desirable to afford a suggestion of some means by which evenness and exactness of distribution can be obtained mechanically. The illustration given in Fig. 193 represents a very simple contrivance for the purpose of seed sowing. It consists of a small box of wood, about 2 inches square and 6 inches long for small seeds, and about 3 inches square and 9 inches long for larger seeds, such as peas. There is a bottom, two sides cut in a shoe-like form, and an end, which must be firmly bradded together, and the thickness of the wood need not be more than ⅛ inch or 3/16 inch – in fact, an old cigar box will furnish excellent material of which to make the hopper. Then between the sides a slanting piece of wood is inserted, in such a manner as to leave an open space at the top, through which seed may be introduced into the hopper, and a very narrow slit at the bottom through which the seed may emerge and fall over the front edge of the bottom into the drill. The hopper is held in the right hand, and is gently shaken as the operator passes from one end of the drill to the other, so as to ensure an equal flow and an equal spreading of the seed. If the side of the box were made a little thicker, so as to admit of being grooved, the slanting piece forming the front of the hopper could be made to slide stiffly in the grooves, and thus the opening for the egress of the seed might be regulated to suit seed of any size.

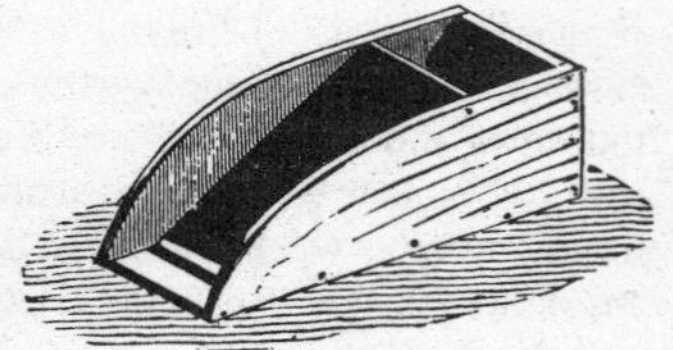

FIG. 193 *Seed hopper*

504 Those who do not care to take the trouble of making the contrivance described in the preceding section, and who desire the aid of a more perfect appliance, should provide themselves with the Hand Seed Drill, supplied by Messrs Deane and Co., 46 King William Street, London. This drill is represented in Fig. 194. It consists of a hopper, supported on a light frame, and having a wheel with rounded circumference in front. A long handle is attached to the drill, by which it may be pushed along. The seed is put in the hopper, and falls into a shallow trench that is marked by the wheel in its onward course. An appendage in the rear of the hopper draws the surface mould over the seed as it falls from the hopper and is deposited on the surface of the trench. The machine will be found a convenient appliance by those who cannot sow seed in the usual way by hand. The price of the drill is 10s. 6d.

FIG. 194 *Hand seed drill*

505 *The Dibble or Dibber* This is an indispensable tool in any garden where much planting out is done, and must be called into requisition for the transference to open ground or other quarters of most plants that are grown in seed beds originally, and then planted apart at regular and wider intervals. The best form of dibble is shown in Fig. 195. It may be described as a short piece of rounded wood, terminating in a blunt point at one end, and a handle like that of a spade at the other; indeed, the handle of an old spade is one of the best and most handy things possible for conversion into a dibble. The pointed end is thrust into the earth to a sufficient depth, and the root of the plant, whatever it may be, is thrust into the hole, and the earth brought round it by two or three thrusts of the dibble into the soil at a short distance from the plant itself. When it is desired to make holes of a certain depth, or to make a number of holes of uniform depth, an iron socket should be made, with a projecting piece on one side and divided on the other, with a plate on each side of the division, which may be tightened or loosened by the action of a thumbscrew, so as to admit of the socket being easily shifted up and down the stem of the dibble, or being held immovable in position, as may be found requisite. This is the principle of the potato dibble, which, however, is longer, and in which the projecting piece at the side is fixed at a certain distance from the point. There are other forms of dibbles, but this is the most common, the most useful, and generally preferred by gardeners.

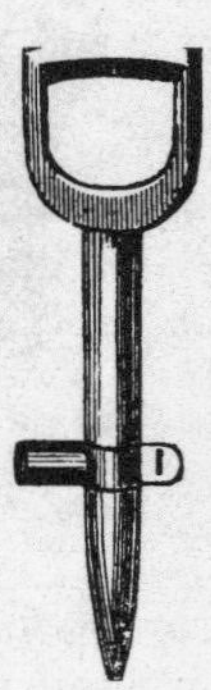

FIG. 195 *Dibble*

Let me take the opportunity to protest against the use of the dibble in planting potatoes. The action of the instrument is to consolidate the soil immediately surrounding the hole that is made, and when a seed potato or a set is dropped into the hole, it is pretty certain that there is a cavity below it and hard earth around it, neither of which can benefit the growth of the tuber, but, on the contrary, rather retard it. And this practice is frequently followed in stiff land, or in soil which quickly dries, being soon deprived of its moisture by a non-retentive subsoil. Potatoes, when planted, should be set in trenches, the small potatoes or sets being placed on and along the bottom of the trench. A liberal supply of light and well-rotted farmyard manure should be shaken over the potatoes as they lie in the trench, and the mould should then be pulled over the manure. In setting potatoes in this way, it saves time if the earth that is taken out of one trench is thrown over the potatoes and manure that have been previously laid in the trench that has been made immediately before the trench that is being taken out next to it.

506 *Munro's Perforator* This is a kind of dibble used for tree planting, which was first described in the *Gardener's Magazine*. It is, of course, only used for planting large tracts with small tap-rooted trees, for whose reception it is not necessary to dig a hole, or even to make one of any size. Its form and dimensions are shown in front view at A, and in side view at B, in Fig. 196. It partakes very much of the character of the spade in its construction, consisting as it does of a steel blade attached by straps to a crutch-headed handle of some length. It has a tread also, but here the similitude ceases, for the blade, instead of being broad and square at the bottom, is wedge-shaped, and tapers to a point. Loudon, speaking of this implement, says: 'In using it, one man employs the instrument, while another man or boy holds a bundle of plants. The first man inserts the instrument in the soil, holding it up for the reception of the plant; round which, when introduced, he inserts the iron three times in order to loosen the soil about the roots; then treads down the turf, and the plant becomes as firmly set in the ground as if it had been long planted. Two men will set in one day from 500 to 600 plants with this instrument, at 1s. per hundred, whereas by digging holes the expense would be 3s. per hundred, and the planting not done so well.' The cost of labour has increased since this was written, but the ratio between the cost of planting with the perforator and of digging holes remains the same.

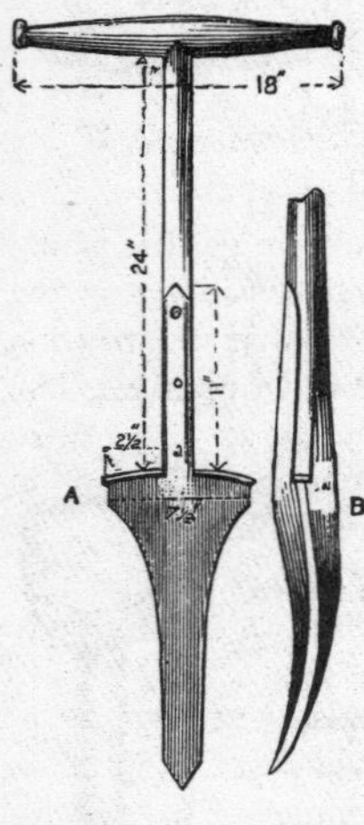

FIG. 196
Munro's perforator

507 *The Trowel* This is a tool that no one can possibly do without, as it is frequently required both in planting and transplanting and in potting. It consists of a shovel-shaped blade, with the sides turned up, so as to better hold and retain anything that may be taken up in it. A bent neck, with a tang to it, is riveted to the top of the blade in the centre, the tang being inserted in a neatly-turned handle, with a ring round the part at the entrance of the tang to prevent splitting. Garden trowels are classified as 'light', 'strong', and 'best', and are made in sizes of 5, 6, 7, and 8 inches in length. The fern trowel is longer than the ordinary garden trowel, and the blade is also curved from top to point, as shown in Fig. 198. They are made in one size only. In transplanting small seedling plants and cuttings the utility of the trowel is very great, for a hole may first be made in the soil with it for the reception of the plant, and the plant may then be lifted bodily, with the soil about its roots undisturbed, and gently deposited in

FIG. 197 *Garden trowel*

FIG. 198 *Fern trowel*

the hole made for it. The prices of garden trowels are as follows: Light, from 6d. to 1s., according to length; strong, from 9d. to 1s. 2d.; best, from 1s. to 2s. Fern trowels are 1s. 6d. each, or in leather case, 2s.

508 *The Transplanter* It is almost superfluous to say that the instruments chiefly used in small gardens for transplanting seedlings from one part of the garden to another are the trowel, the short-handled weeding fork, and the dibble. There is, however, an appliance by which plants of considerable size and well advanced in growth may be removed from the spot in which they are growing and transferred to another situation without sustaining the slightest injury, even though they are in flower. It consists of two semi-cylinders of iron, each of which is furnished with a handle, as shown in Fig. 199. The earth is removed at some little distance from the plant all round it, and the irons are then pressed towards each other, after being placed in the trench in the proper positions, and brought together so as to encircle the roots of the plant, and to press the earth about them with tolerable firmness. Portions of the side of one semi-cylinder overlap the other, and slits are cut in the overlapping portions so as to allow of the entrance of eyes fixed in the other semi-cylinder. Eyes are also fixed in the overlapping parts, so that when the two semi-cylinders are brought together they may be secured by pins passing through the eyes, as shown in the illustration. Thus enclosed, the plant may be safely carried to the place in which it is intended to plant it, and there deposited in a hole made for its reception. The pins should be first withdrawn and the earth drawn round the sides of the cylinder. This done, the two parts of the cylinder may be drawn away from the plant, and the earth again pressed round the soil that has been removed, together with the plant itself.

FIG. 199 *Transplanter*

509 For smaller plants an instrument is used in France and England which in some measure resembles a pair of sugar-nippers. Forms of these are shown in Figs. 200, 201, and 202, which are taken from McIntosh's *Book of the Garden*. They are useful in transplanting cabbages, turnips, etc., because the former sustain no check when transferred from place to place by these means, while turnips could not well be transplanted by any other way. These instruments may be said to be modifications to a great extent of the form or type described above. Fig. 200 shows a useful transplanter, consisting of two trowel-shaped blades affixed to iron handles, which are combined towards the top, and set in a handle of **D** form, similar to those attached to spades and forks. The irons diverge outwardly, and on them moves, by means of rings attached to its ends, a piece of wood. When this slider is drawn to the top the blades separate to their utmost extent, but when it is pushed down they are drawn together. The instrument, when the blades are apart, is pushed into the soil, enclosing the plant to be removed between the blades. The slider is then pushed down, and the instrument is withdrawn, the plant being held firmly between the blades. The pointed

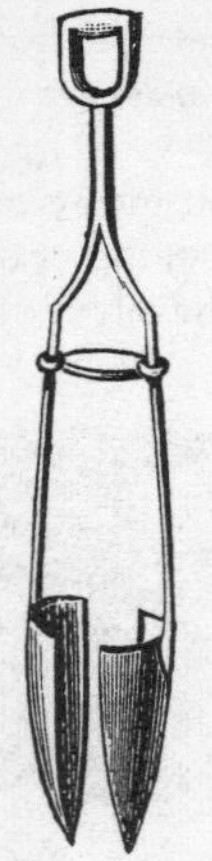

FIG. 200 *Small transplanter*

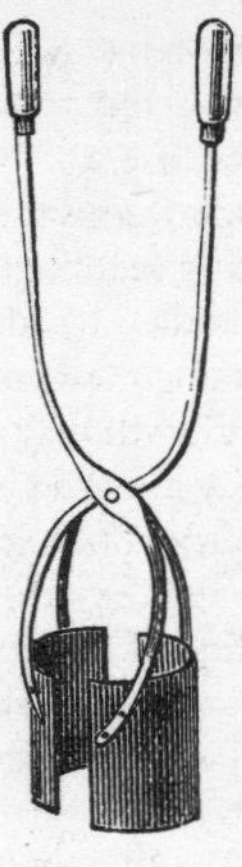

FIG. 201 *French transplanter*

FIG. 202 *M'Glashan's transplanter*

blades, when brought together, form a species of dibble, which may be thrust into the ground wherever it may be desired to do so, carrying the plant with them. The slider is then drawn up, and the blades move apart sufficiently to allow of the easy withdrawal of the transplanter, leaving the plant behind it. Fig. 201 shows the French form of a transplanter of this kind, in which the blades are semi-cylindrical, and are drawn together or pushed apart by pressing the handles in contrary directions. Fig. 202 represents M'Glashan's Transplanter, which differs in many respects from those shown in Figs. 200 and 201. The blades are semi-cylindrical, but are narrower, and smaller at the bottom than they are at the top, exactly resembling, in fact, the two halves of a flower pot from which the bottom has been removed. The handles have the same inclination as the blades to which they are attached. A transverse rack is attached to one handle by a pin, and passes through a slot in the other and over a pin. When the blades are brought together, they are held in place by the pressure of the tooth of the rack which has last passed over the pin, and both plant and soil surrounding it are grasped firmly, the flower-pot-like construction of the blades preventing any chance of that which is between them slipping through.

510 For transplanting shrubs and small trees with as much soil as it is possible to retain about the roots, another plan was devised by Mr M'Glashan, the illustration of which, exhibited in Fig. 203, is also taken from McIntosh's *Book of the Garden*. The general principle on which this contrivance is based is the same as that of the smaller transplanter by M'Glashan, already described. First of all, a strong frame, A, A, constructed in such a manner that it may be opened, is placed on the ground round the shrub or tree to be removed. In order to provide for the opening, one side is movable, being fastened to one adjacent side by a hinge or joint at one end, and attached to the other by a fastener. This done, four spades with broad blades, either of wood or iron, are forced into the ground within the frame in the position shown. The blades form a kind of box, and are pressed inwards at the bottom by passing bars through the handles of opposite pairs of spades, which has the effect of thrusting the handles outwards, the handles being prevented from returning to their original position by pins thrust through holes in the bars. The roots of the tree and the soil about them being firmly clasped by this means, strong iron hooks are passed under the frame at one end and over a bar at the other, so that a couple of bars, one on either side, may provide the means of lifting the mass of earth with the frame, and the spades that hold it from its position, and of transferring it wherever it may be determined to replant the tree. Of course, it would not be worth while to go to the expense of providing an appliance of this sort for an ordinary garden, where but little transplanting is done, and that in the ordinary way; but in removing shrubs an appliance of the kind described may be easily extemporised by four boards cut in the form of the blade of the spade shown in Fig. 203 – that is to say, narrower at the top than the bottom, and held together by a frame passed round them about the middle, the earth having been removed all round the plant, and the soil about the roots, to admit of placing the boards in the proper position. A frame must then be placed round the boards, and this should be in four parts, as shown in Fig. 204, two parts being like A and two parts like B. The tenons in B are passed through the slots in A, and fastened in place by iron pins. To save time and trouble in cutting the slots and tenons, it is as well to make the sides of the frame of three thicknesses of wood firmly screwed together. The inside edge of each side of the frame should be slightly bevelled, as shown in section at C, the bevel being the same as the inclination of the sides of the boards. Provision for carrying the whole by bars, as shown in Fig. 203, may be made by passing eye-bolts through A, as shown in the illustration, through which hooks can be passed, the other end of each hook being put over the bars.

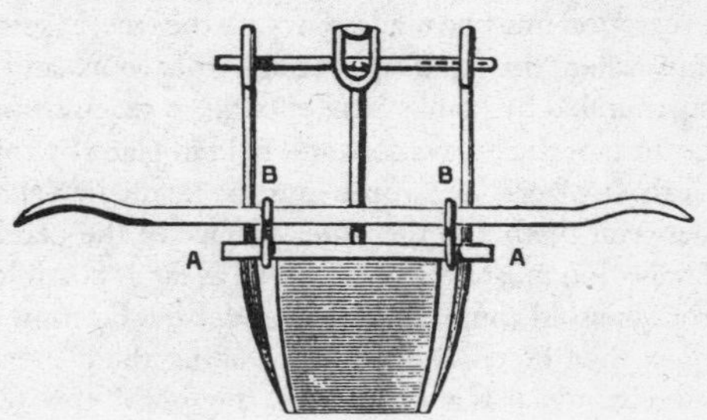

FIG. 203 *M'Glashan's shrub transplanter*

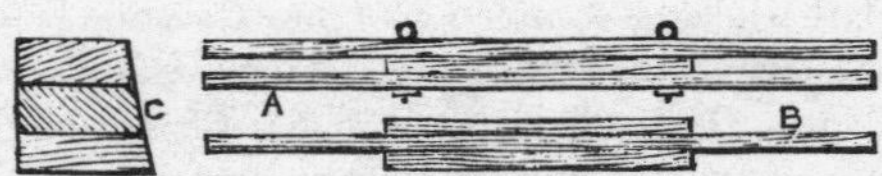

FIG. 204 *Mode of making frame for extemporised transplanter*

511 In landscape gardening it is sometimes found necessary to remove trees of considerable size. Various machines have been devised for effecting this with as little injury to the tree as possible by Messrs Saul, M'Nab, Barrow, M'Glashan, and others, but the principle pervading the whole of these contrivances is much the same, and this need only be described to enable anyone of ordinary ingenuity to put it in force should occasion require it. Of course, it is utterly impossible that a tree of any size can be removed without some injury to its roots, and all that can be done is to limit the injury as much as possible, and retain in position as much as can be managed of the soil in which the fibrous roots in the immediate vicinity of the tree are embedded. First of all, then, an excavation must be made all round the tree, at some little distance from its stem, and when this is deep enough the roots and soil about them should be surrounded by planks long enough to reach from the surface of the soil to the bottom of the excavation, and held in place by ropes placed round them in two or three places. The ropes must be firmly tied and tightened by driving wedges between them and the outer surface of the planks which they surround. The excavation must now be extended as far as possible under the tree, and chains or ropes passed round the mass, under the bottom, and over the top. Long levers must then be taken and passed under the chains, the ends of the levers being directed towards and resting at the foot of the stem of the tree. Fulcrums must be placed on either side of the pit to sustain the levers, and then by pressure attached to the other end of them the mass must be raised gradually, and held in place while the completion of the excavation below the tree is being carried out. Meanwhile, the earth should be removed on one side of the excavation, so as to form an inclined plane from the surface of the soil to the bottom of the excavation, and when all is free below the mass, and the tree has been raised as far as possible, a cradle, formed by more planking and ropes, should be passed under it to retain the earth in place, and a truck with low wheels passed down the incline and under the tree, which may then be lowered to rest on the truck and secured in position. Thick planks should be laid on the earth to form a sort of tramway for the truck, to prevent the wheels from sinking into the soft soil under the weight of the superincumbent mass. When all is ready, the truck and tree must be hauled up on level ground and drawn to its new position. Here a pit must have been dug to receive it, into which the truck must be backed. The tree must then be lifted off the truck by the same means by which it was lowered on to it, and the truck drawn away from under it, to admit of the tree being lowered into the position it is to occupy. Before this is done, however, the cradle at the bottom must be released. When the tree is placed in the pit, all that remains to be done is to remove the ropes and planking that surround the mass and to fill up the pit. In the foregoing description it has been sought to explain the general principle to be followed rather than to describe any special piece of machinery devised for the purpose. No difficulty will be found in carrying out the process with any simple means at command, provided that the directions given are carefully followed. Where much of this kind of work has to be done, and the trees are of considerable size, special machinery will have to be provided for the purpose, which is too elaborate to be described here. But even in this the principle adopted will be found to be the same.

In transplanting trees of any kind, it is better, when putting them in position in their new quarters, to let the sides of the tree retain the aspects to which they have been severally accustomed in the places that they have already occupied – that is to say, the side of the tree that has already faced the north should still be turned towards the north, and so on. It is said that trees make less growth on the side turned to the cold quarter than they do on that which faces south, so to alter the position of a tree would cause a change in its habit with regard to climatic influences, which could not fail to exercise a retarding effect on its growth for some little time, until it had become accommodated to its change of position.

512 *Appliances Required for Potting, etc.* These are by no means numerous, although the various appliances of each class may differ very widely from each other in special features, as, for instance, an ordinary earthern flower pot differs materially from a wooden box, though both may be, and indeed are, used for the same purpose. In considering these appliances we must regard them in two classes, namely, the receptacles themselves and the means that are used to fill the receptacles with soil and to place the plants in them. But before this it may be useful to make a few remarks on the *modus operandi* of potting, as far as its general principles are concerned.

513 *Potting: Its General Principles and their Application* In potting it is always necessary to make provision for the escape of surplus water – that is to say, water which, when given to the plant in the pot, cannot be retained by the soil in which it grows. For the purpose of providing drainage, every gardener keeps by him a store of fragments of broken pots and saucers, oyster shells, and even broken pieces of soft bricks, which are useful in certain cases where much drainage is required. The oyster shell, or indeed any shell, such as that of the clam, mussel, or limpet, is useful for placing over the hole at the bottom of the pot, and surrounding this and above it may be placed small pieces of broken pots, technically called 'crocks'. For cuttings which are not intended to remain in the pot for any length of time after they have rooted, a single piece of crock is sufficient, but when the time of tenancy is likely to be prolonged to months, and perhaps even years, it is necessary to fill one-sixth, and in some cases as much as one-fourth, of the entire depth of the pot with broken potsherds – that is to say, if a pot be 6 inches in depth the crocking should be from 1 inch to 1½ inch in depth. If possible, it is desirable to give a conical form to the crocking placed in the pot: this may be done by placing a piece of potsherd or a shell at the bottom of the pot as already directed, and then placing other pieces round it and leaning against it, the whole being capped by another and longer piece. This provides for the gradual descent of the water from the centre to the sides of the pot, and its escape through the hole in the bottom. Secondly, the pot being crocked, it is considered desirable by some to place a little moss or cocoanut fibre, or even a few leaves, over the crocks before putting in the soil, so as to prevent the interstices between the crocks being choked by aggregation of the finer particles of earth that may be carried down from time to time by the water during the process of watering. There is, however, no absolute need to do this, as the very presence of the shells and potsherds at the bottom of the pot secures the escape of surplus water, even though a little earth be carried down among them. The better course is to place a little coarser mould immediately over the crocks, and use finer soil for placing immediately around the roots of the plant and filling the pot. Thirdly, in potting, the crocking being done and a little coarse mould thrown over them, some fine mould should be put in and shaken together by gently knocking the edge of the bottom of the pot against the potting bench, or by striking the sides of the pot gently with the hand. If the plant is well rooted, and most of the old earth surrounding the roots has been removed, draw up the mould already placed in the pot in a conical form, so that the plant may be placed on the apex of the cone, and the roots disposed about its sloping sides. Then fill up the pot by throwing soil over the roots with the hand or the trowel, consolidating the earth by knocking the pot as before, and pressing it round the sides with a potting stick or with the thumbs, which is most convenient when dealing with the smaller sizes of pots. Also press the earth firmly about the collar of the plant with the thumbs. With the generality of plants it is desirable to pot firmly, not to ram the earth down hard, but sufficiently firm to find that the plant offers resistance if slight pressure be applied to it to pull it upwards. Lastly, never fill a pot with earth right up to the edge, but only to about ½ inch below the edge of smaller pots, and 1 inch for larger pots. This should be done in order to afford sufficient room for water when the plant is watered.

514 *Potting Stage or Bench* To every greenhouse of sufficient size a potting shed should be attached, furnished with a shelf or stage of suitable height, on which plants can be potted or repotted, as the case may be, before removal to the greenhouse. This should be of sufficient height to prevent stooping; the height must of course be regulated by the height of the person who mostly uses the stage; it will vary from 2 feet 6 inches for short persons to 3 feet for tall persons. In a potting shed it is convenient to place drawers below the shelf or stage to contain a sufficient supply of potting materials for immediate use, such as silver sand, peat, loam, cocoanut fibre, crocks, etc., etc. Rough boxes, such as those in which tinned lobster and salmon and Swiss milk are sent to this country, will answer the purpose as well and better than those made by a carpenter, because they cost little, and can be renewed at pleasure. All that is necessary is to put up a framework to suit the size and to furnish runners on which the boxes may be drawn out and pushed in as required. Of course, contrivances of this kind must be suited to the space at command. When much potting is done out of doors, as will be the case sometimes, especially when there is no potting shed, or when it is more convenient to do what has to be done at some distance from the potting shed, it is desirable to have a portable bench on which the work can be

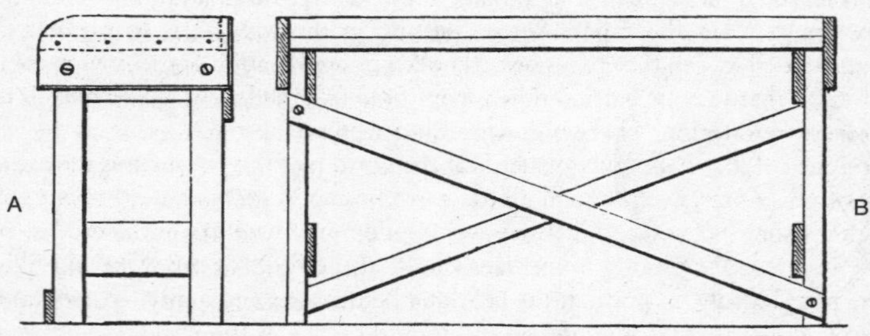

FIG. 205 *Potting bench: A – end elevation; B – front elevation*

conveniently carried out. It will be more convenient, perhaps, if this bench is made so that it can be taken to pieces and put together again quickly and without much trouble. The first thing to be done is to make a couple of strong trestles, as shown in the end elevation of the bench in Fig. 205. These may consist of two uprights of inch stuff with transverse rails screwed to them *on the inside* of the uprights, the upper rail flush with the top of the upright, and the lower one about 6 inches above the lower ends of them. This is all as far as the trestles are concerned. Next, a board or shelf must be provided about 15 inches wide and 3 feet 6 inches long, or, at all events, about 2 inches wider than the width of the trestles. To the back of this a narrow piece of wood must be nailed, and two broader pieces at the sides, as shown in the illustration. This must be placed on top of the trestles and the broad side pieces screwed to the top of the uprights as shown. Stability may be given to the bench by screwing on two diagonal pieces to the trestles, one in front and one behind, as shown. A bench thus made will be found to be firm and stable. It requires only eight screws to hold it together; and the various component parts, five in number, namely, the shelf or top, the two trestles, and the two diagonal pieces, may be put together or taken apart in a very few minutes. When not in use they can be put away in any spare Corner.

515 *The Screen and Sieve* Where much potting is done, and compost for potting is mixed in large quantities, it may be found necessary to screen or sift it, and for this purpose an article called a screen, or riddle, is necessary. This is a large square sieve, similar to that used by builders for sifting ingredients that are to be made into mortar, etc. It consists of a square frame, wired as shown in Fig. 206, and provided with two narrow sides. It is supported on a stick in the position shown, and the workman who has the stuff to be sifted near him takes it up, shovelful after shovelful, and, standing in front of the screen, throws the compost against it. All that is fit for potting passes through the wires and falls in a heap behind. The coarser portions are stopped by the wires, and fall in front in a heap at the foot of the screen. It is not desirable to render potting earth too fine, for if this is done it is apt to cake together, and harden when dry, and when all the fine stones, etc., are removed, the earth is deprived of substances which keep it open and assist in keeping it drained and aerated. For the same reason it is not desirable to be too particular in removing stones from borders, etc., provided that they are not large, and therefore not in the way, like stones such as flints, etc. For ordinary work on a limited scale, a common garden sieve, as

FIG. 206 *Screen*

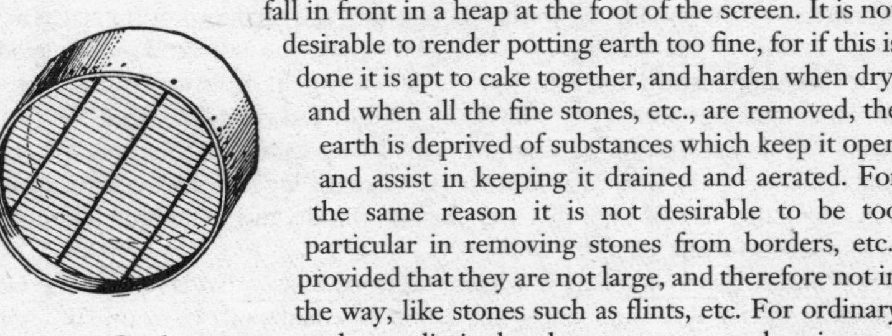

FIG. 207 *Garden sieve*

shown in Fig. 207, may be used for sifting compost. They may be bought at prices ranging from 1s. upwards, according to size. This appliance is made of a broad hoop of tough wood, traversed in one direction by three or four stout wires, and in the other, at right angles to the stout wires, by finer wires about ¼ inch, or ⅜ inch apart, which are bound to the stout wires by fine brass wire or copper wire, which is both tenacious and pliable. A handy man can easily make a sieve for his own use, but those who attempt to do so will find a square frame more convenient for their purpose than a round hoop.

516 *Pots and Water Saucers* These are too well known to need much description, as far as the ordinary description of flower pot is concerned. The majority of those in use are unattractive in form, if convenient, and are made of common potter's clay, similar to that which is used for making the better and softer kinds of bricks. The best, perhaps, that can be had are those made at the Potteries at Weston-super-Mare, which are good and cheap. The shape of the common pot and water saucer are shown in Fig. 208. Pots should always be unglazed, to admit of the escape and absorption of water when necessary; but the interior of the water saucers should always be glazed to prevent absorption of the water that escapes into them. It is convenient, indeed, to fill the saucers, in which the pots are standing, with water, in hot weather, when the water will ascend in the sides of the pots by capillary attraction, and keep the roots and the earth that surround them moist and cool. This may be better effected by standing the pot in which the plant is placed within another just large enough to receive it. It is better to treat in this manner all plants that require plenty of water, especially during the summer, such as arums, when they cannot be transferred to the ground in the open air, oleanders, etc. Pots that have been used should always be well cleansed by washing before they are used again, especially when they have been put by for some time. It is absurd to advise amateurs not to use or buy old pots, for when they have been well soaked for a few hours in cold water, and then well washed and scrubbed in hot soda water, they very nearly recover their original colour, and are as serviceable as when they were purchased new from the maker. Pots should always be soaked and washed before they are used for potting: even new pots should be put in water, for the porosity of the pot renders it a ready absorbent of moisture, and a dry pot will draw away the moisture from the earth in which a newly-potted plant has been placed, and therefore from the plant itself. Another reason for potting plants in clean pots is, that the roots will seek and travel along the sides of a clean pot far more readily than they will, or indeed can, along the sides of a pot that is encrusted with dry dirt left within it after the removal of a former tenant.

FIG. 208 *Ordinary flower pot*

517 Pots are generally made in what are termed casts – that is to say, a certain quantity of clay is taken, from which one pot is made, or two, four, six, eight, twelve, sixteen, twenty-four, thirty-two, forty-eight, sixty, or eighty; and pots are therefore known to gardeners as ones, twos, fours, etc., according to the number of pots made from a single cast. This nomenclature is always puzzling to the amateur, who never knows precisely what number he wants, and so can best express his wants by measuring the outside diameter of the sized pot he requires and mentioning the number of inches to the nurseryman, who is at once able to tell what his customer wants, being thoroughly conversant with numbers and their sizes. It would be more convenient if the old system were abandoned altogether, and if numbers, from No. 1 onwards, were used to indicate successive sizes. This may be done at some potteries, for at different potteries different practices prevail; but the Chiswick standard, as it is called, is that which is most generally adopted for distinguishing the sizes of pots, and it will be convenient, as this is in most general use, to give this, with the diameter and depth of each size, *inside measurement*, and the price, singly and per dozen.

Sizes	Top Diam in ins.	Depth in ins.	Price Singly	Price Per Doz.
Thimbles	2	2	½d.	3d.
Thumbs	2½	2½	½d.	4d.
Sixties	3	3½	¾d.	5d.
Fifty-fours	4	4	¾d.	6d.
Forty-eights	4½	5	1d.	9d.
Thirty-twos	6	6	1½d.	1s. 3d.
Twenty-fours	8½	8	2d.	2s. 0d.
Sixteens	9½	9	3½d.	3s. 6d.
Twelves	11½	10	4½d.	4s. 6d.
Eights	12	11	6d.	6s. 0d.
Sixes	13	12	10½d.	10s. 6d.
Fours	15	13	1s. 6d.	17s. 6d.
Twos	18	14	2s. 6d.	30s. 0d.

The above measurements may be taken as the general average of each size, and every pot in a cast will approximate very closely to the size given. Indeed, it is wonderful to find how similar pots belonging to a cast are in form and dimensions, considering that they are not moulded, but fashioned on a wheel. The above sizes, as it has been said, and the numbers also, are according to the Chiswick standard, which is understood and followed by nurserymen; the prices per dozen and singly are nurserymen's prices, or may be taken as a fair scale of the prices one would expect to pay if buying of a nurseryman and not direct from the maker.

518 The Chiswick standard, indeed, is very generally followed, but at different potteries different practices prevail. Thus, by Mr John Matthews, The Royal Pottery, Weston-super-Mare, Somerset, the following are the numbers adopted, with the sizes, showing the clear inside diameter at top and the prices per dozen.

It will be noted that the graduation of the sizes is effected with greater regularity of progression, and that instead of thirteen sizes only, as given in the above table, under the system of making in casts, there are twenty-three sizes, five of which are larger than the largest size according to the old system:

No.	Clear inside diameter	Price per dozen	No.	Clear inside diameter	Price per dozen	No.	Clear inside diameter	Price per dozen	No.	Clear inside diameter	Price per dozen
1	1¾ in.	3d.	7	5½ in.	1s.0d.	13	11 in.	7s.0d.	19	20 in.	4s.6d.
2	2¼ in.	3d.	8	6¼ in.	1s.6d.	14	12½ in.	10s.6d.	20	22 in.	9s.0d.
3	2¾ in.	4d.	9	7 in.	2s.0d.	15	14 in.	14s.0d.	21	24 in.	12s.6d.
4	3¼ in.	5d.	10	8 in.	2s.6d.	16	15 in.	17s.6d.	23	26 in.	17s.6d.
5	4 in.	6d.	11	9 in.	3s.6d.	17	16 in.	21s.0d.	24	30 in.	25s.0d.
6	4¾ in.	9d.	12	10 in.	4s.6d.	18	18 in.	2s.6d.			

The following table, showing the weight of pots sent out in quantities, and the number of pots to a ton approximately for each size, will be useful to buyers on a large scale:

No.	Quantity	Approx. Weight Tns/Cwt/Qrs	Approx. No. of Pots to Ton	No.	Quantity	Approx. Weight Tns/Cwt/Qrs.	Approx. No. of Pots to ton	No.	Quantity	Approx. Weight Tns/Cwt/Qrs.	Approx. No. of Pots to ton
1	1000	– 1 1	16,000	**9**	500	– 17 0	600	**17**	100	2 0 0	50
2	1000	– 1 3	12,000	**10**	500	1 4 0	400	**18**	12	– 5 2	46
3	1000	– 3 0	6,500	**11**	500	1 13 0	300	**19**	12	– 7 2	34
4	1000	– 4 0	5,000	**12**	500	2 5 0	225	**20**	12	– 10 0	24
5	1000	– 6 3	3,000	**13**	100	– 12 0	170	**21**	6	– 6 0	20
6	1000	– 10 0	2,000	**14**	100	1 0 0	100	**23**	6	– 7 0	17
7	1000	– 17 0	1,200	**15**	100	1 10 0	66	**24**	6	– 9 0	13
8	1000	1 0 0	1,000	**16**	100	1 12 0	62				

519 The diameter of the saucer over the top, inside measurement, should be the same as the pot which it is intended to place it in, and this will serve as a guide when purchasing saucers to suit particular sizes of pots. Saucers cost the same as the pots which they are intended to accompany, for although less material is used in their manufacture they are more difficult to make and are not so much in request, therefore, as a matter of necessity, their prices rule higher.

520 There are other kinds and forms of pots which must be mentioned, but of these it may be as well to say that their prices may be best learnt of the nurseryman who sells them or of the manufacturer by whom they are made. Among these may be specified as being most noteworthy:

1 *Long Toms* – Pots without rims, made only in the smaller sizes – that is to say, from about 2½ inches to 5 inches in diameter, and about half as deep again as ordinary pots, with diameters ranging between these two extremes. They are

not so shapely in appearance as the ordinary pots, nor so convenient for general purposes, but they are serviceable for growing hyacinths and other bulbs.

2 *Oxfords* – These are pots with broad rims pierced with holes, which afford the means of tying down the branches of plants that require training of this description the better to exhibit their blossoms, etc. The holes are also useful for holding the points of wires to which trellises are attached, or to which plants or their branches may be tied.

3 *Pots with Double Rims* – Pots so called resemble the Oxford pots in so far that the rim is utilised for a special purpose by increasing its breadth, so that both kinds, in point of fact, are really pots with broad rims. In the class of pot now under consideration the rim is not pierced as in the Oxford pots, but is grooved in order to receive the edge of a bell glass to be placed, if necessary, over any plant or cuttings in the pot. By this mode of construction plant space within the rim of the pot is not abridged, and cuttings can be placed close to or against the sides of the pot, which is not possible if the covering glass stands on the soil. The double-rimmed pot, therefore, possesses special advantages as a propagating pot, and if water or wetted sand be placed in the grooved rim, and the edge of the bell glass be covered by one or the other rising above it, the pot will be converted for the time into a miniature Wardian case, as no air can find its way into the interior of the glass under its edges.

4 *Pots for Orchids* – The conditions under which orchids grow and are grown differ in many respects from those under which ordinary plants are cultivated in pots. As a general rule, the roots of plants do not seek egress from the pot, unless they find themselves cramped too closely within its limits, and make their way through the drainage and out of the hole at the bottom of the pot to seek nutriment from any moisture that there may be in the saucer and from the air; they do not court exposure, otherwise than this, to the air and light. The orchid, however, delights to thrust its thick and fleshy roots into the air, and requires aeration in the soil more than any other class of plants. Orchid pots or pans are therefore perforated with holes of various shapes, both in the bottom and all round the sides from bottom to rim, and provision is frequently made by holes just below the rim by which they can be suspended from the roof, etc., of any building. Through these holes the air can easily obtain access to the roots of the plants, and the roots can as readily make their way into the air. Some orchid pots are made with false bottoms, removable from the pot at pleasure, and also perforated. Orchids require thorough drainage, as well as aeration of the material in which they grow, and this is also provided for by the structure of the orchid pot.

Orchid baskets, which are of the greatest importance and utility in orchid growing, are supplied by Mr J. E. Bonny, Downs Park Road, Hackney, London, in sizes ranging from 3 inches to 12 inches in diameter, and at prices ranging from 4s. 6d. per dozen for the smallest size named to 25s. per dozen for the largest. Rafts and boats for these beautiful plants are supplied by Mr Bonny at 1d. each the former and 1½d. each the latter, and cylinders at 2d. per inch run. This will furnish the grower with some idea of the cost of the appliances necessary for this branch of gardening.

5 *Double Pots for Alpine Plants* – Pots of this description are manufactured in pairs, the outer vessel forming a receptacle for the inner vessel, in which the plant itself is set. The inner pot is made in the usual way, with a means of escape for surplus water at the bottom, but the outer pot is not. Thus, water or damp moss or cocoanut fibre may be placed in the outer pot, and thus the roots of the plant in the inner receptacle and the soil in which it grows may be kept cool and at an equal temperature, even in the heat of summer. The material of which these double pots are made is better than that which is used for ordinary pots, and not nearly so porous, and this prevents any considerable absorption of water by the inner pot.

6 *Seed Pans* – Earthenware pans for raising seed and for striking small cuttings are similar in shape to saucers, but are, of course, very much larger. They are usually provided with three holes in the bottom for drainage, and are made in different sizes.

7 *Ornamental Pots, Vases, Baskets, etc.* – These are generally made in terra cotta, and are attractive in appearance, though of no greater utility than the ordinary flower pot. They are produced in various forms and shapes, from that of the ordinary flower pot and seed pan, relieved with bands disposed in imitation of trellis work on the exterior, to the rustic jardinière, which is usually fashioned to resemble the trunk of a tree. This receptacle for plants is open at the top and pierced with holes at the sides, whose sides project from the main structure after the manner of boughs that have been sawn off short.

8 *Propagating Frames* – These are earthen pans, square in shape, and having a slanting top after the manner of a cucumber frame. The rim is rebated, to have recourse to a term used in carpentry – that is to say, lowered in a step-like form along the inner edge of both sides and the bottom, so as to afford support for a sheet of glass placed over the interior. They are more handy than seed pans, because the means of covering seeds and cuttings placed within them is far more simple and less costly than the bell glass with which the seed pan must be covered if it be necessary to afford protection to any seeds that are being raised or cuttings that are being struck in it. These propagating frames were introduced by Mr Looker, and are manufactured by all the leading makers of coarse earthenware, and notably by Messrs F. Rosher and Co., Upper Ground Street, Blackfriars, King's Road, Chelsea, and Kingsland Road, who will forward an illustrated price list post free to any applicant. Seed pans, measuring 9 inches by 6 inches by 3 inches, or in other words, 9 inches long, 6 inches wide, and 3 inches deep, are supplied by Mr Tippetts, Aston, Birmingham, at 5s. per dozen.

9 *Prices of Pots, etc.* – The prices of ordinary pots have been given. With regard to Long Toms, their price is much the same as the common pots. Oxfords, double-rimmed pots, Alpine pots, and orchid pots and pans cost from half as much again to twice as much as the ordinary pots. Seed pans are about the same in price as pots of the same diameter. Ornamental pots command much higher prices, which vary according to size. Small quantities of pots may be bought by the amateur of the nearest nurseryman, but gardeners and all who require them in large quantities will go direct to the manufacturers. Before

giving an order it is desirable to procure the price lists of manufacturing firms, such as Mr John Matthews, Royal Pottery, Weston-super-Mare, who supplies a useful guinea crate of pots, especially suitable for amateurs, and who will send his price list to any applicant free, or furnish a book of designs for 1s., or a sheet of designs for 6d., in which all his specialities are carefully illustrated. Buyers in London and neighbourhood should visit the depots of Messrs F. Rosher and Co., at Upper Ground Street, Blackfriars, King's Road, and Kingsland Road, who also send illustrated price lists free on application. The firms just mentioned supply everything in garden ware, both useful and ornamental, including tiles, vases, fountains, baskets, arborettes, jardinières, etc., which are far too numerous to be specified here, with prices of various qualities, sizes, etc. In addition to the guinea crate sent out from the Weston-super-Mare Potteries, it will be useful to mention that Mr H. Goddard. Pottery, Dennett Street, Queen's Road, Peckham, London, sends out, free to rail for cash, a useful case of pots for 7s. 6d., containing 12 8-inch pots, 20 6-inch pots, 50 5-inch pots, 50 4- inch pots, and 50 3-inch pots – in all, 182 pots; and Mr Henry Wainwright, 8 and 10 Alfred Street, Boar Lane, Leeds, sends out for 10s., package included, 60 3½-inch, 54 4-inch pots, 48 4½-inch pots and 36 5-inch pots – in all, 198 pots.

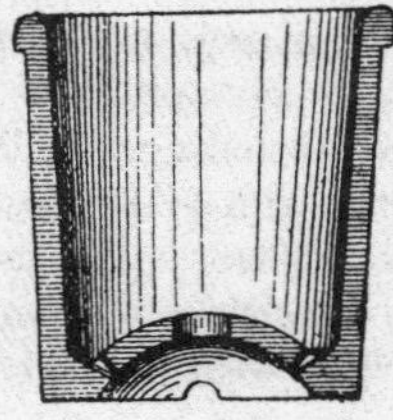

FIG. 209 *Section of pot, showing interior and from of base*

521 *Crute's Patent Concave Flower Pot.* – This new flower pot forms a very desirable addition to existing garden and greenhouse appliances of this kind. The flower pot itself is well made, to judge from the specimen before me, and differs from the ordinary earthen flower pot in being straighter in the sides, deeper and wider in the base; consequently, if one of the Concave Flower Pots be taken and one of the ordinary shape, both being the same in diameter at the top, the former will be both longer and larger at the bottom, and therefore afford more room for mould and the roots of the plant. This will be seen from Fig. 209, which gives a sectional view of the pot, and shows its interior and the structure of the bottom, which is concave, like the bottom of a wine bottle, and is perforated with a large hole in the centre and three smaller holes at the sides, which afford an immediate escape for any surplus water when it reaches the channel that encircles the bottom of the pot inside. Fig. 210, which exhibits a view of the exterior of the bottom, shows the relative position of the holes just described and three grooves in the edge of the bottom, which facilitate the passage of the external air into and

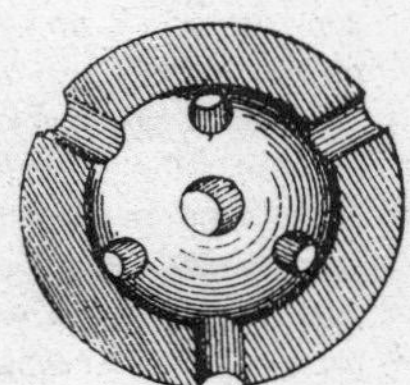

FIG. 210 *Plan of view of outside of bottom of pot*

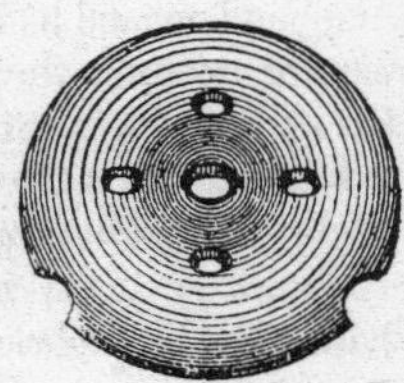

FIG. 211 *Patent cap, used as substitute for crocks*

upwards in the pot, thus ventilating its centre, and tending to induce vigorous plant growth. The pots may be obtained of any florist and seedsman in the United Kingdom, or of the patentee, Mr James Crate, 14 Knightrider Street, London. The sizes and prices of pots per dozen are as follows: 4½ inch pots at 9d.; 5½ inch pots at 1s.; 6-inch pots at 2s.; 7-inch pots at 3s.; 8½-inch pots at 4s. 6d.; 10-inch pots at 6s.; the size, in every case, being the top diameter. The larger sizes are sold singly – 12-inch pots at 1s.; 14-inch pots at 1s. 6d.; 16-inch pots at 3s. 6d.; 18-inches pots at 6s.; and 20-inch pots at 10s. 6d.

522 *Crute's Patent Cap* The Patent Caps, which are shown in Fig. 211, and which resemble small saucers, pierced with five holes at the bottom, and grooved in three places in the upper edge, are used instead of crocks, and before potting any plant one of these is placed inside the pot, on the bottom, and immediately over the large hole in the bottom of the pot itself. The caps may be used with ordinary pots; they induce perfect drainage, save crocking, a troublesome proceeding to many amateurs, and facilitate repotting, for when a stick with a diameter larger than the hole in the bottom of the cap is pushed through the hole in the bottom of the pot, cap, mould, and plant are lifted out of the pot altogether, and may be easily transferred to another and larger pot, or placed in the ground. The caps are supplied at 6d. per dozen.

The merits claimed for Crute's pot and cap are that by their use flowers and plants may be grown to perfection without trouble, that perfect drainage is provided, the use of crocks is greatly abridged, if not saved altogether, ventilation and aeration in the interior of the pot is secured, and evaporation lessened. It is further stated that insects and worms, through the peculiar construction of the bottom, are prevented from entering the pot; but I venture to think that this is doubtful. It is certain, however, that the construction of the bottom will prevent clogging where the pots are plunged in earth, and thus the pots are therefore especially well suited for plants that are kept within doors during the winter and spring, and plunged in the open ground in summer and autumn. In repotting from these pots, when patent caps are used, the plant remains erect, and is not turned upside down, or very nearly so, as is the case in taking plants out of ordinary pots. All that is necessary is to place the pot over an upright stick, which should pass through the bottom, when with gentle pressure the plant with the earth intact remains in the hands, the empty pot sliding down the stick.

523 *Pots for Blanching* Before quitting the subject of pots, it is necessary to state that pots of coarse earthenware are made and supplied for covering up sea kale and rhubarb in the winter months, in order to induce growth in the latter and to blanch or whiten the growing heads of the former, which would otherwise be tough and uneatable. These pots are placed over the plants named, and litter, or manure in which straw abounds, and leaves, are placed around and above them. Thus the temperature within the pot is raised, the plant is started into growth, and the exclusion of the light prevents the stalks and leaves from assuming the colour they present when growing in the open air. Blanching pots for rhubarb are long and comparatively narrow, something like a chimney pot of common shape; pots for seakale are wider and shorter, and rounded at the top. Both are open at the top as well as at the bottom, and provided with covers, which can be taken off when it is desired to inspect the growth of the plant within. These pots cost, for rhubarb, 12 inches diameter, 18s., and 16 inches diameter, 24s. per dozen; for seakale, the same sizes, 12s. and 18s. per dozen.

524 Pots are absolutely necessary to all who take to pot culture of plants for greenhouses, conservatories, and window gardening, and their low price brings them within the reach of all. For everything else the amateur, the cottager, and the professional gardener of limited means may easily provide a substitute. For the double pot, one plunged within a larger one will answer the purpose. This outer pot may have the hole in the bottom plugged with a cork, or otherwise stopped, and the inner pot may be raised within the other, so as not to rest on the bottom, by a wire trivet, a few crocks, or even a small saucer turned upside down, so that space may be obtained between the outer pot and the inner pot wherein to put water or any substance that is retentive of water. An ordinary flower pot may be converted into an orchid pot by making holes in it with a brace and small bit, enlarging them, when bored through the ware, with a rose bit. A soft pot should be chosen for this kind of work, and when boring the holes the interior of the pot should be filled with some soft substance, say, felt rags, tightly stuffed within it. The operation is perhaps somewhat difficult and tedious, but it can be done. Orchids, moreover, will grow in baskets made of wire, or even of bits of stick or wood strung together on wires that are first passed through a wooden bottom, or otherwise connected. The use of the double-rimmed pot is advocated for the better growing of cuttings, because the cuttings can be placed against the side of the pot, but anyone may do as well without them as with them by resorting to a contrivance such as exhibited in Fig. 212. In this the outer pot is partially filled with mould or compost of a light and porous nature, and a small pot, whose bottom has been plugged with cork so as to fill the hole in it, is placed on the mould so that its rim is about an inch above the rim of the outer, pot. More soil is then put in the outer pot until it is from 1 inch to ½ inch below its rim, and by doing this the inner pot is partially buried. The inner pot is then filled with water, and the cuttings are placed round it. A bell glass is then placed over the whole. The cuttings are kept moist by absorption of the water in the inner pot through its sides into the soil without, and there is no necessity to water them or the soil in which they are set. Sometimes the inner pot is filled with mould and the cuttings are placed round its edge; when this is done, the outer pot should be filled with cocoanut fibre or sand, and this should be kept moist.

FIG. 212 *Simple contrivance for striking cuttings*

525 For propagating boxes, any of the boxes, large or small, in which articles of various descriptions, such as cocoa, starch, mustard, tinned salmon and lobster, Swiss milk, etc., are sent in bulk to grocers, may be easily adapted to suit the purpose in view, and they can be easily cut so that the top may slant in one direction, as in Fig. 213, or both ways, like the roof of a house, ledges being nailed externally to sides and bottom to form a rebate to receive the glass. If the box be deep enough, triangular pieces must be cut off each side and the front reduced in order to give the proper inclination to the glass, but if the box be shallow triangular pieces may be added to the sides, and the back raised as shown by the dotted lines in the illustration. Seed pans may be formed out of the bottoms of butter tubs and mustard tubs, both of which may be bought for a few pence of any grocer. And these tubs, when of sufficient size, answer every practical purpose for forcing rhubarb, while half-tubs will be large enough for seakale.

FIG. 213 *Box converted into propagating case*

526 *Tubs, Boxes, and Window Boxes* For growing large plants and shrubs that cannot conveniently be grown even in pots of the largest size, tubs and boxes must be used. Sometimes the larger butter tubs from the grocer will be found sufficient as far as size goes, but it is desirable to have them girt with iron hoops, as the wooden hoops frequently give in a short time by the swelling of the wood of the tub by the moisture absorbed from the soil within when the plant is watered. Strong tubs, such as halves of wine casks, etc., may be obtained of the cooper. Boxes of any kind and size may be made by the gardener if he can turn his hand to the execution of a little simple carpentry. It is not possible, however, to dwell at any length on the construction of such appliances here, though it is necessary to call attention to them as being among the numerous appliances of various kinds that are used in gardening, and may be required at some time or other by every gardener.

527 *Appliances Necessary for Watering, etc.* The rain, when it falls, washes the leaves of plants in its descent, clearing the surface of these organs from dust and all impurities that may have been deposited upon them in dry weather, and so enabling them the better to discharge their especial functions, which they cannot do when their pores are clogged and choked with dust and dirt. The rain further enters the soil, and in its downward passage conveys to the roots the moisture which is necessary for the sustenance of plant life and for the assimilation of the nutriment that they derive from the soil itself and manures of every kind. To assist Nature in the open ground of the garden, *when* the rain does not fall as frequently as the growing plants and trees may require, and *where* the rain cannot fall, as in glazed structures, to imitate Nature is manifestly the duty of every gardener; and to carry out this task, which is imposed on him by the exigencies of plant life and plant culture, he must avail himself of certain contrivances for the conveyance and distribution of the refreshing life-giving fluid. The chief and most necessary of these are the water pot and the syringe, and next to these the hydropult and garden hose and its carriage, which partake more of the nature of the latter than of the former.

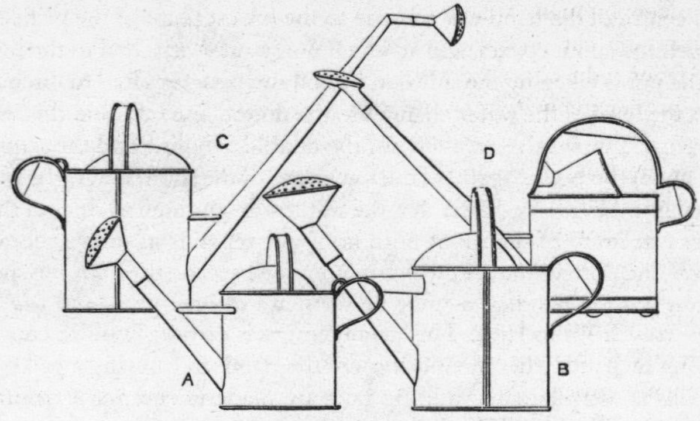

FIG. 214 *Different forms of water pots*

528 *The Water Pot* The principle of the water pot is the same in every case, but the forms of these appliances differ slightly one from another. They are made of tinplate and zinc, and unless lightness is a desideratum those of zinc are preferable, because they are more durable than those of tinplate, though they are heavier to carry. Zinc pots are generally sold unpainted, but those of tinplate are supplied in two colours, red and green, the red being the cheaper. The Paxton pot, supplied by Messrs Deane and Co., 46 King William Street, London Bridge, London, is painted blue. The body of the water pot is cylindrical in form, with a flat bottom, with three bosses or feet of metal attached to the larger and better kinds to keep the bottom from touching the ground when out of use, and partly covered with a crescent shaped, slightly domed top, the object of which is to prevent the escape of the water over the brim of the cylindrical body when tilted, as it would do if there were no cover. Some of the different forms are shown at A, B, C, D, in Fig. 214, in which A represents, the ordinary form, with the rose attached in the usual way; B, a pot of the same construction, with the rose reversed on the spout, so as to distribute the water over a larger area; C, the same construction, with a long spout and fine rose; and D, the Paxton pot, in which the form of the handle is altogether different, as well as that of the rose and the semi-cover. In the ordinary form of pot the handles are disposed as in Fig. 215, a diagram which is given for the purpose of clearly showing the utility of construction. The handle across the top is for conveying the water pot from one place to another, the handle at the side for holding the pot while discharging its contents. In carriage the surface of the water is parallel to the bottom of the pot, but in watering the level changes and maintains a position always at right angles to the dotted line that runs

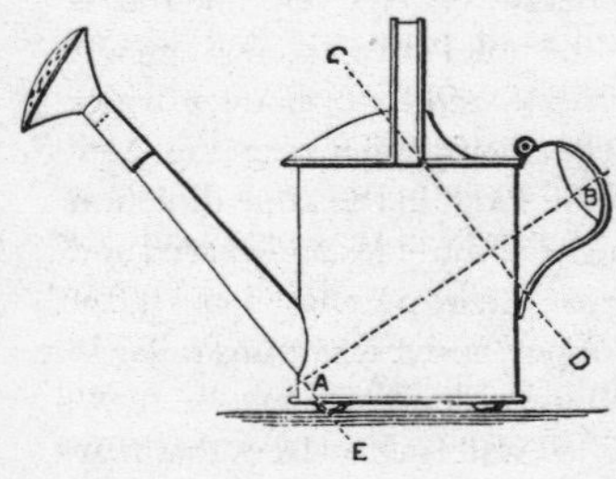

FIG. 215 *Construction of water pot*

from the centre of the handle at the side to the lowest point of the orifice in the body which the spout covers, and at which the spout is attached to the body. As soon as the pot is taken by the side handle and the vessel is tilted to discharge its contents, the level of the water changes to the dotted line CD, and this, without further remark, shows the necessity for the double handling and the semi-cover over the top of the body. Again, as the lower line of the spout is at right angles to the dotted line AB, it is manifest that the water will continue to run out through the upper extremity of the spout until no water remains in the vessel except a little below the dotted line AE, which cannot well escape through the spout. In the Paxton pot the handles, as may be seen, are in one piece, and run in one direction from front to back. This arrangement is obviously more convenient for carrying by hand, when the position of the hands in carrying a pail of water or two pails is considered. Watering pots are made in seven sizes, numbered respectively from 0 to 6. Those that are painted red are always cheaper than those that are painted green, because red paint is cheaper than green paint. Red watering pots range in price, according to size, from 1s. 2d. to 5s. 9d., and green watering pots from 1s. 6d. to 6s. 6d. Green watering pots with a long spout and fine rose are supplied in sizes 0, 1, 2, 3, at from 1s. 9d. to 4s., but if a brass screw rose be supplied the price of each size is 1s. more. The Paxton watering pots are made in six sizes, from 1 to 6, and are sold at prices ranging from 3s. 3d. to 9s., according to size. Special pots for watering strawberries are supplied in sizes 1, 2, and 3, at 1s. 8d., 2s. 4d., and 3s. 3d. respectively.

529 That the orifice of the spout when the rose is removed should be above the level of the top of the cylinder that forms the body is easily understood, when it is remembered that water, both in body and spout, will rise to the same level during the process of filling the pot, and that if the spout were too short it would not be possible to fill the pot. The longer the spout, the more convenient the water pot becomes for watering plants standing to the rear of others, especially in greenhouses, windows, etc. Roses are of different shapes, the most common form being circular, as shown in A, B, and C, Fig. 214. The finer the holes in the rose, the more gentle will be the shower of drops that will be scattered from it on the plants below. When a very fine rose is required, the best material for the plate in which the holes are pierced is brass. A flat, upturned rose, as shown with the Paxton pot, tends to cause a wider distribution of the water, and this may also be effected by a flat rose, Fig. 216, which is a sort of continuation and expansion of the spout in the same direction by two plates, connected by a narrow band, straight at the sides and curved and perforated in front. I do not say that this kind of rose can be purchased, but it can easily be made by any tin-man to suit any kind of pot, and it is not unsimilar in construction to those attached to hydropults and to garden hose.

FIG. 216 *Flat rose*

530 *The Garden Hose* The water pot is intended for watering surfaces that may be broadly characterised as horizontal, in opposition to the perpendicular surfaces of walls or the interior surfaces of roofs, for which the syringe is required

FIG. 217 *Garden hose*

It is impossible to water a perpendicular surface with a watering pot with any degree of ease and comfort to the operator; it is true that a tree may be sprinkled by tossing the pot to and fro in upward, downward, and lateral directions, but the operation is too fatiguing to be continued for any length of time and therefore effectual. The garden hose, however, here comes in opportunely as a means by which the surface, both of ground and of walls, may be readily watered at one and the same time, and by which, in gardens of moderate size, the trouble of carrying water from its source, whatever it may be, to the spot where it is required, is altogether obviated. The ordinary garden hose consists of vulcanised india rubber tubing, which is usually supplied in sixty-feet lengths, with brass union joints, tap for controlling the issue, and spreader for dispersing the water when the tap is turned on, as shown in Fig. 217. The better way of using the hose is to connect it by the junction shown in the centre of the illustration to a tap fixed in a pipe attached to some cistern above the level of the ground or top of the wall it is proposed to water. The fluid will then find its way by pressure from above through the hose, and escape in a widely-spread shower through the spreader when the tap is turned on. For the safe keeping of the hose when out of use, and for its easy conveyance from one part of the garden to another, wherever it may be required, hose reels of galvanised iron are supplied, as shown in Fig. 218. This consists of a frame with a cylinder, having broad plates at each end, and a handle by which the hose may be wound and unwound between the plates at pleasure, with wheels at one side of the bottom of the frame on which it rests when the upper end of the frame is depressed, and by which the whole machine can be wheeled about at will, the upper part of the frame acting like the handles of a wheelbarrow. Patent vulcanised garden hose is supplied, with the necessary unions, taps, and spreaders, at the following prices

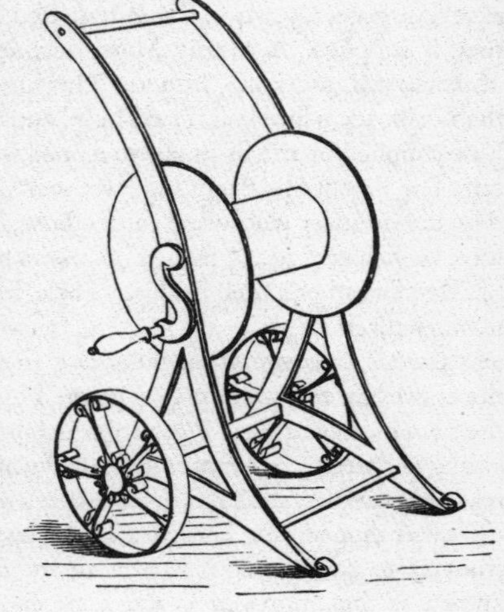

FIG. 218 *Iron hose reel*

per yard, the prices being regulated by the character of the hose, as 2, 3, or 4-ply:

Diam.	2-ply	3-ply	4-ply	Diam.	2-ply	3-ply	4-ply
½ inch	1s. 3½d.	1s. 4½d.	–	¾ inch	1s. 8d.	1s. 11d.	2s. 0d.
⅝ inch	1s. 5½d.	1s. 7½d.	1s. 9d.	1 inch	2s. 1d.	2s. 4d.	2s. 6d.

Galvanised Hose Reels, to carry 100 and 200 feet of ⅝-inch hose, are supplied at 16s. and 18s. each, respectively. Messrs J. J. Thomas and Co., 87 Queen Victoria Street, London send out some excellent wrought iron hose reels at the following prices: 17 inches diameter and 11 inches wide, to carry 200 feet of ½-inch hose, at 13s. 6d.; 17 inches diameter and 13 inches wide, to carry 200 feet off ⅝-inch hose, at 15s. 6d.; and 18 inches in diameter and 14 inches wide, to carry 200 feet of ¾-inch hose, at 18s. 6d.

531 The Overspun India Rubber Garden Hose is considered superior to the ordinary vulcanised garden hose, on account of its being lighter, more pliable, and stronger. It consists of a casing of textile material, woven over a thin tubing of india rubber. The lessened bulk of the india rubber tubing renders the hose lighter, which makes the handling easy when great lengths are brought into use, and the combination of thin tubing and the woven outer coating causes it to be more pliable. The outer webbing with which the rubber tubing is encompassed takes off much of the pressure of the water, and renders the latter less liable to burst through pressure in any spot that may be weaker than the rest of the hose. Its strength, indeed, is said to be about eight times as great as ordinary hose, while its weight is less than half. This hose is manufactured at the Irwell India Rubber and Gutta Percha Works, Limited, Salford, Manchester, and 6 Billiter Street, London, and is sold by all nurserymen, seedsmen, and ironmongers. An excellent hose, known as the Patent Red Rubber Garden Hose, with suitable reel, is supplied by Messrs Merryweather and Sons, Fire Engine and Hose Makers, 63 Long Lane, London This hose has the advantage of being lighter than ordinary white vulcanised hose, and is said to last four times as long. All hose supplied by the firms above named is thoroughly tested before being sent out. The Patent Overspun India Rubber Garden Hose is a little higher in price than the ordinary vulcanised garden hose, ½-inch hose being supplied at 6d per foot, ⅝-inch at 7½d., ¾-inch at 9d., ⅞-inch at 10½d., and 1-inch at 1s. The cost of Merryweather's Red Rubber Hose may be learnt by application to the manufacturers.

532 *Garden Engines and Water Barrows* In a large garden the labour expended in the conveyance of water is very great. This may be reduced by the adoption of the swing water barrow, Fig. 219, which consists of a cistern of galvanised iron, swung in a strong wrought iron frame furnished with wheels in front, legs in the rear, and handles, so that it can be wheeled from place to place as requisite, and the water dipped out. These water barrows are made in different sizes, to hold from 15 to 40 gallons. A barrow of the largest capacity, namely, 40 gallons, known as the Improved Water Cart and Barrow Combined, is supplied by Messrs Deane and Co., of 46 King William Street, London. In this contrivance

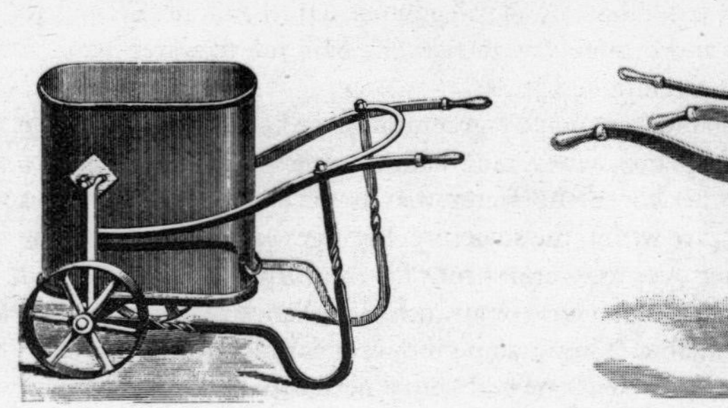

FIG. 219 *Swing water barrow*

FIG. 220 *Garden engine*

the handles are riveted to the sides of the cistern, which is covered in at top, part of the cover lifting up. It is supported on a frame with wheels 2 feet in diameter. In front is a valve, to which a spreader in the form of a cylinder pierced with holes can be attached when the barrow is required for watering lawns, or from which the water can be drawn in a pot or pail placed under the valve, the height of the wheels permitting this to be done with ease. The garden engines, Fig. 220, are similar in form to this last made machine as far as the position of the handles and wheels is concerned, but the top is perforated, and it is furnished at the top with a pillar, to which an outlet pipe furnished with a tap and spreader is attached, through which the water is forced by a small pump within, worked by the handle shown at the top. The garden engines are made in iron, galvanised and japanned, to hold from 12 to 30 gallons; two sizes, holding respectively 14 and 24 gallons, are made of oak instead of iron, a wooden tub being substituted for the cistern. As labour saving contrivances, where much water is wanted at a considerable distance from the source of supply, the water barrows and garden engines are most useful. Water barrows, with galvanised iron cisterns hung on wrought iron frames, are supplied by Messrs J. J. Thomas and Co., 87 Queen Victoria Street, London, to hold 12 gallons, at 31s. 6d.; 20 gallons at 42s., and 30 gallons at 50s. A barrow with wood tank or tub, to hold about 40 gallons, is supplied at 42s. Powerful garden engines may be had fitted to the above barrows at 42s. An excellent and cheap swing water barrow is manufactured and supplied by Messrs Barnard, Bishop, and Barnard, of Norwich. The tub is of oak, 36 gallons, and is mounted on iron wheels 22 inches in diameter. The water can be dipped out, and by merely lifting the handles the tub can be placed on the ground anywhere, and the frame detached. The barrow costs 42s., and it may easily be converted into a garden engine by introducing into it one of the small French portable engines which can be purchased of any ironmonger for 12s. 6d. American Lawn Sprinklers, which scatter the water in every direction like light rain, may be had, with four arms and fountain ball, at 21s., or with eight arms at 25s The prices of Messrs Deane and Co., 46 King William Street, London, are lower, their swing water barrows being supplied as follows: To hold 15 gallons, 30s.; 20 gallons, 36s.; 30 gallons, 46s.; and 40 gallons, 54s. Garden engines with barrows are sold, to hold 12 gallons, £5 3s.; 16 gallons, £4; 24 gallons, £5; and 30 gallons, £6. Portable Lawn Fountains, with Barker's Mill Jet, to water from 10 to 25 square feet in area, are supplied at 24s.

533 *Syringes* It is impossible to manage a greenhouse without a syringe where with to sprinkle growing plants, vines, etc., with a refreshing shower, and to inject into all parts of the house the water that is necessary to maintain a sufficient degree of moisture within the structure. Syringes are also useful in the garden for throwing water over trees and shrubs for the purpose of washing and refreshing the foliage when garden hose or any other appliance that may be used for the purpose is not available. They assume different forms, the cheapest and simplest being a zinc pipe, closed at one end with a perforated disc, and open at the other, into which a rod of wood, with a turned handle and a piece of felt or coarse woollen stuff wrapped round the opposite end, is introduced to act as a piston to draw in the water through the holes in the closed end, and to drive it out when full by thrusting the rod into the pipe. A syringe of this kind has its merit in being cheap and serviceable, but it is inconvenient on account of the tendency of the water to reach the hands both from the outside and the inside of the tube. This is obviated to a great extent by the use of a brass syringe, which, although the principle of action is precisely the same, is nevertheless more carefully constructed, being closed by a cap at both ends – that at the upper end consisting of a fine spout for the emission of water in one jet which diverges when it leaves the orifice, or of a rose for its wider dispersion. Instead of the thick wooden rod of the zinc syringe, a smaller metal rod is attached to a wooden handle, the rod passing through a hole in the cap at the lower end, and terminating within in a suitable piston. Syringes of this description are made in various sizes, and supplied at prices varying from 1s. to 19s.

534 *Cooper's Patent Protector Syringe* Of the various syringes that have hitherto been introduced for garden and greenhouse use, Cooper's Patent Protector Syringe, manufactured by Messrs Nettlefold and Sons, Birmingham, and 54 High Holborn, London, and sold by all ironmongers, appears to be the most desirable, partly on account of the numerous spray jets and fittings that may be had with certain sizes of it, and partly because, by reason of the peculiarity of its construction, all back water or drip is prevented from running down the hand, arm, or sleeve of those who use it. A representation of this syringe is given in Fig. 221, and a sectional view, showing the interior of the tube and handle and the piston, is exhibited in Fig. 222. It is made in six varieties, distinguished by size or

FIG. 221 *Cooper's patent Protector syringe*

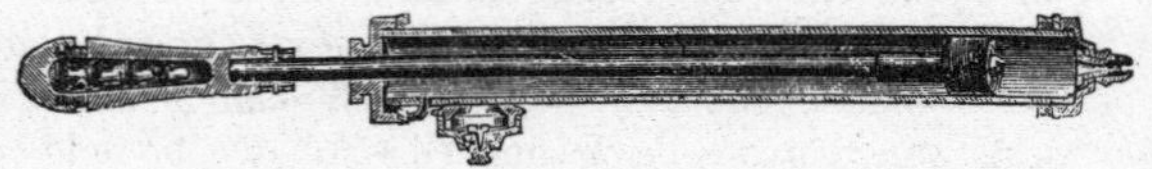

FIG. 222 *Cooper's patent Protector syringe. Section*

the fittings that accompany them. The best of them, perhaps, is No. 1, on account of the duplex spray jets or nozzles, five in number, supplied with it, which divide and distribute the water as it issues from the syringe in showers of different densities. By means of these jets moisture may be thrown in all parts of a greenhouse and on ferns and orchids in fine dew-like showers, closely resembling a very fine and almost impalpable mist. The jets that are not in use are stored away in the handle, which has a screw top, and is made hollow in order to form a receptacle for them. The numbers of the Protector Syringe from No. 1 to No. 6, showing the fittings supplied with each, and the sizes in which they are made, may be tabulated as follows:

Size	**No. 1**	**No. 2**	**No. 3**	**No. 4**	**No. 5**	**No. 6**
Length x diam	Duplex five sprays, valve, rose jets	Valve, rose and jet	Reid's ball valve two roses, and jet	Best plain two roses and and Jet	Plain rose and jet	Special Ladies' conservatory with duplex spray, rose, and jet
14in x 1in	—	—	—	—	4s. 0d.	—
14in x 1⅛in	—	—	—	—	—	6s. 0d.
16in x 1¼in	10s. 0d.	7s. 9d.	–	7s. 9d.	6s. 6d.	—
18in x 1½in	12s. 6d.	9s. 6d.	15s. 0d.	9s. 3d.	7s. 6d.	—
20in x 1¾in	15s. 0d.	12s. 6d.	18s. 0d.	12s. 0d.	—	—

535 *Protector Hose Director* The principle of the Protector Syringe has been applied to hose directors to prevent backwater or drip from inconveniencing the operator. In the simplest form the water issues through a rose, and is turned on and off by means of a stopcock. Another form, also fitted with a rose only, is contrived to regulate the stream, the issue being lessened or increased by a small lever attached to the tap, and actuated by the thumb of the person who holds it. The Combined Protector Hose Director, under which name a third form is known is fitted with a rose having a jet in its centre, and with this the stream may be regulated, and a change made in the issue of the water from rose to jet at pleasure and vice versa by a lever, which moves transversely to the pipe of issue, but which, like the other, is also moved by pressure of the thumb. Each kind is made in three sizes, namely, ½-inch, supplied at 3s., 3s. 6d., and 4s., according to variety; ⅝-inch, at 4s. 3d., 4s. 6d., and 5s.; and ¾-inch, at 5s, 5s. 6d., and 6s.

FIG. 223 *Combined Protector hose director*

536 *Hydropults and Hydronettes* These as the names imply, are contrivances for drawing into a pipe water contained in a pail or any similar receptacle, and driving it out with force to a considerable distance. Like the syringe, the simplest and cheapest form of this appliance is made in zinc. There is a vertical pipe, like the tube of a syringe, which is placed in water; at the lower end is a valve through which the water is drawn into the pipe by the upward action of the piston, which in itself also resembles the piston and rod of the syringe. When the piston is pressed downward the valve at the bottom is closed, and the water is driven upwards through a smaller tube at the side of the larger one, terminating in a spreader, which is flat in form and bent slightly outwards, so that water may be thrown against any object towards which the spreader is directed, and to some height. They are made in different sizes, as are also the Patent Hydronettes, which throw a stream of water to distances varying from 30 to 60 feet, and are supplied in four sizes, namely, No. 1, 20 inches long; No. 2, 24 inches; No. 3, 28 inches; and No. 4, 31 inches. Warner's Patent Aquaject (Fig. 224) is a similar contrivance. Above a cast iron stand, on which it is supported, rises an egg-shaped receptacle, upon which is a vertical tube, in which works a piston, surmounted by a D handle. A flexible pipe of some length, through which water is drawn into the receptacle by the action of the piston, enters the upper part of this cavity; and attached to the main pipe is another tube, also flexible, and terminating in a spreader, through which the water is ejected. From the description that has been given of these appliances, it will be seen that any amateur gardener who can use a pair of zinc shears and a soldering iron can do much to help himself, by turning out home-made articles of this class. The sizes and prices of hydronettes are as follows: No. 1, 20 inches long, 12s. 6d.; No. 2, 24 inches, 15s.; No. 3, 28 inches, 18s.; No. 4, 31 inches, 22s. Warner's Patent Aquaject costs £1 12s. 6d. These articles are supplied by Messrs Deane and Co., 46 King William Street, London.

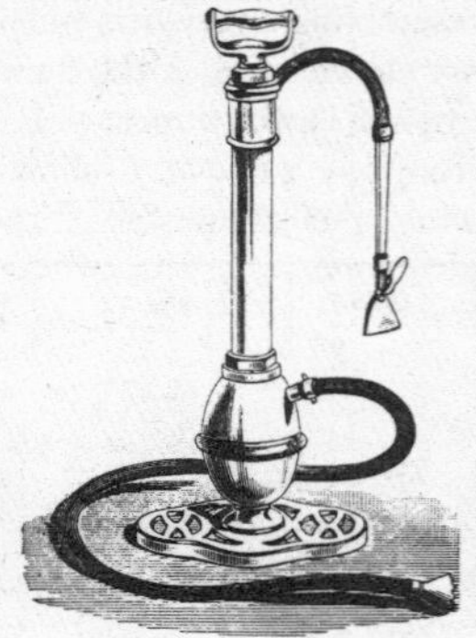

FIG. 224 *Warner's patent aquaject*

537 *The Water Witch Garden Engine* A useful and efficient means of distributing water in gentle showers in the garden, especially suitable to amateurs by reason of its cheapness, is to be found in the Water Witch Garden Engine, which is manufactured by Messrs Joseph, Brothers, 271 Liverpool Road, London, and sold by all ironmongers. This appliance is shown in Fig. 225. It consists of a tube, in which is a plunger or piston at the upper end worked by a handle, and having a strap or stirrup of iron attached to it at the other end, in which the foot of the operator is placed when working the apparatus, in order to keep it steady. From the front of

FIG. 225 *Water witch garden engine*

the main tube proceeds a piece of hose for delivery of the water, 2 feet in length, and fitted with a jet and spreader, and to the bottom is attached a suction hose, also 2 feet in length, with a perforated ball of brass at the extremity, which is placed in a pail of water, and through which water is drawn into the main tube before delivery. The engine is made of brass and wrought iron galvanised, but, if preferred, it may be had with the iron portions japanned in colours instead of being galvanised. With the jet attached to the delivery hose a continuous stream of water can be thrown to the distance of 30 feet, and with the spreader, a gentle, showery spray can be thrown over lawn and plants. Nor is its use confined to the garden only, for it is serviceable also for window cleaning and in cases of incipient fire in places where it may not be possible to throw water on the flames from a bucket. The price of the engine complete is 12s. 6d.

FIG. 226 *Maranta rosea-picta*

CHAPTER 14

Garden Tools, Implements and Appliances Required for Support and Training for Pruning, Grafting and Budding, for Designation and for Protection against Weather

538 The long array of requisites necessary for carrying out the various operations included under the broad and comprehensive term 'Gardening' are many in number, indeed, and calculated to appal the amateur, at all events, when he considers how numerous they are in the first place, the space that is required wherein to put them away when not in use in the second place, and in the third, the sum that would be swallowed up in acquiring them if all were purchased. It is necessary to mention as many as possible, for the benefit of all readers, because what may suit one may not suit another, and because when one may be content with a single watering pot, a man with ample means will provide himself with garden engines, hose and reel, and other expensive appliances, which abridge time and labour, although they cost money. In the articles that have been described in the previous chapter, it has been well nigh impossible to suggest any home-made appliances which may be manufactured by those who are able and willing to aid themselves, except in two or three cases; but we are now entering on a description of a class of articles of which many may be made with ease by the gardener himself, and which will answer the purpose for which they are intended to serve as well as those which may be purchased. It must always be borne in mind that it is not in the number of tools, implements, and appliances at a man's command that success lies, but in the care, skill, and perseverance that he displays in the prosecution of his work.

539 *Appliances for Support of Plants and their Training* These are numerous and various, composing as they do flower stakes and sticks, poles, sticks for peas and beans, stakes for espalier-trained trees, trellises of all kinds, with wire cordons stretched along the ground, or on stakes, or in advance of the surfaces of walls, with the holdfasts and straining apparatus necessary for keeping them in position and drawing them out to a necessary state of tension. Of these, some are made both of wood and iron, and some of iron alone. It will be more convenient to deal with the simple forms first of all.

540 *Natural Supports for Climbing Plants, Trailers, Trees, etc.* These are to be obtained in the country from the cuttings of hedges, the lopping of trees, and the thinning of the undergrowth in woods and coppices; but dwellers in towns of any size must seek them from the woodyard, whither they are brought from the country at certain seasons of the year and stored by the owner of the yard partly for these purposes and partly for the purpose of making wooden hoops for casks. For the support of pea vines, or for sticking small patches and rows of sweet peas, the flat spreading boughs of the birch are the best when they can be obtained, or the larger and almost as flat boughs of the beech, hazel, etc. The flatter the boughs, or in other words, the more the branchlets of the boughs extend from the main stems in the form of a fan when spread out, and in the same plane, the better and the more useful they are, because the sides of the rows of sticks, when thrust into the ground, will be more regular in appearance, and can be more trimly arranged. For scarlet beans or scarlet runners, large sticks of this description are extremely handy, when they are allowed to climb as high as they will, but for beans the more usual course is to stick them on each side with a row of slender poles, about 1 inch or a little more in diameter at the bottom, tapering to about ½ inch at the top, and about 6 feet in height, or a little more. The pea sticks are supplied at about 9d. to 1s per bundle, and the long bean sticks at 1s. 6d. per bundle. The latter may, when fairly straight and cut in two, be utilised as flower sticks. All pea sticks, bean poles, and other poles used for the support of trees and plants, should be sharpened at the bottom before being used, and dipped in tar or a preparation of coal dust, mixed to the consistency of cream and applied like paint, to preserve the ends from the effects of damp absorbed from the soil. These slight poles, when split, are useful for the ornamentation of summer houses, vases, window boxes, etc., in rustic mosaic, portions sawn to the requisite lengths being disposed over the surface in regular arrangement, so as to form patterns of different kinds. The poles can be further utilised as supports for patches of *Convolvulus major* and other climbers of a kindred nature. For supporting young trees when newly planted, stakes nearly as thick as the wrist at the bottom, and about 7 feet long, are required. The thick end of these, when sharpened, should be thrust into the ground, into a hole made with a crowbar for the purpose, in a slanting direction, so that the upper part may be brought close to the young standard that it is desired to stake, the object being to prevent the roots of the tree being too much shaken by the action of the wind on the head of the tree: the steadier a young and newly-planted tree is kept, the more readily will it take hold of the soil by its roots. These thicker poles are sold at from 1s. to 2s. per dozen, according to size.

541 *Artificial Supports of Wood* There are many plants in the garden besides climbers and trailers that require support, and it is desirable, if possible and practicable, that these supports should be formed of the natural woods, in the form of sticks that are as straight as it is possible to get them, protected from the weather by a coat of hard white varnish applied over the bark. Failing these, flower sticks must be used that are cut out of wood. These are usually kept in stock by nurserymen, painted light green, and sold according to size. The amateur may make them for himself out of laths and boards of different thicknesses. Laths used by plasterers are easily split, and if straight in the grain will separate into three, or even four, light but rough sticks, strong enough for carnations and the smaller kinds of plants when blooming. Other sticks may be sawn out of planks varying from ⅜ inch to ⅛ inch in thickness. The planks should be divided into as many spaces as their width will admit, each space being equal to the thickness of the board in width, with an allowance for the breadth of the saw-cut. The object in doing this is to render the sticks as nearly square in form as possible. When the strips have been cut into suitable lengths, the rough exterior should be lightly taken off on all sides with the plane, and the sticks painted, after being sharpened at the bottom and cut into pyramid form at the top. For stakes 1 inch square and upwards it is as well to get the boards cut into lengths at the sawyard, for sawing thick boards is hard work, as is well known by everyone who has tried it. Brown is a better colour for sticks than the pale green that is generally used. It does not contrast so conspicuously with the colours of the leaves and flowers, and is more in accordance with the less obtrusive hue of natural sticks.

542 *Means of Attachment of Plants to Supports* As regards the means of attaching plants to sticks and supports of all kinds, if it be a tree to a stake, or the stem of a hard-wooded plant, such as the honeysuckle, etc., that may be tied without danger of injuring the bark, tarred cord may be used. Of course, climbing plants may be tied loosely so as not to cut into the bark or stem in any way; but when a tree is tied to a supporting stake, it must be bound to it tightly. To prevent injury to the bark, something soft must intervene between the string and the tree and the stake. There is nothing better for this purpose than a piece of old Victoria felt carpeting, a strip of which may be wrapped three or four times round the stem, as shown at A in Fig. 227, or folded to form a wad, and placed on the side of the tree opposite to that on which it is touched by the stake, as at B; but if the latter mode be adopted, it is desirable to place another thickness or two of the felt between the tree and the stake, to prevent them from being in absolute contact. The tarred cord may then be tied as tightly as it is possible to tie it. For tying plants and blooms of plants to sticks, etc., bast was formerly used, obtained from Russian matting made of the inner bark of the lime or linden tree. It was necessary to soak this to render it tough enough for the purpose, for when dry it is extremely brittle. Of late years it has been superseded by raffia, a material obtained from the leaves of a palm. This is sold by all nurserymen and seedsmen, at about 6d. per pound. It is very light, and the long strands are plaited together in lengths of about three feet, or a little more. The plait should be undone and tied at the thick end, to render the strands ready for use. The fibre is extremely tough, and can be used just as it is without soaking, which is a great convenience.

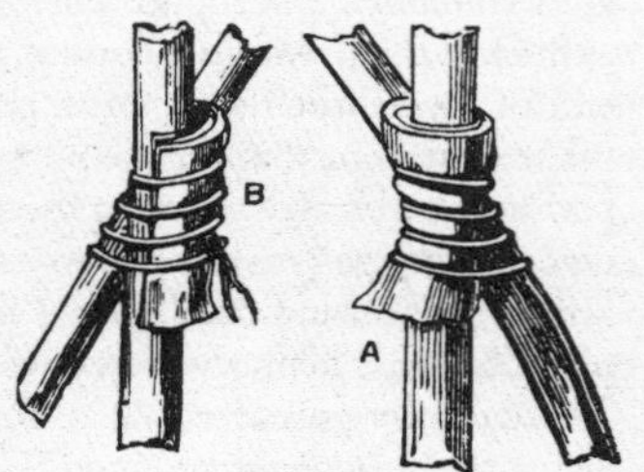

FIG. 227 *Modes of tying tree to stake*

543 *Espaliers* Both natural and artificial sticks, or sticks that are made by hand, may be used for training trees as espaliers. When natural stakes are used, they should be about 1½ inch in diameter at the bottom, and 1 inch at the top; but when made stakes are used, they should be not less than 1¼ inch square throughout from top to bottom. These sizes are, of course, for trees: they should be firmly set in the ground at a distance of from 12 inches to 15 inches apart, and their height above ground should be from 3 feet 6 inches to 5 feet, according to position and circumstances. It is not desirable that an espalier-trained tree should be more than 5 feet in height; and possibly many would consider this too high. Apples and pears are the trees that are most generally trained in this fashion. Espalier training is well adapted for gooseberries and currants. Stakes about 1 inch in diameter should be used, and these should be set in the soil about 4 inches apart, and driven in so that all may be of the same height, say, from 3 feet to 3 feet 6 inches above the soil. When the tops are level, as they should be, additional stability may be imparted to them by nailing pantile laths, 1 inch wide and ½ inch thick, along the tops from end to end. Gooseberries and currants, trained on this principle, should be planted about 4 feet to 5 feet apart, and lateral boughs first trained along the bottom in each direction, from which vertical boughs should be carried up the stakes from the laterals. Far finer fruit can be produced in this manner than on the bush system, and it is a more handy way of bordering pieces of garden ground than by apple and pear trees.

544 *Iron Flower Stakes* These have been introduced of late years as being more desirable and ligter in appearance than wooden stakes; but as they are considerably less in diameter than wooden sticks and stakes that would be used for the same plants, they are not possessed of so much holding power, as it may be termed, in the soil. For example, an iron rod ½ inch in diameter, though stronger and more lasting than a wooden stake of double its diameter, or even more, will not present so much resistance to the wind and weight of the plant that is tied to it as the latter, owing to the small amount of surface to press against the soil, and it would soon become loosened by the swaying to and fro of the plant in a tolerably high wind. In order to counteract and overcome this manifest inconvenience, iron flower stakes of this description, which, by the way, are only used for the larger kinds of plants, are furnished with a tripod-like foot, as shown at A in Fig. 228, By this contrivance a sufficient degree of stability is attained, and the stake itself may be brought close to the plant without any chance of injuring it in its main roots by the bottom of the stake when driven into the ground. The amateur who is desirous of utilising iron rods or even iron wire not less than 3⁄16 inch in gauge for flower sticks may gain stability for them by fitting the lower end into such a wooden foot as is shown at B in Fig. 228, which, from the extent of its surface, will afford enough resistance to the surrounding soil, and be sufficiently resisted by it to prevent any undue loosening, however high may be the wind that blows against the plant that is tied to it.

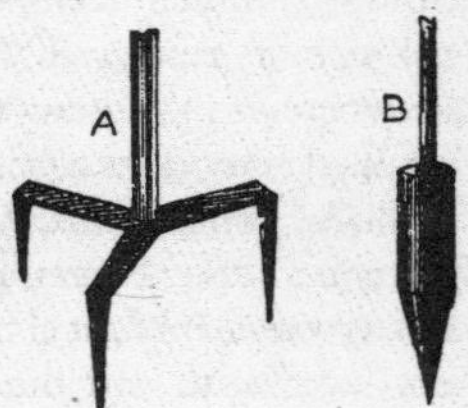

FIG. 228 *Feet for iron flower stakes*

545 An ingenious and useful appliance for sustaining plants and blooms has been introduced by Messrs Williams Brothers, Pershore Street and River Street, Birmingham, in Williams' Patent Improved Flower and Plant Supports, which do away with the necessity of securing the plant to the stick by bast or raffia. They can be quickly adjusted or removed, which renders them specially useful; and are made of the best tinned wire. The support consists of two parts – firstly, a wire with bent head that is stuck in the earth or pot, and secondly, a wire with two loops in it through which the ground stake is passed before it is thrust into the ground, and a coil at the top into which the stem of a plant or the flower stalk is introduced. The prices per gross of these supports, which are done up in 3-dozen bundles, are – 9-inch, 9s.; 12-inch, 12s. 6d.; 15-inch, 10s.; 18-inch, 10s. 6d.; 21-inch, 11s. 6d.; 24-inch, 12s.

546 *Tubular Standards* It is well known that a hollow column will support as great a weight, and be equally as rigid and unbending under a superincumbent mass, as one that is solid. It combines, in fact, strength with lightness. This is taught us by Nature in the hollow stems of cereal plants and reeds that grow in marshes. This fact has been taken advantage of by Messrs Edwin Lewis and Sons, Patent Iron Tube Works, Wolverhampton, in the formation of the tubular or hollow standards that they manufacture as supports for all kinds of trees, plants, and shrubs, and especially for standard roses and raspberry canes. These rods are of wrought iron, and are pointed in form at the bottom. It is alleged that they cannot be broken, while of the neatness of their appearance there can be no question. The diameter, externally, of these rods ranges from ⅜ inch to ¾ inch; their length is from 4 feet to 8 feet; and their price from 2s. 9d. per dozen for the smallest and shortest to 7s. 6d. per dozen for the longest and thickest.

547 *Strawberry Supporters* The contrivance shown in the annexed illustration, Fig. 229, for keeping strawberries from contract with the ground when ripening, is one that will be found useful in all gardens where strawberries are largely grown and highly prized. It is very simple, consisting only of a ring of galvanised wire supported on three stakes of the same material, which are thrust into the ground. They are manufactured and sold by Messrs Reynolds and Co., wire-work manufacturers, 57 New Compton Street, London, at 1s. Per dozen, or 11s. per gross. Improved strawberry and seedling supports are also supplied at moderate prices by Messrs Williams Brothers and Co., Pershore Street and River Street, Birmingham.

FIG. 229 *Strawberry supporter*

548 *Wooden Trellises* These are too well known to require illustration, though it is desirable to give some description of them. The simplest kind of support for creepers or plants trained by trellis against the wall of a house consists of vertical uprights from ½ inch to 1 inch in thickness, and from 1½ inch to 2 inches broad, according to circumstances, with horizontal bars 1 inch wide and ½ inch thick, nailed horizontally across them from 4 inches to 6 inches apart. The branches of the plants are then tied to the horizontal bars as they grow upwards. If a closer trellis than this is desired, it may be made by attaching vertical uprights to the walls as before, and then nailing thin laths to them diagonally, one set in one direction and the other set that surmounts them in the other direction, the laths crossing each other at regular intervals so as to form a pattern of diamonds,

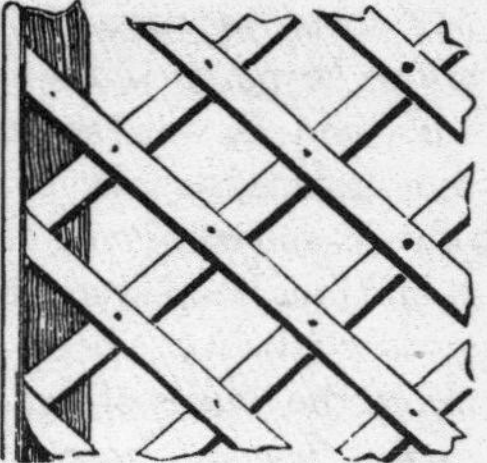
FIG. 230 *Bead on outside edge of trellis*

larger or smaller in size, according as the laths are placed further apart from or closer to each other. If it is not considered desirable to attach the trellises directly to the walls in this simple manner, trellised frames of the requisite size should be made, which may be fastened to the walls by short wall hooks sparsely used. To impart neatness to a trellis made on the wall itself in the manner described, a narrow bead should be nailed on the outer vertical uprights, close to the edge, as in Fig. 230. It is not possible to enter here more closely into the mysteries of trellis making, which belongs to carpentry rather than to gardening, but sufficient has been said to intimate the *modus operandi* to any amateur who may desire to affix such supports to his walls by his own hands without the aid of any professional carpenter. And trellis work, it may be said, is about one of the most expensive articles in carpentry that a man can indulge in when made by a professional hand, owing to the labour and length of time involved in cutting and planing the laths. Expanding trellis, however, of which the laths are nicely planed, and which will therefore take the paint readily, may now be obtained of most dealers in timber and those who sell garden requisites, at an average price of rather more than 7d. per foot superficial when closed. Rough and unplaned trellis work may be obtained at lower rates, but there is no economy in buying it, especially if it be intended to paint it, because rough stuff will always absorb, and therefore use up, more paint than wood that has been planed. The following shows the sizes in which this trellis is made, and its dimensions, both closed and open, and its price per piece:

No.	Closed.	Open.	Price per Piece	No.	Closed.	Open.	Price per Piece	No.	Closed	Open.	Price per Piece
	Feet	Feet			Feet	Feet			Feet	Feet	
1	2½ x 1½	12 x 1	2s.3d.	**6**	2½ x 4½	12 x 3½	7s.	**11**	2½ x 8	12 x 6	12s.
2	2½ x 2	12 x 1½	3s.0d.	**7**	2½ x 5½	12 x 4	8s.	**12**	2½ x 8½	12 x 6½	13s.
3	2½ x 3	12 x 2	4s.4d.	**8**	2½ x 6	12 x 4½	9s.	**13**	2½ x 9	12 x 7	14s.
4	2½ x 3½	12 x 2½	5s.2d.	**9**	2½ x 6½	12 x 5	10s.				
5	2½ x 4	12 x 3	6s.0d.	**10**	2½ x 7	12 x 5½	11s.				

The above prices may vary slightly with different makers; but as far as calculating the cost of covering any given area goes, they will be found to be sufficiently approximate. Trellis or lattice work, suitable for climbing plants, lawn tennis borders, ornamental arches, etc., is manufactured and supplied by Mr W. Burley, 4 Tower Buildings, London Wall, at the following prices: 50 square feet, 10 feet by 5 feet, will expand to 15 feet, unplaned at 3s., and planed at 4s. Nothing cheaper than this is in the market.

549 *Minor Trellises and Trainers for Plants* These are to be purchased for a few pence, when in wood and of a small size for pot plants; but when they assume the form of balloon trainers, made of wire, and consisting of this material disposed round four hooped standards, or rather a pair of standards bent in a hoop-like shape, whose ends afford the means of fixing the appliance in the earth, they are more costly. Trainers of this form range from 15 inches to 36 inches in height, and from 2s. 6d. to 7s. each, according to size. Being globular in form, they present a surface on and over which a climbing plant, such as *Tropaeolum Canariense* or *Maurandya Bardayana*, may be trained so as to exhibit its leaves and flowers to the best advantage. The balloon trainers are shown in Fig. 232; they are useful both for greenhouse decoration and for use in the open ground. The small trellises used in pot culture for sustaining such plants as the Ivy geranium, and even the tree carnation, are flat in form, as shown in Fig. 231, which is given as a general type of the whole. This consists of three standards of wood, one upright in the centre and two inclined to it, one on either side, in the inclination generally given to the sides of a flower pot. These standards should be about ¾ inch in width and ⅜ inch thick for ordinary use. Holes are then bored through the standards, through which wires about ⅛ inch in diameter, or even a little slighter, as 3/32 inch, are inserted in the manner shown in the illustration. The standards in such a composite structure as this present the narrower sides to the front and back. Useful supports may be made in this manner from 18 inches to 36 inches in height, for indoor or outdoor use. For smaller supports, the two slanting standards only need be used, and these may be placed so as to present the broader sides in front and to the rear, and connected by slips on wood laid across them, and secured in place by small brads. A pretty form of flat trellis or trainer, made entirely of wire, may be made by bending a long piece of thick wire in the form shown by the exterior outline of Fig. 233, and then attaching straight pieces of thin wire to this main support, crossing them after the manner of ordinary wooden trellis work. A structure of this kind is all the stronger if the wires are interlaced. If this is not done it is necessary to fasten them at the points of crossing with thin binding wire.

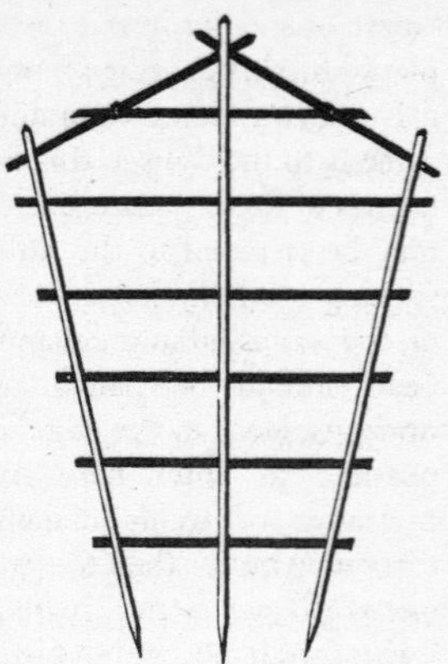

FIG. 231 *Composite trainer*

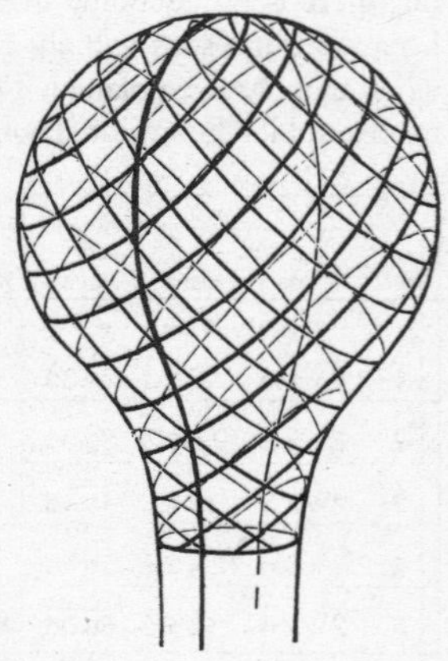

FIG. 232 *Balloon trainer*

FIG. 233 *Diamond wire lattice*

550 *Wire Lattice* There are many, perhaps, who will prefer wire lattice for training climbers to wooden trellis work, because it is more easily removed, and presents a lighter appearance. The nature of this lattice may be best understood from the accompanying representation of it in Fig. 233, which clearly exhibits its formation. As it is generally required to cover spaces of certain dimensions, it is made to order in pieces of any size that may be required. When the pieces contain four square feet superficial measurement, or more than this, they are charged according to measurement at per square foot; but when the pieces do not contain four square feet, they are charged for by the piece. The following table exhibits the prices per square foot for this kind of lattice, made in different gauges of wire and in different sizes of mesh, from ½ inch to 6 inches. The size of the mesh is according to the measurement across the diamond horizontally, and not according to the longer or vertical measurement. This should be remembered in ordering wire lattice, which will be found of special service for training climbing roses, vines, and any kind of climber that requires support of this kind. But it is necessary now to give the prices at which it is supplied. There may be a slight difference made by different makers, but these are the prices of Messrs J. J. Thomas and Co., 87 Queen Victoria Street, London, and 285 and 362 Edgware Road, London.

Size	Nos. of Wire Gauze							
of mesh	15	14	13	12	11	10	9	8
¾ in	1s.4d.	1s.5d.	1s.6d.	1s.7d.	1s.9d.	2s.0d.	—	—
1 in	10d.	1s.0d.	1s.1d.	1s.2d.	1s.5d.	1s.8d.	2s.0d.	—
1¼ in	—	1s.11d.	1s.0d.	1s.1d.	1s.3d.	1s.6d.	1s.9d.	—
1½ in	—	9d.	10d.	11d.	1s.0d.	1s.2d.	1s.5d.	—
2 in	—	6d.	6½d.	7d.	8d.	10d.	1s.0d.	1s.4d.
2½ in	—	—	—	5½d.	6½d.	8½d.	10d.	1s.1d.
3 in	—	—	—	5d.	5½d.	6½d.	8d.	10d.
4 in	—	—	—	4½d	5d.	5½d.	6d.	8d.
6 in	—	—	—	—	4½d	4d.	5d.	7d.

551 *Pea Trainers and Supports* Of late years wire supports have been introduced for peas, to supersede sticking the rows with the fan shaped branches of trees already described. They consist of wire hurdles, so to speak, 6 feet long and 4 feet high, and are supplied at 4s. each. As regards construction, they are formed by three wire uprights, one at each end and one in the centre, and two horizontal

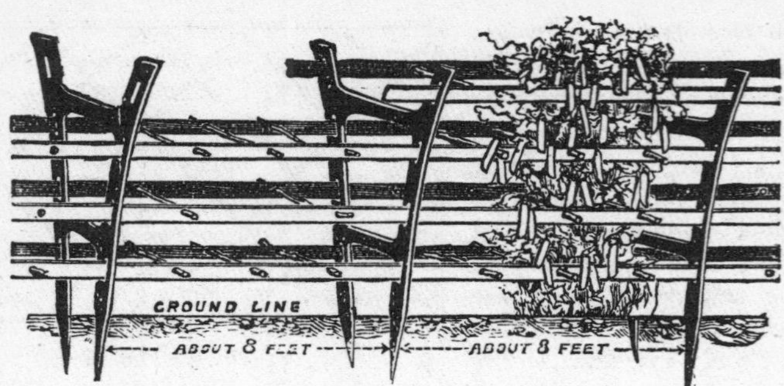

FIG. 234 *Harlow's patent pea sticks*

bars, one at top and one at bottom. On this framework, diagonal wires are stretched in each direction, forming a mesh of about 9 inches. They are far more costly than sticks, even though they are more durable. If used on both sides of the row, it would cost £2 to support a row 30 feet in length, and if only one set of hurdles are placed along the centre of the row, the trainers would cost £1, and much labour in supporting the pea vines by tarred cord, or some such material, as the vines increase in height. A good example of the pea trainer is found in Harlow's Patent Pea Sticks, an illustration of which is given in Fig. 234, and which are manufactured by Mr B. Harlow, Macclesfield. The supports are made of iron, and the laths, which are passed through holes made in the supports for their reception, are of wood. Cross bars of iron are put transversely through the laths, and the entire structure, which is very durable and may be easily fixed by any labourer, forms an admirable support for the growing pea vines, and one which admits of gathering the crop without any impediment. The average price of supports and laths is 2s. 2d. per yard. The supports are placed in the ground at about 8 feet apart.

552 *Pea Guards* The wire coverings known as pea guards, and used for the protection of the young crops from birds during their early growth, consists, as will appear from Fig. 235, of two pieces of wire bent in semicircular form, connected by two horizontal bars, one on either side, the whole being covered with galvanised wire netting of ¾-inch mesh. These protectors are made in 3-feet lengths, and are supplied at 7s. 6d. per dozen lengths, including two stop ends to every dozen, so as to prevent ingress of birds at the extremities of the rows if left open. These appliances are most useful, and can be employed with advantage to protect other seeds that are likely to receive injury from birds.

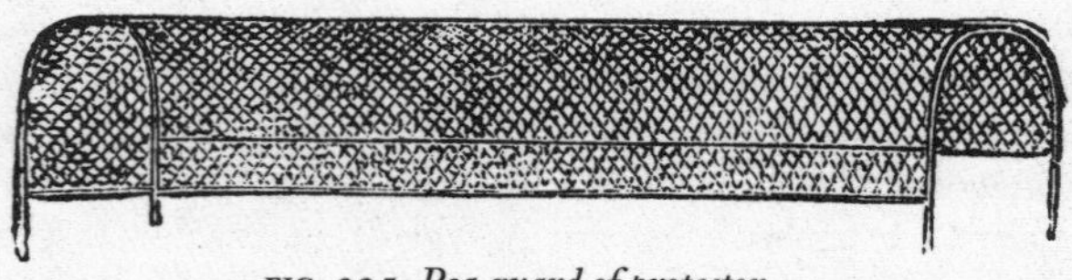

FIG. 235 *Pea guard of protector*

The following simple and easily-constructed substitute for pea sticks and pea hurdles is thus described by a writer in *Gardening Illustrated*, who says: 'Having found some years ago a difficulty in getting pea sticks while in Guernsey, I tried the plan of an old French gardener, and have done it ever since with every success. First, get some square garden stakes (these I have now had for three years) of the height of your pea – we will say 3 feet; then with a sprig bit place holes at about 6 inches apart, beginning at the top, leaving 1 foot to go into the ground (the stake should thus be 4 feet in length); then make your trench, say 1 foot wide; plant your peas, and when just appearing drive your stakes in along each side, say about 8 feet apart; drive in two strong pieces of wood, one at each end, get some strong twine that will go through the holes you have made, wax it well, put it through your holes, and secure it at one end, running it through the holes made in the stake at the other end. I do this every year with the same stakes and string so that the first is the only cost. I have tarred the ends of the stakes. Between every other two stakes I place a piece of wood (say pieces of sawn lath) to keep them in position when I tighten the string, which I do every two or three weeks.' The sprig bit mentioned above is merely a narrow bit that will bore a hole ¼ inch or ⅜ inch in diameter. Those who have no bit and brace may drive in small staples such as are used by bell hangers to retain bell wire in its place, about 6 inches apart, on one side of each stake, the staples to face outwards when the stakes are driven into the ground. And instead of twine, tarred cord, to be bought of the ropemaker or oilman, may be used with advantage, the lengths being joined together with a sailor's knot, which will pass through a hole of f inch diameter, or the eye formed by a staple whose inside measurement is ⅜ inch.

553 *Galvanised Wire Arches* It is not possible, within the compass of a work like this, to enumerate all the various appliances in wire that are supplied as garden requisites, and may be used with advantage in all gardens for the purposes for which they are designed. For example, wire hurdles for the protection of gardens from poultry, or even for dividing one part from another, are often required; but when anything of this description is needed, an application to any of the makers or dealers mentioned in these pages will soon procure the necessary information as to size, price, etc. It is necessary, however, to call attention to an attractive means of embellishment for gardens, which is found in the galvanised wire arch, which forms an admirable means of support for roses or any climbing plant that it is desired to train over a garden path, or in any position in which an arch can be made available. A type of these arches is shown in Fig. 236, which represents the so-called flat arch, the plainest form that is made. It consists of two arched supports, connected at intervals by horizontal bars, terminating in four stakes on each side to enter the ground,

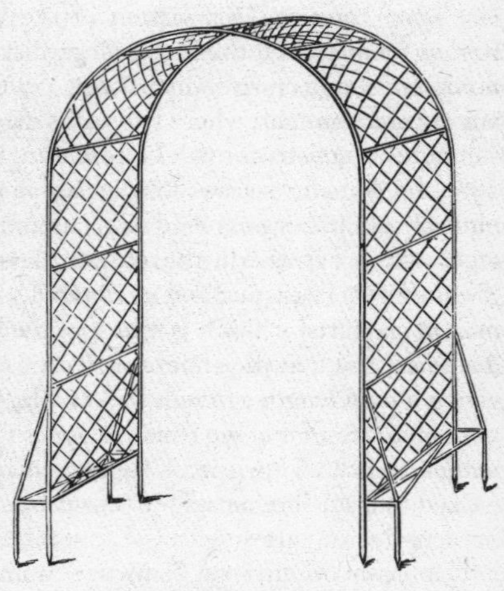

FIG. 236 *Flat galvanized wire arch*

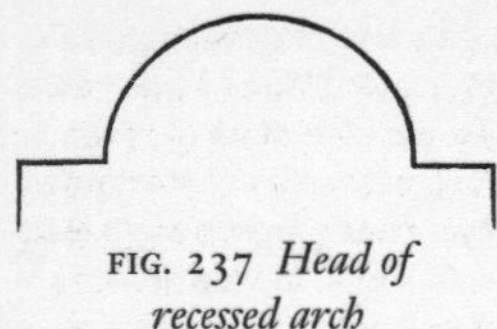

FIG. 237 *Head of recessed arch*

strengthened by diagonal stays, the whole forming a skeleton support, which is covered with galvanised wire netting. An arch of this kind, measuring 7 feet in height above the ground in the centre, 4 feet wide, and 18 inches deep, is supplied for 16s., but narrower arches can be purchased for less money. These arches are furnished with a border of wirework, on one or both sides, at a cost of 23s. for single border, or border on one side only, and 27s. for double border. The borders have their use in preventing the climber from drooping over the edges of the arch to too great an extent. In the recessed arch, the top is formed in the manner shown in Fig. 237. An arch of this description, of the dimensions given for the flat arch, with the exception of being 4 feet 6 inches in width instead of 4 feet, costs 22s.; but they cannot be considered as being as stable as the flat arch, as they have only two points to enter the ground on each side instead of four, and the shape is by no means as attractive as that of the plain arch. These arches are made to order to any size and of various designs, and before giving an order, the width to be spanned and other details with regard to position, requirements, etc., should be submitted to the manufacturer, who in his turn will submit suitable designs and give an estimate for the work to be done.

554 *Rose Temples* This section of the work would be incomplete without passing mention of the ornamental garden structures known as Rose Temples, a domed structure of wire which forms a suitable embellishment for the garden in any conspicuous part where two paths meet and cross, or any position which is suited to its construction. The rose temple consists, as may be seen from Fig. 238, of a domed structure in wire lattice work, surmounted by an ornamental pinnacle of the same material, and entered on each side by a highly-ornamental arch, styled an annexe by the makers, Messrs J. J. Thomas and Co. Some idea of the size of this structure and its suitability for training roses and other climbers may be gathered when it is said that the body of the temple itself is 8 feet in diameter, and that the annexes or entrances are 2 feet 6 inches in depth, thus giving a total length through the temple, from the outer face of one annexe to the outer face of the one which is opposite to it, of 13 feet. It is painted in two shades of green. The price is £45. It is made to take to pieces, so that it may be packed in a small compass for transit by ship or rail. Smaller structures of the same character, but without the annexes or arched entrances, from 9 to 11 feet in height, and of different diameters to suit pathways from 4 to 6 feet in width, may be had at prices ranging from £4 4s. to £7. These are open on four sides, the width of the trellises that support the dome varying from 9 to 15 inches. The openings may be filled in with trellises to form an enclosed summer house at an additional cost to the prices already named of from £2 2s. to £3 10s.

555 *Wires and Fittings for Training Trees on Walls* There are many who do not think it to be to the advantage of a trained tree that its branches should be pinned closely to the surface of the wall by nails and shreds, while others, again, do not care to have nails driven into brickwork. There is something to be said, no doubt, against both these methods of procedure, but it is improbable that ither of them will ever be entirely abandoned, as they possess advantages as well as disadvantages. For those, however, who have a decided objection to them, a substitute can be found in the form of wires stretched horizontally along the surface of the walls from end to end, at a little distance from it. The wires may be placed at such distances apart as may be deemed suitable to the trees that are to be trained on them; but it is not desirable that they should be closer than 6 inches or farther apart than 12 inches, or, taking a brick wall as our guide, that they should not be closer than the width of two bricks with the intervening layer of mortar, or farther apart than four bricks. The appliances that are required for stretching wires over the surface of walls are simple in themselves. First of all, there is the wire itself; secondly, the holdfasts for taking the fixed end of the wire; thirdly, the driving eyes; and lastly, the holdfasts that are used as strainers to draw the wire tight, and to afford the means of tightening it at any time should it have become slack from any causes that may tend to stretch it or cause it to expand. In Fig. 239, illustrations are given of the necessary fittings. At A the form of the ordinary holdfast is shown, which is galvanised, and sold at the rate of 2s. per dozen; and at B an improved form, also galvanised, and sold at 2s. 6d. per dozen. Each of these appliances consists of a piece of pointed iron to be driven into the wall between any two courses of bricks, and a projecting flange near the outer end, pierced with a hole to take the fixed end of the wire, which is passed through it and fastened by twisting the free end round the wire. At C a representation of the driving eyes is given. These eyes are driven into the wall at distances of about 10 feet, and serve to guide the wire in its course along the walls from end to end, and to support it, as without such means of sustaining it at intervals a

FIG. 238 *Rose temple*

considerable length of wire would unavoidably sag or hang down in the centre, presenting a curved line instead of a straight one. These eyes are made in lengths varying from 1½ inch to 6 inches, and are sold according to length, at prices ranging from 2d. to 1s. 6d. per dozen. At D is shown the method for fastening and straining the wires. A holdfast, similar in form to A and B, but having a hole through it large enough to take a slight bolt threaded at one end with a screw instead of a pierced flange, is driven into the wall in the proper position, the wire is twisted into an eye at the end of the screw bolt, and the threaded end is passed through the hole in the holdfast, and a nut worked on to the screw. By turning the nut with a small wrench the wire can be drawn to a sufficient degree of tightness. The terminal holdfasts are supplied – A at 2s. and B at 2s. 6d. per dozen; the straining bolts and holdfasts at 3s. 3d. per dozen; and the wire, which is galvanised and of the best quality, at 1s. 9d., 2s., and 2s. 6d. per length of 100 yards, according to size. When gardens are fenced with wooden palings, or enclosed by boarding nailed to posts and rails, it is better to adopt this mode of training trees, stretching the wire from post to post. When this is done, staples may be used instead of holdfasts and driving eyes.

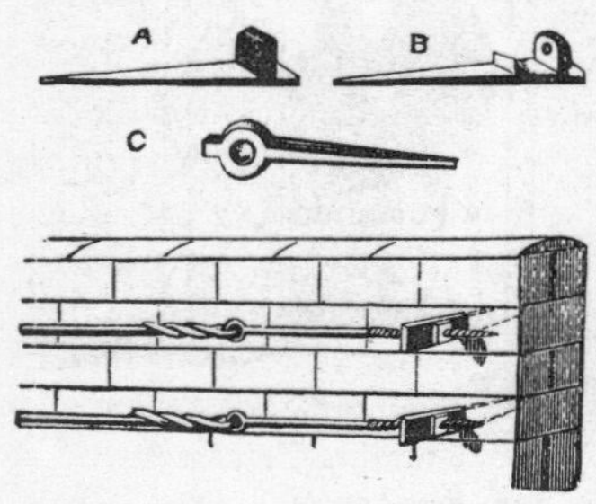

FIG. 239 *Fittings for wiring walls*

556 Materials for wiring garden walls are also supplied by Messrs Bayliss, Jones, and Bayliss, Victoria Works, Wolverhampton, and 3 Crooked Lane, King William Street, London. The galvanised eyes and holdfasts, with winders or strainers, are very much like the eyes and holdfasts shown in Fig. 239, but they are somewhat different in form to those that have just been described, although they perform the same functions. The eyes are supplied at 7d. per dozen, the holdfasts at 7s. per dozen, and suitable wire at 2s. per 100 yards.

557 *Espaliers of Wire* Wire fencing has long been used for the separation of the lawn proper from the surrounding park or grass lands, and for the division of fields and large extents of arable and pasture land, instead of hedges or solid fences, and it is not surprising that an adaptation of it has been made for garden use, for the purpose of training trees. The appliances required in the formation of espalier fencing and the mode of putting it up are shown in Fig. 240. On the left is the terminal post, two of which are required for each length of fencing. They are made open, consisting, as it were, of two flat parallel bars, with round bars running transversely across from side to side, affording convenient means for attaching the ends of the wires at starting, and also for drawing them tight at the other end. The terminal posts thus form an upright bar rising from a square foot, with a strut having bearing against the upright at two points, and terminating also in a square foot. This strut prevents the post from being drawn out of its upright position by the tension of the wire. The bars in the terminal post at the other end can be turned so as to strain the wire, but in other respects its construction is the same. They are made in heights ranging from 4 to 7 feet, and are sold at prices from 9s. to 16s. each if painted, or from 14s. to 23s. each if galvanised, according to height. The wires are further supported by intermediate standards with anchor feet, as shown, and generally placed about 10 feet apart. Like the terminal posts, they are made in heights of 4, 5, 6, and 7 feet, and are sold at prices ranging from 1s. 5d. to 2s. 2d. each if painted, and from 2s. 1d. to 3s. 9d. each if galvanised, according to height. Those who do not care to go to the expense involved in iron espalier fencing may erect terminal posts and standards of wood, disposing the struts in the same manner, with extended bearing for the end in the earth, obtained by butting it against a flat stone placed so that its surface may form a plane at right angles to the direction of the strut. The wires may be fastened with staples to one terminal, and strained on the other terminal by eye-bolts passed through holes bored through the post, carrying nuts on the threaded ends. A more simple way of straining wires is shown in Fig. 241. In this a few links of a light chain are attached to the free end of the wire, and passed through a hole in the post large enotrgh to admit of its easy passage. The wire is then drawn as tight as it is possible to strain it, and secured from returning by a nail or piece of stout wire passed through the link projecting beyond the surface of the post opposite to that at which the chain has entered it.

FIG. 240 *Espalier iron fencing for fruit trees*

FIG. 241 *Simple mode of straining wire*

558 *Wire Netting* Before quitting the subject of wire and various articles made of wire for garden use, it is necessary to call the attention of the reader to wire netting, which is machine made and supplied in various sizes of mesh and strength of wire according to the purpose for which it is to be used. The form of mesh is hexagonal in all cases, from the smallest to the largest. The following table gives the prices of this netting per yard in rolls of 50 yards in length, and in various sizes of mesh; but it must be borne in mind that if a less quantity than 50 yards is required, the price per yard is increased one halfpenny. So this must be taken into account when buying or ordering.

Width of Netting	Width of Mesh			
	½ inch	1 inch	1½ inch	2 inches.
18 inches	6d.	4d.	2½d.	1½d.
24 inches	8d.	5d.	3d.	2d.
30 inches	10d.	6½d.	4d.	2½d.
36 inches	1s. 0d.	7½d.	4½d.	3d.
48 inches	1s.4d.	10d.	6d.	4d.

The first use of this netting is as a protection to flower beds, seed beds, etc., from the inroads of cats, etc., or for light fencing for separating one part of a garden from another. When used in this way, iron stakes or standards are necessary as supports, unless wooden stakes be used, along which the wire may be stretched by the aid of tenter hooks or small staples. Stakes of galvanised iron suitable for the purpose, with a foot at right angles to the stake, bent at each end to enter the soil, as shown in the illustration, are supplied in lengths to suit the width of the netting used, at the following prices per dozen, namely: 18 inches, 5s.; 24 inches, 5s. 6d.; 30 inches, 8s. 6d.; 36 inches, 9s.; and 48 inches, 12s. 6d. The increase of price according to increase of length may appear disproportionate; but it must be remembered that the longer stakes are much stouter than the smaller sizes, and therefore are much heavier in weight in accordance to the length.

559 *Home-made Substitutes for Trellises, Pea Guards, etc.* Now, it will be at once apparent to any man who is self-helpful, how very easily wall trellises, trainers, protectors, and pea guards may be contrived by the aid of wire netting. For trellises it is sufficient to nail vertical strips of wood to the wall it is sought to cover, at widths suitable to the width of the netting to be used, and then to strain the netting on them by tenter hooks, staples, or clout nails. A great advantage is afforded by trellis of this description in the fact that if the strips of wood be sufficiently thick to keep the wire, say, 1½ inch or 2 inches from the wall, the climbers will grow between the wall and the wire, and send out branches and tendrils through the wire, falling in natural festoons over it, and concealing it from view in a great measure, if not entirely. Again, protectors for patches of seed may be easily made of wire of narrow width, by forming a cylinder, supported by stakes of wood or wire to fasten it to the ground, and covering it at top with a piece of netting cut to shape. Pea guards also may be contrived by bending the netting and supporting it on wires bent in the form of an arch; and trainers for sweet peas and other plants requiring support may be made, as shown in Fig. 242, by attaching a cylinder of wire to stakes or sticks to support and secure it.

FIG. 242 *Wire frame for sweet peas, etc*

560 *Instruments for Pruning, Grafting, Budding, etc.* Under this heading must be comprehended all the appliances that are used in any operation connected with fruit culture in the first degree, and flower culture in the second. First of all, we have the knives used in pruning, grafting, budding, etc., and the scissors used in thinning fruit and cutting flowers. Next, the larger articles that are required for trimming trees, cutting off boughs, and cutting them down altogether, must be mentioned in detail; and, lastly, the movable subordinate appliances that must be called into requisition in training trees, the fixed appliances for training, such as the wires extended along the face of a wall, wire espaliers, and fences of various kinds suitable for this purpose, having been already considered in this and preceding chapters.

561 *The Common Garden Knife* This is a knife for all ordinary purposes which should be carried by every gardener. It may be had with or without a joint, as preferred; but one with a broad and strong curved blade, set in a buckhorn handle with a slight curvature in the opposite direction, without a joint, and carried in a stout leather sheath, is preferable. This kind of knife is shown in Fig. 244. The handle, as will be noticed, is larger at the bottom than at the top, from which the blade issues. This enables the operator to hold the knife with a firmer grip, and to apply more force or power when cutting away a bough of some size from a shrub, etc., as he often must do. There is a flat plate at the bottom of the handle, which may be utilised for loosening old garden nails, or even for driving in a garden nail on an occasion when no hammer is within reach, or it is not worth while to fetch one.

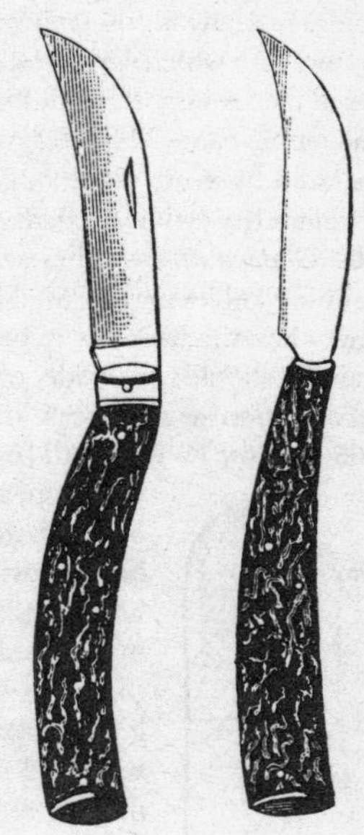

FIG. 243 *Pruning knife* FIG. 244 *Garden knife*

562 *The Pruning Knife* This description of knife is shown in Fig. 243. It should be furnished with a buckhorn handle of the same form, or very nearly so, as that of the garden knife; but it should be made with a joint, so as to be closed when out of use, and it is not amiss if the spring at the back be so constructed as to prevent any chance of the knife closing when the operator is using it. The edge of the blade should be straight, or all but straight, from haft to point. The blade, moreover, should be of the best steel, and kept scrupulously keen. It may be asked why one knife will not serve for all purposes. The reply lies in the fact that in pruning it is necessary to make a clean cut across the bough or branchlet that is severed from the tree, and that the bark should be cut all round as cleanly as the wood that it encloses, without leaving any shreds or stripping when the cut is made, which shows that the knife is blunt or not so sharp as it ought to be, or that the operator is unskilful in the use of his tool, or has not made the cut at the proper angle, which is an angle ranging from 30° to 45° to the axis of the branch that is cut. The greater the angle, the less the chance of making a clean cut and of leaving a little flap of bark at the upper end of it stripped from the portion that is cut away. It is undesirable to use a knife for which sharpness is indispensable for any other purpose than pruning, and hence an ordinary garden knife should be kept for rougher work. The blade of the pruning knife is not so large, broad, and heavy as that of the garden knife. Good garden knives and pruning knives may be bought at prices ranging from 1s. to 3s.

563 *Hone for Sharpening Knives* As it is always desirable to have the means of putting an edge to a knife at any time and at any place, the gardener should carry in his pocket a slip, as it is called, for this purpose, if his work be such that the knife is called into frequent use. A piece of good Turkey stone, to be procured from any ironmonger, is generally used; but no one will do amiss in furnishing himself with one of the Tam O'Shanter Hones, prepared by Mr John C. Montgomerie, Dalmore Hone Works, Stair, Ayrshire. This hone is accounted to be as good as, if not better than, any other for sharpening all kinds of edge tools. It needs no oil, and requires to be moistened with saliva only, or a little water, with which simple lubricant it puts on a keen, sharp edge. It can be had in small pieces, expressly cut for the pocket, when desired. Every hone or slip bears the name Tam O'Shanter, which is a mark of its genuineness. It is, or ought to be, sold by every ironmonger; but anyone who finds a difficulty in getting it through the ordinary channel should write direct to the works.

564 *Grafting Knives* These are similar in form to pruning knives, and, indeed, pruning knives may be used for this purpose. Keenness of edge is indispensable, and when the bark has to be lifted, as is the case in some kinds of grafting, the handle should be made of some smooth material and with a wedge-like termination, as in the case of the budding knife.

565 *Budding Knives* In the operation of budding, the bud has to be prepared for insertion, and the necessary incision made in the stock and the bark raised for its reception, and therefore the form of the blade must be adapted for these purposes, and the form of the handle as well. The shapes in which budding knives are usually made are shown in Fig. 245. Strength is not required in them, therefore they are altogether smaller in size than pruning knives; but although the blades are small, they must be very keen and adapted for making a clean incision as well as for making a clean cut. For this purpose the blades of both the knives that are figured in the illustration are well adapted; but perhaps the form of the smaller one is preferable. The handle is of bone or ivory in every case, these materials being of a smooth surface, and capable of being reduced to a thin spatula-shaped termination, suitable for lifting the bark on either side of the incision for the insertion of the bud. A heart-shaped termination, such as is found in the knife known as Goodsall's Budding Knife, is perhaps the most convenient for accomplishing the purpose for which it is specially required. Budding knives cost from 3s. to 4s. 6d.

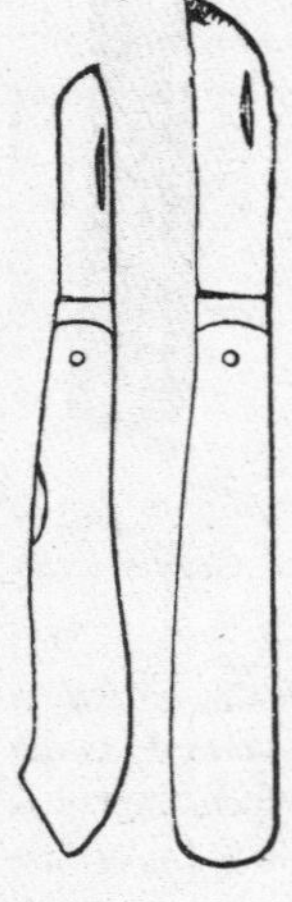

FIG. 245
Budding knives

566 *Asparagus Knife* Where asparagus is largely grown a special kind of knife is desirable for cutting it. If an old kitchen knife is used for the purpose, the back should be blunted and the point brought in a long and gradual curve from the edge in front to the blunt back. When thrust against the root, the cut is delivered from extreme point to the front edge by downward pressure, and injury to any other shoot in the vicinity of that which is cut is guarded against. Asparagus knives, specially prepared for the purpose, are either chisel-shaped – that is to say, with a blade blunt on both sides and sharp at the edge only, which is straight across the end of the blade like that of a chisel – or slightly curved, and made like a saw along the inner or cutting edge, although the teeth are sharp. With the chisel knife the cut is made downwards; with the saw knife the cut is made upwards, the instrument being thrust into the ground by the side of the shoot to be severed. The asparagus knife costs about 1s. 3d.

567 *Scissors for Pruning, etc.* The necessity for scissors in gardening is so palpable that it is not requisite to enlarge much on the minor operations for which they are called into action, namely, those of cutting flowers and foliage in the garden and in the greenhouse. It will be sufficient to observe that for the preservation of flowers, fronds of ferns, etc., in water, it is always better to snip them from the plants that bear them than to break them away. For cutting flowers any ordinary kind of scissors will do; but for the more important operations in which their aid is sought, namely, pruning and thinning fruit, scissors of a different form and description are required. Types of desirable forms are shown in Fig. 246, in which A shows a pair of scissors adapted for general purposes. The pointed shape shown in B is preferable for thinning grapes, the pointed termination of the blades rendering their introduction between closely-packed berries far easier, and with far less chance of injury to those that are to remain, than blades with broad and blunted points. For pruning, an operation for which scissors have been coming more and more into use since the trimming and forming of trees by pinching has been adopted, an instrument with short, broad, strong blades is necessary. Of pruning scissors, the ordinary kind is shown at C, and an improved kind at D. In the former, a semicircular notch is made in one blade to hold the shoot while the sharp blade is being brought down upon it and forced through it; in the latter, the sliding action that is imparted to the blade turned towards the spectator causes the cut that is made by it to partake in some degree of the drawing action of the knife blade, and to exert less of the direct and downward pressure of the ordinary scissors. Pruning scissors cost from 2s. to 3s. 6d. per pair; but the Improved Sliding Pruning Scissors cost 5s. per pair.

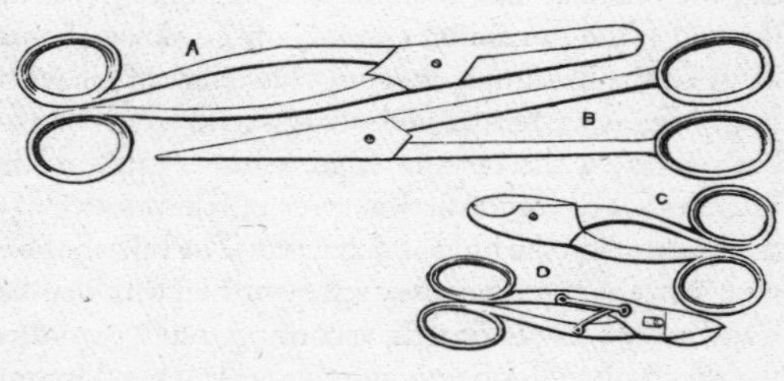

FIG. 246 *Scissors for pruning, etc*

568 *The Chisel* Sometimes old trees of considerable size are renovated by cutting off the head and inserting grafts into the stumps of the branches that are left on the main stem or trunk. The branches are first removed with the saw; but as a saw cut is ragged, and a clean, smooth cut is always necessary for the quicker and more effectual healing of the wound thus inflicted, the rough surface produced by the abrading action of the teeth of the saw must be smoothed over with a chisel. For this purpose the ordinary carpenter's chisel will do, always provided that it is at least one inch in breadth, and very sharp. Sometimes the chisel has to be called into action to slit or notch a stock for the purpose of grafting, and for this purpose a chisel termed the garden chisel is used, which differs from the carpenter's chisel in being wedge-shaped by bevelling on both sides instead of on one only. There is a strong chisel, known as the forest chisel, used in forestry for separating small branches close to the bole or trunk with a clean cut. The blade is broad, and sometimes has projections curving backwards on both sides, which are usually called ears; the handle is from six to ten feet in length, so that branches that are some distance up the trunk of a tree can be lopped off with facility. The edge of the chisel is placed under the branch, and the end of the handle is then struck with a mallet. In pruning orchards, a variety of the forest chisel is used, having a guard at a little distance from the edge of the blade to prevent it from penetrating into the wood beyond a certain distance, and thus causing an injury which was never intended. With a chisel of this kind a large bough may be severed by carrying the chisel cuts round it; but any necessity for its use is obviated by using the saw and smoothing the cut over with a chisel afterwards.

569 *Bill Hooks and Pruning Bills* These implements are used in pruning trees and trimming hedges rather than for fruit trees, although they may be utilised for cutting off the boughs of large trees in orchards, in which apple trees, pear trees, cherry trees, and the trees that are usually found in orchards, have attained such a growth and require such lopping as may be fairly effected by means of these implements. The common forms of billhook are represented in Fig. 247, A having a square-shaped broad blade, rather wider at the top than at the bottom, and slightly curved or hooked at the extremity, and B having a sickle-shaped blade of the form of a crescent. The edge of blades of both types is wedge-shaped – that is to say, bevelled on both sides to the cutting edge in the centre of the thickness. This construction gives greater facility of penetration to the edge of the blade when the blow is delivered. The bills in the illustration are represented with short handles; but they are furnished with handles ranging from 9 inches to 5 and even 6 feet in length, according to the work that is to be done with them, the shorter handles being more suitable when lopping off large boughs, and the longer handles for trimming and pruning hedges. There are various shapes of blades in use for this implement, but the principle in all is the same. In some,

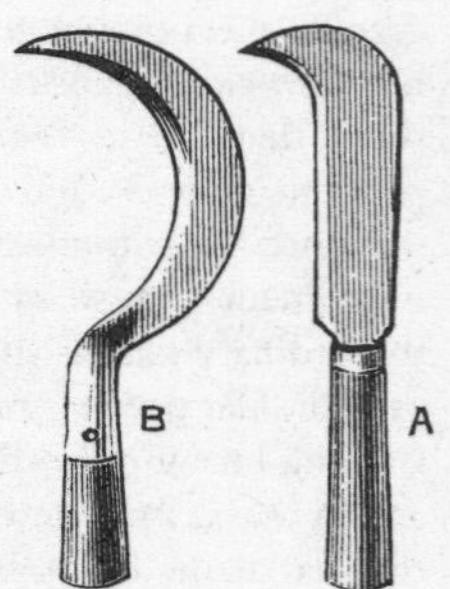

FIG. 247
Common forms of billhook

FIG. 248 *Deane's improved pruning bill*

however, the back is serrated to form a saw, in which case the bill is adapted to do the duty of a pruning saw. An example of this kind of instrument, in which the cutting edge of the ordinary bill and the edge of the saw is combined, is shown in Fig. 248, which is a representation of an Improved Pruning Bill, manufactured and sold by Messrs Deane and Co., 46 King William Street, London. In this tool the lower edge is toothed for sawing, and the upper edge sharpened in wedge-shaped form for chopping; the hook near the point is also sharpened for cutting, and adapted for pulling down boughs that it may be desired to hold, when chopping, within reach and grasp of the left hand. Common billhooks cost from 2s. 3d. to 3s. 3d., according to size; the Improved Pruning Bill, 5s.

570 *The Pruning Saw and Pole Saw* Ordinary saws are constructed for cutting dry wood, while the saws used in gardening and forestry are used only for cutting green wood. Thus, an ordinary saw, although green wood may be, and frequently is, cut with it, is liable to hang in the damp timber, and get choked with the moist fragments that are torn away by the action of the teeth, because the blade is thinner and far more flexible than that of the pruning saw, while the teeth are not so widely set apart as those of carpenters' saws. Sometimes the pruning saw, especially when wanted for the severance of small boughs only, is in the form of a knife, the blade being made to close up into the handle. They are chiefly useful for sawing off boughs in positions such that they cannot be conveniently operated upon by the pruning knife or billhook. When the saw is used, it must be remembered that it is necessary for the well being of the tree to smooth over the cut with a chisel or sharp instrument. Pole saws are longer and wider in the blade, and have the blade, as the name implies, at the end of a pole or long handle, for the purpose of getting at boughs that otherwise would be out of reach without a ladder. Saws for green wood, it should be added, when the bough to be cut is on a level with the arm and hand of the operator, cut equally well whether pulled towards him or thrust from him; the teeth rub away the fibres of the wood. The ordinary saw, on the other hand, cuts only on the downward stroke, although the saws used by Japanese and Chinese carpenters cut when drawn upwards across the wood. Pruning saws cost 2s. and 2s. 6d. each.

571 *Averruncators and Similar Tree Pruners* In order to enable persons engaged in pruning parts of trees at some distance above them with precision, and without the use of a ladder, a contrivance known as the averruncator has been introduced. The principle of this instrument is shown in Fig. 249, in the three different forms depicted therein. All agree in the fact that the cutting part of the instrument is fixed at the end of a pole or handle ranging from 5 to 10 feet in length, and actuated by a cord held and worked by one hand, while the instrument is sustained and directed by the other. In A, the immovable part of the shears – for in point of fact the averruncator is nothing more than a pair of

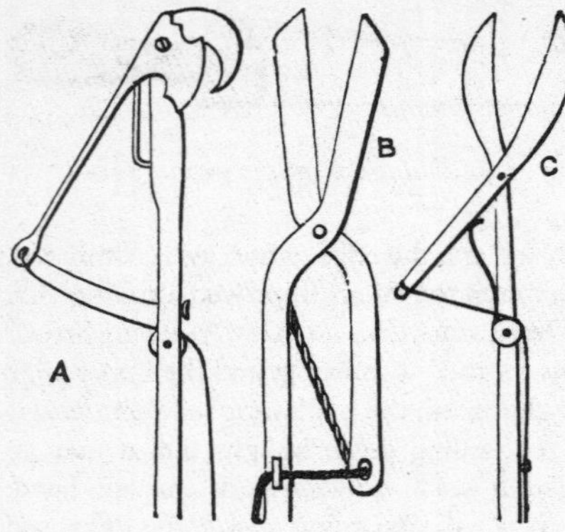

FIG. 249 *Averruncators of different kinds*

shears so fashioned as to effect the purpose for which it is wanted, namely, to lop off boughs and branches of some little thickness when out of reach of ordinary hand tools – consists of a hook, whose inner edge serves to secure and hold the bough; near the outer edge of this hook a hatchet-shaped blade is fixed by a rivet to the hook itself, and on this rivet it can move freely. A guard behind the hook serves as a guide to keep the cutting blade in position when brought into operation. At the lower end of the cutting part is a hole, through which passes a strong cord, one end of which is fastened to the pole, while the other runs over a pulley also set in the pole as shown. When the bough has been hooked the cord is pulled, and the sharp edge of the movable part of the averruncator is brought against the bough, which it severs with a clean cut. The form shown in B is a closer adaptation of the ordinary shears used, as Loudon states, by Dutch gardeners for cutting off young shoots in summer; and C exhibits a similar contrivance, with this difference, that the jaws of the shears are held apart when not in use, and forced apart after the cut is made and the tension of the cord relaxed, by a spring. Averruncators cost 21s. each.

572 *Patent American Tree Pruner* The latest form of the averruncator, and possibly the most serviceable and convenient for use, is the Patent American Tree Pruner, an illustration of which is given in Fig. 250. As the entire instrument is shown in this representation of it, the means by which this and the averruncators previously described are actuated will be readily perceived and understood. There is the hook at the end of the pole immovably fixed, and attached to the hook by a pin, on which it can move freely, is a cutting blade, at the further end of which is a hole for the attachment of a cord or wire. This, in its turn, passes through eyes fastened into the pole, and is fastened at the other end to a short bar, which is also attached to the pole. The cutting blade forms a lever, moving on the pin by which it is attached to the hook, as a fulcrum. When the power is applied by pressing down the bar below, the long arm of the knife is pulled downward, and the short arm which

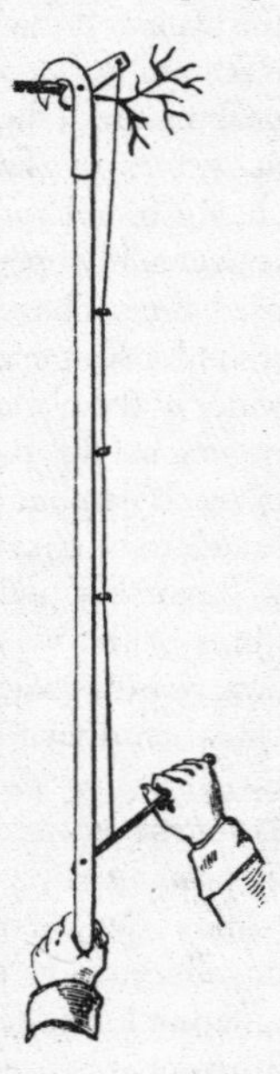

FIG. 250 *Patent American tree pruner*

terminates in a cutting edge is pressed upward against the bough which represents the weight and which is severed by it. These pruners are supplied by Messrs Deane and Co., 46 King William Street, London. They are supplied in different lengths, ranging from 2 feet to 10 feet, the progressive difference in length being 2 feet. The weight varies from 2½lb. for a tree pruner 4 feet long to 4½lb. for one 10 feet in length; and the price ranges from 4s. 6d. to 8s. 6d. Extra knives are supplied at 1s. each.

573 *Pruning Shears* The ordinary shears will be described presently among the tools and implements that are designed for shearing and clipping. In the ordinary shears the blades move on a common centre, but in the pruning shears, as in the Improved Sliding Pruning Scissors shown at D in Fig. 246, there is a movable centre for one of the blades, or, in other words, there is a longitudinal slot in one of the blades, by which it can be moved on the central pin for a distance equal to the length of the slot. The illustration given in Fig. 251 shows the construction of the pruning shears. The broad and straighter lower blade has a slot in it, through which the pin is passed that is rivetted to the upper blade, the upper cutting part of which is curved. When the bough is grasped by the shears and the handles brought together, the upper blade is thrown upward by the action of the bar by which it is further attached to the lower blade, and delivers a drawing cut instead of a crushing cut, which has the effect of leaving a clean smooth surface after the severance of the bough. Shears for pruning purposes are made in different forms, but as the principle is the same in all it is unnecessary either to describe them or to specify them. Pruning shears cost from 6s. to 8s. each.

FIG. 251 *Diagram showing construction of pruning shears*

574 *French Secateur* This is an instrument for branch pruning which is very commonly used in France. An illustration of it is supplied in Fig. 252, from which it will be seen that it is a pair of shears of great power. In the instrument figured, the blades are both falciform or curved, and the edge of each is bevelled in the opposite direction, so that the flat parts of the blades may work smoothly one on the other. They are fastened together by a rivet, on which they turn. When not in use they are held together by a strap at the ends of the handles, as shown; when open, the blades are forced apart and held in this position by the spring between the handles. Secateurs cost 3s. 6d. and 4s. each, according to size. Sometimes they are made with a movable centre, and sometimes one blade is hooked, as in the illustration, while the edge of the other is convex or rounded in form from heel to point. When made in this way, the cut that is made is cleaner than when both edges are straight or curved inwards. They are recommended by Loudon for pruning vines.

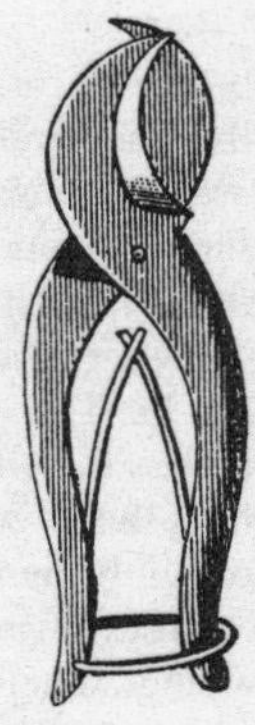

FIG. 252 *French secateur*

575 *The Axe* This is a powerful tool which is too well known to need much description. It is used chiefly in forestry, in felling trees and in cutting through the large roots when the portion underground below the collar is under removal. It varies in size from the ordinary small hatchet to the woodman's axe, which consists of a broad, wedge shaped blade, set on the end of a handle from 2½ feet to 4 feet long. It is useful rather in landscape gardening than in gardening proper, or horticulture. Hatchets cost from 2s. to 2s 9d each; axes, about double as much.

576 *Hammer and Tools, etc., used in Wall Training* The hammer used by the gardener in training trees on walls is, from its shape, usually known as a claw hammer. It has a striking face on one side or at one end, and the other is slightly curved and divided, so that it may be used for extracting nails in walls, by grasping the head of the nail in the cleft and pulling the handle backwards. By this means the nails are easily lifted out of the bricks in which they are driven, but before applying leverage to the nail by means of the hammer, it is desirable to give it two or three light taps on the head. This enables the nail to be withdrawn more easily, and without bringing away a part of the surface of the brick, which has the effect of leaving an ugly mark upon it. The head of the claw hammer is attached to the handle by two straps, one each side, and held in place by rivets passed through straps and handle. If the hammer used is not a claw hammer, the nails should be withdrawn with a pair of common pincers, and worked gently backwards and forwards before any attempt is made to remove them. The gardener's hammer should be tolerably heavy, and shorter in the handle than one which is used in carpentry. A hammer weighing about 1lb. or 1½lb. will be found sufficiently weighty for nailing trees to walls. The gardener's claw hammer may be had for 1s. or 1s 6d.

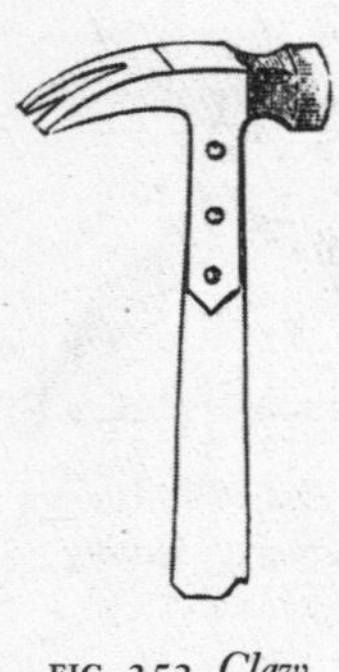

FIG. 253 *Claw hammer*

577 *Garden Nails, Shreds, etc.* The garden nail, or nail for brickwork, is made of cast iron, and is square in form, as shown in Fig. 254. It is the only kind of nail that can be driven into brickwork, wrought nails being useless for this purpose. As garden nails are of cast iron, they are brittle, as may be supposed, and will easily break if not struck fairly and directly on the head, or if the point encounters any hard substance in the brick. They are usually made in two sizes, and are sold at from 2d. to 3d. per lb. The cast iron nails, though excellent for brickwork, are useless for wood, and if trees have to be nailed to wood, wrought nails should be used, nails having a head, or clout nails, as they are called, being the best for the purpose. *Shreds* may be made out of the list of flannel, or from any odd pieces of woollen cloth or old clothes. They should be cut in strips from 2 to 4 inches long and from ½ inch to 1 inch in breadth. When greater holding strength is required than a single thickness will give, a larger shred should be cut, and a double thickness used, either in length or in breadth. Leather nailing bags, for holding shreds and nails, cost 3s. 6d. each.

FIG. 254 *Garden nail*

578 *Ladders* The garden ladder should be light arid portable, and that the utmost lightness as well as a maximum of strength may be attained, it is desirable that the sides should consist of the best red deal or pine sawn and planed, connected with oak rungs or staves, and having three rungs in the form of iron bolts with nuts, as shown in Fig. 255. These iron rungs should be placed one in the centre and one at each end, so as to form the end rungs but one in each case, the end rungs being of oak. The iron bars, as may be seen, are made with a shoulder at each end, against which the sides of the ladder are butted, and the ends are screw-threaded to carry nuts. When the bars, both of wood and iron, are all placed in position, the nuts are screwed up, and the ends of the oak staves are cut off close to the outer surface of each side of the ladder, and split and wedged up. The object in view in making a ladder in this manner is to produce a perfectly rigid framework of the greatest possible strength compatible with the dimensions of the sides, the length of the ladder, and the lightness necessary to ensure portability. The sides of the ladder, at least, should be painted, and the bars, both of iron and wood, may be treated in the same manner. From 10 to 15 feet will be found a convenient length for an ordinary ladder, although in the case of large fruit trees covering the end of a house or building, one of even greater length will be necessary. It is desirable to have two or three ladders of various lengths, from 6 or 8 feet upwards, for short ladders will often be found useful in dealing with fruit trees and climbers on walls of moderate height, and they are always more convenient than steps, and can be lodged against a wall with less chance of injury to trees, etc.

FIG. 255 *Iron rung of garden ladder*

579 *Fruit Gatherers* These are various in form, but the main object in all is the same, namely, to detach from the tree fruit which is out of reach without having recourse to ladders, and, at the same time, to catch it in some receptacle attached to the fruit gatherer, or to hold it fast by some contrivance so as to prevent it from falling to the ground when detached, which would only result in bruises and injury. It is manifest that the principle on which all fruit gatherers are constructed involves the use of a long pole with a cap or receptacle of some sort at the end of it. The very simplest mode of gathering fruit otherwise out of reach is to take a long stick with a hook at the end of it and to pull the branches down to such an extent that the fruit may be easily plucked, but this is not practicable in every case, and great care must be used in the operation to prevent injury to the branches. The next step in advance is to be found in the simple appliances used by the Spanish fruit growers to gather oranges and by the Swiss to gather apples, pears, walnuts, etc. Loudon describes the first of these as a rod with a cup at one end, from the edge of which project tongues of metal or plate iron, as shown in Fig. 256, these tongues being somewhat sharp at the edges. The cup is thrust upward until the fruit rests in it, and a slight twist is then sufficient to detach the fruit, the stalk being caught between the tongues attached to the cup and broken off by pressure. The Swiss fruit gatherer, shown in Fig. 257, consists of a pole with a basket attached to it

FIG. 256
Spanish orange gatherer

FIG. 257
Swiss fruit gatherer

FIG. 258
Funnel for gathering peaches, etc

FIG. 259
Funnel for gathering pears, etc

constructed on the same principle and acting in a similar manner, the projections above the horizontal basket work affording the means of breaking the stalk and detaching the fruit which remains in the basket.

580 Contrivances similar to the above in general construction and purpose have been long used in this country for gathering wall fruit, such as peaches, nectarines, apricots, and plums with as little injury as possible to the bloom that is on them. For the fruit just mentioned a tin funnel is used, which may be held in a ring of metal at the end of a long rod. The funnel is placed under the fruit and the edge brought gently against it in order to detach it. It then drops gently into the funnel and remains there for removal by the fruit gatherer. This kind of fruit gatherer is shown in Fig. 258; another of a similar kind is illustrated in Fig. 259, but in this the edge of the cone or funnel is notched, in order to a better means of detaching fruit with tougher stalks, such as pears. This fruit gatherer is useful for gathering mulberries. In the illustrations the handles are shown at right angles to the axis of the funnels. Such a position is well enough for gathering fruit on ordinary walls, but when the fruit is at some distance above the gatherer, as is the case with pears, apples, and mulberries, the pole must either be in the same straight line with the axis, or, in other words, must have the funnel fixed directly on its end, or must be slightly inclined to it. It is better, perhaps, to have the ring that holds the funnel as near the rim as possible, and to attach it by a flange to a cap on the end of the handle, so that it may be brought to any desired angle to the handle and retained in that position.

581 *Grape and Berry Gatherers* In the fruit gatherers that have been just con sidered, the fruit has been merely detached and prevented from falling by its reception in a cup, basket, or funnel. We now come to the more complicated grape gatherer in which the means of severing the bunch from the stalk is combined with the means of holding it fast when severed. It is necessary, therefore, to have an instrument which shall act as scissors and pincers at the same time. It is clear that if there is a projecting flange within the edge of the cutting blade, against which the other blade – which in itself is also of some thickness – can be brought, the bunch to be severed will be gripped and held just below the part that is cut. This is effected by the instrument shown in Fig. 260, which consists of a pair of scissors constructed on this principle. One arm is fixed on the end of a long handle, and the other is movable. The blades are closed by means of a ring or collar, which is pushed up as far as the projection on the right

FIG. 260 *Grape gatherer*

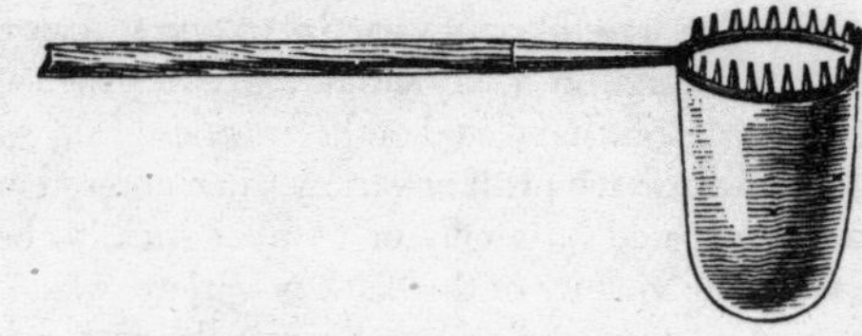

FIG. 261 *Amateurs' fruit gatherer*

of the illustration when it is sought to open the blades, which are pressed apart by the action of a spring when the collar is placed in this position. The instrument is then placed so that the stem of the bunch to be cut is enclosed between the arms or blades of the scissor-pincers, and the collar is pulled down. The pressure of the collar acting on the lower part of the movable arm closes the blades, and the bunch is cut and held by the pressure exerted by the machine on the extremity of the severed stalk. *Berry Gatherers*, for gathering gooseberries, raspberries, strawberries, etc., are merely scissors made on the same principle, the handles terminating in loops or rings, into which thumb and finger are thrust in order to work the instrument.

The accompanying illustration for a fruit gatherer for amateurs is taken from *Gardening Illustrated*. It is easily made and equipped, which is its great merit. The iron part, consisting of a ring set round with teeth or strong wires, and fixed in a socket, into which a wooden handle of any length may be inserted, can be made by any blacksmith; and the bag that is attached to the ring can be made of calico, muslin, or even netting, which will do quite as well, and be stronger. The fruit is pulled off by the teeth and caught in the bag. A hoop six inches in diameter would be large enough for all purposes, and handles of different lengths might be kept for use with it, the socket being held tightly to the handle either by a pin passed through holes made in-the socket and handle for its reception, or by a thumb screw entering the handle.

582 *Appliances for Distinction and Designation* No one will be inclined to dispute the desirability or question the necessity of marking plants and trees of all kinds set in a garden in such a manner that the names and varieties may be immediately ascertained, if memory prove treacherous, as it too often does. It is necessary to mark plants in such a manner, indeed, that the gardener, whether grower or amateur, may be able to distinguish them when recently planted, when growing, and when at rest, in which case, especially with regard to bulbs and herbaceous plants, that die down and grow again once in every year, to show the positions they occupy, that they may be left undisturbed when digging or pointing the borders, or easily taken up for removal to another place. There are various modes in vogue for distinguishing and designating plants, of which the principal are the tally or number stick, the name stick, and the plant label.

583 *Tallies with Notches* Supposing that an amateur gardener has a number of various plants growing in his garden, some dormant or in hibernation, some starting into growth, and others in full growth, but not yet in blossom, or that a grower has a number of varieties of one species of plant that it is necessary for him to distinguish, a very simple and easy plan is to make a register of the plants, etc., on the one hand, and of the varieties of any species on the other, and to affix a number to each plant or variety when entered in the register, which number is to be repeated on a tally or number stick, to be placed in the ground in the immediate vicinity of the plant or variety, whatever it may be. There was, and indeed is, a system of notching sticks with a knife in such a manner as to represent the Roman numerals, but this, after all, is a troublesome method, and one that is likely to lead to confusion if the system of marking for high numbers happens to be forgotten, as it very probably may be. It is desirable, therefore, on this account, to abandon signs and symbols combined with Roman numerals altogether, and to adhere to the Arabic numerals, 1, 2, 3, 4, 5, 6, 7, 8, 9, 0, in common use, which everybody knows, and whose use and application everybody understands, as a means of numbering plants, and making reference to them at any time at once simple and easy. The notched tally was all very well when education was less general and less thought of than it is now; but in the present day the notched sticks and botanic and Roman tallies, described at length by Loudon, may be regarded as things of a past age, and deserving no more than a mere passing reference here.

584 *Number Sticks* Supposing that a register of plants, varieties of plants, trees, etc., is made and kept in the manner indicated above, all that is necessary here is to see by what means of a simple character sticks bearing numbers corresponding to the register may be prepared, so that they may be placed close to the plants, etc., which the numbers indicate. It may be said at once that number sticks suitable for the purpose may be bought of the nurserymen in bundles of 100 each, with the face of each rubbed over with white paint, at from 6d. per bundle upwards, according to size. Sticks, however, of a very small size, such as are sold at 6d. per hundred, although large enough for pot culture, are not of sufficient length for setting in the open ground, and should not be purchased for this purpose. For cheapness sake, it is better to get a bundle of laths from the lath-render, and to cut these up into lengths varying from 5 to 10 inches long, and to smooth the face or front and sharpen the point, as shown in Fig. 262. The upper part on both sides should then be well rubbed over with white lead, or dressed with white paint, and the number written on the face with a tolerably hard lead pencil, cut to a broad point. The bottom of the stick should then be dipped in coal tar, or painted with a composition made of boiled linseed oil, thickened by the introduction of finely-powdered coal dust, until it is brought to the consistency of thick cream. Number sticks prepared in this way will last for a considerable time.

FIG. 262 *Simple number stick*

The following is an easy and inexpensive method of making plant and shrub labels: 'Take common bricklayers' laths of the *double size* or thickness, and cut into required lengths of 10 to 12 or 14 inches: smooth the *sides* with as little waste as possible, and shave off smoothly about 6 or 8 inches of the best front face with a sharp knife, finishing the lower end by cutting the sides to a short, sharp, wedge-like point, and then bevel it off reversely, by cutting it from the front and back face, which is better than leaving it with a sharp, wedge-like point. Procure a few pounds of pitch or tar, and form a brisk fire between loose piled bricks, upon which boil the tar, and dip the lower ends of the labels in the tar, whilst boiling, to the depth required of the labels to enter into the ground (6 or 8 inches). Allow the pitch to dry, and then surface the smooth face of each with a thin coat of well-mixed paint, and lay them by till required. When used, the smooth surface requires a second coat of paint, which should be written upon within a quarter or half an hour after being applied, otherwise it is difficult to make the writing legible. When the second coat of paint is allowed to dry, it is impracticable to impress writing, and in such instances the labels must be refaced. The best round carpenters' or joiners' pencils should be used for prominent plain figures or letters.'

585 It is possible, however, that it may be desired to make number sticks which shall be more durable than those just described, and on which the numbers may be marked in such a way as to render them incapable of obliteration by any other means than that of cutting them away or destroying the stick. When sticks of this kind are needed they should be made of red deal, or even of oak, and the numbers burnt in with hot irons, in the same way as the names of their owners are marked on tools and other things. Small branding irons of this kind, if not procurable of an ironmonger, are easily made by a smith, and with ten of them, for the nine figures and cypher, any combination representing any number, however high, may be made. When the number has been indelibly burnt into the wood the top of the stick may be painted white, and the end that is to enter the earth painted with boiled oil and coal dust, or dipped in tar, or even charred at pleasure, or the whole of the stick may be dressed over with the oil and coal dust, for as the number is burnt in it will be easily deciphered whatever may be the colour of the stick itself.

The following recipe for the preservation of wooden labels, number sticks, etc., is given in *Gardening Illustrated*: Thoroughly soak the pieces of wood of which they are made in a strong solution of sulphate of iron; then lay them, after they are dry, in lime water. This causes a formation of sulphate of lime (a very insoluble salt) in the wood, and the rapid destruction of the labels by the weather is thus prevented. Bast, mats, twine, and other substances used in tying or covering up trees and plants, when treated in the same manner, are similarly preserved.

586 *Number Tallies of Metal* The same end may be attained in the case of trees and shrubs by stamping numbers on small pieces of lead or zinc used as tallies, or even on pieces of tinned iron, obtained by cutting up old cans in which tinned meats have been preserved. Stamps for impressing the numbers on the metal must be obtained, and the pieces when stamped must have a hole punched in them through which a piece of copper wire may be passed in order to attach the label to the plant itself. The method to be followed in doing so will be clearly understood from an examination of Fig. 263, which represents a tally and wire prepared for attachment. Copper wire is recommended for this purpose, because it is more

FIG. 263 *Metal tally attached to branch*

ductile and far more easily bent than iron wire. One end of the wire must be twisted to form a loop: the wire must then be passed round a branch of the plant, or its stem, and the other end passed through the loop. This end must then be passed through the hole in the tally and bent in such a manner that the tally cannot be detached and removed without unbending the wire. The amateur gardener who is fond of helping himself and of making appliances for garden use for himself may learn from Fig. 264 how to divide a slip of lead or zinc or tin into tallies of convenient shape without any waste. In this diagram the outline of the tallies is shown by different modes of marking. Thus the portion of the strip that is shown in the figure is divided by perpendicular lines consisting of dashes into four squares, by dotted lines into seven triangles and two semi-triangles, and by a serpentine line of dots and dashes and perpendiculars, let fall from this line to the apex of each triangle, into seven labels of rectangular oblong form with curved top and two semi-labels of the same kind. For the suspension of these labels holes must be made in the centre close to the top or bottom or in any corner of each square (in which latter case the tally will hang diamond fashion), in the apex of the triangles, and in the rounded tops of the oblong labels. The numbers should be impressed on the widest parts When these metal tallies are used for plants to which they cannot be affixed as shown in Fig. 264, they may be attached in the same manner to a stick, which may be thrust into the ground close to the plant.

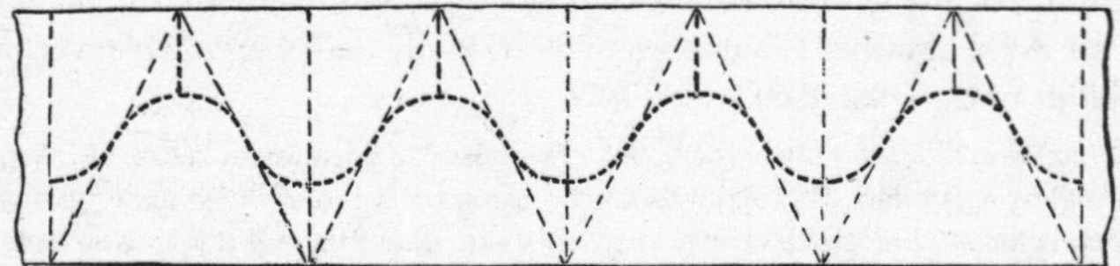

FIG. 264 *Diagram showing methods of cutting strip of metal into tallies without waste*

587 *Other Kinds of Tallies* For nursery use, and for amateurs too, cast iron tallies are made and sold in the form of a pointed stick, with an expansion of various forms at the top, on which numbers may be written. They are 6 inches in length, and are supplied at the rate of about 30s. per hundredweight, which contains about 1600 tallies, or perhaps more; the price, however, of these tallies will vary slightly according to the prices of iron and labour. *Murray's Tally*, described by Loudon, consists of a cast metal standard with a square head in the form of a box, into which a piece of wood or metal may be put with the name of the plant written on it, and a piece of glass placed over it, which must be puttied in like a pane of glass into a window, to keep the ticket intact from wet. *Glazed Number Bricks* are sometimes used, made of common earthenware glazed, and having numbers stamped on them before burning. These are made by Messrs Doulton and Co., of the Pottery, Lambeth, London. In some nurseries a brick is set on end in the ground, and the upper end is painted in black or white, and the number in the reverse colour to the ground colour.

This is convenient for marking spots in which a number of plants of the same kind are growing.

588 *Name Sticks* These are identical with number sticks, and are prepared for use in precisely the same manner. The only difference between the number stick and the name stick is that the former bears a number only and the latter the name of the plant to which it is affixed. Name sticks are used rather within doors in pots than out of doors. In all cases it should be sought to render the name as indelible as possible. This may be done as described above by rubbing the stick with white lead, and by writing on the surface thus produced with a lead pencil. An excellent kind of pencil for this purpose is Woolff's Indelible Pencil, which is prepared especially for this purpose, and sold by all nurserymen at 2d. each.

589 *Plant Labels* Plant labels of metal, for suspension to the plant itself, or for attachment to a stick to be placed close to the plant, have already been described, but these may be made of deal, earthenware, horn, bone, ivory, and even leather, as well as of metal, and attached to trees and plants capable of bearing them, or to the wall or supports on which the trees are trained. A convenient size for such labels is 3 inches long and 1 inch broad. When made of any of the materials specified these labels are distinguished as *permanent* labels, in contradistinction to *temporary* labels, which are made of cardboard, or coarse linen, with a face that can be written on, and having a brass eyelet hole, through which a piece of string or raffia may be passed for attachment to the plant. These temporary labels are soon destroyed by exposure to the weather, and therefore are suitable only for attachment to plants during transit from the grower to the buyer. A label of more than usual strength and endurance is sold by Messrs Dennison and Co., Shoe Lane, Fleet Street, London.

590 *Zinc Garden Labels* Lastly, we come to some labels of comparatively recent introduction, that are made of zinc, and used, according to their make, either for placing in the ground or in pots, or for attaching to the branches of trees, sticks, espaliers, rafters, etc. These are made of different shapes, and some of different sizes of the same shape. The outlines of some of them are given in Fig. 265, but other patterns are to be procured of Messrs Deane and Co., 46 King William Street, London Bridge, and of all nurserymen by whom they are sold. The label shown at A. is 4¾ inches long and 3½ inches broad, and is used for pots and borders by sticking the narrow part in the ground, or it may be reversed and hung on the edge of pots and shallow pans by bending the narrow part into the shape of a hook. The forms B and C,

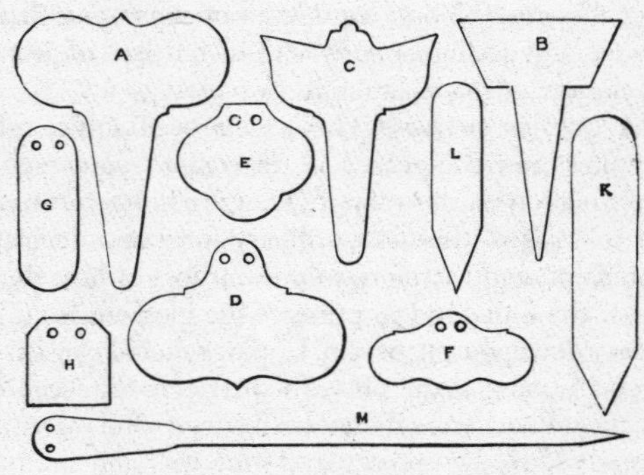

FIG. 265 *Zinc garden labels*

which measure respectively 4 inches by 2¾ inches and 4 inches by 3 inches, are intended for the same purposes, and are used in exactly the same manner, as A. The forms marked D, E, F, G, H, are perforated at the top with holes, and are used for suspension to trees, plants, etc., by wire, or for nailing to rafters, sticks, etc. Then dimensions are as follows: D, 3½ inches by 2½ inches; F, 2¼ inches by 2 inches; F, 2¾ inches by 1¼ inch; G, 2 ¾ inches by 7 ⅛ inches; H, 1½ inch by 1¼ inch. The labels K and L resemble name or number sticks in shape: K is made in different sizes, namely, 9 inches by 1¼ inch for nursery use, and 6 inches by 1 inch and 5 inches by 1 inch for pots and borders; L is 4¼ inches by ¾ inch, and is intended for use in pots of small or medium size. At M is shown a border standard or rafter and wall pin in galvanised iron. It has a head like the handle of a fiddle-pattern spoon, and pierced with holes to allow of the attachment of a zinc label by means of wire. These standards are made in any length, from 4 inches upwards. The following are the prices per 100 at which these articles are supplied: A, 3s. 6d.; B, 2s. 6d.; C, 2s. 9d.; D, 2s. 9d.; E, 1s. 9d.; F, 1s. 8d.; G, 1s. 8d.; H, 1s. 2d.; K, 1s. 9d.; and I, 1s. 8d. Yeats's Indelible Ink, an ink expressly prepared for writing on zinc labels, is supplied at 6d. per bottle. Metal labels possess an advantage over wood labels in being very much more durable, and therefore cheaper in the long run.

591 *Appliances for Protection against Weather, etc.* These appliances resolve themselves into four classes, namely, copings or solid structures affixed to the top of valls, and projecting to some little distance over the vertical surface of the wall; textile materials, such as canvas, tiffany, netting, etc., which are hung in front of trees when in bloom in order to protect the blossoms from the blighting effects of cold winds, frosts, etc.; shelters, such as wattled hurdles, straw mats, etc., designed as temporary protectors against cold winds for growing crops and plants, and against the ill effects of frost when put over frames and glazed structures; and, lastly, small glass appliances, whether wholly or partly of glass, that are used either to protect plants from the weather, or to preserve a more equable temperature within than exists without, so as to assist the formation of callus and rootlets in cuttings that are placed under them, or for shading them from the rays of the sun. They are some what numerous when taken altogether, but they may be best considered by separating them into classes, as indicated above, and dealing *seriatim* with each means of protection, whether for shelter, exclusion, or shade, under its own class.

592 *Copings for Walls* These have been sufficiently discussed in a previous chapter, and the reader is referred to paragraphs 302–4 for all necessary information on this subject. They are protectors easily made and fixed even on or to walls of the most ordinary form and description. Their function is to intercept, and therefore to prevent loss of heat during the night by radiation from the walls, and to preserve the blossom from injury from any direct and heavy downpouring of rain. Copings should consist, when practicable, of glazed wood framing, as this proves no barrier to the access of light to the upper surface of the wall, whereas if they are made of solid material, and are comparatively of great width, the upper part of the wall and the parts of the trees which are trained on this portion of it are plunged in shadow, which is not a thing to be desired or sought after. A wooden framing, moreover, affords a convenient bearing in which to insert tenter hooks, etc., on which canvas or netting may be suspended for further protection of the bloom during frosty nights and dull, cold, rainy weather. The illustration given in Fig. 266 shows a useful form of wooden coping for walls in late winter and early spring. It is made simply of boards – weather boarding, or feather-edged boarding, as it is sometimes termed, is as good as any for the purpose – screwed on to transverse slips, and connected by a ridge, which may be also of wood, or of metal, if preferred. Iron stays are screwed to the under part of the coping, which rest against the wall, and afford support to the coping, and means of attachment to the wall itself if necessary. The coping, as will be seen, is removable at pleasure, and by inserting eyes along the edge in front, or in the under side at a short distance from the edge, any protecting material may be suspended in front of the trees, if the weather be so severe as to render this additional safeguard necessary. The width of the coping from ridge to front edge should be about 18 inches, but this will be regulated by the thickness of the wall.

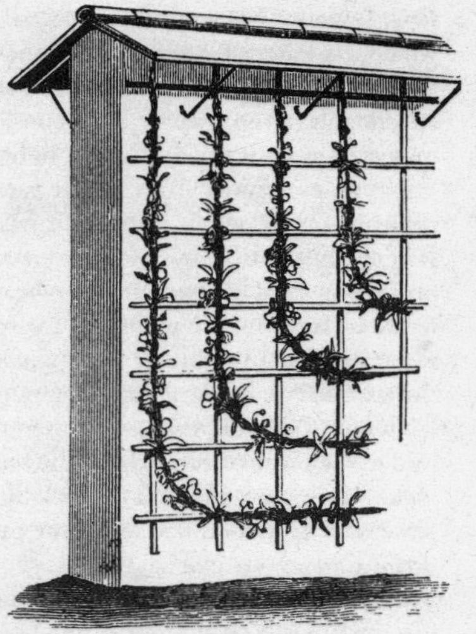

FIG. 266 *Coping for walls in front garden*

593 *Canvas, Netting, etc., for Protection of Blossom and Fruit* The method of attaching canvas to walls, and of forming screens to pull up and let down after the manner of blinds and curtains, has been described when treating of copings, and the reader is again referred to paragraphs 301–4 and following pages for information on this branch of the subject. It is chiefly requisite here to mention the different kinds of material that are used for protection and shade, and to give some idea of the prices at which it can be obtained. These materials may be procured of Mr Benjamin Edgington, 2 Duke Street, London.

1 *Patent Cotton Net* – This is a material that is extensively used for the protection of fruit trees when in bloom and tender plants from frost, hail, and wind, and ripening fruit nearly approaching maturity, from the attacks of wasps and other insects. It is also used as shading for greenhouses, but it does not answer for this purpose as well as other materials about to be described. The price is subject to slight variation, according to the cost of the raw material employed in its manufacture, but it may always be ascertained by application to the maker. It is made in pieces 50 yards in length, in three qualities, known as Nos. 1, 2, and 3. The width of the material is about 52 inches, but when a greater width is required, it may be easily joined with a needle and strong thread, like any ordinary textile fabric.

2 *Frigi Domo* – This is another material used for precisely the same purposes to which the Patent Cotton Net is applied. Being made from prepared hair and wool, it is a perfect non-conductor, and wherever it is used tends to preserve an equable temperature. It is considered to be one of the best covering materials that is made, being light as well as warm, and by no means susceptible of injury from wet. It is easily spread over greenhouses and glass structures, and in this position it has been found to effect a great saving in artificial heat. Its heat-saving properties render it especially well adapted for protecting cold houses and low-heated glass structures in cold and frosty weather. It is made in widths of 2 yards, 3 yards, and 4 yards: its price may be ascertained at any time by making application to Mr Edgington, who is now the manufacturer, or of any nurseryman or seedsman.

3 *Tiffany or Cotton Bunting* – a material also much used for shading, is usually sold in the piece of 40 yards, or the half piece of 20 yards. Its width is about 38 inches. It is generally kept in stock by nurserymen or seedsmen, of whom the prices can be ascertained, or of the proprietor.

4 *Scrim Canvas* – a material employed for greenhouse shading, 36 inches in width, can be obtained from Mr Edgington, at 6d. per yard. A new kind of material of this description has been introduced under the name of the Willesden Rot Proof Scrim, which, from its water-repelling qualities and consequent durability, seems likely to supersede ordinary scrim in popular estimation. It is treated by a patent process which makes it proof against injury by damp or water, and renders it twice as strong as untreated scrim. Its approximate width is 56 inches, and it is sold in four different qualities at 1s., 1s. 3d., 1s. 6d., and 1s. 6½d. per yard, the quality being regulated by the distance intervening between the threads of the canvas. It is used for protecting fruit trees when in blossom, roses, and tender plants and shrubs against frost, wind, and insects, and for shading greenhouses, conservatories, and all kinds of glass structures. It may be procured of nurserymen, seedsmen, etc., or at the Willesden Depot,. 34 Cannon Street, London, where the Willesden Roofing for outside roof covering of horticultural, farm, and other buildings, poultry houses and runs, etc., etc., can also be obtained. Useful horticultural shadings, which afford thorough protection for wall fruit, dwarf trees, plants, etc., against frost, hail, cutting winds, and the attacks of birds, although affording free access to light and air, and furnish admirable material for greenhouse blinds,, are supplied by the Moorhey Mill Company, 13 Ward's Buildings, Manchester, in any length above 10 yards. These shadings are 54 inches wide, and are made in four qualities, namely, No. 1, sold at 7½d. per yard run; No. 2, 6d.; No. 3, 4½d.; and No. 4, 3d. Shadings are also obtainable of Messrs Rigby, Wainwright, and Co., Neptune Works, Manchester, who will furnish samples and prices to any applicant.

5 *Old Bunting* – wholly made of wool, a material of which flags are made when it is fresh from the makers' hands, can be bought at 6d. per yard. This material is very narrow.

6 *Netting* – may be bought either new or second-hand. New netting, prepared

for use and rendered more durable by tanning, is made in two sizes of meshes – one large and the other small – the former at 6d. per yard run, or 36s. the piece of 90 yards; the latter at 9d. per yard run, or 50s. the piece of 90 yards. Its width in either mesh is 2 yards. Second-hand netting, carefully prepared, and suitable for protecting wall fruit, bush fruit, ground fruit, such as strawberries, and seed beds, from birds, is usually supplied in two widths – one of 2 yards, at 2d. per running yard, and the other of 4 yards, at 4d. per running yard. Covering for surface of this kind is therefore obtainable at a little more than 1d. per yard, for persons ordering netting are directed to observe that all netting, whether new or old, is always measured through the hand, and that if the netting is required to be stretched to its full width, about one-fourth extra in length should be ordered. Thus, if it be required to cover a space 20 yards long and 2 yards wide, 25 yards should be ordered. Tanned Garden Netting of the best qualities, and all the materials used for the protection of trees, etc., and shading glass horticultural structures, Archangel mats, raffia, etc., may be obtained of Messrs John Edgington and Co., 19 Long Lane, West Smithfield, London, who will send prices and samples on application.

594 As it is always desirable to know the prices of other makers and vendors when ordering materials of the kind described above, it may be as well to state that the following are the prices at which netting of all descriptions is offered by Mr W. Cullingford, Forest Gate, London. Cotton netting, 9 meshes to the square inch, 1½ yard wide, 7d. per yard run; extra stout strong tanned netting, 2 yards wide, 1½d. per yard, or 10s. per length of 100 yards; or 4 yards wide, 3d. per yard, or 20s. per length of 100 yards. This material is second-hand, but new twine netting is supplied by the same maker in any quantity – 1 yard wide at 2d. per yard; 2 yards wide at 4d.; 4 yards wide at 8d.; and 12 yards wide at 2s. per yard.

595 *Shelters for Growing Plants* Under this heading we may consider the means of protecting plants growing in the open ground temporarily from the adverse influence of frost and cutting winds from any particular quarter, and simple structures and appliances for the protection of cold frames, etc., and their inmates. For obtaining protection against winds there is nothing better than a line of hurdles, whether of wood or iron it matters little, with brushwood, gorse, or even light faggot wood, interlaced vertically between the horizontal bars. This affords a rough but very effective shelter, and, if no hurdles are at command, it is easy enough to knock up a few frames of rough wood for the purpose by nailing to three or more uprights, according to the length, transverse bars, at a distance apart ranging from 6 inches to 9 inches, or thereabouts. When the position of the garden is such that shelters of this kind may be frequently desirable, it is as well to give a permanent character to them by constructing wattle hurdles, which may be put away under shelter in some out-of-the-way corner or spot fitted for the purpose, and brought out for use as occasion may require. There is no difficulty in making a hurdle of this description, such as is shown in Fig. 267. The first thing to be done is to obtain a piece of wood, about 3 or 4 inches broad and the same in thickness, and to draw a line down the centre of the uppermost side as a guide for boring holes in it, about 6 inches apart,

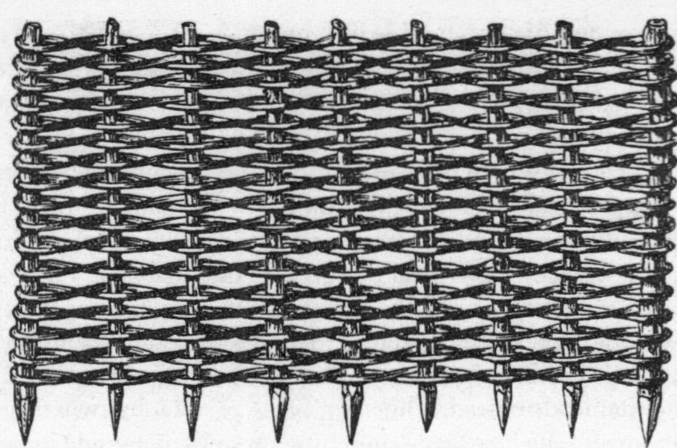

FIG. 267 *Wattle hurdle*

FIG. 268 *Frame for wattle*

which may be done with a brace and 1-inch bit, or a 1-inch auger. The holes at each end should be rather longer, say from 1¼ inch to 1½ inch in diameter. This piece of wood, which may be of any length deemed most convenient for the purpose, and which is shown in Fig. 268, serves as a frame or foundation for the hurdle. The next step is to get some stakes to serves as uprights, those intended for the ends being of the diameter of the holes made to receive them, and the intermediate stakes only 1 inch in diameter, and to sharpen one end of each. They should be about 6 inches longer than the height to which it is proposed to carry the interlacing that forms the hurdle. The stakes being sharpened must then be set in the frame, and the work of making, or rather completing, the hurdle entered on by interlacing rods of willow or hazel, or any suitable material between the uprights. Such hurdles are most useful in breaking the force and mitigating the rigour of a cold and boisterous wind.

596 *Mats for Cold Frames* Straw mats for covering frames and minor glass structures in frosty weather, and for shading them in the heat of summer, are easily made, and may afford profitable employment in the winter season at the time when nothing can be done in the open ground. The proper kind of straw for making mats of this description is wheat straw or reed, as it is called in Devonshire, and which is always combed to clear it of the withered leaves that adhere to it. Enough to make a small bundle of about 1 inch or 1½ inch in diameter is grasped in the hand, and some tarred twine is brought round in three places, or more, if thought desirable, as shown in Fig. 269. Successive bundles of straw are added until the required size is obtained, the strings which are under in one layer being brought over for the next layer. When the last layer or bundle has been added, the strings are securely tied and the ends cut off. In making a

FIG. 269 *Straw mat to project frames, etc*

mat for a frame 6 feet in measurement from top to bottom, it will be found necessary to make each layer of two portions of straw, having the ends turned outward and the heads brought together in the middle, but when a narrow mat is made, the ends of the bundles should be disposed on one side in one layer and on the opposite side in the layer next to it. It is better also to make the mat so that the straw may be arranged longitudinally from the top to the bottom of the light, and not transversely, as in this position the rain that may fall on it will be conducted more readily from top to bottom.

597 *Shelters for Early Peas, Potatoes, etc.* It will be seen from that which has been already said on this subject, that hurdles, mats, etc., thus constructed, may be easily made available for the protection of early peas, potatoes, etc. For rows of peas, the hurdles may be placed against one another on each side of the rows, meeting at the top in this form, **Λ** , which is the form of the letter **V** inverted. Two and perhaps even three rows of potatoes may be covered in the same manner, or if the potatoes are growing in short rows in a south border, a rough frame may be knocked together and placed over them to carry the straw mats, which must be laid on the frame and tied to it to prevent any chance of removal by the wind.

598 *Plant Covers or Protectors* These are equally well adapted in the larger sorts and sizes for protecting half-hardy plants and shrubs in the winter season when the weather is more than usually inclement, or for protecting plants from the sun in summer, in the smaller sorts, when recently transplanted and in absolute need of shade until new rootlets have been formed, and the plants have thus acquired a fair hold on the soil and the means of extracting moisture and nutriment from it. Sometimes the plant cover takes the form of a basket, old hampers answering well for the purpose if they be large enough, but if not, a frame may be made of osiers, or of wooden laths, about 1 inch wide and ½ inch thick, neatly framed together and covered with canvas, matting, or even with netting. It may also take the form of a wooden box or frame, covered with oiled paper, which will be found equally useful for protecting lettuces, cauliflowers, etc., in the winter, or for striking cuttings in the summer. For the latter purpose, indeed, they are well suited, because the semi-transparency of the paper affords shade to a considerable extent as well as protection, as it admits an imperfect light only, and not full light, as glass.

599 *Plant Shades* Among these appliances, Loudon describes a *plant umbrella*, which is exactly like an ordinary umbrella in form, but, instead of the usual handle, has a pointed stick, shod with iron for insertion in the ground. 'It is used,' he says, 'for shading tender plants from the sun or sheltering them from the rain. For both purposes it is convenient to have a joint in the stem so as to incline the cover according to the situation of the sun and the direction of the rain.' Amateurs should therefore take care of old frames and frames with broken handles, for they can easily be covered with green or white calico, or strong brown linen, to afford an agreeable medium for imparting shade without intercepting the light entirely, and the sticks can be jointed without much trouble to a stake or rod to be inserted in the ground, in the manner shown in Fig. 270, in which A is the handle of the umbrella, rounded at the bottom, that it may be readily turned in any direction, and B the stake to which it is attached by a pin or screw. The stick and the rod are 'halved together', as it is technically called, as shown in the side view at C. It must be borne in mind that the upper part of the rod to which the stick of the umbrella is attached should be rounded. If not rounded in the manner described, the lines of contact between stick and rod at the joint should be slanting, but care must be taken to make them parallel. When this plan is adopted, the umbrella shade can be moved in one direction only, whereas, when the ends are rounded, as shown in the illustration, the shade will turn freely in either direction about the pin or rivet that holds stick and rod together. Small shades for the partial protection of tender plants are sometimes made of wire or wicker work, in the form of bowls, cylinders, and cones, to be placed over the plants. Bell-shaped covers of earthenware, pierced with holes, are sometimes used as shades, and earthern shelters in the form of a flower pot or nearly so, with a piece taken out of one side, so that the opening can be turned to the opposite quarter to that from which an inclement wind or the sun's rays are proceeding. The nature of such a shelter may be gathered from Fig. 271, in which a flower pot with a large piece broken out of its side is utilised for this purpose. When a large pot is broken in this manner, it is better not to reduce it to fragments for crocking, but to reserve it for the purpose indicated in the illustration. An unbroken flower pot also makes an excellent shelter.

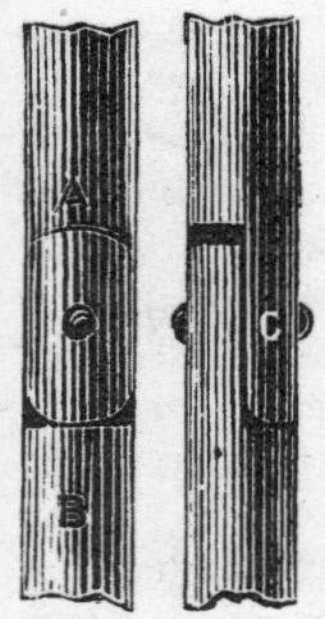

FIG. 270 *Joint in stick of plant shade*

FIG. 271 *Broken flower pot utilized as shade*

600 *Small Glass Shelters and Hand Glasses* These differ essentially from all kinds of glazed structures, from the small garden frame with a light over it, or the different kinds of plant protectors of this character that have been introduced of late years, and which must be described in another chapter. They are comparatively small in size, and are extremely portable and easily shifted from place to place. There are two types of these shelters or hand glasses, differing from each other in their construction; one type consisting of entire glasses, mostly bell-shaped or cylindrical, and the other of small frames, usually of lead or cast iron, in which flat pieces of glass are set. The old leaden hand light was used by every gardener when leaden casements were in vogue, but it is very seldom seen now, having been supplanted by the stronger hand light of cast iron or zinc, which is far less liable to injury from a chance blow, and can be glazed again and again when the glass gets broken.

601 *The Bell Glass or Cloche* This appliance is much used by French gardeners for the protection and culture of lettuces and small vegetables of this character during the winter and early spring. Its form may be seen from Fig. 272. It is usually made of a greenish kind of glass, and may be had in various sizes, large enough, in fact, to cover a cauliflower. Bell glasses, or hand glasses, are made in different shapes, some being of the form shown in the illustration, some cylindrical, some tall and narrow, and others broad and shallow; but whatever may be their form the purpose to which they are put, namely, that of covering and protecting tender vegetables, seedlings, etc., cuttings, and patches of seed that have not yet germinated, is in all cases the same. They may be obtained of Messrs James Carter and Co., 237 High Holborn, London, or of Messrs Breffit and Co., 83 Upper Thames Street, London, by whom they are manufactured. Useful sizes may be bought at 10d. and 1s. each. Bell glasses of all kinds may also be purchased of Mr Tatum, 31 Holborn, London, (corner of Fetter Lane), or of Messrs Eade and Son, 130 High Holborn, London, who will send prices on application. It must be remembered that no means of ventilation are provided in bell glasses, and that as growing plants require air the bell glass should be tilted when the weather admits, and supported on a stone or notched stick.

FIG. 272 *Bell glass or cloche*

602 *Hand Lights* The forms of hand lights are various, for they are made in all shapes – square, and with six or eight sides. Some have a movable top, while others again are made all in one piece. One feature is common to all, and that is that they are pyramidal in form, and most of them terminate in a ring or button at the top, by which the whole structure, if in one piece, or the top if in two pieces, can be lifted and moved from place to place. The form shown at A, Fig. 273, represents W. J. Barns' Patent Cap Glass, one of the best and cheapest plant protectors in the market, and much used by market gardeners. The frame is made of zinc, and the glass is octagonal in form. The 20-inch cap is supplied at 30s. per dozen, or singly at 2s. 6d.; and the 21-inch cap at 36s. per dozen, or 3s. each. An extra strong cap of 21 inches is sold at 48s. per dozen, or 4s. each. It is a useful hand light, but from the fact that its sides slant all the way from top to bottom it is better calculated as a protector for single plants than as a cover for cuttings, because the cuttings cannot be placed so close to the edge of the frame as they can in the form shown at B, as there is no head room for them when in this position, and in consequence of this a considerable portion of the space that is covered by the glass is comparatively useless. The hand light shown at B

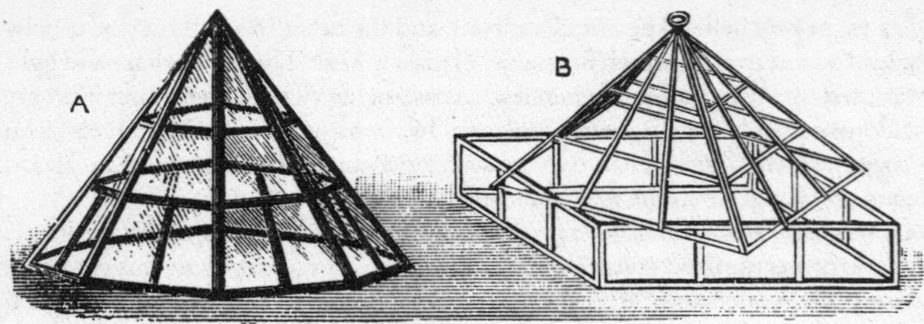

FIG. 273 *Various forms of hand lights*

consists of a cast iron frame, square and rectangular in shape, with a pyramidal four-sided top. The sides of the lower part are in separate pieces, connected at the corners by small bolts and nuts. The top is a frame of the same material, which exactly fits over the bottom, and, being movable, air can be admitted at any time in favourable weather, which is one of the greatest advantages attaching to this form. The cap glass shown at A requires tilting on one side when it is desired to admit air.

603 *Patent Square Hand Glass* The frame that has just been described is strong and durable, but owing to the material of which it is constructed it is heavy and cumbersome. It has, however, the advantage of being easily taken to pieces, and thus put away when out of use in a small space. It is superseded, however, to a great extent, if not entirely, by Barns' Patent Square Hand Glass, illustrated in Fig. 274, the frame of which is made of strong corrugated zinc, and is therefore lighter and more portable. The glazing is effected with zinc slips, and no putty is required for this operation, which is thus rendered as simple as possible, any necessary repairs or replacement of broken panes being effected in the shortest possible time by any inexperienced hand by lifting the slips that secure the pane, taking out the fragments of glass that remain in the grooves, introducing the new pane, and pressing down the slips once more, all of which can be done in a minute or two. The advantages presented by the Patent Square Hand Glass are that every inch of the area it covers can be utilised for cuttings, that it is extremely portable, and combines with these features strength and durability. Every frame is alike in size and shape, and therefore spare glass can be kept at hand for repairs, and, as will be seen from the illustration, only three sizes of panes are required, *one* for the sides and *two* for the top. The frame will retain its original shape and strength should all the glass be broken, and the glass can be removed speedily from one frame and put into another without damage, all glass being interchangeable, and every frame of

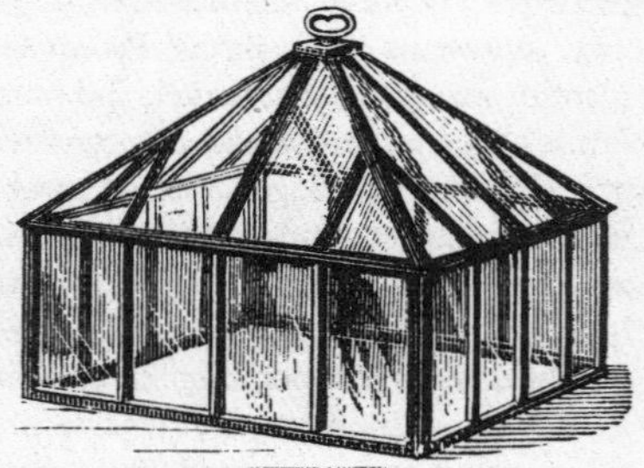

FIG. 274 *Barn's patent square hand glass*

the same size alike. The frames are made in five sizes, 12, 14, 16, 18, and 20 inches square, sold respectively at 5s, 7s., 9s., 10s. 6d., and 12s. 6d. each.

604 It is scarcely necessary to remind amateurs who can use the soldering iron and zinc shears that the zinc strips of various forms which are sold for the manufacture of ferneries and aquariums can be easily utilised for making home-made hand lights of any shape and form. There is no real difficulty in contriving anything of this kind, and it is as easy to made an octagonal light, top and all, with zinc strips, as it is to make a square one. Even the woodworker may serve his purpose by making four frames for the sides, with rebates to take the glass, which must, of course, be puttied in, the frames being attached in rectangular form by screws. A top, fixed or movable, may be added at pleasure, the simplest and easiest made consisting of two sides, upright like the gable of a house, with rectangular pieces of glass between them, one on either side, sloping like the roof of a house.

605 While the subject of hand lights is under consideration, it will be useful to draw the attention of gardeners, and especially of amateurs, to the specialities of Mr C. Frazer, Horticultural Builder, Norwich, in this direction. This maker sends out what may be termed nests of hand lights, which are convenient because they cover conjointly a large superficial area of ground, and may be put away when out of use in a space no larger than that which is covered by the largest, because they can be placed one within the other, from the smallest of the set to the largest. The set of New Improved Hand Lights, the largest of which is shown in Fig. 275, comprises six lights, which cover altogether 17 square feet of ground. They are made in diminishing sizes, are painted with three coats of paint, glazed with 21-ounce glass, and sent carriage paid to any town in England and Wales, or to Edinburgh, Glasgow, Dublin, or Belfast for £2 7s. 6d. The mode of affording ventilation is shown in the illustration.

FIG. 275 *Frazer's new Improved hand light*

606 *Gilbert's Registered Hand Light*

This useful hand light, whose form is shown in the accompanying illustration, is admirably adapted for all purposes for which hand lights are generally used, whether for raising seedling plants, for striking cuttings, for protecting young plants, such as celery and cauliflowers when taken from the seed bed and pricked out for the first time, for putting over lettuces and cauliflowers in the winter season and over cucumbers and marrows in the summer, and even over strawberry plants to accelerate the ripening of the fruit. The frame is made of wood, strengthened at the bottom by corner pieces of iron, and at the top by a plate of wrought iron, which is screwed to the sides and back and is turned over at the top so as to form a groove for the reception of the glass. An iron rib also runs across the frame from front to back, and this is similarly grooved, so that two pieces of glass are used to cover the hand light instead of one, which is economical in case of breakage. To this rib a handle is attached by which the whole frame can be lifted bodily and removed from place

FIG. 276 *Gilbert's registered hand glass*

to place at pleasure. The glass is slipped into the grooves in the ironwork, and each pane is kept in place by a button attached to the front part of the light. When ventilation is necessary the buttons can be turned and the glass drawn down. As no putty is used in the glazing, a broken pane of glass can be immediately replaced without any trouble. These lights are made in sizes ranging from 12 to 22 inches square, and are glazed with 21-ounce glass.

A writer in *Gardening Illustrated* gives the diagram shown in Fig. 277, and the following description of a hand light that he has found useful at all seasons, but especially in spring and autumn for striking cuttings. 'It is formed,' he says, 'of ¾-inch deal board. The pieces are not framed together, but simply nailed so that they can be easily taken apart if it is thought desirable to do that either for removal to a distance or to stow away. The back projects beyond the sides ½ inch to make the nails hold firmer, and the narrow piece in front and the sides are secured by being halved to each other. Small strips of wood are nailed to the front ends of the sides, which, with the addition of another inside, form a groove for the front pane of glass to slide in. The pane at top is supported by a rabbet, formed by other and wider strips fastened to the sides about half an inch from the top, and the front of the pane rests on the glass below, overhanging it by about ⅛ inch. The frames are made to suit the dimensions of the panes of glass used in my greenhouse, a supply of which is always kept in case of accident. The dimensions are 14 inches by 12 inches, and one cut down the middle lengthways makes two front panes, so that one of them will supply glass for two frames. The front pane slides down the grooves on either side, and rests on the wooden base below. The best thing for the frame to stand on is a piece of flat stone or slate, or some material which will not be affected by the damp. On this I place a layer of wet cocoanut fibre and silver sand, and hereon stand 12 3-inch cutting pots. Such frames are easily made, cost but little, and give free admission to the sun's rays, and this is especially beneficial when it is thought desirable to shade the foliage of the plants by placing a piece of paper or other material on the glass at the top. They will also be found to afford temporary spring protection to vegetable marrows and other plants when first turned out of their pots and placed in the open borders; but for that purpose the frames are best made to allow the glass to cover the back board by making it ½ inch less high, and shortening the lengths of the sides in the same proportion. The ends of each piece should be painted before they are nailed together, and the whole should have at least two coats of paint, if they are intended to be used in the open air. Two such frames, and that is all I have at present, will be found to do the work of many bell glasses, and do it more effectually. It will be seen that to get at the plants inside you have only to raise the top pane of glass.' As the dimensions of the glass used are given, the dimensions of the frame can be readily determined.

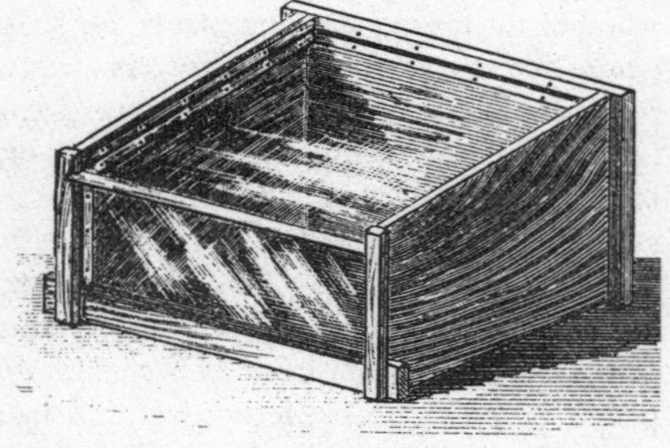

FIG. 277 *Amateur's hand light*

CHAPTER 15

Garden Tools, Implements, and Appliances Required for Shearing and Clipping, for Carriage and Transfer, for Protection against Animals, etc., and for Miscellaneous Purposes

607 The long list of appliances of all kinds that must be, or may be, used in the garden is not yet exhausted, and to do this will require yet another chapter; but it must not be thought that too much space is devoted to this portion of necessary garden lore and teaching, for, indeed, twice as many pages as have already been devoted to the subject and are yet to come might be given with advantage to the reader. And, again, it must be borne in mind that the subject matter comprised in these chapters is not a dull, long catalogue of tools and implements whose names alone are given, but that their uses and the purposes they serve are fully described, that means are often brought under the reader's notice by which home-made substitutes for many of them may be contrived and manufactured, and that advantage has been taken of their mention to introduce collateral information, as it may be termed, on a variety of subjects connected with them more or less directly, but which could not have been dealt with as conveniently in any other part of this work. It has been sought throughout to show how garden work may be done economically as well as efficiently, a point which has never yet been aimed at in any existing work on gardening, but which is as necessary to the gardener as careful management of money and stores is to the householder and housekeeper, and thrift to one and all.

608 *Instruments and Tools for Shearing, Clipping, etc.* In connection with this portion of the subject, we have to consider the implements that are used for keeping the lawn in order, and cutting the grass both on lawn and edges when they are formed of turf. We have, therefore, first, to glance at the appliances that are used for cutting the grass itself, among which the scythe, the mowing machine, and the shears take the lead; then we must consider the tools that are used for maintaining the direct line of the turf edges without and within the edge, or, in other words, next to the path on one side and the border on the other; and then the besom, or broom, with which the cut grass is removed, weeders of different kinds that may not have been already mentioned, and the roller, which is useful both on paths and lawn in preserving a smooth and even surface on each, although that surface is of necessity rounded or sloping in the former and flat for its entire extent in the latter.

609 *The Scythe* Since the introduction of the mowing machine, the scythe is comparatively little used, and is regarded rather as an agricultural instrument

FIG. 279 *Boyd's patent scythe*

than a gardener's tool. But even now there are times when the use of the scythe on a lawn is necessary, and that is when the grass has been allowed to grow to too great a length to permit of its easy and ready removal with the mowing machine. This happens when a lawn or grass plot has been neglected owing to the house to which it is attached being without a tenant, or when the grass has been left too long in the previous autumn, not having been cut to the latest possible date as it should have been. The scythe may be described as a long curved blade, thin at the edge and for the greater part of its breadth, but having a back of considerable thickness, projecting on the side that is uppermost when the scythe is in use, like a flange. This blade is set at the end of a long handle, the handle being bent in such a way as to enable the operator to maintain a semi-upright position, and attached to the handle by two iron rings are two short and upright cylinders of wood, by which the instrument is grasped and worked to and fro with a swinging motion of the body. The edge is soon dulled, and requires sharpening from time to time with a scythe stone, a round stone of coarse grain, like the spoke of a ladder in shape and costing about 4d. Scythe blades are supplied separately at 3s. 6d. each. It should be said that blades are cranked or not cranked; when cranked, there is a hinge between the blade and the socket, into which the end of the handle is put. A lawn scythe, not cranked, costs 5s. 6d., but one that is cranked, and notably the Vulcan, supplied by Messrs Deane and Co., 46, King William Street, London Bridge, costs 1s. more. Boyd's Patent Scythe, which is illustrated in Fig. 279, is cranked so that the blade may be brought close to the handle; it costs 8s. 6d. complete, but it possesses an advantage which other scythes do not, namely, that of being adjustable for use by either a tall or a short man. Warren's Cast Steel Scythes, an excellent kind of scythe blade, of superior quality and highly tempered, are supplied by Messrs John G. Rollins and Co., Limited, American Merchants and Factors, Old Swan Wharf, London Bridge, in sizes from 32 inches to 44 inches, at 42s. per dozen, or 3s. 6d. each. American Scythe snaths, or handles, are supplied by the same firm in two kinds – the ordinary handle at 2s. 6d. each, and the Patent Loop handle at 3s. 6d. each.

610 *Mowing Machines* These are as numerous as sewing machines, and where there are so many that are good, it is difficult, if not impossible, to assign the palm of excellence to any particular machine. All, then, that can be done here is to describe the principle on which the mowing machine acts, and then to give the names of some of the principal machines that are now in use. There are many machines in existence, manufactured and sold by as many makers. To single out any individual machine for commendation would be invidious, and utterly beyond the province of this work. It must, therefore, be understood that those that are named are not introduced through special preference, and that those which may be omitted are not left out with any intention of imputing inferiority to them. The special object here is to place a few names of machines at the disposal of the reader, not to direct or influence him in making a choice. It will be better for anyone who is about to purchase to make personal examination of a few machines before buying, and then to select that machine which, in size, capability, and price, appears to be best suited to his purpose. There is no matter on which all men think alike, and no article that all men regard with the same degree of favour; and this holds good with regard to mowing machines as well as to other machines and appliances that are designed to accomplish a certain purpose.

611 *The Principle of the Mowing Machine* In order to arrive at the principle of action of any class of machines, it is as well to select one whose construction is of the simplest character, as it can be more easily described and the description more readily understood. The Climax, a machine manufactured by Messrs Follows and Bates, Manchester, is perhaps the most simple and least complicated of all the machines that have been in the market, and will, therefore, be better for consideration and for arriving at the principle on which it works than a more elaborate one. This mowing machine, like all others that are driven by hand, consists of a frame formed by cast-iron sides, each terminating in a convenient handle at the upper end, and connected and strengthened by transverse bars. The lower part of this frame is shown in Fig. 280, the principal part of it being A, to which the cutting part of the machinery is attached, and the arm B, at right angles to A, or nearly so, made in the form of a **Y**, in order to strengthen the entire framework, by causing the attachment to be at two points instead of one only. The arm B carries at its lower extremity a small wooden roller, C. The object of this is to afford support for the machine, and to keep it in the proper position when in use, and not, as some might imagine, for the purpose of rolling the turf, for which purpose it would be useless, on account of its lightness. The machine is supposed to rest on the base formed by the wheels in front and the roller in the rear, and should be kept in this position when it is at work.

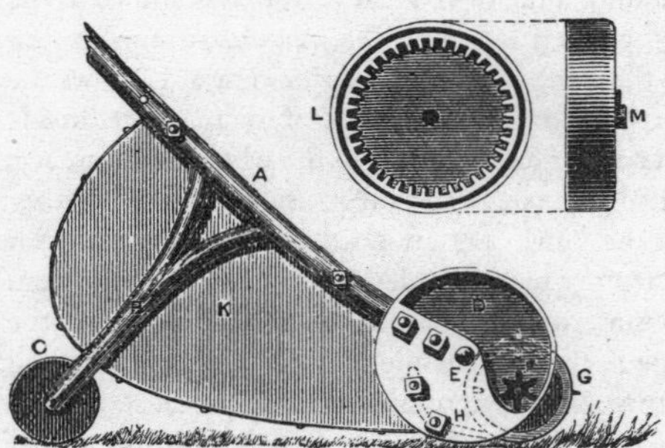

FIG. 280 *Diagram illustrative of general principle of mowing machine*

612 The end of the part A of the framework is secured by two bolts to a strong circular plate, D, the upper part of which is formed so as to present a shallow indentation, as shown in the illustration. The object of this is to make the plate as light as possible, and to throw the strength into the lower half, where it is most needed. This half, accordingly, is of the thickness of the rim of the entire plate. Through the centre of this plate an axle, E, passes, the axle being in no way fixed to the plate, but working freely through a hole made in the plate for its reception. Another axle passes through another hole in the plate at F, terminating in a small cogged wheel. This axle carries the discs, G, on the edges of which the knives or cutting irons are set diagonally to the planes of the discs. The grass is caught by the revolving knives, and drawn by them against the sharp edge of a piece of iron, H, that stretches transversely from plate to plate, and has an arm on either side, which is secured to the plate by a couple of bolts and nuts. The grass, when severed by the action of the knives passing over the edge, is carried by the whirl of the wheel that sustains the knives over the plate, H, and into the box, K, behind it, which is a trough of metal, nailed to wooden sides, which in their turn are attached to the lower portion of the frame, A, by bolts. The machine may be used with or without the, box as found convenient.

613 The question now arises – How are the knives of the machine actuated, and the machine driven? and this must be explained. On the projecting ends of the free axle, E, two cast-iron box wheels are placed and fastened to it by a pin passing through a boss in the centre of the exterior of the wheel and into or through the axle. The axle and the wheels thus attached to it are, to all intents and purposes, one piece, and as the machine is pushed forward the wheels and axle turn, facilitating the progress of the machine, which thus moves on these wheels in front and the roller behind. The form of these wheels is shown in the illustration, an interior view being given at L, and the side elevation, showing the pin that fastens the wheel to the axle, at M. The interior view at L shows the construction of the inside of the wheel on the right hand of the machine. Inside the rim of the wheel is a circle of cogs or teeth, which, as the wheel revolves, acts on the cog wheel at the extremity of the axle F, and causes the cylinder, or rather the skeleton cylinder, to which the knives are attached, to revolve with great rapidity. In the small machine from which this description has been written, there are 51 cogs round the circumference of the box wheel, and 9 cogs on the wheel at the extremity of the axle F, therefore while the box wheel turns round once, the cylinder carrying the knives will turn round $5\frac{2}{3}$ times, because $51 \div 9 = 5\frac{6}{9}$ or $5\frac{2}{3}$. Thus the speed of the cylinder is very nearly six times as great as that of the wheels on which the machine is carried and driven.

614 *Care of Machines* Being brought into contact with wet or damp grass, the machine and all its parts should be kept scrupulously clean and well oiled. The knives should be kept free from dirt, with which they will inevitably become clogged in course of use, and at intervals they should be sharpened, for they require sharpening as much as a scythe or any other cutting instrument, but not so frequently. There is a hole in the wheel on the right-hand side through which the cog wheel and axle of the cylinder that carries the knives can be oiled, and the axle of the driving wheels can be oiled by pouring a little oil on the ends of the axle. But it is also desirable that the machine itself should be taken to pieces occasionally, and the various parts well and thoroughly cleaned. This will cause the machine, be it what it may, to work more pleasantly and perform its duty with less labour on the part of the person who is driving it.

615 *The Challenge Lawn Mower Sharpener*
Apropos to sharpening the knives of the lawn mower or mowing machine, it is probable that many gardeners, both amateur and professional, have found themselves at a loss for the means of doing so. It may, therefore, be useful to say that with the Challenge Lawn Mower Sharpener, sold by Messrs Churchill and Co., Importers of American Tools and Machinery, 21 Cross Street, London, at 4s. each, any man can sharpen his own mower without taking it apart, and, further, it requires a few minutes only to sharpen a machine, which can thus be always kept in perfect cutting order. It is adjustable to any lawn mower that is in the market, and needs to be adjusted but once for any particular machine. It cannot get out of order, and is so simple that anyone can use it. This appliance is illustrated in Fig. 281. The file carrier, the end of which is seen projecting at the front, is cylindrical in form, and is held in place by a set screw, shown at the top. By loosening this screw the file carrier can be turned till the file is properly adjusted to the angle or bevel of the knife to be sharpened. The file is a three cornered file, held in place by a set screw at each end. By means of the hook-shaped guide shown at the bottom of the illustration to the left, and which is adjustable up or down, or may be swivelled either way, it can be adjusted to any of the lawn mowers that are made. The gauge, which is worked by the large screw shown to the right, is intended to touch the back of the knife and steady the sharpener. When properly adjusted, it is in such a position that the little machine may be rapidly moved along the face of each knife, one after another, so as to sharpen their edges whenever it may be necessary, with very little trouble.

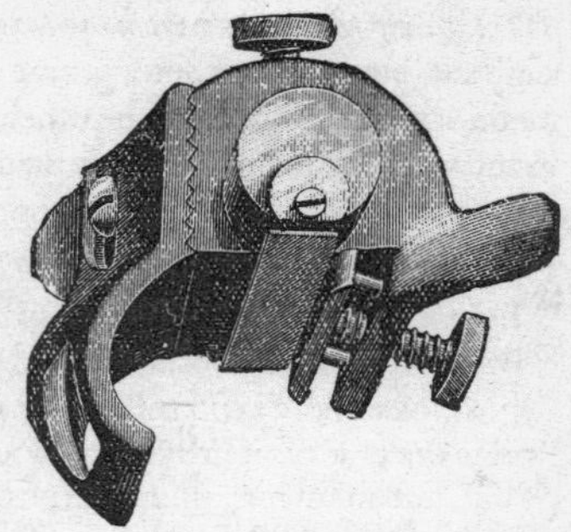
FIG. 281 *The Challenge lawn mower sharpener*

616 *When to Use a Mowing Machine* A scythe works better in the morning when the dew is on the grass, or when it has been wetted by a slight shower of rain, so when mowing is effected by means of the scythe it is better to get the work done early in the morning. The mowing machine, which works on an entirely different principle, acts more smoothly and pleasantly when the grass is dry, and may therefore be used even at midday, when the sun is at its hottest. Neglected lawns that it is sought to bring into better order should first be cut with the scythe early in the morning, and run over with the mowing machine later in the day. With some machines it is said that any kind of grass can be cut, whether long or short, but with the generality of machines it is better to deal with short grass than with long. To produce a soft elastic velvet-like surface of fine short, close grass, a lawn should be run over with the machine at least once a week. Constant cutting at regular intervals carried on as long and as late as possible into the autumn will, in time, render even coarse, broad-leaved grass finer and closer than it is by nature.

617 *Mowing Machines now in the Market* It must be repeated that there is not the slightest intention of setting any one of the kinds of machines now to be mentioned before or after the other. It is only sought to name a few that are now in the market, and to leave it to the intending purchaser to choose for himself of these or others, of which space forbids the mention.

1 *The Archimedean American Lawn Mower* This machine is said to be extremely light in draught, simple in construction, well made, and not likely to get out of order. It cuts long or short grass, wet or dry grass, with equal facility, and does not clog. There is no roller in front of the cutters, and the machine therefore cuts the grass as it grows, and does not miss the bents, It works well on slopes and embankments, under shrubs, and close up to trees. It may be used either with or without the grass box, as may be desired. These machines are supplied by all ironmongers, and by Messrs John G. Rollins and Co., Limited, Old Swan Wharf, London , in sizes and at prices as follows:

6 in.	for small plots	£1 5s.
8 in.	for small plots	£2 2s.
10 in.	for lady or boy	£3 3s.
12 in.	for lady or boy	£4 4s.
14 in.	for man	£5 0s.
16 in.	for man on level	£6 0s.
18 in.	for man and boy	£7 0s.
20 in.	for man and boy	£7 0s.

FIG. 282 *Archimedean American lawn mower*

Grass boxes are charged extra, 6 inches to 12 inches, each, and 14 inches to 20 inches, 10s. each. An illustration of this machine is given in Fig. 282.

2 *The New Automaton Lawn Mower* A representation of this machine, which was awarded a silver medal at the Inventions Exhibition of 1885, is given in Fig. 283. It is graceful in design, easy to work, and cuts without ribbing, producing a fine velvety surface. It rolls the whole of the lawn, no further rolling being required, and has a large open cylinder with patent single screw adjustment. The gearing is simple, quiet, and certain, is completely covered, and allows free motion to the knives. The machine has the best materials and workmanship, and highest finish, will give satisfaction for years, and can

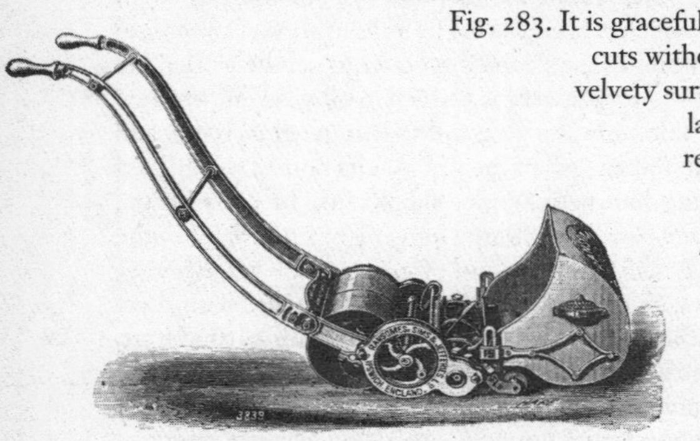
FIG. 283 *Ransome's New automation lawn mower*

be easily repaired. It is usually sent with a grass box, but can be used without if preferred. The sizes and prices are as follows:

8 inch £2 15s. 0d.	14 inch £5 10s.0d.	20 inch £8 0s. 0d.
10 inch £3 10s. 0d.	16 inch £6 10s. 0d.	
12 inch £4 10s. 0d.	18 inch £7 10s. 0d.	

3 *The Coventry Lawn Mower* This lawn mower is so called because it is manufactured at Coventry, by Messrs Nettlefold and Sons, the well known makers of garden tools and appliances, builders' ironmongery, nails, screws, etc., of Birmingham, and 54 High Holborn, London. Its component parts are formed of the best English steel and iron, and it contains all the improvements which have been recently introduced into machines of this kind on both sides of the Atlantic. Its great merits are its cheapness and the lightness and ease with which it can be worked; it will cut wet or dry grass of any length, and can be turned in its own width. The appearance and construction of the machine is shown in Fig. 284. It is made in five sizes, but the largest size is said to be so easy in its working that a lady may manage it. The following table exhibits the sizes in which it is constructed, and the prices at which they are sold, with or without rollers, as may be preferred; the grass boxes and front wooden rollers for cutting verges are charged as extras:

FIG. 284 *The Coventry lawn mower*

Width of Cutters	8 inch	10 inch	13 inch	15 inch	18 inch
Machine only, with or without Rollers	£2 2s. 0d.	£3 3s. 0d.	£4 4s. 0d.	£5 5s. 0d.	£6 6s. 0d.
Grass Boxes	6s. 6d.	7s. 0d.	7s. 6d.	8s. 6d.	9s. 0d.
Front Wooden Rollers for Verges	2s. 6d.	2s. 9d.	3s. 0d.	3s. 6d.	4s. 0d.
Total, if complete	£2 11s. 0d.	£3 12s. 9d.	£4 14s. 6d.	£5 17s. 0d.	£6 19s. 0d.

4 *The Easy Lawn Mower* This lawn mower has acquired its peculiar name from the facility with which large sizes can be worked on account of its lightness. This lightness arises from its make, which reduces the weight of metal employed in its construction to a minimum. The roller, as may be seen from Fig. 285, is an open one, being made of wheels connected by steel bars, the

whole revolving on a strong axle. The knives are bent to greater extent than is usual with the cutters of mowing machines, and are set on curved irons radiating from the axle, and each attached to each cutter at different points of its length. These lawn mowers were originally made with three cutters, but are now furnished with five, thus bringing more shearing power to operate on the grass to be cut, and reducing the work to be effected by each cutter, and consequently the resistance offered by the grass to the machine. The sizes and prices, inclusive of grass boxes, are:

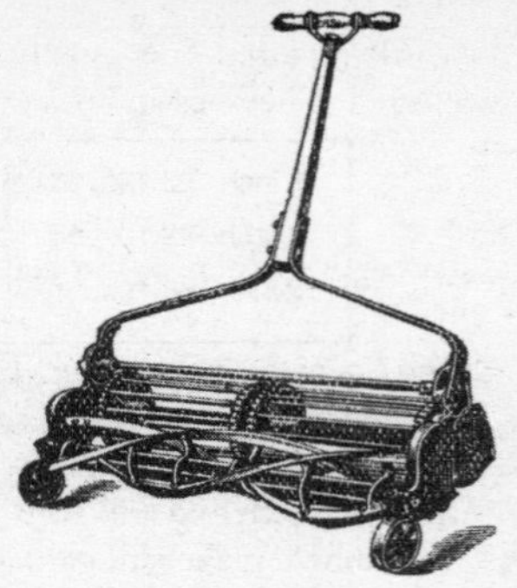

FIG. 285 *The Easy lawn mower*

10 inch	£3 10s. 6d.	16 inch	£5 5s. 0d.	24 inch	£8 5s. 0d.
12 inch	£4 2s. 6d.	18 inch	£5 17s. 6d.	30 inch	£16 10s. 0d.
14 inch	£4 15s. 0d.	20 inch	£6 7s. 6d.	40 inch	£25 0s. 0d.

These machines are supplied by all ironmongers, or by Messrs Selig, Sonnenthal, and Co., 85 Queen Victoria Street, London.

5 *The Patent Excelsior Lawn Mower* This is an American machine, manufactured at Newburgh, New York, by the Chadborn and Coldwell Manufacturing Company, whose London offices are at 223 Upper Thames Street, London, Superiority is claimed for this machine on the score of simplicity of construction, lightness of draught, ease of adjustment, and the variety and quality of the work that is done by it. It is favourably spoken of by those who have had it in use, and it is said to be specially suited for large lawns, lawn tennis grounds, etc., on account of the closeness and evenness with which the mowing is done, and the rapidity with which the work is got through. Another good feature in this machine (Fig. 286) is that if any part is broken a similar part to take its place can be supplied separately. The prices, exclusive of grass boxes, which are extra, and which are charged at 5s. for 8-inch and 10-inch machines, 7s. 6d. for 12-inch, 14-inch, and 16-inch machines, and 10s. for 18-inch and 20-inch machines, are:

FIG. 286 *The patent Excelsior lawn mower*

8 inch	£2 5s. 0d.	12 inch	£4 2s. 6d.	16 inch	£6 2s. 6d.	20 inch	£7 10s. 0d.
10 inch	£3 5s. 0d.	14 inch	£5 2s. 6d.	18 inch	£7 0s. 0d.		

A horse lawn mower is also supplied on this principle, which is light in draught and easy to work. It is supplied in four sizes, at prices as follows, including grass collecting box:

25 inch – £14	30 inch – £18	35 inch – £25	40 inch – £30

With these horse mowers £4 extra is charged for shafts, seat, and castor wheels. Practically the smaller machines of this class may be worked by a man and a boy or two men, as well as the larger sizes of other hand machines. An illustration of the horse lawn mower is given in Fig. 287, from which its nature and construction may be easily seen.

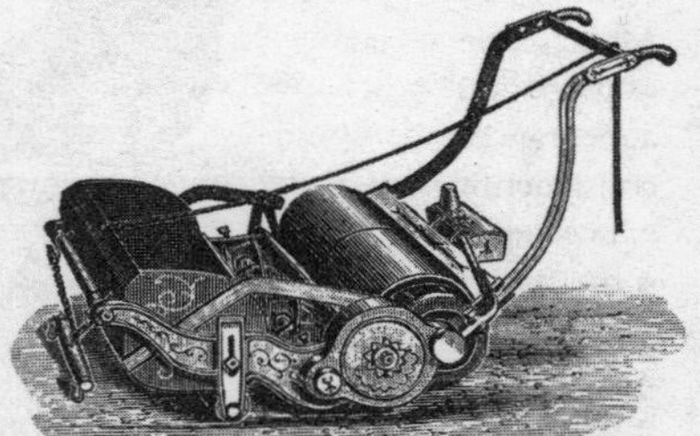

FIG. 288 *The Excelsior horse lawn mower*

6 *The Excelsior Junior Lawn Mower* This machine (Fig. 288) is of the Climax type – that is to say, it is a machine in which the actuating power that sets the cutters in motion is placed within the side wheels. It is stated be light in draught, and thoroughly efficient. The knives attached to the cutting apparatus are of steel of excellent quality, and the patent improved ratchet with which it is fitted is self-cleansing, and therefore cannot clog. There are no springs in it, or any parts that are liable to get out of order. The smallest size is recommended for amateurs, and appears to be desirable for small lawns. It is manufactured and sold by the Chadborn and Coldwell Manufacturing Company, the makers of the larger Excelsior machines. The sizes and prices are as follows: 10-inch, £2 10s.; 12-inch, £3 15s.; 14-inch £4 2s. 6d.; 16-inch, £4 14s.; 18-inch, £5. The machine is light in appearance, and seems eminently well calculated to do the work required of it.

FIG. 288 *The Excelsior junior lawn mower*

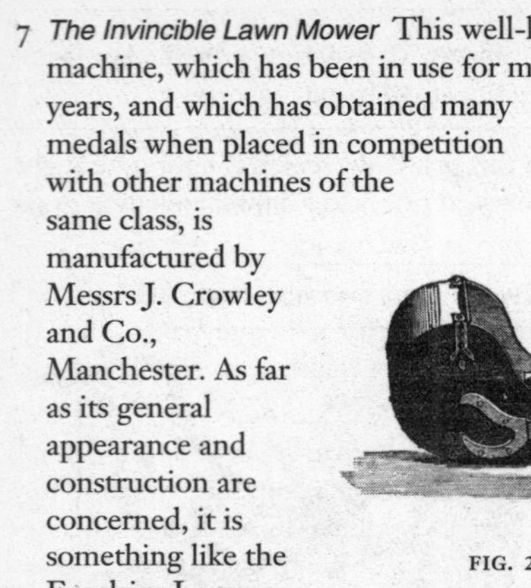

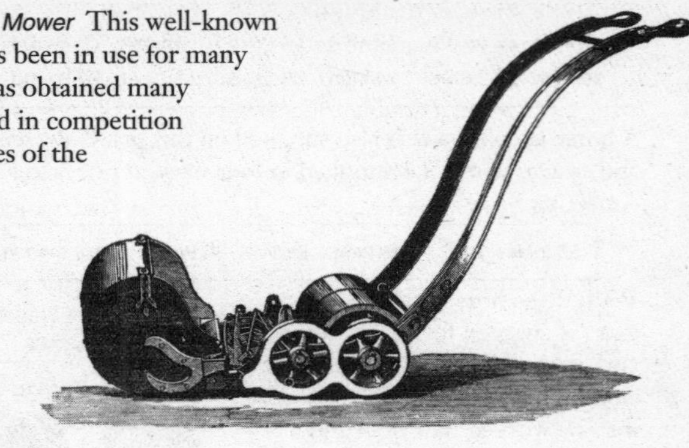

FIG. 289 *The Invincible lawn mower*

7 *The Invincible Lawn Mower* This well-known machine, which has been in use for many years, and which has obtained many medals when placed in competition with other machines of the same class, is manufactured by Messrs J. Crowley and Co., Manchester. As far as its general appearance and construction are concerned, it is something like the Excelsior Lawn Mower, the grass box being in front, the rollers behind, and the cutters between them, but the handles by which the machine is held and propelled are different, both in form and construction. It may be said that one of the points for which superiority is claimed for this machine lies in the long wood rollers being placed behind the cutters, so that no pressure is brought to bear on the uncut grass before it is seized and severed by the revolving knives. This is a point of considerable importance, as it seems undesirable to flatten the grass before the cutters reach it. An illustration of the machine is given in Fig. 289. The following are the sizes and prices at which it is supplied, grass collecting boxes included

10 inch	£3 10s. 0d.	14 inch	£5 10s. 0d.	18 inch	£7 10s. 0d.
12 inch	£4 10s. 0d.	16 inch	£6 10s. 0d.	20 inch	£8 10s. 0d.

The Invincible Horse Lawn Mower, constructed on the same principle and supplied with the necessary appliances for traction by animals, is sold in four sizes at the following prices, namely, 24-inch, £14; 30-inch, £22; 36-inch, £26; 42-inch, £30.

8 *The Patent Monarch Lawn Mower* – This is one of the numerous machines manufactured under one or other of Green's patents by Messrs T. Green and Son, Limited, Leeds and London, all of which, it may be said, are well worthy of notice. It is claimed for this machine that, although it is not so easily worked as the Silens Messor, which will be mentioned presently, it is well adapted for cutting long, coarse, rough, and wet grass, and

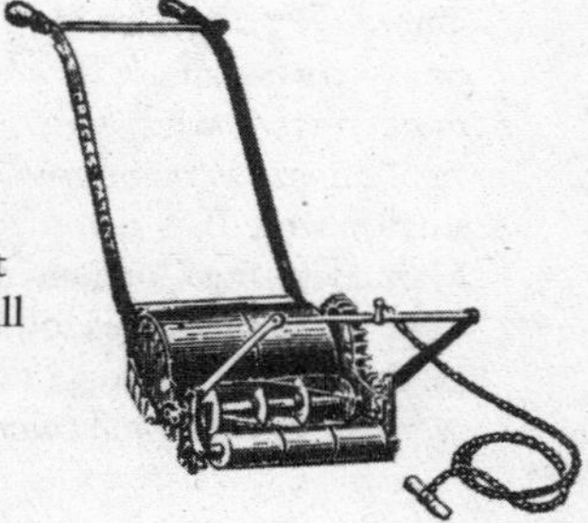

FIG. 290 *The patent Monarch lawn mower*

that it is strongly made and does its work efficiently, cutting nearer to any object than any machine extant. Its form and construction may be seen from Fig. 290, which shows it to have a series of small wooden rollers in front of the cutters and a double roller behind them. The sizes in which it is made and their prices respectively are as follows:

Single Handed – 6-inch, £ 1 15s.; 8-inch, £2 10s. (sizes suitable for lady); 10-inch, £3 10s. (for strong youth); 12-inch, £4 10s.; 14-inch, £5 10s. (for man).

Double Handed – 16-inch, £6 10s. (for one man on even lawn); 18-inch, £7 10s.; 20-inch, £8; 22-inch, £8 10s.; 24-inch, £9 (for man and boy). The 22-inch and 24-inch sizes are supplied in a stronger make, with appliances for donkey, at 30s. extra.

Horse Power Machines – 26-inch, £14; 28-inch, £16 30-inch, £18, the first of these sizes being suitable for a donkey, the second for a pony, and the third for a small horse. The following sizes require to be drawn by a large and strong horse: 30-inch, £22; 36-inch, £26; 42-inch, £30; 48-inch, £34. Leather boots for animals, to prevent cutting the turf with their iron shoes, are supplied – for donkey, at £1 per set; for pony, at £1 4s.; and for horse, at £1 9s.

9 *The Patent Multum-in-Parvo Lawn Mower* – This machine is specially recommended to those who stand in need of a small mower for personal use, as being one of the best of its kind that has yet been produced. It is, moreover, low in price, and therefore combines cheapness with excellence. Its form is shown in Figs. 291 and 292. It is simple in construction, easily adjusted and easily worked, and well adapted for cutting small plots, borders, verges, round flower beds, and the edges of walks. The following are the prices and sizes at which it is supplied by all ironmongers, and Messrs T. Green and Son, Limited, Leeds and London, the manufacturers:

To cut 6 inches without grass box	£1 1s. 0d.	with grass box	£1 5s. 0d.
To cut 7 inches without grass box	£1 8s. 0d.	with grass box	£1 13s. 0d.
To cut 8 inches without grass box	£1 15s. 0d.	with grass box	£2 0s. 0d.

FIG. 291 *The patent Multum-in-parvo lawn mower. (Right side, without grass box)*

FIG. 292 *The patent Multum-in-parvo lawn mower. (Left side, with grass box attached)*

10 *Shanks' Patent Lawn Mower* – Lawn mowers are very much alike in general appearance, and that this machine, manufactured by Messrs Shanks and Co., Arbroath and London, is no exception to the rule, may be seen from the illustration which is given of it in Fig. 293. One great merit attaching to the machine is its cheapness in all sizes. It is said to work with ease and facility in all situations, whether on broad lawns and pleasure grounds, or between flower beds and over narrow verges, and to cut wet grass and dry grass equally well. Sizes and prices of hand machines are as follows, including grass boxes:

6 inches	£1 5s. 0d.	12 inches	£4 10s. 0d.	19 inches	£8 0s. 0d.
8 inches	£2 5s. 0d.	14 inches	£5 10s. 0d.	22 inches	£8 10s. 0d.
10 inches	£3 10s. 0d.	16 inches	£6 10s. 0d.	24 inches	£9 0s. 0d.

Horse Power Machines – Machines for horse power are sold at the following prices, the first three sizes being suitable for a donkey or pony, the last four for horses:

25 inches	£13 0s. 0d.	30 inches (horse)	£32 10s. 0d.	42 inches	£28 0s. 0d.
28 inches	£15 15s. 0d.	36 inches	£24 0s. 0d.	48 inches	£32 0s. 0d.
30 inches	£17 0s. 0d.				

With these machines patent delivering apparatus is supplied at an extra charge, namely, 25-inch, 25s.; 28 and 30-inch, 30s.; 36 to 48-inch, 40s.

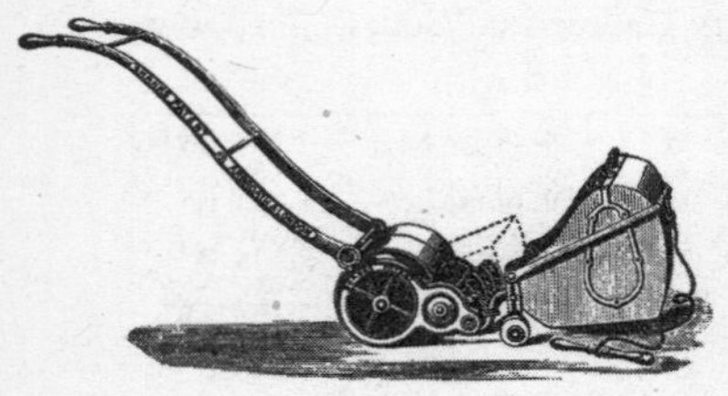

FIG. 293 *Shank's patent lawn mower*

FIG. 294 *The patent Silens Messor machine*

11 *The Patent Silens Messor Machine* – This lawn mower (Fig. 294) is perhaps the best known and most justly celebrated of the various machines manufactured by Messrs T. Green and Son, Leeds and London. They have stood the test of many years' experience, and are held in high estimation by those who have used them. They possess a peculiar advantage over the machines of other makers, namely, that of being self-sharpening, for when the cutters have become blunted by running round in one direction, the cylinder can be reversed, and the blunted edges of the knives working against the bottom blade or plate, which is met by them when cutting the grass, will

be sharpened in a short time. Thus the work of sharpening the edges that are brought into contact with the grass is effected in and by the machine by a simple reversal of the cylinder, which can be effected in two or three minutes' time even by an inexperienced person. Horse-power machines of the same construction are supplied by the makers and all ironmongers. It is unnecessary to repeat sizes and prices, as they are precisely the same as those in which the Patent Monarch Lawn Mower is made, which is manufactured by the same firm, and to the description of which the reader is referred. In this machine, it should be said, the cutter is driven by a solid-link steel chain.

12 *The World Lawn Mower* – In general appearance this machine (Fig. 295) very much resembles the Patent Excelsior Lawn Mower. It is said to be especially adapted for cutting long grass, and to combine the particular features of the American machines with the more accurate fitting and general durability of the English machines. This machine is imported from America, and sold by Messrs J. J. Thomas and Co., 87 Queen Victoria Street, London. It will cut any kind of grass in any condition – that is to say, whether long or short, wet or dry – with equal facility, and moves with such ease and rapidity that a large amount of work may be accomplished with very little labour, comparatively speaking. The sizes and prices, carriage paid, are as follows: 8 inches, £2 2s.; 10 inches, £3 3s.; and so on at an additional £1 1s. for every additional 2 inches up to 20 inches. An extra charge of 5s. is made for grass box for 8-inch machine, 7s. 6d. for 10 and 12-inch machines, 10s. for 14 and 16-inch machines, 12s. 6d. for the 18-inch, and 15s. for the 20-inch machines.

FIG. 295 *The World lawn mower*

13 *The Noiseless Lawn Mower* – While noticing machines of this class, reference must not be omitted to the Noiseless Lawn Mower, manufactured by Messrs Barnard, Bishop, and Barnard, Norwich Iron Works, Norwich. *This machine differs from all other lawn mowers in being constructed without either gear wheels, chains, or levers, the power being transmitted to the cutters by a loose* intermediate wheel, with an india rubber tyre, which is placed between a plain-faced driving wheel and pinion; it is very certain in action, and at the same time so simple that it cannot be deranged. When the machine is drawn back, the intermediate wheel throws itself out of work, and the cutters cease to rotate. The cutters have steel on both sides, and when blunt can be reversed, bringing the sharp edges forward. It is perfectly noiseless, both in its forward and backward action, and works with considerably less power than any other machine yet introduced for the purpose. The india rubber tyre will last from

one to two seasons, and can be replaced at the cost of a few pence. An extra tyre is sent with each machine. The iron grass box is galvanised, which prevents its being destroyed by rust, to which this part is so liable from its contact with damp grass. The machine is kept supplied with oil by a new and simple method. The sizes and prices of Messrs Barnard, Bishop, and Barnard's Noiseless Lawn Mower are as follows:

8 inches	£2 15s. 0d.	14 inches	£5 10s. 0d.
10 inches	£3 10s. 0d.	16 inches	£6 10s. 0d.
12 inches	£4 10s. 0d.	18 inches	£7 0s. 0d.

618 Packing cases for machines are supplied by most of the makers, some making an extra charge and some not. In transit by rail, etc., these are absolutely necessary for the preservation of the machine; and when it has reached its destination the case should be preserved, and the machine always kept in it when not in use, in order to prevent rust, which is detrimental to the works and knives of any machine, and injury from blows, etc. Garden tools of every description require care and to be kept clean, and this is necessary for the mowing machine to a greater extent than any of them.

619 *Patent Grass Edge Clipper* The clipping of the edges of lawns and grass plots, and the mowing and cutting the edges of grass on verges, is usually effected by the ordinary shears, but this is an operation which is both tedious and laborious. In order to get through this part of the gardener's work with greater expedition, Messrs T. Green and Son have devised the machine represented in Fig. 296, by which the overhanging grass on the edges of walks, borders, flower beds, etc., may be cut with facility and rapidity, as well as the grass itself that is in the immediate neighbourhood of the edge. The cutter, like those of the Silens Messor machines, is driven with a chain, which effectually prevents any clicking or sticking fast of the cutter, which is speeded to revolve at a rate three-and-a-half times quicker than that at which the cutter in geared machines moves. The cutter, indeed, moves so rapidly that the clipping required may be done easily at an ordinary walking pace, and when this is considered in comparison with the time taken up in clipping with the shears, it is manifest that a great expenditure both of time and labour is saved by the use of this machine, which works steadily and with ease. It is made in one size only, namely, 8 inches, and is sold for £1 10s.

FIG. 296 *The patent grass edge clipper*

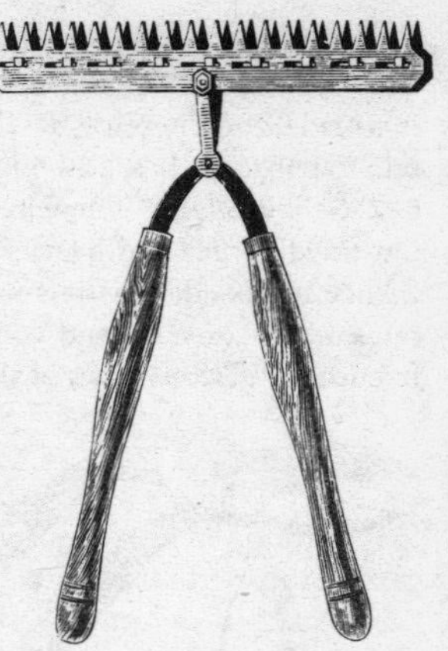

FIG. 297 *Ridgway's patent grass cutting machine*

620 *Ridgway's Patent Grass Cutting Machine* This clever machine bears about the same relation to the common scissors or shears that the Gatling gun or mitrailleuse bears to the ordinary rifle, inasmuch as the action of the single pair of scissors by two blades that alternately part and meet is multiplied some sixteen or eighteen times in the compound machine. The handles, as far as the pin or pivot on which the blades work, are the same as ordinary shears, but here the resemblance ends, except in so far that the blades of the scissors are supplied by two short arms of flat steel, which work one on the other. To the end of each arm, as shown in Fig. 297, a long horizontal blade is fixed, with triangular spikes projecting at intervals from its upper edge. These two plates, when the handles are moved to and fro, also work to and fro on each other, and in a horizontal direction – that is to say, horizontal in relation to the direction of the handles – progress in either direction beyond a certain extent being prevented by stops, which are fixed in the lower of the two blades, and pass through slots cut at intervals in the upper blade. The consequence of this action is that the triangular projection on the edges of the blades work over one another, their edges meeting like the blades of scissors, and severing anything that may get between them. Thus, this machine becomes a substitute for the small mower on the lawn, for by its use the grass is caught between the opposing edges of the projections and cut off. This machine is made in various sizes, with long and short handles, and is supplied with either bright polished or black blades. The sizes and prices are as follows: *Best polished*: To cut 10 inches, with short handles, 4s. 6d; to cut 14 inches, with long handles, 9s. 6d.; to cut 18 inches, with long handles, 10s. 6d. *Black*; To cut 10 inches, with short handles, 3s. 6d.; to cut 14 inches, with long handles, 7s. 6d. This last-named size is much improved, being made of the best steel, and may be recommended to those who are inclined to make trial of this very useful and serviceable machine.

621 *Ridgway's Patent Hedge Cutter* The machine that has just been described completes the list of the contrivances that are sold and used for mowing grass on lawns, etc. It may be regarded as a connecting link between the scythe and the mowing machine on the one hand and the shears on the other, effecting the purpose of the former by the *modus operandi* of the latter. It must be added that the province of the shears for clipping hedges has been encroached on to the same extent as that of the scythe and mowing machine has been interfered with by the grass cutting machine by another of precisely similar make, but heavier and stronger in its parts, and furnished with short handles like those of common garden shears, that it may be powerful enough to do the work of severing small boughs and branches from the plants on which they grow. Ridgway's Patent

Hedge Cutter, as this machine is called, can be used with great rapidity, and does the work of clipping and shearing neatly and efficiently. The sizes in which it is made, and the prices at which it is sold, are as follows: To cut 12 inches, 10s. 6d.; to cut 18 inches, 12s. 6d.; and to cut 24 inches, 15s. 6d.

622 *Garden Shears* These instruments are made on the principle of the scissors, but much larger and heavier, the blades being thick at the back and bevelled thence to the edge, with is perfectly straight from heel to point in most kinds, but curved convexly and concavely in others, in order to give greater power in cutting. Various types of shears are shown in Fig. 298, in which A represents the common garden shears, used for all ordinary purposes of clipping grass and hedges. In B a form is represented that is used in trimming the edges of lawns, beds, verges, etc., being furnished with long handles, so that the necessity of stooping on the part of the operator is entirely obviated. At C a form is shown which is used for branch pruning: in this type, which is furnished, like B, with long handles, a heavy blade with a rounded protuberant edge is brought against one that is hollowed out in the same degree. Shears for ladies' use, similar in form to A, except that they are much lighter, are also sold; but clipping with shears is a kind of work ill adapted for ladies, however light the shears may be, on account of the power that must be exerted in order to use them with effect. Garden shears are made in sizes of 7, 8, 9, and 10 inches, the length of the blade only being taken into account. The form shown at A is sold in these sizes, at 3s., 3s. 6d., 4s., and 4s. 6d., respectively, and notched shears at an advance of 6d. on these prices. Ladies' shears of light make are sold at 3s. 6d.; edging shears, as at B, at 6s.; and branch pruners, as at C, at 6s., 7s., and 8s., according to size.

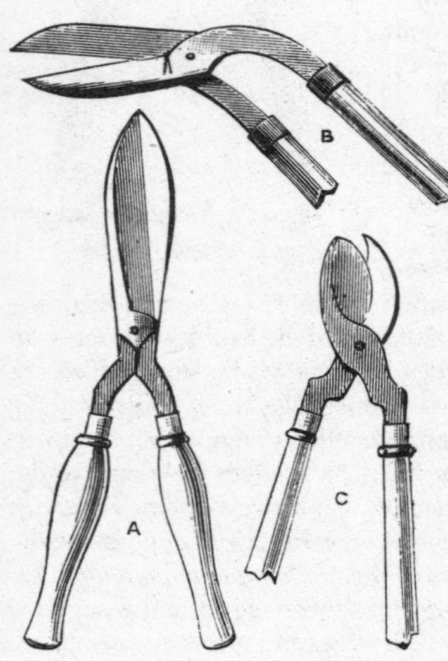

FIG. 298 *Garden shears*

623 *Spring Hand Shears* Everybody who has lived in a grazing district and in most agricultural districts has at some time or other witnessed the operation of sheep shearing, and knows how deftly and quickly the sheep shearers can divest a sheep of his fleece with the shears. The spring hand shears shown in Fig. 299 are somewhat similar to them, although the blades of the sheep shears are in the same plane with the handles, and not inclined to them at an angle, as in the accompanying illustration. They are grasped by the hand across and over the handles, and the blades are brought together by the pressure exerted on them. It requires considerable strength of wrist to use them for any length of time, but they are extremely handy for cutting grass on narrow verges, for trimming edges, and for cutting round shrubs and plants in places where the mower cannot reach. They are sold according to length of blade, namely, 5½ inches, 1s. 9d. 6 inches, 2s.; 6½ inches, 2s. 6d.; and 7 inches, 3s. The amateur gardener will find an old pair of sheep shears almost as useful in a garden, and as they may be bought very cheap at the marine store dealer's sometimes, he should never pass by an opportunity of picking up a pair. They can be sharpened with a rough whetstone.

FIG. 299 *Spring hand shears*

624 *Turf Rasers, Verge Cutters, etc.* A turf raser or verge cutter, also called an edging iron, is an instrument that is used for cutting the edge of turf to be taken up in rolls from grass land for the purpose of laying down on lawns, or for cutting the edges of lawns already laid, turf verges, beds, etc. The simplest form of raser is shown in Fig. 300. In this, a stick or handle, bent at the end, so that the horizontal part may rest flat on the turf when held by the operator, has a coulter-shaped knife or cutting iron inserted close to the bend. An iron ring should be put over the handle on each side of the blade, partly to strengthen the tool and partly to keep the cutter in position. When pushed along in front of the workman the blade cuts the turf in a line of any length, and to the depth at which the knife is set. It is useful only for cutting turf to lay down on lawns. In Fig. 301, an ordinary tool for cutting the edges of lawns, etc., is represented. This consists of a crescent-shaped blade, with an iron socket in the centre, into which the handle is put, The manner of using it is obvious. An edging iron of this description costs 2s. when measuring 8 inches from point to point of the crescent; 2s. 9d. when 9 inches wide; and 3s. when 10 inches wide.

FIG. 300 *Turf raser*

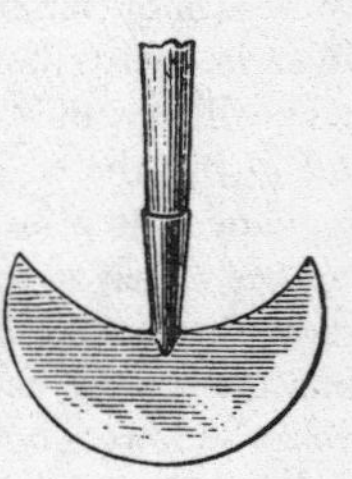

FIG. 301 *Verge cutter*

625 *McIntosh's Verge Cutter*, sometimes called the wheel verge cutter, although this name is generally applied to a circular iron plate with a sharp edge, set in the end of a long handle, has a small flat stage, as shown in Fig. 302, at the end of a handle terminating in a bar set at right angles to it or in a **D**-formed handle, like a spade handle. In the central line of this platform is a slot in which a wheel works, as shown in the illustration, and on either side is a projecting piece, in which a coulter-shaped iron is inserted. When this machine is wheeled along close to the edge of a lawn or bed, the knife will take off all projections and rough grass and reduce the edge to a well-defined line. The coulters, however, soon get blunt, and require frequent changing and sharpening.

FIG. 302 *M'Intosh's verge cutter*

626 After all, the edge of a sharp, well-worn spade is as good a means as any for cutting the edge of a lawn, verge, bed, etc., and in nine cases out of ten a skilful gardener will use this in preference to any other, following curved lines with his eye, and regulating a straight line, especially when of considerable length, by stretching the garden line from end to end of it. It is better to avoid the cutting of grass edges as much as possible, because an interval of bare earth, which is scarcely ornamental, is thus left between the grass and the path. It is preferable to see the edge gently rounded, so that the grass may meet the gravel without any break. Such an edge may not be so easy to mow with the appliances ordinarily used, but at all events it can be easily finished with the shears, the appearance it presents amply compensating for the small amount of extra trouble and labour involved.

627 *The Garden Roller* The roller is a machine that is absolutely indispensable in every garden, whether large or small, being required both for the lawn and for garden paths, especially when gravelled. Ordinary garden rollers are of two kinds, known as single cylinder and double cylinder rollers, so called because the cylinder of the former is one and the same piece of metal from side to side, whereas in the latter it is in two equal and similar parts. There is a third kind of roller, known as the water ballast roller, which is so constructed that the interior can be filled with water, thus considerably increasing its weight when necessary, and giving the owner the advantage of using it either as a light or heavy implement at pleasure. The best rollers of all kinds are made with balance handles – that is to say, there is a weight attached to the lower part of the framework and placed within the roller – and this weight being much greater than that of the handle and framework attached to it taken together, always seeks the lowest point, and thus keeps the handle upright, a great advantage, both in placing the handle out of the way when the roller is stationary on the lawn or elsewhere, and in keeping it in this position when out of use and put away in the tool house or wherever it may be kept. The principle of the construction of the garden roller will be understood from Fig. 303, in which the framework that connects the handle with the axle on which the roller revolves, and the balance weight depending from the axle within the roller, are clearly shown. The chief objection to the ordinary roller is that the edges of the cylinder are sharp, and therefore are apt to cut into grass or gravel when greater weight is thrown or pressure exerted in the direction of the edge, as will always happen in turning the roller, and another is the projection of the axle and frame to an undue extent, although the width of the frame in its greatest part must be greater than that of the cylinder in order to clear it. These faults have been reduced to a minimum in the double cylinder rollers, which are generally made with rounded edges, and thus turn more easily and without injuring either grass or gravel by cutting into them. The improvement in this necessary direction is carried

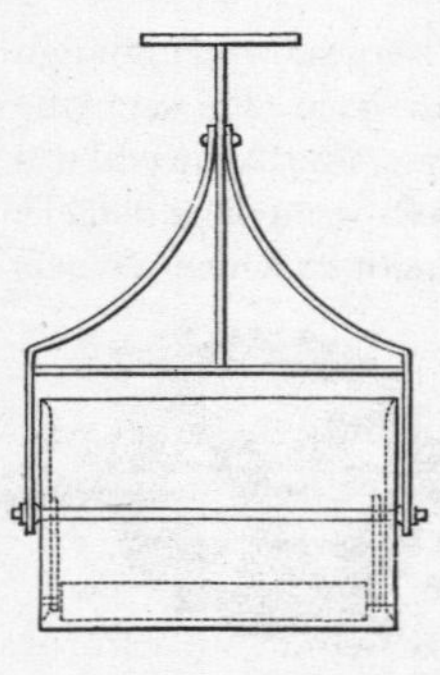

FIG. 303 *Construction of garden roller*

to the greatest extent in the patent rollers manufactured by Messrs T. Green and Son, Leeds and London, one of which, a double cylinder roller, is represented in Fig. 304. In this, the edges are rounded to a very great extent, and the plates which afford a bearing for the axle are deeply recessed, so as to admit of the bending of the frame over and round the edge of the cylinder, and its recession within it so that the outermost point of the axle does not protrude beyond the edges. In the rollers that are ballasted with water, and in some cases with sand, the interior is closed at a little distance within the edges on each side with plates, forming a hollow drum. Bosses with projecting pins are fastened to these plates to form the axle, and on these the frame and its balance weight swing. There is an aperture in the roller which can be opened or closed at pleasure, through which water is introduced by aid of a funnel, and through which it can be discharged when it is thought fit to empty and lighten it. Rollers are made on the ballast principle for large lawns and field work, to be drawn by horse power, which will be found useful for large parks and road making. In the smaller rollers of this description the curved shafts by which they are drawn are attached to the axle, but in the larger ones the shafts are perfectly straight, and are attached to parallel bars fixed to and connected with the axle by a triangular framing, which affords the bearings in which the axle revolves. With Green's Patent Rollers a weight box is supplied, which is placed on top of the shafts immediately over the roller, and which can be filled with stones, gravel, or sand, acting in the same way as sand or water ballast within the roller.

FIG. 304 *Green's patent garden roller*

628 *Weights, Sizes, and Prices of Rollers* The following is a synoptical table of the dimensions, weights, and prices of garden rollers as generally supplied. Prices of various makers and dealers may differ in some respects, but these will form a fair guide to those who may wish for particulars on these points as far as a fair average can be ascertained. The particulars are gathered from Messrs Deane and Co.'s price list:

From this table (*see over*) it will be seen that the sizes of the water ballast rollers are for the most part intermediate to those of the ordinary kind. The larger sizes of the water ballast rollers as given above may be had fitted with shafts for pony at an extra charge.

Excellent garden rollers of great weight for the size, fitted with balance handle, and having the edges rounded, and made in two parts, or in other words, being double cylinder rollers, are supplied by Messrs J. J. Thomas and Co., 87 Queen Victoria Street, London, as follows, carriage paid (*see over*):

Width and diameter	Single cylinder		Double cylinder		Water ballast		
	Weight	Price	Weight	Price	Weight empty	Weight full	Price
in. x in.	cwt.qrs.lb.		cwt.qrs.lb.		cwt.qrs.lb.	cwt.qrs.lb.	
16 x 16	1 3 0	£1 12s. 0d.	—	—	—	—	—
18 x 18	2 0 0	£1 15s. 0d.	2 2 0	£2 12s. 0d.	2 2 0	3 3 0	£3 0s. 0d.
20 x 20	2 3 0	£2 5s. 0d.	2 3 21	£3 0s. 0d.	—	—	—
21 x 21	—	—	—	—	3 1 0	5 1 0	£4 0s. 0d.
22 x 22	3 1 0	£2 12s. 0d.	3 1 14	£3 10s. 0d.	—	—	—
24 x 24	4 0 0	£3 3s. 0d.	4 3 20	£4 0s. 0d.	4 1 0	8 0 0	£5 0s. 0d.
26 x 26	5 1 0	£4 0s. 0d.	6 2 21	£4 10s. 0d.	—	—	—
27 x 27	—	—	—	—	6 2 0	12 0 0	£7 0s. 0d.
28 x 28	6 1 0	£4 15s. 0d.	7 0 14	£5 15s. 0d.	—	—	—
30 x 30	—	—	—	—	8 2 0	16 0 0	£10 0s. 0d.
36 x 36	—	—	—	—	11 2 0	20 0 0	£15 0s. 0d.

Dimensions	Weight	Price	Dimensions	Weight	Price
in. x in.	cwt. qrs. lb.	£ s. d.	in. x in.	cwt. qrs. lb.	£ s. d.
18 x 16	2 1 4	£2 1s. 0d.	24 x 22	3 2 26	£3 12s. 0d.
20 x 18	2 2 14	£2 11s. 0d.	26 x 24	3 3 14	£4 3s. 0d.
22 x 20	2 3 20	£3 0s. 0d.	30 x 26	6 3 7	£5 5s. 0d.

The prices of Green's Patent Rollers are as follows: *Hand Rollers in One Piece*: Diameter 16 inches by length 17 inches, £2 15s.; 20 inches by 22 inches, £3 15s.; 24 inches by 26 inches, £5. *Hand Rollers in Two Pieces*: 16 inches by 17 inches, £2 15s.; 20 inches by 22 inches, £4; 24 inches by 26 inches, £5; 30 inches by 32 inches, £9. This last-named size, when fitted with shafts for pony or horse, costs £12 or with iron weight box in addition, £14 10s. Rollers for horse power, 30 inches in diameter, range in width from 32 inches to 72 inches, and in price from; £12 to £22, the weight box in every case being an extra, and ranging from £2 10s. for the smallest size to £5 for the largest size as specified.

629 *The Turf Beater* This is a rough and ready implement used for beating turf into shape when the grass in the turf of a fresh-laid lawn has sent out fresh roots, and has caught the soil on which it has been placed, or for beating down any part of a lawn that appears to be above the proper level. All beating must be done when the grass, or rather turf, is wet. The beater itself is a square piece of elm or oak, with a long handle inserted in the block at an angle as shown in Fig. 305. The tool is raised as high as the operator can manage to lift it, and is then allowed to fall flat on the turf. Of course, the higher it is lifted, the heavier will be the blow that is given. The work is laborious in the extreme. Sometimes an upright pole is inserted in the block, and to this two handles are attached, transversely, one a little above the other, and the tool is then used like a pavior's rammer. It stands to reason, however, that when the tool is made in this way, it cannot be so effective as when constructed in the manner shown in the illustration.

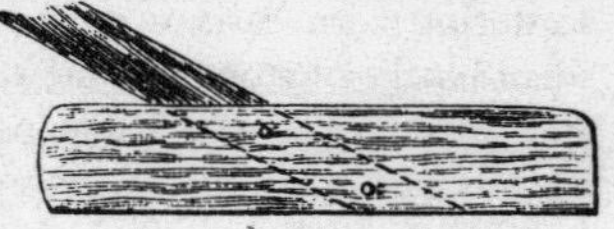

FIG. 305 *The turf beater*

630 *The Turf Scraper* In order to disperse and get rid of worm casts in the spring before the grass begins to grow again, it may be found desirable to go over the turf with a turf scraper. This is nothing more than a piece of board, or even iron, fixed to the end of a long handle, after the manner of a hoe. A well-worn birch broom, however, will be found equally effective for scattering worm casts.

631 *Weeders* Tools for the extirpation of daisies, docks, etc., have been described in a previous chapter (see paragraphs 406–7), and there is no necessity to repeat here the information that has already been given on this subject, all tools of this kind being of the same character, and in the form of pronged forks and levers by which the weeds and roots are raised from the ground.

A useful tool, called the Guernsey weeding prong, is described by Loudon, who appears to have derived his account of it from the *Gardener's Chronicle*, Vol. I, p. 66. He says: 'The head of this implement is in the shape of a claw hammer, with one end flattened into a chisel, one inch wide, and the forked or clawed end consisting of two sharp flat prongs, by which the weeds are grubbed up and lifted at the same time. The length of the head from the extremity of the chisel end to that of the pronged end is 9 inches, and it is attached to a handle 5 feet long. A great part of the labour of weeding may in most gardens be performed by women and children, and it will not only be lightened but their hands will be kept clean by the adoption of the Guernsey prong.' A representation of the iron of this weeding tool is given in Fig. 306. It is nothing more than a small hoe or grubbing axe, of narrow width, and can be made by any village blacksmith. The chisel end is used for cutting off weeds whose roots will perish and not sprout again when thus treated, and the pronged or claw hammer end for grubbing up or seizing and lifting out of the ground such weeds as dandelions and docks, whose roots will send up growth however deep below the surface of the ground they may be cut.

FIG. 306 *Iron of Guernsey wedding prong*

632 *Brooms* The ordinary birch broom, which is made of a number of small branchlets of birch, cut very nearly to one length, and bound together about the sharpened end of a wooden stick which serves as a handle, and which is driven into the centre of the mass after the ends have been cut even, in order to render this part of the broom, which has been already bound up as tightly as possible, still more tight, is the best for all garden purposes, as it is useful in all its stages from its first state to its last. When new, the fine ends of the twigs render it an excellent implement for sweeping turf and gravel walks, and when these ends are worn away and the broom has become stiff and stubby, it is still useful for scattering worm casts on grass and for sweeping up paths and courts paved with small blocks of stone, cobble stones, or pebbles. For hothouses greenhouses, and structures in which flat paving or tiles is used as flooring, a broom of whalebone or bast, inserted in small bundles, in a rectangular piece of wood, and fastened in with wire after the manner of a brush, is most suitable. Inferior brooms of this sort are made by putting the bast into the holes made for its reception, and fastening it in with hot pitch; these may do good service for a short time, but they are by no means durable, and therefore are not cheap. Brooms of iron or copper wire are sometimes used for mossy lawns, paths overgrown with moss, and for clearing moss from the trunks of trees, but they are seldom if ever seen now. A birch broom costs from 3d. to 6d., and a good bast broom from 1s. 6d. to 2s.

633 *Appliances for Carriage and Transfer* These are requisite to a greater or less degree in every garden, according to its size and the work that is to be done in it. First, and most important of all is the wheelbarrow, used for the conveyance of mould, manure, weeds, litter, etc., from one part of the garden to the other, and from the stable yard and manure heap to the garden and vice versa. Next in importance to the wheelbarrow is the handbarrow, of which there are different forms, calculated to serve different purposes. Then come smaller articles, serving for conveyance of earth, manure, pots, flowers in pots, etc., and weeds and litter, from place to place, among which are the mould box or scuttle, the pot carrier, and baskets of all kinds used for carriage, and, lastly, measuring baskets.

634 *The Wheel Barrow* These are made both in wood and iron, and it must remain entirely with the purchaser to determine the sort he will have, as a barrow is absolutely necessary in a garden, and with regard to material it is simply a question of price. The wheelbarrow may be described broadly as a box, open at the top, supported behind by two legs and in front by a wheel, on which it may be driven forward when the legs are lifted off the ground by means of the handles that project from the hinder part of the barrow, either from the top of the box, when the handles are merely a prolongation of the sides, or from the bottom, when the handles form part of a framework on which the body or box is supported. Illustrations of the wooden wheelbarrow and iron wheelbarrow are given in Figs. 307 and 308, which will serve to show their construction. In Fig. 309, a barrow of the old-fashioned type is represented. In this the handles by which it is raised and driven are formed by the reduction of the hinder part of

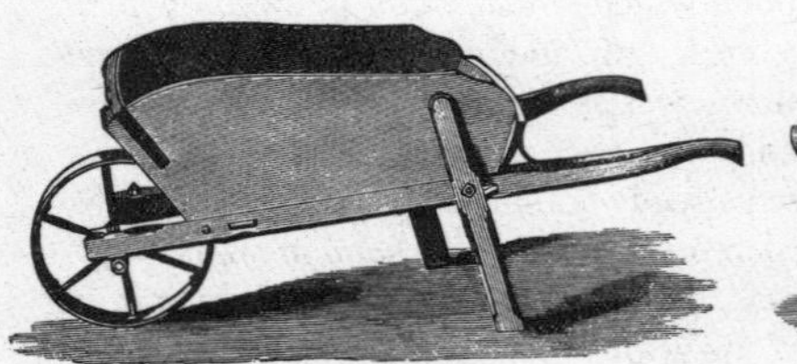

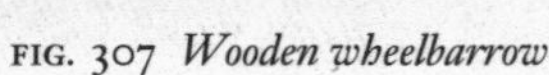

FIG. 307 *Wooden wheelbarrow*

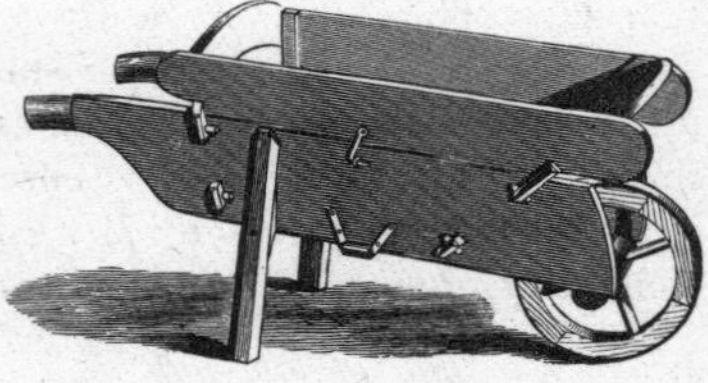

FIG. 309 *Wood barrow with movable top*

each side to dimensions of convenient size for grasping with the hands. A prolongation of the sides to the front further serve as supports for the axle of the wheel on which the machine is propelled. The ends are attached to the sides by tenons passing through mortises cut in the latter and secured with pins; both ends slope from top to bottom, so that the space enclosed at top is much wider than that enclosed at bottom, but the slope of the end in front is much greater than that of the end behind, to afford room for the free play of the wheel, and yet to render the capacity of the barrow as great as possible. The ends are rounded at the top, both in front and behind, so as to afford supports to manure, soil, etc., when heaped up in the barrow in a ridge-like form. The bottom is cut to shape and dropped into the barrow between front, back, and sides, all of which are nailed to it. The bottom is further supported by a transverse bar of wood, supported by iron stays screwed to the sides of the barrow. The wheel is of wood, bound with an iron tyre, and the axle is of wood also, furnished with pins at each ends, which work in iron sockets screwed to the inside of the sides. In order to increase the capacity of the barrow as much as possible for carrying litter, leaves, and any light stuff, as the haulms of potatoes, the cuttings and clippings of plants, grass, etc., a movable wooden frame is supplied, which fits over the top of the barrow and is kept in place by pieces of wood nailed in the corners within and hooks and eyes of iron without. The cost of such a barrow is 24s. without the top, or 28s. with it. It is supplied by Messrs Deane and Co., 46 King William Street, London. An excellent garden wheelbarrow of wood is supplied for 20s. by Mr Henry Wainright, Wholesale Glass Warehouse, 8 and 10 Alfred Street, Boar Lane, Leeds.

635 To return to the wooden and iron barrows represented in Figs. 307 and 308. The former is a barrow of considerable strength, made of well-seasoned elm and ash, and its naturally strong construction is further strengthened by stays and bands of iron, put on wherever occasion may require. Like the iron barrow, it is made on the principle of modelling the handles and support for the wheel into the form of a frame, on which the body or box is placed. The wheel is entirely of iron, formed of a wrought-iron tyre with flanged spokes. The price of this barrow, which is supplied by Messrs J. J. Thomas and Co., 87 Queen Victoria Street, London, is 37s. 6d., or 53s. including shifting top boards and irons for fixing them, in order to increase the capacity of the barrow. An American folding wood garden wheelbarrow, made of well-seasoned elm and ash, with wood wheel and iron tyre, that will fold up into a compact form when not required for use, is supplied for 35s. Amateurs who may be skilful enough to make barrows for themselves – and they will have little difficulty in so doing from the examples given in the illustrations – will find the wrought-iron wheels with flanged spokes manufactured by Wrinch, of Ipswich, and supplied by Messrs J. J. Thomas and Co., most useful for this purpose. The peculiarity in these wheels consists in the outer ends of the spokes being turned at an angle to the spoke, and fastened to the tyre with rivets instead of passing through a hole made in the tyre to receive it. These wheels are made 12, 15, 18, 21, 24, and 30 inches in diameter, and are sold at 4s. 6d., 5s., 6s. 3d., 7s. 6d., 8s. 6d., and 14s. 6d. each, according to size.

636 The iron barrow is made on the same principle as the wooden barrow just described constructed with stays in all parts in order to increase the structural strength. It is made of wrought iron, and the body is surrounded with a strip of metal at top and bottom and at the sides behind, both being riveted together. The thickness of the material in these parts is thus doubled. The wheel is made of cast iron. The barrow is fitted with a loose front board for convenience of emptying, and is painted black and green. The size of the body is 27 inches by 22 inches, and it is sold at 35s. Lighter barrows, having a better appearance perhaps, but not possessed of such strength, are supplied in the following sizes, namely, 17 inches by 16 inches, at 10s. 6d.; 23 inches by 19 inches, at 18s. 6d.; and 26 inches by 22 inches, at 25s. These are supplied by Messrs J. J. Thomas and Co. Strong galvanised iron wheelbarrows are supplied by Messrs Deane and Co., 46 King William Street, London, in three sizes, at 22s., 26s., and 30s., and one that they call the Gentleman's Barrow – size, 25 inches by 30 inches, with galvanised body and tubular frame, combining strength with lightness – at 16s. 6d.

FIG. 308 *Iron wheelbarrow*

637 *The Hand Barrow*, in its simplest form, is a frame of wood consisting of two long pieces disposed lengthways, with the ends fashioned into handles, and three shorter pieces placed transversely and tenoned into the longer pieces, as shown in Fig. 310. On the frame thus formed some half-inch boards, or even thicker boards if thought requisite, are nailed, the whole forming a strong and solid platform, on which large plants in tubs or pots, whether quiescent or in blossom, or when fruiting, if the plants in the pots be fruit trees, may be carried from one place to another by two men without injury. Various modifications may be made in the handbarrow. As shown in the illustration, it is most convenient for the carriage of large plants, because it can be laid on the ground, and the pots or boxes lifted on to it without raising them from the ground more than four or five inches. When a great many plants or pots have to be carried at one time, it is better to add legs to the frame, and place a low railing round the platform, so that those near the edge may be saved from being thrown off by any mischance. For carrying litter, leaves, the haulms of potatoes, old pea vines, etc., a convenient form is found in a box whose bottom and sides are made open, consisting of bars at about an inch distance from one another. If inch laths are used to form the box, the weight is reduced nearly one half. Long bars, as shown in the illustration of the handbarrow, are attached to the sides of the box at the top to afford means of transportation.

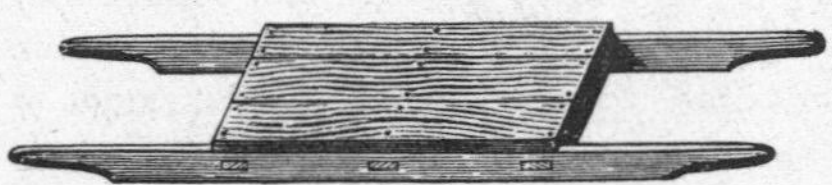

FIG. 310 *The handbarrow*

638 *Substitute for Wheel Barrow* In some cases the gardener is too poor to be able to afford a wheelbarrow, and in others an impromptu means of conveying mould, gravel, sand, etc., that can be hastily knocked together, is desirable. All that is to be done is to procure a strong box from the grocer's – those in which Swiss milk, tinned lobsters, and tinned meats are sent to this country, are most suitable for the purpose – and two long slips of wood are then screwed to the box on the outside of it, one on each side, to form handles by which it can be carried from place to place. Fig. 311 shows how a box of this kind may be converted into a handbarrow, and Fig. 312 further shows how a similar box may be converted into a wheelbarrow – a most necessary proceeding when one is single handed, for it requires two to carry a handbarrow. In doing this, nothing but straight slips of wood about 1 inch thick are required. Of these, two are screwed to the box on the top as shown to form the handles, and two at the bottom to form supports for the wheel. Before these are put on, short pieces must be screwed to the end of the box to form legs. The construction of the wheel is simple enough. Two circles, or pieces to form circles (Fig. 313), are cut out and screwed to each other, the discs being applied to each other so that the grain of one piece runs in a transverse direction to that of the other. This done, a square axle is thrust through a square mortise cut in the centre of the wheel, and an iron pin is put into each end of the axle, and passes out through the slips that serve as supports for the wheel. The strength and durability of the wheel will be increased by nailing a piece of iron hoop round the edge as a tyre. Half-inch stuff or three-quarter stuff should be used for the wheel. If time presses, or if the maker is not skilful enough, or has not the appliances for cutting out circular discs, he may get the tops and bottoms of the cheese boxes in which cheeses are sent to this country from America and Canada, and utilise these by screwing *three* discs together. The trouble and difficulty of cutting out two similar circles will thus be obviated. To some such details as these may appear trivial or unnecessary, but it must be remembered that this work is intended for the amateur and cottager as well as for the more wealthy or the more experienced, and information must be given which will be useful to and appreciable by all.

FIG. 311 *Box converted into handbarrow*

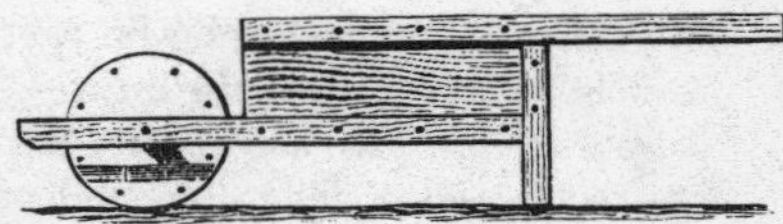

FIG. 312 *Box converted into wheelbarrow*

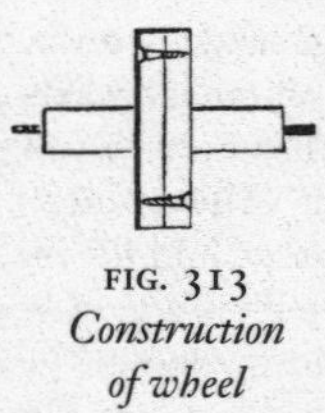

FIG. 313 *Construction of wheel*

639 *Mould Scuttle* All kinds of carriers are desirable and necessary for garden use; and for carrying sifted mould from one place to another, either for potting or for lightening or altering the character of soil in a spot in which it is desired to place any particular plant, and which cannot be approached by the wheelbarrow, there is nothing more handy than a wooden box – whether round or square, it matters little, that is to say, whether it be a box or a pail – with a piece of strong wooden hoop nailed across it to form a handle (Fig. 314). This contrivance is handy, and all the more so because it is shallow, and the earth, if necessary, easily taken out with a trowel. It will suit many an amateur who is anxious to help himself, but in these times, when galvanised iron pails are sold at such a low rate, some will prefer to buy and utilise these as mould scuttles, instead of putting a handle to a box to fit it to serve as one, The ends of the hoop should be turned under the bottom of the box and nailed to it.

FIG. 314 *Mould scuttle*

640 *The Pot Carrier* A box as shallow but larger than that which is used to make a mould scuttle, but furnished with a handle in a similar manner, will be found useful for carrying plants, when newly potted, from one place to another. Two boxes will be found sufficient for the conveyance of from eight to twelve pots, and this is as much as anyone should venture to carry at one time. The cheese boxes mentioned in a previous section may be utilised for this purpose, the covers furnishing a circular tray, with a rim about 3 inches high, in which pots may be conveniently carried. For the transfer of cuttings in very small pots, trays of this description will be found extremely useful.

641 *Baskets* Some may be inclined to say, Why not use baskets as mould scuttles and pot carriers? and the reply must be that mould and sand are apt to escape through the interstices of a basket when made of osiers, and that baskets, unless specially made for the purpose in a tray-like form with a narrow rim, would be inconvenient on account of their shape and depth. The ordinary baskets used by market gardeners for the purpose of measurement, and for the conveyance of some kinds of fruit and vegetables, are always handy in a garden, sometimes for gathering and harvesting fruit and roots, and sometimes as receptacles for rubbish, weeds, stones, etc., into which these things may be thrown when weeding or pointing a border, instead of letting them lie on the path, which necessitates the further labour of sweeping or raking the path when the work of weeding, etc., is finished. One of the most useful baskets for garden use is that which is usually known as the Sussex Basket, and which is illustrated in Fig. 315. This basket is almost square in form as far as the edge is concerned, though the bottom is rounded. It is made of broad laths of wood fastened to a narrower lath, which forms the edge of the basket. Another lath is bent over the basket and securely fastened to it to form the handle, and ledges, curved above to fit the bottom and flat below, are nailed to the bottom in order that it may stand steady when placed on the ground. Being made of solid

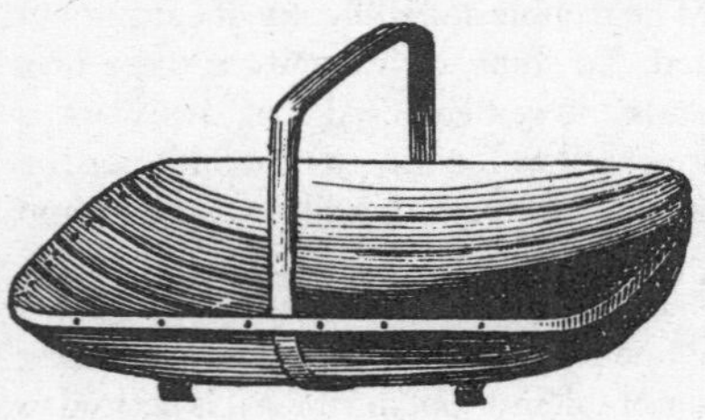

FIG. 315 *Sussex basket*

wood, these baskets may be used as mould scuttles or carriers, for collecting weeds and stones, for gathering the firmer kinds of fruit, such as apples and pears, and for the reception of vegetables when picked or cut, and roots when taken from the ground. They are, in fact, serviceable for every kind of garden work. They are made in various sizes, and are sold by ironmongers, as, for example, Messrs Benetfink and Co., Cheapside, London, and by nurserymen and seedsmen, at prices ranging from 1s. to 2s. 6d., according to size. These baskets are also known as trug baskets, but it is difficult to trace the origin of the name.

642 *Baskets used as Measures, etc.* The following are the names and sizes of baskets used as measures for fruit and vegetables by market gardeners and in the London markets. These being made either of wicker work or deal shavings, vary triflingly in size more than measures made of less flexible materials:

1 *Seakale Punnets* – These are 8 inches in diameter at the top and 7½ inches at the bottom, and 2 inches deep.

2 *Radish Punnets* – These are 8 inches in diameter, and 1 inch deep, if to hold six hands; or 9 inches by 1 inch for twelve hands. The term hand applies to a bunch of radishes, which contains from twelve to thirty or more, according to the season.

3 *Mushroom Punnets* – These are 7 inches in diameter by 1 inch in depth.

4 *Salading Punnets* – These are 5 inches by 2 inches.

5 *Half Sieve* – Contains 3½ imperial gallons. It averages 12½ inches in diameter and 6 inches in depth.

6 *Sieve* – This contains 7 imperial gallons. The diameter is 15 inches, the depth 8 inches. A sieve of currants contains 20 quarts.

7 *Bushel Sieve* – This contains 10½ imperial gallons. The diameter at top is 17¾ inches, at bottom 17 inches; the depth is 11¼ inches.

8 *Bushel Basket* – This, when heaped, ought to contain an imperial bushel. The diameter at the bottom is 10 inches, at top 14½ inches; the depth is 17 inches. It may be said that walnuts, nuts, apples, and potatoes are sold by measure. A bushel of the last named, cleansed, weighs 56lb., but 4lb. additional are allowed if they are not washed. Grapes are put up in 2lb. and 4lb. punnets; new potatoes, by the London growers, in 2lb. punnets. Apples and pears are put up in bushels, sieves, or half sieves. A hundredweight of Kentish filberts is 100 lb. Weights are always 16 oz. to the pound.

9 *Pottle* – This is a long tapering basket that holds rather over a pint and a half. A pottle of strawberries should hold half a gallon, but never holds more than one quart; a pottle of mushrooms should weigh one pound.

643 *Appliances for Protection against Animals, Vermin, etc.* The animals that are accounted to do mischief in gardens are various, though, perhaps, not many in number, unless insects are included in the list. At all events, it is only possible here to dwell for a brief space on those for whose exclusion, alarm, or destruction special appliances have been contrived. Birds, cats, moles, mice, wasps, snails, slugs, caterpillars, earwigs, beetles, and ants are the intruders whose visits are most dreaded and least welcomed, but special notice of most of these, and the method of counteracting and guarding against the ill effects produced by their inroads, must be deferred to another part of this volume.

644 *Birds and Buds* The vexed question whether or not birds do injury to the buds of trees and bush fruit is one that has never been satisfactorily cleared up, some declaring that they do, and others as positively averring that they do not. That certain kinds of birds eat and destroy cherries, etc., cannot be denied; but whether, those which are seen about the branches of trees at the end of winter and in early spring are destroying the buds, or clearing off insect life that will be detrimental to the buds, blooms, leaves, and fruit in after time, is an open question. If they are clearing the branches of insects, they are doing good; if they are destroying the embryo buds and all that will issue from them, they are doing harm. Those who maintain that birds do harm to trees at the time of year just mentioned recommend dusting the branches with a dressing of lime and soot, and allege that the *taste* of the lime and soot operates against further injury from the birds. With regard to this, however, it may be said that the organ of taste in birds is not sufficiently developed to cause them to object to, on the one hand, or to relish, on the other, any peculiar flavouring that may be mixed with their food, and, secondly, that the functions of birds that visit gardens seem to be beneficent rather than injurious, or, at all events, that the balance is in their favour as benefactors, when it is remembered how instrumental they are in keeping down insects, which, if left without check, would soon increase in such quantities as to utterly destroy the fruits of the gardener's labour. And, further, as soot and lime are known to be detrimental to insect life, it is as likely, when dusted on trees and bushes about to burse into bloom and leaf, that they destroy the insects that would otherwise consume these, if the birds do not do so, as many believe. The writer can only say that in his own garden the birds are always fed, and never appear to do injury to the buds, although they pitch upon and frequent the trees.

645 *Bird Traps* These are of two kinds, namely, the traps in which birds are taken and crushed to death, and those in which they are taken alive. The diagram given in Fig. 316 shows the principle of setting traps to *kill* birds. A peg, slightly rounded at the top, is driven into the ground as at A, to afford a solid support for the contrivance immediately above it, which consists of a short piece, B, a forked twig, C, and a longer piece of wood or stick, D. Of these, B is placed on A, and D immediately above B, the forked twig, C, being interposed between B and D, as drawn. A heavy stone, slate, or brick is then placed on D, the whole being carefully balanced. The corn, or whatever may be used as bait, is scattered under the stone between B and the edge of the stone touching the ground. In approaching the bait the bird will at first light on the

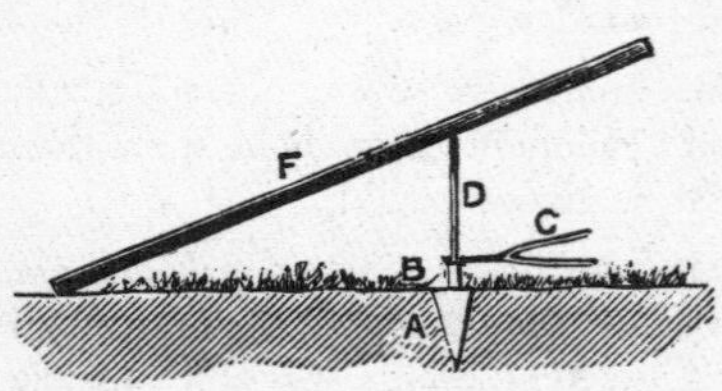

FIG. 316 *Diagram showing principle of trap to kill birds*

forked twig, C, when its weight will destroy the balance, displace the sticks, and bring down the stone. When it is desired to entrap the bird alive, four bricks are used – one on each side, one at the end, and the fourth in the position shown for the stone F in Fig. 316. The means used to prop up the fourth brick are precisely the same, but when the sticks are displaced and the brick falls, its edge is caught by that of the brick at the end, and the bird is secured in the cavity formed between the four bricks. A sieve propped on a stick, with a string tied to it, affords another kind of drop trap in which birds may be taken, but this necessitates long watching on the part of the person who has to let the trap down by pulling the string, and therefore need not be described further.

646 *The Springle* Birds do more injury to seeds when first sown, and even when in the early stages of growth, than to buds, and the most effectual protectors are pea guards and wire protectors of this kind, which have already been described. One means of catching birds engaged in depredations on seeds is to tie a long string to two pegs, and drive the pegs into the ground so as to tighten the string in one long straight line; pieces of horsehair are then attached to the string at intervals, with a running noose at the end of each. In hopping about the feet of the birds get entangled in the nooses, and as they proceed the noose is gradually tightened and the bird caught. But all these things occasion alarm, terror, and injury to birds past conception, and prevention is better than destruction any day. 'Surely,' says Solomon, 'the net is not spread in vain in the sight of any bird'; and we can always take advantage of the rooted, perhaps instinctive, aversion on the part of birds to anything in the form of a net or approaching to it, to work upon their feelings, and to warn them off the ground. A simple seed protector can always be provided by making a few frames of half-inch laths, by halving and nailing pieces together in the manner shown in Fig. 317. Some iron tacks or small clout nails are then nailed on the sides of the triangle and at the head of the central spike, and these being placed, one at each end and others at intervals of 6 or 8 feet, fine twine or coarse white knitting cotton is stretched from end to end over and round the nails, the whole when finished offering an appearance sufficient to frighten the boldest of birds that disport themselves in gardens.

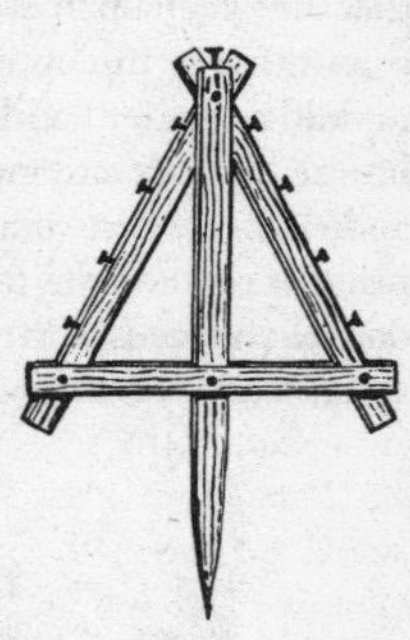

FIG. 317 *Seed protector*

647 *Basket Traps* Bird traps may be procured at the basket makers, circular in form and the top funnel shaped, having a small wicker door on one side. Corn is strewn at the bottom of the basket as bait. The bird forces its way into the trap to get at the corn, and cannot get out again through the ends of the opposing osiers. *Facilis descensus Averno*; *sed revocare gradum*, etc. It is doubtful, very doubtful, if the birds will forsake the tempting inducements in the ground, that can be obtained without difficulty, for the equally tempting enticements in the trap, which cannot be secured without trouble, imprisonment, and perhaps ultimate destruction; for what is to be done with them when caught but to wring their necks, for if they are let go they will be as mischievous as ever on the morrow, and the trapper will have spent his money and had his trouble all to no purpose. The basket trap is shown in Fig. 318.

FIG. 318 *Basket trap*

648 *The Cherry Clack* With birds, as with human beings, it is found that too much familiarity breeds contempt, and that however cleverly scarecrows may be constructed their want of motion begets suspicion in the birds that they are intended to alarm; and finding eventually that the supposed guardian of the seed or fruit, as the case may be, remains silent and motionless, they draw nearer and nearer, and ultimately hop round it and about it, treating it with the contempt that it fully deserves. Motion, noise, and glitter are the things which birds mostly dislike. They will avoid pieces of paper and feathers tied to string or twine and stretched over seed beds, though the string, if plainly discernible, will keep them off, even without paper or feathers attached to it. The fluttering of the paper is strange to them, the net-like cords abhorrent, and so they keep away from the spot that is thus protected. Figures of soldiers and sailors, whose arms end in fans that are turned by the action of the wind, formed in the semblance of broadswords, are disliked by the birds on account of the whirling and twirling that they keep up in every direction, according to the way of the wind. But worse than these is the appliance known as the cherry clack, which turns about as rapidly as these, and keeps up a perpetual rapping in even a moderately brisk breeze, with its castanet-like fittings. The cherry clack is illustrated in Fig. 319, and consists, first of all, of a long axle, having four fans, slightly inclined to a plane at right angles to it, placed at one end. When the wind blows, its pressure on the fans causes the axle to revolve with greater or less rapidity. The axle is sustained by a framework, consisting of an upright piece fitted to another piece of wood, which is bored through to receive a pin set on a pole on which the whole affair will turn. A broad piece of wood is mortised to the first piece, and placed in a horizontal position, and from the end of this rises a small support to carry the other end of the axle. At a point intermediate between the supports a framing in the form of a cross is fixed, and to the end of each arm a piece of hard wood is loosely jointed by a pin on which it turns freely. As the fans turn, carrying with them the axle and the cross that is fixed on it, the pieces of wood knock in succession against the horizontal piece of the support, and keep up a rattle that is anything but pleasant to those who are within earshot of it.

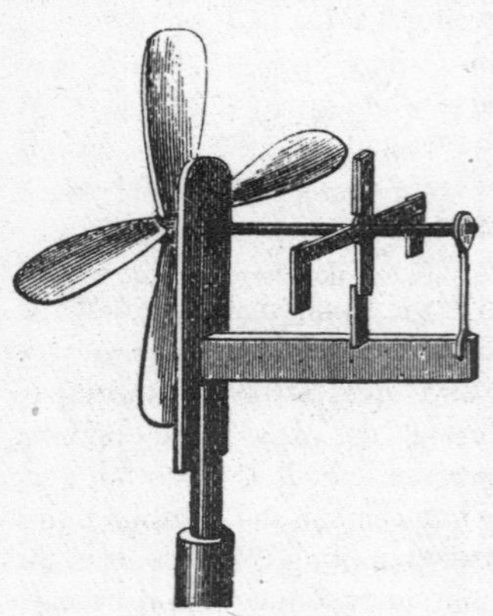

FIG. 319 *The cherry clack*

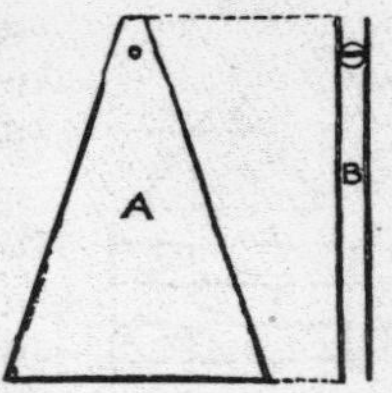

FIG. 320 *Bird scarer*

649 *Bird Scarers* Equally objectionable as noise to birds is glitter. This may be obtained by suspending small pieces of looking-glass in trees. The bits of glass may be framed in strips of tin, and the framing will afford an easy means of hanging them at an angle, which is better than placing them perfectly straight. Odd bits of bright tin may be utilised in this way by cutting them in the form shown at A (Fig. 320), which represents the front view or elevation of a piece of tin thus treated, and then putting two together as shown at B, which affords an end view of the contrivance. Pieces of tin put together in this way keep up a rattling noise, as well as emit flashes of light as the sun's rays fall on them, and thus constitute cheap but very effective bird scarers.

650 *Cats in Gardens* The burglar's horror *may be* a night-light, but the gardener's horror *is* undoubtedly a cat, which is a very Ishmael among them, for the hands of everyone of them to a man are against this prowling, ubiquitous fiend in fur, while its paws and claws are for ever doing mischief in a variety of ways that it would take too much time and space to reckon up here. There is no animal that does more damage in gardens than the domestic cat, and the enforced respect that one is compelled to entertain for one's neighbours' cats, and the aegis of protection which is held over it by the law, are mysteries of English social life which no gardener, at all events, can well understand. To keep a cat out of a garden is a matter of the greatest difficulty; nevertheless, it is to be accomplished by contrivances which shall now be described.

651 *Defences of Wire* To cover the top of a wall with bits of broken glass and bottles offers no bar to the progress of the adventurous cat. It only compels him to proceed at a slightly slower pace when he is viewed and attacked by the outraged gardener, who is generally restrained from throwing stones by thoughts which occur, or ought to occur, to the minds of all who live in or among glass houses. The tenderest points in a cat are his feet, and he has a decided objection to trust them on wire, and especially on fine wire. He or she, as the case may be, for the ladies are no better than the gentlemen, will climb up wooden trellis as easily and as coolly as a man goes up a ladder, but wire netting pussy cannot and will not climb, out of respect to his poor feet. Therefore, when the walls of a garden are surmounted by wire netting from two to three feet in height, stretched from end to end, supported on iron stakes inserted in the top of the wall, and secured at the bottom to the wall itself at intervals, so that there is no possibility of creeping under it, grimalkin's desire to enter the garden and work his will in it is baulked, and he is effectually prevented from entering it. The netting is too high for him to jump over, and he will not try to climb over it more than once.

652 *Wire Entanglements* Among other modes in which wire and wire netting may be utilised are the following. It would be a good thing if the top of walls were formed on the slant, as in Fig. 321, either on both sides or on one, as shown by the dotted lines. Formed in this manner, the tops of walls might be better utilised for the reception of coping to protect the blossom of the trees in early

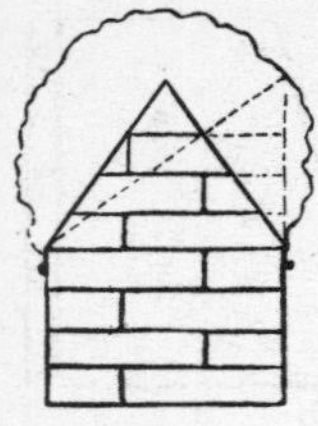

FIG. 321 *Wire netting over top of wall*

spring; and if there be any objection to the limited amount of rain that would find its way down the face of the wall, it could be carried off by very simple guttering. The great object is to make the tops of garden wall as objectionable as possible to the cat as paths and roadways, and, as a matter of course, the more slanting the top of the wall, the less easy will it be for the cat to canter along it. However, his progress may be seriously impeded, if not entirely stopped, by bending a piece of wire netting over the top of the wall from end to end, as shown in section at the top of Fig. 321. What with the slanting top and the wire entanglement, to use a military epithet, into which his legs must be plunged to the whole length at every step that he takes, advance along a wall thus protected would be utterly impossible. Another plan that greatly perplexes poor pussy is to erect broad uprights of wood or iron from end to end of the wall at suitable intervals, and to strain wires along them so as to form a serried fencing. When an arrangement of iron uprights and wires is formed similar to that shown in Fig. 322, the wires being placed about 1½ inch or even 2 inches apart, the wires on the external uprights being opposite to each other, and those in the centre upright just midway between these, a wire obstacle will be formed of such a kind that no cat will be able or willing to force its way through it. Of course there are other means of arranging the wires, but these will readily suggest themselves to an ingenious and inventive mind according to the situation.

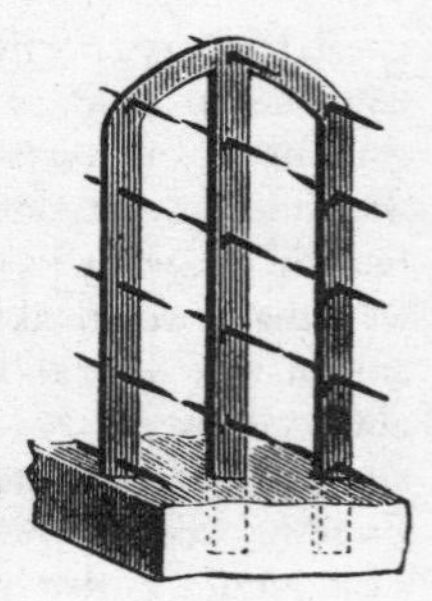

FIG. 322 *Wire obstacle on top of wall*

653 *Cat Teasers of Nails* An effective finish is sometimes imparted to park palings by nailing a strip of wood, bevelled on each upper edge, along the top of the paling, nails about three inches long having been previously put through the strip, point uppermost, at the distance of 1½ inch apart. Such a finish is attended with discomfort to those who attempt to climb over it, especially if the nails be sharp, as they ought to be; but, like the Spartan boy, who preserved an unmoved countenance while a stolen fox, concealed under his robe, was using both teeth and claws to the best advantage, the English boy will endure a great deal in the way of a punctured skin without showing it. If depredators in human form will trespass over the garden wall, the best cure is to smear the top of it liberally with a mixture of *red ochre* and *grease*, which not only spoils their clothes but inevitably leads to their detection if they continue to wear in public the clothes which are thus indelibly marked, for the stain is ineradicable. But let us see how the principle of the bayonet finish to the park palings can be applied to the case of the cat. We must touch his feet again, and make any place that he is accustomed to climb over as uncomfortable to him as possible – indeed, so uncomfortable as to make him reluctant to try the same road again. Cats will run up a fence, or the side of a glass house, or any building that is not too high, and

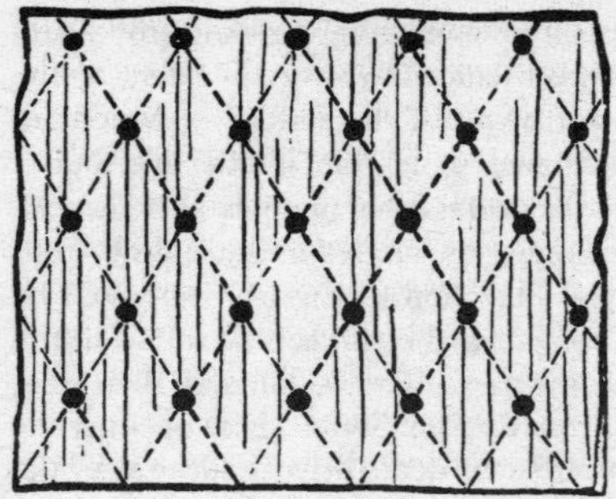

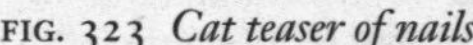

FIG. 323 *Cat teaser of nails*

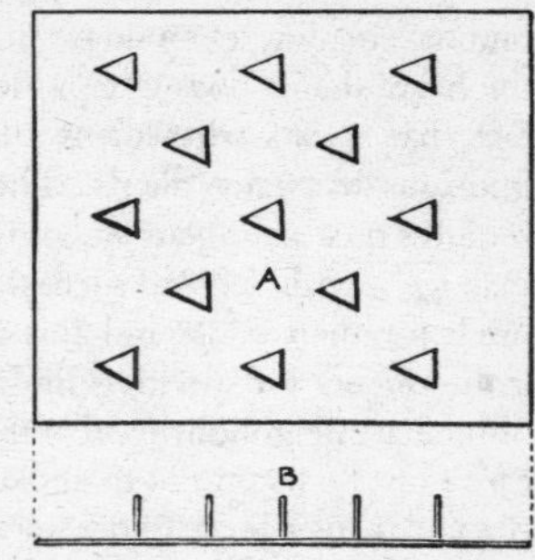

FIG. 324 *Cat teaser of tin plate*

pull themselves on to the roof by placing their feet on the edge before hoisting themselves up. Supposing, for example, we have a wooden paling on the edge of a greenhouse on which cats are in the habit of climbing, and we wish to stop them from doing so, the best thing is to take a single strip of wood, or two strips if the wood coping of the paling slope on both sides, and cut it to suit the width of the coping or edge. The wood should be from ⅜ inch to ½ inch thick, and as free from knots as possible. Plane the wood up on both sides, and then draw diagonal lines all over one side of it, the bottom in fact, as shown by the dotted lines in Fig. 323; then at every crossing insert a 1-inch rivet of the kind used by shoemakers, and which are finer than the French wire nails of this length. When finished, turn the strip up and nail it to the paling or edge of roof, the nails that have been driven into it being point uppermost. I will answer for it that the cat will not relish his reception when he next attempts to come that way.

654 *Cat Teasers of Tin Plate* Many persons, perhaps, will have a number of tin cans that they do not care to throw away, and which they would utilise if they knew how to do so. They may make very effective cat teasers of them by first of all placing the tins on a hot stove to melt the solder and bring them to their pristine condition of flat plates. They must then, with a sharp-pointed tool, scratch small triangles on the surface of the tin, as shown at A in Fig. 324, and with a chisel-shaped punch cut through two sides of each triangle thus made. The triangles must then be turned up on the third side so as to bring the apex of each uppermost, as shown in the side view at B. A piece of tin plate thus treated and nailed on a flat surface will prove most objectionable to the cats; but it is possible that of the two the nails will be found a more effectual deterrent, and certainly easier to make.

655 *Mole Traps* The mole, 'the little gentleman in the black velvet coat' which was instrumental in causing the death of William III, and was thus toasted by the recalcitrant Jacobites, does great damage at times to meadows, grass lands, and gardens, but it is doubtful if the harm done to lawns and meadows is really serious. The hillocks are unsightly, but they can be easily dispersed over the grass, and the runs in their immediate vicinity trodden down. It is in gardens, perhaps, that the mole does genuine harm, when it burrows under pansies, onions, etc., but it can do no injury to potatoes and strong growing crops. And the harm that it does in a garden is counterbalanced to a certain extent by the fact that it eats wireworms and large earthworms, the former of which are injurious to many plants. The old-fashioned mole trap is effective, but it requires nice arrangement, and it is only the professional mole-catcher that can manage it with decided success. The amateur gets puzzled in the endeavour to prick for their runs, and this is an equal objection to the iron trap sold by ironmongers for catching moles at 7d. or 8d. If the run can be found in the immediate neighbourhood of the hillock, the trap can be set; but even then great care must be taken not to choke and destroy the run. Some advise opening the run and firing a piece of rag soaked in paraffin in order to drive them away by the smell, which is offensive to the moles. Others recommend watching for them at about 9 a.m. and 3 p.m., the times when they are said to heave the hillocks that they make, speaking generally, and then to dig under the place sharply and quickly with a fork, and thus eject the mole, and then kill it. But a waiting game is always tiresome, and it is probable that the concussion of the ground under the footsteps of the approaching gardener may frequently scare the mole, and render the plan abortive. When it is desired to get rid of them, the best course is to send for the mole-catcher. When the weather is hot, moles work deeply; when it rains and the worms rise to the surface, the moles work near the surface also. In watching for moles, the rising of worms to the surface is a sure indication of the presence of a mole below and near, and as soon as any motion of the soil is noticed, the fork should be thrust in as deeply as possible, in order to turn out the mole.

FIG. 325 *An effective mole trap*

A writer in the *New York Tribune*, from which source it was transferred to *Gardening Illustrated*, describes a useful method of catching moles as follows: 'Persons who think that moles ought to be caught and destroyed have frequently been exasperated because of the conspicuous failure of traps warranted to catch these little creatures. Now, however, a gardener has hit upon the simplest contrivance in the world (Fig. 325), which he presents to the public for their free use. This is merely a large flower pot – an old tin pail will answer the purpose excellently – sunk beneath the ground upon a level with the floor of the run. A flat piece of board is laid over the run, and the earth heaped upon it so as to exclude the light completely. In the perfect simplicity of the thing its success chiefly lies. The moles, seeing or feeling nothing with the highly sensitive "feelers" upon their snouts, run very readily into the trap, from which there is no escape. Every fresh arrival adds to the company, for there is no resetting required, and there is no disturbance of the ground to excite suspicion. Doubtless the movements of the moles themselves attract other unfortunates to their ruin, for I am assured by one who has tried the trap with eminent success that he caught seven moles the first day, and three the second, after setting it.'

656 *Mouse Traps* Much harm is done by mice in gardens to peas newly sown and just growing and to bulbs, which they gnaw and eat and thus destroy. They are especially harmful to crocuses, and will do injury to most seeds of a large kind, such as the seeds of cucumbers, melons, vegetable marrows, etc. It is supposed that they are guided to the seeds by their acute sense of smell, and it is said that rows of peas covered with a coating of ashes are never touched by them, in which case the ashes will have acted as a deodoriser and destroyed the scent which would otherwise have led the mice to the peas. Some gardeners have found Pullinger's Patent Mouse Trap, which does not require setting, an effectual trap, but this requires protection from the weather. The cost of this trap is 2s. 6d. Others have used the common mouse trap with good effect, oiling the wires to preserve them from rusting, or smearing them with grease. Perhaps the simplest and cheapest trap of any is a pickle jar sunk to the brim, or very nearly so, in the earth, as shown in Fig. 326. The rim and the inside of the jar as far as the shoulder should be liberally smeared with grease, and the jar half filled with water. A little corn, lumps of grease, etc., may be placed on the earth in the immediate vicinity of the jar. The mice, being attracted to the trap by the grease, soon manage to slip over the rim into the water below, from which there is no escape. Another cheap and effective trap may be made of a brick, but as this only disposes of one mouse at a time, and must be re-set before another can be caught, it is not as useful as the jar that has just been described. A piece of slate of the same width as the brick should be obtained and placed on the ground, and the brick then set on edge over the slate, as shown in Fig. 327. The support for the brick is made of a piece of thread about 10 inches long, with a knot at each end, inserted in slits made in the ends of two short sticks, which are stuck into the ground, one on each side of the brick and slate. On the thread two growing peas are strung; or two kernels of nuts, and the thread itself should be well greased. The mouse, standing on the slate, is tempted to gnaw the peas or nuts and the thread between them, the peas, etc., being placed about 1 inch apart; when the string is gnawed through the brick falls and crushes the mouse. The object of the slate is to obtain a solid surface on which the brick may fall; if there was a cavity in the earth the mouse might take refuge therein, and thus make his escape, and otherwise, if the soil were soft, the poor animal might be partly driven into it and its death struggle unduly prolonged.

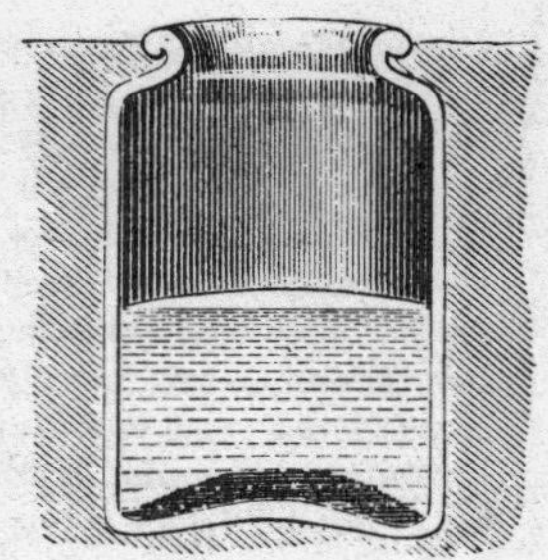

FIG. 326 *Pickle jar as trap for mouse*

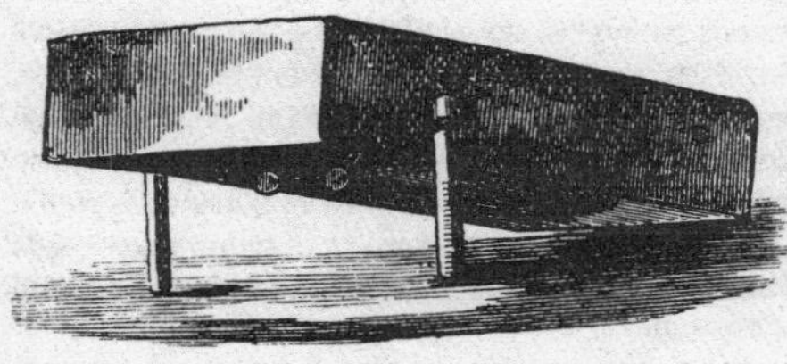

FIG. 327 *Brick as trap for mice*

A writer in *Gardening Illustrated* suggests the following method of dealing with mice: 'More than twenty years ago I had a garden partly surrounded by woods; consequently we were greatly troubled with mice, which made sad havoc with newly-sown peas and other seeds. Fig. 328 is a representation of the trap which I employed for their destruction, and which was eminently successful, for we trapped them by hundreds. I instructed the potter to make me a number of glazed pots, about the size of a 24-inch pot, but 2 or 3 inches deeper. There were four projections on the upper edge, as shown in the sketch, each pair being placed 1½ inch apart. The pots were only glazed inside. The rest of the apparatus consisted of a round stick ¾ inch in diameter, on the centre of which was fixed a turned wooden roller, 3 inches in diameter and ½ inch thick. The round stick being 5 inches longer than the diameter of the pot projected 2½ inches over its outside each way. Four or five baits were fastened on the edge of the roller with tin tacks; the baits consisted of either cheese or bacon rind, or garden beans. Thus baited, the stick was laid between the projections on the rim of the pot, with the roller exactly in the centre. The pots were half filled with water and sunk in the soil, so that the stick, when in position, cleared the ground about ½ inch. A mouse endeavouring to get at the bait has to travel along the stick to the roller, but cannot reach the bait without rising on the roller; when it does this the roller revolves, the mouse loses its balance and is precipitated into the water, leaving the trap ready set for others to follow. The dead mice should be taken out every morning and the roller removed, to be replaced in the evening, for birds sometimes dislodge the baits during the day. A little more water must be put in the pots as required. As many as nineteen mice have been drowned in one of these pots in a single night.'

FIG. 328 *A garden mouse trap*

657 *Precautions against Rabbits* Much injury is done to the bark of trees and many plants by the nibbling of rabbits. The best plan is to keep them out by suitable wire fencing, but this is costly, and perhaps in some places impossible. A safeguard for individual trees is to place boards round the stem or trunk connected with hooks and eyes, so that they may be easily put up and readily shifted, or some sticks, about 1 inch in diameter, may be placed at intervals round and against the stem of the tree, and bound round from the bottom upwards with tarred cord as far as may be necessary. The remedy is an unsightly one, but it has the merit of being effectual.

The above method of protecting trees from the attacks of rabbits is endorsed by a writer in *Gardening Illustrated*, who recommends tarring the stems from the ground to the height of about 20 inches. But he continues, 'If the plants are wanted for ornament, the following plan is better, if the extra expense be no objection. Instead of applying tar to the tree itself, stick three or four stakes round each plant at the distance of 9 inches or 12 inches from it; then tie a bit of fresh tarred line round the stakes at the distance of 9 inches from the ground. The tar which is applied to the trees to protect them from hares and rabbits should be mixed with an equal portion of manure of about the same consistence as the tar, or perhaps it will injure some of the trees.'

658 *Wasps and Flies* Winged insects of this description prove highly destructive to fruit, especially wall fruit, that is approaching maturity. Wasps will eat away the pulp under the skin and round the stone of plums, etc., until little else but skin and stone is left. The best means of protection is the simple contrivance shown in Fig. 329, which represents a bottle containing some kind of syrup, or sugar and beer mixed together, with a piece of string round its neck, from which issue other pieces, attached to hooks of wire, by which the bottle can be suspended to a branch of the tree on which the fruit is ripening. The mouth of the bottle should not be too wide, and it should possess a good shoulder, against which the insects will strike when attempting to fly upwards before getting immersed in the syrup below. As many of these traps may be placed about a tree as may be thought necessary. The same appliance may be used within doors, but for placing on the shelves of greenhouses a glass vessel, shown in Fig. 330, standing on supports and open at the bottom, sold at prices ranging from 6d. to 1s., will be found useful. There is an interior rim rising from the orifice underneath, which, with the external portion of the contrivance, forms a circular trough, in which syrup can be placed. The wasps and flies crawl under the vessel and make their way inwards and upwards, but none that enter ever make their escape. This glass may be suspended in any convenient situation by a piece of string tied round the knot at the top.

FIG. 329 *Trap for wasps and flies in open air*

FIG. 330 *Trap for wasps and flies in greenhouses*

659 *Traps for Earwigs, Beetles, etc.* These insects, especially earwigs, love concealment, and if discovered will make for the nearest hiding place without a moment's delay. Hence they will plunge into the hearts or dahlias, roses, carnations, and all flowers of sufficient size and such a structure as to enable the earwigs to utilise them for shelter. Hence it is that hollow sticks, made of pieces of elder with the pith cleared out, flower pots on the top of a stake, and cabbage leaves, etc., are recommended as means of entrapping earwigs, etc. Cabbage leaves are all very well as tempting cover for slugs, etc., which cannot make good their escape in a hurry, but earwigs can and will, as soon as the leaf, stick, or flower pot is disturbed by the touch of the gardener. The best kind of trap is a wooden or metal box, formed as shown in Fig. 331, and having a hole at the top, in which a funnel-shaped glass is placed. The ear wigs, etc., make their way into the trap down the funnel, but cannot get out again, and when there they may be killed by pouring boiling water on them.

FIG. 331 *Trap for earwigs*

660 *Lime and Soot Dredger* For caterpillars, slugs, etc., a dressing or sprinkling of lime or soot is most useful, either when applied to themselves when visible or to

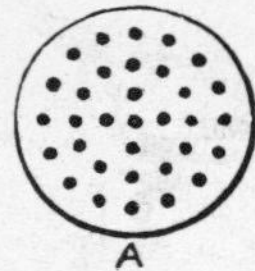

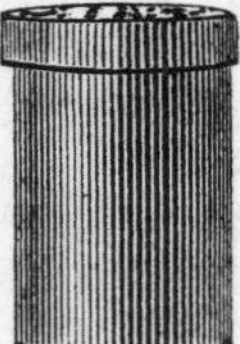

FIG. 332 *Lime and soot dredger*

the plants on which they feed or the plants they frequent. Salt is also a deadly poison to slugs. The difficulty that most people find is in procuring means for the application of the powder. An old flour dredger that is past kitchen use will answer the purpose admirably; but if nothing of this kind is available, a dredger can be easily made out of a cylindrical tin can, as shown in Fig 332. At A the perforated cover is shown in plan. To make this, the cover should be placed on its outer surface on a piece of hard wood or lead, with the inner surface uppermost. Find the centre, and with a pair of compasses trace some fine circles, as shown in the illustration. Then, with an old bradawl that has been sharpened to a point, make holes in the tin along the circles that have been described, driving the bradawl point through the metal by striking a sharp blow on the handle with a hammer.

661 *Appliances for Miscellaneous Purposes* It is difficult to assign to its proper class every appliance that is used in gardening, or even to name everything that may be requisite or desirable at one time or another, so this may be regarded as a kind of refuge for the destitute – a place to which may be relegated instruments and contrivances that cannot be conveniently included under any of the headings that have been already introduced. They are not many, and may be reasonably reduced to instruments of two classes – fumigators and dusting bellows, thermometers, aphis brushes, etc.

662 *Tebb's Universal Fumigator* The object of the fumigator is to apply tobacco smoke to plants infested with insects – aphis, green fly, etc., which are prone to attack the young and tender shoots of many plants, both in the greenhouse and the open air, roses especially suffering from this plague. For the diffusion of smoke in a greenhouse without being present in person – a most disagreeable infliction on those who object to the smell of tobacco – Tebb's Universal Fumigator, which is sold by Messrs Flanagan and Son, 98 Cheapside, London, and all nurserymen and ironmongers, is the best appliance for this purpose that has yet been produced. It is supplied in three sizes, at 3s., 4s. 6d., and 7s. 6d. It will burn any kind of tobacco paper, tobacco rag or cord, tobacco leaf, common tobacco as supplied by tobacconists, cigar ends, or any other fumigating material. When once lit, the fumigator requires no further attention. As no cinders are used in lighting and burning the tobacco, no sulphurous emanations are given forth, but the material gradually smoulders away, the smoke that is given forth rising from it through the holes in the conical top, and gradually pervading the whole interior of the house in dense cool clouds.

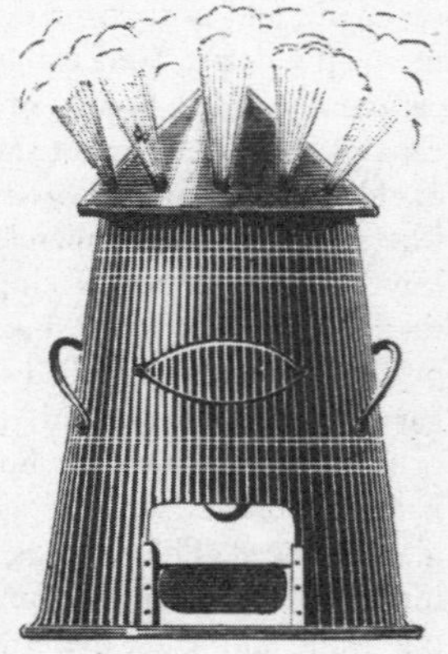

FIG. 333 *Tebb's universal fumigator*

663 *Fumigating Bellows* When there is no personal objection to the smell of tobacco, fumigation can be effected by more simple means, and the smoke brought to bear in a direct current on the infested plants. A small pair of bellows must first be provided, and on the nozzle of this instrument must be fitted a box made of tin, having a pipe at the bottom part for attachment to the bellows, and another pipe issuing through the top part, through which the smoke is driven. This appliance is shown in Fig. 334, in which A is the pipe which fits on to the nozzle of the bellows, B the box in which the lighted tobacco is put, C the cover of the box with a pipe, D, projecting from it, terminating in a small orifice, and E a fine rose which may be placed on D for the dissemination of the smoke in several broken streams or a small cloud, instead of one dense stream. The tobacco being lighted, and the instrument attached to the bellows, a current of air is brought to bear on the burning tobacco by the action of the bellows, and by the same action the smoke is driven out on the plants.

FIG. 334 *Fumigator for attachment to bellows*

The following simple method of fumigation is recommended by a writer in *Gardening Illustrated*: 'To kill green fly on plants, take a short tobacco pipe and attach to the stem any length of india rubber tubing, the size of a feeding-bottle tube; fill the bowl three parts full of strong tobacco, light it, place a piece of muslin or flannel over the bowl, and holding the end of the pipe about 2 inches from the place affected, blow through the tube, when such a dense volume of smoke is emitted from the bowl that in the course of thirty seconds the insects will drop dead or can be shaken off. Great care should be taken that no juice falls on the foliage, or it will destroy it. I have used this method with complete success for years, and it beats everything I know of for cheapness and effectiveness when single plants require fumigating.'

Further, Samuel Wood, in his *Modern Window Gardening*, recommends the following method of fumigating plants, stating it to be especially applicable to calceolarias, which are especially liable to be infested by green fly when placed in the window or conservatory. He says: 'As soon as their presence is detected, the plants, in a dry state, should be placed in tight box or tub, which must also be quite dry. If the box be deep enough, the plants may be placed upright in it; if not, they may be laid down: This done, take half an ounce of tobacco paper, which costs one penny, and will be enough to cleanse a dozen plants; light the tobacco and place it in the bottom, and then as quickly as possible cover the top over with a close damp cloth of some kind, and let the plants remain in for an hour, when they may be taken out and the foliage syringed or watered with a fine rose water pot. Repeat as often as may be necessary, or dust the plant over with tobacco powder when the green fly appears.'

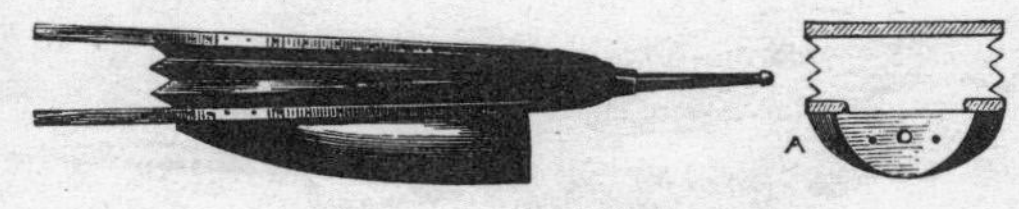

FIG. 335 *Dusting bellows*

664 *Dusting Bellows* Sometimes it is desirable to clear plants of insects by applying to them sulphur, lime, tobacco, etc., in the form of very fine powder, and the dredger described in Section 660 will not be suitable for the purpose, especially if it be desired to scatter the powder on the under part of the leaves. A dusting bellows must then be used. This is similar to the common bellows, but instead of the lower board and leather valve there is a different arrangement. This is shown in Fig. 335, in which the larger illustration exhibits a side view, and the other a view partly front and partly sectional, of this kind of bellows. The bottom board has its central portion taken away, leaving about 1 inch or a little more all round the edge. This serves for the attachment of the leather and of the tinplate receptacle with which the bottom board is covered. This is planished or beaten into a convex form, so that the edges may be attached to the edge of the bottom board or nailed to a ledge screwed on to it. The front of this receptacle, which terminates at the end of the bottom board, is semicircular in form, or nearly so, as shown at A. In the centre is an orifice closed with a cap, for the introduction of the powder, and on each side of this orifice is a small hole and leather valve. When the top board of the bellows is raised the leather valves open and air rushes in, setting the light powder in commotion in the interior of the bellows. When it is pressed down the valves close, and the air and powder in the bellows is driven out on and over the plant to which the nozzle of the bellows is directed.

665 *Sulphurators* These are appliances by which sulphur, either in the form of powder or in a liquid state, is applied to plants in order to kill insects on them or to destroy mildew. Thus it is used for exterminating caterpillars and red spider on gooseberries and currants in a liquid state, and for getting rid of mildew on vines, roses, and other plants, flower of sulphur having been found to be the best remedy for this minute fungus. When the sulphur is used in a liquid form the sulphurator takes the form of a syringe, or, in other words, a syringe is used as the sulphurator; but great care must be taken not to make the solution too strong, as, if so, it will do injury to the leaf. The following recipe for preparing a sulphurous wash for plants is recommended: Two parts of quicklime and one of flower of sulphur, taken by weight, are mixed together with a little water, and allowed to lie for a few hours, at the expiration of which the mixture is boiled for about twenty minutes in water, in the proportion of a pound of the former to a gallon of the latter. The liquid produced is dark brown, approaching to black. For syringing, about a pint of it is put into a gallon of water, this proportion being sufficient; but, before using it, it is better to gather some leaves and dip them into the liquid to test its strength. If the leaves are injured, it is too strong, and some more water must be added. When applied in the form of powder, a pair of dusting bellows is used as a sulphurator.

FIG. 336 *Sulphurator in form of bellows*

The following remarks are made by Mr Thompson on a sulphurator for applying sulphur in powder to plants, in his *Gardener's Assistant*. He says: 'Various kinds have been invented, some working with a wheel on the principle of a fan, others like the bellows. Fig. 336 represents one which answers exceedingly well. The boards forming the sides of the bellows are 7 inches in diameter, forming two-thirds of a circle round the flap opening, then tapering to the place where the nozzle is fixed to the wood. The upper board is cut across, the leather covering over the cut forming the hinge for allowing the board to move up and down. On the upper side of the tube is a circular tin box, 3 inches in diameter and 2½ inches deep, for holding sulphur, which, on being introduced, and the lid fitted on, passes through holes in the bottom of the box and upper side of the tube, from the interior of which it is expelled by the action of the bellows. On the under side will be observed a thin spring strap, bearing at its further extremity a piece of iron, which strikes against the tin tube as the bellows is worked, and shakes the sulphur into the tube when it would not otherwise pass through the holes. The boards are made of thin hard wood about 4/10 inch thick. The leather is also very thin and exceedingly pliable, and to this must be ascribed the superiority in extent of blast which this small apparatus possesses over those of larger dimensions but with thicker leather. The above is a cheap, convenient, and easily worked apparatus. It also economises the sulphur by finely distributing the particles, and, on the whole, is greatly to be preferred to those machines which throw out the sulphur in irregular volumes, and which cannot be controlled to give a well-distributed slight dose when such is required.'

666 *Aphis Brushes* When the aphis, or green fly, collects in great numbers on the end of a shoot of any plant, such as the rose, covering it with a thick external coating of insect life, it has been found that they may be easily removed by means of aphis brushes. These brushes are made in the form of scissors, as shown in Fig. 337. At the end of each arm is a narrow brush formed of soft bristles. The brushes are closed on the infested shoot a little below the insects, and then drawn upwards and along it. Two or three applications of the brush will very nearly, if not entirely, remove all the aphides without doing any injury to the shoot. Sometimes the aphis brush is made in the form of sheep shears – that is to say, an elastic steel bow, with a brush at the end of each arm. Pressure only of the thumb and fingers is required to bring the brushes together, and the shoot is cleared as before by drawing the brushes along it. The cost of an aphis brush is 1s. 6d.

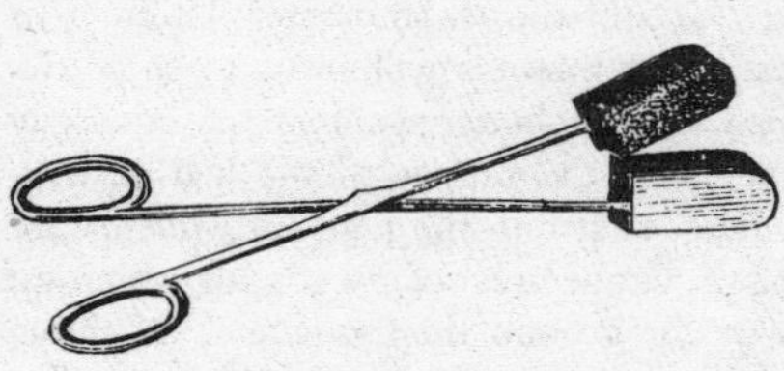

FIG. 337 *Aphis brushes*

667 *Thermometers* The principle of the thermometer is too well known to need any lengthened description here. It is sufficient to say that the ordinary form consists of a wooden frame, in which is inserted a tube of very small bore, terminating at the bottom in a bulb, and hermetically sealed at the top. All bodies expand under the influence of heat, and contract under that of cold; solids, liquids, and gases, the first slightly, the second more than the first, and the third more than the second. Liquids, therefore, having a mean expansion between solids, which do not expand enough for the purpose, and gases, which expand too much, are employed for the medium showing expansion and contraction in thermometers; and of all liquids, mercury or quicksilver is commonly used, because its expansion is more uniform, and the distance between its freezing and boiling points greater than in other liquids, though in some kinds, and especially in self-registering thermometers, spirits of wine is made use of. The mercury having been introduced into the bulb, the freezing and boiling points are ascertained, and the distance between these points is divided into 180° on Fahrenheit's scale and 100° on the Centigrade scale. Freezing point is marked at 32° on Fahrenheit's scale and at 0° in the Centigrade scale, and consequently in the former, boiling point is at 212°. The comparative graduation of the thermometer according to the two scales named is shown in Fig. 338, which does not go up to the boiling point, but which exhibits a range sufficient for all ordinary purposes. Common thermometers sufficiently accurate for all practical purposes in garden work may be bought at 1s., 2s., and 3s. each, but self-registering thermometers, which show the extreme points to which the mercury has fallen by night or risen by day, which are useful in hothouses, cost far more. The price of these may be ascertained from Messrs E. and E. J. Dale, Opticians and Philosophical Instrument Makers, Ludgate Hill, London, or from any makers of instruments of this description, who should be told the purpose for which it is required, and consulted as to which it is best to purchase for the object in view.

668 In ascertaining the temperature of hotbeds, etc., it is as well to place the thermometer in a metal case with one of its sides made of glass, and to make an excavation, in the bed, and lay the box and the thermometer within it in

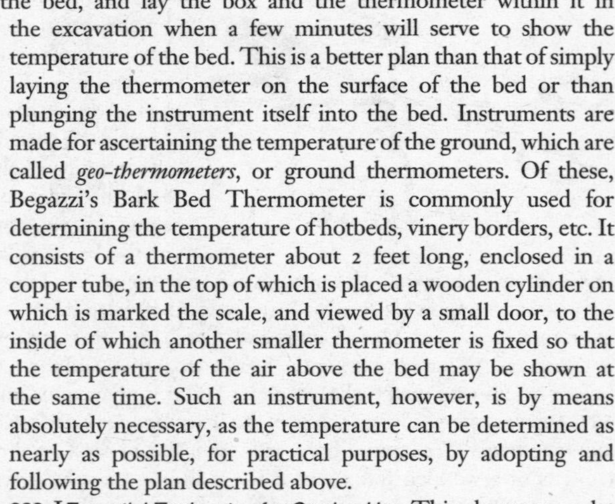

the excavation when a few minutes will serve to show the temperature of the bed. This is a better plan than that of simply laying the thermometer on the surface of the bed or than plunging the instrument itself into the bed. Instruments are made for ascertaining the temperature of the ground, which are called *geo-thermometers*, or ground thermometers. Of these, Begazzi's Bark Bed Thermometer is commonly used for determining the temperature of hotbeds, vinery borders, etc. It consists of a thermometer about 2 feet long, enclosed in a copper tube, in the top of which is placed a wooden cylinder on which is marked the scale, and viewed by a small door, to the inside of which another smaller thermometer is fixed so that the temperature of the air above the bed may be shown at the same time. Such an instrument, however, is by means absolutely necessary, as the temperature can be determined as nearly as possible, for practical purposes, by adopting and following the plan described above.

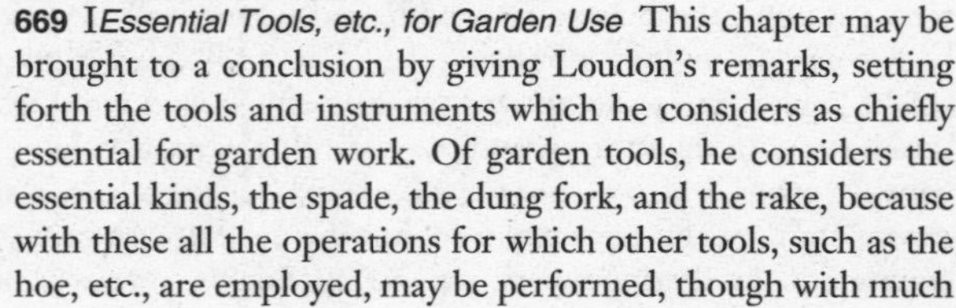

669 I*Essential Tools, etc., for Garden Use* This chapter may be brought to a conclusion by giving Loudon's remarks, setting forth the tools and instruments which he considers as chiefly essential for garden work. Of garden tools, he considers the essential kinds, the spade, the dung fork, and the rake, because with these all the operations for which other tools, such as the hoe, etc., are employed, may be performed, though with much

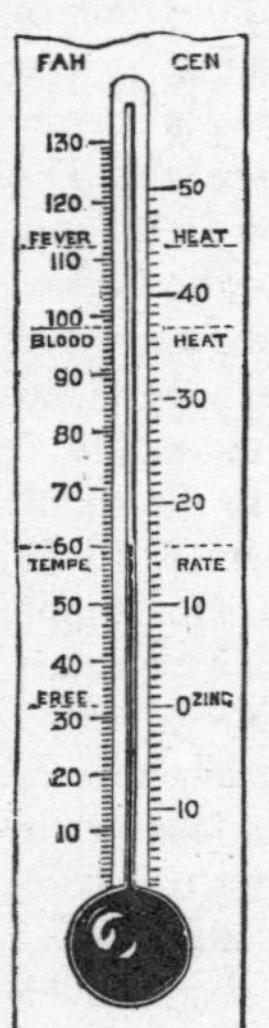

FIG. 338 *Graduation of ordinary thermometer*

less facility, expedition, and perfection. To these, however, must be added the digging fork, which is indispensable. Of instruments of operation, the most necessary are the knife, saw, shears, scythe, and hammer. Of instruments of direction and designation, the garden line, measuring rod, level, and label, of whatever kind it may be, are the most requisite. Of utensils, the most necessary are the sieve, flower pot, watering pot, and hand glass. Of machines for garden labour, the essentials are the wheelbarrow, roller, syringe, and hand forcing pump; and of traps and vermin engines, the mole trap, the mouse trap, the fumigating bellows, and gun. Of course, amateur gardeners will prefer the mowing machine to the scythe, but when the purpose and use of each tool enumerated above is carefully considered, it will be conceded that in the above list are reckoned all that the average gardener absolutely requires, and that none are mentioned which he can do without or which are unnecessary to him.

FIG. 339 *Arutilon Thompsoni*

CHAPTER 16

Glazed Horticultural Structures of the Smaller Kind, Comprising Propagators, Garden Frames, Forcing Pits, and Glazed Covers for Walls

670 A very wide range of buildings and contrivances is comprised under the general terms glazed horticultural structures, and in entering on this important subject it is as well to lay down some broad lines for our guidance on which it may be fairly and sufficiently considered. It is not possible to deal with it exhaustively – that is to say, to touch on everything that might be said upon it, and to enumerate everything that has been done and tried and contrived since the Roman gardeners commenced the work of forcing and protecting with their *specularia*, or frames, in which talc laminae took the place of the more modern panes of glass; and all that can be done at the utmost is to make inquiry into the various kinds of structures now in use, the principles involved, and the purposes aimed at in their construction, the specialities that have been introduced of late years to promote facility of construction, especially with regard to glazing, and the various modes and methods in vogue in the present day for warming, heating, and ventilating. Of these four branches of the subject, three are subsidiary to and spring from the first. By this it is to be understood that, after arriving at some definite idea of the glazed structures that are to be considered, it will be necessary under each separate structure to glance at the distinctive features and peculiarities of its form and the measures that must be taken for the introduction of light, the regulation of the internal temperature, and the free circulation of air when necessary, without draught, which are important factors in the culture and healthy growth of every plant, be it what it may, grown under circumstances which it is no exaggeration to call artificial.

671 With regard to the classification of glazed horticultural structures, let us proceed, because it is the most natural mode of procedure, from the smallest to the greatest. The smallest species of glazed contrivances for plant growing are hand lights, about which enough has been said in paragraphs 602 to 606 of Chapter 14, in which they are treated as appliances used wholly and solely in the garden, which, in point of fact, they really are. They are small movable structures, to be transferred at pleasure from spot to spot at any moment, with no more trouble than the brief labour of lifting each of them from the place in which it is standing, and carrying it to the spot in which it is to stand, until occasion again arises for its removal.

672 The mention of the mobility of the hand light offers at once an easy key to the classification of glazed horticultural structures generally. Broadly speaking, they resolve themselves at once into two groups, one of which consists of frames, mobile and transferable from place to place, like the hand light, and the other of buildings, immovable, fixed to the positions in which they have been raised, and in this respect, as well as many others, unlike the hand light. The structures that are included in each of these groups may be thus enumerated:

1 Propagators and Garden Frames, and Pits of all kinds, with Glazed Covers for Fruit Walls.

2 The Conservatory, the Greenhouse, the Hothouse or Stove, and all kinds of Forcing Houses.

It may be suggested that the forcing pit is a structure that in some cases is partly movable. This is so, it is true, but it will tend to the simplification of the subject, and avoid the introduction of an intermediate class of structures, to consider forcing pits under the latter category. Some forcing pits, in point of fact, combine the mobility of the garden frame with the immobility of the greenhouse, in so far that in the former containing walls of brick are used in substitution for the wooden sides of the latter, as in the melon pit, but the glazed frames that cover in the one and the other are in no way fixtures.

673 Although the terms propagator, garden frame, conservatory, greenhouse, hot house, stove, and forcing pit are at once understood by the professional gardener, there is every reason to believe that the ideas of the amateur as to the last named four are not quite so clear as they might be or ought to be, and that considerable confusion sometimes exists as to the leading purposes and proper functions of each of them; therefore, before entering in each case on the description, either specially or generally, of structures belonging to each class as it comes under consideration in the order already laid down, it will be desirable and even necessary to define their particular purposes and functions with such clearness and distinctness as will altogether prevent misconception, for when these facts are once grasped and thoroughly understood, the knowledge thus gained will pave the way to a more perfect and thorough comprehension of the directions that will be given in future chapters for cultural operations in the different kinds of glazed frames and houses throughout the months and seasons of the year, as they succeed each other in a round which, under God's own promise, can never vary and never be broken (Genesis 8:22), as long as the world on which we live and move and have our being retains its present form. Let us, then, proceed to take the glazed structures in common use in the order in which they have been named, dealing under each head with the various collateral subjects in connection with them that have been already mentioned, or which may suggest themselves while the subject is yet under consideration.

674 *The Propagator* Generally speaking, this is a contrivance of recent introduction, and it will not be wrong to attribute its production to the rapid strides with which gardening has advanced of late years in this country, and the desire which has arisen among those who cannot afford to lay out much in the pursuit of this special hobby to find the means of raising seedlings and striking cuttings on a small scale, on principles identical with those on which the professional gardener raises and strikes these on a larger scale, either for sale to his various customers, or for the embellishment and adornment of private gardens, more or less extensive, of which he has the care. The principle involved in the propagator is the maintenance in an enclosed space of a temperature that will cause the germination of seeds, or the formation of a callus and the subsequent emission of roots at the lower end of a cutting, in less time than that in which germination or rooting could be effected in the open air, or under a hand light at the proper season of the year, or at a time at which natural processes could not take place in the open air, or under the protection that has just been mentioned. The question naturally arises – How is the temperature to be obtained that will promote and effect these natural processes more speedily and at times and seasons otherwise than those at which Nature herself would carry them out in the ordinary course of the seasons and under ordinary conditions? To this the reply is: *By the application of bottom heat*. Here a collateral subject suggests itself, which bears directly on very much that is done in plant culture under glass; and before we can get a step further, even in the matter of propagators, bottom heat, and its application and effect, must be explained and discussed.

675 *Bottom Heat* The application of bottom heat, or heat from sources immediately below and under the roots of plants, is nothing more than the adoption and imitation of a natural process. Between the temperature of the air above and that of the soil below there is always a certain relative proportion, and as the temperature of the air rises and falls so will the temperature of the soil also increase and decrease, as the case may be, and although the increase or decrease of the temperature of the soil is less rapid and far more gradual than the change in either direction in the heat of the atmosphere, yet the former surely follows the latter, and thus the average proportion is maintained and preserved. Bottom heat, then, which, in other words, is heat applied to the soil in which plants are growing, and consequently to the roots of the plants, is an imitation of this natural process in any structure intended to stimulate and hasten the growth of plants. Let us suppose two cases in which the proper average relation in the temperature of the soil and the atmosphere has not been preserved – one in which the temperature of the former is too high, and another in which it is too low, in proportion to that of the atmosphere. Under the first condition, when the temperature of the soil is too high in proportion to that of the atmosphere, plant food will be absorbed by the roots and transmitted to the leaves at a rate faster than that at which the leaves can assimilate it in a proper manner, and the consequence is an overdue development of shoots and leaves, the suppression, if not the absence of, blossom, and a departure from normal healthy progress. On the other hand, under the second condition, when the temperature of the soil is too low in proportion to that of the atmosphere, plant food cannot be absorbed by the roots at the rate that is required by the foliage, stimulated to greater action and consequently greater demands for nutriment by the undue warmth of the air, and in the absence of sufficient support, the leaves will flag, droop, and ultimately wither, and the blossoms, or the fruit, if set, will fall off.

676 *Regulation of Bottom Heat* The regulation of the temperature of the soil under the application of bottom heat, and its modification at all times of the year in due proportion to the ruling temperature of the air, is thus ably explained by a writer in the *Cottage Gardener's Dictionary*, who says: 'Every plant obviously will have a particular bottom heat most congenial to it. Plants growing in open plains will require a higher bottom heat than those growing in the shade of the South American forests, though the temperature of the air out of the shade may be the same in each country. That gardener will succeed in exotic plant culture best who, among his other knowledge, has ascertained the relative temperature of the air and soil in which any given plant grows naturally. At present, such information from actual observation is not obtainable; but it is not so difficult to obtain the maximum and minimum temperature of the air of a country, and, these being obtained, the gardener may adopt this as a safe rule: Let the bottom heat for plants of that country be always 5° higher than the average temperature of each month – that is, if the lowest temperature of the month is 40° and the highest 70°, the average is 55°, and if we add 5° to that, we shall have 60° as the bottom heat for that month. If the average maximum temperature of the air only be known, let the bottom heat be less by 10° than the *maximum* temperature of the air.'

677 From this we may gather that the bottom heat in plant growing, especially as regards exotics, may be and must be suited to the natural climate of the country of which the plant happens to be a native. In raising seeds and striking cuttings of plants which have been brought from other countries, or which, in other words, are not indigenous to our own country, but will germinate or form roots, as the case may be, in the open air in our own land, all that need be done is to raise the temperature to summer heat at the utmost, in order to accelerate growth, which would otherwise take place in the natural way at the normal time. If coldness of soil and coldness of the atmosphere forbid growth altogether, or exercise too great a retarding influence on it, it must be remembered that excess of heat in soil and air will draw up plants in telescopic fashion, like children who have grown beyond their strength, and a forced unhealthy growth will take the place of the short, compact, vigorous growth which is the outcome of proper progress.

As a proof of this, put some seeds of the *Tropaeolum Canariense*, and any others of the varieties of the ordinary climbing Tropaeolum, in a small frame in which the bottom heat is high enough to cause the seeds of marrows, cucumbers, and melons to germinate with sufficient rapidity, and note the result. Long and attenuated growth of the germ of each seed will take place, and presently small leaves of a pale colour will be put forth at the ends of abnormally long leaf stalks, and the stretching out process will be continued from day to day at the same too rapid progress. Tortured into undue growth by improper application of bottom heat, the feeble nurselings are unfit to stand transference into the open air unless measures are taken to slacken the heat gradually, and by a cooling down process to enable the plants to gain strength and tone. Bottom heat is too often applied by amateurs in cases like the above where there is no earthly necessity for it. It is the custom with many to regard the Canary Creeper, as *Tropaeolum Canariense* is familiarly called, as a plant which must of necessity be raised and spend its early days in warmth, and therefore to buy plants in pots for planting out. These seeds may be sown at the end of March, or in April, with every prospect of success, in the open air, and not of necessity in a south aspect. Indeed, this creeper, generally considered so delicate and difficult of culture without heat in its preliminary stage, has been known to grow with the utmost luxuriance in a shady northern aspect never touched by the sun except in early morning and at eventide, and more than this, seeds from the creeper have dropped on the soil, been buried in it, and germinated and grown the following year with all the luxuriance of the parent plant by which they were produced. In fact, they grew so strongly and in such numbers, that the bigger ones strangled the smaller fry, and they went to the wall, and not to the trellis of the porch of the house, recessed between two square bays, up which the strong plants climbed, to let drop festoons of light green palmate leaves, flecked here and there with crested blooms of brilliant yellow. The moral of all this is: Sow the seeds of this plant as you would those of the ordinary Tropaeolum, but if you must raise them in pots, be content with placing the pots in a sunny window, and as soon as the young plants appear above the soil, give them all the air you can from day to day to strengthen them before you turn them out into the open air altogether.

678 *The Principle of the Propagator* The propagator, speaking generally, is a small frame or structure by which plants may be raised and cuttings struck by the application of heat below the seeds or cuttings by artificial means. It generally assumes the form of a miniature greenhouse, with a slanting pane of glass by way of roof, and is divided into two stages, storeys, or chambers – an upper one under the glass, in which the growing process goes on; and an under one, in which heat is generated and applied. It will be understood all the better if we take the simple form of a structure of this kind, which anyone may make for himself at the cost of a few pence and a little thought and contrivance. In Fig. 340, in which this frame is illustrated by means of a sectional diagram, the upper or growing chamber, and the lower or heating chamber, are recognisable at a glance. The upper one consists of a miniature frame easily made out of a box to be bought of the grocer for 2d. or 3d., with the front lowered, the sides cut to slant from back to front, and a ledge nailed round the top at A, A, so that a pane of glass may be dropped into it. The bottom is cut away, as shown at B, B, so as to form another ledge projecting inwards all round, on which a slate or a sheet of metal is dropped, to form a false bottom to the box. If it be asked, Why take the trouble to cut out the wooden bottom when, after all, a bottom is absolutely necessary? – it is sufficient to say that wood is a bad conductor of heat, and slate or metal is a good conductor, and that it is desirable to have the separating medium between the upper and lower chambers of material that is a good conductor, so that the temperature of the air in the upper chamber may be raised with the least possible delay. Fill the bottom of the receptacle thus made with coconut fibre as far as the dotted line C, and nothing remains but to put the seeds or cuttings in small pots filled with light soil, and plunge them in the cocoanut fibre.

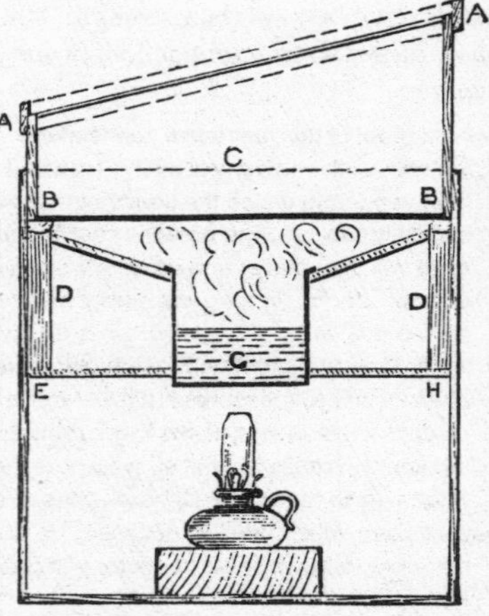

FIG. 340 *Diagram illustrating principle of propagator*

679 The next step is to procure a box, or make a case, of exactly the same dimensions *within* as the growing case is externally, so that the latter may be dropped into it, fitting with tolerable tightness; ledges, D, D, must be nailed to the interior of this case all round, on which the upper box may rest. The front of the case may be open below E to allow the lamp to be taken out and put in at pleasure, and to be visible at all times, so that the oil may be replenished when it gets low. Now get an Australian meat can, G, and having removed the ragged top by cutting a nick on one side with a file and putting it on the hot plate of a stove to melt the solder, put it in the centre of the case as shown, letting the bottom fit tightly into a board with a round hole cut in the middle of it to take the tin, the bottom of which should project beyond the lower surface to the depth of about inch. This board, represented in section by EH, should be dropped on to the ledges D, D, and nailed to them before the tin is put in its place. The upper edge of the tin should rest on boards contrived to slant from the top of the ledges towards the tin, and for this reason a tin that is square in form makes a better boiler than a round one, because it is more easily fixed. The junction between the boards thus put in at top and bottom and the tin must be carefully closed with putty and well painted; the chamber, D, D, surrounding the tin will thus form a hot chamber, which will be of material assistance in preserving an equable temperature should the lamp go out. The lower case being completed, and the tin filled with water, the upper case may be dropped into its place, and all is ready for active operations.

680 Through the open front of the lower case a lamp must be introduced, and so placed on a stand or not, according to circumstances, that the top of the chimney may be about 2 inches below the bottom of the tin that has been utilised as a boiler, and just under its centre. Light the lamp, lay a thermometer on the top of the cocoanut fibre and watch the mercury: it will soon rise and show that summer heat, or there abouts, has been attained in the upper case. Steam has been generated in G, and has risen to the under side of the bottom of the upper case, there to be condensed and fall in drops on the slanting boards round the top of the tin, from which they trickle into the tin itself. The false bottom, being a good conductor of heat, has transmitted the heat derived from the steam generated in the boiler to the air in the box above, and an increase in temperature has consequently followed. This is the whole principle of bottom heating, contained, as it were, in a nut shell, and holds good as an illustration of it whatever may be the heating medium. To be complete in itself, the little propagator described should be furnished with a pipe communicating with the external air, and rising to a level with the topmost edge of the outer case, by means of which it may be ascertained, by the issue of steam or the contrary, whether or not the boiler is empty, and by which it may be refilled; but no attempt has been made to explain this feature, as the boiler can easily be replenished by lifting off the box that covers it in.

681 *Rippingille's Propagating Plant Frame* There are many kinds of propagators in the market, but the principle involved is the same in almost every case, being the communication of warmth to the chamber above by means of water heated until steam is produced in the chamber below. One of the earliest that was introduced is Rippingille's Patent Propagating Plant Frame, manufactured and supplied by the Holborn Lamp and Stove Company, 118 Holborn, London. It has the semblance of a small garden frame raised on four legs, and plants of some size can be grown and kept in it. The heat is applied and maintained by a lamp in which oil is burnt, and which warms a tank of water placed within the plant frame, and immediately under the platform on which a bed of cocoanut fibre or soil is placed in which cuttings may be struck or pots containing plants, seeds, or cuttings may be plunged. The platform, it may be said, consists of slates that are sustained by a ledge running round the inside of the frame, and the water tank is a galvanised iron tray running the whole length of the frame and part of the width. The air enters the box in which the lamp below the tank is placed, through the bottom, and so, however high the wind may be, the flame of the lamp used in those constructed for outdoor purposes can never be blown out. The box can be disconnected from the frame for the purpose of trimming the lamp, which must be done about every thirty-six hours. The cost of oil is estimated at from ¼d. to ½d. per day. The top of the frame slides off either way, and the heat attained in the plant chamber ranges from 70° to 90° Fahrenheit. This plant frame is made and supplied in sizes and at prices as follows, Nos. 1, 2, 3, 4 being for indoor use and Nos. 5, 6, 7 for outdoor use:

No. 1	30 inches long	18 inches wide	11 inches deep	£2 0s. 0d.
No. 2	36 inches long	24 inches wide	16 inches deep with one shelf	£2 17s. 6d.
No. 3	48 inches long	24 inches wide	19 inches deep with two shelves	£3 17s. 6d.
No. 4	72 inches long	30 inches wide	22 inches deep with two shelves	£5 17s. 6d.
No. 5	36 inches long	24 inches wide	18 inches deep with one shelf	£3 5s. 0d.
No. 6	48 inches long	24 inches wide	21 inches deep with two shelves	£4 5s. 0d.
No. 7	72 inches long	30 inches wide	22 inches deep with two shelves	£6 10s. 0d.

A stove for indoor use for fixing to existing frames is supplied at 17s. 6d., and for outdoor frames, with 4 feet water tray and box, at 35s.

682 *Mussett's Excelsior Propagator* This is an appliance of comparatively recent introduction for raising seeds and striking cuttings, and is made in two kinds, which are very similar in appearance, one being intended for indoor use and the other for outdoor use. The chief point of difference between the two kinds is in the construction of the lamp, this feature in the propagator for outdoor use being so constructed that the flame of the lamp cannot be extinguished by the wind even when it is at its highest. The Excelsior Propagator (Fig. 341), which is portable and may be moved at pleasure from place to place, is the patented invention of Mr John Mussett, Winstanley Road, Clapham Junction, London, and is manufactured and supplied by him in six sizes, which, with the prices charged for them, are as follows, including packing:

Number	Size	Price for indoor use	Price for outdoor use
1	24 in. x 12 in.	£1 2s. 0d.	£1 9s. 0d.
2	30 in. x 14 in.	£1 11s. 6d.	£1 19s. 6d.
3	36 in. x 18 in.	£2 2s. 0d.	£2 11s. 0d.
4	48 in. x 24 in.	£3 2s. 6d.	£3 12s. 6d.
5	60 in. x 36 in.	£4 3s. 0d.	£4 13s. 0d.
6	72 in. x 48 in.	£5 3s. 6d.	£6 13s. 6d.

The frame itself is a case of wood, with a slanting glass top and a false bottom, formed by a receptacle for hot water, the whole being supported by four iron legs, which run up the interior of the four corners, thus imparting considerable strength to the entire structure. The frame is painted, varnished, and furnished with handles, by which it may be raised and carried from place to place. The sliding glass top is glazed without putty, so that a broken pane can be at once replaced by a new one should the glass get broken by accident. The hot water apparatus extends all over the bottom of the frame, so that a steady and uniform bottom heat is maintained in every part, and the heat in the plant chamber itself is also steady and equable. A wide tube is attached to the boiler or receptacle for hot water, by which water can be introduced into the latter when necessary, and which is instrumental in maintaining heat in the plant chamber, as it is always charged with steam rising into it from the water. This tube rises inside the case through the mould or cocoanut fibre, or whatever material may be placed on the boiler, which is entirely covered over, and is covered with a metal cap to prevent escape of steam into the plant chamber. Paraffin oil is burnt in the lamp attached to the bottom of the apparatus, and placed close up to the boiler just in its centre. As the lamp is made entirely of metal there is no chance of breakage; the wick needs attention only once in from 20 to 24 hours for the smaller sizes, and once only in twice that time for the larger sizes. The lamp is constructed so as to produce the greatest possible amount of heat from a minimum of fuel, and it is said that the value of the oil consumed in it amounts to no more than a farthing a day. It should be said that the tube rising from the boiler in the interior of the case affords the means of imparting humidity to the air in the plant chamber, if thought necessary, by

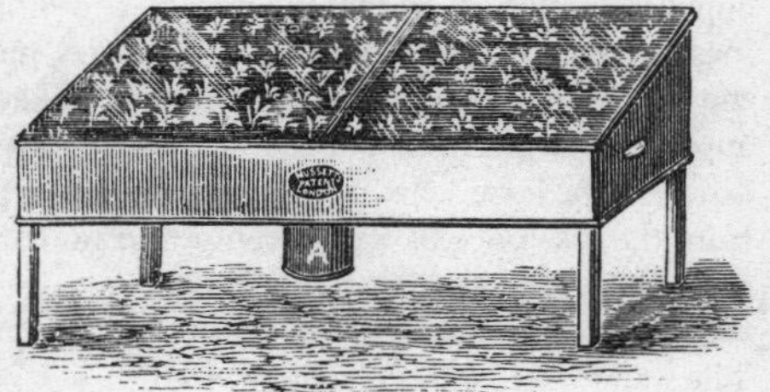

FIG. 341 *Mussett's Excelsior propagator for outside use*

removing the cap and permitting the steam to enter the case. By the aid of this propagator, cuttings may be rooted in from 10 to 14 days. A temperature of 75° or 80° should be maintained for this time, and the heat should then be allowed to decline gradually. This enables the cuttings to become well rooted, and the gradual declension of the bottom heat, accompanied with abundant ventilation, imparts vigour and strength to the plant in all its parts; and these desirable qualities in plant growth are further increased by the full exposure of the plants to the light.

683 *Dobson's Unrivalled Propagator* Amateurs who require a small and handy appliance for raising seeds and striking cuttings will find a very serviceable one on a somewhat different arrangement to those already described in Dobson's Unrivalled Propagator, which is manufactured and supplied by the patentee, Mr H. T. Dobson, New Maiden, London, and at the Surrey Wire Works, 52, 55, and 56 Borough Road, Southwark, London. It is also sold by Messrs Deane and Co., 46 King William Street, London, and by all ironmongers. It is intended wholly for indoor use, and must not be exposed to the rain; it is suitable, in fact, for use in the conservatory or the sitting room, and is well adapted to meet the requirements of window gardeners. It is made of deal, painted, grained, and varnished to imitate oak, and in one size only, namely, 3 feet in extreme height, 2 feet long, and 1 foot 3½ inches deep, outside measurement, the price being £1 8s. 6d. The form and appearance of the propagator may be gathered from Fig. 342, the front of which is partly removed in order to expose to view the plant chamber and the mode by which the bottom heat is applied. It is in the application of the heat that the novelty and simplicity of the apparatus consists, inasmuch as it requires neither oil lamp, gas, manure, skill, or knowledge to set the propagator going and keep it at work. There are two chambers, as in other appliances of this class, but they are entirely separate and distinct one from the other. In the lower chamber there is a kettle of peculiar form, which is removed from the case once in every twenty-four hours, put on an ordinary fire to boil, and restored to its place as soon as the water in it has reached boiling point. The water never wants changing, and addition to it is very seldom required, as but little is lost from evaporation. *Care must be taken to remove the cork in the kettle before it is placed on the fire to boil, and to replace the cork when the water boils and the kettle is taken off the fire.* The tin dish at the bottom must be kept dry. With regard to the plant chamber, drainage may be placed on and over the bottom, and it may be charged with mould in the same manner as an ordinary flower pot, but it is better to use pots for the cuttings, seeds, etc., to stand these on the

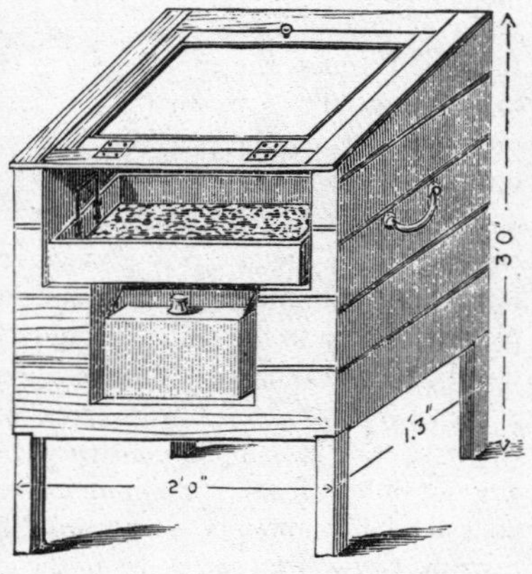

FIG. 342 *Dobson's unrivalled propagator*

bottom, and to pack the intervening space between with cocoanut fibre. Cuttings may be rooted in this case, bulbs forced for early flowering, and seeds that require a high temperature for their germination raised in about five or six days. There is no smell whatever given forth from the apparatus, and there is no liability in its use to derangement in its operation, or to accident, provided always that care is taken to remove the cork before setting the kettle on to boil, for if the orifice were closed the expansion of the steam would drive out the cork with a report that might cause alarm.

684 *The Gardener's Friend Propagator* The propagators that have been described afford bottom heat by means of the agency of hot water, but the Gardener's Friend Propagator supplies this through the medium of hot air, and is extremely simple in its formation and easily managed. It is the invention of Messrs Fletcher and Phillipson, Engineers, Lower Baggot Street, Dublin, who will deliver the entire propagator complete to any railway station, carriage paid, for 20s.; or will send by parcel post for 7s. 6d. the bottom box complete with lamp, the sheet tin for the bottom of the top box, and the **V**-shaped plate in the middle box, as well as a suitable thermometer for the propagator, which is convenient for amateurs, who may prefer to make the more bulky portion of the contrivance for themselves. Its construction is so easy, and Messrs Fletcher and Phillipson bring the means of making a propagator at little cost so completely within the reach of amateur gardeners and cottagers, that a description of it is appended in full.

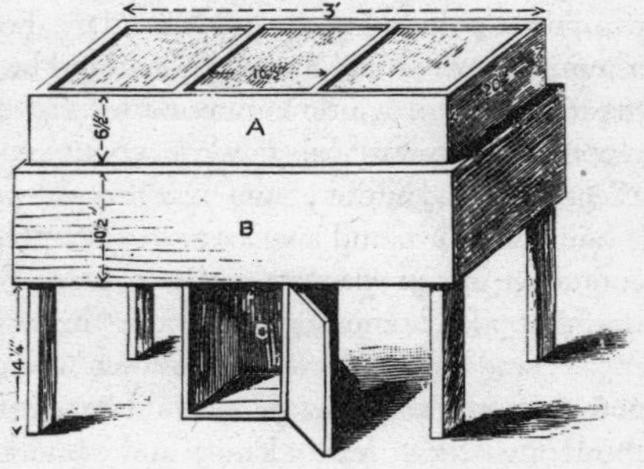

FIG. 343 *The Gardener's Friend propagator. Isometrical perspective view.*

685 The propagator, as may be seen from Fig. 343, consists of three separate parts – namely, A, the upper box; B, the middle box; and C, the lower box. The dimensions of the upper and middle boxes are shown in the sketch, and the lower box is supplied by Messrs Fletcher and Phillipson. The upper box, A, as shown in Fig. 344, which exhibits a sectional view of the appliance, is nothing more than a case or frame of the same depth on every side, rebated in the inner edge at top, and having three slips of wood across it, also rebated, to receive three

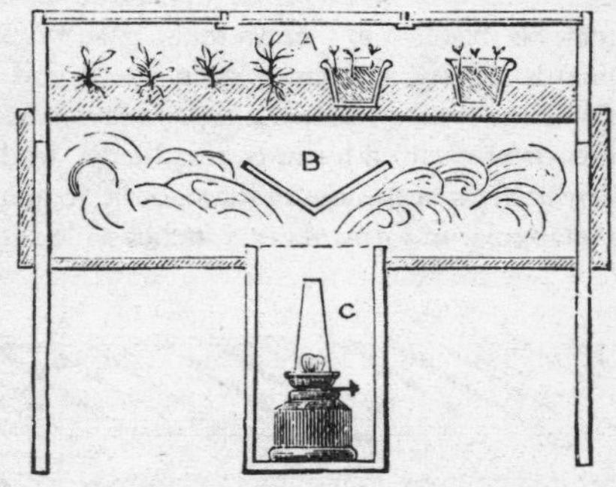

FIG. 344 *The Gardener's Friend propagator. Sectional view.*

panes of glass, by which its interior is covered in. The bottom is formed of sheet tin. It may be filled to the depth of 3 or 4 inches with light mould, or a mixture of two parts of cocoanut fibre refuse and one of silver sand, and in this compost cuttings may be inserted and rooted, and seeds raised in shallow pans or small pots plunged in it. The middle frame, B, is large enough to allow A to fit within it at the top, and four stout legs, 2 inches wide by 1½ inch thick, enter it from below and form supports, on which the corners of A rest when placed within B. The bottom of B is boarded up, but a square hole is cut in the centre, into which is fitted the top of the lower box, C, which contains a small rock oil or petroleum lamp, which, if kept constantly burning, consumes no more than 3d. worth of oil per week. The chimney is of tin, with a mica plate in it to allow of the flame being seen and regulated. The hot air ascending from the top of the chimney into B strikes against the bottom of a **V**-shaped sheet of tin, by which it is divided and compelled to distribute itself equally over all parts of the bottom. To make the upper and middle boxes, nothing more is required than a few feet of ½ inch deal, three panes of glass, and some nails. For striking cuttings and raising seeds, a temperature of 70° Fahrenheit should be maintained in the upper box, but a greater heat must be maintained for stove plants. Cuttings of ordinary soft-wooded plants may be struck in about six days, when the roots will be about ½ inch in length; the plants may then be potted and removed to a cool frame. Thus, by keeping up a succession of cuttings, a great number of plants can be rooted in this propagator in the course of a few weeks. When complete, this useful appliance measures 32 inches in height, the, width of the box being 20 inches, and its length 3 feet, as shown in Fig. 343.

686 *Garden Frames of All Kinds* The garden frame is a glazed structure of moderate height, and of length and breadth generally regulated by the purpose to which it is put. It will be convenient to regard the garden frame as altogether a structure movable at pleasure, and to dissociate it from the immovable forcing pit, whose sides, as it has been already explained, are of brick surmounted by a coping of wood, whereon rest movable lights, precisely similar to those that are used for the wooden garden frame. Long ranges in frame fashion, which must be regarded rather as protectors than as structures in which heat is maintained, may be made in any convenient position and in a sunny aspect by means of boards at front and back placed end to end, those in the rear being wider than those in front, so that the lights may slant from back to front, and closed by boards at each end, the boards being steadied and kept in position by stakes driven in on both sides of them, or, if greater neatness be sought after, by stakes rectangular in form, about 3 inches wide and 1 inch thick, sharpened to a point

FIG. 345 *Long frame or protector, with range of small lights on top*

at the lower end to enter the soil, and screwed to the boards either inside or outside. The frame thus made is then covered in with a row of small lights, say 4 feet long by 3 feet broad, placed side by side, and resting, one end on the board at back and the other end on the board in front. A structure of this kind may be considerably strengthened by nailing strips of wood between each frame from back board to front board, and then by screwing a broader strip to these *underneath*, so as to form a rebate on each side of them, facility may be given for sliding the frames up and down, otherwise ventilation must be effected by raising the frames either in front or at the back, propping them up by supports cut step fashion, as in Fig. 346, so that more or less space may be given for the entrance of air according to the state of the weather. Lights for such a frame as this may be glazed or covered with oiled calico, or even with oiled paper. Such appliances as these are used in market gardens, and by reason of their simplicity and cheapness, and the ease with which they are put up and dismantled, will be found of much use in private gardens for raising and protecting early crops in a warm aspect in the spring, and for obtaining and saving lettuces, etc., throughout the winter.

FIG. 346 *Support for light*

687 *Ordinary Garden Frame* The principle of the garden frame is set forth in the preceding section, and from this it may be seen that the frame itself, be it of what size it may, is always made in the same stereotyped manner, so to speak – that is to say, the back is higher than the front, and the sides are cut so as to slope or slant from back to front in accordance with the relative height of these parts. A good proportion for the relative heights of back and front is 3 parts for the former to 2 parts for the latter – that is to say, if the front board be 12 inches high the back should be 18 inches, or if the front be 18 inches high the back should be 27 inches. These are the heights at which the back and front parts of a garden frame are usually made, their lengths varying according to the number of lights with which the frame is covered; and as garden lights, as a general rule, are 6 feet by 4 feet, so a frame will be 6 feet by 4 feet, 6 feet by 8 feet, or 6 feet by 12 feet, according as it is made to be covered by one, two, or three lights. The best way of making a frame is to construct the sides with tenons of some length, that pass through mortices cut for their reception in the ends of the front and back, as shown in Fig. 347, which affords a correct representation of a two-light garden frame, in accordance with the directions given above. In this, A and B represent respectively the front and back, and C the side nearest to the spectator. The mortices, tenons, and pegs by which these parts of the structure are connected and held together are shown at D, D. Ledges, lettered E, E, are screwed on to the outside of the sides, and front and back are further connected by a slip of wood, F, which should be rebated on each side, or on which a slip should be nailed down its centre lengthways to form a rebate, in order to supply a bearing in which the inner edge of each light may slide up and down. In these bearings and in the top of each side a semicircular groove should be cut from top to bottom to catch and carry off any rain that may find its way in at the edges of the sides of the lights. The lights are made of stuff from 1¼ inch to 1½ inch thick,

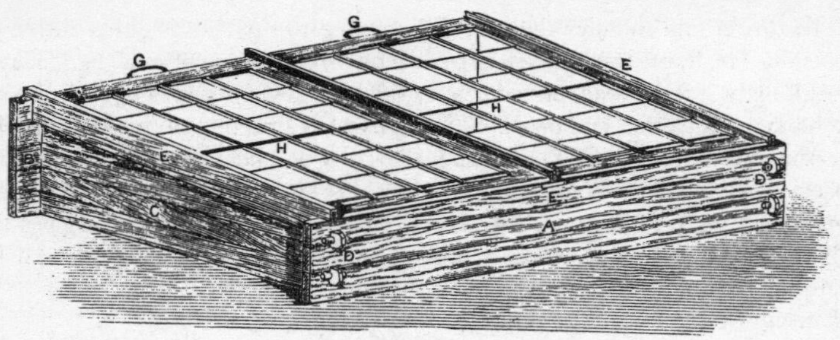

FIG. 347 *A two-light garden frame in isometrical perspective*

and are furnished with three or more grooved sash bars, as shown, and strengthened by a flat iron bar about 1/16 inch thick and 1 inch wide, let into the under side of the framework of the light, and passing through slots cut for it in the sash bars. This bar is shown at H in each light, and at G an iron handle, which is screwed to the edge of the top of the frame to afford means by which it may be more easily pushed down or drawn up into its place when down. Frames should be glazed with 21-ounce glass.

688 *Prices of Garden Frames* These vary according to the makers and according to size. Thus, Mr John Mussett supplies a one-light frame, about 4 feet by 3 feet, for £1 6s. 6d., packing included; a one-light frame, 6 feet by 4 feet, for £1 17s.; a two-light frame, about 7 feet by 5 feet 9 inches, for £3 7s. 6d.; and a three-light frame, 12 feet by 6 feet, £4 13s. 6d. These are noted because they vary from the regulation sizes, as they may be called, and afford intermediate sizes, which some amateurs may prefer. Mr Henry Wainwright, 8 and 10 Alfred Street, Boar Lane, Leeds, supplies strong frames made of good timber, with sashes or lights, in two sizes, namely, 6 feet by 4 feet, a single-light frame, at £1 16s., and 6 feet by 8 feet, a double-light frame, at £2 12s. 6d. These frames and lights are not painted or glazed, but with them are supplied putty, white paint, a paint brush, putty knife, and glass sufficient in quantity to allow for breakage and repairs. The frames are made and put together in the same manner as the two-light garden frame described above; they are put together without nails or screws, a desideratum in articles of this description, which should always be constructed so that they may be soon taken apart and put away when out of use in the smallest possible compass. Among the numerous makers of these specialities that are to be found in all parts of the country, mention may be made of Mr C. Frazer, Horticultural Builder, Norwich, and Messrs Messenger and Co., Loughborough, Leicestershire, who will forward their price lists – the former on receipt of 2d. in stamps, the latter post free to anyone who may care to apply for them. The prices of Mr Frazer's frames, it may be said, are £3 4s. 6d. for a two-light frame, 8 feet by 6 feet, and £4 12s. 6d. for a three-light frame, 12 feet by 6 feet, 5s. being charged for the cases in which they are sent. These frames are painted with four coats of paint, and the lights are 2 inches thick, and glazed with 21-ounce glass.

689 *The Hotbed* The garden frame, when used for forcing and as a means of raising the temperature in the space surrounded and covered by it, takes the same place as the upper plant chamber in the propagator, but the bottom heat is supplied by different means. It can be supplied by hot water, it is true, but when this is done the frame assumes the form of a pit with sides of brick, the consideration of which must be postponed for the present. The garden frame, being movable, may be used in any convenient part of the garden, and the heating material, which must be brought to the spot, consists of dung from the stable yard or farm yard, or leaves or bark from the tan yard in a state of fermentation; thus we arrive at a different means of imparting heat, which may be regarded as a natural means, and differing in this marked respect from the application of bottom heat by the agency of combustion, which, after all, is a purely artificial system.

690 *How to Make a Hotbed* There is no fixed rule as to the best time for making hotbeds: they may be made, indeed, at any time of year, and for any purpose for which they may be required. For example, if it is desired to have cucumbers at Christmas, the bed must be made early in October; if in January, early in November; and so on in proportion, little less than three months being required from the time of planting to the time of ripening fruit at this time of the year. It is immaterial what time of the year is chosen to commence cucumber growing, the only difference being that in the spring and summer months the task is comparatively easy, requiring less labour and less material than in the winter. In the colder months the weather has to be battled with; in the warmer months the weather in a great measure assists. Supposing it is desired to commence in October, let a quantity of stable dung be got together, proportioned to the size of the frame: two double loads for a three-light frame are usually allowed for the body of the beds; but it is as well to add an additional load, in which to start the plants. Having shaken it all together, laid it out for a week, and then turned it over again, take rather less than one load and make a bed for a one-light frame. This may be put together roughly, as it is merely to raise the plants in, and may be pulled to pieces when that is accomplished. The remainder of the dung should be turned over four or five times during a fortnight, and wetted, if dry. This preparation is most important; the inexperienced operator, unless he would run the risk of destroying his plants at the beginning, should follow it to the letter; for, unless the material has been well worked before the bed is made, it is apt to heat too violently, and burn the roots of the plants. In order to avoid this, it is advisable to use an equal quantity of leaves mixed with stable dung for the bed; the leaves give a sweeter and more moderate, as well as more lasting, heat.

691 *Marking Out Bed* When the material is ready, measure the frame, length and breadth, and mark out the bed, allowing 1 foot or 18 inches more each way for the bed than the length and breadth of the frame. At each corner of the bed drive a stake firmly into the ground, and perfectly upright, to serve as a guide to build the bed by. Then proceed to build up the bed, shaking up the dung well and beating it down with a fork. The whole should be equally firm and compact, so that it is not likely to settle more in one part than in another, the surface being quite level. The frame and lights may now be placed in the centre, but the lights left off, so that the rank steam which always rises from a newly-made hotbed may escape.

692 *Putting Soil on Hotbed* When the bed is made, the frame and lights put on, and the rank steam passed off, which generally takes five or six days, let a barrowful of good loamy soil be placed under each light; by the next day this will be warmed to the temperature of the hotbed, and the plants may be planted in it; no matter how small the plants are, it is better than raising them in the bed in which they are to grow, the shift itself being beneficial, and the time saved being rather more than a fortnight.

693 *Making Seedbed* When the dung has lain the first week, the seedbed is made. In three days the rank steam has passed off. A few pots with soil are then put in the frames. The next day the seed may be sown in these, two in each pot; in three days the plants will be up. They need not be re-potted or disturbed, but grown as they are; and, when the principal bed is ready, turned out of the pots with a ball of earth, and sunk in the new soil an inch or so over the ball of earth. If the bed now gives a moderate heat of 75° or 80°, and a sweet steam pervades the inside of the frame, the plants will soon root into the new soil, and grow very fast. Care must be taken, however, that the humidity is not too great, or that, in allowing some of it to escape, cold winds are not allowed to enter; an excellent preventive being to stretch a piece of fine netting or gauze over the opening.

694 *Covering for Lights* In covering the lights, during frosts or rough winds, it is advisable to avoid letting the mats, or what not, hang over the sides, as there is often danger of conducting rank steam from the linings into the frame. Straw hurdles which exactly fit the lights are better than mats. The covering should be used just sufficiently to protect the plants from frost or cutting winds, without keeping them dark and close.

695 *Linings for Maintenance of Heat* The heat of the manure is not lasting; consequently, the bed will require watching. It is advisable to have a thermometer in the frame, and as soon as the heat gets below 70°, apply a lining of fresh dung, which has been prepared as before, to the front and one side of the bed; and when this again declines, add another to the back and the other side. The bed can be kept at a growing heat for any length or time by this means, removing, at first, the old linings, and replacing them by fresh; but after a time, the roots will penetrate the linings, when they must not be disturbed; fresh dung must then be added to them.

696 *Economical Mode of Making Hotbed* These directions for the preparation of the material and making the hotbed apply to all such, whatever the size, thickness, or purpose; consequently, it will be unnecessary to repeat them; but there are other modes of making hotbeds. One is sometimes adopted which is very effective, while it greatly economises the manure. The trimmings and prunings of trees are tied up into faggots, and with these the walls of a pit are built, the exact size of the frame: on this the frame rests. The faggots are fixed by means of stakes driven through them into the ground, the walls being about four feet high. After the frame is put on, the mixture of dung and leaves is thrown in and well beaten down; but the job of building a hotbed is dispensed with. The dung is piled nearly up to the glass to allow for sinking; otherwise, the management is the same as for an ordinary bed. The advantages of this plan are, first, it requires a trifle less manure; secondly, the heat from the linings penetrates through the faggots under the bed, and is found more effective. The treatment after the frame and lights are put on, and the first emanations of steam are allowed to escape, is the same for a bed made on this principle as for any other.

697 The formation of a hotbed as described above for cucumbers is precisely the same for whatever purpose it may be desired. Technically speaking, the heat engendered in the dung when taken fresh from the stable yard for the purpose of making a hotbed is termed sweating, and it is to get rid of this too powerful heat that the manure is frequently turned over and watered before the bed is made. When leaves are added, it is thought better to do so at the last turning but one, when the bed is said to be sweet – that is to say, free from any rank and disagreeable smell. On the contrary, if a handful be drawn from the interior of a hotbed in a proper condition for covering with mould, the smell that it gives forth is agreeable rather than otherwise, and has been described as being like the smell of mushrooms.

A writer in the *Cottage Gardener's Dictionary* has given the following directions for making the hotbed, which are well worthy of attention. Having described the preliminary treatment of the manure as detailed above, he continues: 'All things will now be in readiness for building the bed, and one necessary point is to select a spot perfectly dry beneath or rendered so. It must, moreover, be thoroughly exposed to a whole day's sun; but the more it is sheltered sideways the better, as stormy winds, by operating too suddenly in lowering the temperature, cause a great waste of material as well as labour. The ground plan of the bed or ground surface should be nearly level. A good builder, however, will be able to rear a substantial bed on an incline, and such is not a bad plan, so forming the slope as to have the front or south side several inches below the back, the front being *with* the ground level, the back raised above it. By such means there will be as great a depth of dung at front as back, which is not the case when the base is level, for then, unluckily, through the incline necessary for the surface of the glass, the dung at back is generally much deeper than at the front, at which latter point most heat is wanted. Good gardeners not unfrequently use a portion of weaker material at the back, such as littery stuff containing little power to heat. It is well also to fill most of the interior of the bed after building it half a yard in height with any half-decayed materials, such as half-worn linings, fresh leaves, etc. This will, in general, secure it from the danger of burning, whilst it will also add to the permanency of the bed.

'For winter forcing, a bed should be at least four feet high at the back – if five feet, all the better; and as soon as built, let some littery manure be placed around the sides, in order to prevent the wind searching it. As soon as the heat is well up, or in about four days from the building of it, the whole bed should have a thorough watering. It is now desirable to close it until the heat is well up again, when a second and lighter watering may be applied, and now it will be ready for the hills of soil at any time.

'In making the hills of soil for the plants, in forcing melons or cucumbers, make a hollow in the centre of each light half the depth of the bed. In the bottom of this place nearly a barrowful of brickbats, on this some half-rotten dung, and, finally, a flat square of turf, on which the hillock is placed. It is almost impossible for the roots of plants to scorch with this precaution.

'As the heat declines, linings, or, as they might be more properly called, coatings, are made use of, which consists of hot fermenting dung, laid from 18 to 24 inches, in proportion to the coldness of the season, etc., all round the bed to the whole of its height, and if founded in a trench, one equally deep must be dug for the coating, it being of importance to renew the heat as much as possible throughout its whole mass. If, after a while, the temperature again declines, the old coating must be taken away and a similar one of hot dung applied in its place. As the spring advances, the warmth of the sun will compensate for the decline of that of the bed; but as the nights are generally yet cold, either a moderate coating, about 6 or 10 inches thick, is required, or the mowings of grass, or even litter, may be laid round the sides with advantage.'

698 The making and maintenance of a hotbed may thus be summed up and set forth in a few words. (1) Choose a position that is naturally dry, or can be rendered dry, having a south aspect, situated, if possible, on a slight incline, and sheltered from cold winds in rear and at the sides. (2) The dung having been tempered, or sweetened, sufficiently by turning over and wetting, mark out the space to be occupied by the bed, making it larger by 18 inches every way than the frame that is to stand upon it, or, in other words, that there may be a margin of 18 inches every way all round the frame when the frame is placed on the hotbed. (3) In constructing the hotbed, pile up the dung in such a manner that the manure may be higher at the back than in the front, and beat down the dung with the fork when the bed is made, in order to impart solidity to it. (4) Put the frame on the surface of the manure, but leave the lights off for three or four days to allow the emanations of rank steam to pass off. (5) Cover the surface of the dung with mould in the proportion of a barrow load of good loamy soil to each light, and make the surface of the mould level, covering the dung entirely; or, if preferred, form hillocks for the reception of the plants. As soon as this is done put on the lights. (6) Raise the plants required in pots placed within the bed under the frame, and sunk a little in the mould. When about a week old, turn out of pots and set the plants with the mould from the pots undisturbed in the mould that covers the manure. (7) Maintain the temperature of the air within the frame by mats placed over the lights in frosty or windy weather during the early stages of the bed's existence. (8) 'As the heat of the bed declines, prevent its diminution by coatings of fresh dung, technically called 'linings', piled up round the bed on all sides. (9) If necessary, as time progresses, remove the old linings and replace by fresh manure, but if the roots of the plants in the frame have penetrated into the old linings, they must be allowed to remain where they are, and fresh linings must be again piled up outside the first set. (10) As the temperature of the hotbed should maintain an average of 75°, as soon as it is found to fall below 70° lose no time in putting linings round the bed. (11) It is as well to place mould on the surface of the hotbed *outside* the frame, and to utilise it for growing radishes, lettuces, or small salading, which are all the better for quick growth in a position of this kind.

699 *Three-quarter Span Roof Garden Frame* This kind of frame is of comparatively recent introduction, and for many purposes, and especially for plant growing and plant protecting, it has a decided advantage both in point of shape and general principles of construction over the ordinary garden frame, although it costs more money. Its form is shown in Fig. 348. The proportion of height in front and at back in the ordinary garden frame, it will be remembered, is as three parts at back to two in front, but in the Three-quarter Span Roof Frame a different proportion is observed. In this kind of frame, if the height of the front be taken at one part, that of the back will be two parts, and that of the highest point in a perpendicular, raised at a point three-quarters of the length of the side from the front, will be three parts. Thus, if the height of the front of the frame be 11 inches, that of the back will be 22 inches, and that of the highest point 33 inches, or thereabouts, and these are the general proportions of frames of this description, which are made in various lengths, ranging from 4 feet to 16 feet, the length of the side, as in the ordinary frame, being 6 feet. The prices charged for these frames by Messrs Boulton and Paul and Mr C. Frazer, Horticultural Builders, both of Norwich, with their sizes, are as follows:

Sizes	4ft. long by 6ft wide	8ft. long by 6ft wide	12ft. long by 6ft wide	16ft. long by 6ft wide.
Boulton and Paul	—	£4 5s. 0d.	£6 10s. 0d.	£8 5s. 0d.
C. Frazer	£2 17s 0d.	£4 10s. 0d.	£6 5s. 6d.	—

The frames sent out by both makers are painted within and without with four coats of the best oil colour, and glazed with 21-ounce glass, but there are points of difference in the method of construction. Messrs Boulton and Paul's frames, the lights of which are made to turn over, are supported, when opened for ventilation, by means of iron stays and splines; but those which are sent out by Mr Frazer are marked by certain registered improvements in their construction which render them peculiarly valuable to those who use them. These improvements consist, firstly, of a new method of fastening the frames at the corners; and, secondly, of new set-opes by which the lights are supported, when raised either for ventilation or for attention to the plants that are within the frame.

FIG. 348 *Three-quarter span roof garden frame*

700 With regard to the first improvement, it has been found that the bolts used in fastening the frames by the old method often became completely set fast with rust, thus rendering it next to an impossibility to take the frames apart, either for removal from place to place or for painting. The new Registered Corner Fastenings with which these frames are fitted have been introduced for the express purpose of obviating this difficulty, and consist of a combination of the dovetail and wedge, made of cast iron, with screws to fasten the parts to the frame. Thus there are no nuts and bolts to be lost, no holes to receive and retain moisture, which, if it gets in, is sure to rot the wood.

701 The second improvement consists of the new Registered Set-opes, which will support the lights when lifted in any position, either for the admission of air or for affording that necessary attention to the plants which all plants, whether in frames or out of them, require from time to time. By the use of the old form of set-ope, the lights could be lifted a short distance for ventilation, but not to the extent which the new set-opes allow. Besides this, when it is found necessary to open a frame of this kind wide enough for a man to get inside, which is frequently the case, under the old system a wooden spline is resorted to for the purpose of propping up the light. Now, as this is behind the man, it is very apt to get shifted, and the result is that the light falls, possibly injuring the man, and certainly breaking a quantity of glass. The new set-opes save time, and are economical in preventing the breakage of glass, being much safer than the old ones. When not in use, they fold down into the frame and are no encumbrance, whereas when the old set-opes are not in use, they rest upon the ground outside the frame, and are liable to trip up any person who may be walking past. These frames are made of good red deal, the sides and ends being 1¼ inch thick, and the lights 2 inches thick. The form of the set-ope is shown above in Fig. 348.

702 *Ground Vineries* Some years ago a great deal of interest was shown in viticulture, or grape growing, by means of long ranges of garden frames, or 'ground vineries', as they were then called. The system is too good a one to be permitted to drop out of recollection, and it is noticed here. In point of fact it is merely an adaptation of the principle prescribed in Section 686 of protecting tender plants in winter, or accelerating the growth of early vegetables in spring, by means of lengths of boarding in front and in the rear, closed in at the ends, and supporting garden lights, glazed or covered in with even oiled paper or oiled calico. For grape growing the frames must be of a more solid and finished character, and for those who wish to make them – for it does not appear that they are now supplied by horticultural builders – the following description is given, illustrated by a sectional view of the structure in Fig. 349. The length of the vinery having been determined – and this must be of course regulated by the length of ground at command – two ends must be constructed of the extreme size shown in the illustration – that is to say, of the size shown by the space A, B, C, D, E. A convenient width for the vinery will be 3 feet, inside measurement, timber 1¼ inch or 1½ inch thick being used for the frame, which will bring the outside measurement to 3 feet 2½ inches or 3 feet 3 inches. Two slips of timber of the same thickness as the frame must then be cut out and bevelled, as shown at C, and firmly screwed together, each screw being inserted on the opposite side to that into which the last screw put in has been driven, so that the pieces of wood forming the ridge may be firmly held together throughout its length. Notches should be cut in the apex of each end for the reception of the ridge piece, which need not be more than 2 inches wide in its widest part – that is to say, on the outside from C to the edge F, at which the lights are hinged to it. Before the pieces that form the ridge are screwed together, mortises must be cut in them for the reception of tenons at the ends of strips or bars running at intervals from the ridge to the boards forming the front and back of the frame (or the sides of the frame, if the term be preferred), and to these the other ends of the bars should be firmly screwed down. The form of the connection between ridge and bar and the mortise is shown in Fig. 350. To the bottom or under side

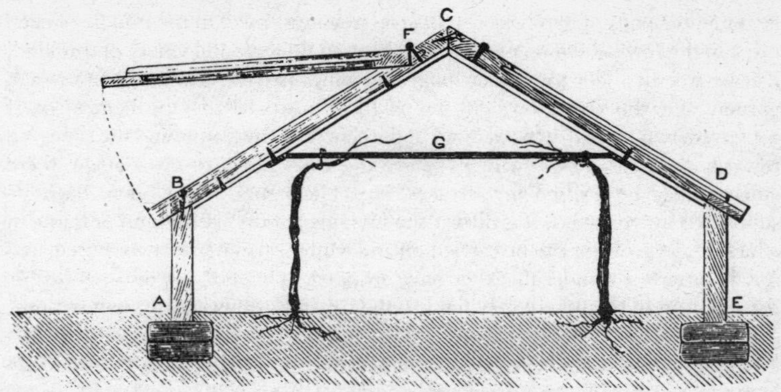

FIG. 349 *Sectional view of ground vinery*

of each bar a slip of wood, 3 inches wide and ½ inch thick, must be screwed, as shown in section at **X**. This forms a rebate to the bar, and forms a support to the sides of adjacent lights when closed down, and a means of preventing the entrance of any water that may find its way in between the edges of the lights and the bar. It will be better if the rebate is grooved along its whole length, and the groove continued across the edge of the boards on which the bars rest. The bar is shown in Fig. 349 by BF, the light being represented as open, so that its position and attachment to ridge and board may be better seen.

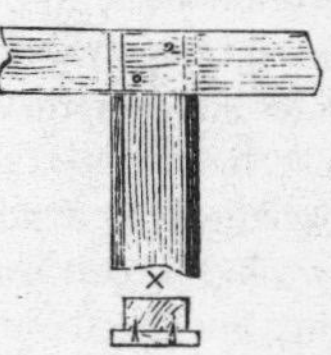

FIG. 350 *Mode of forming and attaching strips to support sides of lights to ridge*

703 These bars may be inserted at distances varying from 3 feet to 4 feet along the ridge, but when the length of the ground vinery is determined it will be better to divide the length into equal spaces, approximating as nearly as possible to 3 feet or 4 feet, or something between them, and then to form the mortises for the bars accordingly. Strength and rigidity may be imparted to the whole structure, and the necessity for any supports for the ridge between the ends obviated, by the use of iron ties screwed to the under side of the bars from bar to bar, as shown at G. These bars may be utilised further for the support of the canes, as shown in the illustration. The frames must be constructed to fit the spaces between the bars, and are hinged to the ridge piece as shown at F. The construction is simple, and as the whole framing is put together with screws, it may be taken to pieces at any time for removal or for putting away if not wanted, but it must be borne in mind that the screws must be well greased before insertion, otherwise their withdrawal will be anything but easy. It is better to rest the frame on a foundation of bricks, placed on a trench taken out for them in the soil. Three rows of bricks placed end to end under ends and sides will be sufficient, or even two, as shown in Fig. 349. They must be put together so as to 'break bond' – that is to say, the ends of two bricks in the top row must meet in the middle of each brick in the row below; no mortar need be used. In a ground vinery of this kind, if it be from 20 feet to 30 feet long, four vines may be planted, one in each corner, and the canes brought in parallel lines towards the centre; or if preferred, two vines may be planted in the centre of the frame, and the canes led towards the ends. In the winter, before the vines begin to grow again, these vineries may be utilised for lettuces, etc. The lights, when open, must be supported by iron stays. It is difficult to imagine a more useful kind of frame in which grape growing can be carried on and winter salading always secured, and it is a matter for wonder that they have dropped, as it were, out of use. Possibly the mention of them here may tend to their revival, especially among amateur gardeners.

704 *Forcing Pits* It has been said that the forcing pit is, as it were, intermediate between the garden frame with its source of heat, the hotbed, and glazed structures which are heated by artificial means. It partakes of the nature of the former in so far that it is used for the same purposes, and chiefly those of growing cucumbers and melons, and is covered in by glass lights; and it partakes of the nature of the latter in being formed of brick, and therefore immovable and not portable from place to place, like the garden frame, and in being capable of heating by artificial means, as well as by the warmth produced by fermenting dung. In its simplest form, it is constructed by digging a pit in the ground about 6 feet in width and 12 feet long, and then lining the pit with containing walls of 4½-inch brick; the depth of the pit should not be less than 3 feet below the ground level, and it may be more than this with advantage. The walls must be brought up to about 2 feet in front and 3 feet behind above the ground level, the sides being gradually sloped from the back wall to the front wall. Upon the wall a kerb of wood is laid, consisting of a timber framework with bars from front to back, in accordance with the number of lights used – that is to say, one bar for two lights, two bars for three lights, etc. The frames and bars are rebated, or slips are nailed on the upper surface of the frame and bars so as to form rebates in which the lights may be moved up and down. The price of a kerb frame, 2 inches thick, with a single light, for a brick pit, as supplied by Mr John Mussett, Winstanley Road, Clapham Junction, London, is £1 1s., and for two, three, or more lights, in proportion.

705 An ordinary forcing pit thus constructed is managed in precisely the same way as a garden frame and hotbed. The dung must first be turned over and sweetened, and when in a proper condition be thrown into the pit and well trodden or beaten down to consolidate it. The rank steam must then be allowed to escape, and when this has been done the mould may be thrown over the dung and the lights put on. There is no means of lining a pit of this description or of increasing the temperature when it is beginning to decline, unless by piling-fresh manure and litter round the walls above the ground level, which would be attended with a certain degree of inconvenience; and any steam which may arise from the dung after the lights are on must naturally find its way into the plant chamber within the frame, between the mould and the glass. The portability of the garden frame is useful, and affords a strong argument in favour of its use; but if it be asked in what points a brick pit is desirable, it may be pointed out that it is generally constructed in a waste corner of the garden, where it is in the way of nothing, always provided that the aspect is a warm one, that it can be filled with more ease and less trouble than to construct a hotbed on which to place a garden frame, and that in the winter, when its work as a forcing pit is over for the season, it can be turned to good account either for stimulating rhubarb and seakale into growth or for protecting half-hardy plants, forming, in fact, an excellent shelter and a miniature conservatory at this season of the year.

706 *Forcing Pit with Linings* It has been said that it is not possible to line an ordinary forcing pit, and by this it is meant that it is not possible to maintain by means of linings the dung that occupies the lower part of a forcing pit built in the ordinary way – that is to say, surrounded by four brick walls – and not that it is impossible to construct a forcing pit in such a way that linings may be added, for it is as easy to put linings to a forcing pit as it is to add them to a common hotbed, but the walls of the pit must be constructed in such a manner that there may be direct communication between the exhausted manure within the pit and the fresh manure that is placed without it in the form of linings. If it be asked if a pit be preferable to a hotbed, the answer is that it is, and further, if the reason be sought, it may be found in the fact that the heat escapes from a pit less quickly than it does from a hotbed, and that a more regular temperature can be sustained in it, which causes all kinds of fruit raised in it to attain greater perfection than it can in the hotbed. The pit itself is constructed in the same manner as the pit described in the preceding section above the ground level, but below this line the walls of the pit itself are built in a different manner, and there are additional brick walls surrounding it at a little distance from it, which renders a forcing pit with linings a more costly structure than a pit without them. Instead of excavating an area sufficient for the pit itself a very much larger one must be dug out, so that when the walls of the pit are built, as at A, A, there is a wide trench all round it, or in front and at back only, as may be desired. The upper walls of the pit are supported on pillars, which serve as abutments to flattened arches, which also lend their aid to sustain the walls above ground. The pillars are shown at B, B, and the arches at C, C Fig. 351 representing part of the end elevation of the pit, as well as a section of it from back to front. The manure is thrown into the pit until it is brought up as far as D, and to prevent undue escape of heat through the arches it is also desirable to fill up the passage round the pit, shown at E, E, between the pillars and the containing walls at F, F, which form the utmost limits of the pit, with spent manure at first. The top of this passage is covered in with thick boards, G, G, or, if preferred, a wood framing may be put over the top of the opening, to which wooden flaps or doors of thick timber may be attached by hinges, which is a neater method of construction, and decidedly preferable. The trench or passage may be made only in the front and rear of the pit, as it has been said, but it is better carried all round. When the heat begins to slacken, the spent manure should be taken out of the trench and fresh manure substituted for it.

707 *The Cold Pit* The forcing pit that has been described above must not be confounded with the common cold pit, which is as different from it as a

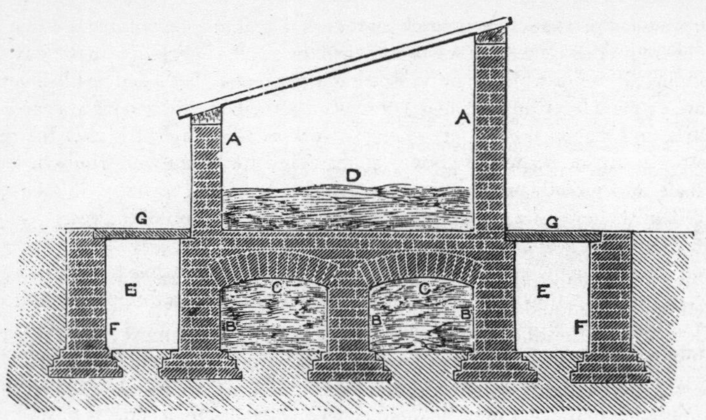

FIG. 351 *Forcing pit with linings*

conservatory or cold house is from a greenhouse or a hothouse, because one class of buildings is heated by artificial means and the other is not heated at all. A very good cold pit may be formed by building containing walls of turf or of earth well beaten together, so that the back wall is higher than the front wall, and the sides sloping from back to front like the sides of a pit or frame, so that lights may be placed over it on frames covered with any protecting material. A cold pit of this kind, well and firmly built, will last a long time, and is most useful in the winter for sheltering vegetables liable to injury from frost, and half-hardy plants, which will do well with this minimum of protection. If the bottom of the pit be sunk below the ground level it will be all the warmer, and the containing walls above the surface of the ground need not be made so high. A cold pit of greater strength and permanence may be made in the same manner by making an excavation in the earth about 2 feet deep, and surrounding it with containing walls about 1 foot above the ground level in front and 2 feet behind, which must be finished at top with a wooden kerb, and bars from back to front, if long enough to require them, to support the lights.

Speaking of the cold pit, Loudon says: 'The cold pit with earthen sides is in part sunk in the earth, and in part raised above it by walls of loam or turf. On these walls glass frames are sometimes placed; and at other times only mats or canvas frames. Such pits are used by nurserymen and market gardeners, and answer perfectly for the preservation of half-hardy plants. A pit of this kind is shown in the annexed illustration (Fig. 352). It is a sunk wall excavation 3½ feet wide, 3 feet deep at back, and 1 foot 9 inches in front. It is covered with movable thatched frames, which are tilted at pleasure by a notched prop. It is used as a kind of store house for all culinary vegetables in leaf which are liable to be destroyed by frost, such as cauliflower, broccoli, endive, lettuce, etc. These, before the winter sets in, are taken up from the open ground with balls of earth, and embedded on a bottom layer of rich soil, filling up the vacancies between and among the stems with old bark or decayed leaves. Air is given on all occasions when it can be done with safety, and in severe frosts additional coverings of litter are put on.' In Fig. 352, A shows a bank of earth thrown up against the back containing wall in order to increase the warmth of the pit, the ordinary ground level being preserved in front; B is the thatched frame in section, supported, when raised to admit air, by the notched stick C; D is the mould in which the plants are set; and E the leaves or bark that should be thrown in between and among the stems of the plants.

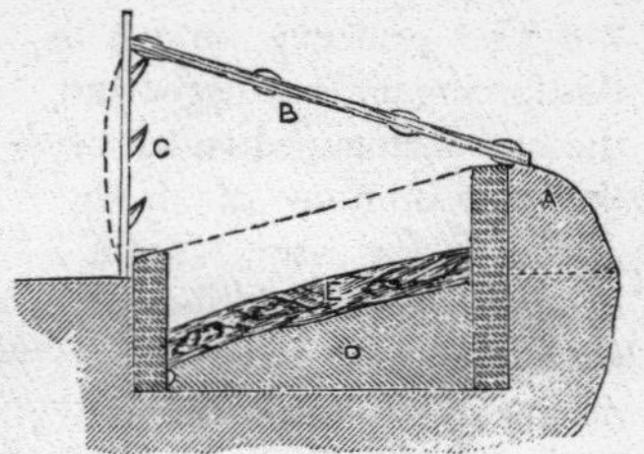

FIG. 352 *Section of common cold pit*

708 *West's Forcing Pit* In the ordinary frame, in which the heating material is thrown directly into the bottom of the pit itself, and the mould is placed upon it, it follows as a matter of course that any steam from the dung must enter the soil, and find its way through this porous medium into the plant chamber between the soil and the lights, and in addition to this there are no means by which the temperature in the pit can be maintained when it begins to decline, as by linings in the ordinary hotbed. It has therefore been sought to obtain means of access to the chamber below in order to take measures necessary to maintain the temperature, thus bringing the forcing pit to the condition of a propagator on a large scale. Among the numerous plans that have been proposed for effecting this, and at the same time utilising dung as the heating medium, the most simple and easily managed seems to be that which is adopted in the structure known as West's Forcing Pit, from the name of its inventor. This, or rather the principle on which the pit is constructed, will now be described; but it should be said that considerable modifications have been made in the original plan, in which entrance into the lower chamber was obtained through doors in the front wall and back wall of the structure, whereas in the modified and improved plan about to be given entrance is effected by doors at each end, and bank of earth may be thrown up against the pit in front and behind, thus preventing the external air from coming into immediate access with the containing walls except at the sides, and above the level of the earth within the pit at front and rear, while in the original plan the air came in contact with the walls all round the pit from base to lights.

709 The entire structure, as will be seen from Fig. 353, consists of two chambers separated by a platform or partition between them, which will be described presently. The diagram exhibits a sectional view of the pit, but this will be sufficient to explain the nature of the structure internally and externally, and the mode by which access is obtained to the lower chamber. It may be explained that, in order to render both the description and the diagram as useful as possible, the latter has been carefully drawn on a scale of inch to 1 foot, so that all its parts are represented in due proportion. The structure is supposed to be of the same size as an ordinary three-light frame – that is to say, 12 feet by 6 feet, external measurement – and as the containing walls are 9 inches thick, it follows that the internal measurement of the lower chamber is feet 6 inches by 4 feet 6 inches, and as its height is 3 feet 6 inches the capacity of the entire space is a little more than 6 cubic yards. The lower chamber is shown at AA, in Fig. 353.

710 The principle on which this forcing pit is managed and the heat maintained is that of the substitution of fresh manure for the spent material, or the addition of fresh dung to it, as soon as a decline in the temperature of the upper chamber begins to show itself. One half of the chamber, AA, is filled length ways with fresh manure at the commencement, and this, if the pit be kept close shut up, will last from twelve to eighteen days, according to the quality of the manure. As the heat declines the other side is filled, and the temperature is further sustained by additions to the top of both as the mass settles. When the heat given forth by the dung on both sides becomes insufficient, the side first filled being cleared, the old manure must be mixed with some fresh dung, and replaced; and this is repeated alternately on either side as often as necessary. The doors by which entrance is gained to the lower chamber are shown by the dotted squares surrounding the letters A, A. They are separated by a pier of brickwork 9 inches square. A framework of wood, rebated to receive the doors, is built into the brickwork on each side of the central pier, and the doors, which should be 2 inches thick, made of two thicknesses of wood firmly screwed together and placed the reverse way of the grain to prevent warping from heat and moisture, are fitted against and into the framework and secured by staples and pins. The construction of the doors is shown in section in Fig. 354, in which Z, Z, is the brickwork at top and bottom, Y, Y, the rebated frame, and X, X, the two thicknesses of which the door is composed. Slots are cut in the doors, through which the staples W, W, are passed, and oaken pins are thrust through the loops of the staples to hold the door tightly against the frame. Fig. 354 is not drawn to scale, but is purposely exaggerated in order to show the construction as clearly as possible.

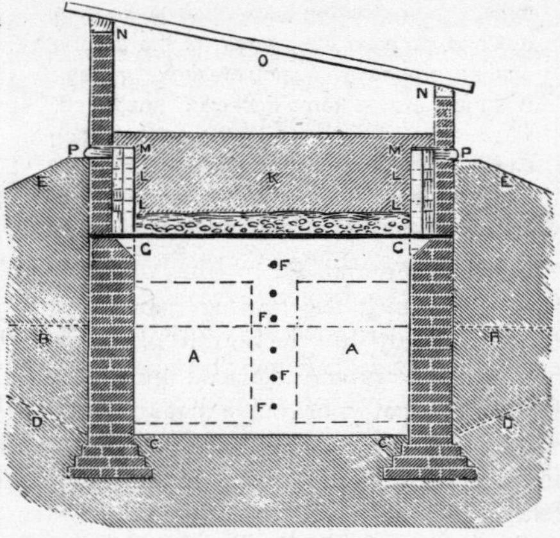

FIG. 353 *Section of west's forcing pit on improved plan. Scale – two-thirds of an inch to one foot.*

711 The dotted line, BB, in Fig. 353 shows the original ground level. From this level on each side of the pit a trench is sunk to the depth of 2 feet, to the level shown by C, C. This trench should be about 3 feet 6 inches wide, and the earth on the side furthest from the pit should be supported by a containing wall of brick. There should be an approach to the trench on each side on a gentle incline, so that barrows may be easily wheeled

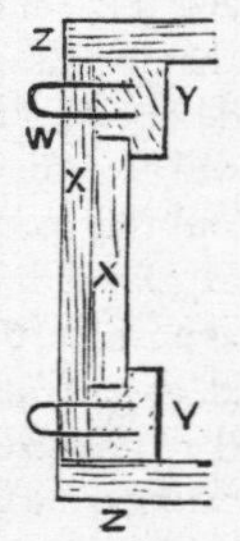

FIG. 354 *Section of door of pit*

up and down, and above the inclines D, D, a containing wall should be built from each end of front and back, to sustain the earth thrown up also at an easy incline against the front and rear wall. The slanting top of each bank is shown at E, E. In order to divide the lower chamber into two parts, iron bars, F, F, are built lengthways from side to side into the brick piers that separate the doors, to form a partition in it, and to serve as a guide and support when packing the dung that is introduced through the doors. When the pit is a three-light pit and 12 feet in length, it will be convenient to have two doors on each side, but if a pit be made on this principle for two lights or one light, two doors on one side will really be all that is necessary, or one door on each side; but when one door on each side is made, care must be taken that they are not *opposite* one another, but placed so that one will afford access to the front part of the lower chamber, and the other to the back part. If the two doors are made on one side, one trench will be sufficient at the end at which the doors are, and a bank may be thrown up against the other end, as at front and rear.

712 The arrangements for the lower chamber are now complete, and the construction of the upper chamber only remains to be described. Up to the height of the lower chamber the containing walls have been built solid, but above this point, up to the level to which the earth is intended to rise, or just the thickness of one brick less, it is to be built hollow, so as to form a flue throughout the walls at front and back and sides, which may be permeated in every part by the steam arising from the dung, in order to impart additional warmth to the mould. In order to do this, bevelled orifices are made at intervals all the way round by cutting away bricks, as shown at G, G, in the last two courses. Should there be any difficulty in understanding this, it will be removed by reference to Fig. 355, which clearly exhibits the construction of the entrance to the flue. The next step is to form the partition between the upper and lower chambers, and this is done by laying a row, of cast-iron bars, 2 inches wide and ¾ inch thick, on the top of the last course of the lower chamber from back to front, as shown by the black line from G to G in Fig. 353. These bars are placed from 9 inches to 12 inches apart, and serve as a support for a layer of small boughs, brushwood, and leaves, which are laid on them at H, to sustain the soil, K, which is thus prevented from penetrating into the lower chamber. Above the last course the wall is built hollow as far as the height to which it is intended to fill in with mould. This is done by building the external part of the wall 4½ inches thick, by laying courses of bricks end to end and flat, and by forming the internal face of the wall of bricks laid on edge, which makes this part of it 2¼ inches thick, leaving a hollow between each part of 2¼ inches. In order to strengthen the structure, tie bricks are laid from face to face of the wall at intervals, as shown by the dotted lines across the flue at L. The shaded part indicates the position and extent of the flue. When the wall has been carried high enough in this manner, a course of thin tiles is laid all round the top in

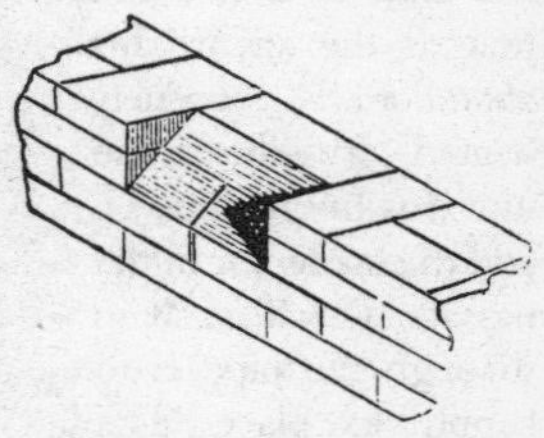

FIG. 355 *Formation of bevelled entrances to flue*

cement, to close in the flue, and the walls are then carried up, brick thick, or 4½ inches thick, to the requisite height, when a wood kerb, N, N, is laid on the top to take the lights, O. The tiles are shown at M, M. Two holes, shown at P, P, should be left in the brickwork, both at front and back, 4½ inches by 2¼ inches, or of the width and thickness of a brick. These must be stopped with wooden plugs. They serve as outlets by which the steam in the flues may be let out, and for the regulation of the temperature by the admission of the external air. By having the doors at front and back, there would naturally be some little difficulty in getting the dung into the chamber and out of it, but by having them at the end, the chamber for the reception of the manure is commanded throughout its entire length, and the dung can be drawn out with a dung rake with a long handle, and packed in as tightly as possible by mean of a pole with a piece of flat board at one end of it, with the greatest ease.

713 *Mitchell's Forcing Pit* If the bottom heat in a forcing pit is supplied by means of hot water pipes, then the circulation of the hot water by flow and return pipes is managed in precisely the same way as that which is adopted for heating hot houses, etc., which will be explained presently in connection with these structures, but before quitting this part of the subject it may be useful to call attention to a form of pit designed and used by Mr Mitchell, formerly of Worsley, which was described in the *Gardener's Chronicle*,' and was spoken of as being the best form that could be employed. The objects held in view when it was planned were: (1) A complete circulation of air without loss of heat. (2) A supply of moisture at command proportionable to the temperature. (3) A desirable amount of bottom heat. (4) A supply of external air, when desirable and necessary, without producing a cold draught.

714 The form of the pit and the principle of construction are sufficiently set forth in Fig. 356, which shows a sectional view of it, and there will be no necessity to give a detailed description of its construction. It will be enough to explain how the four requirements mentioned above are satisfied. The method by which the first is accomplished will be understood by referring to the illustration, in which A represents the flow pipe, and B, B, B, the return pipes in the vaulted chamber below the bed. It is evident that as the air in this chamber becomes heated, it will escape upwards by the pipe C, and the cooler air in the passage D will rush in through the pipe E to supply its place. The ascending current of heated air through C is

FIG. 356 *Sectional view of Mitchell's forcing pit*

cooled by coming in contact with the glass, and descends into the passage D, to pass through the pipe E into the vaulted chamber, where it is again heated, and in this way a constant circulation of air is maintained without loss of heat in the structure. In order to obtain the second object, namely, a supply of moisture at command proportionable to the temperature, the tank and pipe systems are, to a certain extent, combined. The flow pipe A is put to the extent of half its sectional area into a tank shown below it by a black line at F. When water is poured into this tank, vapour is given forth exactly proportionable to the heat of the pipe A and the pit. The third requisition is produced by the surrounding atmosphere and the system of heating employed. The fourth is attained simply by lowering the upper sash: the cold air thus entering at the top only, descends at once into the passage D, and passes through E into the hot chamber below the mould before it rises through C and comes in contact with the plants. When the heat in the chamber is 95°, it is 71° in the open space over the bed, and only 60° in the bottom of the passage D, while in the mould in the bed it is 80°. The amount of vapour is regulated with the greatest facility, even from the smallest quantity to the greatest density.

715 *Glazed Wall Covers for Fruit Walls* In gardens in which fruit is grown on a large scale, glazed covers for the walls are very desirable, if their cost be no bar to their adoption, because, by their use, the fruit crop may be secured, beginning from the unfolding of the blossom to the time when the fruit is fully ripe and ready for the table. It is only for the less hardy kinds of fruit trees, however, that such protection need be provided, as, for example, apricots, peaches, and nectarines: plums and other kinds of wall fruit do not require appliances of this sort, although, even for plums and some kinds of cherries, they may be used with advantage. Due regard being had to the proper management of fruit trees, by pinching and pruning, root pruning, and the judicious administration of stimulants when requisite, in the form of manure, the most necessary things to be kept in view by the fruit grower in order to attain success in his pursuit are the complete protection of the trees from frost, and the proper ripening of the wood. For the first of these, various means have been mentioned in the preceding pages, but none of them can be regarded as being so effectual as glazed covers for fruit walls, by which both objects are completely secured, with thorough ventilation and easy access to the trees at all times for pruning and syringing.

In advantageous positions, even oranges and lemons may be grown and ripened in the extreme south of England, with no other protection than that of the glazed cover, as may be seen in the gardens of Coombe Royal, near Kingsbridge, in the south of Devon. Here, to the right of the house, on approaching it, is a long arcaded wall, having a southern aspect, or very nearly so, forming a series of broad niches, surmounted by depressed Tudor arches, in which orange trees and lemon trees are planted and grown throughout the year in the open air, trained to the wall behind them, with no other protection than the brickwork behind them, between them, and above them, and some glass frames and matting which fit into the front of the niches and are put up during the winter months and early spring in cold and frosty weather. This is a special case, which is well known in the gardening world, but there may be many others in sheltered sunny aspects in the South Hams of Devon and along the south coast of England, from the Land's End to the Isle of Wight, in which orange and lemon culture is carried on in this simple manner.

FIG. 357 *Glazed cover for fruit walls with upright front*

716 *Glazed Wall Cover with Upright Front* Glazed wall covers are made in two forms, namely, with upright front in the one form, and with sloping front in the other. The appearance and construction of the glazed wall cover with upright front is shown in Fig. 357. It may be said that it consists of two parts, namely, the cover or coping at the top and the sash in front, both being removable at pleasure, and capable of being fitted to any ordinary wall, which, however, should be provided with a projecting coping of brick or stone, if not already finished in this manner. The first thing to be done is to furnish support for the glazed continuation of the coping or the covering overhead, by attaching strong iron brackets to the face of the wall, which is done by means of bolts passing through the wall and secured by nuts. On these brackets the glass coping is laid, the brackets being placed under the brick coping in such a manner that the glazed frames may be run up *under* it instead of butting against it. The upright front lights slide behind or in front of each other in a grooved framing, the upper part of which is attached to the iron brackets that support the roof, and the lower part supported on iron standards sunk into the soil. Ends to the covers can be added if desired. The roof lights are so made that they can be secured in position or removed by the insertion or withdrawal of a wedge. The front lights slide on brass rollers and iron runners. The framing is all made of the best red deal, painted with four coats of paint, and glazed with 21-ounce glass. These glass covers, which are cheap, because they will soon repay their first cost by the increase in the fruit crop that is secured by their use, and so simple in construction that any local bricklayer or carpenter can fix them, are manufactured and supplied by Messrs Messenger and Co., Horticultural Builders, Loughborough; brackets, copings, and front sashes complete, at 12s. per foot run for a wall 10 feet in height, ends being charged at £2 10s. each.

717 *Glass Coping* The width of the space between the face of the wall and the upright sash in front depends entirely on the width of the coping used, and as the glass coping or roof light is made in different widths, arrangements may be made by which glazed covering may be obtained of a width suitable to the space occupied by the borders and the size of the garden, though the most desirable width, and that in which the covering is usually supplied, is 4 feet. It may be useful to many readers to know that glazed coping, as shown in Fig. 358, without front sashes, may be had in widths of 2 feet, 3 feet, and 4 feet, at the prices respectively of 2s. 6d., 3s. 6d., and 4s. 4d. per foot run. This affords an effective and by no means expensive method of affording overhead protection for fruit trees, and it may be rendered still more efficient by suspending tiffany, screen netting, or any other protecting material from the eaves or the coping.

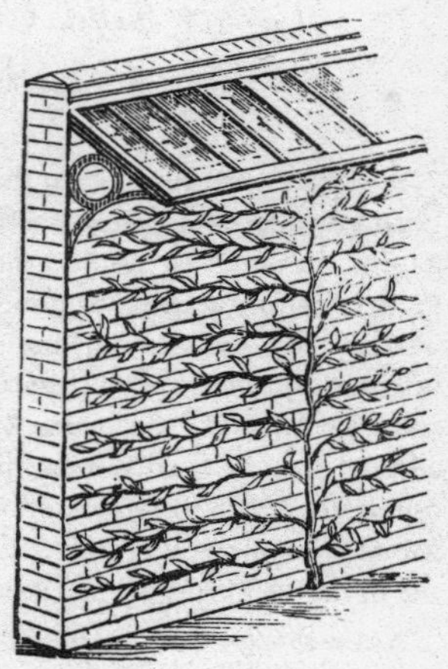

FIG. 358 *Glass coping for walls*

718 *Glazed Wall Cover with Sloping Front* In cases in which space is no object and no regard need be paid to economy, the glazed wall cover with sloping front which is illustrated in Fig. 359 is to be preferred, on account of the extra space which is afforded at the bottom of the space covered in by this means of construction. The width at the top of the front sloping lights is 4 feet in this case, as in the glazed wall covers with upright fronts, but the width at the bottom is extended to 6 feet, thus affording space for a narrow walk from end to end of the enclosure, and room for fruit trees in pots close to the sloping sashes. The foundation of the wall at back is carried to some depth, and prior to making the border, the whole space in front of the wall between the wall and front sashes is excavated to admit of a bottom of concrete, with a layer of rubble above it, being laid in, the front edge of the concrete serving as a foundation for the iron standards or supports on which the runners rest on which the sashes slide. Glazed wall covers of this form, suitable for a wall 10 feet in height, are supplied, complete in every part, by Messrs Messenger and Co., at 16s. 6d. per foot run, ends fitted with a door with lock and key being furnished in addition, if required, at £2 15s. each. Covers of either kind, upright or sloped, may be had for walls of any height, either above or below the height for which prices have been named, at charges proportionate to the height.

CHAPTER 17

Glazed Horticultural Structures of the Larger Kind, Comprising the Conservatory, Greenhouse, and Hothouse

719 Glass structures of even the smallest kind would, a very few years ago, have been considered a piece of great extravagance for any but the affluent. The garden, indeed, may not pay the rent, especially with amateurs, but if owners of gardens who use them to good effect will only debit the garden account with what strictly belongs to it, and give credit according to the market value for the luxuries as well as the necessaries of life they draw from it, they will find that a small garden and greenhouse will not prove an expensive luxury, but a necessary adjunct, which need not be dispensed with on the score of economy; more especially, if either the master or the mistress of the house happen to have a taste for such employment, and does not disdain to undertake, personally, some of the lighter portions of the labour so needful to keep a garden in proper order.

A case strongly in point with respect to this may be mentioned here appropriately enough. A gardener was applied to for advice by a friend, who, through an accident, was precluded from taking walking exercise, and who wished to learn, as he had a marked predilection for gardening, how far its practice would supply him with a proper amount of healthy exercise, without the necessity of walking. He took to the pursuit in consequence, not only practically but theoretically, and studied the physiology of the subject, reduced many of its directions to practice, and in a few years became one of the most successful cultivators of plants in England, and in every respect a leading gardener. He produced seedling plants, which he sold from the very beginning of his career, so as to repay him for his outlay: for the production of seedlings, besides being a very interesting, is a very profitable occupation if followed with judgment; new varieties of pelargoniums, fuchsias, azaleas, and heaths, if tolerably perfect and never parted with until success is achieved, producing a return by no means inadequate to the trouble. Some amateurs have arrangements with certain nurseries, by which their gardens are furnished with all they require in exchange for the pick of their seedlings; and it is said that as much as £100 was paid for the stock of a single dahlia – Queen Victoria; while the Muscat Hamburg grape realised upwards of £800, and the Golden Hamburg double that amount. Facts like these would intimate that gardening pursuits have their blue ribbon, while they yield many luxuries of an inexpensive character.

720 In former times, glazed horticultural structures were not only costly to fit up, but inefficient when erected. The proper principle of their construction was not very well understood; heavy rafters, complicated sashes, at once costly and inefficient, encumbered many a fine garden, as well as gardens of smaller pretensions. To Sir Joseph Paxton, and some other well-known cultivators, the merit is due of breaking through the old system, and proving to the world that light inexpensive structures were not only cheaper, but in every respect better adapted to their intended purpose than the old costly buildings.

721 Before proceeding further with this branch of the subject, it is desirable to pause a moment and gain a clear idea of the difference that exists between the various glazed horticultural structures known as conservatories, greenhouses, and hothouses or stoves, as suggested in the previous chapter, because a knowledge of the difference in the purposes to which they are severally applied will not only afford an easy clue to their management and all that it involves, but will also enable any gardener, and especially the amateur, to decide which will best suit his requirements and come within his capabilities, and so to provide himself with nothing beyond that to which he can pay the necessary attention and devote sufficient time to keeping everything in proper, because perfect, order. Large and extensive ranges of horticultural buildings demand considerable outlay and the employment of much labour, skilled and unskilled, and the maintenance of a small hothouse requires more constant attention and causes infinitely more trouble and anxiety than is involved in the care of a large conservatory. Indeed, as we proceed onward and upward from the construction and management of the conservatory to the formation and maintenance of the hothouse, the cost and labour seems to increase in geometrical rather than in arithmetical progression, or, to use an expression recently imported into matters political by a wondrous master of phrases, 'by leaps and bounds', rather than by a fair rate of advance, with which every one can keep pace without difficulty.

722 As there are three degrees of comparison in adjectives, so are there also three degrees of comparison in glazed horticultural structures, which are distinguished by the amount of heat which can be or ought to be maintained in them, and, as far as mere nomenclature goes, by the terms conservatory, greenhouse, and hothouse. There is no absolute hard and fast definite line of demarcation between the conservatory and the greenhouse, and the greenhouse and the hothouse, but the pairs of structures overlap and run into each other in very much the same way that the bands of primary colours in the spectrum, obtained by the refraction of a ray of light through a prism, overlap each other at the edges, and are interfused, thus forming zones of intermediate and secondary tints. In saying this, there is no intention to imply that there are structures that are intermediate between the conservatory and greenhouse and the greenhouse and hothouse, but that there are varieties in these which are distinguish able from each other in just the same manner that conservatory, greenhouse, and hothouse are distinguished from each other by the degree of heat that is severally maintained in them.

723 *The Conservatory* Speaking generally, the term 'conservatory' denotes a place in which sufficient protection is afforded to plants to shield them from injury from frost and the inclemency of the air in winter, and to enable them to continue growing and putting forth flowers without let or hindrance from the weather. It is a structure, in fact, in which plants that are too tender to stand the severity of winter and early spring may be sheltered, and in which hardy plants, bulbs, etc., may be induced to bloom or to remain in blossom at a time of year earlier than that at which they would flower in the course of nature – a structure in which plants are preserved from being brought into contact with climatic changes out of doors, and in which a temperature is maintained which is more equable and genial than the external air. A conservatory may be without heat altogether, in which case it is known as a *cold* house, or it may be heated just sufficiently to maintain a temperature of 45° by day, subsiding to 40° during the night, and in which the heat may be applied only just when it is wanted in time of severe frost, etc., when it is known as a *cool* house. Under the general term 'conservatory', then, such glazed structures are implied which are without artificial heat, or in which the general temperature, even if heated, should not rise in the cold weather and in the absence of sunshine above 45°, or, at the very utmost, to more than 50°. In the conservatory, moreover, plants may be grown without pots as well as in them – that is to say, in borders formed within the building itself, and this affords another marked characteristic of the conservatory.

A writer in the *Cottage Gardener's Dictionary* says that 'the term "conservatory" is often used synonymously with *greenhouse*, and then it denotes a suitable structure for the cultivation of those exotic plants which are just too tender for our climate, yet do not require the hot temperature of plant stoves, orchid houses, etc., which are set apart chiefly for plants from the tropical regions. With the greenhouse should be associated the idea of plants cultivated in pots or boxes, but with the conservatory we would associate the idea of plants growing in suitable soil, without at least the apparent intervention of pots and boxes, *and the structure connected with the residence*. To keep up the interest of such places, it is necessary that plants in bloom should be introduced: but in every case the pot should be plunged, so that the plant may appear to be growing in the soil. We would only make one exception in the case of very small ornamental plants, or even those not so very small, but to which it is desired to direct particular attention. We would elevate them in groups into ornamental vases or baskets, for which suitable places should be found, and which would be quite as much in harmony in such a place as in ornamenting a regular geometrical flower garden. For several reasons, therefore, the planting out in conservatory fashion – that is to say, in beds and borders within the structure – should not be attempted, except with climbers for the rafters, where the space is but limited, as a few plants, however beautiful at times, lose to a certain extent the power of pleasing when seen every day all the year round in the same position. The having the plants in large pots or tubs enable fresh combinations to be effected at any time. Where the range of glass is varied and extensive, though the plants be chiefly turned out in the soil, the feeling of sameness is not engendered, as the owner may easily enter his house at different points, and in such circumstances the very number of objects will constitute variety.

'Unity of expression is, to a certain extent, maintained by a mixture of the two modes, the centre of the house being supplied with plants that are really turned out, or which, brought for a temporary purpose, appear to be so, while all round the house there is a broad shelf for the accommodation of plants in pots. In saying *all round the house*, we are of course alluding to houses that have glass on all sides. Where there is an opaque back wall, the shelf could only be at the front and ends. However desirable it is to have light on all sides, where expense for heating in winter is no great object, yet very pleasing effects are produced even in lean-to roofs where a little attention is paid to unity of idea.

'With the single exception of planting out, the treatment of the conservatory is similar to that of the greenhouse. Keeping this in mind, good drainage should be secured; and the general soil should consist of two parts of fibrous loam and one of fibrous peat, with pieces of sandstone, charcoal, and broken bricks intermixed to keep it open. The peculiar requirements of each plant, as respects soil and manure, can be attended to in planting. Where the object is merely to preserve the plants during the winter, the general treatment will be similar to that of a cold greenhouse. Where the ideas of comfort, alike for the plants and the visitors, are to be maintained, and flowering plants are to be introduced liberally, in winter the general temperature should not be lower than 45°, and should range from that to 50°, allowing 10° or 15° more for sunshine. In such circumstances, the camellia and the orange will bloom during most of the winter; and acacias, eugenias, etc., will bloom early in spring. The greatest possible quantity of air must be given in summer; but in winter it must be very limited in frosty and dull foggy weather, it being better in either circumstance to keep the house rather close in preference to using large fires. Protecting by covering in severe weather will be of importance. The heating medium, to be most effectual, should be above ground; but, to save room, the flues or pipes may be underneath the pathways, which will also be of importance for keeping the soil in the beds in a nice warm condition, and, in such a house, will render the flowering of many of the hardier stove climbers a matter of certainty. Watering may be given liberally during summer, both at bottom and overhead; but in winter the plants will want little if duly attended to in the autumn, yet what is given should be rather warmer than the atmosphere of the house. In planting, it will often be necessary to make little brick pits for particular plants, to prevent them occupying too much space.'

724 The conservatory may appropriately be termed a winter garden, for such is its most useful purpose; it is really an essentially necessary adjunct to a well-ordered country house of any pretensions, affording means of exercise to the ladies and visitors in inclement weather. In houses of smaller dimensions it is the storehouse for displaying the flowers as they are forced into bloom in the greenhouse or frames, as well as for growing certain climbing and creeping plants festooned and trained under its roof and over its walls, and for other plants only requiring protection from frosts, which occupy its beds and borders. Even in the absence of any heating apparatus, the conservatory, if properly glazed and painted, will bring the temperature of the atmosphere to about the

FIG. 360 *Design for lean-to conservatory*

FIG. 361 *Design for ridge-and-furrow roof conservatory*

degree enjoyed by Frenchmen on the banks of the Loire, 7° farther south, without the great extremes of summer heat and winter cold to which they are exposed. In these days, therefore, of cheap glass, there is no reason why every house, suburban or country, should not have its glass house, proportioned to its size; and it may be added that it is possible to show that an additional rent of 7½ per cent would amply repay any landlord for the necessary outlay.

725 There are some few points which should influence the choice of a site for every kind of plant structure, the first and most important being that it is not over shadowed on the south, east, or west, or exposed to the drip of trees or houses in any direction. A lean-to house, which, however, is the worst form, although, perhaps, in the majority of cases it is the most suitable for the building to which it is to be attached, because the only one which can be adopted, may have any aspect between south and south-southeast – south, inclining a point or two to east, being the best – as it receives the early sun as it gradually rises, without being exposed to its full meridian glare. The span-roofed house would probably be well placed which ranged from north-west to south-south-east also: it would thus receive all the morning sun on one side, while the other would receive the meridian sun slightly oblique, and all the afternoon sun, varying according to the angle of incidence of the roof. This would also be the most favourable aspect for a ridge-and-furrow roof, whether it were supported against a back wall or had a rectangular roof with vertical lights on each side.

726 Conservatories, however, which are appendages to the house must depend for their aspect on the position that the house itself occupies, except where the principal rooms lie to the north. No plant house can possibly prosper in a north aspect, since the house shades it from the south sun; nevertheless, with these rooms it must be connected, or it fails in its object; and a passage or corridor connecting it, covered with glass, must lead to some locality, either to east, or west, or south, where a more genial aspect can be obtained for the conservatory.

Where a glass corridor becomes necessary, either round the house, or as described in Section 174, it should be made subservient to the objects of the conservatory by the introduction of baskets, trailing plants, vases occupying niches, and other attractions.

727 As regards its architectural style, the conservatory should, at least, be in harmony with that of the house: if ornaments are permitted, they should be Gothic, Tudor, or Grecian, according as the house is of one character or the other: in this, as in all other matters, congruity is to be studied.

728 The conservatory, properly speaking, is a house in which the plants occupy beds and borders as in the garden, but on a smaller scale: sometimes the plants are permanent ones, more frequently they stand in pots plunged into the soil, or in tubs standing on its surface, or in vases occupying pedestals. Much has been written on the arrangement of conservatories, and, among others, Mr Noel Humphreys has advanced some excellent ideas and suggestions for their construction and equipment, which would have a very pleasing effect in a house of sufficient size. Among more modern works on this subject, attention may be directed to *Artistic Conservatories*, in which is given a series of designs by E. W. Godwin, FSA, and Maurice B. Adams, consisting of forty photolithographic plates of winter gardens, conservatories, porches, verandahs, summer houses, etc., of a highly ornamental and artistic character, in the Queen Anne and other styles. This work, which is used by Messrs Messenger and Co., Horticultural Builders, Loughborough, and is supplied by this firm, post free, at 6s., cannot fail to be of the utmost use to those who are about to add a structure of this kind to the dwelling-house.

FIG. 362 *Design for ornamental conservatory*

729 For those, however, who may not care to provide themselves with this work, four designs are given in Figs. 360, 361, 362, and 363, which will at least prove suggestive and show how it is possible to make the conservatory simple and inexpensive as well as useful, or to render it a highly ornamental structure, which will add considerably to the appearance of the dwelling house to which it forms an annexe, provided always that it is in congruity with the style of architecture followed in designing the house itself, for this is a *sine qua non*, as it has been already said. Buildings in each of the styles shown are supplied by Messrs Messenger and Co., Loughborough, by whom the designs have been kindly furnished. Fig. 360 shows a lean-to conservatory, simple in character, but effective in appearance, despite its plainness, and suitable for a plain villa residence in suburban districts or for small country houses. It is useful and commodious, and in cases where economy in cost is an object it is the best kind of house to erect, because there is nothing about it that tends to render it expensive. Ventilation is secured by opening the front lights and the narrow lights at the top of the roof. In Fig. 361 is shown a more elaborate structure, with a ridge-and-furrow roof, and having three gables, the central portion being wider than the sides, and thrown out in advance of them. The sashes open on each side of the building to let in the external air, and the hot air which arises to the top of the roof is afforded means of escape by Messenger's improved ventilating apparatus, by which the lights in the roof and lantern may be raised or closed at pleasure. Although the conservatory has the appearance of being highly ornamental, the cost is not so great as might be supposed, the ornamentation being mostly in iron work, and introduced chiefly in the ridges of the roof and the lantern which crowns the central part. The size of the conservatory shown in the illustration is about 22 feet in extreme length from the house to the entrance, 30 feet in width from side to side, and 20 feet in height from the ground to the ridge of the lantern. In Fig. 362 a conservatory of some pretensions is depicted, attached to the side of a house, and intended to be in strict keeping with its architecture. Its construction is clearly shown in the illustration. Like the conservatory in Fig. 361, its roof is a ridge-and-furrow roof, but the central portion is crested with a lantern that is more elaborate in form and ornamentation. The sashes forming the side lights and the front are supported on a dwarf wall, enriched with a course of balustrades, and raised by a pediment above the ground level. The end of the central part farthest from the house, which affords the means of entrance and exit, is semicircular in form, and approached by steps flanked with balustrades on either side. Ventilation is obtained from the side lights and the rows of narrow lights that form the roof of the lantern. A good size for such a house will be 45 feet long, 23 feet wide, and 20 feet high, but these dimensions can be varied to suit the building to which it is to be attached. In Fig. 363 a design is shown for an arched or curvilinear conservatory, in which rows of *flat* lights, disposed in tiers, are fitted into curved ribs, which meet and butt against each other in the ridge at the top. The principle of construction may be seen from the illustration. The form of roof is admirably adapted for the training of creepers, and when covered with them it presents a very effective appearance. It is especially suitable when thorough and

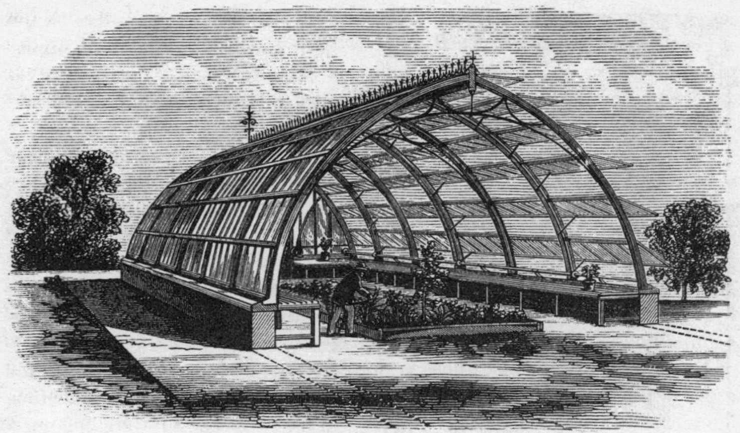

FIG. 363 *Curvilinear conservatory*

complete ventilation is required. This form of structure is well suited for a vinery, either cool or heated with pipes.

730 It is not possible, however, to dwell further here on the varieties of form and construction which may be followed in designing and building conservatories, but it will be useful, before quitting the subject, to bring under the notice of the reader a plan for the erection of a conservatory which is described by Loudon in his *Encyclopaedia of Cottage, Farm, and Villa Architecture*, which he considered to be admirably adapted for a small country mansion. In the plan itself, and in the details of construction, a few slight alterations have been made which tend to improve its appearance as an adjunct to the house, and to increase its utility for the purpose for which it is intended.

731 The conservatory, of which a ground plan is given in Fig. 364, showing its general arrangement, and a section, showing the form of roof, in Fig. 365, is Gothic in style, 43 feet long and 18 feet wide, having two folding doors, D, opening on the grounds and two, D´, communicating with the house – one with the library, and the other with the drawing room. The south end is octagonal in form, having three sashes, one similar sash and a door bringing the house flush with the south-east wall of the house. These sashes or vertical lights are 6 feet 8 inches in width, fitted into a frame and well secured by bolts on each side and at top; two other lights in the lower part of the same frame, turning on a horizontal pivot at its centre, give the means of ventilating the house.

732 A beam 45 feet long occupies the centre of the house, supported by the end walls and three hollow columns, C, 9 feet high; upon this beam the central rafters and lights of the roof rest. The beam is cut out so as to incline towards each of the supporting columns, and covered with lead; thus forming a central gutter to collect the water from the roof, which is carried through the columns into the tank by means of drains. Corresponding beams built into the wall on

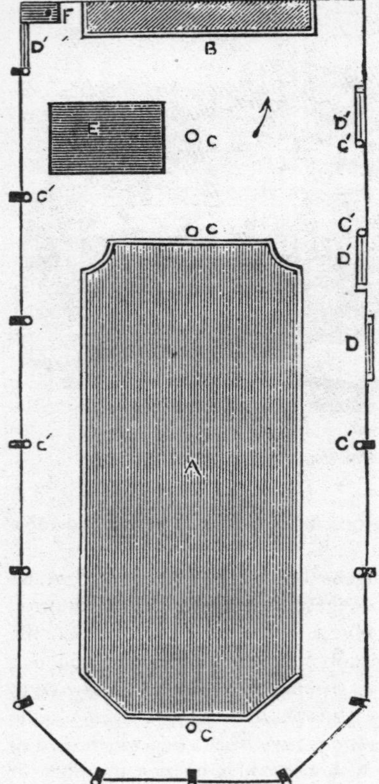

FIG. 364 *Ground plan of conservatory*

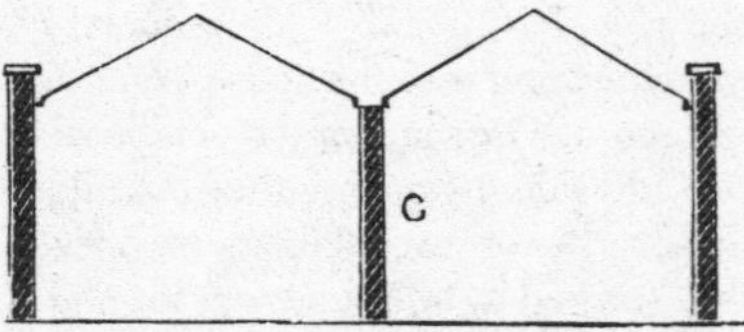

FIG. 365 *Section of conservatory showing form of roof*

each side receive the waters on the right and left by means of similar hollow columns, which serve at once the purpose of drainage and support.

733 The roof, which is rectilinear and double ridged, lakes four sashes 4½ feet in length, with broad gutters at each side and in the centre, and glazed with panes 4 inches by 5½ inches, the laps being ⅛ inch, with putty between; the side lights having glass 4 inches by 4½ inches.

734 As the house was laid out for beds and borders, the foundations of the beds A and B were dug out 6 feet deep, and piers raised to support them. At E is a tank 6 feet by 4 feet for rain water, with perfect drainage for the overflow. A pump connected with the tank occupies the north-west corner at F, and the whole of the beds and borders are surrounded with stone kerbs; and the house paved, full glazed, and painted, cost, at the old price of glass, £250.

735 The elevation of this house, it must be allowed, is not as attractive as it might be: the side lights are in the form of a pointed arch, and the brick piers, as well as the entablature over them, are heavy in appearance, and must have been ill-suited for the purpose. Cast-iron pillars in place of piers, with a light moulded cornice, would have been great improvement, as a matter of taste, besides being much cheaper, and adding from 12 inches to 18 inches to the height and width of the side lights. In this house ventilating shutters were inserted in the roof nearest to the wall of the house. Under the improved system of building, Sir Joseph Paxton's system of ventilating sashes would apply admirably in connection with the lower panes of the side lights; or the patent ventilating ridge of Messrs Messenger and Co., which opens and shuts very conveniently, by means of a rod and lever, working on an endless chain, which will be described presently, might be introduced with advantage.

The great conservatory at Chatsworth is built on the ridge-and-furrow system, as it has been called – a system by which acres of ground may be covered with the greatest ease. It consists of a number of small span roofs joined together, so to speak, and forming one entire roof, of which the length is 97½ feet, and the breadth 26 feet. This roof is supported by rows of cast-iron pillars, one along the centre, the others along the front and ends. These pillars are placed 6½ feet apart in the rows, and are 3 inches in diameter, the front ones being hollow, so as to admit a lead pipe, which carries off water from the roof into a drain in the gravel walk.

The bottom of each iron pillar is formed by a socket let into stone. The sockets and the stones combined form a solid base for the pillars, and the lead pipe is carried through socket and stone into the drain. The height of back wall is 13 feet 6 inches at the lowest and 15 feet at the highest part, or ridge of the angle; the front, 8 feet 6 inches in the valley, 10 feet at the ridge or angle. The lights are fixed-and angular, each 25 feet 6 inches in length, the front and side lights sliding in a double groove; the centre row of pillars, it should be said, are 2 feet 6 inches longer than the front or end pillars. Two feet from the bottom of each a screw passes, to fasten the bearer which supports the central walk; another arched iron support on the top of each rises up to the ridge of each angle. The pieces terminate in small squares, which fix in a similar hollow left at the top of the pillars, into which they are fastened by means of lead run into the interstices. In each valley of the angles two large screws are inserted into the styles of the light to fasten them firmly. Air is admitted by sliding back the front sashes, and by ventilators in the back wall, which swing on pivots and open by means of long iron rods having holes forged and pins driven into the wall, regulating the air at pleasure. Over these a square of trellis work is placed inside. The sash bars are an inch in width, and grooved to receive the glass.

In the ventilation of the forcing houses at Frogmore, an iron rod, which works on brass bearings or chains, runs the whole length of the house about a foot from the wall plate. On this shaft, opposite each light, is a brass pinion working into a toothed quadrant attached to the bottom rail of each light. This shaft is turned by a handle, when the quadrants are either thrown out or drawn in, and the whole light thrown open or shut to the extent required. In the back wall of each intermediate light is a ventilating frame, which is opened or shut by similar apparatus; above these frames over the glass is a corresponding number of open gratings. Flues or chambers in the wall open into the flues at the bottom, while the grating covers the opening at top. When it is desired to thoroughly ventilate the house, the fan lights being open, it is only necessary to turn the screw or worm, which is connected by the rod attached to the lever, and the lever being attached to the end of an iron shaft running the whole length of the house, the whole of the frames are thrown open at once.

736 'There are many modes,' says Mr Humphreys, 'by which the conservatory might be rendered both picturesque and interesting, apart from the actual brilliancy of the flowers, the principal feature being to relieve the spectator, as far as possible, of the idea that he is walking under glass. I propose to do this by making the frame work for receiving the glass of some irregular form, resembling the branches of trees or ribs of large leaves, such as the palms. This would greatly tend to encourage the illusion that the openings between the branches are not glazed.' This Mr Humphreys sought to do by the introduction of a series of light iron arches, meeting at a centre, glazed with curved glass, giving the appearance of a succession of arches half-hid, half-seen through the rich foliage of palms and climbing plants; while ornamental basins and vases fill up the recesses formed by these light airy supports to the roof.

737 Through some of the darker recesses of the house a stream of tepid water might flow amid fragments of rock and boulders, in which aquatics and rock plants from the tropics might be displayed in their natural and wildest habits; while the centre of the building, instead of being choked up with tall shrubs and trees, should be kept open; low-growing plants only being placed in the ground, as in a flower bed, in the central compartment; while some of the finest Ipomaeas and Passion-flowers (*Passiflorae*) should occupy the central beds, trailing round the slight pillars, and forming a matted roof overhead, with the double purpose of giving shade and concealing, at the same time, the artificial nature of the edifice. The side walls should be skirted next the glass by a bank filled with plants in flower, like those in the central beds; while seats of elegant design, either in stone, wood, or iron, should be scattered at intervals amid groups of aloes, arums, and other odoriferous plants in the centre. Of course, such a design as Mr Humphreys has imagined would require considerable space for its development, and for this reason it would only be available in a house of considerable dimensions; but some portions of it, namely, the arrangement of vases and rockwork, might be adopted with advantage for growing ferns and some of the less delicate orchids, even in a small house.

738 *The Greenhouse* The glazed structures to which this name is applied occupy an intermediate position between the cold house and conservatory on the one hand, and the hothouse or plant stove on the other. In the conservatory the heating apparatus need not be always at work, and the temperature will be sufficiently high if maintained at an average of 45°. In the winter and early spring it is necessary to keep sufficient fire going in the greenhouse, or rather in the heating apparatus, to maintain a temperature ranging from 45° to 50° in the night time, rising to 60°, or even higher, in sunny weather. In the conservatory we have plants growing in the ground, in beds formed within the building, but in the greenhouse all the plants by which it is tenanted are in pots or tubs, and platforms and stages are erected within the building, in order to bring them as near to the glass so that they may have the benefit of a full exposure to the light as it is possible to maintain. In the conservatory shade is permissible; in the greenhouse it is not desired, except in the summer, when the sun has acquired so much power that delicate plants would languish and droop under the influence of his heat-laden rays. Amateurs who can have only one glazed horticultural structure will prefer a greenhouse to a conservatory, because, in point of fact, it is more useful than ornamental, the former quality predominating in the greenhouse, whereas the conservatory, or winter garden, would be a failure, unless it were embellished in a marked manner. It has been said that it is difficult to draw a strongly defined line between the greenhouse and the conservatory, and this will now be more apparent to every reader.

739 With amateurs, especially those who are obliged to content themselves with a small house, the glazed structure that will most commend itself to them will be a compound of the conservatory and the greenhouse, partaking as much of the character of the one as of the other, for in it will be found the shelves and stages of the latter, and perhaps a vine or two, while a corner will be found here and there, especially at the back, for climbers to cover the walls and hang in festoons from rafter to rafter, and ornamental baskets filled with suitable flowers will be placed overhead in every available position that can be assigned to them. The fernery partakes more of the nature of the conservatory and less of that of the greenhouse, and will be found most suitable to those who do not care, through lack of time or inclination, to encounter the trouble which is inseparable from a greenhouse and the attention that its maintenance demands. Professional gardeners, too, whose aim is and must be the profit which arises from the exercise of their calling, will also prefer the useful greenhouse to the ornamental conservatory, and for this reason it will be necessary to dwell more at length upon its structure.

740 *Position and Form of Greenhouse* In constructing a greenhouse, the first point to be considered is the position and aspect that can be assigned to it, and the second, its form; of these, the second will be generally, if not always, subordinate to the first. With regard to position, it will be either an independent structure, complete in itself, or a structure attached to and proceeding from some other building – that is to say, a wall of some kind, pre-existent to the greenhouse, whether it be the wall of a house or a garden wall. Putting aside all fanciful outline in the ground plan and ornamental annexes, which belong to the conservatory rather than to the greenhouse, and restricting ourselves to the consideration of rectangular ground plans only, the best form for a greenhouse is an oblong rectangle, and in this shape it may be carried to any length, according to the space that may be available. The roof of such a structure may be in one single rectangular plane, in which case it is what is commonly known as a lean-to roof, or it may consist of two planes, inclined to each other, and meeting so as to form a ridge, in which form it is known as a span roof. If it be more convenient on account of the area of the ground plan to form the roof of a series of inclined planes, forming a succession of gables along opposite sides or ends, it is styled a ridge-and furrow roof. As regards aspect, a greenhouse that is built in the open as an independent structure gets the sun all day, provided that it is sufficiently removed from the neighbourhood of other buildings so as to escape being shadowed by any of them. For a glazed structure thus situated, the best position, perhaps, would be on a line due north and south, the ends facing these aspects, and the planes of the roof, for it should of necessity have a span or ridge-and-furrow roof, facing east and west, so that one would catch the morning sun and the other the afternoon sun. If a greenhouse has a lean-to roof, being built against a house or wall, the north is the worst aspect for it, and the south is the best, or an aspect varying from south-east to south-west. If the house has a north aspect, ferns and plants which thrive in the shade must be chiefly grown in it. In any aspect the roof should have a good pitch or slope, say from 30° to 45°, this being the angle of inclination to the front wall, and if the aspect be from south-east to south-west means should be provided for breaking the force of the sun's rays in summer. Lean-to houses, moreover, should have the front of a fair height, so that the upright glass may catch as much of the obliquely slanting rays of the sun in winter as may be possible. Of the form of a detached greenhouse it is unnecessary to say anything further at present, but of semidetached greenhouses, if the term may be used, it does not follow as a matter of necessity that they must be lean to houses, for they may proceed from the wall to which they are attached so as to have a span roof, the wall in this case forming one end of the house instead of the back, as in a lean-to house, and the other end being gabled. Thus, in the lean-to house, we speak of the containing walls as back, front, and ends, but in the span-roof house, we call them ends and sides.

741 *Size of Timbers, Glass, Containing Walls, etc.* As the method of building a small and useful greenhouse will be given presently, containing all necessary details of construction which may be applied to any form of house, it will only be necessary here to make a few remarks relating to general matters in connection with the erection of glazed horticultural structures. The best mode of building is to set up, first of all, dwarf walls of brick all round the area to be enclosed, from 2 feet to 2 feet 6 inches in height, and then, from the top of the wall upwards, to make the structure of glass and iron, or glass and wood, the latter being more common and more readily obtained. Glass is generally spoken of as 16-ounce glass and 21-ounce glass, by which it is meant that a square foot of glass weighs 16 ounces and 21 ounces respectively. Thus, the heavier glass is thicker and therefore stronger than the lighter, the thickness being in proportion to the weight; speaking in round numbers, the 21-ounce glass is thicker by one-fourth than the 16 ounce glass – that is to say, if the thickness of the latter be represented by 1, that of the former will be represented by 1¼, or very nearly so. There is no advantage gained in using small panes, for the narrower the pane, the greater will be the number of sash bars required to receive the glass, and consequently the less will be the space through which light can enter. Glass is now so cheap that the smallest size used should be 12 inches by 12 inches, and panes of 12 inches in length and from 15 to 18 inches in width, from rafter to rafter, are by no means too large. Ventilation should be carried out, as a rule, by openings immediately below the roof in the back and front wall of a lean-to house, if possible, or, if not possible, in the front wall and along the ridge of the roof; and in a span-roof house, by openings under the roof and at the highest point of the upright walls, and in the ridge, which may, if preferred, be crested with a lantern, as shown in the illustrations of conservatories in Figs. 361 and 362. Modes and methods of glazing, ventilating, and warming, will be dealt with further on.

742 *Tenant Right in Greenhouses* The right of a tenant to take down and remove any glass structure that he may have put up on another man's ground has been, is, and probably will be, a fruitful source of misunderstanding between occupiers and landlords, unless, when building greenhouses, tenants take means to prevent it. The landlord, with that desire for acquisitiveness which seems to be an inherent and pre-dominant quality in all who happen to have, desires to retain *in situ* anything that may have been put up, and which tends to the ornamentation or improvement of his property, and the law lends him all possible aid in sticking to it. The tenant, naturally enough, wishes to carry away with him what he reasonably-regards as being *bona fide* his own, as much as his coat, waistcoat, and trousers, household furniture, or any other part of his personal estate. And the law will lend even the tenant a little help also in the retention of his own, provided always that he knows the difference between that which is a fixture and that which is not a fixture, and between a nail and a screw, and has acted on his knowledge when building his greenhouse. Anything that enters the ground and is immovable, and anything that enters a wall and is immovable, or nailed to a wall and *quasi* immovable, is a fixture, and must not be taken away, but anything that is attached to a wall by screws is not a fixture, and may be removed at pleasure. There is a great deal of common sense in this, because the withdrawal of nails causes considerable injury both to wall and that which is nailed to it, be it what it may, while the withdrawal of a screw can be effected without doing any harm whatever. Of course, what is said here about the construction and removal of greenhouses does not apply to professional gardeners, who are permitted by law to remove any glazed buildings that they may have erected, and any trees, shrubs, etc., which form part of their stock, and which they have planted themselves, whereas the amateur may take away nothing that is a fixture in the soil, whether it be tree, or shrub, or greenhouse.

743 First, then, with regard to lean-to houses. Greenhouses of this form must only be attached to walls or houses against which they are reared by means of screws. Walls may be plugged with wooden plugs, and into the plugs screws may be driven and taken out at pleasure. Nothing, then, is easier than to provide holding for posts and wall plate of roof of a lean-to greenhouse by plugging and driving screws through posts and wall plate into the plugs, but there should be as few of them as possible. Of course, it is supposed that the wall is of brick or stone visible to the eye, and not covered with a coating of plaster, rough casting, or cement, in which case plugging would be impossible, and the tenant builder will have to put a back to his house, which may be done by filling in the spaces between the uprights of the back with wooden panels or boarding. With regard to the foundations of the structure, screws must again be brought into requisition in this wise. Having marked out the area that the greenhouse is to occupy, take out a trench and fill it up to the ground level with a concrete foundation, or a brick foundation of three or four courses. In the upper course of the brickwork, or in the top of the concrete, as the case may be, insert blocks of wood, technically known as wood bricks. All this the tenant will have to, leave behind him, and in leaving it there will be no great loss to him and no great gain to the landlord. All above it he may take, provided that he erects his structure on a substantial wall plate that is held down to the wood bricks and the brickwork or concrete in which they are set by stout long screws that pass through the one and enter the other. On this wall plate the containing walls of the structure may be reared, either in the form of framework screwed to the wall plate and to each other, or by mortising uprights into the wall plate to which the boarding and sashes may be screwed. I use the word *screwed* advisedly, because, the wall plate being screwed down, it is within the power of the tenant to use nails to any extent in making the structure *above* the wall plate; but it would be very undesirable for him to do so, because in case of removal boarding and sashes and everything else would be irretrievably damaged in taking down if attached by nails, whereas if screws are used no harm whatever would accrue to the greenhouse in taking it to pieces.

744 It is not so very long ago that a glasshouse was an object of reverential awe to the mass of the population, when the tax on glass made the smallest conservatory attached to a nobleman's house a thing to look at and talk about but which was far beyond the reach of the average country squire's means. Subsequently, when this tax was removed, greenhouses began to increase in our gardens, but it is only within late years that these embellishments, alike to house and garden, have become as general, nay, universal, as they now are. No allusion is intended to the acres of glass which appear in the extensive gardens of those who can afford them, but rather to the little glass plant house, which, built on to, or apart from, houses of moderate dimensions, keep the plants alive, and the house supplied with flowers during the dreary darkness of our English winter. One of our best poets has said, and most justly, 'Who loves a garden, loves a greenhouse too', and he did not mean a lofty glazed pavilion where the gardener-in-chief reigns supreme, and the owner enters with lowly mein and bated breath, but a snug little conservatory where one may pick this, repot that, tie up the other, grow winter salads, and cultivate one's own vine. To show the amateur gardener how to build such a snuggery for himself, at the cost only of the labour of his hands, his wood, and glass, is the object of the following instructions, and anyone who follows them closely and strictly may be sure of a result which cannot fail to gratify.

745 *A Small but Useful Greenhouse* Before entering further on details, it will be well to say the position best suited for the erection of the greenhouse is one that is dry, and exposed on the east, south, and west sides, but, if possible, sheltered on the north; and as the house is mainly constructed of wood, it should be placed on a bank of earth or masonry 10 inches or 1 foot higher than the level of the surrounding ground, and some 6 or 8 inches wider than the base of the greenhouse.

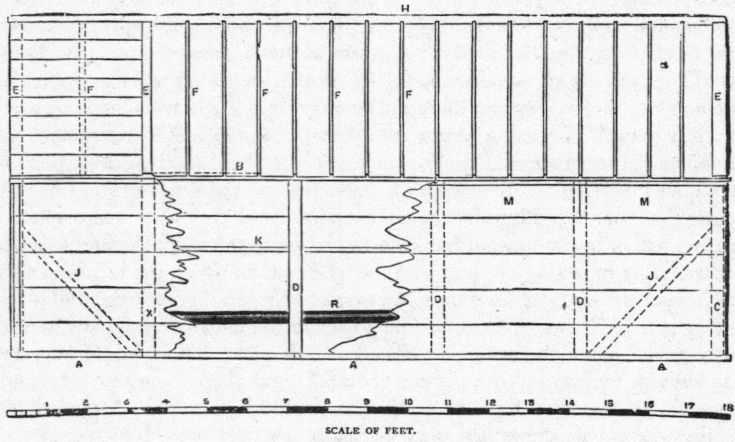

FIG. 366 *Front elevation. Scale of fleet*

746 *Class of Greenhouse* The greenhouse that it is proposed to describe is a small span-roofed one, which is preferable, as being easier to construct than the lean-to or half-span, ones, and more useful when constructed than one of the latter would be. And, more than this, a span-roofed house, when made in the way proposed, may be easily moved at the pleasure of the owner, not being a fixture; so that, should he desire to change his place of residence, his greenhouse need not be left behind, but may be taken, and again erected in another suitable position. It is for this reason that the posts marked C and D – similar parts are similarly lettered in all the diagrams – are mortised in the ground plate shown at A, instead of being driven in the ground, as they would have been had the house been intended for a fixture. But as the framing of it only rests on the surface, it will be necessary to fasten it down by some means, to prevent it being moved by high winds, as it otherwise would be. This will be best done by driving into the

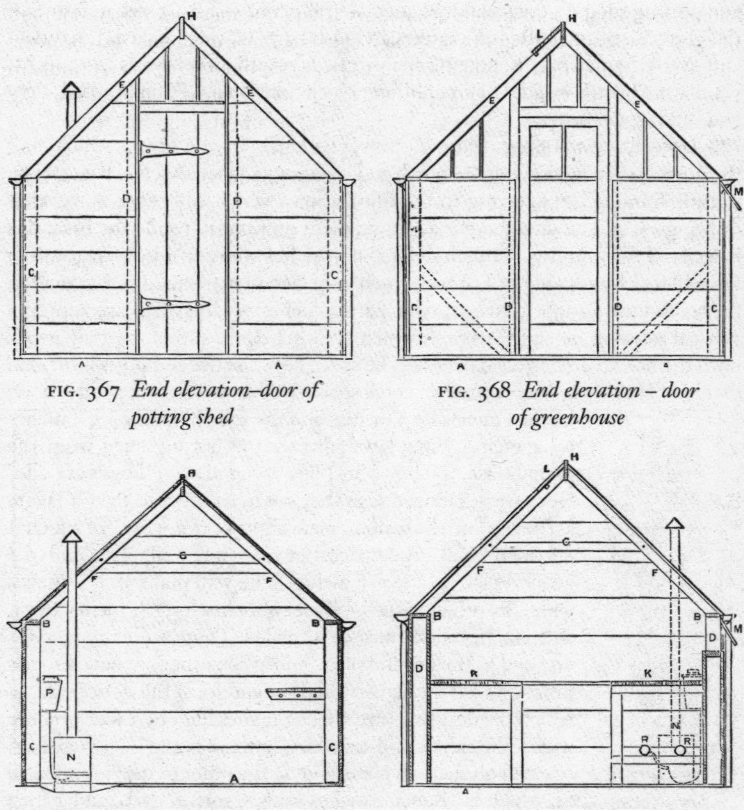

FIG. 367 *End elevation–door of potting shed*

FIG. 368 *End elevation – door of greenhouse*

FIG. 369 *Section of potting shed, etc*

FIG. 370 *Section of house, showing stage, etc*

ground prepared for the greenhouse four posts, so that their heads are level with the surface, each post being about 5 inches square, and about 2 feet 6 inches long. These must be put in such positions that they are under the ground plate, which must be secured to them by four ⅜ coach-screws, screwed through it into the posts. The best position for the posts is near the corners of the house.

747 It has been said that all similar parts shown in the diagrams given in Figs. 366, 367, 368, 369, 370, 371, are similarly lettered. It may be useful to give at this stage of the description the designation of each part to which the several letters refer, as in considering the figures in detail it will render the comprehension of them all the more easy. Thus, A in all cases denotes the ground plate to receive uprights; B, the wall plate on top of the upright; C, the corner posts of the greenhouse; D, the intermediate posts between the corner posts; X, the intermediate posts dividing the potting shed from the greenhouse; E, the large and heavier rafters at the ends and the division of the structure into greenhouse and potting shed; F, the small intermediate rafters or sash bars, rebated to take the glass; G, ties to stiffen the rafters and sash bars; H, ridge board; J, struts to stiffen the framework; K, staging for plants; L, ventilating boards in roof; M, ventilating boards in sides of greenhouse; N, circular boiler; P, tank; and R, flow and return pipes.

748 *Dimensions and Construction* A convenient size for the house – including the potting shed, which is at the north end – is about 18 feet long and 8 feet wide, outside framing. In referring to the illustrations, which will serve as working drawings, it will be seen there is a ground plate running all round the base; this is lettered A, A, and is 1½ inch deep and 5 inches wide, and is formed into a frame 8 feet 1 inch wide and 18 feet 1 inch long. Securely fastened at the corners, there are four upright posts, C, which are 4 inches square; these are kept in a vertical position by eight struts, J, which greatly help to stiffen the framework until the boards are fastened over it. The space between the end posts is divided on either side of the house into five equal spaces by four posts, three of them, D, being 4 inches by 3 inches, and the fourth, marked x, 4 inches by 4 inches. This latter divides the potting shed from the greenhouse, as shown in Figs. 366 and 371. These are all 4 feet 9 inches long, and as they are mortised into the wall plate at the top and the ground plate at the bottom, each of which is 1½ inch thick, the space between the wall plate and the ground plate is 4 feet 6 inches. The wall plate, B, is 4 inches wide. Six other posts, D, 7 feet 4 inches long, 3 inches thick, and 4 inches wide, must be provided. These are all mortised at one end to the ground plate, and at the other are nailed to the rafters, E. Of these, two at either end form the door posts, of which the doorways are 6 feet 3 inches high by 2 feet 3 inches wide. The rafters and sash bars, lettered E and F, are nailed at one end oh the wall plate, and on the other to the ridge board, H, which is 18 feet 3 inches long, 6 inches deep, and 1 inch thick. The larger rafters, lettered E, are 2 inches by 3 inches, and the smaller rafters or sash bars, lettered F, are of the form

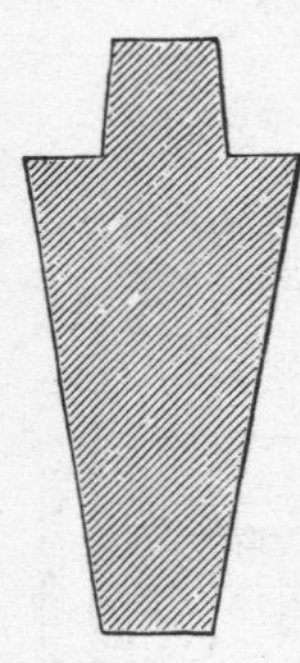

FIG. 372
Transverse section of rafter or sash-bar

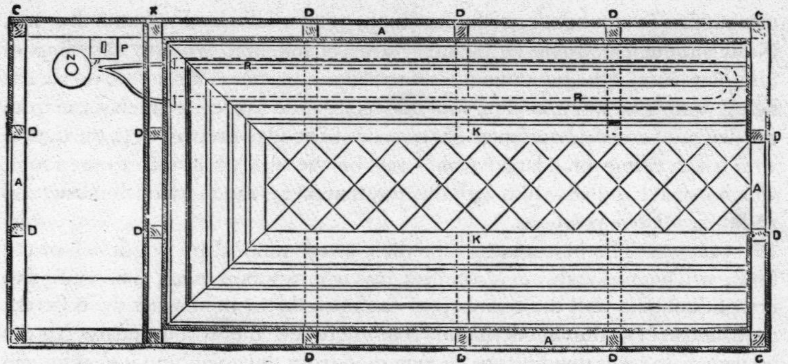

FIG. 371 *Plan of house, showing stage, apparatus for heating, etc*

shown in Fig. 372, which represents the actual size or the section; they are all 4 feet 9 inches long. These rafters can be purchased of the section shown, and should be all carefully placed at equal distances (see Fig. 366), when the width must be measured, and the glass ordered accordingly.

749 *Ventilation* To ventilate the house, about 9 inches next to the ridge board on one side should be unglazed, and the space covered with ½-inch board, hinged in four lengths to the ridge board, and arranged so as to be easily opened from the inside, as shown at L (Figs. 368 and 370), and the same must be adopted at the bottom of the opposite rafters, where four lengths of board, M, are hinged to the wall plate, B. The outward thrust of the rafters over C, X, D, D, D, and C, can be counteracted by pieces of wood used as ties, as shown at G. The house should be glazed with glass 16 ounces in weight to the square foot. With regard to doors, if the amateur gardener is building the house himself, he had better get them made by a carpenter, as to look well they require good work, and they are not expensive. The framing of the sides must be covered with ½-inch or ⅝-inch boarding, tarred or painted on the outside, and the spaces between the inner and outer boards filled with sawdust, which is a slow conductor of heat.

750 Plans and Working Drawings Perhaps some who may be induced to study and act upon this description will require a little explanation with regard to following the drawings in cutting the timbers to the necessary length. To describe the dimensions of every piece of timber used in the framing would be tedious, and occupy too much space, and there would be but very few who would require such minute instructions. If anyone who is in difficulty on this point will look at the illustrations of the plan, front, and end elevations and sections of the house that accompany this paper, he will find that they are working drawings, drawn to scale, and that a scale from which he may ascertain the dimensions of any part of the house, by the aid of a pair of compasses, is given below the elevation of the house in Fig. 366. The proportion in which the scale is drawn is one-third of an inch to a foot – that is to say, every linear dimension, as shown in the illustrations, is one thirty-sixth part of its counterpart in the house itself when built, or of a full-sized working drawing. Now, although it would be possible to make full-sized working drawings of different parts of the building, it is neither desirable nor necessary to do so; but before setting to work, anyone who may determine to erect a greenhouse from the diagrams and description given, is recommended to prepare from the figures working drawings on a larger scale – say, on the scale of an inch to the foot – which would familiarise him with the different pieces required for the structure, and their relative positions.

751 *Materials* The best material for the construction of the woodwork of the house will be thoroughly dry, soft deal, free from knots as much as possible; and it will doubtless save the constructor much trouble if he obtains the different required pieces of the sections shown in the drawing, only a little larger, as he easily can do from saw-mills or elsewhere; so that all he will find necessary will be to plane them, and follow the drawings in cutting them to the required length, and then nail, mortise, or screw them together as shown in the different diagrams.

752 *Glazing and Painting* When all the woodwork has been put together, and is thoroughly dry, the knots must be carefully stopped, and the whole framing given one coat of white lead; this will make the putty in the glazing hold well, if putty be used, but there are methods of glazing without putty, which will be touched on presently. Then the glass must be put on of the required width, the length of each piece being from 12 to 18 inches, and each overlapping the next to it by widths varying from ¼ inch to 1¼ inch, according to choice; the only thing in favour of the broad lap is the additional strength it confers at the junction of the panes. When this is completed, the whole of the inside and outside wood should receive three good coats of paint, of pale stone colour or white; and in doing this, it is strongly advised that the paint used should be rather thick, and well rubbed on, a little only being taken up in the brush at one time.

753 *Heating* The subject of heating the greenhouse is a very wide one, but as it will be treated more at length further on, all that need be done here is to give a brief summary of the chief modes of heating in as few words as possible. There are four well-known methods – namely, heating by brickwork flues, by hot air, by steam, and by hot water. Each of these systems has its admirers, who have, of course, claimed for it the advantages of effectiveness, economy, and equality of temperature, amongst other less important ones, which want of space will not allow being here enumerated. The heating by flues was for many years after the introduction of the others the most popular, but it now is, and has been for some time past, rapidly giving place to the hot water system, which appears to be by far the best arrangement for houses of all sizes.

754 *Heating by Flues* Referring to the different systems in the above order, the chief quality which appears to recommend the use of the old flue method in the small house now under consideration is its cheapness of construction; but this advantage is more than counterbalanced by the fact that greenhouses heated by it are liable to rapid changes of temperature, should the fire (which, therefore, requires constant attention) become either too great or too little, and that should the cement in the joints of the flue crack at all, the house becomes filled with a strong odour of sulphur, which is both unpleasant to those entering and very injurious to the plants inside; besides which, there is the inconvenience of the flues constantly requiring sweeping – an operation which, should the amateur gardener be obliged to do for himself, though not taking long, it is difficult to believe, however enthusiastic a floriculturist he may be, he would not greatly dislike. However should anyone decide, in spite of these objections, to adopt this form of heating his house, it will be well to say that the fireplace, which must be built about ten inches below the level of the flue (and which, of course, is horizontal where it runs through the house), should be 20 inches long, 10 inches high, and 9½ inches wide, into which space must be built the fire-bars. The flue should be about 8 inches square inside, and be fitted with a damper to regulate the draught, and a small wrought-iron or brick chimney at the other end to carry away the smoke.

755 *Heating by Hot Air and by Steam* With regard to the next two systems, those of heating by hot air and by steam, it can only be said both of them are expensive, and generally unfit for a small house.

756 *Heating by Hot Water* The fourth method now remains, which, as it has been said, appears best adapted for all sizes of greenhouses, and this opinion is much strengthened by the numerous boilers of so many shapes, sizes, and principles, which are to be seen advertised in every gardening paper of the present day. In fact, there are so many good arrangements of boilers, that it can only be said the most popular seem to be the horse shoe and saddle types; but of the boilers which have come under my notice of late, the Patent Automatic Coke Boilers, made by Messrs Franklin, Hocking, and Co., Limited, 37 Hanover Street, Liverpool, which are represented as being 'automatic, economic, and efficient', three excellent and desirable qualities, seem to be well deserving of attention and careful trial. The notice of the reader may also be directed to the Loughborough Greenhouse Hot Water Apparatus, manufactured by Messrs Messenger and Co., Horticultural Builders, Loughborough; the Silver Medal Horse Shoe Boiler, made by Messrs Charles P. Kinnell and Co., Iron Founders, Engineers, and Contractors, 31 Bankside, Southwark, London; the Ivanhoe Boiler, made by Messrs Robert Jenkins and Co., Rotherham; and the Champion Boiler, supplied by Messrs G. Wilcox and Co., Hot Water Engineers and Boiler Makers, 85 Old Street, London. In all cases, in ordering boilers of any maker, the length, breadth, and cubic content of the greenhouse should be stated, so that a suitable size and requisite length of pipes, etc., may be obtained.

757 *Fuel* However, in so small a boiler, the best way will be for the amateur to send to the various makers for prospectuses, price lists, testimonials, etc., and fix on one which he thinks is likely to do the work he requires, and is offered at a price he is prepared to give. As is shown in the illustrations, it will be best for him to select some arrangement in which no brickwork setting is required, as it would be more easily moved, and would occupy less room than it would otherwise do. The fuel should be small coke or gas; the latter has been found very convenient in small houses, on account of the little attention which is required in keeping the house at a uniform heat. However, where this means of heating cannot be used, as is generally the case in the country, small coke is the most convenient. This description of fuel will burn for a considerable time, without attention, in any description of boiler in which the upper part is filled with a considerable quantity of coke at a time, which works down, and slowly takes the place of that which has been already burnt.

758 *Boiler, Tank, etc.* In the diagrams are shown a small circular boiler and tank and piping (P, N, R), which are heated by gas, the fumes of which should be carried away as indicated in the illustrations, by a piece of iron stove pipe, capped by a conical covering, raised a little distance above the top of the pipe to prevent the sudden down-rush of any gust of wind.

759 *Size of Pipes, Paving, etc.* For a greenhouse of the size described, the pipes should be 2 or 2½ inches in diameter. The stage marked K is 2 feet 5 inches wide and 2 feet 9 inches or 3 feet high, as will be seen in the drawings. The most important thing in its construction is that it should be made so that the plants may be as near the glass as possible, which will prevent their being drawn into those long, sickly-looking objects one so often sees in conservatories and greenhouses in which the old-fashioned step-stage is used. The centre of the house may be laid with tiles or thick slates, which will help to make it more tidy and cleanly. Slabs of the material known as Croft Adamant, supplied by the Croft Granite, Brick, and Concrete Company, Croft, near Leicester, will be found most useful for this purpose. The slabs may be had to any size required, and are more durable than York Paving Stone, though they cost only half as much.

760 *Guttering, etc.* All minor details which have not been specially described will be sufficiently understood on referring to the drawings, but there is yet one thing to which the attention of the amateur must be drawn, and that is the necessity of providing means for carrying off the water that will fall from time to time on the glass roof when 'the clouds drop fatness', in order to prevent the drip on the earth below, and the disfigurement that it causes if it be allowed either to trickle down the front and back of the house, or to fall and splash against its base. As the house that has been described has a span roof, and a door at each end, zinc or iron guttering, supported on brackets, must be placed immediately under the eaves along the front and back, and two pipes must be provided to admit of the exit of the water caught in the gutters. Had one end of the house been permanently closed, one exit pipe would have been sufficient, as the gutters in front and back could have been connected by a third piece running across the closed end.

761 *Disposal of Rainfall* The next thing to be considered is the provision of means for the dispersion or absorption of the rainfall, or, what is better, for its storage for use in the greenhouse. If it is not to be saved, the pipes must have their lower ends set in drain pipes leading to a pit dug in the earth, and filled to about half or two-thirds its depth with brickbats covered with brushwood to prevent the entrance of the mould with which it is filled in. If the water is to be stored, a brick tank, well cemented, should be made under the potting shed, from which receptacle the water can be raised when wanted by a small pump in the shed itself. A sliding panel in the partition between the potting shed and the house will be found useful for passing in newly-potted plants, etc., without carrying them round in the front of the house.

762 The leading principles which enter into the construction of an ordinary greenhouse have been dwelt on at some length here, because, after all, they appertain to the erection of houses of this description of all kinds, whether large or small. In a work like this, although as much practical instruction is given as it is possible to introduce, yet the whole ground cannot be traversed in this way; nor, indeed, is there occasion to do so, because those who can afford to have extensive glazed houses on a large scale, involving considerable outlay, will, without doubt, call in the aid of the architect, the builder, and the hot water engineer, and they are right to do so. We must now pass on to the consideration of the hothouse and the points in which it differs from the greenhouse and the conservatory, and after touching on structures of various kinds, more particularly suitable for various horticultural purposes, bring this chapter to an end with a few remarks on glass and glazing, ventilation, heating, and warming, and the fittings of glazed houses which could not be conveniently brought under notice of sufficient length in any of the stages through which we have already passed.

763 The greenhouse is essentially the amateur gardener's house, and although in the construction of glazed horticultural structures of this class it is desirable that those who can afford to do so should spare no expense when erecting them, it is necessary for all lovers of gardening and gardens whose means are limited to count the cost before going to work. For such as these, greenhouses that are at all events helpful to the end in view, if not the best possible for the purpose, are offered by good makers at all prices, from £4 10s. upwards. Mr George Dawson, of the Whittington Horticultural Works, Highgate Hill, London, who always has a large stock of houses of all kinds on the premises, supplies a lean-to greenhouse for the price just quoted, and a span-roofed house for £5 5s.; and Messrs T. H. P. Dennis and Co., of the Anchor Works, Chelmsford, have on their list various buildings at equally low rates. Another firm of whom glazed houses can be obtained at low rates is Messrs Alfred Peel and Co., Wood Green, London, or Windhill, Bradford, Yorkshire. The greenhouses made by the makers whose addresses in town and country have just been given are known as the Desideratum. Prices range from 50s. upwards. Mr C. Frazer, Horticultural Builder, Norwich supplies a useful house – a tenant's fixture, 10 feet by 8 feet – for £16 10s., if made entirely of wood, but for £14 15s. if the lower part of the house be constructed of bricks; and a larger size, 12 feet by 8 feet, for £25 3s. in wood entirely, and for £17 15s. in brick – this is also a tenant's fixture. Again, Messrs Deane and Co., 46 King William Street, London, supply a house of a very pretty design, which they call the Gem Conservatory, 10 feet long, 8 feet wide, and 10 feet 6 inches high, with lantern roof, staging, and all the necessary fittings, including a Loughborough Hot Water Apparatus, with 15 feet of 4-inch pipe, for £25, and a larger one of the same kind, 12 feet in length, but otherwise of the same dimensions, for £28. Messrs Messenger and Co., Loughborough, Leicester, who make all kinds of houses, from the cheapest to the most costly, furnish a nice little lean-to house, 10 feet by 5 feet, for £6 16s. 6d., carriage paid, and a larger and better kind of structure, 12 feet by 8 feet, for £12 15s., if with lean-to roof, and for £13 5s. with span roof. Thus no one need be without a greenhouse who desires to have one, for the prices are calculated to suit all pockets.

764 It may be useful to give here an extended scale of Messrs Messenger and Co.'s charges for their Amateur's Lean-to and Span Roof Greenhouses, which will enable everyone to calculate for himself the cost of the house that he requires when he has determined the size. As regards the description of these houses, they are made of well-seasoned red deal, with lights 2 inches in thickness, and ventilators at top and in front. The lights on the roof are glazed with English 21-ounce glass, and the sashes at the ends and sides with 15-ounce glass. Surplus glass is sent with each house to make up for breakages, for which the firm do not hold themselves responsible. The length is 12 feet, the height to eaves 5 feet. There is one door complete with lock and key, one end, gutters, and down pipe. The houses are painted with two coats of the best white lead, and are made either for placing on brickwork, or with boarding below the sill on which the upright lights are placed.

Width	8 feet	10 feet	12 feet	14 feet.	16 feet
Lean-to Greenhouse, 12 feet long					
	£12 15s. 0d.	£15 14s. 0d.	£19 4s. 0d.	£22 17s. 0d.	£26 7s. 0d.
Extra for Boarding under Sill	£2 10s. 0d.	£2 18s. 0d.	£3 6s. 0d.	£3 14s. 0d.	£4 2s. 0d.
Every 4 feet extra length	£2 7s. 0d.	£2 18s. 0d.	£3 7s. 0d.	£3 16s. 0d.	£4 8s. 0d.
Extra for Boarding under Sill	8s. 0d.	8s. 0d.	8s. 0d.	8s. 0d.	8s. 0d.
Stages	£2 8s. 6d.	£3 0s. 0d.	£5 10s. 0d.	£6 12s. 0d.	£7 18s. 0d.
Every 4 feet extra length	15s. 0d.	£1 6s. 0d.	£1 16s. 0d.	£2 4s. 0d.	£2 12s. 0d.
Span Roof Greenhouse, 12 feet long					
	£13 5s. 0d.	£15 14s. 0d.	£17 12s. 0d.	£20 0s. 0d.	£22 6s. 0d.
Extra for Boarding under Sill	£2 18s. 0d.	£3 2s. 0d.	£3 6s. 0d.	£3 10s. 0d.	£3 14s. 0d.
Every 4 feet extra length	£3 4s. 0d.	£3 14s. 0d.	£4 2s. 6d.	£4 14s. 0d.	—
Extra for Boarding tinder Sill	6s. 0d.	16s. 0d.	16s. 0d.	16s. 0d.	16s. 0d.
Extra End	£1 11s. 0d.	£2 5s. 0d.	£2 18s. 0d.	£3 7s. 0d.	£4 14s. 0d.
Extra for Boarding under Sill	16s. 0d.	£1 0s. 0d.	£1 4s. 0d.	£1 8s. 0d.	£1 12s. 0d.
Stages	£2 8. 6d	£2 18s. 0d.	£3 18s. 6d	£4 7s. 6d	£5 5s. 0d.
Every 4 feet extra length	15s. 0d.	18s. 0d.	£1 3s. 0d.	£1 10s. 0d.	£1 15s. 0d.

A wood-slatted walk, 2 feet 6 inches wide, is supplied at 1s. 10d. per foot run for either kind of house. Heating apparatus is not included, but the prices of these will be given farther on, when the subject of heating is under consideration. It may be said, however, that the charge for the lean-to house supplied at £16 6s. 6d. for brickwork, or at £8 8s. with boarding under sill, costs £4 12s. The extras bring up the price of each house according to what is required. Thus, a lean-to house, 12 feet by 8 feet, with a stage, which is absolutely necessary, comes to £13 10s., and then there is the heating apparatus, which is also needful, unless the house be treated as a mere cold house or unwarmed conservatory, and if boarding under the sill is required instead of brickwork, the price would amount for the house only to £16. It is necessary to point out this, that persons may not think they are going to obtain a house complete with every fitting necessary for the sum named in the top line of each class of house.

We have indisputable authority for the worth and utility of a word in season, and it may not be inopportune to give a little advice here. Even in the cheapest house the purchaser will undoubtedly get his money's worth for his money, but it must be borne in mind that the limited sizes of the cheap houses take away in a great measure from their usefulness. No one can expect to do much with a very small house, and if a good and really serviceable one is purchased, it runs into money. The cheapest and most effectual plan of getting a good working greenhouse, is to build it. The materials required – wood, bricks, glass, and a little ironwork – are cheap enough, and heating apparatus of the Loughborough type is by no means expensive. Ornamentation should be sacrificed to utility. Pretty-looking houses and fanciful shapes, with lanterns and scrollwork in iron, and elaborate cresting, are very nice to look at, but the economist must always remember that they add to the cost without contributing in the slightest degree to the leading requirements of plant culture.

765 *The Hothouse or Stove* The absolute line of demarcation between the greenhouse and the hothouse or stove, for structures included in the third class of glazed horticultural structures are known indifferently by these names, between which there is no distinction whatever, inasmuch as they both mean one and the same thing, is as difficult to define as that between the conservatory and the green house. The chief points in which the hothouse differs from the greenhouse is that a higher temperature must be sustained within it and a moister atmosphere must prevail, for it is devoted to forcing fruit or growing plants from tropical climates, and fruit-forcing is best accomplished under these conditions, and the air within the tropics is, generally speaking, warm and laden with moisture, which tends to promote the luxuriance of vegetation, brilliancy of flowers, and flavour of fruit that are found in tropical countries. In structural points, the hothouse differs but little, if at all, from glazed buildings of the other two classes, so that the chief points which will have to be regarded in connection with it are, the means of maintaining a high temperature, and of obtaining that moisture of atmosphere which is so necessary for the well being of its tenants.

766 *Temperature of Hothouse* As a general rule, the temperature of the hothouse may be taken at 80° for bottom heat, with an average of 75° in the part of the house or pit, as the case may be, in which the plants are growing. In the full sunlight, these rates of heat will be increased from 5° to 10°, but no injury will accrue to the plants from this augmentation of heat arising from natural causes. Under the old system heat was induced and a moist atmosphere maintained by means of flues, and bark, and by tanks but at the present time heating is chiefly effected by hot water pipes. These various modes of heating will be described in detail farther on, in that portion of the subject to which they properly belong. At present the attention of the reader may be directed to the structures of this class that have been introduced of late years for fruit culture more especially.

767 *Sir Joseph Paxtons Hothouses* The first steps in the improvement of glazed horticultural structures, in which a temperature could be maintained sufficiently high for forcing fruits and growing tropical plants, were taken by the late Sir

Joseph Paxton, who invented and patented a system of hothouses for fruit culture, at once economical, efficient, and, above all, portable. These houses are both lean-to and span-roofed, and require no masonry or brickwork beyond the piers necessary to support the wall-plate, which is so contrived as to form at once the gutter and groove in which the sashes rest, the plate being grooved so as to agree with the angle at which the sashes are to be placed. The sashes average in width about 4 feet 6 inches, varying in length from 8 to 16 feet; the styles and sash-bars being proportioned to the length, inasmuch as, there being no rafters, the bars and styles supply the place of both, and must, consequently, be sufficiently strong: they are bolted together at the top and bottom.

768 The ventilation, which is the subject of a patent, consists of a smaller sash, 9 inches wide, between each pair, and extending the whole length of the sash, but divided in the centre, the upper half folding upon the lower with a slope, so as to throw off the water. This narrow sash is hinged to the adjoining one, and bolted to the other by a spring when closed. These ventilating sashes may either be worked by an iron rod and pinion, or by the hand. The principle on which they are formed, and the relation which they bear to the larger sashes to which they are hinged, is clearly shown in the two illustrations of the elevation of a lean-to fruit house, and that of a span-roofed vinery and plant house, shown in Fig. 374.

769 The portability of these houses is a great recommendation, where a tenant is building a house on ground of which he has only a short tenure, inasmuch as they can be entirely removed in a few hours, without causing any dilapidation or interfering with the rights of landlords. Strict adherence, however, must be maintained to the method of fixing the removable parts of these structures to those which cannot be removed, as already explained in Section 742.

770 The purposes for which these structures are adapted will be better understood from the following illustrations of houses built on Sir Joseph Paxton's plan, and the description that accompanies and explains the illustrations. In Fig. 373, the section of a lean-to vinery and fruit house is exhibited, which is formed by sashes placed against a wall at an angle of 45°, the sashes being 14 feet in length from top to bottom. By raising the border in the manner shown in the illustration, not only is more space given within, but the practice of planting the roots, as well as the stem, in the border within the glass, is favourable to the vine, and to the production of good-flavoured fruit, while the border itself may be appropriated to vines in pots.

771 Lean-to peach houses may also be formed by 14-foot sashes placed against a

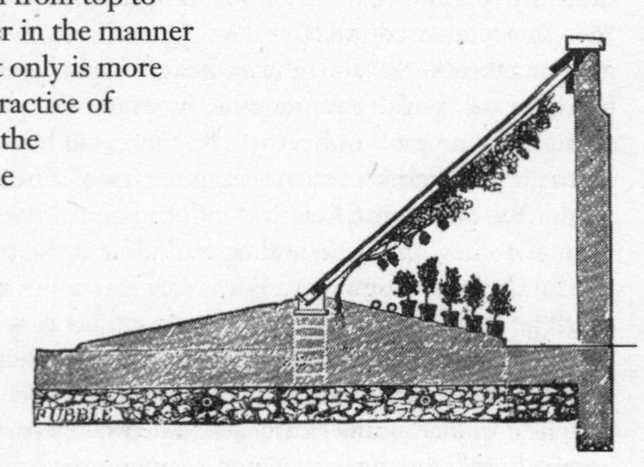

FIG. 373 *Lean-to vinery, in section*

wall at an angle of 40°, as shown in Fig. 374; the peaches being trained against, the back wall, and others planted either in the front border, stand-in pots, or partially trained upon a front trellis, according to the taste of the cultivator. This style of building requires no rafters, framework, or other erection, excepting the fixing of the wall plate in a bed of concrete, at the required angle. A lean-to pinery is formed by laying 14-foot sashes at a proper angle, and arranging the border to suit them, as will be shown farther on.

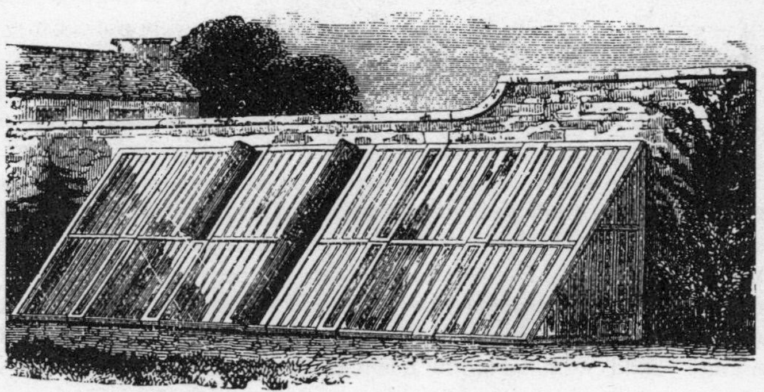

FIG. 374 *Lean-to peach house or fruit house, in elevation*

772 A span-roofed house composed of 10-foot lights, at an angle of 45°, gives an internal width of 14 feet, and forms an excellent vinery and fruit house; the border, both inside and out, being raised . Here the border outside the house has been raised so as to be flush with the wall plate, which rests on piers, or, if the ground is sufficiently solid, the saddles rest on a concrete bottom: the border is prepared for the reception of the several trees or vines intended to be grown in it.

773 The house, however, which Sir Joseph Paxton specially commended to public notice was a span-roof structure, consisting of a range of 14-foot lights, set at an angle of 45° which gives an internal width of 19 feet 9 inches. This house, which is admirably adapted to serve the purpose of a vinery and fruit house combined, is shown in Fig. 376. By raising the borders about 4 feet above the ground level, as represented in Fig. 373, a handsome, lofty structure is formed, capable of producing excellent crops either of peaches, plums, figs, or cherries. In a house of this description, Sir Joseph Paxton raised splendid crops of grapes, ripening through the autumn and winter from October to March, with no more artificial heat than was necessary to keep out frost; the house being placed, however, under a most favourable aspect, ranging from north-west to south-east, and on a mild southern slope, so that each side of the house caught its share of the sun's rays for an hour or two daily, even in midwinter. The vines may be trained on wires, near the glass, in a house of this kind; while standard peaches, plums, and figs may be planted on each side of the central walk at intervals, and dwarf trees nearer the glass, according to their size. The standard trees will spread their heads over the centre of the house: and, if left to their

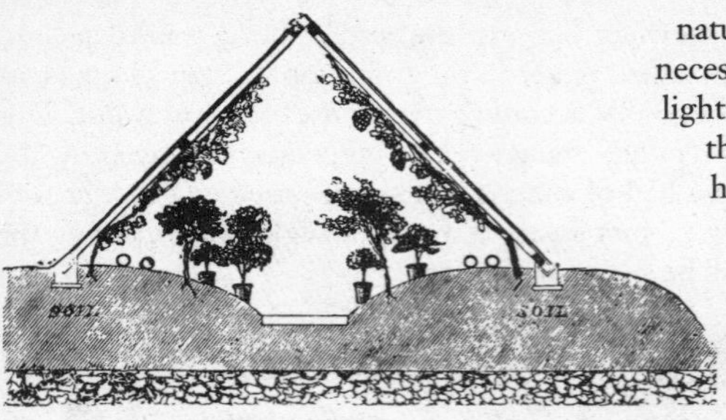

FIG. 376 *Vinery and fruit-house, in section*

natural growth, with only the necessary pruning to admit the light to the centre of the trees, the result will be heavy and highly remunerative crops, success being certain under judicious management. A house constructed, as shown in Fig. 376, of 12-foot lights placed at an angle of 40°, which gives a width of 17 feet from side to side, would form an admirable orchard house, the trees being planted in the soil of the border, and arranged so that those in the back line would be placed in the centre of the openings between those in the front line.

774 Eight-foot lights, when placed at an angle of 30° or 35°, as in Fig. 378, make an excellent house for sheltering bedding-out plants, and, with suitable heating apparatus, would form an admirable cucumber or melon pit. The only arrangement necessary would be to dig out the soil 3 feet below the ground level, to give head room; then lay down half a foot of rubble, for drainage, and fill up to the surface with good sandy loam, leaving a central path 3 feet wide. If this border is made outside as well as in, very good grapes may be grown while giving shelter to the bedding plants, by using the ventilators adapted for wintering the vines, and admitting them after they have ripened their wood outside. Or these houses may be employed for small greenhouses by placing them on side walls from two to three feet high, instead of sinking for a path, and placing flat stages on each side over the pipes on which to stand the pots; and for the pot-culture of strawberries this arrangement answers extremely well. Peach and other trees in pots may be grown when the stages are dispensed with, and thus a very cheap and efficient orchard house on a small scale may be formed. Lights 10 or 12 feet in length, placed at an angle of 35°, give a favourable form of pine pit, as shown in Fig. 378; the 10-foot lights give a width of 16 feet, and the 12-foot lights a width of 19 feet; and if a slightly sunk walk of three feet wide occupy the centre, and a foot and a half at each side, near the glass, is allowed for the hot water pipes, there will be room left for two good pits.

FIG. 377 *Section of pit for bedding-out plants*

FIG. 378 *House suitable for pinery, in section*

775 The erection of these houses is extremely simple, and constitutes one of the many advantages that they possess; the sashes are all made to an exact measurement, each one alike available and interchangeable. The site and the plan of the house being settled, if it is to have a made border outside, a sufficient space of ground is excavated to the necessary depth, and a setting-out rod prepared, which must be of the length of the intended house. This rod is laid on the ground, and on it the exact width of each sash, which should be about 4 feet 8 inches, and a ventilator, is laid out, allowing space for an iron bar gauge, which connects each sash with the other, and receives the ventilating sash between, for which nine inches are required. Having marked the space required for each sash, gauge-bar, and ventilator, proceed to transfer corresponding marks to the ground: the marks thus made are the centre of a series of piers of brick or stone, each 14 inches square, and equidistant, if a lean-to house, from the back wall: if a span-roofed structure, the same is to be done for the opposite side.

776 These piers, if for 16-foot sashes, will be better if made 18 inches thick, and built buttress-fashion – that is, sloping outward to their base, so as to bear better the thrust of the sashes. When the piers have settled sufficiently, the saddles are fixed on them, in a bed of cement.

777 The saddle consists of a block of wood fitting on the piers, the upper surface of which is cut to an angle according with the angle of the house. Upon this saddle another angular frame of wood is placed, which fits the angle of the saddle, and runs along the whole range of piers, performing at once the office of wall plate, gutter, and support to the sashes: for the upper surface is a hollow angle, receiving the lower ends or horns of the sashes, while it is so set on the piers as to have just sufficient inclination to carry off the water to a pipe at the lower end. All the lengths necessary to connect this gutter are joined over the saddles, the joints being made watertight either by putty or cement, and pitched inside and out.

778 In lean-to houses, the top of the sash simply leans against the wall, being bevelled to fit it; they may be covered with cement or not; but in span-roofed houses the sashes are bevelled so as to support each other at the proper angle, and a pair of strong iron hinges sunk into the wood and screwed firmly to the styles of each sash keep them in their proper place; while a ridge or coping of wood, fitting them exactly, covers the whole, and is screwed on to the top rail of the sashes, fitting closely to the upper ends of the ventilators when closed; for these, like the cap, are raised above the surface of the sashes.

779 The ventilators, consisting, as we have already explained, of two smaller sashes, each one half the length of the lights, and 9 inches wide, are hooked on to the left-hand style of each sash by two hinges, the hook being screwed into the style, and the eyes into the lower part of the ventilator, lapping over the right-hand style of the adjoining sash. A stay opens both ventilators at once when required, or the upper ventilator alone may be opened. The upper ventilator falls into the lower by a sloping bevelled edge, and both are hooked together by a hook-and-eye on the lower surface. A small piece of wood sliding in a groove made in the side styles of the sashes protects the house from drip, and the water is carried off into the gutter below by grooves on the upper surface of the styles of the sashes. The ends are fixed under the styles of the outside roof sashes, and secured to each other by means of cross-plates let into each, and firmly screwed up; the doors being hung in the usual manner, and opening to the right or left, or inside, as may be desired.

780 In houses of great length, all the ventilators on one side can be opened at once from one end of the house to the other, by a very simple contrivance. This mode of ventilation has the advantage of avoiding all draughts of wind; for if it is blowing on one side, the opposite ventilators can be open. When the temperature is very hot, perfect circulation of the air is obtained by opening the ventilators on both sides.

781 The cap or ridge screwed on, and the ends properly fixed, it only remains to furnish the houses with such borders as are considered suitable for the trees or plants to be grown in them. The soil of the border, both outside and in, should be flush with the level of the gutter or wall plate, so as to exclude the external air; and it should slope outwardly so as to throw off moisture.

782 When these houses were introduced, they were regarded by practical men as being admirably adapted for fruit cultivation and vineries, or, indeed, anything that requires training parallel with the glass. For potted plants, or shrubs requiring headroom, some consider them objectionable and difficult to manage, the roof springing from the soil of the border rendering it difficult to get at the plants at the sides. This is a well-founded objection, and as the whole argument in their favour is involved in this feature, which gives simplicity and economy to their erection, it is probably calculated to limit their use to vineries and very narrow fruit houses requiring an acute inclination. The simplicity of their structure, and the ease and rapidity with which they can be put up and removed, will recommend them to many who hold their houses on short or uncertain tenure.

783 With this, the remarks that it has been thought necessary to make on the very efficient and inexpensive style of horticultural buildings initiated by Sir Joseph Paxton may be brought to a close. A full description of them has been given, because there will be many, doubtless, who may wish to adopt the ideas set forth and mould them to suit their own special requirements. To some extent they have been superseded by the glazed covers for fruit walls, and especially those with sloping fronts, which to a certain extent are constructed on the leading principles found in Sir Joseph Paxton's houses. The same may be said also with regard to the houses supplied by Messrs Messenger and Co.,

Loughborough, Leicestershire, for fruit culture, which it will be useful to describe here as briefly as possible, following this with a description of some serviceable and desirable lean-to and span plant houses or stoves for forcing, manufactured and supplied by the same firm of horticultural builders.

784 *Messenger's Plant Houses – Principles of Construction* One of the leading features in the construction of the plant houses or stoves manufactured by Messrs Messenger and Co. is the combination of metal and wood, by which, in houses of considerable size the bulk of the latter can be considerably reduced, the strength that is lost by the reduction being more than made up for by the firmness and rigidity imparted by the introduction of the metal. Of course, the use of metal in conjunction with wood increases the cost of the erection in the first instance, but when that strict economy is not necessary the extra outlay brings its full compensation in the imperishable nature of the building and its light and graceful appearance, which combine to render the form of greenhouse that is thus produced the most perfect that can be attained.

Messrs Messenger and Co. thus explain the principles and leading features of their patent method of building greenhouses and hothouses. 'By our patent system of construction,' they say, 'which consists of a special arrangement of iron to carry the woodwork, all strain is taken off the timbers, which are thus enabled to be made of slighter scantlings, offering the smallest possible obstruction to light, an advantage which, every practical gardener will assert, cannot be over-estimated. The natural consequences are: 1st, That the original cost is lessened; 2nd, that durability is gained, as small timbers being more thoroughly dry than large ones, do not so readily decay, and the structure, when placed upon stone or iron sills, and kept properly painted, is practically imperishable. The small timbers and the ornamental ironwork give an elegant and light appearance; economy in cost of maintenance is gained, as the surface of the wood to be painted is small, and the arrangement in ironwork is such, that should a rafter by any chance sink, the screwing up of a nut, which can be done by the gardener, will remedy the defect. It will be obvious-that as all the ironwork is placed inside and covered with woodwork, the disadvantages attaching to iron houses, such as excessive radiation of heat and fracture of glass consequent upon the expansion and contraction of the iron work, are avoided, as are also those of ordinary wooden houses, namely, clumsiness,

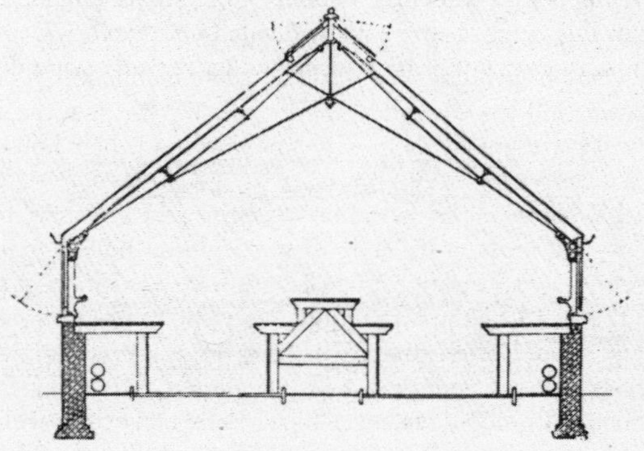

FIG. 379 *Messenger's principle of construction*

obstruction of light, and expense in maintenance. Our patent construction, which is shown in the accompanying illustration (Fig. 379), may be briefly described as follows: Upon a sill of wood, iron, or stone, cast-iron muntins with bracket heads are erected; upon these muntins rests a light plate to receive sash bars and to carry gutter. The rafters are of wood of small scantlings, so as to offer the minimum obstruction to light and sun. The rafters would be by themselves insufficient to bear either the stress of snow, workmen climbing on them for painting, etc., or even a heavy crop of fruit. They are therefore trussed with iron tension rods which are secured to the iron muntins at foot of rafter, and to an iron saddle at ridge, giving to these light rafters as much strength as was formerly obtained by the use of rafters 9 or 10 inches deep. Further, the whole roof is trussed at intervals by light wrought-iron principals.' From these remarks the construction of some of the house now to be described will be better understood and appreciated.

785 *Three-Quarter Span Vinery* The elevation or general view of this vinery, and a view of the interior, showing its construction and all the internal arrangements, are exhibited in Figs. 380 and 381. It is constructed on Messrs Messenger and Co.'s. patent principles of light rafters strengthened with ironwork, iron muntins for the front, etc. This is a good form for a vinery, and requires a lower back and therefore less brickwork than a lean-to. The iron muntins are provided with carriers for the ventilating rod and for the vine wire, which is so arranged that it can be tightened by screwing up a bold the whole being compact and not liable to get out of order. The construction of the inner and outer vine borders are shown very distinctly in Fig. 381, from which it may be seen that the sustaining wall in front is built on a series of arches below the highest line of the border, through which the roots may pass from the inner to the outer border, and thus have free scope for growing. The path through the length of the house may be formed of iron gratings carried on iron kerbs, or of stout wood slats, which, with the hot water pipes, are supported by a series of brick pillars. When any attention is required to the border below, all that is necessary is to lift up the gratings. The lights are continuous to both front and roof, or are made separately, as may be preferred. They are 2 inches thick, and hung by specially constructed hinges, not liable to be set fast by rust, and are opened by improved apparatus, set in motion by the wheels and winches shown close to the door in Fig. 381. Wrought-iron principals are fixed to alternate rafters. The front is 5 feet in height, this height being equally divided between brickwork below and sashes above. Cast-iron guttering is placed under the eaves, and down pipes are

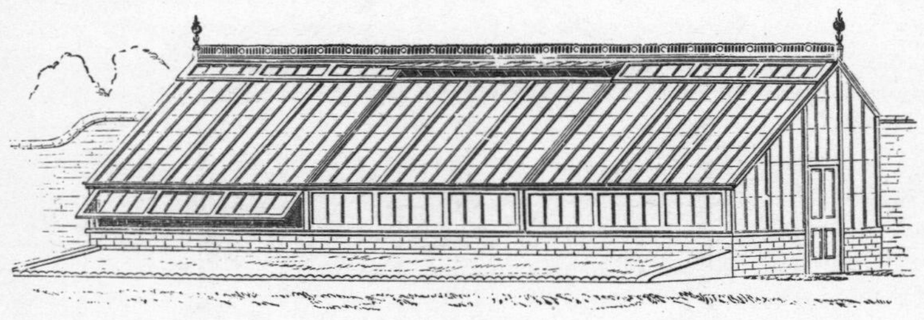

FIG. 380 *Three-quarter span vinery. General view of exterior*

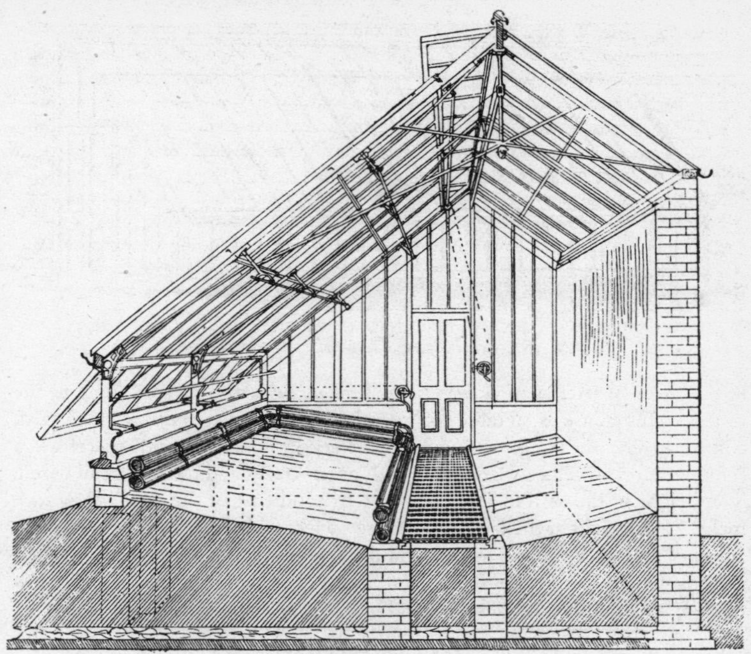

FIG. 381 *Interior view of three-quarter span vinery*

provided to carry off the rainfall. The front and ends are glazed with 15 ounce glass; the roof with 21-ounce glass. The house is as suitable for a plant house as it is for a vinery. The approximate prices for houses in this style in different widths, but in a length of 30 feet, exclusive of brickwork, heating apparatus, iron walk, and wiring to roof, are as follows: 12 feet wide, £59; 14 feet, £63 10s.; feet, £71; 18 feet, £78.

786 *Lean-to Peach House* The form of house exhibited in Figs. 382 and 384 is a good one for general purposes, but especially adapted, as its name implies, for peach culture. The arrangement of the borders and substructure of the front containing wall is similar to that of the vinery described above, but the iron muntins are leaded into a rough stone which is supported on brick pillars about 4 feet apart. The iron muntins have pockets or grooves cast in them, into which self-faced slate fronts ¾ inch thick are dropped, running down to the ground level. The front light is continuous and shuts against the slate front. The peach trellis is bolted to the muntins and slung up to the rafters as shown; it is curved over at the top to allow the trees trained to the back wall to receive the full rays of the sun. The walk is formed of iron gratings on iron kerbs, or of wood slats supported on pillars of brick, about 5 feet apart, an arrangement which leaves the whole of the ground covered by the structure free for the run of the roots, as

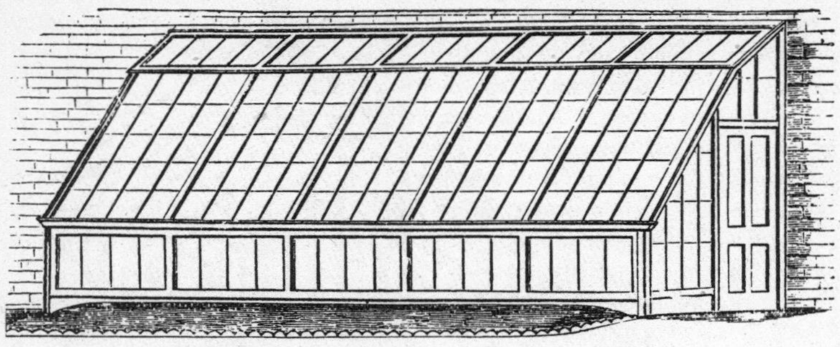

FIG. 382 *Peach house. General view of exterior.*

in the three-quarter span vinery. A shelf for strawberries may be slung to the rafters. This house is suitable for covering long garden walls at small cost, comparatively speaking, and forms a very productive, and therefore a remunerative, structure when fitted with peach trellis and the back wall wired. The height of the sash in front is 2 ft. 6 in., and that of the slate below it, 8 inches. The height at the back for a house 10 feet wide is 10 feet 6 inches; for a width of 12 feet, 11 feet 6 inches; and for a width of 14 feet, 12 feet 6 inches. Approximate prices for houses 30 feet long, and of the widths and heights just named, but exclusive of brickwork and heating apparatus, are as follows:

	10 feet wide	12 feet wide	14 feet wide
Cost of structure, without heating apparatus, etc.	£49 0s. 0d.	£57 0s. 0d.	£67 0s. 0d.
Peach trellis and wiring to back wall	£6 4s. 0d.	£7 7s. 0d.	£8 0s. 0d.
Iron Walk, 2 feet 4 inches wide, on iron kerbs	£7 0s. 0d.	£7 0s. 0d.	£7 0s. 0d.
Wooden slat walk	£2 12s. 0d.	£2 12s. 0d.	£2 12s. 0d.

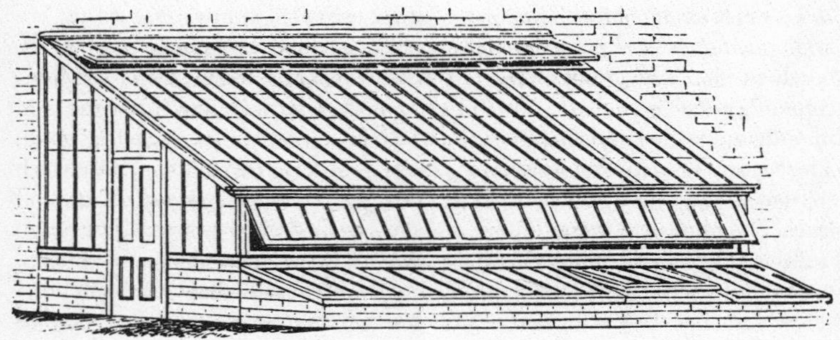

FIG. 383 *Lean-to house with pit in front. General view*

787 *Lean-to Plant House or Stove with Pit* Dwarf houses covered with lights and usually called pits, are sometimes placed in front of lean-to houses, and on both sides of span roof houses, and whether heated by an additional series of pipes or constructed as cold pits for protective purposes only, form a most useful kind of annexe or addendum to the main house. An example of a lean-to plant house or stove with pit is shown in Figs. 383 and 385, of which the former shows a general perspective view, and the latter a view of the interior, with the stages and arrangements for ventilation. It is constructed on the system patented by Messrs Messenger and Co, and already described; and as the illustrations, combined with what has been already said of houses erected on this principle, fully explain themselves, it is unnecessary to say much more about them, except that the pit in front, which is 4 feet in width, will be found of great use, either for hardening off plants or for growing salads in the winter months. The lights are fitted with opening tackle, by means of which they can be set open at any angle, and retained in the position desired; a 2-inch flow and return pipe is carried along the front within. The house is represented as being fitted with wooden stages, but if it is required as a stove, it should have an iron and slate stage, which will be described further on in connection with the subject of stages. The approximate prices for a house of this description, 30 feet in length, but exclusive of brickwork and heating apparatus, in various widths, are as follows: 12 feet wide, £50; 14 feet wide, £57; 16 feet wide, £64; and 18 feet wide, £71. The house may be had with or without pits, an additional charge of £10 being made for a series of pits of the length of the house and of the width stated above.

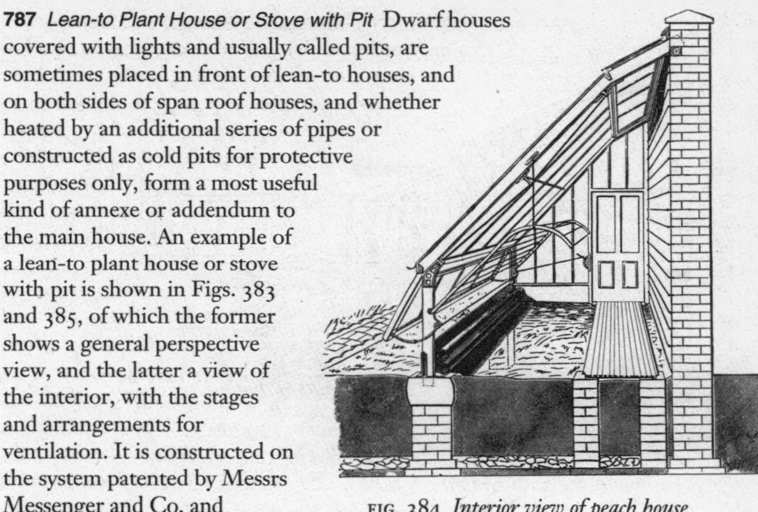

FIG. 384 *Interior view of peach house*

788 *Span-Roof Plant House or Forcing House* In Figs. 386 and 387, are shown views of the exterior and interior of a span-roof plant house, stove, or forcing house, similar in general construction and purpose to the lean-to house just described. It may be had with beds formed on the principle shown in Fig. 387, or with stages on both sides similar to those shown in the interior view of the lean-to house in Fig. 385. It must be understood that the stages are more appropriate for a plant house, but that for a forcing house or stove the iron and slate beds exhibited in Fig. 387 are necessary. The beds are formed of iron framing, carrying strong slates to form the bottom and self-faced slates along the front, back, and ends. Below the beds run the pipes of the heating apparatus. Air flues are arranged at the back, by which means separate pipes for top heat are dispensed with, the heated air from below the bed ascending through these

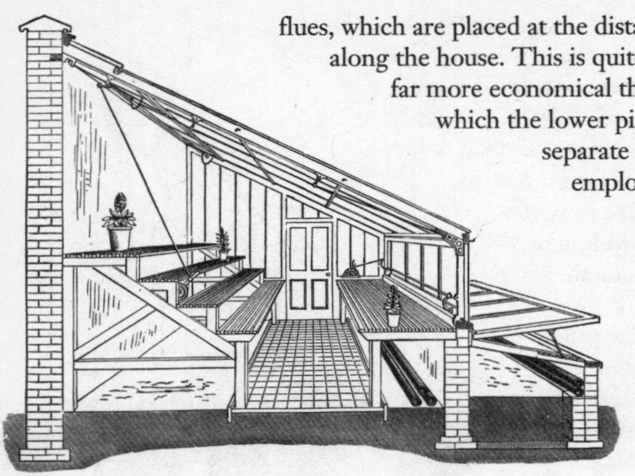

FIG. 385 *Interior of lean-to house with pit*

flues, which are placed at the distance of 2 feet apart all along the house. This is quite as efficacious as, but far more economical than, the old system, in which the lower pipes were buried and a separate system of upper pipes employed for top heat. The prices of the houses, without beds and heating apparatus, brickwork, etc., 30 feet in length, are as follows: 12 feet wide, £56; 14 feet, £64; 16 feet, £72; and 18 feet, £78. Pits can be placed on either side of a house of this description, if required.

789 *Plant Houses without Front Lights* Houses of this description, without any upright sashes whatever in front in lean-to houses, and with none at the sides in span-roofed houses, are much used both as plant houses and forcing houses by market gardeners, and for various reasons are equally desirable for amateurs. In the first place, the cost is considerably less than that of a house of the same area with upright sashes, and by reason of the construction of the house, plants that are placed on the stages within, if it be arranged as a plant house, or in the beds, if it be formed to serve the purpose of a stove or forcing house, are brought as close up to and under the glass as it is possible to place them, and more so in the lean-to form than in that of the span-roof, unless the roof lights of the latter are inclined to each other at an angle greater than a right angle. The construction of these houses is shown in Fig. 388, which presents an exterior view of a lean-to house of this description. In Fig. 389, a section of the lean-to house is shown, fitted with stages and shelves, as a plant house, and in Fig. 390, a section of the span-roof form is

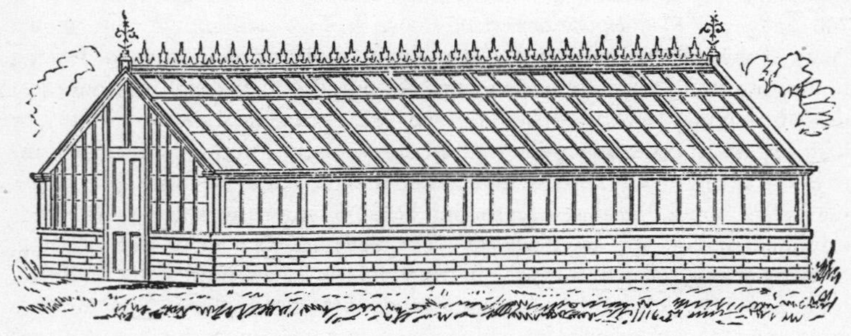

FIG. 386 *Span-roof plant house or stove. Exterior*

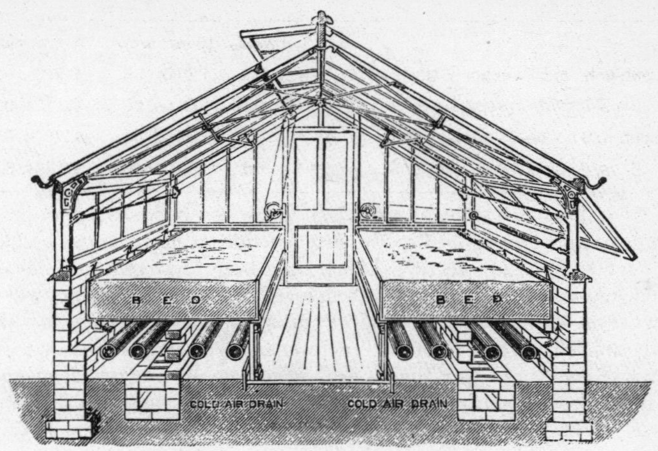

FIG. 387 *Interior view of span-roof plant house, etc*

shown, furnished with beds, so that it may be used as a forcing house or stove. The mode of building is in each case precisely the same. The brickwork is carried up to the height of 4 feet, and into the brickwork, about the centre of the wall, or a little lower in the plant house and just under the wall plate that carries the roof lights in the stove, are built wooden sliding ventilators for the admission of air. The lower ends of the roof lights rest immediately upon the wall plate, without any upright lights intervening. Houses of this description are supplied by Messrs Messenger and Co, either to form permanent structures, or constructed with lights so that they may be taken down and removed at pleasure. The framing is 2 inches thick, and the roof lights are glazed with 21-ounce glass, 15-ounce glass being used for the ends. The eaves are fitted with a half-round gutter, to which a down pipe is attached to carry off the rainfall. The prices of these houses, 30 feet in length, and in different widths of 8, 10, and 12 feet, exclusive of brickwork, beds or staging, and heating apparatus are as follows, taken approximately:

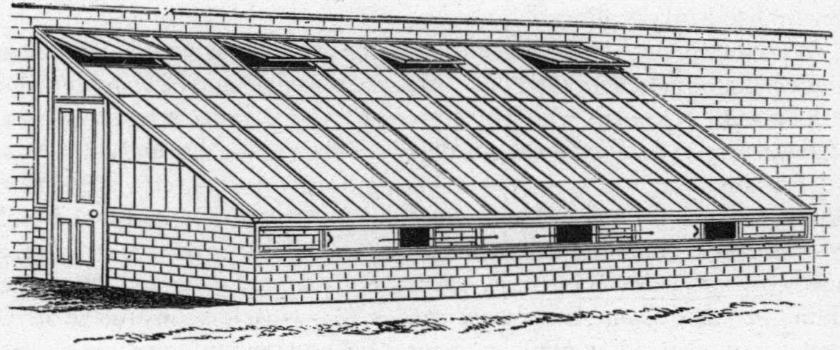

FIG. 388 *Lean-to-plant house without front lights. General view*

	8 feet wide	10 feet wide	12 feet wide
Lean-to house. Permanent structure	£24 0s. 0d.	£30 0s. 0d.	£36 0s. 0d.
Extra, if made in separate lights	£1 10s. 0d.	£2 0s. 0d.	£2 12s. 0d.
Span-roof house. Permanent structure	£27 0s. 0d.	£33 0s. 0d.	£38 0s. 0d.
Extra, if made in separate lights	£1 12s. 0d.	£2 0s. 0d.	£2 10s. 0d.

790 As it has been already remarked, there is no economy in inferior workmanship when applied to the first erection of horticultural buildings. Although the glazed structures which have been illustrated and described include most of those that are at present in use, it is unlikely that they will fully meet the requirements of everybody. Position, aspect, the purpose to which it is to be applied, the area that it is to enclose and cover, and the amount that the intending owner can spend in its acquisition, are all data which materially affect the mode of construction, and must be carefully considered. The proper course for anyone to adopt and follow who wishes to have a hothouse, greenhouse, or conservatory built for him, is to apply to some well-known horticultural builder, unless he is possessed of sufficient technical knowledge and skill to become his own architect, clerk of the works, and possibly his own mechanic, and to ask for sketches, plans, and estimates, submitting at the same time for the guidance of the builder and the hot water engineer such necessary information as to situation and attendant circumstances, the kind of structure required, the purpose to which it is to be devoted, the sum that can be expended on it, and any other particulars that may suggest themselves. In almost every town of importance a horticultural builder will be found who will undertake the work, and carry it out in a proper manner. The nearer the builder is to the locality in which the purchaser resides, the better will it be for the latter, as carriage forms a considerable element in the cost of buildings made at and brought from some distant place. Due inquiry will always produce the desired information with respect to who can build, where he is to be found, and what he is to build for. It may be added that to those who find any difficulty in getting information of this kind, it may be readily found in such yearly publications as Glenny's *Illustrated Garden Almanack*, and the *Garden Annual*, in which lists are given of those who follow the horticultural trade in any and every branch in all localities.

791 With the view to render the information contained on greenhouse building in this chapter as complete as possible, Messrs Messenger and Co. have furnished, for the benefit of readers who may wish to possess a compact range of houses, including stove or forcing house, greenhouse, a plant house, hot and cold pits, and all the necessary adjuncts, such as a potting house, stokery, etc., a design and estimate for such a range, which cannot fail to be generally useful and highly suggestive. As it embodies and includes everything that is necessary for greenhouse work on a moderate scale, it may not inaptly be termed Messenger's Multum-in-Parvo Range. It is almost needless to say that it is constructed on their patent system of building glazed structures for horticultural purposes, in which glass, wood, and iron are judiciously combined, and which has been described in this chapter, and is fitted with their several patented appliances for the regulation of ventilation, heating, etc.

792 In a range of buildings like that which is now under consideration, in which the pits occupy both sides of the house, it is obvious that the nearer they are placed in a direction ranging from north-west to south-east, the more equally will the light and heat of the sun be distributed to them. The site being fixed on, the estimate given includes the foundation walls, and air drains and everything that is necessary for the proper management of the house: external drains are, of course, constructed by the owner at his own expense. The arrangement and relative positions of the different parts of the entire range may be seen from Fig. 391, which exhibits a plan of the whole structure. The entire length of the site that it occupies is 49 feet in length and 26 feet in width, which is thus divided: The central space, which is covered from end to end by a span roof, is 18 feet in width, and of the length already mentioned, and this is flanked on one side by two cold pits, and on the other side by two hot pits or pits warmed by pipes, which are each 4 feet wide and 24 feet 6 inches long, outside measurement. The form assumed by the house and the pits by which it is flanked is shown in Fig. 392, which exhibits a section through the stove or forcing house.

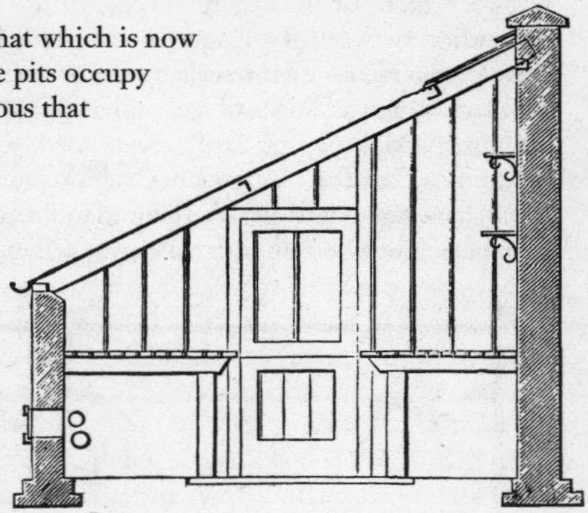

FIG. 389 *Section of lean-to-house adapted for plant house*

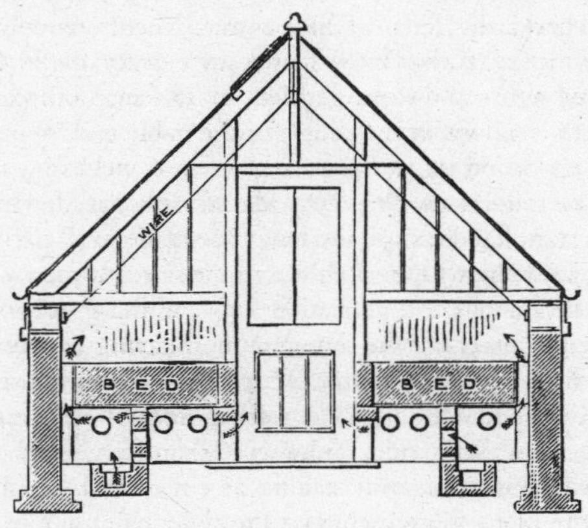

FIG. 390 *Section of span-roof house adapted for stove*

793 The plan and section shown in Figs. 391 and 392 were drawn on a scale of 7 feet to 1 inch, or ⅐ inch to 1 foot, to use another mode of expressing the proportion between the diagrams and the actual house. It is an irregular, and therefore an inconvenient, scale to use, but as the dimensions of the various parts are marked, and as a scale of feet is given by which the dimensions of details that are not marked may be easily ascertained, the inconvenience is reduced to a minimum. Had the diagrams been drawn on a scale of ⅛ inch to 1 foot they would have been considerably reduced in size, and the reduction, perhaps, would have been incompatible with clearness, which is so desirable in all plans.

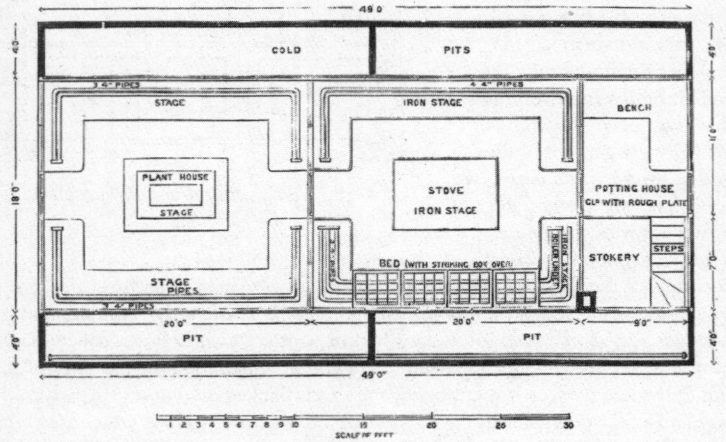

FIG. 391 *Plan of Multum-in-parvo range, exhibiting in combination stove, plant house, cold pits, hot pits, potting house, and stokery*

794 The central part is divided into three compartments, namely, a plant house or ordinary greenhouse, 20 feet by 18 feet, a stove or forcing house of the same size, and a potting house and stokery, 9 feet by 18 feet. Commencing with the plant house, there is a door in the centre of the gable end, opposite which, on entrance, there is a wood stage, measuring 7 feet 6 inches by 5 feet 6 inches. Round this central stage is a walk 3 feet wide, suitably paved, which is bordered by stages on the right hand and on the left, 3 feet wide in all parts, under which run three 4-inch iron pipes. Opposite the entrance already mentioned is another door, affording means of communication between the greenhouse and stove, which is arranged in precisely the same manner, having an iron stage 7 feet 6 inches by 5 feet 6 inches in the centre. This stage is encompassed by a walk or path 3 feet wide. On the left-hand side walking through it towards the potting house, is an iron stage 3 feet wide, under which run four 4-inch iron pipes. On the other side there is some iron staging at either end, but between them, occupying a length of 13 feet 6 inches on the right-hand side of the house, is a bed, with a glazed box above it that is utilised for striking cuttings, etc. Below the

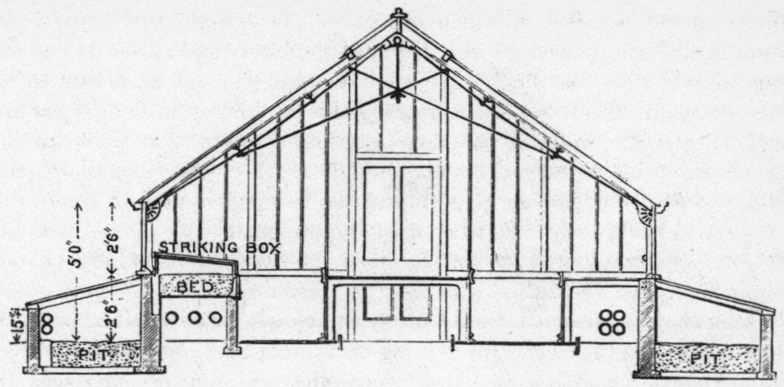

FIG. 392 *Section of Multum-in-parvo range through stove*

bed and the iron staging at either end of it run three 4-inch iron pipes; and below the staging at the upper corner is situated the boiler belonging to the hot water apparatus by which the entire building and the hot pits are warmed. At the upper end of the forcing house is a third door, through which access is obtained to the potting house, which is also entered from the grounds by a fourth door in line with those already mentioned. The portion of the range devoted to this purpose is 9 feet by 11 feet: a bench 3 feet in width occupies one end and part of one side. The potting house itself is glazed with rough plate. From the potting house a flight of steps leads down to the stokery, in one corner of which is the furnace by which the boiler is heated. The hot pits are warmed by two 3-inch pipes running along the front of the pit just inside the front wall.

795 So much for the arrangement of the house in plan. We may now pass on to the consideration of the building as it appears in the section exhibited in Fig. 392. From this it is apparent that the main walls surrounding the plant house, stove, and potting house are of brickwork 9 inches thick, and that the brickwork in front of the pits is of single brick, or 4½ inches thick. From the foundation to the sill of the pit these front walls are 2 feet 6 inches high, half of which is above and half below the ordinary ground level. The brickwork of the containing walls of the main part of the range is 3 feet 9 inches high, of which 1 foot 3 inches is below the ground level, and the remainder between the ground level and sill of the side lights, which are themselves 2 feet 6 inches in height, thus giving a total height of 5 feet from the ground to the roof. A bottom of rubble or concrete is formed for the pits on a level with the foundation, and the space between this and the ground level is filled up with suitable material. The height of the ridge above the ground level is 12 feet, and the doors are 6 feet 9 inches high and 3 feet wide.

796 The method of construction of the roof, the ends, and indeed of all parts above the brickwork which is Messrs Messenger and Co.'s patent method, has been already described, and need not be repeated. The lights of the pits are hinged to slips running the whole length of the house under the sills of the side lights, and can be lifted up when necessary. The upright side lights open outwards, and are opened for ventilation of the house and closed as may be required by an apparatus which will be described when the subject of ventilation comes under consideration. There are also lights for ventilation along the entire length of the ridge, which are actuated by the same means. The results of this system are fourfold, namely, 1, Perfect ventilation; 2, Non-interference with the plants; 3, No risk of broken glass through an inopportune fall of any of the lights; and 4, Exclusion of rain when the lights are open.

797 The glazing adopted for this house is the ordinary putty glazing, but without top putty – a method which can be treated more conveniently in the following chapter, in which it will be fully and clearly described. The panes of glass are curved at the edge, so as to bring the centre of the edge to a lower level than the ends, which has the effect of carrying the moisture produced by condensation to the centre of each pane, instead of allowing it to trickle down the edges.

798 The stages in the plant house are constructed of wood, but those in the stove are formed of slates supported on iron standards and framing. The bed, which combines with the lights placed above it to form a striking box, is also formed of slates, but the compartment below, through which the three pipes that warm it run, is enclosed in front by a 4½-inch brick wall, on which the bottom and front of the bed is sustained. The striking box above is formed of wood covered in by glazed lights. The roof and pit lights are all glazed with 21-ounce glass, but the side lights, ends, and partitions between the different houses are glazed with 15-ounce glass. The woodwork is painted with four coats of the best oil colour.

799 For such a house, or rather range of houses, a wrought-iron saddle boiler is the best that can be used. This also will be described in the next chapter, among the boilers that are now chiefly used for greenhouses, and in connection with the means necessary for heating glazed horticultural boilers. There is no necessity to do more at present than call attention to the description of boiler that is intended to accompany the range.

800 The cost of a block of buildings as has just been described, taken according to its different parts and fittings, will be as follows:

The span houses – plant house, stove, and potting house	£135 10s. 0d.
Wood stages in plant house	£10 10s. 0d.
Iron and slate stages, slate bed, and striking box in stove	£18 0s. 0d.
Pits, inclusive of hot and cold pits on each side of span houses	£25 0s. 0d.
Heating to plant house and stove	£67 10s. 0d.
Heating to hot pit	£8 10s. 0d.
Bricklayer's work to span houses	£57 0s. 0d.
Bricklayer's work to pits	£6 10s. 0d.

The total cost, therefore, would be £328 10s., delivered and fixed complete in any part of England, and therefore inclusive of carriage. The publication of this is authorised by Messrs Messenger and Co., as being their estimate at present prices of material and cost of labour for this very compact and useful combination of greenhouse, stove, hot and cold pits, and potting shed. It is not practicable, nor indeed is it necessary, to carry out this part of the subject to greater length. Few persons will be disposed to build hothouses and greenhouses without proper plans and estimates, and all that it is sought to do in the remarks that have been made is to point out the best modes of construction, the most desirable forms of glazed horticultural structures, and some of the necessary steps to be taken by those who have it in their minds to build.

FIG. 393 *Clerodendron speciosum hybridum*

CHAPTER 18

Modes of Glazing, Ventilating, and Heating Glazed Horticultural Structures; The Various Methods of Heating, and Appliances Necessary for them; Stages and Staging of all Kinds

801 We have dealt with all the varied structures now in use for protecting and forcing plants and fruit with the exception of orchard houses, a subject of such importance to gardeners, both from the pleasure and the profit point of view, that it deserves a chapter to itself, and will accordingly be brought fully under notice a little further on. They have, furthermore, been considered and described as fully and explicitly and as much at length as is possible, having due regard to the various topics that must of necessity find a place in any comprehensive book on the management of the garden. A little has been said about the mode to be followed in building a greenhouse and the principles of construction involved in the provision of glazed structures for special purposes. To enter at length into a discussion on the labour of different kinds that must be called into play in putting them up, or, in other words, to describe the duties required of and the work done by the architect, the engineer, the builder, the bricklayer, the carpenter, etc., in the construction of a glazed horticultural structure of any kind, is foreign to the purpose of the present work, and must, therefore, be left wholly untouched, beyond such casual references and allusions to them which have been already made here and there in the preceding pages.

802 It is impossible, however, to ignore systems on which special kinds of work are done, especially when much importance is attached to each by its different advocates, and to pass over without mention appliances connected with the most important parts of greenhouse building, namely, painting and glazing, ventilation and heating, in which it is necessary to deal with theory as well as practice, and to endeavour to explain why one system appears to be better or worse than a rival system, as the case may be. For this reason, it is necessary to touch, though briefly, on the modes of dry glazing, or glazing without putty, which have been brought into competition of late years with the old system of glazing with putty, which has held its own for so many years, chiefly because no attempt, until recently, comparatively speaking, has been made to supersede it. Nor, in these times, when every gardener wishes to have some glazed structure, however small and restricted in space it may be, at his command, and desires to have efficient means of warming it, is it possible to refuse to accord notice to the various modes of heating that have proved formidable rivals to the old flue system, and the appliances by which they are carried into effect.

803 *Glass and Modes of Glazing* There is not much, perhaps, to be said about glass, but it will be necessary to describe some of the new modes of glazing that have been introduced of late years. The difference between 15-ounce glass and 21-ounce glass has already been explained; and it has been explained that the difference between specimens of glass thus designated consists not in quality but in thickness, and therefore in strength and resisting power. Most oil and colourmen supply glass, as do also painters and glaziers, and will cut it to the size and in the quantity required at about 3d. or 4d. per square foot, and some may do it at prices even lower than these. Belgian and English glass are both supplied, but the latter is preferable if you can make sure of getting it. The following list of sizes and prices of glass per 100 squares, at sizes always kept in stock, is from the price list of Mr Henry Wainright, Wholesale Glass Warehouse, 8 and 10 Alfred Street, Boar Lane, Leeds, and will form a fair guide for buyers, as they are placed as low as they well can be, the quality of the material being taken into account. These prices are for delivery in Leeds only: it must be understood that they do not include carriage to any part whatever, which must be defrayed by the buyer. Packing cases are furnished without charge.

Size	15 oz.	21 oz.	Size	15 oz.	21 oz.
13½ in. by 8 in.	10s. 0d.	14s. 0d.	12in. by 12 in.	13s. 6d.	21s. 0d.
12in. by 9 in.	10s. 0d.	14s. 0d.	15in. by 12 in.	19s. 0d.	26s. 0d.
14in. by 10 in.	13s. 6d.	21s. 0d.	18in. by 12 in.	22s. 0d.	32s. 0d.
15in. by 9 in.	13s. 6d.	21s. 0d.	20in. by 12 in.	25s. 0d.	40s. 0d.

Prices for other sizes are quoted on application. Frames and sashes should be made to suit the size of glass that it is intended to use. Those who make them must, therefore, construct their lights in such a manner, and determine the distance between the sashes, so that the glass may drop easily into the rebates on opposite sides of the opening, and an allowance must be made for laps. Thus, supposing it is intended to use glass 12 inches by 12 inches, and to allow a lap of ½ inch, the length of the opening between sash bars in a light to take eight panes would be 91 inches. As there are eight panes, having a full length of 12 inches each, there will be seven laps of ½ inch each, or 3½ inches, and there will be ½ inch more to be allowed for the groove or rebate at the top of the light and about 1 inch lap over the wood forming the lower rail of the light, making in all 5 inches, and if this be taken from 96 inches, the full length of eight panes, there will remain 91 inches, which will be the length of the opening. Thus it is easy to regulate the lengths of openings to suit the dimensions of the glass, or to determine the sizes of glass suitable for particular pieces of work. In addition to the prices already named, Mr Wainright will supply, for the sum of 10s. 6d., in 15-ounce glass, 300 squares 8 inches by 6 inches, or 250 squares 8½ inches by 6½ inches, or 220 squares 9½ inches by 6½ inches, or 170 squares 9 inches by 7½ inches, or 150 squares 10 inches by 8 inches. Putty is supplied at 1d., and paint, in 1lb., 2lb., 41b., or 71b. tins, at 5d., per lb.

804 *Paint and Putty* The general price of putty for glazing is 1d. per lb., and that of paint, ready for use in tins, at 5d. and 6d. per lb. Paint in large quantities is sometimes offered at lower prices, but the usual charges for paint ready prepared in tins are as just stated. Thus, Messrs A. Leete and Co., Paint Works, 129 London Road, offer paint in all colours for horticultural buildings, greenhouses, wood, iron, and stone work, at 2½d. per lb., or 23s. per cwt., for cash; but this is an exceptionally low rate, and may be taken as the minimum at which paint can be obtained.

805 *Torbay Paint Company's Colours for Conservatories, etc.* Colour for the decoration and preservation of frames and glazed structures of all kinds is a subject that demands the earnest attention of the horticultural builder, for the paint is a most important feature in the internal economy of the pit, conservatory, greenhouse, and hothouse. Indeed, it is by no means an easy matter to get a satisfactory paint for this purpose, as, unless the base be free from lead and other noxious ingredients, it will prove fatal to delicate plants by reason of the fumes which it gives off. It is also difficult to find a material that will not be affected by the steam or vapour that is always more or less present after watering, and especially if the place be heated by hot water pipes. The colours prepared and supplied by Messrs Stevens and Co., of 26 Billiter Street, London, proprietors of the Torbay Paint Company, seem to be especially well suited, both for external and internal work, by reason of the durability of the pigment both in colour and substance. The shades of colours supplied by Messrs Stevens and Co. are most delicate, comprising every grade desirable for conservatories, from white to cream, blue, green, etc., and the peculiar richness of the tints it would be certainly difficult to surpass. There is not an atom of lead in any of their paints, the base being the Torbay oxide found on their works at Brixham, Devon. Being a perfect oxide paint, it does not give off any poisonous vapours or fumes fatal to plant life, as do common paints. By reason of its fineness and finish, a gloss is obtained on the surface which is very little inferior to varnish, and which is in no way affected or impaired by heat or cold, or by the steam generated in a conservatory. It may even be used on the hot water pipes with perfect security, and thoroughly prevent any chance of rust, which is a great desideratum.

806 When put in comparison with lead paint, the price of the Torbay paint is really cheaper, as the covering powers are much greater, whilst it will last three times as long as lead paint, and never lose the peculiar delicacy and beauty of its tint. The colours most suitable for conservatories, and most generally used, are pale cream, pale light blue, white, and pale light stone, either singly or in combination. The white is really a beautiful colour, and, unlike white lead and common white paint, it retains its tone and tint, as it is a chemical impossibility for it to go off colour, as the term goes, and as is the case with other whites. Messrs Stevens and Co. have a pamphlet in which are exhibited seventy different shades and colours of their paint, and they are always pleased to send this pamphlet to anyone who may be interested in the question.

807 Among other specialities in paints may be mentioned the valuable Charlton White, prepared from zinc according to the formula of the inventor, Mr Thomas Griffiths, FCS, by the Silicate Paint Company, J. B. Orr and Co., 46

Cannon Street, London, and so called from the place of its manufacture. This is a brilliant, harmless colour, which may be used without any detriment to health. The damp-proof paint made by Messrs H. Thompson and Co., 95 Merrow Street, Walworth, London, is specially useful for damp walls, and the Magnetic Oxide of Iron Paint, prepared by the same firm, for outdoor or indoor work. These paints are supplied in cans, containing 7lb. at 3s., 14lb. at 6s., and 28lb. at 11s. The colours supplied by Messrs Pontifex and Wood, Shoe Lane, London, Messrs Colthurst and Harding, Temple Gate, Bristol, and Messrs Wilkinson, Heywood, and Clark, Caledonian Varnish and Colour Works, 7 Caledonian Road, King's Cross, London, may be also pointed out as being suitable for all purposes for which paint is used.

808 *Modes of Glazing* It is only of late years – say, since 1850 – that any departure has been taken from the time-honoured mode of securing panes of glass in place either by leads, as in casement and church windows, or by putty when set in rebates cut in sash bars, frames, etc., of wood. Lights for horticultural buildings are generally constructed with long and comparatively narrow openings extending from the top to the bottom rail, and the panes of glass are allowed to lap, each pane in turn over the pane immediately below it. The panes were then bedded in putty, and the angle of the rebate in which the edge of the pane was placed were filled up with putty bevelled in a slope from the upper edge of the rebate to the glass. At present, when putty is used, the panes are bedded in this material as before, and secured with sprigs or small nails, driven in over the lap and at the edge of the squares; and instead of filling the rebate with putty, two or three coats of paint are applied to prevent any moisture from penetrating between the glass and the wood. There are many other systems of glazing in vogue, known as dry glazing, or glazing without putty, some of which will be mentioned presently. None, however, seem to be so efficacious as bedding the panes in putty and securing them with sprigs, as just described.

Messrs Messenger and Co., whose long experience renders them reliable authorities on the subject of glazing, say: 'We do not advocate the system of glazing houses without putty, as we are sure that many advantages that are claimed by the advocates of this system are entirely fallacious, and that the increased first cost will more than counterbalance any advantages that may exist as regards painting, etc. One point upon which great stress is usually laid is that the bars being wholly covered by the glass, no external painting is required. This is only partly true, for it will be seen by anyone examining a house glazed in this manner that in most cases the rafters, stretchers, top ventilators, ridges, the end framing, and, in fact, the greater part of the woodwork, are *uncovered*, and therefore requires painting just as much as a house glazed in the ordinary way, while but very few of these systems are able to make a house as dry and warm as one glazed in the ordinary way. Any gardener who has tried the two methods will admit that a house with dry glazing takes more coal, and requires more pipe, to keep up the necessary temperature during the winter than one glazed with putty. We are convinced from careful observation that the method we pursue, and which is described below, is the best that can be adopted when all things are taken into consideration. We have our putty specially prepared for us, and made only with *boiled oil*, so that we are enabled to ensure a really satisfactory article.

'The system we, from long experience, recommend is to bed the glass firmly on a thin layer of putty, being particular that the glass fits well between the bars, and sprig it – that is, nail it over the lap and at the edge of the squares. The old system of top puttying is expensive, and, what is worse, unsatisfactory, for, unless done in dry weather, the putty does not adhere to the bars, and in course of time cracks away, leaving a slight crevice, which holds the moisture and leads to the decay of the woodwork.'

809 *Forms of Glass for Glazing* That the fullest possible benefit may be obtained for plants growing within any kind of glazed horticultural structure, it is necessary that the glass should be kept clean, and it is recommended that glass in greenhouses, etc., should be thoroughly cleansed on both the inner and outer surface in February and October in each year, with an intermediate cleansing of the exterior only in June. Dirty glass hinders the full entrance of light, and in proportion to the diminution of light plants under glass become *drawn* – that is to say, the leaf stalks are elongated and the leaf surface spread out to an extent far beyond the natural length and area, the larger surface being required in diminished light for the proper maturation of the sap, if the term be admissible – whereas in full light, to which no hindrance in the form of an intervening medium is opposed, the smaller surface accorded by nature is amply sufficient for this purpose. All who have grown plants in a window will understand what is meant by a plant becoming drawn, and will remember how plants in this position grow towards the light, inclining themselves towards the aperture through which the light enters, leaning forward, as it were, to meet it. It may be urged that the hindrance of the entrance of light means shade, but diminution of light caused by dirt at all times as long as it is allowed to remain, and the lessening of the intensity of the sun's rays by shading materials or mediums of any kind when necessary, are two very different things.

810 It is necessary, then, that glass in glazed structures should be kept clean – as clean, in fact, as the windows of the dwelling-house, and that as much width as possible should be allowed between the sash bars in which the panes are placed; and having due regard to economy in case of fracture, it is considered that 12 inches from bar to bar, including rebates, is a sufficient width for the openings, so as to take panes measuring 18 inches long by 12 inches broad. When expense is no object, rough plate glass is recommended, because the roughness of the glass prevents any chance of the leaves getting scorched by the heat of the sun's rays, while it in no way lessens the entrance of light. Panes of glass used in glazing are generally cut perfectly square, as at A in Fig. 394, and when a lap is permitted they lap in the manner shown. The great objection to the lap is that water is apt to rise in the lap between the adjacent surfaces of the panes by capillary attraction, and that the moisture too often takes up dirt with it, which remains behind when the moisture itself has evaporated, giving a dirty and repulsive appearance to the glazing. With the square pane, descending moisture is apt to linger on the edge at the bottom from end to end without, and at the edge of the top within, which gives better opportunity for penetration between the laps of the glass, either by descent from the top edge, or by ascent by capillary attraction from the bottom edge. In order to obviate this, and to carry off the moisture to the sash bar, and induce it to trickle away down this part of the framing as quickly as possible, panes in hothouses are sometimes cut in a rhomboidal form, as shown at B in Fig. 394, and but little lap is given to the panes, say, from ⅛ inch to ¼ inch at the utmost. This form of pane is desirable in forcing houses, in which there is always a large amount of vapour in the air, which condenses and is converted into water on coming into contact with the glass. It has been suggested to form the edges of the panes at the laps as shown at C, but although this may accelerate the downward progress of water on the exterior, it will certainly retard its escape in the interior. The only feasible step in this direction would be to cut the panes in a hexagonal form, as shown in Fig. 395, which would tend to the speedy accumulation and escape of moisture at the lowest point of the panes externally, and from the highest point to the sash bars internally; but any advantage in this respect would be more than counterbalanced by the waste of material in the large rhomboidal lap, and the extra amount of surface afforded for the accumulation of dirt brought in by water rising in the lap by capillary attraction. Of course, in the illustration the lap is shown in an exaggerated form, but this affords no plea in favour of its adoption. If any departure from the common form is made, it must of necessity be as shown at B in Fig. 394.

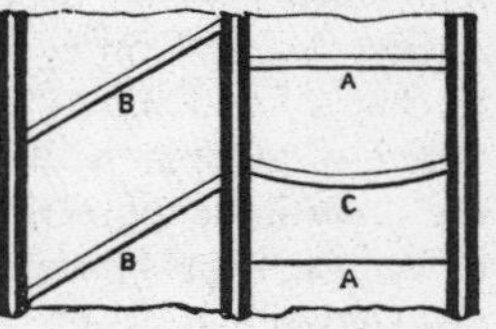

FIG. 394 *Forms of panes used in glazing*

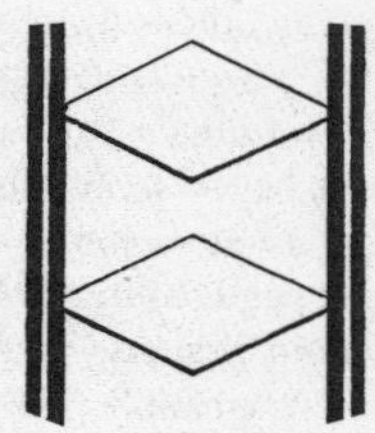

FIG. 395 *Hexagonal glazing for greenhouses*

811 *Glazing without Putty* The chief objections to glazing with putty seem to be that the putty itself, being perishable, requires renewal at intervals or to be protected by the frequent application of paint, and that its use renders the removal of the fragments of broken panes and the introduction of new panes a difficult and tedious operation, and one that frequently tends to the fracture of adjacent panes, and additional cost in replacing them. Systems by which glazing is effected without putty mostly involve an elaborate manipulation of sash bars, whether in wood or metal, to carry off the moisture that must of necessity find its way in between the glass and the wood or metal in which it is laid when no putty is used. The plan of glazing without putty seems to have been originated by Mr Rendle, of the firm of Messrs W. E. Rendle and Co., 3 Westminster Chambers, Victoria Street, London, from whom all information respecting it can be obtained. Many persons have followed in his wake with modifications of the system, all original and ingenious; and among these may be named Helliwell's Imperishable Glazing, 8 Victoria Chambers, Westminster, London, and Brighouse, Yorkshire. The advantages claimed for the various systems of glazing without putty on a large scale, are numerous, and chief among them is the great space that is given for the entrance of the light, the sash bars being small in section, and the purlins on which they rest being a considerable distance apart. Roofs made on this principle are further said to be both windtight and watertight, and attended with considerable saving in maintenance and repair, because no painting is required, and skilled labour in replacing broken panes is not needed.

812 *Causley's Patent Glazing* This is another mode of glazing without putty, and is represented by the manufacturers, whose address is 19 Downs Park Road, West Hackney, London, to be the most perfect system of glazing on this principle now in use. A certificate of merit has been awarded to it by the Royal Horticultural Society. For this kind of glazing a rebate is cut on each side of the sash bar, leaving a projecting ridge along its centre from end to end. Over this a plate is fitted, with the ends turned up on either side to form gutters to carry off drip. The glass is laid on the plate in the angle that fits into the rebate, and is secured in position by a cap which is fastened to the sash bar by screws that pass through capping and plate and enter the sash bar.

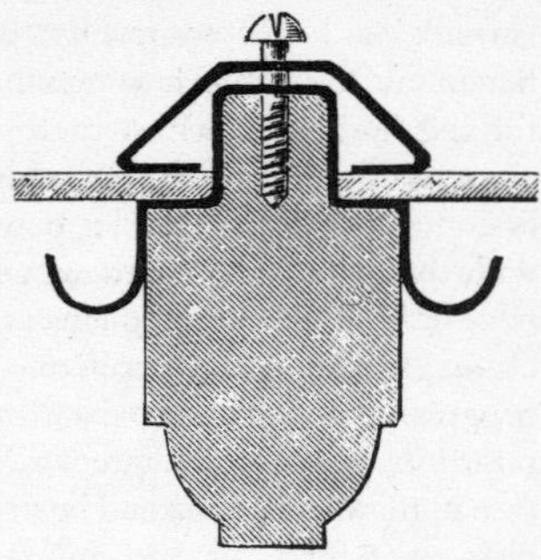

FIG. 396 *Causley's patent glazing*

813 *Crewe's Improved System of Glazing without Putty* In this system, invented and patented by Mr H. J. Crewe, Sunning Hill Road, Lewisham, London, from whom designs, particulars, and prices can be obtained on application, the intermediate bars or rafters have a double groove running from end to end of the upper surface. These bars are placed at such distance apart as may be necessary to allow the ends of the panes to span the space between adjacent bars, and meet on the ridge that divides the double grooving just mentioned. The panes have a narrow lap, and are held in position by a step-shaped clip which is laid on them over the bar where the panes meet. Every clip – those at the sides excepted – thus holds down the four contiguous corners of four adjacent panes. A slot is cut in the clip to admit of the passage of a brass screw which enters the bar, and is screwed down until the clip is held with sufficient tightness. When the clip is withdrawn it is only necessary to loosen the screw with three or four turns of the screw driver, when the head of the screw passes through a circular hole cut in the upper part of the clip at the upper end of the slot. Angular clips are made for securing ends of panes along the side of an end or main rafter. A more simple or effective means of glazing without putty could not be readily devised. The glass can be put on and removed quickly and without breakage by any unskilled hand, and broken panes can be replaced with ease and facility.

814 *Bickley's Patent Horizontal Sash Bars* Before leaving the subject of glazing it is desirable to call the attention of the reader to two modes of glazing which there is every reason to believe are the most simple that have yet been introduced, and in one of which the bars are disposed in a different manner to that which is generally adopted for greenhouses, and in which they run from top to bottom, or from ridge to wall plate. The patent sash bars manufactured by Mr Thomas A. Bickley, 7 Thorp Street, Birmingham, the inventor and patentee, are notably different, as they are placed horizontally from side to side of the roof. By the aid of these bars the amateur may construct a glass roof for a greenhouse without much trouble and without resorting to the use of putty, or finding himself compelled to use overmuch paint. The principle on which these

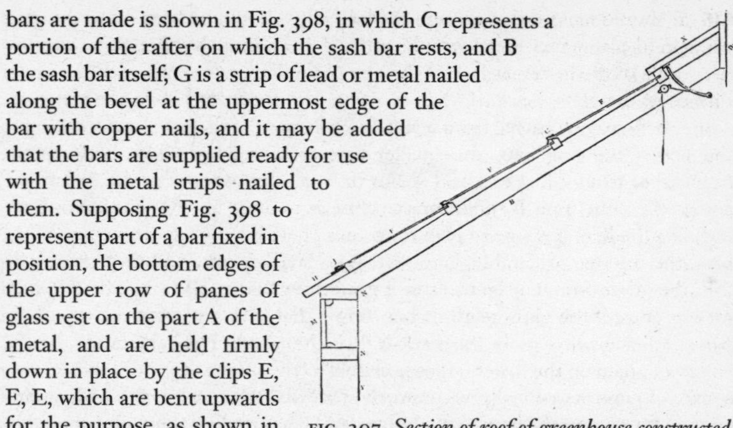

FIG. 397 *Section of roof of greenhouse constructed with patent horizontal sash bar*

bars are made is shown in Fig. 398, in which C represents a portion of the rafter on which the sash bar rests, and B the sash bar itself; G is a strip of lead or metal nailed along the bevel at the uppermost edge of the bar with copper nails, and it may be added that the bars are supplied ready for use with the metal strips nailed to them. Supposing Fig. 398 to represent part of a bar fixed in position, the bottom edges of the upper row of panes of glass rest on the part A of the metal, and are held firmly down in place by the clips E, E, E, which are bent upwards for the purpose, as shown in the illustration. The upper edges of the lower row of panes are laid along the rebate D in the sash bar B, and are held in place by the clips F, F, F. which are pressed down upon them. The clips F, F, F, serve also to carry the water from the upper panes far down on to the next row of panes, and the sloping part G also carries all condensed moisture safely away from the inside of the glass to the next row of panes, thus preventing drip which exists in the ordinary method of glazing.

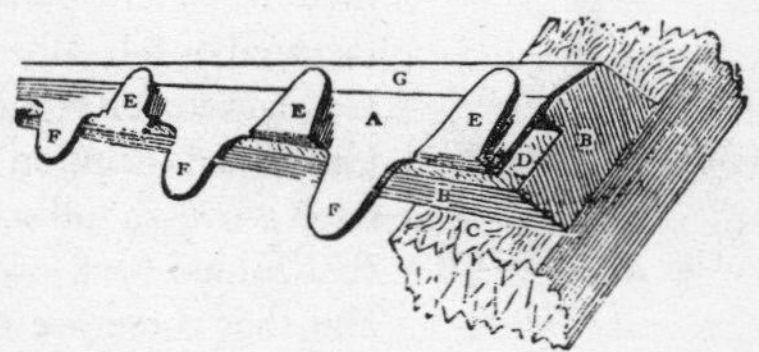

FIG. 398 *Bickley's patent horizontal sash bar*

815 In Fig. 397 the section of a pit or greenhouse roof is shown on a scale of 1 inch to a foot, which exhibits the simplest mode of covering a structure of this kind. B is a rafter 3 inches deep by 1½ inch wide; C is a patent horizontal sash bar let into the rafters by means of notches cut in them ½ inch in depth, and nailed on with wire nails; F, F, F, are sections of panes of glass; H is the eaves board with a strip of patent lead, J, nailed along it to receive and hold down the lower edges of the lowest row of panes; N is the wall plate; M, a hinged flat board, just under the eaves board, for ventilation; X is a hinged flap-board on light for top ventilation; W is the wall against which the structure is built, it being in this case a lean-to; and Y the front wall or row of lights in front, according as the structure is a greenhouse or a pit. The bars are made in various sizes, from 1 inch by 1 inch to 1 inch by 1¼ inch, in section, and are sold at prices ranging from 3d. to 3¼d. per foot run. For small structures the smaller size is sufficiently strong, but for large buildings the larger sizes should be used. The lead plates are made of the weight of 3lb. to the foot super, but they may be had of 4lb. to the foot super at an extra charge of ¼d. per foot run of the bars.

816 It should be said that though the lead clips should be bent on to the glass when in its place, they should not be pressed down in such a manner as to allow the whole of the lower surface of the clip to lie flatly in contact with the upper surface of the glass, because when in this position the lead sucks the water up. The rafters may be placed from 4 feet to 6 feet apart at the utmost, according to the size of the sash bars, the smaller bars requiring less width between the rafters; but from 3 feet to 5 feet seems to be a safer distance as the maximum, and, at the same time, by no means so close as to cause any diminution of light. In fixing the bars it is a good plan to strain a chalk line tightly where one of the bars, the top one preferably, is to be fixed. Having marked all the rafters with this, the other ones may be measured from these marks, allowing about ¾ inch for lap; thus, if the glass be 18 inches long – that is to say, from the top of the pane to the bottom – make the marks 17½ inches apart. The bars should then be nailed on, placing the lower edges precisely to the marks. It is desirable to try a square of glass occasionally as the work proceeds. Wire or French nails should be used for nailing the bars to the rafters, and when nailing them care should be taken to avoid the rebate. The glass should be laid edge to edge, and if it be cut true, so that the edges of adjacent panes meet throughout their length, moisture will not enter. If, however, the glass is not cut true it should be lapped, making the laps towards the south or west, or a strip of glass 2 inches wide may be laid over the joints.

817 *Simplex Lead Glazing* We now arrive at the last system of dry glazing that will be described here, and which, from its great simplicity, as its name indicates, appears to be the best and most perfect medium of its kind that has yet been introduced. It is manufactured on Mr Albert Smith's system by Messrs Grover and Co., Limited, Engineers, etc, Britannia Works, Wharf Road, City Road, London,. In Fig. 399 a section of the lead strip itself is shown full size, from which it appears that the lead is first folded back over itself until the outer portions meet, and that these are then brought against each other in an upright position, so as to form a **T**-bar inverted or turned upside down, and as far as the manufacturers are concerned this is all, for the strips may be bought at the cost of about 4d. per foot run, and nailed down to sash bars by the builder with wrought copper nails, of which sufficient for nailing down 100 feet of lead strip are supplied for 1s. A wooden tool for dressing down the lead on the glass is always sent free of charge. The mode of making the sash bars and laying in the glass is shown in Fig. 400, in which a section of the

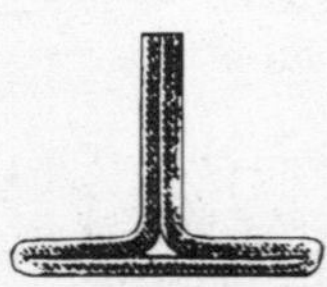

FIG. 399 *Section of strip*

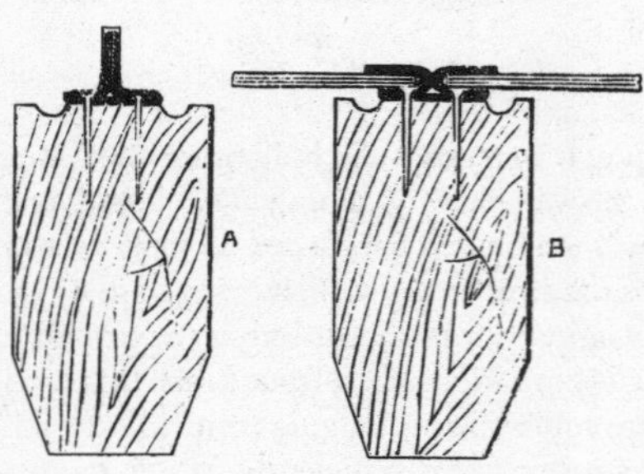

FIG. 400 *Section of strip in original form attached to sash bar (A), and then turned down over the glass (B). Half full size*

sash bar with the lead nailed on is represented at A, half full size, and the way in which the lead is turned over the glass, when placed in position, at B. The shape of the sash bar in the lower part may be altered and moulded according to taste, but the upper part on which the lead is nailed should be perfectly level, with the exception of a groove run along each edge to carry off any moisture that may make its way thither and run down the side of the bar and cause drip if there were no grooves. The copper tacks with which the lead is nailed down to the wood are ¾ inch in length, and the angles of the strips should be payed with thick white lead paint before being dressed down on the glass with the wooden tool which, as it has been said, is supplied for this purpose. In Fig. 401 the adaptation of the strips for glazing upright work, as in vertical sashes, doors, windows, and the ends of glass houses, is shown. The diagram, which is half full size, needs no further explanation. The panes of glass may be lapped or not according to pleasure, but when ordering strips it is necessary to say whether or not the glass is to be lapped, and to mention the thickness of glass that it is proposed to use. To this must be added the lengths of strips required, and the number of strips to each length. The strips, if necessary, can be made 18 feet in length without a joint. The strips can be used for securing the glass in the end bars, and, if required, Simplex capping can be supplied to cover the ridge of the roof, and render it perfectly secure against the intrusion of wet.

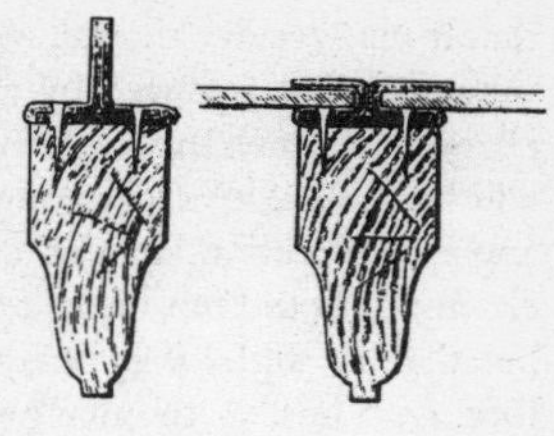

FIG. 401 *Adaptation of strip for upright work in doors, ends, sashes, etc*

818 The advantages claimed for the Simplex Lead Glazing are as follows: 1, No putty is used nor outside painting required, and, externally, nothing but glass and lead are exposed to the action of the weather, which has the effect of reducing the cost of outside maintenance to a minimum; 2, Although no putty is used, the work is airtight, a quality so desirable, and even absolutely necessary, in glass structures in which fumigating must be sometimes resorted to, and which are used for forcing; 3, Repairs of accidental breakages can be easily effected, as there are no fastenings or screws to remove at any time, and no old and hard putty to hack out; and 4, It is equally applicable, as it has been shown, to sloping roofs and upright fronts, sides, and ends of glazed houses.

819 *Inclination of Roofs of Glazed Structures* In the construction of a conservatory or greenhouse, the pitch of the glazed roof, or angle of elevation which the roof forms with a horizontal plane passing through the wall plate to the back of the house in a lean-to, or from wall-plate to wall-plate on the sides in a span-roof house, is an item which requires the attention of the builder. It is desirable that the plants should be as near the light as possible, because the further they are from the glass, the medium through which the light has to pass, the less effective is the action of the light on the foliage, and, vice versa, the nearer the plants are to the glass the more effective the action of the light, because it has less space through which to pass before it reaches them and exercises its influence on them. It is further desirable that the angle of elevation of the roof should be so regulated that it may receive the full force of the sun's rays at that time of the year when they are most required by the plants or fruit in the house, according to the purpose to which the house is devoted. Thus, the higher the latitude, the greater will be the angle of elevation required, and the less the latitude the lower the angle of elevation. In this country it is generally accepted that the angle of elevation should not be, or need not be, less than 30°, and not greater than 40°, but that an angle of 45° may be adopted when the house is required for early forcing. Thus, in the diagram given in Fig. 402, in which AB represents the horizontal plane, AC is inclined to AB at an angle of 30°, AD at an angle of 40°, and AE at an angle of 45°; F, G, and H represent the positions of the sun at periods when the sun's rays strike the planes passing through AE, AD, and AC, respectively, at right angles in the dotted lines F, G, and H. The sun's rays, therefore, exert their full force on a roof at an angle of 30°, with the horizon at an earlier period than on a roof with an inclination of 40°, and still earlier than on a roof with an inclination of 30°. Therefore, it is clear that the earlier and later in the year it is desired to obtain the full effect of the sun's rays, the greater must be the angle of inclination of the roof. From the great distance of the sun from the earth, it must be remembered that, practically, the sun's rays strike every point of a sloping roof at exactly the same angle, and that this holds good for every part of the lines AC, AD, and AE in Fig. 402, as well as for the points on which the sun's rays are represented as falling.

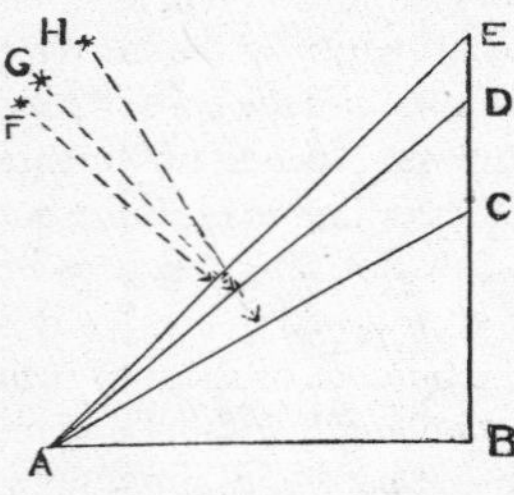

FIG. 402 *Angle of inclination for roofs of greenhouses*

In dealing with the question of the angle of elevation for the roofs of glazed structures, Thompson, in his *Gardener's Assistant*, makes the following remarks with reference to the roofs of lean-to houses. He says: 'As the slope of the roof is dependent on the relative dimensions of the house, and *vice versa*, the following table, which has been constructed to show by inspection the angle of elevation rendered necessary by various dimensions, will prove useful. To use it, look for the width of the house, say 15 feet, and at top for the number of feet by which the back wall exceeds the front wall in height, say 12, and where the two columns intersect will be found 38° 40′, the angle of elevation corresponding with that width of house and height of back wall above the front.' In the table, however, the height of elevation will be found to be 39°, as to render the table as concise as possible degrees only have been given, and where the minutes in Thompson's table are less than 30, or half a degree, they have been omitted, and where more than 30, the number of degrees has been increased by 1. The table is, therefore, approximate only, but sufficiently close for all practical purposes.

Thompson further adds: 'In latitude 54°' – which is about the latitude of York, and about the central latitude of the British Isles – 'the angle of roof may be as high as 74°, or as low as 34°, without the transmission of light being materially affected. Therefore, between these limits we may choose any angle, according as the structure is intended for dwarf or tall plants.' Wilkinson's rule for the construction of a house with an inclination or slope to which the sun's rays shall be perpendicular at any given period of the year, as given in the *Transactions of the Horticultural Society*, Vol. 1, page 162, is as follows: 'Make the angle contained between the back wall of the house and its roof equal to the complement of the latitude of the place, plus or minus the sun's declination for the day on which we wish his rays to strike perpendicularly. From the vernal to the autumnal equinox, the declination is to be added; from the autumnal to the vernal it must be subtracted.' Thompson prefers to find the angle of elevation between the slope of the roof and the horizon instead of the angle between the slope of the roof and the back wall of the house, shown by the angles ACB, ADB, and AEB in Fig. 402, and to do this, he says, 'it is merely necessary to *subtract* the sun's declination from the latitude between the vernal and autumnal equinox, and *add* it between the autumnal and vernal.'

Width of	Height of back wall above front wall in feet													
House	2	3	4	5	6	7	8	9	10	11	12	13	14	15
5 feet	22°	31°	39°	45°	50°	54°	58°	61°	63°	66°	67°	69°	71°	72°
6 feet	18°	27°	34°	40°	45°	49°	53°	56°	59°	61°	63°	65°	67°	68°
7 feet	16°	23°	30°	36°	41°	45°	49°	52°	55°	58°	60°	62°	63°	65°
8 feet	14°	21°	27°	32°	37°	41°	45°	48°	51°	54°	56°	58°	60°	62°
9 feet	13°	18°	24°	29°	33°	38°	42°	45°	48°	51°	53°	55°	57°	59°
10 feet	11°	17°	22°	27°	31°	35°	39°	42°	45°	48°	50°	52°	54°	56°
11 feet	10°	15°	20°	25°	29°	32°	36°	39°	42°	45°	47°	50°	51°	54°
12 feet	9°	14°	18°	23°	27°	30°	34°	37°	40°	43°	45°	48°	49°	51°
13 feet	9°	13°	17°	21°	25°	28°	32°	35°	38°	40°	42°	45°	47°	49°
14 feet	8°	12°	16°	20°	23°	27°	30°	33°	36°	38°	41°	43°	45°	47°
15 feet	8°	11°	15°	18°	22°	25°	28°	31°	34°	36°	39°	41°	43°	45°
16 feet	7°	11°	14°	17°	21°	24°	27°	29°	32°	34°	37°	39°	41°	43°
17 feet	7°	10°	14°	16°	19°	22°	25°	28°	30°	33°	35°	37°	39°	41°
18 feet	6°	9°	13°	16°	18°	21°	24°	27°	29°	31°	33°	36°	38°	40°
19 feet	6°	9°	12°	15°	18°	20°	23°	25°	28°	30°	32°	34°	36°	38°
20 feet	6°	9°	11°	14°	17°	19°	22°	24°	27°	29°	31°	33°	35°	37°

820 *Ventilation of Glazed Houses* With reference to ventilation, or the admission of fresh air into greenhouses, etc., and the facilitation of escape of vitiated air that has been deprived of its oxygen and impregnated with carbon evolved from plants, the great point seems to lie in the proper placing of the apertures necessary for these purposes. Of course, in summer, when the heat is intense, and the air comparatively still, every part of the house that will open may be opened with impunity, but at other times of the year ventilation must be effected with judgment. Draught is as harmful to plants as to human beings, but draught must inevitably occur if, in a span-roof house, vertical sashes are put open on opposite sides, or if, in a lean-to house, the door is

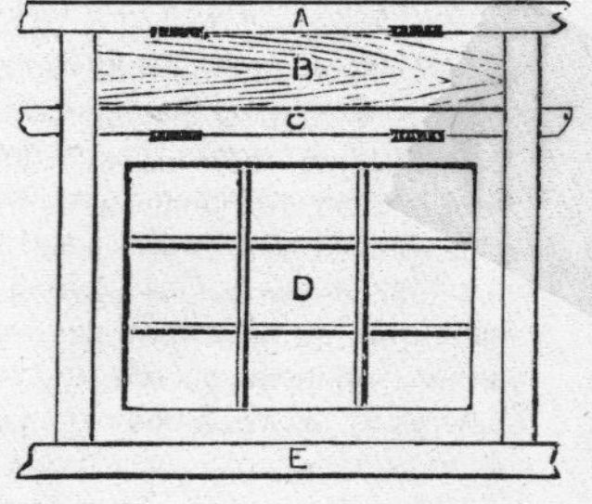

FIG. 403 *Greenhouse ventilation by ventilators under wall plate*

opened at one end and sashes are also put open in the end opposite. It is important, then, never to have apertures opened on opposite sides or in opposite ends at one and the same time, *on the same level*, except in summer, and it is furthermore desirable to have openings for ventilation as high as possible in all parts of the house – that is to say, immediately under the wall plate at the top of the containing walls and in the highest part of the roof; narrow and extending from end to end of a house, rather than to have hinged sashes from wall plate to sill, which let in the air in a considerable volume, and permits it to impinge directly on the plants and the pots in which they are growing.

821 It is unnecessary to look very far for good reasons to support this theory Hot air is light and will always ascend, having suffered expansion by becoming warmer. Cold air, on the contrary, is heavier, and will find its way downwards, pressing the hotter air upwards, as it makes its way into the house. Entering then through apertures immediately below the wall plate, it diffuses itself throughout the lower part of the house without blowing directly on the plants, and it forces the heated and vitiated air upwards, until it finds means of exit in raised sashes in the highest point of the roof, or through a lantern constructed for ventilation along the ridge of the house, and made in such a manner that the vertical sashes which form its sides may be opened, or the sloping lights which constitute its top. This is, without doubt, the proper mode of ventilating, and should be carefully followed in the construction of every glazed structure, and especially in those intended for greenhouses or hothouses. Let those who build greenhouses hang the vertical lights on hinges so that they may be opened at pleasure if they will, but at the same time let the fronts or the sides of the house, as the case may be, be so constructed that it be possible to afford ventilation by a series of narrow openings placed immediately under the wall plate and over the hanging vertical sash. Fig. 403 will show, although in a somewhat exaggerated form, what is meant In this, A is the wall plate, to which the ventilator, B, is hung by means of hinges, C is a rail interposed between the ventilator, B, and the vertical light, D, and to this rail the latter is attached by means of hinges. E is the sill intervening between the lights and the brickwork or boarding below. By adopting this mode of construction, ventilation can be secured at any time by opening B, while in the heat of summer the fullest possible amount of air may be admitted by setting open both the ventilator and the light below it.

Support is given to this theory by the observations made on this all-important subject by a writer in *Gardening Illustrated*, who says: "The object of ventilation is to secure a free exchange of air between the inside and the outside of the house, in order that the air in the house may not become stagnant, over-dried, and overcharged with the vapours and gases exhaled from the plants and from the heating apparatus employed, all of which will act to the detriment of the growing plants. The air of the greenhouse will, on principles well known, be always by day rather warmer, and during the sunshine very much warmer, than the air outside, and the warmest air will rise to the top of the house. There is, therefore, always a bed of foul air lying along the ridge of the greenhouse, whether lean-to or span-roofed, which it is the primary function of good ventilation to remove thoroughly. This can only be done effectually by an opening along the whole length of the roof, by which the hot air will continually and freely pass off. This it will do when there is free admission for the cooler and heavier external air lower down in the house; and this latter is the function of front ventilation. This, I believe, is best effected by an opening also along the whole length of the house, but by no means extending down the whole front sash. On a sunny day, the 'dark heat',' as it is technically called, cannot pass freely through the glass roof, but heats it, and this in turn heats intensely the air in contact with the glass, and unless the air be changed by being kept constantly in motion, it will become so intensely heated as to dry and scorch all leaves which extend near enough to the roof to enter this heated layer. If, on the other hand, we secure a sharp draught along the whole surface of the glass, we shall entirely prevent the formation of this layer, and the air next the glass will not be hotter than that in the rest of the house, even when the stratum of moving air is only a few inches thick; while the air heated by contact with the interior walls and stages, etc., will rise up slowly and join this current along the roof. But will not the plants there be in a thorough draught? That it is my first purpose to avoid, and for this reason the openings top and bottom should never exceed 6 inches in width. This will not affect injuriously even plants trained on the roof, which should never be so near the glass as this. I am sure, two such openings extending along the whole length will be ample to secure perfect ventilation, even in a large house. The opening of the whole front sash, with only limited open lights above, creates a large amount of draught not confined to the roof, and acts injuriously on all plants on the stages near the open sash. This it does, both by unduly drying the earth in their pots to the great danger of small roots, which seek the surface of the porous pots, and also by increasing unduly transpiration (or vegetable perspiration) from the leaves themselves."

The writer then continues with an account of his practical experience in the matter as follows: 'I have long had these views as to ventilation, but have only lately had an opportunity of testing them. Three years ago (1882) I planned a small greenhouse (18 feet by 8 feet) ventilated on the plan described above, but was overruled by my builder and professional garden adviser, getting instead the customary two sash windows below and two above. The result has been that the plants standing opposite the lower sashes have been dried up constantly, while the part of the roof away from the roof sashes gets very deficient ventilation. Last summer (1884) I required to build a new house somewhat larger, and having spare time on my hands I undertook to be my own architect and builder. It is a lean-to, 8 feet wide, 4 feet 6 inches high in front, and about 8 feet at the back. The front I boarded (the whole structure being wood and glass) up to the height of 2 feet 3 inches. On this is a glass sash of 20 inches deep, and above this a sash, opening 5 inches wide, made in four divisions, each 6 feet long, with a 5-inch deal board hinged on to the upper plate, which forms the whole front ventilation and is movable by irons inside. The back is a repetition of the front, except that the glass sash there rests on the top of a wall about 6 feet high. In some of the hot days of autumn I found that when all ventilators were open the temperature inside was even and pleasant and hardly in excess of that outside. Throughout the autumn (from October 1 [1884] to January 20 [1885]), I had the house filled, and in the early part of that period overcrowded, with chrysanthemums, which remained healthy and flowered very well, only one about Christmas showing any trace of mildew, which disappeared of its own accord on removing the plant to a less crowded position.'

822 *Tackle or Ventilators* When ventilators have to be opened and closed one by one, it is manifest that if the ventilation be as complete and thorough as possible, it will take much time to complete the operation going from one to the other, or, on the other hand, if the lights or shutters that will open and shut are restricted in number, the ventilation will by no means be so perfect as it ought to be. It is desirable that every light in the sides of a span-roof house, or in the front of a lean-to house, should open, and the ventilating lights in the ridge of any

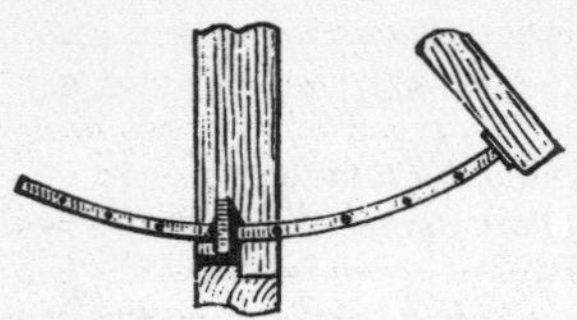

FIG. 404 *Stay for greenhouse light*

house, whether lean-to or span-roof, should extend from end to end. For narrow shutters to be opened one by one, it is sufficient that they be hinged at the bottom, so that they will fall downwards and outwards, and require no stay. They are secured at top by means of buttons when closed. For shutters or lights hinged in this manner and opening inwards, stays must be used, but it is desirable to avoid this mode of opening, unless it be in the case of small narrow shutters whose width is not so great as to prevent putting them down to their fullest extent. Lights and shutters in the front or sides of a house hinged at the top and opening outwards must be secured by stays. Of these, there are many varieties, the most common being a bar attached to an eye secured to the sash, and pierced with holes, fitting over a point attached to the sill or side, so as to permit of opening the window to a greater or less extent, as may be necessary. Another and more convenient variety of this kind of stay is found in a curved piece of iron forming the arc of a circle, and attached by one end to the sash. This iron works in a slot in another piece of iron screwed to the sill, and is held, when the light is opened, by a pin thrust through one of the holes with which it is perforated and through corresponding holes in the iron in which it works. The principle of this kind of stay is shown in Fig. 404. The simple stay formed by a long hook, attached to the framing by one eye, and having its point turned at right angles to its length, to fall into another eye screwed into the light, needs only a passing mention, because by its means a light can only be set open at one width, namely, the length of the stay. For lights that open in the roof, it is obvious that stays such as these cannot be reached, because the lights themselves are out of reach, and the only available plan by which these can be actuated is by a system of cords, with or without pulleys, as the case may be, the cords when not handled for the purpose of opening or closing the light being fastened round a hook like those used for fastening the cords of Venetian blinds.

823 *Messenger's Ventilating Tackle* Now, as it has been said, it is clear to all who consider the matter that a great waste of time must of necessity be occasioned by dealing with every single light for ventilation in front or sides of a house and the ridge; that the apparatus is far from handy and convenient, and in all probability necessitates interference with the plants, and sometimes injury to them, whenever it is desirable to open or close the lights; and that, through want of care in fixing the bars or properly fastening the ropes, a light may fall and cause breakage of glass, and consequently damage to the plants if the broken glass cannot be immediately replaced. It is preferable to have machinery by which not a single light only, but a whole series of lights, from one end of a house to another, can be closed or opened, as the case may be, both speedily and securely. And here Messrs Messenger and Co. step in and offer us machinery, or, as they prefer to call it, ventilating tackle, by which by a mere turn of the hand a whole series of lights in a large house can be opened and closed at once in a few seconds with perfect safety. Indeed, they have several systems of ventilating apparatus,

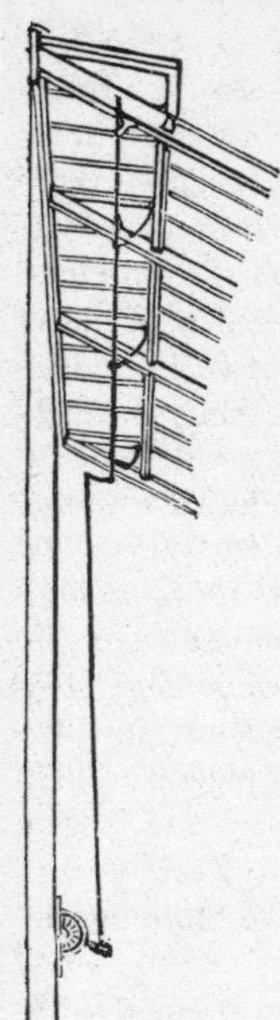

FIG. 405 *Lever tackle applied to lights in ridge of glazed house*

such as the lever tackle, the screw rod tackle, and the chain tackle, each of which has its peculiarities which render it more particularly suitable for the case to which it is applied. In Figs. 405 and 406 the lever tackle is shown, actuating the ventilating lights in the ridge of a house in the former, and in the latter the side lights of a span-roof house or the front lights of a lean-to house. In these, a bar, AB, extending along the entire length of the lights, serves as a fulcrum or centre on which work small bent levers, C, D, E, F, whose other ends are attached to the lights to be actuated. The end of the lever, CA, is extended to G, and connected by the rod H with a handle, K, working in a rack, L. When the handle K is pressed downwards and towards the operator, the end G of the lever is drawn in the same direction, and the end C is pressed outwards. The pressure outwards is communicated to the light through the other arm of the bent lever that is fastened to the light, and the consequence is that all the lights are thrust outwards and opened in a moment. On the contrary, when the handle in the rack L is pushed from the operator, the end G of the lever is pushed outwards, the end C is brought in, and the light is closed. Thus it is plain that a slight movement of the hand, which can be made in a second or two, will open or close all the lights in a row in the same space of time and at the same time. Moreover, the space at which the lights are placed open can be regulated at pleasure. The apparatus can be applied to every light in a row, or only to alternate lights if preferred. For lengths from 8 feet to 20 feet the cost of the apparatus ranges from 22s. 6d. to 36s., and for lengths from 20 to 32 feet, for which a stronger make is required, it ranges from 42s. to 60s. The apparatus can be applied to existing houses.

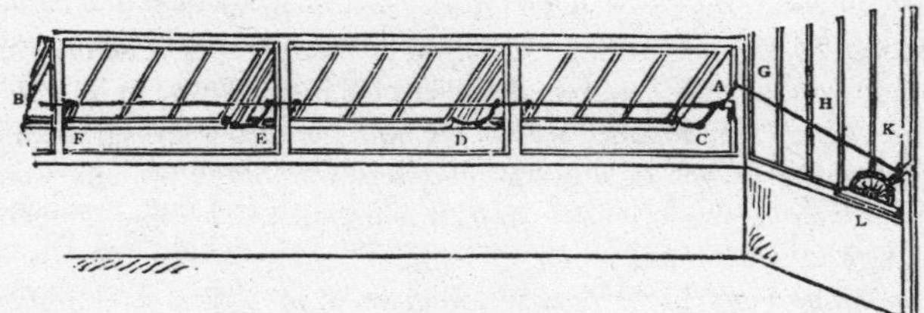

FIG. 406 *Lever tackle applied to front lights or side lights of house*

824 *Warming and Heating of Glazed Structures* In no department of industrial art, perhaps, has more ingenuity been exercised than in applying heat, whether it be to houses or horticultural buildings: stoves, furnaces, and boilers, endless in form and principle – hot air, hot water, and steam – have, in turn, been adopted, approved, and superseded; tubular furnaces, tubular boilers, in an endless variety of forms, have been invented, sometimes with most satisfactory, at other times with doubtful results; and a very close approximation to the truth in all probability will be found in the statement that while all have had, and have, their advocates in the gardening world, no mode of heating is so universally approved as hot water circulating in iron pipes, with bottom heat supplied from tanks heated by the same means. But even to this cleanly and convenient form of heating, however, there are objections: something is wanted that shall simulate the ammoniacal gaseous qualities of the vapour arising from hot dung, in which plants seem so to revel; and various expedients are adopted by which this is partly attained. At Trentham the experiment was tried of introducing into the hot water tanks a mixture of pigeon's dung, in the proportion of an ounce to a gallon of water, to supply this desideratum to vegetation; others, again, tried to attain the end desired by watering the pots and beds with manured water, in varying proportions, according to individual judgment. Mr Beaton suggested the application of vapour impregnated with tobacco or sulphur for the destruction of insects; while Mr McIntosh recommended guano, pigeon's dung, and urine, used in the same manner by means of evaporating pans attached to the pipes, in order to attain the fumes of the old-fashioned dung bed, 'so pre-eminently valuable for the restoration of sickly plants and for promoting the vigorous growth of healthy ones'.

825 We are indebted to the Dutch for the earliest edifices warmed with artificial heat, as for initiation into many other gardening secrets. Their early trade with the East developed a taste for flowers as early as the fifteenth century; and they soon found that their cold, moist atmosphere was unfitted for the successful culture of the delicate plants even of the Levant. They erected houses for their reception, therefore, which they heated with the common earthenware stove of the country, equalising the heat by earthenware pipes carried round the room. In course of time other countries adopted the idea – in our own country by means of open fires outside the building, with connecting flues going round the house inside the walls; and there are not wanting, even now, gardeners who assert that as good crops of grapes were and are grown by these flued walls as can be produced by the modern innovations of hot water pipes. The invention and application was, however, a great discovery for horticulture; and, accordingly, the names which are identified with it are both numerous and eminent in their art. Space, however, will only permit of description of the principles on which the system acts, and a brief mention of a few of the leading appliances for heating now in general use.

826 *Heating by Flues* In the description given in preceding sections of a small and useful greenhouse suitable for amateurs and professional gardeners in a limited way of business, it has been said that the modes of heating are three in number – namely, by brickwork flues, by hot air, and by hot water. Under the method of heating by flues the plan adopted was not unlike the mode adopted for heating the back kitchen copper, to accomplish which a fire is kindled in a small grate immediately under the copper itself, and a strong in-draught being set up, the flame and heat is drawn round the copper, between it and the walls of the structure in which it is set, and through the narrow passage, or flue, with which the cavity communicates with the chimney of a grate not far from it, generally speaking. The flue being narrow is soon choked with the soot deposited by the smoke as it passes through it, and frequently requires cleansing. The same kind of thing goes on in heating by flues in greenhouses, but on a larger scale. A long, but comparatively small and narrow, furnace was erected in a small room, or stoke hole, contiguous to the greenhouse, but outside it, and the heat arising from the combustion of fuel produced within it was drawn into the flues that were made round the house, either in the walls themselves, or under beds and tanks for the purpose of heating the house. But, like the copper flues, these soon choked, and were obliged to be cleared at frequent intervals. The mode of forming flues is sufficiently understood without further explanation. It was an imperfect system of heating at the best, and one that few will care to adopt now. It was necessary that the brickwork should be of the very best, and that the courses that formed the flues should be set in good genuine mortar, if not in cement, for if any joints were defective, the sulphurous exhalations from the coal or coke that was used for fuel would find its way through them into the house, and pervade it, much to the detriment of the plants that were within it.

827 *Heating by Hot Air or by Radiation of Heat* Heating by flues was in reality nothing more than heating by hot air, or communicating warmth throughout a chamber of any kind or size by radiation of heat, for the air that entered the furnace was heated therein, and drawn in its heated state through the flues from the furnace to the point of exit, yielding up its heat to the surrounding brickwork in its passage through the flues, the brickwork in its turn communicating the heat it had absorbed to the air in the chamber as it came in contact with those parts of the wall through which the flues; an. Heating by hot air again, or heating by radiation, is only a form of heating by flues, for the heated air is drawn into pipes or some receptacle constructed to receive and hold it, and its heat passes through the conducting material of which the pipes or receptacle are made into the air which is in the immediate vicinity of either the one or the other, and which by rarefaction is immediately set in circulation. There are various appliances for heating by means of hot air, but it is desirable to describe a few of the cheaper and simpler forms only, for the larger and more elaborate appliances, such as stoves in which solid fuel is burnt, and which consume their own smoke, or are credited with doing so, are expensive to buy and difficult to maintain in action, and as there would be but few, if any, that would care to buy them when more efficient modes of heating are at their command for about the same outlay, space would be wasted in enumerating and describing them. It will be enough to say that under this category – namely, appliances which give warmth by heated air – may be classed all stoves which are heated with fuel of any kind, solid, fluid, or gaseous, but which do not actuate any boiler, but merely give forth dry heat, or, in other words, cause warmth by radiation of heat. Generally speaking, the fumes given forth by the metal – usually wrought iron – of which they are made, are unwholesome and oppressive through their but too perceptible heat. The fuel will often go out when it is most required, and their use, where solid fuel is burnt, engenders much dirt and dust. When a stove pipe is attached to a stove by which smoke and all products of combustion are carried from the stove to the chimney into which it may be led, or to the point whence they escape into the open air, wherever it may be, the heat emanating from the pipe soon deprives the air in the house of all its moisture, and in order to prevent harm to the plants as far as possible from its dryness, it is necessary to keep up the balance, or endeavour to do so, by putting water into a vessel that is brought into contact with the smoke pipe or the stove itself, in order to cause the evaporation of the fluid so that it may restore to the air the moisture that has been drawn from it, a plan which is seldom thoroughly effective, always troublesome, and like nothing so much as that very peculiar process which is known as 'robbing Peter to pay Paul'.

828 With regard to stoves in which solid fuel is burnt, the moral to be derived from that which has just been said is that it is better to avoid all contrivances and appliances of this kind that possess no flues, or which have pipes that convey the smoke and heated air through the house, because fumes are inevitably given forth by both which are highly deleterious and destructive to plant life. It is better to avoid all stoves for heating that possess no flues, and therefore no means of escape into the open air for the products of combustion, if it is wished to keep and maintain plants in health; and if it is absolutely necessary to have any kind of stove burning solid fuel that gives off dry heat, take care to have it outside the house, or, in other words, not in the chamber in which the plants are kept, and see that the joints of the pipes which must of necessity be carried through the house are perfectly secured at the joints with good luting of red lead and oil, so that no crevice or opening may exist in them for the escape of the fumes that pass through the pipe. To prevent fumes from the heating of the pipe itself is most difficult, if not impossible. The best way to do it is to discard the metal piping altogether, and to cause the pipe that carries the heat and smoke through the house to be constructed of pipes of earthenware or stoneware, such as are used for drains, for these fictile pipes are excellent conductors of heat, and may be secured at the joints quite as easily, if not more so, as stove pipes made of sheet iron.

829 Further, as a fixed and settled rule, it is better, unless there be absolute necessity for it from some cause or other which there is no getting over, to avoid having any appliance that is used for generating heat, whatever it may be, in the same part of the house in which the plants are kept. Let the heat generator be always *outside* the plant chamber, in a convenient place where it can be seen to when necessary, and where there is no chance of its emitting fumes which may do injury to the plants. Never have any furnace, whatever may be the heating medium, and whatever may be the means by which heat is imparted to the plant chamber – that is to say, whether by hot air or hot water – within the plant chamber itself, but without it, in what we may call the furnace room or stoke hole, after the manner of the furnace that was used for heating flues in brickwork, which was chiefly troublesome on account of the frequent attention that was requisite in order to maintain the fires and keep them going. Given a heating apparatus outside the plant chamber, and you may use whatever fuel you like –

gas, mineral oil, coke, or coal; that is to say, any apparatus contrived for burning any of these fuels, to use a term that will apply to them collectively – that will do the work and duty that is expected of it in a complete and thorough manner.

830 In the strictures made above on the use of metal pipes for the conveyance of heat, it must be understood that they apply to wrought-iron pipes, or pipes of thin metal, that are used for the conveyance of dry heat, and not to pipes that are made of cast iron, and used as ducts for hot water, Such pipes as these, through which hot water is caused to circulate, seldom, if ever, give forth any smell, and when they do the cause will be found in all probability in some material that has been applied to their external surface, such as paint, Brunswick black, or some varnish for metal, under the idea of imparting a neat appearance to them. The best application for iron pipes, especially those of cast iron, is black lead, well rubbed in and polished, for a surface thus treated is rendered all the more effective for the radiation of heat.

831 We may now pass on to a consideration of some of the minor contrivances and less elaborate means for heating with hot air that are so eagerly sought after by persons having cases in windows of some size, frames used as plant protectors, and small conservatories into which it is desirable to prevent frost from entering. Even a small petroleum lamp or two placed in a small glazed structure of this kind has been found of service, but there is always danger from the escape of smoke from the chimney if the wick is not carefully regulated, and the admission of air to the flame such as to procure complete combustion of the oil. There are many so-called stoves in which petroleum is burnt, but as in the generality of them the heated air from the lamp is allowed to pass into and heat a metal casing in which the lamp is placed, there is the smell that is the natural consequence of confining hot air in a receptacle of thin sheet metal. The contrivances for giving forth heat that are described in the following sections seem to be the best of the kind that have yet been produced for heating with hot air, and may be looked on as being the leading types of all heat generators of their class.

832 *Joseph Brother's Oil Stove* It has been said that two or three small petroleum lamps set about in different parts of a small cold house will raise the temperature of the air sufficiently to prevent the entrance of frost. The question of the utility of lamps of this kind, under the circumstances, lies in the manner in which combustion is effected in them. If the wick is regulated so nicely as not to liberate more petroleum than can be entirely consumed, and if there be free admission of air *below* the flame so as to supply sufficient oxygen for the maintenance of the flame at its proper pitch, and to insure as complete and thorough combustion of the oil as possible, the lamps will be useful, but if the combustion is not perfect, or, in other words, if the wick gets out of order, and the lamp smokes, it will do as much harm as good, if not more. Metal stoves heated with mineral oils give off unpleasant fumes, and soon deprive the air in the plant chambers in which they are used of the necessary moisture, unless evaporation is kept up from water in a little vessel placed on top of them. There is a little oil stove made by Messrs Joseph Brothers, 271 Liverpool Road, London, with a conical metal chimney, that has a 2½-inch wick, which is as useful for a small greenhouse as any that are made. The lamp itself is sold at 3s.

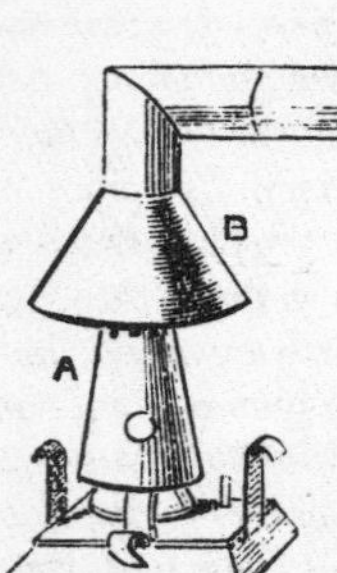

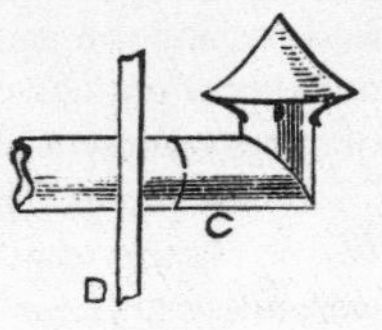

FIG. 407 *Method of catching and conveying away products of combustion from mineral oil lamp*

6d., and the wick at 8d. per yard. To use it effectually it is desirable to intercept the products of combustion as they rise from the chimney in a metal cone or funnel-shaped receptacle, and to let them pass through a pipe proceeding from this receptacle into the open air. By this means no fumes arising from combustion will be given forth, but there will be a smell proceeding from the heated metal which is unavoidable in any case. All appliances of this kind should be treated in the same way, and the products of combustion collected in a hood or cowl, and passed into the open air through a pipe. The mode of doing this will be understood from Fig. 407, in which A is the lamp, B the cowl that intercepts the products of combustion, C the pipe passing through the wall of the house, represented by D, and terminating in an elbow joint, with a cap over it to prevent down draught and the entrance of rain.

A writer in *Gardening Illustrated* thus relates his experience with this identical lamp, and it is introduced here, because it will be interesting to many readers who have small glass houses, and are puzzled what to do to keep out the frost in winter, or at all events to mitigate its severity. He says: "I will give particulars of a little contrivance I have been very successful with for heating my small greenhouse, which is a lean-to, 8 feet long and 6 feet wide. I bought a small oil stove, for which I paid 3s. 6d., also five 2-feet lengths of 3-inch sheet-iron pipe at 10d. per length, and two elbow joints at 8d. each. The stove is different from Rippingille's, as it runs narrower at the top, which has a movable iron ornament. I place the stove at one end near the front of the house, having previously removed the iron ornament, and thus leaving the top of the stove open, 2½ inches in diameter. Over this I place one elbow joint, with three lengths of pipe along the front of the house, at the end of which I fix the other elbow with the other two lengths of pipe. This goes along the end of the house. These pipes carry the heat all round instead of its being in one place, as it usually is with oil stoves. I suspend the pipes with stout wire hooks, which cost 2d., to the lattice stage above. Three or four of these will be sufficient. The stove, when filled, holds about one pint of oil, which will burn for 12 hours. The burner is 2 inches wide, and I can raise the temperature 12° above the outside. Over the end of the pipe I put a flower pot (a 54) which is about 4 inches across the top, and just fits the pipe nicely. This prevents the heat rising and injuring the plants immediately above the outlet, and as there are no fumes that will hurt the plants, there is no need to carry the pipe outside, as you would thereby lose a lot of heat. I have a blind on rollers (outside) to shade the house in summer, and in very severe weather I pull this over the house as an additional precaution. I should think that in a house of larger dimensions, pipes arranged in the same manner, with an elbow at the other end, and another stove placed under it, would answer very well, as, if the weather was not very severe, you need only keep one stove alight. I always take every favourable opportunity to give air, and if the stove is kept clean there will be no smell whatever."

To this it may be added that it is scarcely possible that heated metal should do otherwise than give forth some smell, and that it is safer, even though there be a loss of heat, to carry the end of the pipe into the open air, shielded in the manner shown in Fig.

407. When two stoves are used, the junction of the pipes for each stove should be effected by means of a **T** joint, by means of which another length of pipe may proceed into the open air from the third orifice at right angles to the other two that connect the pipes from the stoves. It is always better to be on the safe side, even though the means of procedure adopted involve a little loss.

833 *Gillingham's Heat Radiator* The appliance for warming a glass structure that has been described above is, perhaps, the most simple form of apparatus that can be contrived for heating with air warmed by its passage through a lamp in which mineral oil or petroleum is burnt. A more elaborate contrivance for gas or oil lamp, which is said to exhibit 'the true and scientific mode of utilising heat and separating the product', and to be 'based on Nature's own laws', is offered in Gillingham's Heat Radiator, invented by the well-known maker of surgical mechanism to replace lost limbs or supply deficient action of the muscles, Mr James Gillingham, of Chard. The machine consists of a horizontal metal tube, supported on two cylinders, as shown in Fig. 408. The cylinders are placed in trays, and are furnished with two outlet pipes, or product tubes, at a little distance above the bottom. In the centre of the horizontal tube there is a funnel-shaped orifice, below which a lamp or gas burner is placed, suited to the size of the tube above. The air is heated in its passage through the lamp, and ascends into the tube or receiver, where it accumulates, no escape for the heated air being possible, as, being lighter than ordinary unheated air, it is kept by the upward pressure of the surrounding atmosphere from making its way down through the funnel. The warming of the chamber, be it what it may, in which the apparatus is placed, is caused by the current which is set up by the heated tube in the air of the room, the particles when heated rising upward to make room for other particles colder than themselves, which take their place, and rise in their turn, after coming into contact with the receiver, and thus the temperature of the entire body of air in the chamber is gradually raised. The course of the heated air from the lamp into the receiver is shown by arrows. The products of combustion which are heavier than common air are separated from the heated air in the receiver, and fall downwards through the cylinders that support the receiver in a course also indicated by arrows. The trays in which the cylinders stand serve to catch the water that is formed in condensation by the union of the oxygen and hydrogen gases evolved, and the carbonic acid gas is

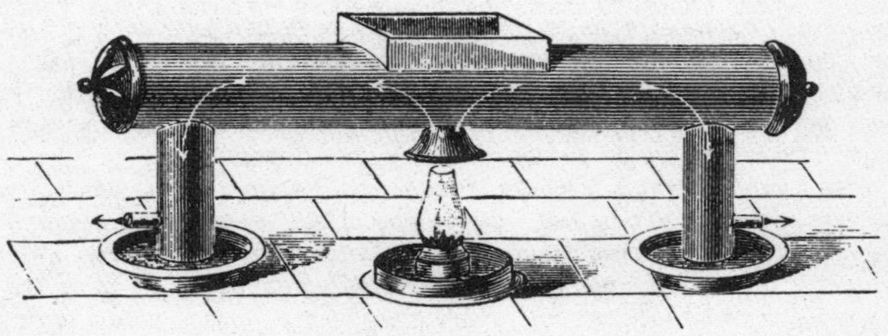

FIG. 408 *Gillingham's heat radiator*

driven out through the small tubes placed near the bottom of the cylinders, its course being also indicated by smaller arrows. If a moist heat is required, an evaporating tray containing water should be placed on the top of the horizontal receiver, in its centre, just over the lamp and opening through which the air enters, as shown in the illustration.

834 The Patent Heat Radiators, or Radiating Heat Generators, as they are sometimes called, are supplied by Messrs Treggon and Co., York Works, Brewery Road, London, and 19 Jewin Street, London, in brass, copper, or iron, at prices ranging from 31s. 6d. upwards, according to size. The cylinders or receivers range in length from 3 feet to 18 feet, and are made in diameters of 4, 4½, 5, and 6 inches. The longer receivers require two lamps. They are supplied with duplex lamp having two metal chimney, a large Cleopatra lamp, or a large oxygen ring gas burner, according to diameter and length of tube or material of which the tube is made. When oil lamps are used with this or any other description of small greenhouse heater, it is necessary to clean them daily, keep them well supplied with oil, and to see that there is always plenty of wick. The lamp must not be started or adjusted until it has done drawing, which should be full ten minutes after it is first lit, or it will smoke. The lamp, or gas burner, whichever is used, should be stood in a tray, and this tray and the stands in which the vertical cylinders of the apparatus are placed should be sponged out daily. Glass chimneys may be used if they are preferred to those of metal. When a gas lamp is used, too much pressure on the burner must be avoided, and a gas regulator should be used. In Gillingham's Oxygen Ring Burner, the button should always be 1 inch above the ring. India rubber connecting tubes should be avoided, and atmospheric burners also, because their use causes great loss of radiant heat and the generation of carbonic oxide. When gas is used, the product should be carried off outside the chamber in product tubes and not allowed to escape, and it must pass off in a rarefied condition, or it will choke the tube. When lamps are used, product tubes are unnecessary, and need not be attached to the apparatus, wherever it may be used

The following notes on the scale of temperature, and the power of Radiating Heat Generators of different sizes, may be useful to readers who may wish to give them a trial. It must be understood that they do not increase the temperature of the chamber in which they are placed to too high a pitch at one time, to fall again to too low a point at another time, but maintain an equable heat and diffuse a soft, genial warmth.

1 A 1-inch Duplex Lamp, or Small No. 1 Oxygen Ring Gas Burner, with 2-inch ring, consuming 7 cubic feet of gas per hour, or less, will serve for a generator from 3 feet to 9 feet long and 4½ inches in diameter, with one supply, or any intermediate length to suit the space in which it is placed, and will be sufficient for a conservatory 10 feet by 8 feet, or even larger, provided there is not too much glass, or for a room 15 feet square, or even larger, if the ceilings are low and the room have a south aspect.

2 A 4-inch Single Wick Cleopatra Lamp, or a No. 2 Oxygen Ring Gas Burner, with 3-inch ring, consuming 10 cubic feet of gas per hour or less, will serve for generators from 4 feet to 9 feet long and 6 inches in diameter. Where 12-feet generators are required, it is better to have two of 6 feet, which can be more conveniently moved from place to place. This lamp or gas burner will be sufficient for a conservatory 15 feet by 10 feet, or even larger, if in a sheltered position, or for rooms 20 feet square, or even larger, if the ceilings are low.

3 A No. 3 Oxygen Ring Burner, with 5-inch ring, burning 4 cubic feet of gas per hour, or less, will serve for a generator 6 feet long and 8 or 10 inches in diameter, and will heat a room 30 feet by 20 feet, containing 600 superficial feet of flooring.

4 Product tubes are not needed in conservatories when oil is used, or in rooms where ordinary ventilation by the usual means is going on, but they are required in conservatories where gas is used, and the products must be allowed to escape in a slightly rarefied condition.

Mr Gillingham, speaking of the experience of those who have used the Generator in conservatories 10 or 12 feet by 8 feet, heated by a duplex lamp, says: "The average temperature was from 35° to 40°, according to situation, with 15° below freezing point outside. The flowers were vigorous, green, and in bloom during the severest frost, and there was no damping off. Why? The temperature was not 70° at night and 30° in the morning, but uniform; the carbonic acid gas given forth from the lamps fed the flowers, and the oxygen given off by the plants fed the lamps."

835 There can be little doubt but that the Radiating Heat Generator is constructed on true principle, and is one of the most effective and useful of all apparatus designed for warming small glazed structures, as by it small conservatories, such as many amateur gardeners possess, can be kept at a uniform temperature at the trifling cost of 2d. per day of 24 hours, or 1s. 2d. per week. The heater requires no attention during that period. Contrivances heated by lamps generally tend to throw burnt and vitiated air into the room, but this heats the air in a room by radiation, and all impurities are deposited in the water automatically condensed. The chief danger lies in any slight imperfection in the apparatus itself which may nullify its utility, and when purchasing one it is desirable to have it tested in every part, with a view of ascertaining its soundness, and therefore fitness for the purpose for which it is required and designed.
For example, a writer in *Gardening Illustrated* complained that although he had closely followed the instructions sent with the Heat Radiator he had not found it possible to maintain an even temperature, the thermometer in the conservatory having fallen below freezing point several times during the winter, and that three times all the ferns and plants in the conservatory, which was 14 feet by 5 feet, and connected with the house, were covered with soot. To this another correspondent replied that he had a greenhouse, 16 feet by 10 feet, full of white chrysanthemums, well-nigh spoiled by a deposit of soot from his Heat Radiator. He found that the cause of this was a minute air hole between the mica window and the copper of the chimney, through which the heat escaped, and also soot from the flame. When a glass chimney was substituted for the defective metal chimney the apparatus worked well enough. He found also that the brass ends of his receiver were burnt through, which was another defect, causing loss of heat, etc. He adds: 'I may mention that the whole apparatus requires a thorough sweeping out two or three times a year, and the water troughs require fresh water once a week.' With these precautions he considers that this kind of stove will always behave in a most exemplary manner.

836 *George's Calorigen* This, as its name implies, is another form of heat generator, but this differs from the Radiating Heat Generator described above, both in its construction and action. The apparatus is contrived so as to admit of oil, gas, or coke being used as the heating power, and is manufactured and

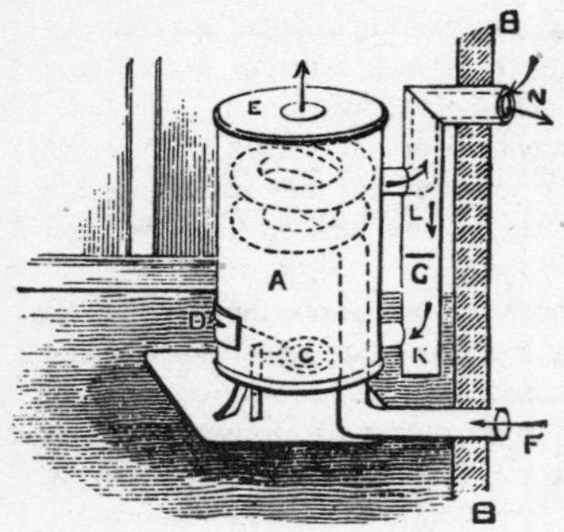

FIG. 409 *George's patent calorigen*

supplied by Messrs, J. F. Farwig and Co., 36 Queen Street, Cannon Street, London. An oil Calorigen 12½ inches in diameter and 25 inches high, and a gas Calorigen 14 inches in diameter and the same in height, cost each £3 3s., but a coke Calorigen 16 inches in diameter and 32 inches high costs double that amount. The construction and action of the apparatus may be readily understood from Fig. 409. In this, A is the Calorigen itself standing in a room, the wall of which, BB, near which it is placed, is shown in section. The heat in the illustration given is supplied from a ring gas burner at C, which is lighted through a door, D. When a lamp is used the form of apparatus is the same, but the door is larger, to admit of the lamp being taken out and replaced at pleasure. The plate at the top of the contrivance is open, and connected with the orifice E, of a coiled pipe, which passes out of it at the bottom and through the wall at F, so that the air enters at F, is warmed in its passage through the pipe, and then escapes in its heated condition into the chamber through E, taking the course shown by the arrows at F and E. At the back of the apparatus is a pipe, G, which is carried through the brickwork, and through its orifice, N, the external air passes in the downward course shown by the arrows, and enters the Calorigen at the small connecting pipe, K, to feed the flame when the burner is lighted. At L is an exit pipe, smaller in diameter than the pipe G, through which it passes to the orifice N forming the means of the escape of the products of combustion into the open air.

837 *Ritchie's Lux Calor* The principle of this stove is somewhat similar to that of the Radiating Heat Generator, although it differs from it in construction, and the apparatus, therefore, will not need any lengthened description. It is so called because it affords light (Latin, *lux*, light) as well as heat or warmth (Latin, *calor*, heat), and is therefore serviceable for illumination as well as heating. Either gas or mineral oil may be burnt in it, and the petroleum lamp or Bunsen burner for gas which is used for it is placed as shown in Fig. 410, in the lower part of the large vertical tube in the centre. On each side of this tube are two smaller ones, into which the heated air, after passing upwards through the central tube to the top of the appliance, is forced by the inrush of air through the bottom and lamp or gas burner into the side tubes where it accumulates. These tubes gradually become heated, and by radiation warm the air of the apartment or conservatory in which the apparatus is placed. The products of combustion, with the exception of the carbonic acid gas, are condensed in

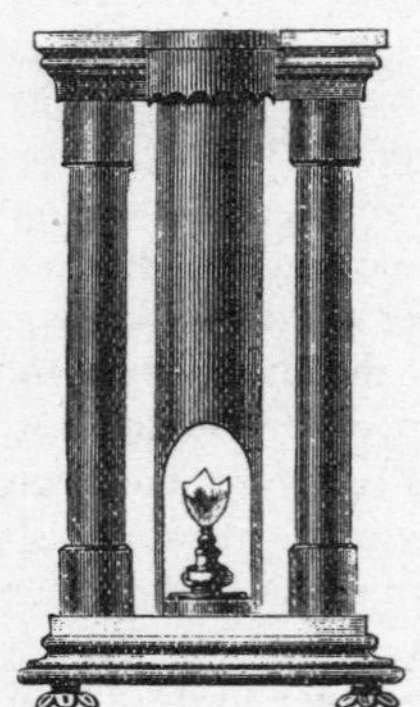

FIG. 410 *Ritchie's lux calor*

the side tubes in the form of water. The great advantage of this heating apparatus lies in the fact that, as its peculiar name implies, it supplies illumination as well as warmth to every apartment in which it may be placed, and that the light afforded, although so near the floor, is sufficient to render everything in the apartment visible. With regard to its capacity for heating, the stove is said to afford sufficient heat to maintain an equal and pleasant temperature in a house about 15 feet long, 10 feet wide, and having an average height of about 6 feet 6 inches, which gives a height of 5 feet in front and 8 feet at back supposing it to be a lean-to, or a height of 5 feet on either side and 8 feet at the ridge supposing it to be a span-roof house. Such houses would have a cubic content of about 1000 square feet.

838 *Heating by Steam* The method of heating glazed horticultural structures by steam was the first advance from the old system of heating by flues. It consisted in the application of steam generated in a boiler, and passed through a steam pipe proceeding from it into chambers placed below the beds into which the plants were plunged or the stages on which they were arranged, or by heating cisterns of water in similar position to the chambers already mentioned, by means of steam injected into pipes that passed through the water in the cisterns, or by allowing the steam to circulate through pipes formed either of earthenware or stoneware or cast iron. When the method was first introduced it was considered superior to that of heating by flues in brickwork, because the heat given forth by the brick flues was a dry heat, while that from pipes, etc., heated by steam was supposed to be a moist heat, and therefore better suited for the encouragement of plant growth. It was found, however, to be an expensive method, and involving more trouble than the mode of heating by the aid of a furnace which was used in connection with brick flues, because the boiler which was required with the furnace involved greater trouble in looking to it, and needed more attention. And for these reasons, although the system was adopted and found to answer well in large establishments, it was never much used for smaller greenhouses and hothouses.

The advantages of heating by steam are thus set forth by Loudon, and may be repeated here with advantage, because, generally speaking, they apply equally to the later and more convenient method of heating by the circulation of hot water through pipes instead of steam. He says: 'Steam affords a simple and effectual mode of heating hothouses, and, indeed, large bodies of air in every description of chamber, for no other fluid is found so convenient as a carrier for heat. Steam was the first improvement on the old mode of heating by flues, and it is still occasionally used, though it has been almost superseded by hot water. The heat given out by vapour differs in nothing from that given out by smoke, though an idea to the contrary prevails among gardeners from the circumstances of some foul air escaping into the house from the flues, especially if these are over-heated or over-watered, and from some vapour issuing from the steam tubes when these are not perfectly secure at the joints. Hence flues are said to produce a burnt or drying heat, and steam tubes a moist or genial heat, and in a popular sense this is correct, for the reasons stated. It is not, however, the genial nature of steam heat which is its chief recommendation for plant habitations, but the equality of its distribution and the distance to which it may be carried. Steam can never heat the tubes, even close to the boiler, above 212°, and it will heat them to the same degree, or nearly so, at the distance of 1000, 2000, or an indefinite number of feet. Hence results the convenience of heating any range or assemblage of hothouses, however great, from one boiler, and the lessened risk of over or insufficient heating at whatever distance the house may be from the fireplace. The secondary advantages of heating by steam are the saving of fuel and labour and the neatness and compactness of the whole apparatus. Instead of a gardener having to attend to a dozen or more fires, he has only to attend to one; instead of ashes and coal and unsightly objects at a dozen or more places in a garden, they are limited to one place; and instead of twelve paltry chimney tops there is only one, which, being necessarily large and high, maybe finished as a pillar, so as to have effect as an object; instead of twelve vomiters of smoke and flakes of soot, the smoke may be burned by using some smoke-consuming furnace. The steam tubes occupy much less space in the house than flues, and require no cleaning; they may often pass under paths where flues would extend too deep; there is no danger of steam not *drawing* or circulating freely, as is often the case with flues, and always when they are too narrow or too wide, or do not ascend from the furnace to the chimney; steam is impelled from the boiler and will proceed with equal rapidity along small tubes or large ones, and descending or ascending. Finally, with steam, insects will be effectually kept under in hothouses with the greatest ease, by merely keeping the atmosphere of the house charged with vapour from the tubes for several hours at a time.'

As a matter of course, the size of the boiler used depended, as in heating with hot water; on the size of the house to be warmed, or rather, the superficial extent of the glass contained in the house, and the following are mentioned by Loudon as the principles on which the sizes of boilers might be calculated for heating by steam: "(1.) For forcing houses under ordinary circumstances, it is found that I square foot of bottom surface of boiler is equivalent to 150 square feet of glass. (2.) Where bottom heat is required, I square foot to 135 square feet of glass. (3.) For greenhouses, 1 square foot is equal to 200 square feet of glass. (4.) For houses that are ill glazed, or placed in an exposed situation, ten or fifteen per cent, may be added to the proportionate surface of the boiler." With reference to furnaces for boilers, it is said that 'the surface of the fire grating should be from one-fourth to one-fifth of the bottom surface of the boiler, according to the strength of the fuel employed'.

839 *Heating by Hot Water* We may now pass on to the consideration of the fourth mode of heating, namely, by the circulation of hot water, which is admitted to be decidedly the best of the four. It will be convenient to take, first of all, the principle of the circulation of hot water in pipes and matters immediately in connection with it, and to follow this with a description of some of the appliances that are used for heating water in order to cause it to circulate through pipes, proceeding from those by means of which this operation is effected on a small scale to the large boilers and apparatus by which hot water is made subservient to the heating of a large greenhouse or forcing house, or even ranges of glazed horticultural structures on a considerable scale. It is manifestly impossible to call attention to, or even to name, every appliance of this kind that may be in the market, but it will be sought to place on record as many as possible, and to select for description from each group one or two that appear to be good representative types of the class to which they belong.

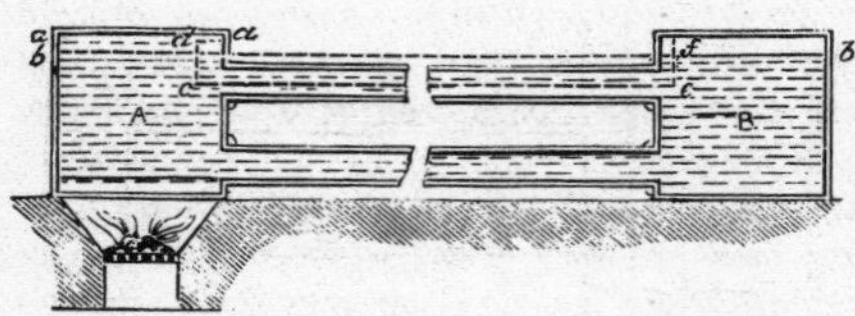

FIG. 411 *Diagram illustrating Tredgold's theory of circulation of hot water*

840 *Principle of Circulation of Hot Water* The principle upon which hot water circulating in pipes is applied to warming houses is that hot water, like heated air, has a tendency to ascend and to fall again as it cools, the denser colder fluid displacing the more rarefied. This principle has been extensively applied to warming public and other large buildings, distance from the furnace and height above the boiler being no obstacle to the circulation of the fluid, the boiler being placed in the basement while a water box is placed at the top of the building, both vessels being closed. The boiler and the water box are connected by two pipes, one of which is called the flow pipe, as by it the water rises or flows from the boiler to the water box, and the other the return pipe, because the water returns through it or descends from the water box to the boiler, and by its greater density displaces a like amount of hotter fluid on the surface. A supply pipe, regulated by the ordinary ball cock, admits cold water into the water box to replace that which has been withdrawn by evaporation, while safety valves, placed on the boiler, guard against too great a pressure from the expansion of the water. This is the principle that is applied in heating glazed horticultural structures by hot water, but as it is seldom necessary to raise the water for this purpose to any great height, the amount of heat required is not so great. It should be said that the principle was applied to heating glazed houses before it was brought into use for warming dwelling houses and other buildings.

841 *Cause of Circulation of Hot Water* Various causes have been assigned for the circulation of hot water. It was held by some that the circulation was caused by the expansion of the water in the boiler under the application of heat, and it was thus explained by Tredgold, and illustrated by him in Fig. 411: 'If,' he wrote,]the vessels A and B, and the pipes that connect them, be filled with water, and fire be applied to the vessel A, the effect of heat will expand the water in the vessel A, and the surface will, in consequence, rise to a higher level, *aa*, the former general level surface being *bb*. The density of the fluid in the vessel A will also decrease in consequence of its expansion, but as soon as the column *dc*, above the centre of the upper pipe, is of a greater weight than the column *fe*, motion will commence along the upper pipe from A to B, and the change this motion produces in the equilibrium of the fluid will cause a corresponding motion in the lower pipe from B to A.'

842 This theory, however, was pronounced to be erroneous by Mr Hood, who proposed in its place a theory of a different nature, which he enunciated and illustrated as follows: 'Let us suppose heat to be applied to the boiler, A (Fig. 412): a dilatation of the volume of the water takes place, and it becomes lighter, the heated particles rising upwards through the colder ones, that sink to the bottom by their greater specific gravity; and they in their turn become expanded and heated like the others. This intestine motion continues until all the particles become equally heated, and have

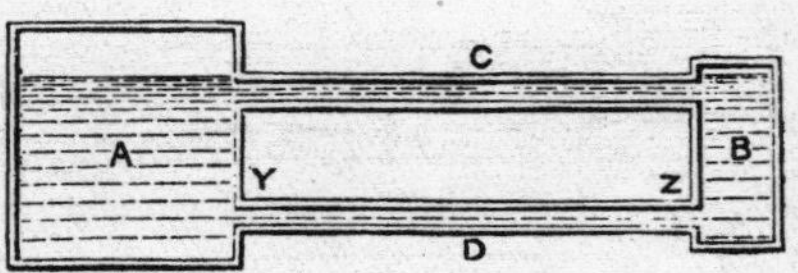

FIG. 412 *Diagram illustrating Hood's theory of circulation of hot water*

received as much heat as the fuel can impart to them. But as soon as the water in the boiler begins to acquire heat, and to become lighter than that which is in the opposite vessel, B, the water in the lower horizontal pipe, D, is pressed by a greater weight at Z than at Y, and it therefore moves forward towards A with a velocity and force equal to the difference in pressure at the two points Y and Z. The water in the upper part of the vessel B would now assume a lower level were it not that the pipe C furnishes a fresh supply of water from the boiler to replenish the deficiency. By means of this unequal pressure on the lower pipe, the water is forced to circulate through the apparatus, and it continues to do so as long as the water in B is colder and heavier than that which is in the boiler; and as the water in the pipes is constantly parting with its heat both by radiation and conduction, while that in the boiler is as continually receiving additional heat from the fire, an equality of temperature never can occur, or else, if it did, the circulation would cease. We see, then, that the cause of circulation is the unequal pressure on the lower pipe of the apparatus, and that it is not the result of an alteration which has taken place in the level of the water, as has been erroneously supposed.'

843 Mr McIntosh, in commenting on this in his *Book of the Garden*, says: 'From this it appears that circulation is really owing to the water in the lower or returning pipe being of greater specific gravity than that in the boiler, and that motion takes place in the lower pipe first instead of in the higher one, as was formerly supposed. The colder the water is in the lower pipe when it enters into the boiler, the more rapid will the circulation be; and as it is desirable to have in most cases a rapid circulation, it follows that the greater the length of pipe employed, the more likely is this to be effected, because the greater the length of the pipe, the more surface is produced for radiation and conduction. Hence, four courses of pipes, as in Fig. 413, will give out more heat than two, and the specific gravity of the fourth, on entering the boiler, will be much greater than at the same end of the second pipe. The water having given out nearly all its heat in the course of a long circuit must naturally absorb more heat from the fire than if it had made a shorter circuit and entered the boiler in a much less cold state.'

844 In actual practice it is not absolutely requisite to have a reservoir or receptacle for water at the ends of the pipes that are removed from the boiler, as shown at B in Figs. 411 and 412, as it is in no way essential to the motion of the water. The reservoir may be utilised for the storage of a mass of hot water that will continue to give forth heat after the fire in the furnace has subsided, and even gone out, or after the flame, be it what it may, by which the water is heated has been extinguished. A bent pipe, such as is shown in Fig. 413, is all that is necessary for carrying on circulation, which, indeed, ought to be more rapid without the reservoir than with it. It has been said that water, when heated, may be caused to rise to any height, and advantage has been taken

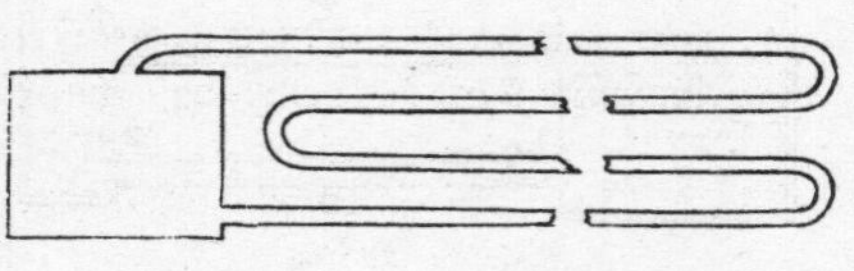

FIG. 413 *Increase in pipes to produce increase in heat*

of this fact to construct the pipes in such a manner that they may be carried, in greenhouse heating, over a doorway if necessary, the pipe being led up one side of the door, across the architrave or lintel, and then down the other side. It must, however, be borne in mind that when the highest point has been reached and the descent has been commenced, the pipes must never be permitted to ascend again, but be carried on either in a horizontal or a downward course, or in both combined, until the lowest level, namely, that at which the water re-enters the boiler, has been reached. To make this perfectly clear, circulation is impracticable in a pipe like A in Fig. 414, because when the water has entered at *a*, risen to *b*, and descended again to *c*, it cannot possibly rise to *d* and find an exit at *e*. But alter the position of the pipe, as at B, and circulation is practicable from *a* to *e*, because the course is level in some parts, and descending in others, throughout its entire length. The part of the pipe which is highest above the boiler should have a small air pipe inserted in it at its highest level, in order to afford means of escape for any air that may have entered the pipe, for should no precaution of this kind be taken, and air find its way in, it would accumulate in the bend, and circulation would be stopped until the pipes had been disconnected, and means of exit thus provided for the imprisoned air.

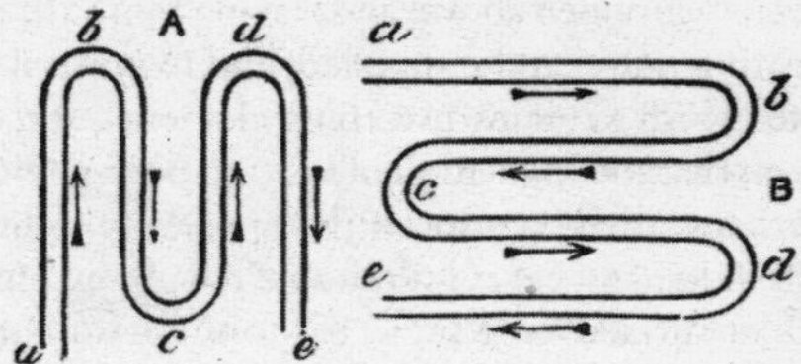

FIG. 414 *Diagram showing practicable and impracticable courses of circulation*

845 *Size of Boiler* In providing apparatus for heating any glazed structure, it is necessary to determine with as much precision as possible what may be most suitable to carry out the end in view. The first thing to be considered is the size of the house itself, its construction and position, and the purpose to which it is to be devoted. Thus, we must calculate the number of cubic feet in the house, the area of glass employed in its construction, its aspect, and its use, for all these separate items will exercise an influence on the temperature required for it and which must be maintained in it. For example, it will make a difference whether the house be larger or smaller, whether it be wholly of glass and wood, of which wood is a bad conductor of heat, or of glass, wood, and iron combined, the last-named metal being a good conductor of heat, and therefore such as would cause more loss than wood. Again, a house having a north aspect would require a greater heating power than a house with a south aspect, the same temperature being required in each; and greater heating power would be required for a house that is to be used as a stove or forcing house than for a house to be used as a cool greenhouse or as a conservatory, the cubic content of each being the same. The construction of the furnace, the height of the chimney, the draught of the flue, the degree of temperature required, will all exert their influence; and taking all these points into consideration, as the deductions to be made fall within the province of the horticultural builder and the hot water engineer, it is better to apply to one of these in any case of importance, submitting such data as have been mentioned above, and leaving him to draw from these conclusions as to the heating power to be supplied, and to prescribe accordingly.

846 With so many disturbing elements, as they may be called, it will be evident to all that the regulation of heating power, and the determination of the size and perhaps of the nature of the apparatus to be supplied, is one of considerable difficulty, and yet it is desirable to submit a formula for determining the size of boiler surface to be subjected to the action of the fire and the extent of the fire grate that may be at once simple and easy of comprehension. Such a formula was propounded by Mr Ainger in the *Gardener's Chronicle* in the following terms: 'Take the cubic content of the house, and for half-hardy plants give to every 100 feet 10 square inches of boiler surface and 1 square inch of fire grate. For tropical plants double these proportions, and for forcing houses take intermediate proportions, according to the temperature required.' This, at all events, has the merits of simplicity and brevity, and, as a general rule, is one that can be followed with safety, and without any possibility of falling into error as far as calculation is concerned.

847 *Size and Extent of Pipes* The pipes that are most commonly used in greenhouse heating are 4 inches in diameter, and are therefore known as 4-inch pipes. As the proportion of the diameter of a circle to its circumference, roughly stated, is 1: 3⅐, the surface of a foot run of 4-inch pipe is a little more than 1 square foot, and it may be taken approximately at 1 square foot if any necessity arises for computation by area of surface of pipe instead of length. Pipes of 3 inches and 2 inches in diameter are also used, and as they are less in superficial area it is manifest that greater lengths of pipe of these diameters can be heated by any boiler than of 4-inch pipe. In point of fact, if a boiler will heat 100 feet of 4-inch pipe, it will heat 133 feet of 3-inch pipe, and 200 feet of 2-inch pipe. Pipes may be placed in a horizontal position, or in positions which involve a gradual rise or even gradual fall from the boiler, but it is necessary that the water should leave the boiler at a higher point and re-enter it at a lower point. It was recommended by Mr Rogers that when 2-inch or 3-inch pipes are used, they should have a uniform rise of 1 inch in 20 feet, while in 4-inch pipes they should fall from the boiler in exactly the same proportion, but the arrangement of the pipes is a matter that affects the velocity of the circulation of the water, a question that need not be entertained here. It may be added, however, that it is better that pipes should rise from the boiler, because this arrangement causes economy of fuel on account of the quickening influence it exerts on the circulation.

848 *Rules to Determine Length of Pipe in relation to Cubic Content of Building* It has been already said that the length of pipe necessary for heating a glazed structure must depend partly upon its size or cubic content, partly (but in a much less degree) upon its form, partly on the superficial content of glass in it, and partly on the construction of the house, whether of glass and wood, of glass and iron, or of glass wood, and iron in combination. It will be convenient to take the rules laid down by Tredgold and Hood for determining the length of pipe required.

1 *Tredgold's Rule* – This authority divides his mode of arriving at the result required in two parts – that is to say, he finds first of all the quantity of cubic

feet of air in a house to be heated per minute, and when this is ascertained he proceeds to determine the length of pipe that is necessary. For greenhouses and glazed structures in which it is not desired to raise the temperature of the house more than 30° above the temperature of the air without the house, he determines the number of cubic feet of air to be heated per minute by adding together 5 times the length of the glass of the roof in feet, 1½ times the whole area of glass in feet, and 11 feet for each door, the total obtained being considered as cubic feet. In the case of forcing houses and stoves, however, where a higher temperature is required, he determines the number of cubic feet of air to be heated per minute by multiplying the length of the house in feet by half the greatest vertical height in feet, and adding to the result obtained 1½ times the whole area of glass in feet, and 11 feet for each door as before. From the total results given by either method, according to the kind of house for which the calculation is made, he deducts one-tenth if the house be built with wooden rafters. He then proceeds to enunciate his rule, which is as follows: 'If the cubic content of air to be heated per minute be multiplied by the number of degrees it is to be warmed, and the result be divided by twice the difference between the temperature of the house and that of the surface of the pipes; the result will be the surface of iron, pipe required in feet.' Or, as it has been already shown, if the pipe be 4-inch pipe, the length in feet and the surface area correspond numerically, the result will be the number of feet of 4-inch pipe required. Thus, if 1000 cubic feet per minute are to be warmed, and the temperature of the external air is 20°, and that to which the air of the house is to be raised is 50°, being 30° in excess of the external air, and 180° the temperature of the pipes in an average state, then the superficial area of pipe required is denoted as follows:

$$\frac{1000\ [\textit{cubic feet to be warmed}] \times 30\ [\textit{difference in degrees between external and required temperature}]}{2 \times 180\ [\textit{average temperature of pipes}]\ \text{minus}\ 50\ [\textit{required temperature of house}]} = \frac{30{,}000}{260} = 116$$

which may be read as linear feet for 4-inch pipes, as well as feet superficial, this being close enough approximately for all practical purposes.

2 *Hood's Rule* – The rule laid down by Mr Hood in his treatise on 'Warming Buildings by Hot Water' is somewhat different and, perhaps, less elaborate. He estimates, first of all, that the quantity of air to be warmed per minute in glass houses of any kind and for any purpose whatever is 1¼ cubic foot for each square foot of glass that the structure contains. The cubic content of air to be warmed being thus determined, he finds the required length of pipe by the following process: 'Multiply 125 by the difference between the temperature at which the structure is desired to be kept when at its maximum and the temperature of the external air, and divide this product by the difference between the temperature of the pipes and the proposed temperature of the structure: then the quotient thus obtained, when multiplied by the number of cubic feet of air to be warmed per minute, and

this product divided by 222, will give the number of feet in length of pipe, 4 inches in diameter, which will produce the desired effect.' Mr Hood assumes 200° as the heat at which the pipes can be easily maintained, and then, taking the other data as given by Tredgold, namely, 1000 cubic feet per minute to be warmed, the temperature of the external air 20°, the temperature to which the air in the house is to be raised 50°, being 30° in excess of the external air, then we get as a numerical expression for the length of pipe required as follows:

$$\frac{125 \times (50\ [\textit{required temperature of house}]\ \textit{minus}\ 20\ [\textit{temperature of external air}])}{200\ [\textit{average temperature of pipes}]\ \textit{minus}\ 50\ [\text{required temperature of house}]} = 25{,}000 \text{ cubic feet to be warmed}$$

then

$$\frac{25{,}000}{22} = 112 \text{ feet of 4-inch pipes required}$$

849 As it has just been said, Mr Hood assumed, as a basis for his calculations, that 200° Fahrenheit represented a degree of heat at which the temperature of the pipes in a house could be most easily maintained, and on this assumption he constructed the following table, which shows the quantity of pipe, 4 inches in diameter, which will heat 1000 cubic feet of air per minute any required number of degrees from 45° to 90°, the external air having a temperature ranging from 10° to 52°, and the temperature of the pipes being, as stated, 200°. In order to ascertain by the table the quantity of pipe that is required to heat 1000 cubic feet of air per minute, find in the column to the left hand the temperature of the external air, or the temperature which approaches most closely to that of the external air, and in the line across the page at the top of the table find the temperature to which it is desired to raise that of the glazed building. Then in the column immediately under this temperature, and on a line with the corresponding temperature of the air without the house, the number of feet of pipe required will be found. The table is calculated, as it has been said, for 4-inch pipes, but if it be required to ascertain the relative quantity of piping required when 3-inch pipes or 2-inch pipes are used, multiply the quantity of feet of 4-inch pipes required for 1000 cubic feet of air by 133 for 3-inch pipes, and by 2 for 2-inch pipes, because, as explained above, the surface of 1 foot of 4-inch pipe is equivalent in superficial area to that of 1½ foot of 3-inch pipe, or 2 feet of 2½-inch pipe.

'There are other rules laid down,' says Mr McIntosh in his *Book of the Garden*, 'for calculating the length of pipe required for heating any extent of hothouses, but although, perhaps, sufficiently correct for ordinary purposes, they are far less scientific than those already noticed. Thus, for example, for a hothouse to be heated to about 60°, divide the cubic content of the space to be heated by 30; when 70° to 75° of heat is required, divide by 20; and when 75° to 80°, by 18: the quotient will give the length of 4-inch pipe required. If 3-inch pipes are used, add one-third; if 2-inch pipes, double the length of the 4-inch pipe.'

Temperature of External Air	Temperature desired for glazed house in degrees Fahrenheit									
	45°	50°	55°	60°	65°	70°	75°	80°	85°	90°
10°	126	150	174	200	229	259	292	328	367	409
12°	119	142	166	192	220	251	283	318	357	399
14°	112	135	159	184	212	242	274	309	347	388
16°	105	127	151	176	204	233	265	300	337	378
18°	98	120	143	168	195	225	256	290	328	368
20°	91	112	135	160	187	216	247	281	318	358
22°	83	105	128	152	179	207	238	271	308	347
24°	76	97	120	144	170	199	229	262	298	337
26°	69	90	112	136	162	190	220	253	288	327
28°	61	82	104	128	154	181	211	243	279	317
30°	54	75	97	120	145	173	202	234	269	307
32°	47	67	89	112	137	164	193	225	259	296
34°	40	60	81	104	129	155	184	215	249	286
36°	32	52	73	96	120	147	175	206	239	276
38°	25	45	66	88	112	138	166	196	230	266
40°	18	37	58	80	104	129	157	187	220	255
42°	10	30	50	72	95	121	148	178	210	245
44°	3	22	42	64	87	112	139	168	200	235
46°	—	15	34	56	79	103	130	159	190	225
48°	—	7	27	48	70	95	121	150	181	214
50°	—	—	19	40	62	86	112	140	171	204
52°	—	—	11	32	54	77	103	131	161	194

Mr Forsyth, when treating of the same subject, says that, viewed in relation to 10 feet of cubic air, or to every 10 feet of cubic air to be heated: 'I consider 1 square foot of pipe (or 1 foot linear measure of 4-inch pipe) necessary for pines; 1 foot in 12 for grapes; 1 foot in 15 for peaches; and I foot in 24 to keep the frost from greenhouse plants when the thermometer in the open air falls to zero.'

Mr Scott, again, writing in the *Journal of the Horticultural Society*, says: 'In stoves of considerable dimensions containing from 50,000 to 60,000 cubic feet of air, having a surface of glass, including rafters and sash bars, in the proportion of 1 square foot of glass to 10 cubic feet of air, the proportion of 1 foot of 4-inch pipe to 5.33 feet of glass, will be ample heating surface to maintain a minimum temperature of 60° during severe weather. But in a house containing from 10,000 to 15,000 cubic feet of air, with a surface of glass in the proportion of 1 foot of glass to 6.75 feet of air, the proportion of 1 foot of pipe to 3 feet of glass will be required to maintain a minimum temperature of 60° to 65°, provided covering be not used. In vineries and peach houses, the quantity of heating surface required will very much depend on circumstances, as whether they are attached or connected in a range, also whether the crop is wanted early or late; but 1 foot of pipe to 4 feet of glass will be a fair average for vineries, and 1 foot of pipe to 5 feet of glass for peach houses, conservatories, and greenhouses, according to size and other circumstances, will require 1 foot of 4-inch pipe to 5 or 6 feet of glass. If flues be preferred, I should consider 1 foot of an ordinary flue equal to 2 feet of a 4-inch pipe. In pits or small forcing houses, where covering can be easily applied at night, the proportion of 1 foot of pipe to 4 or 5 feet of glass will maintain a minimum temperature of 60°.'

850 *History of Heating by Hot Water* To give a full sketch of the rise and progress of heating by hot water would take up too much space, and it is only possible here to dwell briefly, and in a very condensed form, on a subject which is necessarily one of the greatest interest and importance to gardeners of all classes. After this has been done in the manner indicated, a few types of apparatus for heating hot water and promoting its circulation will be noticed, as previously intimated, and the subject must then be dismissed, although it would be possible to occupy an entire volume of large size in giving it full and exhaustive consideration.

On the authority of Seneca, the Romans are credited with initiating the art of causing the circulation of hot water through pipes, called *dracones*, from their serpentine form. These pipes were passed through or round a furnace, and water which went in cold at one end of the pipe came out boiling at the other. Sometimes the pipes were ranged round a furnace, and connected with a tank of water, the upper end entering the tank near the top, and the lower end near the bottom. This arrangement was the first appearance of the coil boiler, introduced in the present century by Mr A. M. Perkins.

From Seneca's time until the eighteenth century, no progress was made in the discovery put in force for the first time, as far as we know, by the Romans, when it occurred to Sir Martin Triewald, a Swede, who resided at Newcastle-on-Tyne, and Sir Hugh Platt, who lived about the same time, that hot water might be made available instead of manure for heating hotbeds, and also for warming greenhouses, but neither of them seemed to have arrived at any practical method of effecting it. Next to them, M. Bonnemain, a Frenchman, took the matter up in connection with the hatching of chickens, and afterwards extended the principle to the warming of greenhouses. He produced his first apparatus, which he called a new water calorifère, in Paris, in 1777, and maybe regarded as being the discoverer of the circulation of hot water. His calorifère was so regulated by the unequal dilation of metals that he could maintain a temperature varying scarcely half a degree of Reaumur. This was the principle of its construction. A rod of iron, screwed to another of brass, was enclosed in a lead tube terminating at its upper end in a ring of brass; the leaden tube was passed through the water in the boiler, by the side of one of the circulating pipes, and the dilation of the lead being greater than that of the iron, and the rod being enclosed within the lead, it was less heated; and the consequent lengthening of the leaden tube brought the brass ring into contact with a claw at the short end of a bent lever; the slightest increase of heat lengthened the tube, and pressed down the long end of the lever, and a wire connected with it opened or closed a valve, regulating the air admitted to the furnace; this, however, is a refinement on heating which is rarely practised or required.

M. Bonnemain's invention was introduced into this country in 1815, by Count Chabannes, who warmed a dwelling house and hothouse at Sundridge, Kent, with water heated on this principle in the following year, but the first actual advance in the attempt to make warming by hot water general in this country was not made until 1822, when Messrs Bacon and Atkinson commenced a series of experiments which attracted considerable attention. Mr Atkinson's idea was evidently founded on the theory of fluids finding their level; for his first apparatus was merely a boiler, from which the water was made to flow and return by means of two pipes on a perfect level. At the extremity of the pipes a reservoir was considered necessary, exactly on a level with the top of the boiler, the reservoir being covered with an iron top, fitting into it with a flange; the boiler with a wooden one. Mr Atkinson afterwards constructed boilers with closed tops; by which means he carried hot water 30 feet above the level of the boiler. An improvement upon this system of heating was attempted upon what was called the siphon principle, which was invented at the same time by Messrs Kewley and Fowler, and it is difficult to say to which of them the credit of being first in the field really belongs. In this system, in an open boiler, the flow pipe being placed a few inches below the surface of the water where it is hottest, the lower, or return pipe, descending nearly to the bottom of the boiler, a small tube or air hole being placed in the upper pipe near to the bend at its highest elevation; the surface water being the hottest, the heated particles are forced into the upper pipe, after dispelling the air, get cooled, and descend again into the lower pipe by the force of gravitation.

Numberless modifications of these principles have been proposed at various times, the chief modifications being in the form of the boiler. After many experiments, Mr Rogers, at a later period, was led to adopt a conical form of boiler, in place of a cylindrical one, the interior or furnace resembling in shape the sugar-loaf cone, supplied with coal from below. The boiler is also slightly conical. Cottam and Hallen, and Burbidge and Healy, have each of them produced boilers extensively in use among gardeners; the object in both instances being to present the largest surface of the boiler to the flames; and both, though by different arrangements, carry the flame up the centre of the boiler. Messrs Cottam and Hallen's boiler, in point of fact, was a saddle-backed boiler, and the first of its kind. That of Messrs Burbidge and Healy was a round boiler in the form of a pail, with a hollow cone rising in the centre, on which the fire acted, as well as on the exterior. The surface of the boiler was corrugated, and it was furnished with a double set of flow and return pipes, which tended to render the circulation more rapid and to increase the heating power.

Where great heat is required, however, from moderate space, the tubular boiler seems to have considerable advantages. Mr Weeks, the founder of the firm of S. Weeks and Co., Horticultural Builders and Hot Water Engineers, King's Road, Chelsea, London seems to have been the earliest adapter of this system, now extensively used in horticultural buildings. Mr Weeks seems to have adopted, and even patented, the well-known principle of the displacement of rarefied water by the pressure of the denser cold water, already explained; but his heating principle was a system of pipes placed round the fire, and communicating with the cistern and with the warming pipes. This he did at first in connection with a boiler; but the tubes were soon found to be perfectly efficient when ranged round the fire without any boiler. This apparatus is now constructed of upright tubes placed over the fire, and united together at top and bottom, the furnace bars being hollow tubes, through which the return water passes before entering the upper part of the boiler; thus producing very rapid circulation, with great economy of fuel.

Another mode of promoting the circulation of hot water was introduced by an American, Mr A. M. Perkins, which may be thus explained. Instead of a boiler into which the flow and return pipes were inserted, a coil of wrought-iron pipes, about 1 inch in diameter, was used, and in this coil the water was heated. The furnace was placed in the interior of the coil, but was encased in brickwork to prevent the fire from being brought into direct contact with the pipes of which the coil was formed, but the brickwork casing was open at the top, so that the heat and smoke might enter the flue in which the coil was placed. The fuel was put in from above, and the ashes taken out below. The tubes Were hermetically sealed, but to counteract the danger that would arise from the expansion of the water in tubes thus treated, an expansion tube was added, which rose above the level of the flow pipe and the point at which the coil was filled, which, of necessity, was also a little above the level of the flow pipe, and afforded scope for the expansion of the water in the form of high pressure steam. The disadvantages attending this mode of heating are the chances of the pipes bursting under pressure of the heated water and steam, the unpleasant smell which is given forth from the pipes at times, the inequality of the temperature maintained, and the rapidity with which they cool when the fire gets low.

851 Practically speaking, there is but one principle of effecting the circulation of hot water in pipes for heating purposes, and that lies in the point that the flow pipe and the return pipe must be inserted into or communicate with the boiler at different levels; and further, there are virtually only three kinds of boilers, namely, the Conical or Cylindrical Boiler, such as those of Rogers, and Burbidge and Healy, in which the fire had access to the whole interior surface of the boiler; the Saddle-Back Boiler, introduced by Messrs Cottam and Hallen, in which the fire had access to the interior surface of the boiler, throughout its entire length, from end to end; and the Tubular Boiler, invented by Weeks, to which the Coil Boiler of Perkins and the modern Coil Boiler may be considered as being analogous, in a great measure. There are many forms of boilers, it is true, but when they are divested of the modifications which give distinction to them, they may all be traced to one or other of the leading principles of construction involved in those which have been mentioned above. And by far the greater number trace back to the saddle back boiler.

852 Before dealing with the larger and more important kinds of boilers which are heated by the combustion of solid fuel, let us just glance at appliances for the circulation of hot water heated by mineral oil or petroleum and gas. It will be understood that it is impossible to deal with every apparatus of the kind that is in the market, and that those which are described are selected because they appear to be good types of their class, and not with any intention of depreciating those which are not described or not mentioned. *Detur digniori* is the principle on which the selections have been made, but intending purchasers are recommended to make inquiries for themselves, and before coming to a final choice, to see each apparatus at work, if possible, so that each may be in a better position to judge which appears likely to be best fitted to meet his individual requirements.

853 *Rippingille's Circulating Hot Water Apparatus* This appliance may be selected as the type of contrivances of this kind for heating conservatories and small glazed structures by the circulation of hot water. Its construction and principle, when considered in connection with the explanation already given of the means by which the circulation of hot water is caused, will be understood from an inspection of Fig. 415, in which A is the stove, made of sheet iron, black japanned, with an ornamental cast iron base, and fitted with a patent sliding tank, shown at the opening below, which is furnished with two 4½-inch burners. Above the stove is the boiler, B, through which a tube passes, which renders assistance in heating the water, and affords means of escape for the products of combustion, as shown at C. The flow-pipe from the boiler is at D, the return pipe at E. The water circulates through the horizontal tubes sustained by supports at either end, the support farthest from the boiler having a tap inserted in it on a level with the return pipe for drawing off the water when necessary. The water reaches boiling point in about two hours from the time of lighting the stove, and can be kept at this temperature for any length of time. The total

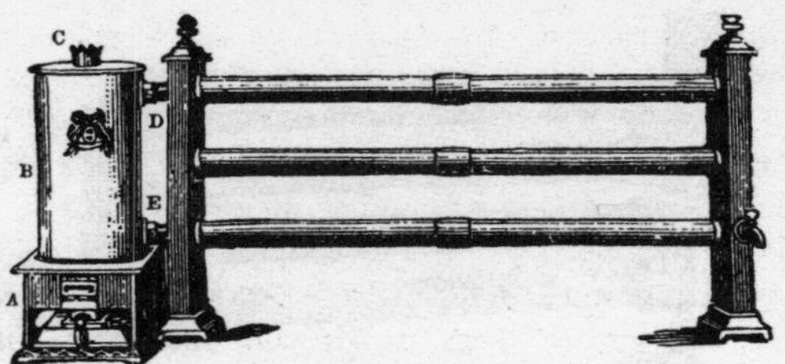

FIG. 415 *Rippingille's circulating hot water apparatus*

length of the apparatus is 6 feet 4 inches, the height 2 feet 9 inches; the supports are 4 inches by 3 inches, and the tubes 2⅜ inches in diameter. It can be purchased of the Holborn Lamp and Stove Company, 118 Holborn, London, for £3 15s. with an iron boiler, or for £5 5s. with a copper boiler. A smaller apparatus, 3 feet long and 2 feet 4 inches high, having a stove fitted with 2-inch burners, and furnished with 2-inch pipes, can be had for £2, or for £3 15s. if fitted with copper boiler. Vapourisers for creating a moist atmosphere can be had at 2s. 6d. and 3s each.

With regard to the cost of fuel, it is calculated, taking the price of oil to be 1s. per gallon, that a 2-inch burner consumes oil to the value of ⅛d. per hour; a 3-inch burner, ⅙d.; a 4½-inch burner, ¼d.; and a 6-inch burner, ⅓d. This gives data for calculating cost of burning according to the price of oil. With regard to heating power or capacity, it is taken as a rule that a single 2-inch burner will effectually warm small greenhouses, unless the cold is very severe. A room having an area of 14 feet by 12 feet, and about 10 feet high, may be warmed with a stove having two 2-inch burners, or one 4½-inch burner, but for greenhouses of the same cubic content a more powerful apparatus would be necessary, because the cold air outside the glass carries off so much of the heat given out. For greenhouses that are much longer than they are wide, two stoves of medium size, placed one at each end, are better than one large one, because the heat is then distributed, and an increased temperature throughout the house obtained more quickly. Proper arrangements should be made for ventilation wherever these stoves are used. Stoves of great power should always be used, because they may be regulated so as to give forth less heat in mild weather and more in very cold weather, when a higher temperature is required.

854 *Mussett's Patent Portable Hot Water Apparatus* This is another good type of boiler and hot water apparatus in which petroleum may be used as fuel, but it may be heated by gas as well, or by common coke, cinders, etc., a suitable heating apparatus being furnished in each case according to the fuel to be used. These apparatuses vary in size and construction. A boiler and hot water apparatus, 4 feet long and 20 inches high, consisting of two cast-iron pipes supported on legs, with a supply cistern at one end and a boiler and paraffin lamp at the other end, connected with the heating apparatus by flow and return pipes, suitable for heating a conservatory about 8 feet long and 6 feet wide, may be had complete for £2 10s. Another size, about 7 feet 6 inches long and 20 inches high, provided with two lamps and boilers, as shown in Fig. 415, at one end, and a supply box at the other, is supplied for £4. 10s. without tap, or for £5 with tap. The best and most efficient apparatus, however, of this class is that

FIG. 416 *Mussett's patent portable hot water apparatus*

which is illustrated in Fig. 416, which consists of a coil of four cast-iron pipes, with supports at either end, and a supply cistern for water at the end opposite to that which is connected with the boiler, or rather boilers, for there are two boilers and two lamps, connected by transverse pipes, from which, from points midway between the boilers, issue the supply or flow pipe, A, and the return pipe, B, which communicate with the heating apparatus. A tap is fixed to the lower pipe between the boilers on the same level as the return pipe, to draw off the water when necessary. This apparatus is about 4 feet long and 2 feet high, and is supplied complete for £5 12s. by the manufacturer and patentee, Mr J. Mussett, Winstanley Road, Clapham Junction, London.

It is asserted that the appliances described above are found to be efficient in maintaining a sufficiently warm temperature in a small glazed house in severe weather, and capable of preventing the ingress of frost. To start the apparatus in the shortest possible time, the water should be drawn off" by means of the tap shown between the lamps and boilers in Fig. 416, and the pipes and boilers completely emptied: These should then be refilled with hot water, introduced through the supply cistern, and as the water is hot the circulation will soon commence. On no account should the lamps be lighted unless the pipes are fall of water. The entire apparatus may be moved from place to place at pleasure, even when the lamps are lighted, for it is not in any way fixed to the ground. It must be remembered that gas and solid fuel may be used to heat this apparatus, but with appliances differing more or less from that shown in the illustration for burning petroleum.

855 *Shrewsbury's Gas Conservatory Boilers* When gas is used as fuel, the gas conservatory boilers and hot water apparatuses manufactured and supplied by Mr G. Shrewsbury, 122 Newgate Street, London, will be found excellent for the purposes for which they are specially constructed. The boilers and apparatus are supplied separately. The former are made in four sizes, distinguished as Nos. 0, 1, 2, and 3, sold at 35s., 45s., 85s., and 110s. respectively. No. 1 boiler will heat from 25 feet to 30 feet of 2-inch pipe, No. 2. from 50 feet to 60 feet, and No. 3 from 100 feet to 150 feet of the same size pipe When extra powerful burners are required with any size of boiler, 5s. must be added to the cost as given above. The boilers require no setting in brickwork, and can be applied to any hot water pipes already in use without disturbing the boiler originally attached to them. They require no attention after the burner is once lighted, and they maintain an equal and uniform temperature. They can be fixed either inside or outside a

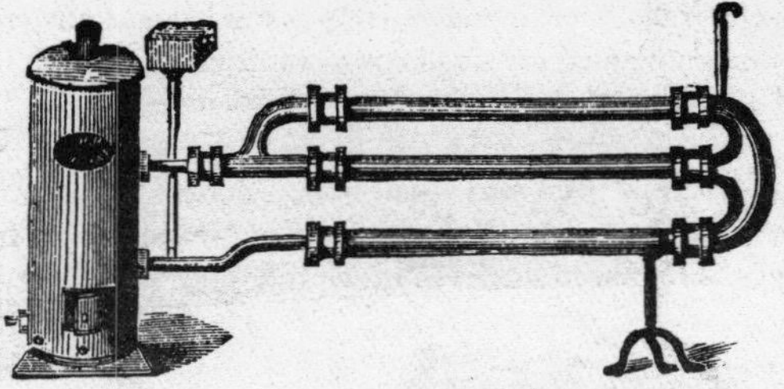

FIG. 417 *Shrewsbury's gas conservatory boiler and hot water apparatus*

greenhouse. The burners turn out of the apparatus for convenience in lighting, and no deposit of soot is caused by the burning as the flame is smokeless. The hot water apparatuses vary in length from 4 feet 5 inches to 8 feet 3 inches, and range in price from £2 15s. to £7 10s., according to size and construction. The smaller sizes are portable and require no supply cistern or air pipe, but some of the larger sizes are fitted with both. They should be fixed in such a position as to be safe against down currents, and the escape pipe from the boiler should be carried into a warm flue or taken through the roof, the end in the air being covered in with one of Shrewsbury's Improved Caps for flue pipes, which cost from 2s. 6d. to 4s. 6d., according to size.

856 The lengths given above for the hot water apparatus do not include the boiler and the connecting pipes between the boiler and the apparatus. In Fig. 417 a representation is given of an apparatus with supply cistern and air pipe intended for fixing inside a conservatory, but when there is a down draught or any risk of it, it is considered better to have the boiler outside the house. The apparatus shown in Fig 418 is made in two sizes, namely, 5 feet 3 inches long, sold for £4 15s., and 8 feet 3 inches long, at £5 15s. The larger size, fitted with No. 2 boiler, supplied together for £9 10s., is suitable for conservatories 15 feet long, to which the length of the boiler and apparatus combined closely approaches. The smaller size, with boiler, is sufficient for a conservatory 10 feet long. Fig. 418 shows an apparatus with boiler and flue cap for fixing outside the greenhouse or conservatory. In fixing, all that is needful to be done is to make two small holes in the containing wall of the structure to admit of the passage of the pipes which connect the boiler and hot water apparatus. The price of the apparatus complete, which is 9 feet in length, including boiler, though the

FIG. 418 *Shrewsbury's hot water apparatus with boiler for fixing outside greenhouse*

apparatus itself is only 6 feet 9 inches, is £4 15s. It has a supply cistern but no air pipe, and is recommended for small conservatories on account of its cheapness and general efficiency. It is suitable for a house about 10 feet long and 6 feet wide.

857 Enough has now been said about boilers actuated by petroleum and gas, and we may now pass on to the larger and more important kinds of boilers, taking as types of the three classes to which reference has been made the Patent Duplex Upright Tubular Boiler of Messrs J. Weeks and Co., King's Road, London, as a fitting representative of that class of boilers in which the water receives additional impetus in its circulation by being compelled to pass through pipes of comparatively small diameter; the Patent Automatic Coke Boiler of Messrs Franklin, Hocking, and Co., Limited, 37 Hanover Street, Liverpool, as a good specimen of the conical or cylindrical boilers; and the 'Loughborough and other boilers of Messrs Messenger and Co., Loughborough, Leicestershire, as good forms of the saddle boiler, which is justly regarded as being one of the best kinds of boilers, if not the very best, for horticultural purposes.

FIG. 419 *Weeks's patent tubular boiler*

858 ***Weeks's Patent Duplex Upright Tubular Boiler*** The construction of this boiler is clearly exhibited in Fig. 419, which represents the size called No. 3 by the makers, which will heat from 600 to 750 feet of 4-inch pipe, according to its construction with or without the patent diaphragm. The boiler, as shown in the illustration, is raised on piers of brickwork, between which the ashes fall from the furnace above them. It is then enclosed up to the top in a setting of brickwork, and this brickwork itself furnishes a furnace in which the flame, heat, and smoke come in contact with the boiler at every point. Every tube shown in the boiler is hollow, and is of cast iron. Even the straight bars running from front to back at the bottom, just above the brickwork, are hollow, and so is the ring on which the vertical tubes stand, as well as the vertical tubes themselves. The fuel is placed under this ring on the hollow furnace bars, and the boiler and pipes being full, the fire is lighted. When the boiler is in action, and the water is circulating, it enters from the boilers at the pipe shown in the lower right-hand corner of the illustration in Fig. 419, which is the return pipe, passes first through the furnace bars, then upwards into the ring on which the vertical tubes stand, and from the ring through these tubes till it reaches the upper part, and thence through the flow pipe in the upper right-hand corner. These boilers are guaranteed for ten years, and will actually last for twice this time. They are perfectly safe, and can be quickly taken to pieces for cleaning or repairing, if necessary, without disturbing the brickwork setting. The larger boilers are made in two sections, which are perfectly independent of each other, and if one section be removed for necessary repairs the other section can remain in position and be kept working. There are seven numbers of these boilers specified, as in the table below, which gives details of heating power with or without the patent diaphragm, which has the effect of increasing the heating capability, and their sizes and prices, with prices of various fittings. Their description, as far as construction is concerned, can be given here instead of in the table. Thus, No. 1 is plain tubular in one ring, with single mud pad and solid furnace bars; Nos. 2 and 3 are tubular, and generally as No. 1, but both are supplied with or without diaphragm, as may be desired, and No. 2 has solid and No. 3 hollow furnace bars. These may be regarded as forming the first group. In the second group they are described as tubular in two rings on the Duplex principle, which refers to their construction in *two* sections. They have four mud pads, hollow furnace bars, and are supplied with or without diaphragm. The only point of difference between Nos. 4, 4A, 5, and 6, size excepted, is that No. 4A has hollow furnace bars of extra size. The first group, it may be added, are without boiler valves, and an extra charge for solid furnace bars is made for Nos. 1 and 2 – namely, 15s. for No. 1, and 20s. for No. 2. With this explanation the tabular statement about to be given will be fully understood.

	Quantity of 4-inch pipes heated without diaphragm	with diaphragm	Average size of boiler when fixed	Price without diaphragm	Price with diaphragm	Price of furnace doors, etc.	Price of boiler valves
1	200	—	3 ft 6 in x by 3 ft 6 in	£4 10s. 0d.	——	£2 5s. 0d.	——
2	300	400	3 ft 9 in x by 3 ft 9 in	£7 10s. 0d.	£10 10s. 0d.	£2 5s. 0d.	——
3	600	750	3 ft 9 in x by 3 ft 9 in	£13 0s. 0d.	£16 0s. 0d.	£2 10s. 0d.	——
4	1,500	1,800	4 ft 6 in x by 4 ft 6 in	£22 0s. 0d.	£26 10s. 0d.	£3 3s. 0d.	£1 10s. 0d.
4A	2,300	2,700	4 ft 9 in x by 4 ft 9 in	£27 10s. 0d.	£32 0s. 0d.	£3 5s. 0d.	£1 10s. 0d.
5	4,000	4,500	5 ft 0 in x by 5 ft 0 in	£38 10s. 0d.	£45 0s. 0d.	£3 10s. 0d.	£1 15s. 0d.
6	10,000	11,000	6 ft 0 in x by 6 ft 0 in	£60 0s. 0d.	£67 0s. 0d.	£5 5s. 0d.	£2 0s. 0d.

859 An Improved Conical Tubular Boiler, with taper tubes, heating rapidly, and well suited to cases in which the fire is required to be maintained for some time without constant attention, is made by Mr W. M. Appleton, Clifton, Bristol, who will send price list free on application. The vertical tubes enter rings at the top and bottom, the flow pipe proceeding from the upper ring, and the return pipe entering the lower ring. The boiler is supported on piers of brickwork, and enclosed in a brick setting. Between the piers, a little below the boiler, are solid furnace bars, door, and ash-pit. Mr Appleton also supplies a Duplex Boiler of good form for gas or oil for greenhouses, complete with four pipes 6 feet in length in all, for £3. The boiler is made in different sizes.

860 *The Coil Boiler* in its most ordinary form is nothing more, as has been already explained, than a simple coil of pipe of narrow diameter enclosed in a setting of brickwork, so that every portion of the pipe is subjected to the action of the flame in the furnace formed by the brickwork, which is fitted with a door and furnace bars. The flow pipe issues from the upper extremity of the pipe, and the return pipe communicates with the lower portion. Means should be taken by the adoption of proper fittings to prevent any chance of accident. George's Calorigen, illustrated in Fig. 409, may be viewed as an example of the coil boiler suited for the circulation of warm air instead of warm water, the air being heated in its passage through the pipe from the lower to the upper extremity. Coil boilers for enclosure in brickwork are made in various sizes by Messrs Charles P. Kinnell and Co., 31 Bankside, London, by whom they are declared to be very efficient, and to show wonderful results when set in a proper manner. The following table shows the numbers in which these boilers are supplied, with dimensions, heating power, and price, and in the last column but one the cost of fitting for coils and smoke pipe, brickwork excepted, in every case.

No.	Diameter of coil	Length of tube in coil	Diameter of tube	Heating power in 4-in. piping	Price of coil	Price of fittings	Total Price
0	9 in.	4 ft 6 in.	¾ in.	24 ft.	£0 10s. 6d.	£0 18s. 9d.	£1 9d. 3s.
1	9 in.	6 ft 8 in.	¾ in.	36 ft.	£0 12s. 6d.	£0 18s. 9d.	£1 11s. 3d.
2	11 in.	8ft 3 in.	¾ in.	48 ft.	£0 15s. 6d.	£1 1s. 3d.	£1 16s. 3d.
3	12½ in.	12ft 8 in.	¾ in.	72 ft.	£1 0s. 0d.	£1 1s. 3d.	£2 1s. 3d.
4	12½ in.	12ft 9 in.	1 in.	100 ft.	£1 2s. 6d.	£1 1s. 3d.	£2 3s. 9d.
5	13½ in.	13ft 0 in.	1¼ in.	150 ft.	£1 7s. 6d.	£1 7s. 9d.	£2 15s. 3d.
6	13½ in.	15ft 0 in.	1¼ in.	200 ft.	£1 12s. 6d.	£1 7s. 9d.	£3 0s. 3d.
7	16 in.	16ft 0 in.	1½ in.	250 ft.	£2 0s. 6d.	£1 16s. 6d.	£3 16s. 6d.
8	16 in.	20ft 0 in.	1½ in.	300 ft.	£2 10s. 6d.	£1 16s. 6d.	£4 6s. 6d.
10	18 in.	24ft 0 in.	2 in.	400 ft.	£3 7s. 6d.	—	—

861 *Hocking's Patent Automatic Coke Boiler* This boiler, which is manufactured and sold by Messrs Franklin, Hocking and Co., Limited, 37 Hanover Street, Liverpool, may be taken as an excellent type of boilers of the conical form, in which the fire is brought into contact with every part of the interior surface of the boiler. Its cheapness, its efficiency, and certain peculiarities in its construction and action, render it well suited for small greenhouses and for all heating purposes for amateur gardeners. The general appearance of the stove from without, and its construction within, are shown in Fig. 420, which affords a view both of the exterior and the interior. The entire apparatus is made of welded wrought iron. In the centre is a large tube called the hopper, shown at AA, which is continued to the lowest level of the boiler, BB. Into this hopper the coke is thrown through the opening in the top, which is fitted with a cover. The bottom is open, and as the coke is gradually consumed, the waste is supplied by fresh coke gradually descending from above. At the bottom at CC is the fire,

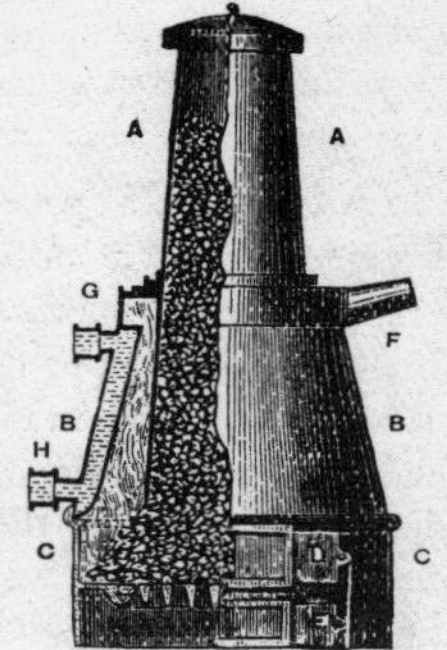

FIG. 420 *Hocking's patent automatic coke boiler*

which feeds on the coke that is supported by the furnace bars below; the fire, as will be noticed, acts all round on the coke, which is in its centre. D is the furnace door, and E a damper below it by which the entrance of air into the furnace, and consequently the action of the fire, may be regulated at pleasure. The flame and smoke play on the whole of the interior of the boiler, and reach the upper part of the interior between the boiler and the hopper, and from this part the smoke finds an exit by the smoke outlet F. The flow pipe, or rather the connection with the boiler and the flow pipe, is shown at G, and that of the return pipe and boiler at H. The apparatus requires no setting in brickwork, and can stand in the open air or in a small stokery, as may be preferred. The whole structure can be taken to pieces in a few minutes for cleaning or repairs. A charge of coke ranging from 45lb. to 50lb. thrown into the hopper is enough to keep up the action of the boiler and maintain a proper temperature for 14 hours. These boilers are good in all respects, and require attention only in the morning and evening of each day as long as the fire is kept alight. They can be fitted to any existing system of pipes at but little expense. The following statement shows the sizes, heating power, and prices of these serviceable boilers:

	Quantity of pipes heated			
No.	2 in.	3 in.	4 in.	
1	180	130	90	£5 5s. 0d.
2	360	240	180	£6 15s. 0d.
3	525	350	260	£10 10s. 0d.
4	690	460	345	£12 10s. 0d.
5	900	600	450	£17 0s. 0d.
6	1125	750	562	£19 10s. 0d.

862 *Messengers Dome Top Cylinder Boiler* Another variety of these independent boilers, so called because they are complete in themselves, and require no setting wherever they may be placed, is to be found in the Dome Top Cylinder Boiler manufactured by Messrs Messenger and Co. The peculiarity in this boiler, as implied by the name, is that the cavity in which the water is placed not only surrounds the furnace within, but is extended in domelike form over the top of it, and has an upright flow pipe issuing from the centre and highest point of the dome. This arrangement adds to the heating surface, and as the flow socket is on the top, there is no risk of steam being generated. The return pipe enters the boiler at the bottom, opposite the door of the furnace; the smoke pipe, or issue for the smoke, is on the same side as the return pipe, but nearly at the top of the furnace. Opposite to it and above the

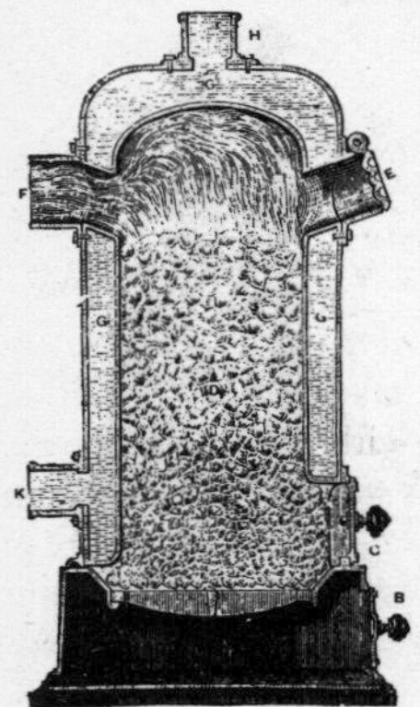

FIG. 421 *Messenger's dome top cylinder boiler*

furnace door is an arrangement for feeding the fire with fuel from above. Below all is a commodious ash-pit. A section of this boiler is shown in Fig. 421, in which A is the ash-pit; B, the door of the ash pit; C, the furnace door; D, the furnace; E, arrangement for the introduction of fresh fuel from above; F, issue for smoke; G, the boiler, with the flow pipe, H, issuing from the top of the dome in an upright position; and K, the return pipe. The following table shows the numbers and sizes in which this boiler is made, with prices and particulars respecting the heating capacity and height of flow pipe. From these, the space required by any size may be readily determined (*see chart at foot of page*).

863 *Saddle Boilers* We may now turn our attention to Saddle Boilers, the chief feature of which is that they are better suited for larger horticultural structures and ranges of glazed buildings, because the length is theoretcally unlimited – that is to say, a saddle boiler may be made shorter or longer, so as to afford a greater or less amount of heating surface, according to the work that is required of it. In Fig. 422, two types of saddle boilers are shown in section, one rectangular and the other cylindrical. The fire is in the centre, and acts directly on the whole of the interior surface of the

No.	Height.	Diam.	Approx. height of flow pipe	Heating power of 2-inch pipe	Price
1	21	13	33	350	£6 10s. 0d.
2	24	13	36	400	£7 0s. 0d.
3	24	15	37	550	£8 5s. 0d.
4	30	15	43	700	£9 5s. 0d.
5	36	15	49	850	£10 10s. 0d.
6	30	18	45	1050	£13 0s. 0d.
7	36	18	51	1200	£13 10s. 0d.
8	42	18	57	1300	£14 12s. 6d.
9	36	21	51	1400	£16 17s. 6d.
10	42	21	57	1600	£18 0s. 0d.
11	48	21	63	1800	£20 5s. 0d.
12	54	21	69	2000	£23 12s. 6d.
14	48	24	65	2400	£27 0s. 0d.
15	54	21	71	2600	£28 15s. 0d.
16	60	24	77	2800	£29 15s. 0d.

boiler. Now, there is nothing to prevent the making of boilers of this description in any length compatible with reason. Practically, the length of saddle boilers and their heating powers are subordinated to the work required of them, as will be seen, but there is no reason why a saddle boiler should not be made to any length that may be required, when placed, as shown in Fig. 422, with the fire below the inner surface. Sometimes, however, this kind of boiler is stood on one end, as in the Loughborough boiler, to be described presently; and the fire is then in an upright or vertical chamber, instead of a horizontal chamber, and then its height is necessarily limited, because it is not so convenient to extend a furnace vertically as it is horizontally.

FIG. 422 *Types of saddle boiler*

864 *The Loughborough Boiler* In accordance with the principle that has been generally acted on in this work, of taking the smaller things first, and leading onward and upward through them to larger articles of like description, we will take the upright saddle boilers first, beginning with the Loughborough Boiler, manufactured by Messrs Messenger and Co., a patent boiler which is largely used, and which has achieved a well-merited reputation. The general appearance of the entire apparatus may be gathered from Fig. 423, which affords an external view of it. A section of the boiler, showing the relative positions of the furnace and boiler, are shown in Fig. 424, and the mode in which it is placed in the wall of a greenhouse, so that although access is given to it from without the house, the whole of the heat generated is available within, is shown in Fig. 425. This boiler is made and supplied in six sizes, which will be mentioned presently. In sizes Nos. 1 and 2, of which the latter is shown in Fig. 423, the front is solid and pierced with three doors, the upper door, open in the illustration, being for feeding, the middle door, shown closed, for raking out the fire, and the lowest, shown open, for clearing out the ashes. In No. 2 and the larger sizes, a water front is added. The point of escape for the smoke, and the smoke pipe itself, is without the building. The boiler is provided with sockets at the back, which are connected at once to the pipes to be heated, without the intervention of mains, and without the necessity of a sunk stoke hole. All that need be done is to make a hole in the brick wall of the greenhouse for the introduction of the furnace; if the containing wall below be of wood, a

FIG. 423 *The Loughborough boiler. External view.*

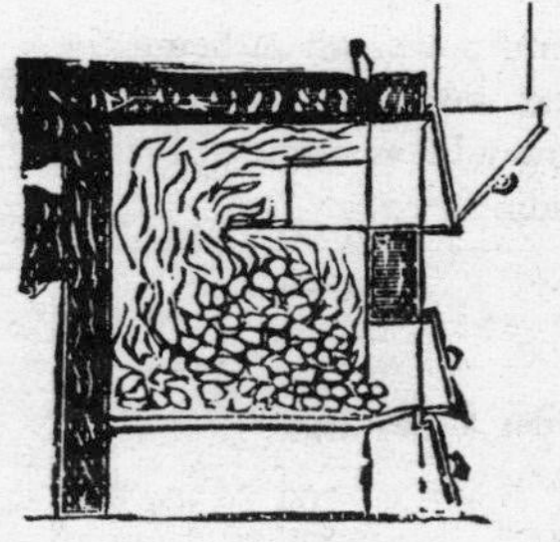

FIG. 424 *Section of Loughborough boiler*

FIG. 425 *Mode of fixing Loughborough boiler*

part of it must be removed, as in the brick wall, but no danger need be apprehended from the proximity of the woodwork to the stove. The pipes, two in number, terminate in an open-feed siphon, which takes the place of a supply cistern and pipe. An arrangement has been perfected by Messrs Messenger and Co., by which the circulation of hot water is managed in a single pipe, so that one 4-inch pipe may be carried round a greenhouse, giving a better distribution of heat than by placing two pipes on one side only. This is effected by a division in the socket on the boiler by which the water is caused to flow along the top of the pipe and to return along the bottom of the same pipe. This, however is only brought into use with the No. 1 size, and with 4-inch piping.

865 The advantages of the boiler consist in its economy, efficiency, and easy management. The whole of the heat from the boiler is utilised in the house, as already stated, the heat in a No. 1 size being about equal to that from 9 feet of 4-inch pipe. No brick setting or iron casing is required, which renders it inexpensive in first cost, while its maintenance costs but little, as there are no surroundings to get out of order. Not being set in brickwork, it is removable, and therefore a tenant's fixture. It is powerful in its heating capacity, and so simple that a woman servant can manage it. There is no stoke hole required for it, the boiler being flush with the wall of the greenhouse, and on the level of the ground. The boiler is not unsightly within the house, being covered with the stage, and as the stoking is all done outside the house, no fumes can enter it to the detriment of the plants. The stove will burn for twelve hours without attention, and as it is constructed on the slow combustion principle, the quantity of fuel required and consumed is comparatively small. The joints to the pipes are put together with elastic rings, which can be fixed by any person, and which obviate the necessity of having recourse to the ordinary method of jointing by rush cement joints and other means.

866 The sizes and prices are as follows, the heating power given being the actual amount of piping that the boilers will heat. The power is given for 2-inch pipes, but the powers for 3-inch and 4-inch pipes may be ascertained for the former by dividing by 1·33, and for the latter by dividing by 2:

	Height	Width	Depth	Heat power in 2-in pipe	Price		Height	Width	Depth	Heat power in 2-in pipe	Price
1	25 in.	13 in.	13 in.	100	£2 12s. 0d.	4	25 in.	19½ in.	21 in.	700	£6 10s. 0d.
2	25 in.	17 in.	13 in.	200	£4 0s. 0d.	5	25 in.	19½ in.	25½ in.	1100	£8 10s. 0d.
3	25 in.	19½ in.	17½ in.	400	£5 10s. 0d.	6	28 in.	19½ in.	25½ in.	1300	£10 0s. 0d.

The boilers can be had with 4-inch, 3-inch, or 2-inch sockets, so in ordering the size of sockets should be stated. It should also be stated whether the sockets are for rush cement joints or elastic joints, or if bosses are required drilled and tapped for wrought pipe, which are supplied at an extra charge of 2s. 6d. If three pipes are desired, another socket can be cast on the boiler at an extra charge of 2s. Socket bends also can be cast on the boiler either at the side or the back at an extra charge of 5s. The flue can be placed at top or in front, or to the right or left hand, as required. In some positions the sockets have to be bolted on to the boiler, the charges for which are – 2-inch, 4s. 6d.; 3-inch, 5s. 6d.; 4-inch, 6s. 6d, for each socket. The price of boiler includes fire bars, ash-pit, and dampers. The prices for elastic joints, which are not included in those named for the boilers are – for 2-inch, 1s.; 3-inch, 1s. 2d.; and 4-inch, 1s. 4d. each. The above prices, it must be understood, are for boilers only. It should be said that a No. 1 boiler, when fitted with the arrangement mentioned above for the circulation of hot water in a single pipe, costs £2 17s., instead of £2 12s.

867 The heating apparatus must not be confounded with the boiler – in other words, it must not be thought that the prices named above for the boilers include every requisite for heating purposes. On the contrary, the boiler is only a part of the whole; the apparatus is the whole, so to speak, and includes the boiler. When an apparatus is spoken of, the term includes a boiler, two 6-feet lengths of 4-inch pipe, feed siphon, and elastic joints, and this is implied in the cost of complete apparatus for houses of various dimensions as given in the following table, the first excepted, in which the pipe is 3-inch pipe. Carriage is included in the prices quoted. A No. 1 boiler is sufficient for houses of the dimensions named, the temperature being reckoned as for a plant house. If a set of stoking tools is required, an extra charge of 5s. is made for them.

Dimensions		Price		Dimensions		Price	
Length	Width	Lean-to	Span roof	Length	Width	Learn-to	Span roof
10 ft	5 ft	£4 12s. 0d.	—	16 ft	10 ft	£6 13s. 0d.	£5 18s. 0d.
12 ft	8 ft	£5 0s. 0d.	£5 0s. 0d.	20 ft	10 ft	£7 10s. 0d.	£7 12s. 0d.
16 ft	8 ft	£5 10s. 0d.	£5 10s. 0d.	16 ft	12 ft	£7 13s. 0d.	£8 3s. 6d.
20 ft	8 ft	£6 6s. 0d.	£5 18s. 0d.	16 ft	12 ft	£6 15s. 0d.	£6 8s. 0d.
12 ft	10 ft	£6 0s. 0d.	£6 8s. 0d.				

The first of the houses named in this table is the Loughborough Six-and-a-half Guinea Greenhouse, which is only made as a lean-to house.

868 *Silver Medal Horse Shoe Boiler* This is another saddle boiler on end, of the class to which the Loughborough Boiler belongs, and although there are many essential points of difference between them, still there is sufficient family likeness on each side to lead a casual observer to imagine that they are precisely the same in principle, though not exactly alike in construction. This boiler is patented and manufactured by Messrs Charles P. Kinnell and Co., 31 Bankside, London, who call attention to the great waste in heating power that arises from the exposure of the boilers themselves or of their front plates to the air when the air carries away the heat from the surface that is thus exposed, and

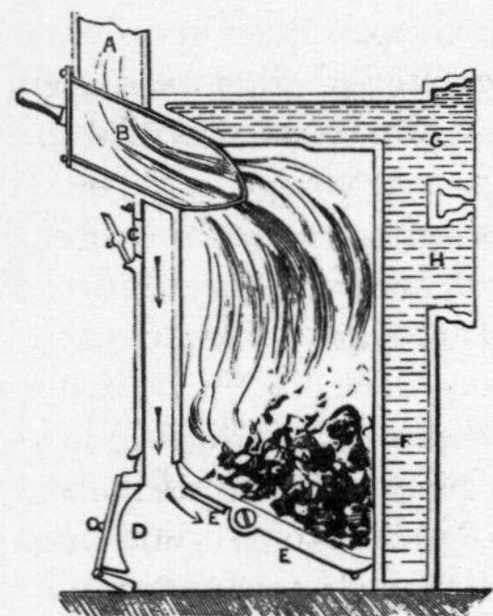

FIG. 426 *Silver medal horse shoe boiler section*

shows that in this boiler the heated air previously wasted is utilised by carrying it into the furnace for the purpose of supporting combustion, thus securing that great desideratum, a hot blast. When the fire is lit the air to support combustion enters through C, and passing downwards through the space enclosed between the outer and inner fronts in the direction indicated by the arrows, passes under the bottom grating into the furnace. The bottom door E is carefully fitted so that the external air cannot find ingress at this point, and is only removed for the purposes of clearing away ashes, etc. The bottom grate E, swings on pivots, but it is so placed that it naturally rests at the angle shown in Fig. 426, which represents a section of this boiler. This arrangement gives greater depth to the furnace, and causes the most intense heat at the back of the boiler, where it is most required, and keeps the fire going as long as any fuel, remains. In order to light the fire the door D is removed, and an iron bar sent with the boiler is introduced into the opening at E, and used as a lever to press the grating downwards. This is easily done, and affords space for inserting fuel. After the fire has been once lit all further supplies of fuel are introduced through the hopper, B, immediately below the smoke-pipe, A. The boiler, F, is continued to the bottom of the ash pit, and forms its own stand, thus effectually preventing the escape of injurious gases into the house. As the flue or smoke-pipe leaves the boiler in the centre of the front and not on one side, equality of combustion is thereby secured in the whole of the internal space which forms the furnace, G and H are the sockets in the boiler for the flow pipe and the return pipe respectively.

869 The automatic draught regulator shown at C obviates any necessity for the use of dampers. 'It frequently happens,' Mr Kinnell points out, 'that after a boiler has been left for the night with the bottom doors and dampers properly regulated for slow combustion, that a change either in the direction or in the velocity of the wind upsets the nicest calculations, and morning finds either the whole of the fuel gone and the fire out through excess of draught, or the fire out and the fuel unconsumed through insufficient draught.' Mischances of this kind are prevented by the use of the patent automatic valve, which acts in such a manner as always to admit sufficient air to keep the fire going properly, and no more or less than is enough to keep the fire burning steadily. The valve, C, which covers the opening in front of the stove below the hopper, B, is formed of a thin steel plate, weighted with lead along its bottom edge, and rests on two small projections in the framework, on to which it fits. A small brass pin, provided with a thread and weighted at each end, passes through the centre of the steel plate, the valve working as in a balance. Screwing this pin outwards increases the draught, screwing it inwards decreases it, but once set, it does not require to be touched afterwards. The amount of piping to be heated governs the rate of combustion required, and the regulating pin is only required to make the boilers suitable for any less amount than their specified power. The pin having been adjusted, and the valve in operation, it will be found that when the fire has a tendency to burn too fast, the current of air passing into the furnace draws with it the valve, closing the orifice, and temporarily checking the supply. As soon as the fire has resumed its normal state, the valve automatically opens, to close again when the inrush of air is so great as to render it necessary to check it.

870 The Silver Medal Horse Shoe Boiler is made in three sizes, as follows, the dimensions of each size being external measurements: No. 1, 27½ inches high and 14 inches wide, heating 70 feet of 4 inch pipe, price £2 15s.; No. 2, 25 inches high and 14 inches wide, heating 120 feet of 4-inch pipe, price £4 5s.; and No. 3, 26 inches high and 22½ inches wide, heating 250 feet of 4-inch pipe, price £5 17s. 6d. A supply tank and expansion box, to be fixed at the end of the apparatus, fitted with sockets to which the pipes are bolted, affords the necessary connection between the flow and return pipes. It also acts as a supply cistern and air outlet, and the portion above the socket which receives the flow pipe affords ample room for the expansion of the water. The cost of the tank is 12s. 6d. There is an additional charge for pipes, joints, etc., but this depends on the quantity of piping and the number and nature of the joints required.

871 Many other boilers of different kinds, but all being variations of the different types of boilers that have been described, are manufactured and supplied by different makers, but it is manifestly impossible to describe them here. With regard to saddle boilers, it may be said that for ordinary use they are made in many sizes, ranging from 18 inches long, 10 inches wide, and 11 inches high, with a heating power of 200 feet of 4-inch pipe, at £2 7s. 6d., to 72 inches long, 24 inches wide, and 21 inches high, with a heating power of 250 feet of 4-inch pipe, at £42 10s. For large ranges of houses, it Is better, in order to find out exactly the size of boiler that is required, to consult any horticultural builder and hot water engineer, who, when he has considered all the attendant circumstances of position, aspect, extent, etc., will point out what is wanted and the best mode of fixing the heating apparatus in its entirety. It has only been sought here to point out some of the boilers and heating apparatus that are in use in the present day for the general run of glass structures used by amateurs and professional gardeners, and this has certainly been done sufficiently if not exhaustively.

872 *Tank System of Heating* It is undesirable to pass from this part of the subject of heating glazed horticultural structures and the appliances for effecting it without reference to the tank system of heating. The mode of heating houses by hot water pipes was long objected to, as most improvements are. Probably the inefficiency of heating power, at first, was at the bottom of most of these objections; but the same objections have never been raised to the various modifications of it applied to heating tanks and gutters. These inventions supplied the gardener with many of the fertilising results he had been in the habit of obtaining from the old dung beds: he could obtain moisture, and, by mixing manure in his tank, he could obtain much of the old ammoniacal essence along with it. He was also enabled to obtain greater uniformity of temperature, for the mass of water contained in the tank was more easily retained at a regulated temperature than could be done in the pipes alone. Mr Rendle, of Plymouth, perhaps did more to introduce this system of heating than any other person.

873 Mr Rendle recommended tanks of yellow deal, 8 or 9 inches deep, for the purpose. The tanks should be made of 2-inch deal, thoroughly well-jointed, as brewers' backs are made, and rendered watertight by red lead or lining with lead: they should be placed upon piers, at the required height, and over the tanks should be placed closely-fitted coverings of slate. Through the tank, either by means of elbow-joints or by perforations in the tank, to be sealed up again by cement, the flow and return pipe should pass with a sufficient coil of pipes to secure the degree of heat to the water which is required. The supply of water, of course, must be regulated by a ball cock, and the usual measures taken to prevent damage by overflow by the use of a waste pipe. Such a tank, coated with lead, would, of course, be more enduring, but not more efficient for the time. It will be obvious that the tank would only perform half the duty that has been assigned to it if it did not, by some contrivance, give out some of its heat and moisture to heat the atmosphere of the house and dispense the necessary vapour and moisture, and it may be necessary to have a coil of pipes available for this purpose, independent of the tank, with a stopcock attached, to turn the hot water on or off at pleasure.

A most efficient range of tanks, fitted up by Mr Rendle for Messrs Veitch and Son, of Exeter, were thus described in the *Gardener's Chronicle*, by Mr Veitch: 'This tank,' he says, 'is formed of brick arches, worked in cement, with brick sides; the whole well coated with cement. The top is of slate, cemented down; the sides of the beds are of brickwork. The material used for plunging is a clear sharp sand, which we find retains the heat for a considerable time. In one part of the bed we have put soil, in which the cuttings planted out have rooted most rapidly. The heated water is regulated by means of a division at the end of each house, through apertures in which communication is preserved by a short piece of 4-inch pipe, having plugs fitted into them. By this simple means, one end, or the half of one end only, may be heated, or each bed may be regulated to a different degree of heat.' The house that was heated by this tank was 51 feet 9 inches in length, 11½ feet wide, and 6 feet 9 inches high under the ridge.

Much as it has been approved by the best practical horticulturists, the tank system has its objections, which are thus stated in the *Gardener's Chronicle*: 'It is well-known,' the writer remarks, 'that by means of a flow and return tank, the degree of bottom heat in the pits can be very steadily maintained. Once the mass of soil on the beds is heated to the required pitch, very little is required to keep it up, and sudden changes of temperature do not much affect it: even such extremes of external temperature as 55° one night and 25° the next will only occasion a few degrees lower temperature in the beds. But the case is different as regards the air of the house itself; for, under the above conditions, it would certainly be affected to a much greater extent – perhaps as much as 20°. Presuming that the temperature of the beds is just what it ought to be, any attempt to counteract the coldness of the air in the pit on a cold night would cause an excess of bottom heat, which, by repetition, must prove highly injurious to the plants. If the communication of heat from the tanks to the surface is only through the soil, the conduction of heat will be very slow, whilst its escape through the glass is rapid.' The remedy for this, the writer goes on to say, is a separate command of heat for heating the house, which he proposes to supply by a 2-inch steam pipe, running from the top of the boiler and ranging along the front of the house, immediately under the glass, terminating at the further end of the return tank. Why steam, he does not say: perhaps a water pipe would be sufficient for the purpose; but such is certainly an objection to which the system is open, and the best means of obviating it is by constructing hot air chambers under the tanks, from which the air may escape into the body of the house, and find its way upwards from all parts to the ridge.

874 *Staging for Glazed Horticultural Structures* There is no necessity to dwell at any length on stagings for greenhouses, etc., and it is not so much the mode of making them that requires remark as their disposition in the house to which they belong; and this must be entirely subordinate to the character and size of the house. The great desideratum in the arrangement of staging of any kind, as far as the plants themselves are concerned, is to bring them as close to the light as possible, so that they may be as fully exposed as they can be to the direct influence of the sun's rays, and, therefore, be enabled to gain the maximum benefit afforded by their light and warmth.

875 *Staging for Lean-to House* In the form of glazed house known as a lean-to, the arrangement that gives the most available space for plant room is a platform or level stage, immediately in the rear of the front lights, and on a level with the sill or nearly so, this platform being turned and continued at the end furthest from the door, until it meets the staging in the form of steps at the back of the house. For example, supposing the house is 8 feet wide, and the entrance is 2 feet 6 inches, including the jambs of the door, the available space for staging will be 5 feet 6 inches, of which 2 feet may be given to the front platform and 3 feet 6 inches to the back staging, or 1 foot 6 inches to the former and 4 feet to the latter, according to preference and the character of the plants to be grown. The shelves for the back staging will be supported on timbers placed aslant and cut step fashion in the manner of those which carry the outer ends of the treaders and risers of a staircase. The number of these supports must be regulated according to the length of the house and the weight of the pots and mould that the stage will have to sustain. Thus, if the pots are large and heavy, the supports must be closer together, and the shelving made of thicker material; if, on the contrary, the pots are small and light, the supports may be placed farther apart or be made of lighter stuff and the shelving of thinner wood. The shelving of a back stage need in no case be more than 12 inches wide or less than 3 inches, according as the house is required for flowering plants or for plants for bedding out. For ordinary purposes, a medium width of 8 or 9 inches will be found sufficient; and to suit all circumstances it will be better to have the lower shelving a little wider and the upper shelving a little barrower. Solid shelves should always be avoided; the shelving is better for all purposes, whether for front stage or back stage, if made of battens, not nailed down to the supports but notched into the horizontal edges of the supports as at A, A, A, A, in Fig. 427, B being a slip of wood screwed to the vertical edge of the support in order to prevent the outer batten that forms the front edge of the shelving from being dislodged. When staging is constructed

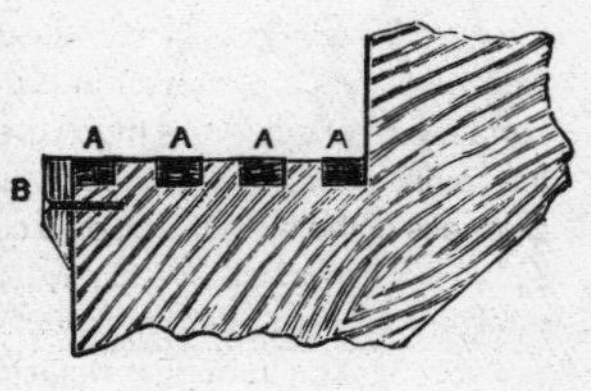

FIG. 427 *Mode of notching battens of staging into supports*

in this manner it can be removed in a short time and without injury for the purpose of cleaning, painting, etc. If the plants to be kept in the house are all very nearly of the same size, it is as well to keep the edges of the supports of the staging as nearly as possible parallel with the roof, but if large and small plants are kept together, the back staging may be so constructed that there is less distance between the glass and the shelving at the extreme rear of the back staging than in the front.

876 *Staging for Half Span and Three-Quarter Span Houses* For houses of this description, the arrangement of the staging will be precisely the same as for lean-to houses, but as houses constructed on this principle get more light than lean-to houses, the parallelism between the supports of the staging and the roof need not and indeed cannot be observed, as it will be necessary so to regulate the height of the rearmost shelf that there may be sufficient space for plants between it and the glass above.

877 *Staging for Span-Roofed Houses* In the generality of houses of this description, and invariably in those in which the roof lights rest on the side walls of the structure, the staging will consist of a level platform on each side of the house. Thus, for example, if a house be 9 feet wide, there will be room for a platform 3 feet 3 inches wide on each side of the house, allowing 2 feet 6 inches for the central passage. If the house be wider, say 12 feet wide, there may be a platform in front of the vertical side lights, of from 1 foot 6 inches to 2 feet, and a platform in the centre of five shelves, one, forming the highest, in the centre, with two on each side of it and below it in pairs, on the same level, from 3 feet 6 inches to 4 feet in width, allowing 2 feet 6 inches for the walks on each side.

878 *Construction of Staging* For all ordinary purposes level staging may consist of battens or narrow slips of wood not less than 1 inch thick and ranging from 1 inch to 2 inches in width, laid on a framework composed of a front rail, supported on posts at intervals, and horizontal pieces running from the front rail to the sill of the front or side lights, according as the house is a lean-to or span. The construction of staging consisting of shelves rising one above another in tiers has been already explained, but the supports must be framed into posts in front in the lean-to house, and on each side in the span-roof house. When the level staging is narrow, iron brackets, plain or ornamental, will be found to form suitable and convenient supports, care being taken to provide for their attachment to the building, either by vertical wooden uprights rising from floor to sill or by wooden bricks built into the brick wall when in course of erection. Of course, if the containing walls are of wood, the attachment of brackets is simple enough. For the support of single shelves along the framing of a glazed structure, iron brackets, screwed to the uprights, are the most suitable. For hanging shelves, pendant from the

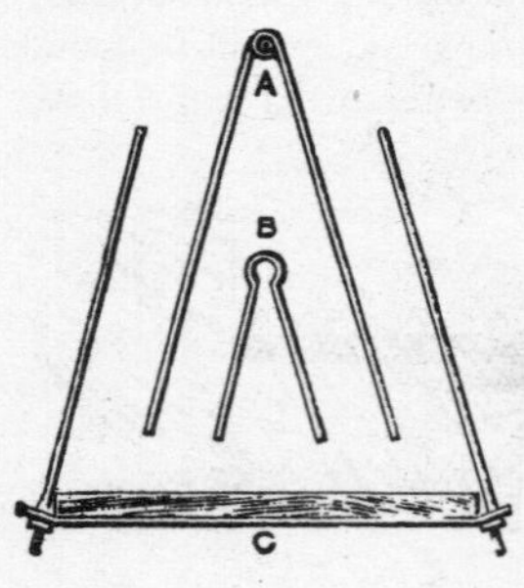

FIG 428 *Support for hanging shelf in greenhouse*

roof, perhaps the best kind of support is a strong wire turned at the top into a loop, as at A in Fig. 428, or fashioned as at B, to hang on a support inserted into the roof timbers. The ends of the wire should be screw cut and pass through the ends of an iron band, slightly turned up and pierced, so that the wire may pass through it at right angles to the bend. A nut is then put on each end of the wire, and screwed up close to the lower surface of the bent end of the band. This affords a support for a hanging shelf which is both stable and safe, a great desideratum in matters of this kind. When staging of great strength is necessary in order to support large plants, it should be made of slates of some thickness, sustained by iron framing, but for this it is desirable to seek the advice and aid of the professional builder. Staging of slate and iron is also desirable for supporting plunging beds of any great extent, and for the formation of hot air chambers below.

879 *Floors of Greenhouses* These may be paved, and indeed generally are paved, but if the floors are made of solid material it is well they should be disposed in such a manner as to facilitate the immediate drainage of any water that may fall on them, and this must frequently occur if the plants in a house are kept properly watered and syringed, and when water is sprinkled over the floor in hot weather to promote freshness and coolness of temperature throughout the house. If it is not thought desirable to construct the floor of the house of paving, gratings of iron supported on brickwork may be used, or it may consist of wooden slats or battens of some thickness supported on sleepers. Even when stone paving is used, it is desirable to lay a wooden grating upon it, similar to the gratings of this material used for bathrooms, in order that it may be possible to walk with comfort from one part of the house to another, even when the watering has been heavier than usual, and the floor has been consequently rendered more than usually wet.

FIG. 429 *Clematis John Gould Veitch.*
Hardy climber, with flowers of a beautiful light blue colour

CHAPTER 19

Orchard Houses: Their Construction and Management

880 From all that has been said in the preceding chapters about glazed horticultural structures, it is evident that when they are built, contrived, and warmed in such a manner as to be of genuine service, their construction at the outset is attended with expense, and their maintenance, and the care and cultivation of the plants that are grown in them, involves continual care and supervision, and thus causes a constant drain on purse and pocket. Of course, in the case of the professional gardener, the outgoings are balanced, and more than balanced, in a pecuniary point of view, by the incomings arising from the sale of plants, flowers, and fruits, but with the average amateur it is not so, for he does not and cannot grow for profit. The rich man, however, does not care what his outlay may be on his garden and greenhouses in the course of the year; he leaves it all to his gardener, or gardeners, as the case may be, and as long as the senses of sight and smell and taste in himself and his family are gratified, and another sense, which may be defined as the sense of proprietorship, is satisfied, he is content. All it costs him individually is represented by a certain sum of money, larger or smaller; he gets his reward or interest on his outlay in the mode and manner just stated, and he is content. The professional gardener invests money, time, and labour in the pursuit of his vocation, but it pays him to do so, because it enables him to live, and in many cases, let us hope, to make money, and he is content also.

881 But with the majority of non-professional gardeners, whom it is convenient to consider and describe as average amateurs – men of modest means, who are compelled, and at the same time pleased, to do their own gardening, with, perhaps, a little extraneous assistance now and then – the case is different. Gardening with them is an amusement pure and simple, and the bulk of it is done, per force, in early morning or in the evening, when the length of the day permits, for in the interval that elapses, say from 9 a.m. to 6 p.m., or thereabouts, they have their business to look after. Now, the care of plants under glass is of such a nature that it demands constant attention, both in summer and winter. The houses must be opened for the admission of air, and closed to maintain the internal temperature, according to the time of day or the variation of the weather, and incalculable and irreparable damage may be caused in a very short time from the neglect to do something that is absolutely necessary at the right time, in the right place, and in the right way, as many may have realised to their cost who have had nothing more important to look after than an ordinary garden frame with cucumbers within it. A gardener, to do his work well and thoroughly, must be always on the spot and as watchful as Argus, but for the ordinary amateur to be always at his post is absolutely impossible, for the reasons that have been given.

882 What, then, is he to do? Give up all thought of indulging in a bit of glass, and content himself with culture in the open air only? By no means; but let him make up his mind to deal only with *unheated* glazed structures, or with such that only require a moderate amount of heating in cold and wintry weather to maintain a temperature sufficiently high to prevent injury to the plants that are kept in it and to exclude the frost. And for fruit growing, in which he may combine profit with pleasure, let him go in for the orchard house, which is essentially the house of the amateur who is bound to look after the main chance and attend to his hobby at odd times only. When orchard houses were first introduced by the late Mr Rivers, of Sawbridgeworth, we used to hear a great deal about them: they are not so prominently brought into notice now because the charm of novelty no longer attaches to them, but this is no reason why the orchard house should be shown the cold shoulder. It is a structure so essentially and intrinsically good in itself, so cheaply and easily constructed, and so simple and unexacting in its management, that the greatest possible prominence is given to it here. Its great value lies in the fact that the fruit crop on trees that are grown within it is sure and certain, and that the cost of the structure is to be looked upon as nothing more than an insurance paid to secure this immunity from loss – an insurance whose amount every year grows less and less, as the original cost gets spread over many years by the lapse of time, and the proportional outlay for each individual year becomes less and less.

In order to make this perfectly intelligible, let us suppose that a man puts up an orchard house, and it costs him, in round numbers, £20. Viewed in the light of an insurance to secure the certainty of a crop, whatever the weather may be and the detrimental influence it may exert on trees growing in the open air, the premium for the first year is represented by the cost of the house, namely, £20, but when the second year has elapsed, the premium per annum has been; £ 10, at the end of the third year, £6 13s. 4d., at the end of the fourth, £5, and at the end of the twentieth, only £1 per annum. It must be understood that this is put forth as a broad and approximate statement only. The interest on the original sum sunk in the building is not taken into account, and the probable amount of annual repairs is omitted, which would tend to raise the yearly premium above the sum stated. The principle involved, however, remains the same. This is said for the confusion of financial critics; and those who know how to use sword and singlestick – a most desirable acquirement – will know what I mean when I point out that it is intended to run on parallel lines with the sharp and rapid twist of wrist and sword, technically known as parrying, which so frequently disarms one's adversary, jerking his weapon out of his grasp and leaving him at his opponent's mercy.

883 The orchard house is a very simple, but, nevertheless, a distinctive structure, perfectly efficient for all practical purposes, and its projector claims for it that it confers all the benefits of a warm climate without their sometimes oppressive heat. Mr Rivers was led to adopt orchard house cultivation by observing the effect produced on some figs in pots, which he had occasion to turn out of a greenhouse, and which were accidentally placed on a border in another house. The roots penetrated through the drainage hole in the bottom of the pot, and spread themselves over the border, giving to the plants an unusually vigorous and healthy growth. In due season the pots were taken up, and the external roots pruned close with a sharp knife, and placed on a shelf suitable for them during their season of rest.

884 The following spring they were placed in the same border, but, by enlarging the drainage hole, an increased growth of the roots was encouraged. The result justified his expectations: an unusual display of fruit followed the experiment. He now reasoned that if figs could be grown in small pots by supplying extra nourishment, why not peaches, nectarines, pears, and other fruit? – and he proceeded to follow up the mode of culture he had accidentally hit on to a large extent, with the certainty of a crop proportioned to his exertions.

885 A visit to Mr Rivers's grounds at Sawbridgeworth, in Hertfordshire, to which all comers are invited, may be at first rather disappointing if made, as it most probably will be, in the summer, and it is necessary to recall the fact, from time to time, that the business of the firm is to grow and sell trees, and not to sell fruit. Nevertheless, in the course of a walk round the grounds, the visitor cannot but be satisfied that all the statements as to the productiveness of the orchard houses can be verified. One of the partners will take you to a small house, which is nothing more than a pit dug in the ground, the soil being a fine rich sandy loam, and over the pit, some 10 feet wide, a range of ordinary frame lights, about 10 or 12 feet long, are raised, so as to form a sort of lean-to roofed house, which probably cost, with the ends and doors, a matter of £10. In such a house as this, simple and unpretending as it may seem, it is possible to have most delicious figs and white Frontignac grapes perfectly ripe in July, which have been grown in it without the slightest aid from artificial heat.

886 In walking through the grounds, the orchard houses that present themselves to view are plain useful buildings, generally span-roofed; but the demand for trees will be found to interfere with their show of fruit, as in the summer season they are all half empty, but they will exhibit enough of the system to satisfy the visitor of what it is capable. It must be added, however, that Mr Rivers is so happily placed in respect to situation that, in his own grounds alone, he has five or six different soils of a most fertile description, in which all fruit trees grow naturally and in great luxuriance, so that with him the system is carried out under the best possible auspices.

887 Mr Rivers has described, as a convenient form of house, a lean-to structure, 30 feet long and 12 feet 6 inches wide, made in the following simple manner: Six posts of yellow deal, 5 inches by 3 inches, or oak posts, 4 inches by 3 inches, and 9 feet 6 inches in length, are firmly fixed, and driven 2 feet into the ground, the lower ends being previously charred and coated with coal-tar, or boiled linseed oil thickened to the consistency of paint by mixing finely-powdered coal dust with it, which is said to be better than tar. This is the back line of posts. Six other posts, exactly similar, but only 5 feet long, are fixed also 2 feet in the ground, forming the front posts of the house – the one rising 3 feet and the other 7 feet 6 inches above the ground level. Two posts at each end occupy the centre, and form the door posts. On the six posts, both in back and front, a wall plate is nailed to receive the rafters, one of which springs from each of the six front posts, resting on the corresponding back post.

888 The rafters are 14 feet long. A 9-inch deal, 3 inches thick, will make four of them. On the upper side of each rafter is nailed a slip of ½-inch deal, 1¼ inch wide, which will leave ½ inch on each side as rebate to receive the glass. The rafters so prepared are fixed in their place to the wall plates by having a piece cut out at each end to correspond with the angle of the back and front plates. They are then firmly nailed, at back and front, by a strong spike nail, leaving a space between each rafter of 5 feet, which is called a bay; this is filled up by smaller rafters or sash bars of a size proportioned to their length and the use they are to be put to – vines trained to them requiring stronger bars. A piece of ¾-inch deal board, 6 inches wide, nailed along the top of each rafter, so as to be even with their upper edges, forms the ridge board, leaving a space between the board and the rafter to receive the upper end of the glass. A similar piece of inch deal, 6 inches wide, let in to the rafters by sawing a piece corresponding to the width and thickness of the board out of each, will receive the glass and carry off the water. The placing the glass is a very simple process: a bedding of putty is first laid in the rebates, the wood having been previously painted, and then, beginning at the top, a plate of glass, 20 inches wide, is laid in the rebates, and fixed in its place by a brad driven into the rafter; and so on till the whole is covered in: there are no laps, but the edges of the panes touch each other, the joints in the glass being what is termed open joints, which are rather advantageous than otherwise, if not too wide. The ends of the houses are fitted up to correspond with the roof, only that above the doorways a small sash is fitted in for ventilation. These sashes at each end, and the other provisions for ventilation to be mentioned presently, were said by Mr Rivers to be quite sufficient; indeed, he pronounced the ventilation perfect. Well-seasoned ¾-inch deal, planed and jointed, nailed outside the posts forms the lower part of the house.

889 In the front wall, sliding shutters, 3 feet by 1 foot, will afford ventilation to the roof; and about 3 feet from the surface of the ground, two similar sliding shutters will ventilate the lower part of the house behind, and on a level with them. Ventilation behind is further secured by shutters 2 feet 6 inches long, and running the whole length of the house under the wall plate; below these shutters the space is filled in with boarding, well painted. In summer, it is impossible to give too much air. The house is now complete, except the door, which must open inwards for obvious reasons, and may be half glass, or otherwise, at the proprietor's discretion.

890 Within the house, a trench, 18 inches deep and 3 feet wide, is formed, to which two steps from the outside will lead. This leaves a platform or border on each side of 4 feet 9 inches; the back border requires to be raised 18 inches above the original ground level, and Mr Rivers suggested that it would be improved by a second terrace behind the first, 14 inches in height, supported by a 4½-inch brick wall, so that the back row of trees need not be shaded while they are brought nearer to the glass.

891 The nature, size, and appearance of the structure that has just been described will be rendered clearer to the ordinary reader by the diagrams given in Figs. 430, 431, 432, 433, 434, and 435. The house itself is a low boarded structure with a glass roof of considerable size, when the height of the building

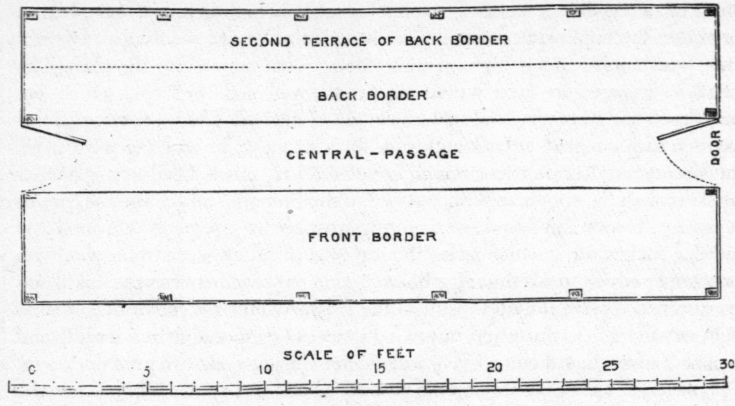

FIG. 430 *Ground plan*

is taken into consideration: it may, in fact, on account of its wooden front, back, and ends, and its glass roof, be looked upon as a cucumber frame on a large scale. The diagrams are all drawn to scale, according to the scale of feet given below Fig. 430. Beginning with this diagram, which represents the ground plan of the orchard house, the dimensions adopted are in accordance with those of the house recommended by Mr Rivers, and the relative positions of the posts of the structure, the central passage running through it, the border in the front and the border at the back, with the raised terrace in the rear, are all shown, with the doorway at each end of the passage. It is always convenient, if situation permit, to be able to go in at one end of the house and out at the other, and having two doors instead of one increases the means of ventilation in hot weather. If it is not possible to have two doors, as may be the case in some gardens, then the door must be made in the end which can be most easily approached. Again, there may be situations – as, for example, at the end of a narrow garden about 30 feet wide, with a fairly good aspect, ranging from south-east to south-west – in which it is desirable to make the house right across the garden without the possibility of having even a single door at one end. In such a case the door must be made in the

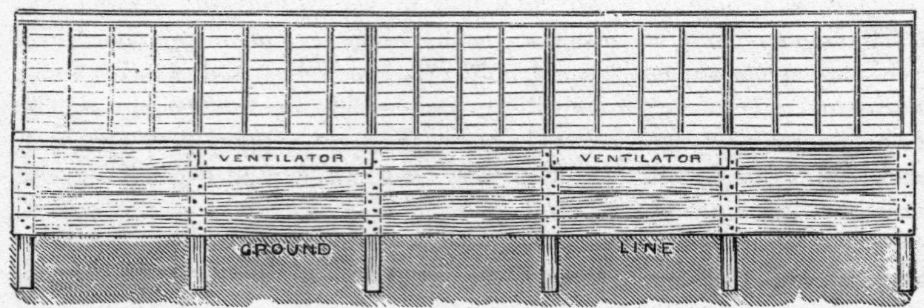

FIG. 431 *Front elevation*

centre of the front, and headway must be gained for entrance by steps without the house leading down to the door, and more steps within to give access to the central path, care being taken to leave room enough for the door to open properly before the ascent is commenced.

892 Here a few remarks are necessary on the construction of approaches to a low house by steps without it leading down from a higher level. Looking at Fig. 436, which represents a section of the approach, it is clear that there will be an enclosed space between the door and the steps and the containing walls that sustain the soil on either side, and this will act as a catch-pit for rain that may fall on it or water that may trickle into it. Supposing the bottom of this tiny court to be a dead level, as shown by the dotted line at A, the water, having no means of escape, or a very slow means of soaking away at the best, will touch the door sill, B, which will swell by absorbing the moisture and cause the door shown in section at C to jam and open and shut with difficulty. Everybody knows what a nuisance a tight door is, so to prevent any annoyance from this cause let the bottom of the court in front of the door slope from the door sill to the face of the bottom step as shown by D. Let there be a small gutter running along the front of the step, to one corner, and there, by means of a drain pipe, shown at E, make provision for the immediate escape of the water into a small cesspit at F, filled with brickbats and large rough stones and clinkers, and covered with brush wood, etc., or two or three large flat stones or slates, if preferred. The cesspit should not be made immediately under the steps, but on one side of them, for obvious reasons. The bottom of the court should be solid and formed of concrete, and it is desirable that the central path of the house should also be of concrete.

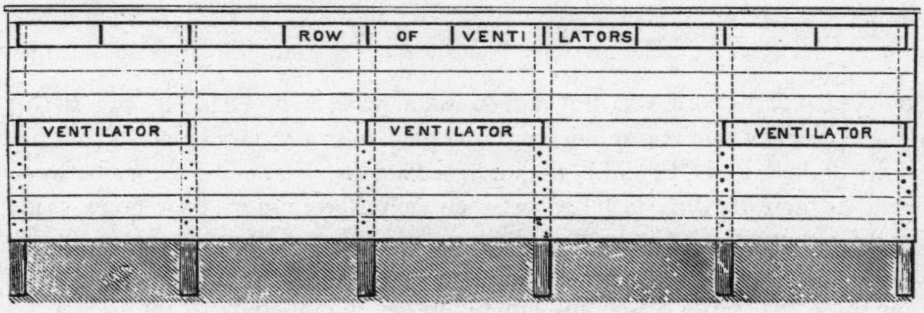

FIG. 432 *Back elevation*

893 To return to the orchard house itself, the front elevation is shown in Fig. 431, the back elevation in Fig. 432, and the end elevation in Fig. 435. From these the mode in which the house is boarded up all round, and the construction of the doors, may be seen and fully comprehended. The position of the ventilators is also shown, there being two immediately under the wall plate in the front, three in the back just above the surface of the terrace of the back border, and a row at back immediately under the wall plate. The best and most simple method of making ventilators is shown in Fig. 437. The ventilator itself is a swing board or shutter hinged to the wall plate or board immediately above it, and secured when closed by buttons screwed to the woodwork on either side of it. If it is not possible to gain access to the ventilators from outside, and it is necessary to fasten them on the inside, the buttons must be attached to the inner surface of the ventilator and turned over the surrounding woodwork. When there is a row of ventilators, as shown under the wall plate in the back elevation, the buttons must be attached to the lower edge of the ventilator. There should be two buttons to every ventilator, one near each end, and not one in the centre only; the use of two buttons tends to prevent warping. When opened, the ventilator may be fixed, as shown in Fig. 438, by means of a stay of iron attached to an eye screwed into the ventilator, and hanging from it when closed, but propped against and sustained by a small piece of iron bent at an angle and screwed to the board below, as at A, a depression being made in the upper part of the iron to receive the end of the stay.

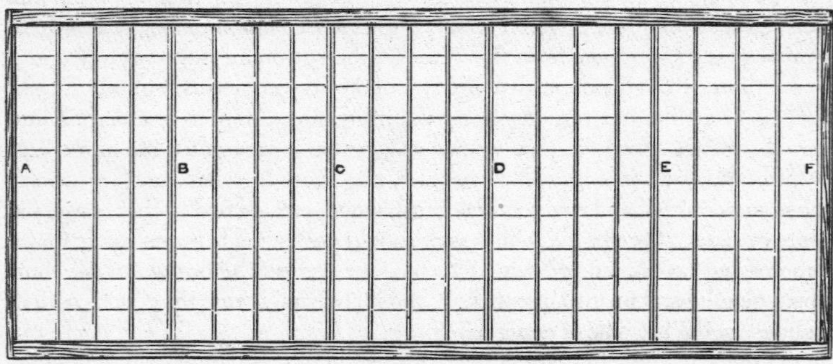

FIG. 433 *Plan of roof*

894 A plan of the roof, also drawn to the same scale, is shown in Fig. 433. In this the six principal rafters running from wall plate in front to wall plate at back are shown at A, B, C, D, E, and F, the intermediate sash bars being shown between them. As there are three sash bars between each pair of rafters, provision is made for the reception of panes of glass about 15 inches broad and the same in length, but, as it has been already said, the number of sash bars, which should not be less than three, may be increased, though it must be remembered that the greater the number of sash bars the less will be the space to be occupied by glass. A useful hint may be given here with regard to glazing. As there are no laps to the panes of glass, the top edge of each pane will about against the bottom edge of the pane immediately above it. The panes are to be secured from sliding downwards by brads driven into the rafter or sash bar, as the case may be. The usual mode of doing this is shown at A in Fig. 439, and under this system there must of necessity be an open space of the thickness of the brad between the edges of the panes. The better plan is to take off the lower corners of each pane, as shown at B. The brads are then driven into the woodwork in the space originally occupied by the corners of the glass, and there is no impediment to pushing up the lower pane so as to touch the edge of the upper pane, so that there will be no appreciable space between them if the edges are properly and truly cut.

895 In Fig. 434, a section of the house is given, showing the borders at front and back, the raised terrace in the rear of the back border, and the central path. The borders must be sustained by containing walls, shown at A, B, and C. These may be – indeed, ought to be – of 4½-inch brick as stated, but the building of such simple walls as these would take a great many bricks and cost money. Concrete slabs screwed to posts would be cheaper than brickwork, and for this purpose the slabs known by the name of Croft Adamant, manufactured and supplied by the Croft Adamant Granite, Brick, and Concrete Company, Croft, near Leicester, will do well. Those, however, who are making a house of this kind as cheaply as possible will have to content themselves with containing walls of rough wood set on end and nailed to a framework set up from end to end of the borders. An excellent appearance, approximating to rustic work, is obtained by the use of fir poles sawn down the middle, which may be cut in lengths and set on end and nailed to the framework in the same manner as the boards. A coping should be formed by nailing lengths of the same material along the top edge of the wooden wall thus formed. With regard to the terrace at the back of the back border, means should be taken to protect the exterior hoarding from decay from the moisture of the earth piled against it by an interior coating of wood, or, better, of concrete slabs. The disposition of the borders is such as to bring every tree as near the light as possible, no matter in what part of the house it may be.

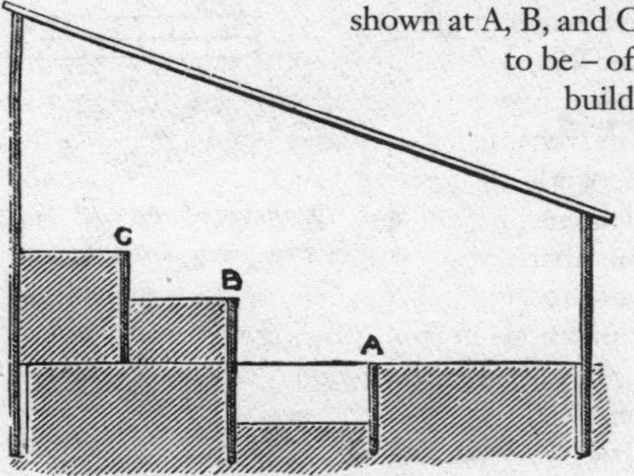

FIG. 434 *Section of house, showing borders*

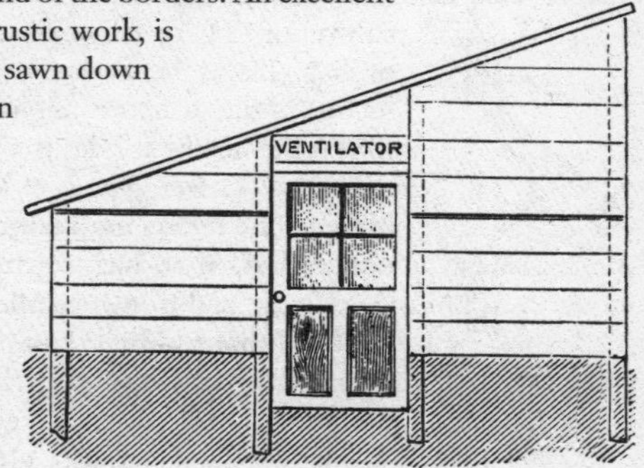

FIG 435 *End elevation*

896 In the case of an orchard house constructed across the end of a narrow garden, with an entrance in front, the cost would be comparatively trifling, because there would only be the front to make, the roof, and the enclosures at the sides, and the portion of the back above the garden wall, supposing this to be of brick. Indeed, it is difficult to think of a more appropriate way of disposing of the end of a long and narrow garden to advantage, especially if the owner of the garden be fond of gardening and of fruit. The house already described may cost from about £15 to £25, or even £30, according to the manner in which it is built, but it is possible that a man who can use his tools and purchase and work up his materials with care and judgment, would construct it, with the hints that have been given, for even less than £10.

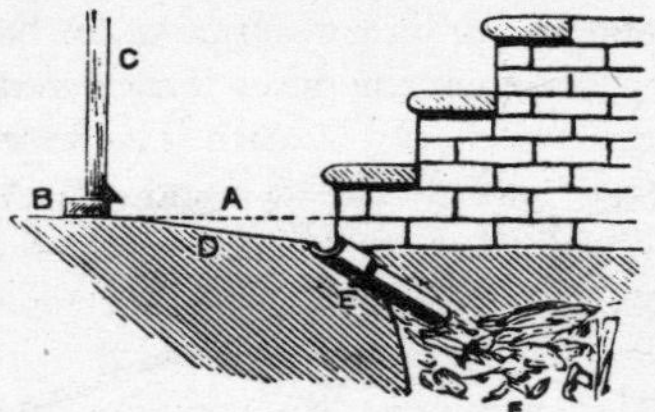

FIG. 436 *Drainage of approach to door by steps from without*

897 With regard to successful operations in fruit growing within the house, everything depends upon the borders; their surface should be loose and open, and formed of old lime rubbish and road sand, mixed with manure laid 4 inches deep, the whole forked over and well mixed with the soil 9 inches deep.

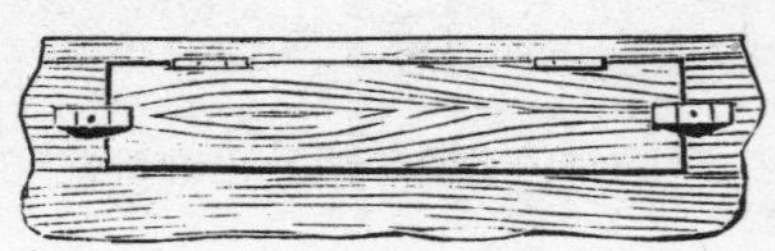
FIG. 437 *Mode of attaching and fastening ventilators*

898 As a lean-to house has been described, it may be useful to supplement it with a brief description of a span-roofed house, which comprises the advantage of border as well as pot cultivation. There will be no need to show every part in detail by diagrams, as the method of building it is the same. A simple section of the structure, as given in Fig. 440, will be sufficient. In this the height at sides is 5 feet; the height of ridge, 9 feet; the width, 14 feet. The roof rests on oak posts 5 inches by 3 inches. The rafters are 20 inches apart; it is glazed with 16-ounce glass, in 20-inch squares. Under the eave boards, the sides, back, and front, are filled in with glass 15 inches deep, joined without putty. Under this is a ventilating board, on hinges, opening downwards; below this are ¾ inch boards, to the ground; the two ends are glazed to the same level as the side lights; the doors, with glass sash, opening inwards. Over the door, an angular space, 9 inches deep, is found sufficient for roof ventilation; the rafters, 3-inch by 1½ inch stuff, are tied at the top with a light iron tie screwed to the rafters. No putty is placed in the laps of the glass, which serves every purpose of roof-ventilation found necessary in this house. The only ventilators are the shutters, 1 foot deep on each side and 2 feet 6 inches from the ground, and the angular opening over each door. Fig. 440, as already said, affords a sectional view of the house and the end elevation also. The

FIG. 438 *Mode of fixing ventilator when open*

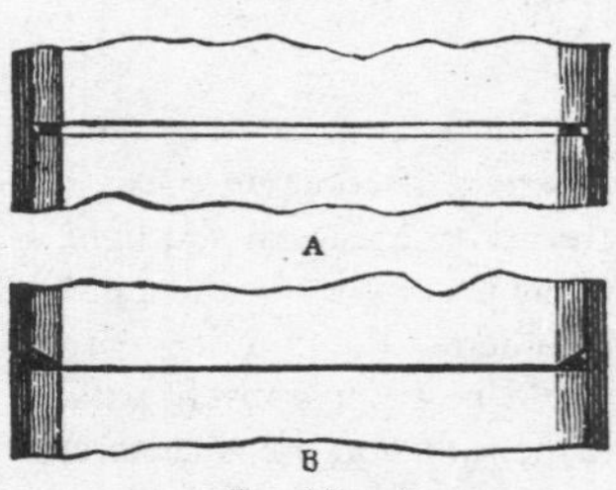

FIG. 439 *Bradding in panes in glazing without putty*

ground line or level is shown by AA. The borders, B, B, are slightly raised above the ground line and level of the central path, being edged with tiles or stones, shown in section at C, C; they are 5 feet 6 inches wide, and the path, D, between them is 3 feet wide. The posts are shown by E, E, surmounted by wall plates, L, L, on which are notched the rafters, M, M, butting against a ridge board, N, above which are the boards which are laid on the rafters to form the ridge and cover the edges of the panes of glass in the highest row next the ridge. From M to M runs the iron tie attached to the rafters to strengthen them. The space COPC in centre, enclosed by dotted lines, represents the door in the end elevation, and the triangle N, just under the ridge, shows the ventilator for the roof, its position when open being indicated by the triangle N′. At H, H, between L and F on each side of the house, there is glass, but the structure is boarded up all round to the height of the dotted line FF. Between F and G are the lines of ventilating boards, the ventilators, K, K, being shown as open: they are hinged to the boards immediately below by the lower edge, and when closed are secured by buttons. This form of house is more desirable than that of the lean-to previously described, and should be chosen in preference to the latter if space will admit.

899 The borders in such a structure as the span-roofed house just described need not be raised, nor the path sunk, except as a matter of choice; they should have a dressing of manure and sand, or manure and burnt soil, or any loose material well forked over, and mixed with a dressing to the depth of 6 inches, composed of the top spit of a pasture of tenacious loamy soil, which has been exposed to the air for the summer months, mixed with one-third of well-rotted manure, chopped up into lumps as big as an egg. In the border thus composed two rows of trees may be placed; the front row 3 feet apart, the second being in the rear, zigzag fashion, but half way between, so that they are each 3 feet from

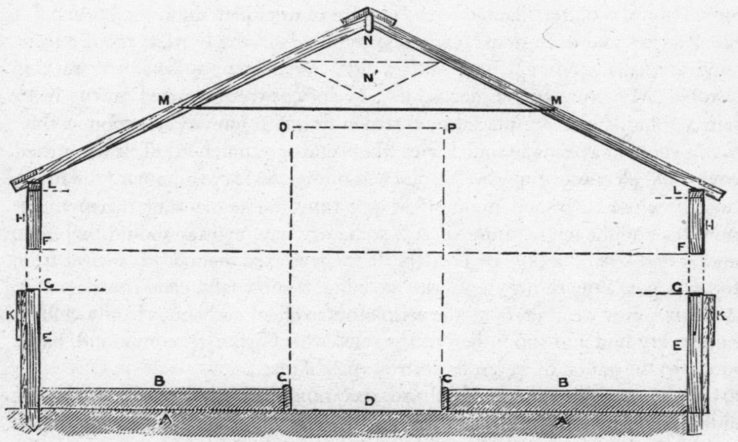

FIG. 440 *Section and end elevation of span-roof orchard house*

stem to stem, and none shading the other. Such a house as this, without artificial heat, is intended for protection only, and not for forcing; but oranges and camellias might be grown with success in it, if the house could be heated in very severe weather so as to prevent it falling at any time below 26°. The heating, however, would be absolutely necessary for the oranges only, as camellias will grow and bloom satisfactorily in the open air, being hardy and as suitable for outdoor culture as for greenhouses. The most severe frost would not injure tea-scented roses so sheltered; but the house is essentially intended for the protection of fruit trees, whether planted in the borders or in pots, and has the effect of bringing us, without artificial heat, to the temperature of Angers, in the south of France, where the royal muscadine grape usually ripens in the open air on the 25th of August.

900 The use to which the lean-to structure may be put with good effect is the culture of peaches, vines, and figs, in pots. Selecting a straight-stemmed maiden peach or nectarine, well furnished with lateral buds, and not more than three or four feet high, it is planted in an 11-inch pot, and each lateral shoot is cut into two buds. As soon as the shoots have made three leaves, the third is pinched off, leaving two, not reckoning, however, one or two small leaves generally found at the base of each shoot. These pinched shoots soon put forth a fresh crop of buds, each of which, and all succeeding ones, must be pinched off to one leaf as soon as two or three leaves are formed.

901 This incessant pinching off the shoots of a potted pyramid tree, in the climate of an orchard house, will, in one season, form a compact cypress-like tree, crowded with short fruit spurs. In spring, these will require to be thinned, and every season the shoots will require to be pinched off as above described.

902 Dwarf pyramidal peach and nectarine trees may also be planted in the border, two feet apart, with excellent results. They require the same incessant pinching, and must be *lifted and replanted* annually in October; but the span-roofed house is better adapted to the culture of trees planted in the borders.

903 Peaches and nectarines, planted as pyramids in the border, require to be lifted annually, and replanted with a little fresh compost the last week in October. Miniature peach, nectarine, and apricot trees, grafted on the black damask plum stock, are placed in a garden frame in January. As soon as their young shoots have made four leaves, their ends are pinched off, leaving their leaves, and all succeeding shoots, pinched off to one leaf. In January the house must be closed day and night. If at any time the registering thermometer indicates a night temperature of 20°, some dry hay or litter should be placed among and over the pots or borders. If the trees are inclined to shrivel from drought, give a quart of water in the morning. If snow falls, clear the glass of it. In bright sunny weather, open the ventilators to check early buds from swelling. Paint every bud and shoot, before it swells, with Gishurst's compound, half a pound to the gallon of water, to destroy eggs of insects.

904 Continuing this mode of culture, recommended by Mr Rivers, from the autumn after grafting till the fourth or fifth year, when the trees are beginning to show fruit buds, these, which it is the object of this training to promote, are distributed along the branches, in their whole length, in spur-bearing fruit, as the apple and pear. In the peach tribe, short spur-like shoots appear towards the end of August, bearing triple buds – a plump silvery one on each side, and a thin one in the centre. This central bud is the terminal leaf bud; the two others, blossom buds, which, in March, will have opened their silvery coat, showing the bright pink of the blossom. These indications appear in the third year after planting. Their development is promoted by carefully watching every branch, checking the more vigorous shoots by pinching off the terminal buds, or by breaking or half-breaking them, so as to check the flow of the sap.

905 The work of pruning begins with the second year's growth. In the winter following, the terminal branches will present a series of small shoots more or less vigorous, and the required pruning will be according to their vigour; repressing the stronger as early as possible by pinching off the leading shoots, and encouraging the weaker shoots; thus balancing the growth of the tree, and suffering no more branches or leaves to be produced than can properly perform their function of elaborating and storing up matter for the production of fruit – a function for which a full exposure of every part of the tree to light and air is quite essential. It is the pruner's work to remove all shoots which do not fulfil this condition by rubbing them off, and arresting the over-luxuriant ones by timely pinching off the terminal bud. Others, suited for his purpose, he leaves at their full length, merely depressing their points, which will induce them to push from every bud fruitful twigs of moderate growth, or he prunes back a weak shoot to two or three buds, raising the point in a perpendicular direction, knowing that the sap may thus be concentrated so as to produce a more vigorous growth. If he wishes to increase the vigour of his trees, he will prune them early in autumn, so that the sap they may accumulate in the winter is not thrown away: he studies, in fact, the ways and means of the tree; nor does he forget that the roots should be under control as well as the branches. The treatment should be preventive as well as remedial; the latter, indeed, as Mr Rivers tells us, 'is out of place in a well-ordered garden – the finger and thumb, and a moderate sized penknife, should do all the pruning required'.

Sir Joseph Paxton's houses, which have been described in the preceding chapter, may be so extended as to form an excellent range of orchard houses at a comparatively small cost, while the crops of fruit and vegetables are not only excellent in quality, but certain in their results, no matter how unpropitious the season. The following is a brief account of a winter garden of this description, on a large scale, which was erected on Sir Joseph Paxton's plan. It consisted of a range of span roofs of 14-foot sashes, which occupied the centre of the garden in the form of a quadrangle, connected with the house by a corridor, formed of sashes of the same dimensions, so arranged with lean-tos against the walls as to form an extensive promenade, several hundred feet in length, terminating in a similar range of lean-tos placed against the outside of the south wall. Groves of fruit trees planted near the side of the walks of the span roofs filled up all the available space; grapes hung overhead, and vines and other fruits in pots were placed in different parts, late and early vegetables forming an important feature during the winter and early spring. The walks were made of neat paving tiles, forming at once a cheap and beautiful tesselated pavement. The whole range of winter gardens, especially when in blossom in early spring, formed, as may well be imagined, a most enchanting scene when contrasted with the appearance of the garden outside, the centre of the quadrangle being treated as an ordinary out-of-door garden.

906 In Fig. 441 an idea is given for a range of orchard houses, which might be of any size required, although for peaches, nectarines, apricots, cherries, etc., 12 feet in breadth would be sufficient, with 12 feet between the rows of houses; this would allow about 6 feet inside on each side, and 6 feet outside for the roots of the trees, which is ample for any sort of fruit tree. The houses should be just sufficiently high in the middle to allow a tall gentleman to walk through upright; thus the trees would be convenient for training without the aid of steps; there would also be every convenience for regulating the roots as well as the branches. The water from the roofs of the houses and the drains might (if there were no other supply) be conveyed into a tank, which might be made large enough to supply the garden. In the illustration provision is made for ventilation at the top by raising the ridge and inserting louvre boards along the sides of the superstructure thus raised. This, with ventilating shutters in the walls under the wall plates, will be sufficient for the admission and free circulation of air. The louvre boards may be set on pivots in the centre of each end, and opened and closed by a cord in the same manner that the top board of a Venetian blind is turned, and with it all the other slips that form the blind.

FIG. 441 *Range of orchard houses*

A correspondent of the *Gardener's Chronicle*, who wrote shortly after the introduction of orchard houses by Mr Rivers, thus recounts his own experience in cheap orchard house building, from which those who may desire to try this method of fruit culture may gain some useful hints. 'I venture,' he says, 'to send you an account of one I raised last autumn, which has certainly the merit of economy – I think also of effective appearance, so far at least as that is necessary in such a structure; and, thirdly, I hope of efficiency in the fruitful work for which it is designed. Being rather crowded with trees, I looked about for a few whose absence would be rather a benefit than otherwise. I soon found an oak, a lime, and sundry Scotch and larch firs. My own men dug a pit in a very short time in a back part of the garden, and three trees were sawed out at an expense of about £2; they served for posts, plates, rafters, purlins, boarding, etc. I purchased and used foreign deal to the value of another £2; nails and screws, 14s.; carpenter's labour, £2 17s.; glass, 400 feet, allowing for breakages, carriage, etc., £4; putty and paint, say £2; but this last is with me a difficult item to reckon, as so much is always being used on the premises. I can make no further charges, for my own gardener and his assistant, with very little hired aid, did the glazing and painting, etc. Pots and plants are expensive, but they vary in different districts; so the mention of mine will not benefit anyone else. The cost of my house then stands thus:

Wood, sawing, nails, etc.	£4 14s. 0d.
Glass, with putty and paint	£6 0s. 0d.
Carpenter's labour	£2 17s. 0d.
Total	£13 11s. 0d.

My house is 30 feet long by 12 feet wide, inside measure; 9 feet high at back; 3 feet 3 inches in front, weather-boarded. The back is tarred; front, sides, and roof, painted with anti-corrosive paint; the inside walls are whitewashed with lime. This rather washes off with hard syringing. I am doubtful whether next season I shall renew it, mixing some flour of sulphur with the lime to keep off the red spider, or whether I shall paint it. The path was dug out to about a foot depth below the door-sill, but nearly filled up again with dry stones, which were well gas-tarred, and then covered with clean gravel. The borders on each side are raised and boarded – the front 1 foot, the back 1 foot 6 inches. This, I think, adds very much to appearance and convenience, the trees coming close up to your hand for the numerous manipulations required, and being seen very much better; they are also nearer the glass, and no shade is thrown from the front border plants on those of the back border. I have four sliding shutters at the back, a board to let down the whole distance in front, also a small ventilator in the boarded side opposite the door. My plants in 16-inch and 11-inch pots stand diamond-wise on each border, and between the large pots at the back I have planted in the border a few trees for training up the back of the house, which I shall keep in check by lifting and root-pruning. I have a ledge for strawberries about six inches below the front shutter, holding about fifty plants, and another hundred are placed between the large pots on the borders; they are blooming and setting fruit abundantly.'

The returns for a much greater outlay than is here contemplated will be gathered from a communition on the subject by Mr Morris, gardener to Mr T. G. G. White, of Weatherfield Manor, near Braintree, Essex. In 1851, an orchard house, 80 feet long by 12 feet wide, was put up, and eleven trees were planted in that space as permanent ones. They began to bear in 1852, and in 1854, just after the gardener had commenced gathering fruit, there could not have been less than 5000 or 6000 peaches and nectarines on the trees, besides what had been removed. In 1858, according to Mr Morris, the trees were still producing heavy crops. So much for trees planted in the open border. To this statement, so creditable to Mr Morris, it was suggested at the time that such a house to a market gardener must be a source of great profit, but 'for a gentleman to surfeit himself and his friends with fruit for eight or nine days in autumn would never do, while his gardener, by potting a few well-grown trees in summer, placing them from time to time in his forcing house, could produce him fine ripe fruit from June to October, by leaving Royal George and Noblesse peaches and Moorpark apricots out of doors in July, so as to retard them.' But the advocate for orchard houses has his answer. There is a range of peach and nectarine houses at Weatherfield for early forcing, but, as a matter of fact, he supplied the family table with fruit from August 9th till November, from the orchard house to which exception is taken, and from trees planted in the border. From the manner in which the trees were planted, two crops were taken from each tree; one side being so placed as to be from 15° to 20° colder than the other; and if he were to add an early York peach to his collection, Mr Morris adds, he could have ripe fruit a fortnight earlier.

907 For more humble gardeners, who cannot afford even one of the very cheap orchard houses that have been described, here is a suggestion which may be adopted and followed with advantage: Take two or three of the lights used in a common frame; support their upper ends against a south wall, on which a full-grown healthy peach or nectarine is trained, just as the buds are swelling and about to blossom. Let the bottom rail stand three feet from the ground and three feet from the wall, supported by a strong stake driven into the earth at each corner. Protect the open spaces at the bottom and ends by mats of wheat straw, made in the manner recommended in Chapter 14, Section 596. Give air on every fine day, and watch the tree so as to supply moisture when required; remove decaying leaves, and guard from insects. When summer is fairly come, let the fruit ripen under a June and July sun, and the finest peach house in the country will not furnish fruit more delicate or in greater proportionate quantity.

908 For the information of those who may not care to build an orchard house of the kind introduced by Mr Rivers, and which has been described in the

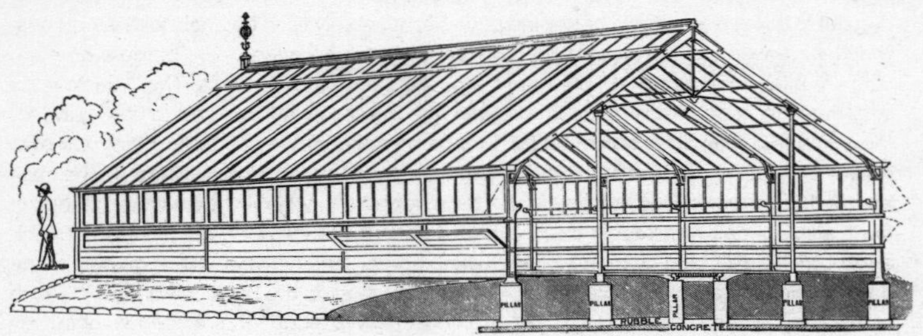

FIG. 442 *Orchard house of glass, wood, and iron*

preceding part of this chapter, and who may wish to have the very best structure of the kind that money can procure, it will be useful to describe and illustrate an orchard house that is constructed and supplied by Messrs Messenger and Co., Horticultural Builders, Loughborough, Leicestershire. The view of the house given in Fig. 442 affords a view of both the sides and the interior of the house, or, in other words, exhibits the elevation and sectional view of it. It is built on Messrs Messenger and Co.'s patent principle of iron muntins and light rafters strengthened with ironwork, which has been described in an earlier chapter. The iron muntins rest on brick pillars built about 5 feet apart, which are based in their turn on a solid bed of concrete, over which a coating of rubble is thrown, which affords drainage for the beds in the interior of the house. If preferred, the muntins or supports for the roof and walls may be carried down 3 feet below the ground level to the bottom of the border, and rest direct upon the concrete, thus dispensing altogether with brickwork. Pockets are cast in the muntins to receive the upper and lower wood sills. The sides are 5 feet in height, and of this the lower half consists of boarded framing, and the upper half of glazed framing. Ventilators are fitted in the boarded framing, hinged at the bottom, and opening outwards. The house is usually made from 16 feet to 24 feet wide, the intermediate widths being 18, 20, and 22 feet. In the larger sizes columns are provided at intervals to strengthen the roof, as shown in the illustration, a provision which is desirable, because as the width of the house is increased the weight of the roof is increased in like proportion. The arrangement of the substructure of the house affords complete communication between the outside and inside borders, so that the roots have free space for growing. Ample ventilation, so necessary in an orchard house, is provided by the ventilating shutters in the boarded framing, by the lights that are hung in the upper moiety of the sides and in the ridge. The lights are 2 inches thick, hung on hinges that are specially treated to guard against rust. Wrought-iron principals are fixed to alternate rafters. The walk through the centre of the house, between the beds on either side of it, consists of iron gratings on kerbs of the same metal supported on brick pillars about 5 feet apart. Wood slats may be substituted for the gratings if preferred. Cast-iron guttering is provided for the eaves and down pipes to carry off the rainfall. The entire work is painted with four coats of colour, the roof being glazed with 21-ounce glass, and the sides and ends with 15-ounce glass. The prices for a house 30 feet long, exclusive of brickwork and heating apparatus, which may be added at extra cost if desired, are – for 16 feet in width, £71; for 18 feet, £77; for 20 feet, £86; for 22 feet, £94; and for 24 feet, £100. For 30 feet of iron grating, 2 feet 4 inches wide, on iron kerbs, the price is £7 2s. 6d. These prices are given approximately only, but will be found near enough for all practical purposes in estimating the cost of a house to cover any specified area.

909 *Furnishing the Orchard House* Full directions for the management of the orchard house will appear in the calendar of operations in the garden for each successive month, and therefore there is no occasion to anticipate them. It will be well, however, to give here a list of such trees as may be introduced into an orchard house without fear of disappointment, for it is hardly necessary to observe that all sorts of trees do not bear the confinement of glass nor ripen their fruit under such circumstances equally well. All the sorts mentioned are of course suited to the table; for no one would take the trouble which an orchard house involves to grow in it any sorts of fruit which are fitted only for culinary purposes.

1 *Apples* – Ribston Pippin, Blenheim Orange, Cox's Orange Pippin, Sturmer Pippin, Golden Reinette, Coe's Golden Drop, Melon, Nonpareil, Margil, Newtown Pippin, Northern Spy, Worcester Pearmain.
2 *Apricots* – Breda, Blenheim or Shipley's Large Early, Kaisha, Gros Peche, Moorpark, Royal, Turkey.
3 *Cherries* – Amber Heart, Adam's Crown Heart, Bedford Prolific, Kentish Bigarreau, Bigarreau Napoleon, Black Eagle, Black Turkey Heart, Early Elton, Florence, Governor Wood, Flemish Red, Kentish Red, Knight's Early Black, May Duke, Old Black Heart, Black Tartarian.
4 *Figs* – Early Violet, White Marseilles, Dwarf Prolific, Hardy Prolific, Osborne's Prolific, Brown Turkey, White Ischia (excellent for forcing, and an abundant bearer).
5 *Grapes* – Black Cluster or Black Burgundy, Prolific Sweetwater, Buckland Sweetwater, Calabrian Raisin, Esperione, Ferdinand de Lesseps, Muscat St Laurent, Royal Muscadine, Trentham Black, Black Hamburgh, White Frontignan.
6 *Nectarines* – Downton, Elruge, Pitmaston Orange, Rivers' Orange Violette Hative, Prince of Wales, Hardwicke Seedling, Pineapple.
7 *The Orange Tribe* – Maltese Common Oval Orange, Maltese Blood Oval Orange, Citron, Lemon, Persian Lime, Silver Orange, St Michael's, Tangerine, Egg Orange.
8 *Peaches* – Acton Scott, Late Admirable, Barrington, Bellegarde or Galande, Crawford's Early, Dr Hogg, Early Alfred, Early Savoy, Early Louise, Early York or Victoria, Royal George, Grosse Mignonne, Malta or Royal George, Noblesse, Red Magdalen, Violette Hative, Walburton Admirable, Hale's Early, Princess of Wales.
9 *Pears* – Doyenne d'Eté, Jargonelle, Duchesse d'Angoulême, Seckle,

Louise Bonne of Jersey, Josephine de Malines, Passe Colmar, Williams's Bon Chrétien, Winter Nelis, Gansel's Bergamot, Crassanne, Marie Louise, Beurré d'Amanlis, Beurré d'Aremberg, Beurré de Capiaumont, Beurré Clairgeau, Beurré Diel, Beurré Easter, Beurré Giffard, Beurré Hardy, Glout Morceau, Bishop's Thumb.

10 *Plums* – Angelina Burdett, Belgian Purple, Coe's Golden Drop, Cox's Emperor, Golden Gage, Green Gage, Guthrie's Aunt Ann, Guthrie's Late Green, Huling's Superb, Ickworth Imperatrice, Jefferson Kirke, Mitchelson's Damson, Orleans, Oullin's Golden Gage, Pond's Seedling, Prince Engelbert, Prince of Wales, Reine Claude de Bavay, Royal Hative, Victoria, Washington, Webster's Gage, Woolston's Black Gage.

CHAPTER 20

Principles of Vegetation and Modes of Propagation

910 Plants may be described as organic bodies, composed of an outer bark or epidermis, and an interior, consisting of an irritable elastic cellular tissue, through which the sap necessary for its support rises from the root towards the upper part, namely, the leaves and flowers. Each cell forms a small closed vesicle, a complete laboratory in itself, through whose membranes the sap oozes by the process of *osmosis*, which may be explained as the tendency of fluids to become diffused through a separating membrane when placed in contact with it, and the action produced by this tendency, which is a pushing action or impulse: the cells stand side by side filled with most different matters, which never become intermixed. Each of these cells extracts from the constantly passing current of sap those constituents required for its own product, and when its allotted elaboration is completed, they either are passed on again in a fluid state, or reserved for the future needs of some other part of the plant, or they are used to repair or increase its own solidity. Plants are thus possessed of a vital principle, only differing in form and intensity from that of animals.

911 The water plants classified as *Characeae*, growing in stagnant waters, always submersed, and often entirely concealing muddy bottoms, of which *Chara vulgaris*, a native of the British Isles, may be cited as a type, are usually advanced as a proof of this. Through these plants the sap may be seen circulating in a current of green globules, rising through one set of transparent cells and descending through another, and this evidence of the circulation of the sap in plants is rendered still more convincing if a ligature be tied round the centre, when the motion continues as before, but is confined to each end – two endless chains being produced in place of one. It was in the *Characeae* that the phenomenon of *cyclosis*, or the circulation of the sap in plants, was first observed, and though the exciting cause of this movement of the contents of the cells of plants is not perfectly understood, still it is now generally allowed that it prevails throughout the whole vegetable kingdom, and characterises the active life of all vegetable cells. Dutrochet, the eminent French physiologist,* who was at one

* René Joachim Henri Dutrochet, who was born in 1776, and died in 1847, a well-known French physiologist and physician, devoted himself, in the latter part of his life, to the study of physiology. An account of his various investigations and discoveries is given in his *Mémoires pour servir à l'Histoire Anatomique et Physiologique des Végétaux et des Animaux*, published at Paris in 1837. His reputation chiefly depends on his researches on the passages of fluids through animal and vegetable substances He applied the term *endosmosis*, or inward impulse, to the passage of a fluid from without, and *exosmosis*, or outward impulse, to the passage of a fluid from within, and these terms are now accepted and applied in these senses by physiologists of later date.

time opposed to the theory of vital force, advocating the theory of electrical action in place of it, finding that the magnet exercised no influence over the circulation in *Characeae*, admitted afterwards the doctrine of vital force, which is now generally accepted, as it has been already said.

The sensitive plant, which shrinks from the touch, the lip of the peculiar and unique ground orchid, *Drakaea elastica*, which closes under similar circumstances, and the snap of the leaf of *Dionaea muscipula*, or Venus's Flytrap, are all arguments favouring the doctrine of *cyclosis*, which is confirmed by the effect of laudanum or arsenic dropped on the leaf of plants, such as the kidney bean or lilac, or two drops of chloroform placed on the leaf of *Mimosa pudica*, or the Sensitive Plant, the leaflets collapsing pair by pair at the extremity, but recovering their sensibility after some hours.

912 In a state of nature all plants are propagated from seed, and the multifarious forms of the seeds and envelopes with which they are provided form one of the many interesting subjects of investigation to the lover of nature. For the present purpose it is sufficient to state that most seeds are covered with a hard shell or envelope, which protects them from external injury, and that within the envelope lies the embryo plant. All seeds in this latent state contain an organ, or Germ, which, under favourable circumstances, shoots upwards, and becomes the stem of the plant; another, called the Radicle, which seeks its place in the soil, and becomes the root; and the Seed-Lobes, which yield nourishment to the young plant in its first stage of growth.

913 Moisture, heat and air, are necessary conditions for the development of all seeds; and most of them require, in addition, concealment from the light. These conditions are found in the open texture of well-pulverised garden soil, through which water percolates freely, and air follows, each yielding their quota of oxygen, hydrogen, and carbon, in a gaseous state, for the support of the plant. The great majority of plants cultivated in gardens are obtained by sowing the seeds in beds suited to their constitution, to be afterwards planted out where they are to grow and ripen their fruits, or seeds, or leaves. Leaves are the first outward sign of germination, and throughout its existence, next to the roots, the most important organ of a plant. The seed leaves, as the buds which first appear above the ground are termed, are of vital importance to the plant, and if destroyed prematurely, the young plant rarely recovers; therefore, the leaves of all young seedlings require protection from insects, worms, and slugs, their most dangerous enemies, as well as from severe weather.

914 *Germination* is the natural process by which the embryo of the seed placed in favourable circumstances – that is to say, surrounded by moisture and heat and shrouded in darkness, throws off its shell or covering, and in course of time becomes a vegetable resembling that from which the seed was obtained. From the time that the acorn of the oak is placed in circumstances favourable to its germination, it absorbs moisture, the cotyledon, A (Fig. 443), swells, the root or radicle, B, is elongated, and the

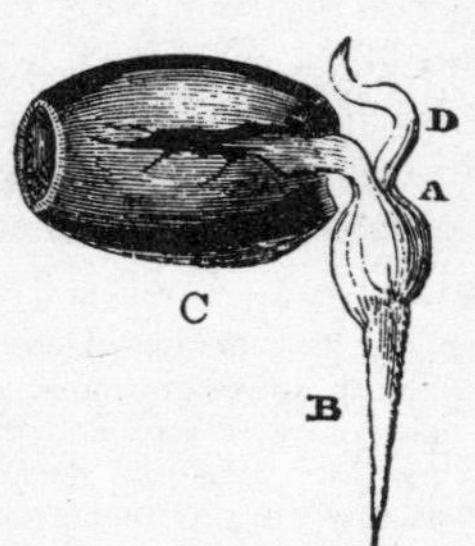

FIG. 443 *Diagram illustrating germination of acorn*

shell or envelope, C, is broken. The root issues by the fissure, and directs itself downwards into the earth; the plumule, D, erects itself, is disengaged from the shell, and becomes the stem, while the cotyledons furnish food to the young plant, until the first leaves develop themselves and the spongioles of the roots are capable of receiving nourishment from the earth.

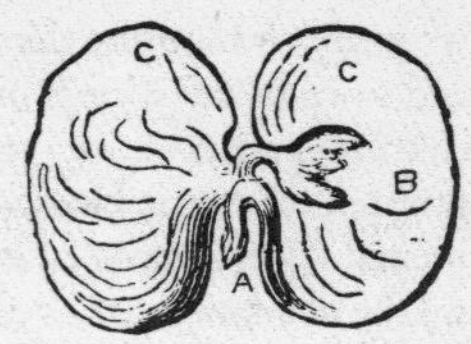

FIG. 444 *Formation of kidney bean*

915 In plants with a soft covering, as the bean, the radicle, A (Fig. 444), is directed to the outside of the seed; it is the rudiment of the root, and this is the first part which develops itself in germinating. The plumule, B, on the contrary, ascends towards the centre of the grain, and becomes the stem, while the two cotyledons, C, C, remain in the soil between the root and stem, yielding nourishment to the young plant until the root can perform that office.

916 It is found, however, that, except in the case of annuals – as plants are called which are raised from seed, which grow, produce their seeds, and ripen their fruit in one year – much time is lost by following this mode of propagation; it is also found that the seed does not always produce the same identical plant; above all, it is found that none of the double-flowering, and few of the herbaceous-flowering plants, with which our gardens are furnished, ripen their seeds in our climate. The observation of this led to other methods of multiplying; for, besides the roots properly so called, which attach themselves to the soil, and draw from it the principal nourishment of the plant, it is found that each branch conceals under its outward covering a bundle of fibre or tissue, which, under favourable circumstances, develops roots, and becomes the basis of an independent plant, identical with that from which it sprang. Many plants have also a crown with buds or eyes, each capable of propagating its species. Every plant with roots of this description may be divided into as many portions as there are eyes, taking care that a few fibres are attached to the root, and each will become an independent plant.

The potato, and all the bulbous and tuberous plants, are familiar examples of this principle of propagation; so are the dahlia and peony, which grow better when the set is confined to a piece of the tuber with one eye attached than when planted whole. So conspicuous is this in the potato, that, where it is planted *whole*, all the eyes except one, or at most two, are scooped out with a sharp knife; and the only argument on which this mode of planting is adopted at all is that it supplies the young plant with more of its natural pabulum while it rooting, and thus increases the vigour of the young plant.

917 A few remarks on the different characters of the roots of plants and the various terms applied to them may not be out of place here, before the description of the different modes employed in the propagation of plants, otherwise than by raising them from seed, is entered on. Plants are broadly classified by the character and permanence of the stem, the stem being *annual* (Latin, *annuus*, yearly, from *annus*, a year), *biennal* (Latin, *biennis*, lasting for two years, from *bis*, twice, *annus*, a year), or *perennial* (Latin, *perennis*, that lasts from year to year, from *per*, through, *annus*, a year) – that is to say, lasting for a year, for two years, or for more than two years. Thus, in an *annual*, the plant is raised from seed sown in the spring, or at the earliest, in the winter preceding the spring, in which it appears above ground, the stem attaining its fullest development in the summer, when the blossom appears and the seed is subsequently produced and ripened. When the seed is ripe, the functions of roots and stem are performed, and the plant dies, to be reproduced from the seed that it has yielded. The various cereals, many vegetables, and all the flowers popularly termed annuals, may be cited as examples of this class.

918 A *biennial*, on the other hand, lives, as the term implies, for two years. The seed from which it is raised is sown in the spring, and during the first year of its existence the plant produces leaves, and in some cases develops a fleshy tuberous *quasi* root, which, though usually called by this name, is not the actual root or roots by which the plant derives nourishment from the soil. In the second year, as spring is ripening into summer, the plant sends up a strong stout stalk, which blossoms and yields seed. As in the annual, when the seed is ripe the work of the root and stem is done, and the plant perishes. Parsley, the carrot, the parsnip, and beetroot afford familar examples of plants of this class.

919 *Perennials* differ from annuals and biennials in the length of their duration. They do not, as might be inferred from the term, exist for ever, but their life as plants is more than two years, to say the least of it, and in some cases has endured for hundreds of years, as is proved by tradition and the venerable aspect of the plants that have witnessed the birth and death of so many generations of men and have outlived and outlasted even the youngest and latest. Among such may be named many ancient oaks and forest trees in various parts of the world, the vine at Hampton Court, and the still more wonderful rose tree at Erfurt, in Germany, which still yields its fragrant flowers in rich abundance, is guarded with vigilant care to prevent its propagation, and has attained an age, it is said, of upwards of eight hundred years. All perennials are not so long lived: they will last a few years, some dying down to the ground and sending up fresh stems yearly, and others retaining their stems and branches, and shedding their leaves at autumn time, or from time to time gradually and almost imperceptibly, as evergreens; but many show deterioration in every way as they advance in age, and ultimately perish or are rooted up to make room for plants of a similar kind in the full strength and vigour of a lusty youth.

920 Advantage has been taken of the varying character of perennial plants to classify them in accordance with their habit of growth and appearance. Thus, plants whose stems are soft and succulent, and contain but little woody fibre, and die down to the roots annually to spring up again next year from buds formed at the base of the perished stems, are called *herbaceous* plants, because their stems partake more of the nature of grass, the Latin term for grass being *herba*. The lychnis, the phloxes, some of the delphiniums or larkspurs, and the Michaelmas daisy, are examples of herbaceous plants. Trees, on the contrary, whose stems are composed of hard woody fibre, are classified as *ligneous* plants, from the Latin *lignum*, wood. Shrubs are ligneous plants, by reason of the hardness and toughness of their stems, although they differ widely in height and dimensions from trees properly so-called, varying in altitude from about 2 feet to 20 feet. The stems of shrubs throw off an undergrowth at their base, which develop into new stems in time and produce flowers. The rose is an example of the smaller kinds of shrubs, the laurustinus of shrubs of intermediate size, and the arbutus of shrubs of large size. Between *herbaceous* and *ligneous* plants is an intermediate link, consisting of plants which partake partly of the nature of each, but are dissimilar to each in some respects. These are termed *sub-ligneous* plants. The hard lower portions of the stems of these are lasting, and send forth fresh shoots every year, but the extremities of the shoots thus sent forth perish year after year, and are again renewed when the plant makes fresh growth. Among these may be named sage, rue, and southernwood.

921 Returning to the consideration of the root of the plant, it must be remembered that it is not always the portion of the plant that happens to grow underground that is really its root. We are accustomed to call potatoes, parsnips, carrots, onions, beetroots, etc., root crops, because the parts of them that we eat grow under the earth's surface, or nearly so, but in reality the parts of the potato that we use as food are tubers; the carrot, parsnip, and beetroot, as well as the dahlia, are tuberous roots; and the onion, in common with the lily and the hyacinth, is a bulb. What, then, is the root? The root or roots of a plant are offsets from that portion of the plant which is below the earth's surface, in the form of threads or filaments, terminating in soft little organs called *spongioles*, through which moisture and the various elements that combine to form the structure of the plant are absorbed from the earth. In the case of the tree, as the plumule develops into the hard stem, so the radicle branches into roots, which ultimately assume the form of subterranean branches, that afford safe anchorage to the tree itself, but at the extremities of these, and at the ends of branch-lets which issue from them, are bunches of fibrous roots terminating in spongioles, through which the nourishment of the tree is derived from the earth, to be carried upward to the extremities by the branches that we familiarly call roots below ground, through the stem and branches above ground.

922 Similarly in the onion and all bulbs, the roots are not the bulbous portions which are produced and matured below the surface of the soil, but the coronal of fibres which issue from the edges of the circular patch at the bottom of the bulb. In the potato, the tuber, rich in starch and nutritive matter, is not the root, but the fleshy string-like fibre issuing from the tuber, through which the food stored up within it has been gathered from the soil by means of the fibrous roots. The junction of the old root with the tuber may be readily distinguished on an examination of any tuber, for it differs from the eye in exhibiting no signs of vitality. It will be understood that this fleshy string-like fibre of which I have spoken is the emanation from the root proper at the end of which the tuber has taken its origin, and that it acts as a medium of connection between the root and the tuber, and a channel for the conveyance of nutriment from the soil through the roots to the latter. Again, the real roots of the parsnip, the carrot, and the beetroot are the threadlike fibres which issue from the fleshy tuberous root on all sides, and especially at the extremity of the tuberous root, which is commonly called the tap root.

923 We are now in a better position to understand the various natural means by which the propagation of plants is effected. Popularly speaking, the root of a plant is considered to be that part of the plant which is below ground, and which commences just where the stem ends. This junction of root and stem is usually called the collar, and in planting, due regard should be had to keeping the collar in its proper position, for if it be too low – that is to say, underground – the portion of the stem that is buried will be liable to canker, especially in the case of worked trees, where the junction is close to the ground, and if it be too high, a portion of the plant that ought to be below ground will be above it, and will suffer from the exposure. This, however, as we have seen, is not the case with every plant, and we know that the rootlets or fibres which are sent forth anew by the parts underground are put forth for the collection of nutriment from the soil in the same manner as leaves are put forth by the parts above ground for the reception, aeration, and maturation of the sap, when it is brought to them from below by the system of circulation which carries the sap through the plant, in a manner analogous though not similar to that in which the blood is carried through the arteries and veins of animals by the action of the heart.

924 Sometimes the underground portion of a plant assumes the form and functions of a stem to a certain extent, running sometimes above ground and partly below ground, but generally the latter, and sending up shoots into the air from the upper surface and roots into the ground from the surface below. When the stem assumes this rootlike form, as it does in ginger (*Zinziber officinale*) and Solomon's Seal (*Polygonatum*), it is called a *rhizome*, from the Greek *rhizoma*, which means 'that which has taken root'. The primrose and kindred plants are also an example of natural propagation by rhizomes, for the stem of the primrose, instead of being upright and ascending as in the great majority of plants, and attached to the roots below ground by a collar, is an underground stem, or nearly so, thrust forth laterally from the plant, and from this the leaves and blossoms immediately grow, and the roots issue, taking a downward course into the earth.

925 In other plants, Nature has resorted to an entirely different kind of propagation. In these, a loose trailing branch or stem, called a *stole* or *stolon*, from the Latin *stolo*, a twig or shoot springing from the stock of a tree, is sent forth from the plant at the summit of the root, just where the leaves spring from the stem. This branch or stem proceeds from the original plant to some distance, and then takes root downwards and sends forth leaves upwards, frequently continuing its growth beyond the first attachment to the soil, and rooting at intervals, forming a new plant at each rooting. Plants that propagate themselves in this manner are called *stoloniferous*. The strawberry affords a familiar example which is known to everyone, and another is found in the Trailing Saxifrage, *Saxifraga sarmentosa*, sometimes called Mother of Thousands, one of the prettiest basket plants that can be found, with its green foliage, nearly round in shape and flecked with white, its pyramidal spikes of white flowers, and its deep red stoles, which hang on all sides over the basket, from 18 inches to 24 inches in length, breaking out at intervals into miniature reproductions of the mother plant.

926 Speaking broadly, natural propagation is effected by the development of a bud which proceeds from some portion of the plant, either root or stem, as the case may be, that is below the surface of the ground, or from the stem proceeding from it at a point just above the surface. Examples have been already given. No matter what may be the mode of propagation that Nature selects, the offset, when ultimately separated from the parent plant, assumes a separate existence, and becomes an independent plant similar in every respect to that from which it sprang. Thus, the suckers thrown up from the root of a rose or any shrub that throws up shoots of this kind from below ground, when detached, with a portion of the root, will speedily form new and strong plants. The rhizome of the primrose, polyanthus, etc., may be removed from the parent plant, and will soon send forth roots under favourable circumstances, if it be not already rooted before removal; and when the new plant springing from the stole of the strawberry is once attached to the soil by roots of its own, the connecting link between parent and offspring may be cut away, rendering the latter dependent on itself for obtaining a supply of nourishment through its own roots. Every plant is provided by Nature with a suitable means of reproduction, whether by seed, or sucker, or stole, or rhizome.

927 Mention has been made of bulbs and tubers and tuberous roots, but their nature has not been exactly explained. A bulb may be best described as an underground bud, which it is, in point of fact. Its name is obtained from the Greek *bolbos* or Latin *bulbus*, meaning a globular root. The coronal of fibrous roots by which the bulb derives its nourishment from the soil are sent out annually, and wither and die annually when the year's work is done and the bulb proceeds to take its annual rest. While in activity, the bulb takes in a store of sap, which is elaborated within it, and remains in reserve during the dormant season until the vital powers of the plant are roused once more into action, and it sends forth leaves and blossoms afresh. Bulbs are not all alike in form: some, like the onion and hyacinth, consist of successive concentric layers from the heart to the exterior, like a nest of boxes; others, like the white lily (*Lilium candidum*) and many others of the lily tribe, are formed of scales that overlap each other, and which may easily be detached; in other plants, again, such as the crocus and gladiolus, the bulb or corm, as it is properly called, from the Greek *kormos*, a stem or log, is neither in layers nor in scales, but solid. The cyclamen is another familiar example of this kind of bulb. All these different forms of bulbs vary in their mode of reproduction: the bulb in layers sends forth bulblets from the main bud, just above the root coronal, which may be separated and nursed into perfect plants; the bulb in scales will also send forth bulblets similar to itself, but if the scales be detached from the main bud, every scale will in time form a separate and perfect plant; lastly, the solid bulb or corm reproduces itself by forming similar bulbs on the top of the original bulb, as may be seen on examination of a crocus corm when its flower has perished and its long grasslike leaves decayed. But in addition to root bulbs, Nature in some cases has provided plants of this kind with means of reproduction in the form of stem bulbs, or caulinary bulbs, as they are sometimes called, from the Latin *caulis*, or stem or stalk. The stem bulb is formed for the most part of scales firmly packed together, and assumes an ovate or conical form. It keeps its connection with the parent plant until it has reached maturity, and then it falls to the ground, sends out roots from the base, and assumes a separate existence. Examples of stem bulbs are to be found in the Bulb-bearing Toothwort (*Dentaria bulbifera*) and several kinds of lilies, in which they originate in the axils of the leaves, and in the Tree or Canada Onion (*Allium proliferum*), in which they proceed from the base of each umbel of flowers.

928 Bulbous-rooted plants may be propagated by seeds as well as by offsets in the form of bulblets or little bulbs, for the term is by no means to be restricted to tiny bulbs formed in the axils of the leaves of plants, as some are inclined to think, and tuberous plants also are propagated by seeds as well as by means of their tubers. With such plants, however, propagation by seed leads to the production of new varieties, while propagation by bulb or tuber must of necessity be resorted to in order to ensure the maintenance of the same variety. Thus, new varieties of the potato are produced by hybridisation from seeds, but if any variety raised from seed exhibits qualities which render its preservation and propagation desirable, this must be effected by offsets from its tubers. The dahlia is a tuberous plant, which is increased by offsets from tubers, or even by cuttings of sprouts from tubers, but new varieties must be raised from seed. Tubers, a term obtained from the Latin *tuber*, a hump or protuberance, from *tumeo* I swell, are expansions of underground stems studded here and there with eyes or buds, and stored with starchy or feculent matter, which affords nourishment to the buds until their root growth is sufficiently progressed to admit of their deriving support direct from the soil. The turnip, parsnip, carrot, beetroot, and radish should be termed tuberoids rather than tuberous roots; they resemble genuine tubers in many points, but they are not reproduced from offsets cut from them but wholly from seed.

929 To sum up in as few words as possible that which has been advanced in the preceding remarks, propagation by natural methods, or methods that are adopted by Nature, are six in number, namely – (1) by seed; (2) by germs or bulbs, or, in a more comprehensive term, by offsets; (3) by slips; (4) by division of the plant; (5) by runners; and (6) by suckers: and under each method a special mode of treatment is not only desirable but necessary, thus:

1 ***In Propagation by Seed,*** it is requisite to use seed the vitality of which is unimpaired. Under certain circumstances, the vitality of seed will endure for thousands of years, as is apparent from the so-called Mummy Wheat, which was grown from a grain of wheat found in the swathings of a mummy of the body of an Egyptian that had been embalmed and shrouded in its cerements for burial perhaps four or five thousand years ago, or even longer. When placed in the soil this wheat corn germinated and reproduced itself in great abundance. The maintenance of vitality was due in this case to the exclusion of the external air and moisture. Generally speaking, seeds retain vitality for one or two years only under ordinary circumstances, and from this we gather that:

(a) *It is better to sow seed saved during the previous season, or, at the utmost, not more than two seasons old; and*

(b) *If it be desired to preserve the vitality of seed for a longer period than two years', it is necessary to keep it in airtight receptacles, or, at least, to exclude air from the receptacles in which they may be kept as far as it is possible to do so.*

In addition to age, due regard must be had to soil, season, and other circumstances. As a general rule, it may be laid down that seed should not be buried below the earth's surface at a depth greater than its own thickness of diameter, though it may be safely assumed that the depth may be increased with perfect safety in the case of seeds of leguminous plants, which are large and bulky in comparison with the generality of seeds. Thus, the tiny seeds of the auricula should be sprinkled on the surface of the soil in which they are sown, dusted over with a little fine soil and sand sprinkled on them by means of a tin pepper-box, a little moss being laid over them until they have germinated, in order to promote and preserve surface moisture. Larger seeds should be strewn on flattened surfaces prepared to receive them, and sprinkled over with a light covering of soil. Such seeds as onions, carrots, parsnips, etc., should be sown in drills made in the earth with the end or back of the rake, and have the ridge that is thus thrown up drawn over them. Peas and beans may be set at a depth several times their thickness or diameter in a shallow trench made for their reception by the end of the blade of the hoe. The smaller the seed, the finer should be the soil in which it is grown. The soil in which seed is sown should be tolerably dry – dry enough to crumble lightly when worked with the hand, and not to clot together in a pasty mass. Therefore, dry weather should be chosen for seed sowing, and if seed can be sown just before a gentle shower, or when the weather bids fair to be showery, so much the better. Of course, there is a proper time for sowing for every kind of seed, but this cannot be specified in a series of general instructions which apply equally to all. Place or position – that is to say, whether in the open air or under protection – also forms an important factor with regard to time.

2 *In Propagation by Germs, Bulbs, or Offsets*, all bulblets, whether they proceed from the stem of the plant or from the parent bulb, immediately above the part from which the fibrous roots emanate, should be placed in light soil, at a depth equal to their own height below the surface, immediately after removal from the parent plant, otherwise they will dry up under exposure to the air and lose vitality. By some a distinction is drawn between the terms *bulbs* and *offsets*, the latter being applied to bulblets thrown off by the main bulb. But this is a nice distinction which is scarcely requisite. All bulblets are of necessity offsets.

3 *In Propagation by Slips*, it must be explained that slips are young shoots which spring from the collar or upper portion of the roots of herbaceous plants, as in the auricula or chrysanthemum, or from shrub-like plants, as thyme and sage. In some plants the shoot or slip may be stripped from the upper part of the stem. When the lower part is sufficiently firm and ripe, the slip is stripped away from the parent plant in such a manner as to bring away a heel or projecting piece of the old wood, whether stem or root. The edges of the heel should then be trimmed with a sharp knife, and inserted in suitable soil, and shaded until it has commenced to send out roots. When slips are taken from the collar, they will often have roots already sent forth, or exhibit the rudiments of roots. These will of course grow more rapidly. Want of success in many cases may be traced to neglect in trimming the heel or base of the slip, as a callus is produced more quickly on a smooth surface than it is on a ragged one.

4 *In Propagation by Divisions of the Plant,* the original plant is broken up into pieces, and each piece, which will be found to consist of stem, leaves, and roots, maybe planted separately, and will soon form a young and vigorous plant. This mode of propagation is resorted to in the case of all plants proceeding from rhizomes, as the daisy, polyanthus, Solomon's Seal, etc., and in all herbaceous plants. Solomon's Seal, for example, may be cut into pieces, provided that each piece has an eye or bud from which it may sprout upwards, and roots below. Herbaceous plants should be divided in the spring, when growth is commencing. They will then separate readily into portions, each replete with buds for its upper growth and roots for its growth below ground.

5 *In Propagation by Runners,* all that has to be done is to peg down the runner, or place a weight on it so as to prevent it from being moved by any cause, and to give the young plant that issues from any knot or division an opportunity of rooting itself in the soil. When sufficiently well rooted, the young plant can be removed. This has been explained in speaking of plants that propagate themselves by stoles or runners like the strawberry.

6 *In Propagation by Suckers,* which in point of fact are underground runners, all that is necessary is to dig them up with care and to cut them away as near the parent plant as possible, so as to retain the roots which have issued from it between its point of issue from the main root, and that of its appearance above ground. All suckers should be headed back from one-fourth to one-half their length immediately after separation from the parent plant, to lessen the demand on the roots for nutriment.

930 *Mode of Sowing Seeds* In the majority of instances, the following treatment is recommended as the best in such situations where soil, locality, and other causes require care; otherwise, in favoured sheltered positions, the plants may succeed with more hardy treatment. Small seeds should only be lightly covered with soil, and if unusually dry weather prevail, as light surface protection with moss or similar material is beneficial until the seeds have well germinated. The scale of humidity and temperature adapted to the germination of seeds and rearing of young plants is regulated by the temperature plants are capable of bearing in their mature growth. The hardier the species, the lower the average temperature required for germination, and *vice versa*, allowing for the artificial stimulus naturally required for establishing young plants in their primary stages of growth. The absence of surface or bottom heat may in some measure be compensated by early ventilation, if required; and, where compatible, closing up pits or houses with a high degree of sun heat and artificial moisture. As a uniformly modified degree of moisture in the soil is indispensable to the successful germination of seeds, it is important that the seed stores or pots should never remain parched or dry overnight; such omissions, when repeated often, prove injurious to the vital germs, and cause the eventual loss of the produce.

931 *Preparation of Seeds before Sowing* The following instances will serve as types of the treatment of different sorts of seeds. The seeds of Martynia, abronia, and tropaeolum generally require peeling previously. Cobaea seed is best planted edgeways; geranium seed pricked in, leaving the feathery tail or pedicle out. Calceolaria seed germinates best without heat. The seeds of ipomaea and convolvulus, when very dry or as old imported seed, often refuse to vegetate: they should be taken up and slightly cut on the surface, or on the edge, apart from the eye or vital speck (where it exists outwardly), which should be preserved from injury. Rhodanthe and other seeds of similar character should be well soaked in water before sowing. Cyclamen should be sown as soon as ripe. Orchid seed may be sown on a rough-barked block, and suspended in the shady humid atmosphere of a tropical stove or orchid house; warmth and continued moisture are essential. Fern seed should be sown on the surface of rather coarse heath soil, without further covering of soil; place over it a flat square of glass, or a bell-shaped one; place the pot in a dish, and keep the surface soil uniformly moist and covered until the plant germs are well developed, after which very gradually admit air. Seeds of *Clianthus Dampieri* should be sown singly, each in small pot. Mistletoe seeds should be inserted within the bark, on the under side of the branches, to prevent the birds from feeding upon them.

932 *Soil for Surface Covering* In the sowing of exotic seeds in pots, especially those of a small and delicate structure, and those in which germination is slow and irregular, one very essential point consists in obtaining the most suitable quality of soil for surface covering. Whilst it is important that the bulk of soil used in such operations should be well pulverised, and proportionately porous throughout, in order to admit of a free and quick growth during and after germination (which a too retentive and close quality is unfavourable to), it is still more important that the soil with which the seed is covered should not only be well pulverised but also rendered less retentive of moisture; for effecting which, where prepared soils are not at hand, that which is intended either as mixture or otherwise should be passed through a suitable sieve, and also be thinly spread in the open air, or exposed to the influence of artificial heat until thoroughly dry or parched. To admit of using the soil thus dried for covering seeds, it is readily sprinkled with pure water, and passed through the hands until it admits of being easily spread. By thus reducing the retentive quality of the soil, it admits of a more uniform and healthy circulation of moisture during the first growth of the young seedlings, and, moreover, preserves the surface soil from becoming stagnant by the incipient germination of moss, etc., brought on in unprepared soils by repeated after waterings. Two very important benefits arise from using a less retentive quality of soil for covering seeds: first, in admitting of a proportionately greater depth of soil upon the seeds, and yet being equally pervious to the atmosphere, thus acting as a preserving medium in the case of small and delicate seeds exposed to extreme alternations of temperature; secondly, by dispensing to a great extent with the excess of sand in mixture, which is too often used in covering seeds generally. Beyond the requisite amount of sand as a mechanical agent or force in modifying too retentive soils, it only impoverishes in proportion to its bulk. The more nutritive the elements of soil for the growth of plants, the less they are subject to injury by extremes of temperature, other conditions being equal, and vice versa.

933 *Watering Seeds* In all cases where rare or delicate bodied seeds, uncertain in their periods of germination, are covered with prepared soil, as described in the foregoing remarks, it is requisite that the pots or seed pans thus sown should be care fully well watered immediately after, to settle the soil down to a uniform surface, suitable for after waterings. As all seeds lie dormant in the soil for given periods previous to the swelling of the inner substance, which is the first evidence of their fermentation, it is not safe to give successive heavy waterings for a short time after the first application, as referred to. Even the softest seed should be but gradually moistened, and not repeatedly gorged with water, before they able to digest or decompose it through the medium of living organs; and from this fact it is legitimately inferred that there should always be a due period allowed between the first repeated watering of seeds, to admit of a healthy evaporation from the surface soil at each watering, especially where the material for covering seeds has been indiscriminately applied, without previous exposure to the ameliorating and purifying influences of sun and air. Daily or alternate waterings are essential, as required, first known by the gradual upheaving of the surface soil, and secondly, by the bursting or expansion of the seed-lobes above the soil. Water may always be given more freely with advancing growth to the most delicate germs, admitting a healthy evaporation or dryness of surface as the test of a further supply. The importance of uniform attention to watering may be best learnt by experience and observation; but the inexperienced cultivator may be reminded, that to omit a single watering overnight of young plant germs from seed, when in a parched state, often leads to the eventual loss of the whole, and, in many individual instances, is the incipient cause of constitutional debility throughout the entire life of the plant.

934 Hitherto we have been considering and dealing with the means of propagation that Nature herself affords, but there are others in which Nature requires the aid of Art. One of these modes is propagation by layers, which consists in taking means to arrest the circulation of the sap on its return from the extremities to the roots. In this operation an upward slit is made half across a joint; and when the part so cut is fixed in favourable soil a callus or callosity (from the Latin *callus*, hard, thick skin) is formed. This hardening of the surface arrests the sap, and after a brief period roots are thrown out, and the branch becomes an independent plant. This process is adopted with pinks, carnations, roses, and many other plants. It is, however, a very-important operation in gardening, and should be neatly executed. The *modus operandi* is so simple that it really requires no illustration to show how it is to be carried out. Indeed, no one who carefully considers it, aided by the following description, can possibly fail in performing it in a perfectly satisfactory manner. Choosing the suitable branch of a carnation, for instance, which is first stripped of all leaves below the joint selected, and being furnished with a very sharp knife, the operator begins to make an incision in the under part of the branch a quarter of an inch below a joint, passing the blade upwards through the joint in a slanting direction to a quarter of an inch above, taking care that the cut terminates as nearly as possible in the centre of the stem: the tip of the tongue thus made is cut off with a clean sharp cut, and the layer pegged down in a little fine rich mould, but not more than an inch under the soil. In the case of carnations, the plant is in a fit state for the operation as soon as the flowering season is over. No stem which has already produced flowers should be employed for the purpose.

935 It has been said that the layer should be pegged down in the mould. This has the effect of opening the incision which has been made in the under part of the branch or grass, as it is technically called, for when pressure is brought to bear on the upper part of the branch, between its junction with the stem and the incision that has been made in it, it must of necessity force the cut open and cause the tongue to recede from the part from which it has been severed. The part that is cut will form a callus far more readily than if the sides of the incision were permitted to remain in contiguity. Some gardeners, indeed, in order to prevent this and keep the cut open, insert a little piece of tile, slate, or stick, etc., but this is not absolutely necessary, as the pressure of the peg, as it has been already said, is sufficient to keep the cut open. It is said that the presence of this extraneous substance acts on the plant as a stimulus to the production of roots, and experience has shown that this is the case, though it is by no means easy to assign a satisfactory reason for it. Pegs for keeping down layers may be cut from pea sticks or old birch brooms, as shown in Fig. 445, or hairpins may be used, provided they are sufficiently stout. When neither of these can be procured, some wire can be cut into pieces about 4 inches long, and turned so as to resemble a hairpin. Care must be taken not to break the branch thus layered or layed down by exerting too great pressure on the peg or pin, and when this part of the operation has been successfully carried out the mould should be pulled over the branch and pressed about it with tolerable firmness.

FIG. 445 *Crook and hairpin for pegging down layers*

936 In the case of roses and other shrubby plants, all that is required is to run the knife through a joint sufficiently so to make an opening or crack near it, and plant it three inches below the surface of the soil, securing it there with a peg, pressing the soil firmly round it, but leaving that part of the branch above the soil as erect as possible. The roots will soon form, when it may be separated from the parent tree and planted out.

937 With regard to the proper season for layering plants, Loudon tells us that 'in general the operation of layering in trees and shrubs is commenced before the ascent of the sap or delayed till the sap is fully up, and hence the two seasons are early in spring or at midsummer.' This is applicable rather to trees and hard wooded plants which are propagated by layering rather than to carnations and pinks, which are layered after the plants have done blossoming – that is to say, from the middle of July to the middle of August. Ivy, jasmine, the wistaria, and many other plants of the kind, may be propagated by layers if necessary, though the last-named two send out suckers. Ivy will take root readily if merely pegged down, but it will root even more quickly if a notch or slit be made at the joint in which the trailing stem is brought into contact with or buried under the surface of the soil. Jasmine should be cut partly through a joint when laid down for propagation. The wound intercepts the flow of the sap backwards to the root, and the accumulation of the sap at the callus that is formed tends to promote the formation of roots. This is the main principle of propagation by layers.

938 The sap ascends from the roots to the stem, branches, and leaves of the plant by the woody fibre enclosed by the bark, but it returns to the root through the bark itself. Advantage has been taken of this to promote root growth in the case of hard wooded plants which are difficult to deal with in this manner by an operation which is known as *ringing*, and which consists in removing a small narrow ring of bark all round the stem in the place in which the formation of roots is desired to take place. Care must be taken not to cut deeply into the stem – indeed, it is better to peel off the bark only, and not cut into the inner wood at all, for thus no hindrance is offered to the ascent of the sap. A callus is formed on the bark which forms the upper edge of the ring, and this thickens as time goes on, and ultimately emits roots. Branches and trailing stems operated on in this way should be firmly pegged down, and earth should be drawn over the incision. Layers should be brought into as erect a position as possible, and they may be shortened back. When layers are made from plants in pots, the layers should be pegged down in the soil in the pot in which the parent plant stands, or in separate pots properly supported. The layers should be watered occasionally, whether in pots or in the open ground. The autumn is the best season for the removal of well-rooted layers.

> Loudon says: 'The Chinese method of propagating trees by first ringing, or nearly so, a shoot, and then covering the ringed part with a ball of clay and earth covered with moss or straw, is evidently on the same general principle as layering, and is better effected in this country by drawing the shoot through a hole in the pot, ringing it to the extent of three-fourths its circumference near the bottom or side of the pot, and then, the pot being supported in a proper position and filled with earth, it may be watered in the usual way. Some plants difficult to strike, and for which proper stocks for inarching are not conveniently procured, are thus propagated in the nursery hothouses.'

939 *Propagation by Cuttings* We may now pass on to propagation by means of slips or cuttings. Every tree or shrub which produces buds possesses also the incipient root fibre already mentioned. The young twigs and branches of such trees, if placed in the ground and properly treated, will readily develop these roots, and become, in course of time, vigorous as the parent plant. This mode of propagation by *slips* or *cuttings* is applied to almost every description of plant, but especially to those which refuse to ripen their seed with us, or which consume years in attaining maturity, as the ordinary fruit trees do. To be successful in the operation, the cuttings should be made just at the point where the wood of last year's growth terminates and that of the current year begins; it should be removed with a clean, sharp, sloping cut just below a bud, for there lies the latent root.

940 In propagation by slips or cuttings, warmth, moisture, and air are as essential as with propagation from seeds; and shade is a requisite also. In layering, shade is not essential, for the branches are still connected with, and derive nutriment from, the roots of the parent plant. These conditions must be supplied by means of bell glasses, shaded from the sun, and slightly tilted for the admission of air, where the young cuttings occupy pots, and by hand glasses when it takes place in the open ground, care being taken that the cuttings are not planted too deep.

941 Cuttings in general may be considered as of two kinds – matured wood and young green shoots. The former, whatever they may be, strike readily, and with very little care. A plan of striking cuttings which has been practised with success is to lay them in slightly-damped moss, or to drop them lightly into a wide-mouthed bottle, having a piece of damp sponge at the bottom and a covering of muslin over the top. In either of these methods a callus is soon formed, and the cuttings readily throw out roots. Cuttings of young green shoots, however, require a very different treatment: they must be so managed as never to be allowed to flag, and the following appears to be the best method that can be pursued. Put silver sand about an inch deep into shallow pans (common saucers answer every purpose), and in these plant the cuttings. Then pour carefully upon the sand enough water to make a thin sheet about it. The lower leaves of the cuttings are to be removed before planting, and the stalk fixed firmly into the sand before the water is poured on. These tender young green shoots, or cuttings, will be better for a little shade and heat. A piece of thin muslin or tissue paper will provide the former, and heat may be had by placing the pan of cuttings over a basin of hot water, re-filled twice a day. These cuttings will be rooted and ready for potting off before the water in which they are grown has dried up.

942 Cuttings of hard wooded plants, such as the heath, myrtle, etc., are more difficult to strike than those of soft wooded plants, such as the geranium, etc. Free-growing hardy plants, such as the gooseberry and willow, strike freely without care or attention after inserting the cuttings in the soil. The side shoots of plants, low down in the stem, are the best for cuttings, and should be taken when the sap is in full motion, because its return by the bark tends to form the callus, or ring, of granular matter between the wood and the bark from which the roots proceed. Cuttings should be taken of wood which has ripened, or which is beginning to ripen, because in wood which is attaining or has attained maturation the callus so necessary to root formation is more readily induced to show itself. Never cut off the leaves of a cutting except so far as may be necessary at its base in order to insert it in the soil. Formerly it was the fashion to top the cuttings, or pipings, as they are technically called, of pinks and carnations in a manner similar to that of docking a horse's tail, but this unreasonable mutilation both of leaves or tail has now gone out of date. The leaves are the lungs of plants, and if they be cut the sap that they contain will be lost to the cutting, and prevented from passing downwards to form the callus. Cuttings of plants that are difficult to strike may frequently be induced to do so by making a ring round them, or tying a piece of string round them for a short time before they are taken from the parent plant. The downward flow of the sap is arrested by the cut ring or tightened ligature, and a swelling is caused, which forms a callus, from which roots are soon emitted. The cutting must be severed from the parent plant just below the ring or band, and the callus must be covered with soil.

943 Cuttings strike more readily when placed at the side of a pot, touching the pot, than when placed in its centre and surrounded with soil. Some kinds of cuttings will strike more freely when the lower end is placed in contact with gravel or crock drainage placed at the bottom of the pot. Cuttings of the mulberry and orange may thus be struck with comparative ease. It has been said that the great art in striking cuttings of the orange is to place them to touch the bottom of the pot; they are then to be plunged in a bed or hotbed, and be kept moist. Different kinds of cuttings require different management, and no hard and fast rule can be laid down for all. No cutting should be set too deeply, but, as in the case of seeds, the depth will depend mainly on the size of the cutting. No leaves should be permitted to touch the soil; if they do they will damp off, or, in other words, perish by rotting and fall off. Plants with hollow stems, as the honeysuckle, should have both ends of the cutting inserted in the soil; if both ends root, the plant can be easily divided, and will then form two Loudon tells us that too much light, air, water, heat, or cold are alike injurious to cuttings. An equable temperature should be maintained, and a moderate degree of moisture, and this is best attained by covering them with a bell glass, and shading them, if not placed in a shady situation, which is the best possible for them. Myrtle and camellia cuttings require but little heat; those of the heath, dahlia, and pelargonium require more. Special directions for the management of cuttings of special plants will be given hereafter, when the culture of these plants is under consideration. For the present, the general rules laid down will suffice, with an intimation that, after all, experience is the best guide in these as in most other matters.

944 *Propagation by Pipings* This method is applicable to plants with tubular jointed stems, such as the pink and carnation, though the latter are chiefly propagated by layering, as it has been said. It will be remembered that the stem of the pink consists of a series of successive joints or knots, a pair of leaves proceeding from opposite sides of each joint. In order to take the piping, the upper extremity of the shoot is held in the right hand and the lower end in the left hand, and the upper portion is gently pulled till it comes away, exhibiting a tubular or pipe-like termination at the end of the portion of the stem that is thus removed. The pipings are set in fine earth up to the first joint above the fracture, the soil is pressed firmly round them, and they are then sprinkled with water from a fine rose, and covered with a hand light.

945 Even the leaves of many kinds of plants will emit roots and a stem, and become independent plants. This is especially the case with succulent plants, such as the crassula, sedum, houseleek, portulaca, cactus, and others. These will never root when laid on the surface of soil in a warm and moist atmosphere. The leaf should be taken off with the petiole or stalk entire. A callus is eventually formed at the base of the petiole, from which roots and leaves eventually emanate. It has been found from experiment that even portions of leaves will root and form plants, the roots in the upper portion of the leaf proceeding from the mid-rib.

946 Silver sand is perhaps the best medium in which to strike small cuttings. A light free soil, through which the air can pass freely, is essential to the well being of all cuttings. That aeration is necessary is proved by the fact that cuttings will strike readily in cocoanut fibre, a material which is extremely pervious to air, and retains moisture for a considerable period. Powdered charcoal also forms a good medium. Perhaps the free access of air through the drainage is the reason why cuttings root more freely when placed close to the side of the pot.

947 In the case of camellias, fruit trees, and hard wooded plants generally, as well as roses, more elaborate processes, called inarching, grafting, and budding, are adopted. By these processes old fruit trees which have lost their bearing wood, or whose constitution qualifies them for growing varieties of fruit better in quality than that native to the tree, may be renovated by grafting the desired variety on its principal branches, and heading them down by degrees, until none of the old tree remains above the graft. But the chief use made of the principle of budding and grafting is to prepare young trees for planting by grafting the more delicate varieties on hardier stems of the same species, where that course is necessary, and by grafting trees of too vigorous growth on stocks which will check their vigour when it is desirable to do so. Thus, most kinds of pears, when grown on a free stock, as the native pear produced from seed is called, have a great tendency to make wood: this tendency science has checked by grafting the pear on a quince stock. In the same manner the apple is grafted on the wild crab, and for dwarf trees on the Paradise stock, and the peach and nectarine on that of the wild plum and almond, the result being that when grafted on native stocks the apple and pear are of more vigorous growth and the trees of longer duration, while those grafted on the quince and Paradise stock come more rapidly into a fruiting state. The first mode is also preferred for dry and less fertile, and the second for more rich and fruitful soils; there are also some varieties that in all cases do best on the free stock. These processes are extremely interesting in themselves, and a general knowledge of their principles indispensable to an acquaintance with the art of gardening.

948 Before anyone can hope to attain success in the operations known as grafting and budding, it is necessary that he should have a clear conception of the structure of the part that is operated on, and of the functions of the various parts of which the stock and scion are composed at the point of operation. When the stem or branch of a tree is cut across transversely, it exhibits a central mass of woody fibre within, surrounded externally by a ring-like covering or coating, which we term the bark. The woody portion in the very centre is the pith or medulla, which is supposed to possess the function of nourishing the buds until they are sufficiently advanced in growth to obtain nourishment for themselves. From the pith the medullary rays extend themselves through the woody fibre from centre to circumference, acting, according to Dr Lindley, 'as braces to the woody and vasiform tissue of the wood', and conveying 'secreted matter horizontally from the bark to the heart wood'. These rays connect the pith and the bark, and form the medium of intercommunication between the pith within and the buds without. Broadly speaking, the sap ascends in spring from the roots through the woody fibre that is covered by the bark; in autumn, having been matured in the leaves, it descends once again to the roots through the bark, or passes horizontally into the stem.

949 The bark may be at any time separated in a mass from the woody stem, but this may be done more readily in spring or autumn, when the sap is ascending or descending. Looking at it casually, it appears to be a coating of homogeneous substance, rough and hard without when exposed to the air, and smooth and moist within at its contact with the woody stem. The coating, however, which we call the bark, is composed of tissues of widely different natures, and is composed of different layers, each of which possesses its especial function. First comes the epidermis, corresponding with the outer or scarf skin of the human body, often called the epidermis also, which is perishable and renewable. The removal of this bark is in no way injurious to the tree, and often it will split as the tree increases in size, and come away itself. Next to this outer coating is the true bark, consisting of two layers known respectively as the outer and inner layers. Within this is another bark, called the *liber*, or inner bark, composed of bundles of woody fibre. In the lime or linden tree this *liber* is present in considerable quantities, and supplies the material for mats which we call bast, useful for tying up plants. Within this third bark, intervening between it and the woody stem, is another layer of mucilaginous, viscid matter, called the *cambium*, more abundant and more active in spring than at any other time. It is uncertain whether this belongs properly to the stem or the bark. It is certain, however, that it is a connecting link between them, that both bark and stern are increased from it, and that it plays a most important part in the plant as a living, organised structure.

950 To all appearance the *cambium* is the chief means by which the growth and increase of the tree is maintained, the organ from which the growth and increase of the tree proceeds. *In grafting and budding, it is absolutely necessary that contact be effected between the cambium of the stock and the cambium of the scion.* If this be secured, the well-being and junction of scion to stock is certain; if not, the graft will fail. Hence it appears how necessary it is that this should be known to and recognised and understood by those who attempt grafting and budding. It is to insure a good contact between the cambium of the bark that contains the bud and the cambium of the stock that the old wood taken away with the bud is removed before the latter is applied to the stock, and it is because the contact of cambium of scion and stock is rendered more complete in budding than it is in grafting that the former operation is performed more frequently with success by amateurs than the latter.

951 Gardening ingenuity has invented many kinds of grafting, but it will be sufficient to describe a few only of these processes, in order to explain their principle. The first thing to be done is to select a suitable stock, whose height will be according to the purpose for which it is intended, and also a graft, which should be from an early branch of the previous year's wood which has ripened under an August sun, so that the wood has been thoroughly constituted before the early frosts set in. It should also be selected so that the graft is in the same state of vegetation with the intended stock. Where the texture of the wood is less advanced in the graft than in the stock, the latter intercepts the descent of the pulpy sap, and forms the bulging on the stem which is observable on many trees that have been subjected to the process of grafting. When the case is reversed, the swelling occurs in the branch above the graft; for the principle of the union is that the pulp from the scion descends to the point of junction, where, being shut in by the ball of grafting wax, which surrounds it, and thereby secluded from the light and air, it forms woody fibre in place of the roots which it would have formed in the soil; in the meanwhile, the sap from the stock rises into the graft, where, it is elaborated into pulp by the action of the leaves, and returns again, but in a more consistent state. It is necessary, therefore, where the graft selected is in a more advanced state of vegetation, to detach it from the parent stem, and bury it in the ground, under a north wall, until both are in a similar state: in this position the graft will remain stationary while the stock is advancing.

952 *Grafting and Budding* In gardening nomenclature, the term stock or subject is applied to the tree on which the operation is performed; that of graft, and sometimes scion, to the portion of the branch which is implanted on it. The implements necessary for the operation are – a handsaw, sometimes made with a folding blade, the peculiarity of which is that the blade should be thin at the back, with very open teeth; a grafting knife, with a chisel and mallet bevelled on both sides, used where the graft is too large to be cut by the knife; and a supply of small quoins, or wedges of hard wood, to keep the slit open while the graft is preparing. The grafting knife is furnished with a smooth spatula, of hard wood or bone, at its lower end. Tools of this nature, however, have been described and illustrated in a previous chapter (see paragraph 565), to which the reader is referred. A bundle of coarse hemp, or worsted thread, or of willow bark which has been softened and rendered pliable by being soaked in water, and some composition which shall protect the graft from the atmosphere and from rain, are also necessary, and these complete the appliances necessary in grafting.

953 With regard to grafting wax, as these compositions are generally called, there are various preparations sold in the shops, some of which are composed of ingredients that are kept secret; but many good gardeners are contented to use well-tempered clay – that is, clay of which the silicious or calcareous particles have been washed out, and pure clay only left. French gardeners use a paste composed of 28 parts black pitch, 28 parts Burgundy pitch, 16 parts yellow wax, 14 parts tallow, and 14 parts yellow ochre. This mixture is applied in a hot liquid state, but not so hot as to affect the tissues of the trees; it is laid over the graft in coatings by means of a brush, until sufficiently thick for the purpose.

There is a composition of this kind, called the Invicta Canker, Pruning, and Grafting Paint, prepared and sold by Mr H. M. Clements, Seedsman, Canterbury, in the form of paint and powder, at 2s. 3d. per pint tin, and 3s. 6d. per quart tin, each tin being accompanied with a tin of powder. In budding and grafting, as soon as the bud or graft is inserted, paint before the bast is tied on, and then put on the bast, covering it well with paint and powder. The paint should only be used in dry weather to prevent its being washed off before it is set. In pruning trees and vines, and also in heading down old trees, immediately paint and powder the parts cut, which will exclude the air, prevent bleeding, and cause the parts that are cut to be soon covered with new bark. In propagating by cuttings, dip them in the paint, and allow them to dry before planting. To renovate unhealthy trees, scrape off the diseased bark and apply the paint and powder to the spot. If a tree is bark bound, draw a knife from the top of the trunk to the bottom, cutting through the bark, and immediately paint and powder the incision thus made. In cankered trees, first cut away all the dead wood, leaving the surface smooth; round off the edges of the bark; paint the part thus prepared, using a small brush, and then shake over the paint a good dusting of the powder. When the growth of the new wood, gradually advancing from both sides of the wound, almost meets, cut off the bark from the approaching edges, and the bark will join, the wound being thus filled up and covered with a new bark.

954 *Cleft or Tongue Grafting* In this mode of grafting, the crown of the stock is cut across, and a longitudinal wedge-shaped slit, C (Fig. 446), is made about 4 inches long, according to the size and vigour of the intended graft; this cleft is kept open by a wooden wedge until the scion is prepared. The scion is then selected, having a bud, A, at its summit; and the lower part of it is shaped with the knife so as fit the slit in the stock. The double-tongued graft only differs from the first in having two grafts in place of one; and it is preferable, when the size of the stock permits of its use: the wound heals more quickly, and the chances of success are greater than in the single graft. In placing the graft, it is to be observed that the top, whether single or double, should incline slighty inwards, as at E (Fig. 447); thus leaving the lower extremity slightly projecting, as at F, in order that the inner bark of the graft and stock may be in direct contact with each other. Finally, bind the whole, and cover it over, from the summit of the stock to the bottom of the cleft, with clay or grafting paste.

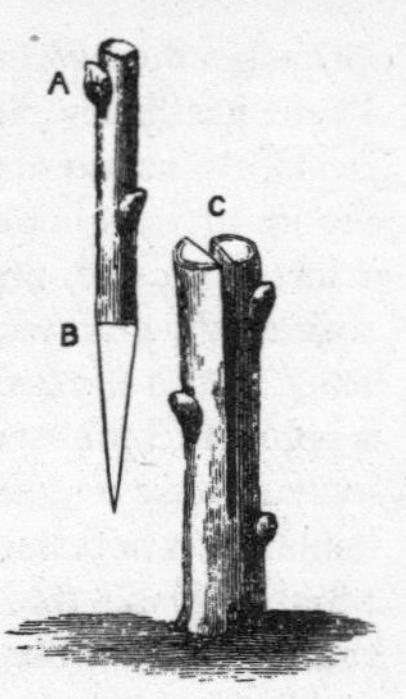

FIG. 446 *Diagram exhibiting mode of cleft grafting*

955 *Double Grafting* When two grafts are inserted in the stock, and they both take, it is necessary to suppress the least vigorous as soon as the wound is completely closed, especially in the case of standard trees; otherwise the head gets formed of two parts completely estranged from each other. During the first twelve days after the operation, protect the head from the action of the air and the heat of the sun by some kind of shade. A square piece of paper, twisted into the shape of a bag, such as grocers use for small quantities of sugar, answers very well for this purpose, protecting it at the same time from the attacks of insects. When the grafts, whether double or single, begin to grow, protect the head from being disturbed by the wind, or by birds lighting on it, by attaching it to some fixed object. A perch formed of an osier rod, having both ends tied firmly to the stock, and having the young shoot attached to it, as in Fig. 448, will serve both purposes.

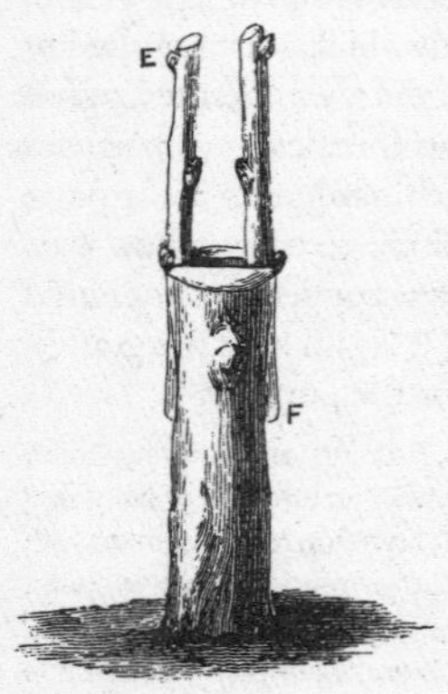

FIG. 447 *Position of double graft in cleft grafting*

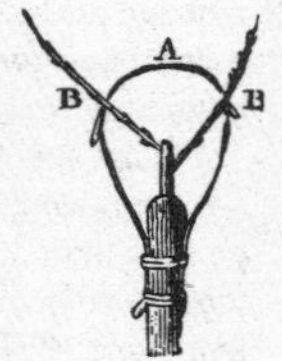

FIG. 448 *Mode of securing graft from disturbance by birds, winds, etc*

956 When the young scion begins to grow, it is necessary to suppress all buds which develop themselves on the stem below it, beginning at the base, and advancing progressively towards the young scion, but in such a manner as not to destroy those near to it until it has thrown out branches an inch and a half or two inches long.

957 *Bertemboise Grafting* A very neat mode of grafting, called by the French the Bertemboise graft, is described and figured by M. Du Breuil. Cut the crown of the stock at a long bevel, leaving only about an inch at the top square, cutting out an angular piece to receive the graft, and operating in all respects as in the former instance. When the stock is not large enough to receive a graft on each side, this mode is preferred, as forming the neatest union, as well as the most rapid; for all the ascending sap is thus drawn to the summit of the bevel on which the graft is placed.

FIG. 449 *The Bertemboise graft*

958 *Crown Grafting* This mode of grafting, which has been dignified with the name of Theophrastes, is sometimes practised on trees having healthy roots, where it is desired to improve the fruit. Having cut the stem of the tree itself horizontally, or selected a single branch to be operated upon, about twenty inches from the principal stem, three vertical cuts are made in the bark, at equal distances from each other, about an inch long. Then, having selected three or more grafts, A (Fig. 450), and shaped their lower extremities into a tongue somewhat like the mouthpiece of a flageolet, with a neck or shoulder at the upper part, introduce a graft under the bark of each vertical cut, raising the bark for that purpose with the spatula of the grafting knife, and placing each graft in such a position that the inner bark of the graft is in immediate contact with the inner bark of the tree. When neatly arranged, bandage the whole, and cover with grafting paste.

FIG. 450 *The Theophrastes graft*

959 *Slit Grafting* In place of the vertical cut through the whole of the stem, in this process a triangular cut is made in the side of the stock, as in Fig 451; the lower end of the graft is then cut so as to fit exactly into the gap made, so that the inner bark, or liber, meets in contact at all points; this done, it is covered with clay or grafting paste, and bound up until amalgamation takes place.

960 *Shoulder Grafting* A strong and efficient mode of cleft grafting, to which the term shoulder grafting may be appropriately applied, is represented in Fig. 452. Make an elongated bevelled cut in the proposed stock from left to right; make another vertical wedge-shaped cut, three inches long, from left to right, leaving a narrow shoulder at the top on the left side, and terminating in the centre of the stock, so as to resemble that in the illustration. Take the intended graft, of the same diameter as the stock, and shape its lower extremity so as to fit into the cleft thus made; bind

FIG. 451 *Slit grafting*

FIG. 452 *Shoulder grafting*

up in the usual manner, and cover the joint with grafting paste. This forms a very strong and very useful graft in species which unite slowly.

961 *Herbaceous Grafting* This method of grafting, which was initiated by Baron Tschoudi, consists in choosing branches still in active growth. Pines, walnut trees, oaks, and other trees which are multiplied with difficulty by other processes, are easily produced by this one. The mode of operating differs slightly, according to the species.

962 In the case of pines and resinous trees, when the terminal bud of the subject, A (Fig. 453), has attained two-thirds of its growth, make a horizontal cut at D; then make a slit downwards to the point where it begins to lose its herbaceous character in the ligneous consistence of the tree, stripping the part of its leaves, and leaving only a bud or two at the top to attract the sap. The graft, B, is now prepared, having a cluster of young buds at its summit, and its lower extremity shaped to fit into the slit, where it is so placed that the upper part projects over the cut in the stock. It is now covered with grafting clay, and bound, beginning at the top, below the bunch of leaves left on the stock, so as to avoid disturbing the leaves, and working downwards. This done, break off, an inch or so from their axils, the branches, C, C, of the stock below the graft. When operating on delicate species, it may be desirable to envelope the graft in a covering of paper, to preserve it from the over dry atmosphere or the heat of the sun, for ten or twelve days after the operation. Five or six weeks after grafting, the union will be complete, and the bandage may be removed, or at least relaxed; and when the suture is perfect, the leaves at D may be removed, other wise they will originate buds and branches from the old tree.

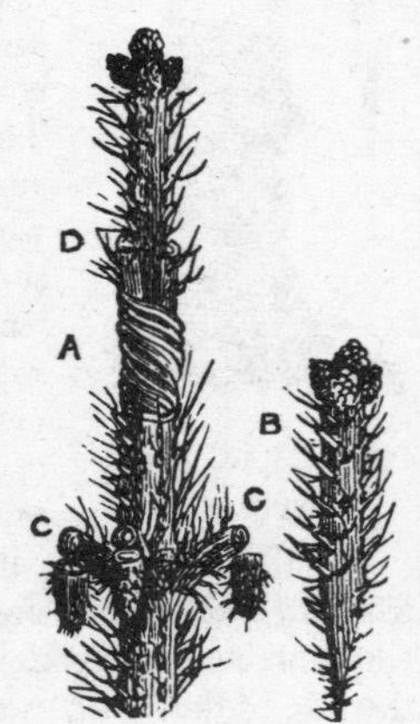

FIG. 453 *Herbaceous grafting in the pine*

963 In other species proceed as follows: Towards the end of May, when the terminal bud of the tree is in a state of active vegetation, make an incision, crossing the insertion of the petiole of the third, fourth, or fifth leaf, as at B (Fig. 454), penetrating half the diameter of the stem; the choice of the particular leaf depends upon its state of vegetation as compared with the proposed scion If the axil of the leaf A is examined, it will be observed that it has three eyes, or *gemmae*, the centre one being most developed; it is between the axis of the central eye, at B, and one of the lateral ones, that the oblique cut is to be made, stopping in the centre about half an inch below the axil of the leaf. The graft, C, consists of the fragment of a branch of the same diameter as the stock, and in the same state of

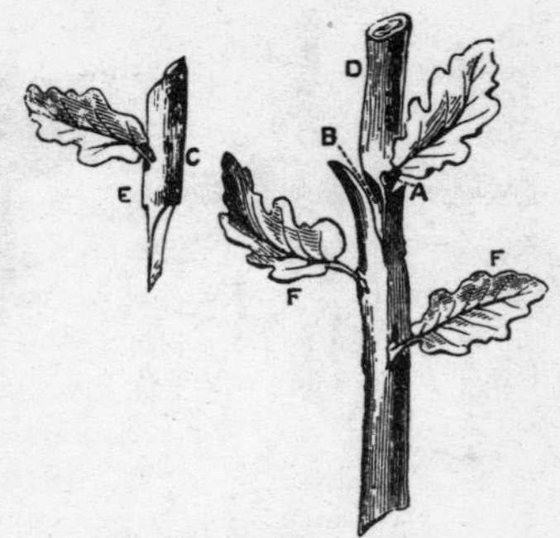

FIG. 454 *Herbaceous grafting in the oak*

vegetation; it is cut to the same length as the prolongation of the stem, D; it is wedge-shaped, fitted to the slit, into which it is inserted, bound, and covered with some grafting paste. The leaf A is left on the stock to draw the sap upwards for the nourishment of the graft. The leaf of the graft, E, assists in the process by absorbing it to the profit of the young scion. The fifth day after the operation, the central eye at A is suppressed; five days later, cut the disk of the leaves at F, F, reserving only the median nervure, rubbing off at the same time the eyes at the axil of these leaves, repeating the same suppression ten days later. At this time, also – that is, twenty days after the operation – cut the disk of the terminal leaf, A: these several suppressions will force the sap progressively from the roots into the graft. Towards the thirtieth day the graft enters on its growth: at this time remove or relax the bandage, protecting it by a paper coronet from extreme drought and the sun.

964 *Side Grafting* In this mode of grafting it is not essential, as in other groups, to amputate the head of the stock, the graft being attached to the side, as its name indicates. Having made a cross-cut into the bark of a tree, as at B (Fig. 455), and a vertical incision in the bark from its centre, thus marking a cut in the form **T**, each cut penetrating to the liber or inner bark; having also prepared the scion, A, by a longitudinal sloping cut of the same length, as BC, and raised the bark with the spatula of the grafting knife, the graft is introduced, and the whole bandaged in the usual manner. This kind of graft is particularly useful in replacing branches on fruit trees which are necessary to complete the symmetry of the tree for horizontal training.

FIG. 455 *Side grafting*

965 *Root Grafting* In this kind of grafting the roots are operated on as the stems have hitherto been. Although it is by no means in common use, this mode of procedure will be found very convenient on some occasions. Having laid bare the roots to be operated on, shape the graft, A (Fig. 456), by cutting its lower extremity into a shape resembling the mouthpiece of a flageolet, with a tooth or shoulder, D, in its upper part. Cut the root across as at the dotted lines, and make a vertical cut in the separated part to receive the tongue of the scion, with an opening also corresponding to the tooth in the scion. Bring the scion and vertical cut together, so that all the parts cut meet and cover each other, meeting just below the last bud on the scion. This root being already fixed in the soil, will serve to multiply plants which do not even belong to the same species.

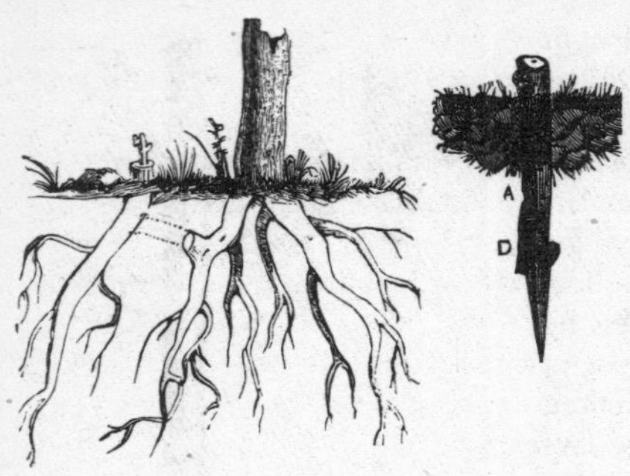

FIG. 456 *Root grafting*

966 *Budding or Shield Grafting* Grafts of this description present the following characters: They consist in raising an eye or bud with a piece of the bark and wood, and transferring it to another part of the same plant, or any other plant of the same species. Budding is chiefly employed on young shoots or trees from one to five years old, and which bear a thin, tender, and smooth bark. The term shield grafting is applied to it from the shield-like form of the base of the bud, which is inserted into the cleft cut for its reception in the bark of the stock.

FIG. 457 *Budding—preparation of bud*

967 The necessary conditions are, that the operation takes place when trees are in full growth, when the bark of the subject can be easily detached from the liber, and it may be performed generally from May to August. The bud adapted for the operation should present well constituted eyes or gemmae at the axle of the leaf; if they are not sufficiently so, it is possible to prepare them by pinching the herbaceous extremity of the bud, thus producing a reflux of the sap towards the base, and in about twelve days' time the eyes will have become sufficiently developed: then detach the bud from the parent tree. Suppress all leaves, only reserving a very small portion of the petiole, or leaf-stalk, C, as in Fig. 458.

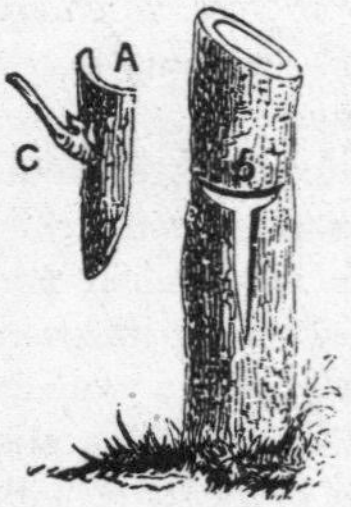

FIG. 458 *The operation of budding*

968 Having fixed upon the intended stock and bud, take a sharp budding knife, and with a clean cut remove the bud from its branch, with about a quarter of an inch of the bark above and below; remove all the wood without disturbing the inner bark of the eye, for it is in this liber, or inner bark, that the vitality lies. Now make a cross cut in the bark of the intended stock, and also a vertical one, **T**, and shape the upper part of the shield, or bud, A, so as to fit it exactly. Having fitted the parts correctly, raise the bark of the stock gently with the budding knife and insert the bud; afterwards bandage lightly above and below the eye, bringing the lips of the bark of the stock together again over the bud by means of the ligature, in such manner that no opening remains between them, and, above all, taking care that the base of the eye is in free contact with the bark of the stock.

969 Some weeks after, if the ligatures seem to be too tight, they may be untied and replaced with smaller pressure. When the operation takes place in May, the scion will develop itself as soon as the suture is completed. In order to provide for this, cut the head of the stock down to within an inch of the point of junction immediately after the operation.

970 When the operation takes place in August, the head is never cut till the following spring, when the scion begins to grow. If the same practice as in earlier budding were followed, the consequence would be that it would develop itself before winter; but the bud, having no time to ripen its new wood, would perish, or at least suffer greatly. When the buds begin to grow, they require to be protected from strong winds; otherwise they would be detached from the stem. This is done by driving a stake firmly into the ground, attaching it by a strong cord to the stem of the stock above and below the junction, as in Fig. 459, and tying the shoot of the young scion firmly to the stake above, protecting it by a bandage of hay or other substance, to prevent the bark being injured.

FIG. 459 *Mode of supporting growing scion by stake*

971 Shield grafting is also usefully practised on the root in some cases even where the stock and scion are not of the same species. To discover the larger and better roots, trace them with the finger, and graft upon them in the spring, leaving the spot A (Fig. 460) occupied by the cushion or shield of the bud uncovered. In the following spring, when the graft has pushed forward, separate the root from the parent tree. A new individual is thus easily obtained.

FIG. 460 *Budding applied to root grafting*

972 *Circle Grafting* This kind of budding is sometimes called ring or flute grafting. The grafts are composed of one or many eyes or buds, carried by a ring of bark including the liber. They are applied generally to the multiplication of certain large trees, as the walnut, chestnut, oak, and mulberry. Towards the decline of autumn, as the sap returns to the roots, choose a mild day, free from rain. From the tree to be operated on

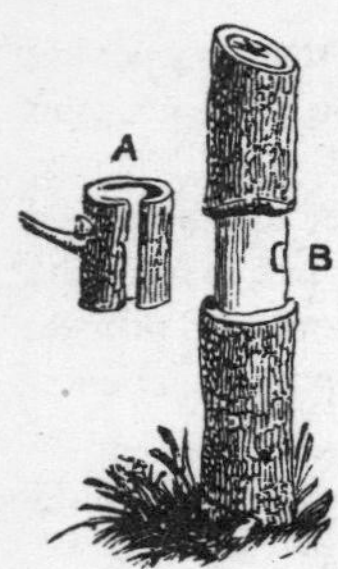

FIG. 461 *Circle grafting*

select a branch of the same size as the scion, having well-formed eyes. Upon this branch raise a ring of bark, A, as in Fig. 461, without detaching the branch from the tree, making two circular incisions all round it, and another vertical incision afterwards on one of its sides, and removing it gently. Detach from the intended stock another ring of bark of the same size, and place the ring of the graft in its place at B, in Fig. 461, and the ring of the stock on the place whence the scion was taken; bind up and cover the joinings with grafting paste. 'In the following spring, if the graft has taken, cut the head of the stock immediately above the rings, which will favour the development of the buds which they carry.

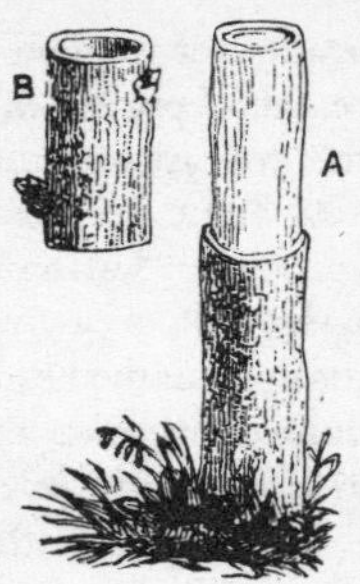

FIG. 462 *Another method*

973 Another application of this mode is carried out in the following manner: When the spring sap is about to rise, cut the head from the tree to be operated on, and remove a ring, B, from the top, A (Fig. 462). Choose a tree of exactly the same size, on which the operation is to be performed; detach from it a ring furnished with two or three eyes, as B, and of the same length. Adjust this cylinder in the place of the ring detached, making it coincide exactly at its base with the old bark, and cover the whole with grafting paste. Of all these grafts this is the most solid, and least subject to be disturbed by the wind; but even this requires protection, so that it is not shaken in its place till a complete suture has been formed.

974 *Inarching or Approach Grafting* This mode of joining stock and scion, which is troublesome though certain of success, must be performed in the spring. Supposing the stock to be planted, and the scion in a pot, as in Fig. 463, make a longitudinal cut in the stock, of such extent as to reach the medullary canal at A, and leave a corresponding notch in the scion at B, but in such a way that in the scion it is less deep at the base, B; while, on the contrary, the cut in the stock is less deep at the summit, C. Bring the two cuts in contact, so that the liber, or inner skin, of each meets the other; then bind them. The consequence of these unequal incisions will be, that in separating the head at the point D of the graft and A in the stock, there will be less deformity left in the tree.

FIG. 463 *Inarching or approach grafting*

975 In the preceding example of approach

grafting, the parts of the branch operated upon should be of the previous year's growth at least. It is sometimes desirable, however, to apply the principle to branches of the same year's growth. Accident may deprive a tree of the branches necessary to its symmetry, and a year's growth be saved by applying a herbaceous or green graft to supply the deficiency, if there happens to be a lower branch of the same tree available for the purpose. Let us suppose that a void exists at A, A, A. (FIG. 464), on an otherwise healthy peach tree, and that side branches, or fruiting spurs, are required at these points to balance the tree and restore its symmetry, and that a lower branch from B is available to supply them any time between June and August. Supposing the shoot to have attained sufficient length, an incision is made in the branch, about a quarter of an inch long, with a cross cut at each extremity, deep enough to penetrate to the inner bark; the bark is raised from the wood on each side of the longitudinal cut by means of the spatula at the end of the budding knife. A thin slice is now cut out of the shoot B, on the lower side, and opposite to a leaf bud, corresponding in length with the incision on the branch. The parts thus laid bare are brought together, the lips of raised bark brought over the shoots, and the parts are again bound together. The process is continued as often as is deemed necessary, or the length of the shoots will permit, taking care that in each case a leaf bud is left above the point of union, and that it is left uninjured by the ligature, but leaving eight or ten days between each operation. In the following spring the union will be complete; but it is better not to separate the grafts till the second spring. At this time cut each shoot which has furnished the graft immediately below the ligature, and submit each of the new shoots to the usual training.

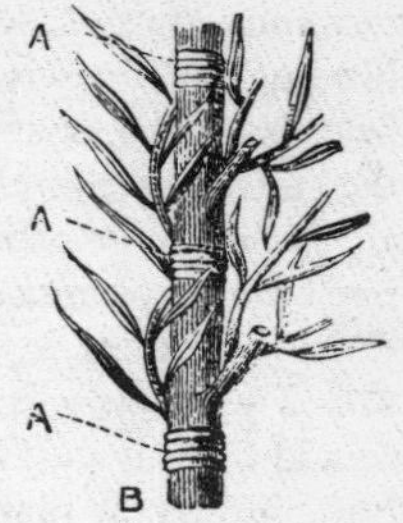

FIG. 464 *Inarching applied to herbaceous grafts*

976 The weather most suitable for budding is a subject of dispute among practical men. Cloudy weather has generally been preferred by gardeners, but many are in favour of warm sunny weather, provided the stock and buds are in proper condition. 'In warm weather,' says Mr Saul, 'the sap is more gelatinous, and the bud, on being extracted and inserted in the stock, quickly and properly tied, soon takes. On the contrary, in wet, cloudy weather, the sap is more thin and watery, and the bud will not unite so freely; besides this, a fall of rain, after the buds are inserted, likely enough, in such weather, will fill up the interstices and rot the buds before they have time to unite with the stock.'

977 American gardeners have questioned the necessity of extracting the wood from the eye of the bud. With regard to this, however, Mr Saul points out that it may suit their hot, dry climate, but that he gives the preference to the English system of extracting the wood from the bud, not only for roses, but for fruit, ornamental, and forest trees. In rose-budding, he adds, the bud in the shoot should be commenced with, cutting out from it about ⅛ inch below the bud or eye, to about ½ inch above it. Take out the wood without touching the liber or inner bark; next make an incision in the branch on which the bud is to be placed quite close to the main stem, half an inch long, with a cross cut at the upper extremity, thus, **T**. Raise the bark with the end of the budding knife, without bruising it, and insert the bud, tying it well with worsted thread, giving one turn below, and two, or at most three, above the eye of the bud. Worked in this way, they grow out from the axil of the branch, and look neat and workmanlike; and after a season or two, when headed back and healed over, the head presents a fine bushy appearance, growing apparently out of the main stem, without scars, wounds, or knots.

978 The shoots selected for budding or grafting, whether for fruit or rose trees, should be firm and well ripened; watery shoots, or watery buds, are valueless. For grafting, the branches should be of the preceding year, well ripened under an August sun – *Auguste*, as French fruitists say.

979 The stock should be in a state of vegetation slightly in advance of the graft; otherwise, the flow of the sap is insufficient to supply the wants of the scion. In order to provide for this, the graft may be removed from the parent branch a little before the operation, and buried under a north wall: there it remains stationary, while the stock is advancing to maturity.

980 It frequently happens that grafted fruit trees, some at one period of their age and some at another, cease to assimilate themselves with the stocks upon which they have been worked. This is to be seen by a thickening of the tree just about the place where it has been worked. This thickening, which in some parts of the country is called a burr, is always to be regarded as an effort of nature to throw out new roots and preserve life, and should be treated accordingly. If the tree has originally been worked, and the burr consequently shows itself at some distance above the ground, a large box should be provided, and placed round the burr in such a way that it may contain a quantity of soil into which the tree can strike out its new roots. This soil should be a light loam, and always kept moist. In the second or third year new roots will have been formed, and the tree may safely be separated by a saw from the old stock, and let down into the earth beneath. When the tree has been worked close to the surface, a place about a yard square may easily be built up with bricks or tiles, and filled with light soil a few inches over the burr, to receive the new roots. By a somewhat similar process, the healthy branch, B, of a favourite tree may be preserved by layering it in a box or pot, A, supported on a stake and slab, C, as shown in Fig. 465.

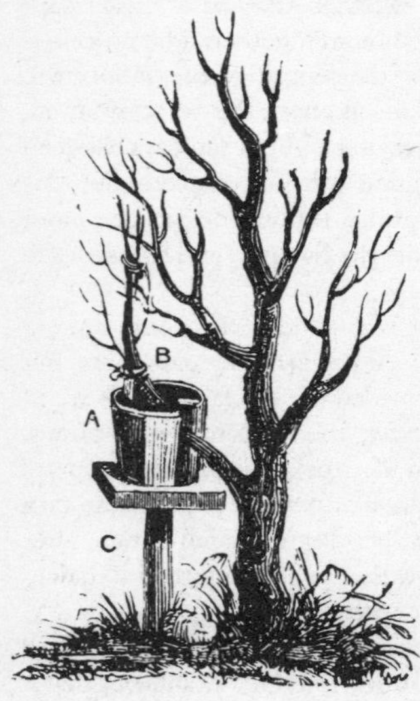

FIG. 465 *Provision for preservation of healthy branch by rooting*

981 This is an effective mode of treatment by which the healthy branches of a worked tree may be preserved, when it is found that the stocks to which they have been attached have not sufficient power to sustain them. There is another, whose object is to utilise the roots and stem of an old tree which is in a failing or even perishing condition; and although it belongs properly to the renovation of old trees, a subject which has been already touched on, yet it may be fairly described here, as it is intimately connected with the operations under consideration.

982 The final cause of the languishing state of a tree in this condition is the absence of vigorous young shoots and the imperfect organisation of the cambium and liber, and, finally, the abortion of its root fibres in consequence, and it can only be restored to health by the production of more healthy and vigorous organs, which may be done by concentrating the whole energy of the tree on certain points. This is done by amputating the principal branches, A, A, A, as shown in the annexed example of a decayed pear tree in Fig. 466, about 7 or 8 inches from their base at c, the branches B being left entire for the present, the amputations being so made that the branches left are not required to carry out the new system of training to be adopted, passing, in all cases, the four largest branches. These branches are retained for the present, it being yet doubtful if the tree has strength to develop upon the old bark the new buds necessary to fulfil the functions of the roots; for if the buds perish, and there is no outlet for the rising sap, the tree dies. By preserving these branches, their leaves and shoots provide against such accidents. To facilitate the issue of buds on the tree, the hard dry bark should be removed by means of a plane, or by paring it away with a sharp knife, and its place covered by a coating of chalk and water, a covering which will stimulate the vital energy of the living bark, and protect the tree from the sun's rays.

983 Following this operation, it is found that the sap when concentrated on

FIG. 466 *Renovation of decayed pear tree*

only a few branches acts with great energy upon the cellular tissues of the bark nearest to the summit of the cut branches. It determines towards these points the formation of buds, which soon develop vigorous branches. Towards the middle of June, choose such shoots as are best suited to form the principal branches for horizontal training, as C, D, E, F, G, H, in Fig. 467. The others are cut towards the middle of their length.

984 The year following, in the spring, train the principal branches according to the plan laid down; for example, in the fan shape, as in the engraving, break the tender branches close to their junction with the stem or main branch, and, during the summer, pinch the leading shoots off, so as to convert into fruit spurs the shoots not intended to form main branches.

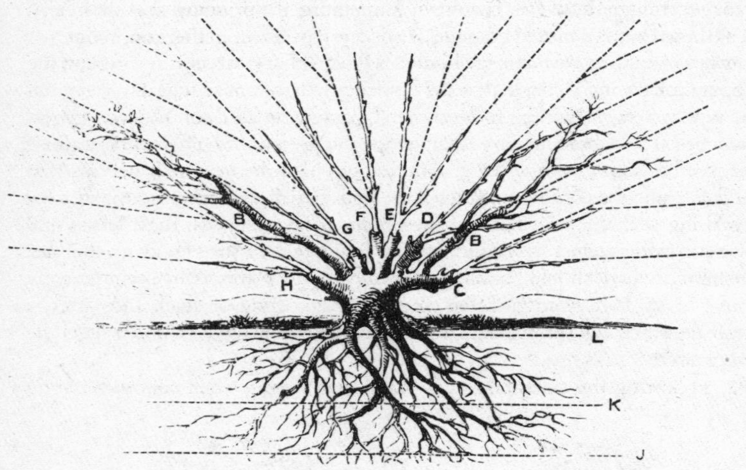

FIG. 467 *Regenerated pear tree*

985 In the following spring the tree will have assumed the form represented in Fig. 467. At this time, the branches, B, B, left for precaution, may be entirely suppressed, the several cuts being covered with grafting paste. As these new suppressions will tend to increase the energy of the young branches, they will hence forth grow with great vigour, and will soon replace the branches that have been removed from the ancient tree.

986 In the same proportion in which the stem is operated upon, so must the roots be. As soon as buds begin to appear upon the portion of the branches left, the leaves which are developed send towards the roots a quantity of ligneous fibre and corticle, or wood fibre. In its course towards the roots, this sap meets with beds or layers of cambium and liber, through which they extend themselves in a languishing state, since it is now deprived of the fluid which facilitated its passage, taking their natural direction, and penetrating the cells in the bark upon the roots, they give place to new organs, at once more nourishing, more healthy, and more vigorous than the old roots. If, after three or four years, a tree operated upon as we have indicated is transplanted, it will be observed that the lower half of the old roots, comprised between the lines J and K, are decayed, and that young roots, comprising those between K and L, have been thrown out. The tree has reached the state represented in the engraving, and is supplied with young, healthy, and vigorous roots, as well as more vigorous branches, with new layers of cambium and liber. It is, in reality, a new tree, which has taken the place of the prematurely old one, whose organs have ceased to live.

987 Analogous treatment to that which we have indicated for espalier trees may be followed with standards and pyramid trees; removing the objectionable branches eight or ten inches from the stem, and placing a crown or cleft graft on each, if it is considered necessary, but taking care to leave a fourth of the old branches, till the branches cut down have thrown out young shoots. In the second year, the remaining branches may be removed altogether, the extremity of the severed cuts, when made perfectly smooth, being covered over with grafting paste.

988 By these processes, it is possible, except in cases of complete decay, to restore the tree to its first vigour, especially in the case of pip fruit, as the apple and pear. In stone fruit, the success is less assured; above all, it is doubtful in the peach, which scarcely ever produces buds on the old wood; and the application of grafting is had recourse to when it is desired to regenerate the tree, or to graft an improved variety of the same fruit on an old but healthy stock. In this case, crown grafting is adopted, and a graft placed at the extremity of each branch, which is cut down in the manner already described, favouring, in the meanwhile, the development of young wood at the base of the tree, by short pruning, and pinching off the buds at the summit.

FIG. 468 *Giant emperor aster*

CHAPTER 21

The Selection, Planting, Pruning, and Training of Fruit Trees

989 The propagation of different kinds of fruit trees by grafting and operations that are closely akin to it naturally enough demanded consideration in a chapter devoted to an exposition of the principles of vegetation, and the various modes of increasing and multiplying various sorts of plants and trees, and was appropriately followed by hints and directions for the renovating old and worn-out trees, and bringing them once again into bearing. As we have made a beginning with this part of the wide and comprehensive subject of gardening, it will be well to continue it forthwith with a consideration of the equally important matter of selecting fruit trees for the garden, planting them, and then pruning and training them.

990 *Selecting Trees* In selecting trees for planting, it is important to note their different seasons for ripening, and to select the sorts, so that a continuous supply may follow. There are some kinds of fruit which must be consumed when ripe, or preserved in sugar or otherwise, which altogether changes their character. Besides, only a moderate supply of apples and pears need be provided in summer or early autumn, when peaches are in season. Nevertheless, it would be a great mistake to overlook summer apples and pears altogether: many of them are of excellent quality, and form an agreeable addition to the dessert, as well as for kitchen use, even in houses well supplied with peaches, nectarines, and apricots. In arranging the quarters of the fruit garden, therefore, leaving the walls for the more tender peach, nectarine, apricot, and more delicate French pears, the espaliers, dwarf trees, and pyramids should be arranged so that out of every hundred trees, whether pears or apples, a tenth might ripen early, a fifth ripen in October, a fifth in December, and the remainder – long keeping sorts – in the winter. This proportion might be adopted in the largest establishments, and even in the orchards of the cider counties, where the system about to be described might be acted upon with great advantage to the owners. In smaller gardens, with which this work has more immediately to do, the proportion of apples, pears, and plums will be decided by individual taste. Perhaps the best course would be to divide the garden, one half, or thereabouts, into apples and pears; and to plant the outside of the wall borders next the walks with espaliers, for apples and pears of the finer sorts.

991 *Planting Trees* The time for planting may be in any month from October to February inclusive, but many arguments may be brought forward in favour of the month of November, if the weather be open and free from frosts. Spring is always a busy season in the garden; digging, sowing, grafting, and pruning are then in full operation. 'And why should planting be added to the number?' asks

Lawrence. 'It makes part of the wise man's pleasure and diversion to have always something to do, and never too much. Amusements and recreations of all kinds should come to us in regular and orderly succession, and not in a crowd; besides, some intervals of time for meditation between different kinds of work in a garden are very desirable to a good and thoughtful man.'

Planting, without doubt, is best performed in November, for every kind of deciduous tree and shrub, and for most evergreens, although it is possible, with care, to plant and transplant evergreens in almost every month in the year. Whatever variety of opinion may exist in reference to evergreens, there is no doubt whatever that the planting of all deciduous trees, fruit trees included, and shrubs should cease by the middle of December. This work should therefore be pushed forward in mild weather. One great point of success is to keep the roots of the plants as little exposed as possible: a dry wind or a cutting frosty air is fatal to them. The tops of plants are endowed, even when in a dormant state, with a wonderful power of resisting cold. As Nature never intended the roots to be exposed, and does not needlessly squander her resources, it is obvious that this power of resisting cold is not extended to them. Therefore, all newly-planted shrubs and trees should also have their roots protected during the first winter with long litter, to prevent their being injured. When placed close together in nursery lines, plants shelter and protect each other, and the massiveness of their tops, and possibly their summer leaves, shield their roots from the frost. Their condition is widely different when placed thinly, in newly formed shrubberies. Hence the propriety, and in many instances the necessity, if their lives are to be saved and their health preserved, of what is termed *mulching* – that is, covering the surface with some good non-conducting material. The next point of most importance in planting trees or shrubs, especially of large size, is to firmly secure the top to a strong stake, or by any other method, so as to keep it immovable in one spot. When it is otherwise, the trees, both top and root, are the sport of every fresh breeze; and the probability is that after the roots have made a feeble effort to grow, and been forcibly wrenched from the soil, they will perish.

992 The pear loves a silicious earth, of considerable depth; plums flourish in calcareous soils, and the roots seek the surface; the cherry prefers a light silicious soil; and all cease to be productive in moist, humid soils. The apple accommodates itself more to clayey soils, but does best in a loamy soil of moderate quality, slightly gravelly. In preparing stations, therefore, suitable soils should be supplied to each. The station is prepared by digging out a pit about three feet square, and the same in depth, in ground that has been well drained. In the bottom of this pit lay 10 or 12 inches of brick or lime rubbish, the roughest material at the bottom, and ram it pretty firmly, so as to be impervious to the tap root: the remainder of the pit must be filled in with earth suitable to the requirements of the tree. When the surrounding soil is a tenacious clay, the roots of the young tree should be spread out just under the surface, and rich light mould placed over them, forming a little mound round the roots; but in no case should the crown be more than covered: deep planting is the bane of fruit trees.

993 The stations being prepared, and the trees having arrived, it is necessary to prune the roots, by taking off all the small fibres, and shortening the larger roots to about six inches from the stem; and if any portion of the roots has received any bruise or been broken before the trees have reached their destination, that part of the root should be removed entirely, by a clean sharp cut. Two or three spurs are sufficient, but if there be more good ones, they may remain, after being carefully pruned. The rapidity of railway conveyance will secure the trees from injury, especially if they are carefully packed in mould, and matted; but it may be a proper precaution against carelessness at the nursery, if the roots are laid in milk and water or soap suds a few hours before they are planted.

994 The process of planting will differ, according as it is intended to be a dwarf, a standard, a pyramid, or a wall tree. If for a dwarf, standard, or espalier, after cutting away the tap root, except in the case of the peach, which, having a tendency to throw up suckers, should have the roots directed downwards, place it upright in the centre of the station; spread the roots carefully in a horizontal direction, and cover them with prepared mould to the required height, supporting the young plant with a strong stake, driven firmly into the ground, and tying the stem to it, after surrounding the stem with hay or straw, or even a wrapping of old felt carpet, so that the string may not bruise the young tree or cut into the bark, pressing the soil gently, but firmly, over the extended roots. When the operation of planting is finished, cover the ground all round the tree with a layer of half-rotten dung. This process, called mulching, consists in spreading a layer of short half-rotten dung five or six inches thick round the stem, in a radius six inches beyond the extremity of the roots. The mulch should be spread evenly with the fork, and gently pressed down by the back of the spade, or, if exposed to wind, pegged down to prevent its being blown away. If a wall tree, let the root be as far from the wall as may conveniently be, with the stem sloping to it, the roots being extended and covered in the same manner with the soil. The way in which this should be done is shown in Fig. 469. The object is to give the roots as much room as possible in which to ramify.

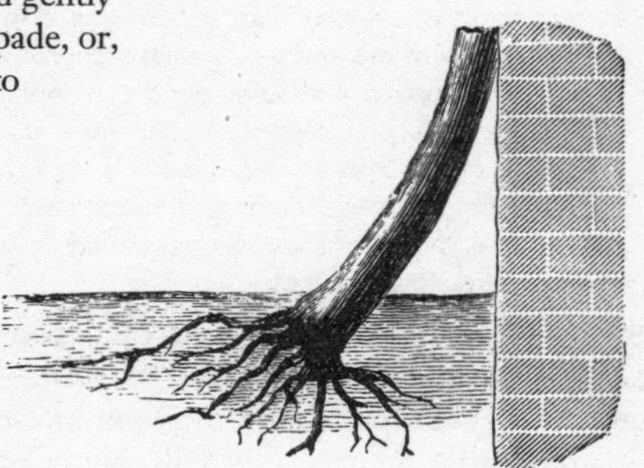

FIG. 469 *Mode of placing tree in position against wall*

995 The nature of the soil is to be regarded, and the tree planted at a greater or smaller elevation above the level of the surrounding soil, according to its nature. Where the subsoil is a stiff clay, the mound in which it is planted should rise from nine to twelve inches; in a warm dry soil, a very gentle elevation suffices. The roots should be planted in the richest mould; and various expedients, to which reference will be made presently, should be used to keep them moist and cool, and free from canker. The mould requires to be pressed gently and closely round the roots with the hand, so that the soil may be closely packed round them; with these precautions no fear need be entertained of productive fruit trees being obtained.

996 And now, the trees being planted, the wall trees nailed to the wall to prevent their being shaken by the winds, the standard and dwarf trees firmly attached to a strong stake for the same purpose, let us consider the various expedients which have been adopted, from time to time, to protect the roots of the young trees from the frosts of winter and the scorching heats of summer. For this purpose, layers of straw or of ferns, five or six inches thick, laid in circles three feet round the stem, have been recommended, and the nurseryman should have very special directions to have them carefully taken up, with every root and fibre as entire as possible, and to pack them carefully in damp moss, or any other material that will retain moisture, the stems and branches being well tied in, and wrapped up in straw inside and mats outside. On their arrival, if the weather continues open, they are to be carefully unpacked, and laid in by the heels, as gardeners term the operation of laying them in a temporary trench.

Lawrence, who has been so often quoted, very much approves of the ferns and mulching during violent frosts; but the straw and dung, he thinks, encourage worms, ants, and other vermin very injurious to the young roots; therefore, he adopted, as equally effective, more sightly, and free from that objection, the plan of placing a layer of sand in a circle round the tree, covering the sand with small round stones, which is neat and attractive to the eye, and equally effective in protecting the roots, keeping them, at the same time, cool, and admitting of the necessary percolation of moisture.

997 *Pruning Trees* The principles of physiology, briefly sketched in a former page, are applied to the pruning of fruit trees, with the following results:

1 It imposes on the tree a form in keeping with the place it is intended to occupy.
2 It leads to the principal branches of the tree being furnished with fruiting branches in all its extent.
3 It renders the fructification more equal, by suppressing superabundant flower buds, and encouraging new ones for the following year.
4 It determines the production of larger fruit, and of better quality, by regulating the supply of nourishment to the fruit-bearing branches.

998 In fruit trees in a state of nature the sap is distributed equally, because the tree follows its natural tendency, which is to develop perpendicular branches; and as the tendency of the sap is to ascend to the loftier branches, the ramifications of the base of the stem come to languish, and finally dry up altogether into hard wood; it is, therefore, indispensable to the production of fruit to overcome this natural tendency of the sap. Let us imagine an espalier-trained tree in which the equilibrium of vegetation is broken. We know that the sap is attracted by the leaves, and that by suppressing a sufficient number of the leaf buds upon the branches, growing with superfluous vigour, the sap flowing into them will be diminished, and an increased quantity will fall to the weaker branches, whose leaves are kept untouched; therefore suppress, as early as possible, all useless buds on strong branches, and retain them as long as possible on weak ones.

999 The sap acts with greatest force upon the shoots thrown out by vertical branches; weak branches will be assisted, therefore, by being placed in a vertical position, and strong ones repressed by being trained horizontally, or by having their extremities arched downwards.

1000 In removing the leaves from a strong shoot, in order to restore the balance to a weak one, it is necessary to remember that without a due proportion of leaves to attract and elaborate the sap, the branch will perish: the leaves removed, therefore, must be sufficient to restore the equilibrium, and no more; and they must be removed in such a manner as to preserve the petiole, or leaf stalk, on the branch.

1001 Fruit has the property of attracting sap, and elaborating it for its increase; and it follows that a superabundance of sap will be drawn to the stronger branches. Leave all the fruit possible on the strong, and suppress them upon the weaker branches.

1002 A solution of sulphate of iron, in the proportion of one grain to a pint of water, applied after sunset to the green leaves and leaf buds of weak branches, is rapidly absorbed by the leaves, and powerfully stimulates their action upon the ascending root sap of fruit trees.

1003 By detaching weak branches from the wall or espalier to which they are fixed, they receive an increased amount of light and air on both sides. As light is the chief agent employed in the elaboration of the sap, its energy will thus be largely increased. But this must not be done until the end of May, when any danger from frosts may be considered as past. The same result is obtained by covering the stronger branches from the light.

1004 The sap develops itself much more vigorously under short pruning than under long branches. If, then, it is desired to obtain wood branches, prune short: when the branches are vigorous they develop few flower buds. On the contrary, if it is desired to develop fruit-bearing branches, prune long: the less vigorous branches develop abundance of flower buds. Another application of this principle, to re-establish the vigour of a tree exhausted by a heavy crop, is to prune it short the following year. This may appear to be a contradiction of a maxim previously laid down, to prune short an over-vigorous branch and leave the weak ones long. The contradiction is only apparent: the one applies to a whole tree, which is to be treated alike in all its parts; the other to a tree whose equilibrium is to be restored – the one to the production of wood, the other of fruit.

1005 The tendency of sap to flow to the extremity of the branch leads to a more vigorous development of the terminal bud than of the lateral buds: accordingly, where it is desired to obtain an elongation of the branch, it is necessary to prune back to a vigorous wood bud, and to leave none beyond it which can interfere with the action of the sap.

1006 *The more* the sap is retarded in its circulation, the smaller is the force with which it acts in developing branches, and the greater its action in producing *flower buds*. Trees only begin to develop flower buds when they have reached some maturity, for it is necessary for the production of flower buds that the sap should have attained some consistency, and circulate slowly. This elaboration is assisted by the extended course it has to run in the lengthened branches; it is also assisted by broken and interrupted lines. This well-known principle has been taken advantage of to check the sap by pinching and torsion, and even partially breaking over-vigorous branches. These mutilations have been found to diminish the vigour of the shoots and branches, by forcing the sap into new branches while the older branches are elaborating their fruit buds.

1007 *Late Winter Pruning* When all other methods of checking the superfluous vigour of a tree fail, late winter pruning is sometimes practised, when the shoots have attained a length of one-eighth of an inch, when the sap has already reached the summit of the branches, and the buds near the base push less vigorously. Another expedient is to apply side grafts to the branches, the grafts being fruiting buds. When they blossom and fructify, the fruit absorbs the superabundant sap of the tree: this, however, is only applicable to the apple and pear and other pip fruit.

1008 In the case of pyramid trees, the vigour of the tree is diminished by arching all the branches, so that their extremities are directed to the ground; this is done by surrounding them with a cord, pegged down a short distance from the ground, and attaching the tips of all the branches to it.

1009 *Root Pruning* The pruning or cutting back of the roots of trees is a never failing remedy for over luxuriance and reluctance to produce fruit; but the remedy is a severe one, and it may be doubted if it should be lightly performed. A less violent mode of treating the roots is sometimes tried with advantage: the soil is removed from one entire side of the tree, and the roots laid bare, and left exposed during the summer to the effects of air and light. This has the effect of diminishing the vigour of the tree, and throws it into bearing; or, if it fails, the same treatment pursued in the following spring will probably be effectual. Should it fail, recourse must be had to root pruning. This is performed by digging a trench round the tree so as to keep clear of all the roots, at the same time laying them all open about three feet from the stem of the tree; then, with a sharp axe, or chisel and mallet, cut through a portion of the strongest roots, according to the requirements of the tree. If the tree is extremely vigorous, without producing fruit, two-thirds of the stronger roots cut through in this manner will probably restore the tree to a state of perfect bearing; the trench being filled up with fresh virgin mould, and the tree left at rest for a year. The proper season for root pruning is the autumn, when the roots will send forth small fibrous spongioles, which elaborate the sap, and form blossom buds. Should this operation fail to check the superfluous vigour of the tree, the roots may be again laid bare in the following autumn, and the remaining large roots cut away, avoiding, as much as possible, all injury to the smaller fibres which have pushed out from the previous operation. Should the tree still present an over-vigorous growth, it must be taken up entirely, and all the strong roots pruned in, then replanted, taking care that in replanting the tree is raised considerably above its former level – a severe operation, but certain to be successful in reducing the tree to a fruitful state.

1010 *Transplanting* is another remedy recommended for over-luxuriant growth; it is, however, only applicable to young or dwarf trees. It is performed in autumn; the roots being trimmed and shortened, and the tree carefully replanted in a suitably-prepared station. The check is usually followed by an ample abundance of fruit buds the following year.

1011 *Winter Pruning* The process of pruning fruit trees is performed at two seasons – winter and summer. Winter pruning should be performed while vegetation is entirely at rest – the period which follows the severest frosts, and which precedes the first movement of vegetation – that is to say, the end of February or the very beginning of March in ordinary years. If trees are pruned before the strong frosts of winter set in, the cut part is exposed to the influence of the severe weather long before the first movement of the sap takes place which is so necessary to cicatrise the wound, and the terminal bud is consequently often destroyed. Equally troublesome are the wounds made during frosts: the frozen wood is cut with difficulty; sometimes the cuts are ragged, and they do not heal; mortality attacks the bud, and it disappears. To prune after vegetation has commenced, except where summer pruning is to be pursued, is not to be thought of; therefore, let it be done in February, if the frost has disappeared, more especially for the peach, whose buds, placed at the base of last year's shoots, are particularly exposed to the action of the ascending sap. Summer pruning will be best treated of under the particular species, each of which require to be attended to at different periods.

1012 *Process of Pruning* The instruments required in pruning are a hand saw, a pruning knife, a chisel, and a mallet. For garden trees the knife is the most important; it should be strong and of the best steel, with a considerable curve, so as to take a good hold of the wood. The way in which to perform the operation requires attention. The amputation should be made as near as possible to the bud, but without touching it; the cut should begin on the opposite side, and on a level with its lower part, made at an angle of 45°, and terminate just above the bud, as at A in Fig. 470, which shows the right mode of cutting a branch in pruning, and which, with the accompanying illustrations at B, C, and D, is reproduced from Du Breuil's work on the culture of fruit trees. When cut as at A, the amputation is made as close as possible to the bud, but not so near as to injure it. The pruning knife is placed exactly opposite the bud, and cut in a slanting direction upwards, in the line *ab*, coming out a little above the bud. By this means the bud remains uninjured, and more readily bursts into growth when the time comes. In B, the branch is cut in the line *ab* too far from the bud, and the consequence is that the wood dies down to the line *c*, and the dead stump has to be cut away the following year. In C, the cut *ab* is too slanting, and commenced too far down the stem on the side opposite the bud, and the consequence is that the bud is weakened and its growth rendered less vigorous.

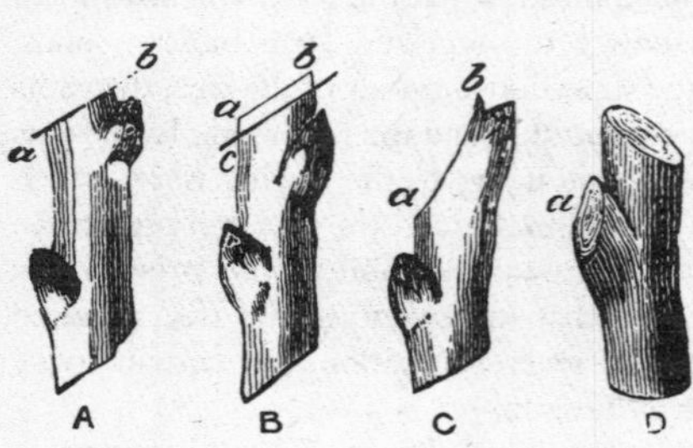

FIG. 470 *Right and wrong modes of pruning*

1013 If it is necessary to cut away a branch altogether, a small portion of it should be left on the stem, as at *a* in D, and the cut should be a smooth one, slightly bevelled, presenting the smallest possible extent of wounded surface,

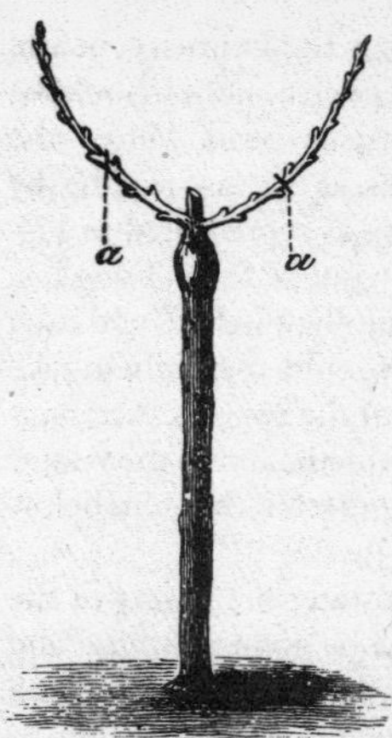

FIG. 471 *First year's pruning of standard*

when the healing of the wound will be quicker than it would have been had the cut been made nearer the stem. If amputation of a larger branch is made with the saw, the cut should be made smooth with the knife or chisel, and covered with grafting paste.

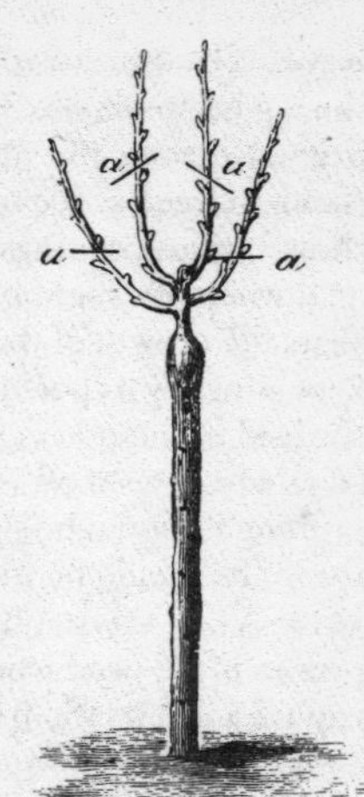

FIG. 472 *Second year's pruning of standard with two shoots*

1014 The first object in pruning a standard tree is the formation of its head. The first pruning must take place at the end of the first season after grafting, when the scion has made its growth, as represented in Fig. 471, and when two shoots have sprung from the graft. To form a full round head, the two shoots should be pruned into *a*, *a*. The year after, the tree will present the appearance represented in Fig. 472; or, if three shoots have been left the first year, and the whole three headed in, in the following year they will appear as in Fig. 473, each shoot having thrown out two new branches. The one tree now presents a head of six, and the other four shoots. At the end of the second year both are to be headed back, the one to the shape indicated by the crossing lines *a*, *a*, *a*, *a*, the other as nearly as possible to the same distance from the graft.

1015 Another year's growth will, in each instance, double the number of main shoots, which will now be eight and twelve respectively. If a greater number of shoots appear, or if any of them seem badly placed, their growth should be prevented by pinching off the tops when young, and pruning them clean off when the tree has shed its

FIG. 473 *Second year's pruning of standard with three shoots*

FIG. 474 *Appearance of standard in third year's growth*

leaves. The time for winter pruning is between November and February, before the sap begins to stir. Those trees which have produced twelve shoots should be pruned exactly like those with eight, to form a compact head. When the standard tree has acquired eight or twelve main branches, as the case may be, by these various prunings, it has attained its full formation, as represented in Fig. 474, where the eight branches have assumed a circular, cuplike form. For a few years the growth of these eight branches should be carefully watched, and each kept as nearly as possible in an equally vigorous state. Should any of them take the lead of the others, so as to threaten the symmetry of the tree, its extremity should be nipped off in such a manner as to check its growth, and at the winter pruning it should be shortened in considerably. All shoots from the stem below the grafts should be rubbed off as soon as they appear.

1016 When the standard tree has reached its bearing state, the object of the pruner is the production of fruit, which is best attained by giving a round and cuplike form to the tree. If the branches are too rigorously shortened, strong useless wood will be produced, without fruiting spurs. If the branches are well placed, let them have their free course, and they will throw out bearing spurs to the extremity of the branches. Little more need be said on the subject, except that all unproductive wood, crowded sprays, and decayed branches, that cross each other, should be cut out, the tree kept open in the centre, and the open cuplike form rigorously maintained. These remarks apply chiefly to apples, pears, and other trees which bear their fruit on spurs. These spurs will in time become long and scrubby, with many branches, as in Fig. 475, in which a spur is shown which has grown beyond due limits. No fruit spur should be allowed to grow beyond 2 inches in length, and to bring back the spur in Fig. 475 to its proper position, cut away neatly the upper shoot at A, when the small buds will push out and form blossom buds the following year.

FIG. 475 *Fruit spur too long and with too many branches*

1017 *Breaking Young Shoots* When a tree is very vigorous, the buds will break strongly and run into wood too strong to form blossom buds. The remedy in this case is to break the young shoot near the third bud from the main branch, leaving the broken part hanging down. The time for this operation is about the middle of March. The broken part, while it droops, nevertheless draws up a portion of the wood sap. The following winter, when the buds are turned into blossom buds and become fruitful, the hanging shoot should be neatly pruned away, when a fruitful bearing spur will be formed. But this brings us to the consideration of pinching and twisting shoots for the production of fruit spurs.

1018 *Pinching: its Purpose and Utility* The work of pruning is done chiefly with the view of regulating the shape and growth of a fruit tree and the formation of wood: the promotion, however, of the growth of fruit branches is effected by another kind of operation, to which the name of pinching has been applied, as it is done with the forefinger and thumb, the thumb nail being the agent or instrument by which the tender shoot is shortened or nipped back. The end of the shoot is taken between the thumb and finger, and a portion of it removed by pressing the nail into and through its stem, which is supported as by a cushion by the finger.

1019 In a standard, pyramid, or espalier tree, the fruit branchlets will grow along each branch from its junction with the stem to its terminal point, and are disposed all round the branch, radiating from it at different points; but in trees that are trained against a wall the fruit spurs will grow from the branches in an upward, downward, or outward direction: there will be none developed on the side that is turned to the wall. Fruit branches are generally in bearing the third year after their first development. They should be kept, says Du Breuil, 'as short as possible, that the fruits may be close to the principal branches; they will then receive the most direct action of the sap, and become larger than if placed at a further distance from its source.'

1020 The following account of the *rationale* and mode of pinching, and the illustrations that accompany the text, are taken from Du Breuil's work, although the exact wording of his remarks and instructions has not been always followed: 'Fruit branches,' he explains, 'are developed from the less vigorous buds upon the wood branches. In order to obtain a continued series of fruit buds upon the entire length of a branch extension, it is necessary to cut back a little of the branch, otherwise the wood buds on one part, towards the base, should be cut back according to their degree of inclination.' At this point the question naturally will arise to what extent and in what manner the degree of inclination must influence the shortening. In Fig. 476 there are three branches which are supposed to emanate from the same point. Of these, A is vertical, B at an angle of 45°, and C horizontal. Now, in A, owing to its upright position, the sap will run to the extremity with the greatest vigour, and be most active in the buds between *a* and the terminal bud, but between *a* and the point of issue from the stem, two-thirds of the length of the entire bough, the buds will remain dormant. In order, then, to cause a proper development of the lower buds the branch must be shortened back to *b*, which is by just half its length. In B, the progress of the sap is not so rapid, and the buds from *c* to the extremity will become tolerably well developed, while those between *c* and the point of issue from the stem will remain dormant. In order, then, to promote the due development of buds near the bottom of the branch, it must be shortened to *d*, a distance of one-third its entire length. In C, the bough in a horizontal position, the sap will act with equal force at every point of its length, and there is no need to shorten it at all. If we suppose branches D and E growing in intermediate positions, the points at which they are intersected by the arc XY, which passes

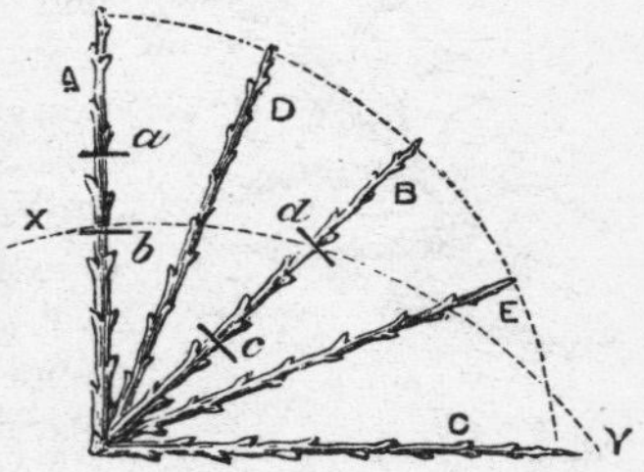

FIG. 476 *Diagram illustrating shortening of branches according to inclination*

through *b* and *d*, will show the extent to which these branches ought to be shortened. In this lies the whole matter of shortening the yearly extensions of wood at the proper time for doing so.

1021 To return to the fruit buds. 'Suppose,' says Du Breuil, 'the pruning has been duly performed upon the branch extension, by the beginning of May the branch will be covered with buds upon its entire length. The vigour of the buds will be greatest as they approach the highest part of the branch, and those quite at the extremity, will, unless arrested, acquire great development. Now, it is only the weak buds that become fruit spurs: it is therefore important to diminish their vigour. This result is obtained by pinching. As soon as the buds intended to form fruit branches have attained a length of about four inches, they must be pinched off with the nails.' In Fig. 477 the right and wrong place at which to pinch a shoot is shown, the former being at A and the latter at B. When pinched in the proper place, fruit buds will be developed along the shoot from its base to the extremity; but if too much has been taken off, leaving only three or four leaves between the new extremity and the base, the piece that remains may cease altogether to grow, and ultimately perish, leaving a bare space the next year, or if it does not do this, in a year or two years after the pinching buds may appear on each side of the base of the suppressed shoot, which after the lapse of two or three years more develop into flower buds. Sometimes premature buds will spring from the axils of the lower leaves immediately after the excessive pinching, which may develop into fruit spurs, but which never set for fruit so freely as spurs from branchlets that have not been shortened to more than three, or at the utmost, two inches.

FIG. 477 *Mode of pinching to from fruit spur*

1022 In pinching, then, everything depends on the time of growth at which each shoot is shortened, and the extent to which the shortening is carried. It has been shown that when the shortening is too great, the shoot may perish altogether, or that years may elapse before proper fruiting takes place on it, or that the fruit buds that are immediately developed are weak and far from being as productive as they ought to be. In the first case, there is loss of material, in the second, loss of time; and in the third, loss of power and vitality.

1023 When any shoots have been allowed to grow without pinching until they have attained a length of from 8 inches to 12 inches or even more, they must not be pinched off at about four inches from the base, because this would tend to cause the buds at the base or axils of the leaves to develop into branchlets in due time; but they should be twisted round without snapping them off at the distance of four inches from the base, and the extremity of each shoot nipped off.

1024 With regard to subsequent treatment, in the second year it will be found that the shoots on the branch which has been shortened and pinched in the manner described will have developed into a series of small branches, of which those on the lower third of the shoot are very short, and those on the middle third only a little longer than those on the lower third: these may be suffered to remain as they are, as they will develop into fruit branches without any further treatment. The shoots on the upper third, although repeatedly pinched during the summer, for the shoots near the ends of the boughs do not take their pinching so quietly as the lower shoots, but put forth fresh growth, will have formed shoots, more or less vigorous, according to their position, towards the end of the bough. The less vigorous ones must be broken right off just above a bud, at about three inches from the base, and the more vigorous partly broken through at the same distance from the base as the less vigorous, and the shoots that have been twisted the previous summer should be broken off at the twist. Longer shoots at the very extremity of the branch which may have escaped pinching and have attained a length of from 12 to 18 inches, and are more or less thick, may be let alone to form additional wood for laying in, or broken off at four inches from their base, if not too strong, or if very vigorous, they may be broken at this distance from the base, and then snapped off at about the same distance beyond the first fracture.

1025 In the third year, the minute branches at the lower third of the main branch will have developed into fruit buds, and will bear fruit, now becoming fruit spurs. The fruit buds may be easily distinguished from leaf buds, as they are very thick and full at the upper part when compared with the latter, which are slighter and more elongated. The longer shoots in the intermediate third have also formed minute branches, and so have the stronger and shortened shoots at the extreme third, and fructification will ensue. When after the lapse of years the fruit spurs become too large and require pruning, they must be cut back as already explained in Section 1016. Sometimes it will happen that fruit spurs are permitted, through want of care, to attain too great a size. They must then be shortened back gradually, portions furthermost from the base being taken off the first year, then other portions in the second year, reserving the final shortening for the third year, because, if they were cut back to the full extent that is necessary all at once in the first year, the consequence would be that the spurs thus shortened would put forth vigorous shoots which would assume the character of wood branches.

1026 *Training of Fruit Trees* Let us now consider briefly the forms in which trees may be trained. We may best do this by first turning our attention to the modes and conditions under which trees must, of necessity, be grown. These narrow themselves, in point of fact, to two – that is to say, a tree may be grown naturally, so to speak, without any support, save and except its own stem or trunk, from which proceed the branches; or it may be grown artificially – that is to say, by the aid of artificial supports, in the form of stakes, wires, and walls, which enable us to give whatever direction we please to the branches, and otherwise mould them to our purpose by the processes of pinching and pruning, which have been already explained.

1027 By a rough and ready form of classification, then, all fruit trees maybe grouped in two divisions, as those that are grown *without* artificial supports, and those that are grown *with* artificial supports. These divisions overlap each other, it is true, inasmuch as any fruit tree may be grown in either way, the conditions being favourable under which they are grown, but each method of growing is more favourable to some descriptions of fruit trees than to others. For example, we find in this country apple trees, pear trees, cherry trees, and plum trees grown in orchards, but peaches, nectarines, and apricots require the shelter and warmth afforded by a wall with a south aspect, to enable them to bring their fruit to perfection when grown in the open air. Yet there is nothing to prevent the growth of the trees named in the first group on walls and other kinds of support; nor, on the other hand, is there anything that militates against the culture of the trees in the second group under the form prescribed by nature, when we give them the protection that they require in our climate by means of orchard houses, in which they may be grown in pots or in borders in the pyramid or bush form.

1028 The arrangement proposed may, therefore, be regarded as a conventional arrangement – that is to say, an arrangement which, if not absolutely in keeping with nature, is at least convenient for the treatment of the subject. We say, then, that, broadly speaking, trees may be grown *without* artificial supports, or *with* them; and taking this general view, we find that the trees that are grown without artificial supports are the apple tree, the pear tree, the cherry tree, and the plum tree. Under this condition, the forms assumed by these trees are the *standard* and the *pyramid* or *bush* form, the former being more suitable for culture in isolated positions or in orchards, and the latter for gardens and smaller areas of ground and for orchard houses. All the trees mentioned, and the peach, the apricot, and the cherry, may be grown by aid of artificial supports. When recourse is had to artificial support, the support assumes the form of a vertical stake or a horizontal line, either singly or collectively, or of a plane surface, though, in point of fact, a row of vertical stakes set in line, or a series of horizontal wires one above another, are tantamount to a vertical plane surface as presented by a wall. But this brings us to the fact that trees may be trained on a single horizontal wire on what is called the *cordon* system, a system which we shall see presently may be carried out with equal facility on walls, or they may be trained on a plane surface, with branches radiating from the main stem on each side of it. The various forms adopted in and suitable for this mode of training will be mentioned presently.

1029 *The Standard Form* This form, as it has been said, is best adapted for orchards and for fruit trees in isolated positions, hedges, etc., in which fruit trees ought to be found far more frequently than they are, and doubtless would be if the eighth commandment were more generally respected, and the law of trespass more rigidly enforced. The ideas of the British black sheep with regard to *meum* and *tuum* are woefully contracted, and his insolent disregard of the rights of property prevents the doing of many things that might otherwise be done in hedgerows and elsewhere. But what has been and is in this way will continue to the very last line of this chapter of Earth-Life, until the Mystery of God is finished. To return, however, to the subject in hand, the standard form of growth, which is the most natural form, is too well known to need further explanation, and the process of pruning necessary to control and induce this growth in its best form has been explained in Sections 1012 to 1016.

1030 *The Pyramidal Form* No form in tree growth is more graceful, perhaps, than that known as the pyramid, and it is profitable as graceful, inasmuch as double the number of trees may be planted in the same space without crowding. This mode of training is now extensively adopted in small orchards and gardens, with pear trees, apples, cherries, and plums, and with the more delicate kinds of fruit trees in orchard houses. The form is, of course, the result of pruning, as well as training, a young tree with a single strong leader, which may be obtained at any of the nurseries, though the best and surest way would be to plant stocks where the trees are to stand, and graft them with suitable varieties for the purpose, taking care that one shoot only is allowed to spring from the graft.

1031 If the newly-grafted trees are procured from the nursery, plant them in properly prepared stations, as already described, supported by a strong stake driven firmly into the soil, and leave them for a year, in order that the roots may have a secure hold of the soil, and send up plenty of sap, when the growth commences, to push the buds strongly. We will assume that the young trees have plenty of buds, nearly down to the graft; then, in the following autumn, cut off the top of the shoot at A, in Fig. 478, about 18 or 20 inches from the ground, with a clean cut. 'The terminal bud reserved at the top,' says Du Breuil, should be on the side opposite to that on which the graft has been placed upon the stock at B, in order to maintain the perpendicular direction of the stem. At the end of the second year it will have made several shoots, and will probably, in many respects, resemble Fig. 479; but as we still require vigorous growth, it will be necessary to cut in again severely at A and B, B. The summer following, the side shoots will spring forth with great vigour, spreading on all sides; and now the first foundation of the pyramidal form is laid, by extending the shoots horizontally, and tying them firmly to stakes so placed that the range of branches forming the bottom of the pyramid should project away from the tree

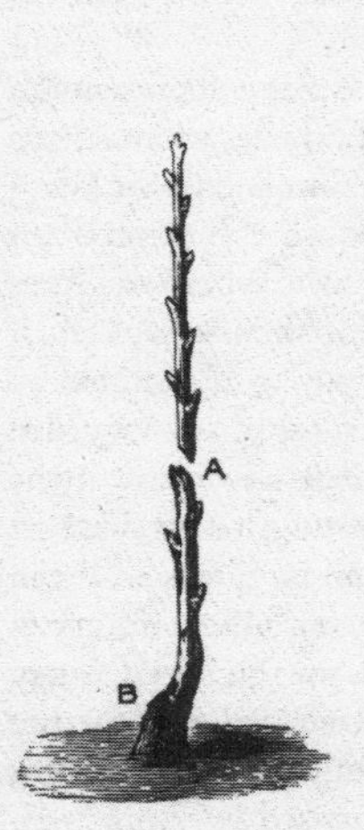

FIG. 478 *Pyramid in first year*

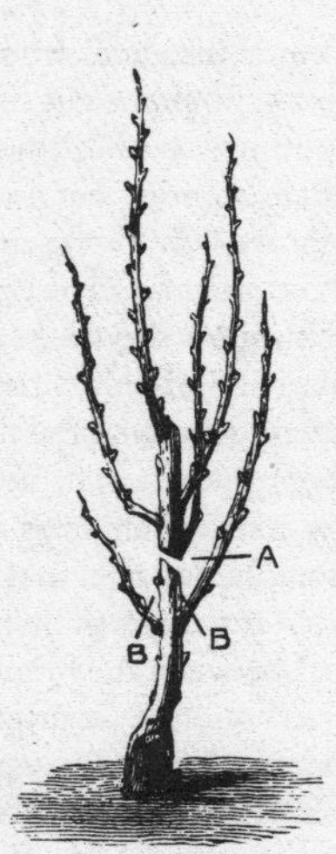

FIG. 479 *Pyramid in second year*

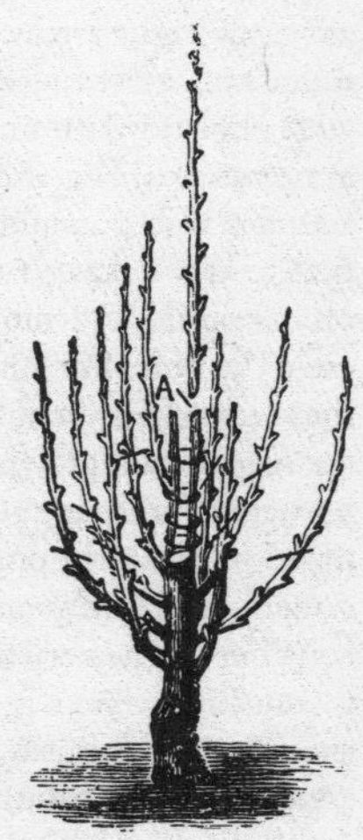

FIG 480 *Pyramid in third year*

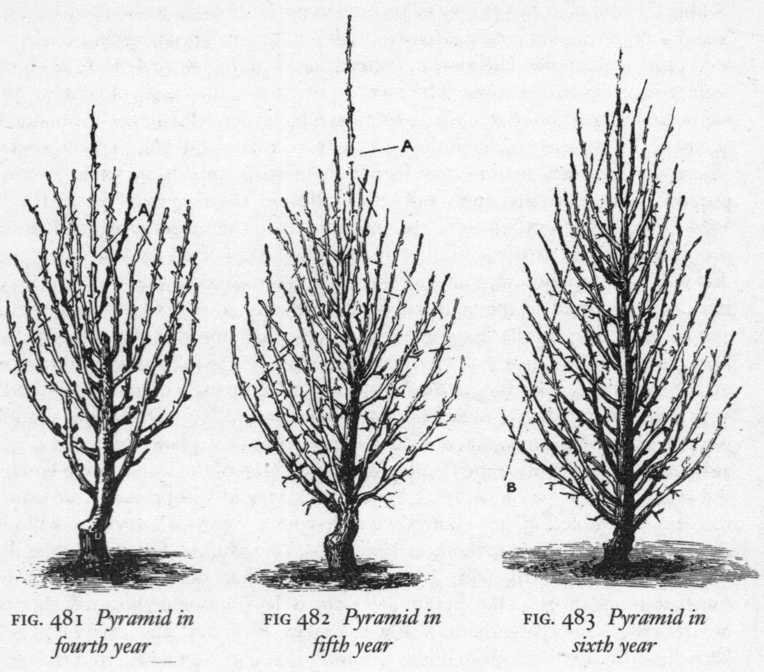

FIG. 481 *Pyramid in fourth year*

FIG 482 *Pyramid in fifth year*

FIG. 483 *Pyramid in sixth year*

at nearly right angles, and at equal distances from each other. If they are too numerous, the superfluous shoots should be cut off.

1032 The third summer, if it continues in a healthy state, the tree will present the appearance of Fig. 480, with this exception, that the lower branches will be more horizontal in position than they are here represented in consequence of being tied to the stakes. If some of the branches have grown more vigorously than others during the summer, such shoots should be pruned in to where the lines cross the branches. On the other hand, should others develop themselves feebly, they should be left at their full length, so that the descending sap, elaborated by the leaves, should deposit a larger amount of cambium. Strong shoots may also have their vigour modified by making an incision immediately below their junction with the stem, just before the sap rises in the stem; and if a desirable bud remain dormant, it may be forced into growth by making an incision just above it. Where a large vacancy occurs between the branches, then a side graft, in the manner illustrated in Fig. 455, should be inserted to fill up the space. They should again be cut at A, and in the fourth year the tree will present the appearance represented in Fig. 481, when the main stem should be again cut at A, and the lateral branches at the points at which they are crossed by short lines. The branches will then most likely begin to throw out fruiting spurs; these should be carefully encouraged, for on the number of spurs which a branch exhibits it entirely depends whether the tree is to bear a good show of fruit or not.

1033 The tiers of branches, as they advance in height, should be regulated so that every side is furnished with an equal number of branches. In the autumn of the fifth year the form of the tree will resemble that which is shown in Fig. 482. The pruning is now confined to shortening the leading shoots and the laterals, as before, where the lines cross the branches. The spurs should be carefully examined, and if any of them get long and branching, prune them in, as described and illustrated in Fig. 475.

1034 In the sixth year, the tree, continuing its progressive growth, presents the appearance represented in Fig. 483. It is now a tree of considerable size, and requires, besides the regular annual pruning of the leading shoots and spurs, that the lateral branches should be cut in a line as nearly as possible to that indicated by the dotted line AB. We see in the figure some short lateral shoots crowding towards the centre: all these, if present, should be pruned away. After this, careful pruning is all the tree requires, taking care that the lower branches are not shaded by the upper ones, which is attained by pruning them at greater length than those above; for it is one of the great principles on which this mode of training has been advocated, that the trees should be so managed that the advancing tier of branches shall not interfere with the swelling and ripening of the fruit on the lower tier by overshadowing them. During every summer all superfluous shoots should be rubbed off as they appear, and all strong shoots in the spurs should also be stopped during that season, in order to insure vigorous action in the remaining buds, while the base of the pyramid is to be extended as far as is consistent with the development of fruit-bearing habits: and this will probably be best attained by making it a rule that as soon as a shoot has extended from eight to ten inches, the point should be cut. By this practice the more powerful shoots are checked and the weaker shoots encouraged.

1035 The advantages derived from this system of training may be summarised as follows: (1) An increased number of trees in the same space. (2) The trainer has his trees more directly under control. (3) Increase of crops. (4) Ornamental and uniform appearance.

1036 *Conversion of Tree into Pyramidal Form* Any large and straight tree that has been allowed to grow in a wild manner may, by grafting, be converted into the pyramidal form, like that illustrated in Fig. 484. By a process of this kind, following the directions already given for side grafting, fine new varieties of fruit may be raised in a comparatively short period, and a comparatively lifeless tree converted into an object of great beauty. A similar mode of treatment must be followed for small pyramidal or bush fruit, as they are sometimes called, grown in pots and borders in orchard houses. This disposes of the modes of training trees without artificial supports.

Supports, however, are sometimes pressed into the service even for trees grown in the pyramidal form. Some years ago, M. Cappe, a gentleman of very great experience in the management of fruit trees, and curator of the gardens belonging to the Museum of Natural History in Paris, devised a modification or the pyramidal form, which secures a more complete diffusion of light and air in the interior of the trees, causing the centre of the tree to be more fruitful, and the fruit to ripen and colour more perfectly. He terms it the

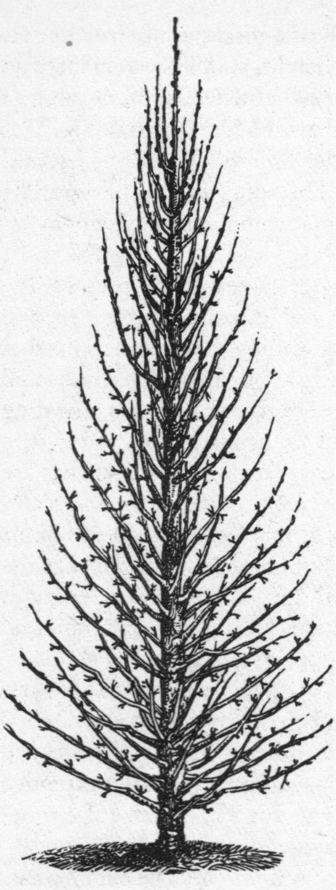

FIG. 484 *Straight tree converted into pyramid*

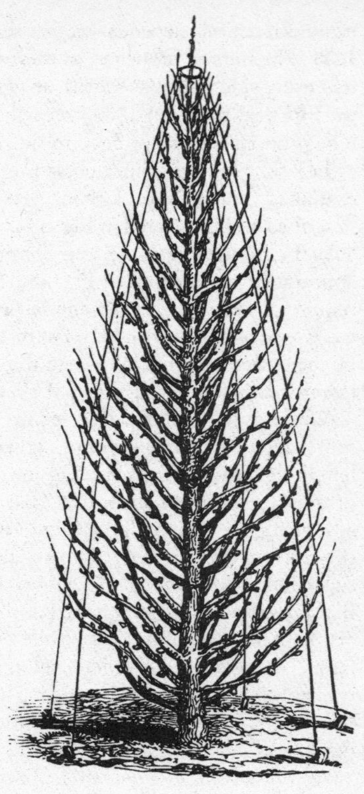

FIG. 485 *Cappe's winged pyramid tree*

winged pyramid, and certainly a tree so managed exhibits the highest skill in pruning and training, and is, independently of its fruit-bearing qualities, a most beautiful object. In adopting this system of training, a long pole of oak, or some other imperishable wood, some 30 feet in length, and charred at the lower extremity for about four feet, is employed. The charred end is driven firmly into the soil, close to the stem of the tree. At the upper extremity of the pole is fixed a strong iron ring or hoop, perforated with five holes equidistant from each other; five strong stumps of oak, charred like the pole, are driven into the earth, at spots corresponding with the holes in the hoop, the tops being four inches above the ground, and having a strong staple attached to them. Five iron rods with hooks are attached to the staples at one end, and to the holes in the hoops at the other: this is the framework of the winged pyramidal tree. These preparations being completed, the tree is planted in the soil, and on a station previously prepared for it, and pruned annually, so as to produce lateral branches in the manner already described. The branches are to be trained in right lines, slightly rising at the points towards the iron rods. It is evident that there will be regulated lines or openings between each of the five rods, into which light and air penetrate without obstruction, the openings also enabling the operator to reach every part of the tree with great facility; for the radiating branches should not be too close together in trees trained in this manner: 20 inches would be a proper distance, though that would greatly depend upon the habit of the tree. In one of vigorous growth, that distance would not be too great; but for one of delicate growth, 16 inches would probably be better. In Fig. 485 is shown a tree trained by this ingenious method, which exhibits at once the form and the means by which it has been attained. In reducing it to this shape, the various points of pruning and training, which are identical with those already described, must be rigorously followed.

1037 We now pass on to the various methods adopted for training trees on supports, which for the most part involve differences in form rather than differences in system of training. All trees, whatever they may be, must be subjected to the same discipline of pruning and cutting back, in order to induce the branches to break where they are wanted, and to take the directions that are required. And here again the methods may be narrowed down to two – namely, the *Cordon* system, which is virtually a tree with a long stem and no branches, the branches having been converted into, or having had their places taken by, fruit spurs; and the *Palmette* or *Fan* system, in which the main branches radiate from the tree on all sides, like the ribs of a palm leaf, the sticks of a fan, or even the fingers and thumb of the human hand.

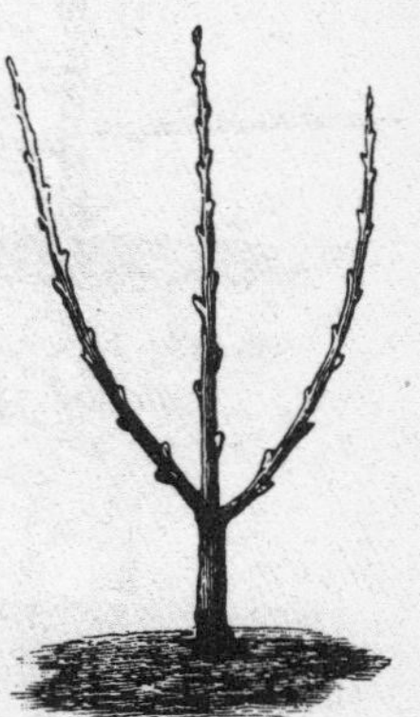

FIG. 486 *Palmette or fan before commencement of training*

1038 *The Palmette or Fan System* Let us take this system of training first, because it is the form of training most commonly exhibited on garden walls, on wires strained on posts, and on rows of stakes in the same straight line, usually spoken of in this country as espaliers, although this term is applied by the French to trees trained on any plane surface, whether it be solid, as in the case of the wall, or a skeleton surface only, as with strained wires and stakes in rows. After the pyramid form, there is no better mode of training apples in gardens, as the apple tree is usually impatient of training against a wall. The stakes, whether rough from the coppice or hedgerow, with the bark on, or of timber 1½ inch square, well planed up and painted, are driven into the ground at equal distances, and capped or not at pleasure by a horizontal rail at the top to steady them. The tree is planted in the centre of the space allotted to it, and it is then trained in the way about to be – described, so that lateral branches may be induced to run at regular intervals in horizontal lines at right angles to the stem. The same style of horizontal training is often adapted for pear trees on walls and on the sides of buildings.

The espalier system, such as is described above, namely, training on rows of stakes, is one of the very best that can be adopted for gooseberries, because the fruit on trees grown in this manner is better exposed to the influences of light and air than when grown on bushes, and can be manipulated and thinned all the more easily by picking in a green state. The mode of training is very easy. Rough stakes are driven into the ground at the distance of about 3 or 4 inches apart, and connected at top with a capping of the same. Two lateral branches are then led from the main stem, one in one direction, and the other in the opposite direction. From these laterals, which were close to the ground, branches were led upwards vertically, a branch on each stake. I never saw this mode of growing gooseberries carried out in any garden but one, and that was in a garden close to the Grammar School at Kingsbridge, in South Devon, which for many years was tenanted by the late William Carwithen Ford, a skilful surgeon and an enthusiastic gardener, the Lawrence of his neighbourhood in everything except that he never took pen in hand to write of the pleasures and profits of his garden. About a mile to the north of Kingsbridge is Coombe Royal, which has been already mentioned in this work, and which is justly famed for its gardens and arcade of oranges and lemons.

1039 In the Palmette or Fan system, whatever may be the direction that the branches are ultimately compelled to assume, the system of training to be carried out in the infancy of the tree, so to speak, is the same. The tree is subjected to this training when it has attained a central stem and two lateral branches, as in Fig. 486. In the autumn or winter pruning of the following year, the two side branches are trained horizontally, as in Fig. 487, and pruned back to about two-thirds of their length, with a bud immediately below the cut. The stem itself is pruned back to about 18 inches above the side branches, taking care that there are three buds immediately below the cut – one on each side, well placed, and a third in front to continue the stem.

FIG. 487 *First pruning or palmette of fan*

FIG. 488 *Palmette in second year*

FIG. 489 *Pruning of palmette in second year*

With the fall of the leaf in the following year the tree will be as represented in Fig. 488, with two horizontal shoots, a central stem, and two other untrained side shoots. When the pruning season arrives, the same process of cutting back takes place, each of the new side shoots being cut back to two-thirds of its length, the two lower branches to two-thirds of the year's growth, and the stem to within 18 inches of the second pair of laterals, leaving three well-placed buds immediately below, as before, to continue a third pair of side branches and the stem. It will be seen at once that this is the treatment required to induce the horizontal growth for apples and pears for walls and espaliers, as shown in Fig. 489, while Fig. 487 represents the commencement of a tree trained on the fan system, with this exception, that the lowermost branches on each side should have a direction slightly inclined to the stem, and not perfectly horizontal.

1040 A clever modification of the palmette or fan form was introduced by M. Verrier, the manager of the fruit farm at Saulsaye, in France, whose name was given to it. With the fifth year's growth the lower side branches will have attained as much horizontal extension on the wall or espalier as M. Verrier felt disposed to give them. When he had nailed the branches to the wall, or tied them to the trellis, as the case might be, he gave the end of each terminal shoot a gentle curve upwards. Continuing the usual annual process of cutting back after each year's growth, in some eleven years from the graft the tree will have covered a wall 12 or 14 feet high and 6 feet on each side of the stem; each side shoot, when it is within 18 inches of the one immediately below it, receiving an upward direction, until the tree has received the form shown in Fig. 490. The stem, as well as the side shoots, having reached the top of the wall, the extremities of the branches are pruned back every year to about 18 inches below the coping, in order to leave room for the development of the terminal bud, which is necessary to draw the sap upwards for the nourishment of the fruit. After 16 or 18 years a healthy tree, properly trained on this system, presents a surface of upwards of 60 square feet of young fruit-bearing wood. The symmetry of the tree is pleasant to look at, and it is certainly admirably balanced for vegetation, and consequently for fruit bearing.

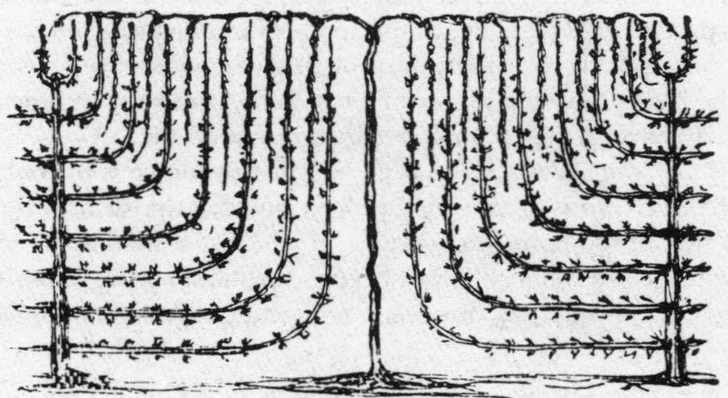

FIG. 490 *Combination of vine and pear grown on Verrier's system*

1041 One objection to this peculiar modification of the fan system is that the buds do not always occur at the right spot for projecting new side shoots. When this is the case, the process of shield budding is had recourse to, in August. In other respects, the same principle of pruning is adopted as in pryamid-trained trees, the only modification being the removal of the spurs thrown out between the tree and the wall. Another objection to the system is the time which must elapse before the wall is covered; but this is inseparable from any mode of growing apples and pears on walls, and may be met by planting vines between each, running a central rod of the vine to the top of the wall, as shown in Fig. 490; stopping it there for the first year, and carrying a shoot on each side under the coping, with descending rods at intervals, calculated not to interfere with the side shoots of the pear tree. The gain, however, if it be gain at all, is more than counterbalanced by the ugliness of the arrangement and its contrariety to nature in all trees except those of the weeping class, such as the weeping ash and the weeping willow, in forcing the branches into a downward position and compelling the sap to travel to the extremities in a downward direction. And, besides this, if the vine is allowed to remain after the shoots of the pear reach nearly to the coping, the space becomes too crowded, as may be seen from the illustration. There is, however, small chance of the plan being adopted to any extent in this country, because vine growing on unprotected walls is by no means remunerative from any point of view.

1042 *The Cordon System* This system of growing and training trees on supports is applicable to the apple in open ground, and to pears, peaches, nectarines, apricots, plums, and cherries on walls or wires. When a tree is said to be trained on the cordon system, it means that its growth is restricted to the stem only and the fruit spurs which issue from it, or to two branches, which leave the stem at a short distance above the ground, and are trained in directly opposite directions or in parallel lines. The cordon assumes three directions – the horizontal, the vertical or upright cordon, and the oblique cordon, which is mostly grown at an inclination of 45° to the ground level. When a wall is covered with cordon trees, the trees are planted about 18 inches apart, and the stems are trained in parallel lines. By a judicious system of pruning, based on the mode already described in this chapter, the growth of lateral branches is prevented, and the formation of fruit spurs promoted. The utility of this mode of training rests on the fact that the wall is more quickly covered by the growth of many trees than by that of one, and that the fruit-producing power of a tree is concentrated and focused as it were far more effectually in a small tree than in a large one.

1043 *The Apple as a Cordon* It has been said that the apple is the only kind of fruit tree that is grown as a cordon in the open, and that the form most generally adopted is that of the horizontal cordon, in which it is used as an edging for borders, being grown about 12 inches from the artificial edging of the border or piece of ground. Strawberries, however, may line the edge, and the apples be put

FIG. 491 *Low cordon for edging of border in winter*

FIG. 492 *Low cordon for edging of border in summer*

a little further back. Posts must be set in the ground at either end of the line that the cordon is to take, and intermediate posts set between them at the distance of about 12 feet apart from post to post. Galvanised iron wire is then strained from end post to end post, as shown in Fig. 491, which shows the appearance of the tree in winter, and supported by or fastened to the intermediate posts. Small trees grafted on Paradise stocks, and planted about 4 or 5 feet apart from end to end, are recommended. At the first planting about one-third of the stem is cut away, and the tree is left in a vertical position. The following winter the stem is bent and fastened to the wire, which should be about 18 inches above the level of the ground. In the second year, all vertical shoots are removed, and horizontal and lateral shoots pinched and pruned in order to convert them into fruit spurs; the leader or terminal shoot is allowed to grow about 18 or 20 inches beyond the stem of its next neighbour, and at a fitting season, namely, March, the leader of one tree is connected with the stem of the next tree a little beyond the bend by inarching. Thus, a connected row of little trees is obtained, in which uniformity of growth is promoted and maintained by an equal distribution of the sap throughout every tree. Sometimes two shoots are allowed to spring from the stem and are trained in opposite directions, as shown in Fig. 492, which exhibits the appearance of the cordon apple tree in summer.

1044 *The Pear as a Cordon* The oblique cordon is considered the best form for the pear, and indeed for all kinds of trees that are trained on this system on walls and wires, but sometimes the vertical form with two branches is adopted, as shown in Fig. 493, which is sufficient to show the manner in which the training and pruning is effected. In order to render the method of growing pears, and indeed all other fruit trees on the cordon system, as complete and as intelligible as possible, the following is taken from the instructions given on the pruning and training of the pear by Du Breuil, the eminent French authority on the culture of fruit trees, to whom allusion has been frequently made.

> 'Choose,' says M. Du Breuil, 'healthy and vigorous young trees of one year's grafting, carrying only one stem. Plant them 16 inches apart, and incline them one over the other at an angle of 60° Cut off about a third of the length just above a front fruit bud. During the following summer favour as much as possible the development of the terminal shoot: all the others must be transformed into fruit branches, by the same means as described for pyramidal trees.
>
> 'The second pruning has for its object to transform the lateral Shoots into fruit spurs;

the new extension of the stem must be cut back a third. If the terminal extension has grown but slightly and shows signs of weakness, the cut must be made lower down on the two years' wood in order to obtain a more vigorous terminal shoot. Apply the same treatment to these young trees during the summer as during the preceding one.

'By the time of the third pruning the young stem has generally attained two-thirds of its entire length; it must then be inclined at an angle of 45°; the terminal shoot and side branches must be pruned in the same manner as for the preceding year. If the stem had been inclined in this manner at the first, the consequence would have been a growing out of vigorous branches at the base of the stem, to the injury of the terminal shoot. The new shoots must be treated as usual.

'There is now nothing more to be done than to complete the tree by continuing the same treatment until it reaches the top of the wall. Arrived at its final height, it must be cut every year about 16 inches below the coping of the wall, to allow space for the growth of a vigorous terminal shoot every year, which will force the sap to circulate freely through the whole extent of the stem.

'If the wall run east and west it is not important to which side the stem is inclined, but if the wall extend north and south it should be inclined to the south to afford as much light as possible to the under side fruit branches. When the wall is built on the descent of a hill the trees should be inclined towards the summit, or their growth will be too soon arrested by the top of the wall. The trees being planted 16 inches apart and each developing a single stem, the result will be a parallel series of slanting trees having a space of about 12 inches between each stem.

'Wall trees trained in this way attain their full size in five years – a gain of at least ten or twelve years compared with other methods. By this plan trees become fruitful in the fourth year, and attain their maximum in the sixth year, while other and larger forms require twenty years to attain their maximum. If the extent of wall is limited, only a small number of varieties can be planted by the ordinary method of growing large trees, while the method now described allows of a considerable number of varieties being planted, their fruit ripening throughout the season.'

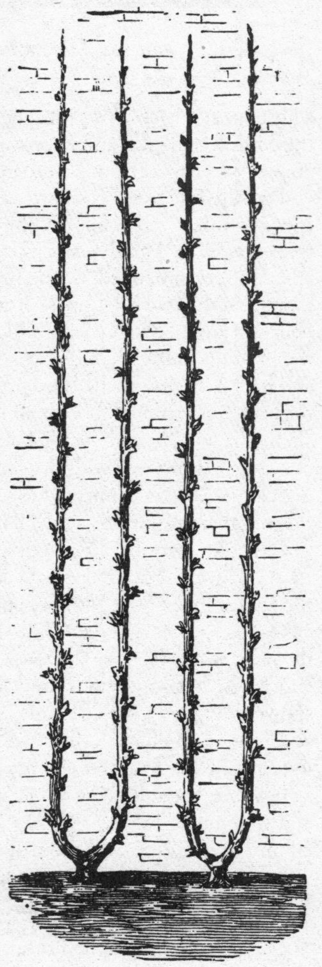

FIG. 493 *Pear as double vertical cordon*

1045 It will have struck the thoughtful reader that if a wall be covered with a row of oblique cordons, there will be a triangular space, extending to the upper corner of one end of the wall and the lower corner of the other, which will be uncovered. It may be filled by working the first and the last trees

FIG. 494 *Treatment of first and last trees in row of oblique cordons*

of the series in the manner shown in Fig. 494. From the base of the last tree to the right, a shoot, A, is allowed to grow, and is carried up at an angle of 45° parallel to the principal branch or stem: from the bend of A, a shoot, B, is trained in the same manner; a third shoot, C, from the bend of B; and so on until the terminal, D, completes the series, and covers the remainder of the right-hand lower corner of the wall. The same process is followed with regard to the first tree on the left, but in this case the shoot A is led from the upper side of the cordon instead of the lower side, as in the tree to the right. From the bend of A, which is turned into a direction parallel with the cordon, a second shoot, B, is led, and from the bend of this a third shoot, C, and so on until the terminal shoot, D, completes the series.

1046 *Training of the Peach, etc.* Enough has been said in the directions given above for the pruning and training of pears and apples to guide the gardener in work of this kind when carried out on other kinds of fruit trees, but it will be necessary to make a few brief remarks on the treatment required by trees that bear stone fruit and not pip fruit, as apple trees and pear trees do. Peaches and nectarines, to be brought to perfection in this country in the open air, require walls with a southern aspect, or south with a slight turn east or west. The trees that bear them are obtained by budding on a plum stock, that of the Muscle plum being the most suitable for the purpose. They may be trained in the fan or inclined cordon form, but the main branches must be disposed in such a manner and at such a distance apart as to leave room for lateral shoots to be laid in on each side of the main branch, because it is on the new or young wood that the fruit is produced, and not on permanent fruit spurs as in the pear and apple. Thus, although the branches of a trained pear or apple need not be more than 12 inches apart, the branches of a peach or nectarine must be from 20 to 24 inches apart in order to give room for laying in the lateral fruit-bearing shoots that proceed from the main or wood branch. For the same reason, although pears in the oblique cordon form may be planted 16 inches apart, so that their branches when inclined are about 12 inches apart, yet the trees in a row of oblique cordon peaches must be planted from 24 to 30 inches apart in order that there may be an interval of from 20 to 24 inches between them when inclined.

1047 That there may be no misconception of that which has just been said, Fig. 495 will give a rough idea of the training of the peach and nectarine in fan form, the tree being represented in the form that it assumes in the fifth year of its training and the sixth year of its growth after planting, for peaches and

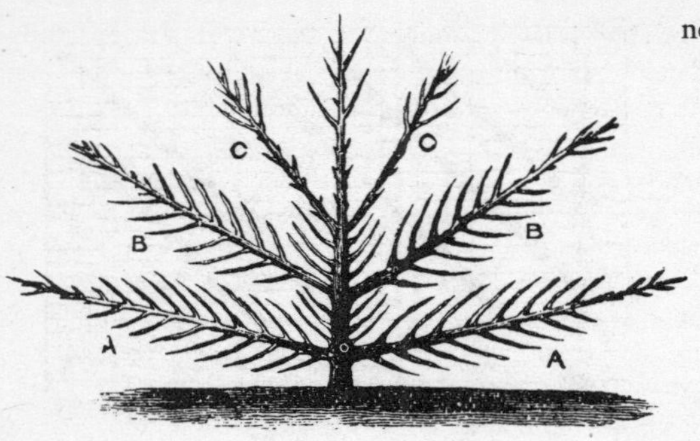

FIG. 495 *Peach tree trained on fan system*

nectarines should not be pruned during the first year of their growth. At the end of the first year the tree should be cut back to about 18 inches, or even less, from the ground, in such a way as to leave three buds on the stem – two on opposite sides of the stem, about 12 inches above the ground level, and one in front: from the side buds the branches A, A, are obtained, while the front bud affords the continuation of the stem. The second year the new shoots that spring from the three buds must be cut back about a third of their length, and at the third pruning the main stem is again cut back in order to allow the lowest branches, A, A, to gain in size and strength and to develop lateral shoots. It is not till the fourth year that the branches B, B, are allowed to grow. In the fifth year the upper branches, C, C, are developed from buds left below the point at which the stem has been last cut, and at the end of the summer the growth of the tree is as shown in Fig. 495. In the meantime, the side branches and the lateral fruit-bearing shoots have been cut back year after year in order to secure the proper extension of both. In the peach and nectarine the fruit branches – they can scarcely be termed spurs – are new every year; that is to say, the branches which have borne blossom and fruit one year, and will bear no more, must be replaced the next year by fresh branches from new buds at the base of the shoot.

1048 *Training of the Apricot* All that has been said with reference to the peach and nectarine applies equally well to the apricot, which is also budded on a plum stock. It requires a warm and sheltered situation, and in this country must be grown against a wall whose aspect may be towards any point of the compass between south and east or south and west.

1049 *Training of the Plum* Plum trees are obtained from grafts on stocks raised from plum stones, or by budding on stocks also grown from plum stones. The treatment of the plum in training and general management is similar to that which has been described for the pear. It may be grown in any form, but the best fruit is obtained from trees trained on walls or from those grown in orchard houses.

1050 *Training of the Cherry* The cherry is propagated by budding on stocks usually obtained from the stones of the wild black cherry, or in the case of standards, by grafting on stocks of the wild cherry. Trees for training on walls are generally worked on the St Lucie plum. Its treatment, like that of the plum, is precisely the same as that laid down for the training of the pear. It may be grown in any form.

1051 This chapter may be appropriately brought to a close with a table setting forth the soil that is liked best by each kind of fruit tree that is adapted for training, and other particulars with respect to its culture, propagation, training, etc.

Apple *Soil:* Rich, moist soil, or cool, sandy soil, of medium consistency; *Mode of Propagation:* Grafting on stocks from pips, or on Paradise stocks from layers for dwarf trees, cordons, etc., or on Doucin or French Stocks also from layers; *Time:* March and April; *How Grown:* Standard, Pyramid, Espalier, *i.e.*, trained with horizontal branches on stakes or wire; Single or Double Cordon, also horizontal; *Aspect: Any* aspect; does best in open.

Apricot *Soil:* Clay soil, open and calcareous, and not deep; *Mode of Propagation:* Budding on plum stocks; *Time:* July and August; *How Grown:* Pyramid in Orchard House; Fan or Oblique Cordon on wall; *Aspect:* Any aspect from east (by south) to west.

Cherry *Soil:* Dry and light sandy loam on dry subsoil, or chalky soil with chalk subsoil; *Mode of Propagation:* (1) By budding on small stock or St Lucie Plum (2) By grafting with Cleft or Crown graft on wild cherry stock; *Time:* (1) July and August (2) March; *How Grown:* Standard, Pyramid, Double Vertical Cordon, Single Oblique Cordon and Fan; *Aspect:* Any aspect, but chiefly east, west, and south for trained trees.

Peach and Nectarine *Soil:* Open soil, deep, fairly consistent, calcareous, and not too moist; *Mode of Propagation:* Budding on plum stock; *Time:* July; *How Grown:* Pyramid or bush in Orchard House; Fan and Single Oblique Cordon on wall; *Aspect:* South-east is best, but any aspect from east to south-west will do.

Pear *Soil:* Deep clay soil, containing flints; cool, but not too moist; *Mode of Propagation:* (1) Grafting on stocks from pips or on quince stocks. (2) By budding on smaller stock; *Time:* (1) March and April (2) August; *How Grown:* Standard, Pyramid, Espalier, Fan, branches horizontal; Vertical and Oblique Cordon, single and double; *Aspect:* Any aspect, but east and west are most suitable for trees trained on walls.

Plum *Soil:* Clay soil, open and calcareous, and not deep; *Mode of Propagation:* (1) Budding on plum stock (2) Grafting on plum stock; *Time:* (1) July (2) March; *How Grown:* Standard, Pyramid, Fan, and Single Vertical and Oblique Cordon; *Aspect:* Any aspect, but chiefly east, west, and south for trained trees.

CHAPTER 22

The Garden and Its Work in Every Department in January

1052 Up to this point the management of the garden has been treated generally, and it has been sought rather to show how to get a new piece of ground into fitting order for garden work and culture, and how to give a fresh aspect to a garden that is old and worn out, and to impart new youth and fertility to trees that are going out of bearing through age and neglect, than to deal with special work to be done at particular times. We know now what must be done to get a garden, whether new or old, into order, and how to keep it in order, and we know what appliances are necessary for every kind of garden work. The knowledge thus gained must now be turned to account for everyday work in the garden in all its various departments. We are acquainted with all the leading processes that are called into play in gardening, the various conditions and procedure of plant growth, how to raise, propagate, pot, and transplant all kinds of flowers, and how to plant, prune, bud, graft, and train our fruit trees, and how to grow our vegetables. Knowing *how* to do all these things, it is clear that the next step will be to note *when* to do them, so that everything that has to be done may be done at an appropriate and fitting time, and just at the periods when the doing is likely to be followed by the most profitable results.

1053 There is no better – indeed, no other – way of doing this than by tracing the work of the garden throughout the year from month to month. Properly speaking, for the gardener the work of the gardening year commences in November, that being the first of the three months of preparation in which most things must be done that will impart character and lend beauty to the garden during the nine months that follow, but to begin a Calendar of Garden Work with all that is to be done in November would seem to some perhaps like beginning near the end, to say nothing of the middle; so to avoid any imputation of having done this it will be desirable to commence with January's work. Let us take, then, each month singly, and consider its aspect and character and the work to be done in it, and let us view the various kinds of work to be done, each in accordance with its nature. By adopting this course it will be found that some degree of classification can be imparted to the parts that combine to form the entire subject. It is manifest that there are only two conditions under which plant culture is carried on, namely, without protection, or with protection – that is to say, in the open air, or under glass. It is equally obvious that there are three descriptions of plants that command the gardener's attention and demand his consideration, namely, flowers and flowering trees and shrubs, vegetables, and plants and trees that yield fruit; and that each class is subject to culture, more or less, both in the open air and under glass. The main divisions of the subject arrange themselves, therefore, in this manner:

I – Plant Culture in the Open Air

1 – The Flower Garden and Shrubbery.

2 – The Vegetable or Kitchen Garden.

3 – The Fruit Garden and Orchard.

II – Plant Culture under Glass

1 – Flowers, etc., in Conservatory, Greenhouse, Stove, etc.

2 – Plants under Glass in Hotbeds, Frames, etc.

3 – Fruit under Glass, Heated and Unheated.

1054 Even these divisions seem to overlap a little, for it may be urged that the growing of vegetables under glass belongs properly to the work of the vegetable or kitchen garden. It does so, without a doubt, but it is impossible to deny that hotbed and frame cultivation, carried on as it is either in the kitchen garden or in a quarter immediately contiguous to it and set apart for the purpose, is plant culture under glass, and it must therefore be placed under the second of the principal headings that indicate the chief or primary divisions of the subject. In this and the eleven chapters that follow it will be sought to show *when* it is necessary to perform the various operations that make up the sum total of gardening in their proper sequence throughout the year.

FIG. 496 *Winter aconite (Eranthis hyemails)*

The work to be done will be specified in general terms, but as full instructions have already been given in the preceding chapters for the preparation of the soil, and the various modes by which plants and trees are raised, propagated, and trained, there will be no difficulty in applying them to the culture of any flower, fruit, or vegetable, although the remarks on each special kind must of necessity be brief.

FIG. 497 *Christmas rose (Hellebrous niger)*

1055 *Aspect and Character of the Month* January is the first month of our civil year, the second of winter, and the third of the gardener's year. The average temperature is 39° during the day and 32° during the night, and the mean temperature, during an average of many years, does not fall below the freezing point; severe frosts, and frosts of long continuance, occurring in January, are therefore exceptional occurrences in our climate.

> Regarded from a less prosaic point of view, January is the Gate of the Year, 'the Entrance-hall of the Seasons', as it has been called, whose portico, supported by glittering pillars of ice, leads through long vistas of leafless snow-laden branches and frosted work of silvery tracery,
>
> Of what may seem the sparkling trees
> And shrubs of fairy land,
>
> to the vernal glories of spring, the flowery landscape of summer, and the russet and golden tints of autumn. Even at this dead season of the year,
>
> When icicles are hanging
> Like spears from every tree,
> And beautiful to gaze on
> Is the frost-work tracery,
>
> a few flowers venture to put forth their blossoms: the garden anemone, the yellow crocus, and the herb rosemary, for remembrance, the winter aconite (Fig. 496), the Christmas rose (Fig. 497), with its white petals and yellow anthers and dark green leaves. The mezereon and the laurustinus enliven the otherwise deserted winter garden, and the snowdrop, in particular, the first pale blossom of the unripened year – all these are found in secluded and sheltered spots in the garden, and under the hedgerows, towards the end of the month, in our less exposed counties.

1056 In the garden, January is the last month of preparation: the processes of vegetation will soon be in full progress; for 'Nature even in her sleep is never still,' and even now the sap is stirring in her veins. The good gardener who has husbanded his time may now, in some measure, slacken his efforts, and look forward to the results that the future has in store for him, although he has still some work of preparation to complete. But what of him who has neglected to take time by the forelock? He must toil after the old scythe-bearer in a vain struggle to overtake him, for time once lost can never be recalled; and there is much to be done in the garden in autumn which cannot be done so well in any other season. There are, however, many things which may yet be done towards recovering lost time. Among these may be included all organic changes, such as taking in new ground, making new walks, draining, planting, and, if the weather continues mild, pruning.

I – Work to be Done in the Garden in January

1 – The Flower Garden and Shrubbery

1057 *Work that Must be Done* The gardener's attention must now be concentrated on the future rather than diverted by the past. All arrears of labour due to the past year must at once be discharged. Nothing tends more to mar the success of gardening operations than dragging through the necessary work three weeks or a month behind the time proper for its performance. Not only our comfort, but our success, demands that we become thorough masters of our work, instead of allowing our work to master us. The peculiar fickleness of our climate renders gardening precarious and difficult enough with every advantage of judgment and foresight. It will be well, therefore, to bear in mind that the work can only be done, weather permitting. For instance, it is impossible to dig, plant, or sow, when the frost has set its strong seal upon the earth. It is bad practice to dig in snow, and worse than useless to attempt anything on the surface of the ground when an excess of moisture has converted it into mud. It may thus occasionally happen that a part or the whole of the work prescribed for one month may have to be deferred to another, and thus a double portion fall upon one or any of the winter or spring months. In such cases, extra labour must be employed, or diverted from other departments, until the whole of the work indicated is completed.

There is a difference of several weeks in the climate of different parts of the country, so that operations that should be performed at once in the south may thus generally be deferred for several weeks in the north. The seasonal directions that are given here for garden work are calculated for the latitude of London. It may be useful to those who are located north or south of this latitude, to quote the comparative heat of the sun at various degrees of latitude, from Lawrence's *Pleasures and Profits of Gardening*, 1000 being the unit, or full measure of heat, of which the following are parts:

Places	*Latitude*	*Heat June 10*	*Heat April 10 & August 12*	*Heat March 10 & September 12*
Lyons	46°	880	711	516
Paris	49°	814	631	431
The Lizard	50°	800	614	413
London	51½°	777	597	388
Bedford	52°	770	579	379
Northampton	52½°	767	574	375
Boston	53°	757	561	362
Lincoln	53½°	753	555	357
York	54°	742	543	346
Newcastle	55°	726	524	320
Edinburgh	56°	711	506	312

The term flower garden seems almost a misnomer at this season. But now is the time to consider what can be done to prepare the garden for the re-appearance of our favourites. Is its form in any way objectionable? Let it at once be altered and brought into conformity with a design that cannot fail to satisfy and please the eye. Is it too small? Enlarge it, if possible. Is the soil exhausted? Renew it. Is it naturally poor? Enrich it. Is the situation bad? Select a better, if space permits. In a word, do any and everything that industry suggests, foresight approves, and enlightened judgment commands, to furnish the plants on their re-appearance with all that is needful to add additional beauty and glory to their lives.

1058 *Trenching Borders, etc.* All new flower gardens must, of necessity, be trenched, and the same treatment may be prescribed for old ones. No soil, however rich in quality, will go on producing flowers in perfection for years, with an annual digging in autumn or spring and frequent hoeings and pointings in summer: this practice soon exhausts the best soil. Nothing benefits old gardens more than the entire removal of the old plants, trenching up the soil to the depth of three feet, liberally manuring it, and replanting. Gardens, or rather beds and borders in which the bedding-out system is put in force, should be trenched every fourth or sixth year. The plants would then be much less at the mercy of the extremes of drought or wet, and have a more copious supply of suitable food.

Trenching is not a process to be carried out every year: it should be carried out in the flower garden at long intervals, as indicated, but when it is done, it should be done properly and effectually. The operation of trenching, simple as it appears, is often so indifferently performed as to be of doubtful utility. Sometimes the best soil is thrown into the bottom of the trench, and a foot of sterile clay brought to the surface. Such practice is to be avoided; for while most soils are improved by a slight admixture of the subsoil, such a mode of procedure as that to which allusion has just been made would prove a quietus to the productive powers of many soils for many years. The process of deepening shallow soils must be gradual. The best mode is to bring up, say 6 or 8 inches of the subsoil, and mix it with the top soil; then dig up the bottom of the trench a spit deep, place a layer of manure on the bottom so loosened, and proceed filling up with the next trench, mixing the soil as much as possible, and incorporating the manure with it as the process goes on. The operation is performed by first digging out a trench 3 feet wide and 3 or 4 feet deep, and wheeling the soil taken out to the other end of the ground. Then spread a layer of manure from 9 to 12 inches thick upon the next yard of ground, dig up the bottom of the open trench, divide the yard of ground already manured in the middle, throw part of the manure from its surface into the bottom of the open trench, and then proceed right down the entire depth with this half trench. Keeping the ground in the half-filled trench at a rough level, proceed to fill up with the 18 inches left; the result will be that the top and bottom earth will not be simply inverted, but will be mixed with manure and thoroughly incorporated together. The next time the ground is trenched, the bottom spit of subsoil will be mixed with the other soil, and another turned up and manured as before. In this way, soil that was only from 15 to 18 inches in depth will gradually be deepened to 3 or 4 feet, which is requisite to grow most plants in the highest perfection.

1059 *Rough Digging* The moment that flower beds are cleared of their summer occupants, they should be dug up as roughly as possible. But rough digging, while it can never present a *smooth*, may always exhibit an *even* surface, and, in that case, it is not unsightly. Besides, the objections against it would generally be silenced if its obvious importance were understood. It would be difficult to say whether the mechanical or chemical influence in enriching the quality of the soil is the most important. Certainly, both are of the highest value, and their influence will be powerful, or the reverse, in exact ratio to the quantity of *fresh* surface exposed to atmospheric influence. Hence the importance of rough digging or forking over ground in frosty weather; resulting in that finely pulverised, mellow, genial soil in spring, in which plants delight to grow.

1060 *Pointing Surface of Borders* Next in importance to draining, trenching, and manuring, and often of greater moment than any or all of them put together, is the frequent digging, forking, and scarifying of the surface; and from December to April are the months specially adapted for these operations. It must be remembered that deep digging is not intended, but merely the stirring of the surface soil with a fork or hoe. Working the surface of the ground with a fork is the operation which has been already mentioned as pointing, and is so called because the stirring of the ground is effected by the introduction of the points of the fork. Pointing should not be carried beyond a depth of 2, or at the utmost, 3 inches. The object of it is to loosen and break up the surface and admit the air. Deep digging when plants are growing is simply ruination to them, especially to those whose roots seek the surface. Borders which are stocked with herbaceous plants should only have the surface well broken.

1061 *Manuring for Bedding Plants* To grow bedding plants in perfection, the beds should have a dressing of manure annually, or a heavier application every second year. It would be almost as reasonable to attempt to grow two crops of cabbages in succession without enriching the soil as two crops or bedding plants. Many of them exhaust the soil more than any crop whatever; and to grow them rapidly, and in perfection, the beds must be liberally manured.

1062 *Dressing Shrubberies* Shrubberies on poor soils are much benefitted by manuring. The practice of raking every weed and leaf off the surface, and cruelly disrooting the plants by a deep winter or spring digging, is altogether a mistake. Once shrubberies are properly established in good soil, no rake should ever cross their surface, and every leaf that falls upon them should be merely dug in at any time from December to April, but the earlier the better. Leaves are Nature's means of sustaining the fertility of the soil, and whenever or wherever they are removed and no substitute for them takes their place, the soil rapidly inclines towards sterility.

1063 *Planting Trees and Shrubs* November is undoubtedly the proper month for planting and transplanting every kind of deciduous tree and shrub, and evergreens as well; and, if possible, the planting of all trees and shrubs should be carried out by the middle of December. This kind of work should, therefore, be pushed forward in mild open weather. All newly-planted shrubs and trees should have their roots protected with long litter or manure to preserve them from injury. This surface dressing is called *mulching*: the litter or manure being a non-conductor tends in winter to shield the roots from frost, and to protect them in summer from the parching influence of the sun's rays. All trees and shrubs, especially those of large size, when newly-planted, should have the top firmly secured to a strong stake, so as to keep it from swaying to and fro when the wind is high. If this precaution be neglected, the rootlets, which have begun to take hold of the soil, will be dragged from their moorings, and the first efforts of the freshly-planted tree to take anchor in its new position will be rendered of none effect. Beds of hyacinths and tulips, in whatever part of the garden they may be, should be protected during severe weather, as the spikes of leaf and bloom are often injured when coming through the soil. Mats supported on hoops may be used, or the surface may be covered to the depth of a few inches with coconut fibre.

1064 *Hardy Bulbs* During this month plant crocuses and any other hardy bulbs for succession, the main crops having been planted in October or November. The usual mode of planting crocuses is to set them in the soil in patches, varying from half a dozen to a dozen. They are also highly effective in rows or ribbons of different colours.

1065 *Pruning Shrubs, etc.* All deciduous shrubs may now be pruned, and hedges consisting of privet, beech, the white thorn or hawthorn, etc., should be pruned and trimmed, if this has not been already done, and the bottom cleared of all weeds and rubbish. Climbing roses, tea roses only being excepted, jasmines, clematises, and other climbing plants may now be pruned and trained.

1066 *Snow on Trees, Shrubs, etc.* When a heavy fall of snow occurs, dislodge it from ornamental and flowering trees, shrubs, etc., by shaking them with a rake or pole like a clothes prop, with a fork at the top, to prevent them from getting broken by the superincumbent weight.

1067 *Carnations in Pots* Especial care should be taken to protect carnations in pots from heavy rains, hard frosts, cold winds, or snow, by means of frames, hand lights, etc. The carnation is perfectly hardy, though liable to injury from deep planting and excessive moisture, and can stand the winter in the open ground, but by protecting the choicer sorts in bad weather they are preserved in strong condition for blooming in good order at the right time. Those in frames should be examined frequently and watered with care if necessary. Pinks and carnations in beds should also be examined, and if any are heaved up by the frost they should be pressed firmly down in the soil.

1068 *Layering* Provided the weather is open, layers may be made of the young branches and shoots of hardy shrubs, to raise a supply of new plants. The branches should be laid into the soil three or four inches deep, and be tightly pegged down, the top in each case being left out of the soil and brought as far as possible into an upright position. These layers will be well rooted by the following autumn and fit for transplanting.

1069 *Suckers* Rooted suckers, or rather suckers that can be taken from the mother plant with a portion of root to it, may now be removed from roses, lilacs, and other shrubs, and transplanted so as to enter on a separate existence. The larger ones may be planted at once in the borders wherever it may be intended for them to remain; but the smaller ones should be placed in rows in the nursery or reserve garden, to make good strong plants in about two years' time.

1070 *Cuttings of Shrubs* Cuttings of the young shoots of many sorts of hardy deciduous shrubs may likewise now be planted in open weather, inasmuch as they will be sure to take root in the spring and summer, shoot at the top, and form strong plants, with plenty of fibrous roots, by the autumn.

1071 *Annuals and all Seedlings* Autumn-sown annuals in the reserve garden in the open ground should be protected by having some boughs stuck among them, or by being covered with mats, canvas, etc. Beds intended for the main sowing of hardy annuals should be prepared for this purpose. Pans, boxes, or pots of any tender or choice kinds of seedlings in pits or frames, should be covered up in event of frost, either with mats, long litter, or some similar material, which should be laid over them to the depth of say 9 inches, and close round the sides of the structure.

1072 *Ranunculuses, etc.* – Beds intended for choice ranunculuses and anemones should receive a liberal dressing of two-year-old cow dung, and be laid up rough, so as to be ready to receive their singular-looking corms and tubers in the following month.

1073 *Auriculas, Polyanthuses, etc.* These plants, if protected by frames, should be examined from time to time and watered with care. Early blooms must be removed from polyanthuses.

1074 *Roses* Hardy roses may still be planted, and all weak plants requiring it may be pruned. Tea and China roses should be protected above the surface of the ground by boughs, the roots being shielded from harm by heaping up spent tan, cinder ashes, etc., over the roots and round the stem. Stocks should be obtained from the hedgerows for budding if this has not been done in November or December. All ground occupied by roses should be well manured, and care must be taken not to injure the roots when digging in the manure.

1075 *Herbaceous Plants* It will be found that many kinds of herbaceous plants, and such flowers as aubrietias, arabis, alyssum, carnations, daisies, forget-me-nots or myosotis, pansies, pinks, primulas, phloxes, polyanthuses, violets, etc., and growing bulbs planted in the autumn, will be somewhat raised out of the ground or above the ground level by the action of the frost. These must be firmly pressed down into place and a little fine mould drawn round them. Hoe or point the surface of the soil between the flowers when it is dry enough.

1076 *Alterations of Borders, Walks, etc.* All alterations in the form of flower beds or the direction of walks, if not already carried out in the autumn, may still be made, and all vacant ground dug over and thrown up into ridges. The surface of old walks may be renewed by skimming off the surface to a depth ranging from 1 to 3 inches, according to circumstances; with the spade, and turning it over so as to bring the part that had previously been below uppermost, to form a new and fresh surface, which must then be raked even and rolled.

1077 *Grass Lawns, Walks, and Verges* These should now be kept neat and trim by frequent rollings, which should be performed in open dry weather, when the surface is not too moist; and by equally frequent mowings, which should be done the first thing in the morning, when the dew is on the grass. Turf may be laid wherever wanted, provided that the weather is favourable, and grass plots in a dilapidated condition may be relaid or patched. The best turf for gardens is to be met with on commons or downs where sheep are pastured. A fine dry day should always be selected for cutting turf for lawns.

1078 *Transfer of Earth, Turf, etc.* Earth may be carried from one part of the garden to another, turf brought in, and manure wheeled to its destination, when the surface of the ground is hardened by frost, but when the frost is over and the ground begins to give, or, in other words, to soften, and lose its rigidity, boards should be laid down to prevent the wheel of the barrow from making deep ruts in the paths. Boards should also be laid down on lawns if it be found necessary to take anything over them in the wheelbarrow.

1079 *Rockeries, etc.* Old structures of this kind may now be repaired and renewed, and new rockeries may be formed of materials that have been collected for the purpose. Stones are the material that is to be preferred for ornamental work of this description, but as they cannot be got everywhere and anywhere, and as the desire to have a bit of rockwork in one corner or another of the garden is general, clinkers, débris of stone ware, bricks, cement, chalk, concrete, and even rough pieces of timber, may be utilised for the purpose. The patent blocks for rockwork, supplied by Mr W. H. Lascelles, builder, 121 Bunhill Row, London, at 9d. each, are picturesque in form, of pleasing colours, light, durable, and from their porosity well calculated to encourage plant growth on themselves. They are large in size, so that a few of them go a long way.

1080 *Removal of Litter* Nothing, perhaps, is more objectionable even in the winter months than an untidy garden. Leaves and all litter of dead and dying plants should be collected and carried away, and neatness and order should everywhere be apparent.

2 – The Vegetable or Kitchen Garden

1081 *Work Dependent on Weather* The work to be done in the kitchen garden in January depends altogether on the weather. In open frosty weather no opportunity should be lost for wheeling manure on the vacant ground. All the refuse about the grounds should be collected and added to the manure heap, and that burned or charred which will not readily decompose, and added to it.

1082 *Forecast of Operations* This is also the season when the forethought of the gardener may be exhibited. He has to lay down his plan of operations for the year, or at least for the next three months; and on his judgment in doing this much of the successful cultivation depends. If he cover too much ground with early crops in these three months, not only will great waste arise, but he will have forestalled the space required for the main crops in April, May, and June, when some of the most important crops are to be sown. He should make his calculations now, so as to secure a constant succession of the various products as they are required, but leaving little or nothing to run to waste.

It is a good practice, in going through the orchard, bush fruit, and trees generally, to cut off all spare wood at this season, assort them as to size and shape, and tie them up in bundles ready for use as pea sticks and other purposes.

1083 *Crops for the Month* The crops to be got into the ground this month are – (1) Peas and beans, radishes, lettuces (the black-seeded cos does well if sown early), Walcheren or early Cape broccoli, and cauliflower, in the open ground or in cold frames; (2) Early horn carrot and potatoes on a slight hotbed of two feet or so in height. A little parsley sown now on a slight hotbed will be useful for planting out early. A little celery should be sown for an early supply, and a little cabbage also, should these be scarce, or to fill up in case of the main crop, if thinned out by severe frosts.

At this season it is necessary to be provided with mats or litter to cover the glass, in case of sharp frost; for, though most of these crops are hardy, yet, when young and growing, they are not unlikely to be cut off by frosts. They are also much strengthened and hardened by exposure to the air in mild weather. A warm shower is also beneficial; but too much wet is injurious, especially in cold inclement winds.

1084 *Early Peas* Early peas may be got in any time this month, if the weather permits. Where the ground is tolerably porous and well drained, and a warm border, well sheltered on the north, is available, nothing more is required than to sow them in rows, 5, 6, or more feet apart, the rows running north and south; for dwarf peas, 5 feet will suffice. In warm situations and light soils, early peas will probably have been sown in October. As they spear through the ground, some light litter should be placed over them in frosty weather, but this should be removed in mild weather: by this treatment they will come in very early. Where the soil is light it is very necessary to mulch early peas; it protects the young roots from frost, and saves watering and manuring the ground for the next crop. It tends, also, to produce a better and much earlier crop of peas.

About London it is the custom to sow spinach between the rows of peas, the spinach coming off in time to be replaced with broccoli before the peas are over; but there is nothing lost by sowing spinach apart, and leaving the spaces between the peas till the time for planting potatoes, French beans, and other open ground crops, taking care to leave sufficient space for the main crops.

1085 *Beans* Beans, like peas, can be sown in October, where the soil is light or well drained and well sheltered. Where the ground is heavy, they may be raised in a pit or frame. To do this a number of 4-inch pots should be obtained, and the beans placed three in each pot. Beans thus sown in January may be planted out in March. Beans, and peas also, that are sown in January must be protected against the depredation of mice by suitable traps, and against severe frosts by mulching or covering with long litter, or by covering the ground with branches of spruce, fir, and similar material, or by protectors specially devised for the purpose.

1086 *Lettuces* In every garden it should be possible to obtain a salad at any season of the year, but to do this, and to maintain a constant supply, recourse must be had to frequent, say fortnightly, sowings. Sow this month in a warm border under a south wall or fence. They are better if sown at this season in a frame, if one can be spared; even a hand-light is better than no protection at all. Wanting either, it is advisable to cover the seed when sown with straw or light litter, taking it off sometimes to give a dusting with lime, in case any slugs may be harboured. The ground should be well dug over one spit deep, a dressing of manure being turned in, as lettuces require a rich soil in order to grow them to advantage. Advancing crops must be well protected.

1087 *Endive* Full-grown plants should be well covered with slates, tiles, or even pieces of board, and litter heaped over all, in order to blanch and preserve them. Crops for succession should be placed under protectors; and fresh sowings should also be protected. It is better and safer to sow on a slight hotbed. An example of winter endive is given in Fig. 498.

FIG. 498 *Fine curled green winter endive*

1088 *Celery* Sow a small pinch of celery seed in a patch, for the purpose of flavouring soups in the early part of summer, when full-grown sticks cannot be had. Earth up celery as it advances in growth, and when performing the work see that the soil is well broken up and laid round the plants lightly, that they may not be crushed or bruised, raising the earth very nearly to the top of each.

1089 *Spinach* Sow a row or two between such crops as beans, peas, and the like, as in such situations there will be a good chance of obtaining an early crop.

1090 *Asparagus* The surface soil should be raked away, and a fresh top dressing should be spread over the beds, consisting of half-rotted farmyard manure from 4 to 6 inches thick.

1091 *Carrots* A little seed may be sown on a hotbed for an early supply, and *radishes*, *kidney beans*, and anything else that is likely to be needed before the time that it will arrive at perfection in a natural way, may be similarly treated. If no hotbed is available, the seeds may be sown in the ground in a south border or some sunny spot, under protectors, frames, or even hand-lights.

1092 *Broccoli* Early varieties, such as the Walcheren (Fig. 499) and others, when nearly fit for table, should be taken up before the central leaves unfold and placed in a shed or cellar, where they may be preserved from frost until they are required for use. If the flower of the broccoli, which is the part that is eaten, is exposed to even a slight frost when it is in a wet condition, it is fit for nothing. Hence the utility of plant protectors for broccoli, which at all events shield them from wet, although they do not exclude frost.

FIG. 499 *Early Walcheren broccoli*

1093 *Protection* This is essentially a month in which protection is required for growing crops as well as those which have not yet germinated. *Globe artichokes* and *parsley* require protection as well as the crops already indicated, and *celery* and *cauliflower* are all the better for it. It will be sufficient to throw a covering of long litter over globe artichokes and celery, but for parsley and cauliflower, plant protectors are more suitable, with a lining of dung placed along the sides, and branches or straw mats over the glass.

1094 *Cleanliness and Order* Remove all stumps of broccoli or cabbage as soon as used, and gather up all dead and decaying leaves. If weeds are perceptible among growing crops, run the hoe over the ground, that the weeds may be cut up and so perish.

1095 *Trenching and Digging* All ground that is yet unoccupied by crops, and has not been already trenched, should be trenched and thrown up into ridges at once, in order to expose as much surface as possible to the air, and to let in the frost between the clods of earth, for the surface should be left as rough as possible. Ground intended for *Parsnips* should be trenched this month.

1096 *Roots in Store* Whether in cellars, or in pits or caves formed of straw or litter and covered with a coating of earth, all roots, such as potatoes, parsnips, carrots, beetroot, and onions, in store, should be looked to, so that decaying roots or bulbs may be removed, and to ascertain that the pits or caves are impenetrable to frost.

1097 *Mushrooms* Mushroom beds, in general, should be carefully attended to at this season – that is to say, they should have sufficient covering to defend them effectually from frost, should there be any, and from rain or snow. This covering should not be less than a foot thick, and if rain or snow should have penetrated quite through it, it should be removed immediately, or the spawn will be in danger of perishing. Replace it with another covering of clean, dry straw, and to defend the bed more effectually from wet and cold, spread large mats or canvas cloths over the straw. New beds may be made, if required, as they will afford a full crop in the spring and early summer months, though perhaps not so large a one as the beds made in the autumn.

3 – The Fruit Garden and Orchard

1098 *Work that May and Must be Done* In January, planting *may* be done, but pruning ought to be done, or, to speak in even stronger terms, *must* be done. It is better, in fact, to prune now than at an earlier period, because pruning, when deferred till January, retards flowering, and the later the flowering the more certain is the crop.

1099 *Planting* Planting in this month is not safe – less safe, perhaps, than in February. For preference, November is the best month for planting fruit trees, and December the second best, and before Christmas comes all planting should be done. If it is absolutely necessary to do any work of this kind in January, open weather should be selected for the operation, and no longer time than is absolutely necessary for the transfer of the trees from one place to another should be allowed to elapse between the taking up and the replanting, so that the roots may not be long exposed to the chilly air and cutting wind, which are most injurious to them, although they are in no way detrimental to the parts that are always above ground. When the work of planting is complete, and the trees have been staked, cover the ground over the roots with a thick mulching of warm litter.

It may be well to remind the reader here of the fruits that are usually grown, and of the forms they assume, and the modes of growing. Of the smaller kinds of fruit, *strawberries* are usually spoken of as *ground fruit; gooseberries*, *currants*, and *raspberries* as *bush fruit.* Of the larger kinds, the sorts that may be grown as *standards* are the *apple*, *pear*, *plum*, *cherry*, *quince*, *medlar*, and *mulberry*. Of these, the first five are suitable for *espaliers*, or training in the open on rows of stakes or on stretched wires; further, among *wall fruit* may be reckoned the *pear*, *plum*, and *cherry*, but walls are essential for the *apricot*, *peach*, *nectarine*, *vine*, and *fig*. It must be borne in mind that this classification relates to fruit grown in the open air. Under glass, or in the orchard house, it is possible to grow any and every kind of fruit in pots in the bush or pyramid form.

1100 *Pruning* The pruning of all the hardier kinds of trees, whether standards, espaliers, wall trees, or' pyramids, should be carried out during January. Among the hardier trees are included all except those of a more tender character mentioned in detail below.

1101 *Apricots* The pruning of these is better deferred to the end of the month, or even to February. At all events, the pruning of the hardier sorts should be completed before these are touched. These directions apply equally to the *peach* and the *nectarine*.

1102 *Figs* Fig trees may be pruned this month, but, as in the case of the apricot, peach, and nectarine, it is better to postpone the work till after other trees have been pruned, or to leave it even till February. If, however, the work is done in January, merely leave a sufficient number of last summer's shoots from the base to the extremity of the tree in all parts where possible, and cut out the ill-placed and superfluous ones. Also cut away a portion of the aged bearers and long extended, naked old wood, so that in training plenty of room may be commanded for such shoots as are retained.

1103 *Vines* Grapevines in the open air should be pruned as soon as the leaf falls, and the work, if not done already, should be completed this month. The reason why pruning of vines should not be too long deferred is that as soon as the sap begins to rise the vine bleeds most profusely from its wounds, and this causes a useless, and in some cases, fatal waste of vital force. The young shoots of last summer are the only bearing wood on the vine. If the pruning is done on the spur system, one bud, or at the utmost two, should be left at the base of the shoot, and all the rest should be cut away. If the shoots are laid in to cover wall space, the young branches and shoots should be trained very carefully at a distance of 10 or 12 inches apart, either horizontally, obliquely, or vertically, as the space of wall at command may allow. Therefore, in pruning, care must be taken to leave a sufficient supply of last year's shoots, that every part may be abundantly furnished with them.

1104 *Scions for Grafting, etc.* When pruning, save all scions of vines and other trees, which may be required for grafting. Put them in by the heels in a sheltered and shady place. Success in future operations with the scions mainly consists in keeping them dormant, as, if they can be kept in a state of quiescence until they are wanted, the better are the chances that they will grow.

1105 *Strawberries* Point the surface of the ground between the rows of plants with a light fork, and then, if this has not been done already, give the strawberries a plentiful mulching with long litter, which will form a clean and suitable bed for the fruit to rest on while ripening, and keep it from coming into contact with the ground or getting spattered with mud during a heavy fall of rain. The leaves of strawberries should not be cut off, and digging between the rows must be avoided, as it injures the roots.

1106 *Raspberries* Fresh plantations of raspberries may now be made, young stools being chosen that are furnished with several strong canes or shoots of last summer's growth. These may always be obtained in sufficient quantity from an old plantation, as an abundance of young growth is always sent up by the old stools. Preference should be given to the stools which have good fibrous roots: those which have naked and woody roots should be rejected. In planting, cut off the weak tops of the shoots and any long straggling fibres of the roots, and plant in trenches taken out with the spade in rows, about 4 feet apart from row to row, and 2 or 3 feet apart in each row.

1107 *Gooseberries and Currants* Cuttings of these may now be taken with the view of obtaining young plants. The cuttings should be from 12 inches to 18 inches long. Do not pick off any buds until the shoot has rooted, because the bursting and growth of the bud acts as an incentive to root formation. Place the cuttings in rows from 18 inches to 24 inches apart, planting them about 3 or 4 inches deep, with a distance of about 6 inches from cutting to cutting. The ground about gooseberries and currants should on no account be dug over, as this mode of treatment injures the roots. If not already mulched, the ground should be covered with a coating of half-rotten manure, and the surface soil lightly raised and stirred with a fork to incorporate it with the manure.

1108 *Stems of Old Fruit Trees* These should now be scrubbed with strong brine, and dressed after scrubbing with paraffin oil, in the proportion of 1 part of the oil to 100 parts of water, in order to remove the dead bark, and to clear the trees of all insect life that may be lurking in the cracks of the bark. Some recommend a compound of lime, cow dung, and soot, mixed up to the consistency of thick paint, and applied to the stems and principal branches with a brush. This preparation is certainly detrimental to insect life, but it is by no means attractive in appearance.

1109 *Fruit in Store* All fruits that are kept in store during the winter months require frequent examination as they come into season for the removal of any that may show symptoms of decay, etc. The maturity of fruit for table use is hastened by placing it in a warm and dry atmosphere for a few days before it is required.

II – Work to be done under glass, etc.

1 – Flowers in the Conservatory, Greenhouse, Stove, etc.

1110 Without protection of some kind during the winter months no collection of plants can be kept together; but when mere protection is all that is sought, it is easily obtained. A trench 2 feet deep, dug in the ground, if the soil is dry, and a drain at hand to carry off surface water, will suffice, if covered with frames, straw, hurdles, or other efficient covering; for it is ascertained by numerous experiments that the earth at 2 feet deep is warmer by two or three degrees than the surrounding air in winter. A vacant frame, a cold pit, a greenhouse, or a conservatory, will also either of them serve the purpose. On the other hand, where plants of a warmer climate or season are to be forced into early bloom, or where exotics are cultivated, artificial heat must be applied, not only to keep out the cold, but to simulate their native climate and atmosphere. It will be useful in treating this part of the subject to endeavour to group the instructions given for plant culture under glass as far as possible in accordance with the uses of the different glazed structures devoted to this purpose, which may be specified as the Hothouse, also known as the Plant Stove or Forcing House, the Greenhouse, and the Conservatory.

1111 The arrangements to effect the culture of plants under glass are usually confined to the greenhouse, generally a lean-to structure placed against the wall of some other building, heated by flues or hot water apparatus, to pits of various constructions, or to simple frames adapted for heating by hot dung; while places of greater pretensions add to this a conservatory, which is a structure of the same character as the greenhouse, but larger and more ornamental, being, in fact, the show room of the establishment, to which the finest plants are removed when coming into bloom. A complete range of houses, however, would include, in addition to a conservatory, a place of exhibition for flowering plants when at their best.

1 The Hothouse, devoted to the cultivation of orchids, for which it is admirably adapted, or to the production of roses, melons, cucumbers, vines in pots, or, in fact, anything to which it is applied.
2 The Greenhouse, in which a lower temperature is maintained than in the hothouse or plant stove, but, still, one that is sufficient for all purposes of plant culture and the protection and propagation of less hardy plants.
3 The Warm Pits, heated by pipes, but to a less degree than the greenhouse, in which may be placed flowers such as roses, achimenes (Fig. 500), *Poinsettia pulcherrima*, cinerarias, heaths, epacris, primulas, azaleas, acacias, camellias, arums, chrysanthemums, mignonette, cyclamens, and other plants required at this season for the windows, the conservatory, and for cut flowers, or which may be devoted to any other of the multifarious uses to which a pit can be applied in winter. There will be no necessity to allude otherwise than casually to the warm and cold pits. It will be sufficient to confine the remarks that will be made, as far as flowers are concerned, to the three principal structures specified above, namely, the Hothouse, the Greenhouse, and the Conservatory.

FIG. 500 *Varieties of achimenes*

4 The Cold Pits, usually adjoining and outside the greenhouse, not heated by pipes, but very useful for growing mignonette, violets, stocks, and other things which only require protection.

1112 *The Plant Stove or Forcing House* The routine business here during the month commences in earnest in January. A few plants of all kinds for ornamenting the house and conservatory should be introduced and started gradually; Indian azaleas, bulbs, roses, and lilacs, if already somewhat advanced, should have others brought forward to succeed them.

In the warm pits or frames attached to the hothouse, a good stock of pinks, sweet williams, lilies of the valley, etc., may be started towards the end of the month.

1113 *Temperature* The temperature of the forcing house should not be suffered to fall below 50°; and as the days lengthen, the temperature should be increased 4° or 5° until it attains a minimum temperature of 60° and a maximum of 70° by artificial heat, and an increase of 10° by sun heat; giving air daily, even if for a short time only, and keeping the atmosphere always moist and genial by syringing or watering the pipes and flags.

1114 *The Greenhouse* With the opening year and the lengthening day the busy season in the greenhouse commences; plants of all kinds begin to move, and most of them may now be assisted with a little heat. Soft-wooded plants may be stimulated by it, and, when they begin to grow, moved into the larger pots in which they are to flower, while those which are more advanced and showing bloom may be introduced into a warmer place.

1115 *Temperature* In the greenhouse maintain a temperature of at least 40° by night and 50° by day, which will keep the plants from being excited unduly. The warmth at either period should not be suffered to go below the heights stated.

1116 *Cinerarias* Many cinerarias are now in bloom, and may be removed to the window or conservatory, while those reserved for blooming in May and June should still be kept in cold pits or frames, taking care to guard them from severe frosty weather, and especially from moisture.

If large cinerarias are required, shift a few into larger pots, and pinch off the tops to produce a bushy head, tying or pegging down the side shoots to keep them open, keeping them supplied moderately with moisture, and giving air on every possible occasion. As cinerarias begin to throw up their flower stems, they should be removed to a house where a very moderate heat can be kept up. They do not require much warmth, it is true, but at the same time they would produce but a very poor display of bloom were they allowed merely to take their chance.

1117 *Fuchsias* Fuchsias maybe started this month, and large early flowering specimens produced by cutting down the old plants and shaking the roots out of the old soil as soon as they have broken, re-potting them in a good rich compost, with sufficient drainage. Strike cuttings for bedding plants as soon as the shoots are long enough. To start them, place them in the light, and water moderately.

1118 *Calceolarias* Calceolarias require great attention as to watering. Remove all decaying leaves as they appear, peg down the shoots to the soil, that they may root up the stems and thus strengthen the plant. As seedlings advance, shift them into larger pots, and prick off those sown for late blooming. In potting, use a compost of light turfy loam, well-decomposed manure and leaf mould, and a liberal portion of silver sand, with an ample drainage of potsherds and charcoal, and keep them free from insects.

1119 *Pelargoniums* Pelargoniums (Fig. 501, *see over*) which are strongly rooted may be shifted into larger pots and stronger soil, using silver sand freely, taking care that the pots are clean and dry and the drainage good. Stop some of the plants required for succession, remove decaying leaves, and thin out weak shoots. Stake and tie out the shoots of those sufficiently advanced to admit air to the centre. In plants of dwarf habit, peg the shoots down to the edge of the pot to encourage foliage. Stir and top dress the soil from time to time, if required: a watering once or twice with lime water and soot imparts a rich dark colour to the foliage, and destroys worms in the soil.

Where early flowers of the pelargonium are required, and a stove or hothouse or other forcing convenience is at hand, remove a few plants of early flowering sorts thither from the greenhouse for forcing.

FIG. 501 *Varieties of the pelargonium*

1120 *Management* Should frost appear or the weather prove damp, light the fires in the afternoon, and shut up the house before the sun disappears, keeping the heat as low as is consistent with excluding frost and dispelling damp, giving all the air possible in fine weather. Water those plants which have become dry, but water them copiously. The fancy varieties, being the most delicate, should be kept in the warmest parts of the house, and their foliage thinned out occasionally. Fumigate occasionally to prevent the appearance of the green fly. All watering should be done in the morning, and none should be permitted to fall on the leaves of the plants. Give air when the external air shows a temperate of 40°. If the temperature without is below this, and the weather dull, air may be admitted without injury to the plants through the top ventilators for a short time by raising the fires so as to produce a few more degrees of warmth in the house, so that the air admitted may be more rapidly warmed. In watering, especially at this time of the year, it is better never to water any plant until it is dry, and then to give the soil in which it is growing a good soaking, and then to refrain from watering until it is dry again. The faster a plant grows, the more water it requires.

A constant and ample supply of compost, well turned and thoroughly dry, should now be prepared for spring potting, and the pots washed and dried for use when wanted. Advantage should now be taken of any enforced abstinence from outdoor work to prepare stakes, labels, compost, etc., and everything that, will be required by and by as the season advances.

1121 *Hard-Wooded Plants* It is usual, where circumstances permit, to grow hard-wooded plants, such as heaths, azaleas, camellias, and others of similar habit, in a separate house; and some cultivators go so far as to recommend those having limited accommodation to confine their culture to one family, contending that it is better to have a houseful of finely-grown heaths, geraniums, or camellias, as the case may be, than a miscellaneous collection of indifferently cultivated plants. This, however, must be a matter of taste.

Care should be taken that hard-wooded plants do not suffer from the absence of moisture at the roots. After severe frosts, when the fires have been used, the evaporation by the sides of the pots is very great, while the surface seems to be moist enough: this should be seen to. Among the hard-wooded plants the same remarks respecting heat are applicable; a temperature of 40° should be aimed at during the night, rising a little by natural causes during the day. Air should be given from above, or by means of ventilators, without exposing the plants to cold draughts, and a moisture encouraged by sprinkling the floor, flues, and pipes, when warm, with water.

1122 *Heaths* With heaths, guard against mildew, but water moderately. Avoid artificial heat if possible, but keep out frost; and, if heat becomes necessary, remove such plants from its influence as are required for later flowering.

1123 *Camellias* Camellias should now be advancing into full bloom, and the young expanding buds should be protected from cold currents of air, but without much fire heat. With camellias and other plants of similar habit advancing into bloom, occasional doses of manure water in a tepid state should be given, and the plants syringed with tepid water every other day, until the flowers begin to expand. Camellias should not be watered too liberally when coming into flower or when in bloom. It is after they have flowered and are making wood that they require most water.

1124 *Azaleas* Azaleas should now be growing freely, if they were shifted and promoted to a warm place last month. To get early flowering plants, some of the more advanced specimens should be introduced to greater heat, while others are retarded for a succession, to supply the conservatory or window cases.

1125 *Position of Plants in Greenhouse* Bulbs, such as hyacinths, crocuses, narcissi, etc., should be placed in positions that are warm and sheltered, and also shady. All plants should be kept from draughts, which are as injurious to them as they are to human beings. Hard-wooded plants may be placed in the coldest parts of the house. Soft-wooded and herbaceous plants should be placed in the warmest parts of the house and close to the glass.

1126 *Cleanliness* This is specially required in plant houses of every kind. No litter should be suffered to remain on the floor, stages, or shelves, and every dead leaf should be removed from the plants before it falls.

1127 *The Conservatory* This structure being only a more ornamental variety of the greenhouse, the general directions for the management of the plants that are housed in it are the same as those given above for the latter. But as the conservatory is generally a lofty building, it is not so well calculated for growing plants unless they be of a climbing habit, when they may be displayed to great advantage.

Everything here should now look fresh and healthy. Acacias should be advancing into bloom. Camellias are either out or advancing rapidly into bloom: to promote this, see that they do not want for water. If there is a forcing house in the establishment, orchids, hyacinths, arums, tulips, and other bulbs transferred thither from it, with heaths and epacrises from the greenhouse, will render the conservatory both gay and fragrant; and if only a frame is available, cinerarias, violets, and mignonette will afford a good display.

1128 *Management* To preserve flowers in bloom in the conservatory for the longest possible period is now the principal object in view. To do this, keep the atmosphere moist and genial, but not wet. Water the plants regularly when necessary, especially the bulbs, giving as much water, of the same temperature as the house, as they can assimilate. Keep the temperature about 40°, rising a few degrees from sun heat during the day, ventilating daily, if only for a short time, but avoiding cold draughts of air.

The foregoing observations comprise all necessary instructions as to the work which should go on in the forcing house, the greenhouse, and the conservatory during January; but no doubt the reader will like to know how a greenhouse may be made gay while nature wears its wintry aspect. A little care and attention are all that is requisite to accomplish this, for there is a great abundance of plants which may be brought into flower at this season. By depriving them of their flower buds during summer and autumn, any of the Zonale Geraniums may be made to blossom all the winter, and these alone, by their rich foliage and freedom of flowering, will keep a house gay. A good stock of Primulas also should be provided for this period, and Calceolarias and Cinerarias must not be omitted. The Coronilla, with its profusion of yellow blossoms, may now be had in full glory, provided it has been well pinched in during the summer months. Of the genus *Epacris* there are many interesting varieties which will bloom on from December to May. Among other beautiful flowering plants may be named *Cosmelia rubra*, closely resembling the *Epacris*, but with flowers larger and more deeply coloured; *Chorozema*, *Fabiana imbricata*, and *Eutaxia myrtifolia*, a most beautiful plant, with blossoms of an orange colour. To grow this in perfection, every new shoot during summer and autumn should be stopped as soon as it has made two or three eyes. In this way it is kept as a compact dwarf shrub, and becomes a profuse bloomer. Then again, *Diosma ericoides*, and plants of the genus *Pimelea*, with their full heads of pink, white, and red flowers. All these plants do well in a sandy peat. They should, while growing, be frequently stopped and kept moist. In addition to these may be mentioned the tender sorts of *Genista*, *Kennedy a monophylla*, a beautiful climber, bearing large racemes of blue and white pea-shaped flowers; the *Boronias*, which, with a little management, may be made to flower thus early; with *Oxylobium retusum*, *Oxylobium obovatum*, and *Polygala latifolia*, and others of this last named genus. Any good gardener could make large additions to this list; but here, surely, are enough, if all the plants are flowering at the same time, to render even a very large sized house as gay as it can be.

2 – Plants under Glass in Hotbeds, Frames, etc.

1129 The cultivation of plants in hotbeds, frames, pits, etc., which are heated mostly by farmyard manure, occupies an intermediate position between plant culture under glass in hothouses, greenhouses, and conservatories, and plant culture in the open air. As far as flowers are concerned, it bears the same relation, or very nearly so, to the more advanced kinds of plant culture under glass that the reserve garden bears to the principal flower garden, as pit, frame, and hotbed serve very much as nurseries for the greenhouse and conservatory, and as a nursery for the flower garden too, in propagating and hastening the rooting of slips and offsets of many of the less hardy tenants of the latter, so as to render them fit to take part in the floral display of summer at an earlier period than they would without the stimulating action of gentle heat and the protection that is afforded by the appliances named above. This brings under notice another of the overlappings of the subjects comprised under the general headings of the divisions into which these cultural directions for the months are divided, for on account of the nature of the appliances used it will be impossible to dissociate some few flowers from the vegetables and fruits which occupy the chief place in this section. Let us deal with the flowers first.

1130 *Verbenas* Place verbenas that are to be propagated from into a gentle heat, and prepare a slight hotbed for striking cuttings of these or any other bedding plants. All bedding plants will bear a much stronger heat while they are striking in the spring than in the autumn, and verbenas will root in a week, placed in a close pit, with a bottom heat of from 80° to 90°.

1131 *Dahlias* Place scarce varieties of dahlias in heat for the purpose of securing plenty of cuttings. Proceed with potting off singly all cuttings in store pots, using 48-sized pots for geraniums, and large 60 for verbenas, etc., where abundance of space is available. Where this is not the case, the potting off must be deferred till another month.

Dahlia roots should be examined very carefully, in order to ascertain whether or not they are becoming decayed. If symptoms of decay are apparent, the affected parts should be removed without loss of time. Tubers of dahlias, as it has been said, are placed in heat for the purpose of inducing growth from which cuttings may be made. This need only be done when a large number of plants are needed. If only two or three plants of each variety or sort are required, it will be sufficient to part tubers of each sort into as many pieces as are required of each particular variety, just as you would divide potatoes, with an eye to each set.

1132 *Management of Pits and Frames* Such plants as pinks, carnations, picotees, auriculas, polyanthuses, etc., may be kept through the winter in pits and frames without any artificial heat. Calceolarias also – that is to say, herbaceous calceolarias required for bedding out – need no artificial heat. Frost must be kept out of the pits or frames in which cinerarias, pelargoniums, and verbenas are wintered by putting a lining of long farmyard dung against the sides and covering over the glazed lights with mats. Air should be admitted freely between 10 a.m. and 1 p.m. when it is not freezing. All watering should be done early in the day, and care should be taken not to wet the leaves of the plants when watering.

1133 *Vegetables, etc., in Hotbeds and Frames* No appliances are more useful than garden frames, yet none are more generally misapplied in small gardens; many gardeners considering them as proper only for the growth of the cucumber and melon, when, in fact, these should be considered but of secondary importance. Of course, whatever is grown in them is entirely a matter of taste, and, as a general rule, that may be considered most profitable which is most in request. The chief object in calling attention to the fact that other things besides cucumbers and melons may be grown – and grown with profit – in hotbeds is to get rid of the idea so generally prevalent that they can be used for no other purpose than that of growing these delicious members of the great gourd family.

1134 *Cucumbers* These may be had in hotbeds, or under glass in properly heated structures, at any time of year, and all the year round. The main thing to be borne in mind is that when cucumbers are wanted in winter, three months are required from the time of planting the seed to that of cutting the fruit ripe and ready for table. Therefore, if cucumbers are wanted in the middle of January, the hotbed should have been made and in a proper condition for the reception of the seed by the middle of October. If they are wanted in March, the bed must be ready, and the seed planted, in December, and so on.

It is immaterial at what time of the year cucumber growing is commenced, but in spring and summer the culture is attended with far less trouble, because less labour is required and less heating material than in the cold months of autumn and winter; the weather tending to retard the growth of the plants at these seasons of the year, but to accelerate it in the former seasons. The routine of culture is the same all the year round, and consists in regulating the growth of the plants. When they have made two leaves, pinch out the point above the second. Two lateral shoots will then be sent out above the second leaf, which must be pinched in a similar manner. After that stop above every fruit, adding fresh soil of the same temperature of the bed from time to time, until the whole surface is level. Between the months of October and April, when the fertilisation of the female blossom by bees is suspended, the fecundation must be effected by the grower by applying the farina or pollen of the male flower to the female flower.

1135 *Melons* The rules to be observed for the culture of melons are precisely the same as those for growing cucumbers. Ventilation is necessary for growing plants of both kinds, in order to prevent too great humidity within the frame or pit, and consequent injury to the plants; but in allowing this to escape, cold winds and draughts must not be permitted to find their way in: the best way to prevent this is to stretch some protecting material, such as tiffany, scrim canvas, etc., over the opening.

In covering the lights during frosts or rough winds, it is advisable to avoid letting the mats or other material used for protection hang over the sides, as there is often danger of conducting rank steam from the linings into the frame. Straw hurdles which exactly fit the lights are better than mats. The covering should be used just sufficiently to protect the plants from frost or cutting winds, without keeping them dark and close.

1136 *Seakale* This vegetable may be successfully forced in the frame and melon pit in the winter months, and a commencement may now be made. The usual plan is to make up a 3-foot bed, and cover it with 3 inches of loamy soil, before putting on the frame; this allows more space inside. When the frame is on, and the bed of a right temperature, a little soil is put at the back of the frame, in the form of a bank, about 6 inches high, and sloping to the front. On this bank, place a row of seakale roots, laying them almost flat, as this admits of covering them without an undue thickness of soil. When the first row of roots are laid, cover them with a few inches of soil, and make another bank 6 inches from the first, on which lay another row of roots; and so proceed till the frame is full. A gentle heat must be maintained, but the light should be excluded entirely from the frame, otherwise the growth that is induced will not acquire that whiteness and delicacy for which forced seakale is valued.

1137 *Early Potatoes in Melon Pit* – For growing very early potatoes, nothing is more suitable than a broad roomy melon pit. The potatoes will be fit for use about the time for planting out the melons. About the beginning of January, let some middling-sized tubers be laid in a warm and moderately dry place, well exposed to the light: here they will make short plump shoots by the time the bed is ready. Prepare a quantity of dung sufficient to make a bed 3 feet 6 inches in depth. By the end of the month the bed will be ready; then lay on 3 inches of soil, and place the potatoes 15 inches apart, covering them with 6 inches more of soil. Some seed of the scarlet short-top radish may be scattered over the surface. As these begin to grow, give abundance of fresh air in mild weather, so that neither potatoes nor radishes be drawn up; and as they come up, remove the radishes from immediately about the crowns of the potatoes: earthing up the latter will not be required. The radishes will be ready to draw in March, the potatoes early in May.

1138 *Early Potatoes in Frame* When potatoes are grown in a frame, the treatment is much the same as before; but some grow them very successfully in this manner: The frame being placed on a level piece of ground, the soil within is dug out to the depth of 2 feet, and banked round the outside of the frame. The pit thus formed is then filled with prepared dung; on this 3 inches of soil is placed, then the potatoes, then 6 inches more soil. The potatoes, when planted, should be just starting into growth, but the shoots should never be more than half an inch from the tuber, or they do not grow so strong. It is advisable to pick off some of the shoots; three on each tuber is sufficient.

1139 *Radishes in Frame* To grow radishes in a separate frame, make up a hot bed 2 feet in height, on which place a two-light frame. Over the hotbed place about 10 inches of loamy soil, on which the radishes are sown broadcast or in rows, the former being preferred; press the seed in with the back of the rake. This may be done from the beginning of January to March; but if begun very early, a little auxiliary heat, by means of linings, is required as that of the bed declines.

1140 *Early Carrots* These may be grown as directed for radishes on a hotbed 2 or 3 feet high, covered with about 10 inches of soil, which should be perfectly sweet, and free from the larvae of insects; a bushel of pounded chalk mixed with it will be advantageous. The early horn variety is the best for early culture; but, as the seed is very light, and hangs together, it requires, for the purpose of separating it, to be rubbed up in a peck or so of tolerably dry soil, which will help to bury it when sown, using the rake to press it in. When up, and sufficiently large to handle, the plants should be thinned to 2 inches apart, and plenty of air given, or they will be drawn all to top.

> Leaves, tan, or a small quantity of hot farmyard manure will give sufficient heat for potatoes. When the heat begins to come through, place light soil to the depth of 12 or 14 inches on the heating material, and plant the potatoes immediately. Give air whenever the weather permits, and take care that the plants are not drawn up when young, as this renders them weak and unhealthy. Do not let the temperature of the bed fall below 40°. Beds prepared in the same way will do well for radishes and carrots.

1141 *Mustard and Cress* This small salading is usually sown round the edges of carrots or potatoes, or, indeed, in any such space that offers; but, where a succession is required, it is worth while to give it a frame to itself. On a one-light bed 2 feet high let the seed be sown, and, when that is up, sow another light; when the first is all cut, pare off the soil containing the roots, replace it with new soil, and sow again, either in drills or scattered evenly, but thickly, over the surface and pressed into the soil.

1142 *Kidney Beans* These beans may be grown on a hotbed, but they are better raised in pots, or they are apt to run all to haulm and leaf. In an ordinary hotbed, as if made for cucumbers, place as many 6-inch pots as will stand 15 inches apart. These pots being filled with good loamy soil, in each plant, triangularly, three beans of any sort, of dwarf habit. As they grow, give them regular waterings, and do not let the heat fall below 60°. Kidney beans are very susceptible of frost, and will require careful protection. Nothing can be better for covering the lights than hurdles made of lath and straw. If sown in January or February, they will bear in April or May. They sometimes require supporting with sticks.

1143 *Strawberry Plants* These may now be potted up, or the runners laid into pots, and placed in a frame: they will bear much earlier than in the open ground, and if treated occasionally to liquid manure they will bear as abundantly.

3 – Fruit under Glass, Heated and Unheated

1144 *The Vinery: Vines in Ground already Started* Vines, where they form a feature in the cultivation, are usually cultivated on some principle of succession, either by dividing the house by partitions or by having a succession of houses. Supposing the plants to have been started in October, they would break last month with a temperature in house of about 70° This should now be the point aimed at, the minimum being 60° during the night. The actual heat, however, should be regulated by the state of the external border. If the heat is falling there, then fresh heating materials must be applied there; for on that depends the result. Later sections may follow for succession, beginning at a lower temperature, and increasing the heat gradually as the vines break and advance.
1145 *Vines in Pots already Started* – Vines in pots, if started in October and exposed to regular heat, will now be setting their fruit. They may be pushed on vigorously; for the roots being entirely under control, there is less danger of the plants being injured by over-forcing. Fresh plants should be brought forward. This maybe done by plunging them into a hotbed and frame, and adding linings to keep up the heat until they break, when the heat of the vinery will be found sufficient. The plants showing fruit should be assisted by occasional applications of manure water in bright weather.
1146 *Vines yet Dormant* The stems of vines not yet started should be kept dry, but the roots which are not in a quiescent state, but growing, must be kept moderately moist. To retain the vines in their present state of rest, plenty of air must be given when the weather is mild, and the temperature of the house should not be raised above 40°, nor permitted to fall below 32°.
1147 *The Orchard House* What is applicable to one kind of fruit tree in the orchard house is equally applicable to all, whether apricot, peach, nectarine, plum, cherry, pear, or apple. A very moderate degree of heat is sufficient to promote activity in all trees of this kind when under glass; therefore, the care of the gardener should be to keep the buds of the trees at rest as long as possible at this season. Air should be admitted freely at all times, and although frost will not injure the trees, it is desirable that it should be excluded, and a temperature maintained ranging from 32° to 40°. It is better to keep the roof of the unheated orchard house covered with mats by night and some shading material by day, to protect the trees from excessive cold, should severe weather over take us in the former time, and in the latter to shield them from the stimulating influence of the sun's rays when the weather is bright. If the ground in the borders or in the pots in which small bush or pyramid trees are planted appears too dry, give the roots a good soaking with water occasionally.
1148 *Cleanliness* Insistance on cleanliness in all glazed structures is absolutely necessary: house and plants should alike be kept clean. Scale and green fly should be treated with Gishurst's Compound as soon as any show themselves.

CHAPTER 23

The Garden and its Work in Every Department in February

1149 *Aspect and Character of the Month* The mean temperature of February is nearly two degrees higher than January – that is to say, about 41° during the day, and 34° during the night – and the average number of frosty nights is about eleven. Less rain falls this month than in any other, and hoar-frosts at this season generally precede it.

February has been called the reviving month, but it is best when its vivifying influence is confined: to the roots of plants, as a mild February is often the precursor of a fruitless, flowerless summer. No matter, then, if our favourites are arrested in their efforts to grow by the hard vicelike grip of the frost, or hidden from view beneath a fleecy covering of snow. If we cannot see them, we know that they are safe, and are compensated for their absence by the spiritual-like beauty, grace, and grandeur of every twig, laden with its pure white covering of snow, or silvered over with a frost-work of glittering glory. As the sun rises on such scenes:

> Every shrub and every blade of grass,
> And every pointed thorn seem wrought in glass;
> In pearls and rubies rich the hawthorns show,
> While through the ice the holly-berries glow.

Gratitude and admiration of the beauty within our reach will be the best preparation for hard work when labour becomes possible, and for appreciating the beauty of the flowers, as they awake and come forth from their winter's sleep.

Slow but sure is the progress Nature is making; first a bud or two of larger size than usual appear, then we discover another already silvered over with its greenish-grey, and after a shower and a day of sunshine, it is wonderful to witness the bulk some of the more favourably-situated blossoms have attained. On the south walls, at the end of the month, in well-sheltered places, the pale blossom of the apricot may be already distinguished through its bursting envelope. The gooseberry bushes show a glimmering brownish-green, more like the reflection of a colour than the real hue it will presently assume. In sheltered beds, St Valentine's flower, the crocus, blue, yellow, and white, already show themselves, and the snowdrop lifts its modest head, inducing one to ask:

> What impels, amid surrounding snow
> Congealed, the crocus' flamy bud to glow?
> Or what retards, amidst the summer's blaze,
> The autumnal bulb till pale declining days?

Winter and the first dawn of spring offers the best opportunity for witnessing the rich effects produced by moss and lichens upon the trees; and even ivy-covered trees are a pleasing variety at this season, with their gaudy mingling of green and orange and silvery hues, although lichens, moss, and ivy are fatal to the hopes of fruit from tree, and must be ruthlessly expelled from the habitat they have selected. Among the flowering shrubs, the mezereon and spurge laurel show a few flowers, the lingering Christmas rose will still appear, and some of the veronicas will now show their welcome blossoms, indicating that spring is close at hand.

I – Work to be done in the Garden

1 – The Flower Garden and Shrubbery

1150 *Work that Must be Done* Any contemplated alterations in the form and arrangement of the garden which have not been carried out must of necessity be completed in February, and as early in the month as possible. Vacant spaces and flower beds intended for the reception of bedding plants at a later period must be dug over; and all composts and manures should be carried to and placed on the ground over which they are to be spread. Wherever turf is to be laid, it should be done before the month comes to an end. New edgings of any kind may yet be laid or set, to divide borders from walks, and the borders may be pointed and receive a coat of top dressing, if this has not been given at an earlier period, and the walks, if of gravel, can have the top surface turned, and then be raked and rolled.

1151 *Hardy Roses* Tender sorts of Bourbon, China, Noisette, and Tea-scented roses are better if planting is deferred to the end of March or the beginning of April; but all the hardy varieties may be planted this month. The planting, however, should be finished as soon as possible.

1152 *Pruning Roses* It is not a good practice to prune roses when planted. The tops of newly-planted roses should be left on for a month or six weeks after the operation; they should then be cut back and headed in to three or four buds from the stock. This will insure a healthy, vigorous growth. After the plants are established, the shoots may vary in length from 4 to 16 inches. The weaker the growth, the closer roses should be pruned, and vice versa. Established plants of hybrid perpetuals and summer roses should be pruned at once; the more tender varieties will be safer if left unpruned for another month or six weeks. Roses in borders should be staked anew and fresh labelled, if necessary. Hardy climbing varieties may be trained and trimmed. Banksian roses should have had the old wood cut in when they went out of flower. The growth of last summer will bear blooms this season and must be left untouched. Thin out the weakly shoots of Austrian, Copper, Persian Yellow, and other briers of the same class, shortening the stronger ones but very slightly. Treat some of the stronger Teas and Noisettes, as Maréchal Niel, Celine Forestier, Solfaterre, and Cloth of Gold, in the same way.

1153 *Dressing Roses* The rose is a gross feeder, and requires a liberal amount of manure in order to induce it to bloom effectively. Roses should have a plentiful top dressing in February. Nothing is too rich for the rose; even night-soil may be applied as well as farmyard manure of any kind. Cow dung is, above all manures, preferable for roses. Those who keep fowls and pigeons will find the droppings of the birds, stored in a proper receptacle and soaked with urine, a useful dressing. Manures should not be applied in a perfectly fresh state to roses; but if it is necessary to use them in this condition they should be mixed with equal quantities of good loam or charred earth to lower their strength.

1154 *Treatment of Beds and Borders* Where the beds are filled with shrubs in winter, they should be hoed deeply several times during the month, to expose a fresh surface to the air. Beds occupied with crocuses and snowdrops should have the surface broken with a rake occasionally, or, what is better, gently stirred with a fork before the plants appear. Borders similarly furnished require the same treatment. This not only imparts additional neatness, but, by breaking the crust, enables the plant to appear more easily and speedily, and in dry weather it considerably modifies the power of the frost. Beds planted with herbaceous plants, as well as herbaceous borders, would be benefitted by similar treatment, provided they were dug early in November. Finish digging among herbaceous plants, circumscribing, dividing, rearranging, and replanting all where necessary, during mild weather.

The old-fashioned way of arranging these according to their height is still the most effective. The modern bedding system well nigh banished herbaceous plants from our gardens, when everything else had to give place to it, but it is now properly confined to certain positions and situations for which it is peculiarly well suited, and herbaceous plants may now be said to have risen once more in popular favour and esteem. Many of them are very beautiful, and a collection containing Phloxes, Asters, Campanulas, Delphiniums, Aconite, Pentstemon, Hellebore, Aquilegia or Columbine, Cheiranthus, Gentian, Iberis, Lathyrus or Everlasting Pea, Lupines, Monardia, Peonies, Potentillas, Primulas, Salvias, Saxifrages, Sedums, Silene, Spiraea, Iris, Statice, Chelone, Lychnis, Alyssum, Acanthus, Fraxinella, Achillea, Orobus, Yucca, Scabius, Oenothera, Dianthuses, Dielytra, Veronica, Myosotis, Sachys, etc., etc., arranged according to their height, colour, and time of flowering, and intermixed with bulbous-rooted plants, such as the Crocus (Fig. 503), Narcissus, Hyacinths, Cyclamen, Oxalis, Tulips, Ornithogalum, Scilla, Fritillaria, Lilium, Cypripedium, Gladiolus, Allium, Anemone, Ranunculus, Galanthus, Tritonia, Orchis, Colchicum, Pancratium, and Tigridia, would make a very fine display.

FIG. 503 *Varieties of the crocus*

1155 *Turf and Gravel Walks* Sweep and roll turf and gravel; finish laying turf; top dress, turn, renew, and relay the edgings of walks; and let cleanliness and neatness compensate as far as possible for the absence of floral beauty.

1156 *Shrubberies* Push forward the digging and clearing of shrubberies. The great point in the management of shrubberies, however, is so to plant, prune, and train the shrubs, as to render these operations unnecessary. The raw edges and masses of bare soil that render digging and cleaning an injurious necessity, also mar the beauty and grandeur of masses of shrubs. As a rule, their branches should never be attempted among them.

Where digging has to be performed, it should assume the character of pointing. Among shrubs, this operation should be performed by running the spade along the whole length, about 3 inches beneath the surface, and inverting t. This process buries the leaves and rubbish without injuring the roots. The growth of shrubs should also be regulated by pruning and training as the cleaning proceeds. Common laurels and lilacs will often be found overriding rhododendrons or other shrubs. The most worthless should always be removed or boldly cut in. Rhododendrons are often very effective as margins to masses of other shrubs, and they are invaluable in groups by themselves. No collection of shrubs is complete without them.

1157 *Precautions against Effect of Frost* The earth round the collars of all plants is loosened by frost, and when the frost has been severe and lasting, some plants will be found even to be raised slightly out of the ground when a thaw takes place Therefore, after frost, press the earth firmly about carnations, pinks, pansies, primroses, polyanthuses, aubrietias, daisies, arabis, myosotis, and all plants of this kind, and hardy autumn-sown annuals.

1158 *Reserve Garden* If the weather continues open, the following hardy annuals should be sown during the month:

Alyssum calycinum (*Sweet Alyssum*)
Bartonia aurea
Calandrinia speciosa
Calliopsis bicolor atrosanguinea
Calliopsis Drummondii
Chrysanthemum coronarium
Collinsia bicolor
Collinsia grandiflora
Erysimum Perofskianum
Eschscholtzia Californica
Eschscholtzia crocea
Eschscholtzia crocea alba
Eutoca Manglesii
Eutoca viscida
Gilia tricolor
Gilia alba
Gilia rosea
Iberis coronaria (*Candytuft*)
Iberis odorata
Iberis umbellata
Iberis alba
Leptosiphon androsaceus
Leptosiphon densiflorus
Leptosiphon flore arbus
Limnanthes grandiflora
Nemophila atomaria
Nemophila discoidalis
Nemophila insignis
Nemophila maculata
Schizanthus pinnatus (Fig 504)
Schizanthus pinnatus Priestii
Schizanthus pinnatus porrigens
Silene pendula
Sphenogyne speciosa
Viscaria oculata

There are many other beautiful hardy annuals, some of which, such as the lupines, had better not be sown till March. Only half the packets of the above seeds should be sown in February, and the other half reserved for a second sowing, either in the reserve garden or on the borders and beds where they are to bloom. Those sown during March or the beginning of April are more to be depended on than the earlier sowings. However, the above will prove quite hardy in ordinary seasons, unless the frost is very severe just as they are coming through the ground; in that case, some slight protection should be afforded them. Hence one great advantage of sowing all early seeds in the reserve

FIG. 504 *Schizanthus pinnatus*

garden, where any, necessary shelter may easily be provided. With the exception of ten-week stocks, which should be sown in pots or a frame at once, the sowing of all other tender or half-hardy annuals may safely be deferred to next month.

1159 *Transplanting Annuals* If the weather continues mild, autumn-sown annuals may be transplanted during the month; from 2 to 4 inches square, according to the size and habits of the plants, will be a proper distance apart.

1160 *Tulips, Hyacinths, etc.* Guard choice tulips, hyacinths, etc., against the attacks of mice and snails. An endless variety of traps have been invented for the former: no trap is more efficient for the latter than leaves of the cabbage tribe, laid flat on the ground, and carefully examined every night; if left till morning, possibly the leaves will be eaten, and the snail hid beyond our reach. In order to protect tulips from the ill effects of severe frosts and heavy rains, hoops should be placed over the beds, and mats laid on the hoops. The mats should be removed at the approach of finer and less inclement weather.

1161 *Crocuses* At this period, mice and sparrows will do much mischief to crocuses, and care must be taken, by plunging jars, half filled with water, in the earth, to serve as traps for the former, and spreading light netting or other protecting medium over the surface to keep off the latter, to protect the corms from injury in this respect as far as possible.

1162 *Anemones, Ranunculuses* If not already planted, the planting should not be longer deferred. Good soil is desirable for ranunculuses, and it should be enriched by the addition of well-rotted cow dung. Anemones do not require so rich a soil, but the blooms will be all the finer if the ground is well dressed with the same kind of manure.

1163 *Lawns* Ground that is to be sown for lawns, etc., should now be well trenched and drained if necessary. If the soil is poor, the incorporation of some well-rotted manure with the top spit will improve the quality and luxuriance of the grass in time to come.

2 – The Vegetable or Kitchen Garden

1164 *Work to be Done* The operations in the kitchen garden in February will depend very much on the weather, and must be regulated by it. It is useless to attempt to dig, plant, and sow in wet weather, for the ground will cling in masses to the feet of the workman, and the time spent in the vain attempt will be altogether lost. The hand of the gardener must be withheld until drier weather prevails and the surface of the soil is fairly dry. Then no time must be lost in preparing the ground for, and getting in, the crops for the coming season. Continue to wheel manure on to vacant ground, and get all digging, trenching, and in fact all ground work, as forward as possible, bearing in mind that much of the success of the season depends upon it; and how important it is to have the ground prepared a week or two before cropping, especially where it is heavy or retentive, for none but a practised workman can appreciate the advantage of having the surface in that finely-pulverised condition that follows sharp frost and drying winds.

1165 *Radishes* In mild, open weather, a sowing of radish is made, and to protect them from birds and frost, cover lightly with straw or fern, uncovering the beds occasionally in mild weather. Although they are best when sown in frames, they do very well on a warm border.

Chaffinches are very fond of pulling up these and other seeds, as they appear through the ground; so that they should not be left unprotected. Netting stretched over them will admit light and air, and exclude the birds; white worsted will keep them off for a day or two, but they soon get used to it, and scarecrows are equally ineffective. A covering of tiffany, canvas, or calico, stretched on laths, will be effective, and resist the March winds more than straw or fern; they need be but a few inches from the ground. If the ground is in condition for treading, it is best to do so, as, indeed, it is with nearly all seeds; but if the ground is apt to clod or bind, it should by no means be trodden, but covered with light soil or pressed in with the rake. The ground, in such cases, should be marked into beds of convenient width, allowing a foot or 15 inches between, for alleys, to stand in, never treading on the beds. This comes naturally enough after a little practice; but experience is a dear school to learn in, and the most inexperienced, by following some such directions, may avoid failure as certainly as the most practised. Some gardeners, whose ground is limited, are in the habit of sowing parsley, carrots, onions, leeks, or some such crop, which takes longer to grow, along with radishes, sowing both together, the radishes coming off soon after the others are up. This may be a saving of time or room; but where there is plenty of space, it is not advisable to sow two crops together, but let every crop have the best chance of doing well.

1166 *Cauliflowers* These, which will be under hand glasses, should have all the air, sun, and light possible, and gentle showers in mild weather, where they are protected from frost, cold winds, or heavy rains. Dust them also occasionally with lime, to destroy slugs, and stir the earth about the roots.

1167 *Peas* Crops which are advancing should be earthed up, both to protect and strengthen them. A dusting now and then with lime will protect from birds and mice; or white worsted stretched along the rows will do so, if rightly managed. Dwarf peas may always be grown advantageously where sticks are an object, and these may be sown closer together; but where sticks or hurdles can be obtained, it is no saving to grow without them, for the taller sorts, which grow six or eight feet high, bear most enormously if in good soil and mulched.

One way of protecting peas by lines of cotton or worsted is to have some half-circular pieces of board, a foot wide, with pegs nailed to them to thrust into the ground; then have five or six small nails on the upper edge at regular distances; these are fixed into the ground at each end of the row, and as many lines of worsted as there are nails passed over the peas. This covers them completely in. Others lay branchy sticks over them. Some sow rather thickly and leave them fully exposed, affirming that by allowing for loss, the others are not drawn up, thus avoiding more covering than is necessary to insure a good crop.

1168 *Broad Beans* A sowing of any sort of these beans should be made this month, in order to provide for a proper succession of this crop. About the end of the month is the best time for getting in the main crop of this useful vegetable. They may be planted among early cabbages or between rows of potatoes.

1169 *Cabbages* Look over the rows of cabbages, and see if any are eaten by vermin. A dusting of lime when the ground is wet, or early in the morning, will destroy slugs. Another good plan at this time of the year is to let a few ducks into the kitchen garden for half an hour or so every morning; they will destroy immense quantities of slugs, snails, worms, and grubs. Replace all the plants that have been destroyed by frost or otherwise, and draw earth up to the stems.

1170 *Cabbage Crops to be Sown* It is advisable to sow under hand glasses a little cabbage, of some quick-heading kind, as Early York or East Ham, or indeed any sort: they will follow those which have stood the winter, and be very useful in July, August, and September. Some Brussels Sprouts may be sown; also Purple Cape and Walcheren Broccoli, for autumn use.

1171 *Broccoli* In time of frost, place a few boughs or some protective medium of this sort over broccoli. The plants should be frequently examined, and the leaves bent inwards over those that are showing blossom. Those that are fit for use should be cut as soon as ready.

1172 *Parsley* This may be sown in drills, or broadcast, or as edgings, or between dwarf or short-lived crops. The seed should be but slightly covered, trodden or pressed in, according to the state of the soil, and raked evenly. It takes several weeks to germinate at this season of the year.

1173 *Carrots* Short-horn carrots, if sown on a warm border now, will come into use in May, and be very sweet and good. Sow rather thickly, and thin to two inches apart.

> To produce carrots and parsnips of an extraordinary size, make a very deep hole with a long dibble; ram the earth well round it while the dibble is in, and when it is removed, fill up the hole with fine rich earth. Sow a few seeds on the top, either parsnips or carrots, as may be required, and when up, draw out all except the one plant nearest to the centre of the hole. Prodigious carrots and parsnips may be produced by this means.

1174 *Onions and Leeks* Onions for salading may be sown on a warm border. A small sowing of leeks may be made at the same time and in the same manner, but not quite so thick. The ground for the main crops should now be thoroughly trenched and heavily manured, the surface being left rough so that the frost may act upon it. A top dressing of soot once a fortnight, or even oftener if the weather be rainy, will have a very great effect upon the onion crop, and will prove an effectual remedy against the maggot at the root, which so often destroys the entire crop, especially on highly-manured land. Some will sow onions in February, and later in the season, when they are large enough, they will transplant them from the seed bed to the prepared ground. It is far better to sow in drills, and then to thin the crop at intervals, for the thinnings are always useful as salading, etc.

1175 *Shallots, Potato Onions, etc.* The bulbs may now be set for multiplication by offsets in ground not too heavily manured. Shallots should be set in rows 12 inches apart, 8 inches between each plant, and 2 inches below the soil. Potato onions should be placed at the same depth, but the distance between the rows should be 15 inches, and between the sets 9 inches.

> In Devonshire it is the generally-received rule to plant these bulbs on the shortest day, which is St Thomas's Day, namely, the 21st of December, and to take them up for storage on the 21st of June, the longest day and St John Baptist's Day.

1176 *Red Beet* This root, familiarly known as beetroot, if sown now, will be very useful in the summer. Sow in drills 9 or 10 inches apart.

1177 *White Beet* This may be sown now for the sake of the leaves, in the same manner as red beet. The leaves are used in summer as a substitute for spinach.

1178 *Early Potatoes* may be planted on a south border, or under a wall having a sunny aspect. At this time it is well to plant middling-sized tubers whole. The early tops are apt to get cut off by spring frosts; but they bear none the less for it, and they may be recovered, if not too severely frozen, by watering with cold water before the sun is up. When planting at this season, it is better to place the tubers at the depth of 6 inches below the surface, and, if the weather be very frosty, to spread thick litter or boughs over the ground. It assists very much to throw the ground up in ridges running east and west, and to plant on the south side of the ridge.

1179 *Lettuces and Small Salading* Lettuces should be sown now for succession. Mustard and cress may be sown under hand glasses. American cress, which is much the same as watercress, may also be sown on a sunny border; it is very useful for salading, and easily cultivated. Lettuces in the open ground under walls should be protected against injury from slugs, birds, etc.

1180 *Pot Herbs* Chervil may be sown about the end of this month, and also other pot herbs, as savory, marjoram, coriander, and hyssop: unless it is desired to have them very early, however, it is as well to defer sowing these till next month. They are mostly very slow in germinating.

1181 *Scorzoneras, Salsafy, Hamburg, Parsley, etc.* A little of each of these may be sown now, but it is as well to defer sowing main crops of these things till next month.

1182 *Jerusalem Artichokes* This useful vegetable (Fig. 505), an excellent accompaniment to roast beef when nicely boiled in milk, may be planted this month. The tubers should be set at a distance of 18 inches apart every way in any piece of waste land or corner of the garden that happens to be suitable for them. It is as well to appropriate a special piece of land for their cultivation, because when they have been once planted it is difficult to get rid of them, owing to the growing of the young tubers which are left in the soil when the roots are taken up for use.

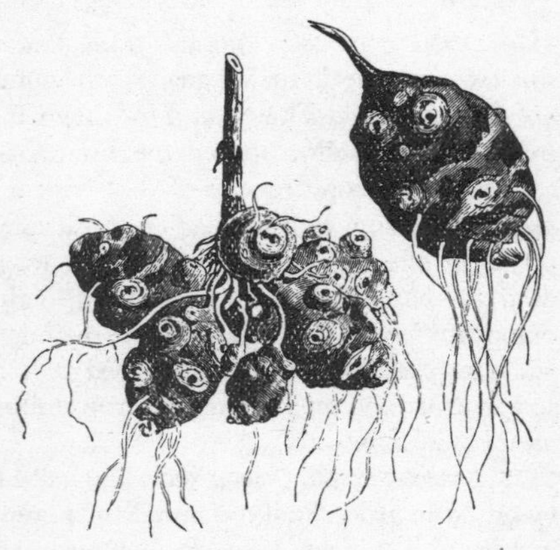

FIG. 505 *Tubers of Jerusalem artichoke*

1183 *Seakale* This maybe planted now in the open ground, the plants being set 15 inches apart in rows 30 inches from each other.

1184 *Rhubarb* Fresh plantations of rhubarb may be made now, the roots being placed at least a yard apart every way, if more than one row of roots is wanted.

1185 *Horseradish* The smallest piece of the pungent acrid root known as horse-radish will grow, but it is better to set the crown with a small portion of the root attached to it. The ground must be dug very deeply, and the sets placed in rows about 18 inches apart and 9 inches from each other in the rows. Deep holes are made in the newly-dug earth at these distances, and the sets dropped into them; after which the holes are filled up with sand.

1186 *Judicious Apportionment of Ground to Crops* The advantage of having early crops is great, but they should be proportioned to the extent of room, the time they last, or the wants of the family. A square rod of ground will generally be sufficient for early sowings of most of the principal crops, but herbs and salads will do with less, and it is best to look forward to what is to be done during the whole season, and calculate to a nicety what can be grown on every part without wasting room, or crowding and over-cropping, and exhausting the soil beyond the power of manure to restore it. It may seem advisable to make early use of the ground, and get it three-parts cropped in February; but in May and June it will be seen that a fatal error has been committed.

3 – The Fruit Garden and Orchard

1187 *Strawberries* If it is desirable to make new plantations of strawberries at this time, it may be done by taking up runners with a trowel, and planting them 18 inches apart. It is easy to select plants that will flower and fruit the same year by the crowns, which, if plump and full, indicate flower buds. After planting, mulch with dung: they will bear much more freely, and it is important to do this early. Old plants should be cleaned and mulched.

1188 *Raspberries* These should be pruned without delay, if not done before. Cut out all the old canes, and thin out the new to four or five; shorten them one-third, and, if necessary, support them with sticks, rails, or by arching them together. If this is done carefully, only tying two together, it will answer better than by tying them to stakes.

1189 *Gooseberries and Currants* The bushes of both kinds should be pruned where formerly omitted. In pruning gooseberries, the object is merely to thin out and regulate the shoots, which need not be shortened except to keep them off the ground. In pruning currants, the object is to produce short fruit-bearing spurs, so that all the shoots, except the leaders, should be cut in three-fourths, the leading shoots about one-half, or rather more.

1190 *Black Currants* Pruning must not be carried to so great an extent for black currants; indeed, these should scarcely be cut at all, for they do not bear so well if much pruned; so that a little thinning or reducing into shape is all that ought to be done.

1191 *Apples and Pears* Finish pruning all fruit trees this month, whether standards, espaliers, dwarf bushes, pyramids, pillars, or trained on walls. In pruning these, the main object is to produce short fruiting spurs, so that all vigorous shoots should be shortened in; but the stronger the shoots the less they should be cut; for too close cutting throws them into the production of wood and leaf, and not fruit.

1192 *Figs* Figs on walls should scarcely be cut at all: in fact, no trees should be cut in frosty weather.

1193 *Peaches, Apricots and Nectarines* on walls ought to be un-nailed and pruned this month. Thin out the shoots till they lie about 6 inches from each other, and shorten or not according to the strength of the tree or shoot; if very strong, shorten little or none; but if the end of a weak shoot terminates still more weakly, cut back to a double bud – that is, one leaf bud between two flower buds: prune neatly in this way, and tack them up again with fresh nails and shreds. The trees should be done over in this way every winter, but it is important that the shoots be thinned out and disbudded in summer time.

1194 *Plums and Cherries* These should be treated in a manner similar to that which has been prescribed for other kinds of fruit trees.

1195 *Root Pruning* This should have been done in October and November, and unless the need be very urgent, it had best be left till the end of the autumn again comes round. Otherwise it may be done in open weather, and when there is no immediate fear of severe frost.

1196 *Pruning and Training* These necessary operations should be carried out, and the hardier kinds of trees should be finished this month. It is necessary to see that the trees are perfectly clean, and free from dirt and canker, and that the walls, etc., be clear of insect life. Trees that are bark bound, and in which the bark refuses to expand with every fresh deposit of woody fibre, must be relieved by dressing the bark with linseed oil, and then drawing the point of a sharp knife longitudinally down the stem and through the bark of the part affected. Care should be taken to undo every ligature or shred that is too tight for the branch it holds and is cutting into the bark, or is likely to cut into it as the tree grows. It is impossible to be too careful in looking to old ties, shreds, and nails, in order to obviate any drainage that may arise from neglect of injuries that have arisen, or are likely to arise, from them.

1197 *Stocks for Grafting* These, if not done already, may be headed back this month, but they should not be left too long, as the sap is already beginning to move upwards.

1198 *Scions for Grafting* Those already taken off should still be left where they were placed when cut off – that is to say, in the earth, under a north wall. Any not yet taken from the parent tree should be removed at once and treated in a similar manner.

1199 *Materials for Grafting* Everything necessary for grafting in March should now be got ready, such as tow, grafting wax, etc., so that opportunity may be taken when a favourable time comes to enter on the work without delay. Clay for grafting should have been prepared by successive beatings and kneading together, and the removal of all small stones and hard particles that may be in it. It is prepared finally for use by thoroughly incorporating it with fresh horse dung or cow dung in the proportion of one part of dung to three parts of clay.

1200 *Manuring Borders, etc.* Borders containing fruit trees may now be covered with a mulching of good farmyard manure, or a coating of fresh loam may be used as a top dressing for the borders and stimulants given in the form of liquid manure. It is beneficial at this time of year to all kinds of trees, bush fruit, and ground fruit, because it affords plant food that will be taken in and assimilated by the roots, and will impart vigour to the plants and increase the quantity and quality of the fruit.

The urine of any animal, when diluted with water to the extent of three parts of the latter to one of the former, forms an excellent liquid manure for trees, gooseberries, currants, raspberries, and strawberries. The slops of the house are also useful, and require little, if any, dilution. Sewage water and liquid manure from the farmyard may also be used to advantage at this time of year.

II – Work to be done under Glass, etc.

1– Flowers in the Conservatory, Greenhouse, Stove, etc.

1201 *Classification and Management of Glazed Structures* Plant houses obviously divide themselves into houses for *show* and houses for *growth*. The former should be devoted to plants in flower, or comparatively perfect plants, with handsome foliage; the latter to plants in their incipient preparatory stages. The object in the show house or houses is to preserve the plants in the *same state* as long as possible; the aim in the other houses will be to urge the plants forward as rapidly towards perfection as may be consistent with their well being. Diametrically opposite means must be employed to secure these nearly opposing results. Hence the necessity of the division indicated. A comparatively dry, cool, well-ventilated house tends to prolong the blooming period of plants to the utmost; a moist, warm, close house is best adapted to secure rapid expansion and perfect growth. The term Conservatory, as it has been already said, is generally given to a house for preserving plants in flower; the Greenhouse being a house devoted chiefly to Cape heaths and other hard-wooded plants, in complete establishments in which geraniums, fuchsias, and other soft-wooded plants have separate houses devoted to them. In places where two or more houses exist for the culture of stove plants, one of the houses should be a *conservative* and the other a *progressive* stove; and if an intermediate one could be provided to receive the plants as they go out of flower, the trio would complete a most useful cultural circle.

1202 *Hothouse or Plant Stove* Maintain a temperature of from 60° to 65° fire heat. Start the first batch of achimenes, gesnerias, gloxinias, etc. A good variety of the gloxinia is illustrated in Fig. 506. Prune plants of allamanda, dipladenia, clerodendron, etc. Pot *Gloriosa superba* during the month; it thrives best plunged in a brisk bottom heat. Many ferns, begonias, and other plants should also be potted, and started into fresh growth. Some of the dendrobiums, stanhopeas, and maxillaras should now be watered and pushed into flower.

FIG. 506 *Gloxinia hybrida erecta*

1203 *Routine Work in Hothouse* Prepare plenty of good peat and loam broken potsherds, charcoal, etc., etc., for a general potting of all plants that require it. Hunt for and destroy mealy bug and scale, and maintain the semblance of health and reality of cleanliness throughout the whole of the plant structures.

1204 *Forcing Pit* This is an indispensable adjunct to a well-kept conservatory, and should now be occupied with bulbs for succession, rhododendrons, azaleas, Ghent and Indian (most of which, especially *Azalea Indica alba*, force admirably), roses, lilacs, Anne Boleyn; white and other pinks, carnations, cloves, etc. Maintain at a genial growing temperature of 55° to 65°; on very cold nights, however, it may fall 5° or 10° with impunity.

1205 *Greenhouse* More air may be given to, and 5° less heat will suffice for this house than for the conservatory. Now is a good time to examine and clean the whole stock of plants. Many of the acacias and epacrises are apt to become infested with scale.

So liable to this pest are many acacias and epacrises, and, indeed, many other plants, that it seems to be a constitutional tendency; its eradication, too, is very difficult. Prevention is the only remedy, for experience tends to prove that a perfect cure is impossible. So doubtful is this point, that I would rather spend a week in looking over an entire collection without finding a single scale, than an hour in trying any nostrum upon a single infected plant. Experiments with every kind of preventive and so-called cure, Gishurst's Compound included, for scale and bug, go far to prove that there is no remedy for these pests but removing and destroying them. Spirits of wine, indeed, will kill the latter, but it is powerless upon the former. It has also the great drawback of killing some of the tender leaves.

1206 *Heaths and Azaleas* If any dust or soot has accumulated on the leaves of heaths and azaleas, they will be much benefited by a good washing. Water with care, examining carefully the balls of the plants, which, in heaths, sometimes becomes so hard and dry that the water refuses to pass through. They should never be allowed to become so, but if found in this condition, they should be plunged into a pail of water for 12 or 24 hours, until the ball is thoroughly soaked. Pick off the flowers of winter-blooming heaths as soon as their beauty has faded. Carefully watch weak downy-leaved varieties for the first symptoms of mildew, and refrain from syringing any of them overhead in dull weather.

The best mode of washing is to hold the plant on one side over a tub of water, turning it round in all directions, while an assistant dashes the water violently upon it with a syringe. Very dirty plants may sometimes require to have their leaves sponged with soap and water in addition to this.

1207 *Plants requiring Shifting* Towards the end of the month several species of greenhouse plants, such as kalosanthes or crassula, baronias, chorozemas, dillwynias, pimeleas, and azaleas, may be shifted into larger pots. Most of these thrive well in good fibrous peat and a little loam, liberally intermixed with sharp silver sand and charcoal.

One of the chief things to attend to before placing any plant whatever, but especially any hard-wooded plant, into a larger pot, is to see that the old ball is in a nice healthy growing state. The extremities of the roots should also be carefully untwisted or unwound, to induce them to start at once in the fresh soil. The new soil must also be pressed firmly into the pots, or the water will pass through it, instead of penetrating through the old mass of roots. More hard-wooded plants are destroyed through inattention to these points than by all other sources of mismanagement put together.

1208 *Green Fly* At this season of the year green fly often attacks pimeleas, leschenaultias, and other plants; let them be destroyed at once by fumigation with tobacco smoke, applied by the agency of a fumigator. They also put in an appearance on calceolarias and cinerarias, of which they are particularly fond; as soon as their presence is detected they must be destroyed.

1209 *Pelargoniums* These plants now delight in a temperature of from 45° to 50°, with 10° increase by sun heat. Scarcely any rise of temperature should be permitted, however, before the house is slightly ventilated. The sun's rays striking upon plants with any drops of condensed moisture on the leaves is certainly one cause of the *spot* on these plants. Cutting draughts of cold wind are doubtless another cause of the same disease. This must be specially guarded against on bright days, when the air is keen and harsh.

1210 *Management of Pelargoniums* Shifting the young successional stock should now be completed. The soil they delight in consists in two parts good turfy loam and one of leaf mould, with a slight admixture of thoroughly decomposed cow dung and a liberal sprinkling of silver sand. The chief work here at present will consist in stirring the surface of the large plants, staking, training, and watering. The water should be, say, 5° warmer than the temperature of the house, and in dull weather, or indeed any weather at this season, the foliage must be kept dry.

1211 *Achimenes* These plants are especially useful in small greenhouses. They may be propagated by small tubers or cuttings in bottom heat. The best material to grow them in is a compost of leaf mould, peat, and a little well-decomposed cow dung with some silver sand. For flowering in June, plant the small tubers in pans in February, and in succession for autumn flowering. When about an inch high, transplant into pots or pans, several in each, shifting them when full of roots. After flowering, the plants should be kept growing till the foliage decays, that the tubers may become ripe and perfect. Then place the pots or pans in a warm place, to be kept dry till the tubers are wanted.

1212 *Tydaeas* Allied to the achimenes are the tydaeas, which produce beautifully spotted tube-shaped flowers. These, however, require more heat.

1213 *Gloxinias* These are flowers of the same class as the achimenes and tydaeas. The tubers should be potted in February or March. The soil best suited for growing them is composed of rich loam, leaf mould, and peat, in equal proportions, to which should be added a good quantity of Reigate or silver sand. Place in a little heat to start them into growth, and water sparingly till the plants are well established. When in bloom, bring them into the conservatory or drawing-room. After the plants have done blooming, dry gradually off by withholding water from their roots; afterwards remove them to a warm place, to be kept dry till the tubers are wanted.

1214 *Fancy Pelargoniums* These will bear a temperature of 5° or 10° more than the other varieties. They should be potted in lighter soil, and even more carefully watered, as altogether their constitutions are more tender. The shoots will now require thinning and training.

1215 *Calceolarias and Cinerarias* These now enjoy a temperature of from 45° to 55°. Well-rooted plants of the former should be shifted into the compost recommended last month; and plants for very late flowering of the latter may also be shifted The earliest cinerarias will now be opening their flowers in the conservatory, and a succession coming on to supply their place.

1216 *Fuchsias* These, after re-potting, thrive best if plunged in a gentle bottom heat. Water carefully until fresh roots are emitted; shade in bright sunshine to prevent flagging. Thin out plants that have been cut down to a single shoot, if the pyramidal shape is desired; if bushes are wanted, leave three or four, and maintain a genial temperature of from 50° to 60°.

Never cut down and shift fuchsias at the same time, nor shake them out for re-potting before they have again begun to grow. After cutting down, allow the shoots to grow two or three inches; plants that have not been cut down must fairly *break* before they are re-potted. The young top growths will then hasten the emission of roots, and the plants, with a moist atmosphere provided for a few days, will scarcely sustain any check. When re-potting, use a smaller pot than that in which the plant has been growing. A suitable soil for fuchsias is composed of two parts of turfy loam to one of peat, with an admixture of bone dust and charcoal.

1217 *Watering Plants in Greenhouse* Water may be given freely to heaths, epacrises, and azaleas coming into flower, but camellias, on the contrary, must have but a limited supply. Chinese primroses require a liberal supply of water, but care must be taken not to let any fall on the hearts of these plants.

1218 *Conservatory* Here camellias, arums, epacrises, *Salvia splendens*, Chinese primroses, a few heaths, lachenalias, and perhaps forced lilacs, azaleas, rhodo dendrons, hyacinths, narcissuses, jonquils (Fig. 507), crocuses, and other bulbs, will now be either in flower or coming into flower bud. Keep a night temperature of from 40° to 45°, allowing a rise of 10° with sun heat. Unless during very severe frost or cutting winds, give air daily, if only for an hour at noon, to change the atmosphere of the house and dry up drip.

FIG. 507 *Jonquil (Narcissus Jonquilla simplex)*

1219 *Management of Conservatory* Prune and destroy scale and other insects on climbers and other permanent plants. All plants should be carefully examined before they are introduced into this house, in order to prevent an importation of insects, as smoking with tobacco, or other insect-destroying processes, are not only very disagreeable, but are most inimical to the beauty and long continuance of the flowers. Examine, water, and top dress, if necessary, any of the borders. Remove all plants back to their respective quarters as soon as their flowers fade, and introduce fresh supplies from forcing pits, greenhouse, or stove, and let no dead leaf, or flower, or dirt of any description, be allowed to mar the sense of delight which this house and its occupants should ever be calculated to inspire.

2. Plants under Glass in Hotbeds, Frames, etc.

1220 *Propagation of Flowers for Bedding Out* The great business of propagating tender plants for furnishing the flower garden must now be vigorously prosecuted. Stock must be taken, calculations made, judgment and foresight exercised, and activity displayed, if the garden is to be liberally filled next May. For the last few months, the great object has been safely to keep what we have. During the next three, the plants we have must be used to furnish what is required to fill the garden next May.

If the bedding system is carried out, the garden must be filled with *flowering plants* by the end of that month. To effect it, verbenas must be planted 4 inches apart, and geraniums from 6 to 8 inches. Measure the superficies of your beds; calculate at these distances, and increase your stock accordingly. With the exception of calceolarias certainly, and probably geraniums, nearly all other bedding plants grow and flower as well, if not better, when propagated in the spring as in the autumn. Geraniums grow equally well; but I think autumn-struck cuttings flower more freely, and certainly two, three, or four-year old plants flower more freely than any cuttings whatever.

1221 *Geraniums* Boxes of geranium roots that have been stored in cellars through the winter may now be brought out into the light of day, and, if they have been carefully managed, the whole surface will be alive with buds and shoots. A hundred such roots will furnish a thousand well-rooted plants before bedding-out time, and leave the old roots still available – the best of all plants for the centres of beds. For this purpose, however, they must be placed in bottom heat until the shoots are two or three inches long. Then thin the *stools* by heeling off the cuttings – that is, taking them off quite close to the old stems. Place the cuttings singly in small 60-sized pots, or three round a large 60, or in pots or boxes of any size; place them in a house or frame with a temperature of 60°, and in three weeks they will be well rooted. If a frame is used, it must have a little air night and day, as geraniums are very impatient of a close atmosphere.

Those who happen to have a spare house in which bottom heat under slate can be obtained may use it for propagating bedding plants. On the top of the slate two inches of rough leaf-mould is strewed for drainage; over that, three inches of sandy loam; and on the top of the loam, half an inch of common pit sand. The cuttings are inserted with a small dibber in this prepared bed, the surface watered until it is perfectly level – a point of great moment. A temperature of 60° should be maintained, and the house never shaded. In less than a month, thousands of plants may be rooted in this way with very trifling loss.

1222 *Verbenas* Verbenas also root well in the same way; but in bright weather they require shading. However, for verbenas, ageratums, pelargoniums, heliotropes, fuchsias, lantanas, petunias, etc., in the spring, no place is better than a pit or frame with top or bottom heat of from 60° to 70°. If any or all of these have been gradually hardened off in the winter, the store pots ought to be now plunged into a temperature of 50° or 60°, for a week or fortnight before the tops are removed for cuttings. Within certain limits, the more tender the shoots of such plants are, the more rapidly they will emit roots.

1223 *Dahlias* Place dahlia roots, also, in heat at this time, to excite healthy growth for cuttings.

1224 *Seeds for Bedding Out* Seeds of lobelia, pyrethrum, Golden Feather, and any other plant required for edgings and bedding out in quantity may now be sown. Tender annuals and climbing plants may now be placed in cold frames.

1225 *Auriculas, Pinks, Carnations, etc.* These may have as much air as it is possible to give them, provided always that the temperature of the external air is not lower than 35°: draughts must be avoided, and water given but sparingly and when the weather is mild.

1226 *Re-potting and Shifting* Cinerarias and calceolarias in frames may be re-potted or removed to glass house. Pelargoniums should now be shifted for the last time before blooming, into the pots in which they are to blossom.

1227 *Vegetables in Hotbeds and Frames* Cucumbers in full growth require every attention. See that the heat of the beds does not fall below 70°: apply fresh linings as soon as this is the case. Attend to stopping and setting; allow no more than two or three cucumbers to grow at the same time on one plant; admit air in sunny weather, but not enough to produce a draught; give all the light possible, but cover at night with mats or straw, and add fresh earth if required.

If it is desired to start more beds, the dung may be got ready and treated as formerly described, during which time the seed may be sown in pots and placed in a bed in full operation; or those who have not yet begun may proceed as described last month. Good loamy soil is best to grow them in, so that it is warm enough before planting. Place two plants on a mound under each light; as they grow, add fresh soil till the bed is level. Peg the bines down as they grow. If a proper temperature and sweet dewy atmosphere pervade the frame, they will never be troubled with insects or mildew; but if they are chilled or over heated these will soon follow. If mildew attack them, sprinkle with water and dust with sulphur, if green fly or thrips, fumigate with tobacco.

1228 *Melons* The directions given for cucumbers apply equally to the culture of melons; but, before planting the latter, make the soil pretty firm. Melons require the same temperature as cucumbers, and great care as regards watering: if too dry, they are apt to become infested with red spider; if too wet, they are subject to canker. In the former case, apply sulphur, or syringing; in the latter, apply soot about the collar. Set many fruits, but allow no more than two, or three at the most, to swell off at once; and cut away, or rather prevent, all superfluous growth, by pinching out every new shoot that is not wanted. Attend well to the application of fresh dung. Nothing can succeed unless the heat can be maintained.

1229 *Watering Plants in Hotbeds* Water of the same temperature as the bed is absolutely necessary in watering cucumbers and melons, which should be done over the leaves, as well as at the roots, about twice or three times a week, which is as often as they are likely to want it. Still evaporation proceeds, and it is sometimes necessary, therefore, to make good the consequent loss; but in watering forcing beds a fine rose should be used, so that the surface of the soil be not beaten down in the process. The water should be of a temperature nearly equal to that of the bed – rather above than below; and if liquid manure is used, it should be rather weak: for asparagus and seakale, a little salt, about a tea-spoonful to the gallon, may be advantageous. It is decidedly better to water effectually at once than to water little and often, because the latter is apt to keep the surface slimy and soddened, with no benefit to the plants, but rather the contrary. It is advisable to be cautious in watering forcing beds in the colder months, as I consider that a properly made-up bed should contain moisture in itself sufficient, or nearly so, to nourish it.

1230 *Seakale* Some families like to have seakale (Fig. 508) in by Christmas; but at whatever time it is in request, the process is the same. It may be forced in a frame or pit, or put in pots made for the purpose, having covers to exclude the light, and these pots placed in a frame, pit, or warm greenhouse.

The most common method is to place seakale pots over the crowns, and cover these pots with fermenting dung or leaves. Leaves are the safest, not in too great quantity, or mixed with grass which is too wet. If stable dung is used, it should be well prepared by turning and allowing the rank heat to pass off. Too great a heat is likely to destroy the crop for the season, and the plants permanently. If left till March, the open ground culture is best. Then a little sand or ashes placed over the crowns, and banking over as we would earth up celery, is sufficient. When the kale is fit to cut, it will be indicated by the plants.

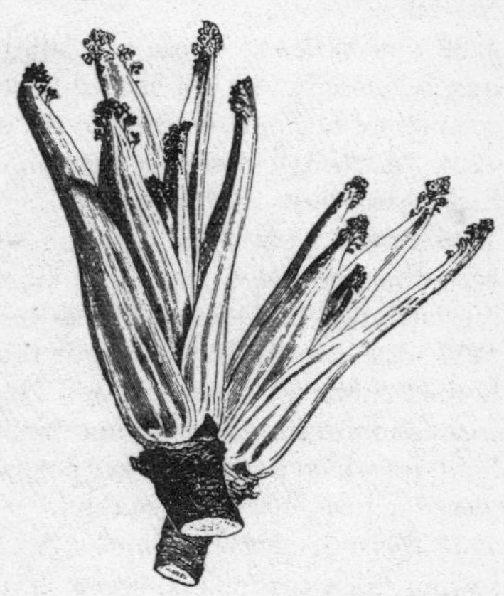

FIG. 508 *Seakale (Crambe maritime)*

1231 *Asparagus* Early asparagus is forced in the following manner with most satisfactory results. In an ordinary melon pit, about the beginning of February, a quantity of stable dung is set to work by turning and shaking in the ordinary way to sweeten and regulate the heat. By the middle of the month, as much of this is thrown into the pit as will fill it to within a foot of the glass. Two days afterwards, this is covered with a layer of 3 inches of mellow soil. On a mild day previous to this, a quantity of asparagus roots should have been grubbed up from an old bed – these are the best plants for forcing – and placed ready. As soon as the fermenting material has arrived at a safe temperature, about 80°, these roots are packed thickly together on the 3 inches of soil, and more soil thrown on them, just sufficient to cover them, without increasing the weight too suddenly or too greatly. This precaution is necessary, because the addition of 10 inches of earth would cause a rapid sinking and proportionate rise in the temperature of the dung, to the injury of the roots. Four days after planting, sufficient earth is put on to cover the crowns about 6 inches. In ten days the crowns begin to appear.

When the crowns appear, settling of the dung has brought the surface of the soil 18 inches from the glass. Nothing more is required to be done than to cover them from frosts and give them an occasional watering, with a little salt in the water. This bed will continue to produce largely till the time asparagus is plentiful out of doors. Asparagus may be forced any time during the winter; but to have it earlier than February, a frame and dung bed is better than a melon pit, since the necessary heat must be maintained by means of outside linings. In other respects the treatment is much the same.

1232 *Frame Potatoes* It is now a good time to put some potatoes in a little heat. An excellent plan is to pare the soil off an old cucumber or melon bed; add 3 inches of fresh earth, then set the potatoes 15 inches or so apart, and cover with 5 or 6 inches more earth; put on the lights, and then give a good lining of prepared dung; this will cause heat, and the potatoes will root into the dung of the old bed and be very fine. Give them plenty of air, but never allow them to get frosted.

1233 *French Beans* These may still be sown as described last month, or they may be placed in an old hotbed fresh lined. As the season advances, they will require less heat, but will not do out of doors yet.

1234 *Radishes* Radishes, if sown now on a slight hotbed, will come in much earlier than those in cold frames.

1235 *Early Carrots* These maybe sown, for succession, on a slight hotbed, and very dwarf peas also, which may be treated in the same way as French beans, mustard cress, and lettuces, for succession.

1236 *Mint, Horseradish, etc.* Some roots of mint may be potted and placed in a hotbed. Some use them as salads. Horseradish, dandelion, and chicory may be treated in the same way. All but mint should be blanched by covering from the light, for which purpose flower pots will do. Some parsley roots, potted up and placed in heat, may also be useful.

1237 *Ridge Cucumbers, Marrows, etc.* Now is the time for making a hotbed for sowing ridge cucumbers, vegetable marrows, tomatoes, capsicums, and such plants. Those who have hotbeds in operation may sow these seeds in pots, and put them in the frames; otherwise it is necessary to make a bed for them.

Although it is advisable to get the dung or begin to prepare it this month, it is not desirable to sow the seed till March, and even the third or fourth week is time enough, for these cannot be planted in the open air till quite the latter end of May, unless hand glasses are used to cover them, and they are planted in a little heat, when they may be trusted out earlier; but March is quite early enough to raise them.

1238 *Seedling Beds* Cauliflower, lettuce, cabbage, broccoli, radish, carrot, onions, beet, etc., may now be sown in the cold pit or frame; they will not come on so quickly as those sown in heat, but will be earlier than those sown outdoors. It is not well to begin too early with seeds of this kind, unless an abundance of manure is at hand, for the earlier the beginning, the more dung to maintain the heat will be required.

1239 *Strawberries* Plants in pots placed in heat now will fruit in April: they will want liquid manure occasionally to keep them in vigour. Plants in cold pits or frames should be looked over often, dead leaves picked out, slugs and other pests destroyed.

1240 *Cauliflowers, Lettuces, etc.* Cauliflowers, corn salad, parsley, endive, lettuces, etc., in cold frames, should have the earth stirred between them occasionally; they should have every ray of sunshine, and be uncovered entirely in mild weather. Pick out dead leaves, and water if needful, but beware of over-wetting.

3 – Fruit under Glass, Heated and Unheated

1241 *The Vinery: Vines in Houses* Vines in houses, started in October, will now be swelling their fruit. Thin in time, and maintain a steady growing temperature of 65°. Those started in January will show their bunches this month, and a temperature from 55° to 60° will be suitable. Some prefer leaving the disbudding until the bunches show, and then leave the best. This is safe practice, and the buds up to this stage do not exhaust the vine much.

1242 *Starting Vines* In many places the first or second house will be started this month. See that all loose bark is removed from the vines, that they are thoroughly cleaned with soap and water, and painted over with a thick coating of equal parts of sulphur, soot, lime, and cow dung, made into a paste with strong soap suds, previous to starting them. Begin with a temperature of 45°, and slowly and gradually increase it during the month 10° or 16°. Maintain a genial atmosphere in all the houses by sprinkling the paths, syringing, etc., and give as much air as the weather will permit, allowing a rise of 10° or 15° during sunshine.

1243 *Vines in Pots* Grapes grown in pots require the same general treatment as those planted out. It will very much hasten the ripening of the fruit if the pots are maintained in a steady bottom heat of from 70° to 80°.

1244 *Pines* From 65° to 70° should be the minimum temperature during the month; the bottom heat may range from 5° to 10° higher. During dull weather a dry atmosphere must be preserved. The plants should be carefully examined previous to watering, and this operation, whenever necessary, performed so as to prevent the water getting into the axils of the leaves. Plants swelling their fruit should be placed at the warmest end of the house, and those intended for autumn or winter fruiting kept steadily growing, carefully guarding against any sudden check. Succession plants in pots must be kept rather dry, and the linings and coverings carefully attended to.

1245 *Peaches, Nectarines, etc.* In their early stages these are very impatient of heat. Begin with a temperature of 40°, and gradually rise to 50°. This should not be much exceeded until the fruit is set; then, by gradual ascent, from 5° to 10° may be added; and this is the maximum of fire heat for peaches until the ticklish period of stoning is over. Syringe twice daily in bright weather, except when the trees are in flower. The borders should have a good soaking, if dry, before forcing commences. Give as much air as the weather will permit at all times.

Unless bees make their appearance, the trees should often be gently shaken when in flower, and the pollen distributed by a camel-hair pencil to insure the fructification of the blossoms.

1246 I*Figs* will bear a higher temperature than peaches, and may be started at 50°. The terminal buds of the young shoot should be removed to insure a good crop. Maintain a moist atmosphere, and water copiously when necessary.

1247 *The Orchard House* Orchard houses should stand open night and day, unless during severe frosts. Plants in pots must not, however, be allowed to become too dry, because dryness at the roots of trees weakens the buds and renders them less capable of proper expansion under the influence of the rising sap when it reaches them. The trees will benefit if painted over with a similar composition to that recommended above for vines. This would tend to prevent the attacks of insects, kill all moss and fungi, and render the buds safe from the ravages of birds, which often play sad havoc with trees in orchard houses.

It is a good plan to look through every part of the house at this time of year before the buds break, and clean it in every part, fumigating it and applying an infusion of Gishurst's Compound in the proportion of ¼lb. to 2 gallons of water to walls and trees, in order to get rid of insects that might otherwise prove troublesome as the year advances.

1248 *Caution respecting Forcing Fruit Houses* During dull weather, care must be exercised not to force the fruit houses too rapidly, or the trees will be induced to make elongated spongy growth at the expense of future strength and fruitfulness.

FIG. 509 *Hypocyrta brevicalyx (Gesnerance)*

CHAPTER 24

The Garden and its Work in Every Department in March

1249 *Aspect and Character of the Month* The increased temperature during March is chiefly observable during the day. It is still variable, advancing as it were by starts, but the mean temperature of the month is about six degrees higher than February, although the thermometer still ranges from 28° to 53°, including the night and day temperature, the mean maximum being 49° 9', and the mean minimum 40° 49'.

The trees are still leafless, and the only things really vernal are the evergreens about the grounds; but there is that about a mild sunny day at the close of March which tells us that vegetable nature is once more alive: there is a murmuring of life in the air, which was so silent while the trees and fields bore their 'beards of icicle and shroud of snow'. The winding hedgerows have a summer look; under the hedges, and on the sunlit bank, the silent progress of spring makes itself visible; violets and primroses peep out, the starry celandine opens its golden rays. The first bee comes blundering forth from its winter den; well it knows, however, where the finest primroses and sweetest violets blow, and soon finds the broadest yellow blossom of the furze bush, in which it can bury itself while it rifles it of its richest pollen.

Though still leafless, many trees and shrubs are just bursting into leaf. In the words of good Bishop Mant, the poet of the months, on:

Currant and prickly gooseberry,
Along the hawthorn's level line,
On bush of fragrant eglantine,
On bramble, and pithy elder pale,
On larch and woodbine's twisted trail,
And willow lithe, there's flush of green;
The forward sycamores display
Their foliage; and the shining spray
Of chestnut, to the sun protrude
His lengthen'd and expanding bud,
Which once unwrapp'd, in vain would Art
Fold it anew.

In the garden many floral ornaments begin to appear; the spring adonis peeps out in the herbaceous border; the fritillaria, or crown imperial, exhibits its drooping bells; the periwinkles open their bright blue eyes in old gardens, reminding us that Chaucer sang of its beauties along with the violet in his parterre:

There sprang the violete al newe,
And fresh pewinké, rich of hewe.

The delicate blossom of the almond perfumes the air with its fragrance, precursor of the apple, pear, and cherry; and others, which we need not name, admonish us 'that the winter is past, that the rain is over and gone, and the flowers appear on the earth; that the time of the singing of birds is come, when the voice of the turtle is heard in our land.'

March, while treading thus on the flowery borders of spring, does not fail to remind us that it was not without sound analogy that the name of the roughest of the fabled Olympian deities was given to it by the Romans. The stormy winds of the vernal equinox render it both boisterous and cold. These gales are distinguished from those of autumn by their greater dryness, during which evaporation takes place with great rapidity. The moisture engendered by the heavy snows and rains of winter exhales; 'the dry winds of March come strong and thirsty, and drink up the dregs which winter has left in the cup'; and the earth is thus prepared for the seed about to be committed to its bosom. Hence the old rural proverb, which declares 'a measure of March dust to be worth a king's ransom'. Another homely adage is old enough among us to be embodied in verse by one of our poets:

March, though his early mood
Is boisterous and wild, – feeling that shame
Would follow his fell steps, if spring's young brood
Of buds and blossoms wither'd where he trod, –
Calms his fierce ire, while the blue violets
Wake to new life.

I – Work to be done in the Garden

1 – The Flower Garden and the Shrubbery

1250 *Protection of Plants in March* This is generally a busy, but by no means a genial month. The winds are generally rough and biting, harsh and boisterous, and especially severe upon weak and tender plants; indeed, trees, plants, and shrubs that may have borne the rigours of winter with impunity often succumb beneath the chilling blasts of March. Therefore, if any plant, not quite hardy, has not hitherto been protected, that protection should now be afforded.

The precaution is all the more necessary in seasons in which there has been little or no early winter, followed by periods of intense cold and frost, which too often leave impaired constitutions and sickly growths. When weakened by previous disease, mismanagement, or disaster, and when the winter has been exceptionally severe, such trees as *Araucaria imbricata*, *Cedrus Deodara* (Fig. 510), *Pinus insignis*, and *Sequoa sempervirens*, may require slight protection with mats and boughs in the spring. Sickly hollies, succulent growths of sweet bay, and laurustinus, may be saved by similar treatment. Magnolias, delicate roses, and other scarcely hardy plants on walls, should receive some shelter from the stern bite of March frosts and winds. Care must be exercised not to keep them too close and warm, or the remedy will prove more disastrous than the evil. For walls, nothing answers better than a thin layer of straw, covered over with a mat, and kept dry, if possible. This not only keeps *out* the cold, but keeps *out* the heat. Protection against the exciting energy of the sun's rays during this month is almost

FIG. 510 *Cedrus deodara*

of equal importance to warding off the effects of extreme cold. The later in the season tender plants can be kept in a *dormant* state, the better, and nothing secures this object more effectually than a thin covering of *dry* non-conducting material, such as straw. The utmost caution must be exercised in removing protection from plants. Uncover them *a shred at a time*. Nothing effects them more injuriously than sudden transition from semi-darkness to perfect light, or from kindly shelter to full exposure. Often such a shock to the vital energies induces either death or constitutional debility, puny growth, and lingering disease.

1251 *Grass Lawns, Walks, etc.* The increase of floral beauty in all parts of the garden points out our duty and defines the routine work for the month. The more beauty in the garden, the better it must be kept; for slovenliness and dirt are never so intolerably hideous and unbearable as when seen in juxtaposition with their opposites. Therefore, grass lawns must be frequently swept and rolled; gravel walks turned, fresh gravelled, raked, rolled, and swept; edgings cut, planted, or altered; and all planting, pruning, and digging finished as soon as possible. This is also a good season to remove plantains and daisies from the turf, and to sow grass seeds for new lawns. If the weather be mild, grass lawns and verges may have a first mowing during the month.

1252 *Herbaceous Borders and Flower Beds* Fork over flower beds on frosty mornings, to expose a fresh surface to the atmosphere, and provide a finely pulverised soil for the roots of bedding plants. Stir the surface by flat hoeing, or deep raking among borders of annuals and bulbs. Remove all prunings and winter rubbish, to be either rotted or charred, and see that the entire garden has a cared-for appearance.

1253 *Tulips, Hyacinths, etc.* Tulips in beds must be protected from severe frosts, and crocuses from the depredations of birds. Hyacinths and narcissi should be tied to short sticks, so that the blooms may not be broken down by the wind.

Crocuses are now in full glory, and a brilliant display they make; while tulips, narcissi, crown imperials, cyclamens, ixias, scillas, and hyacinths hasten forward to uphold the matchless supremacy of bulbs as the most beautiful of all spring flowers. The double-blossom furze, deciduous yellow jasmines, scarlet ribes, almonds, heaths, daphnes, snowy mespilus, *Magnolia conspicua*, holly-leaved berberry, saxifrages, orobus, calycanthus, etc., etc., weave a floral garland of which any month, not excepting June even, might be proud.

1254 *Pruning Climbers* Complete pruning and training clematises, jasmines, bignonias, and other creepers on trellises.

1255 *Roses* Finish planting all hardy roses at once, if bloom is expected this season. The excited state of the shoots from a mild winter must not arouse impatience to finish pruning. The more excited they are, there is the greater necessity for delay, as the expenditure of the sap in the terminal buds will preserve the buds near the base of the shoots the longer in a dormant state; and it is upon these buds we are dependent for next year's blossom. Towards the end of the month, perpetual roses may be pruned. In pruning roses, it must be remembered, as a general rule, that it is the weakest growers that must receive the most severe pruning, because their bearing powers are considerably less than those of the strong growers. Look to the stakes and supports to see that they are firm and sound, and look to the ties as well; point the borders in which roses are growing, and give a top dressing of well-rotted manure if necessary. Nothing but roses should be allowed to grow in rose borders, as the presence of any other flower will absorb plant food, which otherwise would go to the roses, which want all the nourishment they can get.

In pruning roses, every bit of old wood, loose bark, etc., should be carefully removed, as it is exactly amid such *débris* that the larvae of caterpillars, aphides, etc., are deposited. Whenever trees have been much affected with these pests, they might be coated over with a similar mixture to that recommended for vines (see Section 1242). This would remove all moss, etc., from the stems and branches, and prove an effectual preventive and eradicative measure; it is less troublesome and unpleasant than hunting throughout the summer for green caterpillars, buried deep in rosebuds or wrapped up in leaves, and driving away the delicious perfume of the roses with the noxious fumes of tobacco water or other disagreeable compounds. When the green fly does make its appearance, a strong infusion of carbonate of ammonia (smelling salts) is the only remedy that ought to be admitted among choice roses in bloom. This will not only destroy the aphis, but supply the plants with useful food, and heighten, by its volatile aroma, if that were possible, the perfume of the rose. In small gardens, a number of trees might quickly be cleaned with the aphis brush, as illustrated in paragraph 665, figure 337. The shoot, with its living freight, is firmly grasped between them, the brushes are gently drawn along the shoot, and the insects carried off by the bristles and consigned to a well-merited death.

1256 *Gladioli* This is the proper month for planting all the hardy gladioli. If they were taken up in November and kept in a proper temperature, they will now be *starting*, and should be planted at once. They grow well in any light, rich garden soil. In growing them *en masse*, drills should be drawn on beds or borders about four inches deep, the bulbs inserted, and covered over with the soil. Stakes about two feet high should be put in at the same time, as, if inserted afterwards, they might injure the bulbs. The distance between the bulbs should be from nine inches to a foot. Nothing can exceed their brilliancy when in flower. They present a beautiful appearance when in flower if planted in lines or in clumps of three, but in this case the three corms should be of the same colour.

1257 *Hardy Annuals* In addition to the sowing of annuals named last month, the following should at once be sown either in the reserve garden, or in beds, rows, or patches where they are intended to flower. The figures indicate height in feet. Seeds that are sown now should be sown, if possible, in warm and sheltered beds. If the weather is fine and open, advantage may be taken of it to transplant annuals sown in the autumn, but if it be wet or frosty, the sowing and transplanting had better be put off to the following month. In less favourable situations the sowing of annuals may remain until next month, and biennials and perennials may also be left till then.

Adonis flos (or aestivalis) (1) – deep crimson.

Amaranthus caudatus (*Love Lies Bleeding*) (2 to 3) – long drooping crimson flowers; greenish white.

Amaranthus hypochondriacus (*Prince's Feather*) (2) – upright crimson flowers.

Calliopsis bicolor (or **tinctoria)** (2) – yellow, with purple-brown blotch at base.

Calliopsis bicolor nana (1) – similar to preceding.

Calliopsis coronata (2) – orange, spotted brownish purple.

Calliopsis Drummondii (1) – orange-yellow, with crimson-brown eye.

Campanula Loreyi (or ramosissima) (1) – bluish violet.

Campanula speculum (*Venus's Looking Glass*) (½) – blue and white.

Centaurea Americana (3) – red.

Centaurea cyanus (*Bluebottle* or *Cornflower*) (2 to 3) – blue, white, crimson-brown.

Centaurea depressa (1) – blue, with brownish-red centre.

Chrysanthemum coronarium (2) – yellow and white.

Chrysanthemum tricolor (2) – yellow round purple disc.

Chrysanthemum Burridgii (2) – yellow centre and pure white edge, with bright crimson band intervening.

Clarkia elegans (1½) – crimson, rose, and white.

Clarkia pulchella (1) – purple, rose, white.

Collinsia bicolor (1) – lilac and white.

Convolvulus tricolor (or minor) (1) – yellowish centre, white and blue, purple, white striped, etc.

Coreopsis. *See* **Calliopsis.**

Delphinium Ajacis (*Rocket Larkspur*) (1 and 2) – blue, pink, red, white, single and double.

Delphinium cardiopetalum (1) – dark blue.

Delphinium Sinense (2) – brilliant blue.

Erysimum Perofskianum (1) – orange.

Eschscholtzia Californica (1½) – brilliant yellow, orange towards centre, orange, pale primrose approaching white.

Eschscholtzia tenuifolia (¾) – pale yellow.

Eutoca viscida (1) – blue with white eye.

Godetia Lady Albemarle (1½) – large rosy-crimson blooms.

Godetia Lady Satin Rose (1½) – deep rose pink, with satiny surface.

Godetia The Bride(1½) – white with purple eye.

Helianthus annuus (*Common Sunflower*) (6) – yellow.

Helianthus argophyllus (5) – yellow, silvery leaves.

Helianthus Californicus (7) – orange.

Helianthus centrochlorus (4) – yellow, green centre.

Helianthus cucumerifolius (3) – golden yellow, purple centres.

Helianthus globosus fistulosus (5) – saffron, double.

Helichrysum compositum (*Everlasting Flower*) (1½) – various colours.

Iberis amara (*Candytuft*) (¾) – white.

Iberis amara hesperidiflora (*Rocket Candytuft*) (1) – pure white.

Iberis umbellata (1) – purple.

Larkspur. *See* **Delphinium.**

Lathyrus odoratus (*Sweet Pea*) – various colours, as Invincible Black, dark rich colour; Invincible Scarlet, intense scarlet; Crown Princess of Prussia, lovely blush; Clarke's Hybrid, rose, blue, and white; Painted Lady, red and white.

Linaria triornithophora (2) – *Antirrhinum* like flowers, reddish violet and purple, spotted yellow.

Linum grandiflorum (1) – blue flax plant.

Linum rubeum (¾) – crimson.

Lupinus (1 to 3) – many varieties, purple, lilac, white, violet, yellow, blue, red, and brown.

Malope grandiflora (*Mallow*) (3) – red.

Malope alba (3) – white.

Malcolmia maritima (*Virginian Stock*) (1½) – white, red; useful for margins.

Matthiola (*Stock*) – Dwarf German Ten-Week, (¾), various colours; Large Flowered German Ten-Week (1¼), various colours; New Autumnal (1¼), various colours.

Nigella Hispanica (*Love in a Mist*) (1½) – dark violet.

Oenothera bistorta Veitchiana (½) – lemon colour, with blood-red spot at base.

Oenothera Drummondii nana (1) – golden yellow.

Oenothera Lindleyana (1) – white and red.

Oenothera rosea (1) – purplish rose.

Omphalodes linifolium (*Venus's Navel-Wort*) (1) – white spikes of bloom.

Papaver caryophylloides (*Carnation Poppy*) (2½) – various colours, and crimson scarlet.

Papaver Marsellii (2) – white tipped, blood crimson.

Papaver Rhaeas plena (*Dwarf French Poppy*) (2) – various colours; double flowers.

Perilla Nankinensis (1½) – pink, with maroon- bronze foliage.

Phlox Drummondii (1) (Fig. 511) – pure white, pink, buff, purple, crimson, some with eye in centre, and some striped.

Rhodanthe atrosanguinea (1¼) – magenta-purple.

Rhodanthe maculata – deep rose with yellow centre surrounded by crimson ring; white.

Rhodanthe Manglesii (1) – silvery rose, with yellow centre.

Saponaria alba (½) – white.

Saponaria Calabrica (½) – pink, compact.

Sunflower. *See* **Helianthus.**

Schizanthus Grahami (1½) – red and orange, with purple streaks.

Schizanthus pinnatus (1¼) – purple and white, spotted red.

Schizanthus retusus (½) – red and yellow.

Schortia Californica (¾) – yellow, with dark centre; useful for masses; better sown later in the season.

Silene pendula (1) – rosy pink.

Statice Bonduelli (1½) – golden yellow.

Tagetes signata pumila (¾) (Fig. 154) – excellent as bedding plant, yellow with brown spots; better sown in April.

Stock. *See* **Matthiola.**

Sweet Pea. *See* **Lathyrus.**

Venus's Navel Wort. *See* **Omphalodes.**

Virginian Stock. *See* **Malcolmia.**

Veronica Syriaca (*Syrian Speedwell*) (¾) – blue; pretty for margins; sow where it is to flower.

Viscaria elegans picta (1) – crimson and scarlet, with white edge.

Viscaria oculata (¾) – pink, dark eye.

Viscaria oculata coccinea (¾) – scarlet, dark eye.

Viscaria splendens (1) – rose pink.

FIG. 511 *Phlox Drummondii*

The above list comprises an excellent variety of hardy annuals, and, if not absolutely exhaustive, is sufficient for all general purposes. For other sorts, reference must be made to the catalogues of the leading seedsmen. They are beautiful for masses in borders, edgings, small beds, patches, and single lines. A few cultural remarks on some of them may be useful. By cutting off the flowers of *Erysimum Perofskianum* as soon as they fade, and thus preventing it from running to seed, it may be kept in bloom throughout the summer. The varieties of *Clarkia* are so beautiful that all mentioned above should be grown. *Convolvulus major* is not included in the above list, because it is best raised in heat with the half-hardy annuals.

1258 *Winter-sown Annuals* Stir the soil among these in the reserve garden, and transplant them, weather permitting, to their quarters in the flower garden in which they are desired to bloom.

1259 *Ten-Week Stocks* Prepare a sunny bed in the reserve garden, and sow ten-week stocks for succession to those already raised in heat.

1260 *Anemones* Prepare a piece of ground in the reserve garden for sowing anemone seed; *Anemone hortensis*, *A. coronaria*, and *A. rectifolia*, are the most useful varieties. Rub the seed clean in sand; sow in shallow drills nine inches apart, and cover with fine sifted leaf mould and sand.

1261 *Biennials and Perennials* Get ground in readiness for a general sowing of all biennials and perennials next month. The oftener it is forked over, the more thoroughly pulverised it will be; consequently, the better adapted for raising seeds of every description.

1262 *Protection of Seeds* Protect seeds from birds, which are most destructive just as the seeds are vegetating.

1263 *Beds for Bedding Plants* Enrich the hooped beds designed for the temporary protection of bedding plants next month with a liberal dressing of manure, and get everything in readiness that the approaching busy season will demand.

1264 *Protecting Bedding Plants* It is always desirable to get bedding plants out as early as possible, and yet there is much danger both from wind and frost in so doing. It is an excellent plan to stick sprays of evergreens, Scotch and spruce firs, in different parts of the beds as a protection. By this means the force of the wind is broken, and the plants take hold of the ground sooner; the tender leaves also are saved, which otherwise not unfrequently turn brown, and fall off, retarding the growth of the plants.

1265 *Carnations, Pinks, etc.* Carnations and picotees should now, if the weather is mild, be placed in their blooming pots, and sheltered under glass during bad weather. They should be potted firmly, care being taken to keep the soil out of the axils of the leaves. Pinks in pots or open borders should be top dressed with a mixture of fine loamy soil and half-rotten manure.

1266 *Shrubberies* Let all planting and alterations cease for this season at once. Finish digging and clearing all this department, and manage to have a clean home for the shrubs before they robe themselves in their beautiful flowers. Attend to staking, tying, and mulching all newly or recently-planted trees and shrubs before the March winds tear them half up by the roots. Choice specimens, recently moved, would be much benefitted by a copious syringing with the engine, on the evenings of dry, pinching days, to check perspiration, and husband the scanty juices of the plants.

1267 Top dress rhododendron beds with equal parts of cow dung (thoroughly decayed; say four years old) and leaf-mould. On poor soils this imparts a rich gloss to the foliage, and causes luxuriant healthy growth. Where such material is not procurable, a thick layer of leaves may be *pointed* in with excellent results.

2 – The Vegetable or Kitchen Garden

1268 *Work to be Done: Cropping* During this month the great operations of the year are commenced, and most of the principal crops got in. Hitherto, warm and sheltered spots and borders have been appropriated, but the larger quarters have been dug up into ridges, and as large a surface as possible exposed to atmospheric influences. Now the whole garden is to be cropped upon a carefully-considered plan, so that no crop of the same character should follow on the same spot; but having once laid down a well-devised plan for the season, the operations should become comparatively easy. Assuming, therefore, that previous directions have been attended to, that the soil was turned over in autumn, that it has been frozen, the surface turned over and frozen again, and dried by the winds which generally occur early this month, it is now ready for cropping.

Where any of the Brassicae, or *Deteriorators*, were grown the previous season, follow them with *Preparers*, which are mostly root crops, as potatoes, carrots, parsnips, onions, scorzoneras, salsafy, etc. These, again, should be followed as far as possible by *Surface Crops*, which are mostly the shortest-lived of any, and include all saladings. Indeed, it is possible to go further, and include among surface crops pot or sweet herbs, and also medicinal herbs, besides some of the shorter-lived vegetables, as spinach, coleworts, French beans, early carrots, and the longer-lived sorrels, and even strawberries; so that surface crops comprise a group equally copious with exhausters or preparers. Map out the garden, therefore, and give each crop its proper position and space, and note the time of its duration as a guide for selecting its successor; this applies to kitchen gardens of any extent, but more particularly to those which are limited, because it economises the room. These crops, called *Deepeners*, on account of the depth and richness of soil they require, and their long occupation of the same spot, comprise but a small portion, comparatively, of the occupants the kitchen garden, and cannot be used in the same proportion, although their office in respect of deepening the soil is important; but where bush fruits are grown largely in the kitchen garden, they may be added to the group, and managed in the same way – that is, plant a certain number every year and remove an equal number of old ones: by this a fresh piece of soil can be devoted to grosser-feeding crops, which has long been innocent of them. The principal point of culture for the *Deepeners* is that the ground must be deeply worked, both at planting and taking up, For the *Preparers* the ground should be trenched two spades deep, chiefly bastard trenching, with plenty of manure of good sound quality, or mixed with maiden earth. For the *Surface Crops*, merely pointing or forking manure into the surface, or top six inches of soil, will suffice; after which, if again trenched two spits deep, adding no fresh manure, the ground will be in excellent condition for the most scourging of all crops, the *Exhausters*; namely, broccoli, Savoys, Brussels sprouts, cabbages, borecole, etc. By working on some such principle as this, the soil may be kept in a state of fertility for ages without fear of those vexations and disagreeable results which arise from want of method and forethought.

It should be observed, that to carry out this system of grouping and rotation there must be no edging of beds with parsley, chives, or other dwarf plants, for appearances; no devoting particular corners perpetually to sweet herbs for convenience; no edging the quarters with strawberries, or what-not; but every plant must take its place and turn as part and parcel of the whole; every variety and species must perform its part in preparing the ground for a successor. It may appear difficult, but it is practicable.

1269 *Seakale* This still requires some covering, but less than last month, blanching being now the main object of it; and sand, ashes, or leaves will effect the object. When the kale is past blanching, its use does not end here: the leaves may be eaten all through the summer and autumn while they are green, merely dressing them in the same way as winter greens. Thus it will be found a very profitable crop for cottagers; it grows well in shady places, and is not particular as to soil, and will stand a cold, bleak climate. A top dressing of very rotten dung, of any kind, is suitable for this plant, but it is rendered more efficacious by the addition of a little salt, about a pound to the barrowful of manure; wood ashes are also beneficial, and may be added in any quantity.

1270 *Asparagus* Those who wish to raise asparagus for planting out in beds should sow now. Rich soil is required, and the seed should be sown in drills about 15 inches apart.

1271 *Celery* It is too early yet to sow the main crop of celery, but a little may be sown for early use. First sowings may be sown in seed pans; but for the main crop, it is preferable to shake together a small heap of stable dung, just sufficient to give a slight heat; spread three inches of soil on it, sow the seed, and cover with a hand glass. The plants come up much stronger by this method. The seed takes a long while to germinate compared to some: that sown in March will be ready to transplant in April.

1272 *Jerusalem Artichokes* should be planted not later than this month. The ground for them should be rather deeply worked, which gives them a firmer hold; for, the plants growing tall, are exposed to rough winds, which they resist better where they root pretty deeply.

Almost any part of a tuber will grow and form a plant; but it is advisable to select middling-sized tubers, planting them a foot or 10 inches deep. This may be done as the ground is dug or trenched; or they may be planted with a spade or trowel, making a hole for each set. They should be not less than a yard apart; four feet is better. The more open the spot, the more likely they are to prosper. As a rule, they produce a great number from each set. No other treatment is required than to keep the ground well stirred about them, and prevent the growth of weeds. Cut them down when the leaves are decayed, but not before; other wise the tubers will cease to grow.

1273 *Globe Artichokes* will be making offsets about the end of this month, or during next; these should be taken off for propagation. They bear best the second or third year after planting; so that it is advisable to plant one or more rows every year, and remove the same quantity of old roots. The ground should be deeply worked and well manured; let the manure be incorporated with the soil, not laid in a mass at the bottom of each trench. Fig. 512 exhibits an example of the variety known as the Large Paris Artichoke.

FIG. 512 *Large Paris artichoke*

It is better to trench the ground first, and fork the manure well into the surface spit, which gives the plants a better chance of immediately profiting by it. The offsets may be dis-severed with a knife, or slipped off and cut smooth afterwards, and planted with a dibber. Some plant in threes, a yard apart, and 4 feet from row to row, or they may be planted singly, 2 feet apart in the row, and 4 feet from row to row. They should be well watered, and the ground kept loose between.

1274 *Cardoons* are not so generally cultivated now as formerly, especially in small gardens, on account of the space they require. The seed is sown in March, in a warm sheltered spot, or under a hand glass or frame. When large enough, they are planted 8 or 10 inches apart, in rich or well-manured soil. Then again, they are planted in rows or trenches, after the manner of celery, only at a much greater distance from each other. During the autumn, earth up to blanch.

The plant grows very large, after the manner of the globe artichoke. Much room is required for banking up; accordingly, some gardeners recommend placing them 5 feet apart at the final planting; but the crop can never pay for this enormous extent of ground.

1275 *Potatoes* About the beginning of this month is the time to get in early potatoes. Some recommend planting them in October, placing them deep enough to be out of the reach of frost. In porous, well-drained soils this answers admirably; but the advantage is not so great as to recommend it for general practice. To insure a good crop, the ground should be bastard trenched in October or November, and left in ridges; in February levelled, and some thoroughly-decomposed manure forked in. In March the frosts will have left it well pulverised, and ready to receive the sets. Some prefer middling-sized potatoes for setting, planting them whole, scooping out all the shoots except one or two; others prefer large ones, cut in two or more, assuming that a large potato makes stronger shoots, capable of standing erect in full light of day.

When planting later in the season, it is enough to cut the potato into pieces, having an eye to each piece. The writer treated a pound of Early Rose potatoes in this manner, and found that the haulm was strong and vigorous, and that there was plenty of it. The produce of the single pound cut up in this manner, when taken out of the ground, weighed 48 lb.

1276 *Carrots* Some seed may be sown early this month, but the main crop should be deferred till the first week in April. Such sorts as the Intermediate may be sown in the four succeeding months; they will be useful to those who like to have this vegetable fresh and sweet from the ground. The ground should be deeply dug or bastard trenched in autumn, left at first in a rough state; but when it has been well frosted, stir and level it in January or February.

For the purpose of doing this the Canterbury hoe (that is, a hoe having three prongs instead of a blade) is a very useful implement. This treatment of the soil applies in all cases of spring sowing, especially if the ground is heavy or retentive; in that case it will not fall to pieces, unless it has been frosted and dried by winds. In preparing the ground for carrots, no manure should be applied; it is known that it induces them to fork, and they are more likely to become grub eaten. A dressing of sand is advantageous.

1277 *Parsnips* The main crop should be sown this month. For culinary purposes the roots will be large enough if the seed is sown in drills 15 inches apart, and the young plants thinned out to 10 or 12 inches apart. The Hollow Crowned variety of this root is the best, but by many the Guernsey is accounted equal to it, if not superior.

1278 *Cabbages* It is advisable to sow some cabbage seed of a quick hearting sort to follow those raised in January, or that have stood the winter. They will be of great service in July and the following months. The Early York, Large York, Nonpareil, Matchless, or indeed any sort, will do for the purpose. Sow broadcast on a warm sheltered spot, and protect from birds with light litter or netting; but, if covered with litter, it must be uncovered to admit light and air, or the plants will be drawn up weak.

Avoid planting cabbages when the ground is soddened after heavy rains. The soil is best when tolerably dry, and the state of the weather most favourable is a dull day preceding rain. It is an excellent plan at all times to mulch the roots of the young plants in a compost of soil and soot, wetted to the consistency of thick paste. This saves a great deal of trouble in watering afterwards, and in the driest weather will generally prevent flagging. Broccoli plants so treated will be found very free from clubbing. All young plants should be set deep, certainly to within an inch of the first leaf.

1279 *Cauliflowers* Cauliflower seed sown now will furnish plants for planting out in May and June; it may be sown in the open ground or in a frame or hand glass. Sow on the surface, tread and rake, and protect with litter or netting.

1280 *Broccoli* Such sorts as Walcheren, Purple Cape, or any sort that heads in autumn, should be sown at this time in the same manner as cabbage or cauliflower. They will be ready to plant out for good in May or June, or will be very useful at a time when summer crops are over and winter crops not ready.

1281 *Brussels Sprouts, etc.* Let a sowing be made on a fairly warm border at the end of the month. Sowings should also be made of Scotch Kale, Savoys, Sprouting Broccoli, and other winter greens.

1282 *French Beans* These may be sown towards the end of this month, choosing an early dwarf sort; but the principal sowing should be deferred till next month. Those sown this month should be in a border, sheltered from cold winds, but open to the full sun. This crop is less hardy than most others, being often cut off by late spring frosts, of which it is very susceptible; for that reason it is advisable to sow rather sparingly this month, and also to sow rather thickly.

In sowing, draw some drills 2 feet apart and 2 inches deep; drop the seeds 1 inch from seed to seed, and draw the earth in a ridge 2 inches high, which will cover the seeds 4 inches; when up, thin to 3 or 4 inches. But it often happens that early sowings do not all come up, or come thick in parts, leaving others bare; so that, to regulate the crop, it is necessary to thin out where they are thick and plant the thinnings to fill up the vacancies. This should be done in mild weather, or in the morning, so that in watering, to settle them in the ground, they may get warm before night.

1283 *Peas* Fresh sowings should be made this month, as formerly directed, and coal ashes scattered at the roots of those coming up, to prevent their destruction by slugs, sowing a row of many-leaved spinach between the rows.

1284 *Beans* The chief crops of this useful vegetable should be sown this month; sowings of the Green Windsor Broad Bean and Long Pod Bean being made.

1285 *Onions* The main crop should be got in this month. Sow in drills from 6 to 9 inches apart, and about ¼ inch deep when covered in. The White Spanish, Deptford, and James' Keeping are accounted good sorts.

1286 *Leeks* A sowing should be made in a small bed not later than the middle of the month, to be transplanted, when large enough, into well-manured trenches for winter use.

1287 *Radishes* may be sown thinly between the rows of the more enduring crops, such as onions.

1288 *Spinach* A crop of summer spinach should be sown in drills on open ground, or between growing crops suitable for the purpose, in the first and third weeks of the month.

1289 *Turnips* For use in haricots, etc., in late spring and early summer, a bed of some good early turnip, such as the Early Red Dutch, should be sown.

1290 *Small Salading* Mustard and cress should be sown in small quantities every week, to keep up a proper succession of small salading.

1291 *Rhubarb* If fresh plantations of rhubarb are required, and have not yet been made, it is desirable to form them without delay.

1292 *Basil and other Sweet Herbs* Basil, burnet, and other herbs, require to be sown at this season on slight hotbeds of about two feet in depth; but many cultivators leave them till next month, and sow in the open ground, unless they are wanted early. Thyme, marjoram, savory and hyssop, chervil (Fig. 513), and coriander, may be sown this month in dry, mild weather, to be transplanted by and by.

Sow them moderately thin in drills or beds (each sort separated) in good light soil; if in drills, 6 inches apart: some of the plants to remain where planted, after a thinning for early use; others to be planted out in the summer.

1293 *Mint* may also be propagated this month by separating the roots and planting them in drills drawn with a hoe six inches asunder, covering them with an inch of earth, and raking smooth. They will quickly take root, and grow freely for use in the summer. This method may be applied to the several sorts of spearmint, peppermint, and orange mint.

The herb garden in the present day is somewhat neglected, and yet the culture and curing of simples was formerly a part of a lady's education. There was not a lady in the kingdom but made her dill-tea and diet-drink from herbs grown under her own eye. Thyme, sage, spearmint, and marjoram are all pretty, and a special quarter should be set apart for them in our gardens. This would probably recover, for our soups and salads, some of the neglected tarragons, French sorrel, purslain, chevril, dill, and clary, which are only found now in the pages of the old herbals. Laid out after a simple geometric design, the herb garden might be rather ornamental than otherwise. Most of the herbs are propagated by slips in the autumn. The whole family of borage, burnet, clary, marigolds, orach-root, carduus, dill, fennel, buglos, sorrel, and angelica, may be sown about the middle of March, when the weather is open.

1294 *Parsley* Full crops of parsley should now be sown in drills along the edges of one of the borders. The quantity sown must be regulated by the requirements of the household; in the summer months it is frequently in request for garnishing cold meats, etc.

FIG. 513 *Curled or double chervil*

3 – The Fruit Garden and Orchard.

1295 *Work to be Done* Generally speaking, the pruning and nailing will be finished, but the trees should be washed with the garden engine or syringe, using tepid water, with solution of sulphur and soot, or lime wash, as a protection against scale and other insects. If there are any fruit growers who still doubt the efficacy of protecting the blossoms of apricots, peaches, and other wall fruit, this month will test their faith. To those who will be guided by reason, we say, Apply the most efficient protection within your reach.

This will probably be found in temporary wood copings, projecting 10 or 12 inches from the wall, with canvas curtains attached, which can be readily removed in fine weather; next to the coping, worsted netting is, perhaps, the most efficient defence against severe weather, with the least obstruction to the necessary circulation of air, light, and rain. Those who have curtains will do well to use them, not only against frost, but against the extreme ardour of the noonday sun, which will at once retard and strengthen their blossom.

1296 *Apples and Pears* Pruning these should now be finished, and this is the last month for planting until the autumn; the various operations of grafting and budding are now in full progress. This is especially the season for crown grafting, where it is desired to use some vigorous old tree bearing an indifferent fruit. In this case, the grafts should be taken from the trees before the buds begin to swell.

There should be no delay in setting about the operation of grafting wherever it is to be carried into effect. Trees that are most forward should be treated first, and these will be found to be the cherries and plums, for which grafting is as well as budding, though many are of opinion that all trees bearing stone fruits are better budded than grafted. The stock, as it has been said before in these pages, should be in an active state before the scion or graft, which has all the better chance if it remain dormant till the last moment. In fact, the buds of the scion should not be showing signs of swelling before the operation of grafting is completed. The cuts should be clean, as they will be if they are made with a keen knife. The cut parts of stock and scion should be brought into contact immediately after the cut is made, taking care that the cambium or inner bark of the one is brought into contact with the cambium of the other. This done, the stock and scion must be bound together firmly, but not so tightly as to bruise or injure the bark in any way, and the whole plastered over with a mixture of clay and cow dung, or some kind of grafting wax, to exclude the air from the recently cut surfaces.

1297 *Trained Trees* Trained trees not already disposed of should now be pruned and dressed at once; to delay till the buds swell is to endanger them in the process. In all cases, plums and cherries should be taken first; then the early pears, and afterwards late pears. Peaches and nectarines should always be left till the last.

1298 *Apricots* The apricot, the fruit of which is held in such high estimation, has a tendency to die prematurely – first a branch, then a side, until scarce a vestige remains of the tree; and this generally occurs on fine sunny days in spring and early summer – supposed to arise from the sap vessels being excited too early and rising too rapidly; so that they are in too watery a state to resist the severe frosts which sometimes follow. Every possible protection should be given to these delicate trees, and, perhaps, planting them in a border, where they would be less exposed to the action of the sun, would help to retard the rising of the sap till the season was more advanced.

1299 *Blossoms of Wall Trees* Birds that frequent the garden, or, at all events, the smaller kinds of these birds, are credited with doing much mischief with a will to the buds and blossoms of all fruit trees. Injury from this cause may be obviated by sprinkling the buds, etc., liberally with dry soot applied with a dredger.

1300 *Plums and Cherries* With the exception of pruning, grafting, and taking precautions to protect the buds and blossoms from the ill effects of inclement weather and the attacks of birds, nothing is wanted for these trees but the ordinary routine work.

1301 *Peaches and Nectarines* The same may be said with reference to these trees, whose pruning and nailing, as it has been said, should be left until the last.

1302 *Strawberries* Such sorts as British Queens, hitherto protected, should be uncovered now, and the beds weeded and the plants trimmed; the soil stirred round the roots with a fork without disturbing the dung. Runners placed in a nursery bed last autumn should now be removed to where they are to remain for fruiting.

Where fruit of a large size are required, open a trench, as if for celery, filled half up with well-rotted dung, and dig it well into the bottom of the trench, and fill in the soil previously taken out, and plant immediately. Where they are planted between dwarf fruit trees, it is good practice to keep each plant or stool separate for the first two years, and then allow them to cover the ground. Where plants have been growing in the same place for several years, weed the beds well before they begin to grow, stir the soil, and sow some guano over them in showery weather.

1303 *Gooseberries and Currant Trees* bear on the young as well as on the two-year-old wood, generally upon small spurs rising along the sides of the branches. In autumn or winter, when digging between the bushes, sow fresh-slaked lime copiously over the whole ground, more particularly round the stems and about the roots, before forking it over. About the latter end of March repeat the operation, raking the ground afterwards. In a fortnight or three weeks this liming should be repeated, and, except under extreme circumstances, no future attacks from caterpillars need be apprehended.

1304 *Pruning Gooseberries, etc.* In pruning gooseberry trees, for which January is a favourable season, keep the tree thin of branches; but let those left be trained to some regular shape, and never permitted to grow ramblingly across each other, but radiating in a cuplike form from their common centre, so as to be six or eight inches apart at the extremities and hollow in the centre. Prune out all worn-out branches, retaining young shoots to supply their places, retaining also, where practicable, a terminal bud to each branch while shortening long stragglers. The same remarks apply to currant trees. Young gooseberry trees designed for standards should be pruned back to a clean stem for 10 or 12 inches, retaining the best properly placed shoots to form the head, cutting out all irregularly-placed shoots, keeping them, as nearly as possible, of the same length and form.

1305 *New Plantations of Bush Fruit* In making new plantations, place the bushes 8 feet apart each way, if in continuous rows; if intended to be placed round the quarters, or to divide the ground into compartments, prune them up to a clean stem 12 or 14 inches high; otherwise the foliage will impede the growth of the crops sown beneath them.

The best mode of growing gooseberries is as espaliers or as standards. If grown as standards in the form of a low bush, the bushes should be trained 3 feet high before they are suffered to form a head. According to the ordinary system of training, the branches are borne to the ground by the weight of the fruit, and its bloom is destroyed by being draggled on the soil and splashed by heavy rains.

1306 *Filberts* At this time of year, while the male flowers, familiarly known as catkins, are in blossom, the trees or bushes should be shaken frequently, in order that the small female blossoms may be fertilised by the pollen that falls on them from the former.

II – Work to be done under Glass, etc.

1 – Flowers in the Conservatory, Greenhouse, Stove, etc.

1307 *Hothouse or Plant Stove* Keep a nice growing temperature of from 65° to 70°. If the sun continues very bright throughout the day, houses containing variegated plants will require shading for a few hours about noon. This will be the more necessary after re-potting. Clerodendrons, allamandas, stephanotis, ixoras, etc., should now be pushed forward in a sharp bottom heat. They may receive a liberal shift, and be allowed to grow rather loosely for a time, to encourage a rapid extension of parts. Ferns should now be thoroughly overhauled, examined, shifted into larger pots, or reduced, as circumstances may require; nice fibrous peat, leaf mould, sharp sand, and broken sandstone, suit them well.

1308 *Scale* Now is the time to destroy scale, so troublesome on the beautiful and graceful plants named above. It has been said in advice already tendered on this subject, that removal by hand is better than the application of any composition yet devised for this purpose.

1309 *Forcing Pit* Introduce fresh batches of azaleas, lilacs, rhododendrons, roses, etc. Remove pinks, as soon as they fairly show flower, to a cooler house. Hydrangeas introduced now will force well, and make useful plants for the conservatory. Part of the pit should now be devoted to sowing tender annuals in pens or boxes – a first sowing of balsams, amaranthus, egg plants, mesembryanthemum, ipomea, thunbergias, *Primula Sinensis*, humea, etc.

1310 *Management of Roots for Cuttings* Dahlia roots, and roots of Marvel of Peru, *Salvia patens*, and old pelargoniums may now be placed in a warm part of the pit, in order to stimulate them into growth for the sake of obtaining cuttings from them.

The following instructions for the management of cuttings from roots thus stimulated into growth may be useful: When the cuttings have reached a length of from 1 to 2 inches, cut them from the parent stock with a sharp knife in such a manner that a heel maybe left to them, the heel being part of the old growth. Insert these cuttings in smaller pots singly, or in twos or threes, or in numbers in shallow pans or boxes. When a sufficient number have been obtained, the roots themselves may be cut into pieces, each piece having a shoot growing from it.

1311 *The Greenhouse: Shifting Plants* Proceed with the shifting of all plants requiring it. Free-growing plants, such as leschenaultias, boronias, etc., may be treated on what is termed the one-shift system, provided they are very healthy and the after treatment is skilful. They require turfy peat, well coloured with gritty silver sand, and a fourth part of clean leaf mould. Much of the dirty putrid water and tannin that is used under this designation is enough to kill most plants, and is certain death to hard-wooded species. Therefore, unless the leaf mould is really good, add none to your compost for hard-wooded plants.

In shifting any of these plants or heaths from a 48- to a 16- or 12-sized pot, the soil should be used in a much rougher state than for ordinary potting. The draining must also be more liberal, say at least four inches deep, and besides the materials for drainage, pieces of broken potsherds or charcoal should be mixed freely with the soil in the process of filling up. The soil should be so dry as never to stick to the fingers, but by no means *quite* dry. It should also be well consolidated as the work goes on, and rammed in with a small rammer, or the bottom of a pot of about the same size, before the plant is inserted. If the soil is of the proper texture, and in a right condition in reference to moisture, it will be almost impossible to make it too firm in potting. The roots of hard-wooded plants seem unable to get hold of loose soil. Much that is far from being to the point and purpose has been written about stirring and patching the surface of soil. When plants are properly rooted, this operation is alike unnecessary and impossible. To secure plenty of roots, thorough drainage is the first desideratum, proper compost the second, firm potting the third, careful watering the fourth, and proper top management the very last point for consideration. Keep the new soil *level* with the top of the old ball. The collar should not be raised above the general level, but to depress it beneath is certain death to hard-wooded plants. All plants, however hardy, should be kept warm and moist for a few weeks after re-potting, especially if they have received a large shift. The growth of the roots is thus promoted – a point of great importance at this stage. At first, before the roots have taken good hold on the earth, the plant is easily expelled by accident or disease; but after it has filled every available space with its roots, it requires a violent wrench and the application of much force to remove it.

1312 *Heaths* The preceding remarks on potting are applicable to heaths as well as to other free-growing, hard-wooded plants. The potting of all the specimens in the house should now be proceeded with in accordance with the instructions given.

1313 *Pelargoniums* These, whether show, fancy, or zonal, will now require careful training. Remove every dead leaf, thin out superfluous shoots, and keep the plants scrupulously clean. Maintain a temperature of 50° to 55°; syringe on fine, bright mornings. If the weather is fine towards the end of the month, sprinkling may be repeated in the afternoon, and the house shut up about four o'clock. Keep the plants close to the glass, and admit air in quantity proportioned to the mildness of the external air. Tie into shape, stop and shift plants for the latest bloom, and put in the toppings for cuttings. Fancy pelargoniums require the same general treatment, but even more care in ventilation and watering. Scarlet and variegated geraniums require shifting, training, and stopping.

1314 *Cinerarias* Keep clean, remove decayed leaves, and throw away all but the most choice varieties as soon as they have finished flowering. Save the best sorts for seed or suckers, and sow seed at once for the earliest plants.

1315 *Calceolarias* Thin out the worst of the crowded leaves; peg down the shoots to increase the strength of the plants, and sow seed for next year.

1316 *Fuchsias* These must be shifted now, and stopped and get into shape as necessity may require and direct.

1317 *Azaleas and Camellias* should be shifted into larger pots, either as soon as they have flowered or when the new growth is formed. Care must be taken not to allow any water to fall on the petals of camellia flowers, for their beauty and brilliancy is considerably marred thereby. And they must be sedulously kept out of draughts.

1318 *Climbing Plants* These must be neatly tied in as they grow, and nicely trained to suit the position in which they are placed.

1319 *Temperature* The temperature of the greenhouse during March may range from 45° to 50°. In fine, open, sunny weather air may be freely admitted; but it is better to let the temperature of the house run up even to 65° or 70° under the influence of the sun's rays than to run the risk of chilling the plants by letting a rush of air too cold for them into the house, with the view of lowering the temperature. In March, as well in April and even May, a hot sun with a cold wind too often prevails.

1320 *Watering* The plants will begin to look out for more water now, as the sun gains power, and a moist and genial atmosphere should be maintained by sprinkling the path, etc., with water, rather than by watering the plants themselves too much, and, worst than all, letting water fall on the leaves.

When plants appear to wilt, as the Americans have it, or, in other words, to droop, the drooping is caused rather through want of shade than want of water. Over-much watering is good for no plants, except sub-aquatic plants. Hard-wooded plants, such as heaths, camellias, azaleas, etc., require more water when they are growing than when they are flowering A too copious supply of water when about to flower, or when flowering, often makes the camellia cast its buds. Soft-wooded plants, such as fuchsias, geraniums, etc., grow and bloom at one and the same time.

1321 *The Conservatory* The interest and beauty of this house will now increase day by day. Let a minimum temperature of 45° be maintained, allowing for a rise of 10° from sun heat, and give as much air as the state of the weather and the maintenance of a kindly genial atmosphere will permit. The less fire heat that is used, the longer will the flowers continue in blossom; therefore, in very cold weather, suffer a depression of 5° from the above, rather than increase by artificial heat.

Keep the heating apparatus cool in the morning if there is the slightest chance of bright sunshine. Nothing destroys flowers so fast as the sun shining upon a house while the pipes or flues are also in operation: this remark applies to all heated flue structures, although specially so to conservatories. Flowers reveal its effects sooner, but it is doubtful if they suffer more from this cause than other plants in full growth. In the one case, the effect is apparent at once, in showers of dead flowers; in the other, it is hidden for months, but not the less potent and injurious, except on dull, wet days, than when fires are necessary to expel damp and maintain the temperature while air is freely admitted. Lay it down as a rule, that the conservatory fire is drawn right out, or shut off by the valves when that cannot be done, on every morning promising sunshine.

1322 *Camellias* Camellias in full flower in the conservatory must not be too liberally watered at the roots; although during the expansion of a heavy crop of buds, the demand on their roots is very great. Clear, weak manure water will excite them gently; it must, however, be both clear and weak, or it will do harm rather than good, for they seem to have no power of assimilating gross food.

The blossoms, as it has been said, must on no account be rubbed, touched, or wetted: they show at once any bruise or spot of water on their clear and distinct and delicate petals. Two buds can scarcely be held in the hand at the same time without injury. In cutting the flowers, therefore, each should be placed separate in a basket divided into small compartments, or in pots filled with sand.

1323 *Inarching* Immediately after camellias have flowered is the best time for inarching any indifferent or worthless variety with a good sort.

The operation of inarching is very simple. Merely partly cut through the bark into both stock and branch, and unite the wounded parts, binding them tightly together, and fix them securely in one spot, excluding the air from the united part: in two months they will be united for better or worse. At this time, cut the head off the stock, and leave it a few weeks longer to make sure that the junction is perfect. Then cut off the branch, and place the stock with its new head amongst the others as an independent plant. The operation is now completed. Large branches from 3 inches to 3 feet high can be attached in this manner, in the course of three months, and most valuable plants secured at once. The stock and branch must always, however, bear a proper relation to each other, and the latter, as a rule, should never exceed the former in thickness.

2. Plants under Glass in Hotbeds, Frames, etc.

1324 *Flowers in Hotbeds and Frames: Half-hardy Annuals* If the frame has been prepared as recommended last month, lose no time in sowing the following half-hardy annuals. Other varieties may be deferred until next month, when a descriptive list will be given.

The following cultural directions will be found useful: Place a layer of 4 inches of leaf mould on the top of the hotbed, then a layer of the same depth of fine sifted soil, consisting of equal parts loam, leaf mould, peat, and sand. Sow the seeds in drills, formed about a quarter of an inch deep, with the point of a stick (for very small seeds ⅛ of an inch will suffice). Carefully sow, label, and cover the seeds as you proceed. If the soil was in a proper medium state in reference to moisture, and it is shaded from the midday sun, no water will be necessary until the seeds appear. The frame must not be allowed to rise above 45° or 50°, and should never sink below 40°. The atmosphere should be changed daily by the admission of air, and the surface of the soil looked over frequently, to see if any *mould ox* fungus is making its appearance on the surface of the soil. This must be at once removed, and the spots where it appeared dusted over with quicklime. With proper treatment, most of the plants will appear in from a week to a fortnight of the time of sowing.

1325 *Half-hardy Annuals for Bedding* The following are extensively used for grouping purposes, and where this is intended, they should be pushed on and potted singly into small 60-sized pots previous to planting. Some of them are very neat continuous flowering plants, and if cut back several times during the summer, form nice compact masses of bloom.

Ageratum Mexicanum (2) – lilac blue, white. Half-hardy annual out of doors, perennial in greenhouse, provided that seed is not allowed to ripen. The best dwarf varieties produced by cultivation for bedding purposes are:

Cupid (½) – deep rich blue, free flowering.

Imperial Dwarf (¾) – porcelain blue.

Lady Jane (¾) – porcelain blue, free flowering.

Queen (¾) – silvery grey.

Snowflake (¾) – white, free flowering.

Swanley Blue (¾) – very deep rich blue.

Anagallis grandiflora (⅓) – deep blue and vermilion red.

Anagallis linifolia or **Monelli** (¾ to 1) – many varieties, blue, red, maroon, scarlet, purple with yellow eye, etc.

Canna Indica (or **Indian Shot)** (mostly 3 to 6) – various, of many different colours, scarlet, yellow, etc., and remarkable for foliage. Among these, *C. I. Bihorelli and C. indiflora Ehemanni* may be specially recommended.

Datura ceratocaulon (2) – white, tinged with rose.

Datura fastuosa (2½) – purple, red and white, etc.

Datura humilis flore pleno (1½) – yellow, flowers double and scented.

Datura stramionium (*Thorn Apple*) (1½) – white.

Datura tatula (2) – deep lilac.

Datura Wrightii (or **meteloides**) (2) – white, bordered with lilac.

Dianthus Sinensis (*Indian Pink*) (1 to 1½) – various. The variety known as *D. S.* (or *Chinensis*) *Heddewigii* is perhaps the best.

Helichrysum bracteatum (*Everlasting Flower*) (2 to 3) – yellow, orange, brown, and all shades of red.

Helichrysum orientale (*The French Immortelle*) (2) – primrose-yellow.

Ipomaea bona nox (Tall climber, as are all the Ipomaeas) – rose, deepening to violet.

Ipomaea coccinea – scarlet. There is a yellow variety.

Ipomaea purpurea (*Convolvulus major* or *Morning Glory*) – white, striped, red, purple, etc., in all shades and tints.

Lobelia speciosa (¾) – beautiful deep blue.

Lobelia pumila (½) – deep blue. Many varieties produced by cultivation, but perpetuated by cuttings to preserve strain.

Perilla Nankinensis. *See* List of Hardy Annuals.

Phlox Drummondii. *See* List of Hardy Annuals.

Ricinus Africanus (*Castor Oil Plant*) (8) – remarkable for beauty of foliage.

Schizanthus. *See* List of Hardy Annuals.

Stocks. *See* List of Hardy Annuals.

Zinnia elegans (2) – red and various colours.

Zinnia Mexicana (1) – bright orange.

1326 This is the best month for increasing dahlias (Fig. 514) by cuttings. If the old stools were placed in a warm pit or house, as recommended last month, cuttings three or four inches long may now be secured. Cut them off close to the stem, if you can find as many as you want by this mode; if not, leave one or two eyes on the old stool, and in

FIG. 514 *Varieties of the double dahlia*

another week these eyes will furnish two, four, or six more cuttings. Place them in light sandy soil; plunge the pots in a bottom heat of 80° and a top heat of 60°: in a week or ten days they will be rooted.

The white, scarlet, yellow, and purple bedding sorts should be placed into heat, where an increase of stock is required. The dwarf whites will be found to be much more difficult to increase than the other colours: nothing can look richer than rows of these dwarf dahlias in ribbon borders, or groups of them in front of shrubberies.

1327 *Calceolarias* Cuttings of these kept in cold pits during the winter for bedding out purposes in the summer should have plenty of air daily when the temperature is above 40°, by withdrawing, during the day, the light by which they are covered. The tops should be pinched off to encourage the formation of side shoots, and to render them strong bushy plants for flowering.

1328 *Auriculas* As the power of the sun increases, if the weather continues mild, these plants might now have the benefit of warm showers. The light should be drawn off daily on fine days. When the weather is rough and boisterous, avoid cutting draughts. See that the plants have plenty of water, as they will now be throwing up their flower stems. The plunging material may be sprinkled, to keep up a moist genial atmosphere. Cover up securely from frost, and shade for a few hours on bright days: take off offsets, and insert in a close frame; water with care until rooted.

Plants intended for showing should have seven pips as level as possible, round and well-shaped: any ill-shaped small pips may be cut off to avoid crowding.

1329 *Balsams* These beautiful flowers, with coxcombs, thunbergias, rhodanthes, primulas, etc., may now be sown in pits or frames.

1330 *Vegetables in Hotbeds and Frames: Cucumbers* Where cucumbers have not already been started, it should be done now, as formerly described, the manure being shaken and turned over three or four times; for on this everything depends, the heat lasts longer, and the plants are not exposed to violent and irregular heating.

When the bed is made, some gardeners recommend its being left a short time to settle before putting on the frame and lights, in order to prevent violent heating and rapid sinking, from the additional weight of the frame; but if the bed has been well turned and beaten down in the process of making this will hardly be necessary. If the frame is not put on at once, however, it is advisable to cover the bed with litter or mats, in case of heavy rains, which would reduce the temperature of the bed.

1331 *Temperature* After the frame is on, place about a bushel of loamy soil under the centre of each light – too much soil at once would induce too much heat. It is an old-fashioned but safe plan to thrust a pointed stick into the bed. By drawing it out occasionally, the temperature of the bed can be ascertained by feeling it: if more exactness is desired, a ground thermometer might be plunged into it. If the plants have been raised in a temporary bed, they may be planted five or six days after the bed is made: they will thus be ready to start into active growth at once.

If no plants are ready, sow two seeds each in 3-inch pots, only half filled with soil at first, and add fresh soil as the plants grow. The soil in which they are to grow should be rather coarse, and by no means sifted. The after treatment is the same as that described in January.

1332 *Asparagus* Slight hotbeds should still be made for forcing asparagus, or the roots may be placed on an old bed; the old lining removed, and fresh but prepared linings applied to give the necessary heat. If they are forced in a pit, let the dung be well worked, laid in carefully, levelled and beaten down, and filled high enough to allow for sinking. At this time of the year, no other heat than that supplied by the dung in the pit will be necessary; for late spring forcing, brick pits are preferable, on account of their cleanliness.

1333 *Seakale, Potatoes, French Beans, etc.* The same means as those prescribed for forcing asparagus may be also taken for the vegetables named here.

1334 *Vegetable Marrows* The seeds should be sown in threes in pots, and placed in a cucumber or melon frame. When up, they are separated and planted out, two or three in a 4-inch pot, where they may either continue till their final planting out, or separated again, and potted singly, to prevent their getting pot-bound. At the end of the month, or early in April, plant them out on a bed of manure of sufficient heat to start them, covering them with hand glasses. In May, plant them out, without any such stimulus, on ridges in the open ground.

1335 *Salading, Radishes, etc.* Radishes may still be sown in frames or in the open air. Mustard and cress should be sown for succession every week. Chicory planted in a hotbed and blanched by excluding the light will be found useful as salading.

1336 *Mint, Parsley, etc.* Some roots of mint and parsley planted in this month in a hotbed will soon produce young shoots or leaves available for culinary purposes.

1337 *Tomatoes, Capsicums, etc.* These may be raised in the same manner as directed for vegetable marrows. They may be eventually planted out under a south wall, or grown on and ripened in pots, frame, pit, or greenhouse during the summer.

1338 *Melons* This is a good time to make up hotbeds for melons, to ripen in June and July. The soil should be put into the frame at once to the depth of 8 or 10 inches, and trodden or pressed rather firmly, if the dung has been carefully turned and the bed well beaten down in the making. Two plants should be planted under each light, the vines radiating from the centre; or place them further apart, and train the vines back and front, picking off all superfluous soil, and leaving only sufficient to nourish the fruit.

Where a cucumber or melon bed is in full operation, the other seeds may be sown in pots, and placed in them; and when up, re-potted, and grown till the beds destined for them are ready: a great saving of time and material is thus effected. Where a good sort is growing, which it is desired to increase, it may either be done by plunging some pots filled with soil, and laying shoots of the vines into them, or by taking off cuttings, and placing three or four round the edge of a pot; they will strike root readily in about the time it takes to raise plants from seed, and bear rather quicker than seedlings.

1339 *Maintenance of Hotbeds* At this time, as formerly, dung beds must be lined with prepared dung, to maintain the heat; for any decline below the point of safety, which is about 70°, will check the growth of the plants, and throw them back considerably. This applies to the culture of cucumbers and melons, and of forcing plants generally; but, in the case of plants which are to be turned out later in the season, it is necessary to inure them, by a gradual decrease in that of the frame, to the natural temperature of the air.

1340 *Strawberries* Advantage may be taken of frames and hotbeds which are not in immediate use, or which are not completely filled by other tenants, for forcing some strawberry plants and procuring some fruit at an earlier period than that at which they will have ripened in the open ground. There is no better position for these plants during winter than the floor of an orchard house, cool, dry, and free from frosty which preserves them in a healthy, dormant state. They may now be looked over, top dressed, raked, and plunged in a pit with a bottom heat of 50°, giving air in sufficient quantity, dry and bright, to keep the top for another fortnight at 40° to 45°. This will secure a root action in advance of the top; so that, when the top *moves* and the trusses appear, plenty of active roots may be ready to minister to its wants. After that period, the temperature in the pit may be raised from 45° to 55°; and this should not be much exceeded until the fruit are set. They will then bear ten degrees more heat during the ripening period.

Plants may also be introduced upon shelves in vineries, etc.; but a pit for themselves is the best place for them. For succession, introduce a fresh batch of plants every fortnight. Dr Hogg, Black Prince, and Garibaldi, otherwise Vicomtesse Hericart de Thury, are useful, early sorts. Nothing, however, is better then Keen's Seedling for the early, and British Queen for the late crops.

3 – Fruit under Glass, Heated and Unheated

1341 *Difficulties of Culture: Ventilation* March is a peculiarly trying month for forcing. The extreme changeableness of the weather, varying almost every hour, from the fiercest sunshine to the bitterest cold, and both these forces to contend against at once, render the utmost attention necessary. This is the more essential, as at this season the young foliage and fruit are so easily injured. Perfect ventilation may be said to constitute the main feature of successful cultivation throughout the month.

The powerful rays of the sun compel us to give air; the keen withering wind says, Do it at your peril. Both must be obeyed; but a skilful balance, resulting in a genial atmosphere, must be struck between these contending forces. The moment, too, that one ceases to act, the other must be checked. Does a genial, mild March day for once occur, then you have only to guard against the sun's rays. Is there no sunshine, then you have the cold air only to combat. This principle must be applied to hours and minutes, as well as days. The moment a black cloud intervenes between your glass and the sun, the air must be excluded; no sooner does the sun emerge from the other side, than air must be admitted. Hence the extraordinary attention required and labour involved in ventilating houses during the month.

1342 *Moisture* March winds are not only cold, but dry. In fact, in mercy to the comfort of men and the well-being of plants, it has been ordained that the colder the air the drier it is. This fact renders it of the utmost importance that every space in forcing houses should be kept damp during bright weather in the spring month. The inside air is not only to be warm, but it must be kept moist.

Every particle of outside air admitted becomes charged with humidity, exhausting the moisture so necessary to the existence of the plants, extracting the water out of the leaves, and leaving them thin, dry, and parched. Lay it down, then, as a principle of universal application, that the less of the cold air admitted this month, consistent with the maintenance of a proper temperature and a change of atmosphere in the house, the better, and that the more you are compelled to admit, the more water must be used to supply the demand that cold air makes for water. This principle reduced to practice will secure in every plant structure at all times that greatest of all cultural desiderata, a genial, kindly-growing atmosphere.

1343 *The Vinery: Grapes in Early Stages* The above remarks are peculiarly applicable to grape vines in the early stages of their growth. When fully expanded, the leaves will bear the strongest sun, and exposure to a cold air in the autumn, without inconvenience; but when young, they are very easily injured. The earliest grapes may now be stoning. Don't attempt to hurry them during this process; for, in the first place, you will not succeed, and, in the second, you will certainly weaken the vines. This process occurs when the grapes are about three parts grown, and often causes vexation and disappointment to young beginners. The grapes make no *visible* progress for six weeks or two months. They are, however, progressing within, forming their seeds, or stoning, as it is technically called. A temperature of 60° at night is enough until this work is completed. Vines should gradually be disbudded, if necessary, when the shoots have attained a length of 2 or 3 inches. By doing this the vine grower is enabled to retain the best for future bearings.

1344 *Ventilation and Syringing* The utmost care should be taken to prevent draught, especially a thorough draught passing right through the house. To insure this, ventilators should never be opened at opposite sides of the house at the same time – that is to say, the top and bottom ventilators, or front and back ventilators, should never be open at the same time. The surface of the floor should be sprinkled several times in the course of the day with a watering pot fitted with a fine rose, and the vines should be syringed twice daily. The most suitable hours for syringing are between 8 and 9 a.m. and between 4 and 5 p.m.

1345 *The Pinery* Many of the fruiting plants will now be showing flower. Maintain a minimum temperature of 70°, allowing a rise of 10° or 15° in the sun, and a rather dry atmosphere, until the blooming period is over. Drip, or too much water on the blossom, will prevent it setting. Unless it *set*, that pip will not swell, and one pip vacant in a pine destroys the beauty and symmetry of the finest fruit. Water with water at 80° immediately after potting, to prevent the roots receiving a check from the cold soil, and maintaining a nice growing heat of 65° to 70°.

1346 *Peaches* Guard against sudden or great variations of temperature and cutting draughts; and syringe morning and evening as soon as the fruit is set. Begin to disbud the more forward wood-buds, leaving the strongest and best-placed shoots. This disbudding should be done very gradually: say at five or six periods, during the early stages of growth. Early peaches, after they are stoned, will bear a temperature of 70° with safety. They should be exposed to all the light and air possible, consistent with the principles enunciated in the preface to these instructions.

1347 *Nectarines, etc.* The instructions given for the management of peaches apply equally to nectarines and all fruit of this class, subjected to forcing under glass.

1348 *The Orchard House: Temperature* In this department a temperature ranging from 45° to 50° will be sufficient, as the fruit trees here will be in blossom, and too great a degree of heat is detrimental at this stage. Ventilation, as much as can be safely given, is absolutely necessary, but in the *heated* orchard house as well as in the heated vinery thorough draught must be avoided throughout the whole of March. In the *unheated* orchard house, thorough draught is rather desirable than otherwise, because in a house of this description the trees are not yet in bloom, and a full flood of air into the house from all quarters retards the blooming.

1349 *Watering* Plenty of water should now be given, to prevent any dryness at the roots. By this it must be understood that copious watering is necessary only at such periods when the earth appears dry, and not as a matter of everyday occurrence. Syringe the trees twice daily in fine weather, but not on dull and cloudy days.

1350 *Fertilisation* If bees are about, they will accomplish the work of fecundation in the most effectual manner; but if the weather is not such as to admit of the appearance of these useful little insects, apply the pollen of the stamens to the pistils of the flowers with a camel hair pencil, or shake the trees gently, that the pollen may be dispersed and set free to do its mission.

1351 *Birds, Green Fly and Ants* Dust the front buds with a plentiful dressing of soot, to keep intrusive birds from feeding on them. Green fly should be killed off before the trees are in full bloom by tobacco smoke, dispersed through the house with a fumigator, or by means of Gishurst's Compound. If fumigation is resorted to, the ventilators and all apertures should be carefully closed, so that the smoke may effectually perform its death-dealing mission. Ants may be destroyed by pouring boiling water on the nest, or by a mixture of sugar and beer, in which arsenic has been mixed. Chloride of lime will drive them from their haunts.

FIG. 502 *Primula cortusoides amoena alba*

CHAPTER 25

The Garden and its Work in Every Department in April

1352 Aspect and Character of the Month The variations in the temperature are still very great, even in April, the thermometer ranging from 75° to a degree or two below the freezing point in the meridian of London; the mean maximum of an average of ten years being 57·82° in the atmosphere, and the mean minimum being 35·33° the temperature is lowest at sunrise; and there are, on an average of ten years, six frosty nights in the month. An unusual fall of rain in April is supposed to indicate a dry season for the harvest.

The *Aprilis* of the Latins, from *aperire*, 'to unveil oneself', fairly lands us amidst the glories of spring, 'with wreaths of the rainbow and sandals of green'. The opening buds and blossoms respond to the returning warmth of the sun, although in our northern and sea-girt climate there is, perhaps, little of that genial temperature which suggested the name to the Romans. However, many a grassy lane and green bank, and unfolding blossom, many a daisied lawn and meadow, profusely embroidered with the white blossoms of the snowflake and windflower, indicate the presence of spring. In the garden, the delicate blossoms of the almond, as yet unrelieved by other foliage, are its solitary harbingers; but, before the end of the month, this will be varied by the still more beautiful blossom of the apple, and the walls will be enriched by the opening blossom of the peach and apricot and the whole of their fellows. The blossoms of the fruit trees render the April garden a very grove of flowers, not the less welcome that they hold out promise of a fruitful autumn.

All Nature stirs: slugs leave their lair;
 The bees are stirring; birds are on the wing;
And Winter, slumbering in the open air,
 Wears on his smiling face a dream of Spring.

The elm trees are now assuming their new and graceful garment of leaves, the blossoms of the horse-chestnut are expanding in their fanlike sheath, and the cone-shaped terminations of the lilac are swollen almost to bursting in every shrubbery. Many wild auriculas are now in flower, the double furze is now in all its brightness, and the wild hyacinths abundant in many a wooded dell.

Shade-loving Hyacinth, thou com'st again,
And thy rich odours seem to swell the gale.

The biting, shivering winds of March are forgotten as we bask ourselves among the warm and cheerful beams of the April sun. During this month, in the language of Dickens, slightly altered, a celestial presence brightens everything. After April's quickening showers, the cornfields, hedgerows, checkered roofs, steepled churches, leaping streams, gladdened gardens, all spring out of the gloomy darkness smiling. Birds sing sweetly, flowers raise their drooping heads, fresh scents arise in the air, and a rainbow spirit of all the colours that adorn the earth and sky spans the whole arch with its triumphant glory.

Muttering magic and playing earth-spells,
Mixing her charms over woodlands and bowers,
Throwing her seeds in, and taking out flowers,
Nursing the blooms that she seeth not fade,
For she passeth away ere a bud has decay 'd.

I – Work to be Done in the Garden

1 –The Flower Garden and the Shrubbery

1353 *Shrubberies* The directions for this department of the garden during April are necessarily short, all cultural work that must be done in the early part of the year in the shrubbery having been carried out by this time. If there is any planting to be done during this month it must be accompanied by copious watering.

1354 *Rhododendrons* These beautiful shrubs, whose blooms are at the finest in June, may well be planted either singly or in masses in April. The rhododendron likes a loose, peaty soil, and plenty of peat should be mixed with the earth in which they are planted.

1355 *Seed Sowing* All seeds intended to flower during the summer should be sown during this month. Lists and descriptions have already appeared of hardy annuals. In places where they are extensively grown, another sowing might be made this month. It would be best to sow now where they are intended to remain. The modern system of furnishing the flower garden has limited the use of annuals. In gardens, however, where the family may not be always at home, or where the proprietor is indifferent to more permanent and durable flowers, a very brilliant display may be made for several months with annuals.

FIG. 515 *Ten-week stock*

1356 *Half-hardy Annuals* Seeds of all sorts may now be sown in warm, sunny borders, giving them the protection of hoops and mattings at night and in severe weather, and hardier sorts in the beds and borders, in small patches, where they are to flower, observing that their position is to be regulated according to their height and colour. The mode of sowing is to form a shallow basin in the soil, such as might be made with the convex side of a breakfast saucer; in this hollow sow the seeds, and sift half an inch of fine earth over them. Thin out the patches as the plants begin to grow.

1357 *Mignonette and Ten-week Stock* Seeds of these fragrant flowers may be sown in patches or beds for transplanting on a warm border in the same manner. The blossom of the ten-week stock is shown in Fig. 515.

1358 *Perennials and Biennials* All kinds may still be transplanted. Among these we may name the whole tribe of Convolvulaceae, rockets, lychnises, Caryophyllaceae, and most fibrous-rooted plants. The whole may still be increased by dividing the roots, and by offsets, or by seeds, either sown on borders, in beds, or in pots; watering the patches moderately in dry weather.

1359 *Carnations* Carnations in pots should have the surface stirred, and a little new compost added, and watered with lime water, to destroy any worms in the soil. Sow seeds in pots or boxes during the month, place them in a west aspect, and cover them with a sheet of glass.

1360 *Pansies* These will now be interesting. Water the fresh-potted plants sparingly, until the roots reach the edge of the pots. Top dress the beds with rotten manure; look for and destroy black slugs; plant out seedlings, and put in cuttings.

1361 *Tulips* Tulips must now be protected with canvas or mats in frosty, snowy, or very wet weather, exposing them entirely during every hour of genial sunshine. They may be protected from cold winds and frosty nights by netting thrown over hoops, and by mats in severe weather, leaving plenty of light and air. Stir the surface soil, watch for mice and other marauders, who seem as fond of the sweet roots as man is of the gorgeous flower of this splendid bulb.

1362 *Hollyhocks* Hollyhocks kept in pots during the winter should now be planted out, about 6 feet apart, in deep rich soil. Cuttings of choice sorts are more tender than seedlings, and would be safer with a little protection for six weeks after planting. Seed may also be sown now in the reserve garden for autumn flowering.

1363 *Polyanthuses* Polyanthuses require protection from cold winds and sudden storms, which are apt to do them considerable injury, and break stalks crowned with heavy trusses of bloom. Polyanthuses in pots will now require plenty of water.

1364 *Auriculas* Auriculas are now come into bloom, and require great attention; the trusses thinned, and deformed pips removed. Weak manure water should be applied in the mornings, shading the plant afterwards from the sun. Seed should now be sown in shallow pans, and lightly covered with soil, and the pans placed in some gentle heat.

1365 *Dahlias* Dahlia roots may now be planted out on the beds, 3 or 4 inches deep, and 5 feet asunder.

1366 *Ranunculuses* Ranunculuses require the soil to be loosened as they come up, and watering with weak manure water. A watering with lime water will destroy any worms in the beds.

1367 *Pose Garden* All pruning and any planting not done last month must be finished early in this, and all recently-planted trees copiously watered, and the ground stirred, but left rough, at least unraked. Beds for tea-scented roses prepared for planting towards the end of this month or in May. The following descriptive list of a few Noisette, Bourbon, China, and Tea-scented roses, with be found excellent.

1368 *Noisette Roses* Of all the Noisette roses, nothing can equal Cloth of Gold, Solfaterre, and Maréchal Niel. The first does not bloom so freely as the other, but it is superlative when it does bloom. Both Cloth of Gold and Solfaterre do best when allowed to grow freely without much pruning; and, unless in the extreme south of England, both require a wall with a south or west aspect. During severe weather they should also be protected. Marechal Niel will do well in some warm localities out of doors in a south aspect, but is better under glass. The following list comprises the best roses of this class:

Aimée Vibert – a universa favourite, white, small but full flower in large clusters, very hardy.
Bouquet d'Or – deep yellow, copper-coloured centre, large, full, climbing habit.
Celine Forestier – rich yellow, deeper in centre, very hardy, fragrant and good bloomer, good for south wall or conservatory.
Cloth of Gold – sulphur-yellow, deeper in centre, shy bloomer, requires south wall.
Fellenberg – bright crimson, brilliant and free bloomer.
Jaune Desprez – fawn and yellow, tinted with rose, very fragrant.
Lamarque – very fine, pale lemon, very large when fully expanded.
Lily Mestchersky – violet red, medium size, but good form, good pillar or climbing rose.
Madame Alfred Carrière – fresh white, salmon-yellow at base of petal, large and well shaped.
Madame Auguste Perrin – pale rose, petals whitish at back, medium size but well shaped.
Madame Caroline Kuster – pale lemon, with canary-yellow centre, fine large bloom.
Maréchal Niel – rich brilliant yellow, large, deep, full and well-formed, good for conservatory.
Ophirie – very peculiar-formed and unique-coloured rose, bright salmon and fawn.
Perle des Blanches – pure white, bloom perfect in form and of full medium size.
Rêve d'Or – deep yellow, sometimes with coppery tinge, large full bloom, growth vigorous.
Solfaterre – sulphur-yellow, strong, large bloom.
Triomphe de Rennes – fine canary-yellow, large and full.
Unique Jaune – coppery-yellow, shaded with vermilion, clusters of bloom, full, but of medium size.
William Allen Richardson – orange-yellow, large well-formed flower, vigorous growth.
Yellow Noisette – lemon centre, flower large and very double.

1369 *Bourbon Roses* These bloom more freely in the autumn than even the hybrid perpetuals, and most of them are quite hardy even in the extreme North of England. They are deficient generally in shape and fragrance, but brilliant in colour. They are extremely well adapted for planting in large masses, as half standards or dwarfs, or for furnishing complete beds of one colour. Several of these, such as Souvenir de Malmaison, Catherine Guillot, etc., have also a good form. Souvenir de Malmaison, a large bright flesh-coloured flower, is exquisite in bud, and one of the very best roses grown. The following are good Bourbon roses:

Acidalie – blush-white, large and globular, does not expand well on some soils.
Armosa – very free bloomer, pink.
Baron Gonella – deep rose, approaching cherry colour, shaded with rosy bronze, bloom large and very double.
Catherine Guillot – carmine rose, bloom large, well formed, and full.
Emotion – delicate rose, free bloomer, flowers of excellent form, cupped and double.
Jules Jurgensen – deep velvety carmine rose, with slaty reflex in centre, large and well formed.

Louis Margottin – very pale rose, hardy, and of robust habit, flowers beautifully formed.
Madame Isaac Pereire – glowing carmine, large and perfect bloom, vigorous habit, and hardy.
Malmaison Rouge (sport of *Souvenir de Malmaison*) – deep velvety red.
Queen of Bedders – deep crimson, free and continuous bloomer, good for bedding.
Queen of the Bourbons – fawn, shaded with rose, most abundant bloomer, beautiful in bud, and highly fragrant.
Rev. H. Dombrain – fine dark crimson, medium size, good for potting.
Setina – silvery pink, of fine form, from United States, profuse bloomer, climbing habit.
Sir Joseph Paxton – brilliant rose, shaded crimson, robust grower.
Souvenir de Malmaison – flesh, very large and full, a charming rose.

1370 *China Roses* The common and crimson China roses are very beautiful, grown either in beds or on walls. Among groups of bedding plants mixed with geraniums, the common China rose, edged with the crimson, and surrounded with a white band of Alyssum or *Cerastium tomentosum*, is very effective, distinct, and striking. Towards the end of May or the beginning of June, they will be in full beauty, and the mass of blush pink, with the setting suggested, is peculiarly soft and beautiful. By cutting off the flowering stems as soon as they begin to fade, a succession of flowers will be secured throughout the summer. If, however, a short hiatus should intervene, the geraniums will fill up the gap. Several other China roses form beautiful groups for the flower garden. The best of them are, perhaps, the following:

Abbe Mioland – purplish crimson, shaded.
Alfred Aubert – bright red, growth vigorous, free bloomer.
Archduke Charles – rose, changing to crimson, very large and full.
Clara Sylvain – pure white, large.
Cramoisie Supérieure – bright crimson.
Duchess – pure white, medium size, but of excellent form, free bloomer.
Fabvier – beautiful scarlet crimson.
Mrs Bosanquet – pale, delicate flesh, free bloomer.
Old Blush – very free-flowering. This is the original China rose.
Old Crimson – deep bright crimson of a dark shade, free grower.

1371 The whole of the China roses require some protection in winter. Nothing is better than some coal ashes over the roots, say eight inches thick, and a quantity of boughs of spruce, etc., bent over the tops, from six to eight inches in thickness.

1372 *Tea-scented China Roses* With this protection, many of the following tea-scented China roses may be grouped in beds, in a similar manner to the common China roses. The best and hardiest of these delightfully sweet-scented roses is Gloire de Dijon, a large buff-coloured rose, with orange centre. It resists frosts, both on walls and as standards, when hundreds of the hybrid perpetuals will be killed:

Abricote – bright rosy fawn.
Alphonse Karr – purplish red, shaded crimson, large and well-formed, vigorous habit.
Belle Lyonnaise – deep yellow, changing to salmon, large and finely formed.
Bougère – deep rosy bronze, large and double.
Catherine Mermet – rosy carmine, flower large, full, and beautiful.

Cheshunt Hybrid – cherry carmine, large and full; good climbing rose.
Gloire de Dijon – fawn shaded with salmon, flower very large and fragrant, vigorous habit.
Goubalt – bright rose, buff centre, robust grower.
Isabella Sprunt – sulphur-yellow, back of petals white, habit vigorous.
Madame Damaizin – pale rose and salmon, free bloomer.
Marie von Houtte – yellowish-white, striped and edged with bright rose, large and full bloom.
Perle des Jardins – varying from pale yellow to deep canary, splendid well-formed bloom.
Pink Gloire de Dijon – deep shade of pink, but otherwise similar to *Gloire de Dijon*.
Reine Marie Henriette – beautiful reddish-cerise, flowers like those of *Gloire de Dijon* in form, very vigorous.
Reine Maria Pia – deep rose, crimson centre, large bloom, vigorous habit.

1373 The very best of the tender tea roses is Devoniensis, a creamy white, large, truly magnificent variety; for beauty of bud, size, consistence, and perfume of flower, it stands unrivalled. It has a peculiar odour, all its own, and may be known out of a hundred by the scent alone. The leaves, too, are beautiful and glossy, the habit good, and for a tea rose it is a robust grower. It will do well in a sheltered situation out of doors in summer, and a clean sunny window will be the spot for it in winter, failing a little greenhouse. The following are also beautiful varieties of this interesting class:

Adam – rose large and splendid.
Alba Rosea – white, tinted with rose, a beautiful flower.
Barillet Deschamps – pale lemon, large.
Baronne de Sinety – deep yellow, back of petals rose, blooms fine and well formed, habit very vigorous.
Bouton d'Or – deep yellow, small bloom.
David Pradel – pale rose and lavender, very fine.
Devoniensis – creamy white, a beautiful rose.
Devoniensis, Climbing – creamy white, like preceding, but vigorous climber.
Gloire de Bordeaux – fawn shaded with salmon, blooms very large and fragrant, vigorous habit.
La Boule d'Or – rich golden yellow, large and full.
La Pactole – lemon, small blooms in clusters.
Madame Bravy – French white, rosy centre, beautiful, large, and full.
Madame Eugene Verdier – rich chamois, very fragrant, seedling from *Gloire de Dijon*.
Moire – rosy fawn, beautifully shaded.
Niphetos – pure white, large and round in form.
President – pale rose, shaded with salmon, fine form, large, and double.
Princess of Wales – rosy yellow, centre rich golden yellow, flowers large and well formed, habit moderately vigorous.
Rubens – white, tinted with rose and fawn, blooms large and well formed.
Safrano – bright apricot, changing to fawn, very beautiful.
Souvenir d'un Ami – deep rose, large and full, one of the best, good shape.
Souvenir d'Elise – creamy white, with blush centre, large and full.
Vicomtesse de Cazes – beautiful bright orange-yellow, with deeper centre shaded with copper, delicate habit.

For planting out in conservatories, covering walls in arcades, or heated walls covered with glass out of doors, these roses rival the camellia in beauty of tint, and some of them almost equal it in shape; and nothing can equal their perfume. They also form excellent pot plants for adorning the greenhouse or conservatory throughout the summer; and in warm conservatory, they can be had in flower at almost any time. Their *tenderness* excepted, they require the same general treatment as other roses. They thrive well in a well-drained compost, of equal parts loam, leaf mould, and peat, and a sixth part broken charcoal and gritty sand. Before starting them in the spring is a good time to pot them; and if they could be plunged for a few weeks after this operation in a gentle bottom heat of 50°, so much the better. They could then be placed fully exposed to the light on a greenhouse shelf. The pots should be placed in a larger-sized pot, with a layer of moss between, to protect the roots from the heat of the sun. After flowering, the shoots should be cut back to two or three eyes, and any weak old shoots cut entirely out. They will break again directly, and flower several times throughout the season. After their last flowering in September, they may be placed for a month or so exposed to the sun out of doors, to give them a season of rest, and be kept dormant until wanted again in the spring. If required for winter flowering, however, they must be moved out of doors, and a rest, *if possible* (for it is not always possible), secured earlier; or they may remain under glass to ripen their wood; be pruned at the end of September or beginning of October; kept in a genial temperature of from 50° to 60°, and they will be in flower at Christmas. When growing freely, they enjoy *weak* manure water; but they are very impatient of an excess of moisture or *gross food*. They are, perhaps, less liable to the attacks of insects than other roses; but if they appear, they must be at once destroyed, as nothing should be allowed to tarnish the beauty of their exquisite foliage, which constitutes one of the chief charms of this delightful family of roses.

1374 *Gravel Walks and Lawns* Walks should be broken up and turned, if not done last month; if turned then, roll twice a week at least. Lawns should now be mown once a week, and carefully; for nothing looks worse than the marks of the scythe on an otherwise smooth lawn. All gaps in box edging should now be made good, well watered, and trimmed. Place stakes to all such plants in the beds as require support, bearing in mind that as the twig is bent the plant inclines; fix the sticks firmly in the ground, bring the stalks to the stake, and tie them neatly but firmly to it, without galling the plant, removing all straggling, broken, or decayed shoots, and keeping all clear of weeds, and raking smooth with a small rake.

2 – The Vegetable or Kitchen Garden

1375 *Disposition of Crops* Although this subject and that of rotation of crops has been treated at length in another part of this work, it may not be without its use, even at the risk of a little repetition, to show how a garden, or a piece of ground devoted to gardening purposes, may be apportioned and suitably cropped. The quantity of ground under consideration here is an acre, but smaller plots of ground may be treated in like manner, due regard being had to the proportions of the different parts into which they are divided.

1376 Suppose Fig. 516 to represent an acre of ground, the length to run east and west, which gives the advantage of a good peach wall at *a*. The line beyond which it is not advisable to crop is shown by *b*. A border 12 feet wide, which may be devoted to early crops, or espaliers, pillar, or bush fruits, is denoted by *c*. The same may be said of the borders *f* and *g*. The east and west walls may be devoted to trained plums, cherries, and pears; *i* is supposed to be a low wall, fence, or hedge; *h*, a border, where late fruits or salading may be grown during the summer time, when a little shade is an advantage to them; *d* is the main walk, 6 feet wide, running round the quarters; *e*, cross walks, 4 feet wide between them. The main body of the kitchen garden is divided into eight squares, two of which are devoted to each group of plants, namely, Deepeners, Exhausters, Surface Crops, and Preparers. Let 6 be planted with (1) asparagus, (2) globe artichokes, (3) seakale, and (4) rhubarb. Of course, the space for each will be determined by the requirements of the family; but the proportions indicated may serve as a guide. Let 5 be planted with bush fruits, as currants – including red, white, and black – gooseberries, and raspberries, and, it may be, root-pruned trees. Horseradish may be planted between these. To keep all these in proper condition, a few of each should be removed every year; the asparagus, seakale, and rhubarb for forcing; the artichokes can be separated for propagation; and the raspberries divided and replanted. The parts numbered 7 and 8 are supposed to be planted with *preparers*, which comprise beet, celery, carrots, turnips, leeks, onions, peas, scorzoneras, salsafy, beans, cardoons, Jerusalem artichokes, potatoes, parsnips, scarlet runners; these are some of the principal kitchen crops, and comprise about one-fourth. Then, again, let 1 and 2 be devoted to *surface crops*, which, for the sake of equalising them with the other groups, will comprise numerous light crops, as salads, sweet herbs, and similar crops; the *exhausters*, comprising another fourth of the whole – broccoli, cabbage, Savoys, Brussels sprouts, cauliflower, kale, or borecole. These will occupy 3 and 4. As these two squares become vacated, the *deepeners* may fill the space left by them, until, in course of time, 3 and 4 become filled with the latter. The *exhausters* will have taken the place of the *surface crops* on 1 and 2; the latter will be transferred to 7 and 8, previously occupied with *preparers*, which have followed the *deepeners* on 5 and 6; and thus a perpetual rotation may be maintained, which will improve the ground instead of impoverishing it.

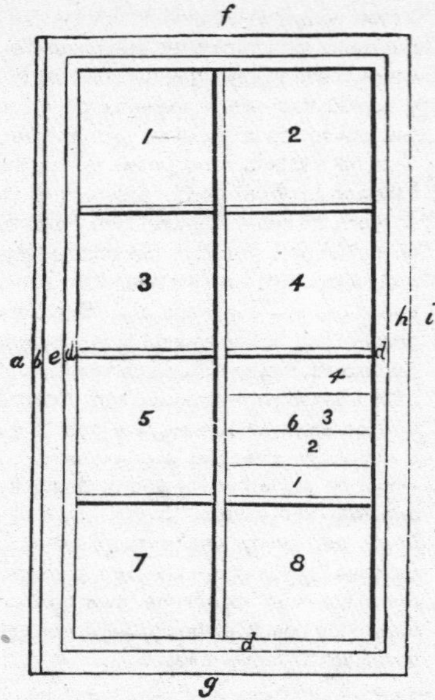

FIG. 516 *Disposition of crops in kitchen garden*

1377 *Hints on Sowing Seeds* There are two points in connection with seed sowing which are of paramount importance to the success and vigour of germination and the regularity, strength, and luxuriance of the crop, besides that of having good and perfect seed. These are, the proper mechanical condition of the soil, and the regular and uniform depth at which the seed is sown. The presence of air, moisture, and a certain degree of warmth, is essential to the germination of seeds. In the absence of these agents the process of germination will not go on. The soil is the medium by means of which a supply of air, moisture, and warmth is kept up; but, unless the soil be in a proper condition, it cannot supply these. If it be very dry, it contains too much air and too little moisture. The proper condition of the soil is when it is neither very dry nor very wet; it is then moist, but not wet; it has the appearance of having been watered, and is easily crumbled to pieces in the hand, with its particles adhering together.

A state of too much dryness seldom occurs in this country; but the presence of too much water is not uncommon; it is, however, remedied by drainage. The grand point is to get the soil thoroughly well pulverised, by means of which, with proper drainage, it will be in a condition favourable to germination of seeds. Temperature exercises a powerful influence over the time required for germination, and, within certain limits, the higher the temperature is, the more rapidly does germination go on. The soil receives its heat through the medium of the air; consequently, the surface soil is more quickly heated than that lower down. Whenever the air is warmer than the soil, the surface will be warmer than that below; when, on the other hand, the air is cooler, the surface will, by contact, cool much more rapidly than that below the surface. From this it follows the more rapid germination will occur at about 1 inch below the surface, to which depth the heat will soon penetrate, and which, nevertheless, will not be so readily cooled during the night. Seeds on the surface will generally grow most rapidly, and the germination of others will occupy more time as the distance from the surface is increased. It is owing to this fact that seeds too deeply sown do not grow at all, the temperature not being sufficiently elevated, and the supply of air being too limited to set the chemical process at work which is essential to germination.

1378 *Asparagus* When it is determined to raise plants from seed, the seed should be sown on ground that has been well dug, but not manured, at any time from March to June, but April is considered the most suitable time. Beds to be filled with roots should have been deeply trenched and heavily dressed in the winter. The ground must now be levelled and forked over, a liberal dressing of rotten manure being incorporated with the soil at the same time, and the roots then set in the ground in rows 24 inches apart, and at the distance of 8 or 10 inches from each other in the rows.

1379 *Celery* Seed may be sown during this month for a late supply. Plants raised early in the year in pots should now be pricked out and pushed on by affording them some slight protection, so that the plants may not experience too severe a check when the time arrives for them to be transferred from temporary to permanent quarters.

1380 *Jerusalem Artichokes* The tubers may still be planted where not previously done. Let there be a space of 3 or 4 feet between the rows, if a large piece of ground is planted with them, and about 3 feet between the sets, which, however, may be placed 18 inches apart, if a single row is planted at the foot of a wall or wooden fence to serve in some measure as a screen. Planting should not be delayed after the first week in April.

1381 *Globe Artichokes* These may be propagated by offsets taken from them in April or May, and planted on deeply trenched ground in rows 5 feet apart, and 3 feet apart in the rows.

1382 *Horseradish* This, if not already planted, may also be planted this month in an open spot. The ground should have been already deeply trenched, and prepared for the crop. To obtain sets, cut off the crowns of old roots taken up for culinary use, and put them into holes 2 feet deep, and 2 feet apart in rows 3 feet apart.

1383 *Spinach* This delicious vegetable is always welcome at table, and is also useful for colouring green pea soup in the summer months. Seed may still be sown, and if sown in a shady spot the crop will last longer.

1384 *Potatoes* The main crop should be got in this month. As the ground is more likely to be dry at this time, they may be dibbled in whole, thus yielding food for the young shoot till it can find its own – a most reasonable assumption, and one worthy of adoption. When potatoes are cut, it is best to expose them for a day or two to render the surface of the cut callous by giving the faces of the severed parts of the tuber time to dry.

There are better modes of planting potatoes than by dibbling, which is not a desirable method, if the soil is inclined to be heavy, or has a tendency to dry and harden into cakes and clods in dry weather. One of these modes, in which the soil is disposed in a series of ridges, is shown in Fig. 517. A shallow trench is taken out with the spade about 6 inches deep, and from 20 to 24 inches in width, and the tubers are set along the centre of each successive trench about the same distance apart. The earth taken out of the next trench fills up the trench just furnished with tubers, and prepares the trench for the next row just as the earth from A has filled up B, the earth from B having filled C, and so on for D, etc. The trenches should run from east to west, if possible, and the soil disposed in ridges so as to present a short, steep slope to the north, and a longer incline at a more gentle gradient to the south. When the young shoots make their appearance above ground, the crest of each ridge affords useful protection to them until they have out-topped it. The soil is lightened by being broken thoroughly and thrown up with the spade, and in this condition permits more readily the entrance of air and moisture.

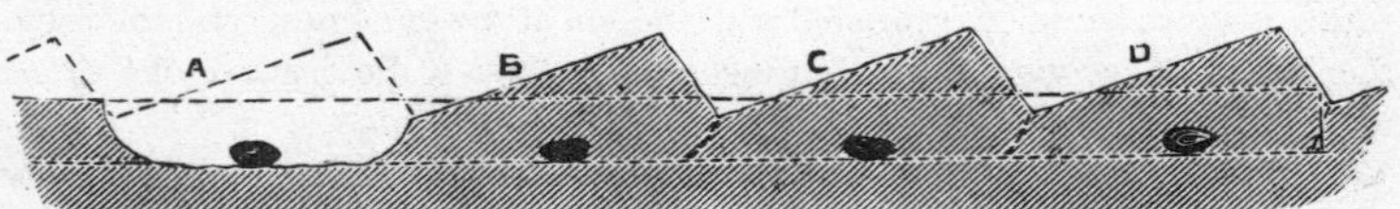

FIG. 517. *Diagram illustrating method of planting potatoes.*

1385 *Turnips* A sowing of early Dutch turnips may be made in this month. This crop is very apt to run to seed instead of swelling at the root, if sown too early, but a great deal depends on the kind of soil in which the seed is sown. It does best on a rather retentive soil, but should be in an open and unshaded piece of ground, for turnips never do much good if shaded or overhung with trees. A dressing of soot at the time of sowing makes a vast difference in them on their first appearance through the soil, and seems to benefit them greatly. The Red Stone is a sweet and good early sort.

1386 *Carrots* The main crops should now be sown, and those who know the sweetness and delicacy of the short-horn kinds in their young state will take care to have a supply of them. The Early Horn may be sown for succession till the end of July.

1387 *Parsnips* The sowing of parsnips should be completed this month, as they require a long time to mature their growth. The seed should be tolerably deeply buried, say as much as 1 inch below the surface of the soil.

1388 *Onions* Sow the main crop by the third or fourth week in this month, if not already done in March, which is a better time. For salading and for pickling they may be sown at any time up to June for use in the summer and autumn, but if the main crop be sown later, a deficiency in weight will be the result.

1389 *Leeks* For the main crop leeks may be sown this month in a bed for transplanting into trenches later on. Sometimes a sprinkling of onions is sown with them, to be drawn, when very young, for salading.

1390 *Red Beet* Red beet, or beetroot, as it is frequently called, should be sown at the beginning of the month. The ground should be open and exposed to the sun's rays, and such that no shade from trees can fall on it.

1391 *White or Spanish Beet* This may be sown now, though it is usually sown in March, and allowed to grow large: the leaves are eaten in the same way as spinach. It is a useful summer crop, because spinach soon runs to seed in that season, when this beet makes a very good substitute, and may be grown advantageously by those who desire to have a continuous supply of vegetables throughout the season. An illustration of this plant is given in Fig. 518.

1392 *Cabbages* The first week in this month is a good time for sowing the various sorts of cabbages for main crop, selecting the beginning of the month for the meridian of London, and a fortnight later north of Cheshire and Lancaster. If sown earlier, except for early use, they are apt to make a deal of superfluous growth, and grow up lanky, in place of being firm and stocky. This applies to borecoles and Savoys, coleworts, and all greens usually regarded as cabbages.

FIG. 518 *White of Spanish beet*

1393 *Cauliflower* A small sowing of seeds for planting out early may now be sown in any warm spot in the garden.

1394 *Peas* Seeds for late crops may be sown any time this month, and even later, for maintaining a succession as late as possible into the year. The medium and tall-growing sorts are the best to sow now, and if sticks are plentiful, perhaps the tall sort should have the preference. If on good soil, and well mulched, they will yield far better than most of the shorter varieties, but the rows must of necessity be further apart.

1395 *Broad Beans* A few rows of any good dwarf variety, or even a row or two of Green Windsor beans, may be sown for succession.

1396 *Kidney Beans* Seeds may be sown at the beginning of the month in pans, and under hand-lights, and at the end of the month in the open ground, for transplanting. Scarlet runner beans, the most profitable, and perhaps, the most palatable of this class of beans, should be remembered. This is a most appropriate vegetable for cottage gardens, and has a good appearance when sown at the foot of a fence or palings, which its exuberant growth, when it has well started, will soon hide from view.

1397 *Rampion* may be sown about this time, either in drills a foot apart, or on the surface broadcast, treading and raking it in: in either case it may be thinned to 8 or 10 inches apart, and may be used in the summer and autumn in the same way as spinach, and the roots as a winter vegetable.

1398 *Salsafy* may be sown about the end of this month, or beginning of next. It is best to sow this seed in drills 15 inches apart, or thereabouts, and thin to six inches in the row. The roots of the plant (Fig. 519) are usually eaten in the same way as radishes, being often a substitute for them during the winter: in the spring time, the young shoots are blanched and used as seakale. Let the ground be deeply worked, but add no manure. Sow in drills 1 inch deep and 15 inches apart, and tread and rake the ground even after sowing.

FIG. 519 *Salsafy*

1399 *Scorzonera* This is sown in the same manner; and, by some, is much esteemed. To have it large, it should remain over the second season. It seldom grows large enough for use the first year, but is none the worse for remaining two or even three years before using. The mode of culture is the same as that given for salsafy.

1400 *Lettuces* Lettuces should be sown for succession; the large Drumhead, or Maltese, does well sown at this time. Cos lettuces are generally preferred, as being considered most crisp; but any sort will do sown at this season.

1401 *Chicory* This is used both as a salad in spring and also the roots as a vegetable: it should be sown late this month and the two following. Sow in shallow drills a foot apart, and thin to 8 or 10 inches in the row: they need not be disturbed again until taken up for use, or to put in a frame to blanch the tops; but, in common with all crops, they must be kept clear of weeds.

1402 *Radishes* These should still be sown in the open ground for succession. They do best if the beds are hooped and netted.

1403 *Small Salading* Herbs used for this purpose will do best if under hand glasses; but they will do if wholly uncovered.

1404 *Mint* should be transplanted as soon as the shoots are 3 inches high; if it is to be increased, merely pull up the shoots with a piece of root, and dib them in 9 inches apart, and water them.

1405 *Sage* is easily propagated by slipping off young shoots, and dibbing them

in where they are to remain. They will want watering, but no shade or covering.
1406 *Thyme, Marjoram, Pennyroyal, etc.* may be increased by dividing the roots or slipping off pieces of the plants with roots to them, and planting with trowel or dibber, taking care to water well. Sweet or knotted marjoram must be sown every year in the same way as basil; but if sown on the open ground this month, they do well, although they are a long time coming up.

Nearly all sweet and pot herbs may be raised from seed if sown now, and some of those used medicinally, as horehound, camomile, etc. Tansy, wormwood, etc., are best propagated from offsets.

1407 *Parsley* This may be sown at any time, but a principal sowing is usually made now. Some prefer sowing in shallow drills, 8 or 10 inches apart; but an even broadcast sowing is preferable, at least if the ground is in condition to be trodden, which appears to fix the seed in its place, and, after raking, leaves a firm, even surface, more comfortable to step on afterwards. Use the small hoe as soon as up, and thin out gradually, till the plants are 10 inches or a foot apart.
1408 *Chervil* is sown and treated in a similar manner to parsley, and is much used in some families. See that a good curled sort is sown.
1409 *Marjoram*, of the sweet or knotted kind, is usually sown this month, on a clear open spot; the seed is small, and should be sown on the surface, trodden, and raked evenly, and watered in dry weather. In common with most herbs, it takes a long time to germinate; so that care should be taken that it is not choked with weeds, which, being of much quicker growth, are likely to do so if not destroyed. They should be removed by the hand, until the plants are large enough to use the small hoe with safety.

Pot marjoram, winter and summer *savory*, *thyme*, and other herbs, may be sown and treated in the same way; but savory and indeed most culinary herbs may be propagated by slipping of young shoots and planting them as directed above for sage. *Dill*, *fennel*, *horehound*, and other herbs not specified, may also be sown about the end of April.

3 – The Fruit Garden and Orchard

1410 *Planting* Planting of all kinds, except in cases of absolute necessity, should now be over for the season. Should, however, it still be necessary to plant, precautions should be taken to protect the tender roots, while they are yet foreign to the soil, both from frost and heat, by mulching with long stable manure, or, as some recommend, by laying a layer of pebbles over them, laid on a bed of sand, and covering that, during the spring months, with ferns, haulm, or other attainable rubbish.
1411 *Pruning* All winter pruning – that is to say, cutting off portions of last year's wood where necessary – should be completed as early in the month as possible, if not already finished in March. During April, disbudding should be resorted to wherever it may be needful, and to the method of performing this process it is necessary to call attention.
1412 *Disbudding* Stone fruit, such as apricots, peaches, nectarines, plums, and cherries, bear chiefly on the wood of the preceding year, and on these fruiting shoots are left from 12 to 18 inches in length. On such shoots it will be found

that there are many wood buds that will break into full growth as the sap rises, and deprive the fruit buds of the nutriment that would otherwise fall to their share. At the end of the month, therefore, some of these wood buds should be gradually removed, say two at a time at intervals of six or seven days, leaving those that are best placed to afford fruit-bearing shoots next year. The end shoot of the branch, which is the main shoot in continuance of it, should also be stopped, in order to divert the sap into the fruit buds and wood buds that are left.

1413 *Peaches and Nectarines* Peaches and nectarines are advancing towards blossom, and apricots, on a south wall, will be showing their bloom. These now require the greatest attention. If the autumn and winter months have been wet and cloudy, the fruit-bearing branches will be weak and watery. Every protection from spring frost should be given to the tree under these circumstances. In such seasons, especially in the months of August and September, the young shoots being unripened in the previous autumn, the trees are subject to the ravages of the green fly. If not observed at once, they commit very serious damage. Tobacco water, in the proportion of 2 ounces of tobacco infused in a quart of boiling water, is a remedy as well as a protection, when applied cool to the tree with a brush. A weaker decoction may be applied with the syringe with advantage.

The question of protection is one on which the authorities are by no means agreed; but Mr McIntosh and some of the best gardeners recommend temporary projecting copings to the walls, and canvas or calico curtains depending from them. Others find a worsted netting of small mesh and thickish thread a sufficient protection, while it leaves a freer play to the natural atmosphere round the trees; and many good authorities favour this view. Another object of protection in the early spring is to retard the blossoms by shading from the sun. For this purpose, canvas, suspended before them during the heat of the day, is the most efficient.

1414 *Fruit Buds on Peaches, etc.* The perfect bearing shoots of the peach and nectarine are known by their buds towards the base of the shoots. Some of these are pointed, single buds, with a brownish envelope; these are leaf buds. Next to these, and higher up the shoot, are triple buds; a plump, silver-coated one on each side, and a thin one in the centre. This central one is a leaf bud, the outer two are blossom buds; and it should be the aim of the pruner to cultivate as many of these as possible.

1415 *Apricots* The directions given for peaches and nectarines apply equally to apricots. On these trees, branches, sometimes of considerable size, will suddenly wither and die. When this happens, the dead limbs should be cut away as near the base as possible.

1416 *Apples and Pears* These trees, which bear their fruit on spurs, when cultivated in gardens, are usually trained as espaliers, as pyramids, or dwarf bushes. We have already described the training and pruning these trees undergo. In the mature state they require care in selecting the shoots to be retained, preferring ripe, short-jointed, brownish shoots, shortening back those to a bud which will extend the growth of the tree, studying, first, the production of spurs; second, to keep the heart of the tree open; third, as the finest fruit is borne on the extremities of the branches, to keep these within as compact a range as possible.

In order to keep back the bloom to as late a period as possible, the pruning of apples is frequently put off to the end of April. The buds at the end of the spur will now be breaking into leaf, retarding those at the base, but when the end of the shoot has been cut away, and the more precocious buds with it, the buds at the base will be brought into bloom at a later period, when injury from spring frosts is reduced to a minimum.

1417 *Vines* Outdoor vines are now pushing forth their young shoots in great numbers. At this season only those which are obviously useless, and especially those issuing from old wood, unless wanted for future years' rods, should be rubbed off with the finger and thumb close to the stem. The useless ones being disposed of, those left should be trained close to the wall, at regular distances apart, so that all may enjoy the light, heat, and air.

1418 *Strawberries*, which have been under mulch all the winter, should now be uncovered; the old foliage would be cut down in March, as directed; and after clearing away all weeds and useless runners, a spring dressing of half-decayed material from the cucumber frame, mixed with soot and decayed leaves, will be useful, watering frequently towards the end of the month.

1419 *Gooseberries and Currants*, pruned in January and top dressed in March, by removing an inch or two of soil and replacing with a compost of loam and decayed dung, in equal proportions, extending to the extremity of the roots, will now require little attention till the fruit begins to form. The ground between bush fruit should be kept clean and free from weeds and grass at all times, and it is better to abstain from planting between the rows unless they are unusually far apart.

II – Work to be done under Glass, etc.

1 – Flowers in the Conservatory, Greenhouse, Stove, etc.

1420 *Hothouse or Plant Stove* During the warmer months of the year, the routine work, etc., of the hothouse and greenhouse for flowers, etc., is identical, or very nearly so, and for the present no distinction need be made between them. The chief difference is in the temperature, which always rules higher than in the greenhouse. In the plant stove, a moist, growing atmosphere of 70° to 75° should be maintained as a general rule.

1421 *Orchids* As soon as these begin to grow, a general potting should take place. The beautiful palm-like leaved Cyrtopodiums should be shaken out and potted in a compost of equal parts loam, leaf mould, turfy peat, sand, broken crocks, and charcoal. They are noble looking plants. Bletias may be treated in the same manner, using more loam, how ever, for them and the beautiful dove plant, *Peristeria elata*. Plunge Aerides, Vandas, etc., in water, when their flower stems appear, until they are thoroughly soaked. Shift into fresh baskets Laelias, Brassias, Cattleyas, etc. Keep Oncidiums rather dry at present. The beautiful old *Goodyera discolor* will now be in full blossom. Its striking dark purple-veined leaves, and noble heads of pure white blossom, make it still a charming object Clean all plants when in a dormant state, and secure a moist growing atmosphere of 70° to 75°, as already directed.

1422 *Begonias* Most of the variegated varieties do best treated as half deciduous. Retaining a few plants for winter decoration, the main stock should be compelled to rest for the winter; that is, they are kept warm and very dry, so that many of the leaves fade. Now is the time to shake over the dry soil, re-pot, and plunge into a bottom heat of 75° or 80°, or they will start very nicely on a stone shelf. The rapidity of the change from semi-death to vigorous life is very striking. This treatment suits begonias admirably. An example of the begonia is shown in Fig. 520.

1423 *Caladiums* Start a few pots of caladiums. Their adder-tongued-looking leaves have a striking effect, and, with foresight, some may be had throughout the year. Keep dormant plants quite dry. In this state they are liable to damp and rot. The beautiful Argyrites is often killed by attempting to keep the plant in leaf all winter, and by watering it to secure this object. Nature tells them all to rest for three or four months, and they will sooner perish than grow.

FIG. 520 *Begonia hybrida erecta superba*

1424 *The Greenhouse* Slight shading is desirable at this period of the year for every kind of plant, pelargoniums excepted, which should be placed near the glass and fully exposed to the sun's rays. As the days grow longer, and the heat of the sun increases, watering must be resorted to freely, and the air of the house moistened by sprinkling the floor, and, on hot days, even the stages and shelves, liberally with water from a pot with a fine rose, or with a syringe. By this means undue detraction of moisture from the pots and plants by the heat of the sun's rays will be prevented.

1425 *Temperature* The shading to which reference has been made is chiefly necessary, it should be said, to plants in blossom and coming into bloom, and to those making young growth after flowering, pelargoniums excepted. Air should be given freely, due care being taken to prevent all draughts, which tend to check plants that are exposed to them. A minimum temperature from 40° to 45° should be maintained, rising from 50° to 60° under the influence of the sun's rays. It must be borne in mind that this is the temperature to be maintained *with* admission of air and shading.

1426 *Routine Work* All dead leaves should be removed from growing plants, and if moss appears on the surface of the soil in any of the pots, clear it away and replace with a little fresh mould as top dressing. Keep all shelves and stages well scrubbed, and the entire house as clean as possible, to keep down insects, etc., and to preserve a neat appearance throughout.

1427 *Fumigation* Insects, and more particularly the troublesome green fly, will find their way into every house, and the latter will infest the succulent ends of shoots, robbing them of their sap and moisture. To clear them off every crevice must be closed, and the house filled with tobacco smoke, generated by a fumigator, until a cloud is formed so dense that it is not possible to distinguish any plant in the structure. Let this state of things continue for a few hours, the fumigating being done in the evening; and next morning well syringe the plants, in order to clear away the dead insects. The smoke will do no injury to the plants.

1428 *Classification of Greenhouse Plants* These divide themselves into hard and soft-wooded plants. Among the former are boronias, hoveas, acacias, and chorozemas, Epacridse, Genistas, and Pultenaeas, which will now be coming into bloom, if well managed.

1429 *Azaleas* Late-blooming azaleas will be coming forward. Where there is a good stock of plants, the bloom of some should be retarded by placing them on the shaded side of the house. Plants that have been forced should have the seed vessels picked off, and shifted, if the pots are tolerably full of roots.

1430 *Heaths* These plants in full growth require an astonishing quantity of water at this season of the year; mere driblets are certain death to them. When the pots are full of roots, they should be gone over two or three times a week, and filled to the brim with water. The longer it is in passing through (provided the drainage is all right), there is the greater necessity for repeating the dose, as dry peat earth is one of the worst conductors of water. When the water remains longer than ten minutes on the surface, a cold bath for twenty-four hours is the only remedy. Unless the soil is hopelessly dry, this will cure it, and it must not be watered again until the ball is turned out and examined. The evil of excessive dryness is often increased by excessive drainage. Heaths, while they cannot endure stagnant water, like a moist genial soil when making rapid growth. They resemble neither epiphytes nor orchids, and some of them naturally inhabit almost swampy districts. Give air more liberally as the sun strengthens and the days lengthen, but avoid the cutting draughts so characteristic of the month.

1431 *Pelargoniums* These and other soft-wooded plants, now growing rapidly, require every attention. Water carefully, so as to avoid any check in their growth, using manure water occasionally, composed of equal parts of sheep, cow, and horse dung, and a little lime. Fill up the tub with soft water, and mix it well, and draw it off clear, when settled, into another tub; to this mixture add two parts of soft water to one of the liquid, and water once a week with it during the growing season. Ventilate freely on warm sunny days, and syringe with water of the temperature of the house.

1432 *Scarlet Geraniums* These require similar treatment to promote their growth. Cuttings struck now in 48- or 32-sized pots will fill the pots with roots by the autumn, and bloom through the winter months.

1433 *Calceolarias* These should now have a final shift. Use a light rich compost, and peg the plants down to encourage roots up the stem. Water cautiously when dry, and fumigate for green fly. Ventilate freely whenever suitable opportunity offers.

1434 *Fuchsias* This is a good time for buying in plants, and for striking cuttings, which should be inserted in pots filled with loam and leaf mould, or peat and silver sand, plunged in a bottom heat of about 60°. In three weeks' time the rooted cuttings may be potted into 3-inch pots, and replaced in the same bottom heat, until the end of June, when they may be shifted into pots for blooming, 6- or 9-inch pots being used if it be intended that they shall bloom in July, and 12-inch pots for September or October flowering.

1435 *The Conservatory* While any probability of spring frosts remains, ventilation must be cautiously given, especially with newly-potted plants and tender flowers from the stove or forcing house. As they begin to grow, air should be given whenever it can be done with safety. Where artificial heat is used, ventilation may be rendered safe by using extra firing.

1436 *Camellias, etc.* Camellias and other plants with large coriaceous leaves, if not perfectly clean, should be washed with sponge, and, if necessary, with soft soap, to eradicate the haunts of insects; and a moist, genial heat maintained by sprinkling the floor, stage, and pipes.

1437 *Boronias, etc.* Boronias, leschenaultias, chorozemas, and tropaeolums – an example of which (*Tropaeolum Lobbianum*), exhibiting its habit, is shown in Fig. 521 – will now be fit to remove from the hothouse or forcing pit to the conservatory. Place them in as airy a situation as possible, maintaining a temperature of 45° to 50° at night, rising 10° or so from sun heat.

It may be partly on the principle of contrast with the dormant state of plants out of doors, but chiefly on account of the intrinsic beauty of its occupants, that the conservatory is so much more beautiful for the next three months than it ever is afterwards throughout the year. There is a delicacy and fragrance about spring flowers that never seems equalled afterwards. In addition to the plants named last month, this perfume will now be enlivened by the lily of the valley, roses, sweet-briar, and violets. Either is exquisite alone; but, all combined and added to the odour of lilacs, hyacinths, narcissi, and other spring flowers now filling with fragrance an artificial, partially confined atmosphere, constitute a delicious odour.

FIG. 521 *Tropaeolum lobbianum*

2 – Plants under Glass in Hotbeds, Frames, etc.

1438 *Flowers in Hotbeds, etc.* The culture of flowers in beds of this description will be mainly confined to the treatment of tender annuals for transfer to the open air as soon as the temperature of the air out of doors permits.

1439 *Sowing Tender Annuals* Tender annuals should now be sown in heat, and half-hardy ones in cold frames. Pot or prick off any that may be up. Balsams, cocks-combs, and globe amaranths, still require heat, and should be kept near the glass, to prevent being drawn up.

1440 *Transplanting Tender Annuals* Plants from seed sown last month should now be pricked out three or four inches apart on a fresh hotbed; on this they will grow without interfering with each other for three or four weeks. At the end of this time they must either be transplanted to a fresh hotbed, or thinned by removing every second plant. Shade from the sun till rooted, after which give air every day, and water whenever the plants seem to flag. As the plants approach the glass, let the frames be raised about six inches, repeating the operation from time to time, so as to keep the plants a few inches from the glass.

A hotbed for this removal, made as before directed, should have seven inches' depth of earth laid equally over it; the plants carefully removed with a ball of earth round the roots, and replanted six inches apart, or singly in pots, to be plunged into hotbeds; the whole being lightly watered to settle the earth about the roots.

1441 *Bedding-out Plants* Cuttings of all soft-wooded plants should now be struck in great numbers for bedding out. They root and grow freely in hotbeds.

1442 *Calceolarias, Verbenas, etc.* In gardens where there is no greenhouse, and recourse is had of necessity to the hotbed and frame for rearing and maintaining bedding plants wherewith to furnish the garden in the summer, the pits, etc., will probably be full of calceolarias, verbenas, and geraniums. But other things are wanted besides these, and when March has come to an end, the calceolarias and verbenas, at all events, must be transferred to cold frames, which will afford sufficient protection to them until the time comes for their final transfer to the beds and borders.

1443 *Petunias, etc.* Thus will a portion of the available pits and hotbeds be set at liberty for raising any of the tender annuals, as *Phlox Drummondii*, ricinus, amaranthus, portulacas, zinnias, and *Perilla Nankinensis*, and for raising from seeds or multiplying by offsets, lobelias, petunias, etc. An example of the double petunia is given in Fig. 522.

FIG. 522 *Double petunia (Petunia hybrida flore pleno)*

A word or two on the mode of sowing these seeds may not be out of season. Light sandy soil should be used, placed in a pot filled to one-third of its height with crocks broken up small, over which a little moss or a few dead leaves should be placed to prevent the earth from filling up the spaces between the pieces. Fill the pots to the brim, and press down the earth to render it as firm as possible, and see that the surface is level. Sprinkle a little seed over the surface thus prepared, sift a little fine earth over the seed, and again press the surface with the bottom of a pot or saucer. Give no water until the plants appear, and then sprinkle the young plants with a very fine rose, so that they may not be washed out of the soil, or their hold of it loosened, by heavy drops of water falling on them. A suitable temperature for such seedlings is from 55° to 60°. Give air freely on hot days, and on cold nights prevent the reduction of the temperature to an undue degree by covering the glass with mats.

1444 *Dahlias* These may still be started in hotbeds, in order to get cuttings, and the young plants should be obtained in this manner before geraniums, pelargoniums, etc., which may wait for propagation until May, if there be lack of room, as there doubtless will be in small gardens.

1445 *Auriculas, Carnations, Pansies, Polyanthuses* All these flowers, when grown in pots in pits and frames, will require abundant ventilation in fine weather, with a little shade when the sun's rays are hot. Liberal watering will be required, especially for polyanthuses.

1446 *Vegetables and Fruit in Hotbeds* There is no necessity to discriminate between vegetables and fruit raised in frames, for the fruits that are raised by this mode of culture are but few in number, and widely different in character from tree fruit.

1447 *Asparagus* This should be watered with weak liquid manure; but care should be taken not to overdo it. Be rather sparing of stimulants than otherwise.

1448 *Seakale* When cut, the roots should be removed, and planted in the open ground, if required for increase.

1449 *Potatoes* Plants in frames may be tried by scraping away the earth near the collar. The largest tubers are near the surface generally, and may be removed without disturbing the plants, which should be left to perfect the smaller ones. Water, if required, but liquid manure is not necessary.

1450 *Salading* Lettuces may still be sown in cold frames, and a good plan is to move the frames from place to place, merely using them to protect the seeds from birds.

There is no limit to the utility of cold frames in the garden. A frame placed over rhubarb will bring it on fast. Lettuces, etc., may be urged on in the same way.

1451 *Cucumbers* Plants in growing condition require more air in the daytime as the sun acquires more power. Healthy plants will bear the full light without shading; if they droop under its influence while air is given freely, something is wrong at the roots or collar, and fresh plants should be raised to supersede them, provided they do not recover. Air should be admitted, in proportion to the weather, and as this varies every day, more or less, watchfulness and care are necessary. Peg down the bines, and pinch off shoots that are not wanted, and all shoots above the fruit; add fresh soil and fresh linings outside as required. Fresh cucumbers should be started for successions.

1452 *Melons* Syringe occasionally with water of a temperature rather higher than that of the bed; pinch off all shoots not wanted, so that the strength of the plant can go into the fruit. Fresh melons should be started for successions.

The heat of the dung now lasts longer, and is not counteracted by severe frosts, and the sun begins to yield more heat; the days also are longer; the plants receive more light, and consequently are likely to be more stocky and short-jointed, the dung, however, being well prepared, as formerly described. Much time is saved by raising the plants in pots upon the fruiting bed already going; if none are in operation, make a small bed with part of the dung, and cover it with a small frame or hand glass, as formerly described. Hotbeds at this time of the year are of the greatest importance in gardens where other appliances for raising seeds are limited. The most tender plants may be raised from seed, and cuttings of almost all plants strike root most readily in them. A melon pit, divided into compartments of two or more lights each, will be useful at this time, and will answer most of the purposes to which frames are applicable.

1453 *Vegetable Marrows, etc.* Vegetable marrows, ridge cucumbers, tomatoes, capsicums, chillies, tea plants, and egg plants may be sown and raised with the aid of manure, managed as for melons. April is a good time to raise all these, or to pot them and plunge them in the dung, if already raised.

1454 *Mushroom Beds* may be made out of doors this month. Prepare the dung by turning it over five or six times; mix a portion of loamy soil with it, and some recommend a sprinkling of salt; build the bed up in a ridge of 4 feet high and 5 or 6 wide; dig a trench round it to drain it; beat it firmly, and when about 80°, spawn it by making shallow holes with one hand, thrusting pieces of spawn into them with the other. Some recommend waiting a day or two after making the bed, asserting that the weight of the casing, as it is called, causes a rise in the temperature, which might endanger the spawn. It is as well to be cautious. Case the bed with 2 or 3 inches of loamy soil, rather stiff, and cover with 6 or 8 inches of clean straw; and to keep this in its place, cover it with mats, This will protect it from winds and rain.

Mushrooms are sometimes grown in large pots, boxes, or baskets. In either case the process is this: Prepare some stable dung as for making a mushroom bed. When well worked and sweetened, fill the pot, etc., five sixths, and press it firmly down; then lay in pieces of spawn, and top with loamy soil, placing it in a warm place, as under the stage in a warm greenhouse or stove, forcing house or pit, or even a hotbed frame. They come into bearing rather quicker than on a bed in a mushroom house; they are often grown on shelves, the house being quite dark and furnished with hot-water pipes. This is the most satisfactory mode of growing them, the other being a makeshift. In this case a mixture of horse, cow, and sheep dung, loam, and road sand, is well worked together, and placed on the shelves, mixed with pieces of spawn, and the whole pressed firmly down, and heat applied of an average of 70°. Vapour troughs should be provided, for the mushroom will not bear a dry heat. Water should be applied when required, but very gently, and rather sparingly than otherwise, and of a temperature rather above that of the bed at the time.

3 – Fruit under Glass, Heated and Unheated

1455 *April Troubles in Temperature* The changeable temperature of the early spring months is a source of immense anxiety to the gardener. From cloud to sun shine, and from sunshine to storm; warm days succeeded by frosty nights, and cold winds by perfect calms, are constant occurrences, and keep the gardener and his assistants continually in a state of uncertainty.

The changeable temperature of the month is one of the greatest trials to a master, as men will often look up to the sky, measure the size of the cloud, and calculate *time* in favour of their own indolence. It is a good plan to make youngsters fetch a pair of steps, and thrust them up among vines, figs, and strawberries, to enable them to feel what the plants are enduring. Five minutes' penance in such a position, without hat, cap, or coat, proves a very efficient lesson to young gardeners. By all means scan the sky, measure the size and observe the direction of these black clouds, heavily laden with their freight of hail or snow, but only for the purpose of being on the spot the moment they impinge on the sun's rays, and of being at your post before they have quite passed over.

1456 *Management of Ventilation* With every attention and skill, proper ventilation is a work of great difficulty, from the fact that on the brightest days the air is often only a few degrees above the freezing point. Unless provision is made for introducing the external air through a heated chamber, no *front* air should be admitted until the end of April or beginning of May. In fact, it is better not to give direct air in front of vineries until the fruit is ripe. In the absence of some better means of partially heating the air admitted at the back or top of the house, before it reaches the plants, a close woollen net, or some protective material of this kind, might be fixed over the ventilators or open spaces where the lights run down. The force of the current would be broken, and the air would be partially heated as it was *sifted* through the fine meshes of the netting. If it were practicable to keep this netting wet, the rapid evaporation from it would tend largely to moderate the temperature of the air, and prevent its being so rapidly raised by the influence of the sun. But an equable temperature is scarcely more important than the amount of moisture contained in the air. Hydrometers, although not yet common, will soon be felt to be as necessary as thermometers.

1457 *The Vinery* As soon as the grapes begin to swell again, a rise of 10° may take place, which may be continued until the first spot of colour appears. The minimum may then be from 60° to 65°, with a *little air constantly* in the house, never omitting to close it at night.

1458 *Vines for Succession* Successional houses will now require great attention, disbudding, thinning, and tying the shoots, etc. Raise the temperature, through the different stages, as recommended last mouth. Stop the young shoots a joint beyond the bunches, excepting always the leading shoots on young vines. After a few stoppings, if the leaves become crowded, take the young wood off at the same point at every stopping, as two or three large leaves beyond the bunch are sufficient to supply its wants, and more useful than a number of small ones.

1459 *The Pine House* Shift all the succession plants as soon as possible. It will facilitate this operation very much if one man places his arms carefully round the leaves and another slips a tie of soft matting round the plant, sufficiently tight to compress, without bruising, the leaves. This will render the plants manageable, and enable the potting to be done without *gloves*; for it is very doubtful if anyone can pot a plant properly with gloves on.

1460 *System of Potting* Do not follow the barbarous disrooting system. If the plants have been properly kept during the winter, remove the crocks, gradually unwind the roots, take away as much of the old soil as possible, pull off from three to six inches of the bottom; place the plant two or three inches deeper in the new pot than it was in the old, as pines root up the stem, and have no permanent collar, press in the earth firmly, and the work is complete.

Turfy loams, mixed with a little charcoal and broken bones, is the best compost, enriching it with manure water during the rapid growing and fruiting stages.

1461 *Renewal of Bottom Heat* If fern or leaves are used for bottom heat, this will now require renewing. This work should proceed at the same time as the potting, so that the plants may at once be removed back to their proper quarters. Keep the plants level during the process of plunging the pots, and after two rows are plunged, cut the ties and arrange the leaves of the back row; plunge another row, then cut and arrange the second row; and so on throughout.

> A mild day must be chosen for shifting and renewal of bottom heat, as five or six hours' check from cold will often throw a whole pit of succession pines into premature fruit – one of the greatest calamities that can happen to the cultivator.

1462 *Figs* A dry close atmosphere often causes the embryo fruit to drop. Dryness or excessive moisture at the root may produce the same results. When the fig is in full growth, the latter evil is almost impossible; but there appears to be but little demand upon the roots for moisture until the leaves are fully expanded. Maintain a temperature of 60°, and syringe the leaves daily.

1463 *Strawberries* Give plenty of air when in bloom, maintaining a drier atmosphere during that process. After they are fairly set, they will bear a temperature of 70° to swell off; but 60° to ripen, with abundance of air, is quite enough. When on shelves, place each pot in a pan, or within a second pot half filled with rotten manure. Water with manure water, syringe twice a day, and keep the plants clear of insects.

1464 *Orchard House* Unless this is heated, keep it constantly open when the outside temperature is above 32°. Success here depends upon retarding the trees as much as possible. If they start now, and there happens to be a sharp frost in April, the chances are that the crops will be lost. If a pipe runs round part or the whole of a house, it may now be allowed to move at a temperature of 40° to 45°. Place plums, apricots, and cherries in the coolest part, nearest the ventilators. See that the trees in pots and borders are well watered previous to starting, and give all the air possible to keep down the temperature during frosty weather.

FIG. 523 *Nierembergia Veitchii. Hardy dwarf perennial (Solanaceoe, or nightshades), suitable for border of rockwork.*

CHAPTER 26

The Garden and its Work in Every Department in May

1465 *Aspect and Character of the Month.* – The average temperature of May is from 8° to 10° above that of April – that is to say, the mean height to which it rises throughout the month may be taken at from 66° to 68°, speaking in round numbers. The maximum average of heat in May, taken over a period of ten years, was found to be 65·36°, the minimum 41·73°, and the average mean 53·54°. It presents, however, an increased variation in its extremes of heat and cold over April, which renders it very dangerous to the tender flowers and fruits of spring, which now, in consequence, require increased care in protecting them from cold frosty nights, and shading them from the sun's heat.

May, the Milk-month of our Saxon ancestors, is said to have derived its name from the pastoral custom of English maidens – the Mays of our older authors – of rising early on May morning, and proceeding to the meadows to milk the cows, and elect the most beautiful of their companions as the Queen of the Mays. In process of time, when the name was established, and the custom in which it originated had become a tradition, another Mayday custom had crept in, when, according to old Herrick,

> Not a budding boy or girl that day,
> But is got up and gone to bring in May.

May, however, so poetical in the origin of its name, is one of doubt as to its true season: is it the first month of summer or the last month of spring? It probably rests between the two seasons. It is certainly the month when the renovated earth appears again in its peculiar honours clad. Its mean temperature, on an average of years, is higher; but it still ranges from 33° to 70°, and severe frosty nights are by no means uncommon. It is, however, very nearly the driest month of the year, although warm sunny showers are also frequent, and under their balmy influence the garden now displays itself, decked in its gayest attire. The tall and shapely Asphodel, or Jacob's Rod, and the double red peony, now burst into bloom, while the rose-coloured double white varieties open their more delicate blossoms. The mountain or tree peony, from the distant Chinese mountains, once rare, and a fertile subject of gardening controversy, is now by no means uncommon. The milk-white balls of the Guelder rose, the lilac, and all the magnificent American plants, are now glowing in the fullness of their beauty.

> Laburnums rich
> In streaming gold, syringas ivory pure,
> The scentless and the scented rose, – this red,
> And of a humble growth, – the other tall,
> Her silver globes light as the foaming surf;
> The lilacs – various in array, – now white,
> Now sanguine; the beauteous head now set
> With purple trusses pyramidal.

Nor are the more lowly flowers, native to the soil, less lovely even in the parterre: the lily of the valley, which art has taught how to retain its bloom far into summer, is always lovely, and the marigold, the golden flower of older poets, whose

Winking Mary-buddes begin
To ope their golden eyes.

All the orchis tribes native to our woods are now in full bloom; the saxifrages belong to this month, during which the woods and hedgerows will be found highly productive in native flowers this month, for the Ranunculaceae, the Cruciferae, the veronicas, violas, euphorbias, and wild geraniums, are now in full blossom; the air resounds with the hum of bees, and the groves re-echo with the notes of our feathered favourites.

I – Work to be done in the Garden, etc.

1 – The Flower Garden and Shrubbery.

1466 *Routine Work: Lawns and Walks* Grass lawns and gravel walks should now be kept in high order, the grass well mown once a week if possible, and kept clean and orderly; gravel walks kept free from weeds, and well swept and frequently rolled, especially after heavy rains; borders, beds, and shrubberies free from weeds, and where vacancies in the beds occur, let them be supplied; let the earth be clean and well raked, and the edgings, whether of turf or box, be kept in perfect order.

One of the principal points in pleasure-ground scenery is the beauty of the turf, which should be kept at all times well cut, but more particularly when, by cutting the grass as low as possible, the foundation of a close-bottomed turf will be laid for the season. On poor sandy or rocky soil, the verdure must be maintained by occasional waterings with liquid manures, or dressings with guano, leaf mould, or decayed dung.

1467 *Clipping Hedges and Evergreens* This should receive attention before the young growth has made too much way. AH evergreens and hedges, especially evergreen hedges, should be cut to a point pyramidically; for if the top be allowed to overhang the bottom, the lower shoots will invariably die off. With hollies and laurels, use the knife in pruning, to avoid the rusty appearance of the withering of half-cut leaves. Privet and thorn may be clipped with the garden shears.

1468 *Planting Shrubs* When autumn planting has not been effected, Portugal laurels, evergreen oaks, red cedar, arbor-vitae, etc., etc., and hollies, have been found to take root more freely now than when planted earlier in the spring. If, therefore, any positive need exists for doing any planting of shrubs of this kind, it may be done now.

1469 *Thinning Out for Bloom* Large plants of some genera, as phloxes, asters, etc., generally throw up too many flowering shoots: where such is the case, thin them out at once, so as to obtain not only fine heads of bloom but increased strength to the remaining shoots, to enable them to need less assistance from stakes.

1470 *Hollyhocks* Hollyhocks for late blooming (Fig. 524) may still be planted, as it is better, where they are grown extensively, to plant at two or three times to insure a succession of bloom.

1471 *Hardy Annuals: Their Treatment* Continue to prick off annuals raised in frames into small pots, and harden such as are established preparatory to their turning out into the open ground. Those which have been potted some time should have another shift, rather than allow them to become stunted in their pots. Another sowing of annuals may now be made either in an open border for transplanting, or on small squares of turf, grassy side downwards. When the plants are up, the pieces of turf with the plants may be removed to their final quarters. As the planting season approaches, have everything ready by hardening the plants, that they may experience no check by removal, and turning over and well working the soil to get it into a proper state for planting. Lupines, Flos Adonis, lychnis, mignonette, and many others, may still be sown in beds or patches where they are to flower, watering them after sowing and in dry weather.

FIG. 524 *Hollyhock (Althoea rosea)*

1472 *Perennials: Their Propagation* Perennials may now be increased by cuttings of the young flower stalks; double scarlet lychnis will grow freely so propagated. Divide the young flower stalks into lengths, each having three or four joints, and plant them in a shady border of rich light earth about four inches asunder, two joints of the cuttings being in the ground: press the earth round the stem, and water them moderately, covering them with hand glasses, and shading from the midday sun.

All the fibrous-rooted plants may be increased by this method, as well as by separating the roots, the only methods by which the properties of the double-flowering species can be propagated.

1473 *Seedling Perennials and Biennials* All seedling perennials and biennials should now be planted out if sufficiently advanced; the others pricked out in nursery beds. Dig up a piece of clean ground for this purpose, and divide it into beds 3½ feet broad; rake level before planting, and prick the plants out by line six inches apart each way. Seeds of gillyflowers, wallflowers, sweetwilliams, Canterbury bells, and most other sorts, may still be sown in beds of mellow ground not too much exposed to the sun.

1474 *Annuals, etc., for Succession* Plant out in rich soil a good supply of stocks and asters for the autumn; and sow a succession of annuals for making up any vacancies which may occur, and likewise another sowing of mignonette in pots for rooms or for filling window boxes.

1475 *Bedding Out Plants* As the soil and weather will now be in a fit state to commence bedding out, a start should be made with the half-hardy plants first; as antirrhinums, pentstemons, etc., which may be followed by calceolarias and verbenas; reserving heliotropes and the more tender kinds of geraniums for the latest planting.

1476 *Plants Necessary for Bedding Out* Where bedding out is practised, this is a busy month. Let all be done according to a well-digested plan, in which the height and distance, as well as the colour of every plant and every bed, are previously determined; for the next few weeks will be devoted to filling up the flower garden beds and clumps intended for the summer and autumn display. Every exertion should be made to get the planting out completed with all possible despatch; and, premising the plants intended for each bed have been previously determined and hardened off, no great difficulty will now be met with in filling them up. If an early display is wanted, they must be planted rather thicker, and need not be stopped; if not before a later period in the summer, plant somewhat thinner; and the flower buds should be pinched off as they appear, till the plants have filled the beds.

A flower garden is only interesting as a whole when the beds are distinctly seen; any gradations, therefore, produced by mere colouring and shading in one bed by plants closely approaching each other in the colour of the flowers, and perhaps height too, is lost, because the eye gets entangled by one colour after the other, and the whole effect is a series of impressions so slight as to be scarcely felt – the shades of difference are too minute for effect. If you would leave a pleasing and lasting impression, therefore, plant your flower beds with decided colours, and leave to Nature the task of shading them off.

1477 *Staking and Pegging Down* It is always desirable to stake or peg down such plants as may require it as the planting proceeds, or the wind may break many things off.

Various expedients are resorted to by gardeners to peg down the different sorts of bedding plants – verbenas, petunias, etc., etc. Some use ladies' hairpins, and some use small pegs made of hazel or other wood; but pegs that are at once neat, cheap, and most efficient may be cut from the brake, a wild fern which grows freely in every lane and on almost every common in England.

1478 *Violets* Select a shady border, and give it a good dressing of rotten dung or leaf soil; slightly fork in for planting with the runners of the different kinds of violets for forcing. The Neapolitan is the best for frames or pots, and the runners will now be found in a proper state for removing: plant them 8 or 10 inches apart, water them abundantly in dry weather, and pinch off the runners as they appear: if the soil is rich and open, they will grow into stout bushy plants by the autumn, and may then either be potted or planted into pits for forcing.

1479 *Bulbs and Tubers* Bulbous roots and tubers intended for removal should be taken up as their leaves decay. Even those which are usually left in the ground should be taken up every two or three years, and their offsets, which will have grown into large bunches, should be separated, if large and handsome flowers are desired. When the offsets are detached from the principal bulb, it is desirable to give it a season of rest. This treatment is necessary for all bulbs. The principal one, planted in its season, flowers with renewed vigour; and the offsets, in time, form new plants. The proper time for removing the various narcissi, jonquils, irises, tulips, and hyacinths, and all other bulbs, is the season when the leaves and stems begin to decay; for then the roots are in a state of rest: if left in the ground three or four weeks later, they put forth fibres and buds for the following year's bloom, thus wasting their strength fruitlessly.

Be careful to give a good dressing of well-rotted manure, and as much mulching from the liquid manure tank as can be spared to all choice bulbs while their leaves are in a growing state; for it is at this time that Nature is making her greatest efforts, and will require, of course, the greatest support. Those who wish to increase the size of any single bulb, and so insure an extra fine flower for another year, will do well to cut off the flower stalk as soon as it appears this season; but by no means to pluck or injure the leaves. In the case of all bulbs, the leaves should be suffered to die away naturally, notwithstanding the beds where they grow are not improved in appearance while the process is going on. In crocusses and narcissi for edgings the dying leaves may be curled round and made neat; but they must on no account be shortened or cut off. Nothing in the spring of the year makes a more effective display in a garden than different sorts of bulbs round the edges of the different beds, now of necessity empty of everything else. Yellow, purple, white, and variegated crocuses, may each have its own edging of a bed allotted to it – the little single daffodil, the winter snowflake, and hoop-petticoat narcissus, may be placed around others; but if these are to flourish and do well, they must not be disturbed; they must be well manured when in a growing state, and their leaves not removed until they have died down.

1480 *Hyacinths* Hyacinths and tulips, ranunculuses and anemones, formerly the glory of our garden as so-called florists' flowers, are now in full bloom; and although the roses, fuchsias, and a thousand rivals, contend with them for pre-eminence, they have still their phalanx of admirers. The more valuable hyacinths and tulips are planted in beds defended by hoops, which, in hailstorms and heavy frosts, are covered with mats. These protecting coverings are now only kept at hand ready to throw on when their shelter is required either from the sun or from sudden showers and hailstorms. By this means the blooming season for these flowers may be prolonged for a fortnight or three weeks, and their brilliancy increased.

1481 *Tulips* Tulips beginning to show colour should be shaded by an awning or otherwise, but not too soon; neither should it remain after the sun has begun to decline. Watering round the beds will keep them cool, and protract the blooming season.

1482 *Treatment after Flowering* When these choice bulbs are past flowering, and the leaves begin to decay, let the roots be taken up and spread out to dry and harden in some dry shady place for a fortnight or three weeks; the roots trimmed, cleaned, and deposited upon shelves or in boxes, till required for replanting in autumn. Others recommend that the bulbs should be recommitted to the earth, not planted out, but placed on their sides in a bed of dry soil, and the roots covered for two or three weeks, during which the moisture of the bulbs will gradually exhale, and the bulbs dry and harden without shrivelling or rotting. From this bed they are removed in a dry day, the stalk leaves trimmed off, and the bulb well cleaned, then spread out in a dry shady place till perfectly dry, when they are put away till required.

1483 *Crocuses, Snowdrops, etc.* Spring crocus, snowdrops, crown imperials, and all other flowering bulbs, should also be taken up when the leaves decay. It should especially be practised in the case of bulbs which have remained in the ground two or three years and increased by offsets into large bunches. These offsets are detached from the principal stem, and each planted separately. The larger roots, planted again, bloom the following year, and offshoots will probably bloom the year after.

1484 *Autumn-flowering Bulbs* This month, or the following, it will be proper to remove the autumn-flowering bulbs, such as the colchicums and autumnal crocus, which have now ceased to grow. All these removals must be made in dry weather, and the offsets carefully separated, and either planted again immediately, or spread out to dry, and stored till August, when they are to be planted again.

1485 *Dahlias* Dahlias potted off last month, and hardened by exposure, may be planted out about the third week. If the pots are getting too small for the growing plants, it is better to repot them in larger pots than to plant out too early.

1486 *Auriculas* Auriculas (Fig. 525) going out of bloom should be placed in a shady place, if in pots, and receive shade from the sun, if in beds.

FIG. 525 *Auricula (Primula auricular)*

1487 *Ranunculuses* These should have the soil pressed round the collar and watered when the soil becomes too dry.

1488 *Phloxes* These, whether in pots or beds, should be watered occasionally with liquid manure.

1489 *Carnations, etc.* Carnations and picotees in pots should at this time have every assistance given them; sticks should be placed to support the stalks towards the end of the month, the plants watered in dry weather and kept clean, the soil occasionally stirred, and kept free from dead leaves, and a sprinkling of fine fresh soil added occasionally. All the side stalks rising from the stem should be taken off, leaving none but the top buds, shading the pots from the midday sun. Pinks, as well as carnations and picotees in beds, require the same treatment.

1490 *Pansies* These may be planted for successional beds in a north border, in which spring seedlings may be used. Plants in bloom should be shaded at noon in sunny days, and well watered in the evenings. Blooms not required for seed should be cut off as they fade, and side shoots taken off and struck.

2 – The Vegetable or Kitchen Garden

1491 *Asparagus* New plantations of asparagus may still be made, but it must be well watered, unless rain occurs. Sow asparagus seed where it is to grow, and thin the plants to the proper distance. Beds that are in bearing should be kept clear of weeds, and the ground stirred occasionally, adding a sprinkling of salt, which improves the flavour. In cutting, use a rough-edged knife, and insert it close to the head to be cut, to avoid cutting others in the process.

1492 *Seakale* This should now be cleared of the litter used in forcing, and the ground forked between the rows, and kept clear of weeds till the following

December, unless the season should prove a dry one, when one or two copious waterings should be given, especially to newly-raised plants, the roots of which are yet shallow. If the leaves are used, they must not be thinned too much.

1493 *Artichokes* Stir the earth well about them, and reduce the shoots to three, and draw the earth well about the roots. The offsets taken off may be planted in threes, 4 feet apart one way and 5 another, giving a copious watering till they have taken root.

1494 *Celery* Prick out that sown in March, giving 6 inches distance from plant to plant. In order that they may get strong, let plenty of good rotten manure be worked into the soil. An excellent plan is to cover a hard surface with 4 inches of rotten dung, over this 3 inches of soil, which having trodden and raked even, prick out the young plants the same distance apart, and water plentifully; they will form a mass of fibres, and may be cut out with a trowel for planting in the trenches. A little shade will benefit them in sunny weather.

1495 *Cardoons* These may be treated in a similar manner to celery; and may yet be sown – they will grow large enough for every purpose: there is no advantage in having them over large.

1496 *Peas* To sow now, use any good medium or tall sorts in good soils. Even in poor soils the tall peas, if mulched with good sound manure, will yield immensely. Observe the same rule in sowing these as regards distance as laid down below for scarlet runners. Earth up and stick any that may be advancing, as they grow quicker now than in former months: this must be done in time, or they will fall over. Dwarf sorts will not require sticks, and are very useful in some localities.

1497 *Beans* These may still be sown; about the end of this month some will be in full bloom; pinch out the tops of such to hasten the setting of the flowers. Black fly frequently infest the tops of the beanstalks, and this renders their removal all the more necessary. Indeed, it is the only way to get rid of the fly.

1498 *French Beans* These may be sown plentifully this month; they will be found exceedingly useful, as they follow the main crops of peas, and are both delicate and wholesome. Sow in drills 3 inches deep and 3 feet apart. Earth up those that have made a pair of rough leaves, after thinning to 4 or 5 inches. These should have no manure, as that is likely to make them run all to haulm.

1499 *Runner Beans* May is the best month for sowing runner beans in open ground. Being climbers of very quick growth, they must have plenty of room. Sow in rows 7 feet apart, or sow 10 or 12 feet from row to row, which will allow of planting ridge cucumbers between: drill them in 4 or 6 inches deep, or dib them in clusters or circles, of five or six beans in each cluster; these being 6 feet apart, they may be grown with fewer sticks, and look more natural. The Giant White and other varieties have all the same habit; but that most usually grown is the Scarlet Runner, which is unsurpassed either for flavour or productiveness.

Scarlet runners may be planted at any time in April or May. The seed should be dropped about 4 inches apart, and if a line be selected along the two sides of a walk in the kitchen garden, a very pretty shady avenue may be made. Plant stakes 7 or 8 feet high in the row where the beans are; set 2 or 3 stakes to the yard, and bend them over at the top to form arches. In the spaces between the stakes place pea sticks, to which the runners may at first be trained. The stakes should also be tied together by wands arranged longitudinally, one along the top, and one halfway up each side. When this framework becomes covered with scarlet runners, a very pleasant shady walk will be formed. With a little care in manuring and watering, the runners may be kept green and in bearing till killed by the autumn frosts. The runners will blossom and bear much more freely if the old beans are all removed, and they are not allowed to ripen seed. A mixture of the white Dutch runner with the scarlet runner gives to the avenue a very pretty effect.

1500 *Carrots* that are advancing should have the small hoe employed between them, as nothing benefits these more than continually stirring the surface of the soil: thin them to the proper distance. Fresh sowings may still be made. *Early Horn Carrot* sown now will be very useful in the autumn, and should be sown thicker than larger sorts.

1501 *Parsnips* Thin out to a foot apart at least; 18 inches is not too much.

1502 *Onions* Seed may still be sown, more particularly for salading, for which purpose thin out the earliest sowings and clear from weeds: drenching the soil with liquid manure occasionally will benefit these. Give a dredging with soot occasionally, and sprinkle the bed with a dressing of washing soda crushed to powder just before rain, if possible.

1503 *Leeks* Thin where forward enough, and plant the thinnings a foot apart, in rows 2 feet from each other. Give liquid manure to those that remain, and stir the ground between.

1504 *Potatoes* Continue to plant if desirable: no fear need be entertained of their doing well. Several good late sorts do as well planted this month as earlier. Earth up those that are forward enough, but not too much: more earth than is just sufficient to cover the tubers is likely to prove injurious to the crop.

1505 *Turnips* These may do well sown now, if wet or showery weather occur; sow broadcast, tread the seed in, and rake soot in with it. This seed germinates very quickly at this time, especially if sown on fresh dug ground. Such as are up should be hoed between and thinned out immediately. Doing this early will be of great advantage to the crop; the oftener it is done the better.

1506 *Lettuce* Sow in drills, a foot or rather more at this time of the year, especially on light ground: let as many as possible continue where sown. Those transplanted had better be in drills, for the greater facility of watering, an abundance of which they must have in dry weather, to insure that crispness and milky flavour which indicates a well-grown lettuce. The soil for these cannot be too rich. The large heading kinds of cabbage lettuce are proper to sow this month, but cos lettuces do equally well. Tie up cos lettuce about a fortnight before using.

1507 *Endive* The Batavian may be sown now; it may be useful to use in the same manner as spinach; treat in the same way as lettuce.

1508 *Beet* Sow the white as a substitute for spinach, and also silver beet to be used as seakale; treat same as the red.

1509 *Spinach* This may yet be sown for succession; but as it is apt to run very quickly, it is advisable to sow on a north border. Give plenty of room; it is less likely to run than when crowded.

1510 *Radishes* Sow for succession. These must be well protected from birds, as they are immoderately fond of pulling them up as they begin to grow. They must be well watered, to prevent them becoming hot and woody. A good retentive soil suits them best at this time.

1511 *Cress and Small Salading* American, Normandy, and Australian cress, and corn salad, to come in in August, should be sown now in shallow drills or broadcast, treading the seed firmly in before raking; these also will require copious waterings.

1512 *Cabbage* To hasten the hearting of those that have stood the winter, tie them in the same way as lettuce. Plant out early sown ones, and sow again for succession.

1513 *Couve Tronchuda* This plant (Fig. 526) is much esteemed in some families for the mid-rib of the leaf, which is used as seakale. Treat as directed for cabbages generally. All the members of this group like a retentive soil, highly enriched with manure; but the latter is best given in the form of mulch. They then throw out root fibres on the surface of the ground and grow luxuriantly.

FIG. 526 *Couve Tronchuda*

1514 *Broccoli* This being a good time for sowing late sorts, as Purple Sprouting, Miller's Dwarf, etc., care should be taken to have a good supply of them; they are invaluable in the early spring time. Give them an open situation; sow broadcast, each sort separately, and rather thinly. Walcheren sown now will be very useful in the autumn; plant out early sorts that are large enough before they get shanky.

1515 *Brussels Sprouts and Borecole* Seed of these varieties may yet be sown; treat these in the same manner as broccoli.

1516 *Savoys* This useful vegetable may yet be sown, since moderately-sized heads of good colour are better than large white ones – the result of too early sowing. The main point in their culture, in common with the rest of this group, is an open situation and plenty of room – 2 feet each way is none too much; they must also receive their final planting before they are drawn up in the seed bed.

1517 *Cauliflower* Plant out early-sown 18 inches apart. Those that have stood the winter should have liquid manure, or, at least, plenty of water, unless they were previously mulched, which prevents evaporation, and also feeds the plants. Break the centre leaves over any that may be heading.

1518 *Scorzoneras*, *Salsafy*, and *Hamburg Parsley* may still be sown, the treatment of these being very much the same. Sow in drills 15 or 18 inches apart, and thin to about 9 inches when up. Their culture is very simple, merely requiring the hoe between them during the summer. It is as well not to give manure before sowing.

1519 *Sweet Herbs* Balm, mint, marjoram, savory, thyme, and other sweet herbs of this description, may be increased by slips, offsets, or divisions of the roots; at this time they grow quickly after the operation. They must be well watered. Other herbs, as basil, knotted marjoram, fennel, dill, etc., may be sown on the open ground. They are not generally subject to the attacks of birds, as many other seeds are.

1520 *Chervil and Parsley* These sown now on a sunny border will be useful in winter. Sow either in drills or broadcast; tread the seed in before raking; thin out that which is sufficiently advanced to 9 inches; plant out the thinnings to the same distance – they are said to curl better when planted out.

1521 *Indian Cress* Nasturtiums, or, to use their proper name, Indian Cress, are often grown as salad, and also for the seeds, which in the young state are useful for pickling. Sow in drills in the same manner as peas; or at the foot of rustic fences, hurdles, etc., which they will soon hide with a highly-ornamental covering.

1522 *Rhubarb* The roots may yet be divided and planted 4 feet apart; it is a good practice also to sow the seed, which may be done at this time. Sow broadcast, and leave the plants till the following spring, so as to judge of the earliest, so that thinning is unnecessary till this is ascertained. Roots for forcing may be raised thus in abundance.

1523 *Horseradish* Pinch out the tops where running to seed, and use the hoe freely all the season through. It will require little other attention the rest of the season.

1524 *Watering* It is not accounted a wise proceeding to begin to water vegetables, for if you begin to do so you will have to continue it. Some vegetables, too, will present a very bad appearance under intermittent watering, as, for example, onions, whose tube-like leaves will turn yellow at the top, if water is given to them and subsequently withheld. Nevertheless, all transplanted vegetables must be watered plentifully, and even shaded if facilities exist for affording them shelter from the sun's rays, in order to prevent too great a check to their growth.

3 – The Fruit Garden and Orchard.

1525 *Disbudding and Stopping* As the health as well as the symmetry of the trees depends in some degree on judicious and timely disbudding and stopping nothing should interfere with their performance this month, bearing in mind that as peaches, nectarines, and cherries bear their fruit on shoots of last year's growth, new wood, both present and prospective, is absolutely required. If these operations are properly done now, and to a sufficient extent, any extensive use of knife and saw may be dispensed with.

1526 *Summer Pruning* Weak trees will be strengthened, and fruitfulness promoted in vigorous ones, by summer pruning; and the outward sign of good management is exhibited in trees equally balanced both as to their young wood and fruit-bearing branches. Any departure from this equilibrium must be remedied by one or other of the expedients already described. Remove all fore-right and misplaced shoots, unless there is fruit at the base, when they should be stopped, only leaving two or three leaves. Thin the fruit slightly, if crowded. At the end of the month all protection may be abandoned. If insects infest the trees, wash with soapsuds from the laundry, or soft soap prepared for the purpose, and syringe with tobacco-water: a little flour of sulphur added is a preventive of mildew.

1527 *Inspection of Wall Trees* Towards the middle of the month all wall trees should be carefully inspected. Where it is necessary to remove nets or other shelter to accomplish this, they should be kept ready at hand, and in order for being replaced, should any indications of low temperature or spring frosts show themselves. The object is now to search for insects and disbud superfluous shoots, especially where the trees are old and walls indifferent. This can only be accomplished by examining them tree by tree and branch by branch.

1528 *Treatment of Wall Trees* In this search, all decaying branches must be cut back to a healthy bud; all discoloured and unhealthy leaves and all dead blossoms removed; nails and shreds in the way of young wood loosened and placed in a more accommodating place, and the leaves and branches well syringed with soapy water. Should any appearance of the fly or scale present itself on the leaves, they should be hand-washed and sponged with tobacco water, or some other composition, and the whole syringed with clean tepid water. This will give even clean and healthy trees a healthier appearance. The fruit, which will now be of some size, thus cleared from all decayed or decaying matter, will have a fresh and healthy appearance.

The object of disbudding is to remove all useless spray not required for next year's branches, or which would not, from its position, ripen into desirable fruit-bearing wood; it is, in fact, to relieve the tree from nursing wood that must be cut away in the autumn pruning; but it must be the care of the operator to avoid removing well-placed shoots for future branches, or which would expose the tree to too severe a trial of its vital power.

1529 *Apricots* Stop all leading shoots, and pinch off to a few buds all shoots not required to fill up vacant places on the wall. Thin partially all fruit where it is thickly set, but reserve the final thinning until the fruit has stoned.

The apricot, and especially the Moor Park, the finest of them, is subject to a sudden paralysis, in which first a branch, then a side, dies away, until scarce a vestige of the tree is left; and this generally occurs on fine sunny days in spring and early summer, when the sap vessels are young, and the sap easily exuded by a few sunny days. In this state a frost occurs, the sap vessels are burst by the thawing of the frozen fluid, and the whole economy of the plant deranged. Under these circumstances a warm sunny day occurs; the injured limb, having consumed the sap, can draw no further supply; it yields to the solar influence, languishes, and dies. Such is supposed to be the cause of the disease under which this delicate tree suffers. The remedy is to retard – or rather prevent – premature vegetation, and when that can no more be done, protection; for which is recommended netting made of sedge, of about 4-inch mesh, with which the main branches should be enveloped. This treatment has been attended with favourable results.

1530 *Peaches and Nectarines* The directions given for the treatment of apricot trees apply equally to peaches and nectarines.

1531 *Apples*, *Pears*, *Plums*, and *Cherries*, on walls or espaliers, should also be divested of all useless wood during this month, and the useful shoots trained in, regularly removing all shoots produced in front of the trees close to the stem. In summer pruning, leave side shoots in different parts convenient for training for the production of future fruit-bearing spurs. By stopping these side shoots when they are a few inches long, the trees, whether espalier, dwarf, or wall trees, will be brought into a moderate state of growth favourable for the production of fruit, with less use of the knife.

1532 *Gooseberries and Currants* At this period of the year great injury accrues to gooseberries and currants from the attacks of caterpillars, which, if left to themselves, will soon strip a bush of every leaf, leaving only the mid-rib and stalk to show where a leaf has been. To prevent their inroads, the trees, when the shoots are yet young and uninjured, should be well dusted with dry lime, soot, and guano, mixed together in equal proportions, and sprinkled by means of a tin dredger. Tobacco water and soapsuds may be used, but the dry mixture described above is thoroughly effective. If the young shoots of any fruit tree show the presence of green or black fly, they should be liberally dredged with the powder, in order to dislodge them, or dressed with Gishurst's Compound, infused in water in the proportion of 2 oz. to the gallon, and applied with a syringe.

Quassia water is an effectual means of getting rid of these pests, and is less offensive to use than those already described. It is made by boiling quassia chips in water, in the proportion of ¼lb. of chips to a gallon of water, for a quarter of an hour. Soft soap should then be added to the decoction in the proportion of ¼ lb. to a gallon.

1533 *Strawberries* Towards the end of the month lay clean straw or fern between the plants to keep the fruit clean and prevent evaporation; water the plants copiously in dry weather while in flower, and remove all runners not required for propagation.

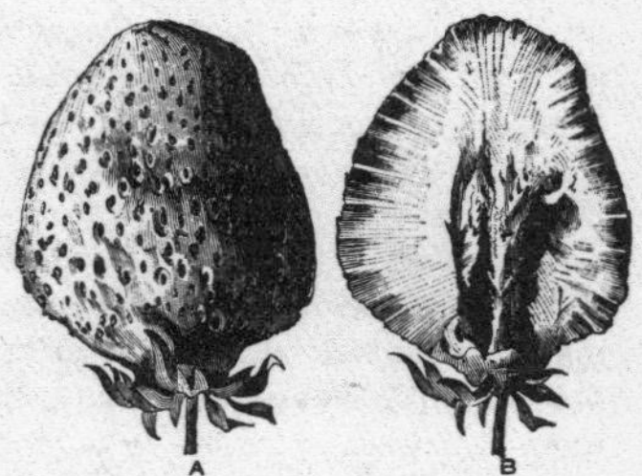

FIG. 527 *Strawberry (British queen). A. Fruit. B. Section*

1534 *Watering* If the ground be very dry, and it is possible to convey water to the spot, it is desirable to give a plentiful watering to fruit trees and bushes, or, what is better, to keep the roots cool and fresh by a thick mulching of well-rotted dung, coconut fibre, tan, moss, or any material that will prevent the drying influence of the sun's rays on the soil, or the exhaustion of water from it by the same means.

1535 *Vines on Walls* With regard to the general routine, the treatment of vines on walls is much the same as that of other trees, as far as the training and pruning goes, and with careful culture it is impossible to doubt that fruit of good size and of a delicious flavour may be obtained in the open air, at all events in the southern parts of England, provided that they are grown against walls that reflect the light and heat, and are properly cultivated and protected.

The culture of the Chasselas de Fontainebleau, at Thomery, and other places in the vicinity of Paris, is the best example of open-air culture anywhere to be found; and this variety, more generally known in England as the Royal Muscadine, is also far the best for culture in the open air in this country. Therefore, an account of the Thomery system from the pen of the best grower there may be very useful to those who wish to try grape-growing out of doors.

At Thomery the soil is of a sandy and clayey nature, and mixed with pebbles in those parts which are near the river. The soil is at all times easy to work. Near the Seine it lacks depth – so much so, indeed, that before cultivation it has to be dug and trenched, so as to remove some of the stony subsoil. Everywhere else the layer of vegetable mould measures from 4 feet 6 inches to 6 feet in thickness. This layer lies on a reddish clay of about the same thickness, and beneath the clay a broken-up stratum of building stone, filled with fissures. This building stone is easily extracted. The grapes ripen a fortnight earlier in the flinty districts than in those parts in which the soil is deeper and richer. The gardens at Thomery, taken altogether, present much the appearance of those of Montreuil-sur-Bois. There is nothing but walls in all directions, distant from each other about 40 feet, and 10 feet high. When this mode of viticulture was first commenced the walls were rarely higher than 6 feet or 7 feet. The change in height, however, has been advantageous for two reasons – first, the grape growers have been able to increase the space required for their purpose by taking possession of a larger portion of air, instead of having to bring fresh ground; and, secondly, the high walls are found to improve the appearance and quality of the grape. The walls are built of hard stone, quarried in the neighbourhood, the stones being laid with mud only. The face of the wall is then covered with a mortar made of lime and sand, and is finally covered with the same material thinned to a cream. Every wall is topped with a roof of pantiles, surmounted by a row of gutter tiles. These roofs project about 10 inches, and below them are fixed at every yard iron rods, inclined slightly downwards. These supports project about 20 inches beyond the edge of the tiles, affording altogether a support of at least 2 feet 6 inches wide. Upon this is fixed, when occasion requires it, a strip of bitumenised felt, or, where economy is necessary, a piece of thin plank. The bitumenised felt is stretched on frames of wood, about 10 feet long and 18 inches wide, by means of small nails. These frames are only used when the grapes are perfectly ripe, which is generally about September 15, or when there is danger of the fruit being spoilt by heavy rains. Formerly, before these methods of shelter were employed, large quantities of grapes were continually lost through becoming rotten with the wet; but since the adoption of the frames there is no fear of such a result. The size of the frames to be used is always dependent on the aspect and height of the walls. With walls facing the south, and 10 feet high, frames containing felt at least 30 inches in width ought to be used. With a western aspect, they ought to be even wider, in order to avoid all danger from the heavy rains. With the old low walls, frames 24 inches wide for the south, 28 inches for the west, and 16 inches for the east, were found to be quite sufficient. It is almost needless to give the preparation of the soil, pruning, etc., these are so simple. Nobody should plant in soil over-rich, cold, or wet. The pruning may be performed in the ordinary spur fashion – the shoots being trained erect on the walls, much as they are up the roof of a vinery. The really important points to bear in mind are – firstly, the warmer the exposure is, the better for the grape; secondly, that as the walls are white, or nearly so, the vines get more heat on them than they do on dark ones and are maintained in better health; and, thirdly, that wide and efficient copings are used to permit the fruit to thoroughly ripen in autumn, and prevent its being spoiled by heavy rains. It must also be borne in mind that higher walls possess advantages over lower ones, as already explained. After selecting a proper position and soil, the most important point is the sulphuring, to prevent the oïdium, a disease peculiar to vines. Under sunshine the oïdium may be totally destroyed in one hour – a result that may be attributed to the speedier disengagement of sulphuric acid gas by the heat of the sun. It is even possible to save the produce of a neglected vine, provided that the ends of the grape have not been blackened by the disease.

II – Work to be Done under Glass, etc.

1 – Flowers in the Conservatory, Greenhouse, Stove, etc.

1536 *Hothouse and Greenhouse* Like human beings, the flowers so long pent up in their warm quarters begin to look for change at this time of year, and many of them which have done flowering are transferred to cool and shady positions in the open air, to recruit their wasted energies, and to prepare for another year, while those that yet remain in bloom, and are retained in the house for its embellishment, require as much air as it is possible to give them, but always without draughts. During the month of May the hothouse or stove may be kept at a temperature necessary for the plants that are kept within it, but that of the greenhouse should not be lower than 45° or higher than 50° during the month, an equality of temperature being carefully maintained, as sudden fluctuations are always harmful to flowers. Plants must be freely watered, and sprinkling and syringing the house in all parts frequently resorted to, in order to keep the air moist and cool. With regard to ventilation, the amount of air given must always depend on the temperature of the external air: for example, if it be 40°, the house should be kept closed; if 45°, air may be admitted freely; and if 50°, all the ventilating sashes may be put open, provided always that there is no strong wind blowing at the time.

1537 *Azaleas* Azaleas as they go out of bloom should be attended to, the old flowers and seed vessels picked off. Should they require repotting, it should be done when the new growth begins; the strong shoots of young plants stopped, except one, to form a centre for a tall pyramidal-shaped plant, the best form for this beautiful tribe of flowering plants.

1538 *Pelargoniums* These, when trussing up for flowering, require particular attention. Tie out the shoots as far apart as possible, to admit air freely to the heart of the plant, keeping the pot covered to its rim with foliage; give liquid manure two or three times a week, and fumigate for protection from the green fly; give all the ventilation possible, and water sufficiently to prevent the lower foliage losing colour.

1539 *Scarlet Geraniums* These should be encouraged to grow by liberal shifting, and when established water freely, giving liquid manure to those fully rooted. Stop those that are growing freely, that they may become compact and bushy plants.

1540 *Fuchsias*, like geraniums, require liberal shifting in order to grow them properly. Select strong plants of either, and shift them into a sufficiently large pot filled with a good rich compost, and, if convenient, place them in a gentle bottom heat. Shade them from the sun, and syringe occasionally, to keep up a moist atmosphere. If they are required to be large plants, pinch out the first flower buds and place stakes a foot higher than the plants, to tie them to as they grow. When well established, give liquid manure and ample ventilation during the day; but shut up early to promote vigorous growth.

1541 *Calceolarias* Herbaceous calceolarias, either in flower or coming into bloom, require watering freely. Pick off all decayed leaves from calceolarias and other shrubby plants, and peg down, to furnish the surface of the pots.

1542 *Heliotropes, Alonsoas, etc.* These, like fuchsias, require liberal shifting to enable them to grow well and make fine plants. The treatment should be precisely the same, due regard being had to the different habits of the different plants.

1543 *Heaths* These, with epacrises, ferns, lycopodiums, and any other greenhouse plants that appear to require it, may now be shifted, as it is a good season for thus treating any that seem to require more root room.

1544 *Hyacinths, Tulips, etc.* These bulbs and others that show signs of fading may be removed out of doors as soon as they have done flowering, and the contents of the pots emptied out and placed – soil and all – in the ground, to allow the leaves to die away, and the bulbs to recover themselves for the next year.

Bulbs that have been flowered under glass naturally have more taken out of them than if they had bloomed in the ordinary way; but if placed in the earth as enjoined they will form nice clumps for the garden, and in two or three years' time recover themselves and send up nice trusses of flowers.

1545 *Coronillas and Cytisuses* These plants will now be in bloom, and should be placed well in the light, and have a good supply of air. A look out must be kept for the appearance of green fly on them, which must be immediately checked by fumigation.

1546 *Chinese Primroses* When these have finished flowering, keep close for a short time, and when the young growth has appeared, and is sufficiently large, take off the offsets, or shoots, and pot separately in small pots, well drained, in a compost of peaty loam and silver sand. Keep the cuttings in a close pit or frame, until well rooted, when they may be shifted into larger pots.

1547 *The Greenhouse in Summer* If the greenhouse is not much used during the summer months – and this is frequently the case with small houses found in small gardens – advantage should be taken of the temporary absence of the plants to scrub, cleanse, and newly paint the exterior and interior before the return of its inmates.

It by no means follows that the greenhouse must of necessity remain empty during the summer season. It has been well said that 'all glass houses in villa gardens should have one or more creepers or strong growing plants on the roof, such as *Passiflora caerulea*, *Dolichos Agnosus*, some of the clematises, tacsonias, such as *Van Volxemii*, *Mandevillea suaveolens*, *Cobaea scandens variegata*, or even jasmines, tall fuchsias, myrtles, *Plumbago capensis*, and heliotropes. These should be encouraged to grow freely, and if a few hanging baskets of *Lobelia speciosa* and *Paxtonii*, fuchsias, thunbergias, petunias, ivy-leaved pelargoniums, achimenes, and ferns are suspended from the roof, the whole will have a pleasing effect without much trouble. A good deal may be done to furnish a house with even commoner things than these, such as maurandyas, canary creepers, tropaeolums, convolvolus major, ipomaeas, verbenas, petunias, sedums, saxifrages, echeverias, and such annuals as nemophilas of sorts.'

1548 *The Conservatory* A watchful eye must now be kept on all house plants for insects, or the labours of months, perhaps even years, will be lost. Ply the syringe diligently upon all plants not in actual bloom, to keep away the red spider; wash off the scale with soft soap, and fumigate for aphis and thrips. Where fumigation is necessary for a few plants only, perhaps they can be removed to a close room and subjected to that process. The house must be kept thoroughly ventilated and moist.

1549 *Roses, etc.* The occupants of the greenhouse are now being transferred to the conservatory, rendering its appearance gay and lively. Roses especially will be coming forward from the forcing houses.

1550 *Camellias* Camellias, their season of bloom being past, are now in their full growth, and will be benefitted by being shaded from the bright sunshine. An application of weak manure water will now be of great use to them if the surface soil is getting dry. Those that require it should now be transferred to larger pots. All of them, whether shifted or not, should be placed in a cool and shady part of the house till their growth is finished, and the buds for next year's blooms formed on the ends of the shoots. To complete their growth, camellias may be taken from the conservatory into a cool house or even into the open air.

The camellia is, perhaps, the most beautiful flowering shrub which enters the conservatory; its dark glossy leaves are beyond description magnificent when well grown, and are almost as attractive as the plant in flower. Every year the collections are enriched with some new variety which surpasses its predecessors; but it is also important to preserve the few old favourites, by inarching them on strong, healthy plants, bearing inferior sorts, a process which is best performed while both are in vigorous growth after flowering. According to Glenny, a perfect camellia should be round in outline, the petals smooth on the edges, and thick and firm in texture; each row of petals should rise sufficiently above the other to form a globular face; and, as a consequence, perfect symmetry, uniformity, and order should pervade the plant. In order to secure these points, the plant should be grown bushy and short-jointed, shrubby, and with foliage compact and close down to the rim of the pot; the blooms encouraged at the end of the shoots fairly beyond the foliage, which should conceal the stems and present a bright surface of dark green.

1551 *Climbing Plants* Climbers must now be attended to, kept from confusion and from intermingling with each other, and neatly trained.

1552 *Lily of the Valley* By a little management now, that universal favourite, the Lily of the Valley, may be retarded in its bloom till June. Keep the pots perfectly dry and in a cool, shady place until their natural season is past; by watering they soon come into foliage and flower, their white bells being especially welcome among the dazzling and gay-coloured flowers of June.

2 – Plants under Glass in Hotbeds, Frames, etc.

1553 *Flowers in Hotbeds, etc. – Tender Annuals* Cockscombs, balsams, amaranths, egg plants, and others, wanted early or in large plants, should now be shifted to another hotbed previously prepared for them, either on the surface of the ground, or in a trench of the size of the frame. When ready, plunge the pot into the soil, cover the bottom with the proper drainage, and half fill it with fresh compost; then take the plant from the old pot with its ball of earth, and place it in the centre, filling it in all round with fresh earth to within half an inch of the top, and water moderately. When the lights are put on, tilt them a little for ventilation, and to let the steam escape, and shade from the noonday sun. As the plants increase in height, raise the frame a little: many expedients for doing so will readily present themselves to a thinking man.

1554 *Celosias, Coxcombs, etc.* These always do best when plunged in heat and grown in a frame or shallow pit. Advantage should be taken of a frame from which early vegetables have been removed for growing these with balsams and similar plants, the hotbed having been relined, and the old soil removed and new soil introduced.

1555 *Bedding Stock* Frames are also excellent for hardening off all sorts of bedding stock for the flower garden; the lights can be pulled quite off, and the plants are thus inured gradually to the open air.

1556 *Half-hardy Annuals* Those intended for beds and borders should now be planted out in the ground, others potted or pricked out on a slight hotbed; and those pricked out last month will now be fit to transplant, having been gradually inured to the open air; for this purpose let them be taken up with the roots entire, and carefully planted with their ball of earth in the places where they are to remain. Ten-week stocks, mignonette, and China asters, may still be sown in a bed or border of rich ground; but a gentle hotbed will bring them forward so as to flower a fortnight earlier.

1557 *Tuberoses* Tuberoses planted now will bloom in autumn if the pots are plunged in a hotbed: they require no water till the roots begin to push, when they should be watered every second day.

1558 *Auriculas, etc.* Pits and frames that have been cleared of tender and half-hardy annuals, arid which are otherwise unoccupied, may be devoted to the propagation of auriculas, polyanthuses, etc., from offsets taken from the old plants, or even by seeds.

1559 *Vegetables and Fruit in Hotbeds* Hotbeds may still be made for starting cucumbers and melons with greater certainty of obtaining fruit, and also with far less labour and material than formerly, the weather being much warmer, and the sun aiding by his rays the efforts of the cultivator; but the same directions apply now as before for making the beds, excepting that they need not be quite so high; 3 feet or rather more will be sufficient.

Beware of building hotbeds with long or insufficiently-prepared dung: the violence with which it ferments will destroy the plants or lay the foundation of a weak, sickly growth, accompanied by mildew and other pests. Great caution is necessary, because over-heating is more likely to occur, and is less easily detected now than in colder weather. Wait a week, or even two, rather than build with insufficiently-prepared dung. Sow the seed and raise the plants as already directed, and treat in nearly all respects in the manner described.

1560 *Cucumbers: Shading and Repotting* Shading will be necessary for newly-removed plants, if the sun is powerful; but plants can be repotted, or planted in such a manner that they do not in the least miss the moving: let the pots be thoroughly clean before using them, and the plants will turn out without breaking the ball of earth or disturbing the roots.

1561 *Ventilation* Give plenty of air to growing plants, particularly in sunny weather. Neither cucumbers nor melons should be shaded; it is necessary that the stems be matured and ripened, in order to secure a good bearing condition; plants that are vigorous and healthy will bear the full light of the sun, if air is admitted proportioned to its influence.

1562 *Pinching Back and Watering* Attend well to pinching back under-growth, and pegging down the stems; they will root at every joint by so doing, and continue bearing much longer. Water must be given more freely as the weather gets warmer; but see that the plants are not chilled, which will be the case if the water is not of a temperature nearly equal to that of the bed.

1563 *Closing Frames* Shut up the lights about 4 or 5 p.m., and open as early in the morning as the weather will permit, and water before closing in preference to other times, as during the night the plants revel in a moist, dewy atmosphere.

1564 *Melons* The principal summer crop of melons should be got out this month; and here the ordinary melon pit will be brought into requisition.

Let a good quantity of well-prepared dung be ready. The pit should be about 4 feet deep in front, rising at an angle of 45°, or thereabouts, of the most simple construction, no other appliances being necessary; but it should be broad and roomy, both on account of holding sufficient dung to maintain a lasting heat, and also that the plants may have sufficient room to trail; but they must not be allowed to ramble at pleasure, but kept within bounds by stopping and pinching. Let the dung be thrown in evenly, and worked about with the fork, so that it may not sink more in one place than another; allow it to settle; throw on 6 or 8 inches of good loamy soil, which tread over. When of the right temperature (about 80°) the plants may be put in, settled with warm water, and afterwards watered about twice a week, but not overhead when about setting the fruit; stir the soil and pour it between the roots at that time.

1565 *Fertilisation and Management* Bees will find their way into pits and frames at this time of the year, and fertilise the fruit blossoms, although some growers, to make doubly sure, still perform that task. Melons in full growth must have plenty of fresh air to insure that dark healthy greenness in the foliage indicative of vigour in these plants. Close before the air cools too much, and open in the morning before the steam shows on the glass: both are important, because, if the lights are left open late, the air inside is chilled, and rendered unsuited for healthy respiration; whereas, in the morning, if kept closed too long, the plants sweat, and are less able to bear the sunlight. Shading is unnecessary, except in case of fresh planting: if properly treated in other respects, they will be able to bear the sun's rays.

1566 *Watering* Melons now swelling will require a moderate amount of water. If the plants are growing in mere loam, liquid manure should be given. Be particular that the bottom is maintained at a steady point; a deficiency or excess of heat at this stage would most materially interfere with the swelling of the fruit. To preserve the soil in a medium state of dryness, and to save frequent waterings, the surface of the bed may be covered with common flat tiles or broken brickbats. Great attention must be paid to preserve the principal leaves from injury.

1567 *Melons on Trellises* The fruit of plants growing on trellises should be placed on a thin piece of board suspended under the plants. After the fruit is three parts swelled, a fresh growth may be permitted if the plants are intended to produce a second crop.

Cucumbers and melons may be grown under hand glasses, if managed in some such method as the following. The plants are supposed to be raised in March or April, and potted singly or in pairs, and kept growing till the beginning of May. A trench is marked out, 4 feet wide, and dug out to the depth of 15 or 18 inches, throwing the earth equally on each side; then throw in dung which has been previously prepared, sufficient to form a bed at least 3 feet deep; on this throw hills of soil – if good garden soil, that thrown out of the trench will do – at intervals of 4 feet from each other. The only reason for making small hills of 8 inches high or so, is to avoid the rapid sinking consequent upon adding too great a weight all at once, which would cause a proportionate rise in temperature – a circumstance to be avoided, because the greater the heat the sooner it is over. Place a hand glass on each hill – those with iron frames and portable tops are best. When the rank heat has passed, put in the plants, two under each hand glass, and shade if necessary. When the fibres begin to appear through the soil, add more earth till the whole is level. The heat is maintained by placing more dung, first on one side and then on the other. By that time the weather will be sufficiently warm to keep them growing. As they begin to trail, lift the lights on bricks or inverted flower pots, before they run any length. It is advisable to mulch with light litter; watering will be sometimes necessary, but it should be administered warm, and not too often; stopping and pinching must also be attended to. If several ridges are ranged together, leaving 4 feet clear between, this can be filled in with proper dung, and the whole levelled for the plants to trail on.

1568 *Vegetable Marrows* Vegetable marrows and gourds may be planted under hand lights, in somewhat the same manner as that described above, if done before the last week in this month; but let the bed be broader than for cucumbers and melons, and not quite so high, placing about a foot of soil on it; all that is necessary is a slight heat to start them, and covering with hand lights.

1569 *Renewal of Frames for Tomatoes, Capsicums, etc.* Frame potatoes, carrots, cauliflowers, etc., will be fit for the table this month, and may be replaced by any of the above, taking out the old soil and replacing it with fresh, and applying new linings. Such are also very useful for growing capsicums and tomatoes, either for fruiting or merely preparatorily to planting them under a wall; in either case they should be grown in pots.

3 – Fruit under Glass, Heated and Unheated.

1570 *Red Spider* The great enemies of fruit-forcing are insects. Strict watch must now be kept for the red spider; if allowed to establish itself on the vines now beginning to ripen their fruit, it will seriously compromise next year's crop. The thrip is a still more insidious enemy, and its destruction is both difficult and expensive. On large-leaved plants, such as the vine, if not very numerous, it may be kept down by carefully washing the infected leaves with weak tobacco water, using a soft sponge for the purpose, that the leaves may not be injured; but on peaches, strawberries, and even when numerous on the vine, nothing will serve to destroy them but repeated fumigations with tobacco.

1571 *Brown Scale* The brown scale is sometimes troublesome to peaches, and should be brushed off with a small painter's brush dipped in strong soapsuds; but this pest seldom occurs if the proper dressing were applied to the trees before forcing. French beans, strawberries, and the like, must be removed from houses occupied by other crops as early as possible, as they are generally the means of introducing some of these insect pests.

1572 *The Vinery – Earlier Crops* The earlier crops now coming forward will be colouring: they must be kept perfectly dry, and have as much air as can be given safely, the temperature of the house being maintained at 65° or thereabouts. The most important part of the vine's growth is between the breaking and the setting of the fruit; for the formation of sound, healthy wood and perfect bunches, they should be assisted by artificial means during that stage of their growth.

When the grapes in the early house are cut, great care should be taken to preserve the foliage in a healthy condition for the next three months, by frequent syringing, to keep down the red spider, which the dry air of the house during the ripening of the fruit will have encouraged. The success of next season's crop will mainly depend on this after-treatment. If the foliage is unhealthy, or the vines weakly, and new wood is required to furnish healthy leaves, the growth should be stopped when three or four joints are formed. Abundance of air and light are indispensable auxiliaries. Keep the houses containing grapes ripe or ripening very dry, and admit air liberally.

1573 *Later Crops* Hamburgs, and the more hardy grapes, will require to be kept near 65° as a night temperature as they approach the time of flowering; but the more delicate varieties will require an additional 5° as they get into bloom; and this heat should be maintained till the berries are wholly set, when a slight diminution of temperature may take place, according to the time when the crop is wanted.

1574 *Management of Growing Vines* Regulate the growing vines so as to keep them as evenly balanced as possible. To effect this, keep the lower spurs on a par with the upper ones, and allow them to grow for some time before they are stopped; this will help to counteract the flow of sap upwards, and to balance the growth of the tree. Thinning, stopping, and tying in should now be done daily, watering freely, and some sorts with more delicate foliage require shading for a few hours about noon. About the middle or end of the month remove any fermenting material which may have been left on the borders of the early houses, and give a dressing of decayed turf or rotten dung, spreading it over the surface to preserve the roots.

1575 *Vines in Pots* Where it is intended to grow vines in pots, select the necessary plants now; those raised from last year's eyes being best for forcing. Cut them down and pot them in 12- or 14-inch pots, using a compost composed of good turfy loam, mixed with a little rotted dung. Place them in a cool house or pit to break; afterwards place them in a house where they can be trained near to the glass.

1576 *The Pinery* Keep the atmosphere of the swelling fruit humid, and the earth about the roots moderately moist, using occasionally weak manure water. Where extra heavy fruit is desired, all suckers should be removed as they appear. On warm afternoons syringe copiously, and close up with a temperature of 90°, giving air again towards evening. When there are indications of changing colour, withhold water, and see that the bottom heat is kept steady at about 85°.

1577 *Pines for Autumn Fruiting* The plants intended for autumn fruiting should now be shifted into their fruiting pots. The best pines for swelling their fruit in winter are the Smooth-leaved Cayenne (Fig. 528) and the Black Jamaica, with a few Queens. To insure these showing fruit within the next two months, it will be necessary either to remove them into a house with a drier atmosphere, or to apply it to them where they are growing. They should now have filled their pots with roots, and should have larger pots without delay. Let the pots be large enough to allow a good portion of turfy loam round the ball; pot them firmly, and rather deeper than the previous potting. On plunging them afresh, allow them considerably more room, and bring them near the glass.

1578 *Pines in Open Beds* Pines planted out in open beds must also have the roots kept in a moist state by waterings, which at this period may be given overhead, provided the pits are closed up at a high temperature.

FIG. 528 *Pine apple (Smooth-leaved Cayenne)*

1579 *The Peach House* The fruit on trees put forward in December will now be approaching maturity, and the house should be kept rather dry, giving all the air possible. At this stage they will bear forcing freely; keep, however, the syringe at work twice or thrice daily; tie in the shoots as they advance, and expose the fruit to the free action of light, if a high colour is wanted. In the succession house the borders should be kept well watered. Some varieties are very subject to red spider to keep this down, ply the syringe well till they are in bloom after the fruit is set; the inside walls of the house should be washed with a sulphur mixture.

That the ripening fruit may enjoy all the advantages of light and air, tie close in the shoots intervening between the trellis and the glass, and take off any leaves shading the fruit from the sun. Give air freely to peaches during their last stage, to improve the colour and flavour, and allow them plenty of time to ripen, which will improve both their size and appearance. Suspend a net loosely underneath the trees before the crop is ripe, to receive any fruit overlooked in gathering.

1580 *Figs* These will now be ripening, and in this stage watering should be discontinued, as it injures the flavour of the fruit. When in tubs, however, and a second crop is coming on, manure water should be given in moderation.

1581 *The Orchard House* Ventilation must still be strictly attended to. Open all ventilators during the day, except in fierce north and east winds. Worsted netting of ½-inch mesh may be placed over the ventilators in severe weather. If the caterpillar attacks the young shoots of the apricot, the ends must be pinched off and crushed.

1582 *Summer Pruning* Summer pruning of trees to be so treated to commence early this month. In pyramids, apricots, as soon as the shoots have made six or seven leaves, must have the sixth leaf with the end of the shoot pinched or cut off with a penknife, leaving only five main leaves. From this leading shoot two or three will break: in like manner, when they break, all but one of these are to be pinched down to five leaves. When this one has made ten leaves, pinch down to nine. With pyramidal peaches and nectarines, as soon as the shoot has made three leaves, pinch off the third leaf with the end of the shoot, leaving two principal ones. These pinched shoots will soon put forth fresh shoots, which, with all succeeding ones, must be pinched off to one leaf as soon as three are formed.

1583 *Watering* Trees in pots will require watering daily, but trees planted in borders will require water at intervals of a week or a fortnight, according to the state of the weather and the temperature of the external air. Thus the trees will require water more frequently if the weather be hot and dry than if it be cold and wet, because the beds will not lose their moisture so rapidly under the latter conditions as they will under the former. A regular and sufficient supply must be maintained; the trees will be injured if water is given too copiously at one time and withheld altogether at another. It is better to water equably and regularly than in doses of different calibre – sometimes much, sometimes little – administered spasmodically. Liquid manure should not be given until the stone begins to form in the fruit, and then it must be very weak. When the fruit is swelling, its strength may be increased, but at no time should very strong manure water be given to fruit trees.

CHAPTER 27

The Garden and its Work in Every Department in June

1584 *Aspect and Character of the Month* In June the direct power of the sun's rays is at its maximum, although the radiation of heat from the earth's surface, which decides the temperature of our atmosphere, does not attain its highest point till August. The variation of the temperature is still great, ranging, according to local circumstances, from a few degrees above freezing to 90°, the mean heat being 58°. The average mean temperature at Chiswick, for a period of ten years, at 2 feet below the surface, was 58°, at 1 foot 60°, and on the surface, 60° 45´; the mean maximum and minimum of the external air being respectively 81° 13´ and 45° 10´. The dryness of the atmosphere is also at its height in our moist climate, and vegetation now depends on the dew – the moisture with which the atmosphere is laden, and which being condensed, every blade of grass and leaf is saturated with it in the form of dew, an hour or two after sunset and sunrise.

1585 *Formation of Dew* Beautiful indeed are the mornings and evenings of June, when the dew hangs upon leaf and blossom, and beautiful the economy of Nature as displayed in this arrangement; for the formation of dew is an illustration of the law of attraction. The aqueous vapour held in suspension by the atmosphere coming in contact with leaf or blade of grass, or other non-conducting body of a slightly lower temperature than itself, is attracted to it and condensed. The temperature at which this phenomenon occurs is called the dew point, and the moisture thus deposited is an important portion of the food of plants at this period of their growth.

Summer has now fairly thrown open her doors of green, the whole landscape is at last fringed with foliage, the fields are ankle-deep in flowers; wild flowers are, indeed, too plentiful to be named here. The garden, also, is in full bloom – roses of a hundred hues, the fragrant honeysuckle and jasmine, load the air with their perfume.

> Now broad carnations, and gay spotted pinks,
> And showered from every bush, the damask rose,
> Infinite in numbers, delicacies, scents,
> With hues on hues, expression cannot paint.

June is indeed the 'leafy month of roses', during which the oak, the elm, and other 'green-robed senators of mighty woods', are clothed in all the beauty of their summer array, while the honeysuckle, with its streaked, spider-like flowers of white, red, and yellow, and the fragrant wild rose, flaunt their blossom from a thousand hedgerows, and mingle with the pale golden flowers of the woodbine and the drooping crimson blossoms of the foxglove, lighting up with their brilliancy the green masses of the underwood,

> Under the oak, whose antique roots peep out
> Upon the brook that brawls along the wood.

I – Work to be Done in the Garden

1 – The Flower Garden and Shrubbery

1586 *Routine Work* The most pressing work about the middle of the month is that of keeping the place in order. The edgings, whether of grass or box or other evergreen, should be repaired or clipped now. The effect produced at this season will amply repay the trouble; and in flower gardens the effect is excellent. Evergreen hedges clipped now have time to make and mature a new growth before winter, while the season is far enough advanced to prevent them from growing much out of shape.

1587 *Bedding Plants* Until the individual plants in the beds are sufficiently grown to meet one another, and intermingle their foliage, the beds cannot be expected to harmonise perfectly; but this period of their growth is approaching, and some judgment may now be formed of the taste with which their arrangement has been carried out. The growth of some of the bedding plants will be promoted by slight shading from the noonday sun; others, as the verbenas, grow faster when exposed to dry cool air; and all grow faster and fresher when watered occasionally. This should be done in the evening, and copiously, but not too often, stirring the soil amongst calceolarias, pegging down the lateral branches of verbenas, ageratums, petunias, and anagallis, so as to cover the ground.

1588 *Management of Beds* The newly-planted beds require constant watching. All failures should be instantly made good, and the tying and staking of everything requiring support attended to. Where an early display of flowers is not wanted, the buds may be pinched off. Pansies, anemones, double wallflowers, and other spring plants, should be removed as they go out of bloom, to make room for autumn-flowering ones, the beds being made up with fresh compost, in planting the later.

1589 *Surplus Bedding Stock* As soon as the beds, borders, etc., of the flower garden are finished, the baskets and vases filled, and the general spring planting out brought to a finish, the remaining stock of bedding plants should be looked over. A portion will be required for stock; and as a considerable number of plants will in all probability be required to make failures good, or to replace beds now occupied with short blooming plants, and other demands through the season – these, with few exceptions, had better be kept in pots; and, therefore, if any unpotted cuttings yet remain, let them be potted off into clean pots. Repot others, also, getting too full of roots, plunging them afterwards in ashes, in a cool shady situation, and pinching off all early or premature blooms: they will soon be ready for turning out.

1590 *Annuals* Watch the different annuals as they come into flower, and mark those varieties whose superior habit of growth, size of flower, or brilliancy of colour, makes it desirable to procure seed from them. Destroy inferior sorts as soon as they expand their first flower.

1591 *Annuals to Replace Failures* A few kinds of annuals should also be sown on a light soil in a shady border to take the place of those which may have failed. By frequently transplanting and stopping, their tendency to bloom will be encouraged, and the formation of roots promoted, and they will soon bear removing to the permanent beds without injury.

1592 *Vases and Basket Plants* It will add much to the effect of vases, etc., if, after they are filled, a few trailing plants are put in to peg over the surface of the mould, and ultimately to hang over the sides. For the larger ones the different kinds of maurandyas and lophospermums are well adapted, while for the smaller vases, baskets, etc., dwarf loosestrife and plants of similar habit will add much to their beauty. Moss, which we so frequently see used for the purpose, can never present so elegant an appearance. Those plants which interlace the meshes of basket-work require continual attention now, covering over the soil with some of the spreading lobelias, whose colours, when in bloom, harmonise with the trailing plants, and have an excellent effect.

1593 *Iberis Saxatilis* Cuttings of *Iberis saxatilis* root readily under a hand glass at this season; when placed in a shady situation, they form a beautiful edging, and may be cut like box for a week or two, to encourage the plants to cover the ground.

1594 *Creepers and Climbers* Creepers against walls or trellises should be gone over and tied or nailed in.

1595 *The Shrubbery* In the shrubbery, tying up and mulching is the chief employment of the month. As the rhododendrons and other American plants go out of bloom, remove the seed vessels and soak them well with manure water prepared from cow dung, mulching the roots.

Among the evergreen plants which are suitable for the shrubbery or border, none can excel the camellia; and any of the varieties of this beautiful shrub will do well in the open ground, or against a north wall or upon a north border. The soil in which they are planted should be a mixture of peat, leaf mould, and cow dung, about 2 feet deep. Great care should be taken that the plants never suffer from drought. After flowering they should be freely watered with liquid manure, especially if the season be dry. The surface of the ground just round the stems of the plants may frequently, with very good effect, be covered with small stones, which assist in keeping the roots cool and moist. As a general rule, the borders on which camellias are planted should not be disturbed more than is necessary to remove the surface weeds. A top dressing of fresh soil may with advantage be given to them every winter. So treated, the sorts of camellias mentioned above will be found as hardy as most of our common evergreens, and require no protection, except, perhaps, in an unusually severe winter, when a few fir boughs may be placed before or around them. The snow should never be allowed to rest upon their branches. Some growers of camellias in the open ground bind straw round the stems of their plants, about 5 or 6 inches from the ground. When winter sets in, this is found a very efficient protection against frost.

1596 *Watering and Mulching* In dry weather frequent and copious waterings must be given, not only to the recently-planted trees and shrubs, but to the bedded plants, annuals, etc. Mulching, wherever practicable, should be adopted, as well as damping the foliage of newly-planted shrubs every evening.

1597 *Herbaceous Plants* Carnations, picotees, and herbaceous plants, with the taller growing bedding plants, should be staked and tied up, to prevent injury from high winds. About the second week, hollyhocks, phloxes, delphiniums, asters, etc., should have the shoots thinned out before being tied up, to prevent an appearance of overcrowding, as well as to improve the size of the flowers.

1598 *Box Edgings, etc.* When showery weather occurs, let the box be clipped.

London pride, thrift, daisies, etc., used for edging, should be taken up once in two years, divided, and replanted when the blooming season is over.

1599 *Hyacinths, etc.* By the end of the month the last of the spring-flowering bulbs should be ripe enough to take up; and if the plants intended to occupy their places have not been already introduced between them, they should at once be planted, altering or improving the soil of the beds to suit the habits of the fresh plants.

1600 *Peonies* For late spring or early summer flowering, few plants are more useful than peonies. Every flower garden should have some of them. They are mostly very hardy, and in colour vary from pure white, blush, salmon, and rose to the most intense and brilliant scarlet. The Chinese tree varieties (*Paeonia Moutan*) are also hardy and early flowering. Bedded upon lawns they have a beautiful effect. In a shrub-like form they rise from 3 to 5 feet in height, and branch out in a good rich soil to 10 or 18 feet in circumference. There are many varieties, and the colouring is extremely rich. They are most of them profuse flowerers.

1601 *Roses* Standard and pillar roses should likewise be looked over to see that they are properly secured to their stakes. This being the month in which roses are in their glory, care should be taken that their effect is not destroyed by imperfect buds or deformed flowers. Weak-growing shoots should be tied up and regulated, and all fading flowers and seed vessels removed, cutting back the perpetual or autumn-flower kinds, as soon as all the flowers of the branch are expanded to the most prominent vertical eye, stirring the ground and saturating it with manure water, or sprinkling the ground with guano and watering with soft rain water.

1602 *Budding Roses* Towards the end of the month many shoots will be firm enough for budding, and some sorts work best on the flowering shoots, provided the buds are taken before the flowering is over.

In selecting buds, take those of moderate size: clean off the thorn, cut the leaves off, leaving only about half an inch of the stalk or petiole to hold by; then with a sharp knife take out the bud, beginning half an inch above the eye, and bring the knife about the eighth of an inch below; with the point of the knife separate the wood from the bark, without interfering with the wood which remains in the eye, leaving it so that, when inserted on the stock, the wood left may be in immediate contact with its wood.

1603 Having removed the thorns on the intended stock, open the bark at the most convenient spot for the insertion, by drawing the point of the knife down the centre of the shoot, and by a cross-cut, where the other begins, raise the corners of the bark sufficiently to introduce the lower end of the bud. Press it down till it is opposite to the corresponding bud on the stock, and bind it up with a piece of fine bast or worsted thread, leaving the eye so that it is just visible. After three or four weeks it should be examined, and the band loosened a little. In cases where the bud does not separate freely from the bark, the wood may be tied in also; but the operation is both neater and more sufficient when all the wood except that in the eye is removed. Cloudy weather is generally recommended for the operation; but some operators prefer bright, warm, sunny weather, provided the stocks are in proper condition. This operation may be performed any time from June to September, and even as late as October, August being suitable for the greatest number of roses, the test being of course the maturity of the shoots.

1604 *Rose Maggot and Green Fly* Close watching is now required to prevent the ravages of the rose maggot, washing daily with the syringe. To dislodge the green fly, a little ammonia or tobacco mixed with the water is useful.

1605 *Tulips* Tulips (Fig. 529) will now require the chief attention; and by proper care and protection their season of bloom may be considerably prolonged. The beds should be gone over carefully, and memoranda made of the style or character of the flowers individually. For instance, tall flowers should be marked to go in the fourth or middle row, whilst the height of others should be noted, in order that a proper degree of uniformity may be attained at next planting.

FIG. 529 *The tulip (Tulipa gesneriana)*

All flowers stained at the base should be excluded in collections intended for exhibition; for, though they may mark prettily, this defect is fatal to competition: those having long disproportioned cups or pointed petals are also defective for that purpose. Whenever addition is made to the bed, make the selection when they are in bloom. By this means you are certain of the strain. If seed is required, let the hybridising or crossing be done now, selecting finely-formed and pure flowers on both sides; do not, however, cross a rose or byblomen with a bizarre. It may be well to explain that a *rose* tulip is white, with marks of pink, scarlet, or crimson; a *byblomen*, white, marked with lilac, purple, or black; and a *bizarre* tulip, yellow, with coloured marks on its petals.

1606 *Management of Bulbs on Covered Beds* About the second week, the awning may be taken from the tulip shed, and the foliage of the plants exposed fully to the action of the sun and rain. Offsets in warm situations will require taking up before those on the main bed; as soon as the foliage turns yellow, they may be removed with safety. Seedlings which have grown one year should be allowed to remain in the ground during the first winter; when two years old they may be lifted and kept separated.

1607 *Management of Bulbs in the Open* Offsets and bulbs in exposed beds should be taken up at an earlier period than those that have been covered, choosing a dry day for the purpose, as soon as the foliage begins to change. They should be stowed away in some dry airy place, where mice cannot have access to them, leaving them there till the bulb is thoroughly dry, the fibres, husk, and skin remaining also.

1608 *Saving Seed* Sorts which it is desirable to save seed from should have the seed-pods covered with a piece of glass placed in a notched stick. This will preserve the crown from receiving moisture, and prevent decay. Remove the seed vessels of all others, as the bulbs become ready to take up sooner than if they were allowed to remain on.

1609 *Dahlias* Dahlias already planted out should be watered in the evenings with soft water overhead, the soil being previously stirred, and others planted out for later bloom, taking care, in hot weather, to mulch round the roots, where it can be done without being unsightly, with short well-decomposed dung. As the shoots advance, train and tie them up carefully, and search for earwigs and slugs in the mornings. A ring, or circle of copper, placed on the ground round the stem, it appears, will prevent this latter pest from approaching the leaves of plants.

1610 *Ranunculuses* These will be making rapid growth. Always water in the evening, and with water which has been exposed to the rays of the sun. When they begin to show colour, the awning, or other shade, should be placed over them: a few hoops extended over the bed, with mats on the sunny side, for a few hours in the middle of the day, will suffice, and greatly prolong their beauty. While the bloom is fresh, give water; but as it fades, discontinue it, and keep them from rain.

1611 *Carnations*, *Picotees*, and *Pinks*, as they advance, should be tied to their stakes, reducing the number of the shoots according to the strength of the plant. Care should be taken that the flower pods of pinks do not burst; and those having ligatures round them will require easing and retying. Shade any forward flowers, giving plenty of water and liquid manure. The distinction between the carnation (Fig. 530) and picotee (Fig. 531) maybe gathered from the accompanying illustrations.

1612 *Propagation of Carnations, etc.* The larger stalks of the pink, or grass, as it is technically called, when separated from the parent plant, may be piped now –

FIG. 530 *The carnation (Dianthus caryophyllus)*

FIG. 531 *The picotee (Dianthus caryophyllus)*

that is, the upper part of the stalk may be drawn out of its sheath or spathe, and struck in light sandy soil under a hand glass. This being done for the larger stalks, the plants will put out abundant stock for later cuttings. At the end of the month, or early in July, the main crop of pipings or layers should be got in. See this is done by making a slight hotbed, and covering it with 6 inches of sandy soil, in which the cuttings or rooted pipings may be planted, covering them with small hand glasses, or they may be struck on a shady border.

1613 *Fertilisation for Seed* The delicate operation of fertilising should be per formed on such as it is desired to keep for seed. This is the only true way of getting first-class seedlings, and both parent plants selected for experiment should be the most perfect of their kind.

1614 *Auriculas and Polyanthuses* These should be removed into a northern aspect, all decayed petals taken away from the seed pods, and as the capsules turn brown, they should be gathered. Water as they require it, and keep the pots free from weeds.

1615 *Hollyhocks* Stake and water hollyhocks freely.

1616 *Pansies* Plants struck from cuttings in April and May will produce fine blooms if planted in shady situations, or potted into 6-inch pots, and shaded in very bright weather. Cuttings may still be taken from promising plants. Mark all seedlings having good or singular properties. Though a flower may not be of good form, still, if it have any novel traits of character, it will be advisable to save seed from it, in order to perpetuate or improve both these and its form. At the end of the month, side slips may be taken and cut down. Strong straggling plants will afford a good supply of rooted cuttings for making up autumnal beds.

1617 *Cuttings for Spring Blooms* A shady piece of ground in the reserve garden should now be prepared for cuttings of double wallflowers, rockets, sweet-williams, pansies, and other plants required for next spring's bloom. Aubrietias and many other spring-flowering plants may also be divided and planted out this month.

1618 *Annuals in Reserve Garden* Beds of annuals to be transplanted for autumn flowering should be sown in the space left vacant by the removal of zinnias, china asters, and marigolds planted out.

2 – The Vegetable or Kitchen Garden.

1619 *Overcropping in Spring* Many principal crops come in this month, and, following suddenly upon a time when the supply from the kitchen garden is somewhat scanty, show the real effect of cropping too abundantly in the early part of the year. Peas, beans, cauliflowers, carrots, potatoes, and many other vegetables, come in all at once, that could not be produced earlier in the open ground. All show the propriety of dispersing the crops more regularly through the season.

The young gardener should make a note of this, and endeavour to manage so that there is no flush of vegetables at one time and a dearth of them at others. Particularly let it be borne in mind that we have long cold springs, in which the weather is exceedingly variable and mostly ungenial, when vegetation makes very slow progress indeed: it is then that root crops and Brassicae come in so useful; then that Brussels sprouts, kale, and broccoli, yield a succession of sweet wholesome sprouts, that grow almost in the coldest weather, and form the principal supply from Christmas to May. It is now the time to look forward to that time and be well prepared for it, so that available space should have been left in which a plentiful supply of the above-named can be grown. Ground that has been lying fallow since the winter can now be turned to good account; and be it remembered that fifty firm stocky plants of broccoli will yield a better supply than a hundred plants that have been drawn up between other crops or been crowded.

1620 *Watering in June* This month being generally a dry one, the watering pot must not remain idle; many kitchen crops will not do well if kept dry. Most kinds of salads are worthless if stinted of water; and as a rule, a judicious application of it will amply repay the time and labour; but let it be applied copiously, for mere surface watering only attracts the roots to the surface, to be burnt up by the sun.

1621 *Asparagus* Water newly-planted beds, and keep clear of weeds. Beds in bearing will be benefitted by an application of liquid manure. Do not cut too closely, but leave a few heads to expand and communicate with the light of day.

1622 *Seakale* Thin out the crowns where they are anyways thick. A few strong heads are better than many weak ones: young seedlings will be benefitted by a sprinkling of wood ashes. As it is a marine plant, salt may be strewn between the rows. Keep the young plants well watered, and hoe frequently between.

1623 *Peas* After the second week this month, it is not advisable to sow strong growers. Before then such sorts may be sown to advantage; but after that it is best to sow shorter sorts. The time from sowing to bearing is less, and proportionately certain of yielding a crop.

1624 *Beans* The last sowing of these should be made for the season; they seldom pay for sowing later. Top those in bloom before they become infested with aphis. This pest adheres to the young tops; consequently, remove that, and the insects have no place suitable for them. If topped as soon as the first flower opens, the crop will be as large as if allowed to continue growing, and they set much earlier. Mulching will increase the quantity and quality of the crop.

FIG. 532 *Garden French bean*

1625 *French Beans* Sow a few rows of these for succession. There are many varieties; but it is immaterial what sort is sown, except on the question of flavour or productiveness. The Canadian Wonder, the Long-podded Negro, and Newington Wonder, and Canadian varieties, continue in bearing a long time. Thin to 4 or 6 inches, and earth up, but give no manure.

1626 *Runner Beans* These do well sown any time before midsummer. On light ground they may be dibbed in, an expeditious method. Some recommend soaking them in water for a day before sowing, which may be advantageous in hot, dry weather; but it is as well to water the drills or holes at the time of sowing. Those sown last month should be earthed and staked before they begin to run.

1627 *Carrots* Thin without delay, but not too closely, as some are apt to run, even under the best culture. From 9 inches to a foot is a good average. A succession may be sown any time before midsummer.

1628 *Celery* will probably be in condition for final planting towards the end of this month; the main crop had better be deferred till next month.

Celery is generally considered a gross feeder, requiring a rich, highly-manured soil and abundance of water. It certainly cannot be grown to perfection without both. In order to give it the best possible chance, it is usually grown in trenches from 6 inches to a foot deep. The trenches are marked out 4 or 5 feet apart, and the top spit thrown out, and also the loose soil. For single rows a foot will be sufficient, but for double rows the trenches must be 18 inches wide. Having thrown out the soil, put 6 inches of good rotten dung in the trenches, and fork it well into the bottom; if then left till a shower of rain, so much the better; for that reason it is advisable to get the trenches ready early. The plants should then be planted with a trowel, and well settled in with water, which must afterwards be used unsparingly. Another way is to plant on the level ground, it having previously been well manured and trenched. Plant 2 feet or 18 inches apart, to blanch it; when drain pipes are used, the pipes should be filled in with sand. This being the cleanest method of growing, celery, it is well worth adopting. A far greater number of plants can be grown on a given space than by the ordinary method. It is also an advantage that the plants can receive the benefit of rain and liquid manure after earthing up, which cannot very well be done in the ordinary way. But if by any chance the sowing was not accomplished in April or May, it may be done early this month, with every chance of success, by sowing some large-growing sort. This will get a moderate size by October; and as it is not desirable to have it over large, such sorts are as well deferred till late before sowing; those already up should be thinned as soon as possible, leaving the best coloured plants.

1629 *Onions* should receive a final thinning, allowing 8 or 9 inches for the main crop. Use the small hoe as often as possible, and keep them clean. Onions for salading may still be sown. A shady border on the north side of a wall will suit them. Tree onions, potato ditto, and those planted for seed, will require some support-Drive a few stakes round them, and pass strings from one to the other, or tie to single stakes. If they are allowed to break down, they receive a permanent injury, and the yield is reduced or altogether prevented.

1630 *Leeks* Plant in deep drills, to admit of earthing up; give an abundance of water in dry weather. Soot dredged over them will stimulate them, and prevent the attacks of insects in a great measure.

1631 *Potatoes* Earth up before they get too tall, but leave the top of the ridges nearly flat, so that the tubers are not buried too deeply. It is a great error many fall into of drawing the earth as high as possible up the stems. They do not bear so well, from the greater exclusion of air from the roots. Potatoes that have been retarded may be planted this month; they will yield new potatoes in the autumn.

1632 *Turnips* Sow a good breadth of these; they will come in well and be very useful in the autumn. Sow immediately after rain, or, if the ground is light, immediately after digging. They grow very quickly; but some slight protection from birds will be necessary the short time they are germinating. White worsted will generally be found efficient. Tread the seed in well, or use the wooden roller after vowing, but finish off with a rake.

1633 *Scorzonera, Salsafy, Hamburgh Parsley, etc.* Thin to about 10 inches or a foot, and stir the ground well between them.

1634 *Lettuce* Sow on a north border, but plant in an open situation. It is necessary to sow often to insure a succession. Water the ground thoroughly, or not at all; surface watering is very injurious.

1635 *Endive* maybe sown this month, as it is less likely to run now than formerly. This seed grows very quickly, and birds do not seem to care about it; it may therefore be merely sown broadcast, trodden, and raked. Plant out early to insure a good curl in the leaf.

1636 *Vegetable Marrows* and *Pumpkins* should be got out early this month. If good strong plants, they may be merely planted on a sunny border; but they are much better for having a little dung heat; or dung without heat will suit them, for they delight in a loose bed of light but well-rotted dung that they can root into easily. Give plenty of water if the weather holds dry. Fig. 533 is an illustration of the long white variety of vegetable marrow.

FIG. 533 *Long white vegetable marrow*

1637 *Capsicums and Tomatoes* At the beginning of the month plant out these against a south wall if possible, otherwise against a sloping bank. The full sun is necessary to induce these to bear well. Vacant wall spaces under and between wall trees, where there may be any, are well filled up by them.

1638 *Cress* Sow American and Normandy for succession.

1639 *Broccoli* Defer not later than the middle of this month the final sowing of late sorts. Walcheren sown now will very likely come in during the winter. Plant out those that are ready and never allow them to draw up in the seed bed, but prick them out temporarily; they will pay for it. If there is no room for them otherways, transplant in drills made for the purpose.

1640 *Brussels Sprouts, Borecole, and Savoys* Get these planted for good as early as possible; plant in drills 2 feet apart, and water freely. Puddling the roots in clay and soot mixed in water may be good for them and prevent clubbing in a great measure. Plant between rows of peas and beans that will soon be off the ground, no matter how firm the ground is. Experience has tended to show this group do best if the ground has not been dug for several months before planting. Watering once a day or oftener will be necessary in dry weather.

1641 *Cabbages and Cauliflowers* Plants of different kinds should also be put out when strong enough. The latter will prove very useful in August and September. A succession of these is an important matter.

1642 *Mushrooms* Mushroom beds may be made at this time out of doors; they will come into bearing in August. Horse droppings, or good short stable dung, mixed with one-third loamy soil, and well worked together till it gives a gentle heat, afford the best material for making the bed; it must not be heaped up too high, or in too great a body, or it is apt to ferment too violently. Let the bed be firmly put together in a ridge, of conical or pyramidal form, of sufficient pitch to prevent water getting into it; a trench dug round it will take the rain. The bed must be protected at all times from rain before spawning and before casing, and afterwards covered with about a foot of clean straw, and this, again, with something to keep it together; mats, netting, sticks, or hurdles, will do, although garden mats are preferable. Beds previously made should be looked over occasionally, and, if dry, watered very gently with water equal at least in temperature to that of the atmosphere.

Some old cultivators, who have no idea of the use of a thermometer, are very successful in the culture of the mushroom, and inform us that the best time to spawn a bed is when it feels of a temperature equal to that of newly-drawn milk. Certainly a proper temperature at the time of spawning is of the first importance: if too cold, the spawn will not work; too great heat destroys it at once. 34 or 85°, perhaps, ought to be the maximum, and 65° the minimum point.

3 – The Fruit Garden and Orchard

1643 *Treatment of Insect Pests* The beginning of the month is a busy period in this department, and much vigilance and perseverance will be requisite to keep pace with the advancing growth, in preventing and keeping down the different pests. Tobacco water must be instantly applied directly the black or green fly makes its appearance, endeavouring to make it act on the underside of the leaves. When the foliage becomes curled, insect larvae are present; a good sulphurator, charged with snuff and a small portion of sulphur, will be found the most effectual implement. Before using this, damp the trees with the syringe, and apply the snuff before the tree becomes dry, that it may more effectually adhere to the leaves. Dislodge the maggot, which coils itself up in the foliage, and not unfrequently spoils some of the finest fruit.

1644 *Pruning and Training of Trees* The occupants of the fruit garden will be either dwarf standards, apples, pears, cherries, or plums, espaliers or pyramids, all of which have undergone a special course of training and pruning suitable to their habits; or peaches, nectarines, and apricots, on the walls, with the usual arrangements for bush fruit; and the skill of the gardener is now best displayed in selecting the shoots to be retained or encouraged for extending the trees. They should be short- jointed and brown-coloured, and should now be stopped and laid in.

1645 *Apricots* These will now require their final thinning, and stopping, and watering, also followed by mulching, which is important at this time for all fruit trees where evaporation is active.

1646 *Peaches and Nectarines* Where the leading shoots of peaches or nectarines are growing too vigorously, stop them, in order to encourage lateral shoots, by pinching off the leading bud. Unless this operation is performed early in the season, the shoots do not get properly ripened. If the fruit seems setting too thickly, let it be partially thinned, reserving the main thinning, however, till after it has stoned. The trees will have been mulched last month to prevent evaporation, and should now be watered, and that so copiously that it does not require frequent repetition, pouring the water into the roots.

1647 *Pears and Plums: Disbudding, etc.* In disbudding pears, plums, and cherries, the fore-right shoots, and those not wanted for laying on, should remain for the present, as stopping them at this time would only cause a fresh breaking into wood, either of the eyes at the base of the stopped shoot, or some portion of the spurs. As they, however, look unsightly on well-regulated trees, it will be better to tie them slightly to the main branches for the present; this will give a better appearance to the trees, and bending the shoots will in some measure stop the over-free flow of the sap, and so help the object in view. The precise time at which shoots should be shortened must be regulated according to the vigour of the tree, and should be deferred till all danger of the remaining eyes again breaking into wood is over.

1648 *Cherries* Cherry trees now progressing towards maturity should be gone carefully over, the shoots stopped and laid in, and the trees netted, to save the fruit and protect it from birds. If the black fly appears, cut off the ends of the shoots, unless it is more convenient to wash them in tobacco water.

1649 *Vines* These will require going over. Thin out what wood is not wanted for bearing, and stop the bearing shoots at one joint above the shoot; nail in the leading shoots close to the wall. Where the long-rod system of pruning is adopted, a shoot must be selected and carried up from the bottom of each stem, to furnish bearing wood for next year. By careful attention to the vine border and to pruning, the vine on open walls may be made much more productive, as well as ornamental, than it usually is.

1650 *Figs* Stop all except the leading shoots when they have made three or four joints, and lay on leaders and shoots required for filling up. Watering the roots with soapsuds is found greatly to benefit the fruit.

1651 *Gooseberries and Currants* A wash of lime or clear soot water may be applied with advantage to gooseberries and currants infested with the caterpillar. These increase so rapidly that a constant watch must be kept up for some time. Pinch back all shoots off the currant trees not wanted for wood. The fruit of gooseberries will be considerably improved by summer stopping the young wood.

The earth immediately under the trees should be watered and beaten firm, which will prevent more of the larvae from rising to attack the shoots. Where the earth is very light, a coating of clay or loam, the consistence of mortar, should be spread under the trees, and made firm to prevent their escape from the earth. If these precautions are taken on the insects' first appearance, they are more easily kept from doing mischief.

1652 *Raspberries* Remove useless suckers from raspberry plantations, to admit more sun and air to the fruit.

1653 *Strawberries* Begin to layer strawberries in 60-pots directly runners can be obtained for next season's forcing. Let the soil used be rich and rather light, to encourage the runners to root freely; when layered, do not let them suffer for want of water. Place straw or some similar material between strawberries now in bloom, to preserve the fruit clean in heavy rains, and to keep the ground moist. Alpines and other late sorts should have all the flowers pinched off this month.

To grow this fruit in perfection, it is necessary to keep the roots moist while it is swelling, either by mulching, which prevents evaporation, or by watering, when it is necessary to give a liberal supply. To accelerate the ripening process, lay some pieces of slate or tiles under some of the best fruit. Where expense is no object, tiles may be obtained cut so as to join round the roots of the plant and fit together; but their light colour and greater porosity increase evaporation, and slates are preferred, and where they are not obtainable, straw or coarse hay (not lawn grass) will retain the heat and moisture and keep the fruit free from grit. This is a fruit requiring very careful packing when sent to a distance. When hampers are to be sent the fruit should be packed in smaller baskets with lids, 5 or 6 inches square, which will pack conveniently in the larger hamper. Having placed some young strawberry leaves in the bottom and round the edges of the basket, fill up the remaining space with fruit and leaves alternately – not in layers, but intermixed with the fruit, and cover the top with leaves, over which place the lid. The fruit selected for packing should never be over-ripe, and all bruised berries should be thrown out.

1654 *Treatment of Forced Plants* Where a large number of strawberries are yearly forced, the plants, after the fruit is gathered, will be found valuable for planting out, producing a most abundant crop the following year: the later-forced ones will answer best, as they are not so liable to bloom again in the autumn. Turn the plants into rich soil, and if they are only to remain one year, they may be planted pretty thick. Water them till they get established.

II – Work to be done under Glass.

1 – Flowers in the Conservatory, Greenhouse, Stove, etc.

1655 *The Hothouse and Greenhouse* At the latter end of the month, as the solar light will be approaching the maximum point, and solar heat also, fires may be discontinued in the orchard houses, except on the evenings of wet days, when a little fire will be necessary to allow of admitting air freely in the morning. As plants at this season will be making way fast, air must be admitted liberally, which, in conjunction with light, will help to arrest the rapid growth of those plants whose disposition to bloom mainly depends on a free exposure to both at the same time.

1656 *Prolongation of Blooming Period* Remove to houses with a north aspect, or under the shade of a north wall, any plants whose period of blooming it is desirable to prolong.

1657 *Chrysanthemums* Place in their blooming pots the principal stock of chrysanthemums, using for potting a rather heavy loam with a portion of well-rotted cow dung.

1658 *Orchids* Orchids will now be making free growth, and as solar light and heat are approaching the maximum point, an atmosphere humid in proportion must be maintained. The paths, walls, etc., should be frequently damped on bright days, and the plants gently dewed over once or twice daily. Air may now be given more liberally, moderating its admission, however, so as to prevent strong currents of air blowing on the plants. Shade regularly in bright weather, placing such plants that bear a pretty free exposure to the sun's rays in the lightest part of the house. Make it a rule to examine plants in baskets, etc., that the necessary dampness of the growing material may be uniform, for nothing tends more to check the growth of orchids than want of attention to this in the growing season. Zygopetalums, Cyrtopodiums, and other terrestrial genera, will be benefitted by being plunged in bottom heat during the season of active growth.

1659 *Climbing Plants* About the second week, stove and conservatory climbers will require attention to keep the current year's shoots within proper limits. Avoid anything like formality in arranging the branches. If at the winter regulation of the plants the main shoots were trained to occupy the desired position, the young wood may be allowed considerably to follow its natural mode of growth, if this does not create confusion, which is equally as much to be guarded against as a strict formality. Hardenbergias, Kennedyas, etc., may slightly be cut back, after blooming, to induce a new growth.

1660 *Balsams, etc.* The stock of balsams and other annuals grown for filling the vacant places in the greenhouses, etc., should be encouraged by frequent shifts; keep them in bottom heat, and near the glass; pick off the early-formed bloom buds, as the plant should attain a considerable size before being allowed to bloom.

1661 *Kalosanthes or Rochea* Continue to train these neatly, and water with liquid manure occasionally.

1662 *Scarlet Geraniums* Specimen scarlet geraniums should likewise have liberal encouragement to grow them on.

1663 *Pelargoniums* Common and fancy pelargoniums for late blooming will thrive better in a somewhat shady situation, and (the latter especially) where they can at the same time be protected from heavy rains. Fumigate whenever green fly appears; for, if suffered to get the upper hand, it soon disfigures the plant.

1664 *Fuchsias* These, if not in their blooming pots, should be potted at once. Train in the desired form, and pinch back weak and straggling shoots.

1665 *Japan Lilies, etc.* The glass must be taken entirely off Japan lilies – of which *Lilium auratum* (Fig. 534) affords a good specimen – gladioli, etc., unless very early blooms are desired. Keep a portion in the shade of a north wall for a succession of

FIG. 534 *Lilium auratum*

bloom. Take care the plants stand on a bottom carefully prepared, to prevent worms getting into the pots. The more tender kinds should be placed under a slight framework, with oiled canvas or tarpaulin attached, to protect them during heavy rains. When the greenhouses are thus partially covered, a portion of the more hardy stove plants may be introduced. This exposure, during the hot months of summer, to a large portion of air, will benefit the growth of many soft-wooded plants, particularly of such as are being grown for blooming late in the autumn.

1666 *Achimenes, Gesnerias, Gloxinias, etc.* Achimenes, gesnerias, gloxinias, etc., as they begin to show for bloom, should be moved to more airy quarters, keeping them, however, partially shaded for a time. Achimenes must be carefully attended to with water while growing.

1667 *Camellias and Azaleas* Keep a damp growing heat to camellias and azaleas making wood; the latter are very liable to become infested with thrips, which can only be kept down by fumigating with tobacco alternate nights for a week, and syringing at the same time with diluted tobacco water, until the appearance of the pest is gone.

The utmost vigilance will now be required in keeping the more choice plants in a healthy growing state, and at the same time preserving the proper uniformity of growth to insure perfect and well-bloomed specimens. The precise time when the active growth should cease, and its energies be directed to maturing the current year's wood, can scarcely be laid down as a rule – the habit of the plant must be taken into consideration. It will, however, be safer, in general, to get the wood of delicate plants especially ripened early; for though they may not get to be such large plants, they will be better able to resist the attacks of mildew in the ensuing winter, and the disposition to form bloom buds is always greater in plants ripening their wood early. Young plants growing into specimens, and where for a year or two bloom is no object, may, after their first growth is over, and being allowed a month's rest (during which time keep them rather dry), be started into growth again, giving them a larger pot, if such is necessary, and paying the same attention to the second growth, by stopping, training, etc., as directed for plants in general.

1668 *Chinese Azaleas, etc.* At the end of the month, Chinese azaleas and camellias intended to bloom early next season, and which have by this time nearly completed their growth, should be exposed to more light and air, to harden their wood before setting them out of doors. As soon as the wood is somewhat firm, and the buds for next season make their appearance, is a favourable time for repotting such as require it, and if caution is used to prevent exciting them into a second growth, the blooms will be finer than when the plants are potted before the year's growth commences.

Plants intended for forcing should on no account be over-potted at any time, and both camellias and azaleas are often shy of bloom when forced after a large shift. Another advantage in keeping plants for forcing rather under-potted, is that they are often required to be turned out of their pots to fill vases, tazzas, etc., in the drawing-room, when in bloom, which can be done without much injury to plants when they have completely filled their pots with roots.

1669 *Orange Trees* Large orange trees grown for the flower garden or grounds during the summer months may now be moved to the places they are to occupy. If they have been kept cool and airy, they will not have commenced their new growth, which should not take place till they are out of doors. Examine the roots to see that the drainage is perfect, and that in watering the water passes freely through the ball. They should have a free sunny exposure, but they must be protected from high winds.

1670 *Treatment of Plants when Placed Out* Plants, when placed out, should be plunged in ashes, or have the space between the pots filled with moss; and those plants in the house which have their pots most exposed should be inserted in larger ones, and the space filled with moss, sawdust, etc. This will prevent excessive evaporation from the soil containing the roots, through the sides of the pots, and will save many plants from being lost during very hot weather.

1671 *Syringing and Sulphuring* Stove plants should be closely watched (particularly those with large soft leaves) for the red spider, which is encouraged by dry weather. Syringe frequently to keep them in check, and plants much infested with them should be dusted over with dry sulphur by the sulphurator. Let the sulphur remain on the plants for a day or two, carefully shading them from the sun, and, if possible, keeping them in a close place. Particular care should likewise be taken in supplying this class of plants regularly with water; a short supply causes the leaves to get flabby in dry weather, and the plant is sure to be laden with the red spider.

1672 *Plants Going Out of Bloom* Specimens and choice plants nearly done blooming should have the faded blooms picked off, and be well washed with the syringe; they should be placed in a cool shady situation to recover themselves before potting, which, as before advised, should on no account take place until a fresh growth has commenced.

1673 *Shading, etc.* Shading will be necessary to all descriptions of plant houses, unless the roofs are covered with creepers; paths, floors, etc., keep damp by throwing water over them, to preserve something like humidity in the atmosphere of the house, which, under the extreme dryness of the external air, is extremely difficult to keep up.

1674 *The Conservatory* The difficulty of furnishing the conservatory is now one of taste and selection. Every floral tribe will now be ready to furnish its quota, and discrimination only is required in selecting and arranging them. Avoid crowding; encourage variety and harmonious contrast in colour; remove all decayed or decaying blossom, and guard against insects of all kinds by cleanliness and timely fumigation. Regulate the luxurious growth of creepers and border plants, watering copiously, occasionally using liquid manure. Water should now be given liberally to plants in the open borders of the conservatory, excepting, perhaps, plants very recently planted.

1675 *Ventilation* Proper and systematic ventilation is now of the utmost importance, but it must be regulated in proportion to the state of the external air. Air should be admitted night and day, except in cold gloomy weather, and shading from the burning sun attended to for an hour or two daily.

2 – Plants under Glass in Hotbeds, Frames, etc.

1676 *Flowers in Hotbeds, etc.* As regards flowers, there will be few, if any, under bottom heat in hotbeds at this period of the year: those, indeed, that are under glass at all will be in cool frames, and will require abundance of air and judicious shading.

1677 *Seedlings for Winter Blooming* Seedling Chinese primroses, cinerarias, and other plants required to furnish the winter supply of bloom, should now be forwarded by shifting into pots. Keep them in a cool frame where a slight shade can be given them in hot weather, or else turn the frame to the north. Look to the stock of plants out of doors in showery weather, to see they are not suffering from imperfect drainage. Throw screens over delicate plants during heavy rains, especially such as have been recently potted.

1678 *Vegetables, etc., in Hotbeds* Making hotbeds is seldom deferred till this time of year; yet it may be done advantageously. Both cucumbers and melons, if started this month, will pay for cultivating: the directions for doing so, being the same as in former months, it is unnecessary to repeat; but common brick pits will be very suitable for the purpose.

1679 *Cucumbers in Advanced Stage* Cucumbers in an advanced stage will want clearing of dead leaves, and the soil stirred about them, and probably fresh earth added. A toad kept in a frame will destroy a great many woodlice and other insects, and keep the plants cleaner than they otherwise would be. The presence of insect pests in the culture of cucumbers or melons is chiefly, if not wholly, the result of mismanagement; but where they do appear it is advisable to get rid of them as soon as possible. Red spider and mildew are counteracted by sulphur, thrips and aphis by fumigating with tobacco, which is the safest means; but more credit is due to the cultivator who, by judicious care and management, keeps his plants clear of them.

1680 *Management of Cucumbers* Cucumbers at this season of the year do best with a considerable amount of shade; this should be attended to, and the necessary bottom heat and moisture kept up. Keep the vines thin and regular by frequent stopping. In planting out at this season use a rather poor, in preference to a rich soil, which in cold wet seasons produces canker. An illustration of the Telegraph Cucumber is given in Fig. 535.

1681 *Cucumbers on Trellis* Cucumbers are sometimes allowed to trail over a trellis. By this means the fruit is suspended, and no glass tubes are required to keep them straight; some, even when grown on a bed, are tied up with sticks for the same purpose. When tubes are used, it is

FIG. 535 *Telegraph cucumber*

sometimes necessary to watch them, in order that, during the swelling of the fruit, they are not wedged into the tubes so tightly that they are difficult to withdraw. Care should be taken that the bloom which adorns the fruit is not removed in cutting them. In the application of lining, to maintain the heat, in watering and giving air, etc., proceed as before.

1682 *Cucumbers in Open Ground* Plants intended for open-air culture, if sown last month, will be ready for ridging out. A south border, or between rows of tall peas or scarlet runners, ranging north and south, will suit them. Open a trench 4 or 5 feet wide, and fill with prepared stable dung to the thickness of 3 feet; cover this with a foot of soil; place the plants 5 or 6 feet apart, two or three together, and cover with hand glasses.

1683 *Melons* These may be started for succession; for, as melons are not generally continuous bearers, nothing is gained by endeavouring to induce old plants to bear again. It is more satisfactory to raise fresh plants and make new beds for them, unless, indeed, they are planted on old beds newly lined. With a tolerable bottom heat, the growth of these plants is very rapid at this time of the year; and though they may be grown without it, still, for the production of fine fruit, heat is indispensable.

1684 *Management of Melons* Where the fruit is swelling off, the roots will most probably have penetrated the lining; if so, this must not be disturbed, but fresh dung added to it; but care must be taken that the rank heat has passed from the new lining, or the roots will be injured. It is advisable to raise the fruit on tiles or slates, or some such material; boards are not so well, as they are more likely to harbour woodlice under them. Pinch back all useless shoots, but keep the plants regularly furnished with healthy leaves.

1685 *Melons in Open Ground* Melons, like cucumbers, may be grown on ridges. Some of the Cantalupe varieties do very well this way; but it is advisable to get the plants strong before turning out. Grow them in frames till they are established in 32-pots; then plant them in the same way as directed for cucumbers, making the soil rather firm, and protecting with hand glasses.

1686 *Vegetable Marrows, etc.* If ridges are prepared in the same way, vegetable marrows, gourds, etc., may be planted on them, or the seed may be dibbed in at intervals of 6 or 8 feet; they will grow and be in time to bear in August; they like a light rich soil, and grow very fast after midsummer. The ice plant, which is sometimes used for garnishing, may be treated in precisely the same manner.

1687 *Lawn Mowings as Mulching* Many growers make use of lawn mowings for lining hot beds. Now, although it may be useful in a certain manner, it is far from being a proper material: it heats too violently, and the roots of plants recoil from it. It also has the very disagreeable property of breeding swarms of insects; it is, therefore advisable to avoid using it about frames. It may be used more advantageously as mulch for kitchen crops, strawberries, or ridge cucumbers or melons: laid on the surface of the ground, and spread out, it is soon dried, and loses its power of doing harm.

1688 *Capsicums, Chilies, etc.* Capsicums, chilies, egg plants, etc., should be repotted into larger pots. This will probably be their final shift. They may then be plunged in a moderate heat, and as they grow taller the frame can be lifted on bricks or flower pots, working the linings up to it. Many tender plants may be treated in the same way, and thus prepared for autumn decoration of the conservatory.

3 – Fruit under Glass, Heated and Unheated.

1689 *Vines: Preservation of Foliage* Supposing a crop of grapes to have been gathered from early-started vines, it is still very important to keep the foliage in a green and healthy state for the next two or three months, when they shed them. This should be so done, however, as to prevent a second growth taking place; the borders should be gently watered, the red spider kept down by using the syringe, and air given on every possible occasion; the leaves may thus be kept in a healthy state, highly useful to the vine while it ripens its wood. By this means, vines endure early forcing for many years without much diminution of their energy.

1690 *Vines for Late Crops* Where vines have been retarded for late grapes, by being turned out they should now be brought into the house and trained to the trellis or rafters, and invigorated by syringing, to encourage the growth of young wood.

1691 *Ripened Crops* Houses where the grapes are ripe should be kept dry, and succession crops encouraged by a little heat, according to their several stages.

1692 *Artificial Heat* Although the nights are now getting warm, it will still be necessary to apply artificial heat, both in houses ripening and in later crops now in bloom, especially where Muscats and other shy setters are grown, as they rarely form perfectly- shaped bunches without a warm and dry atmosphere, which in our climate requires fire heat. In thinning the later crop of grapes, lay out the bunches well, and leave the berries thinner than the early ones; the grapes will keep all the better from not being too thickly set in the bunch.

1693 *Stopping, Ventilating, Sprinkling, etc.* Stop all lateral shoots in the succession house after thinning the crop, that nothing may interfere with the swelling of the fruit. As the season advances, air must be given in abundance, the ventilators being left partially open by night. To prevent the atmosphere from becoming too dry during hot weather, keep the floors, interior walls, paths, and pipes, damp by sprinkling several times a day. This will also assist to keep in check the ravages of the red spider.

1694 *Planting New Borders* Where new vine borders have been made in the spring, the present is a favourable time for planting, if the vines have been started sufficiently long to have a shoot of moderate length, In planting, liberate the roots freely, and spread them in the direction of the border, giving a slight watering, and mulching the surface. The house should be kept rather closer for a few days, shading the newly-planted vines, if disposed to flag, until they show indications of starting, when the usual routine must be followed, preserving the young vines from injury by tying and training the leader up the roof.

1695 *Keeping Grapes* When grapes require to be kept for some considerable time, they must be shaded during bright weather, otherwise the fruit will become shrivelled. If the shoots have been stopped at one or two joints above the fruit, the laterals (which should be taken clean out up to the bunch), should be stopped back to one joint, unless the previously-formed leaves are already sufficiently close together, when they should be stopped close back. All after-growths are injurious when not required for shade.

1696 *Management after Removal of Crop* As the crops are cut, let the vines be cleaned and syringed, to destroy any red spider established since the ripening of the crop; they may be easily eradicated now. Both inside and outside borders will require water occasionally. Admit air freely at all times. The object now is, by careful management, to preserve the foliage in a healthy state for the next two months,, that a supply of properly-elaborated sap may be stored up for next season.

1697 *Vines in Pots* Vines training in pots for next season's fruiting require daily attention and stopping; when they have attained a proper length required for fruiting, stop the laterals and expose the principal leaves to the light. Water with liquid manure when the pots are full of roots.

1698 *The Pinery* The principal crop of summer pines, now swelling their fruit, must be encouraged by frequent waterings, using liquid manure alternately. Support each fruit in an upright position, and remove useless gills and suckers, reserving only sufficient of the latter for stock. Shade with some light material during the middle of bright sunny days, unless vines are grown over them; bearing in mind that, the more light they get, the better will be the colour and flavour of the fruit.

1699 *Ventilation* Give air early, increasing it as the day advances, and close early in the afternoon, at which time the plants, beds, and interior walls should be damped over. When the nights become warmer, a little air may again be put on, which will assist the colouring of the fruit. To insure strong sturdy plants, maintain a uniform bottom heat of 90° during the season of active growth. The frosty nights which occasionally occur, and cloudy or rainy days, require that this temperature should be kept up by fire heat.

1700 *Management of Ripening Fruit* Withhold water from fruit directly a change of colour is discernible. If the fruit is growing in pots, lift them on the surface of the bed, which will help to improve both colour and flavour. Fires will be required, to allow for extra ventilation, which at this period of the crop's ripening is more than ever necessary. Do not allow the bottom heat to decline.

1701 *Plants for Autumn Fruiting, etc.* That portion of the fruiting stock which did not show fruit in February will now be most likely to show. These should be taken care of, as they will bring heavy fruit in October. To assist them, remove the suckers and gills, and keep them regularly supplied with weak manure water, and frequently damp with the syringe. Plants which have been kept back for autumn supply should now be induced to fruit, backward plants being dry for that purpose, and exposed to the light. When the fruit appears, shift plants requiring more pot room, and place them where they are to ripen. The most suitable sorts for autumn and winter use are the two varieties of Cayenne, Black Jamaica, and Queens.

1702 *Early Pines for Spring* When ripe fruit is required next April or May, a portion of them should now be selected, and have their final shift. The best early pines are the Old Queen's, Prickly Cayenne, and the Black Antigua.

1703 *Treatment of Succession Pines* Succession pines should, at the end of the month, be growing very fast, and require air in liberal quantities, both back and front. Water as they require it, using liquid manure occasionally, clarified, to prevent its choking up the drainage properties of the soil. Maintain a steady bottom heat, and pot the suckers of the plants from which the fruit is cut. As the stools are removed to make way for other plants, all succession plants requiring repotting should now be shifted. When replunged, leave plenty of room for the foliage to spread out, and place them near the glass, watering with weak manure water once a week or fortnight, according to their requirements.

1704 *The Peach House* The ripe fruit should be looked over each morning, to gather such as are likely to ripen in a day or two. The fruit will be higher in flavour than when allowed to ripen on the tree, and will save them from getting bruised in falling, to which heavy fruit of the peach is very liable, with the best contrivances to catch them. As the crop is gathered, the young wood should be so exposed as to ripen well; on this depends next year's success, in a great measure. Not a single unnecessary shoot should be retained. The tree should be well washed with the syringe, and all foreign matter removed from the leaves.

1705 *Ventilation, etc.* Give all the air possible to ripe fruit, and shade where it is desirable, to prolong the season. Bring on the second house by an increased temperature; keep damp by the frequent use of the engine, and sprinkle the floors, etc.; at closing time give the inside border a good soaking with weak manure water. Keep a moist atmosphere where the fruit is swelling; water freely; give plenty of air, especially in the forenoon.

1706 *Cherries in Pots* About the second week turn out cherries in pots into an open quarter of the garden, placing some turfy loam round the balls. This will invigorate them much better than keeping them in pots through the summer.

1707 *The Orchard House* In hot and dry weather trees will require watering abundantly every evening; in all weathers syringe morning and evening at 7 a.m. and 6 p.m. Indeed, trees in pots whose fruit is now swelling may require watering morning and evening, unless a heavy mulching is placed on the top of the soil to prevent evaporation as far as possible. If the surface of the soil in the pots or border be dry, a new top dressing may be added. Thin the fruit, pinching in all shoots to the third leaf. Ventilate freely, and continue syringing until the fruit begins to colour.

1708 *Red Spider* The red spider will now make its appearance on the tender part of the peach leaves, and must be extirpated by syringing; if that fail, by lime or sulphur. The house being closed, take some large flower pots filled with unslaked lime, and saturated with four or five gallons of water; over this strew a handful of flour of sulphur, and leave it in the house all night. The next morning syringe the house thoroughly. This will destroy red spider and many other pests of the garden.

1709 *Removal of Trees into Open Air* Remove plum trees and apricots into the open air to ripen their fruit. On the 10th, and again on the 25th, lift up the pots in order to break off the roots which have protruded through the drainage holes, and attend to summer pinching of pyramid and bush trees. The ripening of peaches, apricots, and nectarines may be retarded by removing into the open air.

1710 *Summer Pinching and Pruning* Pinch the laterals, and at the end pinch off all leading shoots. Summer-pinch pyramidal peaches.

Fruit trees in pots require watering to a considerable extent, because the sun and heated air exerts a drying influence on all sides of the pot as well as on the surface of the soil in which the tree is growing, thus causing much moisture to evaporate that would otherwise go to the nutriment of the plant. To retard and counteract undue evaporation, and to keep the roots cool, which is a great desideratum, it is useful to plunge the pots into tubs, or half tubs, which may be obtained from the grocer, butterman, and dealer in flour, and to pack the interval between the exterior of the pot and the interior of the tub with coconut fibre, grass, straw, or any substance that will absorb and retain moisture.

FIG. 541 *Leaf of zonal geranium*

CHAPTER 28

The Garden and its Work in Every Department in July

1711 *Aspect and Character of the Month* The month of July is the hottest in the whole twelve, the mean temperature being 61°, although the thermometer ranges from 82°, and sometimes falls to 42°. The high temperature is chiefly occasioned by the increased radiation of heat at the earth's surface; in consequence, the nights are much warmer than those of June. A period of rainy weather usually occurs about the middle of the month, accompanied by thunderstorms, which have given rise to the popular tradition respecting St Swithin, who is supposed to baptise the apples in this series of rainy days.

It is now summer everywhere; in the deep woods, beneath the shady hedgerows, even in dell and dingle, where twilight reigns at noonday, the warm breath of summer penetrates – the fertilising showers have fallen. The fragrance of the meadow-sweet mingles with the aroma of the sweet-scented briar and of new-made hay. On flowery banks and hedgerows the graceful convolvulus climbs and flowers. The wild briony throws its glossy tendrils round everything it comes near. Wherever the eye alights, the ground is covered with flowers:

Here mantling snug beneath a verdant veil,
Bright creepers draw their horizontal trail;
Wide o'er the bank the slender tendril bends, –
Adown the bank the rooty fringe depends.

'The weeds of one country,' as Dr Edward Daniel Clarke remarks, 'are the flowers of another'; and truly a glance at our garden parterres serves to carry us in imagination to many a distant clime. The damask rose, now in the fullness of its bloom, grows wild in the sunny plains of Syria. The hollyhock, once known as the Foreign Rose, and now common in every cottage garden, is of Eastern origin. Fuchsias, which now have their crimson and purple bells in every garden, were brought by enterprising travellers from the depths of untravelled Mexican forests, where also was found the passionflower, whose type of Christianity, to the imaginative and superstitious Spaniard, demanded of him the conversion of the country, to accomplish which he waded through seas of blood. The jasmines, among the oldest and sweetest of our garden flowers, especially the night-blooming jasmine,

Which keep
Their odour to themselves all day;
But when the sunlight dies away,
Let the delicious fragrance out
To every breeze that roams about,

are still in great request among the women of the East, who are accustomed to decorate their hair with their flowers.

And then the verbenas – brightest ornaments of the parterre – for which we are indebted to the New World, both North and South – how vivid their colouring. In fact, the East and the West have been ransacked to deck our flower beds. 'China and Cathay, and the further Ind' – no country under the sun is unrepresented in them. The frozen plains of Siberia send us larkspurs, golden California her clarkias, and Brazil the petunias.

The early garden fruits are also now in perfection: the black currant hangs like glittering rounded jetty beads beneath its fragrant leaves; the gooseberries can scarcely contain themselves within their hairy husks of green and red; white and red currants hang like pendant pearls and corals from their broad-leaved boughs, and strawberries, ripe and ready for the banquet, peep from under their triple leaves.

I – Work to be done in the Garden

1 – The Flower Garden and Shrubbery

1712 *Borders, Beds, and Shrubberies* Order and neatness should now reign in the beds and borders; weeds should be rooted out as they appear, by hoeing or hand weeding; each individual flower carefully adjusted, the beds and borders, where not covered with plants, neatly raked, forming a clean and even surface, gently sloping to the edges, the clumps and evergreens free from confusion, unless the effect intended is a thicket of underwood. If the shrubs stand apart, let the ground be hoed and neatly raked; all flowering shrubs and evergreens pruned of all straggling shoots, and put in order; all herbaceous plants staked and tied in a neat and regular manner; and all decayed flower stalks, flowers, and leaves, be cut down or removed.

1713 *Shrubs in Eccentric Forms* Shrubs grown to embellish Italian and geometric flower gardens, terraces, etc., should now likewise be cut into the figures they are to assume; in many cases wires will be necessary to keep the branches in their proper places at first; afterwards the knife and shears will suffice to keep them in their proper form. Portugal laurels, cypresses, arbor-vitae, yews, bays, and tree box, are the plants best adapted for this purpose; and when cut into architectural figures, they form fine accompaniments of the above style of gardening. They should be clipped in two or three times during the season, to preserve correctly the required outline.

1714 *Hedges* Quick and privet hedges should be closely cut in with the shears; let them bend off a little towards the top, which gives them a better appearance. Hedges of large-leaved plants, such as laurel, Turkey and Lucombe oak, and sweet bay, must have the young wood cut back by the knife, as the shears would destroy the beauty of their leaves by cutting them.

1715 *Bedding Plants* The first week or so will be chiefly occupied by the usual routine of pegging down plants intended to be kept dwarf, tying others up, and keeping the surface of the beds free from weeds until it is covered by the growing plants. If any bedding out plants still remain in the nursery beds, they should be taken up with as much of the soil as possible, and planted in their allotted place – in showery weather, if possible; if in dry weather, water copiously after transplanting. Beds of verbenas, and similar plants require occasional syringing with weak tobacco water.

1716 *Carnations, Pinks, etc* If these flowers are attacked by wireworm, place pieces of potato just below the surface of the soil. Examine these every morning, and a great number can be thus caught and destroyed. Carnations and pinks should now be propagated by pipings, and carnations by layering. Tie carefully the spindling shoots of carnations and picotees – not too tightly; keep the pots free from weeds, and in dry weather do not let them suffer from drought. Attend to the fertilisation of pinks; a very little attention to this interesting operation will insure a good crop of seeds, and by selecting only excellent varieties, instead of trusting to chance and gathering promiscuously, a much more abundant success will be the result. Disbud carnations and picotees when necessary to insure fine blooms, and give occasional doses of liquid manure.

1717 *Cuttings of Roses, etc.* Cuttings may likewise be put in of tea and China roses, selecting wood of the present year when it becomes a little firm at the base.

1718 *Reserve Garden* Where a nursery or reserve garden exists for supplying the more common kinds of plants, the propagation of various things can now be proceeded with. Keep the smaller and seedling plants free from weeds, and lose no time in sowing perennial and biennial flower seeds for blooming next season.

1719 *Bulbs* Bulbous plants which have flowered should now be removed, the offsets separated from them and placed in dry earth to ripen; and prepare for planting again in October the small offsets planted in a nursery bed, there to remain for a year or two till they reach maturity. Roots, bulbs, anemones, tulips, crocuses, scillas, tritilerias, etc., which have been out of ground some time to dry, should be properly labelled, and put by till autumn.

1720 *Asters, etc* All strong-growing plants, such as asters, helianthuses, and solidagos, or golden rod, should be attended to, so that they all grow together.

1721 *Hollyhocks* Hollyhocks planted on the lawn, whether singly or in groups, should be staked in time; in fact, they should be staked when planted, and the leaves and plants kept in a healthy state by watering and syringing in hot and dry weather. Some hollyhocks will now be in bloom, and others advancing rapidly to flower. Mulching will afford considerable assistance in prolonging the blooming period.

1722 *Cenotheras* Tie up cenotheras neatly. *Cenothera speciosa*, planted pretty thickly over the beds, will produce a fine mass of white flowers, if trained so that they have plenty of light and air, and watered abundantly in dry weather; *Cenothera macrocarpa*, and many other varieties of this plant, better known as the Evening Primrose, also, will well reward the labour.

1723 *Tender Annuals* Cockscombs (Fig. 536), balsams, and other curious annuals, may now be brought out of the frames, cleaned, and top dressed, and tied to suitable sticks, and copiously watered all over, the leaves syringed, if needful, and the plants placed where they are to stand and flower.

FIG. 536 *Cockscomb (Celosia cristata). Dwarf variety*

1724 *Annuals and Biennials* Annuals for autumnal flowering may now be sown, and perennials and biennials sown in March transplanted Stocks, gillyflowers, sweet-williams, Canterbury bells, scarlet lychnis, and others of the class, may now be transplanted into nursery beds prepared for the several sorts; or any of them may be planted at once in beds or borders where they are to remain.

The angularity observable in recently planted-out flower beds is wearing off as the plants approach each other, and harmony begins to prevail as the symmetry of the design develops itself; for here, as in other works of art, the object is to conceal art. If the several parts harmonise imperfectly with one another; if the curve of the outline by which the beds are confined is too sharp; or if, on the other hand, disorder and irregularity meet the eye, and the parts jar with each other – then the design is incomplete, and something is still required to bring all its parts into harmony.

1725 *Autumnal Roses* Autumn-flowering roses now require a liberal supply of liquid manure; guano sown on the ground, and thoroughly soaked with rain water, will serve the purpose. Remove faded flowers and seed capsules every morning; plants which have flowered in pots, keep growing freely, as the future bloom depends on their vigorous growth at this season.

1726 *Climbing Roses* Climbing roses should now be pushing out strong shoots from the roots and main stem; if not required for future training, these should be taken off entirely, or have their tops pinched off a foot or so from the stem.

1727 *Budding and Cutting Back Roses* Budding should now be in full operation, watering the roots and plants freely in dry weather, both before and after budding. Cut back perpetual blooming roses, and water them with the richest manure water to encourage a second growth and bloom.

1728 *Baskets, Vases, etc.* Baskets, vases, etc., will require an occasional regularing: those having plants in them requiring to be tied up should be examined for the purpose; afterwards they may be allowed to grow in a freer style.

Convolvuluses, maurandyas, lophospermums, etc., after being pegged over the surface of the soil, should be left to grow over the sides of the vases, or allowed to ramble among the more formal plants which fill up the centre. Baskets, cases, or other contrivances containing plants in bloom, will require frequent attention to keep them fresh. Remove everything in the shape of decayed bloom or leaves, and take advantage, when a number of fresh plants are wanted, to effect a change in the arrangement, which will be found more pleasing than adhering to one plan. For the same reason, plants under verandahs, or arranged for effect near the house, when undergoing revision for the purpose of adding fresh plants, will be more interesting when variety in arrangement, or in the kind of plants, is introduced as often as they are changed.

1729 *Fuchsias, Geraniums, etc.* Fuchsias, geraniums, and other plants in flower, now require regular supplies of water. Fuchsias going out of flower now, if the leading shoots are shortened and the plants placed in a cool place in the shade, will obtain a temporary rest and strength for putting forth a fresh set of blooms in autumn.

1730 *Tulips* Take up tulips whenever the weather will permit. When lifted, do not separate the offsets from the parent bulb, or remove the roots or skin: these had better remain till a later period. When lifted, ridge up the soil of the beds for exposure to the air. In taking up seedlings, great care must be used, as their bulbs will often strike down from 4 to 6 inches. If possible, keep the stock of each separate; this will save an immense deal of trouble hereafter.

1731 *Ranunculuses* By the end of the month, seedling ranunculuses should be taken from the pans or boxes in which they may have been grown; but as many are so minute, and so like the colour of the soil, that without great precaution, some may be overlooked, the best way is to put soil and roots together in a fine wire sieve, and by holding it under a tap, or pumping into it, the soil will be washed away and the roots left; they must then be placed in the sun for an hour, and afterwards removed to an airy shady place to dry gradually. The large roots of named varieties must be taken up at once, if not already done: for should they start again, which they are very apt to do previous to their removal, their death is inevitable.

1732 *Dahlias* Attend sedulously to dahlias; tie as they require it, and give a good supply of water.

2 – The Vegetable or Kitchen Garden

1733 *Preparation for Winter Crops* Probably this is the busiest month of the year in the kitchen garden, both on account of everything growing so fast, and because many crops have ceased to be useful, and must be removed and give place to others. We have to look forward to a long winter and spring, when vegetation is stationary or very slow: yet at that time it is necessary to have suitable crops; and now is the time to prepare the ground and get them in their places. Stiff soils should be dug some time previous to cropping, especially for sowing small seeds, as turnip. The soil will dry in hard lumps at first; but advantage must be taken of the first shower that wets the soil through, as it will then readily fall to pieces under the rake. On light soils this is of less consequence, and it is as well to sow immediately after digging, as the seeds vegetate quicker.

It is proper to observe that where rows of vegetables have previously grown, the ground is usually dry and hard. However moist the season has been, it will always be found different to that 18 inches or so on either side; it is not, therefore, advisable to crop immediately over the same spot; the difference will soon be observable between the rows planted exactly where peas have grown and those planted at the distance indicated. I have found it best not to plant winter crops on ground that has been newly dug or trenched, and never knew broccoli do so well as when planted on hard ground that had not been dug since February; but when the plants had taken hold, and began to grow, the ground was forked over, and a dressing of manure worked in. I have also been informed by practised gardeners that Brassicae are far more liable to club on loose or newly-trenched ground; but much may depend on the nature of the soil.

1734 *Weeds* During this month it is very necessary to keep the weeds down, as their growth is very rapid in showery weather; it is also beneficial to crops to keep the ground stirred between them, and collect all useless matter as fast as possible.

1735 *Asparagus* Cease cutting early this month, unless some parts can be spared for late use, when it must have a rest the following season. Late cutting has the effect of weakening the roots, but they will recover after a season's rest, if they have not been cut too closely. Hoe frequently between the rows.

1736 *Seakale* should have an abundance of water, particularly young plants. Soot or wood ashes strewn about them will, in a great measure, prevent the attacks of insects.

1737 *Artichokes* will now be in bearing. Cut when the heads are about three parts open. These root deeply, and scarcely require water.

1738 *Peas* If any are sown this month, let it be sorts that bear equally, or the shortening days will prevent their bearing at all. Dwarf early sorts are good to sow this month. Clear away any that have ceased to be productive, and stake any that are just above ground. As they grow quickly at this time, any delay in this respect will be inconvenient to the grower as well as damaging to the crop. Copious waterings will greatly benefit those coming into flower, but may be discontinued when they begin to pod, excepting tall sorts, which continue bearing and flowering at the same time.

1739 *Beans* Pull up early crops as soon as they have done bearing; those advancing will produce better for being well watered, for which purpose make a groove each side of the rows, and give enough to soak the ground to a considerable depth; they had better be left alone than inefficiently watered.

1740 *French Beans* A late sowing of these may be made any time this month; for which purpose dwarf kinds, as the Newington Wonder, are best. Sow on unmanured soil; thin out those sufficiently above ground to 4 or 6 inches apart, and draw plenty of earth up to the stems, which will stay them in windy weather.

1741 *Runner Beans* Apply strong sticks, if not already done. These may be kept dwarf by picking off the runners as fast as they appear; but it is much better to let them have full play by providing supports - the produce is tenfold greater.

1742 *Celery* During this month the main crop should be got out, directions for which were given last month. If this is planted where peas had previously grown, make the trenches between, not on the rows where the ground has been heavily drawn, or the crop will not be so good. It is very proper to give early crops plenty of room, so that, should they not be ready to clear away, such crops as this may be planted between while they are growing.

1743 *Cardoons* (Fig. 537), like celery, should be got out in the trenches, remembering that these crops require a soil highly enriched with manure; they should also have plenty of room and abundance of water. Be not hasty in earthing up.

1744 *Beet* See that this crop is properly thinned, and keep the ground well hoed between.

1745 *Carrots* Seed may be sown any time this month, as its produce will be useful in winter and spring. Sow on an open spot, and do not dig the ground deep. Look over the main crop, and pull up any that are running to seed; they will be of no use if left. Take care that no weeds are allowed to grow amongst them.

1746 *Onions* These may be sown now as

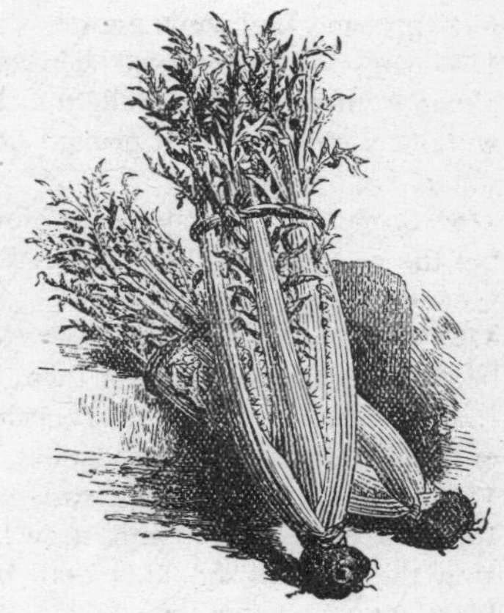

FIG. 537 *Cardoons*

an ingredient of salads in the autumn. Towards the end of this month some of the main crop will be showing signs of maturity, when they may be pulled up and laid on their sides, and thick-necked ones may be pinched; but this should not be done hastily, and probably had better not be done yet.

1747 *Leeks* Plant out the main crop on well-manured ground; plant in deep drills or shallow trenches for the convenience of earthing. This is a strong feeder, and should be well watered.

1748 *Potatoes* Pick off the flowers, if possible; if the potato-apples, which contain the seed, are allowed to form, it is said to diminish the produce, the tubers growing less in proportion to the quantity of seed allowed to ripen. Some advise cutting off the haulm as soon as the disease becomes apparent. Of the efficacy of this remedy there is much doubt, but it may, in a measure, stay the progress of the disease, although at the sacrifice of size in the tubers.

1749 *Turnips* At the beginning of this month, a principal sowing should be made for autumn and early winter use; and again, towards the end, another principal sowing should be made. These will be useful in winter and following spring. It is better to sow broadcast, and not in drills, and to use the large hoe continually till the plants meet. Some, however, recommend sowing in drills a foot apart, and sowing soot, wood ashes, superphosphate of lime, and other ingredients, at the same time. The seed must be protected from birds.

1750 *Lettuce* sown now will do well on a shady border, provided the spot is not too much overhung by trees. An open, well-manured spot is best for them if kept well watered.

1751 *Endive* Two sowings of this should be made this month; one at the beginning, another towards the end. Sow in the same way as lettuce, and plant out as soon as large enough to handle.

1752 *Tomatoes* should be carefully trained, and stopped as they grow. Stop just over a bunch of flowers, and leave no more shoots than can be conveniently trained. Unless the ground is very dry, they do not require watering, and will most probably do best without it.

1753 *Vegetable Marrows* will be in active growth; and where they are planted on a manure heap, or if liberally mulched with it, they will grow freely enough without watering; but, if planted on the common soil, they should be freely watered in the morning.

1754 *Spinach* It is not advisable to sow this month, unless for particular purposes; but the ground should be prepared for sowing next month, particularly if the ground is heavy.

1755 *Broccoli, Brussels Sprouts, and Savoys* The principal crops of these should be got out this month. Plant them in drills 2 feet apart, and 18 inches in the rows. If liable to club, dip the roots in a puddle of clay and soot before planting, or fill up the holes with wood ashes, which will prevent it in a great measure.

1756 *Cabbage* Sow for coleworts early this month, and for early cabbaging about the end of this month; strew lime or soot over the young plants to drive away the fly. This should be done in the morning, while the dew is on them. Plant out for autumn use.

1757 *Cauliflower* sown now may be useful late in the autumn.

1758 *Sweet Herbs* Mint and suchlike herbs should be cut for drying just as they begin to flower; savory, sage, and others, may be now propagated by cuttings or division; parsley and chervil may be sown now for winter use.
1759 *Mushroom Beds* These may yet be made out of doors, providing plenty of clean straw and mats to protect them. Some gardeners make a practice of spawning melon beds, either while the fruit is ripening or after they are cleared off. It is done in this manner: Clear off the old soil, break the spawn into small pieces, lay it regularly over the bed, and cover it with about 2 inches of horse droppings or very short dung. This, again, is covered with 2 or 3 inches of good loamy soil, and all trodden down and made firm. Heat is applied by means of fresh linings of well-worked dung.

3 – The Fruit Garden and Orchard

1760 *Summer Training, etc., of Espaliers* Espaliers and dwarf fruit trees should receive attention with regard to summer training and pruning. This is of the greatest importance, since, when a bud or small shoot is taken off now, the wound is soon cicatrised, and no harm need be apprehended, while this is not always the case as regards the cuts produced in winter pruning.
1761 *Pruning Standards* Standard trees are usually left to take care of themselves and their fruit during the summer time; but good gardeners attend well to them, as to wall trees; nor is there any reason why this should not be done.

Judicious pruning or stopping, and removing superfluous wood in July, would prevent, in a great measure, gumming, canker, and immature decay in standard trees. Towards the middle of this month, apples are well washed by the showers which usually take place now; still, it is worth while to do this artificially with the barrow engine, and endeavour to keep the foliage and bark clean, and wash away insects, which are sure to swarm about them, although invisible. Time will also be well spent in thinning out the fruit, if too thickly set. It is a grievous sight to a good fruit grower to see the limbs of a tree borne down with the weight, which forebodes several unproductive seasons to come.

1762 *Peaches and Nectarines* These should receive their final thinning this month, if not done before. Some prefer allowing them to get large enough to use for pies, etc., before doing so; but the sooner the surplus fruit is taken off, the better for the crop. Nail in neatly all the young wood, and give the fruit the slightest shelter of the leaves, and no more; too much shade deteriorates the flavour of the fruit, while none at all is apt to produce a premature ripening of it.

Some little judgment should be exercised in thinning both wood and fruit; the object being to regulate both, so that a fair balance is maintained. If too much fruit is left on, the present year's crop will not be so good, nor will the strength of the tree be maintained for future bearing; if too much wood is left, the fruit is too much shaded, and the wood itself becomes weak: regulate both, so that the present crop of fruit has a fair chance of doing well, and just about enough wood is left to furnish the tree for another year without having recourse to much pruning in the winter.

1763 *Apricots, Plums, Cherries, and Figs* All trees on walls should be carefully looked over, and all shoots that are not really useful, or any that are ill placed or cannot be properly nailed in, should be removed. It is important to do this in time, because, if neglected till the fruit begins to ripen, the real advantage of doing it is lost; and it is necessary to be long sighted, and have an eye to future crops as well as the present one; and if they are not nailed in, the disbudding ought in no case to be deferred. Figs, especially, are apt to make strong superfluous wood, the leaves of which throw a dense shade over the fruit, while the heat of the sun is so necessary to its ripening.

1764 *Washing Trees* The garden engine should be played freely over wall trees about two or three times a week, as this would wash off dust and insects, and maintain that cleanliness so conducive to health.

1765 *Vines* Vines out of doors should be closely stopped and trained in. All the heat of the sun is necessary to the well-doing of this fruit, which cannot be expected to ripen in our short seasons, unless every care is taken to secure them all the light and warmth of the sun.

1766 *Gooseberries, Currants, and Raspberries* Where the fruit is left to ripen, it is often necessary to give it some protection from birds. Nothing is better for the purpose than tanned netting or an old herring net, spread over and round the tree, completely covering it in; if any opening is left, the birds will get in. Blackbirds are very bold and eager after these fruits, and are sometimes entrapped by this means.

1767 *Caterpillars on Gooseberries, etc* Caterpillars are often abundant on gooseberry and currant bushes, and various ways are propounded for destroying them; as spreading old tan under the bushes, and, at a certain time, burning it to destroy the larvae. Some use no other means but picking them off, or shaking them on to a cloth or sheet, and by this means they have been freed from them, while others have had the foliage of their bushes completely eaten up by them. A little practice in gathering them will enable the operator to destroy thousands in a very short time.

1768 *Strawberries* This is by far the best month of the year for making new plantations. There are various methods of doing this, but, perhaps, the best is as follows: The earliest runners are laid in 3-inch pots; they are fixed in their place by means of small pegs; in three weeks they have rooted into the soil with which the pots are filled. During that time they require an occasional watering, but may be planted out permanently as soon as rooted, placing them 18 inches apart, in rows 3 feet apart. This is a clean and expeditious mode, and I find they bear the following year better than old plants. This is also the best mode of obtaining potted plants for forcing the following winter or spring. If for this purpose, they should not be dis-severed from the old plants till they are well rooted. They should then receive good culture till the autumn, when they may be stored in frames.

1769 *Modes of Growing Strawberries* Strawberries are sometimes grown on permanent beds 4 feet wide, and I have known them bear well for several successive years on heavy soils in this manner. Another method is to have them in narrow beds, 2 feet wide, with 2-foot alleys between. When they have ceased bearing, the runners are allowed to trail over the alleys, and when they are well covered, the old beds are dug in. Next year the same is repeated; thus a succession of young plants is kept in bearing with very little trouble.

There are times when the earth about the roots of fruit trees, etc., becomes parched, so that the fruit is not properly nourished in the process of swelling or stoning. In dry seasons, this is a fertile cause of fruit being small or ill-flavoured. The following mode of remedying this evil, especially in the case of vine borders, cannot be too strongly recommended: Perforated pipes are laid about a foot or 18 inches below the surface of the soil – in the case of strawberry beds about 6 inches; from these a tube is carried to a convenient place for filling with water or liquid manure, with which they are charged twice a day or as often as it is considered necessary. By this means a thorough moistening of the roots is effected, greatly to the improvement of the crops of fruit.

II – Work to be done under Glass

1 – Flowers in the Conservatory, Greenhouse, Stove, etc.

1770 *The Hothouse* Such stove plants as are intended to flower in the winter, as Justicias, *Eranthemum pulchellum*, Euphorbias, Jasmines, etc., should be looked to. Many of these things require to be kept in small pots, and should be watered with liquid manure to grow them on without getting into too large pots. Encourage plants now established by using liquid manure. Young plants growing into specimens will require constant stopping and trying to get them into proper form. In shifting for the season, many conservatory plants will now be in the open air; but some of the New Holland, such as *Boronia pinnata* and *B. serrulata*, still require a little heat and pretty free stopping to insure handsome plants.

1771 *The Greenhouse: Treatment of Plants after Blooming* Greenhouse plants, after they have done blooming, should have a comparatively cool temperature, and no structure presents so many advantages for this purpose, as well as for growing delicate-leaved plants through the summer, as houses having a north aspect; while for the purpose of retarding plants, or for preserving them in bloom, it is indispensable. Such plants, therefore, as Epacrises, Leschenaultias, Pimeleas, Aphelexis, and others of similar habit, which have been kept for late bloom and are now over, should be placed in a house of the above description, or in deep frames, with the sashes turned towards the north, having first picked off the old remaining blooms; here, with gentle syringing once or twice daily, the plants may remain till the new growth commences, when any pruning they may require may be given, and afterwards placed in a more favourable situation for ripening their wood. The flowers of heaths and other plants that have done flowering should be removed, and all straggling branches stopped.

1772 *Ventilation* At this season all the air possible should be given to the greenhouse and most stove plants, keeping it on all night.

1773 *Hard-wooded Plants: Repotting* Hard-wooded plants, including most of the genera from New Holland, which bloom early in the spring, will about the middle of the month be so far advanced in their new growth that any requiring repotting should at once have a shift. After turning them out, loosen the outside roots before placing them in their new pots, to enable them to take up the fresh soil more readily. Keep them close for a few days, especially if the roots have been much disturbed, and damp them once or twice daily overhead.

1774 *Heaths, etc., for Winter Blooming* Attention at this season should be directed to the stock of plants intended to furnish the supply of bloom through the winter, as it is requisite plants should complete their growth early for this purpose

Among heaths, those which flower through the winter should be encouraged to complete their growth.

At no period of the year do heaths and hard-wooded plants in general require more care than the present, more particularly such as have been recently potted. To keep the old ball sufficiently moist to preserve the plant in health in the high temperature without getting the new soil in a sour state, requires great nicety in watering, supposing the plants to be under glass.

1775 *Epacrises* Keep epacrises under glass till their growth is complete; but more air and light must be allowed them, increasing as the wood gets firmer. Towards the end of the month they may be placed out of doors in an open situation, where they can be protected from heavy rains. Young specimens should be carefully trained, the shoots neatly tied down or pegged, to insure a close compact habit.

1776 *Achimenes, Gloxinias, Clerodendrons, etc.* Achimenes, gloxinias, etc., out of bloom should be removed to a pit to ripen their bulbs. Clerodendrons, etc., in the same way may be transferred to vineries, or any place where there is a dry cool atmosphere.

1777 *Shifting and Repotting* Fuschias, geraniums, achimenes, and salvias (Fig. 538) requiring larger pots, should now be shifted, removing the entire ball, and placing in the centre of the new pot, properly drained and half filled with fresh compost, having first trimmed the roots and removed the outside soil; the pot is then filled with compost, well watered, and put away in an airy but shaded situation to settle.

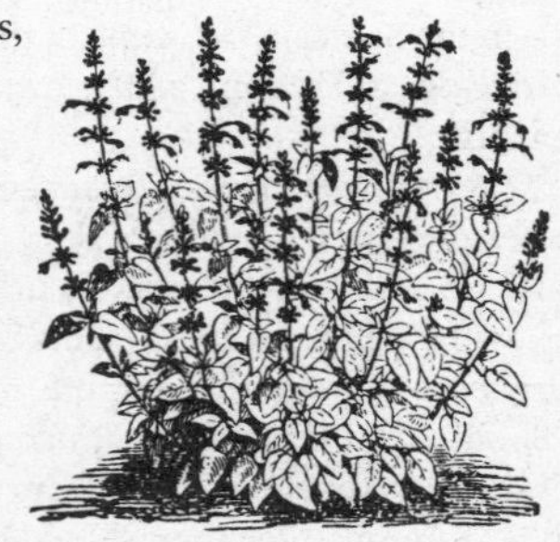

FIG. 538 *Salvia coccinea*

1778 *Oranges and Lemons* Orange and lemon trees will now be in bloom, and should be supplied with water at least three times a week in dry weather, and be occasionally supplied with liquid manure after stirring the surface of the soil and top-dressing. Orange trees when too full of bloom should have the flowers thinned out. They are always in request for drying or distilling. The young fruit when too thickly set should also have a thinning. In order to procure dark glossy foliage, water with clear soot water.

1779 *Budding and Grafting Oranges, etc* Oranges, camellias, azaleas and other hard-wooded plants, can now be budded or grafted; and in the beginning of the month, myrtles, oleanders, and jasmines propagated by layers. All pots and tubs, especially orange and lemon plants, require stirring on the surface of the soil, and top dressed and watered when required.

The stocks for budding orange trees are raised from seeds sown in March or April in pots of rich earth, and plunged into a hotbed. In five or six weeks the plants will come up, when they are planted singly in thumb pots, and plunged into a fresh hotbed, raising the frame as the plants increase in height, to encourage their growth. In August they will be 18 or 20 inches high, when they may be removed into the greenhouse, placing them near the lights. In March or April shift them into larger pots, and plunge again into a hotbed, gradually exposing them to the air towards the end of May, to harden them, turning them out from June till August. In the third summer they will be fit for budding, for which they are prepared by removal into the greenhouse, giving them plenty of air and light, but turning the side on which they are to be budded from the sun, and shading the whole plant from its fiercest heat. Three weeks before budding, the plant may be plunged into a moderate hotbed of tanner's bark, where it can have free ventilation.

1780 *Azaleas* Chinese azaleas should be turned out. Unlike camellias, they require full exposure to sun and air, and should be placed in an open situation, that their wood may become thoroughly ripened. It will, however, perhaps be necessary to place them for a week or two in a partially shaded situation, to harden their foliage sufficiently to bear the full sun, or the sudden change from a house to full sunshine might cause their leaves to turn brown or burn.

1781 *Camellias* Camellias, whenever the young wood appears getting ripe, may be removed to the open air; they thrive best in the shade; they must be placed on a dry bottom to prevent worms from getting into the pots.

1782 *Brugmansias* Brugmansias, and similar plants of vigorous habit, should be frequently assisted with manure water; as they are often troubled with the red spider, the engine and syringe must be kept constantly at work to keep them down, taking care, however, not to injure the fine foliage.

1783 *Chorozemas* Propagate by cuttings sometime during this month, or in August. These greenhouse plants are useful additions to the tenants of any house, because they remain in bloom for the greater part of the year, and more especially in winter and early spring. The plants themselves are easily managed, and the flowers are desirable for decorative purposes and bouquets. For soil, use a rich turfy peat, mixed with fibrous loam, leaf mould, and gritty sand. When freshly potted, they should be put in a close pit or the warmest part of a greenhouse, and be sparingly watered at the roots until they get into free growth. When thoroughly established they may be watered twice a week with clear liquid manure.

1784 *Cactuses and Succulents* Succulent plants, as cactuses, euphorbias, cereuses, sedums, and others of similar habit, require to be abundantly supplied with water, and also a full exposure to the sun, in order to obtain a fine bloom. Offsets of these plants may now be struck in beds or pots of light compost, without the aid of artificial heat, but they root more readily in bark, or on a hotbed under a frame.

1785 *Annuals for Indoor Blooming* Balsams, thunbergias, and other annuals intended to decorate the conservatory and show house for the next two months, should be finally potted, using soil of a light and rich description. Keep down spider with the syringe.

1786 *Creepers and Climbers* – Ipomaeas, thunbergias, passion flowers, and all other creepers, should be neatly trained to their respective trellises as they advance, keeping them fresh and healthy by frequent watering, and by picking off all decaying leaves; and, where the plants are flagging, water them with very weak liquid manure.

1787 *Pelargoniums* June and July are the best months for increasing this plant. Cuttings struck at this season from plants which have been forced, and the wood thoroughly ripened, produce fine plants for autumn flowering and early spring forcing, supplying the want of flowers in the conservatory in winter and spring.

Having prepared the pots in the usual manner, and put in crocks and other loose material for about one-third the entire depth of each pot, fill them up with a compost composed of equal parts of turfy loam and silver sand well mixed, and sifted so as to keep back the large lumps. Then select cuttings from strong short-jointed shoots 3 or 4 inches long, removing the lower leaves so as to leave the base of the cuttings clear; place them round the edge of the pot about an inch or an inch and a half deep. When planted, water freely to settle the soil round them, and place them in a cold pit or frame. Sprinkle them occasionally overhead till rooted: afterwards give air gradually to harden them for potting off into 3-inch pots. When well established in the small pots, and about 6 inches high, stop them, that they may throw out lateral or side shoots. When they have made their shoots, repot them in 48s in a compost of turfy loam, peat, and decomposed cow or stable dung in equal parts, with a good proportion of road or river sand, the pots being thoroughly drained with potsherds or oyster shells. Thin out the leaves and small shoots occasionally, in order to throw the whole sap into the shoots which are to produce flowers. When plunged into the border to flower, these plants will be benefitted by being lifted occasionally to prevent them from rooting through the bottom of the pots. Those for spring forcing will require a further shift in September; and the fancy varieties, being more delicate growers, will require more drainage; and a little charred cow dung in rough placed over the potsherds will be found beneficial.

1788 *Pelargoniums for Autumn Blooming* When autumn-flowering plants are required, take cuttings in early summer, when they will strike freely; fill the pot half full of broken potsherds, and fill up with a compost of equal parts of good turfy loam, peat, and well-decomposed cow dung and leaf mould, with a good portion of silver sand. By the end of July the plants will require to be repotted, taking care that this is repeated as often as roots fill the pots. As the season advances, a little heat will make them expand their blossoms more freely.

For large fine-grown specimens select a strong plant, and pot in a compost consisting of two parts good turfy loam, one of leaf mould, one of well-decomposed cow dung, and a good portion of silver sand. After a summer's free growth, assisted by frequent watering, about the beginning of July begin to diminish the quantity of water, so that the wood may be thoroughly hardened before cutting down. By the end of July the plants should be shaken clean out of the soil, the roots pruned at the points, and repotted in the same compost. The plants, being thoroughly established, should be repotted in November, in pots of suitable size, in the same compost as before. In February they will require a second shift, when each shoot should be

FIG. 539 *Cineraria (Cineraria cruenta hybrida grandiflora)*

stopped at the fourth joint, to induce lateral shoots, tying each out horizontally. When the lateral shoots are of sufficient length, stop a second time. If intended to flower in May, stop after they are cut down in July; if in June, stop in January; if in July, stop in February.

1789 *The Conservatory* Remove from the conservatory or show house those plants which show, by their faded blooms, that they are past their best: their prolonged presence would detract from the freshness essential to beauty and good order. The 'sere and yellow leaf' is now apparent here; the work of decay has commenced; exotic bulbs have nearly finished flowering, and require now to be in a state of rest; those whose stems are still green should have water, in order to mature the bulbs. When done flowering, keep them in dry earth or sand, and in a warm situation, to ripen.

1790 *Cinerarias and Calceolarias* Cinerarias and calceolarias require as cool an atmosphere as the house admits of; those which have flowered, cut down, and plant out in a light loamy border; sow seeds of both for flowering in spring.

2 – Plants under Glass in Hotbeds, Frames, etc.

1791 *Flowers in Hotbeds, etc.* Such hotbeds and frames as are devoted to flowers will now be employed only for the purpose of ripening bulbs, etc., and maturing plants for late blooming, or for striking cuttings. Cuttings of geraniums and most greenhouse shrubs may now be struck, and forwarded by plunging in a gentle hotbed, taking as cuttings only strong and healthy shoots 3 to 5 or 6 inches long, according to the size of the plants. These cuttings should be planted in pans, boxes, or pots of rich light compost, a few inches apart, moderately watered, and placed in a frame shaded from the midday sun till they are rooted. Soft-wooded plants like the geranium hardly require such delicate treatment, although they strike sooner under it.

1792 *Propagating Roses, etc.* Many gardeners make hotbeds at this time for propagating plants, as roses and greenhouse plants, and also for other purposes connected with the flower garden, etc. Hotbeds made in the ordinary way are very suitable, and have their advantages, and where the material is plentiful, they are probably the best: but a very useful bed for propagating and raising seeds, etc., is made as follows: Having prepared the dung as usual, lay the foundation as for an ordinary bed, but commence from the bottom an opening which leaves the bed hollow in the interior, the sides and ends of the bed being sloped upwards all round from a point in the centre; drain pipes are laid to conduct the heat from the linings into this hollow, which is covered by boards laid across, on which the frame rests; the boards may then be covered with soil, ashes, tan, or dung; while the heat of the bed lasts the pipes must be plugged up, but opened when lining is applied, to conduct the heat into the bed.

1793 *Purposes and Management of Hotbeds in July* The purposes of hotbeds are limited at this time of the year, at least in most places. Cucumbers, melons, etc., are usually grown in houses and pits that are otherwise unoccupied at present; and as their culture is more cleanly, and with greater comfort that way, hotbeds may be dispensed with for a time; but those already in operation will require attention. The weather is usually hot this month and next, but is often changeable, and the manager of frames must be ruled by it. We sometimes have sudden and heavy showers, which would drench the plants and beds through if they were uncovered, probably to the destruction of the plants; yet plenty of fresh air is necessary; and the sudden changes produced by the sun being obscured by clouds for a time, and then bursting forth hot and fierce, must be provided against. It is in such cases that a little shade may be advantageous; but it must be very slight, and not be left on a moment longer than is really required.

1794 *Cucumbers* Plants in bearing should be copiously watered occasionally: if the soil shows any symptoms of dryness underneath, they should be moistened overhead every day; but this keeps the surface moist, while beneath it the soil may become dry. This being, frequently the cause of plants going off, it should be guarded against by examining the soil before syringing. If the soil is not sufficiently moist, take care to water plentifully, as at this time of the year there is less danger of over-watering. If the weather is hot, and not too dry, the lights may be pulled quite off for an hour or two before 8 a.m. and after 5 p.m.; but see that the plants are not chilled before closing. A sowing of any good house or frame cucumber may now be made for autumn supply.

1795 *Pickling Cucumbers* Pickling cucumbers may be planted in the open ground at the beginning of this month; the soil should be well dug, and made pretty firm again, and well mulched after the plants are put in. Choose a warm sheltered spot for them, and place hand glasses over them if they can be spared. The work of stopping, pegging down, etc., for these is precisely the same as for ridge and frame cucumbers. They will do on ridges put out at the beginning of this month.

1796 *Melons* Plants raised at the beginning of this month may be put out in the ordinary manner in a common melon pit, with a good body of dung; but, if planted later, it must be so that heat can be applied to ripen the fruit, which, occurring in the shortening days, will want assistance from artificial heat. Plants that are ripening their fruit must have very little water. For melons and cucumbers in houses, etc., keep up a steady bottom heat and afford free ventilation, more especially in wet weather. Keep the strictest watch for red spider and mildew; for both of which, sulphur, properly applied, is the best preventive, in addition to keeping the roots in action by a well-adjusted bottom heat.

FIG. 540 *Cantaloup melon (variety De Bellegarde)*

1797 *Tomatoes, Capsicums, etc.* These, when in fruiting condition, should remain in the pots, and be plunged in the bed; the roots will ramble through the pots, but are more likely to bear than if planted in the bed.

1798 *Strawberries for Forcing* Proceed to pot strawberries for forcing; as soon as the pots in which the runners were layered become filled with roots, pot them in 6- or 7-inch pots, using rich loam of medium texture and well-rotted dung, and drain well. The kinds intended for early forcing need not have quite such large pots as those intended for a later supply. When potted, place them in an open situation exposed to the sun, placing them on boards, or a prepared bottom, to prevent worms from getting to the roots.

3 – Fruit under Glass, heated and unheated

1799 *The Vinery: Shading, etc.* Ripe grapes, if required to be kept, must be shaded during hot sun, to prevent their becoming shrivelled. The Muscat, Sweetwater, and Frontignan, having tender leaves, are most liable to burn, either from bad glass or imperfect ventilation; in which case they must be well watched, as the injury done to the foliage not only affects the present crop, but the succeeding one as well. Any heat given now should be given during the day, in order to their getting well forward before the season gets too far on. Under this treatment they all keep longer and have a finer flower, keeping the outside borders of the late crops watered and well mulched.

1800 *Ventilation* As the houses are cleared of their fruit, and the wood is ripened, it will be much benefitted by having the lights off, and by being freely exposed to the atmosphere for a time. Air must be given in abundance by night as well as day, and the necessary stopping of lateral growths and thinning of the fruit in the last house proceeded with. Watch for mildew, which is caused by excess of moisture, and must be checked by the sulphur remedy, which consists in dusting all affected parts with sulphur in the form of a fine dry powder. The disease shows itself in spots or blotches on the leaves, and a dirty, unwholesome thick dust or mould, which spreads itself over the branches and berries. This, as it has been said, is the consequence of an excess of moisture; too little moisture, on the other hand, will produce red spider, which may be checked by fumigation with sulphur, or prevented, which is better, by maintaining a suitable moist condition of the air of the house, a happy medium, in fact, between insufficiency of moisture and a superabundance of it.

1801 *Vines in Pots* Vines in pots intended to fruit next season should now be well supplied with manure water, to swell out and perfect their buds.

1802 *The Pinery: Plants Ripening Fruit* Still continue to supply fruit swelling with water, and syringe frequently, but not during bright sunshine, unless the shading is immediately put on. Young plants growing fast will require liberal waterings, in addition to air in large quantities by day: the temperature will allow them to have a good portion by night. During hot weather forced fruits of all descriptions will be benefitted by this practice.

1803 *Plants for Autumn and Winter Fruiting* About the second week, the plants selected in the spring for autumn and winter fruiting will be showing fruit; and if they are in a pit by themselves, will require, if a steady bottom heat is kept up, but little attention for some time, except slight shading, plenty of air, and a liberal allowance of water.

On no account let the plants be wetted while in bloom. Some pines having large flowers, as the Jamaica, etc., frequently cut up with black spots in the middle, although apparently sound outside, which arises from a small quantity of water passing through the bloom to the fruit cells, and causing the latter to decay.

1804 *Succession Plants* Let succession plants have abundance of air day and night, to encourage a stocky growth, and water freely when the pots become full of roots. Keep the bottom heat steady. At this season the young staff may be potted whenever they require a shift. Where it is intended to plant out the fruiting stock for next year, a sufficient quantity of loam, peat, and sand should be in readiness for use. Directly the present crop is cut, the stump should be cleared out, and either all or part of the soil removed, according as it may appear exhausted.

1805 *Management of Pits* As soon as the principal part of the present crop is ripe, the pit will be required either for fruiting the winter stock, or for the succession of next season's fruiting. Fruit may yet remain to ripen should be carefully removed to one end of the pit, unless circumstances enable you to transfer them to a house devoted to fruiting the autumn and winter supply, in which case the house may be cleared whenever the principal part is cut. The bottom heat must be freshened up by the addition of fresh material, and made ready for plunging the new stock of plants as they are placed in their fruiting pots.

1806 *Repairing House* In the meantime advantage should be taken of putting the house in repair, if requisite, and the heating apparatus in a state of efficiency, as no such favourable opportunity will occur again for a twelvemonth.

1807 *Peaches and Nectarines* – Any tendency to decay of the leaves when the fruit has been gathered should be prevented by syringing and watering the roots. Fruit coming to maturity will be all the more delicious for a comparatively cool temperature while ripening. Examine daily and gather before it is over-ripe. The great object now is to get the wood properly ripened; and that will be best promoted by a full exposure to the sun, the air, the rain, and the dews, by removing the sashes and top lights.

1808 *Figs* Trees that are swelling off their second crop should be assisted with liquid manure freely, more especially if growing in pots or tubs. As the fruit ripens, care must be taken to preserve them from damp, which the frequent syringing to keep down insects induces; it should, therefore, be a rule to look over and pick the ripe fruit every morning, and syringe directly afterwards. Admit air freely, and pinch out the points of the young wood when grown sufficiently long. This will assist the swelling of the fruit, and produce useful spurs for bearing next year. It should be a rule so to manage figs during the summer, that nothing further than a slight thinning out should be wanted in the winter pruning.

1809 *Orchard House* Ventilation is now the greatest care; fasten back and front shutters down, so that they cannot be closed; syringing night and morning, and watering copiously when dry. If any trees are growing too rapidly, tilt up the pots, and cut off all the roots on that side which are making their way into the soil. A week later, serve the other side in the same way. If the surface is getting hard from watering, place some fresh compost loosely on the surface. Pinch in all lateral shoots to within two buds of their base. On the 10th and the 25th lift the pots in order to break off the roots.

1810 *Ripening Fruit Out of Doors* Remove all trees into the open air, to ripen their fruit in a sheltered sunny spot. This gives them a piquant and racy flavour, unknown to fruit gathered from wall trees. Summer pinching of pyramids and bushes requires rigid attention.

CHAPTER 29

The Garden and Its Work in Every Department in August

1811 *Aspect and Character of the Month* August, the eighth month of the Julian year, received its name from Augustus Caesar, as July commemorated that of the greater Julius. Less rain falls this month than in July, according to the ordinary course of Nature, and the mean temperature is a little higher than in that month, the nights being certainly hotter. In continuation of the experiments at Chiswick to ascertain the average mean temperature in each month at the surface of the ground, and at the distances of 1 foot and 2 feet below the surface, the average mean temperature for August in the positions stated was found to be 61·98°, 61·80°, and 61·26°, respectively. The surface of the earth has been receiving and absorbing the sun's rays during the hot months of June and July, and now it begins to give back a portion of its heat by radiation in place of absorbing it, as in the earlier months of the year.

In fact, Nature's tide has turned and the ebb has commenced; the leaves of the earlier deciduous trees and shrubs begin already to change, their edges are tinged with yellow, and others are just beginning to assume their autumnal tint of russet, brown, and green.

As thou listenest, thou shalt hear,
Distant harvest carols clear,
Rustle of the reapèd corn,
Sweet birds antheming the morn.

But for the crop of young leaves, indeed, which still continue to present themselves on the trees, mingling with those of older growth, and blending in one harmonious whole, the glories of mature summer foliage – the 'sere and yellow leaf' of autumn with the delicate tints and tender foliage of spring – we should have very decided indications of the fading year.

As it is, the dark green masses of the woods are already relieved, and their edges lighted up by the russet, brown, and yellow, which, under the broad rays of the sun, glitter in golden splendour in the landscape. And then the deep azure of an August sky, and the silvery clouds which float about, and the profound repose which has been so frequently sung and said as the distinguishing feature of the month, both by naturalist and poet, when

All heaven and earth are still, though not asleep,
But breathless, as we grow when feeling most.

The broad fern now arrests the eye with its russet-coloured leaves; the autumnal crocus, with its saffron-coloured petals, is now in bloom, and the lilac-coloured flowers of the wild mint are found in moist and shady places. The pinky petals of the lavender plant are now in full blossom, filling the air with their sweet perfume; the air is also musical with the hum of bees; the pearly blossoms of spring have disappeared from the hawthorn hedgerows, to be succeeded by its fruit of pendant rubies. The brilliant dahlia, the gorgeous sunflower, and the lordly-looking hollyhock, have taken the place of the lilies, associated with the magnificent perpetual blooming roses, and the splendid flowers of the Amaranth family:

Immortal Amaranth, a flower which once
In Paradise, fast by the Tree of Life,
Began to bloom.

And, diffusing fragrance in every part of the garden where it has been sown in spring, is the humble blooming but fragrant mignonette (*Reseda odorata*), a native of Northern Africa, whence it was brought by some flower-loving Frenchman, to find its way soon after into England, where it has become a universal favourite with high and low.

I – Work to be done in the Garden

1 – The Flower Garden and Shrubbery

1812 *Importance of August* In the garden, also, August is the pivot of the year – the month in which the gardener may see the full fruition of his hopes, or console himself as best he may for any measure of disappointment, by preparations for the future. His beds are now in full bloom, the foliage in its perfection; and under the most perfect arrangement, a fastidious eye will remark deficiencies to be supplied in next year's arrangement; in fact, August is the month when the man of taste must settle his plans for next year.

The advantage of decided colours in the massed flower garden will now become obvious. As the beds get filled up by the extending foliage, the taste of the designer now becomes apparent, not only in the individual beds, but in the general design, which is now perceptible even to the most unobservant. Clear, simple, and intelligible colours, and regular, well-connected figures, are required in geometrical flower beds; and this is the season when the intelligent gardener can most conveniently reconsider his design, and perfect his arrangements for next year's operations. It was said by the late Mr Errington that one of the first essentials in the massing or bedding system is to keep up the idea of distinctness; confusion of forms being totally out of place. 'Let the brambles,' he observed, 'and dog roses in the wilderness intertwine and smother each other; but distinctness, I say, for the parterre: and the first principle of *distinctness* is to keep every individual flower separate – no two allowed to touch. I feel persuaded that where flower beds are well conceived, the plants individually healthy and blossoming freely, the relief afforded by intervening portions of cleanly-raked soil is just the sort of relief that suits the eye. With those who require to be taken by surprise through a prurient and false taste, why, mere blazes of colour and sparkling contrasts must be the order of the day. Next to the individuality of plants in a bed, I would suggest that edgings or borderings will be found a useful adjunct in promoting beauty of outline. No flower bed ever looks satisfactory to me without at least two, if not three, distinct heights, the lowest at the extremity of the bed. Here an edging makes an elegant and artistic finish, especially if it forms a continuous belt, which is easily accomplished by pegging down the plants during the earlier stages, allowing the

FIG. 542 *Pansy (Viola tricolor – large-flowering garden variety)*

points to rise in relief as soon as the object has been attained. To put a case: suppose a long oval bed, standing in considerable relief. A row of scarlet cupheas as an edging, no part of them allowed to approach the outer edge of the bed nearer than four inches. Let a row of variegated geraniums be planted in a parallel line, and the interior furnished with *Lobeliafulgens*, planted in groups of five: this bed would always give satisfaction, as far as form is concerned. There are many other dwarf flowers, however, better adapted than the cuphea for this purpose; verbenas, Kaulfussias, leptosiphons, pansies, heliotropes, and petunias, are all equally or more suited for forming a continuous band like that indicated.

'High keeping, however, is, after all, the chief element of success in flower gardening: no combination of form or colour can give satisfaction, if neglect is apparent. The rake should be in frequent use where bare soil is shown. Weeds should never be seen; all disproportioned foliage should be removed. Pegging down should be done early in the season, in order that trusses of flowers may stand fairly in relief, and dress naturally with an air of freedom, combined with neatness. Tying up also requires nice handling; the sticks, while uniform, should be inconspicuous. Flowers once suffered to become crooked are long before they regain their position, and the finest flowers look most inelegant if suffered to get into *deshabille* through lack of this needful operation.'

1813 *Borders and Shrubberies* Flower borders and shrubberies now require the most vigilant attention; the borders should be gone over with the hoe and rake; all weeds being raked off, and straggling shoots either removed, shortened, or tied down, and dead footstalks and flowers removed. In shrubberies prune off all exuberant branches, keeping up a dwarf and full foliage, and watering where required.

1814 *Grass and Gravel Walks* Roll lawns well, and meet the rapid growth by frequent mowing. Grass walks and lawns require mowing once a week or fortnight, according to its growth, keeping it short, thick and even, and choosing dewy mornings for the operation. Grass walks should be rolled and kept clean, and free from weeds. Gravel walks will likewise require frequent rolling, and surface weeding, in shady places especially, will be required, or the application of salt and water, to eradicate the smaller weeds, mosses, etc., after which they should be well rolled to make the surface firm and even.

1815 *Routine Work in the Flower Garden* The flower garden will now be in its greatest beauty, and every means must be taken to keep turf, gravel, and edgings of all kinds in the neatest order; dead flowers should be picked off daily, and stray growths reduced within proper limits. Trailing and climbing plants should frequently be gone over to keep them neatly trained and secure after high winds; for the same purpose examine hollyhocks, dahlias, and other tall-growing plants. After removing the dead flowers from roses, encourage the production of autumn blooms in the perpetuals, by watering with liquid manure, and mulching the surface of the ground where practicable.

1816 *Propagation of Plants* Continue the propagation of plants for next season, in which no time must be lost with the more delicate pelargoniums, in order to get them established before winter. Plant out all recently struck pinks, double wallflowers, and pansies, keeping a few of the latter in pots for protection during the winter.

1817 *Geraniums* Now that the planting-out season may be considered over, attention should at once be directed towards furnishing a supply of plants for another year. The class of plants which will require propagation first are geraniums, of which both the fancy and common bedding kinds must be struck in time to get established in small pots before winter, and the different scarlets and horseshoe and zonal sorts. There is no plant more useful for decorative purposes; many are, besides, deliciously fragrant, and there is none whose cultivation is more simple.

Geraniums may be propagated by thinning out the beds here and there, without much injury to them, and inserted in small beds on a south border, putting a little silver sand in the holes made to receive the cuttings.

1818 *Intermediate and Ten-Week Stocks* Intermediate stocks should be sown early in the month, and ten-week stocks of various colours before the middle of the month. The intermediate stocks must be kept in pots throughout the winter for spring flowering. Pot a quantity of Bromptons for the same purpose, planting the remainder in a sheltered spot to take their chance through the winter.

1819 *Propagation of Perennials* All double-flowering perennials done flowering may be propagated by slips, and parting the roots towards the end of the month, taking up the whole plant, and dividing it into as many separate plants as there are roots with buds, eyes, or stems. Let every root be trimmed by cutting off the straggling parts or injured roots, picking off all dead leaves, planting them in some shady border, and giving some water.

FIG. 543 *Mesembryanthemum tricolor*

1820 *The Saxifrages* Many varieties of Saxifrage may now be propagated: the offsets rise from the sides of the plant, and may now be taken off and planted either in borders or pots. Among these may be named *Saxifraga crassifolia*, *S. granulata flore pleno*, *S. peltata*, *S. sarmentosa*, and *S. umbrosa*, or London Pride. *Saxifraga cotelydon* must also be added to the number, which throws up a fine pyramidal spike of blossom 12 inches high. These plants may be propagated by division in spring as well as in autumn.

Many of our most beautiful flowering plants may be propagated this month; other varieties may remain for a week or two longer. With the above may be classed crassulas, lantanas, hydrangeas, mesembryanthemums, etc., as they all should be struck early, to flower freely the following season. Petunias, verbenas, heliotropes, salvias, and lobelias, may be taken in hand next, reserving calceolarias to the last, as they strike better during the cold weather of autumn than earlier in the season. Verbenas and calceolarias may be struck under hand glasses or in a cold frame. Geraniums, including the scarlet varieties, will, as it has been said, strike freely on a south border inserted in sandy soil. Anagallis, maurandyas, and lophospermums may be rooted in sandy soil, if placed in a cold frame, and shaded in bright sunny weather. *Maurandya Barclayana rosea* is an abundant flowerer, but of undecided colours.

1821 *Roses* Perpetual flowering roses in dry weather require copious supplies of water. If mildew appears, forming white spots on any of them, syringe the plant with soft water in the evening, and dust the affected parts with flour of sulphur. Towards the end of the month any roses budded last month may have the bandages removed and the place examined, to see that nothing has interfered with the bud, and the bandage restored.

1822 *Cuttings of Roses* Cuttings of Tea-scented, Noisette, China, Bourbon, and Hybrid perpetuals, may be struck in light sandy soil over a gentle hotbed. When rooted, pot off and replace in the frames for a few days till the roots begin to move, when they are to be removed and hardened off.

1823 *Shoots from Bottom of Stem of Roses* The Ayrshire, Boursault, Sempervirens, and other climbing roses, frequently send out very luxuriant shoots near the bottom of the stem. These, if not wanted to cover some weak part of the plant, should be removed.

1824 *Roses in Pots* Roses standing in pots should never be crowded, but constantly watered and kept in a growing state.

1825 *Autumnal Bulbs* Colchicums, narcissuses, Guernsey lily, and amaryllia may still be planted in borders, beds, or pots, in light sandy loam.

1826 *Carnations and Picotees* These should now be layered, but without shortening the grass. Where seed is required, pick off all decaying petals, to prevent damp injuring the pods. If not wanted for seed, cut down the stems. First-struck pipings may now be planted out, potting a quantity in order to fill up vacancies which may be caused from the ravages of the wireworm, etc.

1827 *Dahlias* These plants now require constant watering and attention to tying out lateral shoots, removing superfluous ones, and relaxing the ties. Stir the soil, but not deeply, and give special attention to seedlings, selecting those worth preserving, and throwing away worthless varieties. Attend to the training and thinning of the shoots of dahlias: place small inverted pots, with a little dry moss in them, on the top of stakes, for a trap for earwigs.

1828 *Hollyhocks* require the same attention as to staking and selecting.

1829 *Pansies* Make pansy beds of cuttings, etc., that have been struck at earlier periods of the year. Cuttings may still be struck.

1830 *Tulips* Clean and prepare tulip beds, and arrange the plants in their drawers, discarding stained varieties, and adding new ones in their place.

2 – The Vegetable or Kitchen Garden

1831 *Garden Pests: Caterpillars* The gardener who would have everything thrive and prosper must exercise the greatest vigilance during August. Apart from the necessity of cropping and removing such as have ceased to become profitable, his attention is drawn towards the multitudes of garden pests, which exhibit their effects at this time of the year more than any other. Caterpillars should be looked for, and destroyed as quickly as they can be discovered – at least, before they fatten on the produce of the garden, which they will do to the deterioration of the crops in a very short time, if not prevented. The ravages of these insects produce an effect at once unsightly and discreditable. Savoys and cabbages riddled by caterpillars are at once unpleasant to the eye and suggestive of neglect. A free use of lime, which should be scattered over the plants on dewy mornings, will, in a great measure, save them; the insects should, nevertheless, be hunted and destroyed on every possible occasion.

1832 *Wireworms* The wireworm and other insects become troublesome at this time, and may be trapped by means of potatoes cut in half, and the cut sides laid downwards. It is a good plan to trench all the vacant ground at this time of the year; grubs and wireworm are then buried deep enough to destroy them.

1833 *Clubbing* The effects of the club become apparent in hot sunny days: cabbages, etc., hang down and turn blue, and often become infested with aphis. This disease is, perhaps, the most vexatious with which the gardener has to deal. How far it may be prevented by the use of wood ashes, etc., is a matter of doubt. The most prominent causes of clubbing seem to be: firstly, an injudicious application of manure in small gardens that are already too manured – the most prevalent cause; and, secondly, the exhausted state of the soil, arising from the too unvaried use to which it is put; either of these circumstances tending to foster the insect to whose work the clubbing itself is certainly due. The plants that are subject to the disease are strong feeders, and exhaust the soil very much; but it is reasonable to suppose they leave food suitable for other plants. Instances have been of ground being left to weeds for several years, when, although cabbages clubbed badly before, they did not after the rest from cultivation that it had experienced; the ground showing a fertility that would justify anyone in believing that weeds have a wonderful faculty for restoring ground that had been exhausted by kitchen crops.

It is the practice in some gardens to have the orchard, or at least the fine fruit garden, within the walls of the kitchen garden, and even to form edgings to the vegetable quarters with them, and this is a time of preparation for planting. As the kitchen garden is usually enclosed by walls, it may be desirable to adopt this arrangement; but the edging system should be avoided, and fruit trees, as well as bush fruit, have a quarter appropriated to themselves. Selecting a piece of ground which has been continually cropped, proceed to plant the young bushes of currants, gooseberry, and raspberry, in rows of about 8 feet apart for gooseberries and currants, and 6 for raspberries, and about 2 feet less in the rows. While the bushes are very young and small, the ground between the bushes may be cropped with almost anything required, but may be particularly useful for raising asparagus or seakale plants for forcing, or it may be planted with strawberries. As the bushes increase in size, let them have all the room they require; plant nothing between that will crowd them, for the nearer the roots of these-bushes approach the surface, the better and more abundant will be the fruit. It is not advisable to dig the ground where the root fibres are likely to be; after a time, therefore, the ground should never be disturbed, and where manure is required let it be applied as mulch – that is, lay the manure on the surface, and the bushes will receive the benefit of it as much as if dug in. Of course, weeds will grow, the chief of which are grasses, and they are to perform an important part in restoring the ground to fertility. They should be mowed occasionally, to prevent them getting too tall, so as to interfere with the trees, and in a measure to prevent seeding. These bushes will bear fruit in great abundance for eight, ten, or twelve years; by that time the bushes will be nearly exhausted, and the ground restored to a fertile condition for kitchen crops. Brassicae which formerly went off with the club, and peas which turned yellow before their time, will grow now in perfection; and if the ground is kept in order by flat digging or by bastard trenching, cabbages will be less likely to club. The probable causes of the origin of this disease have been mentioned above; overmanning and exhaustion the soil both tending to the production and encouragement of the insect by which the mischief is undoubtedly wrought. But, whatever may be the actual cause, clubbing has been found to be the bane of most old gardens, the only remedy being a judicious system of rotation cropping, with moderate and systematic manuring.

1834 *Asparagus* Keep the beds clear of weeds, especially young plants, which are soon overrun by them. Unless seed is wanted, it is advisable to cut off most of the bearing heads, which would, if left, exhaust and weaken the roots in ripening the seed: it is, however, as well to sow every year, and some of the seed may be left for the purpose.

1835 *Artichokes* Cut these down as the heads are gathered, and fork the ground between: they will come up again before winter.

1836 *Peas* Pull up as soon as all are gathered: it is not advisable to leave them a moment longer. The haulm may be dried in the sun, and will be useful in winter for covering and protecting many things from frost. The sticks should be tied in bundles, and stowed away. Succession peas that are coming on for late crops should be sticked and earthed up.

1837 *Beans* Pull up the haulm of any that have done bearing; lay the stalks together, and they will soon rot, or dry them, and they will burn. Some may be cut in lengths, and dried for earwig traps, to place among flowering plants.

1838 *French Beans* A row or two should be left for seed. It is not advisable to leave any to ripen on bearing plants, as they cease to yield for the table while ripening seed.

1839 *Runners* These should be stopped after reaching the top of the sticks: they will set quicker than if left to grow as they please. Give plenty of water at the roots if necessary, but none overhead.

1840 *Celery* This may be got out in any quantity. If young plants are used, and kept growing, they will stand the winter well, but must not be earthed up till November; that put out in June may now be earthed up for blanching. It is not advisable to earth up too quickly, or too much at a time; but there is less danger of doing harm by it now than in cold or wet weather. As it grows quickly at this time, three weeks will blanch it; but it should be quite moist at the roots before being banked up. The early crops of celery should be carefully examined for slugs before earthing up; if any appear, a dressing of soot or lime will remove them. A piece of ground may still be prepared for a late crop, if desired.

1841 *Cardoons* These will soon require earthing up.

1842 *Carrots* Early sowings may be taken up and stowed away for use; but if the ground is not particularly wanted for other crops, it is quite as well to let them remain till required. A little *Early Horn Carrot* seed may be sown early in August, to stand the winter; they will be useful in the spring, when the winter store is exhausted.

1843 *Parsnips* Stir the ground well between, so that the rain may penetrate quickly. Destroy weeds, and keep the crops clean.

1844 *Onions* These, in all probability, will now be arriving at maturity, and as soon as this is the case, they had better be pulled up and laid on their sides. Green thick- necked ones had better be turned down at the collar, and should be used first. It is necessary to ripen onions thoroughly before storing them away. Sow Tripoli, globe, or Welsh hardy, to stand the winter, for planting out in spring, or for salading: a warm sunny border is the most suitable place for sowing them.

1845 *Potato Onions* These should be taken up as soon as the stalks have decayed.

1846 *Garlic, Shallots, etc.* These will most likely be fit to take up this month, and may be treated in the same way as onions – that is, ripened in the open air, and stored away in a dry airy shed, or left beyond the reach of frost.

1847 *Leeks* These may still be transplanted, but the sooner the better, or they will not get any size before winter. Plant in deep drills 2 feet or so apart, and water freely: draw earth up to those in full growth. Liquid manure given occasionally will benefit them.

1848 *Potatoes* Early crops will be ready for taking up; but they will take no harm if left in the ground till wanted. If the disease appears in the haulm, remove it instantly from late crops, if it is desired to save the tubers; they will not be so large, but small and good roots are better than large and bad.

FIG. 544 *Large flag or London leek*

1849 *Turnips* may be sown any time this month: they will not, probably, grow large, but will be useful in February and March for the early greens which they yield; they may be left thicker than early sowings. Continue to use the hoe unsparingly among advancing crops, for this is most important in the culture of the turnip.

1850 *Lettuce* The first week in this month sow cabbage lettuce for winter use. From that time forward, both cos and cabbage lettuce may be sown to stand the winter for spring use: sow rather thin on an open spot, as it is proper to have these as stout and as strong as possible; they will stand the weather much better.

1851 *Endive* Sow early this month for the last time this season; plant out as soon as large enough to do so conveniently; a good watering now and then, after planting, is all the attention they require. When they are ready for blanching, use inverted flower pots with the hole stopped; but by no means tuck the leaves into them; merely place a 24-pot over the centre. This is the best way of blanching them

1852 *Spinach* About the second week in this month sow the main crop of winter spinach; where a good supply of this is wanted, it would be best to sow every week this month. The earliest sown will grow quickly, but the later will stand the winter best, and prove valuable in the spring; sow in drills a foot apart, or sow thinly, broadcast, treading it in either case.

1853 *Radish* may be sown any time this month. The Black Spanish should be sown early this month for winter use. It takes rather longer than other sorts to arrive at a useful state, but may be treated in the same way as the other sorts, excepting that more room should be given to them.

1854 *Tomatoes* Attend to these as directed last month. To have these bear well in our short seasons, it is necessary to aid them as much as possible by pinching out all superfluous growth, exposing the flowers well, and training as close to the wall as possible.

1855 *Ridge Cucumbers, Vegetable Marrows, etc.* The directions given for the management of tomatoes apply equally to these.

1856 *Broccoli, Brussels Sprouts, etc.* These should begot out as soon as possible. It is useless to plant them after this month. Broccoli that are about heading should receive plenty of water and liquid manure two or three times a week, to insure their being fine.

1857 *Cabbage* Sow early this month for a full crop of summer cabbage. Sow thinly on an open spot, that they may come up strong, and scatter lime on the ground to protect from birds and insects; also dust the young plants when up.

1858 *Coleworts* Get out a supply of early coleworts: they will most likely make small heads in November.

1859 *Cauliflower* Some seed should be sown two or three times this month; if sown at the beginning, about the middle, and at the end of the month, it will give a succession. Sow in the same way as cabbage. It will be necessary to give cauliflowers the protection of frames or hand lights during the winter; but the sowing may be in the open ground.

1860 *Sweet Herbs* The gathering and drying of herbs should proceed with all possible dispatch, and should not be left later than this month. The propagation of herbs, if not done before, should be finished up this month; they will do little good if disturbed after.

1861 *Mushrooms* To make a bed for a good supply of these in the autumn, it should be done in a shed or some dry airy place. Let a good quantity of short stable dung be got under cover, and mix about one-third the quantity of soil with it. Let the mixture be worked backwards and forwards at least a fortnight; if for a longer time, it will be better, for the material cannot be too short; but take care never to lay it together, for the

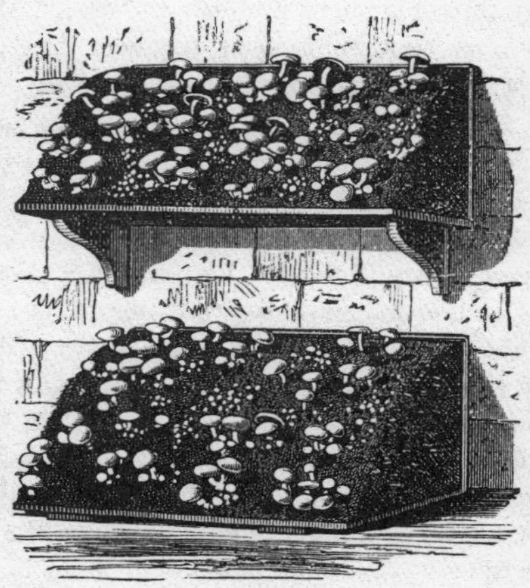

FIG. 545 *Mushrooms on shelves in shed or cellar*

increased pressure causes a rank, fetid smell, which is by all means to be avoided, since it would be destructive to the crop. Never lay it above 4 feet in height – rather less than otherwise: when ready, proceed to make the bed in a ridge or conical form, as this gives the greater surface for the crop. Beat the dung well in the process, and, when finished, let it remain for a day or two; then ascertain the temperature, either by placing a thermometer in it or thrusting a stick into it; if, after remaining a day or night, the thermometer should indicate not above 80°, or the stick on withdrawal feels comfortably warm, it is time to spawn it.

Much has been said about letting the bed all but cool before spawning: it is better, perhaps, to choose a high rather than low temperature, because the spawn sets to work more freely and rapidly, and the mushrooms come up more uniformly over the bed. The process of spawning has been already described. It is not advisable to case the bed (that is, putting a case of good fresh loamy soil of about 2 or 3 inches in thickness all over it) immediately after spawning; but cover thinly with straw for a day or two, or till the spawn just begins to take hold of the dung; then case it, beating the soil firmly, and, lastly, put on straw enough to exclude the light; and as the weather and the bed cool, increase the covering and add garden mats. In making mushroom beds, much depends on the quality of the spawn. Good spawn, which ought to be procured at all nurseries, etc., is full of fine downy-looking threads, and smells exactly like mushrooms; it is sometimes found in plenty in heaps of old manure that have been several years without being disturbed.

3 – The Fruit Garden and Orchard

1862 *Fruit Pests: Snails, Wasps, etc. Keep* a sharp look-out over wall trees; for snails, wasps, and flies are as fond of choice fruit as man himself. Snails will attack peaches, nectarines, etc., before they are ripe, and spoil the appearance of every fruit they approach. Finding out their haunts, and picking them out with the hand, is the best mode of dealing with them; they are then easily destroyed by throwing them into salt and water. Wasps and flies must be trapped in bottles, containing sugar and beer dregs, hung about the trees in different places; or the trees must be covered with suitable netting.

Apricots, as soon as they happen to crack, are sure to be attacked; and a sometimes happens before the fruit is thoroughly ripe, it is always advisable to cover them, even if other fruits are left without protection.

1863 *Nailing in Wood* Nail in all useful wood this month without fail; trees will scarcely require it after. Remove every shoot that is not really wanted: this may as well be done now as at any other time.

1864 *Aphis on Trees* As it is not proper to drench the trees when the fruit is ripe or ripening, any shoots infested with aphis should be cleaned with a brush, or by dipping in thick puddle.

1865 *Blighted Fruit on Standards* Standard trees, where a regular thinning is not adopted, should be shaken occasionally, to bring down any fruit that may be blighted. These can be no good on the trees, and the sooner got rid of the better.

1866 *Budding Fruit Trees* July and August is generally the time for budding fruit trees: if any stocks are to be budded with different or better sorts, it should be done without delay. Any peaches, nectarines, or other wall trees that are scanty, or unfurnished with wood in any part, may be altered considerably by the insertion of a few buds.

1867 *Apricots Peaches, and Nectarines* These are now ripening rapidly, and should be exposed to the sun as much as possible to give them colour. Keep the shoots laid in closely, and remove obstructing leaves, always leaving enough for the elaboration of the juices of the tree. Suspend nets, supported by short stakes, beneath the tree, as the ripening period approaches, to catch any falling fruit, with some soft material in the net to soften the fall. Netting of a fine mesh is also used successfully to keep off the attacks of wasps and flies. Strong shoots that have been stopped have now thrown out laterals, which should be thinned to the number required to cover their allotted space, so that the wood may be thoroughly ripened in the August sun. Should mildew appear, dust with flour of sulphur. If attacked by insects, wash the trees with soapsuds, syringing afterwards with clear water.

1868 *Apples and Pears* Trees that happen to be heavily laden require to have their branches supported; those against walls and espaliers should be pretty closely stopped.

1869 *Cherries* As the fruit is gathered from the earlier sorts, remove the nettings, and wash the trees well with the engine: cover Morello cherries on north walls with nets.

The modern fruit gardens may be described as orchards in miniature. Certainly they are more manageable, doubly interesting, and equally productive with orchards. In the plan already referred to I have indicated two compartments as *Fruit Garden*. They are intended to be furnished with apples on the Paradise stock, pears on the quince, and cherries and plums on the most dwarf stocks that can be procured. Careful summer stopping, root pruning, and the pyramidal form, describe the main features of their treatment and training; and abundance of good fruit is, of course, the ultimate object. They may be planted in rows from 7 to 10 feet apart, and the same distance between each plant. On good soils they succeed well on the level of the ground; on heavy clays, or other unfavourable bottoms, the ground can be thrown into this form. This is better than raising a separate mound for each tree. The bottom of these mounds may be occupied with a standard gooseberry or currant, which bear admirably trained a single stem in this manner, and the sides can be occupied with salading. A fruit garden thus formed is quite a scene of beauty when the trees are in flower, and very enjoyable at all times. Gooseberries and currants present a better appearance when trained as pyramids and on wire espaliers. Trained thus, they look well alternated with apples and pears, or in a compartment by themselves; they fruit quite as finely, are as easily protected, and are much easier gathered.

1870 *Raspberries* Towards the latter end of August, raspberries have generally ceased bearing, and the old canes may be cut down, as they will be of no further service, and are in the way. Their removal gives the new canes a chance to strengthen and ripen the wood. About four or five canes may be left to each stool. This done, it will be advisable to fork the ground over, to destroy weeds and give a fresh appearance, besides admitting rain. All borders about fruit trees should receive a forking about this time. Autumn-bearing varieties must not be treated in this way until the fruit has been gathered.

1871 *Currants* Currants near the ground should be gathered first, as the splashing of rain is apt to spoil them. If trees are netted or matted over so as to be impervious to birds, flies, etc., fruit on them will keep good till late in the year. Black currants will not keep on the trees, and had better be gathered as soon as ripe.

1872 *Gooseberries* The instructions for currants apply equally to gooseberries, of which some varieties, such as the Red Warrington, may be preserved until November, if protected with mats or netting.

1873 *Strawberries* Beds may be planted; but it is advisable to get the planting done as soon as possible, if a crop of fruit is expected the following year. Even now it is a good plan to lay the runners in pots, if it can be done; but, generally, it will be found that strong runners have already rooted by this time, and may be removed with a trowel. Plenty of water is necessary at this time for everything that has been newly planted. If plantations cannot be made now, bed out the plants, so that they may be transplanted during the spring, keeping all the leaves attached to them.

The strawberry requires a deep porous and highly-enriched and well-drained soil. The best natural soil would be what is called a hazel loam – retentive, but not too adhesive – and trenched at least 3 feet deep, and the bottom of each spit enriched with 3 or 4 inches of well-rotted stable manure. This being trenched in in the winter or spring, the land should be kept moved and stirred about as much as possible until the plants are ready for planting.

In the market gardens this planting takes place in June, the market gardeners generally choosing an old celery bed; trenching it deeply, planting immediately, and watering copiously until the plants are established. Where this is not available, the system is to prepare a piece of ground by trenching and manuring as above, and marking it into 4-feet beds, with 15-inch alleys between. In autumn or early spring a row of strong plants are planted in the alleys, and the beds between cropped with summer lettuce. As the strawberries advance in growth, the young plants from the runners are carefully layered among the lettuce, and soon become strong, vigorous plants, producing heavy crops of very large fruit.

In small gardens, strawberry banks or terraces are an excellent device; they are formed as follows: A space of ground of any given length, and 6 feet wide, being marked out, a wall 9 inches high is formed of stones, flints, or old wood, the space between the walls being filled with compost, such as we have described. Upon this compost and 9 inches within the first walls, two more are added and filled up in the same way; and thus the work proceeds, a row of plants occupying the space between each pair of walls, until the space comes to a single row of plants at the top. In a bank of this kind, the walls, if running due east and west, insure both a very early and very late supply of fruit, and it may be planted at any time, taking care, at planting, that the ground slopes inward slightly, so as to secure a full supply of moisture at the roots. Stones, clinkers from the furnace, or other arrangements for preventing evaporation, and providing a clean surface for the fruit to rest upon, are easily applied to this mode of cultivation; while copious waterings with manure water from the time the plants show blossoms until the fruit is ripe, will greatly assist this or any other system of cultivation.

II – Work to be done under Glass

1 – Flowers in the Conservatory, Greenhouse, Stove, etc.

1874 *The Hothouse and Greenhouse* The routine work and management of the hothouse and greenhouse are very much the same, if not exactly, as for the preceding month of July, and therefore need not be repeated.

1875 *Azaleas* Late-flowering azaleas now require shifting and training, so that the foliage draws out properly before winter. On the slightest indication of thrips, fumigate.

1876 *Camellias, etc* These also require shifting, if not done last month. When they have rooted in the new soil, give them plenty of air day and night, and syringe freely three or four times a week in fine weather. *Daphne Indica*, both red and white, as well as *Magnolia fuscata*, are very suitable companions to the camellia, requiring exactly similar treatment and temperature.

1877 *Pelargoniums* Plants which have gone out of flower should be exposed in the open air to ripen their wood preparatory to being cut down in September.

The principal plants that decorate the conservatory at this season will be with some of the more common annuals – fuchsias, scarlet geraniums, with achimenes; and where there is room a considerable number of stove plants and orchids may be safely introduced; and if, in addition, a few palms, etc., be added, they will give the charm of tropical scenery to the house, and render it more attractive.

1878 *Brugmansias* Brugmansias, and other gross-feeding plants, may be liberally supplied with liquid manure to maintain them in vigorous health, and at the same time to prolong the period of their blooming.

1879 *Orchids* Some of the earlier-started orchids will have ripened their growth, and may now be removed to a cooler and drier house, where they can slowly progress to a state of rest.

As the plants approach a state of maturity, more light may be allowed them, which will help to ripen the pseudo bulbs. Continue to plants yet growing the requisite amount of heat and moisture to carry on the present year's growth, but avoid unnecessary stimulants at this season, which might induce a fresh growth, which to many species would be injurious to, their blooming next season. Fires will be necessary during cold nights; but lessen the shade, except in bright weather. Plants suspended on blocks and baskets must be daily examined to see the growing material is kept sufficiently moist, while, at the same time, stagnant damp must be avoided.

As light decreases, shading must likewise be gradually lessened, and in a short time discontinued altogether, except to a section of orchids, which will require it for some time longer. It is highly important that the wood of plants – hard-wooded ones especially, intended to bloom in perfection next season – should be well ripened, and attention is specially directed to this, because the year's growth by this time will, in all likelihood, be completed, and the remainder of the autumn should be devoted to maturing the season's growth. Exposure to the full influence of light and air, which are the principal agents to effect this purpose, is essential; and although water in sufficient quantities must be given to meet the plants' requirements, they should not have more, as an extra supply of water might, in some instances, induce an autumnal growth It will be better to soak each plant well when requiring water, and then allow it to become somewhat dry, than merely to damp the surface only daily, while the principal parts of the roots are suffering.

1880 *Achimenes* These, as they go out of bloom, may be placed in a frame to ripen their tubers, exposing them fully to the sun, but keeping them rather dry.

1881 *Epiphyllum* If the different varieties of epiphyllum have made their growth under glass, they may be removed to a sunny spot out of doors.

1882 *Cinerarias, etc* Pot off seedling cinerarias, Chinese primroses, and calceolarias from the seed pans when the plants are large enough for the purpose.

FIG. 546 *Scarborough lily (Amaryllis vallota purpurea)*

1883 *Amaryllis* Amaryllids which have perfected their growth may be placed in a dry place to winter. An example of the Amaryllids is given in the Scarborough Lily (*Amaryllis vallota purpurea*), shown in Fig. 546. There is one section of this tribe, however, with elongated bulbs, which will not bear to be kept entirely without water, even when in a state of rest. These latter, with *Pancratium speriosum* and *P. fragrans*, etc., should be placed on the back shelves of a vinery, or any house of medium temperature, supplying them only with water sufficient to keep their foliage from dying off.

1884 *Chrysanthemums* Complete the potting of chrysanthemums, and plunge them in ashes or sawdust to save watering. Stake neatly, and stop mildew wherever it appears, by dusting a little flour of sulphur over the infected leaves. Water with liquid manure freely.

1885 *The Conservatory: General Management* Flowers are now so abundant in the open ground that an equal profusion would be in bad taste. Those that remain should now have plenty of room and a free circulation of air. Camellias and acacias now require copious watering, taking care that they are not started into second growth. Sprinkle borders daily, and keep up a moist atmosphere. Train and prune all climbing plants in graceful festoons, avoiding stiff formal tying in, which prevents free flowering in plants of a climbing habit. All plants intended for early forcing should now be placed so that the wood may be thoroughly ripened, for on that chiefly depends the future bloom. Strong growing plants, such as Diosmas, the Epacridae, Coleonemas, etc., which have been in shade to prolong their flowering, should now be placed in a bright sunny place.

1886 *Climbers in Conservatory* The climbing plants will require going over at short intervals to keep the strong growers within limits: any shoots which have done blooming may be cut in, which, in many species, will induce a second flowering. Examine plants out of doors; and any appearing to suffer from rain, etc., should be at once removed under glass.

1887 *Removal of Plants out of Bloom* As stove plants in the conservatory go out of bloom, remove them to a house of medium temperature to ripen, unless they are likely to bloom again, when they should be removed to the stove and be heated, so as to bring on successional flowers. Some of the free-growing stove plants, as Justicias, Eranthemums, etc., may require a small shift, or the foliage is apt to become sickly. Let the whole have air liberally to induce a stocky growth.

1888 *Flowers in Conservatory in August* Towards the end of the month the conservatory and show, house will be gay with the different varieties of *Lilium lancifolium*, fuchsias, neriums, balsams, achimenes, etc., in addition to a selection from the stove and orchid house. As light will now be decreasing, the conservatory climbers may be pruned back, selecting those shoots for the purpose that have nearly done flowering. This will allow more light to fall on the plants below, and will prove advantageous to the ripening of their wood. Vigorous growing plants, whether out in the open border or in pots, must be liberally supplied with water.

2 – Plants under Glass in Hotbeds, Frames, etc.

1889 *Flowers in Hotbeds and Frames: Bedding Plants, etc.* Hotbeds and frames may be utilised at this period of the year for various purposes in connection with the floral department of the garden. It is a good time to strike the winter stock of bedding plants, for raising cinerarias, etc., for which purpose the bed described last month will be useful.

1890 *Annuals in Frames* Frames without the hotbed are also very useful. Mignonette, nemophila, and other annuals sown now in pots, and kept in cold frames, will flower in the winter.

1891 *Balsams and Cockscombs* Plants that are now coming into bloom should be transferred to the conservatory or the window of the sitting-room, and those not yet showing signs of flowering should be pushed on.

1892 *Pelargoniums* Plants that have finished flowering should be placed out of doors for a few weeks to ripen their wood. They should then be cut back to within an inch or two of the old wood, and placed in a cool frame in order to induce them to break. They must then be repotted, and the pit kept pretty close and moist until the plants begin to grow.

The following is the process to be adopted in repotting. First shake away all the earth from among the roots, and remove the soil which still clings to them with a pointed stick. Cut all bruised, broken, and decaying roots away, and shorten those that remain by at least one-third, and repot each plant in a pot one size less than that in which it has been flowering. A suitable compost is composed of 16 parts of turfy loam, to 4 of peat, 4 of leaf mould, and 1 of sharp silver sand. Water the plant immediately after repotting, and then withhold water from the plant itself, until it begins to grow, although the pit must be kept moist.

1893 *Cuttings that may be Struck* Cuttings of pelargoniums, fuchsias, petunias, verbenas, anagallis, ageratums, centaureas, coleuses, etc., may be struck in frames now and potted off when rooted.

1894 *Shifting and Repotting* Seedling plants of auriculas, calceolarias, Chinese primroses, cinerarias, pansies, polyanthuses, etc., may now be shifted into larger pots, using 12 parts of loam to 6 of good farmyard manure and 1 of sharp sand.

1895 *Vegetables in Hotbeds and Frames: Cucumbers* These, as the nights get colder, may have a slight covering, and the bottom heat, if declining, should be renewed. Keep down mildew with sulphur; the covering by night, and the increased bottom heat, will, however, help to keep this in check. These directions are applicable to plants in houses as well as in hotbeds. Cucumbers that have been carefully stopped, trained, and pegged down, will continue in bearing. If mildew appears, sprinkle the leaves, and dust with sulphur; but if very bad it is better to start new plants. If started on new beds now, they will continue bearing until Christmas, and with care all the winter; but they should be on good 4-foot beds, so that good linings may be applied; for, as the season wanes, and the weather becomes colder, heat must be provided accordingly. Give fruiting plants the benefit of watering, either by gentle showers or by artificial sprinkling.

1896 *Melons* The late crop will be advancing, and as light is decreasing, keep the vines further apart, that the leaves, as they are formed, may not crowd each other. Attend carefully to bottom heat, which must not be allowed to decline. Red spider must be kept in check, by now and then washing the interior walls with lime and sulphur. Water cautiously, but do not allow the growing plants to get dry, which would check them and induce the attacks of spider. To grow melons in perfection, they should progress regularly; hence the necessity for steady bottom heat, and close watching as regards watering during the entire period of their growth. These remarks are applicable also to plants in houses. With regard to melons in pits and frames, the same directions apply to them now as formerly. Where the fruit is swelling, keep up a brisk heat and plenty of moisture; but where it is approaching ripeness, let the beds gradually dry off; also, where fruit is setting, maintain a moderately dry atmosphere, as they do not set well if kept damp at the time.

FIG. 547 *Corn salad*

1897 *Early Horn Carrots* Seed sown now in the manner described in January – that is, without making a new hotbed for them, but renewing the soil on an old one – will be useful in the winter. Heat is unnecessary to raise them, but may be applied with advantage in the winter by means of fresh lining.

1898 *Cauliflowers* Seed is often sown in a frame, to save it from birds, etc.; but it is necessary to uncover the young plants as soon as the seed is up, to prevent a spindling growth. It is advisable to look forward to the winter, and sow everything in time to allow of making sufficient growth before winter.

1899 *Salading, Parsley, etc.* Corn salad sown now in a cold frame will be very useful in winter. It is merely necessary to place 16 inches of earth in the frame, and sowing on that, treading or otherwise matting the surface of the soil firmly. Some young plants of parsley planted on the same depth of soil, 6 inches apart, will be also useful in winter.

3 – Fruit under Glass, Heated and Unheated

1900 *The Vinery: Ventilation* Whenever the leaves in the early house show indications of ripening, the sashes should be removed and the vines fully exposed; beyond stopping any late laterals, the vines should not be touched until the leaves fall. While the vines are thus exposed, the sashes, rafters, etc., should be put into a state of repair, and painted, that everything may be in good order when the time for forcing again arrives.

If the sashes are not wanted for repairing, they may be used for a variety of purposes, such as ripening grapes, peaches, etc., against walls, forwarding tomatoes, or to assist in the propagation of bedding stuff.

1901 *Stopping Young Vines* Young vines, planted during the past or present season, should be stopped when once they reach the top of the house. Where the rods, however, are intended to carry fruit next season, and the vines are growing freely, six or eight joints beyond where it is intended to cut them back should be left, as a too close stopping might cause the principal eyes to break, and endanger next season's show of fruit. Lateral shoots, after this, may be kept stopped back pretty close, as the object will now be more to ripen the existing wood than to encourage fresh growth. Besides looking over ripe grapes to remove decayed berries and stopping the lateral shoots as they are formed, there are not many instructions to be given for the vinery this month.

1902 *Muscat Grapes* Fires, especially to houses containing Muscat grapes, should be made each evening and during wet dull days, that abundant ventilation may be kept on.

1903 *Vines in Pots* Vines in pots, intended to fruit next season, must be closely watched to get the wood perfectly ripened. As they have now completed their growth, liquid manure may be given pretty freely to swell out the buds to carry next seasons crop. The plants must be kept close to the glass, and thus exposed to the full influence of light; great care should be taken of the principal leaves as the wood assumes a brown hue. Lessen the water by degrees, and allow (if practicable) a lower night temperature.

1904 *The Pinery: Pines for Early Forcing* As soon as the house for next season's fruiting is ready, the plants should be transferred there at once; the most forward plants should be selected, and have their final shift before removal. When it is desirable to have fruit early, say in April or May, the fruiting pot must not be too large, as it will be necessary to get the plants into rest early. As a rule they should have their pots well filled with roots by the middle of September; and while growing, allow them all the light you can command and a proportionate quantity of air.

The best pines for very early forcing are the black Antigua common Queen and the Providence; to assist them, a few Jamaicas may be started in October, as they take a couple of months longer to ripen.

1905 *Pines for Summer Crop* The plants for the summer crop may remain for a week or two, unless there are reasons for potting them immediately. They may have a larger shift than recommended for the above, and should be kept longer growing in the autumn.

1906 *Sizes of Pots for Pines* As the plants are to ripen their fruit in the pots they are now placed in, the size will be regulated by the kind of pine grown, and in some measure by the size of the plant. For Queens and pines of similar habit, pots of from 12 to 15 inches diameter will be sufficiently large: while pots from 15 to 18 inches will be quite large enough for the largest Providences and Cayennes.

Pots of the largest size are recommended for pines, supposing the plants are well grown and in vigorous health; but nothing but disappointment will follow placing pines in large pots, when the pots in which they are growing are not filled with roots to justify shifting them. Much, however, the easiest and cheapest way to grow pines, is to have them planted on a bed of soil furnished with bottom heat, either by hot water pipes, or by applying hot dung underneath; the soil being supported by brickwork and slates, or rough boards. The bottom heat required will be from 85° to 95°, and the soil may be turfy loam and peat, with sand and leaf mould, varying the latter as the loam is heavy or light. If the plants are growing in pots, they may be turned out into the beds whenever the bottom heat is right; a few of the outside roots being liberated, and the soil carefully packed round the balls as you proceed. The bed should be brought pretty close up to the glass; for as the plants will grow vigorously during the autumn, they will require an abundance of light, assisted by a liberal supply of air, to check vegetation and mature the fruit. In planting out or growing in pots, always allow plenty of room between the plants, that the leaves may spread themselves in a horizontal direction, and thus expose their surface better to the light; and it should likewise be a point that the light and air should reach the lower leaves, which can never be the case when they are crowded together. Directly the succession plants are removed to the fruiting house, the younger plants intended to succeed later next season, and suckers, should be reshifted and plunged to occupy their places. After the suckers, etc., are potted and plunged, keep them rather close for a few days till they begin to grow, after which expose them to light and air.

1907 *Watering Pines* Pines in fruit will require water often, as the pots at this time will be fuller of roots than earlier in the season. Syringe well each; warm, and close the house afterwards. The pines for winter fruiting will now be in bloom, and while such is the case be careful to keep the syringe from the flowers.

1908 *Management of Peaches* As the houses are cleared of fruit, the trees should be gone over, and the wood not required for fruit next season should be cut away; tie the remaining shoots neatly in, without injuring the leaves, removing the laterals as you proceed; this will allow more light and air to reach the shoots intended to carry next season's fruit, and assist towards maturing well-developed fruit buds. To ripen the wood, close up the house early in the afternoon with a temperature of 85°. In the evening again open the house as much as the sashes will allow: fires should be made in wet weather, accompanied by air. The aim should be a dry and rather high temperature by day, and as cold a one by night as circumstances permit. Keep down red spider by well syringing every morning, with air on the house. When the leaves begin to change colour, and the wood becomes brown up to the point, the sashes may be removed.

1909 *Peaches in Pots* Fruit trees in pots, intended for forcing, if the wood is well ripened, supposing they have been growing under glass, may be removed to the foot of a south wall, and in a few weeks to a shady cool place to rest.

1910 *The Orchard House* The general management of the orchard house, as regards treatment of trees, ventilation, watering, and syringing, remains the same as during July. Syringing, however, must be lessened or stopped altogether in cold cloudy weather, lest an excess of moisture induce mildew on the leaves, etc., which must be cleared by producing dryness of the air and by sulphuration. The great thing in the culture of fruit in orchard houses is to give sufficient water, but neither too much lest it produce mildew, nor too little lest it cause fungus. Manure water should be withheld as the fruit approaches ripeness, and given again when the fruit has been gathered.

1911 *Retardation of Ripening* To prevent the entire crop ripening at once and at the same time, some of the trees might be taken out of doors, and placed in the shade, and on north borders; this would promote a succession of ripening fruit, the trees being moved back again to the house as soon as their fruit is wanted. When the crops have been gathered from trees they should be placed out of doors. If any of the trees are still growing, the shoots should be pinched back to three or four leaves.

CHAPTER 30

The Garden and Its Work in Every Department in September

1912 *Aspect and Character of the Month* September 'hath his name as being the seventh month from March', says one of our old writers; 'he is drawn with a merry and cheerful countenance, and in a purple robe'; having reference, doubtless, to the abundance which crowns the year in this its month of maturity:

> Gladdening the farmer's longing sight,
> Blessing him with the harvest light.

The reduction of temperature begins to be felt this month, less, however, by night than by day, the mean temperature of the air at the surface of the ground being 66·14°; at one foot below the surface, 57·54°; and at two feet, 57·89°; being, from this month till April, warmer at two feet than at one foot. The average fall of rain is also increased considerably, falling more in the night than in the day. It abounds, however in delicious autumnal days, when the air, the sky, and the earth seem lulled into universal calm – softer and milder even than in May. The harvest-moon

> With broad-expanded face receives
> The western sun's departing rays,
> And back returns the full-orbed blaze,

There is still much green foliage hanging about the woods, and, as the month advances, the darker masses of the evergreens assume more importance in the garden arrangements. The blue of the sky is disturbed by the equinoctial gales, which drive the white clouds careering before them; but the midday sun still retains much of its ardour. A few fallen leaves are rustling the glades of the forest, but the smaller leaves of secondary growth still retain their freshness; and the woods are now beautiful in their variegated foliage of bright green and russet brown. The colours which distinguish the foliage of different trees in autumn are among the most striking phenomena of the vegetable world; for it is observable that one distinct tone of colour is common to the autumnal leaves of all of the same species. Those of the oak change, in this season, to a yellowish green; the plane tree becomes tawny; those of the sycamore dark brown; the elms take an orange hue; the leaves of the hornbeam assume a bright yellow tint; the cherry becomes red; and those of the beech are dark green, tending to deep orange. The oak, mellowed to a bronzed green, thus blends with the faded yellow of the palmated chestnut-leaves and the deeper hues of the elm, while the darker shadows of the pines are relieved by the lighter tints of the fresh leaves and green underwood. Over the hedgerow trails the rambling briony, the wild bramble of the brake, and the wild rose, some of its fruit becoming tipped with scarlet, mingles with the blackberry, the hawthorn, and the convolvulus – a morning flower, which opens its trumpet-shaped blossom to the morning sun, closing it again with the closing day.

Beautiful are the old English orchards in September. The heavy crop of apples bows down the branches of the trees, and tells of a summer departed.

With ruddy fruit the orchard now is hung;
The golden hop droops pendent in the breeze;
For Autumn from her ample hand hath thrown
Her richest treasures on the laden trees.

Their gnarled and twisted branches and lichen-covered stems, however, are not always indicative of good cultivation, any more than the trim and well-regulated fruit tree forms a picturesque object in the landscape, or adds greatly to the pictorial beauty of the scene. A verdant sward of deepest green, which the shade of the trees keeps moist and fresh all the year round, receives the earlier-ripened waifs and strays, as well as those whose tender lives the 'worm i' the bud' has undermined.

In the flower garden, if the full measure of colour remains, the fragrance of summer is gone. Most of the flowers of August continue to bloom through September; but their number is gradually less as the month advances. The scentless hollyhocks, dahlias, China asters (Fig. 548), and other autumnal-blooming flowers, take the place of the aromatic and fragrant pinks, carnations, and sweet violets:

In colour those, and these delight the smell;

although the tea-scented and perpetual roses still remain to perfume the air with their fragrance, and along with them some very old-fashioned favourites. The arbutus, or strawberry tree, the most ornamental of autumn-flowering shrubs, it remains to add to our Christmas enjoyments, when it shows itself in fruit and flower at the same time. The hydrangea also exhibits its rich clusters of pink flowers. The gentians, too, are rich in the luxuriance of their second bloom in September.

I – Work to be Done in the Garden

1 – The Flower Garden and Shrubbery

1913 *High Keeping* Now that the beds are thoroughly covered, nothing contributes more to that high style of keeping that constitutes the chief charm of every garden than the removal of every dead flower and leaf as fast as it appears; the maintenance of neat edgings and sharply-defined lines of coloured or ribbon borders, or beds planted on the ring principle. Regularity of height is also another desideratum and proof of high keeping.

By regularity of height it is not to be understood that every bed, or every part of a bed, should be of one dead uniform height, but that they should either present a level or an even surface. Suppose, for instance, a bed is raised in the middle, as a rule it should gradually fall towards the sides, and the same parts of the bed should be of the same height. If the edging is 6 inches high, it should be this height all round; if the second row is 9 inches, it should be 9 inches throughout, and so on. Nothing is more indicative of a want of judgment in planting or slovenly keeping than a row or bed 6 inches here, 12 there, and 10 at another point, without regular gradation, or any system whatever. Only of secondary importance to the blending of proper colours is the arrangement of plants according to their proper heights. Of course, the appearance of a weed, great or small, on either beds or ground, is an intolerable intrusion upon, and quite inconsistent with, high keeping. Closely-mown well-rolled turf is like the picture frame's influence upon the picture, and has a powerful influence in exhibiting beauty in the best light. In harmony with all this the walks must be scrupulously clean, hard, smooth, and bright, to afford pleasant facility of access to, and be in character with, the beauty of the objects they are designed to exhibit.

1914 *Propagation* Having thus provided, regulated, arranged, and enjoyed the highest amount of beauty that the garden is capable of yielding, the next point is how all this is to be perpetuated or reproduced another season. This brings us to another great business of the month – propagation. All trimmings of verbenas, ageratums, geraniums, calceolarias, etc., etc., that are cut off to maintain sharp lines, clearly-defined edgings, etc., should be inserted as cuttings. Where enough cannot be thus secured, the thickest parts of lines or beds must be thinned for this purpose; or, better still, plants that were placed in the reserve garden for this object must be cut down and divided into small morsels for cuttings.

FIG. 548 *China aster (Callistephus [aster] sinensis)*

1915 *Cuttings* If any should wish for a definition of a cutting, it may be said that it is simply a part of a branch with two or more joints, leaves, or buds; it must have two joints to constitute a cutting. It may grow if it has only one joint, but then it is called an eye. Generally, cuttings have from three to six joints or leaves: these are enough for a verbena; four to six are good averages for scarlet or zonal geraniums (Fig. 549). Cut the base of the cuttings clean across with a knife; remove the leaves at the base, or not, as you please; insert it firmly in any light sandy soil, covering the surface with fine sand, the more effectually to exclude the air; place it in a position favourable to the retention of its juice until roots are emitted, and then the period of its cutting-hood is over, and it has become a perfect plant.

For cuttings of most flower garden plants at this season no place is so good as a close cold frame. In preparing pots or pans for cuttings at this period of the year, it should first be determined whether they are to remain in store pots for the winter, or be potted off as soon as rooted. If the former, a third of the pot should be filled with drainage; if the latter, a much smaller proportion of drainage will suffice. Cuttings that are to stand in their store pots until next spring must also be inserted thinner than those that are to be potted when rooted. Ten verbenas, or other such cuttings, will be enough for a 48-sized pot to maintain throughout the winter. Twenty might be inserted if they are to be potted off directly. Some cuttings, such as scarlet geraniums, have, however, a superabundance of sap when removed from the parent plant; if placed in the same medium that would suit the tip end of a verbena shoot, instead of forming roots they would decay by wholesale. Various expedients have been recommended to check this tendency – laying the cuttings in the air after they are made, to dissipate their superfluous juices, etc., etc. No practice is,

FIG. 549 *Scarlet and zonal geraniums*

however, so good as removing the cuttings direct from the plants, with all their leaves on, and placing them full in the sun out of doors without any shade or protection whatever. They may either be planted in the natural ground, 6 inches apart, on a prepared border, or in pots or boxes; and success will be alike certain, with less than one per cent loss.

1916 *Dahlias* Dahlias will now require careful tying, disbudding, and thinning of the shoots, where first-rate flowers are required; a good soaking of manure water in dry weather will also be most serviceable to them. The blossoms of dahlias are often infested with and injured by earwigs, which must be trapped by inverted pots filled with hay or straw, into which they will creep, and from which they can be easily removed anddestroyed. Caps of paper may be used to protect choice blooms of dahlias from the intensity of the sun's rays at mid-day.

1917 *Hollyhocks* The blooms of hollyhocks may be much prolonged by similar treatment. Earwigs in hollyhock flowers must be taken and destroyed. Every offset of the best varieties which is found at the base and here and there along the stems ought to be inserted as cuttings. Previously-rooted cuttings of hollyhocks should be planted in the reserve garden.

1918 *Roses* Perpetuals may still be cut back, with the hope of a third bloom; and late-budded plants will require looking after, watering, and training to stakes. Growing shoots that are heavy with buds should be tied in, and thus secured from injury by wind. Suckers should be removed.

1919 *Budded Roses* With regard to the growth of shoots from buds that have been inserted in the stocks early in the season, the ligature that binds the bud should be slackened, so that the growth of the shoot may not be hindered by its tightness; and if the wild shoots from the stock itself happen to be growing very freely, they may be shortened back to, say ten leaves from the bud itself, supposing the bud to be still dormant. Late briars may yet be budded.

1920 *Cuttings of Roses* Cuttings taken and inserted in August will now be rooting, and may be freely exposed to the air, so as to harden them off gradually. Cuttings of perpetual and climbing roses may be inserted in September, but they must be placed in cold pits or under hand lights, and receive protection under glass throughout the winter.

1921 *Carnations, etc.* Pot off layers of carnations as fast as rooted, water sparingly, and place in a cold frame for a few days until they make a fresh start. Choice varieties should be potted in pairs in 5-inch pots, in which they must remain under glass throughout the winter. For rooted layers, pipings, etc., generally a piece of ground should be prepared by deep digging and manuring, and in these the plants should be placed, from 9 to 15 inches apart, according to size, there to remain during the winter and to mature for planting-out in spring.

1922 *Pansies* Plant out in beds early-rooted pansy cuttings, insert a succession of cuttings, and prick out seedlings in the reserve garden.

1923 *Auriculas, Polyanthuses, etc.* Seedling polyanthuses, offsets of these and auriculas should be planted out in the reserve garden on rich shady beds. Shift auriculas and polyanthuses in pots that may require it.

1924 *Stocks* Stocks sown in pans, or in the reserve garden, in August, will now be fit either to pot off and place in frames until established, or to prick out on shady beds in this department.

1925 *Hardy Annuals* The first sowing of hardy annuals to stand the winter in the open air should also be made towards the end of the month.

2 – The Vegetable or Kitchen Garden

1926 *Routine Work* To secure a supply of vegetables in the winter and early spring, all arrangements not already completed should now be made without delay; the growth of those already planted encouraged by hoeing and stirring the earth round the roots; and where slugs abound, their ravages counteracted by sowing soot or lime on the soil.

1927 *Celery* The earthing-up of this useful vegetable now demands special attention. The sowings made in July and August will now be ready for transplanting.

1928 *Asparagus* As this is a permanent occupant of the quarter in the usual mode of management – that is to say, when it is permitted to grow in the ordinary way and to come to maturity naturally at the ordinary time, instead of being removed from the ground for forcing – new plantations may still be made in September on a rich soil, neither wet nor too stiff, but pulverising readily under the spade.

1929 *Seakale* Keep the surface well stirred and free from weeds. As the leaves decay and can be easily detached from the plants, remove them. It will be some time before they are all off; but as soon as this is the case, cover the crowns with ashes or bark from the tanyard till they are required for forcing.

1930 *Cardoons* The early crop is now fit for use; remove the earth carefully, and take up the plant by the roots, which must be cut off. The points of the leaves are also cut off to where they are solid and blanched. These are washed, the parts of the leaf-stalks remaining on the stem are tied to it, and they are ready for cooking.

1931 *Cauliflowers* These may still be sown in some situations, and those sown last month are now ready to prick out under hand glasses or in frames, as they advance: if the season is mild, they may even be planted out under a south wall, provided the plants are not wet at the roots. Plants that are advancing and heading should have the large leaves broken and turned over them, to give shelter from sun and rain, and by having the earth drawn round the stem. The plants sown in May will now be ready for planting out in rows two feet and a half asunder, giving them a copious watering to promote their growth.

1932 *Cabbages, Savoys, etc.* Prepare a piece of ground by deep trenching and copious manuring, for spring cabbages, savoys, and winter greens, and keep it forked over regularly until the plants are sufficiently advanced for planting out. When ready, plant them in rows 2 feet apart, watering them well to settle the earth at their roots. Savoys and spring cabbages, in particular, require a rich soil thoroughly manured with well-rotted dung.

1933 *Broccoli* These also require a good soil, richly manured. Plant them out from the beds in rows where they are to grow, 2 feet apart each way; water as soon as planted, repeating it occasionally till the plants have rooted. It has been found of advantage to dibble large holes to receive the plants, and fill them up with wood ashes or ashes of burnt vegetable matter. This crop may follow peas with advantage, or the plants may be placed between the rows of late sorts. Some seed may be sown to stand the winter, and come up for a late spring crop.

1934 *Brussels Sprouts and Winter Greens* These may now be planted out for autumn use.

1935 *Lettuces* Sow cos and cabbage lettuces in a bed of rich mellow ground; in the first, second, and fourth week, prick out on nursery beds the plants last sown, and plant out the strongest plants in the open ground. Dig neatly and rake evenly, and put in the plants by line 12 inches apart each way; continue to water till rooted.

1936 *Endive* Seed sown now will come in to supply plants for autumn use; the green curled being the best for main crops. Water the beds in dry weather, and tie up to blanch plants advancing to maturity. Dig up a piece of good ground, manure well, and rake smooth. In this plant some strong endive plants a foot apart each way, and water as soon as planted, repeating it in dry weather.

1937 *Small Salading* Sow cresses, mustard radishes, and other small salads, every seven days, choosing a shady border, and sowing in very shallow drills, watering daily.

1938 *Spinach* for winter use, sown late in July or early in August, should now be planted out. The prickly-seeded, or triangular-leaved, is the hardiest for winter use.

1939 *Turnip Radishes,* black (Fig. 550) and white, should now be sown for winter use; and some small Italian radishes, white and red, may also be sown for autumn use.

1940 *Onions* Seed may be sown early this month to afford bulbs to transplant in the spring, for use in salads. The general crop will be ready for harvesting.

1941 *Carrots* Seed should be sown this month in an open situation, and on light soil. The sowing should be done as soon as the bed will work after digging.

1942 *Turnips* Seed may still be sown for autumn and winter use, the Early Stone being a good sort. Sow immediately after digging, and sow thin. Hoe the crops sown in May and June in dry weather, and thin out till the plants are 7 or 8 inches apart.

1943 *Potatoes* As the crops ripen, which may be known by the perishing condition of the haulm and the firmness of the skin of the tubers, which can no longer be rubbed off by the pressure of the thumb, the tubers should be taken up with care, so as to avoid bruising them, and stored away for use, either in cellars or in caves or pits covered in to protect the roots from the weather. The ground from which they have been removed may be planted with broccoli or cabbage, or sown with winter spinach, turnips, etc.

FIG. 550 *Black Spanish winter radish*

3 – The Fruit Garden and Orchard

1944 *Routine Work* The chief work to be done in the fruit garden and orchard is harvesting and preparation for planting, either to replace decaying trees, or for new plantations. In either case let it be understood that, while something of the future success depends on soil, subsoil, and situation, on which subjects we have already remarked, perfect drainage is indispensable. Soil and subsoil may both be corrected by properly prepared stations, if the drainage be sufficient; without it success is impossible.

1945 *Apricots, Peaches, and Nectarines* The trees require to have the future bearing shoots nailed in closely, and all laterals not required removed, so that the fruit may have the full benefit of the sun, from which it derives the colour and flavour. Make a final thinning of the fruit where necessary. A few of the leaves may also be removed, where they shade the fruit too much. As the fruit approaches its ripened state, nets should be extended beneath it to catch any falling fruit. To protect the fruit from wasps, use fine netting, which admits of perfectly free circulation of air, and at the same time keeps off wasps and flies. Should mildew appear at any time, dust the shoots with flour of sulphur; an occasional washing with soap-suds and syringing with pure water will also be useful, avoiding, of course, too near an approach to the fruit with either.

The object of training and pruning is to produce fruit. If this is not specially attended to in the case of the peach and nectarine, the fruit will be small, as well as few and far between. To suffer trees to throw out long luxurious branches, to be lopped off at the end of their growth, reason tells us must be bad management, while Mr Rivers tells us that all the pruning required for wall or dwarf trees should be done with the finger and thumb alone – that is, he would pinch off every shoot not required in the future economy of the tree. By this means he would direct all the sap of the tree to the production of strong young wood and fruit. It is obvious, therefore, that if pruning has been neglected hitherto, no time should be lost in getting them in order now. Let all very luxuriant wood and fore-right branches, as well as all straggling branches, be cut out, leaving ample store of young shoots, however, for next year's use, nailing all in close and regular to the wall at their natural length, so that all branches laid in in former months are firm in their places, and all gross shoots stopped. M. Du Breuil recommends the application of a solution of sulphate of iron dissolved in water, in the proportion of twenty-three grains to two pints of water, to the peach. 'It stimulates the absorbing properties of the leaves, which thus attract more vigorously the rising sap.' He also applies the same solution to the fruit at three different stages of its growth, moistening the fruit with it when it has attained a fourth of its growth, again when it is half grown, and, finally, when at three-fourths of its size. The solution excites its various absorbing organs, attracts to them a quantity of the sap, and greatly increases the size of the fruit.

1946 *Preservation of Fruit from Insects, etc* As the fruit begins to ripen, the attacks of wasps and snails become very annoying. For the benefit of the former, hang up some phials filled with sugared water or beer. This will attract the wasps from the fruit. Snails must be looked for diligently after a shower of rain, and a train of powdered lime round the stem will keep them off in dry weather. Trees are also subject to attacks of the red spider during dry weather. As preventive as well as cure, wash them with water in which flour of sulphur is held in suspension. At the same time give them a good soaking with water at the roots; thick mulching will also strengthen the trees to resist this insidious foe.

1947 *Apples* Apples require very little attention now – only a slight thinning-out of cross shoots, bearing in mind that with the apple, as with all other fruit, the best grown is at the extremities of the branches; therefore, encourage short-jointed wood; and in shortening any of them prune back to a bud which, from its healthy appearance, indicated by its brownish green, promises to extend the tree.

1948 *Pears* The pear requires more energetic treatment than the apple. The young spray requires thinning out towards the end of June, and all watery-looking shoots should then be removed, reserving all of the opposite character for selection in winter. At this time, also, stop all young shoots, except those at the extremities of the branches, by pinching out the terminal bud, and tying down to the rails all such as do not interfere with the fruit spurs, cutting back such as do interfere to two or three eyes. Leave as many leaves as possible round the terminal bud.

Early apples and pears, now coming on, should be gathered a day or two before they are ripe; and it is not unusual to make two or three gatherings from the same tree, for, if gathered too soon, they shrivel; and if suffered to remain on the tree after maturity, much of the best fruit will fall and get bruised while being gathered. As they are gathered, lay the pears singly, and the apples in tiers, of not more than two deep; and separate carefully all bruised fruit.

1949 *Plums* The plum, in moderately rich soil, has a tendency to produce gross shoots between the stem and the extremity of the branches. These, if they have not been removed, now require the pruner's care; where they are not wanted let them be cut away, reserving all short-jointed wood and leading shoots necessary to balance the tree.

1950 *Cherries* With the cherry little or no shortening back is necessary, pruning being confined to thinning away cross and interior shoots on standard trees, and spurring back those shoots which are too close together.

1951 *Budding, Inarching, etc.* All kinds of fruit trees may now be budded; branches may also be added where required, by approach grafting or inarching; trees of healthy growth, but bearing indifferent fruit, may now become the stocks for a fruit of superior quality by the processes already described. All lateral shoots of wall trees and espaliers should be cut pretty closely in, there being no danger now of their breaking.

1952 *Gooseberries* Thin out all overloaded bushes, stop and thin out all shoots, and mat over where necessary, to retard ripening. Look over the bushes for caterpillars, and destroy by every possible means. Many expedients are recommended for the destruction of these pests. Hellebore powder, digitalis, and unslaked lime have been tried; and a layer of tanner's bark laid on the ground in the autumn is said to have had the effect of keeping away insects.

1953 *Currants* Prune away all side spray in currants, and treat generally as directed for gooseberries.

1954 *Raspberries* Stop the canes of raspberries when sufficiently high.

1955 *Strawberries* Alpines are now in full bearing. This is also the season for saving seed, if seedlings are desired for planting. Selecting a few of the finest bearers, let them be fully ripened, and the seed saved. Take the fruit and rub it on a piece of glass or slate, so that the pulp may dry up; when the seed may be rubbed off and preserved till the season for sowing in the spring. Runners, the only means by which plants can be obtained true to the sort, should also be encouraged to grow, but no more than are absolutely required for new beds, as the fruit is always largest and best where the runners are trimmed off.

FIG. 551 *Bush alpine strawberry*

II – Work to be Done under Glass

1 – Flowers in the Conservatory, Greenhouse, Stove, etc.

1956 *Hothouse or Plant Stove* In all glazed structures water should be given in moderation, and only in sufficient quantities to maintain the plants in perfect health. However, the higher temperature maintained in the plant stove, and the difference in the nature of the plants occupying this structure, render a greater amount of moisture necessary than is required in the greenhouse and conservatory; but an autumn – and neither a spring nor a summer – temperature must be maintained.

1957 *Succulents: Caladiums* Plants with succulent leaves must also be gradually inured to as much sunlight as they will bear. This, while it will injure the appearance of some variegated and fine-foliaged plants, will improve others.

Some of the Caladiums, such as *C. pictum*, *C. Newmani*, and *C. bicolor*, assume the most vivid hues when fully exposed to the light. Others, such as *C. argyrites*, *C. Belleymei*, and *C. violaceum*, look most beautiful and delicate when considerably shaded. It is best for the strength and vigour of the roots of all caladiums to have their leaves fully exposed to the sun and gradually matured in the autumn.

FIG. 552 *Caladium violaceum*

This process must, however, go on gradually, and the greatest care must be exercised in getting a plant like *Cyanophyllum magnificum*, for instance, in full vigour, to bear the full blaze of an autumnal sun with impunity. The smallest drop of condensed water on such a leaf, or on almost any begonia leaf, will, in half an hour, do irreparable damage. The heating rays of the sun convert each drop into a burning lens, which quickly parboils the delicate texture of their leaves. Caladiums are not so often injured in this way, as their composition and structure seem specially adapted for throwing drops of water off their surface.

1958 *Winter-Flowering Plant* Clerodendrons, poinsettias, Justicias, euphorbias, begonias, etc., must be grown on freely for winter flowering.

1959 *Climbers and Basket Plants* Stephanotis, passion flowers, jasmines, etc., on the roof, must be carefully trained, cleaned, and regulated. Allamandas often make a splendid display when trained as semi-climbers on the roof of a stove. Achimenes and other plants, suspended from the roof in elegant wire baskets, have a charming effect among climbers, and make the roof at least as showy as either shelf or bed.

These plants, with gloxinias and gesneras, will also make a splendid display here during the month. A proper arrangement of flowering and variegated begonias, intermixed with marantas, musas, palms, ferns, caladiums, and a few other fine-foliaged and flowering plants, will give the house an air of oriental grandeur and magnificence such as our fathers could never have conceived.

1960 *Orchid House* More light and air, and less water, must be the rule here. However, those plants that are in full growth must not be stinted by any means, as the natural growing season of most orchids is the rainy season; the season when it rains and rains every day and night, for perhaps six weeks, without ceasing. Rapid growth, long seasons of perfect repose, and sudden excitement, seem to be the chief essentials to successful orchid culture.

1961 *The Greenhouse* This structure should at once be got ready for its winter occupants. Many of these, such as ericas, epacrises, azaleas, camellias, have probably been in the cold pit or sheltered situations out of doors for the last four months. In ordinary seasons they will be safe enough there until the end of September. Meantime, however, if the house requires painting or cleaning, the sooner it is done the better. Probably the fumes of paint do not injure plants, but they are very unpleasant to plant owners; and the paint stands much better if it has time to become quite hard before the house is used. Greenhouses that have no climbers on the roof should all be fumigated with burnt sulphur several days before any plants are brought into them. This is certain death to all animal life, if all contact with the outer air is cut off, and insures, if the plants are clean when brought from their summer quarters, perfect freedom from insects throughout the winter.

1962 *Temperature* For the plants that will form the chief tenants of the greenhouse during the autumn and early winter, a temperature ranging from 55° to 60° will be found to be in every way suitable.

1963 *Shifting and Repotting* All camellias, azaleas, epacrises, heaths, etc., should be repotted either directly they have done flowering, or as soon as they have finished their growth. Some of the latest, might still be shifted; but this work should have been completed a month ago.

Plants potted so late in the season require special care during the winter. All plants seem to have a firmer hold of health and life when the pots in which they grow are thoroughly filled with roots; hence the desirability and safety of early, and the risk of late potting.

1964 *Heaths* Heaths must be carefully watched for the first speck of mildew, and immediately dusted with sulphur. As this malady often proves fatal among heaths, it should be carefully guarded against. It is generally induced by an excess of stagnant water at the roots, or excessive syringing, heavy rains, or continuous fogs over the tops. Some of the woolly-leaved varieties seem to have a constitutional tendency to it, arising, it is thought, from their peculiar structure, causing them to retain so much moisture on the surface of the leaves. The later the plants are potted, the more they are predisposed to the attacks of mildew.

1965 *Pelargoniums* The grand secret of profuse bloom in pelargoniums is early, strong autumnal growth. The moment pelargoniums begin to fade, they should be placed out of doors in the full sun to ripen their growth. When the wood becomes slightly browned, cut them down to within two, three, or four eyes of the old wood. Leave them in the same position, or place them in a house or pit to break. When the young shoots have advanced from 1½ to 2 inches, shake them entirely out of the pots, slightly pruning the roots; pot them in any light soil in as small pots as the roots can be got into; return them to a close house or pit, and the reduction, repotting, and restarting are finished. All plants intended to flower next May or June should now be ready for removal to their blooming pots. Harden off, cut down, and start

FIG. 553 *Scarlet linum (Linum grandiflorum rubrum)*

afresh, plants for late summer and autumn blooming as soon as they are ripe enough.

1966 *Cinerarias* Pot off suckers from old shoots; prick off, pot, and shift seedling plants, and push forward the first batch for flowering from November to February.

1967 *Calceolarias* Calceolarias require the same general treatment as cinerarias.

1968 *Chrysanthemums* Shift chrysanthemums, liberally water top for late blooms, and stake.

1969 *Primroses and Pansies* Primroses, pansies, etc., must be shifted into larger pots, and maintained in health.

1970 *Plants for Winter Flowering* Provide plenty of linums (Fig. 553), *Salvia splendens*, oxalises, etc., for winter or spring; likewise hyacinths, narcissuses, tulips, etc., etc.; pot the first batch, as early rooting is the only certain foundation for good flowering.

1971 *Tree Carnations* Tree carnations are very useful for the winter decoration of greenhouses and conservatories. They should be kept from flowering during the summer months, and may be treated out of doors, or in a very cool shady house, until well covered with blossom buds for winter. Under glass, in a warm situation, the plants are soon drawn up and the buds are spoiled.

1972 *The Conservatory: Ventilation, etc* For several months past the great difficulty here has been one of selection. Azaleas, geraniums, fuchsias, balsams, globe amaranths, achimenes, liliums, gloxinias, begonias, etc., etc., have been jostling each other for the best place; each form and type of beauty has been striving by turns for supremacy, and it has been unfolded so copiously and rapidly that the great difficulty has been to bring it all into direct proximity with the eye in this house, devoted to the conservation and exhibition of floral loveliness. For the former purpose it can hardly be kept too cool at this season, omitting, however, all draughts upon stove plants; and, for the latter, tasteful arrangement is the most important point. Too many beautiful things crammed together without order or system are never so satisfying as a very few disposed to the best advantage. Good specimens must also have plenty of space if they are to continue good.

1973 *Climbers* During this month the climbers on the roof must be gradually thinned, and the shading partially withdrawn, to allow the wood of both permanent and temporary occupants of the house to ripen well. Much of next season's success depends upon this. Well-ripened wood will also enable plants to pass through the winter better, and to bear a greater amount of cold with impunity.

1974 *Watering* To most plants, except balsams, and fuchsias in small pots, liquid manure must now be given sparingly, if at all. The object now is not rapid growth, but abundance of flowers and matured wood; therefore, even pure water must be given as sparingly as is consistent with good health. In dull weather, sprinkling of paths, and other summer expedients to maintain a humid atmosphere, should also be abandoned. Perfect cleanliness will of course be maintained, as beauty and dirt are not only irreconcilable, but the latter neutralises and destroys the influence of the former.

2 – Plants under Glass, in Hotbeds, Frames, etc.

1975 *Flowers in Pits and Frames: Bulbs* Cold frames will be put in requisition during this month, for passing the first batch of hyacinths, tulips, narcissuses, jonquils, crocuses, snowdrops, and other bulbs, through the preliminary stage of growth that follows immediately on potting, and which consists of the proper development of the roots. A number of 4-, 5-, and 6-inch pots having been obtained and well washed, first fill up each pot to about one-fourth of its depth with broken pieces of pots or potsherds. On these place about the same depth of well-rotted dung, and then fill up with light rich mould. Pot the bulbs firmly, and then place the pots in a frame under glass, standing them on a thick layer of coal ashes, or plunging them in earth or spent tan. Admit plenty of air, but exclude the light as much as possible.

1976 *Annuals* Some pots of mignonette and annuals for winter flowering may be placed in frames in slight heat, for ultimate removal to the conservatory or window.

1977 *Biennials and Perennials* Violets, pinks, carnations, dianthuses, and similar flowers, for winter blooming, should now be potted up and placed in slight heat.

1978 *Pelargoniums* Those potted in August and placed in frames, may now have plenty of air and water, before being removed to the window or the conservatory.

1979 *Balsams and Cockscombs* Plants just coming into flower should be removed into the conservatory or the dwelling-house, where their blooms may be better seen and more highly appreciated.

1980 *Cuttings* Cuttings of various bedding plants may be put in under glass, and all rooted cuttings of geraniums, fuchsias, petunias, etc., should be potted, or, if originally struck in pots, should be shifted into larger pots.

1981 *Cinerarias, Calceolarias, Chinese Primroses, etc.* Seedling plants of these flowers should now be shifted into larger pots in order to encourage and develop their growth.

1982 *Vegetables in Hotbeds, Frames, etc.* Nothing need be added to the directions given last month for vegetables and salading, etc., raised under glass for winter use.

1983 *Cucumbers* The directions already given for preceding months must be acted on, according to the stage of growth that the plant or fruit has attained. Cucumbers should be cut as soon as they are fit; decaying leaves should be promptly removed, and the frames closed early in the afternoon, in order to maintain a suitable temperature within the house, and to promote quick growth.

1984 *Melons* The ripening of fruit not yet ready for the table should be accelerated by placing fresh lining round the hotbeds, etc. Leaves that shade the fruit should be removed, and a temperature of 70° at least maintained at night, the frames being closed between 2 and 3 in the afternoon, and the glass covered with mats as the sun declines. Melons approaching ripeness should be placed on tiles or pieces of thick glass, to keep them from the inroads of insects, and from contact with the earth below.

3 – Fruit under Glass, Heated and Unheated

1985 *Care of Trees* Fruit culture seems almost a misnomer now, as, with the exception of very late crops, the great business at this season is to gather and enjoy the fruit, which has attained full maturity. Nevertheless, the idea of culture must never be lost sight of. This, either in its past, present, or future tense, must ever be present to the mind, if success is to be procured continuous and all but certain, instead of accidental, fitful, and rare. The trees, although their special functions, as fruit producers, have been discharged, still require as much care as ever, particularly with reference to the leaves, which should be kept perfectly clean, that the trees may be preserved in health. Insects are often allowed to perforate, and soot and dust to suffocate the breathing pores of the leaves; and some will even cut off the leaves to allow the sun to shine on the fruit. The conscientious gardener, however, must not allow or do anything of this sort.

The leaves, it must be remembered, are the chief instruments in converting certain earthy and saline matters, and air and water, into the proper food of plants. Consequently, the greater the number, provided they are well exposed to the light, and the more clean and healthy the condition of the leaves, the more rich and luscious will be the fruit, and the more robust the health of the plant producing it. But the leaves perform a twofold function; they do not only ripen one year's crop, but they lay the basis of fruitfulness for another season. No sooner do they mature the fruit for the current year, than they begin to store up organisable matter for the next. The quantity of fruit for the next season depends upon the amount of this organisable matter stored up; and the amount stored is determined by the number of clean healthy leaves that are fully exposed to the light. Hence, the longer the leaves can be maintained in perfect health, the better will be the crop for the ensuing season, and vice versa.

1986 *Thrip on Fruit Trees* Sometimes thrip attacks peaches, vines, etc., when the fruit is ripe. It is then very difficult to eradicate, as either smoking or syringing with any pungent fluid would mar the flavour of the fruit for weeks, if not for ever. The houses should be thoroughly examined before the fruit is ripe, and if a single thrip is visible, it must be at once destroyed. It is a good practice, if there is the least suspicion of their presence, to smoke two or three times in succession to make sure of their destruction.

Notwithstanding all that has been said above about the importance of leaves, as soon as peach leaves will come off with the gentlest touch by drawing the hand up the shoot – not down – they may be partially removed. When their adherence to the branch becomes so slight, their elaborating functions are finished; and as there may not be sufficient wind under glass to shake them off, they may be thus assisted by the hand in parting company with the branch or shoot on which they have grown.

1987 *The Vinery* Care must be taken in preserving the foliage of grape vines, not to allow too many leaves on the lateral shoots. It is the large leaves at the base of the fruiting branches, near to the main stem, that are of most consequence. The buds at their base will yield next year's crop, and the fuller, rounder, and more plump they become, the larger that crop will be. The great point is to maintain these leaves in health without *inducing new growth* or causing the buds to break. A comparatively dry atmosphere and cool temperature are the chief things necessary for this. These are also the main desiderata for preserving grapes as long as possible. An excess of drought and sudden alternations of temperature are, however, almost as injurious as too much water. If the latter induces decay, the former causes the fruit to shrivel, and robs them of that luscious satisfying goodness which is the chief charm of first-rate grapes.

1988 *Mildew on Grapes* Ripe grapes must be frequently looked over, and every specked berry be at once removed. If mildew makes its appearance in the late houses, paint the pipes with a mixture of equal parts lime and sulphur, and sprinkle the infested parts with dry sulphur. Prevention, however, is much better than cure; and experience has shown that a yearly painting of all the pipes in the house with this composition will prevent mildew. The fumes of the sulphur from hot pipes can do no harm; they are not disagreeable, and there is reason to believe that they are a certain preventive of mildew.

Flues, however, must not be painted over near the fire, as the slightest ignition of sulphur produces sulphurous acid, and would destroy every leaf.

1989 *Ventilation* Air should be admitted to all vineries by night as well as day. Except in wet weather, in houses the air is admitted by the roof-lights; but where the ventilation is given by openings in the wall, a little air should be constantly admitted to the house, and fire used in rainy weather to maintain the requisite temperature. For all ripe grapes 60° is high enough; but late Muscats, now ripening, should enjoy a minimum of 70°, rising to 85° or 90° with sun heat. Grapes intended to keep till January, February, or March should be well thinned.

1990 *The Pinery* Keep a genial atmosphere of from 70° to 83° among fruiting plants; water them with clear manure water, and refrain from syringing plants in flower and ripe fruit. Providences, and the black varieties for winter fruiting, would be best in a house by themselves from this time. Maintain a steady bottom heat of 85° to fruiting plants and 75° to succession plants. Where hot water is used this is easily managed; but dung, tan, or leaves require greater caution. However, pines grow better, it is thought, when the bottom heat is derived from fermenting material than from hot water.

1991 *Succession Plants* All the succession plants should have already received their final shift for the winter; those planted out in beds, either fruiting or succession plants, must be sparingly watered from this time, as, if the soil becomes too wet, it will dry slowly at this season of the year. Attend to the making of linings; give as much air as is consistent with the maintenance of a proper temperature; gradually withdraw all shade from this period, and endeavour to secure a firm indurated growth before the approach of winter.

1992 *The Peach House* The lights may now be removed for six weeks from the early peach house; or, if this is not practicable, as much air as possible should be given night and day.

1993 *Figs* These require plenty of water when in full growth; in fact, in this state they may be treated almost like aquatic plants. The second crop of fruit will now be ripening, and those who wish for a third crop in November and December should have stopped the shoots in the middle of August; but where a very early crop is required, the shoots must not be stopped after this period. Great care must be exercised in ripening the wood, and seeing that the embryo fruit buds are formed in the axils of the leaves. Water must be gradually withheld, and a dryish atmosphere maintained for this purpose.

1994 *The Orchard House* This cannot have too much air. Where no fire is used, sometimes late varieties of peaches, etc., are grown here, to come in after the fruit out of doors. Fruit on the north side of an orchard house, with a thorough draught through the house, will be a month or six weeks later than the same varieties on a south or west wall. Maintain all the trees in the most perfect health, and liberally water those in pots with manure water.

FIG. 554 *Flower of Begonia Veitchii.*
One of the finest of the Begonias.
Colour of bloom – vivid vermillion cinnabar red.

CHAPTER 31

The Garden and its Work in Every Department in October

1995 *Aspect and Character of the Month* October, the eighth month from March, the first month of the old Roman year, according to quaint old Peachum, 'is drawn in a garment of yellow and carnation; upon his head a garland of oak leaves, in his right hand the sign of Scorpio, and in his left a basket of services, medlars, and other fruits that ripen late.' The mean temperature of the month is nearly 7° lower than that of September, and frost is by no means uncommon towards the end of the month. The moisture in the atmosphere increases, and evaporation diminishes considerably; the mean average temperature being, at one foot below the surface, 51·52°; at two feet, 52·78°; and at the surface, 49·35°.

The autumnal fall of the leaf, with the change of colour which precedes it, is among the most interesting phenomena of the month. That the latter is due to light was established by the experiment of Mr Macaire Prinsep, who found that the exposed part of the leaf was always the most deeply-coloured portion. In order to determine whether any change of colour took place in absolute darkness, he shaded parts of the branch of a tree, the leaves of which were in three different stages of colour, and found that no further change took place – a green leaf fell off green; a leaf yellow before seclusion fell off yellow; if variegated, the leaf fell off green, yellow, or brown. Seclusion from the light seemed to arrest the natural change which was going on under the action of the sun; but the cause of colour in plants is somewhat obscure. The decomposition of carbonic acid, and the exhalation of oxygen, is productive of a green colour in a ratio proportioned to the intensity of the decomposing cause – light. On the other hand, where water is present in too great abundance in the system, yellow prevails, as if the blue, which is necessary, with the yellow, to produce green, were discharged by the surplus moisture, while the green becomes intense in proportion to the action of light and air. The fall of the leaf itself is a phenomenon not very easily comprehended. 'It is not enough,' says the author of *Observations of a Naturalist*, 'to say that the leaf falls because it is weakened or dead; for if a branch is struck by lightning, detached from the stem by any other cause, the leaves still adhere tenaciously to the dead branch. To produce the natural fall of the leaf, in deciduous trees, the branch must continue to live, while the leaves die.' It is only when it has satisfied the ends of its being, that it is discharged, as it were, from its functions; the sap, which it was called forth to elaborate, is consolidating into wood; and the leaf, no longer required, returns to earth to restore its exhausted powers. It is, therefore, a melancholy sight to witness the falling leaf. We are irresistibly reminded of the holy text, 'We all do fade as a leaf'. In spite of these solemn associations, awakened by the season, however, the varied hues of autumn are beautiful to look upon: all that rendered summer green and lovely is dying by the wayside; but in its place we have a universal and peculiar serenity of atmosphere, a more intensely shining sky, and an impression of ampler expansion; an array of sunny clouds with their silvery lining, the distant horizon, and a landscape of unequalled variety and richness of colouring.

The garden, it is true, begins to look somewhat desolate; flowers which bloomed a few weeks ago – bloomed in numbers innumerable – are now few and far between: but some still linger with us. Dahlias, before the close of the month, are probably touched by frost, and the chrysanthemums and the autumnal roses are the chief ornaments of the garden on which reliance can be placed; but most of the other flowers exist only on sufferance. The first frost will play sad havoc with them, except where they occupy very warm and sheltered spots in the garden. Even there:

> They daily await without terror or grief,
> The summons that tells of the fall of the leaf.

I – Work to be done in the Garden

1 – The Flower Garden and Shrubbery

1996 *Propagation* The great business of propagating for next year should now be consummated. Nevertheless, such things as verbenas, calceolarias, etc., etc., may still be put in with the certainty of success. Sometimes these plants flower so freely that it is almost impossible to get suitable wood for cuttings until the end of September or beginning of this month. It is almost useless to try to strike pieces of the hard flowering wood; the small young shoots, *heeled* off from the flowering branches, constitute the proper cuttings. It is better to wait until now for these than to attempt striking the others in August or September.

The cuttings cannot well be too small if they are long enough to admit of one end being made firm in the soil, and a brace of leaves to breathe in the air; neither is it of the slightest importance whether the leaves at the bottom of the cutting are removed or not, as far as the rooting is concerned. Their retention, in all probability, favours the emission of roots. However, the more leaves retained, the more carefully must damp be guarded against winter, and the greater care must be exercised to guard the cutting, through the preliminary stages from cutting-wood to plant-wood, from an excessive exhaustion of its juices by perspiration. The very effort, however, to perspire causes a circulation of fluids, and when the sap moves, life begins to assert its sway. The leaves are the great agents in maintaining the circulation of the sap; consequently, the more there are retained on a cutting, the more rapid will be the motion of its fluids, and the sooner roots may be emitted. Rapid circulation is good, provided there is a supply to be conveyed; but if a current throughout a plant, or part of a plant – that is, a cutting – is maintained, without the addition of new matter, the period of utter exhaustion, ending in death, will be in exact ratio to the rate of speed. Hence the importance of checking perspiration by a humid atmosphere, and maintaining a proper balance between the supply and expenditure of the organisable

FIG. 555 *Pentstemon gentianoides*

or life-extending, organ-forming matter of the cutting. Free perspiration from geranium cuttings is useful, because they contain more fluid than is necessary to sustain their life until new matter is formed; and the motion of the fluids it induces helps to form such new matter. The same, or half the amount of perspiration, would wither up and destroy verbena or calceolaria cuttings, because they contain less fluid, and are more delicate and fragile in their texture. The juice of the former may, therefore, be freely and liberally expended; the juice of the latter must be carefully husbanded, to guard against death from exhaustion. The whole theory and practice of propagation by cuttings, therefore, turns upon a careful, wise husbanding and expenditure of the sap and organisable matter stored up within the cutting itself. As a rule, the softer the texture of the cutting, the faster it will gravitate towards death, and, of necessity, the more rapidly must the process of rooting be pushed forward; and the harder the texture, the longer the period of probation given, and the slower the process of rooting. All successful practice demonstrates the correctness of this theory; and it is as important to bear it in mind in providing flowering plants as in the higher branches of propagation.

1997 The inexperienced gardener, and especially the amateur, may be led sometimes to inquire what plants are to be propagated at this season besides geraniums, verbenas, and calceolarias. Petunias must on no account be forgotten, and in addition to all these, a greater or fewer number of the following species, according to requirement, should be added to the general stock:

Agathea coelestis, sometimes called Blue Marguerite.
Ageratums.
Anagallis.
Antirrhinums.
Bouvardias.
Centaureas.
Cerastiums.
Cineraria maritima, or Ragwort.
Fuchsias.
Gazanias.
Heliotropes.
Koeniga, also known as *Alyssum variegatum* and *Glyce variegata.*
Lantanas.
Lobelias.
Oenothera macrocarpa, etc.
Pentstemons (Fig. 555).
Phloxes.
Salvias.
Senecios.
Stachys lanata.
Tropaeolums.
Vincas, or Periwinkles.

This list will furnish a pretty safe and correct answer to any inquiry as to the plants that may be propagated. All are beautiful, and if some be thought more desirable than others, there is ample room for choice and selection.

1998 *The Shrubbery, etc.: Transplanting* – Now is the time to look at the shrubbery and pleasure ground, and note what changes are to be effected there, if any are required. It may be that beeches, etc., 20 feet or 30 feet high, are to be moved, to break the prevailing east wind, on the other side of the lawn. Lose no time, then, in preparing the holes, and getting all preliminaries arranged for a heavy job of transplanting. The sooner all deciduous trees are moved, the greater is the chance of success. If the weather continues mild, they will form fresh roots before the winter; and by the time that the spring excites to renewed growth, the roots will be sufficiently restored to perform their important functions without let or hindrance. Large evergreens may also be safely removed this month.

1999 *Turf Laying, etc.* Turf laying, and ground work generally, will also be proceeded with. Where much has to be done, a great deal will be gained by beginning early.

2000 *Flower Garden: Routine Work* Maintain scrupulous cleanliness, and continue the beauty here as long as possible. Prepare pots and space for potting or boxing the chief stock of geraniums, calceolarias, jasmines, etc. If frost should come, get everything you intend to save under cover directly, and proceed to store them away at your leisure.

2001 *Auriculas, Polyanthuses, etc.* Place auriculas, polyanthuses, pinks, carnations, etc., if not already done, in their winter quarters. Give all the air possible, to induce a quick growth.

2002 *Hollyhocks, Dahlias, etc.* Gather hollyhock and dahlia seeds if ripe. Pot choice varieties of hollyhocks, and winter under glass.

2003 *Pansies* Pot up pansies for stores and flowering in pots. Plant out seedlings and put in cuttings.

2004 *Tulips* Prepare beds of good, light, fibrous, sandy loam for tulips, and have all in readiness for planting the main stock early next month. Similar preparations may be made for beds of other bulbs that are to flower *en masse*.

2005 *Reserve Garden* Keep annuals and other plants in beds quite clear. Plant off primroses, polyanthuses, violets, Iberis, and Arabis. Wallflowers may now be removed to flower beds and borders, if these have been cleared of their summer occupants. Increase by division of the roots such herbaceous plants as rockets, lychnis, etc., and plant them in beds in this department. Plant beds of narcissuses, hyacinths, crocuses, etc., either for permanent flowering here, or for removal to the flower garden afterwards.

FIG. 556 *Parma violet (Viola odorata parmensis)*

2 – The Vegetable or Kitchen Garden

2006 *Asparagus* Towards the end of the month the asparagus beds may be cleared of their haulm, but not till it is yellow and the seed ripe, and a portion of the soil forked into the alleys; then mix some good manure with a little salt, and lay a good coating of it over the plants, covering the whole with the soil thrown into the alleys.

2007 *Seakale* This will be ready to force towards the end of the month, either by removal to a forcing bed, or by covering the plants with pots, and these with stable manure on the beds.

2008 *Celery* Earth up as often as it becomes necessary, not only for blanching, but to preserve the plants from injury by frost.

2009 *Cardoons* These should now receive a general earthing up, choosing dry open weather for the operation, first gathering up the leaves and tying them together with a hayband.

2010 *Potatoes* The tubers are now at maturity. Dig them up and store for the winter, so as to protect them from frost. The three-pronged potato-fork, with broad tines, rounded and blunt at the points, is a well-known implement. It is usual, where the haulm is strong, to cut off the tops, and by inserting the fork under the whole plant, turn the whole up in a mass, the potatoes being collected after the digger in baskets; they may either be stored in a suitable room, or stored away in pits in the open ground, properly drained and covered, first with a layer of earth, then with a thatching of clean straw, and then with soil sufficiently thick to protect them from the severest frosts.

2011 *Carrots and Parsnips* These roots are also at their best now, and may be taken up and stored in the manner directed for potatoes. A little carrot seed may be sown on a warm border, with a chance of young carrots in spring.

2012 *Peas and Beans* The peas and beans are now past; let the ground be cleared, and, where vacant, dug or trenched, or ridged up, so that it may have the advantage of fallowing from the sun and air, and salts from the snows of winter. A crop of early peas may be sown, either on a warm south border or under a fence. If the border is 8 or 10 feet broad, let the drills run across, 3 or 4 feet asunder, and so arranged as not to come in front of the stems of the trees on the wall, and 1½ inches deep. Small crops of Mazagan beans may also be planted with a chance of their standing the winter, and coming in in May or June.

2013 *Cabbages* All the cabbage tribes require the greatest attention this month in hoeing, weeding, and warring with caterpillars, which now begin to infest them. Transplant cabbages at the end of the month, choosing the strongest plants. Coleworts should now be planted out for spring use.

2014 *Cauliflowers* Plants from seed sown in August will require pricking out, not less than 4 or 5 inches apart, where some kind of protection can be given them, either under a frame or hand glass; those formerly pricked out and hardened off require planting out under hand glasses to stand the winter, keeping the glasses close till rooted, and then support them on props 2 or 3 inches thick for air.

2015 *Broccoli* All the late-planted broccoli should be hoed in common with cabbages of all kinds, so as to loosen the soil and destroy weeds.

2016 *Lettuces, Endive, etc.* Some lettuces for a spring supply may be pricked out under a frame, though the hardier kinds will frequently stand the winter on a warm border. Lettuce and endive formerly planted out now require tying up. Small supplies of small salading sow weekly in boxes.

2017 *Winter Spinach* Keep winter spinach free from weeds, and thin off where requisite, leaving the strongest plants.

2018 *Radishes* Sow also a small patch of radishes in the beginning, and again towards the end of the month. If the weather proves mild, they will advance, and be ready for drawing in November and December.

3 – The Fruit Garden and Orchard

2019 *Planting Fruit Trees* Planting fruit trees should now be proceeded with if the necessary preparations are made. These preparations consist in draining and preparing stations where planting in the open ground is intended, and preparation of the border where wall trees or espaliers are to be planted.

The most important part in planting, next to soil and subsoil, is to keep the collar of the stem at the surface of the soil, removing all diseased or bruised fibres, spreading the roots out carefully, and putting fine soil over them; keeping the young tree firmly in its place by stakes, without lifting or treading upon the roots. The autumn rains will settle the earth about the roots better than any other means.

2020 *Root Pruning* Root pruning should now be performed, either by lifting the trees altogether and replanting, or by digging a trench round them, and removing or shortening old roots of over-luxuriant or perpendicular growth.

2021 *Apples and Pears* The fruit is now ripening fast. Gather on fine days, taking care that the pears especially are tenderly handled. When laid in the fruit room for a week, it should be carefully looked over; more fruit decays in the first week than for many weeks afterwards, and if not removed, it soon affects others.

2022 *Peaches and Nectarines* The trees should have all superfluous shoots removed, and the young wood left exposed to as much sun as possible, to ripen the shoots, on which the hopes of the following year depend. As soon as the leaves part readily from the branches, sweep them off, but not violently, with a new birch broom. The trees will be benefitted by passing a light broom over the foliage in the direction of its growth. It will detach the ripened leaves, and admit air to the heart of the tree and branches. Root pruning, if thought requisite, perform towards the end of the month.

The sign of root pruning being required is found in over-luxuriant foliage, with an absence of fruit; but it requires to be done with caution. Dig a trench round the tree, 1, 2, or 3 feet from the stem, according to its size, so as to lay open all the roots. All old roots which have ceased to throw out rootlets or spongioles should be pruned away close to the stem, the young roots trimmed, and all having a tendency to tap-root, or descend too deep, should be cut away. This done, fill up the trench with suitable fresh soil or compost. Where extensive root pruning is necessary, it should be done partially in two or three years, removing a portion of the objectionable roots on each occasion.

2023 *Plums* In wet seasons gather the late sorts, with their stalks attached; suspend them in the fruit room, or, wrapped in thin paper, they will keep for several weeks. Quinces, medlars, and all sorts of nuts, are also now fit to gather.

2024 *Raspberries* Canes of the autumn-bearing kinds should now be bearing a good supply of fruit. If the weather be fine, canes which have fruited should be cut out, and the young ones left three or four to a stool; then manure, and dig between them, leaving the young shoots their full length until the spring. New plantations may now be made; the improved mode being to plant single canes about 18 inches apart, and attach them to espaliers, consisting of stakes set in the ground at intervals of 6 or 8 feet, with laths 1 inch broad and inch thick nailed or screwed to the stakes, in a horizontal position, one about 12 inches from the ground, another at the top, and a third midway between the two. This will be found a sufficient support for the canes, which must be tied with bast or raffia to the laths.

2025 *Strawberries* Remove all runners from the plants, and manure and dig between the rows; using the three-tined fork so as to avoid injuring the roots. Runners may be bedded out for new plantations, the formation of which should now stand over, however, till the spring.

II – Work to be done under Glass

1 – Flowers in the Conservatory, Greenhouse, Stove, etc.

2026 *Sheltering Winter-Blooming Plants from Rain* The first, and in many places the chief, duty of the month, is to see that all tender and all hardy plants intended to be bloomed in winter are placed under the requisite shelter. Nothing injures the former, or prevents the perfect inflorescence of the latter, more than being exposed to the chilling drenching rains that often fall at this period of the year. A day or two of such untoward influences will do more harm than months of exposure to genial balmy air and invigorating dews have done good.

It is good practice, in fine weather, to place out in sheltered situations many of our heaths, azaleas, camellias, etc., etc.; but better far to keep them entirely under glass than leave them out too late in the season. It must be regarded as being either the perfection of ignorance or the height of cruelty to leave these plants starving in the cold October blast, while their freshly painted and cleansed winter home is ready to bid them welcome.

2027 *Effect of Over-Exposure* When the plants have all been housed, it is well that their condition should be carefully looked into. If the pots seem heavy, the surface soil somewhat greasy, with an occasional elevation here and there, and some of the leaves present a bluish, slightly-shrivelled, highly-polished appearance, their state is far from being a desirable one. All healthy root action has been paralysed by the combined influence of water and worms, by whose disintegrating and disorganising forces both the quality and texture of the soil have been changed. Keen winds and heavy, dashing, cold rains, or hail, are almost equally injurious. Their influence is less seen and more irremediable at the time; but it is equally potent afterwards. Those blotches, patches, and bruises, so common on leaves and tender branches of plants in winter, mostly originate from keeping them out too late in the autumn. Nothing can possibly be gained – much, yes, everything, may be lost – by the practice. Every prudential, sanitary, and economical consideration urges the propriety of early housing.

While in the open ground, worms are efficient drainers enough; one of the great results of their presence in pots is to render all drainage impossible. They first grind down the soil into small particles, and then work this-finely-comminuted earth down among the drainage. This peculiar process blocks up the outlet for the exit of water, and speedily converts the wet composts into sheer mud. Not only the mechanical texture, but the chemical composition of soils thus water-logged and worm-worked, become so changed as to totally unfit them for the sustentation of plant life. The roots are gorged with crude food, and kept in a dirty bath of muddy water. No wonder, then, at yellow leaves, drooping flower buds, and sickly hues, ending in death.

2028 *Ventilation for Newly Housed Plants* When October comes, every plant to be housed, from the camellia to the humblest denizen of next year's flower garden, should be placed in *safe quarters* at *once* – *safe*, remember, but not *warm*, quarters; because the latter would be most unsafe. Plants that have stood for months in the free air of heaven are most impatient of confinement. Unless the wind is very cutting, or the thermometer is under 40°, the houses should stand open night and day for several weeks after the plants are admitted; otherwise the sudden change of temperature would either cause flower buds to drop or excite to premature wood growth, the probability being that it would do both.

All plants are liable to injury from this cause – camellias, perhaps, more than any other. Sudden transitions from an open, free, to a close, confined atmosphere – rapid alternations of temperature, and either extremes of wet or dry at root or top – are the main, if not the only causes of flower buds drooping in this beautiful species. But the causes that influence this plant so powerfully and suddenly affect all others in a greater or less degree. Hence the importance of adopting, in all changes with plants, the *sliding-scale* system. The change from a low to a high, or a high to a low temperature – from a dry to a moist, or a moist to a dry atmosphere – must be gradual and easy. In one word, the length of the *scale* must be adapted to the extent of the change contemplated; and the smaller the angle of inclination, and the slower the plants progress from one elevation to another, the better the chance of perfect success.

2029 *Cleansing Plants, etc.* When plants are brought within doors for the winter they should be thoroughly cleaned, the pots washed, and the soil top dressed if they require it, as they are introduced into the houses.

2030 *Arrangement of Plants* A great deal may also be done by proper arrangement of the plants when brought into the house to give an air of order and design, which in themselves have much of the charm of beauty. It is certain that there is often more beauty and satisfaction derived from the orderly arrangement of plants than from the plants themselves. The same principles are applicable here that have been laid down for the embellishment of flower gardens. The widely different circumstances will modify the practice, but the same leading objects must be kept in view; and where each different tribe of plants has its special house devoted to its use, the practice in the two cases is not so very widely divergent; but where almost every variety of plants have to be crammed into one house, cultural, rather than artistic considerations, must control the arrangement. A leading point in all cases is to have a system, and to make that obvious. This alone leaves the imprint of superintending care.

The predominance of cultural considerations does not necessarily destroy artistic beauty. The grouping of different species together, so essential to the former, is almost as necessary to the latter. Wherever geraniums, heaths, azaleas, camellias, etc., are not only flowered, but grown in one house, the grouping style is not only the best in a cultural sense, but is the most effective. By placing geraniums and other plants in flower in the warmest end of such a house, and heaths at the very coldest, it is amazing what a difference of climate, succession of bloom, and inexhaustible pleasure may be derived from a single house. But if the plants are crushed together higgledy-piggledy in one house, a suffocating sense of confusion and want of space will be the primary impression received and retained. Even houses of bedding plants may be made interesting by grouping the different species. Edgings and lines of demarcation, and different shapes, groups, or masses, on stage, shelves, or floor, may be

FIG. 557 *Chinese primrose (Primula chinensis fimbriata)*

formed with variegated geraniums, alyssums, cinerarias, etc. Lines of gold or silver-edged geraniums may not only be stored away, but form beautiful objects on conservatory or greenhouse shelves, to contrast with Chinese primroses (Fig. 557), etc.

2031 *Hothouse or Plant Stove: Vincas, etc.* Vincas, clerodendrons, etc., that have finished flowering should now be cut back, and after they have slightly *broke*, be shaken out of the pots, and inserted in as small pots as possible, for they seldom winter well in large pots.

2032 *Watering* Water liberally poinsettias, justicias, begonias, gesneras, etc., coming into bloom; other plants, going out of flower, water scantily. All watering should now be done in the morning; and sprinkling, etc., unless on very bright days, entirely dispensed with.

Drips of water must not be allowed to stand on variegated begonias or other fine-foliaged plants after this period; their impaired vitality, combined with the decrease of solar heat, renders them peculiarly liable to be injured from this cause; the structure of the leaves speedily becomes decomposed, and large blotches or holes appear, in consequence.

2033 *Climbers* Climbers on roofs and all artificial shade must be gradually and finally removed during the month. From this time to the middle of January the utmost amount of solar light attained in our climate is all too little for the natives of tropical climes that generally find a home in our plant stoves.

2034 *Temperature of Hothouse* During cold nights a temperature of 60° will be sufficient, rising to 70° during the day, which must be the utmost maximum of fire heat permitted for the next four months; five or ten higher degrees from solar influences will be very serviceable. However, air must in such cases be given at once, and caution used to prevent the artificial and solar heat exerting their full force simultaneously.

Few plants are proof against the disastrous shrivelling influences of being thus placed between two fires: neither is it at all necessary to give air daily. Often, for a week together, a sweet genial atmosphere may be maintained within, when the outside air is totally unfit for admission. Nothing requires greater practical knowledge and sounder judgment than the ventilation of tropical plant structures in winter; a happy medium between the close glass case and cutting-hurricane system is the grand desideratum, and nothing but enlightened experience, and an innate sympathy with the plants cultivated, can confer the necessary qualifications for the performance of this important operation. It should ever be borne in mind that plants are endowed with the power of purifying their own atmosphere within certain limits; and that, consequently, the incessant admission of ungenial, harsh, external air is not essential to their healthy existence. On the other hand, they rapidly exhaust the supply of carbonic acid gas present in a given quantity of air, and, therefore, an occasional change of air is essential to furnish them with food. Not only that: the quantity of oxygen liberated bears a relative proportion to the amount of carbonic acid gas consumed; consequently, the less of the latter appropriated by plants, the less of the former is given back to the air, and it becomes the sooner deteriorated in consequence. It therefore follows that while for a limited period plants may thrive in the same atmosphere, their constitution and necessary wants demand a change sooner or later. The frequency of the change required will very much depend upon the energy with which the vital force is being expended. In other words, the faster the plant grows, the more fresh air will be necessary. Now, as winter is the dormant period, less external air is requisite in winter than at any other period of the year. The fact thus elucidated is of immense practical importance to the cultivator; for just when it is well-nigh impossible to admit such air, we discover, both by science and experience, that its presence may be largely dispensed with.

2035 *Orchids* The remarks that have been made with regard to the temperature to be maintained and the admission of air are equally applicable to the cultivation of orchids; they even apply with double force to them, for, as most of these will now be comparatively dormant, the orchid house may often remain for a month without fresh air with impunity. The great points are a dry atmosphere and a comparatively low-temperature – from 65° to 70° – and the maintenance of all in a dormant state.

2036 *Expulsion of Insects* Now is the great cleaning season; every scale, bug, earwig, cricket, etc., must now be ferreted out and destroyed, if the house has not already been thoroughly cleaned.

2037 *Forcing Pit* Introduce into the pit the first batch of rhododendrons, kalmias, Ghent and Indian azaleas, etc.; also some tea and hybrid perpetual roses, and early-flowering and sweet-scented geraniums, white and Anne Boleyn pinks, tree carnations, and lily of the valley; also *Salvia Gesnerceflora*, late gesneras, and *Euphorbia splendens*.

2038 *Tulips, Hyacinths, etc.* Towards the end of the month, some hyacinths, tulips, etc., potted towards the end of September, should now be pushed forward in this structure. Procure, and pot forthwith, the whole stock of hyacinths, crocuses, narcissuses, tulips, jonquils, and other hardy bulbs.

2039 *The Greenhouse* Plants brought into or growing in the greenhouse require general treatment similar to that which has been described, but this and any house exclusively devoted to heaths should be kept five or ten degrees cooler than the conservatory. They will also bear sharper currents of air with impunity. Leschenaultias, chorozemas, etc., in the greenhouse, must be carefully examined for green fly. This pest is very prevalent among, and very fatal to, the first-named plants. Sometimes it also suddenly attacks heaths, pimeleas, etc. As soon as one is discovered, fumigate instantly with tobacco paper. This is also a good time to eradicate scale – white, black, or brown – from acacias, clianthus, and any other infected plants. For scale, hand picking is the only effective remedy. Gishurst's Compound, Neal's Soap, etc., may destroy thrip, as well as, perhaps a little better than, a strong decoction of clear soot water in soapsuds. But as for scale and mealy bug, the experience of many tends to show that it is not possible to kill them by dipping or washing in any nostrum whatever. Where plants have become infested very much with either of these pests, the most satisfactory way, unless they are very valuable, is to destroy them. But they ought never to be allowed to become very *bad*. It is in thus attacking insects in time, as soon as one is seen, that the true secret of cleanliness and health lies. Better examine a whole collection and not find one, than allow one to become a million through a month's oversight.

2040 *Benefit of Cleansing Plants* If practicable, no plant should be taken into the house without being carefully examined and thoroughly cleaned. The necessary washings involved in this operation, while essential to cleanliness, have, moreover, a powerful indirect influence in preserving the plants in health. So great is this secondary benefit, that some cultivators have maintained that no collection of stove plants or greenhouse plants can be preserved in luxuriant health without the existence of these aids to successful culture. Doubtless the ablution that their extermination involves enables plants to perform their respiratory functions and work of elaborating the sap with more ease and greater energy.

2041 *Pelargoniums* Maintain a temperature of 45° by fire heat, allowing a rise of 10° by the influence of the sun. No syringing or sprinkling must be permitted here, and care must be exercised in watering, to keep the leaves dry. Give air with great caution, avoiding biting winds and cold draughts. This is specially necessary with *fancy* pelargoniums, which are more tender than either the French or show kinds, as they are termed. Great injury may be done even by keeping the door open a few minutes when the wind is blowing *into the house*, and the plants should never be moved out to the potting shed for shifting after this period. Sudden changes are a fruitful source of that most provoking and troublesome of all diseases to which these plants are subject – *spot*. This disease is practically incurable; if it unfortunately appears, either separate the plant from all the others, or destroy it at once. Green fly is often troublesome, but it is easily got rid of by fumigation, and with good culture no other insect ever attacks pelargoniums.

The disease which is known as spot is considered to be constitutional, hereditary, and infectious. It may also be induced by any of all of the following causes: Imperfect drainage; the use of crude and not sufficiently decomposed manure or leaf mould; the presence of oxide of iron in the soil; sudden draughts of cold air; using water for the plants much colder than the temperature in which they grow; allowing the sun to shine on the foliage, so as considerably to raise the temperature of the house previous to the admission of air in the morning; permitting the drops of cold condensed vapour to drop from the roof on the same leaf, or part of a leaf, for days, perhaps weeks together; over-watering; using too strong manure water; not giving water enough, or dropping water on the leaves; escape of gas from flues; careless fumigation and excess of moisture in the atmosphere of the house, especially if it is cold and close; and, in fine, anything and everything that tends to check the free current of the sap through root or branches, may produce, and always intensifies, the destructive energy of this disease. By carefully avoiding all these causes, the probability is, that you will never be troubled by the spot, and it is certain that your care will be rewarded by healthy and beautiful plants.

2042 *The Conservatory* This structure is always dependent for three-fourths of its charms upon the taste and skill displayed in its arrangement. Beautiful objects beautifully placed, lovely climbers neatly festooned or gracefully trained, and the preservation of all this beauty as long as possible, are the grand desiderata here. Heaths, epacrises, late pelargoniums, scarlet and other fuchsias, geraniums, arums, petunias, salvias, Chinese primroses, Japan lilies, and chrysanthemums, will now constitute the chief display in the conservatory.

2043 *Temperature* As a cool atmosphere is one of the chief means to this end in summer, the mistake is sometimes made of maintaining this structure at too low a temperature. It should never, unless in the severest weather, be lower than 45°. Comparatively few blossoms will expand in perfection, or continue so long, at a lower temperature than this. From 45° as a night temperature to 55° as a day, is a safe range for the next four months with fire heat, 50° being a safe day medium and 55° the maximum by artificial means. If the sun is genial enough to raise the temperature to 60° a few hours in winter, and air is admitted, it will do no harm.

2044 *Ventilation, etc.* In managing the house, two things must be equally guarded against – a moist stagnant atmosphere and a sharp current of frosty air. Although directly contrary in their nature, both are almost alike destructive to flowers; the one rapidly destroys, and the other speedily blasts, their beauty. The proper balancing of air at rest and air in motion, and the right proportion of moisture to be suspended in it, constitutes the true secret of successful conservatory management.

2045 *Light, Shading, etc.* In general terms, it may be stated that the more light that can be secured for the next four or five months the better. Hence, all shading may now be dispensed with, and the foliage of the climbers gradually reduced, however beautiful they may be. They should be gone over two or three times until they are finally cut into the smallest compass by the middle of November. Every ray of light at that period is alike necessary for the health of the plants and the colour of the flowers.

2046 *Watering, Syringing, etc.* Little or no syringing or sprinkling of paths will now be necessary, except a few sprinklings over chrysanthemum and camellia leaves for the first week or fortnight after their introduction from out of doors. Generally, at this season, a sufficiency of vapour will rise from the surface of pots and borders, without having recourse to either sprinkling leaves or paths. Care must be taken not to wet the latter in performing the necessary watering.

2047 *Chrysanthemums* Chrysanthemums will require a liberal supply of clear manure water every day in bright weather, and must never be allowed to droop from the want of it. If they do, their best and finest leaves will be exacted as a penalty for the neglect.

2048 *Chinese Primroses, etc.* Chinese primroses will require the next largest supply of water after chrysanthemums; then early-flowering epacrises, camellias, heaths, etc.

Plants in full growth coming into bloom always require more water than plants past their meridian and waning to decay. Therefore, all the plants already named, and early cinerarias, etc., will require much more copious supplies than late-flowering fuchsias, geraniums, begonias, etc., etc. Semi-stove plants, such as gesneras, gloxinias, globe amaranths, achimenes, etc., which, owing to their great beauty, it is desirable to keep in bloom throughout the month in this house, will now require very little water. In reference to all such, and stove plants in general subject to conservatory treatment, it is of immense importance to bear in mind that the lower the temperature in which they are placed the less *water* they require, and vice versa. Cold, which stimulates man's assimilating organs to the utmost, paralyses those of plants in the exact ratio of its intensity. Hence the necessity of a stinted regimen in cold weather if vegetable life is to be preserved in full vigour. These remarks are applicable to all plant structures, but are particularly applicable to a house where luxuriant health should ever appear adorned with a wreath of floral beauty.

2 – Plants under Glass, in Hotbeds, Frames, etc.

2049 *Flowers in Cold Pits and Frames* Give all the air possible to plants housed in these structures, unless it actually freezes; guard against damp and over-crowding; carefully examine mignonette, stocks, etc., and remove every bit of mould the moment it appears. Provide mats or reed covers in readiness against frost, and keep the glass clean. On mild days remove the glass, in order to render the plants as hardy as possible, a condition which is highly conducive to a safe passage through the trials of winter.

2050 *Pelargoniums* Plants that have been removed from beds and borders, and potted, should be plunged in mild bottom heat on a gentle hotbed to start them into growth. The plants must have plenty of air on mild days and be kept cool.

2051 *Management of Plants in Frames* All such plants as auriculas, polyanthuses, pansies, carnations, pinks, picotees, violets, lilies of the valley, mignonette, hyacinths, and all flowers intended to bloom in pots, are put under glass, rather to preserve them from injury by wind, rain, and frost, than to stimulate them into activity and growth. They must have air whenever it is possible to give it to them.

2052 *Cuttings in Frames* All cuttings, such as those of ageratums, petunias, verbenas, etc., must be kept cool and dry. Calceolarias and cinerarias already rooted must be placed near the glass, but protected from frost by mats, etc. Cuttings of hollyhocks may still be put in, as they will root slowly during the winter, and make nice plants in spring.

The great point with all flowers in frames is to keep them from injury by frost, by covering them up when frost threatens. This applies to roses, strawberry plants in pots, and all the plants that have been mentioned. Protection, and not stimulation, except for pelargoniums and plants that require to be started into growth, is all that is required.

2053 *Vegetables, etc., in Hotbeds* The instructions that have already been given for growing cucumbers and melons in succession in preceding months, apply equally here, and need not be repeated. As already said, hotbeds may be made, seed sown, and plants raised and carried on to fruiting at any period of the year, but more care is requisite to maintain the heat in winter than in summer.

2054 *Melons* With reference to these it may be said that a second or third crop may occasionally be well ripened during this month. If in pits, renew linings, etc., to maintain a brisk heat; if in houses, keep the fires moving to secure a bottom heat of 80°, and a surface one of 70°. Beware of watering to excess, as less can be thrown off by the leaves now than earlier in the season; consequently more must be absorbed by the fruit, which is apt to burst, and often becomes insipid in consequence. With care upon this point, melons may often be ripened as successfully in October as in August.

3 – Fruit under Glass, heated and unheated

2055 *Starting Fruit Trees in Autumn* In our climate, fruit must be cultivated under glass, if at all, at this season of the year; and those who wish for peaches or grapes on their table in May must begin this month. Early work calls for early rest; and where this call is refused, the work will either be badly performed, or the machine will speedily be worn out. Hence, if trees are required to move to any good purpose early in the autumn, they must rest early in the summer. However, if trees have had a good long rest, and if they have first of all finished their summer work well by thoroughly ripening their wood before they went to rest, it is astonishing what an influence a warm bath has in arousing them to vigorous exertion. Only it must not be too warm: water, at a temperature of 50°, applied at first with a syringe all over, in the form of a shower bath, will suffice. A temperature of 45° or 50° being maintained at the same time, and the bath being repeated twice a day, the buds of the trees will soon show signs of expanding out of their case.

2056 *Danger of Checks to Growth* No sooner do they become thoroughly awakened, than they must be provided with work; and one of the greatest mistakes in forcing is to allow them to go to sleep after they have begun to break. Sudden depressions of temperature always have this tendency: they check growth, or, in other words, send them to sleep again; and this sleep in working hours is always fraught with danger, and often produces death: to say nothing of the injurious effects of the stimulants necessary to induce new growth, the mere fact of its forcible cessation, from cold or heat, is pregnant with disease and disaster to plant life.

From the time the bud bursts its horny sheath until the luscious fruit melts in your mouth, all growth and no check must be the stern rule of the successful cultivator. A rapid and vigorous flow of the sap is essential to healthy growth. At this season, unless the sap is urged on with power, the chances are it will not flow at all; but an excess of speed must also be avoided; for what is gained in speed is often lost in safety. But when man undertakes to control the time, circumstances, and results of the motion of the sap in trees, great wisdom and skill must guide his movements, or he is doomed to failure. The first preliminary to success is a clear perception of the object in view – that object is fruit. A too rapid extension of parts is unfavourable to fruitfulness; therefore this must be avoided. The embryo fruits are enwrapped in the buds, and the more vigorously they can be made to unwind themselves, the more robust and vigorous will the young fruit be. Heat in moderation, and a genial atmosphere, favour this vigour; heat in excess, or an enervating atmosphere, destroys it. Hence the importance of striking a balance between opposing forces, and securing a happy medium favourable to our purpose. That purpose is the greatest quantity of the best fruit in the shortest period of time, from the smallest possible space. A thorough comprehension of what is here stated, with the practical instruction already imparted, and yet to be given, will enable anyone who is in earnest to approximate at least towards these desiderata.

2057 *The Peach House: Treatment of House and Borders* Supposing that the fruit was gathered in May or June, the lights removed in July, and the trees pruned in August or September, they may now be thoroughly painted over with a composition consisting of equal parts sulphur, clay, cow dung, and soot. The borders should also be forked up, 6 inches or 1 foot of the old soil removed, if that is practicable, for roots, and the same quantity of turfy maiden loam substituted in its place. Every bit of trellis and woodwork should also be thoroughly washed with soap and water, unless the house has just been painted, the walls whitewashed, coloured, or painted, and the hot water pipes painted over with a mixture of equal parts lime and sulphur. Perhaps it will be as well to omit the painting from the first 12 feet from the boiler on the flow pipe.

2058 *Treatment of Trees* If the roots are at all dry, water with manure water at a temperature of 60°, which will not only moisten, but gently excite the roots, by considerably raising the temperature of the soil. Having thus laid the foundation of success in cleanliness and suitable food, place the lights on, and, if the weather is mild, leave them half down night and day for the first week. If the roof is a fixture, give all the air possible at front and back, and leave the door open. Sprinkle the trees overhead several times a day; sprinkle paths, etc., and maintain an atmosphere like a cool April morning. Proceed thus during the entire month, varying, of course, your treatment, the quantity of air, etc., by the nature of the external atmosphere. A temperature of 50°, however, should never be exceeded by fire heat, if fire becomes necessary, which is not often the case during this month.

2059 *The Vinery: Starting Vines* All preliminary matters may proceed here exactly on the same principle as for the peach house. In all forcing, either of flowers or fruit, let cleanliness, both present and prospective, be the first care. Hence, before the painting, etc., let every bit of loose bark that will rub off with your hand be removed. Severe barking – that is to say, scraping the bark off with knives, etc. – is to be deprecated; as, although vines are endogenous plants – that is, increase from the inside, and not from the out, and their bark is consequently not essential to their healthy existence – still it is useful in retaining moisture on their stems. Nevertheless, tidiness of appearance and the destruction of insects require the removal of that which is loose and easily taken away; to go beyond this, if not certainly injurious, is obviously unnecessary and a tedious loss of time. The varieties best for early forcing are the Royal Muscadine, Duke of Buccleuch, and Black Hambro. Give them the same general treatment as that recommended for peaches during the month.

2060 *Pruning Vines* Prune other vineries as soon as the fruit is cut, if the leaves are thoroughly matured, the wood almost as hard as bone, and they are required to start afresh in January. If neither of these conditions, nor all of them, are present, defer the pruning for another month. Carefully look over grapes twice a week, removing every dead berry or leaf that may have fallen on a bunch.

2061 *Ripening Late Grapes* If late grapes, such as Muscats and West's St Peter's, are not ripe, they must be ripened off with a brisk fire as speedily as possible. If not ripened forthwith, they will not only be deficient in flavour, but will not keep well.

When a bunch of grapes has to be cut at once, either to make room or prune the vines, nine inches or a foot of the branch should be cut with them, and the bunches be suspended in a cool dry room: they will often keep better in such positions than on the vine. In all cases where orange trees or other plants are compelled to be placed in houses containing ripe grapes, it is better that the bunches be cut and thus stored away. Grapes cut for this purpose must never be laid down; cut them carefully, leaving all the leaves on the branch. Hand a couple of bunches, one at a time, to an assistant, and proceed to hang them up. The slightest bruise, by laying them on their side, or allowing two bunches to be carried in one hand, would prevent their keeping. The riper they are, the more care is necessary in this respect. If slightly shrivelled, they keep all the better.

2062 *The Pinery* It is a good plan to cover the pots of succession and other pines (say 2 inches thick) with partially-decayed tan or leaves for the winter. This obviates the necessity of watering through the winter months, and maintains the roots in that medium state of dryness so favourable to the health of the plants during that period. Those planted out in beds might be mulched over in a similar way.

2063 *Watering Pines in Winter* The less water that can be given to pines in any stage during winter, consistent with their health, the better: their peculiar structure renders them especially liable to injury from the accumulation of moisture in the axils of the leaves. Whenever it is necessary to water for the next four months, the water must be applied to the soil only. It is often necessary to use a bent tube, with a funnel at one end, to prevent it falling upon the leaves. If the atmosphere of the house, from the continuance of bright sunshine, or any other cause, becomes too dry, it will be better to secure the necessary humidity by evaporation from the surface of the floor and heating apparatus, rather than by syringing overhead.

2064 *Temperature* After this period maintain a temperature of from 60° to 70° to all pines, the maximum being applied to the fruiting plants. The bottom heat may range from five to ten degrees in excess of the atmospheric temperature. Give a little air when the external air is sufficiently genial; guard against sudden changes, and maintain a growing atmosphere to fruit swelling off.

2065 *Maturation of the Fruit* Cut pines in winter a week before they are ripe, and place them in a hot dry place (near the kitchen fire will do), in a temperature of from 80° to 90°. This will prevent all risk of the fruit decaying, and vastly improves the flavour.

2066 *Figs* These may possibly be ripening their third crop; if so, a brisk temperature of 65° or 70° must be kept up. If the second crop is gathered, and a third is not wanted, reduce the supply of water and the temperature to a minimum, to induce rest or hasten maturity.

2067 *The Orchard House* Unless this structure be used to ripen fruit that has been retarded behind a north wall, it should now stand open night and day, or the trees be removed outside, and the house be devoted for three months to storing bedding plants, etc. If the trees are planted out in the borders, then the lights may be stored away for three months, or used for other buildings. In all cases secure a season of perfect repose for the trees.

2068 *Strawberries* These will or ought to have completed their growth for the season; the sooner they go to rest the better. The floors of orchard houses are the best possible wintering places; as cool as possible, without being frozen, is all the winter treatment they require. Properly placed, it is seldom indeed that they require any water until they are wanted to grow.

2069 *Stacking Strawberry Plants* Lacking the floor or stage of any cool house or cold pit, the next best mode of keeping them is to stack them, not exactly as reaped corn is stacked, with all the heads inwards, but just the reverse – heads out.

The stack can be built on any dry bottom, the best possible position being, however, the south side of a wall or fence. In such a position mark out a place a yard wide or so, and of any convenient length, according to the quantity of plants, and spread upon it a layer of ashes 3 inches thick. Place a row of pots on their sides at the distance indicated from the fence, or nearer, in proportion to the number of plants or height of stack contemplated. Fill up all between the pots, and the space between the bottoms of the pots, with dry ashes or old tan, keeping the side next the wall a little the highest. Then place another layer of plants on the top of the first, about 2 inches further back than the other. Fill up as before, and repeat the filling up, and layers of pots, until this space is occupied, top of the wall or fence reached, or all the plants provided for. The whole will then present a sloping surface to the sun. A boarded roof, 6 inches wider than the bottom rows, should then project over the top, and slightly incline to the back; the front may be supported on stakes driven in at intervals of 6 feet. Always excepting the floor of a cool house, there is no better mode of protecting and treating plants than this. They are kept dry, the frost has little or no influence upon them, for if it is very severe, a thatched hurdle may be laid against them, and both pots and plants are preserved in safety.

FIG. 558 *Victoria aster – larger-flowered dwarf variety. A plant especially desirable for window gardening.*

CHAPTER 32

The Garden and Its Work in Every Department in November

2070 *Aspect and Character of the Month* November, says the old writer already quoted, 'is drawn with a garment of changeable green, and has black upon his head,' to typify the dark and dreary clouds which hang over the gloomy November landscape. The atmosphere during this month is saturated with moisture, dense mists and fogs abound, and gloomy boisterous weather, as a rule, prevails. The mean temperature is about 42° Fahrenheit, but the thermometer ranges between 23° and 62°. The mean temperature of the earth at a depth of two feet is 47·28°; at a depth of one foot, 46·01°; that of the air at the earth's surface being 42·98°.

Everywhere in the woods and coppices and along the hedgerows the blustering roaring of the wind, the rattling of branches, and the swirling flight of falling leaves, which are blown into dark and dreary places, are certain harbingers of winter.

The withered leaves bestrew the garden path,
Made miry with the fall of fleeting showers.

In the garden a great change has come over the scene; even the trimmest of lawns has now a desolate and dreary look; few flowers linger in the beds, and these few seem out of place. But it is not yet entirely bare of flowers; the many-tinted asters remain, the arbutus tree is now conspicuous in its beauty, and a few bright chrysanthemums nod their heads here and there; the brilliant hollyhock still rejoices the eye during the few sunny hours the month affords us, unless frosty weather prevails:

And the blue gentian flower, still in the breeze
Nods lonely, of its beauteous race the last.

But the lover of flowers must now look indoors for his enjoyments – to the conservatory and greenhouse, if he is fortunate enough to possess these, for his flowers. In the open air, if aided by a gloomy imagination, the poet's picture may be nearly realised, and the burthen of the song be:

No sky – no view –
No distance looking blue –
No warmth, no cheerful healthful ease,
No comfortable feeling in any member –
No shade – no shine – no butterflies – no bees –
No fruits – no flowers – no leaves – no buds – No-vember.

Evergreens now become the redeeming element in the shrubbery; the strong viscid juices which bind their leaves to the stem yields a varnish which protects them from the effects of cold and damp, giving them a dark and glossy tint in strong contrast to the deciduous trees around them. These trees are now being rapidly denuded of their leaves. First the walnut becomes naked, then the mulberry, the ash, and the horse-chestnut in their turn. Apple and peach trees sometimes remain green till the end of the month; and trees which have been lopped, as White of Selborne tells us, retain their leaves till a late period.

I – Work to be Done in the Garden

1 – The Flower Garden and Shrubbery

2071 *Routine Work in Garden* The glory of the flower garden is waning, and it will soon be desolate, in spite of the gardener's care. Meanwhile, keep the beds neat by the timely removal of decaying foliage, and keep the grass and gravel walks clean and smooth by frequent rolling. Plants to be taken up and potted should be attended to immediately, or at least protected during the night, for fear of sudden frosts.

Pelargoniums, calceolarias, and similar plants, as noted in instructions given for garden work in previous months, are greatly benefitted by being placed in a gentle bottom heat until the fresh roots break. Now is an excellent time for propagating cuttings of calceolarias and most herbaceous and shrubby plants, if placed in a cold frame. Chinese, Bourbon, and hybrid perpetual roses will now root freely under the same treatment.

2072 *Treatment of Beds: Preparations for Spring* When the beds are cleared, trench them up; manure and add new soil where necessary, and plant the bulbs for spring flowering. Hardy annuals sown last month, if large enough, may be transplanted at once to their permanent beds, with pansies, alyssums, phloxes, primulas, and other herbaceous plants from the reserve garden.

2073 *Alterations in Garden* Where alterations are contemplated, they should be determined on without delay, and proceeded with when the plans are thoroughly matured – not before. To render the grouping system permanently interesting, occasional changes, both in form and arrangement of beds, are necessary; and a retrospective glance, with a view to future arrangements, will be useful now, while the whole effect is fresh in the memory, and when next year's bloom is about to be provided for.

In the selection of plants, it is to be borne in mind that duration of flowering should be the first consideration, for few gardens will afford the time or the cost necessary to carry out the plan of a changeable flower garden, in which the beds are decorated in early spring with scillas, bulbocodiums (Fig. 559), erythroniums, hepaticas, sanguinarias, and other precocious flowers, to be succeeded by autumn-sown annuals, in masses, in the summer months, and autumnal bulbs, dahlias, hollyhocks, and chrysanthemums, bringing us again to the verge of winter. This system of gardening, however attractive when attended with high keeping, is too costly and entails more trouble than proprietors of the ordinary run of gardens will incur; therefore the gardener must have an eye to the means as well as to the end, and arrange his plans accordingly. *Erythronium dens canis, Allium*

FIG. 559 *Bulbocodium vernum*

moly. Anemone Apennina, Sanguinaria canadensis (or Bloodwort), *Scilla Italica, Phlox verna*, and a vast number of other hardy plants introduced now, will add interest to the flower garden by-and-by.

2074 *Collection of Leaves* Now is the best time to collect leaves from lawns and drives, and to stack them in some out of the way place for use. Oak and beech are the most valuable to the gardener, affording the most durable heat. Tread them firmly in the stack, and afterwards thatch them to keep them dry; the remainder may be thrown together for rotting, when they form a valuable auxiliary for potting and composts.

2075 *Lawns* The principal lawns should be swept when leaves are numerous, as well as to remove worm-casts, etc. An occasional rolling will keep the surface in good order.

2076 *Cuttings* The stock of cuttings should be looked over, and additional heat applied, when the roots are not fully formed. In storing the stock away for the winter, endeavour to keep all those plants together which require similar treatment. Some kinds will stand more damp than others, and may be wintered in common frames; but the better kinds of bedding out geraniums, and some other tender things, will require a moderately dry house or pit.

Late geranium cuttings may be removed to the kerbs of the pine pits, which will assist them to make roots. To preserve verbenas, petunias, etc., properly through the winter, they must be kept dry to prevent mildew, to which they are very liable in frames during wet weather. As it is desirable to protect the recently-struck plants from rains, and yet to give them a large portion of air, the sashes must be daily tilted up back and front, to cause a complete circulation. Where room can be found for the bedding stuff in empty vineries, they should be allowed to remain there as long as possible, as in dull weather they become better established than when kept in frames, more especially those only recently rooted.

2077 *Herbaceous Plants* The herbaceous ground will now require a thorough cleaning. Cut down the stalks of plants done blooming, and see to the support of the few things still in flower, as the Michaelmas daisies, and rake and hoe the borders neatly.

2078 *Manuring Flower Beds* During this month the flower beds should be enriched with manure or fresh loam, and the soil turned up before frost sets in; the edges of beds in grass should be gone over with the edging-iron to preserve the form.

2079 *Plants in Pots, etc.* All flowering plants standing in pots or frames should be fully exposed to the sun on every favourable occasion, so as to harden their tissues; and all growing plants, like the verbenas, stopped back to secure a bushy habit by-and- by. Most of the verbenas may be kept in a cold pit, dusting a little slacked lime over the soil in the pots or boxes; applying the same treatment to the shrubby calceolarias. Pot up and cut back the dwarf lobelias and *Oenothera prostrata*, sprinkling a little silver sand among the roots. Lophospermums, maurandyas, and the tropaeolums, require a dry and airy situation in the frame or greenhouse when they are taken indoors.

2080 *Roses* Planting and transplanting are now the chief employment; if very dry during the month, give a good watering to each plant before the soil is fully filled in. Stocks should also be collected and planted for budding on next season.

Prune the old roots close to the stem, cutting all strong shoots close off, When planted, some cut the head down to within four or six inches of the height at which they are wanted, and, having levelled the soil, leave them till spring. The best growers prefer leaving the head full until the plant is thoroughly rooted.

The true dog rose makes the best stock, and may be distinguished from sweetbrier by the large white thorns which thickly cover the stem of the latter towards the base; and from those of climbing habit, by the dark green colour of their bark and weakness in their stem.

2081 *The Shrubbery* should now be thinned out, and other alterations completed, and the formation and repair of new shrubberies brought to a close.

For the purpose of renovation the necessity of a reserve garden cannot be too strongly urged. Most herbaceous plants blossom incomparably finer from young plants propagated betimes than from old and exhausted ones, such as we see generally in the pleasure grounds. With a reserve garden in which the best shrubs are coming forward, alterations are easily made; where overgrown branches have to be cut back and thinned, the operation must be performed gradually, and a portion headed down every season until the whole is renovated and covered with young foliage. When headed down and in a proper state of luxuriance, keep it so. Nothing looks worse than a mass of rambling overgrown shrubs, with large heads and a confused array of naked ugly stems.

2082 *Magnolias* Among the shrubby flowering plants that are only met with in the best gardens, but which might be cultivated everywhere, may be mentioned the magnolias, natives of North America, China, and Japan, which have a noble foliage and wonderfully beautiful flowers, some of them emitting a powerful and most agreeable fragrance. They flourish well in a compost of good loam, peat, and decomposed leaves. *Magnolia grandiflora* and its varieties, all American, are perfectly hardy, flourishing luxuriantly in the open border even when exposed to cold and cutting winds. No garden should be without them.

2083 *Flowering Shrubs. Aralia Japonica* is another splendid shrub from Japan, of rich foliage, and throwing out numerous expanded clusters of bloom of whitish-green colour, each cluster being composed of several spikes of bloom 18 inches long, diverging from a common centre; it requires a sheltered spot in the garden, however. The spiraeas are another highly ornamental family of shrubs, some of them of considerable height, as *S. prunifolia flore-pleno*; others for planting behind smaller shrubs, when the long spikes of bloom bend gracefully forwards, like *S. Lindleyana*; others of the genus are dwarf shrubs of good habit, as *Spiraea* (or *Hoteia*) *Japonica*, and bloom in rich spikes both of white and pink flowers, in great abundance.

FIG. 560 *Spiraea (or hoteia) Japonica*

2084 *Soils for Florists' Flowers* At this season of the year the amateur cannot do better than get together those soils, etc., which are indispensable for the proper growth of his favourite flowers. Where there is an opportunity of so doing, turf, pared 2 inches thick from a loamy pasture or a green lane side, stacked together to decompose, will be the foundation of his composts. A large heap of melon bed manure should also be secured, not forgetting as large a quantity of fallen leaves as possible. A cart load of sharp river sand is an indispensable adjunct, and the florist should look out for willow-dust and decayed and rotten sticks. A quantity of excellent food for plants may be scraped out from hedge bottoms.

2085 *Auriculas* These plants are now in their winter quarters; they require abundant air, and occasional inspection to see that no worms are in the pots, the indications being castings on the surface, if such appear, water them with lime water, or remove them by repotting.

2086 *Carnations, Picotees, and Pinks* Plants layered in previous months should now be potted off and placed in their winter quarters, protection from dampness being the chief consideration; in fine weather let them be fully exposed. Pinks planted last month only require to see that the winds do not loosen them.

2087 *Dahlias* These are still fresh and gay, if the weather has been tolerably mild: but should frost appear, no time should be lost in taking them up, storing them away carefully labelled, stalks downwards, in some place where they can be secured from damp. Seedlings that have bloomed late and weak plants are benefitted by being potted and kept dry through the winter.

2088 *Hollyhocks* Cut down and propagate from the old stools, and by eyes from the flowering stems, as formerly directed, but without forcing.

2089 *Pansies* These should now be potted off as reserves for filling up vacancies, or for new beds in the early spring; the beds should be examined to see that the worms have not attacked them.

2090 *Polyanthuses* Plants in beds will be benefitted if the surface of the soil is stirred, and a top dressing of equal parts maiden loam, leaf mould, and well-decomposed cow dung, applied.

2091 *Tulips* Bulbs not yet planted should be got in without delay, taking care, however, that the soil is not wet; the beds should be hooped over, and matting prepared against rainy weather.

2 – The Vegetable or Kitchen Garden

2092 *Trenching and Ridging* Approaching winter bids vegetation prepare for a rest. In the kitchen garden the crops will make little progress for the four months following this. During that time will be apparent the amount of forethought displayed in summer and autumn cropping. If a fair amount of Brussels sprouts, savoys, and other winter vegetables have been provided, this is the main point; and supposing herbs, salading, and minor crops have been attended to, then, if any ground is unoccupied, lay it up in ridges, having trenched it or dug it deeply, supposing the ground to be light.

There is an objection to laying heavy soil in ridges, except for certain purposes – as for sowing peas, beans, etc. For planting early potatoes, the advantages of ridging are great; but heavy clayey ground does not pulverise easily: the action of frost is wanted on the surface. Of course, the thicker the surface acted upon, the better. In digging heavy ground, lay the soil in solid spits as they are cut out with the spade: the spits should not be broken, but laid roughly together, with plenty of openings for the air and frost to act on them. Ground managed in this way is easier to crop in the spring time than that which has laid in ridges, because, when the ridges are levelled, a new surface is turned up, and the pulverised surface is buried. Ground ridges this month, therefore, should be levelled again in February, and another surface exposed and pulverised. At this time it is very necessary to give attention to the state of the drainage; unless surplus water gets away readily, great inconveniences may result. Heavy rains may make the garden a swamp, and spoil the crops already put in, besides preventing others being sown or planted. The ground, moreover, wherever imperfect drainage exists, is rendered soft and slimy to the feet by heavy rains, and difficult to cultivate.

2093 *Asparagus* If not already done, this should be cut down, and the beds dressed with very rotten dung, which may be forked in or not; it signifies but little, as its fertilising qualities will be washed into the ground during the winter, and the rest will be so pulverised as to fork in all the easier in March; but previous to manuring, all weeds should either be removed, or completely covered by the dressing.

If it is intended to make new beds, no better time can be chosen than the present for trenching the ground. If done now, the new surface will be exposed to atmospheric influences the whole winter long, and, if frequently turned, will be in fine condition for planting the following April.

2094 *Seakale* As the leaves decay and detach themselves, they may be removed; but, unless pots and hot dung are soon to be applied, it is not necessary to remove them; in fact, some gardeners have doubts as to the propriety of doing so.

2095 *Artichokes* A good mulching of leaves will be of considerable benefit to these in protecting the crowns from the frost. Let the ends of the leaves be exposed, and let them be killed. If a good cordon of leaves grows round the collar of each, they will stand better and come in earlier.

2096 *Peas* A sowing may be made now in light soil having a south aspect, but crops are frequently lost during damp winters, and autumn sowing is not recommended to those who have not an abundance of room. Early sorts are, of course, best for sowing now.

2097 *Beans* On light ground and sunny borders, these may also be put in without fear of failure. Without such advantages, autumn sowing of them is not to be generally recommended; the true purpose of it is to have crops a trifle earlier than they would be by deferring the sowing till February; but the loss during the winter counterbalances the advantages in other respects, and sowing now may be left to those who have plenty of room.

2098 *Runner Beans* Pull up these, as they will produce nothing more this season; the haulm may be pulled off the sticks; or, if all pulled up together, the leaves will soon drop off, and the haulm dry, when all may be chopped up together for firewood, or tied in faggots and kept for many useful purposes. Some burn them out of the way at once.

2099 *Celery* It is advisable to give the final earthing up at this time, for celery grows much slower after this month, and must be allowed time to blanch. Besides, should severe frost set in, it might be injured by exposure. Even that grown merely for soups, etc., had better receive a little earthing for protection; and if dusted with lime to destroy slugs, before earthing, so much the better.

2100 *Cardoons* Treat in a similar manner to celery.

2101 *Beet* Get this crop housed or pitted during this month; it will not stand frost without injury. Cut off the leaves without injury to the root, and let them lay a couple of days to heal or callow; then stow them where they will not mould or damp, but can be protected from frost.

2102 *Carrots* Treat in a similar manner to beet. It is advisable to get them housed before there is any danger of very severe frost. Young crops to stand the winter should be carefully thinned and hoed between.

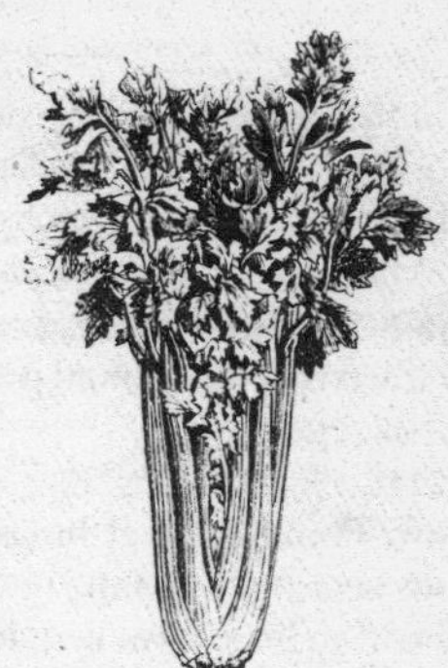

FIG. 561 *White celery*

2103 *Onions* The autumn-sown should be treated in a similar manner to carrots intended to stand the winter.

2104 *Leeks* ought to be earthed up, if not done before, when they can be taken up as wanted. They will continue to grow in mild weather.

2105 *Parsnips* These are as well left in the ground till wanted.

2106 *Potatoes* If any are left in the ground till now they should be taken up without delay, and stored, although they have been known to keep well in the ground by taking up every other row, and placing an additional layer of earth over each ridge.

2107 *Turnips* These should be hoed and kept clean.

2108 *Scorzoneras, etc.* These are best left in the ground till wanted.

2109 *Lettuce* Plants, if tied up for blanching, should be kept dry, if possible, or they will soon rot. The advantage of good cabbaging sorts will be apparent at this time. Some may yet be planted out to stand the winter.

2110 *Endive* Continue to blanch in succession. If this is done with flower pots, these, as they are removed, can be placed on others.

2111 *Spinach* If this has been properly thinned and kept clean, it will continue, to grow, the leaves alone being picked for use. If the plants stand 9 inches or a foot apart, the leaves will be all the better.

2112 *Broccoli* Such as are coming in now should be watched. There is a time to cut them, which is ascertained by so doing. Remove dead leaves, and use the hoe between them.

2113 *Brussels Sprouts, Borecole, and Savoys* are best kept free from dead leaves, which in damp weather become unpleasant.

2114 *Cabbage* These may still be planted out for the next summer's crop; but the earlier it is done now the better. Use the hoe freely amongst those planted last month; they will be much better for it.

2115 *Cauliflowers* Stir the soil about those in hand glasses, and keep the lights off unless frost renders it necessary that they should be kept on.

3 – The Fruit Garden and Orchard

2116 *Care of Fruit* Let the bulk of kitchen and dessert apples in the fruit room be often looked over to remove decaying fruit. In doing this, be careful not to bruise the others, which would induce early decay.

2117 *Clearing Leaves, etc.* Clear off the remaining leaves from wall trees; and now that the greater part of the fruit tree leaves have fallen, the whole should be cleared off the ground preparatory to pruning and turning up the borders rough for winter.

2118 *Figs on Walls* Figs against walls should have any odd remaining fruit taken off. Thin out superfluous shoots, and pinch out the points of the wood selected for bearing, when the branches should be tied together and matted, or protected by haybands, fern, etc., for the winter.

2119 *Shaping Dwarf Trees* Towards the end of the month is the best time to commence pruning dwarf apples and pears. Define in your mind what particular form the young tree should assume when at its full size, whether pyramidal, globular, or spreading. Shoots to form the skeleton of the tree should next be selected. How far these require shortening will depend on their strength and the object wished for. The remaining shoots must then be cut back so as to fill up the figure.

2120 *Large Standard Trees* Orchard trees, where covered with lichens and mosses, should have them scraped off, and a wash of hot lime and water applied to the branches. Apples, pears, plums, and cherries may be taken in the order in which they are named.

2121 *Trees on Walls* Remove all the old shreds where they are used; those that will do another season should be boiled, to destroy the eggs of insects, before using them again. The large wood looks better neatly tied in with osier twigs. Before tying or nailing, examine the trees, and if infested with scale or other insects, dress them with soft soap dissolved in hot water, to which add sulphur, quicklime, and tobacco-water; mix the ingredients well together, which should be of a consistency to adhere to the branches; with this dress the branches, but not during frost.

2122 *Apricots, Peaches, Nectarines, and Vines* These may be left till February or March, when apricots should be taken first, because they are the first to open the flower.

2123 *Plums and Cherries* should all be gathered before the frost sets in, and either wrapped in paper or hung by the stalk in the fruit room. Pruning should follow.

2124 *Currants and Gooseberries* Plant and prune both while the weather is favourable. For the production of large gooseberries, short pruning is necessary. Where quantity is required, and the trees are young, shorten the young shoots one-half or two-thirds. If the trees are of full growth, only take the points off the young shoots, and when the branches are thinned out, cut back to a bud on the upper side of the shoots. When the trees are pruned, lime the ground, and, if necessary, add manure and dig it slightly.

2125 *Strawberries* Continue as directed last month, unless you are inclined to adopt an expedient which has sometimes produced enormous crops, namely, to take up the old plants in spits and plant them again immediately in the same ground. Young plantations of strawberries should have some short dung spread between the rows, to preserve their yet shallow roots from frosts, which otherwise might lift them out of the ground. Look the beds over, and head the ground firmly round the plants. This is more necessary where the soil is light and rich, as the frost will make such ground more porous.

II – Work to be Done under Glass

1 – Flowers in the Conservatory, Greenhouse, Stove, etc.

2126 *General Management of Glazed Structures* During the continuance of characteristic November weather, every glass house should be looked upon and managed as a huge Wardian case, whose first and primary use, under such circumstances, is to keep November outside, while we, the proprietors, are enabled to enjoy spring, summer, or autumn, at our pleasure, inside. It is the height of stupidity and folly to allow a November fog to inundate a conservatory under the pretence of giving air. Such air is as little wanted by the plants as by those who come there to enjoy them, and is equally inimical to the health and well-being of all concerned.

2127 *Ventilation* This is emphatically the dead season. Plants under glass, though in the best possible health, would rather sleep just now than grow; and if a dry atmosphere and rather a low temperature is maintained, houses may be kept shut up close for a fortnight or three weeks together, not only with perfect impunity, but with positive benefit to the plants; but this supposes that the external atmosphere is ungenial. This, however, is not always the case. Embrace every opportunity of admitting the external air to conservatories and greenhouses when it is of a temperature of 45°; also change the air of stoves, etc., during the few hours of sunshine that often come to chase away even a November fog. In fine, the more fresh air the better, provided it be warm and genial; the less the better when it is otherwise.

Plants will live and thrive for weeks in the same atmosphere, when adverse circumstances render a change dangerous, and they will bear this treatment better now than during any other season of the year; and yet, as a general rule, the more fresh air the better.

2128 *Watering* As the quantity of external air admitted may now be safely reduced to its minimum, so may also be the quantity of water. The fact is, the power of a plant to use water to any good purpose chiefly depends upon the intensity of light and heat to which it is exposed. When these agencies exert their maximum power, water is profusely evaporated; when they are weak, as now, evaporation and elaboration are both slowly performed. Even a plant in vigorous growth requires comparatively little water now, while those at rest need scarcely any. It is of the utmost consequence also that what is necessary should be applied only where it is wanted.

2129 *How and When to Water* In watering thirsty roots, see that the flowers and succulent leaves are kept dry. This is a point of considerable importance at almost any season; at this, it is a question of life or death to many plants. Chinese primroses, for instance, double or single, will speedily fog off and perish if the needful water is poured into the centre, or permitted to trickle down wet leaves to the same vulnerable point – no less the centre of beauty than the seat of danger. Other plants suffer in the same manner, although few, perhaps, to the same extent. The water given to plants should always be 5° or 10° higher than the house in which they grow. Never water a plant until it is dry, and then water thoroughly. The quantity given must be regulated by the state of growth and drinking capabilities of each plant. For example, a chrysanthemum coming into flower will require three times the quantity as a camellia in the same state.

2130 *Hothouse or Plant Stove* Here the *Poinsettia pulcherrima*, otherwise called *Euphorbia pulcherrima*, *Euphorbia jacquiniceflora*, *Begonia nitida*, *Gesnera cinnabaranai*, otherwise *Naegelia cinnabarina*, will be lighting up by their dazzling grandeur and enlivening beauty masses of ferns, palms, and variegated plants. Late caladiums must now be watered with great care, as the bulbs are impatient of damp during winter. Those beginning to go off must have scarcely any water, and as soon as the leaves are matured, it should be entirely withheld, and the pots turned on their sides for the winter.

2131 *Temperature, etc.* Remove every dead leaf and flower as soon as they appear; water in the morning for the next three months; keep a temperature of 65°; frequently change the arrangement of the plants, and only admit air in fine weather.

2132 *Forcing Pit: Hyacinths, etc.* The forcing pit, it will be remembered, is an adjunct or accessory to the hothouse, and is artificially heated by pipes. When such a pit as this is attached to the hothouse, introduce into it a few more kalmias, azaleas, rhododendrons, sweetbriers, violets, etc.; and also the first batch of the earliest potted hyacinths, narcissuses, and other bulbs, if the pots are full of roots, otherwise leave them another week or two, plunged in old tan in a cold pit, the best of all positions for them while they are rooting. If the pot (or glass, if the bulbs be grown in glasses) is once full of roots, while the stem is only starting into growth, a good bloom, with ordinary care, is almost certain. In this condition they may be removed to a forcing pit with a temperature of 55°, to a conservatory, shelf, pinery, or peach house at work, or a sitting-room or kitchen window, with almost entire certainty of success.

2133 *Polyanthuses and Narcissuses* These rank only second to the hyacinth for decorative purposes, and totally eclipse it in richness of perfume. They require similar culture to the hyacinth, and will flower in water, sand, moss, etc., but do best in soil.

2134 *Jonquils* These are also beautiful, and effective if half a dozen or a dozen are planted in a single pot; otherwise they are too insignificant. The beautiful large double and single sweet-scented can be bought from 1s. to 3s. a dozen. Culture the same as the narcissus.

2135 *Tulips* Tulips in pots require similar treatment to hyacinths. The earliest are the single and double Van Thols; but any of the early single varieties will force.

2136 *Crocuses* For growing in pots, pans, or baskets, few bulbs can equal crocuses. The pots must be thoroughly drained, as an excess of water is certain destruction to these bulbs; any light soil will do to grow them in. They can also be grown in moss, damp sand, etc., and their general management may be the same as for hyacinths. They are rather impatient of heat, or a close, confined atmosphere, and can seldom be got to flower well before the middle or end of January. Any sort will do for pot culture, either as edgings to pots, vases, or baskets of hyacinths, narcissuses, or tulips, or arranged in contrasting masses by themselves.

2137 *Snowdrops* These must not be overlooked. The best way to succeed with them in pots is to take up patches entire out of the garden, place them in pots, and bring them forward on a warm shelf or with a very gentle bottom heat. Accustomed to the companionship of the biting blast and the cold snow, they will not endure much heat; but gentle, patient treatment will generally be rewarded by the unfolding of their spotless tiny bells.

2138 *The Greenhouse* Greenhouses occupied by heaths, azaleas, etc., not in flower, must be kept cool, dry, and clean. They may also have more air than the conservatory, and a temperature of 40° will suffice.

2139 *Camellias* Where these have a house devoted to them, they require careful management now. The buds will just be swelling, and a sudden change of temperature, a scarcity or excess of water, or a cutting draught of cold air, will often cause the buds to drop. Be extremely careful not to give an excess of fire heat when it becomes necessary, and maintain a genial growing atmosphere of 45°.

2140 *Pelargoniums* A temperature of 45° will suit these during the month. If worms make their appearance in the pots, water three or four times in succession with clear lime water. The repetition is necessary to insure their destruction, as these pests seem to have the power of casting their skins when injured, and so escape. But as they cannot carry on this evasive system indefinitely, a few repetitions of the lime will effectually destroy them. Remove every dead leaf; thin out and train the shoots; shift late-flowering plants into their blooming pots; and give fire heat enough to drive out damp and enable you to change the atmosphere during mild days or gleams of sunshine.

2141 *Pansies* Some of these may be kept and brought into bloom at the warmest end of the house.

2142 *Cinerarias and Calceolarias* Remove dead leaves, if there are any on the plants; there should, however, never be any on them. Shift when necessary into larger pots; pot off and prick out late seedlings; water forward plants with clear manure water; and smoke with tobacco as soon as a single aphis appears.

2143 *Orchids* See that they are clean, dryish, keep in a temperature of 65°, and let them sleep.

FIG. 562 *Giant mignonette*

2144 *The Conservatory* At this season, the conservatory should be well furnished with chrysanthemums, scarlet salvias, geraniums, Chinese primroses, etc., and fragrant with the leaves of a giant mignonette; a few ferns and begonias affording a pleasing contrast to the richness of colour exhibited by the flowers. The charm of the house, however, chiefly lies in the arrangement of the plants, which must be disposed so that the colour of one will be brought out and heightened by the colour of its neighbour.

2 – Plants under Glass in Hotbeds, Frames, etc.

2145 *Flowers in Hotbeds and Frames: Bedding Plants* Where the chief stock of bedding plants is kept in pits and frames, they will require frequent looking over, to guard against damp, careful watering, proper protection from frost, and all the air that the external atmosphere will permit of.

Garden frames are very useful for protecting other plants than those required for bedding purposes. Many plants, as pinks and pansies, stocks and chrysanthemums, and indeed many plants generally accounted hardy when planted in the borders, will, when in pots, require the protection of a frame, or, if planted in a bed of soil placed within the frame, they will flower earlier and stronger.

2146 *Bulbs in Frames* Bulbs may be grown and flowered in cold frames, and will be found to answer admirably when treated in this way. If spring-flowering bulbs are potted and placed closed together in the frames, and covered with about 4 inches of light soil or old tan, and left so till February, they may then be uncovered and exposed to the light; they will then begin to grow and flower to perfection. When plunged in this way, they need not be uncovered until the time stated; indeed, they will flower best if not uncovered till they grow through the covering.

2147 *Cucumbers and Melons* These will require the same treatment as that recommended in January. Heat is most necessary, and, to a certain degree, the more the better. In some families, cucumbers and melons are wanted all the year round. This, of course, necessitates the culture of them at this time of the year as well as any other; and although the difficulty is greater, in proportion to the shortening days and colder air, still they can be grown, and in some cases must be grown.

The main secret in growing cucumbers and melons is a steady moist heat that never falls below 70°, and is better kept up to 80°, and may advantageously be elevated to 90° in the daytime. They must receive no chill; so long as the roots work kindly, and the leaves revel in a sweet moist heat, they will do well. It is needless to repeat directions that have already been given in full; but this much more may be said, the causes of success or failure should be observed or remembered; it is only by so doing that proficiency is to be attained. The best cultivators will tell you that they have had many failures; but failure has given no discouragement, but rather afforded a stimulus to increased effort till success has rewarded their pains.

2148 *Treatment of Vegetables in Cold Frames* Plants in cold frames are often treated as if they were more tender than they really are. The object is not so much to stimulate them into growth, but to protect them from such injury from frost and storms as they would be exposed to in the open air. Corn salad, endive, lettuce, cauliflower, parsley, carrots, radishes, onions, and many more light crops, are not so tender but that they will stand out of doors; but then they keep so much better and fresher under the protection of frames, that it is well worth while to have a few lights devoted to them. They also begin to grow rather earlier in the spring, and continue growing later in the autumn, than they would do if quite exposed.

2149 *Ventilation and Watering* Care should be taken not to keep vegetables in cold frames in any way close, so as to breed mould. If any mouldiness accrue, it is a sure sign that they are kept too close. Let the plants have full exposure as much as possible, just as if the plants were growing out of doors, with just the aid of the lights to protect them in case of sharp frosts, heavy rains, snow, fog, or winds, should they be more than ordinary. Water should be given rather carefully. Avoid giving enough to chill the roots; a medium state, rather approaching dryness, is better than the least over-wetting, especially in frosty weather.

2150 *Seeds in Cold Frames* Seeds of radishes, lettuce, and small salading, may be sown any time during the month or any time in the winter. They will germinate slowly, but may come in very useful in the spring; the latter will be ready in about a month. In frosty weather the protection of a mat will, in addition to the lights, be sufficient protection for most of these things; but if they become frozen, do not expose them too suddenly.

3 – Fruit under Glass, Heated and Unheated

2151 *Preservation of Fruit* In fruit culture at this time one of the chief duties is fruit preservation. November is just the very worst month in the whole year for keeping ripe fruit of any kind, and especially trying for ripe grapes; one speck of decay or mildew will soon become a thousand under the influence of a November fog. Houses of ripe fruit must therefore be examined daily, and every specked berry or decayed leaf removed. Brisk fires must also be lighted in the morning, to enable air to be given both at front and back, to agitate the atmosphere and expel damp. No plant must, on any account, be placed in the house, nor a drop of water be allowed to fall on paths, etc.; neither must the house be shut up close until the heating apparatus is cold.

An increase of temperature in the absence of a current of air is most injurious to ripe grapes, and causes them to decay almost sooner than anything; unless during very cold weather, a current of air should always be maintained through vineries containing ripe grapes. Better that the grapes should be slightly shrivelled than that they should be altogether decomposed. In fact, the toughness of rind induced in the process of shrivelling is one of the surest preservatives against decomposition. If the houses are not waterproof, or plants must be placed in them, the best plan will be to cut and store the grapes as recommended last month.

Another great point in keeping late grapes, is to keep the rain off the borders in which the roots are growing. This is sometimes effected by thatching with straw, sometimes by the use of boarding or tarpaulins, and often by spreading a layer of concrete, formed by mixing six parts of coarse gravel to one of quicklime, over the surface of the border. If the border has a pitch of 3 or more inches from back to front, and this concrete is put on about 3 inches thick, it will furnish a cheap and efficient waterproof covering; it may be removed in the spring or not, at the option of the cultivator. Excellent grapes were obtained from vines in a border thus covered for three whole years. During that entire period they were never watered, and never showed any symptoms of needing it; the surface of the concrete in summer was sometimes so hot that one could scarcely touch it. It never cracked with the sun's rays, however, and early in October it was always covered with strawy litter, to prevent the dispersion of that heat which its absorptive powers had husbanded in the border.

2152 *The Vinery* After taking care of the grapes that we have, the next thing to be done in point of importance is to look after those that are to come. Vines in a vinery started last month will now be breaking, and a genial temperature of 50° to 55° must be maintained. This should not be exceeded during this month: the absence of the sun renders rapid growth now dangerous. What is gained in rapidity will be lost in solidity and strength. If the sun should shine, however, an increase of 10° or 15° will do no harm, but much good. See that the heat of the outside borders is kept regular, avoiding all extremes; it may continue 3° in excess of the inside temperature.

If border heat is maintained by the aid of dung and leaves, frequent examinations and turnings will be necessary to keep it right; sometimes fermenting material is also used to aid other means of keeping up the internal temperature. It makes a good deal of extra labour, but has the great merit of both feeding and warming at the same time. Where it is used, it must be partially sweetened before it is introduced, as too much rank ammonia would prove destructive to the tender foliage of the vines. When this is properly attended to, perhaps no food is so grateful to nor so speedily available for the vines as this. When this material is used beneath healthy vines, it should be turned twice at least in the day.

2153 *Vines in Pots* These may be started in a bottom heat of 53° in dung beds, unless means are found for giving them bottom heat over flues, etc., in the houses in which they are to be fruited. After they have fairly broke, they can be carefully moved to their fruiting quarters; in many places the first vinery will now be started. Proceed as recommended last month.

2154 *Peaches* If these are wanted next May, the house, or trees in pots, must now be started. They should already have been untied, pruned, washed, etc. Examine the borders thoroughly; water, and top dress with good maiden loam, is necessary. See that the house, as well as the trees, is scrupulously clean, so that you do not have to battle with vermin as well as dark skies and inclement weather for the next six months. The Royal George, Noblesse, and Galande peach, and the Red Roman and Violette Hative nectarine, are the best for early forcing. Proceed slowly; give no fire unless compelled, and do not exceed 45° by fire heat during the month.

2155 *The Pinery* Pines swelling off must be assisted by a warm genial atmosphere of 75°, and be watered when necessary. The bottom heat will require to be examined, and fermenting material renewed possibly. Plants intended to fruit next spring and summer must be guarded against any sudden check, be kept rather dry, and rest for the next three months in a temperature of 60° to 65°.

2156 *Succession Pines* Similar treatment, except the resting, will suit the general stock of succession plants. They must be kept slowly moving in a dryish atmosphere.

Much attention will be necessary to renewing linings, etc., to those in pits, to maintain the requisite temperature. Coverings of mats, reed frames, etc., must also be applied in severe weather, and all sudden changes guarded against. Occasionally, too, some of the strongest succession plants will require water at the roots, although the air may be a great deal too damp. The best mode of applying it will be found in the instructions given last month for the culture of pines. This is the most trying month in the whole year for pine plants in pits; hence they must receive extra care and attention.

2157 *Figs* Fig trees grown under glass should never be permitted to be frozen. The embryo fruit will most likely be destroyed, and a whole month's or six weeks' forcing lost in consequence. This is a good time to examine the wood thoroughly for scale, etc., and to paint them all over with the composition that has been recommended for vines.

2158 *The Orchard House* If these are either open or unroofed, see that the hungry birds do not destroy the next year's crop. They seem fond of model standard trees, and in a single day will often mar the hopes of a twelvemonth. The lights should also be placed on these structures, as is it is a dangerous practice to allow standard trees to be much frozen. The cold is also much more intense here than on the surface of a south or west wall.

CHAPTER 33

The Garden and Its Work in Every Department in December

2159 *Aspect and Character of the Month* December, the last month of our year, was, as its name indicates, the tenth of the Roman calendar. Although the thermometer often sinks below freezing point during this month, the frosts are seldom of long continuance. Rain and wind abound:

Sullen and sad, with all his rising train
Of vapours, clouds, and storms.

The variations of temperature are less than in November. The mean temperature of the earth two feet beneath the surface is now 42·83°, at one foot 41·13°, that of the atmosphere at the surface being 38·14°.

December gives unmistakable signs of winter; the last lingering leaf has fallen from the beech and oak, and it will occasion no surprise any morning to find an unvaried expanse of snow overspreading the earth. Nevertheless, a few flowers still linger in the garden; the delicate and fragrant Chinese rose still blooms, if not so rich in hue or powerful in odour as at midsummer, and the absence of other flowers renders its blossoms highly valuable. The starlike anemone, too, sometimes enlivens the December border, as does the laurestinus with its clusters of half-opened flowers; and in the shrubbery the arbutus presents the singular appearance of ruddy strawberry-like fruit on the same branch with delicate trusses of white flowers; and the well-known clematis, the 'traviler's joie' of old Gerard, 'decketh and adorneth waies and hedges where people travell, which is also termed Virgin's Bower, by reason of the goodly shadowe which it maketh with its thick bushing and climbing, and Old Man's Beard from the hoary appearance of the seeds, which remain long on the hedges.' To these we may add the ivy and holly, with its bright red berries, and the mistletoe, and the Christmas rose, which assists at the Christmas garland; but wonderful is the change a few weeks have made.

My very heart faints, and my whole soul grieves
At the moist, rich smell of the rotting leaves,
And the breath
Of the fading edges of box beneath, and the year's last rose.
Heavily hangs the broad sunflower
Over its grave; the earth so chilly;
Heavily hangs the hollyhock,
Heavily hangs the tiger lily.

Apropos to the arbutus and clematis, to which reference is made above, it is much to be regretted that by ninety-nine gardeners out of a hundred, and by about the same percentage of non-professionals who follow humbly and confidingly in the wake of the professional ninety-nine, these names are shamefully ill-treated by being pronounced *ar-bu´-tus* and *cle-ma´tis*, stress being laid with force upon the second syllable of each word, instead of on the first, as it ought to be; the right pronunciation being *ar´-bu-tus* and *clem´-*

a-tis. Gladiolus is another word that is in most cases pronounced *glad-i-o´-lus*, instead of *gla-di´-o-lus.* It is as well to call even plants by their right names, if possible.

I – Work to be Done in the Garden

1 – The Flower Garden and Shrubbery

2160 *Importance of Winter Work* Many amateurs are tempted to desert their gardens until brighter prospects and more genial weather tempt them forth to their usual labours; whilst nothing more liberally rewards proper attention – nothing exacts a severer penalty for neglect – than a garden. A week's cold indifference or studied neglect may counteract the labours of years, and render nugatory most of our future efforts to maintain the beauty of the garden, and especially that portion of it which is devoted to the culture of flowers. In many respects the winter work is even of more importance than that of summer. It is only those who dig, plough, and sow in winter, that have any right to reap in summer or autumn. Now is the time to plan and lay the foundation for the future beauty of the garden. Half the gardens in the country are miserable failures, either because they have no design, or because it is so confused or obscure as not to be perceptible. Advantage, therefore, should be taken of this quiet or *dead* season of the year to remedy any defect or shortcoming that has been brought into prominence by the experience of the preceding summer.

2161 *Preparation of the Soil* Having got the ground into the proper shape, see that it is also made of the best quality. Good, properly prepared soil is of the first importance in the kitchen garden; it is even of greater importance here. The permanent nature of the plants introduced into shrubberies and flower gardens renders the future improvement of bad soil difficult and well-nigh impossible. All who value rapid, healthy growth must see that everything possible is done to ameliorate the soil before planting. November is the best month in the whole year for planting, but if this work has not been done in November, it should be carried out as early as possible in December.

2162 *Laying Turf on Lawns, etc.* November is the best month in the whole year to lay turf, but the work may be done very nearly as well in December. Old common is the best possible place from which to procure it. The most convenient dimensions for turf are a yard long, a foot wide, and an inch thick. This, wound up in rolls, is the best size for carting, unwinding, etc. The ordinary price for small quantities, purchased and delivered, is 1d. per turf, or 3d. per square yard, but it can be taken up at this size at the rate of 8d. per hundred. Thus, enough to cover 100 square yards will only cost 2s. for removal. After all the improvement in lawn grasses, there is no plan of covering a lawn equal to turfing it over; a good, solid, smooth surface is secured at once. Under the most favourable circumstances, three or four years must elapse before the same point could be reached by sowing. All that is necessary is to make the surface of the required shape, unroll the *turf*, placing the pieces close together, beat it firmly down, and frequently roll it, and the work is finished.

2163 *Turfing by Inoculation* The next best method of covering ground with grass is what is termed *inoculation*. Pieces of turf are torn, not cut, into pieces –say 2 inches square – and thrown on to the ground, leaving interstices of the same distance, or less or more, between them. Grass seed is then sown over the ground, and the whole firmly beaten down. It is astonishing how soon a splendid turf is thus formed.

2164 *Pruning Trees and Shrubs* The pruning of deciduous trees and shrubs should also be proceeded with, unless during severe frost. Most evergreens are best pruned in April; nevertheless, as that is a busy and this a comparatively leisure season, the hardiest evergreens, such as laurels, etc., may be pruned now; any, however, that require cutting down, had better be left till that period.

In pruning, it may be said that there are three leading purposes, namely, to improve the shape, curtail size, and to induce a profusion of bloom or fruitfulness. The first is entirely a matter of taste; the second of space; and the third the primary object, for which all flowering shrubs and trees are cultivated. The two first are entirely effected by pruning the top; the last is more effectually secured by cutting in the roots. This latter does not necessarily, however, supersede the former; often both may proceed simultaneously with advantage. One of the chief points in the management of shrubberies is so to prune them and cut down the plants as always to preserve a dense thick bottom.

2165 *Winter Management of Shrubberies* The digging, pointing, top dressing, and cleaning of old shrubberies should also be proceeded with, the turf frequently swept and rolled, the gravel kept scrupulously clean, and every possible thing done to make this outside winter garden attractive and useful during the bleak winter and spring months.

2166 *The Flower Garden* The beds here, disrobed of their summer beauty, will either be furnished with shrubs, herbaceous plants, annuals, or bulbs, or simply roughed up for the winter. Previous to either being done, they should have received a liberal top dressing of manure. It is as vain to expect to grow the majority of bedding plants successively for years on the same soil without enriching it, as it would be successful to produce good vegetables on the same starving regimen; indeed, many of these plants – verbenas, for instance – draw the soil as much as a crop of cabbage.

If every bit of weed, short grass, and other refuse that comes off the garden annually is conveyed to a heap, occasionally turned over and saturated with manure water, a most valuable dressing for the beds will be provided at a cheap rate.

2167 *Roses* Roses may still be planted, although the sooner this work is finished the better for next season's bloom. Plant as many on their own roots as possible they are more durable, and perhaps more beautiful in this form than any other. All newly-planted roses should be mulched over with 3 or 4 inches of light dungy litter on the surface.

2168 *Routine Work* Examine and renew the labels on these and all other named shrubs and herbaceous plants; provide stakes and pegs, and make labels in bad weather. Take stock of, and finally decide on, the disposition of your bedding stuff; sweep, roll, and mow, if need be from the mildness of the season, your turf. Keep your gravel bright, clean, and as hard as adamant, and by such means make the flower garden, even in ruins, a cheerful, comfortable winter promenade.

2169 *Reserve Garden* Annuals, to stand the winter here, will probably require some slight protection. Carefully watch against the inroads of mice, rats, snails,

FIG. 563 *Anemone coronaria (single)*

FIG. 564 *Anemone coronaria (double)*

etc. Not only bulbs, but even young plants, are often devoured by the two former; and in mild winters a little black slug will clear off whole beds of annuals. Let every vacant space be roughly dug up, manured, etc.

2170 *Anemones, etc.* Choice beds of anemones (Figs. 563 and 564), and, indeed, of all plants and bulbs forming entire beds, should be sheltered in bad weather, and the whole examined daily to guard against accident and ward off disease.

2171 *Dahlias* Dahlia roots stowed away in cellars, etc., must be carefully and frequently examined to see how they are keeping, and any scarce sorts placed in heat towards the end of the month, to ensure a large stock before May. Carefully dry dahlia seed preparatory to sowing in pans next month, and see that all the labels are firmly attached to the roots.

2172 *Carnations, Picotees, Pinks, etc.* Pinks and carnations, in beds, will require pressing firmly into the earth after severe frost. Examine the beds for slugs in mild weather, and see that the plants are not destroyed by rats and mice.

2173 *Pansies* The precautions desirable for the preservation of pinks and carnations are also necessary with pansies in beds in the open ground. It is best to keep a stock of autumn-struck cuttings of these in pots to fill up blanks and to make good accidental losses.

2174 *Tulips* If planted early last month, some of these may be peeping through the soil; if so, they may be protected by having a slight pyramid of sandy peat earth or leaf mould placed over them. During very frosty weather the beds or rows must be covered with mats, woollen nets, etc., as nothing injures these bulbs more than severe frosts on their crowns just as they are coming through the ground.

The ground for these bulbs should be trenched from 2 feet to 30 inches deep, mixed with a liberal dressing of well-rotted manure. It is also a good plan to place a layer of manure about 6 inches from the surface, so that it may be readily and speedily available for the roots. The bulbs should be planted 6 inches square and 4 inches deep, and any period from the middle of October to the middle of December will do for planting them.

2175 *Roots and Bulbs* Roots and tubers of Marvel of Peru, dahlias, gladioluses (Figs. 565 and 566), salvias, etc., must be looked to occasionally, to see that they are not affected with damp or becoming rotten in parts that have been bruised or injured in any way. They must be kept in such a way that frost cannot injure them, and the best way to do this with regard to tubers is to store them in dry sand.

2176 *Flowers now in Bloom, etc.* In sheltered positions the yellow blossoms of the leafless *Jasminum nudiflorum* are conspicuous, and *Daphne Mezereum*, *Chimonanthus fragrans*, the laurestinus, and various ericas or heaths, show here and there their pink, yellow, white, and scarlet flowers. *Alyssum saxatile*, *Arabis Alpina*, and *Myosotis dissitiflora* are beginning to open their blooms of yellow, white, and pink; and late in the month *Helleborus niger*, the black hellebore, or Christmas rose, will light up the sombre surface of the nearly flowerless beds with its broad creamy petals.

2 – The Vegetable or Kitchen Garden

2177 *Digging, Dressing, and Trenching* We are now in the dead of winter Vegetation is at a standstill, and whatever seeds or plants are put in the ground now will not move or grow for two or three months to come; but if vegetation does not move, that is no reason why man should not. The experienced gardener knows the importance of winter operations, and knows, in fact, how work, judiciously done now, will save much toil in the spring and summer. Supposing it is only necessary to manure the ground once a year, let it be done in the winter; it is generally most convenient, and the work is better adapted to the season. Digging and trenching is much better done now than in warmer weather, and this more particularly applies to heavy soils some, indeed, cannot be cropped at all unless dug a month or six weeks beforehand, either summer or winter; and it is much more advantageous to move the ground, and let it lie in clods so that the air permeates around them, and the action of the frost brings it into a state easy to work, and better for the seeds, than to leave the work to be done just before the ground is required for sowing.

There is now most likely some portion of ground vacant, and as no general cropping can be done for some time, a little attention can well be given, and would be well bestowed, in considering the important matter of a rotation of crops. If no regular system has been

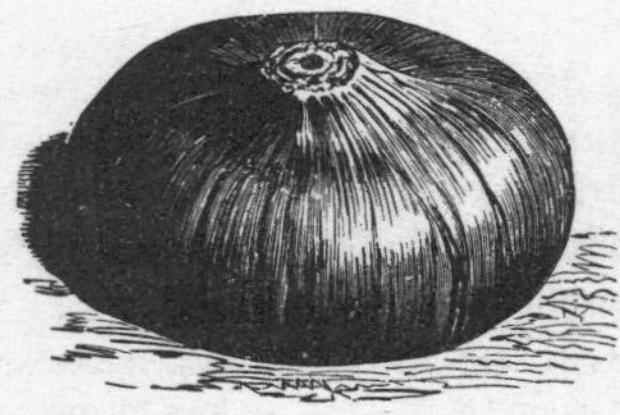

FIG. 565 *Bulb or corm of gladiolus (upper part)*

FIG. 566 *Bulb or corm of gladiolus (under part)*

adopted before, let it be decided at once to begin a systematic arrangement of the various subjects to be dealt with. Much more work may be done under a proper system than by continuing the haphazard style; and not only so, but a great many more subjects **may** be grown on a given space by giving each group its proper place.

2178 *Seeds, etc.* Some attention should be given both to the various stores of seeds and vegetables: the latter should be looked over occasionally, turned, sorted, and cleaned; kept moist without being damp, cool without frost, and where there is a free circulation of air. As to seeds, it is well to have them ready for sowing – that is, thoroughly dried and rubbed out, every particle of husk and light seed blown out, and carefully papered and labelled.

Those that have to be purchased should be procured early. Go to respectable dealers, who can be certain of the sorts being true to name. Note down and procure exactly what will be required for the season, so that no time is lost in running after them the moment they are wanted, and place each sort in its proper drawer or receptacle, that there may be no confusion.

2179 *Garden Tools, etc.* See to the tools or implements, and ascertain that they are in good condition; replace or repair any that are broken; never trust to just the right number if any are not in good condition; keep them dry, and clean well before hanging them up.

2180 *Composts, Manures, etc.* Another thing to attend to is proper composts and manures. These may be collected on a spare or vacant piece of ground in the kitchen garden, where there will be plenty of room to turn it over and where all kinds of woody refuse can be collected and charred and mixed with it. In frosty weather, when the ground is hard, it should be wheeled on to vacant ground.

2181 *Sticks for Peas, Beans, etc.* Much valuable time is saved in the spring and summer, by making a general pruning and trimming of trees at this time of the year. Most trees will be improved by a little cutting out; it prevents them making so much dead wood. Collect all these prunings; take the bill in hand, and look over the sticks; see what are useful for supporting peas and beans. Select them both for tall and dwarf sorts. Keep them all separate; trim them into shape, and point them; tie them into bundles, and store them up in a dry place ready for use, when wanted; the remainder may be tied up in faggots, which are useful for various purposes, or, if chopped short and stored in a dry place, will be useful for lighting fires. Let neither time nor material of any kind be wasted; it is wonderful to what uses a little ingenuity can apply them.

2182 *Seakale* Some may be covered for forcing. Place the kale pot over a bunch of crowns; see that enough is covered; then having previously prepared and shaken out the dung, and got it into a condition to maintain a moderate heat, cover the pots to a thickness of about 3 feet from the ground.

Too great a body of dung is apt to heat too violently, and spoil the crowns; give just enough to maintain a moderate heat, and no more. The seakale will be ready to cut in about three weeks, according to the amount of heat. Some gardeners cover with leaves, which answers the purpose; but in collecting leaves, a great many slugs and other vermin are collected with them. These do mischief to the kale, otherwise the effect is the same.

2183 *Rhubarb* may be treated in a similar manner to seakale, but it requires larger pots, and none but the earliest sorts should be forced.

2184 *Parsnips* These and other crops that remain in the ground ought to be covered with litter or leaves. The slightest covering will make a vast difference in case of sharp frost, which should always be looked for at this time.

2185 *Celery* Cover with litter, if possible, in frosty weather. It will be so much better to take up, besides keeping it fresh and uninjured.

2186 *Lettuces* These should be kept under protectors, cloches, or hand lights. Air is said not to be essential to them, but of this there is room for doubt. When the frost is severe, loose litter should be placed round and over the frames, glasses, etc., to afford additional protection to the plants.

2187 *Endive* Blanch with pots, and cover with litter; and a good supply may be kept up the whole winter without having recourse to frames, the litter helping to blanch it before the pots are put on; but a dusting of lime should be given occasionally to destroy slugs, which are very fond of endive.

2188 *Peas and Beans* of the earliest kinds may be sown on light ground; but it is not advisable to sow many. Those sown in February will be as early within a few days, and much more certain.

2189 *Broccoli, etc.* Heads of Walcheren broccoli should be cut when ready for use, that they may not be injured by frost; or, when ready, they may be pulled up and hung up, just as they are, in a cellar or any place into which frost will not enter. Cabbages, Scotch kale, or curly greens, savoys, Brussels sprouts, coleworts, etc., should all be cut for kitchen purposes when they are in an unfrozen state. If cut when frozen, they should be plunged into cold water and allowed to remain there until all signs of frost and ice have disappeared.

It will now be seen what advantage there is in giving the various sorts of brassicas plenty of room, and also giving them a place to themselves in a clear open spot. Those planted among other crops are shanky, and more exposed to the frost, while those planted open are short, firm, and stocky, and far more likely to stand severe frost. Let this be considered in cropping next year.

2190 *Seed Sowing, etc.* The instructions given last month for provision for early crops apply equally to this month, and need not be repeated.

2191 *Sweet Herbs* Herb beds should be cleared, and made as neat as possible, both for the appearance of the beds and well-doing of the herbs. In order to procure parsley for garnishing, sauces, etc., plant protectors should be placed over a few rows or hand lights over individual plants.

2192 *Alterations and Routine Work* This is the best time to make any general alterations. Where old bushes are to be grubbed up, and the ground prepared for cropping, or where young bush is to be planted, also where drainage is necessary, now is a good time to do it, before the winter rains make a swamp of the garden. Set the edgings and paths in order, and carefully remove any accumulation of rubbish which is likely to harbour vermin.

3 – The Fruit Garden and Orchard

2193 *Preparation for Spring Planting* December is the month of rest here as in other departments of the garden; but there is much to be done which is too often left undone. Planting may now be presumed to be over; at least, unless the weather is unusually mild, it will be well to prepare the ground, and leave the planting until the early spring.

2194 *Management of Wall Trees* Peaches, nectarines, and other wall trees now require pruning, and the shoots selected nailed in; but both operations should be avoided in frosty weather, pruning in such weather being apt to lacerate the sap vessels and destroy the shoots, which die back under its influence.

2195 *Espalier Trees* Espalier trees, and trees planted against a wall for horizontal training, do best when the shoots are tied down; in the absence of trellis on the wall, therefore, studs should be driven into the wall at convenient distances for that purpose, in order to avoid the stiff and formal distortion the branches undergo in the old process of nailing with shreds.

2196 *Standard Trees* Standard apples and pears should now receive their final autumn pruning and thinning out, the latter being chiefly exercised on the interior branches of the tree, so as to admit of a free current of air through it.

2197 *Large Standard Trees* Large standard trees in their prime only require pruning once in two or three years. At these intervals cross-growing or exhausted shoots, especially those in the centre of the tree, require thinning out, bearing in mind that the best fruit grows at the extremities of the branches, and keep those branches under control. In cases where languid growth and barrenness have been engendered by exhausted soil, dig a trench round the tree and lay in some barrowfuls of rich fresh soil; then fork over the surface, and give a dressing of well-rotted stable manure. Where the exhaustion arises from the tap root having penetrated to an unwholesome subsoil, dig a trench deep enough to reach the root, and sever it from the tree if it is one worth preserving, and fill up the trench again with good fresh soil, and top dress with manure.

The modern system of dwarfing fruit trees, by which space is so much economised, is produced by a special course of pruning, commencing a year from grafting, when the apple tree should be pruned back, leaving about eight buds on the shoots. In the second year the head will exhibit eight or ten shoots, and a selection must now be made of five or six, which shall give a cuplike form to the head, removing all shoots crossing each other, or which interfere with that form, thus leaving the head hollow in the centre, with a shapely head externally, shortening back the shoots retained to two-thirds or less, according as the buds are placed, and leaving all of nearly the same size. In the course of the summer's growth the tree will be assisted by pinching off the leading shoots where there is a tendency to overthrow the balancing of the head. At the third year's pruning the same process of thinning and cutting back will be required, after which the tree can hardly go wrong. The shoots retained should be short jointed and well ripened; and in shortening, cut back to a healthy, sound-looking, a dwell-placed bud. After the third year, little or no shortening back will be required, especially where root pruning is practised; the tree should now develop itself in fruiting stems, which will subdue the tendency to throw out gross or barren shoots.

2198 *Gooseberries and Currants* If the bushes have not been pruned in November, let the work be now done and brought to a finish without delay.

2199 *Raspberries* Take up and remove suckers from the stools, but defer pruning till March,

2200 *Strawberries* It is thought that strawberry plants are better for protection during severe winters. A light covering of fern, pea-haulm, straw, or other light material will preserve the plants in vigour at a very slight cost.

II – Work to be Done under Glass

1 – Flowers in the Conservatory, Greenhouse, and Stove

2201 *Routine Work in Glazed Structures* As this is a leisure season of the year, even with regard to work to be done under glass, bring up all arrears of work, so as to start even with the new year. The re-labelling, cleaning, and arranging of all plants should be diligently forwarded, so that every plant should have its proper name attached to it, and look at its best before Christmas. Climbers on roofs and pillars should have their final pruning, cleaning, and tying, if it has not been already done, and every dead leaf and every visible or invisible particle of dirt should be removed.

2202 *Hothouse or Plant Stove* In the hothouse the most conspicuous object will be *Poinsettia pulcherrima*, a plant of whose striking beauty no description can convey a sufficiently strong idea. Half a dozen of them from four to five feet high, and having about eight shoots each, terminated by bunches of enormous scarlet bracts, set off by the peculiar shape and colour of the true leaves, is a sight well worth going twenty miles to see. Anyone who possesses a hothouse may have this treat at home, as few plants are easier propagated or grown. There is a creamy white variety of this plant – *Poinsettia pulcherrima albida* – certainly not to be compared to the other, but still interesting and showy, especially by candle-light. A beautiful companion plant to this is *Euphorbia jacquinioeflora*. For bouquets, vases, or head-dresses, the flower of the euphorbia is one of the finest in existence, consisting, as it does, of a fine spike, 18 inches long, which in itself forms a matchless wreath. The brilliant effect of this plant among begonias, ferns, and other things, must be seen to be appreciated. Some late caladiums, grown for this purpose, will now be intermixing their beautiful leaves with the flower stems of *Gesnera cinnabarina* and others; The bright red berries of *Ardisia crenulata* will also be exhibiting themselves in striking contrast with the shining green leaves.

2203 *Orchids* With these, rest should still be the order of the day; nevertheless, that rest will be partially broken by the flowering of some or all of the following plants, namely, *Phaloenopsis amabalis*, or Butterfly plant, and several Oncidiums, Cymbidiums Epidendrums, Cattleyas, Zygopetalums, etc. Maintain a temperature ranging from 60° to 70°, and avoid all stimulating treatment.

2204 *The Forcing Pit* Keep up a growing temperature of 55° to 60°. Introduce fresh batches of shrubs, roses, bulbs, and everything that will flower early, to supply the place of those drafted off for other service.

2205 *The Greenhouse* Preserve a minimum temperature of 40°; give as much air as possible; see that the stock is kept perfectly clean by occasional smokings, washings, dippings, etc.; put on a fire on dull mornings, to enable you to expel damp; remove heaths, epacrises, etc., to the conservatory as they come in flower; shift young plants of Kalosanthes or Rochea into their blooming pots as they require it, and keep everything in a quiet, semi-dormant state until the new year awakens them to hard work and a new life.

2206 *Pelargoniums* Early varieties for cut flowers maybe forced into bloom in a vinery or peach house at work. The general stock will require careful treatment

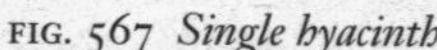

FIG. 567 *Single hyacinth*

FIG. 568 *Double hyacinth*

this month. The latest flowering specimens may receive their final shift, and all will require careful training, a genial temperature of 45°, and great skill in watering and ventilating. Fancy varieties often show a disposition to bloom prematurely. These early flowers must be perseveringly removed, to throw the strength into the shoots, to be husbanded up for a perfect inflorescence at the proper season. Keep the plants within a yard of the glass, if possible, to prevent their drawing, and fumigate as soon as one green fly is visible.

2207 *Cinerarias* The earliest of these will now be in flower, and will have been removed to the conservatory; succession plants will be coming on here.

2208 *General Management, etc.* With regard to general routine work and cultural directions, the instructions given for last month apply equally well to December.

2209 *The Conservatory* Cleanliness, so essential to health everywhere, is especially necessary in the conservatory, where nothing offensive to good taste should ever be seen. The interest of this house is often much increased at this season by introducing some pots of Christmas roses, hyacinths, single (Fig. 567) and double (Fig. 568), narcissuses, etc., from the forcing pit. The edges of the beds, shelves, and vases may also be decorated with variegated and plain holly, and pillars from which fuschias or other climbers have been removed, be wreathed in the same manner. These, with occasional syringing, will keep fresh for six weeks, and very much increase the interest of the house. The chrysanthemums will continue flowering during the month, and camellias be coming on to supply their place.

2210 *Rhododendrons* The tree rhododendron (*Rhododendron arboreum*), grown for several years under glass, will also flower now in the conservatory without any forcing. With a very little forcing, Black-eyed Susan, Bianchi, Brayanum, Captain Webb, Caractacus, Charles Dickens, *R. delicatissimum*, *R. fastuosum flore-pleno*, Iago, Ne Plus Ultra, Nero, Princess of Wales, and The Queen, might be got in flower during the month. With these, and half-a-dozen plants of *R. arboreum*, a magnificent effect during winter and early spring could be produced. The following dwarf hybrid varieties, all of which, as well as the preceding and many other beautiful specimens of this flower, may be obtained from Messrs Richard Smith and Co., seedsmen and nurserymen, *Worcester*, are profuse and early bloomers and admirable kinds for forcing, namely, *R. cinnabarinum*, *R. Dauricum atrovirens*, *R. ferrugineum*, *R. fragrans*, *R. glaucum hybridum*, *R. hirsutum*, *R. lepidotum*, *R. multiflorum*, *R. myrtifolium*, *R. pallidum*, and *R. praecox*.

2211 *Camellias* Next to rhododendrons, or even exceeding them, in usefulness, is the camellia, and December is the month above all others when it is most useful. By inducing early growth and early maturity, it will flower now from habit as well, if not better, than in any other month.

2212 *Azaleas* After camellias, Indian azaleas stand next in order of importance for conservatory decoration; but for flowering in December an early habit must be induced, which may be brought about by merely placing them in the conservatory in the autumn, or by aid of the forcing pit.

2213 *Winter Heaths and Epacrises* The plants, if properly managed after flowering, and removed from the forcing pit to the conservatory late in September, will now be in flower.

2214 *Ventilation, etc.* The same principles will apply to giving air, etc., as in November; only, as we have generally more sun this month, more may be admitted. Care must, however, be taken to prevent a cold draught cutting off the beauty of any plant that may have recently come from a warmer house or forcing pit.

2215 *Epiphyllum* Where a temperature of 45° is maintained, *Epiphyllum truncatum* and other sorts of the Epiphyllum division of the Cactus family, so often met with in stoves in winter, will bloom well in this house. There are now several varieties of this charming winter-flowering plant, grown as dwarfs in suspended baskets, or as tall plants, umbrella fashion, or as pyramids; worked on the Pereskia, or Barba does gooseberry, it is exquisitely beautiful. Perhaps it flowers best in a cool stove, but it will flower for six weeks or two months in a warm conservatory.

Potted in a rough mixture of peat, leaf-mould, loam, brickbats, old plaster, and charcoal, and kept in a temperature of 60°, its progress is rapid. During the summer and autumn months the plants should be fully exposed to the sun in an airy house. Place them in a temperature of 55° towards the middle of October, and now every leaf will terminate in one, two, or three beautiful flowers.

2 – Plants under Glass in Hotbeds, Frames, etc.

2216 *Plants in Cold Pits, Frames, etc.* The instructions given for November apply equally now. As far as general treatment is concerned, water and cover with care; give all the air possible in mild weather. During a severe storm these may remain hermetically sealed for a week with impunity at a temperature of 35° to 40°. After such a long nap, unwrap cautiously, and shade for a few days from the sun's rays. Examine the entire stock every favourable opportunity.

2217 *Auriculas, etc* These, with carnations, picotees, pinks, and polyanthuses, should be kept cool and dry, and have plenty of air in fine, dry weather. They must be kept close whenever fog or frost prevails, and should be placed on a thick bed of cinder ashes.

2218 *Pelargoniums, etc* These, with verbenas and other bedding plants, should be kept warm, but dry. A little water may be required at the roots, but none must be allowed to fall on the foliage.

2219 *Cinerarias and Calceolarias* Of these, cinerarias in pits will be showing flower, and must be watered freely, and kept near the glass. They should not be subjected to a temperature lower than 40°. Frost will not injure herbaceous calceolarias in frames. Care must be taken to fumigate for green fly, if it makes its appearance.

2220 *Bulbs, etc* When bulbs in frames, with violets, forget-me-nots, and plants of this kind, begin to show flower, they may be removed to the conservatory, or window, to come into bloom.

2221 *Cucumbers and Melons* Little can be added to what has been already said. Let the weather be the principal guide as to giving air, etc.; be careful that the frames are ventilated without causing any draught, which might injure the plants considerably. See that the heat is maintained, and cover with mats at night; but do not put on the mats so early as to render the days shorter than they are. The mats should be taken off as soon as it is light in the morning, and not put on till it is getting dark at night, so that they may have all the daylight they can get.

3 – Fruit under Glass, heated and unheated

2222 *The Vinery* The vines have been awake for weeks, and they are now showing branches. By aid of artificial heat, maintain a temperature of 60° by night, and one of 70° by day; admit every possible ray of light; keep the leaves within 9 inches of the glass, and create a midsummer climate in December. Examine frequently the state of the borders, and keep the roots as warm as the tops. Stop the shoots a joint beyond the branches; damp the floors, paths, and pipes, if these are used, during bright days; admit air whenever it is practicable, and try to secure strength rather than length.

2223 *Succession Vines* Where a succession of grapes is wanted, start another vinery; proceed as detailed last month, or, if possible, defer it till the first week of January, when you will receive the full benefit of the vivifying influences, a clearer atmosphere, and more sunlight than falls to our lot in November.

2224 *Preservation of Late Grapes* Continue to look over and preserve late grapes, and maintain a cool and equable temperature of 40° to 50°. If a gentle current of air can be kept up through the houses by night and by day, the fruit will keep all the better.

2225 *Vine Borders* Vine borders may also be formed, or old borders renewed during this month. Old vines may also be taken up where the borders are bad, the roots carefully preserved, a new border made and skilfully planted, and half a crop taken the first season. Young vines may also be planted in a dormant state or first started in pots, and then put in the border in June or July,

The great point in planting at any season is carefully to surround the roots, sprinkle some leaf mould over them, and keep them within 6 inches of the surface. A mulching of dung or some litter will-be necessary to prevent them being dried up; and if the vine is in full growth when planted, the top must be shaded a few days until the roots have laid hold of the soil; then let the top run as far as it chooses. Leave laterals and all on. The more growth for the next four months the better, because the larger the top, the greater the number of healthy roots. Upon the number, nearness to the surface, and strength of these, all future success may be said to depend.

2226 *The Pinery* Keep fruiting pines almost entirely dry if you wish them to start in January. Maintain a day temperature of 70°; night, 60° to 63°. This dryness may be necessary to throw the plants into bloom. Nothing does this more effectually than a check, although the check must neither be too severe nor too long continued. Beware of moisture settling upon any pines that may now be in flower, as it often prevents the proper fructification of the blossoms; and deformed, or not formed, fruit is the consequence. Embrace every opportunity of admitting air when the external atmosphere will permit, and keep the plants within one foot of the glass.

2227 *Succession Plants* Succession plants, if kept tolerably dry, may be wintered in pits, at a temperature of 60°, with perfect safety. Beware of an excess of heat, or any sudden change of temperature, lest you cause premature growth or start them into fruit.

2228 *The Peach House* In many places the fruit house is started this month. For instructions in the preliminary stages, see last month. It is objectionable to allow trees in late peach houses and orchard houses to get frozen. The wood cannot bear cold so well as that nurtured out of doors; therefore, the outside borders of early houses should be protected, as much to keep in as to send in heat.

2229 *Figs* Osborn's Prolific, Dwarf Prolific, Negro Large, and Brown Ischia are among the best sorts grown; but White Ischia, Marseilles, and Black Halicon, or Black Marseilles, are perhaps better for forcing. The plants in trees and pots should be thoroughly cleaned, new borders made, rapid growing trees root pruned, and all top dressed, etc., ready for an immediate start.

2230 *Strawberries* The first batch of strawberries should also be introduced. I find Cuthill's Black Prince the best for the early season, and if they can have a little bottom heat, so much the better. Plants in 48-sized pots also do best for early work, the cramping principle again inducing fruitfulness.

CHAPTER 34

Trees and Shrubs of All Kinds Suitable for the Park, the Pleasure Garden, and the Shrubbery

2231 There is comparatively little to be said respecting the culture of trees and shrubs of all kinds, as it is extremely simple in itself, and confined to raising the plant *in situ* from seed, or transplanting it from the nursery in which it has been grown, and then affording it such protection from animals, and security against injury from high winds and storms, until it is so firmly rooted in the soil, in the first place, or has attained to a sufficient size, in the second place, to render these precautions unnecessary. After this, nothing more is requisite, in the case of trees, than judicious lopping and thinning of branches, and the removal of dead wood when needful. For shrubs, a closer supervision is necessary, combined with pruning and trimming in the winter season, with the clearance of weeds, and the periodical cleansing of the soil in which they are growing, when the shrubs are found in borders and on breadths of ground, which are too large to be regarded as borders, but which are not covered with a carpeting of turf.

2232 It has been said that there are two modes of stocking a park or ornamental pleasure grounds with trees and shrubs, namely, sowing and planting. Let us glance for a moment at the merits and demerits attaching to these two methods. They may be summed up briefly in a very few words. To create a wooded tract of land by sowing is a slow but safe and sure process, but the results desired can only be realised by a lapse of many years. To do so by planting is a rapid but by no means so certain a way of going to work, as transplanted trees and shrubs will often perish, and others must be planted in their place; but when once the plants are rooted and well established, the start they have obtained over those which are raised from seed will obviate the years of patient waiting which must otherwise be endured by those who sow.

2233 In what, then, it will be asked, is the advantage of sowing, and for what reasons can it be recommended? Sowing is cheaper and safer than planting, and is therefore more desirable than planting, when the chief object in view is to transform an untimbered piece of ground into a wood land, or when a person can afford to wait some years before he commences building on the land on which he has sown seeds for the purpose of producing timber. The best writers on arboriculture are agreed on the desirability of sowing, on account of its economy and safety, and declare that trees 'which are transplanted will never arrive at the size of those which stand where they are sown, nor will they last so long'. Planted timber, in fact, has never in any case been found to be 'equal in durability and value to that which is sown', and 'every kind of forest tree will succeed better in being reared from seeds in the place where it is to grow to maturity, than by being raised in any nursery whatever and from thence transplanted to the forest.'

With regard to the growth of trees from seed, Mr Alfred Wallace has stated that 'the Wellingtonia will reach 20 feet in ten years,' and that 'the Douglas Fir grows even more rapidly when young.' The same authority has also pointed out that at Dropmore 'the beautiful grass-green *Pinus insignis* reached the height of 68 feet in thirty-four years,' an average growth of 2 feet per annum.

2234 With regard to the actual operation of sowing, it may be said that for forest trees the same rule holds good as for vegetables, namely, that the depths at which to sow must be estimated by the size of seed, smaller seeds being placed in the soil at less depth than larger kinds. Larger seeds are merely dibbled in; smaller seeds are sown in drills or patches in the spots where trees are wanted, and are afterwards thinned out, ultimately leaving the largest and finest specimen to occupy the site alone.

The seeds of a large variety of trees and shrubs can always be obtained from Messrs Viccars Collyer and Co., Central Hall, Leicester, at rates varying from 4d. to 10s. 6d. per oz. in one case, and 12s. 6d. in another. The price *per packet* for some varieties ranges from 6d. to 2s. 6d. As prices can always be obtained on application, and will in all probability be subject to variation from numerous causes, it is not desirable to state them here at length. The following list of trees, etc, whose seeds may be procured, will, however, be useful. The letters attached to the names bear the following significance: D., best shrubs for growing under the *drip* of trees or in shade; E., *evergreens*; F., *foliage trees*, to be planted for effect; G., best for *game coverts* or underwood; H., specially adapted for *hop poles*, crates, etc.; S., best for growing near *seacoast*; T., best for growing near towns or in smoky districts.

Alder, Common, H.
Alder, Cut-leaved, F.
Alder, Fern-leaved, F.
Arbor Vitae, American, E.F.
Araucaria imbricata (Monkey Puzzle), E.F.
Ash, Common, H.S.
Ash, Mountain, H.S.T.
Aspen (*Populus tremula*), H.
Beech, Common, S.T.
Beech, Purple, F.S.T.
Birch, Common, H.T.
Birch, Silver, or Weeping, F.
Black Thorn, or Sloe, G.
Box Tree, D.E.G.S.
Butter Nut (*Juglans cinerea*).
Cedar of Lebanon, E.
Cedar of Lebanon, Indian (*Cedrus deodara*), E.
Cedar of Lebanon, Red (*Juniperus Virginiana*), E.
Cedar of Lebanon, White, E.
Chesnut, Horse, F.T.
Chesnut, Scarlet-flowered, F.
Chesnut, Sweet or Spanish (*Castanea vesca*), F.H.
Cypress, Lawson's, E.F.
Cypress, Golden, Lawson's, E.F.
Cypress, Scented (*Cupressus fragrans*), E.F.
Elm, English, H.T.
Elm, Wych, or Scotch, H.S.T.
Eucalyptus globosus (Blue Gum), E.F.
Eucalyptus marginata, E.F.
Fir, Austrian, E.S.T.
Fir, Balm of Gilead, E.F.
Fir, Douglas, E.F.
Fir, Scotch (Pinus *sylvestris*), E.T.
Fir, Silver, E.S.
Hawthorn, Thorn, or Quick, G.T.
Hazel, G.H.
Hickory (*Carya alba*).
Holly, Green, D.E.H.S.
Holly, Variegated, E.F.H.S.
Hornbeam, G.
Laburnum, T.
Larch (*Pinus larix*).
Laurel, Common, D.E.G.

Laurel, Portugal, D.E.G.
Lime, Common, Large and Small-leaved, H.T.
Lilac, Blue and White, T.
Locust Tree (*Robinia pseudo acacia*)
Maple, Common or English (*Acer campestre*), H.S.
Maple, Norway (*A. platanoides*), H.S.
Maple, Sugar (*A. saccharinum*).
Maple, Swamp (*A. rubrum*), F.
Myrtle, E.
Negundo, or Box Elder, Variegated (*Negundo Acer variegatum*), F.T.
Oak, English, H.
Oak, Scarlet, F.
Pinaster (*Pinus pinaster*), E.S.
Pine, Corsican, E.S.
Pine, Mountain or Dwarf (*Pinus pumilio*), E.G.
Pine, Nordmann's, E. F.
Pinus insignis, E.F.S.
Plane, **Eastern**, T.
Plane, Western, T.
Poplar, White, H.S.T.
Poplar, Italian, H.
Poplar, Black, H.
Privet, Evergreen, D.E.G.S.T.
Privet, Oval-leaved, D.E.S.T.
Rhododendron Ponticum, D.E.G.T.
Rhododendron Ponticum, **hybridum**, D.E.T.
Spruce, Norway, E.
Spruce, Black American (*Pinus nigra*), E.
Spruce, White American (*Pinus alba*), E.
Sycamore, *Common (Acer pseudo-platanus*), F.
Sycamore, Purple-leaved (*A. p.-purpureum*), F.
Tulip Tree (*Liriodendron tulipifera*), F.T.
Walnut, Common (*Juglans regia*), F.T.
Walnut, Black (*Juglans nigra*), F.
Wellingtonia gigantea, E.F.
Willow, Green, or Osier (*Salix viminalis*) H.S.T.
Willow, White-leaved, S.T.
Willow, Purple-leaved, S.T.
Yew, English, D.E.F.G.
Yew, Irish, E.F.

2235 The foregoing list contains most, if not all, of the trees and shrubs of which seed may be procured without difficulty; but it is desirable to go even deeper into the subject, and to call the attention of the reader more directly to the great facilities which exist in the present day for beautifying our parks, pleasure grounds, lawns, and shrubberies, by the judicious disposal, here and there, of many of those choice evergreens, deciduous trees, conifers, and American plants which of late years have been introduced and become acclimatised, Nature, to a great extent, readily accommodating herself to the requirements of Art in plants as well as with animals.

It will be useful to pause here for a moment and endeavour to associate some of the best-known trees of the world with the latitudes which Nature has assigned to each as its peculiar *habitat*. Those who have visited the countries between the tropics speak with admiration of the luxuriant profusion and rich variety of the vegetable productions of those regions. They tell us that vegetable life is there far more active and vigorous, and that the circumstances under which it goes on are far more favourable, than in our latitudes. Every zone, however, has its peculiar vegetable productions, though some may be more luxuriant and beautiful than others. If we look at the indigenous plants of Asia and Europe, northward of the Equator, we find a very varied succession. At the Equator there are the natives of the Spice Islands, the clove and nutmeg trees, the pepper plants, and cinnamon bushes, which are common in Ceylon. In the East Indies, there are the odoriferous sandalwood, the ebony tree, the banyan, and the teak tree. In the same latitude, in Arabia, we have balm, frankincense, and myrrh, the coffee tree, and the tamarind; while in these countries, at any rate in the plains, the trees and shrubs which decorate our more northerly climes are wanting. At every step we take, the vegetable group changes, both by addition and subtraction. In the thickets west of the Caspian Sea, we read of apricots, citrons, peaches, and walnuts. In the same latitude in Spain, Sicily, and Italy, we find the palm, the cypress, the chesnut, and the cork tree; oranges and lemons perfume the air with their blossoms; the myrtle and pomegranate grow among the rocks. Crossing the Alps, we have the vegetation which belongs to Northern Europe, of which England affords an evidence. The oak, the beech, and the elm are natives of Great Britain. The wych elm is peculiar to the north of England and Scotland. Still further north, the forests change their character. In Northern Russia are found forests of the various species of firs – the Scotch, the spruce fir, and the larch. In the Orkney Islands no tree is found but the hazel, which is also the case along the northern shores of the Baltic. As we proceed into colder regions, we meet with other species, which appear to have been made for their situation. North of Stockholm there is the hoary-leaved alder (*Alnus incana*). The sycamore and the mountain ash grow at the head of the Gulf of Bothnia, and as we pass the boundary line of the spruce and Scotch fir, we come upon those minute shrubs known as the dwarf birch and dwarf willow. Near to, and even within the arctic region, if no trees are to be met with, there are still wild flowers of great beauty, and, when these fail us, there is reindeer moss.

FIG. 569 *Cypress*

2236 *Deciduous Trees* Nature, as it has already been observed, kindly and frequently easily accommodates herself to the wants and wishes, and especially to the industry of man. Our woods, and shrubberies, and gardens, may now be adorned with the vegetable productions of all climates and countries. The Eastern and the Western World, especially Brazil, California, Japan, New Zealand, and Australia, have added many beauties to our scenery which were unknown to our forefathers. The oak, the ash, the elm, the lime, the beech, and the maple, in all parts of the country, testify by their size either to indigenous growth, or to the length of time during which they have been known among us. But then, even these, until comparatively recent periods, were in no great varieties; or, if there were varieties, there was so little specific difference that they were generally regarded as being all of one kind. But the planter, now, who takes up the catalogues of any of our large growers of ornamental forest trees and shrubs, will find that he has a vast variety to select from, and many of them eminently beautiful, while he need not go beyond the old, common, and familiar names. This will be apparent from the following list of forest trees, in which the different varieties are grouped together under the general name of the particular family to which each belongs:

1 *The Oak and its Chief Varieties* – Of the oak, *Quercus*, in addition to the common English oak, *Quercus pedunculata*, there are *Q. variegata*, a beautiful variegated variety, calculated to produce a fine effect in distant scenery; *Q. coccinea* and *Q. rubra*, both scarlet oaks; *Q. nigra*, a black oak, with leaves as

black as the purple beech; *Q. alba*, a white American variety; *Q. macrocarpa*, with its long acorns; and *Q. macrophylla*, with its long leaves. These are only a few among many.

FIG. 570 *Myrtle*

2 *The Ash and its Chief Varieties* – Of the ash, *Fraxinus*, besides *Fraxinus excelsior*, the common ash, there are *F. pendula*, the weeping ash; *F. aurea pendula*, the golden weeping ash; *F. aucubafolia* the aucuba-leaved ash; and *F. crispa*, the curled ash.

3 *The Elm and its Chief Varieties* – Of the elm, *Ulmus*, in addition to *Ulmus campestris*, which is the old English elm, we find *U. foliis variegatis*, a variegated elm; *U. glabra tendula*, a smooth weeping elm; *U. rugosa pendula*, a rough weeping elm; *U. latifolia*, the broad-leaved elm, and many others, all valuable as large trees, for though they require a rich, deep soil, they will live and flourish in the smoky atmosphere of crowded towns.

4 *The Lime and its Chief Varieties* – Of the lime, *Tilia*, the common variety of which is *Tilia Europaea*, there are *T. alba*, the white-leaved and white-wooded lime, and *T. pendula*, the weeping lime, both of which may be planted separately, or interspersed with other trees with very good effect.

5 *The Beech and its Chief Varieties* – Of the beech, *Fagus*, *Fagus sylvatica*, the common beech, is a fine tree and exceedingly useful, as it will grow well in both sandy and chalky soils. It is surpassed, however, by several of its varieties: *F. aspleniifolia*, the fern-leaved beech, and *F. purpurea major*, the large purple beech, are nobler trees.

6 *The Maple and its Chief Varieties* – Of the maple, *Acer*, *Acer campestre*, the common maple, is a showy tree, beautiful in growth and foliage; but there are several others which are even more beautiful: *A. macrophyllum*, the long-leaved maple, is very striking; and so, also, are *A. laciniatum*, the cut-leaved maple, *A. alba variegatum*, the white variegated, and *A. rubrum*, the scarlet or swamp maple; also *A. striatum*, the snake-barked variety, which almost rivals the cork tree.

7 *The Horse Chesnut and its Chief Varieties* – Under the generic name, *Aesculus*, the horse chesnut, we find not only *Aesculus hippocastanea*, the common horse chesnut, but *A. h. flore pleno*, a double-blossomed variety, *A. rubicunda*, with its scarlet blossoms, and one or two others.

8 *The Spanish Chesnut and its Chief Varieties* – The Spanish chesnut, *Castanea vesca*, itself so beautiful in woods and shrubberies, offers an agreeable variety in *C. aspleniifolia*, the fern-leaved chesnut, *C. Knightii*, Knight's Chesnut, and *C. variegata*, the variegated chesnut.

9 *The Poplar and its Chief Varieties* – The *Populus*, or poplar, is a handsome, quick-growing tree under almost any circumstance of soil and climate. Of

this we have several beautiful varieties, of which the most noteworthy are *Populus alba*, the Abèle poplar; *P. fastigiata*, the Lombardy variety; *P. grandidentata*, the large American aspen; and *P. tremula pendula*, the weeping aspen.

10 *The Thorn and its Chief Varieties* – The genus *Cratoegus*, the thorn or hawthorn, is a large one, for which care and cultivation have done much. Flowering and fruit-bearing, various in colour and in growth, the whole family is worthy of a place wherever there is room for planting. So hardy are they, that the most severe frost will never injure them, and so easy of culture, that they do not refuse to grow in almost any soil, and under a smoky atmosphere. Amongst the best and most useful varieties may be named *Cratoegus apiifolia*, the parsley-leaved thorn; *C. Maroccana*, or *Maura*, the Morocco thorn; *C. pendula*, the weeping hawthorn; and *C. rubra*, the red-fruited hawthorn. Of the varieties of the common hawthorn, *C. oxycantha*, *C. o. punicea*, a scarlet-flowered thorn, and *C. o. plena* and *C. o. puniceo flore-pleno*, white and scarlet double-flowered thorns, are deserving of special mention.

2237 *Trees of the Genus Pyrus* Among deciduous trees, the genus *Pyrus* includes apples, crabs, pears, thorns, the service tree, and the mountain-ash – some of the most ornamental of our smaller trees, whether we consider flowers, fruit, or foliage. There are *Pyrus aria*, the white beam tree; *P. prunifolia*, the Siberian crab; *P. spectabilis*, the Chinese crab; and many variegated and weeping varieties, which, as standards upon lawns, form very pretty objects. Anyone who intends to plant cannot do better than select such of these as may suit his garden site, and assist the landscape which he is preparing.

2238 *Deciduous Shrubs* In addition to the deciduous trees under cultivation, the principal of which have been named above, there is a large number of deciduous shrubs which should not be neglected by anyone who wishes to beautify and improve his plantations. Most of these shrubs blossom freely; many are very handsome, and produce an excellent effect when blended with evergreens, of which mention will be made presently. There are different sorts of *Berberis*, or barberry, some evergreens and some deciduous, but bearing in every case a pretty yellow blossom; *Amygdalus communis amara*, the bitter almond; *A. dulcis*, the sweet almond; *Buddlea globosa*, the globe-flowered buddlea, which is very ornamental, with its orange blossoms and lanceolate leaves; the *Daphne Mezereum*, the common mezereum, and *D. M. album*, the white-flowered variety; also three or four varieties of the elegant and free-flowering *Deutzia*. Nor must we omit the different sorts of *Genista*, or broom, the *Robinia*, and the many kinds of *Spiraea*, than which it is hardly possible to find any genus more richly varied and more profuse in flowering. Many other small deciduous shrubs, useful for filling up gaps in plantations and borders, will be mentioned presently.

2239 *Evergreen Shrubs, Hollies, and Evergreen Oak* We must now pass to the description of some of those shrubs of an evergreen character, which are not only highly ornamental in themselves, but so extremely valuable as preserving a fresh appearance in nature, even during the dreary months of winter; also in affording a continual shade and shelter to other things. Chief among these are the *Ilex aquifolium*, the common holly, and *Quercus ilex*, the evergreen oak, both handsome evergreens, and rich in varieties, but preference must be given to the former. Not only is the holly the brightest of all evergreens in the rich green colour of its leaves, but its magnificent scarlet berries give to it an additional charm. There are many varieties of the ilex, and few things are more interesting than a good collection of these within an arboretum, or space so limited as to afford an opportunity for observing their differences of growth and foliage. *I. a. alba-marginata*, the silver-edged holly, and *I. a. aurea-marginata*, the golden-edged holly, are both very beautiful; so also are *I. a. ciliatum*, the hairy holly; *I. a. ferox*, the hedgehog holly; *I. a. ovata*, the oval-leaved holly; and *I. latifolia*, the broad-leaved holly; all presenting a striking appearance. Second only to the *Ilex*, is the genus *Quercus*, *Q. ilex* being the common evergreen oak. When standing singly on a lawn or in a park, *Q. Fulhamensis*, the Fulham oak, is very imposing; and so also is *Q. Luccombeana*, the Luccombe oak, which is of the same character. The acorns of each of these are very handsome, but in some situations these choice varieties do not fruit freely.

2240 *Box Trees* The different sorts of box, *Buxus*, are very ornamental. They do not attain much height; but they grow well in shade, and always look fresh and nice. *Buxus sempervirens* is the common box, to which *B. aurea* and *B. argentea*, the gold and silver varieties, form an agreeable change; *B. Balearica* is a good sort, and so is *B. myrtifolia*. *B. s. suffruticosa*, a dwarf variety of the common box, is the sort that is used for the edgings of borders.

2241 Of *Phillyreas* there are several sorts, all of which, from their dark, shiny leaves, form excellent masses, and grow freely in almost any soil. The *Cerasus* tribe must not be omitted, for to it belongs the common laurel, *C. laurocerasus*, and *Cerasus Lusitanica*, the Portugal laurel, both of which are too valuable to be passed by. *Laurus nobilis*, the common bay, is useful as well as ornamental. In every seaside garden the tamarisk can be grown; and, however smoky the atmosphere, *Rhamnus alaternus*, the common alaternus, and others of the same genus, which are all of quick growth, will live and do well, provided only they have shelter from the wind.

2242 *Conifers and Taxads* There yet remains to be noticed a class of trees, without which it can hardly be said that much has been done in ornamental planting. This class contains the conifers and taxads, which have been so extensively improved and so freely cultivated of late years. The conifers and taxads are considered the grandest of ornamental trees: they are evergreen, thriving, for the most part, in common soil, disliking manure, except in a thoroughly decomposed state. They are best raised from seed, but some kinds are not yet obtainable in that way, and are found to do perfectly well grafted, when united to a proper stock. Where there is sufficient space, the pines and firs should enter largely into the composition of scenery; in more limited grounds the junipers, cypresses, arbor-vitaes, and yews are equally valuable. A few only thrive well in the vicinity of large towns; but as such are very desirable from their distinct and handsome forms, they should not be overlooked when planting.

2243 *Pines and Firs* First among the conifers, let us take the genus *Pinus*. It is hardly possible to do justice to the rich variety which is here included. There are pines adapted to every soil and every situation; also for every purpose of ornament and profit. What more commanding than a fine specimen of *Pinus excelsa*? Then there are *P. Devoniana*, the Duke of Devonshire's pine, *P. insignis*, and very many others. Nor must the magnificent *Wellingtonia gigantea* be omitted, which is certainly a pine, and the noblest and hardiest of pines; nor *Araucaria imbricata*, the Chilian pine, a very distinct variety. Then of the genus *Abies*, the fir, *Abies excelsa*, *A. grandis*, *A. nobilis*, *A. Nordmanniana*, and the Spanish Silver Fir, *A. Pinsapo*, are all eminently noble. The last-named variety, indeed, is a particularly handsome tree, having its numerous branches arranged in whorls in the most perfect order: as a single tree upon a lawn, nothing can surpass it, and in its own country, Spain, it attains a height of 70 or 80 feet. Again, there is *A. Douglasii*, the most distinct and beautiful variety ever introduced. It was discovered by, and named after, the persevering explorer whose name it bears, upon whose authority it is stated to attain the great height of 250 feet, and 12 feet diameter at base. It is thoroughly hardy, of sound constitution, and very rapid in growth. Independent of its great attractions as an highly ornamental tree, its value as timber can scarcely be estimated; it is fine-grained, elastic, strong, heavy, and free from knots, easily wrought, and capable of receiving a high polish, very durable and not subject to split.

FIG. 571 *Pine*

2244 *Cedars* Next in order from which to make a selection is the genus *Cedrus*, the cedar. Among its members *Cedrus deodara* is conspicuous. It should have a place on every lawn which is large enough to admit it, and where it can have shelter from the wind. In its original habitat it attains 120 feet in height, and is frequently 40 feet in circumference. It is distinguished from all others by its handsome pyramidal form and beautiful glaucous green foliage.

In speaking of its excellence as a timber tree, Mr Loudon says, 'The wood is very compact and resinous, and has a fragrant smell, remarkably fine and of close grain, capable of receiving a very high polish – so much so, indeed, that a table formed of a section of a trunk 4 feet in diameter, sent by Dr Wallich to Mr Lambert, has been compared to a slab of brown agate.' Dr Royle says that the wood is particularly durable, and is much used in the construction of Himalayan houses. In Cashmere it is used for both public and private buildings, and likewise for bridges and boats. Strips of it are also burnt as candles.

2245 *Cypresses* Of the cypresses, *Cupressus*, there are many varieties. Conspicuous among them are *Cupressus Lawsoniana argentea* and *C. L. aureo-variegata*, the silver and gold cypresses, varieties of *Cupressus Lawsoniana*, a native of North California, also known as *Chamaecyparis Lawsoniana*. The foliage of these trees clothes the trunk to the very bottom. All the cypresses require a dry soil and situation; if these conditions cannot be obtained, their places would be better occupied by junipers.

2246 *Junipers* The junipers, *Juniperus*, are very similar to the above class, but much hardier. All the taller varieties are striking in shrubberies and plantations, and the smaller very ornamental on grass plots and lawns. Almost all junipers have a close habit, which renders them valuable in small gardens. *Juniperus excelsa*, *J. virginiana*, *J. fragrans*, *J. thurifera*, are some of the best and tallest; *J. Chinensis* is a handsome shrub, and so is *J. Hibernica*, the Irish juniper.

2247 *Arbor Vitaes* Of the *Thuja*, or Arbor Vitae, genus, the varieties are mostly of middle size, varying in colour from a bright yellowish-green to golden. They are very valuable in small gardens, for contrast with shrubs of both a lighter and darker tint. They will grow in any common soil.

2248 *Yews* There yet remains the yew, *Taxus*. Trees of this genus, being generally of the darkest shades of green, may be planted singly for contrast, or in masses to give an effect of shade. They are all very hardy, but with the exception of *Taxus baccata*, the common yew, they do not attain much size. *T. Canadensis* is of a pale colour; *T. b. variegata* and *T. b. foliis-variegatis* have a fine golden tinge.

2249 When time is no object, the advantages to be gained by raising forest trees and shrubs from seed are great, as it has been already shown; but in the great majority of cases it is desirable to produce the effect required in the shortest possible time and in the quickest possible manner, and when the need is urgent and pressing, recourse must be had to planting and transplanting. The proper time for these operations is November, but the work may be done in December with equal safety, and even in January, although it is better to have it done before the new year has dawned upon us. So much for *when* to plant; *how* to plant and transplant is altogether a different matter, and requires careful consideration and instruction in detail. The removal of trees and shrubs of small size is a comparatively easy matter and simple in itself: it is in the case of large trees and shrubs that the work becomes more difficult and laborious.

2250 *Transplanting Large Trees and Shrubs* To gain time, these are largely used in many places. The effect of ten or twenty years' growth is gained on any given spot at once. This is of immense importance in the lifetime of a man, and the practice of transplanting large trees is therefore popular, and highly to be commended; neither is there much risk of failure, as might be thought, with proper caution and skill; and it is not so expensive as many imagine. With the aid of one of McGlashan's Patent Transplanting Machines (see paragraph 509), trees of almost any size may be safely and expeditiously removed; in fact, these machines forcibly remove earth and roots, and all, with the minimum risk of failure. Large trees and shrubs, however, 30 feet high and 20 feet in diameter of top, may be moved with no other machinery than a few strong planks nailed on a low truck or sledge.

2251 In this mode of transplanting, a trench is dug round the plant at a distance from the bole of two-thirds the diameter of the top, and to a depth of 2 to 5 feet, according to the age and size of the tree, character of the soil, depth of roots, etc., leaving a space of from 2 to 3 feet at the back of the tree untouched. A the same time, the front, or part where the tree is intended to come out, should be approached at an easy angle of inclination, extending from 2 to 3 feet beyond the circumference of the trench already begun. The earth is rapidly removed from the trench, the roots being carefully preserved as the operation proceeds. The size of the ball in the centre must be determined by the nature of the soil and size of the plant. Its mere size is of less consequence than the preservation of the roots during the removal of the earth.

2252 A fork must be used to separate the roots from the soil, and they should be carefully bent back and covered over until the work is finished. After excavating from 1 to 3 feet beyond the line of the bole of the tree or shrub, according to its size, introduce into the vacant space a sledge or low truck; cut through the solid part at the back line, and the tree will rest on the machine. This should be furnished with four rings at the corners, through which ropes or cords should be fastened and firmly fixed to the bole of the tree. Of course, some soft substance, such as hay or moss, will be introduced between the bole and the cords, to prevent them from chafing the bark. The tree is then ready for removal; the necessary horse or manual power can be applied; the plant will slide gently up the inclined plane, and may be conveyed any distance desired with facility. Sometimes it may be impossible to fix the cord through the back rings until the tree is out of the hole. In that, and indeed in any case, cords had better be attached to the top, and carefully held by men, lest a too strong vibration of the top should upset the machine or topple the tree over.

2253 If the tree is large the hole in which it is to be deposited should be made in such a manner as to have an inclined plane on each side to enable the horses to walk through with ease. When the sledge arrives at the centre of the hole, the horses must be stopped. If the tree is not too heavy, the truck or sledge is prised up by manual strength, and the plant gradually slid off. If very heavy, a strong chain is passed under the ball, attached to a couple of strong crowbars; the horses are applied to the other end of the truck, and the tree is dropped off into its place.

2254 The roots are then carefully undone, and spread throughout the whole mass of soil as the process of filling up goes on; three strong posts are driven in to form a triangle, and rails securely fixed to them across the ball to keep it immovable, the top reduced there and then in mathematical proportion to the mutilation the roots may have suffered; the whole thoroughly drenched and puddled in with water, and covered over with four inches of litter to ward off cold and drought, and the operation is complete.

If this operation is well performed, the loss will not average more than from five to ten per cent. The principle involved in all planting is the same, and only of secondary importance to securing as many healthy roots as possible. Next in order to this must be placed the stability or immovability of both root and top afterwards. When it is otherwise, every breeze that blows is analogous to a fresh, removal. No sooner do the roots grasp hold of the soil than they are forcibly wrenched out of it again, and the plant lives, if at all, as if by miracle.

2255 The planting of young trees and small shrubs is so simple as scarcely to require instructions. Always make the hole considerably larger than the space required by the roots, whether few or many, so that they may find soft recently-moved soil to grow in; and yet the soil must not be left too loose. If so moist as not to need watering, which will moisten and also consolidate the soil, it may be gently trodden down round the roots.

2256 *Distance between Shrubs* In reference to the proper distance at which shrubs should be planted, much depends upon the object in view. A safe rule, however, is to plant thick, and thin quickly; from 3 to 4 feet is a good average for small shrubs and trees. In three years, two out of three plants should be removed; and in planting it is well to introduce rapid-growing common things amongst choice plants, to nurse them up; only the nursing must not continue too long, nor the nurses permanently establish themselves to the injury of the children. This is too often the case, and nearly every shrubbery suffers more or less to a ruinous extent from this cause.

2257 *Arrangement of Shrubs, etc* But if the mere operation and distance of planting is important, the mode of arrangement is still more so. Nothing can well be more unsatisfactory than the plan of planting at regular intervals on what may be called the dotting system. Perhaps a dozen varieties of shrubs are planted haphazard all over an acre or two of ground. The only principle kept in view is that, strong or weak, they shall be planted at intervals of the same distance. The result is a dreary monotonous maze of tiresome sameness. Whatever the form or extent of shrubbery, the first and leading principle in furnishing it is that it shall be planted in distinct groups, and in masses of shrubs or trees. Single plants, at such distances as to allow them fully to develop their characteristics, are desirable as specimens, and as a necessary and pleasing accompaniment of the gardenesque style; but a shrubbery should be a mass of shrubs, not a congeries of single specimens, however perfect: far less must it be a confused patch of imperfect plants.

Plant everything in groups. Is your shrubbery of serpentine form? Let every separate sweep, as far as practicable, have its specific furnishing. Put variegated holly in that prominence, berberries in that recess; green yew here, golden yew yonder; Portugal laurel in this, in the next box; beyond them common laurel, rhododendrons, arbutuses, junipers, kalmias, azaleas, and heaths, all in their turn. Do the same with deciduous shrubs, which might generally be introduced behind the evergreens; lilacs here, deutzias there; philadelphuses, spiraeas, ribes, and laburniums – all in groups. Is your shrubbery straight? Plant a ribbon border of shrubs, thus: dwarf laburnums, tall standard lilacs, white syringas or deutzias, yews, variegated hollies, box, dwarf golden yews, rhododendrons; and, next to the turf, ericas, or dwarf varieties of *Juniperus sabina*, the common savin. This, and many other arrangements, would look well; only keep the principle of grouping or massing the different sorts together. The same principle applies to trees. The regular pinetum and arboretum have of late years caused us to lose sight of the fact that trees, as well as shrubs and flowers, are most effective in masses. Grandeur is frittered away in the attempt to grow single pretty trees. As an extreme illustration of the meaning of all this, look at a single Scotch fir – how poor the effect! But next look at a forest or a clump of them – how rich and magnificent! To bring out the individual beauties of every tree is a laudable object, and is the chief object of pinetums and arboretums; but it is bad taste to sacrifice the grand effect of masses for the sake of growing single specimens.

2258 *The Golden Rule in Planting* In planting, therefore, except in the smallest places, let it be accepted as the rule – the golden rule, as it may well be termed –

FIG. 572 *Dwarf pine*

that all hardy trees shall be planted in groups or masses by themselves. The different groups can be so arranged, in reference to each other, as to heighten the peculiar characteristics of each. Even in the massing of pines alone, there is scope for considerable judgment and the exercise of great taste; and their relation to other species of deciduous trees may very much make or mar the beauty of all concerned; but it is now time to proceed to answer the question – What am I to plant?

2259 *Conifers for the Pinetum* First, in the pinetum, if space permits, plant any and every pine that will endure the climate of that part of the United Kingdom in which it is situated. If space is limited, and economy to be studied, the following will probably suit, or a selection may be made from them. The names of the trees are alphabetically arranged, according to genus, and except in cases where there is room for doubt, the general limits of height are given, and the name by which each tree is known when it possesses a common name, as well as its botanical name.

CONIFERS AND PINES

		Height in Feet
Abies Canadensis	Hemlock Spruce	50 to 80
Abies Douglasii	Douglas Pine	100 to 180
Abies nigra	Spruce	60 to 70
Abies Smithiana		50 to –
Araucaria imbricata.	Monkey Puzzle	50 to 100
Cedrus deodara	Indian Cedar	150 to 200
Cedrus deodara robusta		150 to 200
Cedrus Libani	Cedar of Lebanon	60 to 80
Cephalotaxus Fortuni.	Japanese Yew	40 to 60
Cryptomeria Japonica	Japan Cedar	50 to 100
Cryptomeria Lobbi		30 to 40
Cupressus Lusitanica.	Cedar of Goa	40 to 50

Cupressus MacNabiana		10 to 15
Cupressus sempervirens	Common Cypress	10 to 100
Cupressus sempervirens horizontalis		10 to 100
Cupressus torulosa		50 to 70
Fitzroya Patagonica		80 to –
Juniperus communis	Common Juniper	3 to 20
Juniperus communis Canadensis	Canadian Juniper	3 to 5
Juniperus communis compressa		1 to 3
Juniperus excelsa		20 to 40
Juniperus prostrata		[6 inches]
Juniperus recurva		5 to 8
Juniperus Sabina	Common Savin	5 to 8
Juniperus Sabina foliis variegatis		4 to –
Juniperus virginiana	Red Cedar	10 to 90
Juniperus virginiana pendula	Weeping Red Cedar	5 to –
Larix Europaea	Common Larch	80 to 100
Larix Europaea pendula		15 to 20
Picea Cephalonica		50 to 60
Picea grandis		100 to 170
Picea nobilis		80 to 100
Picea Nordmanniana		80 to 90
Picea pectinata	Silver Fir	80 to 100
Picea pichta	Pitch Pine	50 to –
Picea Pinsapo	Spanish Fir	40 to 65
Pinus Austriaca	Black Pine	60 to 80
Pinus cembra	Siberian Pine	20 to 30
Pinus excelsa		90 to 100
Pinus Hendersonia		40 to 50
Pinus insignis		40 to 60
Pinus Lambertiana		100 to 200
Pinus macrophylla		30 to 50
Pinus pinaster	Cluster Pine	40 to 60
Pinus pinea	Stone Pine	30 to 60
Pinus ponderosa		50 to 100
Pinus pumilio	Dwarf Pine	10 to 20
Pinus radiata		30 to 50
Pinus Sabiniana		40 to 120
Pinus Strobus	Weymouth Pine	50 to 200
Pinus sylvestris	Scotch Fir	60 to 80
Sequoia sempervirens		– to –
Taxodium distichum	Deciduous Cypress	30 to 70
Taxodium pendulum		20 to 30
Taxusbaccata	Common Yew	20 to 30
Taxusbaccata Canadensis		10 to 20
Thuja filiformis		10 to 15
Thuja occidentalis	American Arbor Vitae	20 to 30
Thuja orientalis	Chinese Arbor Vitae	15 to 25
Thuja Sibirica		20 to 30
Wellingtonia gigantea		200 to 300

It must not be supposed for a moment that the above is an exhaustive list of the various trees that are comprised under each genus. On the contrary, many more will be found under each head in Johnson's *Cottage Gardener's Dictionary* and similar works. It is only sought here to give the names of a few specimens that are possessed of peculiar excellence in one form or another, and, therefore, are especially deserving of notice.

2260 *Distance between Trees* The distance of these trees from each other must be determined by their height, which has been included in the above list for that purpose. For permanent effect, none should be planted nearer to each other than three times their estimated height. This will afford breathing room, and give facilities for seeing them. If the ground can be thrown into rough and uneven ridges, it will show them to most advantage. Nothing can well look worse than the common practice of placing each tree on the top of a little mound, raised on level ground for that purpose. The different classes should be planted in groups, both for the sake of effect and to suit their varying heights; spruces, larches, Scotch firs, junipers, cedars, each having their own compartment in the pinetum. As sometimes the whole of the ground is not moved previous to planting, very large holes will be necessary to secure the well-being of the trees; from 8 to 10 feet in diameter, and from 3 to 4 feet deep, will not be too much for a Wellingtonia. If the soil can be well trenched, mixed, and returned into the hole two or three months before planting, so much the better.

2261 *The Arboretum* The pinetum, as it has been seen, is a piece of ground set apart for the reception of cone-bearing trees and pines, all of which possess a certain degree of similarity. An arboretum is simply an extension of this idea, and in the ground thus called are placed all known hardy trees, and not trees of a single family only. In planting an arboretum, the principles laid down for the pinetum in reference to distance, grouping, etc., will be applicable. The following trees may be planted in the arboretum, either singly or in ornamental groups, at the back of shrubberies, or in parks or pleasure grounds.

EVERGREENS, PARTIALLY OR ENTIRELY

		Height in Feet
Arbutus hybrida		10 to 20
Arbutus laurifolia		8 to 10
Arbutus unedo	Strawberry Tree	10 to 20
Arbutus unedo rubra		10 to 20
Quercus Fulhamensis	Fulham Oak	50 to 100
Quercus ilex	Holly	40 to 60
Quercus ilex latifolia		20 to 50
Quercus ilex variegata		20 to –
Quercus Luccombeana	Luccombe's Oak	30 to 100
Quercus suber	Cork Tree	20 to 30

DECIDUOUS TREES

		Height in feet
Acacia julibrissia	Silk Tree	20 to –
Acer platanoides	Norway Maple	40 to 70
Acer platanoides variegatum		30 to 50
Acer pseudo-platanus	Sycamore	30 to 60
Acer rubrum	Swamp Maple	30 to 50
Aesculus hippocastaneum	Horse Chesnut	30 to 70
Aesculus hippocastaneum flore-pleno		30 to 40

		Height in Feet
Aesculus rubicunda		20 to 30
Ailanthus glandulosa		40 to 60
Alnus cordifolia		15 to 50
Alnus glutinosa	Common Alder	30 to 60
Alnus glutinosa laciniata		30 to 60
Amygdalus communis	Common Almond	10 to 30
Amygdalus communis amara	Bitter Almond	10 to 30
Amygdalus communis dulcis	Sweet Almond	10 to 30
Amygdalus communis flore-pleno		10 to 30
Amygdalus orientalis		8 to 10
Betula alba	Common Birch	40 to 60
Betula excelsa		60 to 70
Betula pendula		30 to 40
Carpinus Americana		15 to 30
Carpinus betulus		30 to 70
Carya alba	Shell Bark Hickory	50 to 70
Carya olivaeformis	Pecan Nut	30 to –
Carya porcina	Pig Nut, or Broom Hickory	70 to 80
Carya tomentosa	Mocker Nut	60 to 70
Castanea vesca	Spanish Chesnut	50 to 70
Castanea asplenifolia		40 to 50
Castanea variegata		40 to 50
Catalpa syringaefolia		20 to 40
Celtis occidentalis	Nettle Tree	30 to 50
Cerasus Padus	Bird Cherry	10 to 30
Cerasus semperfloreus	All Saints' Cherry	10 to 20
Cerasus serrulata	Double Chinese Cherry	15 to –
Corylus avellana	Hazel or Filbert	20 to 30
Corylus avellana grandis	Great Cob Nut	8 to 10
Crataegus apiifolia		8 to 10
Crataegus coccinea		20 to 30
Crataegus Crus-galli	Cockspur Thorn	10 to 30
Crataegus Crus-galli splendens		10 to 30
Crataegus nigra		10 to 20
Crataegus oxyacantha	Common Hawthorn	10 to 20
Crataegus oxyacantha flore-pleno albo		10 to 20
Crataegus oxyacantha praecox	Glastonbury Thorn	10 to 20
Crataegus oxyacantha punicea	Scarlet Thorn	10 to 20
Crataegus oxyacantha rosea		10 to 20
Cytisus albus		6 to 10
Euonymus Europaeus	Spindle Tree	10 to 20
Fagus sylvatica	Common Beech	60 to 100
Fagus sylvatica argenteo variegatis		20 to 40
Fagus sylvatica aureo variegatis		20 to 40
Fagus sylvatica cuprea	Copper Beech	20 to 40
Fagus sylvatica pendula	Weeping Birch	20 to 40
Fagus sylvatica purpurea	Purple Beech	20 to 40
Juglans nigra	Black Walnut	50 to 60
Juglans regia	Common Walnut	40 to 60
Laburnum Alpinum	Scotch Laburnum	15 to 20
Laburnum Vulgare	Common Laburnum	15 to 20

		Height in Feet
Laburnum Vulgare aureum		15 to 20
Laburnum Vulgare Watereri		15 to 20
Liquidambar Styraciflua	Sweet Gum	40 to 60
Liriodendron tulipifera	Tulip Tree	30 to 90
Magnolia acuminata	Cucumber Tree	30 to 60
Magnolia conspicua	Yulan Tree	20 to 50
Magnolia Fraseri		30 to 50
Mespilus Germanica	Common Medlar	15 to 25
and **Dutch**	variety	10 to 15
Nottingham	variety	10 to 15
Stoneless	variety	10 to 15
Morus alba	White Mulberry	20 to 30
Morus nigra	Common Black Mulberry	20 to 30
Negundo aceroides crispum		20 to 30
Negundo aceroides variegatum		20 to 30
Negundo fraxinifolium	Ash-leaved Maple	30 to 40
Ostrya vulgaris	Hop Hornbeam	20 to 30
Pavia rubra		10 to 20
Pavia rubra humilis pendula		5 to 10
Platanus occidentalis	Plane Tree	50 to 70
Platanus orientalis		50 to 70
Populus alba	AbèleTree	30 to 50
Populus balsamifera		40 to 70
Populus fastigiata	Lombardy Poplar	70 to 100
Populus monilifera		60 to 80
Populus tremula	Aspen Tree	40 to 50
Punica granatum	Pomegranate	10 to 20
Pyrus aria	White Beam Tree	30 to 40
Pyrus aucuparia	Mountain Ash	20 to 30
Pyrus aucuparia foliis variegatis		20 to 30
Pyrus communis	Pear (wild)	20 to 30
Pyrus malus	Apple (wild)	20 to 30
Pyrus malus Prunifolia	Siberian Crab	10 to 20
Pyrus sorbus	Service Tree	20 to 30
Pyrus spectabilis	Chinese Apple	18 to 25
Quercus cerris	Bitter or Turkey Oak	40 to 60
Quercus coccinea	Scarlet Oak	40 to 60
Quercus laurifolia		50 to 60
Quercus pedunculata	Common English Oak	50 to 100
Quercus rubra	Champion Oak	50 to 80
Quercus sessiliflora		50 to 80
Robinia hispida	Rose Acacia	12 to 20
Robinia pseudo-acacia	Locust Tree	40 to 60
Robinia pseudo-acacia microphylla		30 to 50
Salix Babylonica	Weeping Willow	20 to 30
Salix fragilis		15 to 20
Sailx Russelliana		30 to 50
Sambucus nigra	Common Elder	15 to 30
Sambucus nigra rotundifolia		20 to 30
Tilia Europaea	Common Lime or Linden	40 to 60
Tilia Europaea rubra		40 to 60

		Height in Feet
Tilia Americana heterophylla		25 to 35
Tilia Americana pubescens		20 to 30
Ulmus campestris	English Elm	60 to 80
Ulmus campestris Cornubiensis	Cornish Elm	60 to 80
Ulmus campestris latifolia		60 to 80
Ulmus montana	Scotch or Wych Elm	30 to 50
Ulmus glabra vegeta		60 to 80

2262 Elms must be introduced sparingly in the arboretum. In the foregoing list the ash is purposely excluded, as its roots run along near the surface, starving every tree in the vicinity, and the top is never sufficiently striking to repay the injury the roots inflict. With the elm the case is different; although a gross feeder, and an indefinite multiplier of greedy roots, its effect in park or pleasure ground scenery is magnificent in the extreme.

2263 Enough has now been said about evergreens and deciduous trees, and it is now necessary to give similar lists of evergreens and deciduous shrubs, merely remarking that as it was impossible to give an exhaustive list of trees, complete in itself and including every variety, so it is equally impracticable to do so in the case of shrubs, and the lists that are given must be regarded as being sufficient and useful representative lists. As many varieties, both of the plain and variegated hollies, should be grown as the space at command will allow. There are about fifty varieties grown in most large nurseries, all beautiful and worthy of cultivation. It is desirable for purchasers, before buying, to ascertain what sorts thrive best in their respective neighbourhoods, and to purchase those sorts only.

EVERGREEN SHRUBS

		Height in Feet
Aucuba Japonica	4 to 8	
Berberis aquifolium	Holly-leaved Barberry	3 to 6
Berberis Darwinii	2 to 4	
Berberis dulcis	4 to 8	
Berberis Japonica	3 to 4	
Berberis Nepalensis	4 to 6	
Berberis Wallichiana	6 to 10	
Buxus sempervirens	Common Box	4 to 8
Buxus sempervirens argentea	4 to 8	
Buxus sempervirens aurea		4 to 8
Buxus sempervirens marginata		4 to 8
Ceanothus azureus		8 to 10
Ceanothus dentatus		4 to 6
Ceanothus Veitchianus		4 to 6
Cerasus Lusitanica	Portugal Laurel	10 to 20
Cerasus laurocerasus	Common Laurel	6 to 10
Cistus Cyprius	Common Gum Cistus	4 to 6
Cistus latifolius		3 to 4
Cistus Lusitanicus		3 to 4
Cistus purpureus		3 to 4
Cotoneaster buxifolia		3 to 5
Cotoneaster rotundifolia		3 to 4
Cotoneaster thymifolia		1 to 1½

		Height in Feet
Crataegus pyracantha	Evergreen Thorn	4 to 10
Daphne cucorum	Garland Flower	1 to 1½
Daphne Indica rubra		3 to 4
Daphne laureola	Sponge Laurel	4 to 6
Daphne Pontica		4 to 5
Helianthemum candidum		3 to –
Hypericum calycinum		1 to 1½
Ilex aquifolium	Common Holly and varieties	10 to 30
Laurus nobilis	Sweet Bay	15 to 25
Laurus nobilis crispa		15 to 20
Laurus nobilis salicifolia		10 to 20
Ligustrum lucidum	Chinese Privet	8 to 12
Ligustrum Japonicum		6 to 8
Ligustrum vulgare cholocarpum		6 to 10
Ligustrum vulgare cholocarpum sempervirens		6 to 10
Mahonia fascicularis		3 to 8
Mahonia Fortunei		3 to 4
Mahonia trifoliata		3 to 5
Phillyrea latifolia		10 to 15
Phillyrea media		10 to 15
Ruscus aculeatus	Butcher's Broom	1 to 2
Ruscus racemosus	Alexandrian Laurel	4 to –
Spartium junceum	Spanish Broom	8 to 10
Tamarix Gallica	French Tamarisk	5 to 10
Ulex Europaea	Common Furze	6 to 8
Ulex Europaea flore-pleno		6 to 8
Viburnum tinus	Laurustinus	8 to 10
Viburnum tinus lucidum		8 to 10
Viburnum tinus lucidum variegatum		8 to 10
Yucca filamentosa		1 to 2
Yucca filamentosa variegata		1 to 2
Yucca gloriosa		3 to 5
Yucca gloriosa fol. variegatis		3 to 5
Yucca gloriosa superba		6 to 10

FIG. 573 *Yucca filamentosa*

DECIDUOUS SHRUBS

		Height in feet
Arabia Japonica		10 to 12
Buddlea globosa		10 to 15
Buddlea Lindleyana		4 to 6
Calycanthus floridus		6 to 8
Calycanthus floridus ovatus		4 to 6
Calycanthus macrophyllus		6 to 10
Ceanothus Americanus		2 to 3
Cnimonanthus fragrans		6 to 10
Cnimonanthus fragrans grandiflorus		6 to 10
Cornus alba		6 to 10
Cornus alba Sibirica		6 to 10
Cornus sanguinea	Common Dogwood	8 to 10
Coronilla emerus	Scorpion Senna	3 to 6
Daphne Mezereum	Mezereum	4 to 4
Daphne Mezereum album		4 to 4
Daphne Mezereum autumnalis		2 to 4
Daphne Mezereum rubrum		2 to 4
Deutzia gracilis		2 to 4
Deutzia corymbosa		4 to 6
Deutzia scabra		4 to 6
Euonymus Europaus		15 to 20
Euonymus Europaus fructu-albo		12 to 15
Euonymus Europaus nanus		2 to 4
Forsythia viridissima		5 to 10
Genista Hispanica		½ to 1
Genista radiata		1 to 3
Genista tinctoria		1 to 2
Hibiscus Syriacus		5 to 8
Hibiscus Syriacus albus-plenus		5 to 8
Hibiscus Syriacus purpureo-plenus		5 to 8
Hibiscus Syriacus ruber		5 to 8
Hibiscus Syriacus variegatus		5 to 8
Hydrangea arborescens		4 to 6
Hydrangea hortensis	Common Hydrangea	2 to 3
Hydrangea Japonica		3 to 4
Hypericum hircinum	St John's Wort and all varieties	2 to 4
Kerria Japonica		3 to 5
Kerria Japonica flore-pleno		4 to 6
Leycesteria formosa		4 to 6
Ligustrum vulgare	Common Privet	8 to 10
Ligustrum augustifolium		6 to 8
Lonicera caerulea	Honey Suckle (Blue-berried)	3 to 5
Lonicera fragrantissima		4 to 6
Lonicera punicea		2 to 4
Lonicera xylosteum	Fly Honeysuckle	4 to 5
Paeonia Moutan	Peony all varieties	3 to 5
Philadelphus coronarius	Syringa	10 to 12
Philadelphus coronarius flore-pleno		8 to 10
Philadelphus coronarius fol. variegatis		8 to 10

		Height in Feet
Philadelphus grandiflorus		8 to 10
Philadelphus latifolius		3 to 5
Potentilla fructicosa		2 to 4
Ribes atro-purpureum		3 to 4
Ribes sanguineum	Red Flowering Currant	4 to 6
Ribes sanguineum atro-rubens		4 to 6
Ribes speciosum and all varieties		4 to 6
Rubus laciniatus	Jag-leaved Bramble	8 to 12
Rubus fructicosus	Common Bramble	8 to 10
Rubus fructicosus flore-roseo pleno		8 to 10
Spiraea ariaefolia		6 to 8
Spiraea corymbosa		2 to 3
Spiraea grandiflora		6 to –
Spiraea salicifolia and all varieties		4 to 6
Syringa Persica	Persian Lilac	4 to 6
Syringa Persica alba		4 to 6
Syringa vulgaris	Common Lilac	8 to 10
Syringa vulgaris alba		8 to 10
Syringa vulgaris alba-plena		8 to 10
also **Syringa alba Charles X** and named varieties		8 to 10
Viburnum dentatum		4 to 6
Viburnum lantana	Wayfaring Tree	8 to 10
Viburnum lantana fol. variegatis		8 to 10
Viburnum opulus	Guelder Rose	8 to 10
Viburnum prunifolium		6 to 10
Weigela rosea		4 to 6

2264 In the following list some choice plants – broadly distinguished as American plants – are named, which will be found useful in the shrubbery, or in any collection of trees and shrubs. They will thrive in any good soil, but will do best in peat earth, or in soil with which peat earth has been plentifully mixed. Rhododendrons, Azaleas, Kalmias, and Daphnes were long supposed to require bog earth for their culture, but they are now found to bloom well in a stiff clay, and such a soil, with a moderate admixture of bog peat and brick and lime rubbish, is admirably adapted for their growth. If in a garden there happen to be a north wall, or wall which faces north and looks towards the house, there is no place more suitable for clumps of American plants. It is well to draw attention to this, even though it is the shrubbery and its tenants that are now under consideration.

CHOICE AMERICAN PLANTS FOR SHRUBBERIES, ETC.

		Height in feet
Andromeda floribunda		1 to 2
Andromeda polifolia	Wild Rosemary	1 to –
Andromeda polifolia grandiflora		1 to 2
Azalea calendulacea		2 to 6
Azalea ledifolia		2 to 6
Azalea Pontica		4 to 6
Azalea procumbens		½ to –
Azalea viscosa		2 to 4
Erica Australia		3 to 6

		Height in Feet
Erica carnea		½ to –
Erica cinerea alba		½ to 1
Erica cinerea rosea		½ to 1
Erica Mackiana		1 to 2
Erica Mediterranea		4 to 6
Erica stricta		2 to 3
Erica tetralix		1½ to 1
Erica vagans	Cornish Heath	1 to –
Gaultheria procumbens	Creeping Winter green	– to –
Gaultheria Shallon		3 to 5
Kalmia augustifolia		2 to 3
Kalmia augustifolia rubra		2 to 3
Kalmia cuneata		2 to –
Kalmia glauca		1 to 2
Kalmia hirsuta		1 to –
Kalmia latifolia		3 to 10
Ledum glandulosum		2 to 6
Ledum latifolium	Labrador Pea	1 to 3
Ledum latifolium Canadense		3 to 6
Ledum latifolium globosum		3 to 6
Ledum palustre		2 to –
Ledum palustre decumbens		2 to –
Rhododendron albi-florum		2 to 3
Rhododendron Catambiense		3 to 5
Rhododendron chamaecistus	Ground Cistus	½ to –
Rhododendron Dauricum		2 to 3
Rhododendron Ponticum		10 to 12
Rhododendron Ponticum odoratum		3 to 4

2265 The plants in the foregoing list all belong to the natural order *Ericaceae*, or Heathworts, and, being thus akin, they require for the most part similar soil and treatment. The soil that is suitable for them has been already mentioned. The Andromedas may be propagated by layers in September; Azaleas by layers in March; Ericas by cuttings consisting of the points of shoots plunged in sand or sandy peat, covered with a bell-glass, and put in a close pit or frame; Gaultherias by layers and seeds; Kalmias by young shoots under hand-lights, by seeds in shallow pans in close frames, or by layers at end of summer; Ledums by layers; and Rhododendrons by seeds in spring sown in shallow pans and kept in close frames, by layers in spring or autumn, or by cuttings of young shoots taken when the base close to the older wood is getting firm, and set in silver sand, placed at first in a close frame, and afterwards subjected to a little bottom heat.

FIG. 574 *Gaultheria procumbens*

2266 It will be remembered that Azaleas, Ericas, and Rhododendrons are frequently spoken of as greenhouse plants used for the decoration of the conservatory. Azaleas are distinguished as Ghent Azaleas and Indian or Chinese Azaleas. The former are seedlings raised from the species named in the above list, and are suited for open-air culture; the latter are varieties raised from the *Azalea Indica*, and are more suitable for forcing and indoor culture. The Ericas are also divided into two classes: the hardy outdoor heaths, natives of Europe, and the Cape Heaths, natives of the Cape of Good Hope, which are greenhouse evergreens. The Rhododendrons are classed as hardy evergreens, propagated and hybridised from *Rhododendron Catawbiense* and *Rhododendron Ponticum*; as half-hardy evergreen shrubs, comprising chiefly plants brought from the south-western slopes of the Himalayas; and as stove evergreens, from Borneo and Sumatra.

No collection of shrubs, and no garden, should be considered complete without an assemblage of hardy heaths. They flower chiefly at the end of summer and during the autumn, and the species *Erica carnea* blooms early in the spring. For beauty of habit, delicacy of tint, sweetness of perfume, usefulness and durability of bloom, they have few rivals. They are also cheap. Good strong bushy plants, of many varieties, can be supplied by most of the leading growers of American plants, at prices ranging from 6d. each upwards, the price for the great majority being 2s. 6d. each. The one great drawback to their culture is, that generally they must have peat-earth to bring them to perfection or maintain them in health, though *Erica carnea*, and several other varieties, do very well in a mixture of loam and leaf-mould. As a rule, however, they all thrive best in a hard, sandy, gritty peat. Bog-peat is hardly fit for their growth, unless it is liberally mixed with sharp sand and the *débris* of freestone rocks. Dryness and hardness of soil seem to be essential to their maintenance in health. No one can have traversed heath-clad mountains without being convinced of this. From 6 inches to a foot of soil is more than most of them find in their natural habitats. It must be borne in mind, however, that in such situations the whole surface is covered with plants; consequently the evaporation of moisture from the soil is checked by the leaves and branches. For their culture in the garden, from 18 inches to 2 feet of such 'soil, resting on a dry bottom, would be desirable. Beds or groups of hardy heaths would make a charming display. Such groups would harmonise well with the different fir trees in or near to the pinetum. Nothing could exceed their beauty, congruity, and adaptability, as furnishings for rockwork. Peat-earth could easily be introduced among the crevices, between stones, etc., and the heaths introduced there. They would thrive admirably in such situations, and contrast well with the ferns and other plants that find a congenial home in such localities.

2267 The named varieties of Rhododendrons are so numerous that full lists of them would occupy some pages of this work. Any one, therefore, who is desirous of forming a collection of these plants, or who requires a supply of Ghent Azaleas, Ericas, Kalmias, and other American plants, is recommended to send for the price list of such large growers as Messrs Richard Smith and Co., Seed Merchants and Nurserymen, *Worcester*, Messrs James Veitch and Sons, Royal Exotic Nursery, 564, King's Road, Chelsea, London, and Mr Charles Noble, Sunningdale Nursery, Bagshot, who pay special attention to the culture of these plants. In these catalogues the names, prices, and colours of the different varieties are duly set forth, with the latest additions, and intending purchasers are thereby enabled to make such a selection as will be satisfactory both as to contrasting tints of blooms and price. It will be as well to add that in purchasing collections of trees, shrubs, and hardy plants, unless the buyer is possessed of sufficient experience to guide him in making his selection, it is desirable to leave the choice of plants to the nurseryman, giving him full particulars as to aspect, site, soil, and the amount which the buyer is willing to expend. Nurserymen invariably behave most generously to their customers on all occasions, and when the selection of plants is left to them the buyer is certain to get the fullest possible value for his money,

The experience of the writer leads him to advise all buyers to send orders for trees, etc., whether fruit trees or ornamental trees, and shrubs, to large growers, especially if they require certain sorts, and desire to get them true to name. Never trust to jobbing gardeners to purchase trees, etc., for you, and beware of nurserymen in a small way, who are often victimised by the men in their employ. The writer, in his time, has trusted to both, and has experienced considerable disappointment, and lost both time and money by doing so. Once upon a time he wanted some very dark roses of the General Jacqueminot type, and some white roses; he left the selection of the former to the nurseryman, and specified white Provence roses for the latter. When they flowered, the bloom in every case was pink. When he gently reproached the employee of the nurseryman for the unexpected result, the said employee, who was supposed to be the nurseryman's right-hand man, confessed that, not having the roses that were wanted, they had been procured elsewhere. And then he went on to say that owing to quarrels between masters and men, the latter frequently took their revenge by mixing the stock, and thus leading the masters unwittingly to disappoint customers, and thus divert their custom to other sellers. By mixing the stock, he probably meant sending out plants that were not those that had been ordered. Whether the allegations of the employee be true or not it is not possible to say. They are, however, borne out to a certain extent by the writer's experience, and he will never again buy trees or anything else but of a nurseryman in a large way of business, on whom he can implicitly depend. *Caveat emptor!* – forewarned is forearmed; and acting on what has been said above, no one need either court or fear disappointment.

2268 In addition to the trees and plants that have been named above, or selections from them, few gardens can be furnished without some climbing or trailing plants to run up trees, scramble over poles and rustic buildings, or to cover walls. The plants that are named in the following list will be found to be well adapted to any of these purposes, being perfectly hardy. To these may be added a whole host of Banksian, Boursault, Ayrshire, and other climbing roses; but attention will be called to these presently, and it is not desirable to waste space by augmenting the list below, when it is intended to mention them in another and a more appropriate place.

CLIMBING AND TRAILING PLANTS FOR WALLS, TREES, BUILDINGS, ETC.

		Height in feet
Ampelopsis hederacea	Virginian Creeper	30 to 50
Ampelopsis bipinnata		10 to 20
Ampelopsis Veitchil		15 to 25
Aristolochia sipho		15 to 30
Aristolochia tomentosa		15 to 20
Bignonia capreolata		12 to 15
Clematis flammula		15 to –
Clematis florida		10 to –

		Height in Feet
Clematis Jackmanni		15 to –
Clematis Jackmanni alba		15 to –
Clematis lanuginosa		8 to 10
Clematis orientalis		8 to 10
Clematis viorna	Leather Flower	10 to 12
Clematis viorna coccinea		5 to 6
Clematis Virginiana	Virginian Clematis	15 to 20
Clematis vitalba	Traveller's Joy, etc	15 to –
Hedera helix	Common Joy	40 to –
Hedera helix Canartiensis	Irish Joy	20 to –
Hedera helix variegata		20 to –
Jasminum nudiflorum	Yellow Jessamine	6 to 18
Jasminum officinale	Common White Jessamine	15 to 20
Jasminum officinale affine		15 to 20
Jasminum pubigerum		10 to –
Jasminum revolutum		10 to –
Lonicera flexuosa	Japanese Honeysuckle	to 5
Lonicera flexuosa aurea reticulata		4 to 5
Lonicera periclymenum	Common Honeysuckle	10 to 15
Lonicera sempervirens	Trumpet Honeysuckle	6 to 10
Passiflora caerulea	Common Passionflower	30 to –
Tecoma radicans		30 to –
Tecoma radicans major		30 to –
Tecoma radicans minor		20 to –
Vitis cordifolia		20 to 30
Vitis vinifera	Common Vine	20 to 30
Vitis vinifera apifolia		15 to 20
Wistaria alba		12 to 20
Wistaria frutescens		10 to –
Wistaria Sinensis		15 to –

It may be well to add that *Clematis Jackmanni* and *Clematis Jackmanni alba*, named in the above list, are varieties produced by cultivation, the one by Mr William Jackman, and the other by Mr Charles Noble, of Bagshot. Of the ivies there are many varieties, distinguished as silver ivies, golden ivies, etc., from the colour of the foliage, which are not named here. In ordering plants of the clematis, ivy, etc., it is desirable to consult the price lists of large growers, as directed above for American plants.

2269 Enough plants have been named in the preceding lists to furnish the largest gardens, and to assist the amateur to a selection of those that he thinks most desirable for his purpose. It is better, however, to plant a considerable number of any one plant that thrives well in the locality, than to grow those, merely for the sake of variety, that do not thrive anywhere and everywhere, as experience has fully shown. Healthy growth of plants, after all, constitutes the chief charm in gardening, and, provided that this be secured, a place furnished with twenty species may be more interesting and beautiful than another that is planted with a thousand.

2270 With reference to the culture of the climbers and trailers mentioned above, the Ampelopsis will grow and thrive in any soil and in any situation, and is propagated by layers and cuttings. The Aristolochia does best in sandy loam, and is propagated by division of the roots, or by layers put down in spring and autumn. The Begonia likes moderately rich soil in a warm or sheltered situation, and is propagated by cuttings of its roots, or shoots, under a hand-glass in spring or autumn. Light loam, or loam mixed with a little peat, suits the hardy forms of Clematis. They are propagated by cuttings of firm side shoots placed under a hand light in summer, or by layers in September. The varieties due to cultivation and hybridisation are usually multiplied by grafting on the common Clematis (*Clematis vitalba*). The Ivies like deep rich soil, but the soil for the tenderer varieties should be fairly light. They may be propagated by layers, or by slips, inserted in a north border in the autumn in sandy soil, which should be kept moist. Good common soil is sufficient for the Jasmines, or Jessamines, which are propagated by means of layers, suckers, or cuttings placed under a hand-light. The Loniceras or honeysuckles are best propagated by layers put down in autumn. They prefer good loamy soil and a shady, sheltered situation. The Passion Flower likes good but somewhat light soil. It requires a little protection by means of matting in severe winters, and may be propagated during the summer by cuttings of young wood in almost any stage, placed in sand under a hand light. Peat and loam suit the Passion Flower, and the Tecoma also, which is propagated by pieces of the roots, or by cuttings of young shoots. The Vitis, or vine, likes a rich, open loam, and is propagated by cuttings and buds of the ripe wood, and by layers. Grafting and inarching are also resorted to for the cultivated sorts. The Wistaria likes sandy loam and peat, and is propagated by layers of long ripened young shoots. Cuttings of strong roots will also serve the purpose, and young shoots getting firm, set in sandy soil and protected by a hand light.

CHAPTER 35

Flower Culture in the Garden and Greenhouse, with Directions for the Special Management of Florists' Flowers, etc., etc.

2271 Broadly speaking, there is not so much difference in the routine to be followed in the culture of different kinds of flowers as may be imagined by those who are unaccustomed to garden work. The preparation of the soil by mechanical means is in all cases the same, and for this ample directions have been already given in the preceding part of this volume. If this were not so, and if every kind of flower that grows required different treatment, it would be necessary for every amateur or grower, in a small way, to confine his attention to two or three special sorts, or to give up gardening altogether, and leave it to those who had time, leisure, money, and space to deal with it in its entirety. Happily, however, this is not the case, for generally plants are grouped into large sections or classes, and the plants that belong to each section will grow together, under the same conditions, subject only to some slight modifications that are produced by artificial means. That is to say, when the soil has been well prepared for the reception of plants by digging, trenching, draining, when and where necessary, all that can be done is to modify it for the plants which are to be grown in it by the addition of manures, natural and artificial, sand, lime, etc., and thus bring it as nearly as possible to the conditions under which plants grow and flourish in their native habitats, or under which experience has shown that they thrive and flourish in the greatest luxuriance.

2272 If, then, we regard the culture of flowers from this point of view, namely, that as regards the management of each great class the system to be pursued is the same for all, and that it is only in some special cases that any departure from the general routine is necessary, it is manifest that our labours will be greatly simplified, and that we shall be better able to turn them to good account when we find and feel that we have to deal with plants broadly and in masses, special treatment being reserved for a few individual sorts only. A few moments' consideration will help us to see how easy it is to arrive at the culture of plants in classes, by looking at their nature and terms of existence. First of all, flowering plants grown in gardens – no reference is now being made to shrubs, which have been dealt with in the preceding chapter – are (1) Annuals, (2) Biennials, and (3) Perennials. To one or other of these three great classes every plant must belong.

2273 We must look, then, at the culture of plants, first of all, with reference to their character and as belonging to the class to which each belongs. We know that some plants are possessed of greater powers of endurance and vitality than others, and thus it is that Annuals are regarded as being ranked in two divisions, *Hardy* and *Half-hardy*; Biennials admitting of the same separation. Passing on to Perennials, we know that there are two sorts, namely, those which are visible above ground, even during the hardest winter, and which do not die down to the ground it autumn and throw up fresh flower stalks in the spring, and those which die down after flowering, to grow again when the time of rest is over, and Nature calls on them once more to exhibit their foliage and flowers. Perennials of the first class partake of the nature of shrubs, but those of the second are known as *Herbaceous Plants*. It is only with the culture of a few of the former that we are particularly concerned, and the latter must be dealt with *en masse* under the special title which belongs to them as a class, namely *Herbaceous Plants*, and under the heading *Bulbs* or *Bulbous Plants*, a name which is applied to them from the peculiar form, not exactly of the roots, but of that portion of the plant which never perishes as long as the plant lives, and which sends out roots below, and leaves and flowers above, in every year at the proper season.

2274 This done, all that remains is to glance at the culture of bedding plants, and the special means adopted for the cultivation of what are generally known as florists' flowers, among which stand conspicuous the Anemone, the Auricula, the Chrysanthemum, the Dahlia, the Hollyhock, the Hyacinth, the Pansy, the Ranunculus, the Rose, the Tulip, and the Violet. The general culture of flowers in the greenhouse must then be looked into, and with this the special treatment of well-known greenhouse plants, such as the Azalea, the Camellia, Cape Heaths, and the Pelargonium.

2275 Although it is desirable in the extreme to give lists of plants as an assistance to the reader, it will be useless to absorb space in setting forth long catalogues of the varieties of any single flower, for more reasons than one. In the first place, new varieties of florists' flowers are brought out every year in greater or less numbers, and are eagerly sought after for a time, to find themselves eclipsed, as years pass on, by new floral gems and stars of a similar character which have been brought into being and under the notice of the public; and in the second place, it is difficult to select a few varieties of each plant with the hope of satisfying every purchaser and grower, for what may suit some will not suit others. Again, when it is said that the known varieties of roses amount to upwards of 2000, and that the varieties of the pansy are numbered by hundreds, it will be seen at once how utterly impossible it is to give complete lists, and how vain and hopeless it would be to attempt to make selections, seeing how tastes differ, and that many a variety that may have been heartily welcomed at its introduction is, so to speak, here today and gone tomorrow.

2276 How, then, it may be asked, are persons to arrive at a knowledge of current sorts when they wish to make purchases and stock their gardens? The answer is simple and easy. Send to any large grower for his catalogue and price list, which is generally sent out twice a year, in spring and autumn, and from the flowers and varieties of flowers that are named therein make such a selection as may be in consonance with your own tastes and wishes.

In no trade, perhaps, are price lists so large and replete with information as in the gardening trade; and growers and nurserymen, although they must expend a very large sum of money yearly in preparing, illustrating, and printing their catalogues, are always ready to send them to any applicant free of cost. Some, it is true, make a charge for their price lists, but in no case does the sum required exceed a shilling, and if purchases to a certain amount are made, the cost of the catalogue is invariably allowed for. Moreover, the information and cultural directions, general and special, that are contained in some catalogues is worth infinitely more than the sums that are charged for them. Indeed, some of them form in themselves a complete guide to gardening.

2277 *Annuals: their Culture and Management* For hardy annuals, and indeed for annuals generally, any ordinary garden soil is good enough, and indeed better than rich soil, for this tends to produce luxuriance of growth, which is incompatible with the production of flowers. Very hardy annuals may be sown in autumn, not earlier than the last week in August, and not later, even in sheltered spots, than the last week in September. Autumn-sown plants, if they survive the winter, will bloom early in spring. Plants of a very hardy nature are indicated thus (*) in the following list of hardy annuals. The situation best suited for autumn sowing is one that is sheltered from strong and cutting winds, but free from shade, and well exposed to the sun. Spring sowings for blooming in summer may be made at any time from the middle of March to the middle of April, due regard being had to situation, and later sowings for flowering in autumn should be made from the middle of May to the middle of June.

2278 *Raising Annuals for Transplanting* When it is desired to raise annuals for transplanting, they may be sown in beds in the reserve garden or elsewhere, and removed, when about half grown, to the positions in which they are intended to flower. The transplanting of annuals, unless very carefully done, is always attended with some danger; but this may be obviated if they are raised in pots, from which they can be turned out without disturbing the roots, or sown on pieces of turf turned grass downwards, the seeds being covered with a thin coating of mould after they have been sprinkled on the turf. Hardy annuals sown in spring, and some kinds sown in autumn, need no protection from the weather.

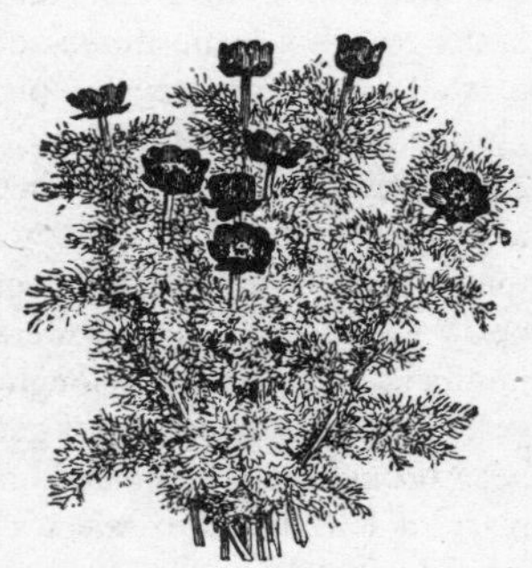

FIG. 575 *Flos Adonis (Hardy annual)*

2279 *Treatment of Half-hardy Annuals* Sow the seeds in March or April, in pots or pans, and shelter them in a pit, or plunge the pots in moderate bottom heat, such as a hotbed that is cooling. The temperature should not rise above 75° by day, or fall below 55° at night. Shade the seedlings from strong sun, give plenty of air when the weather is favourable, and thin out if too close together in the pots. Harden off gradually, and remove to flowering quarters about the middle of May, but delay the removal to the end of the month if the weather be cold and unfavourable.

2280 *General Routine Culture* Before sowing seed, slightly tread or beat the ground, to impart some degree of solidity to it, and prevent it from sinking; rake the surface and sow the seed, sprinkling it evenly over the space to be covered, and complete the operation by scattering or sifting some fine mould over the seed, regulating the depth according to the thickness of the seed, the general rule being that the depth of mould over the seed should in every case be no greater than its own depth or thickness. After the young plants are of a sufficient size, thinning must be resorted to in order to prevent them from being drawn into straggling growth by remaining in too thick masses. Annuals that require support, such as sweet peas, etc., must have sticks placed among or around them, and climbers, such as tropaeolums, convolvulus major, etc., must be supported and trained. In very dry weather a little watering may be found necessary, and withering or withered flowers should be removed, unless it is desired to save seed, in order to induce fresh blooms and to prolong the time of flowering.

2281 The following is a list of hardy annuals, the most hardy having a star attached to them. The ordinary or familiar garden name is given when it can be, with the height in inches, and the colour of the flowers, or colours, when the blooms are not restricted to one tint only, but are of various hues. Strictly speaking, all flowers mentioned in the lists to follow are not annuals in the countries from which they have been first obtained, but they will not survive the inclemency of the British winter, and are, to all intents and purposes, annuals when grown in the open air in this country.

Agrostemma caeli-rosea, 12, rose colour.
Alyssum calycinum (*Sweet Alyssum*), 6, white.
Alyssum maritimum, 8, white.
Amaranthus caudatus (*Love-lies-Bleeding*), 30, crimson.
Amaranthus hypochondriacus (*Prince's Feather*), 30, crimson.
Argemone grandiflora, 30, yellow.
Bartonia aurea,* 15, bright yellow.
Calandrinia grandiflora, 12, rosy violet.
Calandrinia speciosa, 6, violet crimson.
Calandrinia umbellata, 6, rich crimson.
Calliopsis Drummondi, 15, yellow and brown.
Calliopsis tinctoria, 24, yellow with brown eye.
Campanula Attica, 6, blue, with white centre.
Campanula Lorei, 12, blue, white.
Campanula speculum (*Venus's Looking Glass*), 8, blue, white.
Centranthus macrosiphon, 15, red, pale rose, white.
Clarkia elegans, 18, crimson, rose, white.
Clarkia pulchella,* 18, various colours.
Chrysanthemum coronarium, 24, yellow, white.
Chrysanthemum tricolor, 24, variegated.
Cochlearia acaulis, 3, pale lilac.
Collinsia bicolor,* 9, purple and white.
Collinsia grandiflora, 9, lilac and blue.
Collinsia tricolor, 9, purple, lilac, and white.
Collomia coccinea, 12, bright scarlet.
Convolvulus minor, 12, blue, white, and yellow.
Delphinium Ajacis* (*Rocket Larkspur*) 18, various.
Dianthus Sinensis (*Indian Pink*), 12, various.
Erysimum Peroffskianum,* 18, orange.

Escholtzia crocea,* 12, deep chrome yellow.
Eucharidium concinnum, 12, dark red.
Eucharidium grandiflorum, 12, rosy purple.
Eutoca viscida,* 12, blue with white eye.
Flos Adonis,* 9, blood red. (See Fig. 575.)
Gilia liniflora, 12, white.
Gilia tricolor, 12, purple, white, and yellow.
Godetia,* many varieties, 18, rosy crimson, white, etc.
Hibiscus Africanus, 18, pale yellow, with crimson centre.
Iberis amara (*Candytuft*), 9, white.
Iberis umbellata (*Candytuft*), 12, purple.
Lathyrus odoratus (*Sweet Pea*), 50, various colours.
Leptosiphon androsaceus, 9, rose, white, yellow.
Leptosiphon aureus, 9, rich yellow.
Leptosiphon densiflorus, 12, pale purple, white.
Limnanthes alba, 6, white.
Limnanthes Douglasii, 8, yellow and white.
Linum flavum (*Yellow Flax*), 10, yellow.
Linum grandiflorum rubrum, 12, rich crimson.
Lupinus Hartwegii, 24, blue and white, white.
Lupinus nanus, 9, deep blue, white. There are many varieties of the hardy Lupine.
Malcomia bicolor, 6, lilac and white.
Malcomia maritima (*Virginian Stock*), 6, lilac, red.
Malope grandiflora (*Mallow*), 24, dark crimson.
Monolopia Californica, 6, deep yellow.
Nemophila discoidalis, 9, maroon and white.
Nemophila insignis,* 6, sky blue and white. There are other varieties of this plant, variously coloured.
Nemophila maculata, 6, white, blotched with purple.
Oenothera bistorta Veitchiana, 6, lemon yellow.
Oenothera rosea, 9, purplish rose.
Omphalodes linifolium, 12, white.
Reseda odorata (*Mignonette*), 9. Flowers small and insignificant, but remarkable for fragrance.
Portulaca grandiflora, 3, various colours.
Salpiglossis coccinea, 36, various colours.
Saponaria Calabrica, 9, pink.
Schizanthus Grahami, 18, red or orange, streaked with purple.
Schizanthus pinnatus, 15, purple and white.
Schizanthus ortusus, 18, red and yellow.
Schizopetalon Walkeri, 12, white, almond scented.
Schortia Californica, 9, yellow with darker centre.
Silene pendula, 12, rosy pink.
Sphenogyne speciosa, 15, yellow, with purple centre.
Tagetes signata pumila, 9, orange yellow, spotted brown.
Tropaeolum majus (*Common Nasturtium*), 72, many colours, from straw colour to the deepest brown.
Viscaria caeli-rosea, 12, bright rose.
Viscaria oculata, 12, pink, with purple centre.

2282 The best of the half-hardy annuals, which require to be raised either in gentle heat or under protection of some kind, and which should be transplanted to their blooming quarters when the weather permits, are included in the following list:

Abronia umbellata, 6, rosy lilac.
Ageratum Mexicanum, 9, lavender blue.
Alonsoa Warscewiczii, 18, bright scarlet.
Anagallis grandiflora, 6, blue, scarlet.
Aster Sinensis (*China Aster*), 15, blue, red, white. Many varieties variously distinguished.
Balsamina impatiens (*Balsam*), 18, various colours.
Brachycome iberidifolia, 10, lavender, white.
Clianthus Dampierii, climber, scarlet and black.
Clianthus puniceus (*Glory Pea*), climber; scarlet.
Clintonia pulchella, 4, blue, with yellowish eye.
Cobaea scandens, climber sending out shoots 20 to 30 feet long; purplish bell-shaped flowers.
Datura ceratocaulon, 24, white, tinged with rose.
Datura humilis flore pleno, 18, golden yellow.
Datura Wrightii, 24, white, edged with lilac.
Gaillardia picta, 15, rich claret, gold edge.
Helichrysum bracteatum, 30, golden yellow.
Helichrysum macranthum (*Everlasting Flower*), 21, various, but all partaking of a reddish tint.
Ipomaea coccinea, 70, scarlet, yellow.
Ipomaea purpurea (*Convolvolus Major*), 70, various, white, rose, purple, striped.
Lobelia erinus, 6, light blue. Other varieties are *L. e. speciosa*, blue, with white eye, and *L. e. alba*, white.
Lobelia ramosa, 12, deep blue.
Lophospermum scandens, 72, rosy purple.
Mathiola annua (*Ten-Week Stock*), 15, various.
Mathiola Graeca (*Intermediate Stock*), 15, various.
Mesembryanthemum tricolor, 4, rose and white.
Oxalis rosea, 6, bright pink, greenish at base.
Oxalis tropaeoloides, 8, golden yellow, with foliage of a dark brownish purple.
Oxalis Valdiviana, 8, dark yellow.
Phlox Drummondi, 15, various colours; pure white, pink, buff, purple, and crimson.
Rhodanthe Manglesii, 12, rose, with yellow centre. All the Rhodanthes are everlasting flowers.
Salpiglossis coccinea, 36. Flowers funnel-shaped, with ground of whitish yellow, brown, pink, scarlet, or crimson, marked with blue, yellow, or brown.
Senecio elegans, 12, crimson, pink, white.
Tagetes erecta nana (*Dwarf African Marigold*), 9, deep yellow.
Tagetes patula (*French Marigold*), 12, brown and yellow.
Tropaeolum Canariense, 10, canary yellow.
Zinnia elegans, 24, scarlet, with dark purple disc.

2283 *Biennials: their Management, etc.* The difference between annuals and biennials consists in their nature and habit only. The former grows flowers, yields seeds for its reproduction, and dies in the same year; biennials, on the contrary, are sown and grow in the first year of their existence, but do not come to maturity until the second, when they flower, produce seed, and die. It is but few, if any, annuals that can be propagated by cuttings; but biennials, as, for example, the Sweet William, may be preserved, and the possession of any well-marked variety maintained, by pulling down layers and taking off shoots from the base of the plant. Although this and other plants of the same kind, strictly speaking, are biennials, yet, from their capability of reproduction in the manner stated, they are often reckoned among hardy herbaceous plants, and thus it will be most convenient to consider them. Of their culture and management, it is sufficient to say that they are treated in precisely the same manner as annuals. They may be sown, however, at a later period of the year, though not later than the middle or end of September, for plants sown at this time will bloom the following year as freely as those that have been sown at an earlier date. They should be raised in the reserve garden, and planted out in their blooming quarters in the spring.

2284 The following is a brief list of biennials, desirable for the garden and borders. Those that are more hardy than the generality of biennials, and need no protection, are distinguished by a star. Those that are not so marked, should be protected in cold pits or frames during the winter, and not planted out until all fear of injury from frost has passed. Stocks should be placed in a sheltered border during the winter, and kept there at least until April, when they may be removed to their blooming quarters. It is desirable to winter some stocks in a cold frame in pots, lest the winter prove too inclement for them and they be carried off by frost.

Campanula medium* (*Canterbury Bell*), 24, blue-violet, white.
Campanula pyramidalis,* 36, pale blue.
Dianthus barbatus* (*Sweet William*), 15, various.
Digitalis purpurea* (*Foxglove*), 36, white, purple, both marked with spots. Many varieties.
Hedysarum coronarium* (*French Honeysuckle*), 24, purplish red.
Humea elegans, 60, profuse panicles of red colour.
Ipomopsis elegans, 36, orange, bright red.
Lunaria biennis* (*Honesty*), 18, violet-purple. Seed pods used as everlasting flowers.
Lychnis coronaria,* 18, rosy purple. Double variety propagated by division after flowering.
Mathiola incana (*Giant or Brompton Stock*), 24, red, purple, violet, brown, and white.
Oenothera Lamarkiana, 40, yellow.
Oenothera taraxacifolia, 12, trailer, white, tinted rose, and sweet-scented.
Scabrosa dichotoma,* 18, velvety purple.
Silene compacta, 18, rose.
Trachelium caeruleum, 18. Plant suitable for rockwork, yielding small blue flowers.

2285 *Herbaceous Perennials: their Culture, etc.* Any ordinary garden soil is suitable for herbaceous perennials; but soil that is light and easily worked, and is moderately rich in humus, is more suitable for these plants, taken generally, than heavy, lumpy soil, although many will grow even in this. At all events, it may be said that this class of plants, with hardy bulbs, is best suited for gardeners who are possessed of but little experience, and who, for lack of time or other reasons, cannot pay so much attention to horticulture as they might otherwise wish. Some plants of this class are propagated by division of the roots, made in February or March, just as they are showing indications of making fresh growth. Others may be propagated by means of layers or cuttings, or raised from seed. Herbaceous plants are improved, and will be more healthy and sightly, and flower better, if they are taken up every three or four years, divided or reduced in size if needful, and then separated after digging the ground somewhat deeply, turning it over and breaking it up thoroughly. Plant firmly, pressing the earth well round the collar of each plant. The borders in which herbaceous plants are set should be kept clean and free from weeds. The plants themselves should be watered occasionally, if the situation and summer draughts are such as to render it necessary; those requiring support from sticks should be carefully staked, and when the flower stalks and flowers begin to wither, they should be removed. This comprehends everything that is necessary in the treatment of herbaceous plants.

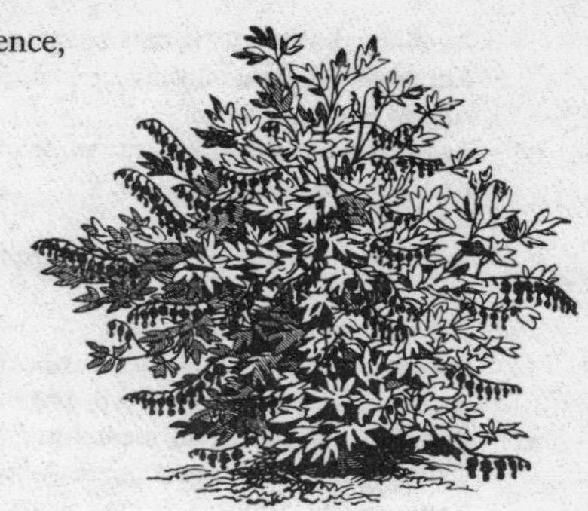

FIG. 576 *Dielytra spectabilis (Hardy herbaceous perennial)*

2286 The following is a list of herbaceous perennials, treated in the same manner as the foregoing lists, and showing, when possible, the familiar garden name, the height and colour of the flowers:

Acanthus latifolius, 48, lilac
Acanthus mollis, 48, lilac.
Adenophora liliflora, 12, blue.
Adonis vernalis, 9, yellow.
Alstroemeria aurea, golden orange. Other varieties of different colours. Plant deep in light soil.
Alyssum saxatile, 6, yellow.
Anemone Apennina, 6, blue, early bloomer.
Anemone coronaria (*Garden Anemone*), 9, various.
Anemone fulgens, 12, brilliant scarlet. Likes calcareous soil.
Anemone hortensis, 9, various.
Anemone Japonica, 24, pure white, red, rose.
Anemone narcissiflora, 12, yellow, white.
Anemone pavonia, 12, crimson, scarlet.
Anemone Pennsylvanica, 12, white.
Anthericum liliastrum, 12, white.
Antirrhinum majus (*Snapdragon*), 24, various.
Aquilegia caerulea, 18, pale blue and white.
Aquilegia chrysantha, 24, yellow.
Aquilegia glandulosa, 18, blue and white.

Aquilegia Skinneri, 18, dark scarlet and yellow.
Aquilegia vulgaris (*Columbine*), 24, various.
Arabis albida, 6, white.
Asclepias tuberosa, 24, orange, scarlet. Likes peat.
Asphodelus luteus, 36, yellow.
Aster Alpinus, 12, lilac blue.
Aster amelloides (*Michaelmas Daisy*), 24, purple.
Aubrietia deltoides, 4, purple.
Aubrietia Graeca, 4, rosy lilac
Baptisia Australis, 30, blue, shy bloomer.
Bellis perennis (*Daisy*), 6, red, white, variegated.
Bocconia Japonica, 60, cream colour.
Calystegia pubescens (Double *Convolvulus*), 60, climber, rose.
Campanula Carpatica, 6, blue, white.
Campanula latifolia, 50, deep slaty blue.
Campanula nobilis, 18, purple, white.
Campanula pumila, 6, greyish blue, white.
Campanula pyramidalis, 45, pale blue, white.
Campanula turbinata, 6, pale blue.
Catananche caerulea, 36, blue.
Centaurea montana, 18, blue.
Cerastium tomentosum, 6, white. Valuable for foliage.
Cheiranthus Cheiri (*Wallflower*), 24, various.
Cistus helianthemum, 9, various colours.
Clematis integrifolia, 36, blue.
Clematis montana, 60, climber, white in clusters.
Clematis recta, 24, white.
Convallaria majalis (*Lily of the Valley*), 9, white.
Convolvulus Mauritanicus, trailer, light blue.
Corydalis bulbosa, 9, purple, rose.
Corydalis nobilis, 12, pale yellow.
Cucumis perennis, large climber, suitable for arbours.
Delphinium cardinale, 24, bright scarlet.
Delphinium Cashmerianum, 15, blue and mauve.
Delphinium formosum, 40, brilliant intense blue.
Delphinium hybridum flore-pleno, 24, various colours.
Delphinium nudicaule, 18, scarlet. Useful for pot culture.
Dianthus caryophyllus (*Carnation*, etc.), 18, various.
Dianthus dentosus, 9, various colours.
Dianthus plumarius (*Pink*), 9, various.
Dianthus superbus, 18, bright lilac.
Dictamnus fraxinella, 30, red, in strong spikes.
Dielytra spectabilis, 21, pink, white. (See Fig. 576).
Dodocatheon Meadia, 12, purple spotted with yellow, white. Like shade and peaty soil.
Epimedium macranthum, 8, white.
Epimedium pinnatum, 10, yellow.
Epimedium purpureum, 8, purple and yellow.
Eremurus spectabilis, 24, yellow.
Erigeron speciosum, 24, lilac blue, yellow centre.
Erinus Alpinus, 6, brilliant violet red.
Eritrichum nanum, 1, sky blue. Suitable for rock work.

Eryngium Alpinum, 24, blue.
Erythronium dens canis (*Dog's-tooth Violet*), 6, rosy purple, deep lilac, white, rose.
Erythronium dens canis Americanum, 6, white, with purple spot.
Erythronium dens canis grandiflorum, 6, yellow.
Ferula communis (*CommonFennel*), 70, yellow. Remarkable for beauty of foliage, and useful for culinary purposes.
Funkia alba, 24, white. Handsome foliage.
Funkia Japonica, 18, greyish white.
Funkia lancifolia, 24, bluish white.
Funkia ovata, 18, blue, dark glossy green leaves.
Gaultheria procumbens, 6, white with cherry-like berries.
Gaura Lindheimeria, 24, rosy white.
Gentiana acaulis, 4, intense blue.
Gentiana lutea, 48, yellow.
Gentiana verna, 4, rich brilliant blue.
Geranium Lancastriense, 3, rose, with darker stripes.
Geranium tuberosum, 15, mauve.
Geum coccineum, 18, bright scarlet.
Gypsophila paniculata, 30, white, beautiful foliage.
Harpalium rigidum, 36, yellow, black centre.
Helleborus niger (*Christmas Rose*), 12, white and various.
Hemerocallis flava (*Day Lily*), 24, soft yellow.
Hepatica triloba, 6, blue, red, white.
Hesperis matronalis, 24, purple, white.
Hieracium aurantiacum, 18, orange.
Hoteia Japonica (*Spirea*), 24, white, pink.
Iberis sempervirens (*Candytuft*), 9, white.
Iris foetidissima (*Stinking Gladwyn*), 30, bluish lilac. Remarkable for seed pods. Likes moist situation.
Iris Germanica (*Blue Flag*), 24, blue and various colours.
Iris graminea, 11, dark violet blue.
Iris Kaempferi (*Japanese Iris*), 18, various colours.
Iris pumila, 10, various colours.
Iris Sibirica, 24, white, with blue veins.
Iris Susiana, 24, greyish white veined with purple.
Lathyrus grandifolius, 45, rosy red.
Lathyrus latifolius (*Everlasting Pea*), 96, red, white.
Lewisia rediviva, 6, pink. Requires sun and dry situation.
Liatris pychnostachya, 3, purple, magenta.
Linum flavum, 10, yellow. Likes sun and dry situation.
Lobelia fulgens, 30, spikes of intense scarlet.
Lupinus polyphyllus, 36, blue, white.
Lychnis Alpina, 6, rose colour.
Lychnis Chalcedonica, 24, scarlet, white.
Lychnis fulgens, 18, scarlet.
Lychnis grandiflora, 12, bright red. Delicate in habit.
Lychnis viscaria flore pleno, 12, purple.
Lysimachia nummularia (*Creeping Jenny or Moneywort*), trailer, brilliant yellow.
Lysimachia verticillata, 12, yellow.
Lythrum roseum, 36, rose colour.
Lythrum salicaria (*Purple Loosestrife*), 36, purple.

Mimulus cardinalis, 24, scarlet.
Mimulus moschatus (*Musk*), 6, yellow.
Morina longifolia, 24, purplish scarlet.
Myosotis alpestris, 3, blue, with yellowish eye.
Myosotis dissitiflora, 9, deep sky blue.
Myosotis palustris, 9, blue, with yellow throat.
Nierembergia gracilis, 6, white, veined with lilac.
Oenothera acaulis, 6, white.
Oenothera Fraseri, 18, yellow.
Oenothera macrocarpa, 12, pale yellow.
Omphalodes verna, 6, blue.
Opuntia Rafinesquiana, 12, yellow, with handsome fruit. A Cactus hardy on dry rock-work.
Orobus vernus, 12, purple.
Paeonia officinalis, 24, crimson, scarlet, pink, white.
Paeonia tenuifolia, 18, deep crimson.
Papaver bracteatum, 48, brilliant scarlet, black spot at base of petal.
Pardanthus Chinensis, 12, orange. Likes shelter.
Pentstemon barbata coccinea, 36, rich scarlet.
Pentstemon Jaffrayanus, 18, blue, with purple stamens.
Phlox decussata hybrida, 30, various colours.
Phlox setacea, 4, pale pink, spotted with purple.
Phlox subulata, 4, pink, darker in centre.
Phlox verna, 6, pucy red.
Phytolacca decandra, 100, white changing to pink.
Platycodon grandiflorum, 30, blue.
Polemonium caeruleum, 24, blue, white.
Polygonatum vulgare (*Solomon's Seal*), 24, white, tipped with green.
Polygonum Sieboldi, 50, white, with large foliage.
Potentilla hybrida, 18, purple, red, yellow, and various colours.
Primula acaulis (*Common Primrose*), 6, yellow, and various colours. Double varieties, white, lilac, crimson, purple.
Primula cortusoides amoena, 1, purple. Better for rockwork or pot culture than for the open border.
Primula elatior (*Polyanthus*), various.
Primula Japonica, 15, purple, crimson, lilac, white.
Pulmonaria Sibirica, 36, blue.
Pulmonaria virginica, 18, blue.
Ramondia Pyrenaica, 6, violet, purple, orange centre.
Ranunculus aconitifolius, 12, pure white and double.
Ranunculus acris, 24, golden yellow, and double.
Ranunculus Asiaticus (*Persian Ranunculus*), 12, various.
Sanguinaria Canadensis, 6, white, with orange stamens.
Saxifraga cotelydon, 18, white, in pyramidal spike.
Saxifraga crassifolia, 9, dark pink.
Saxifraga umbrosa (*London Pride*), 9, white, dotted with pink and yellow.
Scabiosa caucasica, 24, pale blue.
Schizostylis coccinea, 18, scarlet.
Sedum fabarium, 12, pink, in large bunches.
Silene Schafta, 9, rosy purple.
Soldanella Alpina, 3, dark bluish, purple.
Spigelia Marylandica, 12, red, with yellow interior.

Spiraea aruncus (*Goat's Beard*), 60, white, chiefly desirable for its fernlike foliage.
Spiraea filipendula flore pleno, 18, white.
Spiraea palmata, 24, crimson, white.
Statice incana, 18, pink or mauve.
Statice sinuata, 24, blue, in spherical bunches.
Thalictrum aquilegifolium, 36, white.
Thalictrum glaucum, 60, yellow.
Thalictrum purpurescens, 36, yellow.
Thladiante dubia, quick-growing ornamental climber, with bell-shaped yellow flowers.
Tricyrtis hirta, 30, white, spotted with purple.
Trillium grandiflorum, 12, pure white.
Tritoma pumila, 12, orange.
Tritoma uvaria (*Red-hot Poker Plant*), 36, spike bright red at top, orange below.
Trollius Asiaticus, 12, orange.
Trollius Europaeus, 12, golden yellow.
Tussilago fragrans, 12, white.
Valeriana rubra, 18, red.
Veratrum nigrum, 48, white, on straight stem.
Verbascum Phoeniceum, 48, yellow, in spikes.
Vinca major (*Periwinkle*), 18, trailer, bluish lilac.
Viola cornuta, 3, various tints of blue.
Viola odorata (*Common Violet*), 3, various colours.
Zauschneria Californica, 12, scarlet.

2287 *Plants Suitable for Rockwork* All the smaller plants named in the preceding lists, and many of the larger ones, are suitable for rockwork; but at the risk of repetition it will be useful to append another list exhibiting in a collected form the names of most of the plants that are suitable for this purpose, shortening it by omitting heights, colours of flowers, etc.

Achillea tomentosa
Alchemilla Alpina
Alyssum saxatile
Anemone Apennina
Anemone Japonica
Antirrhinum majus
Aquilegia Alpina
Aquilegia Canadensis
Arabis albida
Arabis Alpina
Arenaria Balearica
Asperula odorata
Aster Alpinus
Aster Alpinus albus
Aubrietia deltoidea
Aubrietia Graeca
Brachycome iberidifolia
Calandrinia umbellata
Campanula Alpina
Campanula Carpatica
Campanula fragilis
Campanula muralis
Campanula pumila
Campanula turbinata
Cerastium tomentosum
Cheiranthus Cheiri
Convallaria majalis
Cortusa Matthioli
Corydalis lutea
Corydalis nobilis
Crucianella stylosa
Dianthus barbatus
Dianthus dentosus
Dianthus plumarius
Dianthus superbus
Draba azoides
Epimedium diphyllum
Epimedium macranthum
Epimedium pinnatum
Epimedium purpureum
Eranthis hyemalis
Erinus Alpinus
Eritrichium nanum
Fritillaria meleagris
Fritillaria Persica
Fritillaria pudica
Fritillaria recurva
Gentiana acaulis
Gentiana verna
Gypsophila paniculata
Gypsophila prostrata
Iberis Gibraltarica
Iberis sempervirens
Iris lutescens
Iris pumila
Limnanthes Douglasii
Linaria triornithophora
Linnea borealis
Linum flavum
Lychnis Alpina

Lysimachia nummularia
Mimulus moschatus
Oenothera bistorta Veitchiana
Oenothera macrocarpa
Oenothera rosea
Oenothera taraxacifolia
Omphalodes verna
Onosma Tauricum
Phlox divaricata
Phlox nivalis
Phlox procumbens
Phlox reptans
Phlox stolonifera
Phlox subulata
Phlox setacea
Phlox verna
Polemonium reptans
Potentilla insignis
Potentilla rupestris
Ramondia Pyrenaica
Rhodiola rosea
Rubus saxatilis
Sanguinaria Canadensis
Saponaria ocymoides
Saxifraga caespitosa
Saxifraga crassifolia
Saxifraga hirsuta
Saxifraga oppositifolia
Saxifraga rotundifolia
Saxifraga sarmentosa
Saxifraga umbrosa
Sedum aizoon
Sedum glaucum
Sedum rupestre
Sedum Sieboldi
Sempervivum arachnoideum
Sempervivum globiferum
Sempervivum tectorum
Soldanella Alpina
Soldanella montana
Spigelia Marylandica
Statice incana
Stipa pennata
Trollius Europaeus
Veronica gentianoides
Veronica repens
Veronica saxatilis
Vinca herbacea
Vinca major
Viola lutea
Viola odorata
Zauchneria Californica

2288 *Aquatic Plants: their Culture, etc.* Vegetation of an interesting character will always be found in the neighbourhood of water, and advantage should be taken of all facilities that offer themselves for the culture of aquatic plants. There are, however, many plants which are to be preferred to others in undertaking the culture of aquatic plants in a piece of water, whether large or small, or the margin of a stream. Flowers for water are of two kinds – plants to be placed in the water itself, usually called aquatic plants, and marsh plants to be planted on the banks. Aquatic plants are propagated, some by seed and some by division of the roots. The seeds when sown must be placed under water: in other respects aquatic plants require the same general treatment as other herbaceous plants.

FIG. 577 *Nymphaea alba white water lily (Aquatic plant)*

2289 To those who may be desirous of ornamenting any piece of ornamental water, the following lists will be found invaluable. The situation best adapted for hardy aquatics will be found to be in accordance with their height. Many that are not hardy may be introduced for summer decoration in pots sunk either wholly or half deep in water. These can be removed in winter to warm-water tanks under cover of glass. Every year something new in aquatics is being introduced, for the water plants of the tropics are inexhaustible, and very many of them supremely beautiful. Most of the plants which have been mentioned in the above lists prefer a shady and sheltered situation, and will be found to flourish best when protected by overhanging trees. Rock-work and root-work form admirable receptacles for plants on the margins of streams, and afford all the protection they require when properly arranged. It may be said that aquatic plants out-of-doors flower from May to August. Those that require protection in winter, and that on this account are grown in pots, which are plunged in water, will flower earlier: thus the Arum lily, *Calla Aethiopica*, will flower from Christmas to Easter, within doors. Aquatic plants requiring protection in winter are marked with a star. These plants, whose height is not given, have leaves and flowers floating on the surface of the water.

2290 The following list comprises all the aquatic plants that are most deserving of notice and culture:

Acorus calamus (*Sweet Flag*), 36, yellow.
Alisma plantago (*Water Plantain*), 24, rosy white.
Aponogeton distachyon,* white, marked with black, sweet scented.
Arum Aethiopicum (*Arum or Trumpet Lily*),* 24 to 36, pure white. This plant is sometimes called Calla, or Richardia.
Butomus umbellatus, 24, rose.
Calla Aethiopica. See *Arum Aethiopicum.*
Caltha palustris, 12, yellow.
Hottonia palustris (*Water Violet*), 18, lilac with yellow.
Iris pseudacorus (*Yellow Iris or Water Flag*), 24, yellow.
Limnocharis Humboldtii,* yellow.
Menyanthes trifoliata, white, dark green foliage.
Nuphar advena, yellow, with red anthers.
Nuphar luteum (*Yellow Water Lily*), yellow.
Nymphaea alba (*White Water Lily*), white. (See Fig. 577.)
Nymphaea adorata, white.
Pontederia cordata, blue, in fine tufts.
Ranunculus aquatilis, white.
Sagittaria latifolia, 12, white.
Sagittaria sagittaefolia, 30, white, dashed with pink.
Thalia dealbata,* 40, blue, purple.
Trapa natans, white, with purple claws.
Trianea Bogotensis, fine glaucous leaves.
Vallisneria spiralis, white, with green strap-like leaves.
Villarsia nymphaeoides, golden yellow.

2291 The following are a few marsh plants of handsome appearance that are suitable for planting on the borders of streams and the margins of ponds and ornamental pieces of water:

Arundo donax, 120, remarkable for its foliage.
Hemerocallis fulva, 24, tawny yellow.
Houttnynia cordata,* 12, yellowish green.
Iris faetidissima (*Stinking Gladwyn*), 30, bluish lilac.
Lythrum roseum superbum, 36, rose colour.
Myosotis palustris, 9, blue, with yellow throat.
Oenanthe crocata, 42, white.
Oenanthe fistulosa, 24, white.
Parnassia palustris, 6, white.
Phormium tenax (*New Zealand Flax*), 30, blue.
Senecio paludosus, 42, yellow.
Scrophularia aquatica, 42, red.

2292 Many of the aquatic plants will do well in damp and moist situations, such as *Butomus umbellatus*, *Caltha palustris*, etc., and many marsh plants, as may be inferred from the preceding list, will thrive and flourish in damp, moist, shady spots, in which other perennials would languish and ultimately perish. That this is true is evident from the Arum lily, which is an aquatic plant, or, in other words, a plant that will grow in water, yet it does well as a pot plant set in ordinary soil, provided that it be watered freely, which keeps the soil in a condition similar to that of marsh land, and receives protection in a cool or even cold greenhouse in winter.

2293 *Bulbs: their Form and Classification* The management of some special classes of bulbs, such as the Crocus, the Gladiolus, the Hyacinth, etc., will be indicated further on. At present we have only to consider the culture of bulbs generally, some of which have been already mentioned as herbaceous plants, and which may one and all be classified as such, when we remember that plants of this kind are those in which a new stem is produced, year after year, from a perennial root, and that the term is applicable to any border perennial whose habit is not shrubby. Strictly speaking, the term bulb is applicable only to roots such as the hyacinth, which grows in successive coats superimposed one on and over the other, and the lily, which is formed of scales growing one over the other, as tiles are placed on the roof of a house. From this disposition of the coats in one case, and the scales in the other, of which true bulbs are formed, bulbs following the formation of the hyacinth are said to be *tunicated* bulbs, and those following the formation of the lily are said to be *imbricated*. From this it is evident that snowdrops, daffodils, etc., which are similar in construction to the hyacinth, and all that possess the scale-like formation of the lily, are genuine bulbs.

2294 But what of the crocus, the gladiolus, the cyclamen, and other fleshy roots of bulbous form which have not the construction of either of the classes just described – are they not bulbs? No, not in the strictest sense of the word; but having the form of bulbs they are commonly accepted as being bulbs, and are included in the list of roots called Dutch Bulbs, sent over every autumn from growers in Holland to supply the English market. If the root, say, of a crocus, be divided in any way, whether from top to bottom, or transversely from side to side, it will be found that it is a fleshy root without any division whatever in the interior like the hyacinth, but consisting of one mass throughout like the potato. It differs, however, from the potato in that the roots, by which nourishment is drawn from the soil, are sent forth anew each year, from a ring or circular patch at the base of the bulb (see Fig. 566), and not from eyes, as in the potato, from which stalk and roots both proceed, the former in an upward direction, and the latter downwards. Fleshy masses, like the gladiolus and crocus, are called corms, to distinguish them from the tunicated bulb of the hyacinth and the scaly bulb of the lily, and masses like the potato and dahlia are called tubers.

2295 *Management and Culture of Bulbs* As far as these points are concerned, the treatment of all bulbs in the open air, and indeed in pots, is similar to a great extent for every variety. The more hardy kinds, and notably the common garden lilies, will thrive in any ordinary, garden soil, fairly worked and fairly enriched; but it is necessary for their welfare that it should be well drained, and in no way water-logged. Generally speaking, however, a light soil or sandy loam is preferred by bulbs, and if the soil of the garden be at all inclined to be heavy, it is desirable to lighten it by working in sand, at and around each spot in which a clump of bulbs is to be planted; and to add some leaf mould and manure from a spent hotbed, if the soil be poor. Bulbs, as a rule, should be planted deep, especially crocuses, gladioli, and lilies, because the bulbs are then less likely to suffer from the effects of frost. No attempt should be made, after flowering, to remove leaves or flower-stalks until they have withered and decayed to such anextent that they maybe removed by a very slight effort. The long sword-like leaves of crocuses, hyacinths, etc., should be neatly plaited together, to obviate untidiness of appearance, and allowed to remain until they are quite decayed. The dead flowers may be, and indeed ought to be, cut off just below the spike of bloom, useless it is wished to save seed. This holds good for all bulbs that have a woody or strong flower stem. When the leaves have completely died away, bulbs may be taken up and allowed to dry. They should then be kept in a dry place, to which the air has free access, until the time for planting comes round again, which commences in October for hyacinths, etc., and ends in April for late-flowering varieties of the gladiolus, the period of planting being regulated in a degree by the period of flowering.

FIG. 578 *Fritillaria imperialis (Crown Imperial – bulb)*

Such, briefly, is the accepted creed with regard to the culture of bulbs, and, for sale purposes, it is absolutely necessary that bulbs should be taken up when their leaves are withered and dried, so that transit from place to place may be effected when they are in this condition, and without tender and succulent rootlets to suffer injury by removal and carriage. But in the amateur's garden, bulbs may be suffered to remain where they are from year's end to year's end, provided that the soil is suitable, the drainage sufficient, and that they are planted deep. Bulbs have a tendency to rise to the surface, especially corms, for in the crocus and gladiolus, though not in the cyclamen, the new corms are formed every year on the top of the old corms, which perish. The continuance of bulbs in the places in which they are first planted leads to the formation of splendid masses, from which at the proper season rise glorious flower spikes, rich in colour, and in some cases endowed with delicious fragrance. Flowers are far more satisfying to the senses of sight and smell when in groups and masses, than they can possibly be as single specimens. What can be more desirable than a clump of hyacinths of all colours – red, white, blue, and yellow – or a dozen spikes, four feet in height, of the old but beautiful white and orange lilies?

2296 It is now necessary to give a list of the principal bulbs now in cultivation in gardens, following the form already adopted in the preceding lists of annuals, biennials, and herbaceous plants. It may be considered as a list of perennials, bulbous and tuberous, because it will save space to include the latter kinds without placing them in a separate list. A few plants that might have been included in this list, viewing it as such, have already been named in the lists already given, and it will be unnecessary to repeat them. These are the Alstroemeria, Anemone, Anthericum, Arum, Asphodelus, Corydalis, Dielytra, Erythronium, Hemerocallis, Iris, Lily of the Valley (*Convallaria majalis*), Paeonia, Ranunculus, Sanguinaria, Thladiante, and Tritoma. It is as well to name them, to prevent any trouble, doubt, or difficulty to readers when attempting to determine them. Plants that require protection in the winter, when out of doors, or which are more suitable for indoor culture under glass, are marked with a star.

Agapanthus (*African Lily*), 30, bright clear blue.
Allium azureum, 12, dark blue.
Allium moly, 12, yellow.
Allium Neapolitanum, 18, white.
Allium roseum, 18, claret.
Amaryllis atamasco,* 9, white, with rose stripes.
Amaryllis Belladonna* (*Belladonna Lily*), 18, rosy carmine, scented.
Amaryllis crispa,* 9, lilac. Greenhouse plant.
Amaryllis formosissima (*Jacobaean Lily*), 18, crimson.
Amaryllis longifolia,* 36, rose, scented.
Amaryllis lutea (*Autumnal Yellow Crocus*), 6, yellow.
Amaryllis vittata,* 24, hybrid varieties of all colours.
Anomatheca cruenta,* 12, bright crimson.
Apios tuberosa, climber, brownish purple.
Begonia Froebelli,* 9, scarlet. Greenhouse.
Begonia maculata,* pink, spotted foliage.
Begonia Pearcei, 12, yellow. Out doors in summer.
Begonia Rex,* 18, pink, beautiful foliage. Greenhouse.
Begonia rosaeflora,* 12, carmine rose.
Begonia Veitchi,* 6, orange scarlet. Numerous hybrids from this and *B, Rex.*
Bravoa germiniflora,* 30, scarlet.
Brodiaea coccinea, 11, dark crimson and green.
Brodiaea congesta, 24, blue.
Brodiaea grandiflora, 15. blue.
Brodiaea volubilis, climber, rosy purple.
Bulbocodium vernum, 4, purple.
Caladium esculentum,* 36, fine foliage.
Caladium violaceum,* 24, reddish foliage. Other varieties are strictly hothouse plants.
Calochortus venustus,* 12, various colours.
Camassia esculenta, 18, blue, in spikes.
Canna Indica* (*Indian Shot*), 48, various colours.
Chionodoxa Luciliae (*Snow Glory*), 6, blue, white centre.
Colchicum autumnale (*Autumn Crocus*), 6, lilac rose.
Commelina tuberosa,* 18, rich blue.
Crocus vernus (*Spring Crocus*), 6, various colours.

Cyclamen Coum, 4, purple red, white.
Cyclamen Europaeum, 4, red, white.
Cyclamen Neapolitanum, 6, rose, white, purple throat.
Cyclamen Persicum,* 6, white, rose.
Cyclamen Persicum giganteum,* 8, white rose.
Daffodil. (*See* **Narcissus.**)
Dahlia superflua, origin whence double varieties are derived. These are divided in three classes: Ordinary, 48 to 72; Bouquet and Liliputian, with smaller flowers, bout the same height; and Dwarf, 18 to 36. Useful for bedding; various colours.
Dahlia Mexicana, origin whence single varieties are derived, 36, various colours. Early grown from seed as half-hardy annuals.
Eranthis hyemalis (*Winter Aconite*), 4, yellow.
Eucomis punctata,* 24, pale green, purple centre.
Fritillaria imperialis (*Crown Imperial*), 30, various colours. (*See* Fig. 578.)
Galanthus nivalis (*Snowdrop*), 6, white. There are many varieties of this winter-flowering bulb.
Gladiolus bizanthinus, 18, purple.
Gladiolus cardinalis,* 18, scarlet, white spots.
Gladiolus Colvillei, 18, purple, with white spots.
Gladiolus Colvillei alba, 18, white.
Gladiolus communis, 18, purple-red, rose, white.
Gladiolus florebundus, 30, white or lilac, veined purple.
Gladiolus Gandavensis, 24, various colours. Origin whence hybrids are chiefly derived, among which the most noteworthy is:
Gladiolus Brenchleyensis, 24, intense scarlet.
Gladiolus ramosus, 24, purple, rose, white.
Gladiolus sagittalis, 12, dwarf varieties; various colours.
Gloxinia,* 8, various; for greenhouse only.
Hyacinthus candicans, 60, white in tall spike.
Hyacinthus orientalis, 9, red, white, blue, purple, pink, yellow.
Ixia,* 12, many hybrid varieties; various colours.
Lachenalia,* 6, red, yellow, green, etc.
Leucojum aestivum, 15, white, with green spot.
Leucojum vernum, 6, white.
Lilium auratum, 60, white, gold bands, brown spots.
Lilium Brownii, 36, white, brownish purple outside.
Lilium bulbiferum, 24, orange, yellow, red.
Lilium Canadense, 60, scarlet or yellow, purple spots.
Lilium candidum (*White Lily*), 48, pure white.
Lilium Carniolicum, 30, scarlet, black spots.
Lilium Chalcedonicum (*Turk's Cap*), 36, bright scarlet.
Lilium croceum (*Orange Lily*), 30, bright orange.
Lilium excelsum, 60, soft nankeen yellow.
Lilium giganteum,* 72, white, purplish within.
Lilium Harrissii (*Bermuda Lily*), 36, white.
Lilium Humboldtii, 48, yellow, with brown spots.
Lilium Krameri, 30, delicate pink.
Lilium longiflorum, 24, pure white, scented.
Lilium martagon (*Martagon Lily*), 24, rosy violet.
Lilium pardalinum (*Panther Lily*), 50, scarlet, orange, and yellow, spotted.
Lilium Philadelphicum, 18, orange scarlet, black spots.

Lilium pomponium, 18, bright red.
Lilium pyrenaicum, 36, orange red.
Lilium speciosum (or lancifolium), 36, white, pink spots.
Lilium speciosum album, 36, pure white.
Lilium speciosum corymbiflorum, 54, red, white.
Lilium speciosum punctatum, 36, white, spotted rose.
Lilium speciosum roseum, 36, rose, white edges, crimson spot.
Lilium speciosum rubrum, 36, rose, white edges, purple spots.
Lilium superbum, 24 to 84, scarlet and yellow, spotted with dark purple.
Lilium termifolium,* 15, scarlet, very delicate.
Lilium Thompsonianum,* 24, rose.
Lilium Thunbergianum, 20, red, yellow in various shades.
Lilium tigrinum (*Tiger Lily*), 42, scarlet orange, with dark purple spots.
Lilium umbellatum, 24, orange scarlet.
Lilium Washingtonianum, 48, white, black spots.
Mirabilis Jalapa* (*Marvel of Peru*), 18, red, crimson yellow, white, plain or variegated.
Muscari botryoides (*Grape Hyacinth*), 9, blue, white.
Narcissus bulbocodium (*Hoop Petticoat*), 9, golden yellow.
Narcissus Clusii, 7, white.
Narcissus Jonquilla (*Jonquil*), yellow, many varieties.
Narcissus papyraceus (*Paper White Narcissus*), 12, pure white.
Narcissus poeticus (*Poet's*, or *Pheasant's Eye, Narcissus*), 12, white, with crimson edge to cup.
Narcissus Romanus (*Double Roman Narcissus*) 12, white.
Narcissus tazetta (*Polyanthus Narcissus*), white, with yellow cups, many varieties.
Narcissus telamonius (*Daffodil*), 12, yellow, many varieties.
Narcissus triandrus, 12, sulphur yellow.
Nerine Sarniensis (*Guernsey Lily*), 18, rose, gold spots.
Ornithogalum Arabicum, 12, white; may be grown in glasses like hyacinths.
Ornithogalum fimbriatum, 24, white.
Ornithogalum pyramidale, 12, white.
Ornithogalum umbellatum, 15, white, with green streaks.
Oxalis Bowei, 12, pink or carmine, yellowish centre.
Oxalis Deppei, 12, red, yellowish base.
Oxalis rosea, 6, pink, greenish dot at base.
Oxalis tropaeoloides, 8, yellow, brownish purple leaves.
Oxalis Valdiviana,* 12, dark yellow.
Pancratium Caribbaeum, 18, white, sweet scented.
Pancratium Illyricum, 18, white, yellow inside, scented.
Pancratium maritimum, 12, white, sweet scented.
Polyanthus tuberosa,* (*Tuberose*), 36, white, pink tinge.
Scilla bifolia, 4, blue, purple stamens.
Scilla campanulata, 12, light blue.
Scilla cernua, 6, blue.
Scilla maritima* (*Squill*), 9, blue.
Scilla Peruviana (*Cuban Lily*), 12, blue, white stamens.
Scilla praecox, 6, blue.
Scilla Sibirica, 6, brilliant blue.
Scilla verna, 6, blue, white.
Sparaxis grandiflora,* 12, deep crimson, yellow centre.

Sparaxis pulcherrima,* 40, purple.
Sternbergia lutea,* 6, yellow.
Tigridia conchiflora, 12, yellow, purple spots.
Tigridia pavonia, 12, scarlet, marked with yellow and purple.
Triteleia laxa,* 12, fine blue.
Triteleia uniflora, 6, white, blue, and violet.
Tritonia aurea, 18, spikes of bright orange.
Tritonia squalida, 18, pink, and shades of red.
Tropaeoleum aureum,* climber; azure blue.
Tropaeoleum Jarrattii (or tricolor),* climber; scarlet, black, and yellow.
Tropaeoleum pentaphyllum, climber; scarlet, green lip.
Tropaeoleum speciosum, climber; bright scarlet.
Tulipa gesneriana, 9 to 18. Many varieties, viz.: *Early Single Tulips*, all colours, for bedding, etc.; *Double*, all colours, red, yellow, and variegated; *Late Tulips*, striped, various, show varieties.
Vallosa purpurea,* (*Scarborough Lily*), 18 scarlet.
Veltheimia Capensis,* 12, purple red.
Wachendorfia brevifolia,* 18, yellow.
Zephyranthes Atamasco,* 6, white.

2297 In drawing up the preceding lists much assistance has been derived, especially with regard to plants of more recent introduction, from the *Gardening Guide* issued by Messrs Hooper and Co., the well-known florists and seedsmen, of Covent Garden Market, London.

2298 Among other points about which amateur gardeners are much exercised, is the question as to what plants will do best in the shade. Now, all flowers like a fair amount of light and freedom from shade; but some do not object, like others, to a north or shady aspect and the absence of light and heat, without which the generality of plants would fare but badly. The following list of plants that will thrive in the shade is taken from the volume just named:

Acanthus
Ajuga
Amaryllis lutea
Anemone Apennina
Anemone Japonica
Anemone nemorosa
Anthericum
Aquilegia
Arum
Colchicum
Corydalis
Cyclamen
Cypripedium
Dielytra
Digitalis
Dodecatheon
Epimedium
Eranthis
Erythronium
Gaultheria
Gentiana
Helleborus
Hemerocallis
Hepatica
Hesperis
Hoteia
Iris
Leucojum
Lilium
Lily of the Valley
Lysimachia
Mimulus moschatus
Myosotis sylvatica
Narcissus
Oenothera rosea
Paeonia
Polygonatum
Polygonum
Primula
Sanguinaria
Saxifraga
Scilla
Spirea
Trillium
Trollius
Vinca
Viola

To the above-named flowers reference has already been made in the foregoing list, with but two exceptions, namely, Ajuga and Cypripedium. Of these the first, *Ajuga pyramidalis*, is a hardy perennial, well adapted for rockwork, from 6 to 9 inches high, and with leaves more or less tinted with purple; the second includes

Cypripedium calceolus, *C. macranthum*, and *C. spectabile*, all hardy terrestrial orchids, of beautiful appearance and easy of cultivation.

2299 *Bedding Plants: their Culture and Management* Bedding out plants are plants which will thrive and do well in the open air in summer, but which require protection during the winter. Half-hardy annuals are found among them, but they consist for the most part of herbaceous plants, which are, or may be, propagated by cuttings. The propagation of many of these plants, which are favourite tenants of the greenhouse and conservatory, will be touched on in the special notes devoted to their culture. Speaking generally of their management as a class, it is desirable that all cuttings taken in the late summer to become rooted before the arrival of winter, should be taken early enough to allow of the formation of a good mass of roots before the plants are consigned to winter quarters. Thus, the best time for taking cuttings of geraniums, verbenas, etc., is from the middle of July to the middle of August, during which time they may be struck in the open border or a close frame, but when deferred to September the cuttings should be plunged in slight bottom heat. Calceolarias, however, may be subjected to different treatment. The cuttings may be taken in September, and even later, and they may be wintered with no more protection than that which is afforded by a cold frame.

2300 *Treatment in Winter Quarters* With cuttings of bedding plants under protection during the winter it must be remembered that vegetation is still going on. They are still growing, though not actively, or perhaps apparently, and therefore they must have light constantly and air whenever the state of the weather is such as to allow of its free admission and circulation. If due ventilation and circulation of air is prevented, and the atmosphere of the house, frame, or pit is allowed to get unduly moist, the plants will damp off. The pots in which cuttings are placed for the winter must be well drained, to prevent any stagnation at and about the roots. The temperature should not be allowed at any time to fall below 35°, and in frosty weather it should be maintained by gentle fire heat, which, in combination with the admission of the external air, may be made use of to keep the house dry, even in the coldest weather, the presence of the heat mitigating and tempering the coldness of the air that is admitted.

2301 *Time to take Cuttings, etc.* As a rule, cuttings of all bedding plants, except those to be mentioned directly, are better taken at the time stated for verbenas, namely, from the middle of July to the middle of August. Geraniums may be rooted in the open border in July and August, and in gentle heat in September, in which month cuttings of ageratums, calceolarias, and salvias are best taken, though calceolaria cuttings will root in a cold frame if placed therein even as late as November. For cuttings in early spring, old stocks must be placed in gentle heat and induced to grow, and when sufficiently large the young shoots may be taken off in cuttings, to be rooted also in gentle heat. Half-hardy annuals should be sown in July and August, and kept under protection in frames and pits during the winter.

2302 *Hardening Off and Planting Out* No plant that has been an inmate of a cold frame or glazed structure of any kind during the winter can be removed from shelter at a moment's notice, and placed with impunity in the open air. Before removal from winter quarters into the beds in which they are to bloom, air should be given as freely as possible all day and every day, weather permitting. By this salutary exposure plants will experience no check when moved out. The transfer of bedding plants to the open may begin about the middle of May, or even sooner, if the weather be warm, but if cold and unpropitious, which is often the case in May, it should be deferred till June. Good soil is desirable for bedding plants, but it should not be too rich.

2303 *Plants Generally Used for Bedding Out* The plants comprised in the following list are those which are most commonly used as bedding plants. Of these, some have been mentioned in the preceding lists, and are therefore merely named; but of plants that have not been brought under notice, particulars are given. It will be noticed that the list comprises plants that may be raised from seeds, as well as cuttings, and some that are tender annuals. It may be said that Antirrhinums, Cerastiums, Delphiniums, and Pentstemons, being hardy, require no protection in winter, as do the others.

Ageratums, various sorts.
Alstroemerias, various sorts.
Anagallis, various sorts.
Antirrhinums, of all colours.
Bouvardias, dwarf shrubby plants, scarlet, white, etc., scented. Obtained from cuttings in spring.
Calceolarias, shrubby varieties.
Cerastium tomentosum.
Cineraria maritima, 18, grown chiefly for foliage. Sow under protection in December.
Cuphea platycentra, 12, scarlet, black, and white, with other varieties, from seeds or cuttings.
Dahlias, dwarf varieties.
Delphinium formosum, and other varieties.
Geraniums, all varieties.
Echeverias, perennial succulents.
Heliotropum Peruvianum.
Lantanas, various sorts.
Lobelias, various sorts.
Lophospermums, various sorts.
Maurandya Barclayana.
Mimulus, many varieties.
Nasturtiums, dwarf varieties.
Nierembergias, all varieties.
Oenotheras, dwarf varieties.
Pentstemons, of all colours.
Salvias, many varieties.
Senecio elegans, various colours.
Tracheliums, blue and white.
Tropaeolums, dwarf and double varieties, not climbers. (See Fig. 579.)
Verbenas, various colours.

2304 Lists of various plants of all kinds, and suitable for all purposes in gardening, have now been given, and these, if they are not complete and exhaustive in them selves, are at least sufficient for all practical purposes. It is now desirable to pass on without further delay to the consideration of the culture of some specialities among bedding plants, such as the geranium, and flowers which are generally known as florists' flowers. These cultural notes are in

FIG. 579 *Tom thumb tropaeolum (Annual for bedding out)*

every case as full in detail as space will allow, and afford all necessary information. No attempt at classification has been made, but the plants, whether for garden or greenhouse culture, are taken in alphabetical order. For varieties of each plant the gardener is referred to the price lists and catalogues of large growers, who make the culture of the plants a special feature in their operations.

2305 *The Anemone* Anemones, which are hardy tuberous perennials, are hardier than ranunculuses, have a richer foliage, and their flowers resemble miniature semi-double hollyhocks. They also include most of the colours of the hollyhock, except a pure white or yellow; but to compensate for the want of these, nothing can exceed in loveliness the blue, or in glory the scarlet, of the anemone. And although there is neither a white nor a yellow self among them, for the single *white* is not wholly *white*, yet several of them are beautifully striped with these colours. They may be planted from October to the end of March, and a succession of bloom thus secured, in mild seasons, from February until July. They will flower well in almost any common garden soil, but it is desirable that the ground in which they are grown should be tolerably light (some consider that a calcareous, dry soil suits them best), and that it should be well drained and enriched with decayed manure, or manure from a spent hotbed. The tubers are generally planted in the early part of the year, but the roots can be obtained from September to March, and it is desirable that beds should be formed about October, and the tubers planted immediately after, from 4 to 6 inches apart. If the weather be very inclement during the winter, the beds should be covered with loose litter. The roots may be taken up for removal, or for drying off and replanting in autumn, as soon as the leaves have died off in spring. A change of position is recommended at intervals of two or three years, for the maintenance of the size, beauty, and richness of the flowers; but this may be effected by taking up the roots, digging the bed over, and adding some decayed manure to enrich the soil and nourish the plants in the following spring.

The tuberous roots of the anemone may be obtained from any nurseryman or seedsman from September to March. There are some named sorts, such as the Bride, with white blooms, etc., but for these reference must be made to any dealer's catalogue.

2306 *The Arum* (*Arum Aethiopicum*) This splendid plant, with its snow-white flower, its yellow tongue, and arrow-shaped leaves, is not hardy with us; but it admits of an easy cultivation even where there is no greenhouse, and it is so ornamental in a room or hall, that it is well worth the little trouble which it requires. The arum grows freely from offsets, which are very freely produced. The plants should be repotted every October, in rich light mould, with a few drainers, the offsets having been carefully removed, and all the old soil well shaken from their roots. From this time till June, or earlier, if the plants have flowered and are over blooming, they should have abundance of water; but after this they must be kept quite dry, and may be put away in an outhouse till the following October, when the same treatment should be renewed. The arum, in a growing state, requires so much moisture that it is best to keep the pot always standing in a deep saucer full of water. Under this culture, offsets may be brought into flower in their third year.

Other varieties are *A. crinitum*, *A. dracunculus*, and *A. Italicum*, all hardy perennials, and suitable for outdoor growth, requiring only protection in winter in the form of a little litter thrown over the places where they grow.

2307 *The Auricula* This attractive flower, which is one of those that are popularly known as florists' flowers, has been brought by cultivation to a high degree of perfection. Auriculas are divided into two classes, namely, Show Auriculas and Alpine Auriculas, the latter being more hardy and easier to grow and manage than the former. The distinction between Show Auriculas and Alpine Auriculas is easily explained. Taking a *pip*, or individual flower, from the *truss*, the name given to a collection of pips on one large flower stalk, we find round the central tube, or *thrum*, a circle of white, which is called the *eye* or *paste*; surrounding this is another band, called the *ground colour*, and beyond this again another zone called the margin or *edge*. Show Auriculas are classed according to the colour of the edge, there being *White-edged*, *Green-edged*, and *Grey-edged* varieties. If there be no edge beyond the ground colour, it is called a *self*. Thus there are four classes of Show Auriculas. In the Alpine Auriculas the eye or paste is yellow: there is no edge, but the ground beyond the eye is generally shaded, the lighter colour near the eye deepening in some to a darker colour or shade round the edge.

2308 *Soil, etc.* Various composts have been recommended for the auricula, but the best seems to be a mixture of one part of good fibrous loam and one part of well-decayed spent manure, with a liberal addition of road sand or silver sand, and a sprinkling of charcoal or wood ashes. The pots must be well drained, and small pots should be used, the auricula never doing so well in large pots as in small ones. Thus 4-inch and 5-inch pots are large enough for any full-sized plants. Seedlings and small plants should, of course, be placed in much smaller pots.

2309 *Propagation, etc.* When it is desired to raise plants from seed, the seed should be sown in pans at any time from January to March, on the surface of light rich mould, well drained, or a compost of leaf mould and sand. Moss should be kept over the surface of the soil till the seedlings are up, to prevent it from drying too quickly, and the moss should be kept moist by sprinkling with a fine syringe. When the seedlings have three or four leaves, transplant into 3-inch pots. Propagation by offsets, or division of the roots, may be effected in February or March, when vigorous growth is being made, or in August, just when fresh growth is commencing after repotting. If the offsets can be removed with roots attached to them, so much the better. They may be placed singly in 3-inch pots, or these may be placed in a larger pot at equal distances near the edge.

2310 *Management in Summer* The auricula blossoms and is in full growth from February to June, when the plants should be removed from the glazed shelter under which they have been flowering, and placed in the open air on a shelf or stage having a north or north-east aspect. Under a north wall or hedge is a good situation. The plants should not stand on the ground itself. In August, when the fresh growth, especially the emission of fresh roots, commences, the plants should be repotted, the tap root being shortened with a sharp knife. A depth of 1½ inches should be first filled with small pieces of broken pots, and on this some decayed leaves. The plant should then be introduced, and the pot filled with compost to about ½ inch from the rim of the pot. Care should be taken not to allow the collar of the plant to be below the soil. Press firmly, give a little water to settle the soil about the roots, at the expiration of seven or eight days water again sparingly, and then leave the plants to themselves until November.

2311 *Management in Winter* In November the plants may be removed under shelter, the shelter being merely that of a glazed roof and sides sufficient to prevent wet, but not air, from reaching the plants. When they begin to grow in February, or a little later, they should be watered sparingly, the quantity being increased when the blooming period commences in April. Care should be taken never to allow any water to fall on the foliage, or to settle on the leaves at the base, as this frequently causes decay, and all dead and decaying leaves should be removed from the plants. These directions bear more especially on Show Auriculas, but they are equally applicable to Alpine Auriculas, although these are less susceptible of injury from moisture, and may be grown in the open border. In February, top dress all auriculas in pots.

Alpine Auriculas were a speciality of the late Mr Charles Turner, Royal Nurseries, Slough, Bucks, who also raised some excellent varieties of the Show Auricula. The business is still carried on, and attention is paid to all plants and fruits that seemed to be favourites with Mr Turner.

2312 *The Azalea* The azaleas that thrive out of doors are hybrids from *Azalea viscosa* and *A. Pontica*; they are grown in sandy peat mixed with a little loam, a compost which is suitable for all varieties. For conservatory decoration *Azalea Indica alba* and its hybrids are grown. For flowering in December an early habit must be induced, which may be effected by merely placing them in the conservatory in the autumn. They require a similar growing season, after flowering, to the camellia, which see; and until the shoots are sufficiently numerous, or the plants as large as desired, they can be grown on throughout the entire year, and stopped four or five times during that period. This *pushing* treatment will, however, sacrifice the blossom; but if started early, they can be stopped twice, and yet the terminal buds be sufficiently matured in the autumn to develop flower buds. After the growth is made, the plants should be gradually hardened off, and be placed during September full in the sun's rays out of doors, to thoroughly ripen their wood. Two parts of peat, two of loam, a sprinkling of sand, and one-sixth part of charcoal that has been steeped in urine or other manure water, suits them well. The drainage should be carefully attended to, the pots being filled to at least one-fourth their depth with crocks. While growing, they will also bear watering with clear weak manure water every time that they become dry. Azaleas may be removed from the house in June, and transferred to a cold frame or be plunged in an open border until October, when they should again be brought into the conservatory or cool greenhouse.

Before housing azaleas for the winter, examine the plants, and dip them over head and ears by inserting them into a tubful of equal parts soot water, made by throwing half a bushel of soot in soapsuds and tobacco water. Repeat this dose three times, and every thrip will either take itself off or die. These plants bear forcing well, and either by inducing an early habit, or helping by the aid of the forcing-pit, the luxury of their beauty may be enjoyed in conservatory or sitting-room for six or eight months of the year.

2313 Azaleas should be growing freely in January, if they were shifted and promoted to a warm place in December. To get early-flowering plants, some of the more advanced specimens should be introduced to greater heat, while others are retarded for a succession, to supply the conservatory or window-cases.

Azaleas of all kinds, and especially those for greenhouse culture, may be obtained from Messrs James Veitch and Son, Royal Exotic Nursery, 544 King's Road, Chelsea, London, who grow them in great numbers and variety.

2314 *The Begonia* There are few conservatory plants, perhaps, that are more worthy of cultivation than the begonia, and it is a plant that may be grown with the greatest facility. All it requires is a good rich loamy soil, mixed with a little sand, and a little gentle heat at starting. For this, either hotbed or stove answers every purpose, provided there is a conservatory or greenhouse in which they can be flowered, the chief requirements being heat, moisture, and shade. There is a delicious fragrance about some of the species which renders them particularly well suited for cultivation; others, again, are desirable for their richly variegated foliage and graceful habit.

2315 *Propagation, Management, etc.* Propagation is effected by means of seeds sown in spring in gentle heat, or in the tuberous species by means of division of the roots and cuttings. Plants should be repotted about the end of March, in compost, as described above. The pots should be well drained. When placed in the light, the plants will soon break, and will flower during the months of July, August, and September. They require, as intimated already, plenty of water during growth, and when in bloom it will be found of advantage to water them occasionally with liquid manure. In the winter, the temperature for begonias not in active growth should not fall below 40°, but plants can be kept growing and in bloom during the winter months in a temperature of 55°.

Begonias may be obtained of most nurserymen and growers, and especially of Messrs James Veitch and Son, Royal Exotic Nursery, 544 King's Road Chelsea, London, who have a very large collection, comprising all known varieties and many beautiful hybrids.

2316 *The Calceolaria* Calceolarias consist of two kinds – the herbaceous calceolaria, raised and reared under glass for exhibition purposes, and the shrubby calceolaria, grown for bedding out. The flower of the former, through cultivation, has attained an enormous size and a rich variety of markings, the ground colour being for the most part yellow, blotched, or spotted with brown or crimson. The blossoms of the shrubby calceolaria are small, but very numerous, forming large trusses of flowers, and are either yellow, orange, or a rich dark velvety brown in colour, thus presenting an effective contrast when grown in clumps or masses.

FIG. 580 *Calceolaria hybrida (Herbaceous variety)*

2317 *Propagation of Herbaceous Calceolarias from Seed* The seed of this magnificent greenhouse plant should be sown in July and August, in pans well drained, covered with a little rough turfy loam, making up the surface with a very fine, light, sifted mould and silver sand. Water the pans with a very fine rose; immediately after, sow the seed, no covering of soil being required; then place the pans in a cold frame, or under a hand glass, taking care to keep them from any exposure to the sun. When the seedlings are strong enough, prick them off into pans made up as before, placing them in a close situation. When sufficiently large, pot off singly into 60-sized pots, placing them on shelves near the glass in the greenhouse, where the plants will grow very rapidly.

2318 *Propagation of Herbaceous Calceolarias from Cuttings* Very few people now think of growing a named collection of herbaceous calceolarias, a variety of which is shown in Fig. 580. Those who wish to try must cut them down as soon as they have finished flowering. Place them in a cold pit to break in, lay in the young shoots when 2 inches long, and when rooted proceed as with seedlings; or the whole of the old plant may be kept as a single specimen, and if it does not fog off, it will make a grand display next season.

Green flies hold carnival among the soft delicate leaves of these plants, and unless speedily destroyed will consign the entire stock to the rubbish heap. Fortunately, the flies on these and cinerarias seem to be partially assimilated to the nature of their food, being very soft and easily destroyed.

2319 *Management of Soil, Watering, etc.* Calceolarias require great attention as to watering. Remove all decaying leaves as they appear, peg down the shoots to the soil, that they may root up the stems and thus strengthen the plant. As seedlings advance, shift them into larger pots, and prick off those spwn for late blooming. In potting use a compost of light turfy loam, well-decomposed manure, and leaf mould, and a liberal portion of silver sand, with an ample drainage of potsherds and charcoal, and keep them free from insects.

2320 *Propagation of Shrubby Calceolarias by Cuttings* Take the cuttings early in October, and, having prepared a piece of ground in a north border, the soil of which must be well drained, and made light with a large admixture of sand, place the cuttings in and press the earth well round them, water them well, and cover with a hand glass; or place the cuttings in pots, and having sunk them in a north border, under a wall, place a hand glass or small frame over them. In this way they may be kept without further attention till the following spring, unless the weather should be very frosty, in which case it may be well to throw some covering over the hand glass. In the spring the cuttings should be repotted, and will soon become fine plants. It is to be observed that the state of atmospheric influence most favourable to all cuttings is when a change to moist growing weather succeeds, within two or three days, the warm dry weather during which the cuttings have been taken.

It is a good practice to put calceolaria cuttings into cold pits at once, thus: Place 6 inches of broken brickbats, stones, and charcoal for drainage; another 4 inches of rough leaf mould, or well-decayed light manure; on the top of this, 3 inches of soil, composed of equal parts loam, leaf mould, or peat and sand. Spread over the surface I inch of clean sharp silver or other sand, press it down firm with a spade or other contrivance, and water well to consolidate and settle the whole. Next day commence inserting the cuttings 2 inches apart, taking care to plant them firmly; water the surface, which should have an inclination of 3 inches from back to front, in a pit 7 feet wide, until it is even, and the process is complete. Keep the glass on; shade in bright weather, and give scarcely any air for a fortnight. By this time the cuttings will be partially *callused*, and may be gradually exposed to more air and full sunlight. In a month or six weeks they will be well rooted, after which the glass should be entirely removed, unless during rain, fog, or frost. During winter they must be protected from the frost by a covering of mats or straw. They will require very little water from November to the middle of February. About this period they will begin to grow rapidly, and may either be potted or kept as cool as possible in the pit, and finally transferred to the flower garden in the middle of May. This is the most successful mode of propagating and storing calceolarias. The maintenance of their roots in an equable, cool, and moist condition is the grand secret of success. To have good beds of calceolarias it is also indispensable to strike a sufficient stock in the autumn. They will strike readily enough in the sharp heat in the spring; but spring-struck cuttings seldom flower so well, can scarcely be got forward enough to flower early, and, if subjected to a high temperature, are almost sure to take themselves off suddenly without leave, leaving yawning vacancies behind, at a time when it is often impossible to replace them. For ease, simplicity, and certainty of success, autumn is the season for furnishing the entire stock of calceolarias.

2321 *The Camellia* The camellia is an old-established greenhouse favourite, and at one time it was supposed to be essentially a greenhouse plant. It has been found, however, that it is as hardy as the rhododendron, and as easy of culture out of doors. Its robust constitution, dark glossy foliage, and waxlike flowers, render it essentially a useful plant for greenhouse culture for amateurs; for it will bloom at a time of year when flowers, comparatively speaking, are indeed scarce. December is the month above all others when it is most useful. By inducing early growth and early maturity, it will flower in December from habit, as well as, if not better than, in any other month.

2322 *Culture and Management* The culture and management of the camellia throughout the year under glass may be briefly summarised as follows: Supposing it to finish flowering by the end of December, remove the plant to a peach house or vinery at work as soon as it can be moved from the conservatory. Shift the plant into a larger pot at once if it requires it; at all events, examine the state of the roots, and act accordingly, remembering, however, that the camellia does best to be under-potted. Some prefer not potting until the growth is finished; but when the last flower drops is, perhaps, the best time. Almost any soil will grow camellias. Some grow them entirely in peat, some in strong loam, approaching to clay; and good plants may be obtained in both. The best soil, however, consists of two parts fibrous peat, one part fibrous loam, one-sixth part sharp silver sand, and one-sixth part *rotten wood*, or clean leaf mould. Keep them in a temperature of 55° to 60° until their growth is made and flower buds formed. During this period they should be frequently syringed, and a humid atmosphere maintained. Towards the end of April gradually remove, by easy transitions, to a cool house or cold pit, and the last week in May to a sheltered situation out of doors, or they may continue in the same house or pit throughout the season. The pot must be placed on a hard bottom, to prevent the ingress of worms, and the plant should be watered alternately with clean water and weak liquid manure, and finally removed under glass in October. With such treatment their blossoms will expand in November or December. In January, at the latest, camellias that have been subjected to the treatment described will be in full bloom, or advancing to this point, and then the gardener's care should be to protect the young expanding buds from cold currents of air, and to use as little fire-heat as possible.

Named camellias are to be obtained at moderate rates from any nurseryman or grower in any part of the United Kingdom.

2323 *The Carnation, Picotee, and Pink* The carnation and picotee are varieties of the *Dianthus caryophyllus*, improved and brought into their present condition by cultivation. The pink owes its origin to the *Dianthus plumarius*. The chief distinction between the carnation and the picotee is that the colour of the former is disposed in unequal stripes going from the centre to the outer edge; that of the picotee is disposed on the outer edges of the petals, radiating inwards, and uniformly disposed. Carnations are classified as *Selfs*, *Flakes*, and *Bizarres*. *Selfs* are carnations of one colour only, without marks, and without shading. *Flakes* are those which have the ground colour, be it what it may, striped with one colour only. In these the ground is generally white, and the stripes are scarlet, rose, or purple; and in accordance with the colour of the stripes, they are distinguished as scarlet, rose, or purple flakes. *Bizarres* are those which have the ground marked and flaked with two or three colours, and these are distinguished as crimson, pink, or purple bizarres, according to the predominance of the colour that is found in the markings. The edges of the petals of the carnation are smooth, those of the pink are generally jagged or notched. The pink, for the most part, has a dark eye, and sometimes a zone of the same colour as the eye midway between the base of the petal and the edge. Carnations, picotees, and pinks are propagated by seeds, layers, cuttings, and pipings, the last-named mode being usually adopted for pinks.

2324 *Propagation by Seeds* Sow seeds in May in pots, or small boxes, or seed pans, in soil similar to that which will be described presently as a useful compost for growing carnations, and place in an airy but sheltered part of the garden. When the plants are up, and show five or six leaves, plant out in beds composed of the same rich soil, and about 10 inches apart. Protect during winter with a cold frame. Many of the seedlings will bloom in the following summer.

2325 *Propagation by Layers* The season for propagating by layers is in July and August. The *modus operandi* is very distinctly exhibited in Fig. 581, and may be described as follows: Having selected the shoots to be layered, and prepared pegs for pegging them down, and made a small trench in the soil for their reception, add a little sand where the layers are to be placed, working it into the soil. Prepare each shoot by trimming off all the leaves with a sharp knife, except 5 or 6 inches at the top; then, with a thin-bladed knife, make an incision half through the shoot with an upward cut, beginning below a joint, and passing it through it for about an inch or so. Bend the layer down into the sandy soil prepared for it, pegging it down in that situation in such a manner as to keep the slit or tongue open, and cover it with a rich light compost. Two days afterwards, when the wound is healed, a gentle watering will be beneficial.

2326 *Propagation by Cuttings* Cuttings are made by taking off shoots which cannot be conveniently layered, cutting them right through a joint with an oblique angular cut, and planting them in pots or beds prepared with mixed compost and sand.

FIG. 581 *Mode of layering carnations*

2327 *Propagation by Pipings* Piping consists in drawings out the young shoot from the joints, and inserting it into a light, sandy soil, when it takes root. As it has been said, it is a process more generally applicable to pinks than carnations. Pipings should be struck under a hand glass, and when well rooted, should be planted in a bed, in rows 6 inches apart, and 3 inches between the plants. Supposing the pipings to be taken in June or early in July, they should remain in the bed until September, when they may be transferred to another bed, or to pots, in a compost thoroughly incorporated, consisting of two-thirds loam from decayed turf and one-third well-decomposed cow-dung. If in pots, let them be in 4½-inch pots, having a few crocks in the bottom, and the pots filled with compost. Lift the plants carefully, without breaking the fibres, adjusting the soil so as to place the plant in its proper position, spreading out the roots on the soil, and filling up the pot nearly to the edge. The roots must not be sunk too deep, but the soil on the top must be on a level with the collar of the plant. When gently watered, the pots may be placed in a common garden frame, and the glass closed for twenty-four hours. Throughout the winter the plants give very little trouble, seldom requiring water, but needing all the air that can be given them. In March they should be repotted in the pots in which they are to bloom. These should be 8½-inch pots, with 1 inch at least of crocks for drainage; the soil as before.

Where layers of carnations and picotees are potted, the potting should be done in October, when they will be well rooted. The best plan appears to be to place them singly into small pots for the winter months. In this way they can be packed closely under common frames in old tan or cinder ashes. Let the newly-potted layers have all the air possible in fine weather. If the winter prove severe, it will be necessary to cover the glass with mats, straw, or long litter.

2328 *Soil, etc.* For good compost for carnations, take two-thirds of good loamy soil, the turfy top spit in preference, and add to this one-third of thoroughly rotted cow or stable dung, and one measure of drift sand or other sharp grit, to every ten measures of the compost. The alluvial deposit from water courses, like a mill head, is an excellent substitute for the maiden loam. In preparing the bed for carnations, having filled the bottom with sufficient drainage material, and secured an outfall for the water, fill in the compost till nearly full. On this surface spread out the roots horizontally, and fill up with fresh compost, pressing the whole firmly but gently down in that position. The soil best suited to receive young plants, when potted, is a mixture of good light loam with well-rotted manure from old cucumber or melon beds. This mixture should be made some months before it is required for use, and at the time of potting a little sea sand or fine road sand should be added to the soil.

2329 *Tree Carnations* These are so called from their peculiar habit, the shoots being long and straggling, with an upward tendency, and requiring training on sticks or a trellis of bars between two side pieces. They are also known as *Perpetual Carnations*. They are invaluable for winter blooms. The cultivation and soil are much the same as for the ordinary carnation. The cuttings, which will be furnished by the side shoots, may be struck in July or August in gentle heat, or the old plants may be laid down in a frame in the latter month. When rooted, pot in 4½-inch pots, and winter in a cool greenhouse near the glass. The following summer the plants should receive two shifts, first into 8-inch and then into 10-inch pots. This will repress any tendency to bloom. During the summer the plants should be kept in the open air in a cool position, and carefully trained. Towards the end of September they may be taken again into the house, and watered when necessary with liquid manure; but air must be freely given to them. Under this management they will bloom freely through the winter months.

2330 *The Chorozema* Chorozemas are a most interesting genus of plants from Australia, which bloom almost the whole year, more especially in the early spring, and are consequently most acceptable additions to our greenhouses and conservatories. They are not very difficult to manage, and are alike useful for decoration and as cut flowers for bouquets, at a time when such flowers are valuable. They delight in a rich turfy peat, mixed with fibrous loam and leaf mould and gritty sand. When recently potted, they require a close pit or the warm part of a greenhouse, and cautious watering at the roots, until they get into free growth. When thoroughly established, water with clear liquid manure twice a week.

2331 *Propagation* Chorozemas are propagated by cuttings of the half ripened young wood, taken off in July or August, taking the short, stiff, and weak or medium growth, but avoiding twigs of a robust habit. These, after being trimmed, should be about one inch long, and must be inserted in sand, under protection of a bulb glass. In preparing the pots for the cuttings, take care to drain thoroughly, by half filling them with crocks; then place fibrous peat about an inch deep over the drainage, and fill up with clean sand. After the cuttings are in, place the pot in a close cold frame, water when necessary, and wipe the condensed moisture from the inside of the glass twice or thrice a week. Here the cuttings must remain until they are cicatrised, when they may be removed to a warmer situation, and the pots plunged in a very slight bottom heat, and in a few weeks they will be ready to pot off. If it is late in the season before the cuttings are ready to pot off, they should remain in the cutting pot through the winter, and be potted off in February; but if they are ready for single pots in September, they will be much benefitted by being potted off early.

2332 *Soil, Potting, etc.* Having selected dwarf, healthy, bushy, well-rooted specimens from your stock of young plants, prepare the following compost: Rich fibrous peat, two parts; leaf mould, one part; rich turfy loam, two parts;

clean potsherd and charcoal, broken to the size of horse beans, one part; with sufficient gritty sand to make the whole, when mixed, light and porous. Having prepared this compost, examine the root of each plant, and if it be strong and healthy, prepare for its reception a pot two sizes larger than that in which it has been growing, and proceed to pot, placing some of the roughest part of the compost over the drainage, and fill up with the finer soil.

2333 *Management* After potting, place them in a close frame or pit, taking care to ventilate freely; but keep a moist atmosphere, and shut up for an hour or two every evening, and open it again before retiring for the night. Attention must be paid to stopping the rude shoots, so as to induce close, compact, and healthy growth. If the plants progress as they ought to do, they will require a second shift during the season. The plants should be kept growing until the winter fairly sets in, at which time they should be brought to a state of rest. In the second year some of the plants will produce a nice head of bloom; but in order to produce rapid growth, remove the bloom buds when quite young, and keep the plants vigorously growing through the second season. If the plant is in good health, and the pot full of roots, a shift any time between Christmas and October will not hurt it; but never shift a plant until the pot is full of vigorous roots, and take especial care that the roots do not become matted before you shift.

Manure water in a weak state may be used with advantage; but use it with caution, and not more than twice a week. That prepared from sheep's dung and soot is best, and it *must* be used in a perfectly clear state.

2334 *Treatment for Red Spider and Mildew* Chorozemas are subject to attacks of red spider and mildew. The best remedy is sulphur and water vigorously and plentifully supplied. Take a plant and lay it on its side in the open air, then with the syringe wash it thoroughly: after watering, dust it with sulphur, and repeat the dressing until the pest is destroyed.

2335 *The Chrysanthemum* Although this plant is among the hardiest of the hardy, yet flowering, as it does, chiefly in late autumn and early winter, its beautiful blooms are subject to injury from the weather when grown out of doors, and soon lose their freshness, and are injured in form and dimmed in colour, under the adverse influences of rain and frost. To exhibit their blooms in perfection it is desirable that they should at least have protection overhead, if it be nothing more than an awning of waterproofed calico, with ends of the same, if the pots or border in which they are growing be at the foot of a wall to which the ends and roofing can be attached. The best protection, however, is afforded by a cold greenhouse, a glazed structure without fire heat, because such a building admits of free entrance of light, which the semi-opacity of awning will, to a certain extent, prevent.

November is pre-eminently the month when a conservatory is most needed. When utter desolation reigns without, there is the more need for enthroning the goddess of beauty within. This is comparatively easy with the aid of chrysanthemums, which alone make a brilliant display. November is the reigning season of this beautiful flower, which has been brought to us from China and Japan. If not so refined as some, it is the most strikingly effective of all; even camellias pale their beauty in its presence. Moreover, its cheapness, readiness of increase, and simplicity of culture, bring it within reach of the poorest, and for these reasons it is, and ought to be, sought after here as eagerly as in Japan, where, like the rose in England, the thistle in Scotland, and the shamrock in Ireland, it is regarded as being the national flower and the national emblem.

2336 *Classification, etc.* Speaking broadly, chrysanthemums are classified as Japanese, Reflexed, Incurved, Pompons, Anemones, and Anemone Pompons. The distinction between each class is easily recognised. The *Japanese* variety is marked by its irregularity. The flower forms almost a ball, or at all events a semi-ball, and its petals are tossed wildly about in every direction in charming disarray, which offers a remarkable contrast to the neatness and regularity of arrangement of petals conspicuous in the other varieties. *Reflexed* chrysanthemums are those whose petals are bent back and turn downwards towards the flower stalks. In the *Incurved* varieties the arrangement of the petals is just the reverse, the petals turning upwards and away from the flower stalk, and curving inwards, so that the flower, in many cases, assumes the form of a ball, composed of imbricated petals, or petals so disposed as to lap over one another like tiles on a roof. *Pompons* are varieties that do not attain the height of the tall large-flowering chrysanthemums, and whose blooms are smaller, say about the size of a half-crown, or not larger than a crown piece. When the term *Hybrid Pompon* is used, it is taken to denote varieties which are not small enough to be ranked among the true Pompons, and not large enough to be placed among the large-flowering varieties. The true Pompons, it may be said, are suitable and beautiful for front shelves in conservatories, or for beds or borders out of doors. Being of compact, close growth, and having flowers about the size of very large daisies, and rivalling the large ones in colour, they are at once the neatest and most ornamental plants for furnishing the conservatory. The *Anemone*-flowered varieties differ from all the others, in having a centre of close petals, almost like a sunflower, but still more like an anemone, surrounded by a fringe of edging of large loose petals. The *Anemone Pompons* are merely dwarf varieties of the anemones. Examples of the different varieties are given in the coloured plate of chrysanthemums that appears in this volume.

Further, chrysanthemums of all the varieties named above may be classified according to the time of their flowering, as *early flowering*, blooming from July to October; *semi-early*, blooming in September and October in the open ground; and *ordinary*, or *late-flowering*, blooming in November and December; but this is merely useful as denoting the time when each individual plant will flower.

2337 *Culture, etc.* It will be useful to trace briefly the culture and management of the chrysanthemum throughout the year, beginning from the flowering season. Supposing that plants are brought under shelter late in October, and allowed to flower in the conservatory, they may be removed to a cold frame or sheltered corner out of doors until the end of March or beginning of April. If the latter position is chosen, the pots must be plunged to the rims in cinder ashes, and the tops slightly protected with some dry litter.

2338 *Propagation* In looking the plants over at the time specified, three obvious modes of increase present themselves. The old stools may be divided, they may be planted out as they are in rich soil with a view to layering, or cuttings may be taken off them, and the plants either planted out in the shrubbery or entirely discarded. If division is determined upon, pieces with a single or two or three stems may be chosen, and either planted out into rich soil or potted. If the last-named method be decided on, they should be placed into a close frame for a week to start them, and gradually used to light and air until they are placed in a sheltered situation out of doors.

2339 *Management of Divided Plants* When they have grown 3 inches, stop them, to induce compact growth, if nice plants are your object; but if you grow blooms for exhibition only, never stop them at all. Concentrate the whole strength of the plant into two or three stems, and the strength of these stems into a single bud at the top, and that bud cannot fail to be a prodigious flower. For conservatory plants, however, two or three stoppings will be necessary, and the flowers, if not so fine, will be ten times more numerous; and the leaves will, or ought, to touch the rims of the pots.

2340 *Repotting* As soon as the first pot is full of roots, the plants should be shifted into another, or placed in their blooming pots at once: no soil is better for them than equal parts well-decomposed cow dung, loam, and leaf mould, liberally coloured with bone dust and sharp sand. Neither should there be much drainage, as the roots will speedily occupy the whole mass of earth, and almost prevent the possibility of stagnation. From first to last the plants should never flag, and be constantly fed with rich, clear manure water.

2341 *Training, etc.* In training, the fewer stakes that are used the better, and towards the end of October the plants should be moved under glass. This is a critical change for them, and unless the leaves are kept well syringed two or three times a day for a few weeks, the chances are they will either discolour or fall off.

2342 *Treatment in Open Ground* Pompons, or others to bloom in beds or against walls, may receive the same general treatment in training and watering, etc. It is also a common practice with many to plant out their entire stock, and take up and pot what they require in the beginning of October. This plan succeeds well if the leaves do not wither, as the result of the check of potting.

2343 *Management of Layers* Where layering is determined upon, the stools are planted out in rich soil, and the branches layered into pots about the beginning of July. Very nice plants with splendid foliage may be procured in this manner.

2344 *Management of Cuttings* The favourite mode of increase by the best cultivators is by cuttings. No plant, unless it be couch grass, strikes so easily as the chrysanthemum. In any soil, at any season, put a growing branch in any place where it does not freeze nor scorch, and it is almost sure to root. Nearly all growers differ as to the best time for striking these plants. Some cultivators recommend November; some succeed admirably by inserting them in May. Perhaps it is better to make a compromise between the two extremes by striking cuttings in March. These should be well rooted, and then potted off in April, and receive their first shift into pots 4 inches or 4½ inches across the top, the first week in May. They should then be continued in a temperature of 50° for a fortnight; headed and hardened off, and stood out of doors by the end of May, and receive their final shift a month or six weeks later. By adopting this mode the amateur will not fail to secure good blooms and presentable plants, both essential for conservatory purposes.

No attempt is made to give lists of the different varieties, for reasons already stated, and on account of the enormous number of named plants now in cultivation. Those who desire full information on this matter should purchase the descriptive catalogue issued by Mr N. Davis, Lilford Road Nurseries, Camberwell, London, which may be obtained for sixpence. Mr Davis is one of the largest and most successful growers in this country, and has for years made the culture of the Chrysanthemum his speciality. The number of named plants in his catalogue already exceeds nine hundred.

2345 *The Cineraria* Few plants are so effective for decorative purposes as cinerarias, whose form and habit is shown in Fig. 539. Unless for exhibition, it is best to grow them annually from seed.

2346 *Culture and Management* The first sowing should be made in March, in pans filled with equal parts of peat and loam, and one-sixth part sand. They should be well drained, made firm, and the seed slightly covered, and placed on a slight bottom heat. Keep the pans and young plants, when they appear, partially shaded from the bright sun; put them into 3-inch pots as soon as they will bear handling, return them to the same place, and renew the same treatment until they are thoroughly established in their pots. Then gradually harden them by giving plenty of air, and place them in a sheltered situation out of doors towards the end of May. As the roots reach the sides of the pots, shift them into larger, giving them their final shift in September. The first flower stems should be cut out close to the bottom when large plants are desired. This will induce them to throw out from six to twelve side shoots; these may be reduced, or all left, at the option of the grower. Towards the end of September, they should be returned to a cold pit, and they will begin to flower in October. No soil is better for growing them than equal parts rich loam, leaf mould, and thoroughly rotted sheep or horse-dung, liberally mixed with sharp sand or charcoal dust, and used in a roughish state. They also luxuriate under the stimulating regimen of *rich* manure water. Another sowing may be made in April, and a third in May, for very late plants.

2347 *Treatment of Old Plants* The treatment of old plants may be similar to this. Cut them down as soon as they are done flowering. Shake them out, and pot each sucker separately in March; then proceed as above in every respect.

2348 *Culture of Plants for Conservatory* In August, plants from seed sown in May should be dwarf and compact specimens. Select healthy plants from those potted off in July, which will now be about 3 inches high and well rooted; and shift them into 5-inch pots, in a compost of good turfy loam and well-decomposed cow dung, mixed with a little leaf mould and silver sand, to keep the soil open; giving plenty of good drainage, which is essential to the health of these plants,. When well rooted in the new pots, pinch out the leading shoots. When they have made fresh growth, look carefully over them again, and pinch out all weak shoots, and such of the old leaves as interfere with the free circulation of light and air round the stems, and place them thinly near to the glass in the front of the greenhouse, cold pit, or frame; in the latter case, raising the lights on flower pots to secure free ventilation. When they have made considerable progress, a second shift may be given, using the same compost. In

February give a final shift, when a stronger compost should be used, adding to the former a little well-decomposed night-soil, or an increased quantity of cowdung, with a smaller supply of leaf mould. Continue to thin weak shoots and superfluous leaves, in order to throw the whole vigour of the growth into the leading shoots. When strong enough, stake them, and tie them out as wide as possible. By this means the side shoots will soon fill up the intermediate spaces. Fuinigate frequently, to prevent the green fly, which is the pest of this plant.

2349 *Application of Liquid Manure* When the pot is pretty well filled with roots, water with liquid manure, which will preserve the leaves in a fresh green state, and give additional brilliancy to the flowers.

Seeds sown in the beginning of August, and potted off into store pots when large enough, make good plants for spring purposes. Potting into store pots prepares them for separate potting; their after treatment being the same as above. The process of stopping retards their bloom, and strengthens the flowers: where earlier bloom is required, therefore, a modified treatment is to be adopted. When the flowering season is over, remove them to a shaded place, preserving all the leaves, and watering slightly, guarding them from insects until August, when cuttings may be taken from the old roots. When these are separated from the plant, the roots may also be separated and potted out; every particle of the root being capable, under proper treatment, of propagating a plant; these old ones being the best plants for early flowering, they may be divided even up to October.

2350 *Management in Winter* In January, many plants will be in bloom, and may be removed to the window or conservatory, while those reserved for blooming in May and June should still be kept in cold pits or frames, taking care to guard them from severe frosty weather, and especially from moisture. If large cinerarias are required, shift a few into larger pots, and pinch off the tops to produce a bushy head, tying or pegging down the side shoots to keep them open, keeping them supplied moderately with moisture, and giving air on every possible occasion.

Mr Glenny tells us that 'to make a truly fine cineraria, we must have a white ground, which renders any colours a good contrast, the most striking being crimsons and blues. The edging should be even, forming an even band of colour alike all round, and having a well-defined circle of white surrounding a disc of some determinate colour. This disc, then, should be white on the ground, distinctly banded with a dense colour of some kind, the greater the contrast the better; the disc being small, dark-coloured, or bright yellow; the petals smooth and velvety – no ribs or pinkers; the bloom flat and round; or if they deviate, by cupping rather than reflexing; the foliage spreading, green, and even; above which the flowers should form an even surface of bloom, the flowers setting edge to edge, and perfectly circular; the ends of the petals free from notch, with a distinct edge of colour; thick at the edge, and the flowers opening flat.'

2351 *The Crocus* The chief self sorts of the crocus are white, yellow, blue, and purple; the striped sorts exhibit these colours in every variety of distribution. Size, consistence, shape, and distinctness of colour in the bloom, constitute the chief points in a good crocus. Nothing can be more easy than their culture. They are increased by offsets and seed, the former being the usual mode, as they increase rapidly. Offsets are treated the same as old bulbs, and will bloom the second year. Seed should be sown thinly, in well-drained pans of light sandy loam, as soon as ripe, and placed in a sheltered situation out of doors until late in the autumn. During heavy autumn rains and the cold of winter, they should receive the protection of a cold frame. If sown thin enough, they may remain in the same pans during the first summer. When their foliage dies down in the autumn, they should be shaken out of the soil, and carefully planted in beds of mellow loam in the reserve garden, placing the bulbs about 2 inches apart and 3 deep. Here they will form strong bulbs during the third summer, and a few of them may flower, the most of them, however, deferring to do so until the fourth spring. Crocuses are very accommodating in reference to the depth at which they are planted; from 4 to 6 inches is, perhaps, the best average. When they are planted in beds devoted to bedding plants, they will reach the surface and flower, if inserted four times that depth. As the young bulbs are formed on the top of the old ones, they thus possess a self-elevating power. Crocuses will flower freely for many years without being disturbed. The best growers, however, recommend dividing and replanting every third or fifth year. To secure perfect blooms, the foliage must be left to die down of its own accord.

2352 *The Dahlia* This beautiful flowering plant, named after the Swedish botanist, Dahl, belongs to the same family, and is a native of the same country, as the potato, namely, Mexico, where it was found in sandy plains 5000 feet above the level of the sea. It was sent to Europe in 1789 by Cervantes, then the director of the Mexican Botanic Gardens, who was a Spaniard; Mexico being at that time under Spanish rule. He named it *Dahlia coccinea*. Under the impression that sandy soil was its proper compost, it lingered in our gardens, a miserable scraggy plant, till 1815, when a fresh and improved stock was introduced from France, and it was taken up by the florists. Under the influence of cultivation, it has been so much improved in form as to become one of the finest flowers of the garden, while the shades of colour are so numerous, so diverse, and so opposite, and in so many shades, that it would be difficult to find another plant at once so hardy and so showy.

Probably its importer never dreamed that the naked stem and imperfect flower of *D. coccinea* would, by the efforts of cultivation, become so ornamental in European gardens; nevertheless, such it has become, and few gardens are now without their collection of dahlias, while the nursery lists of named varieties swell into hundreds, of every shade and colour, except the much-prized blue, which was for some years the object of the florist's pursuit.

2353 *Propagation* Dahlias may be multiplied by seed, or by dividing the tuber – every eye, when separated with a portion of the tuber, making a plant. Others, again, cut off the young shoots under the lower leaves, and strike them in small pots filled with sandy soil. Experiments have ever been made to ascertain how far grafting would succeed with the dahlia.

2354 *Seedlings: their Management* – Seedlings are procured by sowing the seeds in shallow pans and plunging them into a hotbed, or by sowing on hotbeds, prepared for the purpose, in March. The soil should be light and sandy, with a mixture of peat mould. The seed should be chosen from the best varieties only; it should be lightly covered with soil. A few days will bring them up, when they require all the air which can be given them safely. In April they will be ready for potting off either singly in the smallest sized, or round the edge of 6-inch pots, which strengthens them for final planting out. Towards the middle or end of August, if successfully treated, they will begin to bloom; at this time they should be examined daily, all single and demi-single blooms thrown away, unless they present some new colour or show some peculiar habit of growth, which may be improved by further cultivation and crossing. Caution in this respect is the more necessary, as it is the habit of the dahlia to improve under a second year's cultivation, some of our finest varieties having come up with indifferent flowers as seedlings. When done flowering, the young bulbs are taken up and treated as old tubers.

2355 *Cuttings: their Management* Cuttings are taken as follows: In February or March, and even as late as the first week in April, the tuber, which has been carefully wintered in a dry place, is placed in soil placed over a hotbed, and in a very short time as many shoots as there are eyes in the tuber make their appearance. As soon as these are 2 inches long, they are taken off just below the leaves, struck singly in small pots, and again placed in the same hotbed. Others prefer cutting up the tuber as soon as the eyes are distinguishable, and replacing them either in the soil of the hotbed or in pots; but to obtain short-jointed, stout, and healthy plants, it is desirable that they should be rooted from cuttings taken off in April, and struck in a gentle hotbed, as cuttings struck in April are more healthy than those struck at an earlier period, and consequently form better flowering plants. As soon as rooted they should be potted in 5-inch pots, and again placed in a gentle heat, but with plenty of air. A week after they are potted they should receive a watering of liquid manure made from guano and powdered charcoal, well mixed with rain water, repeating this occasionally till the time of planting out. Fumigate the frame with tobacco, should there be any appearance of the green fly.

2356 *Bedding Out* Early in May beds are repaired for their reception, if they are to be grown in massed beds. The form of the beds will depend on the general design of the garden; if a portion of the garden is devoted to them, either for the plants or the flowers, they will be best displayed in beds 3 feet wide, with alleys between. The beds being marked by stakes placed at each corner, 4 inches of the surface soil is removed, and 4 inches of thoroughly rotted manure put in its place, and the whole deeply dug and the manure thoroughly mixed with the soil in digging. In the beds thus prepared the plants are placed, the collar, as they have grown in the pots, being on the surface of the beds. The 3-foot beds will receive each a row; the stakes are firmly fixed 4, 5, or 6 feet apart, according to the size of the plants; the plants themselves are planted 4 inches deep, so that the crown of the plant is just above the surface. As the plant increases in growth, tying up commences; at the same time a diligent search should be made for slugs, earwigs, and other pests of the garden. These must be rooted out, or they will root out the dahlias, or at least destroy their flower.

Where any of the plants show a weak and drooping growth, time will be saved by re-striking the top; although they will bloom later, the flowers will be stronger than they would be after the plant has received a check. Another and more common practice in gardens is to place the whole tuber in some warm place in March, and, when the eyes show themselves, cut up the tubers, and in May plant them at once six inches below the surface, in the place where they are to bloom, staking them and leaving them to nature until they are sufficiently grown to compel attention; but even for common bedding-out purposes, and for filling up gaps, the plant is worthy of greater care than this amounts to.

2357 *Management in Summer* During June and July dahlias require careful attention in watering and stirring the soil about the roots. As the lateral shoots attain sufficient length, tie them up so as to prevent their breaking, placing other stakes for the purpose, should that be necessary. The roots should be assisted by stirring the soil with a fork every two or three weeks, and by copious watering, removing all dead or straggling shoots, and keeping the plant trim and well staked. When they are intended either for exhibition or for highly-developed flowers, only one bud should be left on a shoot, and the flower should be protected both from the sun and rain by tin sconces, oilskin caps, or inverted flower pots, placed over the top of the stake to which it is tied. As the autumn approaches, the swelling shoots render it necessary to examine those tied up, slackening the strings, where necessary, to prevent them from being galled.

Light-coloured flowers are confirmed in their beauty by seclusion from sun and air while they are developing their bloom. Darker flowers, on the contrary, lose much of their brilliancy if too much shaded; they should, therefore, only be shaded partially from the direct rays of the meridian sun.

2358 *Soil* Where dahlias are to fill a place in the general arrangement of the garden and shrubbery, care should be taken to supply them with suitable soil. Peat mould, mixed with sand, is useful in developing stripes and spots on the flower.

2359 *Management in Autumn* In October it is necessary to revise the names, and see that they are all correct; and that seed which is to be saved for propagation is secured before it is injured by the frost. It is desirable, also, to provide against any sudden and unexpected arrival of severe weather, by drawing the earth round the stems in a conical form, which will protect the roots from frost while they are yet in a growing state, as well as diminish the moisture, which encourages growth. Even in November, in mild seasons, the dahlia will remain fresh and gay if the weather is open and clear; but in general the earlier flowers will have passed away, and their time for rest will have come. When the frost turns their foliage brown or black, take up the plants and cut off the roots, leaving six inches or so of stem attached; then plunge them into a box of ashes, chaff, or sand, in order to preserve them from damp, frost, and heat, during the winter.

The number of named dahlias in cultivation is very large, but collections may be obtained from any nurseryman or grower. The dahlia was a speciality of the late Mr Charles Turner, Royal Nursery, Slough, Bucks, and buyers may there supply themselves with the very best selection possible, or they may get them from Messrs H. Cannell and Sons, Home of Flowers, Swanley, Kent, who possess a very large stock, both of double and single dahlias, comprising all the newest varieties.

2360 *The Epacris* This is a hard-wooded greenhouse shrub which requires precisely the same treatment as the erica, or heath, which it much resembles, and for directions for its culture and management the reader is referred to those on the erica, which immediately follow. All that it is necessary to say is that all epacrises should be freely cut back as soon as they have done flowering; and after the shoots have grown afresh, two or three inches long, is the best time for potting them; a hard sandy gritty peat is the proper soil. Place them in a close pit, but by no means warm, for a few weeks; gradually inure to the air, plunge in a sunny situation; see that the wood is brown and hard by the end of September. Remove to conservatory shelf in October, and you will have such a charming profusion and succession of tiny tubes of colour, as nothing but epacrises could exhibit.

2361 *The Erica or Heath* This important genus of greenhouse plants includes five or six hundred described species, and as many varieties produced by cultivation, and are the great ornaments of the greenhouse at a time when other flowering plants are scarce; it is therefore impossible to overrate their importance, even were their delicate flowers less beautiful than they are. The genus has, moreover, the advantage of furnishing plants which flower in summer and autumn, as well as in winter and spring.

2362 *Propagation* Heaths are propagated by cuttings formed of the tender tops of the young shoots. The cuttings should be an inch or so in length, and should be tenderly used, so as to avoid bruising any part of the stem, and inserted in pots or pans filled with pure white sand, moistened and firmly pressed down. Having inserted the cuttings, water so as to settle the sand about the roots, and having given a little time for the moisture to subside, cover them with bell glasses, pressing the edges into the sand so as completely to exclude the air, only removing the glasses to wipe off accumulated moisture. They should then be placed in the propagating house, where there is one available, or in a spent hotbed. When they begin to root, which will be seen by the starting of the shoots, they should have air given daily to harden them preparatory to the removal of the bell glasses.

2363 *Soil* The soil best adapted for this plant is that obtained from a locality where the wild heath grows luxuriantly, taking care it is not dug too deep; the turf must not exceed 4 inches – rather less than more; as, if deeper than that, it is more than probable that the good and nutritious upper soil will become deteriorated by an admixture of inert and mischievous subsoil. The summer is the proper season to procure and store up a heap, which may safely be used after having a summer and winter's seasoning. To prepare the soil for potting or shifting, it should be cut down from the heap so as to disarrange it as little as possible, breaking the lumps well with the back of the spade, and afterwards rubbing the soil through the hands, which is far better than sifting, as it leaves more of the fibrous decomposing vegetable matter in it; add to this one-fifth good white sand, and well incorporate the two together.

In selecting plants, it is of the utmost importance to choose healthy, dwarf-growing, robust specimens, taking care to avoid anything like meagre, leggy, stunted plants, which might live for years, but give nothing but disappointment to the cultivator.

2364 *Management, Watering, etc.* To convert plants into handsome well-grown specimens in a moderately short space of time, they must have a liberal shift. A young plant in a 60 or 64-sized pot may be shifted into a 24 or 9-inch pot, taking care that plenty of potsherds are used for drainage. Care must be taken that the soil is thoroughly mixed, by pressing with the fingers in the fresh pot all round the ball of the plant, so as to make it quite firm and close. After being set away in a cool frame or pit, let them be well watered. This is much facilitated by placing a convex potsherd over it, and watering with a spout, leaving the water to diffuse itself equally over the whole soil, which is a means of avoiding what often occurs from watering with a rose – viz., the surface only becoming moistened while the ball remains imperviously dry.

Epacrises and ericas may be purchased of any large nurseryman or grower, who will furnish selections of plants to flower in spring, summer, autumn, or winter, according to the requirements of the buyer.

2365 *The Fuchsia* Whoever has a greenhouse two yards square, or a window free from dust, may grow one or more fuchsias. In fact, it has become quite a window plant, and no plant is better adapted for the purpose. Nothing can be more graceful either in form or flower than noble plants of the fuchsia. They have a grace and beauty peculiar to themselves; and their price is sufficiently low, and their culture easy and simple enough, to bring them within the reach of all. Plants that have been at rest during the winter may be started in January, and large early-flowering specimens produced by cutting down the old plants and shaking the roots out of the old soil as soon as they have broken, repotting them in a good rich compost, with sufficient drainage. Strike cuttings for bedding plants as soon as the shoots are long enough.

2366 *Propagation* Cuttings should be inserted in pots filled either with loam and leaf mould, or peat and silver sand, in equal parts, to within an inch and a half of the top. Place over this three-quarters of an inch of silver sand, and level the surface to make it firm; then insert the cuttings – about 1 inch long is the proper length – and plunge the pots in a bottom heat of 60°, either in a pit or propagating house; if the latter, cover them with a bell glass. In three weeks they may be potted into 3-inch pots, and replunged in the same bed, keeping them at a temperature of from 50° to 60°. As soon as the roots reach the sides of the pots, the plants should be shifted into fresh pots, until they receive their final shift into 6, 9, or 12-inch pots, towards the end of June. The size of the pot must be regulated by the period when they are wanted to bloom. If in July, a 6 or 9-inch pot will suffice; if in September or October, a 12-inch will not be too large.

2367 *Stopping and Training* During the period of growth, the plants will require stopping at least six times, care being taken never to stop the shoots immediately preceding or directly after the operation of shifting into larger pots. If the pyramidal form of growth, which is the best of all forms for the fuchsia, is adopted, the plants, from the first, must be trained to a single stem, and all the side shoots stopped, to make the pyramid thick and perfect. If the bush form is wanted, the whole of the shoots should then be stopped at every third joint, until branches enough are secured to form the bush, and then be trained into the desired shape.

2368 *Temperature, etc.* A regular moist genial temperature must be maintained during the entire period of growth, never exceeding 60° by fire heat. During bright sunshine, the glass should be slightly shaded with tiffany or other material; the delicate leaves are easily injured, and the plant should never receive the slightest check by being allowed to flag.

2369 *Soil and Watering* Fuchsias, while having their preferences, will grow in almost any soil. Garden loam and leaf mould, in equal proportions, with some broken charcoal and sand, do very well. Feeding them with manure water is preferable to mixing manure with the soil. After they are well rooted, they should never be watered with clear water. A carefully-shaded conservatory, guarded against the ingress of bees, is the best place for them when in blossom. In such a situation they will continue in bloom for three months, if the seeds are constantly picked off.

2370 *Hardy Fuchsias* These make the best show when planted together in beds upon a lawn, the colours being judiciously blended. Those fuchsias which trail upon the ground should be grown with a wire hoop, supported by three legs underneath them, so that their branches may be made to bend over the hoop. Several of the more hardy sorts may be trained on one stem, so as to appear as standards in the bed. Many varieties of the fuchsia are hardy, and will stand our winters in the open ground, especially in a well-drained light soil, having a large portion of peat in it; and a great many that are looked upon as tender varieties will be preserved if covered 3 or 4 inches with dry cinder ashes at the first approach of frost. The best plan is to cover the whole fuchsia bed at that time with a good coating. The dead branches should not be cut off, nor should the ashes be removed until the fuchsias begin to shoot in the spring.

2371 *The Geranium* Although the term geranium can be taken to cover both sections of plants to which the names *geranium* and *pelargonium* are usually applied, yet the former is more generally assigned to the hardier sorts, mostly self-coloured, being white, salmon, scarlet, cerise, etc., and single and double, while the latter gathers under it all the show varieties of which the two upper petals are generally distinct in colour and markings from the three below. Many of the varieties of the geraniums are distinguished by the beauty of their foliage, for which, indeed, they are chiefly prized. The fine-foliaged geraniums comprise *Golden Tricolors*, *Silver Tricolors*, *Tricolor variegated*, varieties with *Ornamental Foliage*, such as Happy Thought and Freak of Nature, heavily blotched with white, *Golden Bronze*, *Yellow-Leaved* and *White-Edged Varieties*, *Zonal*, *Ivy-Leaved*, and *Mottled* varieties, with a long train of double varieties distinguished by their colour, which each comprise so many distinct sorts that they can only be described and named in the catalogues of nurserymen who grow them on a large and extended scale. The pelargoniums are well nigh as numerous in their groups, including *French Spotted* and *Early Flowering* varieties, *Fancy Pelargoniums* for exhibition, both large flowering and small flowering, and the magnificent *Hybrid Double Regals* of recent introduction.

Persons who wish to make collections of sorts, whether for bedding out or culture under glass, should, as it has been already recommended, make the selection from a grower's catalogue. If they are at a loss where to go, let them get the illustrated catalogue of Messrs H. Cannell and Sons, Home of Flowers, Swanley, Kent, which will put them in full possession, not only of the names of the different classes under which the varieties are grouped, but also of the names of the different varieties that are comprised in each class. Mr B. S. Williams, Victoria and Paradise Nurseries, Holloway, London, also keeps a very large and extensive stock of all varieties, whether bedding or show, that are in cultivation.

2372 *Bedding Varieties: Striking Cuttings* It is desirable, and indeed necessary, that cuttings of all sorts of geraniums for bedding the following year should be struck early: from the last week in July to the end of the first week in August is very good time. They should be taken in dry weather, when the parent plant' has had no water for some days, and they should be kept to dry twenty-four hours after they have been prepared for potting. The more succulent sorts, and any that appear difficult to strike, may with advantage be touched at the end with a small paint brush dipped in collodion, which will serve to hasten the callus which the cutting must form before it will throw out roots. They may be potted four or six in a pot, according to size. It is essential that the pots be well fitted with drainers, that the soil be light and sandy, and that it be pressed tight round the joint of the cuttings, which should be buried in it as flat as possible. When potted, they may be sunk in the ground on a south border, and well watered in the evening, when the sun is off. They will require no shading, except the sun be very fierce; and, in this case, they must not be kept from the light, but merely screened from the scorching rays of the sun. They may flag a little, but this is of no importance; in two or three days they will recover, and put forth roots. If they grow too freely before it is time to take them in for the winter, the top shoots should be broken off, and in this way they will make strong bushy plants.

2373 *Preservation of Old Plants through the Winter* Take them out of the borders in autumn, before they have received any injury from frost, and let this be done on a dry day. Shake off all the earth from their roots, and suspend them, with their heads downwards, in a cellar or dark room, where they will be free from frost. The leaves and shoots will become yellow and sickly; but when potted about the end of May, and exposed to a gentle heat, they will recover and vegetate luxuriously. The old plants, stripped of their leaves, may also be packed closely in sand; and in this way, if kept free from frost, they will shoot out from the roots, and may be repotted in the spring.

2374 *Show Pelargoniums: their Management* – To secure profusion of bloom, early growth and under-potting are of the first importance. No matter how robustly a plant is grown, one eighteen months old cannot be made to flower so freely as one four or five years old. Whether the closeness of tissue, induced by age, modifies the nature of the sap during its passage or not, I cannot tell. It is probable that the smallness of the vessels may influence, not only the quantity, but the quality of the sap. It is at least certain that age in this and many other species is favourable to profuse inflorescence.

2375 *Early Growth* This is of the most importance. Plants to flower in May should be cut down by the end of the previous June; have broken, been reduced, repotted, and encouraged to grow 2 or 3 inches in a close cold frame, for a fortnight, and have received their final stopping by the end of July, and be placed in their blooming pot by the 1st of November. Success depends upon their chief growth being completed before Christmas. No after management can compensate for the neglect of early growth. Any size of plant or leaf may be obtained at any period; but the flower will be scarce unless early growth is secured.

2376 *Under-Potting* This is the next great point. Plants in general, and pelargoniums in particular, flower best when they are pot-bound – that is, when the roots are trying with all their strength to burst the pot asunder.

The energy they thus acquire appears to rush to the other extremity, and expend itself in flowers. Some varieties will scarcely flower at all unless their roots are in this condition. The reason seems to be, that whatever tends to check the extension of other parts favours the development of flowers. The vital energies, arrested in the formation of wood, concentrate their force in the exhibition of bloom. It would appear as if the vital force in plants was not sufficiently powerful to carry on both these functions simultaneously. At all events, when one is most active, the other is almost passive, and the power of the one is nearly always in the inverse ratio of the other: hence, whatever favours the production of wood (free, large potting for instance), is unfavourable to the production of flower, and vice versa.

2377 *Geraniums from Seed* Provided that good seed can be obtained – and this can be done without much difficulty if application be made to any good seedsman and grower – the following directions from the pen of Mr Shirley Hibberd will be of use. 'If you have plenty of glass,' he says, 'and can keep a few hundred small plants through the winter, sow the seed as soon as ripe, and in due time pot the plants in the smallest pots, and winter them in a warm house near the glass. If not well off in respect of glass, sow in February or March, place the seed pans in a gentle heat, and grow the plants all the summer in a greenhouse or frame, and get them into 60-sized pots before the end of August. In the following March, shift them into 48-size, and as they fill these pots with roots, shift again to 32-size, and in this size let them flower: they are all to be allowed to grow as they please – no stopping, no pruning. In the course of the second summer – that is to say, in about fifteen months from the time the seed was sown – they will flower. All the seedlings should remain one full year in 32-sized pots, and after that time should be shifted into 24-size, or otherwise disposed of as may be considered most expedient. The system of cultivation proposed will produce robust plants, varying from 2 to 5 feet high, with fine heads and abundance of flowers of all colours.'

2378 *The Gladiolus* The hybrid varieties of the gladiolus are very beautiful, and their treatment may be summarised as follows: The grand display of flowers is made by these plants in June and July, and if seed is no object the flower stems should be cut down, or rather shortened, by removing the withered flower spike, when many of the bulbs will throw a second flower stem. The stems should only be cut down as far as the first leaf, as the leaves continue fresh and beautiful,

FIG. 582 *Blooms of hybrid gladioli*

and the second flower stem often proceeds as a lateral from this point. They are easily increased by seed; but, as they are already so numerous, it is as well, perhaps, to leave this mode to the growers. The only drawback is that, in the most favourable circumstances, gladioli will not remain in bloom for longer than two months.

2379 *Propagation and Culture* When taken up in November, they should be put away, with their old fibres and some soil adhering to them, in a dry room, the temperature not being allowed to sink under 40°. Prepare for planting in the following March, by carefully rubbing off the old roots and soil adhering at the bottom of the bulb, and carefully save all this *débris*; you will then perceive that each bulb asks you to divide it into two – sometimes three or four; that is, they will almost split themselves, and will have so many embryo shoots. After dividing and planting your bulbs, examine the *débris*, and you will find hundreds of thousands of little scaly-looking rubbish, which, indeed, are not rubbish, but young gladioli. Pick out the old roots and large particles of soil, draw a drill two inches deep on a bit of rich soil in the reserve garden, sow the scales thinly, and there will be such a crop of bulbs as will astonish every reader. Some of these will flower late in the autumn, many of them the second, and all the third year. These young bulblets require exactly the same treatment as the old ones. They also begin forming offsets at once, and after the second year they divide the bulbs in the same manner.

2380 *Soil and General Management* Gladioli are divided into two sections, namely, the *early-flowering* and the *late-flowering* varieties. The early-flowering varieties, of which *Gladiolus Colvillei* and the Bride may be taken as examples, bloom from the beginning of June to the end of July, but may be induced to flower earlier under glass. These should be planted in October, or, at the latest, in November. The late flowering varieties, of which *G. Gandavensis* and *G. Brenchleyensis* are fitting representatives, bloom in August and September, and should be planted in March. The bulbs, or corms, should be lifted in October or November, and dried off. Gladioli, in common with bulbs in general, like a light rich soil, and if the ground in which they are to be planted is poor, or in any degree heavy, a plentiful dressing of well-rotted manure and some sand should be incorporated with it, and the bed allowed to lie three or four weeks before the bulbs are planted. A warm spot, well exposed to the sun and sheltered from cutting winds, should be selected, and when winter approaches and frost sets in it is desirable to protect beds in which early varieties have been planted by a covering or mulching of litter about 4 inches deep.

Messrs Kelway and Son, seed growers and merchants, Langport, Somerset, are the principal cultivators of the gladiolus in this country, and intending growers should make application to them for their catalogue and price-list, or leave it to them to make a suitable selection from their stock.

2381 *The Hollyhock* There is no finer ornament of the autumnal flower garden than the hollyhock. Its noble, tapering, spike-like stem and rich rosettes of flowers clustering round the foot-stalks of the leaves, and its panicled head and luxuriant massive leaves, render it the most effective occupant of a gap in the shrubbery, or in the back row of an herbaceous border, or even in rows in the flower garden, or in beds by themselves; their variety of colour renders them most attractive objects.

The drawback to the perfection of the hollyhock, for many years after its first introduction, was its coarse habit of growth and thin transparent flower petals, which gave a flimsy appearance to its convolute flowers, and tended to early decay. Much of this objectionable habit has been overcome by the -perseverance of the growers, and under the careful hand of skilful culture the petals have become thicker, and, consequently, the colour is more dense and decided, the centre of the flowers better defined individually, while forming a denser spike of flowers from within a foot of the ground to the summit of the stem.

2382 *Propagation by Seeds* The seed of the hollyhock should be gathered only from the most perfect plants, in which the flowers have been round, the florets thick and smooth on the edge, the colour dense and decided, and the flowers close to each other on the stem. About the middle of March, or not later than the first week in April, the seed bed should be prepared, 4 feet wide, with an alley on each side. The soil should be rich and in good heart; such soil as would suit a cabbage will grow the hollyhock in tolerable perfection. Trench the bed 2 feet deep, throwing the top spit to the bottom, and bringing the second spit to the surface, if both are *of* the same character of loamy, somewhat tenacious soil, breaking up the surface thoroughly. On this bed, raked smooth, sow the seed so thickly as to come up an inch apart, and sift over the seeds some rich dry soil, so as to cover them for about an inch.

2383 *Treatment of Seedlings* When the young plants come up and begin to grow, the weeds must be kept down, and vigorous growth encouraged by watering in dry weather. In June they will bear removal to a nursery bed, prepared in the same manner as the seed bed. If the seedlings have been growing vigorously, the roots will be strong, and must not be broken in taking up; this may be prevented by soaking the bed thoroughly the night previous to removal, and lifting the plants cautiously with a fork inserted under them, as in lifting potatoes. Plant them in the new bed 6 inches apart each way, using a dibber, making a hole large enough to receive the roots, and pressing the earth round them by making another hole on each side with the point of the dibber, watering the bed thoroughly when planted. When dry and somewhat settled, rake the bed smooth, giving the same care as to weeding and watering when dry, as well as destroying slugs, earwigs, and insects.

2384 *Planting in Blooming Quarters* In the autumn they will be strong plants, fit to put out where they are to bloom. If they are intended to bloom in rows where they stand, every other plant must now be removed, so as to leave them one foot apart all over the bed; here they may be supported by strong stakes placed at both ends of each row, and a strong cord carried from one to the other, to which the plants are to be tied.

As hollyhocks come into bloom, in the second year, every single flower which does not exhibit some desirable character of habit or colour should be thrown away before they begin to ripen seed; the majority will be in this category. Those selected for further experiment should be cut down to within 3 inches of the ground, the earth round them stirred with a fork, to loosen the soil and let in the air, having previously named or numbered them in your book, and described the qualities for which they were selected.

2385 *Propagation, by Cuttings* As soon as the first flowers of an old plant open sufficiently to judge of the flowering, the superfluous side branches having no flower buds may be taken off, with two or three joints and leaves. Cut the shoot through with a clean cut, just under the lower joint, leaving the leaf entire; cut it also at about 2 inches above the joint – either joint will do, provided they have growing eyes, with a leaf and piece of ripened wood to support the bud until roots are formed. These cuttings, planted in a light sandy soil, placed under a hand glass, and watered occasionally and shaded from the sun, will require little further care except keeping clear of weeds and dead leaves. When rooted, pot them off in 60-sized pots, and put them in a cold frame where they can remain during the winter. In spring, plant them out in the open ground where they are to flower, the colours being arranged so as to harmonise with other parts of the garden, taking care to furnish the roots with the proper soil.

The old plants in autumn furnish another source for new plants. When the flowers are becoming shabby, cut the plants down, and, beginning at the bottom joints, continue to make cuttings, as described above, until the fibre gets too soft for the purpose – each joint having eyes will furnish a plant; these struck under a hand glass, on a very slight hotbed, will grow vigorously, the soil being gritty sand, loam, and leaf mould, in equal proportions, watering cautiously, but sprinkling the cuttings slightly every day in fine weather.

Seeds of the hollyhock may be obtained from any nurseryman and seedsman, as may seedlings also for planting out. Messrs Paul and Son, Old Nurseries, Cheshunt, Herts, have achieved much celebrity as cultivators of this flower, and Messrs H. Cannell and Sons, Swanley, Kent, possess a good collection of the finest sorts.

2386 *The Hyacinth* Nothing is easier than the culture of hyacinths. The best soil for them, and indeed for all other bulbs, is composed of equal parts of turfy loam and well-rotted cow or horse manure, at least two years old, with a sixth part sharp gritty sand. But they will grow in almost any soil, or indeed without soil at all, in damp moss, cocoanut-fibre refuse, water, or sand.

2387 *Choice of Bulbs: Early Management* The great point is to choose good, firm, well-ripened, rather than *large* bulbs, although, of course, the larger the better if they are also well ripened, and to pot or start them early, say in October, when they should be purchased of the seedsman. Then, by keeping the tops in darkness, and the roots, if possible, a little warmer than the tops, get the roots as much in advance of the *stem* as possible. If the pot or glass is once full of roots, while the stem is only starting into growth, a good bloom, with ordinary care, is almost certain. In this condition they may be removed to a forcing pit, with a temperature of 55°, to a conservatory shelf, pinery, or peach house at work, or a sitting-room or kitchen window, with almost entire certainty of success.

2388 *Potting, etc.* A single bulb in a 4½-inch pot, or one in the centre or three round the sides of a 6-inch or 8-inch pot, look well. Drain the pots well; fill them with the compost, placing some of the richest and roughest lumps over the bottom, and place the bulb on the top, slightly pruning it into the soil. Some recommend a handful of sharp sand to be placed under the bulb to ensure thorough drainage. If the compost is dry, water after planting; if it is in a proper medium state of moisture, this will not be necessary. If water is used, leave the pots for a day or two, to partially dry; then place them in a cold pit, plunged in and covered over the top 3 inches deep with old tan, cinder ashes, or leaf mould: leave them there until they are rooted; then move them to a forcing pit, or anywhere in the light and moderate warmth to bring them into flower.

2389 *Watering, etc.* Hyacinths in pots must never suffer for the want of, nor have an excess of, water; they may have clear manure water alternately with clean, if they are placed where the smell would not be offensive. If grown in the windows of living rooms, they should be placed on the table at night to guard against excessive cold, and also be moved out of the draught when the room is aired. Various ornamental supports are advertised for holding up the flowers in lieu of stakes. In pot culture, stakes are often unnecessary; for glasses, some support is generally indispensable. The supports manufactured and supplied by Messrs Williams Brothers and Co., Pershore Street, Birmingham, in brass wire, at 24s. per gross, are the neatest and most efficient. These are shown in Fig. 583.

FIG. 583 *William's patent support for hyacinths in glasses*

2390 *Hyacinths in Water* Hyacinths in glasses of water require the same general treatment. One of the chief points is to see that the base of the bulb does not *rest in* the water; if it does, the chances are that it will decay before roots are emitted. The water should be changed daily at a temperature of 55°. Sometimes a dozen of bulbs are arranged in a flat glass dish, containing half an inch or so of water, which is speedily occupied with a tangled web of roots: this, as well as placing the bulbs in damp moss in ornamental baskets, affords excellent facilities for tasteful arrangement.

The three striking colours, red, white, and blue, with any good yellow, may be placed in very pleasing and effective contrast, and a bright golden band of glowing yellow crocuses makes a matchless finish to the whole. It is decidedly preferable to grow hyacinths in masses of colour, and they contrast well with narcissuses, tulips, snowdrops, and especially crocuses. In fact, the whole of these bulbs may be grown in juxtaposition to each other in ornamental vases or baskets, and be infinitely more effective than single pots of either dotted about here and there on conservatory shelves.

2391 *Hyacinths in Sand* Any vessel, pot, or pan, may also be filled with damp sand for hyacinths, to be kept damp; and if occasionally watered with manure, they will do as well in it as in any soil whatever. The fact is, the hyacinth is not primarily dependent for its health or beauty on the food or culture we impart: it laid the foundation of both in the rich soil and beneath the warm skies of the plodding Dutchman; and if we will only give it a modicum of light, air, water, and warmth, it hastens to unfold its rich beauty, and diffuse its satisfying fragrance for our gratification and delight.

2392 *Hyacinths in Moss* Fill a china bowl or other vessel with fresh green moss cleared of all impurities. Let this be well wetted, and lightly pressed down; in it plant the hyacinth bulbs, covering them lightly with some of the greenest moss. As soon as the hyacinths are planted, place the bowl in a dark cool place for about three we; keep it near a window, where the bulb will have plenty of light and air. Keep the moss always damp, and that the top moss round the bulbs is changed frequently, so that the surface may be kept green. The moss best suited is that found on banks, or grown upon the roots of old trees.

Every nurseryman and seedsman has plenty of hyacinths for sale at the proper season, namely, early autumn, and in many towns there are sales of bulbs by auction at this time of the year. For named sorts, see the autumn catalogues of the dealers on a large scale, such as Messrs Barr and Son, 12 and 13 King Street, Covent Garden, London, and Mr Thomas Ware, Hale Farm Nurseries, Tottenham, London, who, with Mr William Baylor Hartland, 24 Patrick Street, Cork, make the culture of all kinds of bulbs a speciality.

2393 *The Lily* The liliums, or lilies, now in cultivation are both various and beautiful, and form a class of plants which of late has been largely extended, and which is really very valuable both for the greenhouse and the garden. The culture of these bulbs out of doors has been already described, and the names of the principal varieties have been given in the list of bulbs in paragraph 2296. All then that remains to be done here is to make a few remarks on the treatment of lilies in pots.

2394 *Lilies in Pots* Bulbs grown in pots may be preserved in the dormant state in cold pits or frames until spring, or on the marginal spaces of cold greenhouse paths, or stages where preserved from water drips. In the first position, the pots may be plunged in any dry material, as tan, leaf mould, etc. Many, among which may be named *Lilium Catesboei*, *L. Canadense*, and *L. superbum*, succeed best in a bed of peat or heath soil; and where that is not attainable, equal portions of half-decomposed leaf mould, wood ashes, and decayed branches, thoroughly mixed with river sand to one-third of the whole proportions, is a good substitute. In planting, cover each bulb with a clean stratum or layer of the last-named material. *L. giganteum*, *L. cordifolium*, *L. Japonicum*, and Z. *Wallichianum* or *Neilgherrense* are not as yet proved strictly hardy in all localities, and therefore would be best potted after the blooming season, and preserved in a cold pit or frame, to be again replanted out in the spring. Where this precaution is inconvenient, the surface pots of these kinds in the beds should be covered with a heavy layer of dried tan, wood ashes, or sawdust. The remaining kinds are recognised as hardy species, and will thrive in good sandy loam or a mixture of loam and peat.

Amateurs desirous of purchasing bulbs of lilies, if they are unable to procure the sorts they require of any seedsman in their immediate neighbourhood, cannot do better than apply to any of the growers that have been named in this chapter, or to any nurseryman in our large towns, such as Messrs Richard Smith and Co., Worcester, Messrs Viccars Collyer and Co., Leicester, or to Messrs Collins Bros. and Gabriel, 45 Waterloo Road, London, and Messrs Hooper and Co., Covent Garden, London.

2395 *Mignonette in Tree Form* A plant or two of Tree Mignonette will add greatly to the sweetness of the greenhouse, if made to blossom during winter, which is readily effected by stopping them during summer and autumn. The Tree Mignonette is made by training a vigorous plant for about three years. Sow the seed in April, transplant as early as possible into single pots. In autumn, remove all the lower shoots, and shape the plant into a tree. Somewhat later, shift it into a larger pot in good loam; keep it in a warm greenhouse and growing state all the winter, and remove all flowers. In the spring it will appear woody.

Treat it in the same manner the following year, removing all branches except those that are to form the head of the tree. By the third year it will have bark on its trunk, and form a handsome shrub; and by stopping the flowers as they appear during summer and autumn, it may be made to blossom freely during the winter and early spring. It will continue to blossom for many years in succession.

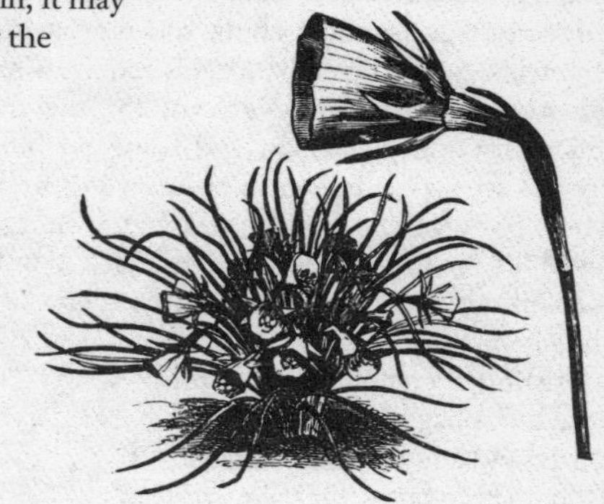

FIG. 584 *Narcissus bulbocodium, or hooped petticoat*

2396 *The Narcissus or Daffodil* The outdoor culture of these has been described in the general instructions for the treatment of bulbs in the open ground. For indoor or pot culture, it may be said that some varieties of the narcissus rank only second to the hyacinth for decorative purposes, and totally eclipse it in richness of perfume. They require similar culture to the hyacinths, and will flower in water, sand, moss, etc., but do best in soil. The Double Roman is the earliest, and may easily be had in flower at Christmas if potted in September.

2397 *Polyanthus Narcissus* To these should be added collections both of narcissus and jonquils. The variety of narcissus best suited for indoor culture is the polyanthus narcissus; and specimens of the common garden Narcissus Bulbocodium, or the hooped petticoat narcissus, should not be omitted. Its rich yellow flowers add much to the gaiety of a greenhouse, and the bulbs do well in pots. Select about a dozen fine bulbs, and plant them singly in 4-inch pots, and a grand display of blossom may be looked for.

The polyanthus narcissus may be ranked with the hyacinth as regards beauty, fragrance, early flowering, and easy culture. The delicate perfume emitted by it resembles that of the jonquil, and its clusters of bloom remind one of the polyanthus. The Double Roman, planted in September, flowers at Christmas; the other varieties, planted in succession, may be had in bloom till May. The pure whites with yellow and citron cups, and the bright yellows with orange cups, contrast well with, and form beautiful companions to, the hyacinth; and, like the latter, they succeed in sand, moss, or water.

2398 *The Jonquil* – Jonquils are greatly prized on account of their delicate fragrance and pretty early flowers. Their culture, as said above, is the same as that which is laid down for the hyacinth and polyanthus narcissus, except that three, four, or five bulbs should be planted together to produce effective display.

Messrs Barr and Son, 12 and 13 King Street, Covent Garden, London, and Mr W. B. Hartland, 24 Patrick Street, Cork, may be said to be the principal growers of, and authorities on, the daffodil and its varieties in the United Kingdom. Each has published a book on its culture and history, which every gardener interested in these bulbs should have. Mr Thomas Ware, Hale Farm Nurseries, Tottenham, London, also grows these and other bulbs on a large scale, as may be seen from his catalogue.

2399 *Orchids* These plants are very beautiful, but singular in appearance, both as regards leaves and flowers, and in many individuals peculiar in habit and manner of growth. They are divided into two classes, namely, *Epiphytes*, or those which grow upon trees – parasites, in fact, after the manner of the Mistletoe; and *Terrestrials*, or ground orchids, which grow on the earth. Coming from tropical countries, the majority of orchids require a high temperature, and are subjects for stove culture, being grown, for the most part, in baskets filled with sphagnum and potsherds, and some on blocks of wood; but the terrestrial orchids are grown in pots in ordinary soil, and in some cases like a stiff loam, in which pot plants, generally speaking, would not thrive. The drainage, in most cases, for orchids should be complete, and in the case of terrestrial orchids, the soil will vary according to the requirements of the individual, from a stiff soil, as already mentioned, to a compost consisting of equal parts of fibrous peat and sphagnum, with a little sharp sand and crushed charcoal.

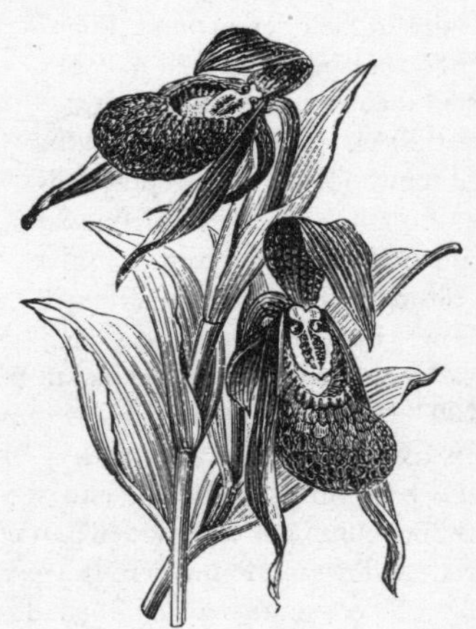

FIG. 585 *Blossom of cypripedium*

2400 *Cypripediums* Of the terrestrial orchids, the Cypripediums, perhaps, are the most hardy, and require the least care in cultivation, as they may be potted in the ordinary way in peaty soil, well drained. They require abundance of water, especially when in flower. The peculiar character of the flower of the orchid will be seen from Fig. 585, an illustration of the blossom and foliage of *Cypripedium macranthum*, kindly supplied by Messrs Hooper and Co., Covent Garden, London, from whom plants may be obtained. The flowers are of a fine crimson colour, beautifully netted, and having the centre brilliantly illumined with golden yellow and white. *Cypripedium calceolus* is also a handsome variety, growing to the height of 12 inches, or 6 inches less than *Cypripedium macranthum*, the sepals being brownish red, and the labellum, or bag-like lip, pale yellow. *Cypripedium spectabile* is another remarkable variety of this species. It is a North American species, growing to the height of 24 inches, and having white flowers, beautifully tinged with rose, the labellum, or lip, being of a deep carmine rose.

It has been said that individual species require individual treatment, and for this reason it is not practicable here to go very deeply into the culture of orchids, or, indeed, to do more than point out one or two of the hardiest of the race. Those who desire to purchase plants, and to obtain information on the modes of treatment that they require, should go to Messrs James Veitch and Son, Royal Exotic Nursery, 544 King's Road, Chelsea, London, or to Mr B. S. Williams, Victoria and Paradise Nurseries, Holloway, London.

2401 *The Pansy or Heartsease* Pansies are of two kinds – the *English*, or Show variety, and the *Belgian*, or Fancy variety. If it be asked what constitutes the difference between a Show and a Fancy Pansy, the answer is that it is in the blotch, or patch of colour immediately in the vicinity of, and proceeding from, the eye, as it were, this being small in the former and large in the latter – the larger, indeed, the better. The Show Pansy is divided into three classes, namely, white grounds, yellow grounds, and selfs. In a white ground pansy, the three lower petals are white or cream, the outer edge surrounded by a belt of darker colour, either broad or narrow, according to the variety. A yellow ground differs from the white ground in the colour only, which is yellow instead of white. The top petals in both varieties are selfs – that is, of one colour throughout – and should be of exactly the same shade as the belt. A self is a pansy of one colour only, the blotch and eye excepted. In very dark selfs no blotch is discernible. The different parts of the pansy, namely the eye, the blotch, the ground colour, and the belt, may be discerned from Fig. 586, in which they are clearly indicated, and which represents a Show Pansy. Pansies may be propagated from seed, or by cuttings, or division of the roots: they are suitable also for pot culture.

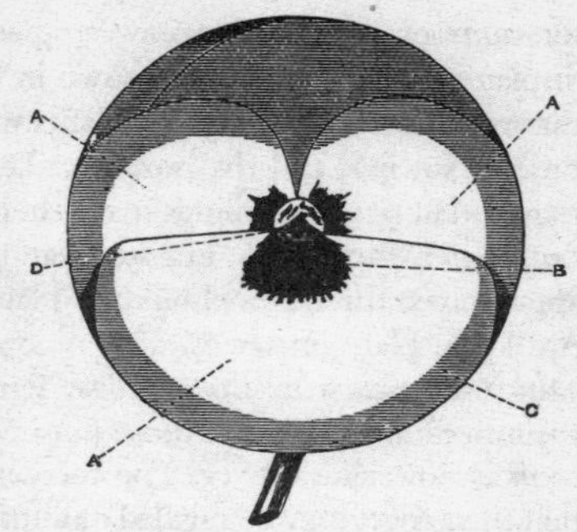

FIG. 586 *Show pansy A. Ground colour. B. Blotch. C. Belt. D. Eye*

2402 *The Soil: its Preparation, etc.* Any ordinary garden soil will do for the pansy; but to grow them for exhibition purposes, it must be properly prepared as follows: Trench the ground two spits deep in October or November, bringing the best soil to the top. If the plants are to be grown in a bed, it should not be more than 4 feet in width. When dug over, the ground will be about 3 or 4 inches above the surrounding ground, and about 6 inches of the top soil should be removed, and replaced by a compost of three parts of good rotten turf, two parts of leaf mould, and one part of good rough sand, white or grey – red sand should never be used, as it contains iron, which is, in some cases, injurious to vegetable life. The compost should be turned over at least half-a-dozen times, and well mixed before it is used. Large lumps should be broken, but the soil should not be made too fine, as when in this condition it is apt to become pasty if the weather be wet. It is better not to put the compost on the bed until spring, or a short time before the plants are set out.

2403 *Propagation by Seeds* Seed that is intended for sowing should be gathered from the best flowers only – that is to say, flowers which are conspicuous for form, substance of petals, size, and good decided colours. It should be gathered just before it is ripe, otherwise the pods burst and the seed is lost, for in hot weather the pods burst suddenly, and the seed is scattered in all directions. When gathered, it should be put into envelopes, sealed down, and put in the sun to ripen fully, When ripe, sow at once if wanted for spring blooming, but for summer and autumn flowering sow in April. Seed intended for a spring display of flowers should be sown in boxes, using good light soil: the same as that recommended above for plants will do very well. If the soil is damp at the time of sowing, and the boxes are kept in a shady place, no watering will be required until the seedlings make their appearance above ground: if the soil be dry, water through a fine rose at the time of sowing. As frosty weather approaches, the boxes should be placed in a cold frame. In the beginning of April transplant into beds.

2404 *Propagation by Cuttings, etc* Pansies require little attention during the autumn months. Indeed, those not intended for propagation may be dug up as soon as flowering is over. The choicer varieties must be taken care of in order that their roots may be divided or cuttings taken from them in April or May, for it is only by such annual renewal that degeneration can be prevented. Propagation by cuttings may take place any time from April to the end of October, although August and September are the best months for the work. The young shoots that spring from the base of the plant make the best cuttings: those that have flowered have generally hollow stems; these do not root so freely, and should not be used unless the variety is extra good or scarce. Cuttings should be taken off just below a joint, with a sharp knife. The soil intended for them should be fine, and a good supply of rough sand thoroughly mixed with it.

Sand is absolutely necessary, as few will strike root without it. The propagator will do well to place some sandy soil round the base of the plants, and also to cover with it all naked stems that are pegged down: the young shoots will root into it, and save the time and trouble of striking after they are separated from the plants. No cuttings of unhealthy plants should be put in, as these seldom do any good. The hardier kinds can be wintered successfully in the open, at the back of a north wall, or any shady nook in the garden, remembering never to put any under trees, as the drips will surely rot them. The best kinds should be wintered in cold frames, each variety being labelled as it is set.

2405 *Culture in Pots* Plants intended to be grown in pots should be struck from cuttings in July or August. When rooted, plant in 4-inch pots with a few crocks at the bottom, using the same kind of soil as for plants in the beds, then place in a cold frame, plunging the pots up to the rims in ashes or coconut fibre; plenty of air should be given, not forgetting to water when required. Keep in the frame until the end of March or the beginning of April, giving plenty of air on warm days. Then shift into 8-inch pots, and plunge in ashes or fibre as before. Keep close for a few days, and then admit air gradually. All plants should have short sticks placed to them, and the shoots tied carefully to the sticks. Plants in pots often furnish splendid blooms for exhibition.

In pansies of all kinds, Mr John Forbes, Nurseryman, Seedsman, Florist, and New Plant Merchant, Hawick, Roxburghshire, has gained a considerable reputation. Persons desirous of purchasing good named sorts should obtain his catalogue, which contains several hundred varieties. Mr Forbes is equally celebrated for his auriculas, dahlias, carnations, hollyhocks, pelargoniums, fuchsias, and hardy perennials.

2406 *The Pelargonium* The culture and propagation of the pelargonium has been described under the heading Geranium, paragraph 2371, to which the reader is referred.

2407 *The Petunia* There is very little difficulty in the culture of this half-hardy, soft-wooded plant, which may be propagated from seeds sown in the spring, and treated in precisely the same manner as that prescribed for raising half-hardy annuals, or it may be grown from cuttings struck in gentle heat in early spring or without heat in August and September. Both single and double varieties are beautiful in appearance, and may be used for borders, bedding-out purposes, and pot culture.

2408 *Propagation by Seeds* The seeds should be sown in light sandy soil that is fairly rich, and sprinkled over with a slight covering of the same mould when sown. When large enough to transplant, shift from the pot or seed pan in which they have been raised into smaller pots; 3-inch pots will do, although even smaller sizes may be used, and in these they may remain until they are required for planting out. If they remain in pots for some little time before they are planted out, they should be pinched in order to induce shrubby habit of growth.

2409 *Propagation by Cuttings* Cuttings taken in August and planted in a south border, in soil with which some sand and rotten manure from a spent hotbed have been incorporated, will soon root and be ready for transfer to pots at the end of September. They should be wintered in a pit or cold frame, round which sufficient litter should be placed, with mats, etc., or other suitable means of protection over the glass, to keep out the frost. When in this position and condition, they will need but little water, for they should be kept as dry as possible, having due regard to the sustention of their vitality. Air should be given when the weather is fine and dry; if any signs of mildew show themselves, they should be dusted with sulphur. Old plants should be subjected to the same treatment to preserve them through the winter. If started in February in gentle heat, they will soon send out shoots which may be taken off and struck in seed pans, well drained and filled with light sandy soil, in warm bottom heat. The soil in which the cuttings are placed should be kept moist.

2410 *Soil, etc.* For a useful compost for petunias, use six parts of rich fibrous loam, two parts of leaf mould, one part of decomposed cow manure, and one part of sharp sand. Incorporate all well together, and let the compost lay by for some weeks before using. Petunias that remain in pots should be shifted in the spring into 6-inch pots, in which they will bloom. Liquid manure may be given when they are about to come into blossom.

2411 *The Poinsettia and Euphorbia* Few plants are more easily propagated and grown than the poinsettia and euphorbia, which can be had in flower from October to March. Their treatment is singularly easy and simple, and may be described briefly as follows:

2412 *Propagation by Cuttings* Suppose the plants flower in December, cut them down to within three eyes of the old wood at the end of January. Put in as many cuttings as may be required, in lengths of from 4 to 6 inches long. They will strike in any vinery or house at work without shading or any attention whatever, except watering. When rooted, pot singly in 48 -sized pots, and return to the same house or a pit with bottom heat. If large plants are wanted, they grow best with the latter treatment. When the cutting has made six inches of wood, stop it, and sometimes it will break into three shoots; and this is quite enough for one-year-old plants. The plants will flower in 8-inch pots, and if they have three good branches, terminating in a whorl of scarlet nearly a foot across, the grower will, or ought to be, more than satisfied.

To attain plants of almost any magnitude, allow the old plants to continue rather dry for six weeks after having cut them down; then water and plunge in bottom heat to break freely. Leave a dozen shoots, and thin off all beyond that, and insert them as cuttings if wanted, to be treated as above. When these shoots are two inches long, shake out the plants, and repot in pots that will just hold the roots, in a compost consisting of equal parts leaf mould, loam, and peat, with a colouring of sand. As soon as these pots are filled with roots, shift into 12- or 8-sized pots, and return them to the same quarters. By maintaining a bottom and surface heat from 60° to 70°, syringing twice or thrice a day, and watering carefully, they may be grown to any size you please. If you start them early, the young shoots may also be stopped, and two dozen flowering shoots secured instead of one. But such a plant well grown would require half an ordinary-sized house to hold it; and, perhaps, plants with three to six blooms are the most beautiful, and certainly the most convenient.

2413 *Management of the Euphorbia* The propagation and culture of the *Euphorbia jacquiniflora* are similar to those indicated for the poinsettia. The euphorbia possesses, however, one peculiarity in the extreme, which the other also has in a modified form. When a young shoot of the euphorbia is stopped, it is seldom that more than a single bud on the stopped shoot will break. By stopping, nothing is gained in advance, therefore, but much time is lost. When bushy plants are desired, from three to a dozen cuttings should be placed in one pot, and grown on into plants without being separated. Cut plants may be treated exactly the same as the poinsettia; but they do not break so freely.

2414 *The Polyanthus* After flowering, divide the roots of the best plants intended for preservation. This operation must be performed every year, or the flowers will soon degenerate. Fresh soil and continual division is the only plan with all florists' flowers which give out offsets. As the polyanthus seeds freely, an infinite variety may be obtained by those who will take the trouble to select or purchase seed, and sow it. The seed should be sown late in autumn, for moderate sunlight only is required to bring it up, and the young plants will not stand the scorching sun of summer. Sow in boxes or pans well drained, filled with light rich mould. The seed must be very lightly covered – indeed, it may almost lie upon the surface. The boxes should be placed under glass, and sparingly watered. They require no artificial heat. When divided in the summer after flowering, the young plants should be removed to the reserve garden, and allowed to remain there until they are removed to their blooming quarters in late autumn or early spring.

2415 *The Primula* The beautiful greenhouse and window plants known as *Primula Sinensis* commence to flower in the early part of November, and, by care, a succession may be kept up till the spring is far advanced. For bouquets also they are almost invaluable. Sow in March, April, May, June, and July, in pots filled to within half an inch of the top with sifted leaf mould, or, what is better, with thoroughly rotted manure, which has been exposed to all weathers for a year or two. The sowing should be carried out with great care, for although the seed is easily raised in the hands of some, it is nevertheless a matter of great difficulty to others, who, in many instances, too hastily condemn its quality. Leave the surface rather rough, and sprinkle the seed thinly upon it, not covering with soil; tie a piece of thin paper over the top of the pot, and place it in a warm house or hotbed. When the soil becomes dry, water the paper only; the seed will then germinate in two or three weeks; after which remove the paper, and place in a shady place, potting off, when sufficiently strong, into small pots, and place near the glass in a frame or greenhouse. The above method of raising the seed is always followed by one of our largest growers for Covent Garden Market, and never fails. One caution is necessary: never use peat mould, or any soil liable to cake on the surface or turn green, as a loss of the seed is a certain consequence.

The foregoing directions for the culture of *Primula Sinensis* are from the pen of Mr B. S. Williams, of Victoria and Paradise Nurseries, Holloway, London, who is noted for the care, assiduity, and attention with which he has prosecuted it. Messrs Carter and Co., the Queen's Seedsmen, 237 and 238 High Holborn, London, are also noted for their magnificent primulas, known as the Holborn Primulas, in all colours – white, vermilion, blue, red, carmine, magenta, and pink.

2416 *The Ranunculus* Next to the tulip, perhaps, ranunculuses are the most beautiful of all bulbs or tubers, if, indeed, their claw-like roots can fairly lay claim to either of these names. They rival the tulip in brilliancy of colour, and many prefer the beautifully-arranged balls of the ranunculus to the stiff formal cups of the tulip; both, however, have their distinctive features of beauty, and deserve a place in every garden. Although, by careful research into the characteristics and qualities of the blooms, it might be possible to increase the number of the varieties of this beautiful flower to five or six, yet at present they are confined to two, namely, the Turban Ranunculus and the Persian Ranunculus (*Ranunculus Asiaticus*). There are classes of the ranunculus known as English, Scotch, and French, but these are merely improvements of the types already mentioned, the last named being a robust variety of the Turban type which has gone back to a semi-double condition, making amends for its retrocession from the close and compact blooms of the Turbans, by increased abundance of flowers and more vigorous growth and habit. The colours of the ranunculus are as numerous as they are beautiful, being in all shades of purple, brown, crimson, scarlet, rose, pink, and yellow, and in black and white, some having the blooms variegated with markings and edgings of another colour.

2417 *Plantings Soil, etc.* The tubers may be planted from October to the end of March, some preferring one period and some another: perhaps no better time could be chosen for planting than the beginning or middle of February. As soon as the beds are in a fit state, lose no time in planting if the weather be favourable; but waiting a day, or even a week, is nothing in comparison with placing the roots in soil in an unfit state to receive them. They are best cultivated in 4-feet beds of rich loam mixed with one-fourth part of decomposed cow dung. The soil should be dug from 2 to 2½ feet deep, and if the situation is moist and partially sheltered, so much the better. A constant supply of moisture is essential to their beauty and growth, although an excess of water would destroy the tubers during the cold of winter and early spring; after their blossom-buds are formed, however, the surface of the beds must never be allowed to become dry; a daily soaking of water will then be necessary in dry weather, not only for the sake of the flowers, but to preserve the roots from injury, these being very near the surface. The roots should be planted about 2 inches deep and 6 inches apart; their claw-like extremities should be pressed firmly into the earth, and the crowns be covered with an inch of sand previous to another inch of soil being spread over them; the beds may then be covered with a layer of spruce branches, straw litter, or leaf mould, to protect them from the frost; this will, of course, be removed before the appearance of the plants above ground.

FIG. 587 *Ranunculus Asiaticus (Double variety)*

2418 *Propagation of Offsets, etc.* Ranunculuses are increased by offsets, dividing the tubers, and seed. The usual mode of increase is by offsets, and these are generally sufficiently strong to flower the first year. Choice sorts may also be divided into several plants; every little knot that appears on the top of a tuber will form a plant if carefully divided, so as to insure an accompanying claw. However, for choice sorts, this mode of increase is not so desirable as propagation by seed, which is more rapid, as well as the only way of securing new varieties. It is said that ranunculuses never come true from seed.

2419 *Propagation by Seed* Perhaps the best time for sowing is the month of January, and the best place a cold frame. Sow either in the frame, or in pots or boxes, on a smooth hardish surface, and barely cover the seed with soil. Exclude the frost, and keep the frame close until the plants show two seed-leaves; then gradually inure them to more air, until May, when the light may be entirely removed. The little tubers may be taken up when the foliage is quite ripened off: they will require the same, or even more attention, in watering than the old roots. Some prefer sowing the seed on beds out of doors in the autumn or spring months.

2420 *Storing Tubers* Generally, ranunculuses will have died down, and be fit for taking up and storing, by the end of June or beginning of July. The place for storing should be dry; a drawer with a bed of sand being the most convenient.

2421 *The Rose* The rose, deservedly called the queen of flowers, some of whose varieties are illustrated in the coloured plate that forms the frontispiece to this volume, is propagated by seeds, cuttings, layers, budding, and grafting, and new varieties are produced by hydridisation – that is, by transfusing the male pollen of one flower into the stigma of another, with the object of producing seed which shall reproduce the best qualities of both the parent plants. The great obstacle to hybridising in our climate is the difficulty found in ripening the seeds. Tea-scented and Chinese roses must be grown under glass to do so; but the seeds of most other varieties will ripen sufficiently out of doors.

2422 *Propagation by Seed* When the flowers have disappeared, and the seed pods begin to swell and ripen, they should be protected from birds; at the same time, the pods should remain on the trees till perfectly ripe and even turning black, when they should be gathered and buried in the earth, either in pots or in the ground. Before sowing, however, the operation of cleaning the seeds is performed by rubbing them out between the hands, preparatory to sowing them in February or March. So soon as the seed pods are broken up, lay the seeds out in the sun to dry, so that the pulp and husk may be entirely removed, and the seeds sifted and winnowed, when they are ready for sowing. Others prefer sowing the seed immediately on its reaching maturity. In this case they come up the following spring, with all the fine growing season before them. The hardier kinds may be sown in the open borders, selecting for the beds a sunny, sheltered spot with an eastern aspect and shaded from the afternoon sun: the more tender varieties require a frame and glass.

2423 *Preparation of Seed Beds* The soil for seed beds should be light and rich; the beds should be dug 18 inches deep, and the top spit broken up fine and raked level. In sowing, let the seed be laid on the top pretty thick, as only a third or fourth of the number sown will come up. Beat the beds smooth with the back of a spade, water, if the weather be dry, and sift over the whole about half an inch of light sandy soil. If the sowing takes place in spring, keep the seed in water for three or four hours before sowing, taking care that the germ of the seed, now developed more or less, is not injured. Seeds of the more delicate roses should be sown in pans thoroughly drained and filled with equal parts of leaf mould and yellow loam well mixed together. Water, as directed above, when the seeds are sown, and cover to the depth of half an inch with the same soil mixed with a little sand.

In each case a sprinkling of soot or lime scattered over the bed will be a necessary precaution against insects and worms, for both of which the tender buds of the rose have great charms. About May, some of the seeds sown in February or March will germinate, and others will come up from time to time till autumn. The growing seedlings will require constant care in shading, weeding, and watering when the soil is dry.

2424 *Propagation by Suckers* Roses (some kinds much more than others) push their roots in a lateral direction underground, and throw up young shoots or suckers from them. These suckers, separated from the parent plant by the cut of a sharp spade, form flowering plants the same season, if separated in the spring and transplanted to suitable soil. When a rose tree is shy with its suckers it may be stimulated by heaping earth round the roots.

2425 *Propagation by Cuttings* Most roses maybe propagated by cuttings; but all are not calculated for being thus propagated, bottom heat being indispensable for the more tender varieties. Summer and autumn are the best seasons for cuttings. The shoot made in spring is taken with a small portion of last year's wood attached, and cut into lengths of five or six inches, selecting such as have two lateral shoots with five or six leaves to each. An inch of the old wood should be inserted in the soil, leaving at least two leaves above. From four to six of these cuttings may be placed round the inside of a small 3-inch pot, in soil consisting of equal parts of leaf mould, turfy loam chopped fine, and silver sand, watering them well with a fine rose, to settle the earth round the stems. When the water is drained off and the leaves dry, remove to a cold frame or place under hand glasses, shade them from the sun, and sprinkle them daily for a fortnight. If threatened with damping off, give air and sun. In a fortnight the stems will have formed a callus. At this time they are greatly benefitted by bottom heat; they root more rapidly, and may soon be shifted singly into 3-inch pots, and removed back to the cold frame, in which they should be kept till spring.

The following directions for striking perpetual and other roses, so as to produce dwarfs on their own roots, may be found useful: Any time from July to October take the matured wood of the current year's growth of perpetual and other roses, having four eyes just protruding; avoid, if possible, blossom-bearing shoots: plant these on a south border, burying two eyes in a sloping direction, from west to east, or, as the gardeners say, in graft. Be careful, also, to press the earth close round their roots, and occasionally look over them, as worms, etc., may loosen the soil. Cuttings are best left for two years, to become well rooted before they are removed to the flower beds.

The following is a method of striking rose cuttings in autumn, which involves but little trouble, and is adapted to all sorts of perpetuals, and other hybrids with hard wood, which are usually considered troublesome to strike. In September or October, when the young wood is well ripened, take off the slips, and cut them, in the usual way, to two or three eyes, according to the distance which they are apart, taking care, at the same time, to retain a portion of the principal leaf-stalk, and some of the stalks of the first leaflets. Put them singly in small cutting pots or in pans, using plenty of drainers, and filling up with peat or with a compost of sand and leaf mould. Plant with a small dibber, pressing the soil firmly to the base of the cuttings; then water, and plunge the pots to half their depth in a bed sloping about six inches, and well exposed to the sun; and cover with a hand glass. In a fortnight or three weeks the cuttings will have callussed and emitted some rootlets. They will not succeed well in the shade so late in the season. An old melon bed is a good situation for them, as it does not afford too much moisture. Shading should be attended to for some time, if the autumn sun has much power. At the end of a fortnight, air must be given by raising the edge of the hand glass on a small pot. When frost sets in, keep the glass perfectly close, and put dry leaves round as high as the top of the hand glass. In April or May the pots will be found well filled with roots, even in varieties most difficult to strike. The young plants should now be gradually exposed more and more to air and sun, till the hand glass is wholly removed. The points of the young shoots should be removed, and all flower buds, if any show themselves, pinched off, so that the plant may gain strength and throw out branches. In June all those which have been struck in the same pans should be separated into single pots and plunged again. They may require shading for a short time, till they begin to grow, but they will soon be well established and fit to plant out.

2426 *Propagation by Budding* The stocks most commonly used for budding and grafting roses on are the common dog rose of the hedges, and the Boursault and Manetti roses, both of which are obtained by cuttings, the former being a good stock for tea-scented and Chinese roses, and the latter for the hardier roses where vigorous growth is required. The dog rose, however, is preferred by many for all purposes. The best time for procuring stocks for planting in ordinary soil is in the autumn, in October and November; but where the soil is inclined to be moist, it is better to obtain them in the spring. The best stocks are those of two or three years' growth, a little under an inch in thickness, with the bark fresh, and having greyish-green stripes. It is remarked that the graft does not take well where the bark is red-coloured. The stock should be of proper length, well rooted in the soil, free from spines, and without branches.

2427 *Time for Budding* The process of budding may be done successfully at various seasons, the first condition being that the branch and stock are in the same state of vegetative progress. The dog rose is in its best condition for operating on in July or August; to operate earlier is considered a disadvantage. Under very favourable conditions of weather, they may be worked as late as September; but vigorous growing roses like the Provence, Moss, Gallican, Damask, Austrian, and other summer roses, are best budded in the former months. Those stocks, on the contrary, which grow luxuriantly and late, as the Manetti and crimson Boursault, are better worked in the beginning of September, provided the stocks are growing freely, and the weather warm and sunny; for in rose budding, where the bud is exposed to heavy falls of rain, it may rot and perish before it is united with the stock. The roses for which these stocks are suited are Perpetuals, Bourbons, Noisettes, China, and Tea roses, and all the autumnal late bloomers. But all these, when budded on the dog rose, succeed best in July and August.

2428 *Conditions for Budding* The conditions required in budding are that the bark should rise freely and that the shoots are getting a little firm; the buds will then take admirably. In budding, the top bud on the shoot should be commenced with, cutting from ⅛ inch below the eye to ½ inch or ¾ inch above it. In removing buds, and especially from the stem, they should be cut very close, and, if large, the wound should be covered with grafting wax or clay. Where branch grafting is to be practised, one bud should be placed on each branch of the stock, and that as near the stem as possible; therefore, when this kind of grafting is resorted to, it is necessary to preserve the equilibrium of the tree by pinching off the leading bulbs of over-vigorous branches. Where stem grafting is adopted, the buds should be placed opposite to each other, one on one side and one on the other, so that one and the same ligature may serve for both. Where this cannot be accomplished, the buds should be placed as nearly opposite to each other as possible. The operation should be performed quickly, and before the sun has time to dry up the juices of the bud; and when circumstances render delay imperative, the bud should be placed in the shade.

2429 *Operation of Budding* The operation of budding consists in transferring from one tree to another a small piece of the bark with an embryo bud, and inserting it beneath the bark of another. The only instrument necessary is the budding-knife. The process consists in making a cross-cut just deep enough to cut through the bark, and a longitudinal downward cut, making the letter **T**. Then, with the thin handle of the knife, raise the inner edges of the bark under the cross-cut: it is now ready to receive the bud. This is procured by first removing the greater part of the leaf from a bud, leaving only the foot-stalk. Now make a longitudinal cut, about an inch in length, beginning below the bud and terminating above it; thus removing the bud with the bark, half an inch above and half an inch below the eye, with a thin slice of the wood: this is the cushion or shield. Having removed the wood as clean as possible, the lower point of the bud is now inserted in the open slip formed by the T, and push in the bud, first on one side and then on the other, pushing it gently under until two-thirds of it are under the bark, so that the eye of the bud is exactly under the opening caused by the raised edges of the bark. The upper part of the bud is now cut across, so as to fit it exactly into the angle at which the bark of the stock was cut; it is now bound up with worsted or cotton thread, previously prepared. Tying commences at the bottom, passing upward until the whole is covered except the eye of the bud; sometimes a little damp moss or a leaf being tied over it for the sake of the moisture it gives out. From three to five weeks after the operation, according to the dryness of the season, it is necessary to examine the buds and loosen the ligature which binds it to the tree, otherwise the growth may be checked.

2430 *Grafting* is performed by cutting the top of the stock to a proper height by a clean horizontal cut, and then make a longitudinal **V**-shaped cut down the centre, one two, or three inches long, according to the size of the stock. In this slit place the graft after having cut the lower end of it to fit the cut in the stock. Having inserted it, bind the whole up with clay or grafting paste, as directed in budding. The best time for grafting roses in pots is January.

2431 *Soil, etc.* The rose grows vigorously in most kinds of soil; nevertheless, it does best in a light free soil, a little fresh, amended from time to time with some well-decomposed manure. A calcareous soil is especially recommended. Delicate varieties do best in fertile, sandy soils and in peat earth. The dog rose grows vigorously in stiff earth. For nearly all roses, however, the soil can scarcely be too rich. They delight in a stiff loam liberally incorporated with manure, and no excellences of variety, climate, or culture can compensate for the absence of this indispensable desideratum. Where the natural soil is light and sandy, the whole bed should be removed to the depth of two feet, and replaced with the richest natural fibrous loam at hand, thoroughly mixed with decomposed dung.

2432 *Planting* At the proper time, having selected the sorts of roses suited for the purpose, and of one or two seasons' growth from budding, and having cut off with a sharp knife all damaged root fibres, we proceed to plant. Good ordinary garden soil will produce the rose large enough for ordinary purposes; but to grow it in perfection, unless a bed has been previously prepared in the manner directed above, a hole in the ground should be opened 2 feet square and a foot deep. This station should be filled with a compost consisting of two good-sized spadefuls of thoroughly rotted dung for each plant, mixing it well with the soil. Upon the soil thus prepared the standard rose is placed, the collar just above the level of the surface, and the fibres carefully spread out over the soil. Fill in the remaining soil and replace the turf, treading it gently until it forms a small mound, out of the centre of which the tree rises. A stake is now driven into the ground, near enough to support the stem, which is tied to it.

2433 *Season for Planting* The season for planting may be any time from the fall of the leaf till the buds again begin to swell, in April or the beginning of May. After that there is danger of the tree dying off.

2434 *Pruning Newly Planted Trees* In pruning newly-planted roses, the object is to balance the head to the vital powers of the fibrous root, which has not yet thrown out its spongioles, and to give a graceful form to the intended head. If there be only one shoot from the bud, cut it down to two eyes; if there be a regular head formed, cut away every shoot down to the lowest eye that points outward or downward, and cut away all weak shoots or thin ones that come in the way of a better, back to their base, leaving only such as are required to form the head of the tree. When the buds begin to break, rub off all that grow inwards, all that would cross other branches, all that are coming weakly, and all that would crowd the head and destroy its cuplike form. It is not a good practice to prune roses immediately after planting them. The tops should be left on for a month or six weeks, and then cut back or headed in to three or four buds from the stock. This will insure a healthy, vigorous growth. After the plants are established, the shoots may vary in length from 4 to 16 inches. The weaker the growth, the closer should they be pruned, and vice versa.

As the growth proceeds, examine every bud, every curled leaf and shoot, for insect larvae; for maggots, if not detected at once, soon destroy the vitality of the flower bud. Do this daily, syringing also with a fine rose syringe, very forcibly applied, which may destroy the green fly, the thrip, and other enemies. If they get established, nothing but hand-picking, washing with tobacco juice, or smoking with tobacco will get rid of them.

2435 *Classification of Roses* Taking height only into consideration, worked roses – that is to say, roses budded on stems or stocks – are distinguished as Standards, Half Standards, Dwarf Standards, and Dwarfs. Of these, *Standards* are on stems from 2½ feet to 4 feet from the ground to the budding; *Half Standards*', from 1½ feet to 2½ feet; *Dwarf Standards*, from 1 foot to 1½ feet; while *Dwarfs* are worked close to or beneath the surface, and form vigorous bushes for winter planting. Dwarfs on own roots are small plants in pots, which should be planted out in early autumn, or kept in frames during the winter and put out in April. In addition to these forms there are *Climbing* Roses, whose habit is obvious from the name they bear. Further, roses generally are divided into two great classes or sections, namely, Summer Roses and Autumnal Roses.

2436 *Summer Roses* The Summer Roses include the Provence Roses, the Striped Provence and French Roses (*Rosa Gallica*), Moss Roses, Scotch Roses, Austrian Roses, and the beautiful double yellow rose known as *Rosa sulphurea*. The Summer Climbers include the Boursault and Ayrshire Roses, some Evergreen Roses, such as Félicité-Perpetué and Banksian Roses. The fine old favourite, the Cabbage Rose, is a pink Provence, the white variety being commonly known as the Provence Rose. Among the striped roses stands conspicuous the old York-and-Lancaster, with white petals, striped and flecked, carnation like, with glowing streaks of red. The Moss Rose, a variety of the Provence Rose, is too well known by its moss-like setting to require further mention. The Austrian Roses are all yellow in colour.

2437 *Autumnal Roses* These roses, which flower from June to December, are many in number, and are classified as Hybrid Perpetuals, divided by Mr Paul into two sections, one comprising roses better suited for exhibition purposes, and the other roses that are more suitable for garden decoration; Macartney Roses, Ramanas Roses, including the beautiful single red rose, *Rosa rugosa*, from Japan, whose large hips look like medlars of an orange-scarlet tint, varieties of the *Rosa Polyantha hybrida*, Musk and Perpetual, Moss and Scotch Roses, Bourbon Roses, Noisettes, Chinese or Bengal Roses, and Hybrid Tea-Scented and Tea-Scented Roses.

2438 *Treatment of Roses* As a matter of course, where there are so many varieties of roses, it may be imagined that the same treatment will not suit them all. The following summary of treatment suited to each class is therefore appended. Its utility is self-evident, as it focuses the special culture of each sort, as it were, and brings the cultural directions suitable for each into the smallest possible space.

1 **Provence, or Cabbage Roses** Prune close, shortening every shoot three or four buds down, one half in April, the other in October, and keep beds of dwarfs clear from weeds. Propagate by budding and layers in July; graft in March.

2 **Moss Roses** require the same severe pruning as the above, and a light rich soil; pruning, one half in May, the other in October, in order to have a succession of flowers. Propagate by layers and budding in July; graft in March. Some of the perpetual mosses are very beautiful: as *Madame Edouard Ory*, dwarf and compact, bright rosy carmine; *Salet*, bright rose, with blush edges. To insure a free bloom in autumn, shift and replant in fresh compost in November.

3 **Hybrid Provence Roses** Prune moderately short; propagate by budding and layers in July, and by grafting in March. Robust, vigorous roses, requiring good soil enriched with manure.

4 **French Rose** (*Rosa gallica*) Prune moderately short, and cut out all spray-like shoots; propagate by budding and layers in July and August; graft in March; mulch round the stems, and water with manure water in dry weather.

5 **Hybrid China** Prune moderately short; shorten strong branches, and cut out the smaller shoots; propagate by budding and layers in July and August, by cuttings from September to November; graft in March; mulch the surface round the stem in winter with good rich manure, adding to it as the blooming season approaches.

6 **Hybrid Bourbons** Prune moderately short; propagate by layers and budding in July and August, by cuttings from November to December; graft in March.

7 **Austrian Briers** Little pruning required; only shorten the shoots and thin out old wood, leaving young wood untouched; propagate by cuttings and budding in July and August. It requires a rather moist soil, and dry pure air, and little manure.

8 **Banksian Roses** bloom on the previous year's wood. Prune in July, when the season is over, and the plant will produce bearing wood in the autumn; propagate by cuttings in May and September. It requires a wall, and should be on its own roots; blooms freely in dry soil.

9 **Hardy Climbing Roses** require little pruning; but thin out old wood as soon as the blooming season is over; the after-growth will furnish bearing wood for next season.

10 **Damask Perpetuals** Prune moderately in June, and again in November; propagate by budding and layers in July, graft in March; a dry soil, with an annual supply of manure on the surface, and the soil just stirred in November.

11 **Hybrid Perpetuals** Prune very close in summer; propagate by budding from June till September, and by layers in July and August; graft in March. In June cut off half the number of clusters showing themselves; these will bloom again in August. Towards the end of February, cut off from each vigorous shoot of the preceding summer two-thirds of its length, and from weaker ones two-thirds, cutting out all superfluous ones entirely. An annual removal is recommended, stirring the bed well and replanting, adding two shovelfuls of equal parts rotted dung and good loam if the soil be poor, and equal parts rotted dung and road-sand if it be stiff.

12 **Bourbon Roses** Prune close to within four or five buds, in April, the more delicate kinds, and moderately all vigorous growers; in summer the ends of long vigorous shoots on standards or pillars should be pinched off. Propagate by buddings, layers, and cuttings, from June to November; graft in March. On Manetti stocks they are

beautiful dwarf standards. They require high culture, plenty of manure water, and a coating of mulch, covered with moss for appearances, and to prevent radiation.

13 **Tea-Scented and China Roses** require little pruning. Thin out old wood about the end of March, and shorten to half its length, to encourage young shoots; propagate by budding, layers, and cuttings, from June till November. The tea-scented roses are more tender than the China, and require more care. On their own roots, and in moist soil, they require a raised bed, made of 9 inches of brick rubbish and 12 inches of garden mould and rotted dung in equal portions, well mixed, adding a little river-sand. In this plant the bushes, 2 feet apart. Protect in winter by green furze or other spray, which will admit plenty of air while keeping out frost.

14 **Noisette Roses.** – Slightly shorten and train the shoots at their full length, and thin out in March; propagate by layers, cuttings, and budding, from June till September; graft in March. When done flowering, cut the shoots close to the ground to encourage others for next season. Tea-scented Noisettes are tender, and require a wall in a warm aspect, or a pillar well sheltered; the soil well manured, and stirred 20 inches deep.

15 **Scotch Roses** will grow almost anywhere, in any soil, in the crevice of a rock, or in a sandy soil, with plenty of air; they require little pruning, and bloom early in the season.

Good roses may be obtained from growers in every part of the country, but among growers of celebrity may be named Messrs Paul and Son, The Old Nurseries, Cheshunt, Herts; Messrs William Paul and Son, Waltham Cross, Herts; Messrs Richard Smith and Co., Worcester; and Messrs Ewing and Co., Sea View Nurseries, Havant, Hampshire. The named roses in cultivation, as it has been said, number over 2000; for a complete list of these the reader is referred to the *Gardener's Magazine* for July 4, 11, and 18, 1885.

2439 *The Tulip* For brilliancy of colour, diversity of height and time of blooming, and striking showiness, we have nothing to equal the tulip. Ribbon borders and masses of colour may be formed of this bulb alone, rivalling and throwing into the shade all our summer and autumn beauties. Of dwarf Duc van Thols alone, we have all the colours necessary to form effective ribbon borders with the exception of blue.

2440 *Tulips in Pots* For winter and spring decoration under glass the tulip may be placed next to the hyacinth. The single and double dwarf Duc van Thol tulips are for this purpose most valuable. There are also several large flowering double tulips, which produce a brilliant display. The former may be planted, six or eight bulbs in a good-sized pot; but of the latter three bulbs will be sufficient. All tulips require a good supply of water when in flower, and to be shaded from the sun. The single Due van Thol is the earliest of all. If these be planted in September they may be had in bloom before Christmas, and by later planting, a succession may be kept up for some time. Of the large double tulips, which are remarkably showy, the best varieties are *Imperator rubrorum*, Duke of York (bronze crimson with a yellow margin), Extremité d'Or (rich crimson bordered with orange), La Candeur (pure white), and Tournesol (scarlet and yellow). The soil and treatment necessary for these, whether grown in pots or in the open ground, are the same as were recommended for hyacinths.

2441 *Show Tulips* Show, or late flowering tulips, of which a single bulb used to be worth a prime carriage horse, are exquisite in shape and colour, and are divided into three classes – *bizarres*, which have yellow grounds, feathered or striped with crimson, purple, or white; *byblomens*, white ground, flaked or striped with black, lilac, or purple; and *roses*, that have white grounds, feathered or striped with crimson, pink, or scarlet. In each of these classes many exquisitely beautiful named flowers exist; but anyone intending to grow these should visit some good collection when they are in flower, and choose for himself.

2442 *Storing Bulbs* Soon after tulips have finished flowering, the leaves will ripen and die off. They should be immediately taken up with all the soil that will adhere to the bulb, slightly dried, and put away in drawers or paper bags, each sort by itself. During the summer they should be frequently looked over to see that they are not decaying. On the 1st of October rub off all the offsets, and plant them by themselves, and prepare for planting the entire stock forthwith.

For the names and colours of special sorts of the tulip, whether dwarf or show, the reader is referred to the price list of any nurseryman and seedsman who provides a large stock of Dutch bulbs for sale in autumn.

2443 *The Verbena* The culture of this useful and beautiful bedding plant, which is serviceable for growing in pots, is precisely similar to that of the petunia (paragraph 2407), to which the reader is referred.

2444 *The Violet* This flower, the emblem of the Bonaparte family, is held in the highest estimation for its exquisite and delicate perfume. There are many varieties, but it will be sufficient to describe the culture of one or two sorts, as from this the treatment of the rest may be readily gathered.

2445 *The Neapolitan Violet: Summer Culture* The Neapolitan violet maybe propagated with advantage in June. When the plants have flowered for the season, remove them from the soil in which they have been grown, and divide them into single crowns, cutting off all runners and selecting the finest flowers only, and plant them out with the trowel 9 inches apart each way, pressing the ground firmly round the roots, selecting for the purpose a rich and well-prepared piece of ground with an east aspect, where they can receive the beams of the morning sun. In such a situation they are said to escape the ravages of the red spider and other pests, and to produce larger and brighter flowers. When the plants show signs of growth, stir the soil about their roots with a small hoe, and syringe them in the evenings of dry hot days with pure water, pinching off all runners as they appear, and keeping the bed free from weeds: nothing more is required for their culture during the summer months.

2446 *Forcing for Winter Supply in Hotbed* When the time arrives for forcing them, prepare the material for a hotbed in the manner already described for making a cucumber bed, either by building it up or by sinking it in the ground two feet, treading down the dung to prevent an over-violent heat at first. Over this place the frame, and cover the bed a foot thick with prepared soil, consisting of the remains of an old cucumber bed with a little leaf mould added. The plants are then carefully removed, with as large a ball of earth round the roots as possible, and planted in rows close together, but not touching each other, and so arranged that the foliage may be close to the glass without touching it, as it will settle an inch or two after the lights are put on. When planted, give them a copious watering, even to saturation, and in warm showers take the lights off and give them the benefit of it: this will give them a clean, healthy appearance. The lights may be kept off all night with advantage when there is no appearance of frost, and all dead, decayed, or turning leaves should be removed as soon as they appear. Plants thus treated will yield a supply of violets from November to April.

2447 *Forcing in Pots* It is immaterial, provided a succession is maintained by separating the crowns as soon as they have done blooming, whether the after culture is on the bed or in pots plunged in the soil. For pot culture, the best compost is formed of half turfy loam that has been turned over two or three times during summer, and half-rotten dung and leaf mould, well mixed together. This should be ready for use by the end of September. At that time the violet plants must be raised from the bed in which they have been growing during the summer with as much earth to their roots as possible. They should then be divested of all their side shoots or runners.

The proper sized pots are 7-inch ones. One strong plant should be put in each pot; but when they are weak, two or three. The pots should be well drained with broken bones instead of potsherds, for the roots of the violets will lay hold of the bones, which gives vigour to the plants and makes them bloom more profusely. The pots have the advantage of being available for the window, garden, or for removal into the drawing-room or hall, as well as for cut flowers.

2448 *Management after Potting: Protection under Glass* Having potted as many as are necessary for the season, a good supply of water should be given to settle the soil well about the roots. A sufficient number of old melon boxes, with the lights belonging to them, should be arranged in a southern aspect, placing the boxes in such a manner that the lights will throw off rain quickly, and thereby prevent drip, which in winter not only rots the plants, but causes the flowers to be produced sparingly. The boxes being placed in position, a layer of old tan should be put into them 4 inches thick: in this the pots should be plunged up to their rims in rows till the boxes are filled. It will be necessary to leave 3 inches space between the pots, where the plants are large, that air may be allowed to pass freely between and keep off damp, which is apt to destroy the plant. If they are so small as not to cover the top of the pots, they may be placed close together.

When the temperature is above 50°, the lights may be removed during the day, and at night they should be tilted up at the back for the admission of air. When the temperature is below 50°, the lights should be left on; but even then air should be admitted from behind during the daytime. When the temperature is below 40°, the admission of air should be very partial, if it be admitted at all. At no time after the plants begin to bloom should the lights be entirely removed, except for the purpose of watering or cleaning the plants, or gathering the flowers. When the weather is cold, coverings of mats should be applied at night. In hard frosts, two mats should be put on as well as litter. The earth in the pots must never be allowed to freeze if it is possible to prevent it. The coverings must be removed in fine days. In March and April, as much air as possible should be given if the weather is fine.

2449 *Watering, etc.* The pots should be examined at all times when the weather will permit. Weeds and decayed leaves must be removed, and a little water given when the soil is dry. Care must be taken to wet the leaves as little as possible. In March and April, if the plants have been properly managed, they will produce abundance of flowers, and consequently will require more moisture than during winter.

Where it is desired to have violets in summer and autumn, runners should be laid either in pots or on a hotbed where they are growing, in February, selecting the strongest runners, and pegging them down, with a little soil over the runner, and keeping them moist: these will be ready to plant out early in April, each with its bundle of roots, and will come in a month or six weeks earlier than the others. But they must be placed in their winter quarters early in September.

2450 *Russian Violets* To have an abundance of fine flowers in the autumn and early spring, these should be planted in beds under a wall, in a warm aspect. The soil should be light, but very highly manured, with a large quantity of sand about 4 inches underneath the top soil. The roots should be planted in rows about 3 or 4 inches apart, and well watered. Every year, in April, immediately after they have done flowering, the beds should be broken up, the soil renewed, and fresh plants put in for another year.

For named varieties of the violet, apply to any of the nurserymen and growers whose names have been mentioned in this chapter.

FIG. 588 *Scolopendrium vulgare*

FIG. 589 *Osmunda regalis*

FIG. 590 *Onoclea sensibilis*

FIG. 591 *Phegopteris vulgare*

FIG. 592 *Athyrium filix foemina*

CHAPTER 36

Vegetables, Culinary Herbs, and Fruits, with Notes on their Culture and Management

2451 With reference to the named varieties of different kinds of flowers, it has been said that it is inexpedient to give long lists of those that are grown and sent out in any year, because many of them that may then stand high in favour will be supplanted in the year following, and in every year to come, by others that will be newly introduced, and may soon drop out of cultivation altogether. Thus a list of varieties which may be everything that can be desired for the year in which it is issued will be almost useless in a few years to come – firstly, because it contains the names of many flowers which cannot be had, and secondly, because it does not contain the names of those which have been brought out since its publication. In the case of vegetables, this does not apply equally well, except, perhaps, in the case of potatoes, because the new sorts and varieties that are introduced are not nearly so numerous, but even in these it is desirable to refer the reader to the price lists issued by seedsmen, in which the best sorts in cultivation are always named and carefully described, and in which the newest varieties always find mention.

2452 It will save trouble, perhaps, and be useful to the reader, to give here the names and addresses of a few seedsmen in London and different parts of the country, placing them in alphabetical order. There are, of course, many others, whom it is impossible to mention through want of space, and the names that are given are inserted merely for the benefit of those who would rather have selections of seeds for use throughout the year in bulk instead of purchasing them as he may want them in his own immediate neighbourhood:

P. Barr and Son, King Street, Covent Garden, London
Isaac Brunning and Co., 3 Regent Street, Great Yarmouth
H. Cannell and Sons, Swanley, Kent
Carter and Co., 237 and 238 High Holborn, London
Carter Page and Co., 53 London Wall, London
Viccars Collyer and Co., Central Hall, Leicester
G. Cooling and Son, Bath
Daniels Brothers, Norwich
W. B. Hartland, 24 Patrick Street, Cork
Hooper and Co., Covent Garden, London
Ryder and Son, Sale, near Manchester
H. Schmelzer and Co., 71 Waterloo Street, Glasgow
Richard Smith and Co., Worcester
Stuart and Mein, Kelso, Scotland
Sutton and Sons, Reading, Berkshire

James Veitch and Sons, **544** King's Road, Chelsea, London
E. Webb and Sons, Wordsley, Stourbridge
B. S. Williams, Victoria and Paradise Nurseries, Holloway, London

To these may be added the name of one foreign seedsman and grower, namely, Chr. Lorenz, 100–103 John Street, Erfurt, Germany. Messrs H. Schmelzer and Co., named above, act, it may be said, as agents for F. C. Heinemann, another seedsman whose seed farm is at Erfurt.

2453 It is not intended here to give minute cultural directions for each variety of vegetables, but merely to indicate the general treatment of the class or species to which each belongs. Before doing this, it will be useful to seek some kind of classification for vegetables, so that the classes, and the kinds that belong to each class, may be taken in order. The classification in sections may be most conveniently effected as follows: 1. *Leguminous Section*, including Peas, Broad Beans, and French Beans, both dwarfs and runners. 2. *Edible Leaved and Flowered Section*, including plants of which we eat the leaves or flowers, or both, being Borecole or Kale, Broccoli, Brussels Sprouts, Cabbages, Savoys, Couve Tronchuda, Cauliflower, Spinach, Asparagus, Seakale, Globe Artichoke, etc. 3. *Edible Rooted Section*, including plants of which we eat the roots or tubers, namely, Beet, Carrot, Parsnip, Turnip, Salsafy, Scorzonera, Leek, Onion, Garlic, Potato, Jerusalem Artichoke, etc. 4. *Edible Fruited Section*, or plants of which we eat the fruit, namely, Capsicums and Chilis, Cucumbers, Vegetable Marrows, Melons, Tomatoes, etc. 5. *Salad Section*, comprising Celery, Endive, Lettuce, Radishes, Corn Salad, Mustard and Cress of various kinds. 6. *The Mushroom*, a nondescript, which cannot be classed under any of the preceding heads, or with – 7. *Sweet Herb Section*, including Parsley and all Pot Herbs, and Sweet Herbs, and Herbs in use for garnishing.

1 – Leguminous Section

2454 *The Pea* This useful and delicious vegetable, which few dislike, may be sown at almost any time throughout the year, or, at all events, from October to May, early sorts being sown in the former month and onwards, being well protected by mulching and litter throughout the winter, and as late as the latter month for crops in autumn. The pea, without being difficult as to the quality of soil, does best on a rich, light loam, and nothing seems to agree with it so well as a fresh virgin soil which has not been cropped for some years before. They may be sown in single rows, or broad drills, not less than 6 inches in width, or, if preferred, in double rows – that is to say, two rows 9 inches apart, and each pair of rows from 3 to 5 feet apart, according to the height of the sort, and for the very tall sorts even 6 feet apart. They should be sown in drills 3 inches deep, and all on the same level, and moderately thick, so as to allow for depredations committed by birds and mice. The subsequent culture consists in hoeing and earthing-up the young peas when an inch or two above the ground, and watering in dry weather; and except in the case of the dwarf sorts, sticking them as soon as they begin to throw out their lateral shoots, choosing sticks with spreading branches, on which the vines may extend themselves.

In sowing peas, they should be scattered evenly, at regular distances apart, so that there may be no crowding; they should be earthed up when about 3 inches high, and the sticks put to them before they begin to be taller on one side than the other, but not till they really require it, as sticks are likely to draw them up weak, especially if they are sown too thickly. After sticking, they should be mulched, spreading the dung over a clear space of 18 inches on each side of the row, to the depth of 3 inches. In sticking peas, plenty of small brush should be placed near the ground, in order to conduct the peas upwards: it is useless to give them support above, and leave them without the means of getting to it. It is very necessary to mulch early crops of peas, especially where the soil is light: it protects the young roots from frost, and saves watering and manuring the ground for the next crop, and tends to produce a better and much earlier supply. Where ground is valuable, and the rows run from north to south, the space between the rows of peas may be filled with cabbages, onions, French beans, and other surface crops; but to do this with good effect there should be plenty of room between the rows. French gardeners sometimes sow peas in clusters, making holes 8 or 10 inches apart in the rows, and planting in each five or six peas. There are various modes of forwarding the growth of peas for early crops. One method is to have some pieces of turf cut very thick, about 8 inches wide, and of any convenient length. Make a groove along the centre, and sow the peas moderately thick in it, cover them with rich light soil, and place the turfs so planted under the stage of a greenhouse, or in a pit or frame. Towards the end of March or beginning of April, plant them out, burying the turfs completely in the soil. A second method is to prepare some shallow boxes, about 6 inches deep, filled with adhesive soil; this soil is drilled or grooved, and in the grooves the peas are planted; the boxes placed, as before, in a frame or under the greenhouse stage. When fully up, cut the soil into portions, each part containing a single row of peas; plant the whole in the open ground, burying the whole of the soil containing the peas. A third method is to use small 3-inch pots, in which clumps of peas are sown, which may be turned out into the ground, without disturbing the roots. Where the garden soil is cold and heavy, it is advisable to adopt one or other of these methods for securing early peas. Early sowing may also be carried out in the manner described below for beans.

2455 *Peas for Autumn Crops* The production of peas in autumn requires considerable attention, especially on light porous soils, and even on soils which produce good spring and summer crops. By the following process fine crops of peas may be produced till October. Manure and trench a piece of ground in the ordinary way, and make a trench 9 inches deep and 15 inches wide; a coating of cow dung 6 inches thick is forked into the trench, and covered with a few inches of soil; upon this soil the peas are sown. If late in the season and in dry weather, soak the peas for a day or two in water before sowing; but for early crops, or in moist weather, the precaution is unnecessary. When in full bearing, a thorough soaking with liquid manure, or a sprinkling of guano over the trenches, and a copious watering with soft water afterwards, will not be thrown away. A row or two of peas, according to length, sown every month until August, will give a plentiful supply for an ordinary family, and good succession throughout the season. Plants sown in August, in pots filled with rich manure planted out on a south border previously trenched and well manured, the whole ground being thoroughly soaked with weak manure water, and mulched several inches thick with well-rotted dung, will yield an excellent crop through October.

2456 *Broad Beans* Beans, like peas, can be sown in October, where the soil is light or well drained, and well sheltered; or, where the ground is heavy, they may be raised in a pit or frame by sowing three in a 4-inch pot now, and planting out in March; but if the soil is cold, and no conveniences are at hand for starting in pots, they may be sown in the following manner: Let the ground be laid in ridges 3 feet wide, and 15 or 16 inches high, ranging east and west; on the south side of each ridge draw a drill halfway between the top and bottom, in which sow the beans about 3 inches apart. By this means they will be above the wet, catch every ray of sunshine, and will be stronger than if raised under glass and planted out. When about 10 inches high, level the top of each ridge to the row of beans behind it; they will not require earthing up again. If sown in October, a succession may be sown in January, in the same manner, and so on once a month till June; they do not bear well if sown after that. Those sown on level ground should have some earth drawn up to the roots when three or four inches high; this induces them to emit fresh roots. They are sown in rows about 4 feet apart, which leaves room for a row of broccoli, spinach, or lettuce between; but those who are not limited as to space had better allow 5 or 6 feet from row to row. On light soils the usual method is to stretch a line along where they have to be sown, and dib holes 4 inches deep, planting a row each side of the line, 4 inches apart, zigzag fashion; but in wet soils it is better to drill them in, laying boards along the row to stand on, so as to avoid clodding the ground by treading on it.

The sort usually grown for first crop is the Early Mazagan, but the Early Long Pod is equally early and prolific, and larger; but whatever sort is grown, the culture is the same, and as it is not a favourite vegetable with many persons, it should be carefully considered how much ground can be devoted to it without encroaching upon the space required for more important crops. A crop which is not required involves a loss of time, space, and nourishment, withdrawn from the soil.

2457 *French or Kidney Beans* These beans, which are sometimes distinguished as haricot beans, require a light, rich, loamy soil, and should be planted in an open situation. In outdoor culture the seed should not be sown until the middle of April in sunny spots, or in the beginning of May in positions not so open to the sun, and from this time crops may be sown in succession once a fortnight, or thereabouts, until the end of July. Plant in rows from 18 inches to 2 feet apart, and from 9 to 12 inches apart in the rows. Put at least three seeds in each patch, lest any should fail; if all grow, two can be removed; if none grow, the deficiency must be supplied by transplanting from a patch sown for the purpose. It is better, however, to sow more plentifully than to transplant, as this operation tends to check the plants. The seed should be dibbled in to the depth of an inch. As the beans grow, draw the soil up round each plant as high as possible.

When forced, kidney beans may be had at any time of year, whether early or late. They may be grown on a hotbed, but they are better grown in pots, or they are apt to run all to haulm and leaf. In an ordinary hotbed, as if made for cucumbers, place as many 6-inch pots as will stand 15 inches apart. These pots being filled with good loamy soil, in each plant, triangularly, three Newington Wonder beans, which is of small dwarf habit and a great bearer, and, as they grow, give them regular waterings; but they need not be removed, and the heat should never fall below 60°. They are very susceptible of frost, and will require careful protection from it, in common with all forcing plants. Nothing can be better for covering the lights than hurdles made of lath and straw. If sown in January or February, they will bear in April or May. They sometimes require supporting with sticks.

2458 *Runner Beans* As these beans grow to a considerable height, they cannot be conveniently forced like the dwarf sorts, though this might be effected by constantly pinching off the leading shoots, and thus compelling it to assume and maintain a dwarf, bushy growth. The soil should be light and rich as for peas and other varieties of beans, and the situation sunny and open. Plant in double rows 9 inches apart, dibbling in single seeds to the depth of 2 inches and 9 inches apart in the rows. At least 6 feet should be allowed between each series of double rows. Means for the plants to climb must be afforded by poles stuck in the ground along each row, inclined towards each other till they cross at the top, and secured by tying with tarred cord to horizontal sticks dropped into and along the crossing of the poles in the earth, from end to end of the row. If there is not much room, the seed may be set in single rows, about 3 feet apart, and kept dwarf by pinching the leading shoots. If this style of growing them be adopted, no sticks will be required. Another mode is to place hurdles along the rows, on which the runners may climb to the height of the hurdles.

Runner beans are often sown in a mass, in a pan or box in richly-manured soil, in the middle of April, and kept under shelter until the middle of May, when they are planted out in the garden. By this means the crop may be obtained a little earlier. These beans are often utilised for covering fences, and yield plentifully when sown or planted in such positions.

2 – Edible Leaved and Flowered Section

2459 *The Cabbage* This section includes the whole of the *Brassicoe*, and many other plants of which we eat either the leaves, as in the cabbage, the flower, as in the cauliflower or globe artichoke, or both, as in the sprouting broccoli. The Cabbage family form, perhaps, the most important and valuable of the different groups of vegetables, for one kind or another may be brought to table all the year round, and even in the depth of winter, when nothing else may be had but roots and bulbs already harvested and stored, it furnishes a welcome and desirable accompaniment to many of the dishes that form our animal food.

2460 *General Treatment* For all varieties of the cabbage the treatment is very nearly the same, and as the directions now to follow will be useful for small seeds generally it will be well to give it, although special instructions for each particular class or variety will be appended. Let the seed beds be open and away from trees or other shelter, and tolerably dry, but not parched, at the time of sowing. Mark out for each sort its allotted space; give plenty of room – at least a square rod; sow the seed broadcast regularly over the ground, so that they do not come up thicker in one part than another; tread it well in, unless the ground is wet and binding; in that case stand in the alleys, rake level, and pat the surface with a piece of flat board: this will press the seed in without hardening the ground. If dry enough to tread, rake the surface even. If the weather is dry, and continue so, it will be necessary to give the seed bed a copious watering to keep it moist, so that the surface does not cake. When the seed is up, keep the beds moist, so as to promote vigorous growth; giving a liberal dusting of lime, salt, or soot now and then, which will benefit the young plants, and prevent the attacks of the fly. When large enough to handle, thin them, and prick out those drawn in nursery beds 5 or 6 inches apart from each other.

2461 *Classification of Cabbage Family* This important family of vegetables are biennial, triennial, and nearly perennial in some of the varieties. They may be divided into:

1 Cabbages proper, which have heads formed of the inner leaves growing close and compactly round the stem, which are thus blanched into a whitish yellow by the outer leaves.
2 Red, or Milan cabbage, which grows in the same form, except in colour.
3 Savoys, distinguished by their curly wrinkled leaves, but retaining the tendency to form a head.
4 Brussels Sprouts, producing the sprouts, or edible part, from the stem in small heads, like very young cabbages.
5 Borecole, of which there are many varieties, has a large open head with large curling leaves.
6 Cauliflower and broccoli, in which the flower buds form a close fleshy head of a delicate yellowish white, for which both are cultivated.

2462 *The Cabbage Proper* Of the first of these there are many varieties, some of them valuable for their precocity, which adapts them for early spring cultivation; others for more enduring qualities. They are all propagated by seed sown for main crops twice a year, namely, in April, for planting out in June and July, for autumn and winter use; and in August and September, for spring use; but it is usual to make sowings of smaller quantities every month for succession.

The Romans propagated the Brassica by seeds and cuttings, by which choice varieties may be perpetuated with greater certainty than from seed. This is done by slipping off the sprouts, which all the tribe produce on the stem, when about 4 inches long; and after exposing it to the air for a day or two to cauterise the wound, it is dipped in caustic lime, and planted where it is to grow. Pliny tells us they are fittest for planting or for eating when the sprout has six leaves.

2463 *Cultivation, Soil, etc.* The seed is sown on beds 4 feet wide, and long in proportion to the sowing – a bed 4 feet by 20 will take 2 oz. of seed. Cover the seed to an eighth or a quarter of an inch with rich light soil, and rake it in: the after cultivation will be gathered from the calendars. They require a rich retentive soil. The whole tribe are improved by early transplanting when about two inches in height. The young plants should be removed into nursery beds thoroughly prepared by digging and manuring, and, if dry, by watering, where they are planted 4 or 5 inches apart. Here the plants remain till well rooted. Their next remove is usually to the place where they are permanently to grow; but they will be rather improved by an intermediate shift to a second nursery bed.

2464 *Planting Out* In final planting out, the ground being trenched and well manured, a drill is drawn, 3 inches deep, at a distance proportioned to the size and habit of growth of the variety; the small or early dwarfs at 12 or 15 inches apart in the rows, the larger sorts at 18 inches. The subsequent culture is confined to weeding and occasionally stirring the earth during summer, and drawing it up round the stem when about 8 or 9 inches high.

2465 *The Red or Milan Cabbage* The red cabbage is chiefly used for pickling. Its cultivation is in all respects the same as the white cabbage, and the vegetable is only gathered when the head is thoroughly formed, and when so gathered the stem is thrown away as of no further value.

2466 *The Savoy Cabbage* This has been in cultivation in this country since the times of Gerarde (1545–1607), by whom it is described. It is distinguished by its curly leaves and deep green colour from the cabbage; like it, however, it grows a compact, well-shaped head, and a plentiful crop of sprouts on the stem during winter. Like the others, it is propagated by seeds and cuttings in the spring, sown on a hotbed in February, or on beds in the open ground early in April. Plants will be ready for planting out permanently in May, June, and July.

2467 *Cultivation, etc.* In all respects the treatment is the same as with cabbages, removing the plants to a nursery bed when two inches high, selecting the strongest plants first. When planted out permanently, they should stand 2 feet apart in the rows and 20 inches between the plants; but it is not unusual to plant them between standing crops of peas or other less permanent crops, whose place they thus occupy when removed.

2468 *Brussels Sprouts* These have the same treatment as other varieties in the seed beds, and in general management; early in April being the best time for sowing in the open ground.

Mr Cuthill thinks March sowing would be better. 'When thus sown,' he adds, 'I have had them 3 feet high, each stem producing a peck of large close sprouts.' The after treatment Mr Cuthill recommends, is to 'select a rich stiff loam, and plant them in rows 2 feet or 18 inches apart, keeping the ground loosened by hoeing; and as soon as the stems reach their full height, which is known by the top beginning to cabbage, it is cut. This throws all the strength of the plant into the sprouts on the stem, and makes the bottom ones as good as the top.' Mr McIntosh dissents from this practice of cutting the top: 'From their form and position,' he says, 'they protect the sprouts during winter, and in wet weather, from frost, snow and rain.'

2469 *Borecole* Borecole, greens, and curlies are a numerous tribe of the *Brassicoe*, cultivated for their leaves in winter and for their sprouts in the spring. The first week in April or May, and again about the second week in August, is the time to sow, using exactly the same precautions as with the others. The borecoles are less exhausting to the soil than the cabbages, and will follow peas without fresh manuring, if the ground is in tolerably good heart; or they may be planted between rows of peas or potatoes, to occupy the ground when these crops are removed.

The varieties of this tribe of the *Brassicoe* are so numerous and so mixed, that the distinction between them is still very indefinite. *Dwarf Curled Greens*, under half a dozen names, are the old Scotch curly, very dwarf in habit, and closely curled – an excellent variety. *The Tall Green Curled*, also under a host of names, grows two or three feet high, stands severe frosts, and affords the most delicate greens when frosted. *Purple or Sprouting Borecole* differs little from the preceding except in colour. Variegated borecole is a mere variety, very useful, and even ornamental, in the mixed garden. *Cottager's Kale* is a variety of the tall cavalier cabbage which was raised at Sherburn Castle, Oxfordshire, from Brussels sprouts, crossed with one of the varieties of kale. It is the most tender of all the greens, and of exquisite flavour. It stands four feet high when full grown, and should be allowed an equal space to grow in, being clothed to the ground with immense rosette-like shoots of a bluish-green tint, which, when boiled, become a delicate green. The seed should be sown late in March or early in April, and when planted out should have a rich deep soil assigned to it.

2470 *Cauliflower* (*Brassica oleracea botrytis*) In the preceding varieties of the *Brassicae*, we find them cultivated for their leaves, growing either loosely on the stem, or forming a round compact head, blanched by being covered with the outer leaves, or sprouting from the stem, sometimes in small heads, at others in separate small slender leaves. We now come to the cauliflower, in which the abortive flowers form a serried corymb, connected with the stem by a thick, fleshy peduncle, the whole thickly interwoven, and forming a compact round head of a creamy white colour, and of great delicacy when properly grown.

2471 *Sowing, etc.* With us the plant is treated as an annual, although it may, like all the race, be propagated from cuttings. In order to keep up a succession, three or four sowings should be made in the season, the first sowing being made on a slight hotbed in February, or very early in March. This is done by digging away a few inches of the soil the size of the intended bed, filling it up to a few inches above the surrounding soil with fresh stable dung which has been well turned, covering the bed with the soil removed, raking it, and patting it smooth with the back of the spade. On this bed sow the seed, raking it in, or sifting fine soil over it, and covering it with hand glasses, and otherwise protecting it when necessary. Early in April a second and larger sowing should be made in the open ground, and a third and last sowing about the middle of August, to stand through the winter.

2472 *Cultivation, Transplanting, etc* All sowings should be made on beds of rich light soil, thoroughly pulverised by digging, and neither too dry nor too moist, 4½ feet wide, and long in proportion to the requirements of the garden, half an ounce of seed being sufficient for a 10-feet bed. In very dry weather, the seed beds should receive a copious watering the night before sowing. When the plants are large enough to be handled, transplant them to nursery beds of rich soil, well manured, pricking them out 4 inches apart each way. Some authorities recommend a second removal when the roots have formed a compact mass, in order to check the growth of stem and promote balling. In June the April sowings will be fit to plant out where they are to grow; in September they will be heading, and will continue to improve up to the frosts of early winter. The after cultivation is very simple; careful weeding, stirring the soil from time to time with the hoe, and drawing the earth about the roots, and copious watering at the roots in dry weather, include the necessary routine.

> Like all the Brassicas, the cauliflower requires a rich, deep soil and an open spot, but sheltered from the north. An old celery or asparagus bed, from which the plants have been lifted for forcing, is excellent: if none such is at liberty, let the ground be well trenched, 3 feet deep, and manured with good rotten dung, thoroughly incorporated with the soil in digging, bearing in mind that the delicacy and freshness of the vegetable depend on its rapid and vigorous growth when once started. On the ground thus prepared plant the young seedlings 2½ feet apart each way.

2473 *Autumn-Sown Cauliflower* The autumn-sown plants are usually pricked out under frames for protection during winter, keeping them clear of weeds and decaying leaves, stirring the soil occasionally, and giving plenty of air in fine weather, protecting them from frost and rain. As they advance, and begin to head under hand or bell glasses, every opportunity should be taken of giving air: in severe weather, protect the frames and hand glasses by packing litter round them. When the heads begin to appear, shade them from sun and rain by breaking down some of the larger leaves, so as to cover it. Water in dry weather, previously forming the earth into a basin round the stem, and pour the water into the roots, choosing the evening in mild weather for so doing, and the morning when the air is frosty.

Mr Henry Baily, of Nuneham Park, a well-known authority, was accustomed to transplant his autumn seedlings, as soon as they had made a few roots, into 60-sized pots, which he placed in an open, airy frame, or other sheltered place having facilities for protecting them from frost. As they filled the smaller pots with their roots, they were transplanted into larger ones, care being taken that the roots never got matted in their pots; and early in February the first crop was placed out on a south border, the holes prepared for them having received a barrowful of thoroughly rotted dung, over which the mould was replaced, forming a little hillock on which the cauliflowers are planted. They were then covered with hand glasses till thoroughly established. By pursuing this course, Mr Baily tells us (*Hort. Trans*, v, p. 103), all check on the vigorous growth of the plant is avoided, while the tendency to increased luxuriance so necessary in plants whose leaves or flowers are eaten, is encouraged.

2474 *Treatment during Winter* On the approach of winter, the plants in flower may be taken up with as much earth at their roots as possible, and planted, or rather laid in by the roots, and lying on their sides, in a light sandy soil, in some warm, sheltered place, where the frost can be excluded. In such a shed or frame they may be kept fresh and in condition for many weeks.

2475 *Broccoli* Broccoli is supposed to be a variety of the cauliflower, from which it differs very slightly, the chief points of difference being that the flower stem is longer and less fleshy, the head less compact, and it rarely attains the size or delicacy of the cauliflower.

2476 *Cultivation, etc* In many respects the culture of the broccoli is the same as the other cabbages. From the middle of April to the middle of May, according to the season and locality, it is sown in beds, or, as some recommend, in the ground where it is to grow, first trenching and treading it thoroughly, and inserting the seeds in rows 2 feet apart from each other, dropping two or three seeds into each hole. In order to prevent early and partial flowering, where this mode of culture is adopted, all but the strongest plant are drawn, when the seeds come up, and either thrown away or transplanted. Where seed beds are adopted, they should be prepared of rich, light mould, well dug, and, if very dry, well watered the evening before sowing. The seeds should be thinly sown, and the beds covered with mats or litter till the plants appear. When the plants are about 2 inches high, prick them out into nursery beds 4 inches apart, watering them in dry weather. In a fortnight or three weeks they will be strong enough for planting out, the ground for them having been prepared by trenching and manuring.

2477 *Soil, Planting Out, etc.* Broccoli succeeds best in fresh loamy soil; therefore, where that cannot be given, deep trenching, by which fresh earth is brought up nearer the surface, is the next best soil for it, adding plenty of manure. According to the size of the plant, they should be planted 18 inches to 3 feet asunder. Knight's Dwarf only require 18 inches; Early White, 27 inches; Purple Cape, Walcheren, and Early White, 2 feet; and the taller sorts should be 3 feet apart. During its summer growth the ground requires to be deeply stirred between the rows, to keep up the action of the air and moisture about the roots.

2478 *Couve Tronchuda* The culture and treatment of this variety of cabbage are the same as for the ordinary cabbage, the seed being sown in March or April, according to situation, and the young plants planted out in June and July. It is fit for use, like savoys, after frosty weather sets in. From the similarity of the leaf stalks to seakale, for which it is a good substitute, it is sometimes called the Seakale Cabbage. The heart may be eaten as well as the leaf stalks, being tender when dressed, and of delicious flavour.

2479 *Spinach* This excellent vegetable requires a light, rich soil, and plenty of moisture, so much so, indeed, that if the ground be dry naturally, or the weather dry in late spring and summer, it should be watered plentifully and frequently, in order to induce a good crop. For spinach in late spring and early summer, sow the round-seeded variety in rows from 12 to 15 inches apart in March, thinning out the plants in rows from 6 to 9 inches apart, repeating the sowing every fortnight for successional crops. For winter use sow the prickly seeded variety in August. Hoe between the rows, and draw the earth loosely about the plants. The outside leaves may be gathered when young, and the heart left to continue sprouting, or the leaves may be cut off altogether, close to the ground – a more desirable method when it is necessary to clear the ground immediately and prepare it for fresh crops.

2480 *New Zealand and Perennial Spinach* The former of these, not being so hardy as ordinary spinach, must be raised in slight bottom heat, and planted out, at the end of May or beginning of June, in light rich soil in a sunny situation in rows, from 30 inches to 3 feet apart, and at the same distance from each other in the rows. It does not require watering like ordinary spinach. Perennial spinach is grown in the same way as red or white beet, which it much resembles in the habit of its leaves, which are stripped from the plant, boiled, and eaten.

2481 *Asparagus* This delicious vegetable is a general favourite; but it is more costly than ordinary vegetables, and for this reason is never greatly in demand. To raise asparagus from seed, which it yields in abundance, if allowed, in the autumn, the seed should be gathered when fully ripe, hung up to dry, and rubbed out when sufficiently so. It may be sown thinly on ground that has been well dug, but not manured, any time from the beginning of March to June. If sown broadcast, it should be scattered thinly and evenly, and trodden in, and the ground raked over; if in drills, they should be about a foot apart and an inch deep, the seeds sown thinly, and pressed and raked over. The plants make more root than top the first year; but if they are kept clear of weeds, and the ground stirred often between them, they will grow vigorously the second year, and be fit to plant out the following spring. Beds of asparagus may be made as late as September.

2482 *Making Plantations* At whatever time it may be determined to make plantations of this vegetable, they should be made on a rich soil, neither wet nor too stiff, but pulverising readily under the spade. On this soil a coating of rich well-rotted stable manure, three or four inches thick, should be spread, after which the ground should be trenched three spades deep, the manure being buried pretty equally at the bottom spit of each trench. The ground being dug and levelled, divide it into 4-foot beds, with alleys two feet wide between each bed.

2483 *Planting* Select strong one-year-old plants without tops, and plant them two rows in each 4-foot bed, the rows a foot from each side of the bed, and the plants a foot apart in the rows. The method of planting is as follows: Strain the garden line longitudinally along the beds, a foot from the edge; then with a spade cut out a small trench or drill vertical to the line, six inches deep. In this trench set the plants upright against the vertical side, so that the crown of the plant stands upright, and two or three inches below the surface of the ground, spreading out the roots against the back of the trench, and drawing a little earth round the roots with the hand to steady them. When the whole row is planted, with a rake draw the earth into the trench, round the roots of the plants; then proceed with the next row in the same manner.

2484 *Management after Planting* As a plantation of asparagus only comes into bearing the third year, it is sometimes customary to sow a thin crop of onions over the beds at the time of planting, afterwards raking the surface of the beds smooth. As soon as they begin to grow, give a good watering with salt-and-water, about the strength of sea-water; then keep the bed clear of weeds, pulling up all onions, or other surface crops, where they come up close to the plants, and the new beds will suffer no injury.

Another practice strongly recommended by some cultivators is to sow asparagus seeds at once on the beds where they are to grow. This requires the same deep trenching and heavy manuring already described. The beds thus prepared, a line is drawn in the 4-foot beds a foot from each edge, and a foot apart. Upon these lines, at every 12 inches, a few seeds are planted about an inch deep. When the seedlings come up, thin out, leaving only one of the most vigorous plants. Abed thus sown, and carefully weeded and manured, and the surface stirred in autumn and spring, will produce buds in the fourth year, and fine large plants in the fifth year, and will continue to bear for twelve or fourteen years.

2485 *Spring Digging and Dressing* Established beds of asparagus require top dressing every spring, and March is the best month for the purpose. This is done by digging in with a three-pronged fork, with short flat tines, a spring dressing of well-rotted manure, which has been laid on the beds in the previous autumn, more or less thick, according to the state of the beds, loosening every part to a moderate depth, but avoiding the crowns of the plants. This gives free access to the light and air, and free percolation for the water. Immediately after this dressing, rake the beds smooth and regular before the plants begin to shoot.

The French practice is to dig a trench five feet wide and the length of the bed, laying aside the best of the soil for surface use. On the bottom of the trench is laid, first, six inches of rich stable manure; above it, eight inches of turf; again, six inches of well-rotted dung, and then eight inches of the reserved soil sifted; over this six inches of thoroughly decomposed manure, and six inches more of the soil thrown aside in making the trench, well mixed together by digging. The beds thus formed are five feet wide, with alleys between two feet wide. The roots are planted in the beds in rows 18 inches apart, and 18 inches apart in the rows; a handful of fine mould is placed under each plant, over which the roots are carefully spread, the crown being an inch and a half below the surface; a spadeful of fine sand is now thrown over the crown, and the operation is completed. In order to procure an early supply of this delicious vegetable, they prepare a moderately warm hotbed in the manner pointed out in paragraph 1231. On this six inches of rich mould is laid, and a sufficient number of asparagus from an old bed planted. Over this lay a few inches of the same soil, covering the whole with sufficient litter to keep out the frost or by mats over the frame. The plants will soon start into growth. A little liquid manure applied occasionally will keep up a vigorous growth, and the plants, if properly managed, will be ready to cut by Christmas.

2486 *Cutting Asparagus* This is an operation of some delicacy. It should be cut with a saw-edged knife, having a straight, narrow, tapering blade, about six or eight inches long, and an inch broad at the haft, rounding off at the point. When the shoots are fit to cut, the knife is slipped perpendicularly close to the shoot, cutting, or rather sawing, it off slantingly three or four inches below the surface, taking care not to touch any young shoot coming out of the same crown.

2487 *Forcing Asparagus* Asparagus is successfully forced in the frame and melon pit; but the plants are not fit to move before February. The usual plan is to make up a 3-foot bed, and cover it with 3 inches of loamy soil, before putting on the frame; this allows more space inside. When the frame is on, and the bed of a right temperature, a little soil is put at the back of the frame, in the form of a bank, about 6 inches high, and sloping to the front. On this bank, place a row of asparagus roots, laying them almost flat, as this admits of covering them, without an undue thickness of soil. When the first roots are laid, cover them with a few inches of soil, and make another bank 6 inches from the first, on which lay another row of roots; and so proceed till the frame is full. To maintain the temperature of the bed, fresh manure should be piled up all round it on every side.

2488 *Seakale: Culture* The best way of raising seakale is from seed, which should be sown in drills, about four or five feet apart, and three inches deep; this should be done about the beginning of April. When sufficiently large to tell which plants are strongest, thin them to about three inches; in July transplant some, leaving them in the rows a foot or 18 inches apart. During the summer and autumn the ground should be kept clear of weeds and often stirred; and in dry weather copiously watered, especially that which has been transplanted.

Some recommend planting these thinnings on ridges raised a foot high or so, placing the plants in threes or fours, the clusters being a yard apart and the ridges five feet. It is affirmed that when heat is applied to seakale planted in this way, the ground gets warmed, so that the plants get bottom heat as well as top. There is, however, no actual advantage in this practice; but it is as well to plant them in clumps of three or four together, a yard apart: in this way a bunch of crowns is formed, over which to place a kalepot, a great advantage in that which is to be forced.

2489 *Management* Seakale is best managed in the open ground, where, if planted on ridges in clusters of three, a yard apart, it may be forced any time in the winter, by putting the pots on, and covering them with about 3 feet of fermenting dung: with a moderate heat, it takes about three weeks, from the time of covering till ready to cut. Never break off the leaves, but leave them to decay naturally, when they may be removed.

Seakale may be grown in about nine months from the seed, in the following manner, in place of the expensive and tedious process now followed: The ground having been prepared in winter, and subjected to a month or two of frost in a rough state, the seed should be sown in the latter end of March or early in April, and even as late as May. Having selected a piece of ground, open but sheltered, trench it 3 feet deep, using plenty of manure – at least a third part – mixing it thoroughly with the soil; when ready, strike the ground into 4-foot beds, and sow two rows of seed in patches 2 feet apart. As soon as the plants come up, thin out to two or three in the patch, and when fairly established, remove all but one. In the course of the season use abundant supplies of liquid manure, and keep the surface well stirred. In autumn the beds will be covered with fine healthy leaves and plump crowns. Pick off the leaves as they decay, and as soon as they are all off, the crowns should be slightly covered with ashes or tanner's bark till wanted for forcing. In November, the plants will be ready for forcing, either on the beds or in some more shaded corner.

2490 *Forcing Seakale* Treated in the manner described above for asparagus, seakale may be produced as a Christmas vegetable, for it may be put in hotbeds for forcing much earlier than asparagus, indeed as early as November. At the same time, it should be said that January is the best month in which to begin forcing seakale, for if forced earlier, it is neither so good nor so abundant, and if left till March artificial heat is almost unnecessary. In forcing seakale the light should be excluded entirely from the frame, otherwise it will not acquire that whiteness and delicacy which it is desirable that it should possess.

2491 *Globe Artichokes* The best method of propagating these is to take offsets from them in April or May, and plant them, 3 feet apart, in a row, and the rows 5 feet apart They bear little or nothing the same season, but produce abundantly the following. To keep them in good bearing condition, it is advisable to plant a fresh row every year, and remove one of the old ones. If they are protected with straw, fern, or leaves, in winter, they bear rather earlier in summer; but many leave them unprotected. They are then killed to the ground, but break up strong in the spring. Before planting them, the soil should be trenched 3 feet deep, and well manured; and as it is advisable to give other crops the benefit of ground vacated by them, it is as well to adopt the above-mentioned rule – to plant fresh rows of them every year and remove some of the old, either for use or forcing.

2492 *Cardoons* A perennial in its native country – the shores of the Mediterranean – the cardoon becomes an annual in this country, the first sowing taking place in the beginning of March, on a very slight hotbed; in April, on the natural ground; and again in June, for next spring's crop. The trenches are dug as for celery, and moderately manured with well-decomposed dung. In sowing, two or three seeds are sown together in a clump, 12 inches apart. Should each vegetate, remove all but one, when 6 inches high. When the plant is 18 inches high, put a stake to it, and tie the leaves lightly to it, earthing up the stem at the same time, like celery. Throughout the summer, water copiously and frequently with soft water and a little guano, to prevent flowering. In September, the early crop will be fit for use; remove the earth carefully, take the plant up by the roots, which are cut off; the points of the leaves are also cut off to where they are solid and blanched. These are carefully washed, the parts of the leaf-stalks left tied to the stem, and they are ready for the cook.

2493 *Rhubarb* Although it is used as a substitute for fruit, and is therefore often regarded as fruit, rhubarb is a veritable vegetable, and must be included among plants whose leaves, leaf stalks, and flowers are eaten. Rhubarb may be planted at any time of the year, although mild weather in autumn or early spring is best; it should be planted on a clear open spot on good soil, which should be well trenched 3 feet deep. The plants should be not less than 4 feet apart; or, where it is intended to take up some every year for forcing, a distance of 3 feet will be sufficient. Before planting, plenty of very rotten manure should be well worked into the soil. When desired to increase the plants, it is merely necessary to take up large roots and divide them with a spade; every piece that has a crown to it will grow and make a plant; and as it grows very quickly, this is as good a mode of propagating it as any. Rhubarb may be forced in a frame in the same manner as seakale or asparagus. If forced on the ground where it grows, nothing more is required than to cover with large pots, or old casks, and stable manure – by this method it is blanched; but when forced in a frame, or otherwise, it is unnecessary to exclude the light, as there is no advantage in blanching it.

3 – Edible Rooted Section

2494 *Red Beet* This vegetable, which is generally known as beetroot, should be sown at the beginning of April, in deep rich ground, fully exposed to the sun, and quite open and away from trees. Sow the seed in shallow drills, 15 inches apart, and drop three or four seeds at intervals of 10 inches or a foot apart, or sow thinly along the drill: cover, tread, thin, and rake the ground roughly with a wooden rake, drawing off large stones, etc., that may be on the surface. Sowing this seed in drills is preferable to sowing broadcast, because it not only gives greater facility for thinning out and using the hoe between, but it insures a regular crop without wasting the seed, the plants being at regular distances. When the plants are about a foot high, thin them to not less than a foot apart, leaving the best-coloured rather than the strongest plants; for the better it is, the less likely it is to grow strong and large. Large roots are not esteemed, being deficient in flavour. The roots should be lifted in October, before the frost sets in, for this is injurious to them. In taking them up, care should be taken not to break the tap root, or puncture them in any way, for damage of this kind tends to deprive them of their colour when boiled. When taken up, the leaves should be trimmed off, and the roots kept in sand, so as to be perfectly dry and free from the hurtful influence of wet or damp.

2495 *White or Spinach Beet* The culture of this variety, which is grown for the sake of its leaves and leaf stalks, that are eaten like spinach in autumn and winter, is similar to that of beetroot or red beet, but a second sowing should be made in July or August, to be available for the winter months and spring.

2496 *Carrots: Solving* Those who know the sweetness and delicacy of the early horn kinds, in their young state, will take care to have a constant supply. They may be sown in frames in gentle heat in January, and in borders from March till the latter end of July. The main crop may be sown from the middle of March to the middle of April, according to situation. Sow broadcast on beds, and thin early horns to 3 or 4 inches apart, as this sort does not require so much room; larger sorts are better sown in drills. If it is preferred to drill the seed in, let the drills be 1 foot or 15 inches apart, as shallow as possible, and sow the seed continuously along the drill, or three or four seeds at intervals of 6 or 8 inches; this economises the seed, and admits of going amongst the plants without treading on them. Light ground should be trodden before it is drilled: the seed hangs together, and should be separated by rubbing it up with soil, if sown broadcast; but this is unnecessary if sown in drills. The seed is very light, so that a calm day should be chosen for sowing: a little wind is apt to blow it anywhere but the right place: it takes one to three weeks to germinate.

2497 *Management* As soon as the seed is well above ground, use the small hoe unsparingly, and thin out to not less than 6 inches apart; as the plants advance, continue using the hoe both to destroy and prevent the growth of weeds, and also for the benefit derived from loosening the ground. They may be drawn for table as soon as large enough; but the main crop for storing should not be taken up till quite the end of October, or even later, unless severe frosts set in.

Early carrots may be grown as directed for radishes: a bed 2 or 3 feet high, about 10 inches of soil, which should be perfectly sweet, and free from the larvae of insects; a bushel of pounded chalk mixed with it will be advantageous. The early horn is the best for early culture; but, as the seed is very light, and hangs together, it requires, for the purpose of separating it, to be rubbed up in a peck or so of tolerably dry soil, which will help to bury it when sown, using the rake to press it in. When up, and sufficiently large to handle, the plants should be thinned to 2 inches apart, and plenty of air given, or they will be drawn all to top.

2498 *Parsnips* The directions given for carrots apply in most respects to the culture of parsnips. Let the soil be deeply worked for this useful vegetable – it possible trenched – keeping the top spit uppermost, allowing it to be well pulverised by frost. Sow drills 18 inches asunder, drop three or four seeds at intervals of 9 inches; when 2 inches high, pull out all but the strongest of each cluster, and use the hoe freely.

2499 *Turnips* These valuable roots prefer a light, rich, loamy soil. Seed for successional crops may be sown in garden ground from February until September; the main crop should be sown for winter use in July. Young turnips fit for culinary purposes may be pulled about eight or ten weeks after the seed is sown; but it must be borne in mind that turnips sown in July will be for use during the winter months, and that those sown later will be for use in early spring. The seed should be sown evenly, but rather thin; a small quantity of it will cover a large piece of ground, but should be regularly scattered. Broadcast sowing is preferable for this crop; but if sown in drills they should be 15 inches distant from each other, and the plants left not less than a foot apart in the rows, or even a greater distance is better, as this crop resents anything like crowding. If sown in drills let them be very shallow – half an inch is deep enough. As soon as they are up, use the hoe unsparingly, and see they are thinned to the proper distance before the roots begin to swell. If attacked with the fly, which happens in dry weather, dust with lime or soot while the dew is on them; on light soils they will repay copious watering.

2500 *Salsafy* This root also likes a light, rich soil, and grows well on ground that has been well manured for the crop that precedes it. The seed should be sown in April, in drills from 12 to 15 inches apart, and the plants should be thinned out to a distance of from 6 to 9 inches apart in the rows. They will be ready for use in the early part of November, when some of the roots may be taken up and stored for winter use in sand, as recommended for beetroot. It is a biennial, and the stalks that it throws up in its second year, and which will ultimately develop into flowers and yield seed, supply a tender and useful vegetable that is not unlike asparagus. The oyster-like flavour of the root when properly dressed has obtained for it the name of the Vegetable Oyster.

2501 *Scorzonera* The culture of the scorzonera is similar to that described above for salsafy, but the rows should be from 15 to 18 inches apart, and the plants from 9 to 12 inches apart in the rows.

2502 *Onions* These are sown either broadcast or in drills; in either case the distance should be not less than 6 inches from plant to plant when they begin to bulb. Sow the main crop the third or fourth week in April: an early sowing may be made late in February or first week in March; and for pickling, or for drawing while young, during the summer and autumn, they may be sown as late as midsummer.

2503 *Sowing: Management* This crop, which is usually considered to be a gross-feeding crop, requires a good rich soil, or one that is made so by proper manuring; and if, in dry weather, they can be well watered, and occasionally with liquid manure, the bulbs will attain a large size and prove a very profitable crop. If sown broadcast, mark the ground into 4-foot or 5-foot beds; sow the seed evenly, tread, and rake. The seed may be sown thickly, if it is desired to draw young onions for the table; or they may be thinned out by this process, leaving those that are to bulb from 6 to 9 inches apart; the same directions apply to sowing onion seed in drills, which should be from 9 inches to a foot apart. The hoe should be freely used among them while growing. When the bulbs are approaching maturity, the stalks should be bent down a little above the bulb. The leaves will then wither more easily, and the bulbs themselves will attain a greater size. When the leaves are nearly withered, the bulbs should be pulled up, and spread out in the sun to dry and harden for a week or two. When drying no rain should be permitted to fall on them. When dry they should be stored on shelves or roped – that is to say, tied with twine round a central core of wheat straw. A sowing may be made in October, to stand the winter, for early spring salading. The silver-skinned variety is usually sown for pickling.

To procure onion-seed, plant some good, sound, full-grown onions in an open situation in March, placing them 6 inches deep and 15 apart. As they grow, protect the stems, which are very brittle, by means of a stake driven into the ground at each end of the rows, and strings passed each side of the stems and fastened firmly to the stakes. This should be done in time to prevent any getting broken, which would reduce the crop.

2504 *The Potato Onion* This onion, which, from its growth and manner of increase is sometimes called the underground onion, is a valuable vegetable, because it furnishes sound, tender, and full-sized bulbs at midsummer, three months before the ordinary onion crop is harvested. It requires a well-worked, moderately rich soil. The bulbs may be planted in warm sheltered situations, such as the south of Devon, in midwinter; but in colder parts the planting must be deferred until late winter or early spring; yet the earlier it can be effected the better. The bulbs should be set in rows from 12 to 15 inches apart, and from 12 to 15 inches apart also in the rows. Each bulb will throw out a number of offsets all round it, which grow and develop into full-sized bulbs, which are taken up and dried when ready for pulling, and then stored for use and for future propagation.

2505 *The Tree Onion* The mode of culture to be followed for this onion is the same as that for the potato onion, from which it differs chiefly in its mode of reproduction, the offshoots being produced in the form of bulblets at the end of what would be the flower stalk in ordinary onions.

2506 *The Shallot* Prepare a bed of light, rich soil, with which a liberal dressing of wood ashes, if they can be obtained, and soot, has been well incorporated. Rake the surface finely, and even consolidate the soil by beating it lightly with the spade. Then set out the bed in rows 9 inches apart, and place the bulbs at the same distance apart in the rows, pressing them firmly into the earth until they are nearly hidden by it. In mild situations, sheltered from the north and east, and in warm positions, the shallot, like the potato onion, may be planted at midwinter; but it is usual to plant them at the commencement of autumn, or at the end of winter or beginning of spring. The subsequent management is similar to that prescribed for potato onions.

2507 *Garlic* This bulb, which, from the strength of its odour and pungency of its taste, requires to be used in small quantities, is propagated, planted, and managed in precisely the same manner as the shallot. A number of bulblets, technically known as cloves, are found grouped together in one whitish integument, or capsule, which holds them, as it were, within a sack. A clove inserted in the knuckle of a shoulder or leg of mutton imparts a slight flavour to the whole joint, and a rump steak is much improved by being placed and eaten on a plate that has been rubbed over for the purpose with a clove of garlic cut in two. In planting, the cloves should be set separately.

2508 *Leeks* These, for the main crop, are usually sown in April, about the same time as onions. Some gardeners sow them with a small sowing of onions, the latter being drawn young for salading, the leeks being left on the bed, or planted out. Some sow them in drills, 18 inches or even 2 feet apart, and thin them to a foot or so apart in the row, planting the thinnings at the same distance. This gives room to draw earth up to them for the purpose of blanching the root and stem. Sow very shallow, tread, and rake, provided the ground admits of it; thin before the plants interfere with each other, and water in dry weather. This crop delights in a light, rich soil, and in moist seasons grows very large. The London Flag is the sort most usually grown; but the Scotch or Musselburg is esteemed by many, as growing larger and better.

2509 *Trenching Leeks* After all, the best way to obtain leeks of considerable size and well blanched is to grow them in trenches, in the same manner as celery; but the trenches need not be more than 8 or 9 inches deep. The trenches should be well manured, but if no manure is added to the soil, a substitute must be found for it in the shape of liquid manure. As the plants grow the earth on the sides of the trench should be raked in, so as to fill it and cover the plants as high as possible, thus blanching them.

2510 *The Potato* The importance of the potato as a culinary root can scarcely be overrated. Since the appearance of the potato disease about 1845, since which time it has never been wholly absent from the United Kingdom, the old sorts which were in cultivation at and before the date just given have almost if not entirely disappeared, and their place has been taken by new sorts raised from seed. At the Potato International Exhibition in 1880, one hundred and seventy-eight varieties were represented, and since that time the number of sorts has been considerably augmented. The best sorts, or those that are considered the best, from year to year, will be found in the catalogues and price lists of the seedsmen and growers. Mr Richard Dean, Ranelagh Road, Ealing, London, is one of the most successful raisers of new varieties.

2511 In growing potatoes it is necessary to look at the work in two aspects, namely, that of growing early potatoes for home use or for market, and that of growing the main crop for use between Midsummer and the next planting season, or indeed till new potatoes come again, and, therefore, for storage during the winter months.

2512 *Early Potatoes in Melon Pits* For the purpose of growing very early potatoes, nothing is more suitable than a broad roomy melon pit – an excellent use to make of it. The potatoes will be fit for use about the time for planting out the melons. About the beginning of January, let some middling-sized tubers be laid in a warm and moderately dry place, well exposed to the light: here they will make short plump shoots by the time the bed is ready. Prepare a quantity of dung sufficient to make a bed 3 feet 6 inches in depth. By the end of the month the bed will be ready; then lay on 3 inches of soil, and place the potatoes 15 inches apart, covering them with 6 inches more of soil. Some seed of the scarlet short-top radish may be scattered over the surface. As these begin to grow, give abundance of fresh air in mild weather, so that neither potatoes nor radishes be drawn up; and as they come up, remove the radishes from immediately about the crowns of the potatoes; earthing up the latter will not be required. The radishes will draw in March; the potatoes early in May.

2513 *Early Potatoes in Frames* When potatoes are grown in a frame, the treatment is much the same as before; but some grow them very successfully in this manner: The frame being placed on a level piece of ground, the soil within is dug out to the depth of 2 feet, and banked round the outside of the frame. The pit thus formed is then filled with prepared dung; on this 3 inches of soil is placed; then the potatoes, then 6 inches more soil. The potatoes, when planted, should be just starting into growth; but the shoots should never be more than half an inch from the tuber, or they do not grow so strong. It is advisable to pick off some of the shoots; three on each tuber is sufficient.

2514 *Potatoes for Main Crop* These should be got in in April. As the ground is more likely to be dry at this time, they may be dibbled in whole, thus yielding food for the young shoot till it can find its own – a most reasonable assumption, and worthy of adoption. When potatoes are cut, it is best to expose them for a day or two, to render the surface of the cut callous. In planting them, let it be in rows 2 feet apart; or, if space is limited, allow 3 feet, which admits of planting later crops between, before they are taken up. Although little is gained by allowing too much room, much is lost by allowing too little; for root crops are apt to run all to haulm or top if too crowded. Two feet from row to row, and 15 inches from plant to plant, is a good average.

2515 *Planting Tubers* If the ground is light or dry, the tubers, either entire or in pieces, as may be preferred, may be dibbled in; that is, a line is stretched where the row is to be, on one side of which the holes are made with a potato dibber – this is a pole or shaft three feet long, having a cross-piece of wood on the top for the handle, and a tread for the foot 8 inches from the lower end, and of sufficient thickness to make a hole that a potato may drop in easily. A potato or set is dropped in each hole, and filled up by drawing a wooden rake over them; but it is objected to this, and rightly enough, that the pressure of the dibber hardens the soil all round, and checks the spreading of the young tubers; making drills with a spade, and planting that way, is therefore preferable; or they may be planted as the ground is dug, merely placing a line, cutting the drill, placing the potatoes 15 inches apart, then digging backward 2 feet, placing the line, cutting another drill, and so on. The main crop may be planted about the end of March or beginning of April, or it may be deferred till quite the end of the latter month, and smaller plantings may be made till midsummer.

If the ground is wet, heavy, or, indeed, under any circumstances, a good plan is to cut a drill with the spade six or eight inches deep. In this place the sets 15 inches apart, then move the line to the next row, cut another drill in the same manner, but fill up the preceding drill with the soil taken out, covering the sets in it. This is an expeditious mode, and will do on any soil. On stiff soils the dibber should never be used, because it forms a basin in which water is likely to stand and rot the potato.

2516 *General Management* – When potatoes have grown 8 or 10 inches high, a little earth should be drawn up to them, just sufficient to cover any tubers that may grow near the surface; but too much earthing up produces luxuriance of growth in the haulm, and is contrary to nature. The ground should be thoroughly drained. It is generally admitted that the disease is most prevalent in wet soils or wet seasons. Some recommend cutting off the haulm as soon as the blight appears; this may save them in a great measure from the rot, but stops the growth of the tubers, and whether any real advantage is derived from it is still undecided. It is advisable to pick off all the flowers, unless seed is wanted, as doing so will throw the strength of the plant into the process of forming tubers. As to sorts, they are sometimes known to change character when transferred to different soils: but, for early crops, the Early Ash Leaf, a kidney potato, is deserving of culture, and all the Ash Leaf varieties.

2517 *Storing Potatoes* When the haulm has thoroughly withered and died down, the tubers are fully ripe, and should be taken up for storage during the winter months. Care should be taken to prevent the frost from obtaining access to the tubers, and if they cannot be put away within doors, which can only be done in the case of comparatively small quantities, the best way to preserve them is in pits covered in, or caves, as they are usually called in the West of England.

To make these, a warm and sheltered position is chosen under a high hedge, and if possible, with a slight fall away from the hedge. A space is then cleared away about 3 or 4 feet in width, and as long as may be necessary, and the roots are then piled up against the hedge, sloping upwards from the outer edge of the space that has been cleared, and they are then covered in with wheat straw, over which a thick coating of earth is thrown, taken from a trench dug out at each end and in front of the cave. When a supply is required one end of the cave is opened and closed again when a sufficient quantity has been removed. When there is no hedge to form a backing, and it is necessary to make the cave on the open ground, the roots are piled up so as to form a ridge like the roof of a house, slanting outwards on both sides from the top. They are then covered with straw and earth as before, the trench from which the earth is taken affording drainage to carry off the water that trickles from the exterior of the cave in wet weather. Roots of all kinds, except onions, perhaps, may be stored through the winter in this manner.

In Hooper's *Gardening Guide* the following is given as 'the result of much experience upon different soils', and will be found a useful guide in suiting the sorts to be grown to the character of the soil in which they are to be planted.

For very light soils. – Try *almost* any kind, avoiding *Magnum Bonum*, *Covent Garden Perfection*, *Alpha*, *Schoolmaster*, and Fenn's varieties generally.

For medium soils. – There is no restriction in this.

For heavy soils. – Choose *Grampian*, *Ash Leaf*, *Schoolmaster*, *Regent*, *Magnum Bonum*, *Covent Garden Perfection*, and *Gordon's Victoria Regent*.

The following is a selection of the best leading sorts of potatoes:

White Kidney
Ash Leaf Kidney
Breadfruit
Breesee's Prolific
Covent Garden
Early King
Fluke
International
Lapstone
Magnum Bonum
Mona's Pride
Myatts's Prolific
Pride of America
Queen of the Valley
Snowflake
Woodstock

Blue Kidney
Manhattan

Red Kidney
Beauty of Hebron
Early Rose
Extra Early Vermont
Superior
Trophy
Wonderful

Red round
Adirondack
Beauty of Kent
Brownell's Beauty
Grampian
Red Emperor
Triumph

Parti-coloured Round
Blanchard
Radstock Beauty

White Round
Alpha
Climax
Dalmahoy
Dunbar Regent
Early Oxford
Gordon's Victoria Regent
Matchless
Paterson's Victorla
Porter's Excelsior
Reading Hero
Schoolmaster
Scotch Champion
York Regent

Blue Round
Forty Fold
Hooper's Round Blue
Vicar of Laleham

2518 *Jerusalem Artichoke* This is a hardy and profitable vegetable, excellent for culinary purposes, and requiring no protection in winter. It likes a light, rich soil, and the ground should be well dug over, and if at all heavy or poor should be lightened by incorporating some sand with it and enriched with well-rotted manure. For planting, small tubers should be chosen, and, indeed, reserved for this purpose when the crop is taken up. These should be set in rows, 3 feet apart, and at a distance of 1 foot from each other in the rows; they should, moreover, be set 6 inches deep. The ground should be kept clean by hoeing, and as the plants grow in height a little earth should be drawn up round the stem.

Jerusalem artichokes afford a useful screen for a wooden fence when planted along the foot of it. When once planted, the difficulty is to get the ground clear of them again, for the smallest tuber will grow. To obviate this as far as possible, it is desirable to endeavour to leave no tubers in the ground when digging the crop. It is desirable to change the ground allotted to their culture about once in three years, for when they are permitted to remain too long on the same spot the tubers deteriorate in size and quality.

4 – Edible Fruited Section

2519 *Capsicums and Chilis* The fruit of these plants are extremely hot and pungent. That of the capsicum is useful for pickling and for eating, when fresh and cut up and infused in vinegar, with roast mutton. Chilis also are used for pickling, and for infusion in vinegar. They are usually grown in the greenhouse, in which the fruit will ripen, and where they present a pretty appearance in contrast with the flowers that are growing there. Their culture is simple and easy: the plants must be raised from seed sown in a hotbed, or placed over gentle bottom heat, and as they increase in size they must be shifted singly into small pots at first, and thence into larger pots, as may be found necessary. Capsicums and Chilis can be used in the green state as well as when ripe and red, and those who are content with the fruit in this condition many set the plants in the open border at the end of June. They will not ripen their fruit in this position.

2520 *Cucumbers: Culture* These can be grown under glass, or on a hotbed, at any season of the year, all that is necessary being to maintain the temperature of the house or frame, as the case may be, at a height ranging from 70° to 75°, but not falling below the former. It is unnecessary to describe the process of making a hotbed here, and for this the reader must be referred to paragraph 689. The seed must be planted in good mould placed in pots, and these pots must be placed in the frame when the rank steam and heat of the bed consequent on its first construction has passed off, and it is in a proper condition for their reception. The seeds may be placed in pots singly, or two or three in a 5-inch pot. Perhaps the former mode is preferable, as the roots are not disturbed when the plants are turned out of the pots to be placed in the soil that forms the surface of the bed. They grow very quickly, and will make their appearance above ground in two or three days.

2521 *Management of Plants in Frames, etc.* When the plants have made two leaves, pinch out the point above the second; each plant will then send out two lateral shoots above the second leaf of each shoot: pick off the top. After that, stop them above every fruit, and, as the plants grow, add fresh soil, till the whole bed is level, taking care that the soil is of the same temperature as the bed before placing it in the frame, or the plants are likely to receive a chill, which throws them back considerably.

2522 *Setting Fruit* It will be necessary, between the months of October and April, to set each fruit as the flower opens. This is done by taking a male flower, and pulling off all but the centre – that is, the stamens supporting the anthers, which hold the farina or pollen – and applying this to the centre of the female flower, which may be distinguished by the rudiment of the fruit supporting it. This, in the warmer months, is the office of bees. Attracted to the flowers by the honey and pollen, they fertilise the female blossom in collecting it; but when there are no bees about, the cultivator must perform the task himself.

2523 *Ridge Cucumbers, Gherkins, etc.* The instructions given above are, as it will be understood, wholly intended for the culture of cucumbers in frames. There are varieties, however, that can be grown in the open air, but the fruit is smaller, and far less wholesome, than that obtained from fruit under glass. The plants are raised from seed placed in pots at the end of March or the beginning of April. The pots are plunged in gentle heat on a hotbed, covered by a frame, and when the plants are up, as much air must be given to them as possible, and they must be stopped at least twice, in order to keep the growth within bounds as much as possible. About the middle of June, they may be transferred from the frame to the open ground on spots prepared for them by digging holes in the earth about 18 inches or 2 feet in diameter, and about 18 inches below the surface of the soil. The earth taken out should be disposed in a hillock over the manure, the top of the hillock being about 9 inches above the ground level, and therefore above the manure also. The ground should be prepared four or five days before the plants are put out.

Cucumbers and melons, it is known, are sometimes grown in pits heated with hot water; the superiority of this plan is so fully established, that none would be troubled with ordinary hotbeds formed of manure after having tried it. The diminution of labour, the cleanliness and comfort, and last, but not least, the ornamental appearance of the suspended fruit, are decidedly preferable to the many inconveniences attached to the management of hotbeds.

2524 *Melons: Culture* The culture of the melon is very similar to that of the cucumber. The preparation of the manure, making the bed, raising the plants, the stopping and setting, are the same; but the soil in which they are finally planted should be trodden down rather firmly; and as the fruit appears all nearly about the same time, it is advisable to have them swell off as nearly as possible together; otherwise, the most forward will take the lead, and become much larger than the other. Two melons on a plant are as much as can be expected to do well; but never more than three should be allowed to remain: pinch off all the rest and every other unnecessary growth. It is important that the plants be not allowed to ramble after the fruit has begun to swell; for this will require the whole strength of the plant. The fruit takes some four or five weeks, occasionally more, from the time of setting to the time of ripening, which is indicated by the stalk appearing to separate from the fruit. They should be cut and used on the day this takes place, or very soon after.

2525 *Production of Second Crop* As soon as the fruit is cut (if it is intended that they should bear a second crop), prune back the shoots to where the fresh growth commences. Two or three inches of fresh loam should be spread over the surface of the bed, which should at the same time have a good soaking with manure water, to assist the plants to make a fresh growth; an additional stimulus at the same time should be given to the roots by slightly increasing the bottom heat. Bring forward the succeeding crops, and take every means to keep down the red spider, which, when once established on the foliage, is most difficult to destroy.

2526 *Regulation of Moisture* Melons, while ripening their fruit, are very liable to crack when exposed to moisture, or when water is supplied too freely to their roots. This is more likely to happen with the higher flavoured ones, from the thinness of their skin. In common frames some difficulty will be found in keeping the air sufficiently dry. To prevent this in moist weather, air must be left on at night both back and front, to admit of a slight circulation; and a little extra heat should be thrown into the bed, to keep up the temperature, by turning over linings. Where, however, melons are grown by the assistance of hot water, an atmosphere can be maintained which will fully carry out the ripening process of this delicious fruit, even in unfavourable weather. In watering melons, great caution must be used in supplying only the exact quantity wanted, as an excess of water at the roots only tends to increase the size and deteriorate the quality of the fruit. The kind of structure the plants are grown in will have some effect on the quantity of water they will require. In lofty pits or houses, where the foliage attains a large size, and where a much drier atmosphere is obtained than in frames and low pits, more water will be necessary, and the surface of the soil should be frequently sprinkled.

An ordinary melon pit is best for a main crop; but, to have them early, a hotbed and frame is the next best thing to hot-water pits. In training them in a frame, have two plants under the middle, and each light placed close together. Stop them at the second leaf, when each plant will throw out three shoots, which are trained fanlike, so that the three shoots from each of the two plants radiate from a centre, and the laterals from these bear the fruit; but never allow more than one to swell off on the same vine, so that each plant has three vines, and each vine one fruit, or six melons from each light. In the pit, which has 6 feet clear space from back to front, the procedure is as follows: About the beginning of May a quantity of stable dung is procured, and prepared by turning and wetting if necessary; this will be about the middle of the month; by that time the pit is cleared of what had formerly occupied it. The dung is then thrown in and levelled; three days after, some good stiff loam is laid on to the thickness of 7 or 8 inches; this is well trodden down, and in three days more the plants are put in a row, about 18 inches from the back, and another about the same distance from the front, the plants being about 18 inches apart. At the second leaf the plants are stopped, and each plant makes two vines, one trained towards the back of the pit, the other to the front. To insure a good crop, any number of fruit may be set; but one to each vine, or two to each plant, is sufficient; no more ought to be allowed to swell, and all superfluous growth should be prevented: the too common practice of allowing the plants to grow and set as they please is not profitable. Both the cucumber and melon grow freely in a moist heat – a certain amount of humidity is indispensable to secure a vigorous and healthy growth; but the melon should be kept moderately dry while setting, and also at the time of ripening the fruit; a copious watering once a week is sufficient for the roots, but the foliage should be sprinkled every day, just before closing up for the night. Early closing is best. Observe that in watering cucumbers, melons, or any plant growing in heat, warm water should be used, otherwise the plants are retarded by the chill imparted by cold water.

2527 *Vegetable Marrows, Gourds, Pumpkins* These vegetables, which produce an immense amount of food, may be profitably and easily cultivated by attending to the following directions: The seed should be sown in April or May, in pots or pans of rich, light soil, and raised in a warm frame. As soon as possible, the young plants should be potted off, and hardened in a cold frame for planting out in the end of May or early in June. The plants may then be set out in the open ground in positions which have been well dug over, and if the land be poor it should be heavily manured. It is desirable to make a trench round each plant when put in the ground, that when water is given – and marrows require plenty of moisture – it may be absorbed by the soil in the immediate vicinity of the plant, and not run off to some distance, as it will when the ground is hard and dry. In planting in the open, at least 6 feet should be allowed every way from plant to plant. Marrows will grow well when placed on a dung hill, or on any hillock formed of stable refuse and covered over with earth. Being a trailing plant, this position suits it, and the hillock will soon be covered with vines. If the vines are pegged down at a joint, and the joint covered with earth, roots will be sent out from the joint, and will afford fresh channels of nutriment for the plant and its fruit. Vegetable marrows, gourds, etc., may be trained on trellises, fences, etc., on which their broad green leaves, brilliant yellow flowers, and fruits of various forms and colours will present an attractive appearance.

> Mr James Cuthill tells us that marrows contain a rich sugary and farinaceous matter, and are a most excellent and nutritious article of diet when dressed in the following manner: Cut the marrows into short pieces, take out all the pith and seeds, and boil them in plenty of water with a little salt. When well boiled, scrape out all the marrow, put it between two dishes, and squeeze out all the water; then mash it well, adding salt, pepper, and a little butter. It is then a dish fit for any table. The cultivation Mr Cuthill recommends is to sow the seed about the first week in May, in the open ground, in a warm corner, transplanted to moderately rich land. 'I can grow,' he adds, 'twenty tons of the marrows to the acre easily; and, when ripe, they can be stowed away anywhere, and will keep good for a very great length of time. In addition to their utility as a vegetable for the table, they form a most excellent and economical article when boiled for fattening pigs.'

2528 *Tomato, or Love Apple* An admirable sauce by itself, it enters largely into a great number of our best and most wholesome sauces. It also may be cooked and brought on to table like other vegetables, in several different ways; or eaten raw, cut in slices like cucumber, but much thicker, and dressed with salt, pepper, oil, and vinegar, in the same way. When prepared in this manner, as a salad, a few slices of onion will be found an improvement. Further, it is extremely palatable when eaten as a fruit, dipped in sugar. Those who have analysed its properties say that the tomato is singularly wholesome, and very useful, especially in cases of bad digestion; still, it is not appreciated or cultivated as it ought to be. There is undoubtedly some little difficulty in our climate in fruiting and ripening tomatoes to perfection; but the following directions will generally be found to succeed.

2529 *Culture, etc.* Sow the seeds in pots, in very rich light mould, in March or April, and place them in a cucumber frame, or other gentle heat. When the second leaf appears, re-pot the plants, either singly or at most two or three together, keeping them near the glass and well watered. In May remove them to a cold frame, for the purpose of hardening them before they are planted out, which should be done as soon as the fear of spring frosts is over, and the earlier the better. The best situation for tomato plants is against a south wall, fully exposed to the sun. The plants should be well watered with liquid manure to keep up a rapid growth. As soon as the blossom buds appear, watering should cease. Stop the shoots by nipping off the tops, and throw out all those sprays that show little signs of fruit, exposing the young fruit as much as possible to the sun and air, only watering to prevent a check in case of very severe drought, of which the state of the plant will be the best index.

In a very dull, wet, cold autumn, even with the greatest care, the fruit will sometimes not ripen as it ought; but in this case it may frequently be made fit for use by cutting off the branches on which full-grown fruit is found, and hanging them in a warm dry greenhouse or elsewhere, to soften and ripen; a cool oven may be used advantageously to effect this. Tomatoes usually require support, which may be afforded by sticks, or by training them against a wall or on trellis. A new self-supporting or bush tomato has been introduced (1886) by Messrs Viccars Collyer and Co., of Leicester, whose stalks are short and stiff, and which sustains itself by growing in the form of a small shrub.

5 – Salad Section

2530 *Celery* As this most valuable vegetable is usually put on table as an accompaniment to cheese in the winter months, during which it is in season, it has been included among those which are comprised in the salad section. It must be borne in mind, however, that it is equally good and useful when stewed and served in white sauce, and that few soups are perfect in which celery or celery seed has not been used as flavouring.

2531 *Propagation, etc.* Celery is propagated by seed, which is best obtained from the seed shops. It may be sown in any month from Christmas to April. To get plants for the table in September, it should be sown in February in pans, which should be placed on a moderate hotbed. In about three weeks they will germinate, and, when about 2 inches high, the plants should be pricked out under glass, either in a frame or in pots, in a compost of loam and three parts well-rotted dung. If in pots, shift them in April, and at the end of May plant them in shallow trenches in a warm part of the garden. If the trenches are dug out to the depth of 2 feet, 6 inches of hot dung placed in the bottom to stimulate the plants, the soil replaced, and the plants put in and covered with hand glasses, an early crop will be the result. A second sowing should be made in March, still on a hotbed or in pans, or protected by sashes and mats until the plants are up; when fit to handle, they should be pricked out on a slight hotbed or on a warm border. After a few weeks they should be again transplanted into a similar bed, and placed 4 or 5 inches apart each way. In July the plants will be fit to plant out in trenches for autumn use; a third sowing in April, treated in a similar manner, will be ready for winter use, pricking them out in fresh loam and decomposed leaf-mould when large enough to handle.

2532 *Planting out in Trenches* The plants are placed 8 inches apart, the rows 4 to 6 feet apart, according to the size of plants required. When the plants are about 18 inches high, blanching commences by throwing the soil round the roots and ridging up, the intermediate ground being planted with coleworts, lettuce, and other light crops likely to be on before the celery requires earthing up.

2533 *Preparation of the Plants* In order to avoid anything approaching a check to the plants, they are taken up and every root and leaf carefully preserved, the bottom of the larger outside leaves carefully examined, and every bud and sucker carefully removed with the point of the knife. Some cultivators go so far as to cut the beds in which the plants are growing into square pieces, and removing the whole mass with the plant by introducing a trowel under it, and planting it bodily in its new abode.

2534 *Watering and Shading* Immediately after planting, a copious watering should be given. In its wild state, celery delights in situations where it can receive an unlimited supply of moisture; and nature is always an excellent guide where cultivation is concerned. Celery trenches should, then, throughout their growth receive abundant supplies of water. When planted, the bed or trench is usually a few inches below the neighbouring soil. The trenches should have some means of shading from the glare of the noonday sun; old lights, bushes of firs, or other dense objects, for a few hours every day, will suffice. Crops of peas are sometimes grown between the rows to afford the required shelter, and there can be no more economical mode of supplying it, provided the rows run from north to south, and are sufficiently apart to admit of it.

The mode of cultivation recommended by Mr Cuthill 'is to dig out a trench two spades deep and five to six feet wide, banking up the mould on either side of the bottom of the trench; fill in a foot of the strongest manure, such as decomposed cow dung, and cover it over with three or four inches of mould for planting in; or if the ground is very rich, half the quantity of manure. The plants are then taken direct from the beds and planted, root and head entire, not trimmed – a plan which ought to be discontinued in everything.'

2535 *Subsequent Treatment* The subsequent treatment of celery is very simple. Remove all side shoots and weeds, stir the earth frequently, and water whenever required, occasionally with weak manure water; sometimes adding a little quicklime to the water for the benefit of worms and slugs. If the celery fly appears, a little soot, applied dry or in water, and sprinkled over the foliage, will be useful. After these waterings, a thin covering of dry soil thrown over the trench will check evaporation. As the time for banking up approaches, it is the practice in some places to tie the plants up with bast strings, partly to keep the outer leaves in proper order, but partly also to assist in the blanching process. When lightly tied up at the top, the centre is encouraged to rise and swell.

With regard to banking up or earthing up celery, it has been a question whether the operation should be performed at once, or progressively, putting it on a little at a time. Mr Judd, a very successful grower, in a report on this subject made to the Horticultural Society, points out 'that it is not well to load the plants with too much mould at once; the first two mouldings, therefore, are done very sparingly, and with the common draw hoe, forming a ridge on each side of the plants, and leaving them in a hollow to receive the full benefit of the rain and waterings. When they are strong enough to bear water, the moulding is better done with the spade, still keeping the plants in a hollow, and continuing the process through the autumn, gradually diminishing the breadth at top till it is drawn at last to as sharp a ridge as possible to stand the winter.' In order to prevent the earth falling on part of the plants, Mr Judd took a long line made of bast, tied the end round the first plant in a row, twisted it round the second, and so round each plant in succession, fastening it to the last in the row. When the moulding was finished, he removed the line. By this means he contrived to earth up the plants without injuring them in any way.

Mr Cuthill performed the operation entirely with the spade; no hand-earthing was employed. Parallel lines were stretched on each side of the row and 18 inches from the plant, and the mould was cut out of the alleys to form the blanching ridge, the whole being effected at three different times, and not commenced until the plants were 18 inches high.

The following method has been recommended for blanching celery, which merits attention. Under this plan the celery is planted out about 15 or 18 inches apart, on a well-manured and well-pulverised piece of ground, and it is allowed to grow to its full size, the ground in the meantime being kept well stirred between. The plants should be freely watered in dry weather, and with liquid manure, unless the ground has been mulched with short well-rotted dung laid between them. When it is desired to blanch it, get a number of 4-inch drain pipes about 18 inches long; place one over each plant, hold the leaves and stalks together, and fill up with sand; it will blanch clean, and is easily taken up. A great many more may thus be grown on a given space, the waste of room between the trenches, as in the ordinary method, being unnecessary. To protect from frost, place litter between; but very sharp frosts alone will injure them. The cost of pipes will be saved in the reduction of the necessary labour. The sand may be collected and used again, or it will be an excellent dressing for the ground, if heavy.

2536 *Lifting Celery* In lifting celery, 'always begin at one end of a row,' says Mr McIntosh, 'taking the plants up by the roots, and carefully avoid bruising the stems or breaking the leaves.' Cut the roots off, and bury them in the trench, but remove the plant to the vegetable house. Remove the outer leaves to be washed, and reserved for soups. The centre part carefully examine, and remove discoloured portions; and when washed clean, dip it in clear salt and water, to dislodge any small worms; this done, it passes out of the gardener's care. As frost sets in, a quantity of the crop for immediate use should be taken up; removing the roots and soil, and tying the leaves together, convey them to the root cellar, and lay them in sand, not too dry. Look to them from time to time, to see that they do not get too dry.

2537 *Lettuce* Lettuces are a surface crop, and light feeders; consequently, by giving plenty of manure, we not only insure good lettuces, but prepare the ground for a grosser-feeding crop, sowing the seed broadcast, and treading it in if on light soil. On wet ground, if apt to bind or clod, this is not to be recommended; but mark the ground into one or more beds, 4 feet wide, with alleys 15 inches in width between. Standing in the alleys, sow the seed, and press it in with the rake, or cover with some light soil.

2538 *Sowing for Succession* Where a succession of lettuces is required throughout the year, it will be necessary to sow once a month till March; after that once a fortnight, or every three weeks; for although a crop may last a month in moist weather, they are soon over in the hot summer months, and it is as well to be provided with plenty of young plants for succession. After August, once a month will be often enough. Sow the seed thinly over a piece of ground sufficient to grow a fortnight's supply; when large enough to transplant, thin them out to a foot apart, and plant the thinnings a foot apart on a piece the same size; those left in the bed come in first, and the others are ready to succeed them. In summer, sow on a larger space, and let them grow where sown.

2539 *Blanching Lettuces* Cos lettuces require tying up to blanch and crisp them. To do this expeditiously, provide a bundle of bast matting, cut to the required length, sling it round the waist, and gathering each plant up, pass the hand rapidly round it. In this way a score or two may be tied in few minutes.

One of the most hardy sorts, and best for sowing at any time, is the black-seeded Bath cos; it is very crisp, and of good flavour. Another good sort is the Moor Park cos, and also the Paris white cos. Of the cabbage lettuces, one of the best, especially for winter use, is the hardy green Hammersmith; but it is apt to run in summer and autumn. The brown Dutch, tennis ball, and Tom Thumb cabbage lettuces are good varieties, and very hardy, the last named being excellent for spring sowing. The Malta, or drum-head cabbage, is a fine large lettuce, and good for summer use, as it is not apt to run if allowed plenty of room. The Neapolitan cabbage is also noteworthy for its great size and crispness. The advantage of cabbage lettuces is, that they require no tying up, which prevents cos lettuces being serviceable in winter, they so soon rot off when tied; but such sorts as the London cos, which turn in without tying, may be grown advantageously in winter.

2540 *Endive* This vegetable is grown chiefly for winter use and for salads in early spring. Sowings in the open ground may be made in April, and continued monthly for succession until August. The seeds may be scattered broadcast over ground prepared as for lettuce, or, which is better, sown in drills, if it is not intended to transplant them. If sown in drills, let the rows be from 12 to 15 inches apart, and thin out the plants to the same distance apart in the beds. If sown broadcast, the plants must be thinned out to the distance of 4 or 5 inches apart, and when large enough transplanted into ground that has been richly manured. The plants should be about 3 inches high before they are transplanted. They should be set the same distance apart as prescribed for thinning out plants sown in drills. Plenty of water should be given when the weather is dry, and liquid manure occasionally.

2541 *To Blanch Endive* Place over each plant, when full grown, a large tile or slate, which will effectually exclude all light, and blanch the endive in a few days. Some gardeners tie the plants up with bast or twine, in the same manner as lettuces; but the plan is objectionable, as in wet weather the rain will run down the endive leaves and rot the hearts of the plants.

2542 *Endive in Frames* Endive may be planted in a frame in September, and blanched for use in the winter by inverting flower pots over each plant – just clapping the pot over the centre of them, but by no means tucking the leaves into it.

2543 *Radishes* If much liked, these may be had ail the year round by sowing in frames from October to February inclusive, and in the open ground during the remainder of the year. They require a light, rich, loamy soil, and if they are grown on ground that has been manured for the crop that has preceded them, so much the better. Sow broadcast, thinly, or in drills from 3 to 4 inches apart for long radishes and the smaller sorts of turnip radishes, and from 4 to 6 inches apart for the larger sorts. Plenty of water should be given to radishes when the weather is dry.

2544 *Culture in Hotbed* Late sown radishes – that is to say, radishes sown in autumn – will need protection at night when frosty weather comes on. To make certain of the crop, it is better to grow them in frames, making up for the purpose a bed of manure about 2 feet in depth. Over the hotbed spread light, loamy soil, to the depth of 10 inches, or thereabout, and then place a two or three-light frame over the bed, as may be convenient. Sow the radishes broadcast, and press in the seed with the back of a rake. This may be done from October to even March, but for sowings in midwinter it will be found necessary to afford auxiliary heat by linings as the heat of the bed declines. When hotbeds are made in early spring for cucumbers, radishes may be obtained more quickly than in ordinary soil by sprinkling seed on the earth that is without the frame.

2545 *Horseradish* This, it is true, properly belongs to the edible rooted section; but, as it is mostly used as an accompaniment to roast beef, rather than as a vegetable in the strict sense of the word, it is more desirable, perhaps, to consider its culture here. Horseradish should be grown on an open spot. It is a mistake to suppose this crop can be stowed away in any corner or out-of-the-way place; it requires high culture to produce it good, and it repays good treatment as well as any crop. The best mode of culture is to trench the ground to the depth of 3 feet, but to be rather sparing of manure, as this produces a tendency to fork; the ground should be well broken any time during the winter. Then take up some old roots, and trim them for the kitchen, cutting off the crowns about an inch and a half long – these latter are for planting. Next, with a dibble, which is marked 2 feet from the lower end – that being the depth the crowns are to be planted – make holes 2 feet apart in rows 3 feet apart. This done, take a lath-stick split at one end, insert the crown in the slit, thrust it down to the bottom of the hole, and push it out by another stick which is thrust down for the purpose. It is unnecessary to fill up the holes, as they gradually fill as the horseradish nears the surface. If a fresh row is planted every year, and another taken up, the crop will be kept in good condition, and a fresh piece of improved ground offered every year for other crops.

2546 *Mustard and Cress* These accompaniments to lettuce, etc., in forming a salad, or saladings, as they are sometimes called, may be obtained by sowing in the open ground in March and April on a sunny spot, and from April to October in a somewhat moist and sheltered situation. The seed should be sown thickly in shallow drills, and a sowing be made every fortnight for succession. The seed leaves only are eaten, because the leaves that show themselves next in order are rough and strong in flavour, For winter use, from October to March, seeds may be sown in boxes filled with light, rich mould, and placed in a greenhouse or window.

2547 *Corn Salad* This ingredient for salad, which is also known as lamb's lettuce, may be had all the year round by sowing in February and March for use in summer, and in September for winter use and for early spring. Sow in drills, about 6 inches apart, in light, rich soil, in a warm situation. The leaves should be eaten when they are young and tender. If the plants show any tendency to run to seed, it is better to take them up and pick off such leaves as may still be eatable, unless it be desired to save seed.

2548 *Rampion* The root and leaves of this plant are both eaten in salads, and in winter, when variety is valued, it forms a valuable addition to the materials in season for salad making. Sowings should be made in March or April for use in autumn, and in May for a winter supply. A rich soil in a shady position is necessary, and the seeds should be sown in drills about 6 inches apart. The plants should be ultimately thinned out to the same distance apart in the rows.

2549 *Chervil* For summer use this salad herb should be sown in March or April, on soil well dug over and manured, in drills about 9 inches apart. The sowing may be made on a warm sunny border; but for winter use a warm and dry situation should be selected, in which a sowing should be made in August. The winter crop will need protection when the nights are frosty; this may be afforded by mats sustained on bent sticks.

2550 *Chicory* The tender shoots of the chicory, whose root when baked and ground is used in the adulteration of coffee, form a useful ingredient for salads in the winter season. The plants from which the shoots are obtained are got from seed sown in the middle of spring, in drills about 9 inches apart, the plants being thinned out to the same distance apart in the drills In the winter the roots should be taken up, and put in boxes in light soil. The boxes should then be placed in any warm position in which the growth of the sprouts from the roots will be excited by the heat. The light must be carefully excluded from the growing shoots in order to blanch them and to keep them in a crisp and tender state.

2551 *Dandelion* The young shoots of the dandelion may be rendered available for salads by treating roots in winter in the manner described for chicory.

6 – The Mushroom

2552 The mushroom is a vegetable requiring a system of treatment peculiar to itself, and so widely different from that of any other that those who do not make themselves acquainted with its nature and mode of cultivation necessarily fail. The first and most important requisite in the cultivation of this plant is good spawn.

Spawn of excellent quality may be made in the following manner: To one barrow-load of moderately strong loam add two of horse-droppings fresh from the stable, and two of cow dung (sheep or deer dung maybe used with equal success). Thoroughly mix these in a dry state, then wet and work the mixture to the consistency of mortar, and spread it over a level floor. When it is set sufficiently firm, cut it into bricks about a foot square; place them on edge in an airy situation, but sheltered from wet; when they become tolerably dry, build them into a square heap, placing a piece of spawn on each brick between every layer, and cover the whole with dry litter. The heap will now require attention, to prevent its fermenting too strongly. If the thermometer rises above 90°, the litter must be removed, the heap flattened and re-covered. Should fermentation not take place sufficiently for the working of the spawn, more litter must be added; too much attention cannot be given at this crisis of spawn-making. If the spawn does not run freely through the whole mass until it becomes of a whitish appearance, it will be of inferior quality; but if it passes this state, and, upon breaking the bricks, long filaments or threads are found, it will be almost useless for the purpose of reproduction. The spring is the best time for this process, as it is easier to raise the temperature than to depress it, and a better opportunity of drying the spawn is gained, which is a matter of vital importance in keeping it for any length of time; but, at the same time, it may be attended with success any time between March and September. Spawn well made, properly dried, and securely stored, will retain its properties for almost any length of time.

2553 *Artificial Culture, Situation, etc.* Mushrooms may easily be had for culinary purposes at any season of the year by adopting an artificial process, and spawning with artificial spawn a bed made as described below. The best situation for the artificial growth of mushrooms is a cellar or underground toolhouse, or any other place where the atmosphere is of that close, damp, foggy character which is always so peculiarly favourable to the growth of fungi. The antechamber or passage to an icehouse is an excellent place for a mushroom bed, and is frequently made use of for this purpose: any shed, however, whether underground or not, may be made available; and, indeed, with a little more care, mushrooms may be grown in the open air, without any roof to cover them at all; but a cellar or underground hole has a decided preference.

2554 *Preparation of Bed* The foundation of the bed must be well-rotted manure from the horse yard, which has been sweetened by being turned over two or three times. It may have a little good loam mixed with it, in the proportion of about two barrows of loam to twelve of manure. The bed is best made on a gentle slope, and the manure should be well and firmly beaten down with a spade. When the heat has fallen to about 75°, the spawn may be put in. This artificial spawn, which is usually made up in cakes, must be broken up into pieces about 2 inches square, and placed all over the bed, upon the surface of the manure, about 10 or 12 inches apart. A covering of 1 inch, or 1½ inch, of good garden loam is then to be placed all over the bed, and the surface again beaten firm with a spade. The whole must then be covered well over with straw or other material, to exclude all light.

2555 *Temperature, Moisture, etc.* The growth of the mushrooms will, of course, depend somewhat on the state of the atmosphere; but in a temperature of 45° to 55° they will usually begin to appear in about six weeks. Little or no water should be given to the bed until the mushrooms begin to come up, as its own moisture and heat ought to be sufficient to start the spawn; but as soon as the mushrooms appear, a plentiful supply of water may be given, and it will be found that a little common salt, or, better still, saltpetre, will have a great effect upon the crop. It is essential that the surface of the bed be kept quite dark. If the bed be made in the open air, it may be necessary, after a time, to give to the spawn a fresh start, by placing a lining of hot manure around it; but on all occasions great care must be taken that the heat of the bed is not so excessive as to burn up the spawn. This, however, can never happen at a temperature of 75°; and when a bed is above this, no spawn should ever be inserted.

2556 *Mushrooms in Baskets, etc.* The *modus operandi* described above shows in as few words as possible the method to be followed in the artificial growth of mushrooms in any situation, whether indoors or out of doors. The process may be carried out as described on either a large or small scale. Indeed, on a small scale they may be grown on shelves, or in wicker baskets, in a cellar, but in any case the preparation of the manure and soil, the operation of spawning, and the subsequent management, are precisely the same.

7 – Sweet Herb Section

2557 *Sweet Herbs* A convenient spot in every kitchen garden should be appropriated to the growth of such herbs as are necessary and useful for culinary purposes. With a little care and management, the herb garden may be made not only useful, but ornamental also. It should, in general, be situated as near the kitchen premises as possible; and each kind of herb should have its own separate bed. If a square piece of land be set apart for the herb garden, the beds may be arranged in some fanciful form, or separated by gravel walks, and having neat box or tile edgings. The most useful and best worthy of cultivation are the following: Parsley, sage, thyme, mint, fennel, rue, basil, tarragon, marjoram, balm, and rosemary.

2558 *Parsley* In order to grow this useful herb in perfection, it is necessary that the roots and stem should be kept in a perfectly dry state; this is indispensable to the health and freshness of the plant. In preparing the beds, therefore, remove the soil to the depth of 6 or 8 inches, and fill in the bottom with the same depth of stones, brick rubbish, and similar loose material. Over this prepare a bed of light rich soil, which will thus be raised considerably above the level of the ground, the bed being raked smooth and level. Towards the end of May, sow some seed of the most curly variety, either in shallow drills, slightly covered with fine soil, or thin broadcast raked in. If the weather continue dry, water frequently: in five or six weeks the plants will have appeared; when large enough, thin them out, so that they may be 4 or 5 inches apart. By the end of autumn they will be large and vigorous plants. At this time, drive a row of stakes or hoops into the ground, on each side of the bed, so as to form arches strong enough to support a covering of mats, which should be laid over them as soon as frosty or wet weather threatens to set in. During intense frosts, increase the protection, removing it partly on fine days, and entirely in mild weather. The soil should be kept dry, and all decayed leaves carefully removed; in this manner this useful vegetable may be available all the winter.

Parsley is a biennial, and as it runs to seed in the second year, even when sown as late as possible in the previous year, it is necessary to make a sowing every year. To keep parsley available for culinary purposes as long as possible, remove the flower stalks as soon as they appear. It should be said that Messrs Carter and Co., 237 and 238 High Holborn, London, supply seed of a new variety, which they call New Perpetual Parsley, and which, they say, has stood for four years without running to seed. Such a kind is certainly preferable to ordinary parsley, because it obviates the necessity of making yearly sowings.

2559 *Sage* will grow freely from slips, which may be taken in the autumn as soon as the plants have ceased flowering, or in the spring of the year. It may also be propagated by layers in spring or autumn.

2560 *Thyme* is easily increased by dividing the roots and planting out the pieces in a bed about 4 inches apart, or it may be raised from seed sown in light, rich soil in April. It may also be propagated by rooted branches, which may be pegged into the earth after the manner of layers, and thus induced to root. April is the month in which old plants should be divided, and rooted branches removed from the parent plant. *Lemon Thyme* is a variety which should be cultivated in every garden on account of its delicious flavour.

2561 *Mint* also grows from pieces of the roots, which spread with great rapidity; for every piece that shows a joint will grow. It requires a moist soil, and the bed in which it is placed should be enclosed with a string, brick, or tile edging, as it is frequently very troublesome in running about. Division of the roots should be made in February or March. When the plants are about to bloom, the stalks should be cut and dried for winter use. Towards the close of autumn all the stalks that remain should be cut down to the ground, and the bed covered with fresh soil to the depth of 2 inches. The varieties of mint grown in gardens are spearmint, peppermint, and pennyroyal, the last-named being used chiefly for medicinal purposes.

2562 *Fennel* may be raised from seed in April or May. The seed should be covered lightly with fine mould; and, when the plants are strong enough, they may be set out in a bed about a foot apart. A good bed of fennel will last for years; but to insure fine leaves, the flower stalks should always be cut off as soon as they appear, so as never to ripen seed.

2563 *Rue* is a medicinal plant, but is sometimes used for garnishing. It may be propagated from seeds or slips sown or taken in March or April.

2564 *Basil* The variety known as Bush Basil is the most hardy. It is raised from seed sown in gentle heat in March. Thin out, and give air freely to harden off the plants, which may be removed to a border consisting of light, rich soil, and in a warm situation, in May or early in June.

2565 *Tarragon* This perennial requires a light, rich, and dry soil, and should be grown in a warm and sheltered position. Propagate by division of roots in March or April, or by cuttings taken in July or August, and struck under a hand light. Cut down at approach of winter, and protect the roots by putting earth and litter above them.

2566 *Rosemary*, although not used in cookery, should be found in every garden. It may be propagated by layers which may be removed in April or May and planted out, or by slips or cuttings taken at the same time, and planted in a situation not too much exposed to the sun. They may be transplanted from the bed in which they have been struck in September or the following April.

2567 *Balm* This may be increased by division of the roots in March or October. It is chiefly useful as a febrifuge.

2568 *Marjoram* This useful herb may be raised from seed sown in April, by division of the roots in April or September, or by cuttings struck under a hand glass in June. The varieties chiefly, cultivated are *Pot Marjoram*, a perennial, and *Sweet or Knotted Marjoram*, a biennial of a delicate nature that will not stand the winter in this country, and must therefore be raised yearly from seed as an annual.

Any of the sweet herbs used for culinary purposes may be preserved for winter use by being cut when in full growth, and dried in the sun. They may then be kept tied up in bunches in a dry room, or rubbed down and bottled, which is far better.

8 – The Best Varieties of Fruits

2569 To give directions at considerable length for fruit culture, would be, in a great measure, to repeat much that has already advanced elsewhere in this volume, in which the culture and the various modes that are adopted in training and pruning trees have been given at some length. Those who require more information in detail on this subject, should consult the excellent and comprehensive treatise, entitled, *Fruit Farming for Profit*, by Mr George Bunyard, FRHS, Old Nurseries, Maidstone, Kent, which will put them in possession of everything they can require, and buyers requiring supplies of fruit trees on a large scale should make application for trees to this successful fruit grower, or to Messrs Richard Smith and Co., Worcester, if they are unable to procure what they require in their immediate neighbourhood.

2570 Although varieties of apples and pears are very numerous, neither these nor the varieties of fruits of other kinds are so many in number as the varieties of roses, chrysanthemums, etc.; nor are new varieties of such frequent introduction. This chapter may therefore be brought to a conclusion with brief lists of the most desirable varieties for general use, which are taken mainly from Mr Bunyard's work named above.

2571 *Early Dessert Apples* The following are thirteen good varieties that ripen their fruit early. They are arranged as far as possible in order of ripening, and those which are marked with a star in all cases may be planted in cold soils:

1 **Red Juneating**
2 **Mr Gladstone**
3 **Devonshire Quarrenden***
4 **Duchess of Oldenburg**
5 **Kerry Pippin**
6 **Summer Golden Pippin***
7 **Worcester Pearmain**
8 **Prolific or Colonel Vaughan**
9 **Pine Apple Russet**
10 **Sugarloaf Pippin**
11 **Red Astrachan**
12 **Stubbard**
13 **Yorkshire Beauty**

2572 *Dessert Apples for Storing* The following are eleven choice varieties for storing:

1 **King of Pippins**
2 **Cox's Orange Pippin**
3 **Blenheim Orange**
4 **Gascoyne's Scarlet Seedling***
5 **Ribston Pippin**
6 **Wyken Pippin***
7 **Golden Knob***
8 **Scarlet Nonpariel**
9 **Sturmer Pippin**
10 **Court Pendu Plat***
11 **Duke of Devonshire**

2573 *Cooking Apples for Immediate Use* The following are the names of twelve good sorts:

1 **Early Julien***
2 **Keswick Codlin***
3 **Manx Codlin***
4 **Cellini Pippin**
5 **Lord Suffleld**
6 **Old Hawthornden**
7 **New Hawthornden**
8 **Cox's Pomona**
9 **Loddington Seedling***
10 **Grenadier**
11 **Warner's King**
12 **Stirling Castle**

2574 *Cooking Apples for Storing* The following are thirteen choice varieties for storing for culinary purposes:

1 **Blenheim Orange**
2 **Small's Admirable**
3 **Golden Noble**
4 **Lord Derby***
5 **Queen Caroline***
6 **Belle Dubois** or **Gloria Mundi**
7 **Winter Queening***
8 **Wellington or Dumelows***
9 **Warner's King**
10 **Beauty of Kent***
11 **Northern Greening***
12 **Smart's Prince Albert***
13 **Norfolk Beaufln**

2575 *Market Pears* The following are thirteen good varieties of pears, arranged in order of ripening:

1 **Doyenne d'Éte***
2 **Lammas***
3 **Jargonelle***
4 **Autumn Bergamot**
5 **Williams' Bon Chrétien***
6 **Colmar d'Eté***
7 **Hessell***
8 **Beurre de Capiaumont**
9 **Aston Town** or **Cresan***
10 **Fertility**
11 **Eyewood**
12 **Bishop's Thumb**
13 **Broom Park**

2576 *Choice Pears* The following are fourteen choice varieties, good as standards or for training on walls:

1 **Souvenir de Congrés**
2 **Beurre d'Amanlis**
3 **Doyen Bussoch**
4 **Durondeau**
5 **Pitmaston Duchess**
6 **Beurre Superfin**
7 **Beurre Hardy**
8 **Beurre Clairgean**
9 **Louise Bonne of Jersey**
10 **Duchesse d'Angouleme**
11 **Josephine de Malines**
12 **Doyenne du Comice**
13 **Beurre Diel**
14 **Marie Louise**

2577 *Plums for all Purposes* The following are thirty excellent varieties of plums. Damson plums are marked D:

1 **Victoria**
2 **Early Orleans**
3 **The Czar**
4 **Mitchelson**
5 **Kent Diamond**
6 **Prince Engelbert**
7 **Golden Purple**
8 **Cox's Emperor**
9 **Rivers' Early Prolific**
10 **Pershore**
11 **White Magnum Bonum**
12 **Pond's Seedling**
13 **Sultan**
14 **Old Greengage**
15 **Coe's Golden Drop**
16 **Autumn Compote**
17 **Belle de Septembre**
18 **Gisborne's**
19 **Prince of Wales**
20 **Grand Duke**
21 **Blue Prolific (D)**
22 **Goliath**
23 **Jefferson**
24 **La Délicieuse**
25 **Old Orleans**
26 **Deniston's Superb**
27 **Kentish Cluster (D)**
28 **Cheshire or Shropshire (D)**
29 **Prune (D)**
30 **Frogmore Damson (D)**

2578 *Cherries of all Kinds* The following are excellent varieties of cherries, arranged, as far as possible, in the order of ripening:

1 *White Heart, Early*
1. **Frogmore Biggareau**
2. **Elton Heart**
3. **Governor Wood**
4. **Adam's Crown Heart**
5. **Bowyer's Early Heart**
6. **Belle d'Orleans**

2 *White Heart, Late*
1. **Kentish Biggareau** or **Amber**
2. **Biggareau Napoleon**
3. **Large French Biggareau**
4. **Florence**

3 *Black*
1. **Werder's Early Black Heart**
2. **Old Black Heart**
3. **Black Cluster or Carone**
4. **Black Biggareau**

4 *Red or Morello*
1. **Kentish.** Excellent for cherry brandy.
2. **Flemish**
3. **Morello.** Good dessert cherry when kept late under net.

2579 *Gooseberries* The following affords a sufficient list for all necessary purposes:

1. **Large White Smith**
2. **Early Sulphur**
3. **Yellow Rough**
4. **Warrington**
5. **Rifleman**
6. **Crown Bob**
7. **Lancashire Lad**
8. **Whinham's Industry**

2580 *Currants of all Kinds* The following is a sufficient list of currants, all of which may be grown in bush form, or trained on walls, trellises, etc. Of the different colours, *black* currants are used for preserves and culinary purposes, *white* for dessert, and *red* for eating, cooking, and preserving:

1 *Black*
1. **Baldwin's Black**
2. **Lee's Prolific**
3. **Black Naples**
4. **Prince of Wales**
5. **Dutch or Old Grape**

2 *White*
1. **Transparent White**
2. **White Dutch or White Grape**

3 *Red*
1. **Cherry Currant**
2. **Knight's Early Red**
3. **La Versaillaise**
4. **Champagne**
5. **Knight's Sweet Red**
6. **Red Dutch or Raby Castle**
7. **May's Queen Victoria**
8. **Long Bunched Red**

2581 *Raspberries The* following will be found excellent varieties of raspberries:

1. **Carter's Prolific**
2. **Fastolf**
3. **Red Antwerp**
4. **Northumberland Fill basket**
5. **Semper Fidelis**
6. **Lord Beaconsfield**
7. **Baumforth's Seedling**
8. **Yellow Globe**
9. **White Antwerp**
10. **Marlborough**
11. **Glenfield**. The Glenfield, the only black raspberry in existence, is a speciality of Messrs Viccars Collyer and Co., Central Hall, Leicester.

2582 *Strawberries* The following are good varieties of early and late strawberries:

Early

1 **Garibaldi** or **Vicomtesse Hericart de Thury**
2 **Black Prince**
3 **Early Crimson Pine**
4 **Keen's Seedling**
5 **Sir Joseph Paxton**
6 **Dr Hogg**
7 **James Veitch**
8 **President**
9 **British Queen**
10 **Grosse Sucreé**
11 **Royal Hautbois**

Late

12 **Sir Charles Napier**
13 **Elton Pine**
14 **Eleanor**
15 **Frogmore Late Pine**
16 **Enchantress**
17 **Roden's Scarlet Pine**
18 **Unser Fritz**
19 **Wonderful**

2583 *Rhubarb* It will be useful to name the following varieties here, although it is *de facto* a vegetable:

1 **Prince Albert**
2 **Johnstone's St Martins**
3 **Marshall's Early**
4 **Hawke's Champagne**
5 **Victoria**
6 **Stott's Monarch**
7 **Crimson Emperor**
8 **Mammoth**

2584 *Cob Nuts and Filberts* The following list is taken from the catalogue of Mr Cooper, FRHS, Calcot Gardens, Reading, who is a specialist in this class of fruit:

1 **Webbs Prize Cob Filbert**
2 **Emperor Cob**
3 **Improved Cosford Cob**
4 **New Cob Daviana**
5 **Prolific Close Head Filbert**
6 **Red Skinned Filbert**
7 **White Skinned Filbert**
8 **Eugenie**
9 **Marquis of Lorne**
10 **Princess Royal**
11 **Garibaldi**
12 **Kentish Cob**
13 **Duke of Edinburgh**
14 **Duchess of Edinburgh**
15 **The Shah**
16 **Cannon**

2585 *Blackberries* A new candidate for a prominent place in the fruit garden has lately been introduced in the blackberry, of which the following are the best cultivated varieties:

1 **Snyder**
2 **Parsley Leaved**
3 **Stone's Hardy**
4 **Wachussett's Thornless**
5 **Brunton's Early**
6 **Mammoth**
7 **Early Harvest**
8 **Taylor's Prolific**
9 **Wilson's Early**
10 **Wilson Junior.**
Best of cultivated kinds.

For the culture of the blackberry, see *All about Blackberries,* Messrs Viccars Collyer and Co., Leicester.

2586 *Peaches* The above lists comprise the chief varieties of the hardier fruits. To these may be added lists of the choicer and more delicate fruits, which require greater care and attention. We will, first of all, take the peaches as recommended by Messrs Richard Smith and Co., Worcester:

1 *Early*
1 **Acton Scott**
2 **Early Albert**
3 **Early Beatrice**
4 **Early Louise**
5 **Early York**
6 **Grosse Mignonne**
7 **Hale's Early**
8 **Noblesse**
9 **Royal George**

2 *Medium*
1 **Barrington**
2 **Bellegarde**
3 **Prince of Wales**
4 **Violette Hative**

3 *Late*
1 **Late Admirable**
2 **Walburton Admirable**
3 **Salway**
4 **Lord Palmerston**

2587 *Nectarines* The following are recommended as excellent varieties of this delicious fruit:

1 **Downton**
2 **Elruge**
3 **Hardwicke Seedling**
4 **Hunt's Tawny**
5 **Lord Napier**
6 **Pitmaston Orange**
7 **Rivers' Orange**
8 **Violette Hative**
9 **Oldenburg**
10 **Old Newington**
11 **Pine Apple**
12 **Victoria**

2588 *Apricots* The following are good varieties for walls or orchard houses, under glass:

1 **Breda**
2 **Hemskirke**
3 **Kaisha**
4 **Large Early**
5 **Moor Park**
6 **Peach**

2589 *Grapes* This fruit pays better under glass than in the open air. The following, however, are most suitable for culture out of doors in favourable situations:

1 **White Sweetwater**
2 **Black Cluster**
3 **Black Hamburgh**
4 **Esperione**
5 **Ferdinand de Lesseps**
6 **Miller's Burgundy**
7 **White Muscadine**
8 **Leicester**

The last-named hardy outdoor grape is a speciality of Messrs Viccars Collyer and Co., Leicester.

2590 *Figs* Of the different varieties in cultivation, the following, perhaps, are the most useful:

1 **Black Ischia**
2 **Brown Ischia**
3 **Brown Turkey**
4 **Marseilles**
5 **Osborne's Prolific**
6 **Castle Kennedy**
7 **Dwarf Prolific**
8 **Hardy Prolific**

2591 *Quinces, Mulberries, Medlars, etc.* Wherever there is room for these fruits, one or two trees of each kind should be planted: the first and last may be placed in the garden or orchard, the second should have grass under it to save the fruit from injury when it falls. In buying fruit trees of any kind, it is desirable to state nature of soil and the position they are to occupy to the nurseryman, and then leave it to him to make the selection.

CHAPTER 37

Gardening in Windows and on Balconies – Ferns and Ferneries

2592 Before this volume is brought to a close, there is yet another form of gardening to be considered, and that is gardening in windows and balconies by the culture of plants and flowers in pots, boxes, baskets, etc., and in window greenhouses.

2593 *Window Greenhouses* It is obvious that these miniature greenhouses may be applied with great ease to any window, for a pair of brackets on a level with the sill will form a stage on which a glazed structure may be easily erected and supported. For the structure itself, all that is required is a glazed frame, from 12 to 18 inches high in front, with glazed sides, rising to the window sash at an angle of 30°, with a framework to receive a sash at the same angle, which may be hinged to the window frame. If this frame extends to three-fourths of the height of the window, it will not interfere very materially with the light of the room. Of course, the plants are watered and arranged from the room within. All manner of ornamental projections may be thus formed in the manner described, and as illustrated in Fig. 593, and when any case outside the window is deemed objectionable, large ornamental bell glasses may be easily adjusted to vases for the hall and drawing-room, in producing which every one will pursue their particular fancy. But whoever would have healthy plants in a sitting-room, of any kind whatever, should provide either a case or vase in which the plants may be provided with an atmosphere suited to them, for the dry air which is agreeable to human beings is unfit for most plants.

FIG. 593 *Glass case or greenhouse for exterior of window*

2594 *Troughs and Boxes* Where a window happens to be in a recess, a wooden trough, lined with lead or zinc, may be used for holding earth, in which climbing plants may be planted and trained about the recess. For this purpose the passion flower is very suitable: if allowed, after crossing the top, to hang down before the window in festoons, displaying its naturally graceful pendulous habit, it will form a pleasant screen for a sunny window.

It is advisable, however, to attempt nothing in this way which cannot be carried out perfectly; a single plant properly grown is to be preferred to the most elaborate attempts the working out of which has not been thoroughly considered; for instance, climbing plants must be very closely watched and carefully trained, or they become so entangled as to be anything but ornamental; they are apt, also, to harbour spiders and other insects, to drop their dead leaves and flowers, and, in common with other plants, they must be watered, which is always inconvenient in a room, for the pots must be well-drained of superfluous moisture, otherwise the earth soddens in the pot. It would never do to let this superfluous water run over the carpet; the pots must consequently have flat basins to receive it, and the water removed from the basins without delay.

2595 *Hanging Baskets* Another feature in window gardening is the introduction of suspended baskets, usually made of wire, for the purpose of displaying to advantage the beautiful habit of trailing plants. These should be potted in ordinary flower pots and surrounded with moss in the basket, the latter being made to hook on to a support in the ceiling, so that it may be temporarily removed when the plant requires water. One of the most suitable plants for the purpose is *Saxifraga sarmentosa*, otherwise known as Mother of Thousands, which does well under ordinary treatment; it is of variegated foliage and highly ornamental. Another suitable plant is *Disandra prostrata*, sometimes called *Sibthorpia prostrata*, with bright yellow flowers,, and pretty foliage like ground ivy. Both these will trail 18 inches or more from the basket in very graceful festoons.

FIG. 594 *Ivy-leaved geranium*

2596 *Planting Baskets: Soil* In planting a basket, if it is to be filled with ordinary soft-wooded flowering plants, that is, geraniums, verbenas, petunias, etc., the soil ought to be two-thirds loam to one of very rotten dung or leaf mould, and a little sand; if planted with ferns or hard-wooded plants, as *Myoporum parvifolium*, *Monochoetum alpestre*, pultenaeas, and the like, the soil should be one half turfy loam and one half peat, using rather more sand than for the freer-growing plants. To those who are not acquainted with soils, it may be worth while to observe that good loam is of a yellowish hue, and feels soft and silky to the touch; it is usually the top spit of meadow land, while peat is obtained in places where heath grows wild.

If the baskets are made of wire and lined with moss, they are sufficiently drained; if of wood, there should be one or more holes in each, to let out surplus moisture. As to soil, those who cannot obtain it otherwise may purchase it at the nearest nursery, properly prepared for the particular kind of plants it is intended for. In filling the baskets, put some rough lumpy soil at the bottom. This should lie hollow, so that surplus water may readily find an exit. The soil should be laid in roughly, with some broken pieces of potsherd mixed with it, when it will keep sweet for years.

2597 *Plants of Trailing Habit for Baskets* Next to fuchsias, the best plants for suspended baskets are ivy-leaved geraniums, one of which is shown in Fig. 594; these being all of a trailing habit, they hang down and flower freely. Petunias and verbenas, also, which are of rich and varied colours, are suitable for baskets, with *Saxifraga sarmentosa*, of variegated foliage and pretty trailing habit, and *Disandra prostrata*, with its pretty yellow musk-like flowers. The common musk is also a very suitable plant; if a bit is planted in the centre, or some small pieces pricked about the surface, it will soon spread out and hang down the sides. Harrison's Giant Musk is also a good basket plant. The common moneywort (*Lysimachia nummularia*) does well and is effective; as is also the trailing snap-dragon, or Toadflax (*Linaria cymbalaria*).

2598 *Hard-wooded Trailers for Baskets* Among hard-wooded plants suitable for suspended baskets, we may reckon *Myoporum parvifolium*, a very neat trailing plant, bearing small white flowers in autumn, winter, and spring; and *Pullenaea subumbellata*, a neat spreading plant, flowering in spring. There are also one or two acacias, as *Acacia rotundifolia* and *A. ovata*, which are of a naturally pendulous habit; and if they can be adapted to the basket, they will be very effective. *Monochoetum alpestre* is a beautiful winter-flowering plant, but will require tying down at first, and training neatly over the basket. In planting the hard-wooded plants, remember what has been said with regard to soil; the softer plants are more easy to cultivate and safer to begin with; but the former are more permanent, and do not so soon outgrow their room.

2599 *Ferns for Baskets* Of a like permanency are ferns, which require much the same soil as the last – that is, equal parts of peat, loam, and sand, having some broken crockery mixed with it. One of the best ferns for baskets is the common polypody, or *Phegopteris vulgare*; this may be planted in nearly all moss, with a small portion of soil. Another excellent fern, and, indeed, one of the handsomest, is *Asplenium flaccidum*, of a beautiful drooping habit, and also viviparous, producing young ferns all over the old fronds. Let this fern be placed in the centre of the basket; it will require nothing more, but will show over the sides and look exceedingly beautiful, being of a bright lively green, and one of the best and handsomest ferns in cultivation. *Pteris serrulata* and *P. rotundifolia* are also good ferns for baskets, and easily grown, being of a free habit. There are several sorts of British ferns which may be grown in this way, particularly the true British maidenhair (*Adiantum Capillus Veneris*), which spreading at the roots, will soon cover the surface of the basket. Next to this may be placed *Asplenium lanceolatum*, which is also a spreader; likewise *A. marinum*.

2600 *Management of Baskets, etc.* Baskets are sometimes managed in the same way as vases, and even troughs. The plants are grown in ordinary flower pots, plunged in moss, placed in the baskets, etc., when in perfection. This plan has its advantages; for as a plant gets shabby, it can be instantly changed for another. All window gardeners who are fortunate enough to possess a frame, pit, or small greenhouse, would do well to adopt this plan; for a plant is not so likely to become one-sided if grown in a frame; the one-sidedness of plants grown in windows being evidence of the advantages to be derived from the possession of other means. But it does not follow that window plants must be ill looking because one-sided; nor should their tendency that way be checked by turning them, as they are weakened thereby. Whether inside or outside a window, plants naturally turn towards the light, as every one knows who has had any practice with them. Whatever means are at command, the main points in window gardening, as in all other plant culture, are perfect cleanliness, a free open soil and good drainage, a fair even temperature, and uniform moisture. Where there is a tolerably clear atmosphere, window gardening may be conducted without glazed coverings, but in the midst of town smoke and dust, glass cases become absolutely necessary.

2601 *Aspects for Window Plants* Of the plants suitable for various aspects, little need be said: the difference is not so great as might be imagined; but it may be taken as a rule, that a sunny aspect is best for all flowering plants, except in the hot summer months, when they last much longer in bloom if kept in the shade. It is possible, however, to have blinds fixed to a south window, by which the plants may be shaded, or not, at pleasure. In the culture of some plants, as the auricula, for instance, it is advisable to give them a sunny aspect from October to May, and a shady one from May to October. Other plants, as ferns, may be constantly kept in the shade, although a little sun does them no harm, but the contrary.

2602 *Influence of Soil* In the choice of soils for pot culture very much depends, but not in the way generally imagined. A few grim, sooty plants may occasionally be seen occupying a window ledge, and their appearance ascribed to the smoky atmosphere. This is, in fact, the case to a certain extent, but not wholly so; they are mostly potted in soil taken from a back yard, impregnated with foul gases, so that plants would not grow in it in the remotest part of the country. In towns, where proper soil can scarcely be met with, it is advisable to purchase it at some suburban nursery; stating the sort of plant for which it is required.

2603 *Suitable Composts for Plants* All soft-wooded plants, such as geraniums, fuchsias, cinerarias, etc., do best in a soil composed of two parts yellow loam, one very rotten dung, one leaf mould, with sand enough to make it porous; but some plants, such as ericas, epacridae, and azaleas, require peat; and others, as the camellia, daphne, and corraea, a mixture of peat and loam. Although the first-named soil will grow almost any plant, still those that require peat must have it, as no substitute will produce the same effects. It should be observed, that soils ought not to be sifted, as a rule; to do so is contrary to what is observed in nature. In borders and ground devoted to the culture of plants of every kind, small stones and individual substances of various kinds are observed. These serve to keep the soil open, and to promote drainage and the admission of air, permeation of the surface soil by air being necessary to the healthy condition of all plants and crops.

2604 *Potting and Drainage* In potting, adapt the pots to the size of the plants as near as possible – or rather, to what the plant is expected to be – as allowance must be made for growth of the root as well as the plant. Let the pots be perfectly clean. Effectual drainage of the pots does not consist so much in the quantity of drainage, as in the arrangement of it. A potsherd should be placed over the hole; some pieces of pot, broken rather small, over that; and these again covered with a layer of peat fibre or rough earth. This gives efficient drainage, and need not occupy more than an inch and a half of the pot. Hard-wooded plants should be potted rather firmly; soft-wooded should be left rather loose and free.

2605 *How and When to Water* In watering fresh-potted plants, it is important that the whole of the soil be effectually moistened, which can only be accomplished by filling up two or three times with water. No fear need be entertained of over-watering; if the plants have been rightly potted, all surplus water, beyond what the soil can conveniently retain, will drain away. Irregular watering is frequently the cause of failure in plant culture, even with experienced growers. A certain amount of tact is necessary in giving plants which have been so neglected just as much water as they should have, and no more.

In watering, much depends on the weather, and also on the season; plants require less in winter than in summer. The proper time to water them in winter is when the plants are in bloom, or growing rapidly – in summer, as soon as the least dryness appears; but a little practice will be more useful than a lengthy description. In giving air, it may be observed that all plants which are not tender – that is, all plants which are natives of temperate climes – may be exposed to the air at all times when the thermometer indicates a temperature above 40°, except in case of rough winds or heavy rains. Hardy plants may be exposed at any temperature above 32°; for, although frost will not kill them, it may spoil their appearance for a time. Plants in bloom should never be kept close, or exposed to wet or wind; the flowers last longest in a soft, mild atmosphere, free from draught. Plants should never be wetted overhead in cold weather, or, rather, while they are in a cold atmosphere, and never, except to wash off dust, should plants having a soft or woolly foliage be so treated; but some plants, as camellias, myrtles, heaths, and others with hard leaves, may be plentifully syringed, or watered over head from a fine rose, in warm weather, especially when in full growth.

2606 *Training and Pruning* When training is required it should be done neatly and tastefully, using thin and pointed sticks, and very fine fibres of raffia, matting, or soft twine; avoid anything like stiffness or formality, which is the opposite extreme to the graceful habit of plants. The same may be said as to pruning. Cut out such shoots as interfere with the symmetrical outline of the plant; but more may be done by timely disbudding than by cutting.

2607 *Management of Plant Frame for Window Plants* I have mentioned plant frames as being desirable, if not indispensable, for window gardeners who have the means of growing a variety of plants to stock their windows at all seasons. In the management of plant frames, nothing is better for the bottom or floor, in spite of all that has been said against it, than finely-sifted coal ashes. The ashes should be firmly trodden down and made perfectly level. So treated, it never gets sloppy, but absorbs all surplus water – a great consideration. Worms or slugs also dislike crawling through or over it. A plant frame generally has short legs projecting below the boarding: these should be sunk in the ground to keep it steady. The glass should be kept clean, and there should be room sufficient to admit of drawing the lights off at the back.

2608 Let us now proceed to consider some flowers that are useful and attractive in window gardening, and the mode of culture that is best adapted to each.

2609 *Hyacinths* These should always find a place in the frame, as much from the certainty of their flowering, as from their rich colour and fragrance and neat habit when in bloom. They should be potted in September, in a mixture of loam and very rotten dung, with a liberal allowance of sand, placing one in a 4-inch or three in a 6-inch pot; if they are potted lightly, with a little sand under each bulb, no more is required than to place them in the frame, watering or exposing them to gentle showers before the soil gets too dry. They will flower in April, if not at an earlier date.

2610 *Tulips* Dwarf and early tulips may be treated in the same manner as hyacinths. After flowering, the leaves should never be cut off until they decay naturally, nor should water be withheld until the leaves begin to turn yellow. When the foliage has thoroughly decayed, they should be kept dry till the same time of the year as they were potted, when they may be repotted or only surface dressed.

2611 *Violets* These may be grown in pots, by placing two or three runners or offsets in a pot in May, and keeping them in the frame slightly shaded from the sun in summer. Loam and leaf mould suits them admirably. Russian violets, and sometimes the Neapolitan, flower all the winter. True violets flower in March and April.

2612 *Pinks, Carnations, and Picotees* These are sometimes grown in pots under frame treatment; they do well in a soil of gritty loam: they flower in May and June, and some sorts even later. The mule pink makes a very pretty pot plant, and so do the Japan and Indian pinks. *Dianthus Heddewegii* makes a fine showy plant when in bloom, and is more permanent than most of them. They are all propagated by seeds or by pipings – that is, pulling off three or four joints of each side shoot, and pricking them into very sandy loam, and keeping them close under glass for a week or two.

The Sweet William (*Dianthus barbatus*) may be utilised for pot culture, but it is apt to grow large and straggling. Pinks (*Dianthus plumarius*) and cloves, carnations and picotees (*Dianthus caryophyllus*), are all desirable for window gardening, especially the Tree Carnation, which blooms in the winter months, and of which there are now many beautiful varieties.

2613 *Pansies, or Heartsease* These may be cultivated in pots; they are often raised from seed, which may be sown at any time from March to October, carefully repotting the young plants as they advance. They are also raised from cuttings or offsets, which strike readily. Pansies flower at almost any time of the year if kept growing, and are very ornamental. Gritty loam is a suitable soil for pansies.

2614 *Cinerarias* are very ornamental while in bloom, and may be raised either from offsets or from seed: if from the latter, sow in July and August, in loam and leaf mould, well sanded; prick off into small pots, and repot as they advance; in winter, protect from frost by means of mats or litter. They will flower in April, May, and June, and often later. If grown from offsets, take them off in September, and pot singly in 3-inch pots; otherwise treat as before. These like frame culture, if protected from frost; in mild weather a slight wetting of the leaves will be beneficial. The seed may be procured at any respectable nursery. Plants raised from seed are sure to flower and look neat; but good sorts must be perpetuated by means of offsets.

2615 *Arums, or Callas* Arums are very ornamental as window plants, on account of their fine foliage, as well as the large and singular flowers; they grow in loam, and require plenty of water; They flower in March, April, and May, after which they die down partially, and should be put aside in the shade till September, when they must be re-potted. *Arum maculatum* deserves to be cultivated on account of its handsome spotted foliage. Arums are propagated by division of the roots in September.

2616 *Lily of the Valley* This fragrant and beautiful little lily (*Convallaria majalis*) should have a place in the window. Where they grow thick in a border, clusters of them may be taken up in November, potted, and placed in the frame; they will flower much earlier than those out of doors. In purchasing of growers, if the plump crowns are picked out and potted, a cluster of flowering spikes may be had in each pot; after flowering they may be plunged in the border again, and will probably flower the following year.

2617 *Stocks* Intermediate stocks will begin to flower in May if sown the preceding July. They may be sown in a shady border at that time, and, as soon as large enough to handle, place three or four round a 3-inch pot; in October, they will be large enough to pot singly into the same sized pots. Stand them in the frame for the winter. As they exhibit buds, the double and the single may be distinguished. Throw away the single unless wanted for seeding. Stocks thrive best in sandy loam.

2618 *Ferns* Many kinds of ferns are very useful in window gardening, especially the Adiantums, or maidenhair ferns, and, most particularly, *Adiantum acuneatum. Adiantum Capillus Veneris* and *A. lucidum* are good for bouquets; *Pteris serrulata* and *P. rotundifolia* for their dark foliage; and even the common Hartstongue (*Scolopendrium vulgare*), if grown in a frame, or anywhere under glass, is very ornamental.

2619 *Orange Trees, etc.* The common orange (*Citrus aurantium*) is worth growing, both for the flowers and fruit, which, in winter, are very effective for table decoration, if cut with foliage attached. The Winter Cherry (*Solanum pseudo capsicum nanum*, Fig. 595) also affords a striking plant for window decoration, with its bright green foliage and scarlet berries – an example of fruit and foliage combined, the one heightening the effect of the other.

FIG. 595 *Winter cherry*

2620 To dwell singly, however, on every genus of plants that is suitable for window culture is impracticable, and the best thing that can be done to afford the greatest amount of assistance to the window gardener in the smallest possible compass is to give a tabular view of some of the plants that are most eligible, showing at a glance a list of the plants themselves, the aspect for which they are best suited, the time during which they are in flower, and any brief cultural observations that may appear necessary. The letters N, S, E, W, denote north, south, east, and west aspects.

TABLE OF PLANTS AND SHRUBS SUITABLE FOR WINDOW GARDENING

Showing aspects, when in flower and cultural notes

Plant	Aspect	In flower
Abutilon – variety Boule de Neige Raise from seed; soil – loam and peat with sand.	S	September–December
Acacia lophanta – tree Soil – maiden loam, sand, and peat, well drained	S	
Achimenes longiflora and **alba** Plant corms in February, in leaf mould and sand	S	June–August
Ageratum, any variety Soil – maiden loam, leaf mould, and sand, well drained	S	June–September
Alyssum saxatile Use light, sandy soil. Useful for rockwork	S	April–June
Anemone coronata and **hortensis** Plant tubers in sandy loam, in October	S,E,W	March–May
Arabis alpina Hardy; use common soil; useful for window sill	S	February–April
Arbor vitae (*Thuja*) – shrub Hardy evergreen; moist soil; from seed or by cuttings	N	
Aster Sow seed in March, in loam light and rich	S	September–October
Arum Lily Sub-aquatic; requires much water sandy peat and loam	N,S,E,W	January–April
Aubrietia Graeca Divide roots in autumn; use good sandy loam	S	April–May
Aucuba – shrub Common soil; from cuttings in spring and autumn	N	
Auricula, Alpine and show varieties Drain well, seed or offsets, in rich sandy compost	N,E,W	March–April
Balsam From seed; pot in rich light mould, from old hotbed	S	July–September
Begonia rex and other varieties Shoots from tuberous plants, in leaf mould, loam and peat	S,E,W	July–September
Box – shrub; golden leaved varieties Division of roots and layers, in good sandy loam	N,E,W	
Cactus, several varieties (Rat tailed Cactus flowers well) Loam, peat, sand, and brick rubbish, well drained; water in summer, but not in winter; offset and cuttings	S	June–July
Calceolaria – shrubby and herb Shrub, from side shoots, in September; herb, from seeds in May	S	June–September
Camellia Place in open air after flowering until October	E,W	
Campanula, many varieties Loam and old manure from hotbed; drain well	S,E,W	June–September

Candytuft	S	April–July
From seeds sown in January in compost of peat and loam		
Carnations, all varieties	S	June–August
Good loam enriched with old manure and some sand		
Centaurea	S	June–September
From seeds in March, in rich sandy loam		
Clematis, any hardy variety	N	April–November
Equal parts of peat, sand, and good loam		
Cockscomb	S	July–August
Seeds in January, in compost of leaf mould, peat, and sand		
Collinsia	S	July–September
Seeds in good loam, sown any time in spring		
Convolvulus major and minor	S	June–August
Seeds in rich, sandy loam, sown early in spring		
Creeping Jenny	E,W	June–September
Offshoots; sandy loam and peat, well drained		
Chionodoxa Luciliae	S	February–March
Hardy dwarf bulb; plant in autumn in common soil		
Chrysanthemum, all varieties	N,S,E,W	October–December
From cutting in early spring; set in good soil		
Crocus, various colours	S,E,W	February–March
Plant corms deeply in light soil in October or November		
Cyclamen Persicum	S,E,W	November–February
Repot corms in August in light, rich, peaty soil		
Cineraria	S	February–April
Sow under glass in rich, light soil from May to August		
Daffodils, various	S,E,W	February–May
Bulbs planted in light, rich soil from October to December		
Dahlia, dwarf varieties	S	August–October
Division of roots and cuttings in rich sandy loam		
Daisy	S,E,W	March–June
Plant double varieties in good rich loam,		
Daphne Mezereum	E,W	March–April
Will grow in any good ordinary soil		
Dielytra spectabilis	S	February–May
Perennial, grown in compost of mould, peat, and sand		
Dodaecathcon Meadia	S	April–May
Division of roots and seeds in good loam, leaf mould, and sand		
Echeveria secunda	S	August–September
Seeds or offsets in good soil; give little water		
Erysimum Peroffskianum	S,E,W	June–September
Sow in September for early blooms in following year		
Erythronium (Dog's-tooth Violet)	S	February–April
Tuberous rooted perennial; peaty soil, well drained		
Euonymus or Spindle Tree	S,E,W	
Cuttings or layers in good loam and sand		
Ferns, any hardy or half-hardy varieties	N,E,W	
Require compost of maiden loam, sand, and old (mortar, drained well		
Forget-me-not *(Myosotis)*	E,W	May–June
Division of roots in autumn in sandy loam and pear		
Foxglove	S,E,W	June–September
Seeds in compost of leaf mould, loam, peat, and sand		

Plant	Aspect	Flowering
Fuchsias, various varieties	S	June–October
Cuttings in spring and autumn in loam and leaf mould		
Gazania pavonia	S	July–August
Side shoots in spring or August in peat, sand and loam		
Genista Cananensis	S	May–July
Will do well and thrive in common loamy soil		
Gentian, various	S,E,W	July–August
Hardy perennials in maiden loam and sand kept moist		
Geraniums, various	S	Mar–October
Hardy, easily grown in leaf mould, loam, and sand		
Geum coccineum and **reptans**	E,W	June–August
Hardy perennials from division of roots in spring		
Guernsey Lily *(Nerine Sarniensis)*	S	September–October
Compost of equal parts of leaf mould, fine loam, and sand		
Gypsophila repens	S,E,W	July–August
Dwarf trailing perennial; grows in common soil		
Heaths *{Ericas)*, various	E,W	December–March
Cuttings in spring in sand under glass ; water well		
Helichrysum (Everlasting Flower)	S	July–September
Seeds in light sandy loam under bell glass in January		
Heliotrope	S	June–September
Cuttings in spring or autumn in light, rich soil		
Hepatica	S,E,W	February–March
Plant tubers in light, sandy soil in October		
Holly tree	N,E,W	February–March
Valuable for berries and foliage; layers in good sandy loam		
Hyacinth, various	S,E,W	January–March
Bulbs; light soil in pots, or water in glasses		
Hydrangea	S,E,W	June–August
Cuttings in sandy loam; when in flower water freely		
India Rubber Plant *(Ficus elastica)*	N,E,W	
Cuttings in sandy peat; grows well in sandy loam		
Ivy, many varieties	N	
Grows in common soil in boxes; require support		
Jessamine, yellow	N,E,W	November–February
Cuttings in light, sandy loam under hand glass		
Jonquils	S,E,W	February–May
Plant from October to December in light, rich mould		
Lachenalias	S	April–May
Bulbs; place three in pot in rich sandy loam		
Larkspur *(Delphinium)*	S,E,W	June–August
Perennials; div, of roots; annuals from seed in rich loam		
Lavender	S,E,W	August–September
Cuttings in light, sandy loam; esteemed for fragrance		
Laurustinus – shrub	N,E,W	November–February
Propagate by layers in good sandy loam in spring		
Lilies, various kinds	S,E,W	June–August
Hardy bulbs grown for the most part in sandy peat		
Lily of the Valley (*Convallaria majalis)*	N,E,W	February–April
Plant in clumps in maiden loam with sand		
Linaria or Toad Flax	N,S,E,W	
Seed or division of roots in sandy loam and peat		

Lobelia	S	June–September
Cuttings in light, rich, sandy soil		
London Pride (a Saxifrage)	N,E,W	April–June
Offsets root readily in common or sandy soil		
Lupines	S,E,W	June–August
Perennials by division of roots; annuals from seed in March		
Lycopods or Club Mosses	N,E,W	
Plant in peat, loam, and sand, and water freely		
Marigold *(Calendula)*	S,E,W	July–September
Seeds in sandy loam in February or March		
Mesembryanthemum, varieties	S	June–August
Maiden loam, peat, and sand; water well in hot weather		
Michaelmas Daisy	S,E,W	September–October
Division of roots in sandy loam		
Mignonette	S,E,W	June–August
Seeds sown in March in light sandy loam		
Mimulus or Musk, varieties	N,S,E,W	April–September
Plant in rich loam and peat; water freely		
Myrtle	S	June–September
Loam and peat mould; cuttings in sand under glass in August		
Narcissus	S,E,W	February–May
Plant from October to December in light rich mould		
Nasturtium *(Tropaeolum)*, varieties	S,E,W	July–October
Seeds in light sandy loam; sow in spring		
Nertera depressa or Bead Plant	N	July–September
Sandy loam; requires shade and much water at roots		
Oleander *(Nerium)*	S	July–September
Sandy peat and leaf mould; requires much water		
Orange	S	May–June
From pips sown in spring in rich sandy loam,		
Pansy or Heartsease	N,E,W	March–June
Seeds and cuttings in autumn in rich sandy loam		
Pelargonium	S	March–October
Seeds or cuttings in autumn; soil, good rich loam		
Pentstemon procerum	S	June–August
Evergreen trailer; grows in good garden mould		
Periwinkle	N,S,E,W	April–June
Division of roots or layers in loose sandy loam		
Petunia	S	June–September
Seedlings and cuttings; soil, good loam and leaf mould		
Phloxes, various	S,W	June–October
Division of roots; plant in light rich soil		
Picotees and **Pinks**	S,W	June–August
Pipings and layers; new varieties by sowing seeds		
Polemonium reptans	S,E,W	April–May
Hardy trailing plant; requires good garden soil		
Polyanthus	S,E,W	March–June
Division of roots in August in good rich loam		
Primroses and **Primulas**, varieties	S,E,W	November–June
Division of roots or seeds; soil, good rich loam		
Pyrethrum	S,E,W	June–August
Cuttings in light sandy loam, or from seeds in January		

Ranunculus	S,E,W	April–May
Plant tubers in well-manured and rich loamy soil		
Rhododendrons, small varieties	N,E,W	April–June
Sandy peat or sandy fibrous loam with clayey loam		
Roses, climbing and small varieties	S,E,W	June–October
Soil, two-thirds rich sandy loam, one-third leaf mould		
Saxifrage	N,S,E,W	May–July
Seeds and div, in spring; sandy loam and leaf mould		
Scabius	S,E,W	June–October
Division of roots or seeds in good rich loam,		
Scarborough Lily (*Vallota purpurea)*	S	September–October
Plant in sandy peat or in good, rich, light mould		
Scilla or Squill	S,E,W	April–July
From seeds; plant bulbs in rich sandy loam		
Sedum or Stonecrop	N,S,E,W	June–August
Divisions and cuttings; dry sandy, loamy soil		
Sempervivum or House Leek	E,W	June–July
Divisions and cuttings; dry sandy soil or sandy loam		
Silene or Catchfly	E,W	June–July
Seeds, division of roots and cuttings; requires rich sandy loam		
Snapdragon *(Antirrhinum)*	S,E,W	July–October
Seeds or cuttings; in dry soil or a sandy loam		
Snowdrop, large and small	S,E,W	January–February
Plant in October or November in light rich soil, loam and leaf mould		
Soldanella	E,W	April–May
Seeds and div, in spring; plant in peat and loam		
Southernwood – shrub	N	
Cuttings or division of roots in light sandy loam		
Spanish Broom *(Spartium)*	N	July–August
Seeds or cuttings in summer; any ordinary garden-soil		
Speedwell	S,E,W	March–May
Division in spring or seeds; good garden soil		
Spergula	E,W	May–June
Division of roots in good, light garden soil		
Spiderwort *(Tradescantia)*	E,W	June–September
Division of roots in light rich mould		
Stock	S,E,W	June–August
Seeds sown in August and September in sand, peat, and leaf mould		
Sweet Peas	S,E,W	June–September
Sow seeds in March, using good maiden mould		
Sweet Sultan	S,E,W	June–September
Cuttings; or seeds in light sandy loam in spring		
Tropaeolum	S,E,W	March–October
Seeds, div, of roots, or cuttings in spring in light rich soil		
Tulips	S,E,W	April–May
Plant bulbs in October or November in rich sandy loam,		
Verbena, various colours	S	July–August
Seeds, div,, layers, and cuttings in rich sandy loam		
Verbena, lemon-scented	S	June–September
Cuttings in spring; soil, rich, well-dressed sandy mould		
Veronica incana	S,W	May–June
Division in spring; requires good garden soil		

Violas or Violets	N,E,W	November–June
Seeds, divisions and cuttings in light rich soil		
Wallflowers	S,E,W	March–September
Seeds in light sandy loam; double vars, by cuttings		

It must not be supposed that these are the only plants suitable for window gardening; there are others,, but in the above it has only been sought to furnish a good representative list of plants from which selections may be made.

2621 *Management of Window Plants* With regard to the general management of window plants throughout the year, the same routine must be followed, with respect to altered circumstances, as in the cool greenhouse and the conservatory, and it will be unnecessary to give a monthly calendar of operations. It will be sufficient to give a few directions for the culture of plants in windows at such times of the year when the greatest amount of care, attention, and assiduity is required from the window gardener, and these times are the months of May, July, and November.

2622 *Window Gardening in May: Ventilation and Shading* Many window plants will be in full bloom at this time, and to preserve their freshness as long as possible, give plenty of fresh air; and though a little sun morning and afternoon is beneficial, still too much is likely to produce a contrary effect, and cause them to fade long before they would with timely and judicious shading.

2623 *Plunging in Ornamental Pots* If the plants are in ordinary pots, which are certainly best, let them be plunged in ornamental pots or vases, and fill up the vacancy between with moss or sand; they will not only look better, but the roots being kept cool, will keep the moisture longer, and less watering will be necessary. This is of some consequence in a room; for although watering will be sometimes necessary, means should be taken to reduce the quantity required, by shading, plunging, and keeping the pots in feeders – that is, pans or saucers, which are made to match with the pots or vases. But this requires a little judgment; it will never do to let the roots of the plants stand in stagnant water. When the pots are placed in the pans or saucers, fill the vacancy with a mixture of silver sand and charcoal finely broken, not powdered; this will absorb the water that runs through the pot, and yield it back again to the plant, besides preventing stagnation.

2624 *Watering Window Plants* The time to water a plant is just when the soil begins to present an appearance of dryness, which is best seen when the surface is pretty firm, although it is advisable to stir it sometimes; but if, after stirring, the plant wants water, give it from a fine rose. This will settle it again, so that it is easily ascertained when the plant wants water afterwards.

FIG. 596 *Sedum sieboli*

2625 *Insects on Window Plants* If any plants are infested with aphis or green fly, brush it off with a small brush, without injuring the plant. A few plants may be kept free from this pest by this means, without fumigating with tobacco.

2626 *Herbaceous Plants on Window Ledges* Various sorts of herbaceous plants may be cultivated outside, on the window ledges. Being hardy, they will stand all weathers, but are best protected from severe frost, and winds, and hot sun; in fact, they do best in a north aspect during the summer, and those who have such situations cannot do better than choose from this class.

Prominent among these are the sedums or stonecrops, many of which are very pretty when in flower, as 5. *Sideboldi* and others. Even the common yellow and white stonecrops are interesting when in flower, and hang over the sides of the pot, completely covering it. They mostly have viscid, fleshy leaves, and stand drought without much injury; consequently they are good things to begin with. The sempervivums, or houseleeks, are much the same in habit and style of growth as some of the preceding; they are equally easy of culture. Then, again, there is the prolific family of saxifrages, which includes the time-honoured London Pride and species far too numerous to mention here, but all of more or less merit for pot culture. Then, again, there are the phlox species, as *Phlox procumbens*, *P. subulata*, etc., which are of dwarf trailing habit, very suitable to hang from a window ledge. Primulas, as the double white, lilac, and red, and also *Primula auricula*, before spoken of, are interesting subjects for practice on the window sill. Many others might be mentioned, as campanulas, particularly *Campanula rotundifolia* and *C. pumila*, irises, brellis, etc.; but the culture for all is much the same. They grow in sandy loam, and should have proper drainage.

2627 *Chrysanthemums* These are very suitable for window culture, and now is the time to propagate them from cuttings or offsets, to make neat, bushy plants for flowering in November. Cuttings strike freely if planted round a pot, and placed in the shade. Offsets may be potted singly. Any that are advancing, and have filled their pots with roots should be put into larger. Such as are growing vigorously may receive liquid manure two or three times a week.

2628 *Turning Window Plants to Light* Fast-growing plants, such as fuchsias, geraniums, genistas, etc., should not be frequently turned, since they always make a face towards the light, and the process might weaken them; it would be better to train them out fanlike, by means of thin painted sticks. Fern cases may be turned occasionally. The plants in these have a like tendency; consequently they show best from the light. By turning the case, the faces of the plants are brought facing the room If they can receive light directly overhead, it will be so much the better.

Fern cases may be planted with most of the British ferns, and a vast number of exotic ones are also suitable. Lycopodiums may be allowed to trail over the surface of the soil. *Pteris arguta* makes a good centre plant for a tall case; also *Adiantum pedatum*, one of the most graceful of ferns, but dies down every winter. The Aspleniums offer an extensive and numerous family to choose from, particularly *A. viviparum*, *A. bulbiferum*, *A. Paniculatum*, and others, producing young ferns on the old leaves, and root in the air. The Scolopendriums are also suitable, and show well their broad shining leaves or fronds.

2629 *Planting and Management of Fern Cases* Both the planting and management of these cases must depend a great deal on the situation or locality. In a dry, warm room many ferns that are considered very tender may be grown successfully; but they will require more water, which should be warm when given, and less ventilation; for the dry air of a warm room, ill suited to most plants, is far more injurious to ferns, and some of them naturally come from warm, humid climates; they must therefore be carefully treated in this respect. If an opening at each end were made, and this covered with fine wire gauze, it would admit air without any of its ill consequences.

2630 *Window Gardening in July: Routine Work* If it is desired to have a succession of window plants in bloom, there must be a certain amount of potting, repotting, and changing; as one goes out of bloom, another is brought in to take its place. By this means a freshness and gaiety may be kept up, and all the necessary work may be done in another place.

2631 *Fuchsias* At this time of the year, fuchsias, pelargoniums, and salvias will be in perfection, and may take the seat of honour while they last; and as most of them are continuous bloomers, will probably last till October, when they may give place to chrysanthemums. Fuchsias, particularly, are adapted for window culture, as they are very clean, and, under good treatment, are little infested with insects.

2632 *Geraniums* The same may be said of geraniums, many an old plant of which has had sole possession for years of the only place the owners had for growing them, *i.e.*, the window. A scarlet geranium trained over the window-sash forms a verdant screen, the only objection to which is that the leaves, being naturally attracted to the light, turn their backs to the interior of the room, nor is it advisable to turn them often; but if trained over a trellis fixed to the pot or box, the plant may be turned to the light in the daytime, and reversed at night.

2633 *Mesembryanthemums* Other plants are suitable for a like purpose; among them must be named the numerous tribe of mesembryanthemums or fig marigolds. These will grow for many years in the same soil, giving little trouble beyond watering. They are well suited for baskets or mounted pots, or vases, where they will hang down and look well. Many of them are very beautiful when in flower, comprising all shades of white, red, and yellow.

> Mesembryanthemums are what are termed succulent plants, having thick fleshy leaves; consequently will bear drought and the heat of a room for any length of time, without injury; and as they require very little water in winter, one objection to their culture is removed. They grow well in sandy loam and leaf mould, in which plenty of broken flower pots, bricks, or charcoal, are mixed.

2634 *Cacti* The various species of cacti are also very suitable as permanent window plants. The varieties of creeping cereus may be grown in suspended baskets, and last for many years without requiring any change in the soil; they naturally droop and hang down, which gives them an interesting appearance. The globular cacti are curious and interesting, and are very numerous.

2635 *Aloes* The smaller kinds of aloes may be grown in the same way. Many of these are curiously and prettily marked, and those who fancy this sort of plant consider them quite as ornamental as flowers. They are all succulent, and may be treated in the same way as the fig marigold, giving plenty of water in hot weather, and little or none in winter, taking care that the soil is well drained.

2636 *Fern Cases* Fern cases should be placed in the shade at this time of the year; if put where they can have light overhead, so much the better. If air can be admitted without dust, let the plants have it; when kept too close, they grow tall and spindling. They should not be allowed to touch the glass, since the condensed moisture rots and disfigures them; but less so when the case is properly ventilated. Water rather freely in the latter case.

2637 *Window Gardening in November: Protection from Frost for Plants on Sills* Window plants now require to be carefully managed as regards exposing them to the open air, and should be adapted to the time of the year. Those who have evergreens for winter, besides flowering plants for the summer, can manage to have the outside sills always furnished; a few of the former will be found very useful, as they are easily managed, and may be placed in the north aspect in the summer, and brought forward in the winter. The best probably are small plants of conifers – that is, pines, cedars, and cypresses – these always look neat, and may be kept small; but other evergreens may also do very well. Aucubas, boxes, and others – above all, laurustinus – in dwarf bushy plants, are invaluable; but then, when standing on a window sill, the pots should not be exposed to frost. During the winter they must be taken inside on frosty nights, or plunged in moss, cocoanut fibre, or some such material.

2638 *Treatment of Indoor Plants* Watering Indoor plants should receive all the light that can be given them; the circumstances of their position, the short days, etc., tend to diminish it; it should not be diminished by placing the plants further from the glass than can be helped. In watering, also, a little more caution must be exercised. Plants are less able to appropriate it now than in warmer weather; it is therefore more likely to stagnate. Examine the drainage, and see that it is sufficient to carry off all surplus water, and allow no dead leaves to mould and disfigure the plants.

2639 *Plants with Ornamental Foliage* Plants having ornamental foliage will be found very useful; they furnish a variety sufficient to satisfy all tastes and conveniences, and many of them are very suitable for window culture. *Farfugium grande* has been already mentioned; it does well in a mixture of peat, loam, and sand, and will always carry a good foliage under ordinary management. *Centaurea gymnocarpa* is a white silvery-leaved plant, which, when properly grown, assumes a palm-like habit, and always looks well. *C. ragusina* is another sort of equal merit. *Cineraria maritima*, otherwise known as Dusty Bob, is somewhat similar, and is often grown as a window plant. These and some others of like 'character will bear the ordinary temperature of the season, and require no more than the mere protection of a dwelling room.

2640 *Bulbs for Spring Flowering* Those who value plants for this quality should have a good supply of hyacinths and narcissuses, jonquils, etc., to flower in March and- April. It is not too late to get them, provided it is done early in the month.

2641 *Chrysanthemums* These will now be in bloom. In order to make them last as long as possible, let them not be kept close or damp; give plenty of free air; water with weak liquid manure. Let them have a little sun morning and afternoon, but not enough to make them flag.

2642 *Ferns and Ferneries* Ferns, as a general rule, require shade and moisture, and they will therefore grow, and may be cultivated with success, in many a dark and comparatively gloomy situation in which flowering plants will not thrive. For an indoor fernery, for example, a north aspect is suitable; while for the majority of plants, whose blossom constitute their chief charm, and which are chiefly in favour during the season in which they are in bloom, it would be objectionable. In the constitution of ferns there is as much difference as in the constitution of flowering plants – that is to say, some ferns, being thoroughly hardy, will do well out-of-doors without the slightest protection; others, again, require shelter, either in a cold greenhouse in which no artificial heat is introduced in the winter season, or a cool greenhouse in which artificial heat is merely utilised for the exclusion of frost; a third class is formed of stove or hothouse ferns, which require heat, and such treatment as may assimilate the conditions under which they are grown as closely as possible to those under which they flourish in their native climes.

2643 *The Out-Door Fernery* The fernery out of doors must be stocked exclusively with hardy British and exotic ferns. Of these none will bear the light and heat of the summer sun in full force, and a situation should be chosen for it which is shady and near water, or in which water can be supplied by artificial means. By this it must not be taken for granted that any moist, dank spot will do for ferns; on the contrary, they like good drainage as well as shade and moisture, and efficient drainage should always be provided. The moisture in which they most delight is a humid atmosphere, and a moisture cunningly created by artificial means, and consisting of drips and splashes that fall in almost infinitesimal quantities on the fronds and sustain their verdure unimpaired.

2644 *Position* A shady bank, or cool spot on the edge of a pond or the brink of a rivulet, is a good position for an outdoor fernery, and admits of treatment by the aid of a few boulders and stones, and even clinkers or masses of vitrified brick, which produce an effect more closely akin to nature than can be attained when the structure is due entirely to art. Failing such positions in gardens and back yards, the best must be done by artificial means, and even under such conditions a fernery that is satisfactory to the eye and suitable in every respect for the plants that are to be placed in it, is by no means difficult to attain or troublesome to manage, provided that the primary requisites of coolness, shade, and moisture are obtainable.

2645 *Construction* When a position that requires little assistance from art can be obtained – such as a cool, shady nook near water, or by a running stream – all that is necessary is to dispose some masses of stone, roots of trees, burrs, etc., in such a manner that they may be partly embedded in the soil, and afford corners, as it were, here and there, in which various kinds of ferns can be judiciously located with regard to their respective habits and appearance and the effect that each is designed to produce. In making a piece of rockwork for ferns, or otherwise *building* a fernery, so to speak, supposing that the work is done on the level do a little below the level of the ground, as may be the case when the upper part of the soil is removed to furnish part of the material for the structure, the first thing to be done is to provide for thorough drainage below the surface by excavating, and filling up the hollow thus formed with brickbats, stones, and other materials which lie together in such a manner as to have interstices of various sizes between them, and thus afford ample room for the escape of moisture from the structure above and its absorption by the soil below. If economy with regard to soil is necessary, a heap of the same material may be thrown up on which to place the compost in which ferns will best thrive, which may be made of good garden soil mixed with leaf mould, some good loam, and a fair proportion of light fibrous peat and sand. Then on the surface of the bank thus formed place stones of various kinds, some on the soil itself and others half buried in it, with roots of old trees, flints, clinkers, etc., disposed so as to leave crevices here and there in which the ferns may be planted.

2646 *Planting Ferns* The fernery, or rockery, being ready for the reception of the plants, put the roots into the crevices provided for them, keeping the crown just above the soil, and pressing the earth firmly about the roots. If the bank of earth below the stones, etc., has been of necessity made of garden earth alone, introduce a liberal quantity of compost of yellow loam, peat, and sand into holes made in the soil to receive it before planting the ferns. Some ferns require a greater depth of soil than others, and some again, such as the Common Polypody and Hartstongue Fern, will grow admirably on a wall, which shows that they require but a minimum of soil in which to root. In planting ferns, the taller sorts should be placed at the back of the bank, those of medium height in the centre, and the dwarf varieties in front.

2647 *Ferns Suitable for Outdoor Culture* The following will afford a list of ferns suitable for outdoor culture, all of which may be purchased at rates ranging from two pence to sixpence each. The ordinary name is appended in most cases, and the letters B, C, F, indicate the position in which the ferns should be placed in the fernery, namely, back, centre, or front. The names of exotic ferns, chiefly of North American origin, are placed in italics:

C	***Allosorus crispus***	Parsley Fern
	Aspidium cristatum	
	Aspidium Noveboracense	
	Aspidium thelypterioides	
F	*Asplenium adiantum nigrum*	Black Maidenhair Spleenwort
F	**Asplenium ruta muraria**	Rue Fern
F	**Asplenium trichomanes**	Common Maidenhair Spleenwort
F	**Asplenium** *thelypterioides*	
F	**Asplenium viride**	Green – stemmed Spleenwort
C	**Athyrium filix foemina**	Lady Fern (Fig 592)
C	**Athyrium** *Michauxii*	
C	**Blechnum Spicant**	Hard Fern
F	**Botrychium lunaria**	Moonwort
F	**Ceterach officinarun**	Scaly Spleenwort
F	**Cystopteris fragilis**	Bladder Fern
F	**Cystopteris** *bulbifera*	
B	**Lastrea aemula**	Hay-scented Fern
C	**Lastrea** *atrata*	
B	**Lastrea dilatata**	Broad Buckler Fern

C	**Lastrea filix-mas**	Male Fern
C	**Lastrea** *intermedia*	
C	**Lastrea** *marginale*	
C	**Lastrea montana**	Mountain Buckler Fern
C	**Lastrea rigida**	Rigid Buckler Fern
C	**Lastrea Sieboldi**	
C	**Lastrea spinulosa**	Spiny Buckler Fern
C	**Lastrea thelypteris**	Marsh Fern
C	**Lastrea varia**	
	Onoclea sensibilis (Fig 590)	
B	**Osmunda regalis**	Royal Fern (Fig 589)
F	*Phegopteris hexagonoptera*	
F	*Phegopteris polypodioides*	
F	**Phegopteris dryopteris**	Oak Fern
F	**Phegopteris phegopteri**	Beech Fern
F	**Phegopteris Robertianum**	Limestone Polypody
F	**Phegopteris vulgare**	Common Polypody (Fig 591)
B	*Polystichum acrostichoides*	
B	**Polystichum aculeatum**	Hard Prickly Shield Fern
B	**Polystichum angulare**	Soft Prickly Shield Fern
B	**Polystichum angulare proliferum**	
B	**Polystichum sestoum**	
B	**Pteris aquilina**	Bracken
C	**Scolopendrium vulgare**	Hartstongue Fern (Fig. 588)

The above list, as it has been said, includes hardy ferns only. Persons wishing to purchase ferns should send for catalogues and price lists to Messrs W. and J. Birkenhead, Fern Nursery, Sale, or to Mr E. Gill, Victoria Fernery, Lynton, North Devon. These nurserymen have a large and comprehensive stock, including every sort and variety suitable for outdoor and indoor culture with lycopodiums, selaginellas, and the hymenophyllums or filmy ferns. Messrs W. and J. Birkenhead also supply an illustrated catalogue of ferns, etc., at is., and suitable fern composts, peat, leaf mould, loam, coarse silver sand, charcoal, virgin cork, and everything that is necessary for the culture of ferns or the construction and decoration of the fernery indoors or out of doors.

2648 *Filmy Ferns* These ferns, which are extremely beautiful in form, are not suitable for outdoor culture, but should be grown under a bell glass or in a Wardian case in a room or greenhouse. The varieties most commonly grown are *Hymenophyllum Tunbridgense*, *H. unilaterale*, and *Trichomanes radicans*. 'They should be grown,' says Mr Gill, 'in seed pans well drained, with good leaf mould, a little loam, and nearly half its bulk of small broken sandstone or soft bricks. The mould should be raised, using little crooks to peg the fern on the mould firmly, leaving room round the sides for the bell glass on the inside of the pan. Some prefer wood to grow them on,, but wood decays, and the whole mass of ferns are disturbed. They require very little water over the fronds, sufficient only to clean them, keeping the glass off for a time to dry the fronds, or they will turn black. Should the fronds look dry or shrivelled at any time, plunge the seed pan in water, letting it stand till soaked.'

2649 *The Indoor Fernery* The construction of the indoor fernery is similar to that of any glazed structure, but its position should be exactly opposite to that of the conservatory or greenhouse – that is to say, it should front to the north,

north-east, or north-west, while the frontage of the greenhouse should be to the south, south-east, or south-west. In the arrangement of the interior, too, there is a marked difference, the greenhouse being furnished with shelves and stages at various heights for the support of the plants, made, generally speaking, of laths or battens, and the fernery with brackets, pockets, platforms, and terraces, to which a rustic appearance is imparted by giving these structures, large and small, an ornamental facing of virgin cork, as this material is generally called, and such forms as may be best calculated to set off the beauty of the foliage of the ferns that are placed in them. Virgin cork may be obtained of most nurserymen and seedsmen at about 3d. per lb., or in bales of 56 11s. us to 12s. 6d. per bale, 112 lb. from 20s. to 25s. It may also be obtained of the London and Lisbon Cork Wood Company, Limited, 28 Upper Thames Street, London, whose wholesale price is 12s. per 112 lb.

2650 *Potting Ferns* When ferns are grown in pots or boxes, care should be taken that the drainage is perfect, and for this purpose a layer of broken potsherds, fragments of brick, and pieces of porous stone should be placed at the bottom, and on this the soil or compost, which should consist of leaf mould, sandy loam, fibrous peat, and silver sand, the first three ingredients being taken in equal proportions, and sufficient of the last named to make its presence apparent through the entire mass when mixed. With the compost should be mixed small lumps of crumbling sandstone or decaying brick, which tends to keep the soil open, and affords a substance to which the rootlets of the fern can cling. All ferns should be potted firmly, and the earth well pressed about the roots just below the crown.

2651 *Watering Ferns* All ferns, whether within doors or out of doors, require their foliage to be kept moist; and some, indeed, such as the Royal Fern (*Osmunda regalis*), will thrive best when exposed to the constant splash of falling water. To afford the proper amount of moisture by artificial means, the best thing that can be done is to syringe them with a syringe having the finest possible rose, from which the water will issue in the form of spray. This mode of watering the fronds should be resorted to both in the open air and in the glazed fernery. With regard to watering the roots, if the surface soil has a dry aspect, it will be necessary to give water. When in pots, the usual test of knocking the pot sharply with a piece of wood may be applied. If the sound is dead and dull, it may then be assumed that the soil is sufficiently moist, but if it be hollow and tolerably resonant, it must be taken to indicate that the ball of earth in which the roots are is getting dry and requires water.

2652 *Raising Ferns from Seed* Mixed varieties of fern seed may be obtained from Messrs W. and J. Birkenhead, Fern Nursery, Sale, at 1s., 2s. 6d., and 5s. per packet. The seeds of ferns, or spores, as they are commonly called, are contained in spore cases on the under part of the fronds, which are green at first, but ultimately turn to a brown colour when ripe. In some ferns the shores have the appearance and shape of long narrow strips; in others they are circular, and look like spots. When the spore cases are nearly ready to burst, the fronds should be cut off and laid on paper, on which the spores will be received when they fall out. Fern spores should be sown on the surface of a compost of sand and loam firmly pressed together at the top, and made moist throughout. A piece of glass should be placed over the top of the pot, and the pot itself placed in a cool and shady place, and water should be kept in the saucer in which it stands, to ensure the continuance of a moist condition for the soil. When the young plants show themselves, air may be given by raising but not removing the glass, and when large enough transplant them into small pots.

Having thus broadly and briefly set forth the principles of fern culture in the open air and the glazed fernery, all that remains to be done is to refer the reader to the price lists of the dealers already mentioned for varieties suited for the greenhouse and hothouse, other than those which have been mentioned already in these pages. These catalogues are supplied gratis, and are far more comprehensive and exhaustive than any list that might be given here, considering the many species that exist, and the number of varieties that are included under each species. Further, mere lists of names are useful only to those who are well acquainted with the different sorts of ferns that are grown, and the habit of growth of each species, and it is difficult for any one who is in ignorance of these to make a selection, large or small, that would be in every way satisfactory. As a parting word of advice to buyers whenever a selection of plants is wanted, no matter what they may be, I cannot do better than recommend them to send the dealer all particulars respecting site, position, and the number and character of the plants required, and then leave the selection to him. In making purchases in this manner, the buyer will never be dissatisfied with what he receives, and he will never be subjected to the disappointment which is often caused by the selection of a number of specimens at haphazard from a mere list of names without description or illustration to help him in his choice.

Index

The figures in this index refer to the numbered paragraphs in the text. Most of the subjects under the headings of 'Gardens' and 'Gardening' are referred to in detail in other parts of the index, under their respective heads,

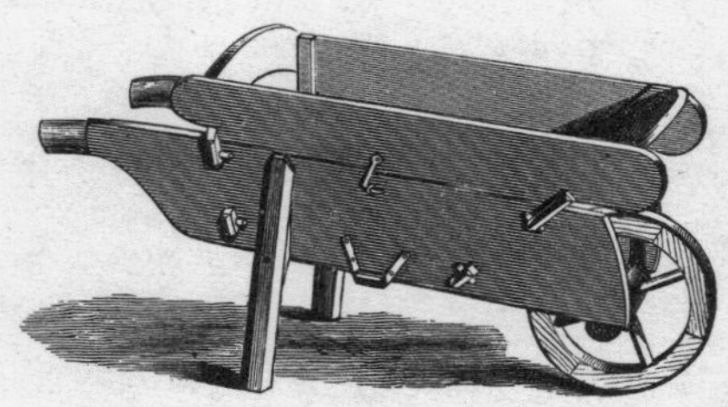